THE OFFICIAL GUIDE TO
AMERICAN HISTORIC INNS

Rated "Outstanding" by Morgan Rand
Winner of Benjamin Franklin Award
Best Travel Guide
Winner of Travel Publishing Ne
Best Travel Reference
Winner of Benjamin Franklin Av
Best Directory

D1514750

Comments from print media:

". . . helps you find the very best hideaways (many of the book's listings appear in the National Register of Historic Places)." — **Country Living**

"I love your book!" — **Lydia Moss, Travel Editor, McCall's**

"Delightful, succinct, detailed and well-organized. Easy to follow style . . ." — **Don Wudtke, Los Angeles Times**

"This is one of the best guidebooks of its kind. It's easy to use, accurate and the thumbnail sketches give the readers enough description to choose among the more than 1,000 properties detailed . . ." — **Dallas Morning News**

". . . thoughtfully organized and look-ups are hassle-free . . . well-researched and accurate . . . put together by people who know the field. There is no other publication available that covers this particular segment of the bed & breakfast industry - a segment that has been gaining popularity among travelers by leaps and bounds. The information included is valuable and well thought out." — **Morgan Directory Reviews**

"This guide has become the favorite choice of travelers and specializes only in professionally operated inns and B&Bs rather than homestays (lodgings in spare bedrooms)." — **Laguna Magazine**

"This is the best bed & breakfast book out. It outshines them all!" — **Maggie Balitas, Rodale Book Clubs**

Comments from innkeepers:

"Your book is wonderful. I have been reading it as one does a novel." — Olallieberry Inn, Cambria, Calif.

"We want to tell you how much we love your book. We have it out for guests to use. They love it, each featured inn stands out so well. Thank you for the privilege of being in your book." — Fairhaven Inn, Bath, Maine.

"What a wonderful book! We love it and have been very pleased with the guests who have made reservations using your book." — Vermont innkeeper

"We have had fantastic response. Thanks!" — Liberty Rose Colonial B&B, Williamsburg, Va.

"American Historic Inns is wonderful! We are proud and delighted to be included. Thank you for creating such a special guidebook." — The Heirloom, Ione, Calif.

"Thanks so much for all your hard work. We receive the largest number of guidebook referrals from The Official Guide to American Historic Inns." — Saddle Rock Ranch, Sedona, Ariz.

"Your book has been invaluable to us." — Ellis River House, Jackson, N.H.

"Your guide has high praises from guests who use it." — The Inn on South Street, Kennebunkport, Maine.

"Thank you for all the time and work you put into this guidebook. We have had many guests find our inn because of you." — Kaleidoscope Inn, Nipomo, Calif.

To Josephine

THE OFFICIAL GUIDE
— TO —
AMERICAN
HISTORIC
INNS

BED & BREAKFASTS AND COUNTRY INNS

SEVENTH EDITION

BY DEBORAH EDWARDS SAKACH

Published By

AMERICAN
HISTORIC
INNS
INCORPORATED

PO Box 669
Dana Point
California
92629-0669
http://bnbinns.com
E-mail:comments@bnbinns.com

FRONT COVER (CLOCKWISE FROM TOP LEFT):

Captain Lord Mansion, Kennebunkport, Maine.
Photo by Warren Jagger Photography, Inc.

Mayhurst Inn, Orange, Va.
Photo by Peg Harmon

Gaige House Inn, Glen Ellen, Calif.
Photo by Richard Jung

Two Meeting Street Inn, Charleston, S.C.
Photo by American Historic Inns, Inc.

BACK COVER (FROM TOP):

The Castle Inn Riverside "The Historic Campbell Castle," Wichita, Kan.

Victoria-On-Main B&B, Whitewater, Wis.
Photo by Peter Hlavacek

Thorncroft Inn, Martha's Vineyard, Mass.
Photo by Robert Schellhammer

Grand Victorian B&B Inn, Bellaire, Mich.
Photo by Don Rutt

Castle Hill Inn & Resort, Newport, R.I.

COVER DESIGN:
David Sakach

PRODUCTION MANAGER:
Joshua Prizer

ASSISTANT EDITORS:
Tiffany Crosswy, Alex Murashko, Stephen Sakach

OPERATIONS MANAGER:
Sandy Imre

DATABASE ASSISTANTS:
Stacey Schweitzer, Molly Thomson

PROGRAMMING AND CARTOGRAPHY:
Tim Sakach

DIGITAL SCANNING:
Dani Coles, Jason Lin, Brionne Longfellow,
Marissa Nunez, Suzanne Sakach

Publisher's Cataloging in Publication Data
Sakach, Deborah Edwards
American Historic Inns, Inc.
The Official Guide to American Historic Inns

1. Bed & Breakfast Accommodations - United States, Directories, Guide Books.
2. Travel - Bed & Breakfast Inns, Directories, Guide Books.
3. Bed & Breakfast Accommodations - Historic Inns, Directories, Guide Books.
4. Hotel Accommodations - Bed & Breakfast Inns, Directories, Guide Books.
5. Hotel Accommodations - United States, Directories, Guide Books.
I. Title. II Author. III Bed & Breakfast, The Official Guide to American Historic Inns

ISBN: 1-888050-07-1
Softcover
Printed in the United States of America.
10 9 8 7 6 5 4 3 2 1

Contents

How To Use This Book

Welcome! You hold in your hands the most comprehensive collection of our nation's best historic bed & breakfast and country inns. Most were built in the 17th, 18th or 19th centuries, but a few inns from the early 20th century have been included. The National Register of Historic Places requires that buildings be constructed prior to 1940 in order to gain historic standing, and we follow this guideline as well.

When you stay at a historic inn, not only do you enjoy a unique getaway, you also promote and support the preservation of our nation's architectural and cultural heritage. Most of these homes are owned privately and have been restored with the private funds of individual families. They are maintained and improved by revenues collected from bed & breakfast guests.

With a few exceptions, we have omitted homestays. These are B&Bs with only one or two rooms, often operated casually or as a hobby.

Accommodations

Among the listings, you'll find B&Bs and country inns in converted schoolhouses, lighthouses, 18th-century farmhouses, Queen Anne Victorians, adobe lodges and a variety of other unique places, both new and old.

The majority of inns included in this book were built in the 17th, 18th, 19th or early 20th centuries. We have stated the date each building was constructed at the beginning of each description. Many of the inns are steeped in the traditions of Colonial America, the Victorian Era, The Civil War, Spanish colonization or the Old West. Many are listed in the National Register of Historic Places.

A Variety of Inns

A **Country Inn** generally serves both breakfast and dinner and may have a restaurant associated with it. Many have been in operation for years, some since the 18th century as you will note in our "Inns of Interest" section. Although primarily found on the East Coast, a few country inns are in other regions of the nation.

A **Bed & Breakfast** facility's primary focus is lodging. It can have from three to 20 rooms or more. The innkeepers often live on the premises. Breakfast usually is the only meal served and can be a full-course, gourmet breakfast or a simple buffet. B&B owners often pride themselves on their culinary skills.

As with country inns, many B&Bs specialize in providing historic, romantic or gracious atmospheres with amenities such as canopied beds, fireplaces, spa tubs, afternoon tea in the library and scenic views.

Some give great attention to recapturing a specific historic period, such as the Victorian or Colonial eras. Many display antiques and other furnishings from family collections.

A **Homestay** is a room available in a private home. It may be an elegant stone mansion in the best part of town or a charming country farm. Homestays have one to three guest rooms. Because homestays are often operated as a hobby-type business and open and close frequently, only a very few such properties are included in this publication.

A Note About Innkeepers

Your innkeepers are a tremendous resource. Most knowledgeable innkeepers enjoy sharing regional attractions, local folklore, area history, and pointing out favorite restaurants and other special features of their areas. Unlike hotel and motel operators, innkeepers often bring much of themselves into creating an experience for you to long remember. Many have personally renovated historic buildings, saving them from deterioration and often, the bulldozer. Others have infused their inns with a unique style and personality to enliven your experience with a warm and inviting environment.

Area Codes

Although we have made every effort to update area codes throughout the book, new ones pop up from time to time. The phone companies provide recordings for several months after a change, but beyond that point, it can be difficult to reach an inn or B&B. Although they are listed by state or province, the new codes were added only in certain sections of the state or province. For example, the new 858 area code in California applies only to certain areas just outside of San Diego.

The following list includes the most recent area code changes that were available at press time.

State/Province	Old Code	New Code	Effective Date of Change
Alberta	403	780	1/25/99
Arizona	602	480	3/1/99
Arizona	602	623	3/1/99
California	805	661	2/13/99
California	619	858	6/12/99
California	909	951	2/12/00
California	619	935	6/10/00
California	760	442	10/21/00
Florida	941	863	9/20/99
Florida	407	321	11/1/99
Georgia	912	229	8/1/00
Georgia	912	478	8/1/00
Kentucky	502	270	4/19/99
Kentucky	606	859	4/1/00
Louisiana	318	337	10/11/99
Michigan	616	231	6/5/99
Michigan	517	989	8/19/00
Minnesota	612	763	2/15/00
Minnesota	612	952	2/15/00
Mississippi	601	662	5/19/00
Missouri	314	636	5/22/99
New Jersey	609	856	6/12/99
New York	516	631	11/1/99
Tennessee	423	865	11/1/99
Texas	512	361	2/13/99
Texas	409	936	2/1/00
Texas	409	979	2/1/00
Wisconsin	414	262	9/25/99

How to Use This Book

Note: We try to keep the use of codes to a minimum, but they help create a more comprehensive listing for each of the inns and B&Bs. We encourage you to read this entire section, as it will help plan a getaway that is just right for you.

Baths

Not all bed & breakfasts and country inns provide a private bath for each guest room. We have included the number of rooms and the number of private baths in each facility. The code "PB," indicates how many guest rooms include a private bath. If you must have a private bath, make sure the room

reserved for you provides this facility. If a listing indicates that there are suites available, assume that a suite includes a private bath. Most cottages also include a private bath, sometimes more than one, but be sure to inquire with the innkeeper about facilities in these units.

Beds

K, Q, D, T indicates King, Queen, Double or Twin beds available at the inn.

Children

Many innkeepers go out of their way to provide a wonderful atmosphere for families. In fact, more and more inns are catering to families.

However, this is always a sensitive subject. We do not list whether children are allowed at inns or B&Bs in this guide because it is illegal in several states to discriminate against persons of any age. Occasionally innkeepers do "discourage" children as guests. Some innkeepers consider their inn a place for romance or solitude, and often do not think younger guests fit into this scheme. Also, many inns are filled with fine antiques and collectibles, so it may be an inappropriate place for very small children. Some innkeepers discourage children simply because they are not set up to accommodate the needs of a family. If you plan to bring your children, always ask your innkeeper if children are welcome, and if so, at what age.

Meals

Continental breakfast: Coffee, juice and toast or pastry.

Continental-plus breakfast: A continental breakfast plus a variety of breads, cheeses and fruit.

Full breakfast: Coffee, juice, breads, fruit and an entree.

Full gourmet breakfast: May be a four-course candlelight offering or especially creative cuisine.

Vegetarian breakfast: Entrees can cater to special vegetarian diets and are created without meat.

Country breakfast: Hearty country fare may include fresh farm eggs gathered on the premises or sausages and cheeses made in the area.

Gourmet lunch: Specially creative sandwiches, soups or other items not normally found in a lunch box.

Gourmet dinner: May include several courses and finer cuisine, usually featuring local produce, fish, fowl, etc. prepared with creative flair.

Teas: Usually served in the late afternoon with cookies, crackers or other in-between-meal offerings.

Meal Plans

AP: American Plan. All three meals may be included in the price of the room. Check to see if the rate quoted is for two people (double occupancy) or per person (single occupancy).

MAP: Modified American Plan. Breakfast and dinner may be included in the price of the room.

EP: European Plan. No meals are included. We have listed only a few historic hotels that operate on an EP plan.

Always find out what meals, if any, are included in the rates. Not every establishment in this guidebook provides breakfast, although most do. Please do not assume meals are included in the rates featured in the book. Occasionally, an innkeeper has indicated MAP and AP when she or he actually means that both programs are available and you must specify in which program you are interested.

Payments

MC: MasterCard
VISA
DS: Discover
AX: American Express
DC: Diner's Club
CB: Carte Blanche
TC: Traveler's Cheques
PC: Personal Checks

Pets Allowed

Under some listings, you will note that pets are allowed. Despite this, it is always wise to inform the innkeeper that you have a pet. Some innkeepers charge a fee for pets or only allow certain types and sizes of animals. The innkeeper also may have set aside a specific room for guests with pets, so if this room is booked, you may not be able to bring your pet along this trip.

Rates

Rates are usually listed in ranges, i.e., $45-105. The LOWEST rate is almost always available during off-peak periods and may only apply to the least expensive room. Rates are always subject to change and are not guaranteed. You should always confirm the rates when making the reservations. Rates for Canadian listings usually are listed in Canadian dollars. Rates are quoted for double occupancy.

Breakfast and other meals MAY or MAY NOT be included in the rates.

Minimum stays

Many inns require a two-night minimum stay on weekends. A three-night stay often is required during holiday periods.

Cancellations

Cancellation policies are individual for each bed & breakfast. It is not unusual to see 7- to 14-day cancellation periods or more. Please verify the inn's policy when making your reservation.

Rooms

Under some listings, you will note that suites are available. We typically assume that suites include a private bath.

Additionally, under some listings, you will note a reference to cottages. A cottage may be a rustic cabin tucked in the woods, a seaside cottage or a private apartment-style accommodation.

Fireplaces

When fireplaces are mentioned in the listing they may be in guest rooms or in common areas and are abbreviated as "FP." A few have fireplaces that are non-working because of city lodging requirements. Please verify this if you are looking forward to an evening in front of a crackling fire.

Historic Interest

Many of the inns included have listed items of historic interest nearby that guests can visit. To help you plan your trip, most of the inns also have included the distance to the sites of significant historic interest.

Smoking

The majority of country inns and B&Bs, especially those located in historic buildings, prohibit smoking; therefore, if you are a smoker, we advise you to call and specifically check with each inn to see if and how they accommodate smokers.

State maps

The state maps have been designed to help travelers find an inn's location quickly and easily. Each city shown on the maps contains one or more inns. As you browse through the guide, you will notice coordinates next to each city name, i.e. "C3." The coordinates designate the location of inns on the state map.

Media coverage

Some inns have provided us with copies of magazine or newspaper articles written by travel writers about their establishments and we have indicated that in the listing. Articles written about the inns may be available either from the source as a reprint, through libraries or from the inn itself. Also, TV coverage, catalogue and movie appearances are included.

Comments from guests

Over the years, we have collected reams of guest comments about thousands of inns. Our files are filled with these documented comments. At the end of some descriptions, we have included a guest comment received about that inn.

Descriptions

This book contains descriptions of more than 2,000 inns, and each establishment was reviewed carefully prior to being approved for this guide. Many inns and B&Bs were turned away from this guide because they did not meet our standards. We also do not allow innkeepers to write their own descriptions. Our descriptions are created from visits to the inns, interviews with innkeepers and from a bulk of other information, including ratings, guest comments and articles from top magazines and newspapers.

Inspections

Each year we travel across the country visiting inns. Since 1981, we have had a happy, informal team of inn travelers and prospective innkeepers who report to us about new bed & breakfast discoveries and repeat visits to favorite inns.

Although our staff usually sees hundreds of inns each year, inspecting inns is not the major focus of our travels. We visit as many as possible, photograph them and meet the innkeepers. Some inns are grand mansions filled with classic, museum-quality antiques. Others are rustic, such as reassembled log cabins or renovated barns or stables. We have enjoyed them all and cherish our memories of each establishment, pristine or rustic.

Only rarely have we come across a truly disappointing inn, poorly kept or poorly managed. This type of business usually does not survive because an inn's success depends upon repeat guests and enthusiastic word-of-mouth referrals from satisfied guests. We do not promote these types of establishments.

Traveler or tourist

Travel is an adventure into the unknown, full of surprises and rewards. A seasoned "traveler" learns that even after elaborate preparations and careful planning, travel provides the new and unexpected. The traveler learns to live with uncertainty and considers it part of the adventure.

To the "tourist," whether "accidental" or otherwise, new experiences are disconcerting. Tourists want no surprises. They expect things to be exactly as they had envisioned them. To tourists we recommend staying in a hotel or motel chain where the same formula is followed from one locale to another.

We have found that inngoers are travelers at heart. They relish the differences found at these unique bed & breakfasts and country inns. This is the magic that makes traveling from inn to inn the delightful experience it is.

What if the inn is full?

Ask the innkeeper for recommendations. They may know of an inn that has recently opened or one nearby but off the beaten path. Call the local Chamber of Commerce in the town you hope to visit. They may also know of inns that have recently opened. Please let us know of any new discoveries you make.

We want to hear from you!

We've always enjoyed hearing from our readers and have carefully cataloged all letters and recommendations. If you wish to participate in evaluating your inn experiences, use the Inn Evaluation Form in the back of this book. You might want to make copies of this form prior to departing on your journey.

We hope you will enjoy this book so much that you will want to keep an extra copy or two on hand to offer to friends and family. Many readers have called to purchase our books for hostess gifts, birthday presents, or for seasonal celebrations. It's a great way to introduce your friends to America's enchanting country inns and bed & breakfasts.

Visit us online!

Would you like more information about the inns listed in this book? For color photos, links to the inns' web sites and more, search our web site at **www.bnbinns.com**. You'll find thousands of inns from the United States and Canada. We think you'll agree it's *"the only online bed & breakfast guide you will ever need.™"*

How to Read an Inn Listing

Anytown ❶ G6

An American Historic Inn

❷ 123 S Main St
Anytown, VT 12345-6789
(123)555-1212 (800)555-1212 Fax:(123)555-1234
❸ E-mail: americaninn@mail.com
Web: www.americaninn.com

❹ **Circa 1897.** Every inch of this breathtaking inn offers something special. The interior is decorated to the hilt with lovely furnishings, plants, beautiful rugs and warm, inviting tones. Rooms include four-poster and canopy beds combined with the modern amenities such as fireplaces, wet bars and stocked refrigerators. Enjoy a complimentary

❺ full breakfast at the inn's gourmet restaurant. The chef offers everything from a light breakfast of fresh fruit, cereal and a bagel to heartier treats such as pecan peach pancakes and Belgium waffles served with fresh fruit and crisp bacon.

❻ **Historic Interest:** Indian Burial Grounds (15 miles), Fort Morgan (30 miles).

❼ Innkeeper(s): Andrew & Chaya Jordan. ❽ $125-195. ❾ MC VISA AX DS PC TC. ❿ TAC10. ⓫ 13 rooms with PB, 4 with FP. 1 suite. 1 conference room. ⓬ Breakfast and afternoon tea included in rates. MAP. ⓭ Types of meals: full breakfast, gourmet breakfast and early coffee/tea. Dinner, picnic lunch, gourmet lunch, banquet service, catering service and room service available. Restaurant on premises. ⓮ Beds: KQTC. ⓯ Phone, air conditioning, turndown service, ceiling fan, TV and VCR in room. Fax, copier and bicycles on premises. Handicap access. Antiques, fishing, parks, shopping, theater and watersports nearby.

⓰ Pets allowed: With prior approval, $50 deposit.

⓱ Publicity: *Beaufort, Southern Living, Country Inns, Carolina Style, US Air, Town & Country.*

⓲ *"A dream come true!"*

---

① *Map coordinates*
Easily locate an inn on the state map using these coordinates.

② *Inn address*
Mailing or street address and all phone numbers for the inn.

③ *E-mail and web address*
Many inns have included their e-mail and web addresses. Use the e-mail address to contact innkeepers regarding reservations or other questions. Often, additional information, including color photographs, can be found on the inn's web site.

④ *Description of inn*
Descriptions of inns are written by experienced travel writers based on visits to inns, interviews and information collected from inns.

⑤ *Drawing of inn*
Many listings include artistic renderings.

⑥ *Historic interest*
Indicates items of special historic significance near the inn's location.

⑦ *Innkeepers*
The name of the innkeeper(s).

⑧ *Rates*
Rates are quoted for double occupancy. The rate range includes off-season rates and is subject to change.

⑨ *Payment types accepted*
MC-MasterCard, VISA, DS-Discover, AX-American Express, DC-Diner's Club, CB-Carte Blanche, TC-Traveler's Check, PC-Personal Check.

⑩ *Travel agent commission*
Indicates the percentage an inn has agreed to offer a travel agent. Example: TAC10=10%

⑪ *Rooms*
Number and types of rooms available. PB-Private Bath FP-Fireplace

⑫ *Included meals*
Types of meals included in the rates. Also may list any meal plans offered by the inn. AP-American Plan, MAP-Modified American Plan, EP-European Plan

⑬ *Available meals*
This section lists the types of meals that the inn offers. These meals may or may not be included in the rates.

⑭ *Beds*
King, Queen, Double, Twin

⑮ *Amenities and activities*
Information included here describes other amenities or services available at the inn. Nearby activities also are included.

⑯ *Pets allowed*
Indicates the inn's policy on pets.

⑰ *Publicity*
Newspapers, magazines and other publications which have featured articles about the inn.

⑱ *Guest comments*
Comments about the inn from guests.

Alabama

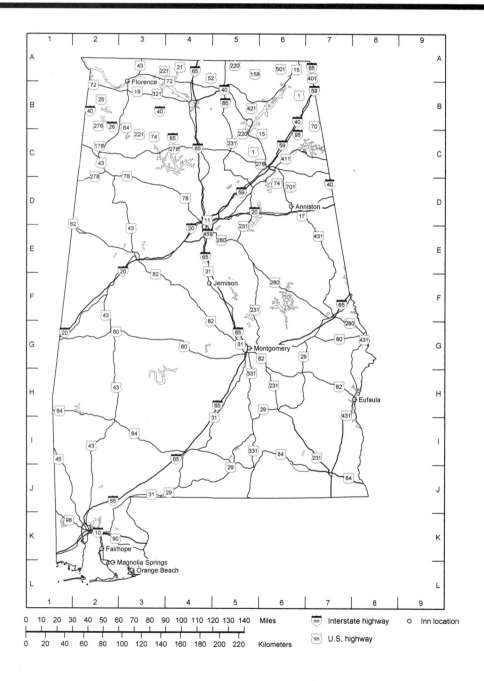

0 10 20 30 40 50 60 70 80 90 100 110 120 130 140 Miles

0   20   40   60   80   100 120 140 160 180 200 220 Kilometers

Interstate highway	○ Inn location
U.S. highway	

Anniston D6

The Victoria, A Country Inn & Restaurant

1604 Quintard Ave, PO Box 2213
Anniston, AL 36202-2213
(256)236-0503 (800)260-8781 Fax:(256)236-1138

Circa 1887. This Victorian estate, an Alabama landmark, occupies almost an entire square block on Quintard Avenue, Anniston's major thoroughfare. The first floor of the main house has four dining rooms, a piano lounge and a glass-enclosed veranda. The guest rooms the house are furnished with antiques, while those in the hotel feature reproduction  pieces. Covered walkways, verandas and gazebos flow among the massive hardwoods, gardens, courtyard and pool.

Innkeeper(s): Beth & Fain Casey, Jean Ann Oglesby. $79-319. MC, VISA, AX, DC, DS, TC. TAC10. 60 rooms with PB, 4 with FP, 1 cottage and 4 conference rooms. Breakfast included in rates. EP. Types of meals: Full gourmet bkfst, cont plus and early coffee/tea. Banquet service, catering service, catered breakfast and room service available. Restaurant on premises. Beds: KQD. Cable TV and phone in room. Air conditioning. VCR, fax, copier and swimming on premises. Handicap access. Weddings, small meetings, family reunions and seminars hosted. Amusement parks, antiquing, live theater, parks and shopping nearby.

Eufaula H8

Kendall Manor Inn

534 W Broad St
Eufaula, AL 36027-1910
(334)687-8847 Fax:(334)616-0678
E-mail: kmanorinn@mindspring.com
Web: www.bbonline.com/al/kendallmanor

Circa 1872. At night, the lights through the Italianate mansion's floor-to-ceiling windows promise a warm welcome. In the National Register, the home's elaborate facade includes columns around the veranda and etched ruby glass. Sixteen-foot ceilings, French gold-leaf cornices, gleaming wood floors, wallpapers, Oriental carpets and appropriate antiques create a comfortable yet elegant decor. Breakfast in the formal dining room may include poached pears in raspberry sauce, pumpkin apple bread, Sunrise Eggs and cranberry coffee cake. Candlelight dinners are available by advance reservation. You may wish to add your name along with those of guests as far back as 1894 onto the walls of the belvedere after enjoying a tour of the home by the gracious hosts.

Innkeeper(s): Barbara & Tim Lubsen. $99-149. MC, VISA, AX, DS, PC, TC. TAC10. 6 rooms with PB, 6 with FP. Breakfast included in rates. Types of meals: Full gourmet bkfst, cont plus and early coffee/tea. Afternoon tea and gourmet dinner available. Beds: KQD. Cable TV, phone, turndown service and ceiling fan in room. Air conditioning. Fax, copier, bicycles and library on premises. Weddings, small meetings, family reunions and seminars hosted. Antiquing, fishing, golf, bird watching, parks, shopping, tennis and water sports nearby.

Publicity: *Country Inns, Travel & Leisure, Southern Living.*

Fairhope K2

Bay Breeze Guest House

742 S Mobile St
Fairhope, AL 36533
(334)928-8976 Fax:(334)928-0360

Circa 1938. A white shell driveway leads to this gracious home, located on three acres of landscaped gardens of camellias and azaleas on Mobile Bay. A wide sandy beach and 462-foot private pier gives guests an unparalleled experience. The pier is popular for waterside picnics, naps, fishing, sunbathing and an occasional barbecue. Furnished with family heirlooms and period antiques, the rooms also offer stained glass, Oriental rugs and quilts. Guests are treated to bountiful breakfasts in view of pelicans in flight or diving into the bay. Southern hospitality is extended in a variety of ways throughout your stay.

Innkeeper(s): Bill & Becky Jones. $100-125. MC, VISA, AX, PC, TC. 4 rooms with PB and 1 cottage. Breakfast included in rates. Type of meal: Full bkfst. Beds: Q. Cable TV and ceiling fan in room. Air conditioning. VCR, fax, copier, swimming and bicycles on premises. Antiquing, fishing, golf, parks, shopping and water sports nearby.

Church Street Inn B&B

51 S Church St
Fairhope, AL 36532-2343
(334)928-8976 Fax:(334)928-0360

Circa 1921. Guests at Church Street choose from three bedchambers, each decorated with family antiques and heirlooms. The home, listed in the National Register, contains many original features, including a clawfoot tub in the Ashley Anne room. Breakfasts offer self-serve deluxe continental. Fairhope, a small town on Mobile Bay, offers a quaint downtown area with galleries, boutiques, antique shops and restaurants.

Innkeeper(s): Marisha Chavers. $85. MC, VISA, AX, PC, TC. 3 rooms with PB. Breakfast included in rates. Type of meal: Cont plus. Beds: KQ. Cable TV and ceiling fan in room. Air conditioning. Antiquing, fishing, golf, parks, shopping and water sports nearby.

Florence A3

Limestone Manor B&B

601 North Wood Ave
Florence, AL 35630
(256)765-0314 (888)709-6700 Fax:(256)765-9920

Circa 1915. Florence's mayor once owned this historic home, which is fashioned out of Alabama limestone. Among his notable guests were Humphrey Bogart, Thomas Edison and Henry Ford. Each has a guest room named in his honor. The

rooms are decorated with antiques, and two include a decorative fireplace. Mornings begin with a candle-lit breakfast. Fresh fruit is garnished with mint from the inn's garden. From there, a savory egg dish is accompanied by a grits soufflé, sausage and homemade baked goods. The National Register home is located in the Wood Avenue Historic district, surrounded by gracious homes and just down the road from the University of North Alabama. The town of Florence boasts more than 400 properties listed in the National Register.

Historic Interest: Helen Keller's birthplace (5 miles), W.C.Handy birthplace (1 mile).

Innkeeper(s): Bud & Lois Ellison. $72-95. MC, VISA, AX, PC, TC. TAC10. 3 rooms with PB and 2 suites. Breakfast and snacks/refreshments included in rates. Types of meals: Full bkfst, veg bkfst and early coffee/tea. Beds: Q. Cable TV and ceiling fan in room. Central air. VCR, fax, copier, library, video library and courtesy refrigerator on premises. Antiquing, art galleries, bicycling, canoeing/kayaking, fishing, golf, hiking, live theater, museums, parks, shopping, sporting events and water sports nearby.

Wood Avenue Inn

658 N Wood Ave
Florence, AL 35630-4608
(256)766-8441 Fax:(256)766-8467

Circa 1889. This historic Queen Anne Victorian was the first home in Florence to boast both indoor plumbing and electricity. The home, which encompasses nearly 6,000 square feet, maintains the original woodwork, a dozen original fireplaces, a grand staircase and many other period appointments. The interior is decorated in Victorian style with antiques and reproductions. Guests can select a room with a fireplace, and two of the bathrooms include a fireplace as

well. Outdoor weddings often are held on the half-acre grounds that include wisteria gardens and a courtyard. Guests enjoy a gourmet breakfast with items such as French toast topped with strawberries, crepes and omelets accompanied by homemade breads and tarts. The inn is less than two miles from the Tennessee River. The Natchez Trace Parkway is 12 miles away.

Historic Interest: Pope Tavern, Indian Mounds, W.C. Handy home, Helen Keller home.

Innkeeper(s): Gene & Alvern Greeley. $66-98. MC, VISA, TC. TAC10. 5 rooms, 4 with PB. Breakfast included in rates. Types of meals: Full gourmet bkfst and early coffee/tea. Gourmet dinner, picnic lunch, gourmet lunch, banquet service and catering service available. Beds: KQT. Air conditioning. Fax, copier and library on premises. Weddings, small meetings and family reunions hosted. Amusement parks, antiquing, art galleries, bicycling, fishing, golf, hiking, Florence Marina, live theater, museums, parks, shopping, sporting events, tennis and water sports nearby.

Jemison   F4

The Jemison Inn Bed & Breakfast and Gardens

212 Hwy 191
Jemison, AL 35085
(205)688-2055
E-mail: theinn@scott.net
Web: www.bbonline.com/al/jemison

Circa 1920. Shaded by tall oak trees, this gabled brick home offers flowers and fountains in the inn's gardens, created by the innkeeper, a certified Master Gardener. The arched, wraparound porch is furnished with white antique wicker and plants. Inside, heirloom quality, turn-of-the-century Victorian furnishings fill the rooms. There are marble top tables and collections of vintage musical instruments, Roseville and Waterford crystal. Whirlpool tubs are available, and an inviting swimming pool is open to guests in summer.

Innkeeper(s): Nancy Ruzicka. $75-135. MC, VISA, AX, DC, CB, DS, PC, TC. 3 rooms with PB. Breakfast included in rates. Type of meal: Full bkfst. Picnic lunch available. Beds: KQT. Cable TV, VCR and one whirlpool tub in room. Swimming on premises.

Publicity: *Southern Living, Birmingham News, Prime Time, Birmingham Post-Herald.*

"I've never had a better breakfast anywhere."

Magnolia Springs   L2

Magnolia Springs

14469 Oak St, PO Box 329
Magnolia Springs, AL 36555
(334)965-7321 (800)965-7321 Fax:(334)965-3035
E-mail: msbbdw@gulftel.com
Web: www.bbonline.com/al/magnolia

Circa 1897. A canopy of ancient oak trees line the streets leading to the Magnolia Springs bed & breakfast. Softly framed by more oaks, and in springtime, pink azaleas, the National Register inn with its dormers and spacious wraparound porch offers an inviting welcome. Warm hospitality enfolds guests in the Great Room with its pine walls and ceilings and heart pine floors, as well as the greeting from the innkeeper. Curly pine woodwork is found throughout the home, which was originally an area hotel. Guest rooms are appointed with a variety of carefully chosen antiques. Breakfast favorites often include pecan-topped French toast, bacon, grits, fresh fruit with cream dressing and blueberry muffins. Guests may also request a special breakfast to accommodate dietary needs. The innkeepers will recommend some memorable adventures, or simply stroll to Magnolia River and enjoy the area.

Historic Interest: Fairhope (15 miles), Fort Morgan (30 miles).

Innkeeper(s): David Worthington. $94-104. MC, VISA, AX, DS, PC, TC. 5 rooms, 4 with PB and 1 suite. Breakfast, afternoon tea and snacks/refreshments included in rates. Types of meals: Full bkfst and early coffee/tea. Beds: KQDT. Cable TV, phone, turndown service and ceiling fan in room. Central air. Fax and copier on premises. Weddings, small meetings and family reunions hosted. Amusement parks, antiquing, art galleries, beaches, canoeing/kayaking, fishing, golf, hiking, museums, parks, shopping and water sports nearby.

Pets allowed: sign waiver and answer pet questionnaire.

Publicity: *Southern Living.*

Montgomery
G5

Red Bluff Cottage B&B

551 Clay St, PO Box 1026
Montgomery, AL 36101-1026
(334)264-0056 (888)551-2529 Fax:(334)263-3054
E-mail: redblufbnb@aol.com
Web: www.bbonline.com/al/redbluff

Circa 1987. This raised cottage sits high above the Alabama River in Montgomery's historic Cottage Hill District. Guest rooms are on the first floor, while the kitchen, dining room, living room, sitting room and music room with piano and harpsichord are on the second floor. An upstairs porch has a panoramic view of the river plain, downtown Montgomery and the state Capitol building. Each of the guest rooms is furnished with family antiques.

Innkeeper(s): Anne & Mark Waldo. $75. MC, VISA, AX, DS, PC, TC. TAC10. 4 rooms with PB and 1 suite. Breakfast included in rates. Types of meals: Full bkfst and early coffee/tea. Beds: QT. Ceiling fan in room. Air conditioning. VCR, library and computer line on premises. Small meetings hosted. Antiquing, golf, ASF Theatre, Robert Trent Jones Golf Course, live theater, parks and shopping nearby.

"This was our first time to a bed & breakfast and I dare say it won't be our last after this wonderful experience."

Orange Beach
L3

The Original Romar House

23500 Perdido Beach Blvd
Orange Beach, AL 36561-3007
(334)974-1625 (800)487-6627 Fax:(334)974-1163

Circa 1924. From the deck of the Purple Parrot Bar, guests at this seaside inn can enjoy a cocktail and a view of the Gulf of

Mexico. Each of the guest rooms is named and themed after a local festival and decorated with authentic Art Deco furnishings. Stained and beveled glass windows add to the romantic atmosphere. A full Southern breakfast is served each morning, and in the evening, wine and cheese is served in the Purple Parrot Bar.

Innkeeper(s): Darrell Finley. $89-129. MC, VISA, AX, PC. TAC10. 6 rooms with PB, 1 suite, 1 cottage and 1 conference room. Breakfast included in rates. Type of meal: Full bkfst. Beds: Q. Turndown service and ceiling fan in room. Air conditioning. VCR, spa, swimming, bicycles and library on premises. Weddings, small meetings and family reunions hosted. Amusement parks, antiquing, fishing, night clubs, seafood restaurants, parks, shopping and water sports nearby.

Alaska

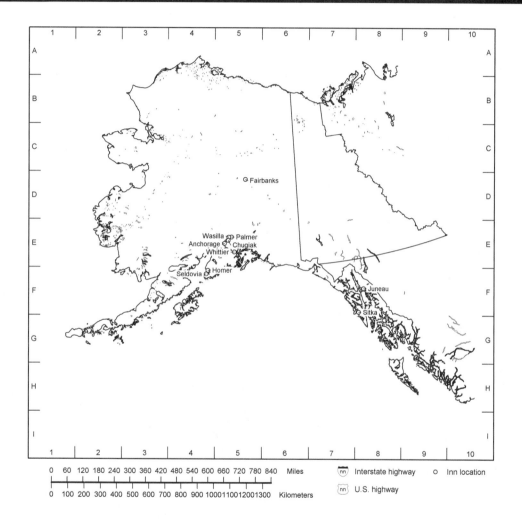

0   60 120 180 240 300 360 420 480 540 600 660 720 780 840   Miles

0   100 200 300 400 500 600 700 800 900 1000 1100 1200 1300   Kilometers

Interstate highway   Inn location

U.S. highway

Anchorage   E5

Alaskan Frontier Gardens

PO Box 24-1881, Hillside & Alatna
Anchorage, AK 99524-1881
(907)345-6556 Fax:(907)562-2923
E-mail: afg@alaska.net
Web: www.alaskaone.com/akfrontier

Circa 1982. Secluded on three scenic acres of woods, manicured lawns and gardens, this lodge-style home offers privacy,
yet is less than half an hour from downtown Anchorage by

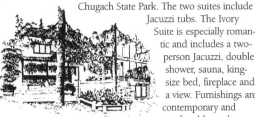

Chugach State Park. The two suites include
Jacuzzi tubs. The Ivory
Suite is especially romantic and includes a two-
person Jacuzzi, double
shower, sauna, king-
size bed, fireplace and
a view. Furnishings are
contemporary and
comfortable, and
guests are encouraged to enjoy the house and relax. Freshly
made Belgian waffles, reindeer sausage, gourmet coffee and
homemade pastries are often part of the breakfast fare.

Innkeeper(s): Rita Gittins. $75-175. MC, VISA, AX, DC, DS, PC, TC. TAC10.
3 rooms, 2 with PB, 1 with FP, 2 suites and 1 conference room. Breakfast
included in rates. Types of meals: Full gourmet bkfst and early coffee/tea.
Beds: KQDT. Cable TV, phone, ceiling fan and VCR in room. Fax, copier, spa,
sauna, library and pet boarding on premises. Handicap access. Weddings,
small meetings, family reunions and seminars hosted. Fishing, golf, parks,
shopping, downhill skiing, cross-country skiing and sporting events nearby.
Pets Allowed.

"A very beautiful spot and wonderful breakfasts."

Juneau   F8

Alaskan Hotel

167 S Franklin St
Juneau, AK 99801-1321
(907)586-1000 (800)327-9347 Fax:(907)463-3775

Circa 1913. This historic Victorian hotel is the oldest operating
hotel in town and was built by gold miners. The accommodations include rooms with private or shared baths and more spacious studios. In keeping with the hotel's Victorian architecture, the owners decorated the place in period style. The hotel
is listed in the National Register of Historic Places.

Innkeeper(s): Beltye Adams. $60-80. MC, VISA, AX, DS, PC, TC. TAC10. 43
rooms, 21 with PB. Beds: DT. Phone in room. Fax and copier on premises.
Small meetings hosted. Spanish and French spoken. Fishing, golf, shopping,
downhill skiing and cross-country skiing nearby.

Palmer   E5

Colony Inn

325 E Elmwood
Palmer, AK 99645-6622
(907)745-3330 Fax:(907)746-3330

Circa 1935. Historic buildings are few and far between in
Alaska, and this inn is one of them. The structure was built to
house teachers and nurses in the days when President

Roosevelt was sending settlers to Alaska to establish farms.
When innkeeper Janet Kincaid purchased it, the inn had been
empty for some time. She restored the place, including the
wood walls, which now create a cozy ambiance in the common areas. The 12 guest rooms are nicely appointed, and 10
include a whirlpool tub. Meals are not included, but the inn's
restaurant offers breakfast and lunch. The inn is listed in the
National Register.

Innkeeper(s): Janet Kincaid. $80. MC, VISA, AX, DS, PC, TC. TAC10. 12
rooms with PB. Type of meal: Full bkfst. Lunch available. Restaurant on
premises. Beds: QDT. Cable TV and phone in room. Handicap access.
Weddings, small meetings and family reunions hosted. Antiquing, fishing,
golf, parks, shopping, downhill skiing, cross-country skiing and tennis nearby.

"Love the antiques and history."

Seldovia   F4

Seldovia Rowing Club Inn

343 Bay St
Seldovia, AK 99663
(907)234-7614 Fax:(907)234-7514
E-mail: rowing@ptialaska.net
Web: www.ptialaska.net/~rowing/

Circa 1930. Majestic mountain peaks and crystal clear waters
serve as the scenery at this bed & breakfast, the first in south
central Alaska. The home is located on the historic Seldovia
boardwalk, just steps from the water. There are two guest
suites; each affords a water view. A full breakfast is delivered to

your room. Innkeeper Susan Mumma has been welcoming
guests for nearly 20 years. Seldovia offers many attractions,
including fishing, mountain biking, hiking, kayaking or just
enjoy the amazing scenery.

Innkeeper(s): Susan Mumma. $100. MC, VISA, AX, PC, TC. TAC5. 2 suites.
Breakfast included in rates. Type of meal: Full gourmet bkfst. Beds: Q. Cable
TV, phone and VCR in room. Library on premises. Handicap access.
Weddings and family reunions hosted. French and Spanish spoken. Fishing,
cross-country skiing and water sports nearby.
Publicity: *Alaska Magazine.*

Wasilla E5

Yukon Don's B&B Inn

1830 E Parks Hwy # 386, 2221 Yukon
Wasilla, AK 99654-7374
(907)376-7472 (800)478-7472 Fax:(907)376-7470

Circa 1971. Decorated with an Alaskan theme, this comfortable bed & breakfast boasts a second-floor room with a spectacular 360-degree view of the Matanuska Valley. Guests can

partake in the continental breakfast bar each morning and also enjoy use of a sauna and exercise room. The inn is about an hour from Anchorage and is on the direct route to Denali National Park, Fairbanks and Valdez. Among its distinctions, Wasilla is the home of the International Iditarod Dog Sled Race, the Reindeer Farm and the Matanuska and Knik glaciers.

Innkeeper(s): Yukon Don & Beverly Tanner. $75-125. MC, VISA, AX, DC, TC. TAC10. 7 rooms, 1 with FP, 3 suites, 1 cabin and 1 conference room. Breakfast included in rates. Types of meals: Cont plus and early coffee/tea. Beds: KQT. Cable TV, phone, ceiling fan, VCR and Moose Nugget Mints on pillow in room. Fax, copier, sauna and library on premises. Weddings, small meetings, family reunions and seminars hosted. Fishing, golf, parks, shopping, downhill skiing and cross-country skiing nearby.

Pets allowed: Limited.

Arizona

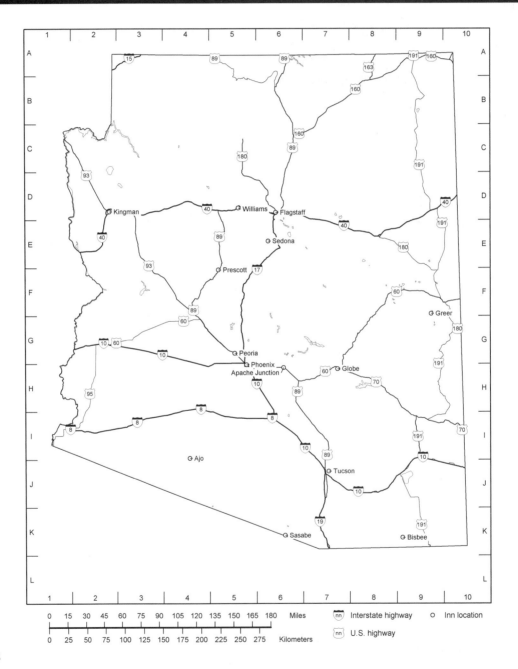

Ajo 14

The Mine Manager's House Inn B&B

601 W Greenway Dr
Ajo, AZ 85321
(520)387-6505 Fax:(520)387-6508

Circa 1919. Overlooking the Southwestern Arizona desert and a mile-wide copper mine pit, the Mine Manager's is a large Craftsman home situated on three acres. Built by the local copper mining industry, it has 10-inch-thick walls. A library, coin laundry and gift shop are on the premises. The Greenway Suite features a marble tub and shower, and one other room has two queen-size beds. A full breakfast is served in the formal dining room.

Historic Interest: The Organ Pipe Cactus Monument, Cabeza Prieta Wildlife Refuge.

Innkeeper(s): Jean & Micheline Fournier. $79-105. MC, VISA, TC. TAC10. 5 rooms, 2 with PB and 3 suites. Breakfast and snacks/refreshments included in rates. Type of meal: Full bkfst. Beds: QT. TV, phone and ceiling fan in room. Air conditioning. VCR, fax and spa on premises. Handicap access. Small meetings and family reunions hosted. French spoken. Parks and shopping nearby.

"The hospitality is what makes this place so inviting! A palace at the top of the hill with service to match."

Bisbee K9

Bisbee Grand Hotel, A B&B Inn

61 Main Street, Box 825
Bisbee, AZ 85603
(520)432-5900 (800)421-1909
Web: www.bisbeegrand.com

Circa 1906. This National Register treasure is a stunning example of an elegant turn-of-the-century hotel. The hotel originally served as a stop for mining executives, and it was restored back to its Old West Glory in the 1980s. Each of the rooms is decorated with Victorian furnishings and wall-coverings. The suites offer special items such as clawfoot tubs, an antique Chinese wedding bed, a fountain or four-poster bed. The Grand Western Salon boasts the back bar fixture from the Pony Saloon in Tombstone. After a full breakfast, enjoy a day touring the Bisbee area, which includes mine tours, museums, shops, antiquing and a host of outdoor activities.

Historic Interest: Located in downtown historic Bisbee, features 110-year-old back bar fixture.

Innkeeper(s): Bill Thomas. $55-175. MC, VISA, AX, DS. 9 rooms and 5 suites. Breakfast included in rates. Type of meal: Full bkfst.

Flagstaff D6

Inn at 410 B&B

410 N Leroux St
Flagstaff, AZ 86001-4502
(520)774-0088 (800)774-2008 Fax:(520)774-6354
E-mail: info@inn410.com
Web: www.inn410.com

Circa 1894. This inn, once the stately family residence of a wealthy banker, businessman and cattle rancher, has been fre-

quented over the years by travelers interested in exploring the Grand Canyon. Today, guests enjoy hospitality, outstanding cuisine and a wonderful home base from which to enjoy Northern Arizona. Each of the guest rooms is individually decorated in a unique style. Eight of the guest rooms include a fireplace, and some offer an oversized Jacuzzi tub. Award-winning recipes are featured during the gourmet breakfasts, and afternoon cookies and tea are served in the dining room. A two-block walk takes guests to shops, galleries and restaurants in historic downtown Flagstaff. Sedona, Native American sites and the San Francisco Peaks are nearby.

Historic Interest: Riordan Mansion State Park and Lowell Observatory both are located in Flagstaff. Wupatki National Monument (Anasazi Indian Ruins) is 35 miles away. Hopi and Navajo Indian Reservations are within 45 to 100 miles away. Walnut Canyon National Monument (Sinaqua Indian ruins) is seven miles away.

Innkeeper(s): Howard & Sally Krueger. $125-175. MC, VISA, PC, TC. TAC10. 9 rooms with PB, 8 with FP and 4 suites. Breakfast and snacks/refreshments included in rates. Type of meal: Full gourmet bkfst. Beds: KQT. Ceiling fan, coffee and tea in room. Air conditioning. Library on premises. Antiquing, hiking, museums, observatory, live theater, parks, shopping, downhill skiing and cross-country skiing nearby.

Comfi Cottages

1612 N Aztec St
Flagstaff, AZ 86001-1106
(520)774-0731 (888)774-0731 Fax:(520)779-1008
E-mail: pat@comficottages.com
Web: www.comficottages.com

Circa 1920. Each of the six cottages has been thoughtfully decorated and features a variety of styles. One cottage is decorated in a Southwestern motif, while the others feature antiques and English-Country decor. Five cottages include fireplaces, and all include kitchens stocked with full equipment and all staples. They also have the added luxury of a washer and dryer. Bicycles are available for guest use, as well as picnic tables, a barbecue grill and picnic baskets. The Grand Canyon and national parks are close by, and the cottages are in the perfect location to enjoy all Flagstaff has to offer.

Historic Interest: The cottages are located near the many activities available in historic downtown Flagstaff. Several Indian ruins are within 50 miles of the cottages.

Innkeeper(s): Ed & Pat Wiebe. $105-210. MC, VISA, DS, PC. TAC10. 6 cottages, 5 with PB. Breakfast and snacks/refreshments included in rates. Type of meal: Full bkfst. Beds: KQDT. Cable TV, phone, ceiling fan, VCR and air conditioning in two cottages in room. Air conditioning. Bicycles, picnic table and BBQ on premises. Handicap access. Small meetings, family reunions and seminars hosted. French spoken. Antiquing, fishing, golf, indian ruins, live theater, parks, shopping, downhill skiing, cross-country skiing, sporting events, tennis and water sports nearby.

Pets allowed: Call and discuss pet with innkeeper prior.

Publicity: *Arizona Republic, Arizona Daily Sun.*

"A delightful stay; and the view of the San Francisco Peaks was gorgeous."

Globe H7

The Foothills B&B

Rt 1 Box 25B
Globe, AZ 85501
(520)425-9422

Circa 1880. Located on more than 72 acres, Foothills B&B was originally built in the 1880s as a copper mining building for managers. It was taken apart board by board and labeled, carted and painstakingly rebuilt on this property in 1920 by the

owner's grandfather. The house is rented to only one party at a time, and since the owners live elsewhere, guests have seclusion and privacy. There's a fireplace, king bed and large porch overlooking the grounds. Breakfast is stocked in the kitchen for your own preparation and includes muffins, juice, cereal, fresh fruit, coffee and cookies. Your horses are welcome to come along and are accommodated in a fenced area, but you need to bring feed.
Historic Interest: Indian Ruins (3 miles), Tonto Ruins National Park (25 miles).
Innkeeper(s): Barbara & Stan Parker. $75. PC, TC. TAC10. 3 rooms and 1 guest house. Breakfast included in rates. Type of meal: Cont. Beds: KD. TV, phone and VCR in room. Central air. Bicycles on premises. Antiquing, bicycling, golf, hiking, horseback riding and shopping nearby.

Gold Canyon H6

Sinelli's B&B

5605 S Sage Way
Gold Canyon, AZ 85219-6872
(408)983-3650 Fax:(480)983-3650

Circa 1981. This B&B is in a Southwest modern style and is located east of Phoenix in the foothills of Superstition mountains. There are hiking trails and riding stables nearby. Both suites and apartments are available. The innkeepers are specialists in alternative building methods and offer this experience in the accommodations. Restaurants and a golf resort are in the area.
Innkeeper(s): Carl & Patricia Sinelli. $55-100. TAC10. 6 rooms, 4 with PB and 2 guest houses. Beds: QT. Cable TV, phone, ceiling fan, VCR and totally furnished apartments in room. Central air. Fax and spa on premises.

Greer F9

White Mountain Lodge

PO Box 143
Greer, AZ 85927-0143
(520)735-7568 Fax:(520)735-7498

Circa 1892. This 19th-century lodge affords views of Greer meadow and the Little Colorado River. The guest rooms are individually decorated in a Southwestern or country style. The common rooms are decorated with period antiques, Southwestern art and Mission-style furnishings. The Lodge's living room is an ideal

place to relax with its stone fireplace. While dining on the hearty breakfasts, guests not only are treated to entrees that range from traditional country fare to the more gourmet, they also enjoy a view from the picture window. The cookie jar is always filled with homemade goodies and hot drinks are available throughout the day. Small pets are allowed, although certain restrictions apply. The inn is near excellent hiking trails.
Innkeeper(s): Charles & Mary Bast. $85-115. MC, VISA, AX, DC, DS, PC, TC. 7 rooms with PB, 1 with FP, 1 suite and 6 cottages. Breakfast and snacks/refreshments included in rates. Types of meals: Full bkfst and early coffee/tea. Beds: KQDT. Jetted tubs in room. VCR, fax, copier and library on premises. Small meetings and family reunions hosted. Spanish spoken. Antiquing, fishing, great mountain hiking trails, shopping, downhill skiing and cross-country skiing nearby.
Pets allowed: One small pet per unit. Must not be left unattended in room.

Kingman D2

Hotel Brunswick

315 E Andy Devine Ave
Kingman, AZ 86401
(520)718-1800 Fax:(520)718-1801
E-mail: rsvp@hotel-brunswick.com
Web: www.hotel-brunswick.com

Circa 1909. Built at the turn of the 20th century, the Hotel Brunswick was, for awhile, the tallest building in three counties. The hotel was built to accommodate the many railroad passengers who traveled through Kingman. Later in the century, the hotel fell into disrepair until the current owners purchased the property, restoring the historic charm. Each of the guest rooms has been appointed individually. Rooms range from the spacious honeymoon suite to the cozy, economical Cowboy and Cowgirl rooms. In addition to the accommodations, the hotel includes a European-style café, Mulligan's Bar, and a full-service business center. Your hosts can arrange a massage service or create a honeymoon package with flowers and champagne. Kingman, a stop along the famed Route 66, maintains many historic buildings and sites.
Historic Interest: Historic Kingman, downtown.
$50-95. MC, VISA, AX, DC, DS, TC. TAC10. 24 rooms, 7 with PB and 8 suites. Breakfast included in rates. AP. Types of meals: Full bkfst, cont plus and early coffee/tea. Gourmet dinner and banquet service available. Restaurant on premises. Beds: QDT. Cable TV, phone and VCR in room. Air conditioning. Fax and copier on premises. Handicap access. Weddings, small meetings, family reunions and seminars hosted. French and German spoken. Antiquing, canoeing/kayaking, fishing, golf, hiking, horseback riding, ghost towns, museums, parks, shopping and water sports nearby.
Pets allowed: seeing eye dogs only.

Phoenix H5

Maricopa Manor

15 W Pasadena Ave
Phoenix, AZ 85013
(602)274-6302 (800)292-6403 Fax:(602)266-3904
E-mail: mmanor@getnet.com
Web: www.maricopamanor.com

Circa 1928. The secluded Maricopa Manor stands amid palm trees on an acre of land. The Spanish-style house features four graceful columns in the entry hall, an elegant living room with a marble mantel and a music room. The spacious suites are decorated with satins, lace, antiques and leather-bound books. Guests may relax on the deck, on the patio, by the pool or in the gazebo spa.

Historic Interest: Arizona Biltmore Resort (2 miles), Heard Museum (3 miles), Pueblo Grand Indian Ruins and Museum.

Innkeeper(s): Mary Ellen & Paul Kelley. $89-229. MC, VISA, AX, DS, PC, TC. TAC10. 6 suites, 3 with FP. Breakfast included in rates. Type of meal: Cont plus. Beds: KQ. Cable TV, phone, ceiling fan and VCR in room. Air conditioning. Fax, copier, spa, swimming and library on premises. Handicap access. Spanish spoken. Amusement parks, antiquing, golf, live theater, parks, shopping, sporting events, tennis and water sports nearby.

"I've stayed 200+ nights at B&Bs around the world, yet have never before experienced the warmth and sincere friendliness of Maricopa Manor."

Prescott   F5

Dolls & Roses B&B

109 N Pleasant St
Prescott, AZ 86301
(520)776-9291 (800)924-0883 Fax:(520)778-2642

Circa 1883. Each of the guest rooms at this historic Victorian is decorated with a rose theme. The English Rose is a spacious room with a sitting area decorated with a loveseat and antique rocker. The Rose Garden has an antique clawfoot tub. In addition to the four rooms in the main house, guests can stay in the guest house. The historic home is decorated in Victorian style with antiques and a collection of porcelain dolls. A full breakfast is served each morning featuring specialty egg dishes, freshly baked pastries, homemade muffins and fresh fruit.

Innkeeper(s): Daryl & Pam O'Neil. $89-109. MC, VISA, PC, TC. TAC10. 5 rooms with PB, 1 cottage and 1 conference room. Breakfast included in rates. Types of meals: Full bkfst and cont. Snacks/refreshments available. Beds: KQ. Ceiling fan in room. Air conditioning. VCR on premises. Weddings, small meetings and family reunions hosted. Antiquing, art galleries, bicycling, fishing, golf, hiking, horseback riding, live theater, museums, parks, shopping, tennis and water sports nearby.

Juniper Well Ranch

PO Box 11083
Prescott, AZ 86304-1083
(520)442-3415

Circa 1991. A working horse ranch sits on the front 15 acres of this 50-acre, wooded property, which is surrounded by the Prescott National Forest. Guests are welcome to feed the horses, and children have been known to take a ride on a tractor with innkeeper David Bonham. Two log cabins and the ranch house sit farther back on the land where families can enjoy nature, "unlimited" hiking and seclusion. A summer house is available for ranch guests. It has no walls, a sloping roof with skylights and a fire pit. Guest pets, including horses, are welcome on an individual basis.

Innkeeper(s): David Bonham & Gail Ball. $100. MC, VISA, AX, DC, DS, PC, TC. TAC10. 3 cabins with PB, 3 with FP. Type of meal: Full bkfst. Beds: QDT. Ceiling fan and full kitchen in room. Stables, library, pet boarding, child care, working horse ranch, unlimited hiking, horse feeding and summer house on premises. Handicap access. Weddings, small meetings, family reunions and seminars hosted. Antiquing, fishing, golf, live theater, parks, shopping and cross-country skiing nearby.

Pets allowed: Well mannered guest pets, including horses, welcome on an individual basis.

Prescott Pines Inn

901 White Spar Rd
Prescott, AZ 86303-7231
(520)445-7270 (800)541-5374 Fax:(520)778-3665
E-mail: info@prescottpinesinn.com
Web: www.prescottpinesinn.com

Circa 1934. A white picket fence beckons guests to the veranda of this comfortably elegant country Victorian inn, originally the Haymore Dairy. There are masses of fragrant pink roses, lavenders and delphiniums, and stately ponderosa pines that tower above the inn's three renovated guesthouses, which were once shelter for farmhands. A three-bedroom, two-bath on-site chalet that sleeps up to eight guests is perfect for a family or group. Eight of the eleven rooms are equipped with kitchenettes and three have fireplaces. The acre of grounds includes a garden fountain and romantic tree swing. A full breakfast is offered at an additional charge.

Innkeeper(s): Jean Wu & Michael Acton. $65-249. MC, VISA. 11 rooms with PB, 3 with FP and 1 guest house. EP. Types of meals: Full bkfst and early coffee/tea. Beds: KQ. Cable TV, phone and ceiling fan in room. Air conditioning. Fax and copier on premises. Small meetings and family reunions hosted. Antiquing, hiking, hiking, live theater, parks and shopping nearby.

Publicity: *Sunset, Arizona Republic News, Arizona Highways.*

"The ONLY place to stay in Prescott! Tremendous attention to detail."

Sasabe   K6

Rancho De La Osa

PO Box 1
Sasabe, AZ 85633-0001
(520)823-4257 (800)872-6240 Fax:(520)823-4238
E-mail: osagal@aol.com
Web: www.guestranches.com/ranchodelaosa

Circa 1830. This adobe, whose 130,000 acres run along the Mexican border, provides a wondrous glimpse back to the old Southwest. The grounds, first settled by Jesuits in the late 17th century, feature a cantina built in the 1700s, as well as the main hacienda, which dates to the 1830s. The interior, with its exposed log beams, thick adobe walls and authentic decor, is reminiscent of Colonial Mexico. Each room includes a wood-burning fireplace. There is a spa, pool and trails for hiking, horseback riding and mountain biking where guests can enjoy the surrounding Buenos Aires National Wildlife Refuge. Rates include breakfast, a Southwestern lunch and dinner. The historic adobe has hosted such notable guests as Lyndon Johnson, Adlai Stevenson, Tom Mix and Margaret Mitchell.

$250-375. MC, VISA, DS, PC, TC. TAC10. 17 rooms with PB, 16 with FP, 6 suites and 2 conference rooms. Breakfast and dinner included in rates. AP. Lunch available. Beds: KQDT. Ceiling fan in room. VCR, fax, copier, swimming, stables, bicycles and library on premises. Weddings, small meetings and seminars hosted. Spanish spoken. Antiquing, bicycling, golf, hiking, horseback riding, live theater, parks, shopping, sporting events and tennis nearby.

Sedona
E6

Briar Patch Inn

3190 N Hwy 89A
Sedona, AZ 86336-9602
(520)282-2342 (888)809-3030 Fax:(520)282-2399
E-mail: briarpatch@sedona.net
Web: www.sedona.net/bb/briarpch

Circa 1943. Getting in touch with nature should come easy at this cluster of cottages found along the lush banks of Oak Creek and located three miles north of the town of Sedona. Fireplaces, shaded patios and privacy help guests relax along with massages offered in your own cottage. Each cottage is different in size, layout and unique decor, which includes Arizona Indian and Mexican art. Healthy breakfasts can be enjoyed by the fireplace in the lounge, on a tray in the cottages or creekside.

Throughout the year, small workshops in painting, Navajo weaving, Indian arts and other self-enrichment classes are given.

Innkeeper(s): Rob Olson. $149-295. MC, VISA, AX, PC, TC. TAC10. 17 cabins. Breakfast, afternoon tea and snacks/refreshments included in rates. Type of meal: Cont plus. Beds: KQT. Ceiling fan in room. Air conditioning. Fax, copier, swimming, library and BBQ area on premises. Weddings, small meetings, family reunions and seminars hosted. Amusement parks, antiquing, fishing, golf, parks, shopping, downhill skiing, cross-country skiing and tennis nearby.

Publicity: *Sedona Magazine, Sedona Visitor Guide.*

The Lodge at Sedona

125 Kallof Pl
Sedona, AZ 86336-5566
(520)204-1942 (800)619-4467 Fax:(520)204-2128
E-mail: lodge@sedona.net
Web: www.lodgeatsedona.com

Circa 1959. This charming lodge, surrounded by the natural wonders of Sedona's red rock and pine trees, was built by the town's first doctor to house his large family. Red rock walls and rough-hewn-beamed ceilings add to the rustic atmosphere of the lodge, which features a glassed-in morning porch, atrium and several fireplaces to enjoy. The grounds include gardens, sculptures and a labyrinth. Expansive, gourmet fare is served each morning, and hors d'oeuvres and desserts are provided later in the day for hungry guests. The Grand Canyon is a two-hour day trip, and the area offers many hiking trails and jeep tours of the surrounding canyons.

Historic Interest: Several Indian ruins are within 40 minutes of the lodge. Prescott, Arizona's first capital and an authentic Western town, is an hour away.

Innkeeper(s): Barb & Mark Dinunzio. $125-245. MC, VISA, AX, PC. TAC10. 14 rooms with PB, 12 with FP, 3 suites and 1 conference room. Breakfast and snacks/refreshments included in rates. Types of meals: Full gourmet bkfst and early coffee/tea. Picnic lunch available. Beds: KQT. Ceiling fan in room. Air conditioning. VCR, fax, copier and library on premises. Handicap access. Small meetings, family reunions and seminars hosted. Antiquing, fishing, live theater, parks, shopping, downhill skiing and cross-country skiing nearby.

Publicity: *Arizona Republic, Sedona, Red Rock News, San Francisco Examiner, Country Register, New York Post, Sedona, Bon Appetit, Mountain Living, Sunset.*

"What a wonderful hideaway you have! Everything about your inn was and is fantastic! The friendly service made me feel as if I was home. More importantly, the food made me wish that was my home!"

Tucson
J7

Casa Alegre B&B

316 E Speedway Blvd
Tucson, AZ 85705-7429
(520)628-1800 (800)628-5654 Fax:(520)792-1880

Circa 1915. Innkeeper Phyllis Florek decorated the interior of this Craftsman-style home with artifacts reflecting the history of Tucson, including Native American pieces and antique mining

tools. Wake to the aroma of fresh coffee and join other guests as you enjoy fresh muffins, fruit and other breakfast treats, such as succulent cheese pancakes with raspberry preserves. The Arizona sitting room opens onto serene gardens, a pool and a Jacuzzi. An abundance of shopping and sightseeing is found nearby.

Historic Interest: The innkeeper serves on the board of directors of the West University Historic District and is full of information about historic sites and the history of the area.

Innkeeper(s): Phyllis Florek. $60-125. MC, VISA, DS, PC, TC. TAC10. 5 rooms with PB, 1 with FP and 1 conference room. Breakfast included in rates. Type of meal: Full gourmet bkfst. Beds: KQ. TV and ceiling fan in room. VCR, fax, spa and swimming on premises. Weddings, small meetings and family reunions hosted. Antiquing, live theater, parks, shopping and sporting events nearby.

"An oasis of comfort in Central Tucson."

Catalina Park Inn

309 E 1st St
Tucson, AZ 85705-7821
(520)792-4541 (800)792-4885

Circa 1927. Classical music sets the mood as guests linger in front of a roaring fireplace at this inn, located in Tucson's West University Historic District. The main house offers a spacious room with mountain views and two rooms with private porches that overlook Catalina Park. Colorful rooms are furnished with antiques and other unique pieces. A bounty of patterned linens, down pillows and comforters dress the beds. The inn is just a few blocks from the University of Arizona and the eclectic shops and restaurants that line Fourth Avenue.

Historic Interest: The San Javier Mission is 10 miles away as is a national park. Closer attractions include the El Presidio and Barrio Historic Districts only a mile away, and the Arizona Historical Society Museum, which is only five blocks from the inn.

Innkeeper(s): Paul Richard & Mark Hall. $75-124. MC, VISA, AX, DS, TC. TAC10. 6 rooms with PB. Breakfast and afternoon tea included in rates. Types of meals: Full gourmet bkfst and early coffee/tea. Beds: Q. Cable TV, phone, robes, hairdryers and iron and ironing board in room. Air conditioning. Fax on premises. Antiquing, live theater, parks and sporting events nearby.

"Our stay here in your beautiful home was wonderful and your hospitality was unsurpassed. Can't wait to return!"

The Congenial Quail Bed & Breakfast

4267 N Fourth Ave
Tucson, AZ 85705-1701
(520)887-9487 (800)895-2047

Circa 1940. At this bed & breakfast, guests can enjoy a soak in the hot tub, rest in a hammock or stroll around the three-acre grounds and watch the sun set. The home features Mexican tile floors and Southwestern decor. Each of the guest quarters is decorated with a different theme in mind. The innkeepers offer bedrooms in the main house, as well as two cottages. Breakfasts feature spicy items such as a Southwestern-style frittata. The Tucson area offers historic sites, shopping and many other unique attractions.

Innkeeper(s): Laurie & Bob Haskett. $65-125. MC, VISA, PC, TC. TAC10. 4 rooms, 2 with PB and 2 cottages. Breakfast and snacks/refreshments included in rates. Types of meals: Full gourmet bkfst and early coffee/tea. Gourmet dinner, picnic lunch and lunch available. Beds: KQDT. Turndown service and ceiling fan in room. Air conditioning. VCR, spa and library on premises. Handicap access. Weddings, small meetings, family reunions and seminars hosted. Antiquing, golf, arts district, world-class museums, live theater, parks, shopping, sporting events and tennis nearby.

The El Presidio B&B Inn

297 N Main Ave
Tucson, AZ 85701-8219
(520)623-6151 (800)349-6151

Circa 1886. The cobblestone courtyards, fountains, and lush gardens surrounding El Presidio are filled with an old-world Southwestern ambiance. The inn is comprised of a Victorian-

Territorial adobe built around a traditional zaguan, or large central hall, plus separate suites in the former carriage house and gate house. Innkeepers Jerry and Patti Toci conducted a 10-

year, award-winning restoration of this inn. Rooms are immaculate, romantic and richly appointed. Gourmet breakfasts are served in a dining room that overlooks the patio. Beverages are served throughout the day. This inn was voted the "Best B&B in Tucson" for 1995-96 and the "Best B&B in Southern Arizona" for 1998. Restaurants and museums are nearby.

Innkeeper(s): Patti Toci. $95-125. 3 suites, 1 with FP and 1 conference room. Breakfast included in rates. Beds: Q. Bicycles on premises. Restaurants, museums, live theater and shopping nearby.

"Thank you again for providing such a completely perfect, pampering, relaxing, delicious, gorgeous vacation 'home' for us."

Hacienda del Sol Guest Ranch Resort

5601 N Hacienda del Sol
Tucson, AZ 85718-5129
(520)299-1501 (800)728-6514 Fax:(520)299-5554
E-mail: hdelsol@azstarnet.com
Web: www.haciendadelsol.com

Circa 1929. What began as a finishing school for girls became a hot spot for Hollywood royalty. In its earlier days as an exclusive resort, Hacienda del Sol hosted the likes of Clark Gable, Kathrine Hepburn and Spencer Tracy. Panoramic views include vistas of mountains, city lights and spectacular Arizona sunrises and sunsets. The lush grounds have a front courtyard with a fountain. Rooms are decorated to look like a Spanish

hacienda with Southwestern accents. Or stay in one of the three private casitas. There is a pool and a tennis court, and horseback riding is available year-round. Although no meals are included in the rates, there is an award-winning restaurant on the premises featuring regional cuisine at dinner. A Sunday brunch also is available.

Innkeeper(s): Steve Musatto. $75-345. MC, VISA, AX, PC, TC. TAC10. 30 rooms with PB, 7 with FP, 5 suites, 3 cottages and 3 conference rooms. Type of meal: Cont plus. Gourmet dinner and banquet service available. Restaurant on premises. Beds: KQD. Cable TV and phone in room. Air conditioning. Fax, copier, spa, swimming, stables, tennis and library on premises. Handicap access. Weddings, small meetings, family reunions and seminars hosted. Antiquing, golf, hiking, 60 miles to Mexican border, parks, shopping and sporting events nearby.

Publicity: *Travel & Leisure, New York Times.*

La Posada Del Valle

1640 N Campbell Ave
Tucson, AZ 85719-4313
(520)795-3840 (888)404-7113 Fax:(520)795-3840

Circa 1929. This Southwestern adobe has 18-inch-thick walls, which wraparound to form a courtyard. Ornamental orange trees and lush gardens surround the secluded property. All the rooms have private entrances and open to the patio or overlook the courtyard and fountain. Furnishings include antiques and period pieces from the '20s and '30s. Breakfasts are served in a dining room that offers a view of the Catalina Mountains. The University of Arizona, University Medical Center, shops, dining and more all are within walking distance.

Innkeeper(s): Karin Dennen. $65-135. MC, VISA, PC, TC. TAC10. 5 rooms with PB and 1 cottage. Breakfast and afternoon tea included in rates. Type of meal: Full gourmet bkfst. Beds: KQT. Cable TV in room. Air conditioning. VCR, fax, library and off street parking on premises. Weddings, small meetings and family reunions hosted. German spoken. Antiquing, live theater, parks, shopping, downhill skiing and sporting events nearby.

The Peppertrees B&B Inn

724 E University Blvd
Tucson, AZ 85719-5045
(520)622-7167 (800)348-5763
E-mail: pepperinn@gci-net.com
Web: bbonline.com/az/peppertrees

Circa 1905. Inside this historic home, you will find English antiques inherited from the innkeeper's family. There is a patio filled with flowers and a fountain. Each of two newly built Southwestern-style guest houses features two bedrooms, two bathrooms, a kitchen, laundry and a private patio. Blue-corn pecan pancakes and Scottish shortbread are house specialties. Peppertrees is within walking distance to the University of Arizona, shops, theaters, museums and restaurants.

Innkeeper(s): Marjorie G. Martin. $75-175. MC, VISA, DS, PC, TC. 3 rooms with PB, 1 cottage and 2 guest houses. Breakfast included in rates. EP. Type of meal: Full gourmet bkfst. Gourmet dinner available. Beds: KQT. TV, phone and ceiling fan in room. Air conditioning. Weddings, small meetings and family reunions hosted. Hiking, live theater, museums, shopping and sporting events nearby.

"We have not yet stopped telling our friends what a wonderful experience we shared at your lovely home."

Arkansas

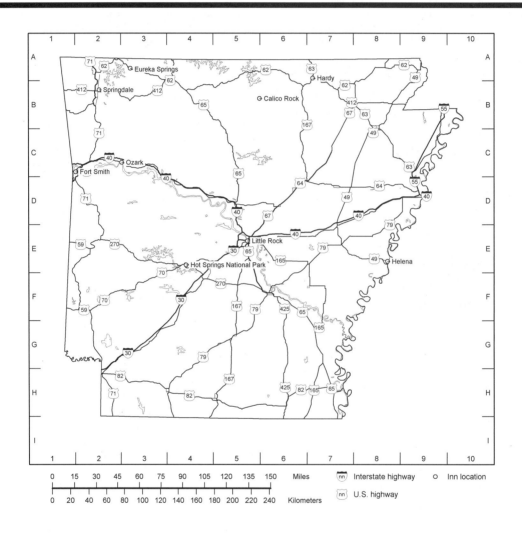

| | | | | | | | | | |
|1|2|3|4|5|6|7|8|9|10|

Eureka Springs
Springdale
Hardy
Calico Rock
Ozark
Fort Smith
Little Rock
Hot Springs National Park
Helena

Interstate highway   ○ Inn location
U.S. highway

0 15 30 45 60 75 90 105 120 135 150   Miles
0 20 40 60 80 100 120 140 160 180 200 220 240   Kilometers

Eureka Springs
A3

11 Singleton House B&B

11 Singleton St
Eureka Springs, AR 72632-3026
(501)253-9111 (800)833-3394

Circa 1895. This pink Queen Anne Victorian is highlighted with bird-shaped exterior brackets. Guest rooms are whimsically decorated with an eclectic collection of folk art and antique family treasures. Breakfast is served on the balcony overlooking a wildflower garden, lily-filled goldfish pond and scenic wooded view. Created by a local artist, the garden features a unique bird-house collection and winding stone paths. Guests may stroll one block down a wooded footpath to shops and restaurants, ride the trolley through town or enjoy a horse and carriage ride through the historic district.

Innkeeper(s): Barbara Gavron. $65-105. MC, VISA, AX, DS, PC, TC. 5 rooms with PB, 2 suites and 1 cottage. Breakfast and afternoon tea included in rates. Types of meals: Full breakfast and early coffee/tea. Beds: QDT. Air conditioning, ceiling fan and TV in room. Phone, fax, copier and library on premises. Antiquing nearby.

Publicity: Arkansas Gazette, The Houston Post, The Wichita Eagle-Beacon.

"All the many little surprises were so much fun. We enjoyed the quietness of sitting on the porch and walking through your garden."

1881 Crescent Cottage Inn

211 Spring St
Eureka Springs, AR 72632-3153
(501)253-6022 (800)223-3246 Fax:(501)253-6234

Circa 1881. This Victorian inn was home to the first governor of Arkansas after the Civil War. Two long verandas overlook a breathtaking valley and two mountain ranges. The home is graced by a beautiful tower, spindlework and coffered ceilings.

A huge arch joins the dining and living rooms, which, like the rest of the inn, are filled with antiques. Four of the guest rooms feature whirlpool spas, and two have a fireplace. The inn is situated on the quiet, residential street at the beginning of the historic loop. A five-minute walk into town takes guests past limestone cliffs, tall maple trees, gardens and refreshing springs. Try a ride on a horse carriage or on the steam engine train that departs nearby.

Historic Interest: Excluding a few new areas, the entire town of Eureka Springs is a National Historic District and filled with beautiful homes, buildings and shops to explore. The Crescent Cottage is listed in the National Register and designated as a state and city landmark.

Innkeeper(s): Ralph & Phyllis Becker. $97-145. MC, VISA, DS, PC, TC. TAC10. 4 rooms with PB, 2 with FP and 1 suite. Breakfast included in rates.

Types of meals: Full bkfst and early coffee/tea. Beds: Q. Cable TV, phone, ceiling fan, VCR and jacuzzi private to 2 rooms in room. Air conditioning. Fax, copier and spa on premises. Weddings and family reunions hosted. Spanish, some Portuguese and little German spoken. Amusement parks, antiquing, fishing, golf, hiking, boating, tennis, live theater, parks, shopping, sporting events and water sports nearby.

Publicity: Country Homes, Country Inns, Minneapolis Tribune, Fort Lauderdale News, America's Painted Ladies.

1884 Bridgeford House B&B

263 Spring St
Eureka Springs, AR 72632-3154
(501)253-7853 (888)567-2422 Fax:(501)253-5497

Circa 1884. Victorian charm abounds at this Queen Anne-Eastlake style home, located in the heart of the historic district. The Southern hospitality begins upon arrival as guests are treated to homemade pecan pralines. Fresh flowers add extra romance to rooms that include a variety of amenities. Several rooms include double jacuzzis, a fireplace and decks. Gourmet breakfasts are served on antique china and silver. The bed & breakfast is just a few blocks from gift boutiques, antique shops, spas, restaurants and much more. The innkeepers offer discounted rates for those who wish to enjoy a spa treatment.

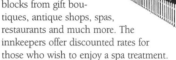

Historic Interest: Pea Ridge National Park (30 min.), War Eagle Mill & Cavern (30 min.), North Arkansas Railway (1 block).

Innkeeper(s): Henry & Linda Thornton. $85-145. MC, VISA, AX, DS. 4 rooms with PB and 1 suite. Breakfast included in rates. Types of meals: Full bkfst and early coffee/tea. Gourmet dinner, snacks/refreshments and room service available. Beds: KQ. Cable TV and fans in room. Air conditioning. VCR on premises. Weddings, small meetings, family reunions and seminars hosted. Antiquing, fishing, golf, live theater, shopping and water sports nearby.

"You have created an enchanting respite for weary people."

5 Ojo Inn B&B

5 Ojo St
Eureka Springs, AR 72632-3220
(501)253-6734 (800)656-6734 Fax:(501)253-8831

Circa 1900. Guests at 5 Ojo choose between lodging in cottages or in one of two restored Victorian homes, the Ojo House and the Sweet House. Rooms are decorated with antiques, but include modern amenities such as refrigerators and coffee makers. Several rooms include whirlpool tubs and fireplaces. The Carriage House Cottage and the Anniversary Suite are ideal places for honeymooners or those celebrating a special occasion. Among its romantic amenities, the Anniversary Suite includes a private porch with a swing. Gourmet breakfasts are served in the Sweet House's dining room, but private dining can be arranged.

Innkeeper(s): Paula Kirby Adkins. $72-139. MC, VISA, AX, DS, PC, TC.

TAC10. 10 rooms with PB, 6 with FP, 2 suites and 1 cottage. Breakfast included in rates. Type of meal: Full gourmet bkfst. Beds: QT. Cable TV, ceiling fan and whirlpool tubs in room. Air conditioning. VCR, fax, spa and library on premises. Weddings, small meetings and family reunions hosted. Antiquing, art galleries, fishing, golf, massage therapy, live theater, parks, shopping, sporting events and water sports nearby.

A Cliff Cottage & The Place Next Door, A Bed & Breakfast Inn

42 Armstrong St
Eureka Springs, AR 72632-3608
(501)253-7409 (800)799-7409
E-mail: cliffctg@aol.net
Web: www.cliffcottage.com

Circa 1892. In the heart of Historic Downtown, this Painted Lady Eastlake Victorian is listed in the National Register of Historic Places. A favorite among honeymooners, accommodations also are available in

a Victorian replica named The Place Next Door. Guest rooms include a double Jacuzzi, mini-refrigerator stocked with complimentary champagne and beverages, and all rooms have private decks. The inn offers gourmet candlelight dinners, Victorian picnic lunches and sunset dinner cruises served aboard a 24-foot pontoon boat, which explores the area's romantic coves. Guests enjoy golf and tennis privileges at Holiday Island, which is located five miles away. The inn recently received the "Garden of the Season" award.

Innkeeper(s): Sandra Smith. $120-195. MC, VISA, PC. TAC10. 5 rooms with PB, 1 with FP, 3 suites and 1 cottage. Breakfast included in rates. Types of meals: Full gourmet bkfst and early coffee/tea. Gourmet dinner, picnic lunch and gourmet lunch available. Beds: KQ. Cable TV, ceiling fan and VCR in room. Air conditioning. Library on premises. Weddings, small meetings, family reunions and seminars hosted. French, Spanish and German spoken. Amusement parks, antiquing, fishing, golf, live theater, parks, shopping, tennis and water sports nearby.

Pets allowed: small dogs only, $20 charge.

Publicity: *Arkansas Democrat Gazette, Country Inns, Modern Bride, Southern Living.*

The Arbour Glen B&B & Guesthouse

7 Lema St
Eureka Springs, AR 72632-3217
(501)253-9010 (800)515-4536

Circa 1879. One might say romance is in the air at Arbour Glen. Guest rooms are decorated in Victorian style with antiques, handmade quilts, luxurious linens and fresh flowers, which create a warm, intimate atmosphere. Some rooms also have double Jacuzzi tubs. There are wraparound verandas to enjoy, and from the porch swing, guests can take in a view of woods and the town's historic district. Gourmet breakfasts are served on the veranda on tables set with china and silver.

Innkeeper(s): Jeffrey Beeler. $85-125. MC, VISA, AX, DS, PC, TC. TAC10. 5 rooms with PB, 2 with FP, 3 suites and 2 cottages. Breakfast and afternoon tea included in rates. Types of meals: Full gourmet bkfst and cont plus. Beds: Q. Cable TV, ceiling fan and VCR in room. Air conditioning. Spa on premises. Weddings and family reunions hosted. Antiquing, fishing, golf, live theater, parks, shopping, sporting events and water sports nearby.

Arsenic & Old Lace B&B Inn

60 Hillside Ave
Eureka Springs, AR 72632-3133
(501)253-5454 (800)243-5223 Fax:(501)253-2246

Circa 1992. This bed & breakfast is a meticulous reproduction of Queen Anne Victorian style, and it offers five guest rooms decorated with antique Victorian furnishings. Popular with honeymooners, the guest rooms offer

whirlpool tubs, balconies and fireplaces. The inn's gardens complement its attractive exterior, which includes a wraparound veranda and stone wall. Its location in the historic district makes it an excellent starting point for a sightseeing stroll or shopping.

Innkeeper(s): Gary & Phyllis Jones. $125-160. MC, VISA, AX, DS, PC, TC. TAC10. 5 rooms with PB, 4 with FP and 2 suites. Breakfast and snacks/refreshments included in rates. Type of meal: Full gourmet bkfst. Beds: KQT. Cable TV, ceiling fan, VCR, private patios and robes in room. Air conditioning. Fax, copier and library on premises. Handicap access. Weddings, small meetings and family reunions hosted. Antiquing, fishing, golf, music festivals, car festivals, passion play, live theater, parks, shopping, tennis and water sports nearby.

Publicity: *Houston Chronicle, Kiplinger's Personal Finance Magazine, Oklahoma Living KLSM-TV.*

"It was well worth the 1,000 miles we traveled to share your home for a short while...thanks for a four-star vacation."

Basin Park Hotel

12 Spring St
Eureka Springs, AR 72632-3105
(501)253-7837 (800)643-4972 Fax:(501)253-6985
E-mail: info@basinpark.com
Web: www.basinpark.com

Circa 1905. This is a historic hotel, located in the heart of the historic downtown area, in a large multi-storied brownstone building that has operated continuously as a hotel for almost a century. Among the hotel's 61 rooms are both Jacuzzi suites and family rooms furnished with some antiques. A Continental breakfast is included in the rates, and the hotel has its own balcony restaurant.

Innkeeper(s): Marty & Elise Roenigk. $72-145. MC, VISA, AX, DS, PC, TC. TAC10. 61 rooms with PB and 28 suites. Breakfast included in rates. EP. Type of meal: Cont. Lunch, banquet service, catered breakfast and room service available. Restaurant on premises. Beds: KD. Cable TV, phone and ceiling fan in room. VCR, fax and copier on premises. Handicap access. Weddings, small meetings, family reunions and seminars hosted. Antiquing, fishing, golf, live theater, parks, shopping, tennis and water sports nearby.

Pets Allowed.

Candlestick Cottage

6 Douglas St
Eureka Springs, AR 72632-3416
(501)253-6813 (800)835-5184
E-mail: candleci@ipa.net
Web: www.candlestickcottageinn.com

Circa 1888. Woods and foliage surround this scenic country home, nestled just a few blocks from Eureka Springs historic district. Guests are sure to discover a variety of wildlife strolling by the home, including an occasional deer. Breakfasts are served on the tree-top porch, which overlooks a waterfall and fish pond. The morning meal begins with freshly baked muffins and fresh fruit, followed by an entree. Innkeepers Bill and Patsy Brooks will prepare a basket of sparkling grape juice and wine glasses for those celebrating a special occasion. Guest rooms are decorated in Victorian style, and some include two-person Jacuzzis.

Innkeeper(s): Bill & Patsy Brooks. $65-109. MC, VISA, AX, DS, TC. 6 rooms with PB. Breakfast included in rates. Type of meal: Full bkfst. Beds: Q. Cable TV and jacuzzi in room. Air conditioning. Weddings and small meetings hosted. Antiquing, fishing, parks and shopping nearby.

The Heartstone Inn & Cottages

35 King's Hwy
Eureka Springs, AR 72632-3534
(501)253-8916 (800)494-4921 Fax:(501)253-6821
E-mail: heartinn@ipa.net
Web: www.heartstoneinn.com

Circa 1903. Described as a "pink and white confection," this handsomely restored Victorian with its wraparound verandas is located in the historic district. The award-winning inn is filled

with antiques and artwork from the innkeeper's native England. Live music is featured: in May, a fine arts festival and in September, a jazz festival. Afternoon refreshments are available on the sunny deck overlooking a wooded ravine. Pink roses line the picket fence surrounding the inviting garden.

Historic Interest: Pea Ridge Civil War Battle Ground (20 miles), War Eagle Mill (20 miles).

Innkeeper(s): Iris & Bill Simantel. $73-129. MC, VISA, AX, DS, PC, TC. TAC10. 12 rooms with PB, 1 with FP, 3 suites and 2 cottages. Breakfast included in rates. Type of meal: Full gourmet bkfst. Beds: KQ. Cable TV and ceiling fan in room. Air conditioning. Fax, spa, massage therapy and gift shop on premises. Weddings, small meetings, family reunions and seminars hosted. Amusement parks, antiquing, fishing, golf, restaurants, live theater, parks, shopping and water sports nearby.

Publicity: *Innsider, Arkansas Times, New York Times, Arkansas Gazette, Southern Living, Country Home, Country Inns.*

"Extraordinary! Best breakfasts anywhere!"

Palace Hotel & Bath House

135 Spring St
Eureka Springs, AR 72632-3106
(501)253-7474
E-mail: phbh@ipa.net
Web: www.palacehotelbathhouse.com

Circa 1901. The Palace Hotel and Bath House has been extensively renovated. The lobby and guest rooms are furnished in Victorian antiques, recalling opulent turn-of-the-century beginnings. Each guest room has a double-sized water-jet tub and a wet bar. Built on the edge of a cliff, the hotel features a lower mineral-bath level. The bath house is equipped with original six-foot-long clawfoot tubs (whirlpool machines have been added), and the Victorian-era Eucalyptus steam barrels are still in service. Each tub is situated in a private alcove.

Innkeeper(s): Steve & Francie Miller. $135-155. MC, VISA, AX, DS. 8 rooms with PB. Type of meal: Cont plus. Beds: K. Spa on premises.

Publicity: *Country Home, Southern Living, Ladies Home Journal, The New York Times, USA Weekend, Washington Post.*

The Piedmont House B&B

165 Spring St
Eureka Springs, AR 72632-3151
(501)253-9258 (800)253-9258
E-mail: piedmont@ipa.net
Web: www.eureka-usa.com/piedmont

Circa 1880. An original guest book from the inn's days as a tourist home is a cherished item here. The Piedmont offers the best views in town and is listed in the National Register. The guest rooms are decorated with antiques and include private exits that lead to the wraparound porches where swings and rockers await. For guests booking a two-night, weekend stay, the innkeepers offer a special moonlight dinner on Friday nights.

Historic Interest: In National Register.

Innkeeper(s): Kathy & Vince DiMayo. $79-135. MC, VISA, AX. 10 rooms, 9 with PB and 1 suite. Types of meals: Full bkfst and early coffee/tea. Snacks/refreshments available. Beds: DT. TV, phone, ceiling fan and antique furnishings in room. Air conditioning. Weddings, small meetings, family reunions and seminars hosted. Amusement parks, antiquing, live theater and shopping nearby.

"Wonderful atmosphere and your personalities are exactly in sync with the surroundings."

Sleepy Hollow Inn

92 S Main
Eureka Springs, AR 72632
(501)253-5561 Fax:(501)253-5561
E-mail: jfdulcimer@aol.com
Web: members.aol.com/jfdulcimer/sleepyhollow

Circa 1904. This three-story Victorian cottage with gingerbread trim serves as an ideal accommodation for honeymooners or those in search of privacy and romance. The innkeepers, a dec-

orator and craftsman of fine musical instruments, showcase their talents and attention to detail in the inn's elegant decor. There are two bedrooms, including a luxurious main suite encompassing all of the second story, and a third-story guest room with a view of the area's limestone cliffs. For the ultimate in intimacy and seclusion, the entire cottage is offered to one or two couples at a time, so they are free to relax and enjoy the home as though it were their very own vacation home. A spacious, well-equipped kitchen is stocked with chilled Champaign, freshly baked pastries and other treats. Guests can soak in the antique clawfoot tub or snuggle up on the romantic porch swing. Red bud trees in a garden setting across from the historical museum shade the inn. Fine restaurants, galleries and shops and the trolley are a short walk away.

Historic Interest: Table Rock Lake (5 miles), Beaver Lake and White River in the Ozark Mountains.

Innkeeper(s): Lavonne. $110. MC, VISA, DS, PC. 2 rooms with PB and 1 suite. Types of meals: Cont and early coffee/tea. Snacks/refreshments available. Beds: D. Cable TV, phone, ceiling fan, VCR and private parking on grounds in room. Air conditioning. Call inn for details on premises. Antiquing, fishing, golf, vintage train rides, live theater, museums, parks, shopping and water sports nearby.

"Truly a delightful experience. The love and care going into this journey back in time is impressive."

Fort Smith
C2

Michael's Mansion

2900 Rogers Ave
Fort Smith, AR 72901-4230
(501)494-3700 (877)439-7147 Fax:(501)494-5674
E-mail: lynn@michaelsmansion.com
Web: www.michaelsmansion.com

Circa 1904. In the National Register, this massive three-story house (10,000 square feet) is a blend of Greek, Romanesque and Renaissance Revival architecture. Located on more than an acre, the inn is known locally as the Horace Franklin Rogers home. Guest rooms are named after the innkeeper's family and decorated accordingly. There are two honeymoon suites with whirlpool tubs for two. One of the suites offers a balcony, while the two-bedroom suite has a fireplace. On most days, a full breakfast is served.

Innkeeper(s): Michael & Lynnette "Lynn" Moore. $57-147. MC, VISA, AX, DC, CB, DS, TC. 5 rooms with PB, 1 with FP, 1 suite and 1 conference room. Breakfast included in rates. Type of meal: Full bkfst. Beds: QD. Cable TV, phone, ceiling fan and VCR in room. Air conditioning. Fax, copier and library on premises. Handicap access. Weddings, small meetings, family reunions and seminars hosted. Antiquing, fishing, golf, live theater, parks, shopping and tennis nearby.

The Olde Stonehouse B&B Inn

511 Main St
Hardy, AR 72542-9034
(870)856-2983 (800)514-2983 Fax:(870)856-4036
E-mail: oldestonehouse@centurytel.net
Web: www.bbonline.com/ar/stonehouse/

Circa 1928. The stone fireplace gracing the comfortable living room of this former banker's home is set with fossils and unusual stones, including an Arkansas diamond. Lace tablecloths, china and silver make breakfast a special occasion. Each room is decorated to keep the authentic feel of the Roaring '20s. The bedrooms have antiques and ceiling fans. Aunt Jenny's room boasts a clawfoot tub and a white iron bed, while Aunt Bette's room is filled with Victorian-era furniture. Spring River is only one block away and offers canoeing, boating and

fishing. Old Hardy Town caters to antique and craft lovers. The innkeepers offer "Secret Suites," located in a nearby historic home. These romantic suites offer plenty of amenities, including a Jacuzzi for two. Breakfasts in a basket are delivered to the door each morning. The home is listed in the National Register. Murder-mystery weekends, romance packages, golf, canoeing and fly-fishing are available.

Historic Interest: Olde Hardy Town 19th-Century commercial buildings (2 blocks), Old Court House and Jail (2 blocks), Railroad Station/Museum at Mammoth Springs (18 miles), vintage car museum.

Innkeeper(s): Peggy Volland. $69-125. MC, VISA, AX, DS, PC, TC. TAC10. 6 rooms with PB and 2 suites. Breakfast and snacks/refreshments included in rates. Types of meals: Full bkfst and early coffee/tea. Picnic lunch available. Beds: QDT. Phone and ceiling fan in room. Air conditioning. VCR, fax, copier, spa, bicycles, library, guest refrigerator and coffee service on premises. Small

meetings hosted. Antiquing, fishing, museums, fly fishing school and guide available, murder mystery weekends, live theater, parks, shopping and water sports nearby.

Publicity: *Memphis Commercial Appeal, Jonesboro Sun, Vacations.*

"For many years we had heard about 'Southern Hospitality' but never thought it could be this good. It was the best!"

Helena
E8

Edwardian Inn

317 S Biscoe
Helena, AR 72342
(870)338-9155 Fax:(870)572-9105

Circa 1904. In his book Life on the Mississippi, Mark Twain wrote, "Helena occupies one of the prettiest situations on the river." William Short, cotton broker and speculator, agreed and built his stately home here. The Edwardian Inn boasts a large rotunda and two verandas wrapping around both sides of the house. Inside are wood carpets and floor designs imported from Germany that are composed of 36 pieces of different woods arranged in octagon shapes. Polished-oak paneling and woodwork are set off with a Victorian-era decor.

Innkeeper(s): Olive Ellis. $65-95. MC, VISA, AX, DC, CB, DS, PC, TC. TAC10. 12 rooms with PB, 3 suites and 1 conference room. Breakfast included in rates. Types of meals: Full bkfst and early coffee/tea. Snacks/refreshments and catering service available. Beds: KQD. Cable TV, phone and ceiling fan in room. Air conditioning. VCR, fax, copier and library on premises. Handicap access. Weddings, small meetings, family reunions and seminars hosted. Antiquing, fishing, golf, live theater, parks and shopping nearby.

"The Edwardian Inn envelopes you with wonderful feelings, smells and thoughts of the Victorian era."

Hot Springs
E4

Vintage Comfort B&B Inn

303 Quapaw Ave
Hot Springs, AR 71901-5204
(501)623-3258 (800)608-4682
E-mail: btberg@ipa.net
Web: www.bbonline.com/ar/vintagecomfort

Circa 1907. This two-story Victorian provides large, comfortable rooms with a charming atmosphere. Honeymooners and romantics will appreciate a getaway package that includes champagne, roses, breakfast, and dinner and dancing on the Belle of Hot Springs. A trip to the Hot Springs Mountain Tower is also included. The Family Reunion Package includes the use of all four bedrooms.

Innkeeper(s): Bill F. Tanneberger. $65-90. MC, VISA, AX, PC, TC. TAC12. 4 rooms with PB. Breakfast and snacks/refreshments included in rates. Type of meal: Full bkfst. Catering service available. Beds: QT. VCR and fax on premises. Weddings, small meetings, family reunions and seminars hosted. Antiquing, fishing, hot mineral baths, live theater, parks, shopping and water sports nearby.

"Our only disappointment, we couldn't stay longer."

Williams House Inn

420 Quapaw Ave
Hot Springs, AR 71901-5201
(501)624-4275 (800)756-4635 Fax:(501)321-9466

Circa 1890. Williams House is a brownstone and brick Victorian nestled among towering oaks and a 40-foot tulip tree. Light and airy rooms are filled with antiques and plants. The carriage house,

hitching posts and mounting blocks are still on the property, and the inn is listed in the National Register of Historic Places. Raspberry French toast is popular for breakfast.

Historic Interest: The inn is located in the Quapaw-Prospect Historic District, and the National Park Visitors Center and Bathouse Row are nearby.

Innkeeper(s): Karen & David Wiseman. $85-125. MC, VISA, AX, DS, PC. TAC10. 5 rooms with PB, 2 suites and 1 conference room. Breakfast and snacks/refreshments included in rates. Types of meals: Full gourmet bkfst and early coffee/tea. Beds: Q. Cable TV and ceiling fan in room. Air conditioning. VCR, fax and library on premises. Weddings, small meetings, family reunions and seminars hosted. Antiquing, fishing, golf, art galleries, horse racing, hiking, horseback riding, parks, shopping and water sports nearby.

Publicity: Los Angeles Times, USA Today, Arkansas Times, Arkansas Democrat, Gazette, Hot Springs B&B.

Little Rock E5

The Empress of Little Rock

2120 Louisiana St
Little Rock, AR 72206-1522
(501)374-7966 (877)374-7966 Fax:(501)375-4537
E-mail: hostess@theEmpress.com
Web: www.theEmpress.com

Circa 1888. Day lilies, peonies and iris accent the old-fashioned garden of this elaborate, three-story Queen Anne Victorian. A grand center hall opens to a double staircase, lit by a stained-glass skylight. The

7,500 square feet includes a secret card room at the top of the tower. The original owner kept a private poker game going here and he paid local boys to keep an eye out for the authorities, who might close down his gambling activities. The Hornibrook Room features a magnificent Renaissance Revival bedroom set with a high canopy. The Tower room mini-suite has an Austrian king-size bed. The two-course gourmet breakfasts are served in the dining room. Enjoy a relaxing and romantic soak in the gazebo hot tub in Eve's Garden.

Historic Interest: At one time it was the first women's college in the state. Arkansas territorial restoration, Old state house, State capital, Villa Marre, MacArthur's birthplace (1-2 miles), Toltec Indian Mounds (5 miles).

Innkeeper(s): Sharon Welch-Blair & Robert Blair. $115-175. MC, VISA, AX, PC. TAC10. 5 rooms, 2 with PB, 1 with FP, 3 suites and 1 conference room. Breakfast and snacks/refreshments included in rates. Types of meals: Full gourmet bkfst, cont, veg bkfst and early coffee/tea. Picnic lunch available. Beds: KQDT. Cable TV, phone, turndown service, ceiling fan, luxury robes, complimentary liquors and antique stove w/gas logs in room. Central air. VCR, fax, copier, library, featherbeds and complimentary liquor on premises. Weddings, small meetings and family reunions hosted. Antiquing, art galleries, bicycling, fishing, golf, hiking, horseback riding, live theater, museums, parks, shopping, sporting events, tennis and water sports nearby.

"Staying at the Empress of Little Rock was a 'dream come true!' We've read about and admired it for years. It was definitely a trip to a more gracious time—one that we should all try to implement more in our daily lives."

Ozark C3

1887 Inn B&B

100 E Commercial St
Ozark, AR 72949-3210
(501)667-1121

Circa 1885. At the foot of the Ozarks, this Queen Anne Victorian inn has been lovingly restored to its natural beauty. The inn's accommodations feature names such as the Anniversary Suite, the Rose Room, the Magnolia Room and the Country Room. Each room includes a queen-size bed, with the exception of the Magnolia Room. This bedchamber includes two double beds. The decor features antique Victorian and country furnishings. Receptions, special events and weddings are popular here. With advance reservations, a special candlelight dinner can be arranged. Less than two blocks away is the Arkansas River.

Innkeeper(s): Kay & Dewayne Jones. $60-75. MC, VISA. 4 rooms. Breakfast included in rates. Types of meals: Full bkfst and early coffee/tea. Beds: QD. Weddings, small meetings and seminars hosted. Antiquing and shopping nearby.

Springdale B2

Magnolia Gardens Inn

500 N Main St
Springdale, AR 72764-1301
(501)756-5744 (800)756-5744 Fax:(501)756-2526

Circa 1883. Even its heyday, it is doubtful that this Victorian was as elegant and unique as it is today. Each of the 10 guest rooms has been individually designed with a different theme. In one cozy room, a handmade quilt and fluffy pillows tops the bed, while ribbon stenciling climbs the wall as a tasteful accent. The Magnolia Chambers room is truly Old South with a lace canopy and antique furnishings. Another room is more Wild West with red walls, a red velvet chair and a brass bed. In still another room, a rustic 150-year-old weaving loom has been transformed into a cozy, quilt-topped bed. In addition to the memorable guest rooms, the 10-acre grounds include ponds with fountains and a stream that runs through the property. The

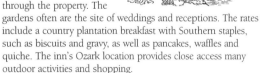

gardens often are the site of weddings and receptions. The rates include a country plantation breakfast with Southern staples, such as biscuits and gravy, as well as pancakes, waffles and quiche. The inn's Ozark location provides close access many outdoor activities and shopping.

Historic Interest: Sea Ridge (Civil War battle), 20 miles.

Innkeeper(s): John & Annette Martin. $85-110. MC, VISA, AX, PC, TC. 10 rooms with PB, 3 with FP, 1 suite and 1 conference room. Breakfast and snacks/refreshments included in rates. Types of meals: Full gourmet bkfst and country bkfst. Lunch available. Restaurant on premises. Beds: QT. TV, phone, turndown service, ceiling fan and VCR in room. Central air. Fax, copier, spa and swimming on premises. Weddings, small meetings, family reunions and seminars hosted. Antiquing, golf, museums and shopping nearby.

California

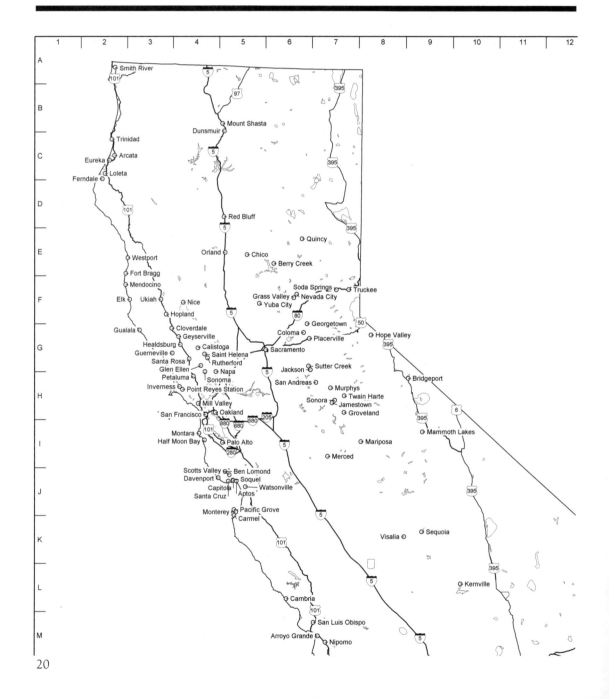

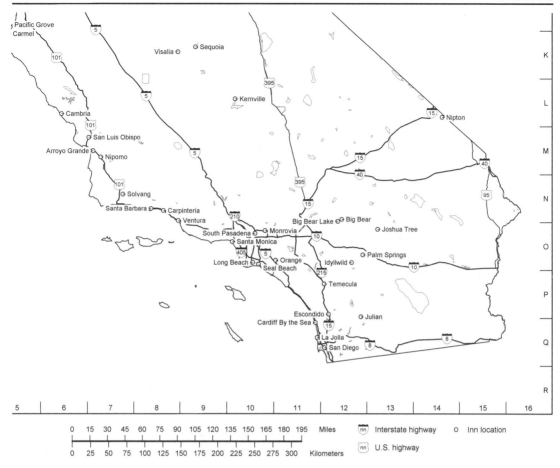

Pacific Grove
Carmel
[5]
[101]
Visalia ○   ○ Sequoia
[5]
[395]
○ Kernville
Cambria ○
[101]
[15]   ○○ Nipton
San Luis Obispo ○
Arroyo Grande ○   [5]
○ Nipomo
[15]
[101]   [15]
[40]
Solvang ○   [395]
Santa Barbara ○   ○ Carpinteria   [15]
○ Ventura   [95]
[210]
Big Bear Lake ○○ Big Bear
South Pasadena ○   ○ Monrovia   ○ Joshua Tree
○ Santa Monica   [10]
[405]   [10]
[5]   ○ Orange   ○ Palm Springs
Long Beach ○   Idyllwild ○
Seal Beach   [215]
○ Temecula
○ Julian
Escondido ○   [10]
Cardiff By the Sea ○   [15]
○ La Jolla
○ San Diego   [8]   [8]

K L M N O P Q R

5 6 7 8 9 10 11 12 13 14 15 16

0 15 30 45 60 75 90 105 120 135 150 165 180 195   Miles   [nn] Interstate highway   ○ Inn location
0 25 50 75 100 125 150 175 200 225 250 275 300   Kilometers   [nn] U.S. highway

Aptos   *J5*

Apple Lane Inn

6265 Soquel Dr
Aptos, CA 95003-3117
(831)475-6868 (800)649-8988 Fax:(831)464-5790
E-mail: ali@cruzio.com
Web: www.applelaneinn.com

Circa 1870. Ancient apple trees border the lane that leads to this Victorian farmhouse set on two acres of gardens and fields. Built by the Porter brothers, founding fathers of Aptos, the inn
is decorated with Victorian wallpapers and hardwood floors. The original wine cellar still exists, as well as the old barn and apple-drying shed used for storage after harvesting the orchard. Miles of beaches are within walking distance of this mini-farm.

The innkeepers were married at the inn and later purchased it.
Innkeeper(s): Doug & Diana Groom. $90-200. TAC10. 5 rooms with PB and 2 suites. Breakfast included in rates. Types of meals: Full gourmet bkfst and early coffee/tea. Afternoon tea and snacks/refreshments available. Beds: QDT. TV and phone in room. Fax, library and pet boarding on premises. Handicap access.

Weddings, small meetings, family reunions and seminars hosted. Antiquing, wine tasting, live theater, parks, shopping, sporting events and water sports nearby.
Pets allowed: Horses in stables, 1 guest room for dogs.
Publicity: *Santa Barbara Times, 1001 Decorating Ideas, New York Times.*

"Our room was spotless and beautifully decorated."

Mangels House

570 Aptos Creek Rd
Aptos, CA 95001
(831)688-7982
E-mail: mangels@cruzio.com
Web: www.innaccess.com/mangels

Circa 1886. Claus Mangels made his fortune in sugar beets and built this house in the style of a Southern mansion. The inn, with its encircling veranda, stands on four acres of lawns and orchards. It is bounded by the Forest of Nisene Marks, 10,000 acres of redwood trees, creeks and trails. Monterey Bay is three-quarters of a mile away.

Historic Interest: Santa Cruz Mission (6 miles).
Innkeeper(s): Jacqueline Fisher. $125-165. MC, VISA, AX. 6 rooms with PB, 1 with FP and 1 conference room. Breakfast included in rates. Types of meals: Full bkfst and early coffee/tea.

Beds: KQT. Refrigerator and phone available on premises. Small meetings, family reunions and seminars hosted. Antiquing, golf, whale watching, elephant seals, live theater, water sports and wineries nearby.

"Compliments on the lovely atmosphere. We look forward to sharing our discovery with friends and returning with them."

Aptos/La Selva Beach   J5

Inn at Manresa Beach

1258 San Andreas Rd
Aptos/La Selva Beach, CA 95076
(831)728-1000 (888)523-2244 Fax:(831)728-8294
E-mail: theinn@indevelopment.com
Web: www.indevelopment.com

Circa 1867. German immigrants built this Neo-Georgian inn, and the innkeepers moved and renovated it in 1997. The home, built just after the end of the Civil War, is a replica of Abraham Lincoln's Springfield home. Four pastoral acres surround the inn, which offers views of the Pajaro Valley. The guest suites and rooms have been decorated individually, and each has a two-person whirlpool tub as well as a fireplace. The décor includes designer linens and canopy or poster beds. Breakfasts include homemade muffins or coffeecake, fresh fruit and entrees such as peach pancakes with scrambled eggs and bacon. Innkeeper Brian Denny is a senior ranked tennis player, and the inn includes two clay and one grass tennis court.

Innkeeper(s): Susan Van Horn & Brian Denny. $150-250. MC, VISA, AX, DS, PC, TC. TAC10. 8 rooms with PB, 8 with FP, 2 suites and 1 conference room. Breakfast included in rates. Types of meals: Full bkfst and veg bkfst. Snacks/refreshments, picnic lunch and catered breakfast available. Beds: KQD. Cable TV, phone, ceiling fan and VCR in room. Fax, copier, spa, tennis, library and child care on premises. Handicap access. Weddings, small meetings, family reunions and seminars hosted. French, German and Spanish spoken. Amusement parks, antiquing, art galleries, beaches, bicycling, canoeing/kayaking, fishing, golf, hiking, horseback riding, live theater, museums, parks, shopping, tennis, water sports and wineries nearby.

Arcata   C2

Hotel Arcata

708 9th St
Arcata, CA 95521-6206
(707)826-0217 (800)344-1221 Fax:(707)826-1737

Circa 1915. This historic landmark hotel is a fine example of Beaux Arts-style architecture. Several rooms overlook Arcata's downtown plaza, which is just outside the front door. A variety of rooms are available, each decorated in turn-of-the-century style. All rooms include pedestal sinks and clawfoot tubs. The hotel offers a full-service, renown Japanese restaurant, offering  excellent cuisine, and there are many other fine restaurants within walking distance. Guests also enjoy free use of a nearby full-scale health club. The starting point of Arcata's architectural homes tour is within walking distance of the hotel.

Innkeeper(s): Virgil Moorehead. $90-180. MC, VISA, AX, DC, CB, DS, TC. 31 rooms with PB, 7 suites and 1 conference room. Breakfast included in rates. Type of meal: Cont. Dinner, lunch, banquet service and room service available. Restaurant on premises. Beds: KQT. Cable TV and phone in room. Fax, copier and free health club privileges on premises. Handicap access. Weddings, small meetings, family reunions and seminars hosted. State parks, beaches, redwoods, rivers, theater nearby, parks and shopping nearby.

Arroyo Grande   M7

Crystal Rose Inn

789 Valley Rd
Arroyo Grande, CA 93420-4497
(805)481-1854 (800)767-3466 Fax:(805)481-9541

Circa 1890. Once the homestead for a large walnut farm, this picturesque Victorian inn features an acre and a half of gardens. The inn is decorated with period pieces and reproductions. The gardens are a favorite setting for weddings. Guests are pampered with afternoon tea, evening wine and hors d'oeuvres and full, gourmet breakfast. The inn also houses The Hunt Club, a restaurant serving lunch, dinner and Sunday brunch.

Historic Interest: Hearst Castle (1 hour).

Innkeeper(s): Bonnie Royster. $95-185. MC, VISA, AX, DS. 8 rooms with PB, 3 suites and 3 conference rooms. Breakfast, afternoon tea and snacks/refreshments included in rates. MAP. Type of meal: Full bkfst. Gourmet dinner, picnic lunch, catering service and room service available. Restaurant on premises. Beds: KQDT. TV and phone in room. Handicap access. Weddings hosted. Antiquing, fishing, wineries, ocean, live theater and water sports nearby.

Publicity: *Los Angeles Times, Daughters of Painted Ladies, Travel, Five Cities Times-Press Recorder, Santa Maria Times, Telegram Tribune, Travel & Leisure, Woman's World.*

"What a wonderful magical experience we had at the Crystal Rose. We chose the beautiful Queen Elizabeth room with the enchanted tower. Our romantic interlude was just perfect."

House of Another Tyme B&B

227 Le point St
Arroyo Grande, CA 93420
(805)489-6313

Circa 1916. An old tree swing sways gently in the breeze in the garden of this grey and white shingled home. A Koi pond, gazebo and a variety of finches add to the garden's interest. There's a stone fireplace and French doors in the living room. Guest rooms feature antiques and comfortable beds. The house is one block from antique shops and restaurants, and nearby is San Luis Obispo and Santa Maria with live theatre. Ask the innkeepers to help you find the swinging bridge.

Innkeeper(s): Jack & Judy. $95. MC, VISA, DS. 3 rooms with PB. Breakfast and afternoon tea included in rates. Types of meals: Country bkfst and early coffee/tea. Beds: Q. Antiquing, art galleries, beaches, fishing, golf, hiking, horseback riding, live theater, museums, parks, shopping and wineries nearby.

Ben Lomond   J5

Chateau Des Fleurs

7995 Highway 9
Ben Lomond, CA 95005-9715
(408)336-8943 (800)291-9966
E-mail: laura@chateaudesfleurs.com
Web: www.chateaudesfleurs.com

Circa 1879. Once the home of the Bartlett pear family, this house offers gables, porches and gardens. The Rose Room has an antique clawfoot tub. A private deck is part of the Orchid Room, which features wicker furnishings and orchid watercolors. Breakfast is in the formal dining room and includes entrees such as cheese blintzes and egg dishes. In the early evening wine and hors d'oeuvres are served in the Gallery.

Innkeeper(s): Lee & Laura Jonas. $110-145. MC, VISA, DS, PC, TC. 3 rooms with PB, 2 with FP and 1 suite. Breakfast included in rates. Types of meals: Full bkfst and early coffee/tea. Beds: KQ. Ceiling fan in room. Air conditioning. VCR, fax and copier on premises. Handicap access. Weddings, small meetings, family reunions and seminars hosted. German spoken. Amusement parks, antiquing, fishing, golf, live theater, parks, shopping, sporting events, tennis and water sports nearby.

Berry Creek
E6

Lake Oroville Bed and Breakfast

240 Sunday Dr
Berry Creek, CA 95916-9640
(916)589-0700 (800)455-5253 Fax:(916)589-5313
E-mail: lakeinn@cncnet.com
Web: lakeoroville.com/lakeoroville

Circa 1970. Situated in the quiet foothills above Lake Oroville, this country inn features panoramic views from the private porches that extend from each guest room. Two favorite rooms are the Rose Petal Room and the Victorian Room, both with

lake views and whirlpool tubs. The inn's 40 acres are studded with oak and pine trees. Deer and songbirds abound.

Innkeeper(s): Cheryl & Ron Damberger. $75-145. MC, VISA, AX, DS, PC, TC. 6 rooms with PB and 1 conference room. Breakfast included in rates. Types of meals: Full bkfst and early coffee/tea. Banquet service available. Beds: KQ. Cable TV, phone, turndown service, ceiling fan, VCR, whirlpool tubs and tape player in room. Air conditioning. Fax, copier, spa, library, pet boarding and child care on premises. Handicap access. Weddings, small meetings, family reunions and seminars hosted. French and Spanish spoken. Antiquing, fishing, golf, live theater, parks, shopping, tennis and water sports nearby.

Pets allowed: On approval.

Big Bear
N12

Gold Mountain Manor Historic B&B

1117 Anita, PO Box 2027
Big Bear, CA 92314
(909)585-6997 (800)509-2604 Fax:(909)585-0327

Circa 1928. This spectacular log mansion was once a hideaway for the rich and famous. Eight fireplaces provide a roaring fire in each room in fall and winter. The Lucky Baldwin Room offers a hearth made from stones gathered in the famous Lucky Baldwin mine nearby. In the Clark Gable room is the fireplace Gable and Carole Lombard enjoyed on their honeymoon. Gourmet country breakfasts and afternoon hors d'oeuvres are served. In addition to the guest rooms, there are home rentals.

Historic Interest: Small Historic Museum in Big Bear City (1 mile) and gold mining.

Innkeeper(s): Trish & Jim Gordon. $125-190. MC, VISA, DS. TAC10. 6 rooms with PB, 6 with FP, 2 suites and 1 conference room. Afternoon tea and snacks/refreshments included in rates. Types of meals: Full gourmet bkfst and early coffee/tea. Beds: Q. Ceiling fan and jacuzzi in suites in room. VCR, fax, spa, bicycles, library and pool table on premises. Weddings, small meetings, family reunions and seminars hosted. Spanish spoken. Fishing, hiking/forest, parks, downhill skiing, cross-country skiing, sporting events and water sports nearby.

Publicity: *Best Places to Kiss, Fifty Most Romantic Places, Kenny G holiday album cover.*

"A majestic experience! In this magnificent house, history comes alive!"

Big Bear Lake
N12

Knickerbocker Mansion Country Inn

869 Knickerbocker Rd
Big Bear Lake, CA 92315
(909)878-9190 (877)423-1180 Fax:(909)878-4248
E-mail: knickmail@aol.com
Web: www.knickerbockermansion.com

Circa 1920. The inn is one of the few vertically designed log structures in the United States. The inn was built of local lumber by Bill Knickerbocker, the first dam keeper of Big Bear. The inn includes two historic buildings set on two-and-a-half wooded acres, backing to a national forest. Although, the inn offers a secluded setting, the village of Big Bear Lake is within walking distance. The village offers shopping, restaurants, fishing, hiking, mountain biking and excellent downhill skiing.

Innkeeper(s): Stanley Miller & Thomas Bicanic. $110-280. MC, VISA, AX, DS. 9 rooms with PB, 2 suites and 1 conference room. Types of meals: Full bkfst and early coffee/tea. Snacks/refreshments available. Beds: KQ. TV, phone and VCR in room. Weddings, small meetings, family reunions and seminars hosted. Antiquing, bicycling, fishing, hiking, live theater, shopping, downhill skiing and cross-country skiing nearby.

"Best breakfast I ever had in a setting of rustic elegance, a quiet atmosphere and personal attention from the innkeepers. The moment you arrive you will realize the Knickerbocker is a very special place."

Bridgeport
H9

The Cain House

340 Main St
Bridgeport, CA 93517
(760)932-7040 (800)433-2246 Fax:(760)932-7419

Circa 1920. The grandeur of the Eastern Sierra Mountains is the perfect setting for evening refreshments as the sun sets, turning the sky into a fiery, purple canvas. The innkeeper's experiences while traveling around the world have influenced The Cain House's decor to give the inn a European elegance with a casual western atmosphere. Travelers can take a short drive to the ghost town of Bodie where 10,000 people once lived in this gold-mining community. Outdoor enthusiasts can find an abundance of activity at Lake Tahoe, which is an hour-and-a-half away.

Innkeeper(s): Chris & Marachal Gohlich. $80-135. MC, VISA, AX, DS, PC,

TC. TAC10. 7 rooms with PB. Breakfast and snacks/refreshments included in rates. Types of meals: Full bkfst and early coffee/tea. Beds: KQ. Cable TV and phone in room. Air conditioning. Fax and copier on premises. Family reunions hosted. Fishing, parks, cross-country skiing, tennis and water sports nearby.
Publicity: *Los Angeles Times*.

Calistoga   G4

Calistoga Wayside Inn

1523 Foothill Blvd
Calistoga, CA 94515-1619
(707)942-0645 (800)845-3632 Fax:(707)942-4169

Circa 1928. The woodsy grounds at this Spanish-style hacienda include a waterfall, which cascades into a picturesque pond. Guests can enjoy the soothing sounds of water fountains from their rooms, which are decorated in a garden theme. The Delaney Room includes a private balcony with wicker furnishings. Down

comforters, special soaps and robes are a few of the thoughtful amenities. The two-course, country breakfast is a perfect start to a day touring the popular Napa Valley. Wine and cheese is served in the afternoon. The Wayside Inn is within walking distance to Calistoga's famed spas. The innkeepers can help guests plan wine-tasting tours as well as glider or hot air balloon rides.
$100-165. MC, VISA, AX, DS, PC, TC. TAC10. 3 rooms with PB. Breakfast included in rates. Types of meals: Full bkfst and early coffee/tea. Beds: KQ. Ceiling fan in room. Air conditioning. Fax and library on premises. Small meetings and family reunions hosted. Antiquing, spas, wineries, mud baths, glider planes, balloon rides, parks and shopping nearby.

"This was my first stay at a B&B and now, certainly the first of many."

Fannys

1206 Spring St
Calistoga, CA 94515-1637
(707)942-9491 Fax:(707)942-4810
E-mail: fannys@webtv.net
Web: sanfrancisco.sidewalk.msn.com/fannys

Circa 1915. In a shingled Craftsman-cottage style, painted forest green and red, this inn offers an inviting shaded porch with swing, rockers and spots for dining. Inside, comfortable interiors include over-stuffed chairs, a fireplace, library and upstairs guest rooms with plank floors and window seats. The innkeeper, a former restaurateur, provides a full breakfast and knowledgeable touring suggestions.
Innkeeper(s): Deanna Higgins. $75-120. PC, TC. 2 rooms with PB. Breakfast included in rates. Types of meals: Full bkfst and country bkfst. Beds: Q. Ceiling fan in room. Air conditioning. Fax and library on premises. Weddings hosted. Antiquing, golf, winery tours & tasting, parks and shopping nearby.

Foothill House

3037 Foothill Blvd
Calistoga, CA 94515-1225
(707)942-6933 (800)942-6933 Fax:(707)942-5692
E-mail: gusgus@aol.com
Web: www.foothillhouse.com

Circa 1892. This country farmhouse overlooks the western foothills of Mount St. Helena. Graceful old California oaks and pockets of flowers greet guests. Each room features country antiques, a four-poster bed, a fireplace and a small refrigerator. Breakfast is served in the sun room or is delivered personally to your room in a basket. Three rooms offer private Jacuzzi tubs.
Historic Interest: Old Faithful Geyser (1 mile), Petrified Forest (3 miles).
Innkeeper(s): Doris & Gus Beckert. $165-300. MC, VISA, AX, DS, PC, TC. TAC10. 4 suites, 4 with FP. Breakfast and snacks/refreshments included in rates. Types of meals: Full gourmet bkfst and early coffee/tea. Beds: KQT. Cable TV, phone, turndown service, ceiling fan, VCR, robes, bottled water, coffee and tea in room. Air conditioning. Fax, copier and library on premises. Weddings, small meetings and family reunions hosted. Amusement parks, antiquing, fishing, wineries, balloon rides, glider port, health spas, parks, shopping and water sports nearby.
Publicity: *Herald Examiner, Baltimore Sun, Sunset, San Francisco Examiner.*

"Gourmet treats served in front of an open fire. Hospitality never for a moment flagged."

Scarlett's Country Inn

3918 Silverado Trl
Calistoga, CA 94515-9611
(707)942-6669 Fax:(707)942-6669
E-mail: scarletts@aol.com
Web: members.aol.com/scarletts

Circa 1900. Formerly a winter campground of the Wappo Indians, the property now includes a restored farmhouse. There are green lawns and country vistas of woodland and vineyards. Each room has a private entrance. Breakfast is often served beneath the apple trees or poolside.

Historic Interest: Old Bale Mill (2 miles), Beringer and Charles Krug Wineries (4 miles), Schramsberg Champagne Cellars (2 miles), Sharpstein Museum (4 miles), graveyard in Boothe State Park (2 miles).
Innkeeper(s): Scarlett Dwyer. $125-185. PC. TAC10. 3 rooms with PB, 1 with FP, 2 suites and 1 cottage. Breakfast and afternoon tea included in rates. Types of meals: Full gourmet bkfst and early coffee/tea. Room service available. Beds: Q. TV, phone and turndown service in room. Air conditioning. Fax, copier and swimming on premises. Small meetings and family reunions hosted. Spanish spoken. Antiquing, fishing, ballooning, gliders, winetasting, parks, shopping and water sports nearby.

"Wonderful, peaceful, serene."

Trailside Inn

4201 Silverado Trl
Calistoga, CA 94515-9605
(707)942-4106 Fax:(707)942-4702
E-mail: h.gray@worldnet.att.net
Web: www.trailsideinn.com

Circa 1932. This secluded valley farmhouse overlooks Three Palms Vineyard and the distant Sterling Winery. Each accommodation is a tastefully decorated suite with its own porch, private entrance, small kitchen, private bath and fireplace. Furnished with country antiques and old quilts, two suites have an extra bedroom to accommodate a family of four. House specialties are banana and blueberry breads, freshly baked and brought to your room. Complimentary wine and mineral water also are offered.

Historic Interest: Robert Louis Stevenson State Park (3 miles), Beringer Winery (4 miles), Calistoga (3 miles).

Innkeeper(s): Randy & Lani Gray. $165-185. MC, VISA, AX, DS. 3 suites, 3 with FP. Breakfast included in rates. Type of meal: Cont plus. Beds: QDT. Phone and complimentary wine in room. Swimming on premises.

Publicity: San Francisco Examiner, Wine Country Review.

"If Dorothy and Toto were to click their heals together they would end up at the Trailside Inn."

Cambria   L6

Olallieberry Inn

2476 Main St
Cambria, CA 93428-3406
(888)927-3222 Fax:(805)927-0202
E-mail: olallieinn@olallieberry.com
Web: www.olallieberry.com

Circa 1873. This restored Greek Revival home features rooms decorated with fabrics and wall coverings and furnished with period antiques. Six of the guest rooms feature fireplaces. Butterfly and herb gardens and a 110-year-old redwood grace the front yard. The cheery gathering room boasts a view of the Santa Rosa Creek. Full breakfast with fresh breads, fruits and a special entree start off the day, and wine and hors d'oeuvres are served in the afternoon. The inn is within walking distance to restaurants and shops.

Historic Interest: Hearst Castle is six miles from the inn.

Innkeeper(s): Peter & Carol Ann Irsfeld. $90-185. MC, VISA, AX, PC, TC. TAC10. 9 rooms with PB, 6 with FP and 1 suite. Breakfast and snacks/refreshments included in rates. Types of meals: Full gourmet bkfst and early coffee/tea. Beds: KQ. Fireplace six rooms in room. Fax on premises. Handicap access. Weddings, small meetings, family reunions and seminars hosted. Antiquing, fishing, Hearst Castle, shopping and water sports nearby.

Publicity: Los Angeles Times, Elmer Dills Radio Show.

"Our retreat turned into relaxation, romance and pure Victorian delight."

The Squibb House

4063 Burton Dr
Cambria, CA 93428-3001
(805)927-9600 Fax:(805)927-9606

Circa 1877. A picket fence and large garden surround this Victorian inn with its Italianate and Gothic Revival architecture. Guests may relax in the main parlor, stroll the gardens or sit and rock on the porch. The home was built by a Civil War veteran and young school teacher. The downstairs once was used as a classroom while an addition was being made in the town's school. Each guest room has a fire stove.

Historic Interest: Heart Castle is six miles away, and further attractions include the San Luis Obispo Mission and San Miguel Mission, both about 35 miles from the home.

Innkeeper(s): Martha. $95-155. MC, VISA, PC, TC. TAC10. 5 rooms with PB, 5 with FP. Breakfast included in rates. Types of meals: Cont plus and cont. Beds: Q. Retail shop in historic 1885 carpentry shop on premises. Weddings and small meetings hosted. Antiquing, fishing, golf, Hearst Castle, wine tasting, galleries, parks and shopping nearby.

Publicity: Cambrian.

Capitola-by-the-Sea   J5

Inn at Depot Hill

250 Monterey Ave
Capitola-by-the-Sea, CA 95010-3358
(831)462-3376 (800)572-2632 Fax:(831)462-3697
E-mail: lodging@innatdepothill.com
Web: www.innatdepothill.com

Circa 1901. Once a railroad depot, this inn offers rooms with themes to represent different parts of the world: a chic auberge in St. Tropez, a romantic French hideaway in Paris, an Italian coastal villa, a summer home on the coast of Holland and a traditional English garden room, to name a few. Most rooms have garden patios with hot tubs. The rooms have many amenities, including a fireplace, white marble bathrooms and featherbeds. Guests are greeted with fresh flowers in their room. Gourmet breakfast, tea, wine, hors d' oeuvres and dessert are offered daily.

Innkeeper(s): Suzie Lankes & Dan Floyd. $195-275. MC, VISA, AX, DS, TC. TAC10. 12 rooms with PB, 12 with FP, 4 suites and 1 conference room. Breakfast and snacks/refreshments included in rates. Beds: KQT. Cable TV, phone, turndown service and VCR in room. Fax and spa on premises. Handicap access. Small meetings, family reunions and seminars hosted. Amusement parks, antiquing, fishing, golf, live theater, parks, shopping and water sports nearby.

Publicity: Country Inn, Santa Cruz Sentinel, McCalls, Choices & Vacation, San Jose Mercury News, Fresno & Sacramento Bee, San Francisco Focus, American Airline Flight, SF Examiner and Sunset Magazine.

"The highlight of our honeymoon. Five stars in our book!"

Carmel   J5

Happy Landing Inn

PO Box 2619
Carmel, CA 93921-2619
(831)624-7917

Circa 1926. Built as a family retreat, this early Comstock-design inn has evolved into one of Carmel's most romantic places to stay. The Hansel-and-Gretel look is accentuated with a central garden and gazebo, pond and flagstone paths. There are cathedral ceilings and the rooms are filled with antiques. Breakfast is brought to your room.

Innkeeper(s): Robert Ballard and Dick Stewart. $90-165. MC, VISA, PC, TC. 7 rooms with PB, 3 with FP and 2 suites. Breakfast included in rates. Type of meal: Cont plus. Beds: KQD. Handicap access. Restaurants and beach and shopping nearby.

Publicity: San Francisco Chronicle.

"Just what the doctor ordered!"

Sandpiper Inn-by-the-Sea

2408 Bay View Ave
Carmel, CA 93923-9118
(831)624-6433 (800)633-6433 Fax:(831)624-5964

Circa 1929. Only a half block from miles of pristine coastline, this early California-style inn is set in a quiet residential neighborhood of million-dollar estates. There are 17 guest rooms, all

individually decorated in English and French antiques. Several offer fireplaces or ocean views. For a more intimate stay, guests can request one of the three cottage rooms. With its beautifully furnished interiors, the inn has been a favorite getaway spot for a host of famous people. An expanded continental buffet breakfast is served in the dining room. In the afternoon, guests are invited to enjoy tea or a glass of imported Amontillado sherry.
Innkeeper(s): Audie Housman. $95-285. MC, VISA, AX, DS, PC, TC. TAC10. 17 rooms with PB, 3 with FP and 3 cottages. Breakfast and afternoon tea included in rates. Types of meals: Cont plus and early coffee/tea. Beds: KQ. Fax on premises. Antiquing, golf, live theater, parks, shopping, tennis and water sports nearby.

The Stonehouse Inn

PO Box 2517, 8th below Monte Verde
Carmel, CA 93921-2517
(831)624-4569 (800)748-6618

Circa 1906. This quaint Carmel country house boasts a stone exterior, made from beach rocks collected and hand shaped by local Indians at the turn of the century. The original owner, "Nana" Foster, was hostess to notable artists and writers from the San Francisco area, including Sinclair Lewis, Jack London and Lotta Crabtree. The romantic Jack London

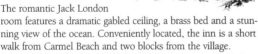

room features a dramatic gabled ceiling, a brass bed and a stunning view of the ocean. Conveniently located, the inn is a short walk from Carmel Beach and two blocks from the village.
Innkeeper(s): Terri Navailles. $159-201. MC, VISA, AX. 6 rooms. Breakfast included in rates. Type of meal: Full bkfst. Beds: KQDT. Weddings and family reunions hosted. Fishing, live theater, parks, shopping and water sports nearby.
Publicity: *Travel & Leisure, Country Living.*

"First time stay at a B&B — GREAT!"

Cloverdale   G3

The Shelford House

29955 River Rd
Cloverdale, CA 95425-3523
(707)894-5956 (800)833-6479 Fax:(707)894-8621

Circa 1885. Shelford House is a charming Queen Anne Victorian with lilac trim. The two-acre grounds are lush and fragrant, and they include a small swimming pool. Guests enjoy

views of surrounding vineyards, and there are more than 150 wineries to visit. The interior of the home is done in period style, with clawfoot tubs and antiques. The innkeepers' latest addition is a 500-square-foot suite with a fireplace and double Jacuzzi. In the evenings, the innkeepers offer snacks for their guests, and in the mornings, entrees such as almond French toast are accompanied by chicken-apple sausage and strawberry parfaits. For an additional fee, guests can enjoy a tour of the area in an antique car.
Innkeeper(s): Bill & Lou Ann Brennock. $105-250. MC, VISA, AX, DS, PC. TAC10. 7 rooms with PB. Breakfast and snacks/refreshments included in rates. AP. Types of meals: Full gourmet bkfst and early coffee/tea. Beds: KQ. Ceiling fan in room. Air conditioning. Fax, copier, spa, swimming, stables, bicycles, ping pong, piano, organ, 1928 Model A and winery tours on premises. Antiquing, fishing, parks, water sports and wineries nearby.

"We just love your beautiful location."

Coloma   G6

Coloma Country Inn

PO Box 502
Coloma, CA 95613-0502
(530)622-6919

Circa 1852. Guests at this country farmhouse will want to take advantage of the nearby American River for white-water rafting. Innkeeper Alan Ehrgott is a veteran hot air balloon pilot and offers flights down the river year-round. Bed, Breakfast and Balloon packages are available at the inn, along with white-water rafting packages. The inn is situated on five, private acres in the middle of the 300-acre Gold Discovery State Park, and guests will feel like they've gone back to the Gold Rush days. A duck pond and gazebo are part of the inn's charm, coupled with antique beds, stenciling and country decor.
Historic Interest: Marshall Gold State Historic Park, Sutter's Mill and the south fork of the American River are among the area's historic attractions.
Innkeeper(s): Alan & Cindi Ehrgott. $90-130. PC, TC. TAC10. 7 rooms, 5 with PB, 2 suites, 2 cottages and 1 conference room. Breakfast and afternoon tea included in rates. Types of meals: Cont and early coffee/tea. Picnic lunch and catering service available. Beds: QD. Ceiling fan in room. Air conditioning. Fishing pond and formal gardens on premises. Weddings, small meetings, family reunions and seminars hosted. Antiquing, fishing, wine tasting, hot air ballooning, live theater, parks, downhill skiing and water sports nearby.
Publicity: *Country Living, Los Angeles Times, Country Inns, Sunset, Motorland, New York Times.*

Crowley Lake   I9

Rainbow Tarns B&B at Crowley Lake

HC 79 Box 1053
Crowley Lake, CA 93546-9704
(760)935-4556 (888)588-6269

Circa 1920. Just south of Mammoth Lakes, at an altitude of 7,000 feet, you'll find this secluded retreat amid three acres of ponds, open meadows and the High Sierra Mountains. Country-style here includes luxury touches, such as a double Jacuzzi tub, queen-size bed, down pillows, comforters and a skylight for star-gazing. In the '50s,

ponds on the property served as a "U-Catch-Em." Folks rented fishing poles and paid 10 cents an inch for the fish they caught. Nearby Crowley Lake is still one of the best trout-fishing areas in California. Romantic country weddings are popular here. Guests are free to simply relax in the peaceful setting, but hiking, horseback riding and skiing all are available in the area. In the afternoons, guests are treated to snacks and wine.

Innkeeper(s): Brock & Diane Thoman. $90-140. PC. 3 rooms with PB. Breakfast included in rates. Types of meals: Full bkfst and early coffee/tea. Beds: QD. Handicap access.

Davenport   J4

New Davenport B&B

31 Davenport Ave
Davenport, CA 95017
(831)425-1818 (800)870-1817 Fax:(831)423-1160

Circa 1906. Captain John Davenport came here to harvest the gray whales that pass close to shore during migration. The oldest building remaining originally was used as a public bath. It later became a bar, restaurant and dance hall before conversion

into a private home. Completely renovated, it now houses four of the inn's rooms. In addition to breakfast, guests also enjoy two complimentary drinks at the bar in the inn's restaurant.

Historic Interest: The Wilder Ranch State Park is five miles away. Davenport Jail, Giovvini Cheesehouse, Old Davenport Pier and the St. Vincent DePaul Catholic Church, built in 1902, are nearby.

Innkeeper(s): Bruce & Marcia McDougal. $89-140. MC, VISA, AX. 12 rooms with PB. Breakfast included in rates. Type of meal: Full bkfst. Dinner, picnic lunch and lunch available. Restaurant on premises. Beds: KQ.

"The warmth of the rooms, the people who work here and the ocean keeps us coming back year after year."

Dunsmuir   B5

Dunsmuir Inn

5423 Dunsmuir Ave
Dunsmuir, CA 96025-2011
(530)235-4543 (888)386-7684 Fax:(530)235-4154

Circa 1925. Set in the Sacramento River Valley, this country-style inn may serve as a base for an assortment of outdoor activities. At the end of the day, guests can enjoy an old-fashioned soda or ice cream cone. Fishing, available in the crystal-clear waters of the Upper Sacramento River, is within walking distance. The innkeepers can suggest hiking trails and driving tours to mountain lakes, waterfalls, the Castle Crags State Park and Mt. Shasta.

Innkeeper(s): Jerry & Julie Iskra. $65-75. MC, VISA, AX, DC, CB, DS, PC, TC. TAC10. 5 rooms with PB and 1 suite. Breakfast included in rates. Types of meals: Full bkfst and early coffee/tea. Snacks/refreshments and picnic lunch available. Beds: KD. Turndown service and ceiling fan in room. Air conditioning. VCR and fax on premises. Family reunions hosted. Antiquing, fishing, parks, downhill skiing, cross-country skiing and water sports nearby.

Elk   F3

Elk Cove Inn

6300 S Hwy One
Elk, CA 95432
(707)877-3321 (800)275-2967 Fax:(707)877-1808
E-mail: elkcove@mcn.org
Web: www.elkcoveinn.com

Circa 1882. This mansard-style Victorian home was built as a guest house for lumber baron L. E. White. Operated as a full-service country inn for more than 30 years, Elk Cove Inn commands a majestic view from atop a scenic bluff. There are four cabins and four new ocean-front luxury suites with large windows, fireplaces, spa tubs and balconies. There is also a new hot tub with a view of the ocean. Most rooms have a fireplace and an ocean view. Antiques, hand-embroidered linens and down comforters add to the amenities. Below the inn is an expansive driftwood-strewn beach. Gourmet breakfasts are served in the ocean-view dining room. Guests can enjoy cocktails, beer or wine in the ocean-front bar. Coffee makers with fresh ground coffee, teas, cider and hot chocolate are available in the rooms.

Historic Interest: Fort Ross original Russian settlement (1 hour away).

Innkeeper(s): Elaine Bryant. $108-298. MC, VISA, AX, PC, TC. TAC10. 15 rooms with PB, 14 with FP, 5 suites and 4 cottages. Breakfast included in rates. Types of meals: Full gourmet bkfst and early coffee/tea. Beds: KQ. VCR, fax, copier and library on premises. Handicap access. Weddings, small meetings, family reunions and seminars hosted. Spanish and Italian spoken. Antiquing, canoeing/kayaking, fishing, golf, horseback riding, whale watching, skunk train, live theater, parks, shopping, tennis and water sports nearby.

"Quiet, peaceful, romantic, spiritual. This room, the inn, and the food are all what the doctor ordered."

The Harbor House Inn

5600 S Hwy 1
Elk, CA 95432
(707)877-3203 (800)720-7474
E-mail: harborhs@mcn.org
Web: www.theharborhouseinn.com

Circa 1916. The Harbor House Inn rests on a cliff overlooking Greenwood Cove and the Pacific Ocean. Built by a lumber company for executives visiting from the East, the inn is constructed entirely of redwood. Most of the antique-filled guest rooms include a fireplace, and some have decks. Guests are treated to both a full breakfast as well as a four-course dinner. A path winds through the inn's gardens down to a private beach below.

Innkeeper(s): Elle Haynes. $195-315. MC, VISA. 10 rooms with PB, 9 with FP. Breakfast and dinner included in rates. MAP. Type of meal: Full bkfst.

Publicity: *Travel & Leisure, California Visitor's Review.*

"A window on love, beauty and the sea."

Sandpiper House Inn

5520 S Hwy 1
Elk, CA 95432
(707)877-3587 (800)894-9016

Circa 1916. A garden path leads Sandpiper guests to a garden sitting area overlooking the California coast. The path continues onward to a private beach. The historic home was built by a local lumber company. The living room and dining room have virgin redwood paneling. Guest quarters are appointed to look like rooms in an English country home. Canopied beds, Oriental rugs and polished wood floors create a romantic ambiance. Rooms offer either ocean or countryside views, and three have a fireplace. Gourmet breakfasts are served on tables set with lace and fresh flowers. In-house massages also are available.

Innkeeper(s): Claire & Richard Melrose. $135-225. MC, VISA, AX, DS, PC, TC. 5 rooms with PB, 3 with FP and 1 suite. Breakfast and afternoon tea included in rates. MAP. Types of meals: Full gourmet bkfst and early coffee/tea. Beds: Q. In-house massage therapy on premises. Fishing, live theater, parks, shopping, water sports and wineries nearby.

Escondido   P12

Zosa Gardens B&B

9381 W Lilac Rd
Escondido, CA 92026-4508
(760)723-9093 (800)771-8361 Fax:(760)723-3460

Circa 1940. Escondido, located in northern San Diego County, is the setting for this Spanish Hacienda. The home rests on 22 well-landscaped acres atop a bluff in the Monserate Mountains. Rooms bear flowery themes. Angel-lovers should try the Angel Room. The Master Suite includes a fireplace. The innkeeper is an accomplished chef, and her cuisine has been featured on the TV Food Network, as well as in Bon Appetit. She serves a full customized breakfast for her guests. In the evenings, gourmet tidbits are served with a selection of local wines. Billiards, hiking trails, a tennis court and massages are available. Golf courses, restaurants and other sites are just minutes away.

Innkeeper(s): Ted & Connie Vlasis. $135-250. MC, VISA, AX, DC, CB, DS, PC, TC. TAC10. 11 rooms, 10 with PB, 2 with FP, 3 suites and 1 cabin. Breakfast and snacks/refreshments included in rates. Type of meal: Full gourmet bkfst. Catering service available. Beds: KQ. Jacuzzi in room. Air conditioning. VCR, fax, copier, spa, swimming, tennis and rental bicycles on premises. Handicap access. Weddings, small meetings, family reunions and seminars hosted. Spanish, Filipino, English and Italian spoken. Amusement parks, antiquing, fishing, golf, Buddhist Monastery, wineries, hot air balloons, live theater, parks, shopping, sporting events, tennis and water sports nearby.

Eureka   C2

Abigail's "Elegant Victorian Mansion" B&B Lodging Accommodations

1406 C St
Eureka, CA 95501-1765
(707)444-3144 Fax:(707)442-5594

Circa 1888. One of Eureka's leading lumber barons built this picturesque home, a National Historic Landmark, from 1,000-year-old virgin redwood. Original wallpapers,  wool carpets and antique light fixtures create a wonderfully authentic Victorian ambiance. A tuxedoed butler and your hosts, decked in period attire, greet guests upon arrival. Croquet fields and Victorian gardens surround the inn. The hosts provide complimentary "horseless" carriage rides. The beds in the well-appointed guest quarters are topped with custom-made mattresses. There is a video library of vintage silent films. The inn has been host to many historic personalities, including actresses Lillie Langtry and Sarah Bernhardt, and many senators and representatives. The Pacific Ocean, beaches

and the Giant Redwoods are only a few minutes away.

Historic Interest: Historic Fort Humboldt State Park, Redwood parks, Clark Historic Museum, Maritime Museum, historic "Old Town" (all within walking distance).

Innkeeper(s): Doug & Lily Vieyra. $85-215. MC, VISA. TAC10. 4 rooms, 2 with PB, 1 suite and 1 conference room. Breakfast, afternoon tea and snacks/refreshments included in rates. EP. Types of meals: Cont plus and early coffee/tea. Beds: Q. Phone, turndown service, chocolate truffles and B&B guidebooks in room. Air conditioning. VCR, fax, copier, sauna, bicycles, library, croquet field, antique automobiles and horseless carriages on premises. Small meetings and seminars hosted. French, Dutch and German and English spoken. Antiquing, carriage rides, bay cruise, horseback riding, sailing, beach, Giant Redwoods, live theater, tennis and water sports nearby.

A Weaver's Inn

1440 B St
Eureka, CA 95501-2215
(707)443-8119 (800)992-8119 Fax:(707)443-7923
E-mail: weavrinn@humboldt1.com
Web: www.humboldt1.com/~weavrinn

Circa 1883. The stately Queen Anne Colonial Revival house features a spacious fenced garden, parlor and gracious dining room. All four guest rooms are furnished with down comforters, fresh flowers from the garden and are decorated to reflect the genteel elegance of the Victorian era. The Pamela Suite has a sitting room and fireplace, while the Marcia Room includes a two-person soaking tub in its private bath. The full breakfast often features home-grown treats from the garden.

Historic Interest: Redwood Forests (30 miles).

Innkeeper(s): Lea L. Montgomery, Shoshana McAvoy. $75-125. MC, VISA, AX, DC, DS. TAC10. 4 rooms, 3 with PB, 2 with FP and 1 suite. Breakfast included in rates. Type of meal: Full gourmet bkfst. Afternoon tea and gourmet dinner available. Beds: KQDT.

"It's a charming inn, warm ambiance and very gracious hosts!"

The Carter House Victorians

301 L St
Eureka, CA 95501
(707)444-8062 (800)404-1390 Fax:(707)444-8067
E-mail: carter52@humboldt1.com
Web: www.carterhouse.com

Circa 1884. The Carters found a pattern book in an antique shop and built this inn according to the architectural plans for an 1890 San Francisco Victorian. (The architect, Joseph Newsom, also designed the Carson House across the street.) Three open parlors with bay windows and marble fireplaces provide an elegant backdrop for relaxing. Guests are free to visit the kitchen in quest of coffee and views of the bay. The inn is famous for its three-course breakfast, including an Apple Almond Tart featured in Gourmet magazine. Restaurant 301 at the Hotel Carter across the street is famous for its award-winning wine cellar and excellent cuisine.

Historic Interest: Redwood forests, historic architecture, wildlife/bird sanctuary, Victorian Sawmill (all within 10 miles).

Innkeeper(s): Mark & Christi Carter. $145-350. MC, VISA, AX, DC, CB, DS, PC, TC. TAC10. 31 rooms with PB, 15 with FP, 15 suites, 1 cottage and 2 conference rooms. Breakfast and afternoon tea included in rates. MAP, AP, EP. Types of meals: Full gourmet bkfst, cont plus, cont and early coffee/tea. Gourmet dinner, snacks/refreshments and room service available. Restaurant on premises. Beds: KQDT. Cable TV, phone, turndown service and VCR in room. Air conditioning. Fax, copier and spa on premises. Handicap access. Small meetings, family reunions and seminars hosted. Italian, Spanish and French spoken. Antiquing, fishing, live theater, parks, shopping, sporting events and water sports nearby.

Publicity: Sunset, U.S. News & World Report, Country Home, Country Living, Bon Appetit, San Francisco Focus, Northwest Palate, Gourmet, Art Culinare, San Francisco Chronicle.

Cornelius Daly Inn

1125 H St
Eureka, CA 95501-1844
(707)445-3638 (800)321-9656 Fax:(707)444-3636

Circa 1905. This 6,000-square-foot Colonial Revival mansion is located in the historic section of Eureka. Enjoy the Belgian antique bedstead, fireplace and view of fish pond and garden from Annie Murphy's Room, or try the former nursery, Miss

Martha's Room, with bleached pine antiques from Holland. Breakfast is served fireside in the inn's formal dining room or in the breakfast parlor or garden patio. In the evenings, wine and cheese is served.

Historic Interest: The Carson Mansion, historic Old Town, Fort Humboldt and a Victorian sawmill are among the nearby historic attractions.

Innkeeper(s): Sue & Gene Clinesmith. $85-150. MC, VISA, AX, DS, PC, TC. 5 rooms, 3 with PB, 1 with FP and 2 suites. Breakfast and snacks/refreshments included in rates. Types of meals: Full gourmet bkfst and early coffee/tea. Beds: QT. Turndown service and antiques in room. VCR, fax, copier and library on premises. Weddings, small meetings, family reunions and seminars hosted. Antiquing, fishing, redwood park, ocean, live theater and shopping nearby.

"A genuine delight."

Old Town B&B Inn

1521 3rd St
Eureka, CA 95501-0710
(707)445-3951 (800)331-5098 Fax:(707)268-0231
E-mail: oldtown@oldtownbnb.com
Web: oldtownbnb.com/eureka

Circa 1871. This early Victorian/Greek Revival was the original family home of Lumber Baron William Carson. It was constructed of virgin redwood and Douglas fir. This renovated inn has been called a "Humboldt County jewel" by the local visitors' and convention bureau. The inn is one of the area's oldest tried-and-true bed & breakfasts, in operation since 1982. Try to time your stay on a day when the Timber Beast breakfast menu is served, and be sure to take home a copy of the inn's cookbook.

Innkeeper(s): Leigh & Diane Benson. $95-185. MC, AX, DC, CB, DS, PC, TC. 6 rooms with PB, 1 with FP. Breakfast and afternoon tea included in rates. Types of meals: Full gourmet bkfst and early coffee/tea. Beds: KQD. Phone, data more-cookies, aspirin and phone available in room. Hot tub (teak) on premises. Family reunions hosted. Spanish and Italian spoken. Antiquing, fishing, hiking, Ocean, Eco-tours, museums, Redwood State National, live theater, parks, sporting events and water sports nearby.

Publicity: *Times-Standard, Country, San Francisco Chronicle, Sunset, San Francisco Examiner, L.A.Times.*

"From the moment you opened the door, we knew we had chosen a special place to stay."

Ferndale   C2

Gingerbread Mansion Inn

PO Box 40, 400 Berding St
Ferndale, CA 95536-1380
(707)786-4000 (800)952-4136 Fax:(707)786-4381
E-mail: kenn@humboldt1.com
Web: gingerbread-mansion.com

Circa 1899. Built for Dr. H.J. Ring, the Gingerbread Mansion is now the most photographed of Northern California's inns. Near Eureka, it is in the fairy-tale Victorian village of Ferndale (a National Historical Landmark). Gingerbread Mansion is a

unique combination of Queen Anne and Eastlake styles with elaborate gingerbread trim. Inside are spacious and elegant rooms including two suites with "his" and "her" bathtubs. The Empire Suite is said to be the most opulent accommodation in Northern California.

Another memorable choice would be "The Veneto", an imaginative experience where guests stay within a piece of artwork. Extensive formal English gardens beautifully surround the mansion and it is a stroll away to Victorian shops, galleries and restaurants. A Wilderness park and bird sanctuary a half mile away.

Historic Interest: Victorian shops and galleries along Main Street, The Ferndale Museum, wilderness park and bird sanctuary (one-half mile).

Innkeeper(s): Ken Torbert. $140-350. MC, VISA, AX, PC, TC. TAC10. 11 rooms with PB, 5 with FP and 5 suites. Breakfast and afternoon tea included in rates. Types of meals: Full bkfst and early coffee/tea. Beds: KQT. Turndown service in room. Library and gardens on premises. Small meetings and family reunions hosted. Antiquing, fishing, hiking, live theater, parks and shopping nearby.

Publicity: *Travel Holiday, Country Inns, Los Angeles Times, Sunset.*

"Absolutely the most charming, friendly and delightful place we have ever stayed."

Shaw House B&B Inn

PO Box 1369
Ferndale, CA 95536-1125
(707)786-9958 (800)557-7429 Fax:(707)786-9958
E-mail: bandb@shawhouse.com
Web: www.shawhouse.com

Circa 1854. The Shaw House is one of the oldest inns in California. It is an attractive Gothic house with gables, bays and balconies set back on an acre of garden. An old buckeye tree frames the front gate, and in the back, a secluded deck overlooks a creek. Nestled under the wallpapered gables are several guest rooms filled with antiques and fresh flowers.

Historic Interest: Listed in the National Register.

Innkeeper(s): Ken & Norma Bessingpas. $85-185. MC, VISA, AX. 8 rooms with PB. Breakfast and afternoon tea included in rates. Types of meals: Full bkfst and cont. Beds: QD. Antiquing, fishing and live theater nearby.

Publicity: *Travel & Leisure, New York Times.*

"Lovely place and lovely people—Willard Scott."

Ferndale (Loleta)   C2

Southport Landing

444 Phelan Rd
Ferndale (Loleta), CA 95551
(707)733-5915

Circa 1890. Situated on more than two acres, this early Colonial Revival with its wraparound front porch offers spectacular views of the hills and Humboldt Bay National Wildlife Refuge. Besides the inn's traditional country manor atmosphere with its period antiques, guests will enjoy the uninterrupted silence and the bounty of wildlife. There are five individually decorated guest rooms all with dramatic views of the hillside or the bay. A third-floor game room features a pool table, ping-pong, darts and cards. The country breakfasts include items such as local sausage, homemade muffins and fresh pastry. Snacks are provided in the evening. Hiking, bird-watching, bicycling and kayaking are offered.

Historic Interest: Redwood forests, Arcata Marsh, Somoa Dunes, Lost Coast are located nearby.

Innkeeper(s): Judy & Dana Henderson. $85-125. MC, VISA. TAC10. 5 rooms, 4 with PB. Breakfast and snacks/refreshments included in rates. Types of meals: Full bkfst and early coffee/tea. Beds: Q. Turndown service in room. VCR, fax, bicycles and library on premises. Small meetings and family reunions hosted. Antiquing, fishing, golf, kayaking, beach, birdwatching, bicycling, hiking, beachcombing, live theater, parks and shopping nearby.

"Our greatest B&B experience!"

Fort Bragg   E2

Avalon House

561 Stewart St
Fort Bragg, CA 95437-3226
(707)964-5555 (800)964-5556 Fax:(707)964-5555
E-mail: anne@theavalonhouse.com
Web: www.theavalonhouse.com

Circa 1905. This redwood California Craftsman house was extensively remodeled in 1988 and furnished with a mixture of antiques and willow furniture. Some rooms feature fireplaces,

whirlpool tubs, or ocean views and decks. The inn is in a quiet residential area, three blocks from the Pacific Ocean, one block west of Hwy. 1, and two blocks from the Skunk Train depot.

Innkeeper(s): Anne Sorrells. $80-145. MC, VISA, AX, DS, PC, TC. TAC10. 6 rooms with PB, 4 with FP. Breakfast included in rates. Types of meals: Full bkfst and early coffee/tea. Beds: QD. TV in room. VCR on premises. Weddings, small meetings and family reunions hosted. Antiquing, fishing, whale watching, Skunk Train, live theater, parks, shopping and water sports nearby.
Publicity: *Advocate News.*

"Elegant, private and extremely comfortable. We will never stay in a motel again."

Grey Whale Inn

615 N Main St
Fort Bragg, CA 95437-3240
(707)964-0640 (800)382-7244 Fax:(707)964-4408

Circa 1915. As the name implies, whales can be seen from many of the inn's vantage points during the creatures' migration season along the West Coast. The stately four-story red-

wood inn features airy and spacious guest rooms with neighborhood ocean views. Some rooms include a fireplace, whirlpool tub for two or private deck. Near the heart of downtown Fort

Bragg, it's an easy walk to the Skunk Train, shops, galleries, a microbrewery and restaurants. There is also a fireside lounge, TV/VCR room and a recreation area with pool table.
Historic Interest: The Georgia Pacific Logging Museum and the Guest House Museum are two blocks away, while the Kelley House Museum and Ford House are a 10-mile drive.
Innkeeper(s): John & Colette Bailey. $90-180. MC, VISA, AX, DS, PC, TC. TAC10. 14 rooms with PB, 4 with FP and 2 conference rooms. Breakfast included in rates. Type of meal: Full bkfst. Beds: KQDT. Cable TV, phone and coffee maker in room. VCR, fax, copier and library on premises. Handicap access. Weddings, small meetings, family reunions and seminars hosted. German, Spanish and Dutch spoken. Antiquing, fishing, whale watching, golf, hiking, bicycling, microbrewery, live theater, parks and shopping nearby.
Publicity: *Inn Times, San Francisco Examiner, Travel, Fort Bragg Advocate News, Mendocino Beacon, Los Angeles Times, Sunset, Contra Costa Times.*

"We are going to return each year until we have tried each room. Sunrise room is excellent in the morning or evening."

Old Stewart House Inn

511 Stewart St
Fort Bragg, CA 95437-3226
(707)961-0775 (800)287-8392

Circa 1876. This is the oldest house in Fort Bragg and was built for the founding partner of the town mill. The Victorian theme is enhanced by rooms that may feature amenities such as a fireplace or spa, as well as period furnishings. Within a three-block area of the inn are the Skunk Train Depot, restaurants and beaches. Nearby are ocean cliffs, stands of redwood, waterfalls and botanical gardens.
Innkeeper(s): Darrell Galli. $75-115. MC, VISA, DS. TAC10. 6 rooms with PB, 2 with FP and 2 cabins. Breakfast and snacks/refreshments included in rates. Type of meal: Full bkfst. Catered breakfast available. Beds: Q. Spa and library on premises. Handicap access. Weddings, small meetings and family reunions hosted. Italian spoken. Antiquing, fishing, golf, live theater, parks, shopping, tennis and water sports nearby.
Pets allowed: in cabins, on approval.

The Weller House Inn

524 Stewart St
Fort Bragg, CA 95437
(707)964-4415 (877)8WELLER Fax:(707)964-4198
E-mail: innkeeper@wellerhouse.com
Web: www.wellerhouse.com

Circa 1886. In the National Register, this three-story Italianate Victorian offers dormers, bay windows, a porch and an unusual historic water tower. Breakfast is provided in the redwood paneled ballroom on the top floor and includes baked goods, asparagus quiche or a variety of other dishes created by your Swedish hostess. Guest rooms are decorated in the theme of a different country and include some furnishings original to the house as well as hand-painted tiles, fireplaces and stained glass. From the water tower, guests enjoy expansive ocean views and often spot whales. The innkeepers are musicians, Ted plays the trombone and Eva plays the bassoon. Ask for directions to MacKerricher State Park, which juts into the ocean and allows close up views of harbor seals or the locals' favorite, Glass Beach.
Historic Interest: Guest House Museum (1/4 mile), Mendocino Village (6 miles).
Innkeeper(s): Eva & Ted Kidwell. $95-175. MC, VISA, AX, DC, DS, PC, TC. TAC10. 8 rooms with PB, 2 with FP and 1 conference room. Breakfast and snacks/refreshments included in rates. Types of meals: Full gourmet bkfst and early coffee/tea. Beds: KQT. Phone in room. Fax, spa and library on premises. Weddings, small meetings, family reunions and seminars hosted. Antiquing, art galleries, beaches, bicycling, canoeing/kayaking, fishing, golf, hiking, horseback riding, live theater, museums, parks, shopping and wineries nearby.

Georgetown   G6

American River Inn

PO Box 43, Gold Country
Georgetown, CA 95634-0043
(530)333-4499 (800)245-6566 Fax:(530)333-9253
E-mail: ari@pcweb.net
Web: www.pcweb.net/ari

Circa 1853. Just a few miles from where gold was discovered in Coloma stands this completely restored miners' boarding house. Mining cars dating back to the original Woodside Mine Camp are visible. The lode still runs under the inn. Swimmers will enjoy a spring-fed pool on the property. There is also a Jacuzzi, croquet field, putting green and complimentary mountain bikes. In the evenings, guests are treated to complimentary wines and hors d'oeuvres. Georgetown was a designated site for the California sesquicentennial celebration.

Innkeeper(s): Maria & Will. $85-115. MC, VISA, AX, DS. 25 rooms, 14 with PB, 3 with FP and 1 conference room. Type of meal: Full gourmet bkfst. Beds: KQ. Fax, copier and spa on premises. Handicap access. Fishing and hiking nearby.

"Our home away from home. We fell in love here in all its beauty and will be back for our fourth visit in April, another honeymoon for six days."

Geyserville G4

Hope-Merrill House

21253 Geyserville Ave
Geyserville, CA 95441-9637
(707)857-3356 (800)825-4233 Fax:(707)857-4673

Circa 1885. The Hope-Merrill House is a classic example of the Eastlake Stick style that was so popular during Victorian times. Built entirely from redwood, the house features original wainscoting and silk-screened wallcoverings. A swimming pool, vineyard and gazebo are favorite spots for guests to relax. The Hope-Bosworth House, on the same street, was built in 1904 in the Queen Anne style by an early Geyserville pioneer who lived in the home until the 1960s. The front picket fence is covered with roses. Period details include oak woodwork, sliding doors, polished fir floors and antique light fixtures.

Innkeeper(s): Cosette & Ron Scheiber. $111-174. MC, VISA, AX, DS, PC, TC. TAC10. 12 rooms with PB, 4 with FP and 1 suite. Breakfast included in rates. Types of meals: Full gourmet bkfst and early coffee/tea. Picnic lunch available. Beds: Q. Ceiling fan in room. Fax and copier on premises. Weddings, small meetings and family reunions hosted. Antiquing, parks, shopping and water sports nearby.

Publicity: San Diego Union, Country Homes, Sunset, Sacramento Union, Los Angeles Times.

Glen Ellen G4

Gaige House Inn

13540 Arnold Dr
Glen Ellen, CA 95442-9305
(707)935-0237 (800)935-0237 Fax:(707)935-6411
E-mail: gaige@sprynet.com
Web: www.gaige.com

Circa 1890. This wine country inn, built in the Victorian style, offers 13 individually decorated guest rooms all appointed in a unique Indonesian plantation style. Rattan pieces, beds topped with lacy canopies and plants adorn the bright and airy guest rooms. The most opulent of the rooms, the Gaige Suite, includes an enormous Jacuzzi tub. The lush grounds feature gardens and a creek meanders through the property. Guests enjoy use of a heated swimming pool and spa. Sonoma Valley's many wineries are near the inn. Restaurants are within walking distance. The innkeepers offer a taste of local wines each evening.

Innkeeper(s): Ken Burnet & Greg Nemrow. $170-395. MC, VISA, AX, DS, TC. TAC10. 13 rooms with PB, 7 with FP. Breakfast and snacks/refreshments included in rates. Types of meals: Full gourmet bkfst and early coffee/tea. Beds: KQ. Cable TV, phone, ceiling fan and CD players in room. Air conditioning. Fax, copier, spa, swimming and library on premises. Small meetings, family reunions and seminars hosted. French and Spanish spoken. Antiquing, golf, parks, shopping and tennis nearby.

Grass Valley F6

Murphy's Inn

318 Neal St
Grass Valley, CA 95945-6702
(530)273-6873 (800)895-2488 Fax:(530)273-5157
E-mail: murphys@jps.net
Web: www.murphysinn.com

Circa 1866. The Gold Rush turned this home's builder into a wealthy man, and he built this Victorian for his new bride. The home is decorated by century-old ivy, and the grounds include a 140-year-old giant sequoia. Guests can choose from rooms with fireplaces or a skylight, and all rooms are decorated with antiques. Two suites are located in a separate house and one includes a kitchen and living room. The Victorian is located in a Grass Valley historic district and is within walking distance to many local attractions.

Innkeeper(s): Ted & Nancy Daus. $115-165. MC, VISA, AX, TC. TAC10. 8 rooms with PB, 4 with FP and 3 suites. Breakfast included in rates. Types of meals: Full gourmet bkfst and early coffee/tea. Beds: KQD. Cable TV, phone, ceiling fan and VCR in room. Air conditioning. Fax and library on premises. Small meetings, family reunions and seminars hosted. Antiquing, fishing, golf, live theater, parks, shopping, downhill skiing, cross-country skiing, tennis and water sports nearby.

Swan-Levine House

328 S Church St
Grass Valley, CA 95945-6709
(530)272-1873

Circa 1880. Originally built by a local merchant, this Queen Anne Victorian was converted into a hospital by Dr. John Jones, and it served the area as a medical center until 1968. Innkeepers/artists Howard and Margaret Levine renovated the house including a printmaking studio and guesthouse. The old surgery is now a guest room with rose-painted walls and octagonal white floor tiles and provides a grand view from the wicker-furnished turret.

Innkeeper(s): Howard & Peggy Levine. $75-100. MC, VISA. 4 rooms with PB, 1 with FP and 1 suite. Type of meal: Full bkfst. Beds: KQT. Fireplace in suite in room.

Publicity: Country Living Magazine.

"You made us feel at home. An atmosphere of open-hearted friendship is rather rare these days."

Groveland H7

The Groveland Hotel

18767 Main St, PO Box 481
Groveland, CA 95321-0481
(209)962-4000 (800)273-3314 Fax:(209)962-6674

Circa 1849. Located 23 miles from Yosemite National Park, the 1992 restoration features both an 1849 adobe building with 18-inch-thick walls constructed during the Gold Rush and a 1914 building erected to house workers for the Hetch Hetchy Dam. Both feature two-story balconies. There is a Victorian parlor, a gourmet restaurant and a Western saloon. Guest

rooms feature European antiques, down comforters and in-room coffee. The feeling is one of casual elegance.

Innkeeper(s): Peggy A. & Grover C. Mosley. $125-200. MC, VISA, AX, DC, CB, DS, PC, TC. TAC10. 17 rooms with PB, 3 with FP, 3 suites and 1 conference room. Breakfast included in rates. Types of meals: Cont plus and early coffee/tea. Picnic lunch, banquet service, catering service and room service available. Restaurant on premises. Beds: QT. TV, phone and ceiling fan in room. Air conditioning. VCR, fax, copier, library, pet boarding and child care on premises. Handicap access. Weddings, small meetings, family reunions and seminars hosted. Antiquing, fishing, golf, parks, shopping, downhill skiing, cross-country skiing, tennis and water sports nearby.

Publicity: *Wine Spectator Award of excellence for our wine list.*

Gualala   G3

North Coast Country Inn

34591 S Hwy 1
Gualala, CA 95445
(707)884-4537 (800)959-4537

Circa 1948. Overlooking the Pacific Ocean, the six guest rooms that comprise North Coast Country Inn are tucked into a pine and redwood forested hillside. Each is furnished with antiques,

and include a fire-place, some wet-bar kitchenettes and private deck. There is a hot tub on the hillside or you may relax in the gazebo. Breakfast is served in

the common room. In the evening, guests are invited to enjoy a glass of sherry. Barking sea lions are often heard in the distance.

Innkeeper(s): Maureen & Bill Shupe. $160-185. MC, VISA, AX, PC, TC. TAC10. 6 rooms with PB, 6 with FP. Breakfast and snacks/refreshments included in rates. Type of meal: Full gourmet bkfst. Beds: KQ. Books and games and ceiling fans in some rooms in room. VCR, spa and library on premises. Small meetings, family reunions and seminars hosted. Antiquing, fishing, golf, hiking, beach combing, parks, shopping, tennis and water sports nearby.

Publicity: *Wine Trader, Motortrend, Los Angeles Times, San Francisco Chronicle.*

"Thank you so much for a very gracious stay in your cozy inn. We have appreciated all the special touches."

Guerneville   G3

Fern Grove Cottages

16650 River Rd
Guerneville, CA 95446-9678
(707)869-8105 Fax:(707)869-1615

Circa 1926. Clustered in a village-like atmosphere and surrounded by redwoods, these craftsman cottages have romantic fireplaces, private entrances, and are individually decorated. The cottages were built in the 1920s and served as little vacation houses for San Francisco families visiting the Russian River. Some units have a kitchen, some have double whirlpool

tubs and other cottages are suitable for families. Guests enjoy use of the swimming pool. The cottages are just a few blocks from shops and restaurants, as well as a swimming beach by the river. A state park and winery tour are within three miles of the cottages.

Innkeeper(s): Anne & Simon Lowings. $69-159. MC, VISA, AX, DS, PC, TC. TAC10. 20 cottages with PB, 11 with FP and 1 conference room. Breakfast included in rates. Type of meal: Cont. Beds: Q. Cable TV in room. Swimming and library on premises. Small meetings, family reunions and seminars hosted. Antiquing, fishing, golf, beach, canoeing, Armstrong Redwater State Park, wineries, parks, shopping, tennis and water sports nearby.

Pets allowed: One per cottage, on leash, clean animals only. $10 charge.

Ridenhour Ranch

12850 River Rd
Guerneville, CA 95446-9276
(707)887-1033 (888)877-4466 Fax:(707)869-2967
E-mail: ridenhourinn@earthlink.net
Web: www.ridenhourranchhouseinn.com

Circa 1906. Located on a hill overlooking the Russian River, this ranch house is shaded by redwoods, oaks and laurels. There are seven guest rooms and a cottage overlooking the rose garden. Guests can relax in the hot tub below the majestic oak trees. The Korbel Champagne cellars are nearby, and it's a five-minute walk to the river. Wineries, vineyards, the ocean and California's famous redwoods all are nearby.

Innkeeper(s): Chris Bell & Meilani Nananjo. $95-145. MC, VISA, AX, PC, TC. TAC10. 8 rooms with PB, 1 with FP and 1 suite. Breakfast and snacks/refreshments included in rates. Types of meals: Full gourmet bkfst and early coffee/tea. Beds: KQ. Cable TV and ceiling fan in room. Antiquing, fishing, golf, live theater, parks, shopping and water sports nearby.

Publicity: *Los Angeles Times, Orange County Register, Los Altos Town Crier.*

"Your hospitality and food will ensure our return!"

Half Moon Bay   I4

Old Thyme Inn

779 Main St
Half Moon Bay, CA 94019-1924
(650)726-1616 (800)720-4277 Fax:(650)726-6394
E-mail: innkeeper@oldthymeinn.com
Web: www.oldthymeinn.com

Circa 1899. Located on the historic Main Street of Old Town, this fully-restored Queen Anne Victorian is known for its aromatic English garden that includes more than 50 varieties of herbs and flowers. Recently redecorated, rooms are furnished with antiques and fine art and are named after various herbs found in the garden. Among the amenities available for guests are double Jacuzzis, fireplaces, feather beds and down comforters. Wine, sherry and snacks are served in the afternoon, and in the morning, enjoy a full breakfast. A beautiful crescent-shaped beach is within walking distance, as are fine restaurants, shops and art galleries. Ask the innkeepers to help arrange horseback riding along the shoreline, whale watching cruises or touring elephant seal breeding preserves.

Historic Interest: San Francisco is just 25 miles away, Filoli Gardens nearby.
Innkeeper(s): Rick & Kathy Ellis. $100-255. MC, VISA, AX, DS, PC, TC. 7 rooms with PB, 3 with FP. Breakfast included in rates. Type of meal: Full bkfst. Beds: Q. Cable TV, VCR and three rooms with Jacuzzi tubs in room. Fax on premises. Small meetings and family reunions hosted. French spoken. Antiquing, fishing, live theater, parks, shopping and water sports nearby.
Publicity: California Weekends, Los Angeles, San Mateo Times, San Jose Mercury News, Herb Companion, San Francisco Examiner.

Healdsburg G4

Calderwood Inn

25 West Grant St
Healdsburg, CA 95448-4804
(707)431-1110 (800)600-5444

Circa 1902. This romantic Queen Anne Victorian is surrounded by lush acres of redwoods, cedars and cypress trees. Each of the six rooms has been decorated with elegant, yet comfortable

antiques. Two rooms offer clawfoot tubs, while others include amenities such as fireplaces and whirlpool tubs. Window seats, down comforters and four-poster beds are some of the romantic touches guests might

find in their rooms. Fresh seasonal fruit and baked goods accompany the morning entree. Appetizers, wine and port are served in the evenings.

Historic Interest: Luther Burbank Home & Gardens, Sonoma County Museum, and a Ripley's Believe It Or Not church, constructed entirely out of one redwood tree, are some of the area's historic sites.
Innkeeper(s): Jennifer & Paul Zawodny. $135-200. PC, TC. 6 rooms with PB and 1 conference room. Breakfast included in rates. Types of meals: Full bkfst and early coffee/tea. Snacks/refreshments available. Beds: KQ. Antiquing, fishing, hiking, gift shop, live theater, water sports and wineries nearby.

Camellia Inn

211 North St
Healdsburg, CA 95448-4251
(707)433-8182 (800)727-8182 Fax:(707)433-8130
E-mail: info@camelliainn.com
Web: www.camelliainn.com

Circa 1869. An elegant Italianate Victorian townhouse, the Camellia Inn has twin marble parlor fireplaces and an ornate mahogany dining room fireplace. Antiques fill the guest rooms, complementing Palladian windows and classic interior moldings. The award-winning grounds feature 50 varieties of camellias and are accentuated with a swimming pool, which guests may use in summer.

Innkeeper(s): Ray, Del and Lucy Lewand. $85-185. MC, VISA, AX. 9 rooms with PB, 4 with FP and 1 suite. Breakfast included in rates. Type of meal: Full bkfst. Beds: QD. Fax on premises. Antiquing and fishing nearby.

"A bit of paradise for city folks."

Grape Leaf Inn

539 Johnson St
Healdsburg, CA 95448-3907
(707)433-8140 Fax:(707)433-3140
E-mail: grapeleaf.inn@cwix.com
Web: www.grapeleafinn.com

Circa 1900. This magnificently restored Queen Anne home was built in what was considered the "Nob Hill" of Healdsburg. It was typical of a turn-of-the-century, middle-class

dream house. It is situated near the Russian River and the town center. Seventeen skylights provide an abundance of sunlight, fresh air, and stained glass. Five guest rooms offer whirlpool tubs and showers for two. The innkeepers make the most of

their wine country location, hosting a wine tasting each evening with a display of at least five Sonoma County wines. Each guest room is named for a wine variety, such as Zinfandel or Merlot. The inn is just a few blocks from many of Healdsburg's restaurants and shops.

Innkeeper(s): Richard & Kae Rosenberg. $105-185. MC, VISA, PC, TC. TAC10. 7 rooms with PB. Breakfast and snacks/refreshments included in rates. Type of meal: Full bkfst. Beds: KQ. 5 rooms have whirlpool tub/showers for two in room. Air conditioning. Antiquing, fishing, over 60 wineries close by, shopping, water sports and wineries nearby.

"It was our first time at a real one and we were delighted with our lovely accommodations, delicious breakfasts and most of all you graciousness in trying to please your guests. Thank you for making our 38th anniversary a very special one that we will always remember."

Haydon Street Inn

321 Haydon St
Healdsburg, CA 95448-4411
(707)433-5228 (800)528-3703 Fax:(707)433-6637
E-mail: innkeeper@haydon.com
Web: www.haydon.com

Circa 1912. Architectural buffs will have fun naming the several architectural styles found in the Haydon House. It has the curving porch and general shape of a Queen Anne Victorian, the expansive areas of siding and unadorned columns of the Neo-Classic style, and the exposed roof rafters of the Craftsman. The decor is elegant and romantic, with antiques.

The Turret Room includes a clawfoot tub and a fireplace. Two rooms are located in the inn's Victorian Cottage, and both have whirlpool tubs. The Pine Room offers a pencil post bed with a Battenburg lace canopy, while the Victorian Room includes fine antiques and a Ralph Lauren wicker bed.

Innkeeper(s): Dick & Pat Bertapelle. $95-175. MC, VISA, DS, PC, TC. TAC10. 8 rooms with PB, 1 with FP. Breakfast, afternoon tea and snacks/refreshments included in rates. Types of meals: Full gourmet bkfst and early coffee/tea. Beds: QD. TV, ceiling fan and double whirlpool tubs two rooms in room. Air conditioning. VCR and fax on premises. Family reunions and seminars hosted. Antiquing, fishing, biking, wine tasting, parks, shopping and water sports nearby.
Publicity: Los Angeles, San Francisco.

"Adjectives like class, warmth, beauty, thoughtfulness with the right amount of privacy, attention to details relating to comfort, all come to mind. Thank you for the care and elegance."

Healdsburg Inn on The Plaza

110 Matheson St, PO Box 1196
Healdsburg, CA 95448-4108
(707)433-6991 (800)431-8663 Fax:(707)433-9513
Web: www.healdsburginn.com

Circa 1900. A former Wells Fargo building, the inn is a renovated brick gingerbread overlooking the plaza in historic downtown Healdsburg. Ornate bay windows, embossed wood paneling and broad, paneled stairs present a welcome entrance. There are fireplaces and the halls are filled with sunlight from vaulted, glass skylights. A solarium is the setting for breakfast and evening wine and hors d'oeuvres. A large covered balcony extends along the entire rear of the building. Shops on the premises sell gifts, toys, quilts and fabric. An antique shop and art gallery can be found there, as well. The surrounding area is full of things to do, including wineries and wine-tasting rooms.

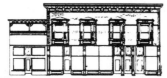

Innkeeper(s): Genny Jenkins & LeRoy Steck. $205-295. MC, VISA. 10 rooms with PB, 9 with FP and 1 conference room. Breakfast and snacks/refreshments included in rates. Types of meals: Full gourmet bkfst and early coffee/tea. Afternoon tea available. Beds: KQT. Cable TV, phone, ceiling fan and VCR in room. Air conditioning. Fax and copier on premises. Small meetings, family reunions and seminars hosted. Antiquing, fishing, wineries, balloon, canoe, historic walking tour, parks, shopping and water sports nearby.

Publicity: *Healdsburg Tribune, Los Angeles Daily News, New York Times.*

"The first-thing-in-the-morning juice and coffee was much appreciated."

Raford House

10630 Wohler Rd
Healdsburg, CA 95448-9418
(707)887-9573 (800)887-9503 Fax:(707)887-9597

Circa 1880. Situated on more than four acres of rose gardens and fruit trees, this classic Victorian country estate originally was built as a summer home and ranch house in the 1880s. Just 70 miles north of San Francisco, Raford House is nestled in the heart of the Sonoma County wine country, minutes away from award-winning wineries and many fine restaurants. Located close to the Russian River, between Healdsburg and the beautiful Northern California coast, the area has scenic country roads and rugged coastlines.

Innkeeper(s): Carole & Jack Vore. $110-175. MC, VISA, AX, DS. TAC10. 7 rooms with PB and 1 suite. Breakfast and snacks/refreshments included in rates. Types of meals: Full bkfst and early coffee/tea. Beds: Q. Fax on premises. Small meetings and family reunions hosted. Antiquing, fishing, live theater, parks, shopping and water sports nearby.

Publicity: *Los Angeles Times, Travel & Leisure, Country. Wine Spectator Magazine.*

"Truly a 'serendipity' experience! Wonderful, welcoming ambiance, great food, lovely hosts. I am 'renewed'."

Hope Valley   G8

Sorensen's Resort

14255 Hwy 88
Hope Valley, CA 96120
(530)694-2203 (800)423-9949

Circa 1876. Where Danish sheepherders settled in this 7,000-foot-high mountain valley, the Sorensen family built a cluster of fishing cabins. Thus began a century-old tradition of valley

hospitality. The focal point of Sorensen's is a "stave" cabin — a reproduction of a 13th-century Nordic house. Now developed as a Nordic ski resort, a portion of the Mormon-Emigrant Trail and Pony Express Route pass near the inn's 165 acres. In the summer, river rafting, fishing, pony express re-rides and llama treks are popular Sierra pastimes. Lake Tahoe lies 20 miles to the north. Breakfast is included in the rates for bed & breakfast units only. All other cabins are equipped with kitchens.

Historic Interest: Alpine County Museum (12 miles), Old Indian Trade Ports, Emigrant Road.

Innkeeper(s): John & Patty Brissenden. $65-350. MC, VISA, AX, DS, PC, TC. TAC10. 30 rooms, 28 with PB, 21 with FP, 28 cottages and 2 conference rooms. Types of meals: Full bkfst, cont plus and early coffee/tea. Gourmet dinner, snacks/refreshments, picnic lunch, lunch and banquet service available. Restaurant on premises. Beds: QD. Copier, sauna and library on premises. Handicap access. Weddings, small meetings, family reunions and seminars hosted. Spanish spoken. Antiquing, fishing, parks, downhill skiing, cross-country skiing and water sports nearby.

"In one night's stay, I felt more comfortable, relaxed, and welcome than any vacation my 47 years have allowed. Thank you for the happiness you have given my children."

Hopland   F3

Thatcher Inn

13401 S Hwy 101
Hopland, CA 95449
(707)744-1890 (800)266-1891 Fax:(707)744-1219

Circa 1890. Elegant Victorian furnishings fill the rooms at this late Victorian manor, which has been restored to its original state. The guest rooms are appointed with floral, Victorian-era wallcoverings and decorated with antiques. The Fireside Library with its rich, wood bookshelves, marble fireplace and highback chairs is an inviting place to enjoy a good book, and there are more than 4,000 volumes to enjoy. A full, country breakfast is served each morning. Special pris fixe dinners are available for bed & breakfast guests Sunday through Thursday. The inn's restaurant, open Wednesday through Saturday, serves a unique selection of Italian and Romanian specialties. Guests also enjoy full bar service featuring Mendocino wines and fine liquors. Plus, the inn is able to host tour lunches, holiday parties and rehearsal dinners, diligently prepared by chefs Don and Marlena Sacca. The innkeepers can help guests plan visits to local wineries, as well as other interesting local attractions.

Innkeeper(s): Don & Marlena Sacca. $115-175. MC, VISA, AX. TAC10. 20 rooms with PB, 2 suites and 1 conference room. Breakfast included in rates. Types of meals: Full gourmet bkfst and early coffee/tea. Beds: KQT. Phone, ceiling fan, hair dryers and bath robes in room. Air conditioning. VCR, fax, copier, swimming and library on premises. Small meetings, family reunions and seminars hosted. Antiquing, fishing, wine tasting, golf, parks and water sports nearby.

"We appreciate your attention to details and efforts which made our visit so pleasant."

Idyllwild   O12

The Pine Cove Inn

23481 Hwy 243, PO Box 2181
Idyllwild, CA 92549
(909)659-5033 (888)659-5033 Fax:(909)659-5034

Circa 1935. These rustic, A-frame cottages offer a variety of amenities in a natural, mountain setting. Refrigerators and microwaves have been placed in each unit, several of which include a wood-burning fireplace. One unit has a full kitchen. A full breakfast is served in a separate lodge which dates back to 1935. The village of Idyllwild is three miles down the road, and the surrounding country offers a variety of activities.

Innkeeper(s): Bob & Michelle Bollmann. $70-100. MC, VISA, AX, DS, PC, TC. TAC10. 10 rooms with PB, 6 with FP, 3 suites and 1 conference room. Breakfast included in rates. Type of meal: Full bkfst. Beds: QT. Ceiling fan and microwave in room. VCR and fax on premises. Weddings, small meetings, family reunions and seminars hosted. Antiquing, fishing, hiking, mountain hiking, live theater, parks, shopping and cross-country skiing nearby.

Inverness   H4

Hotel Inverness

25 Park Ave, Box 780
Inverness, CA 94937-0780
(415)669-7393 Fax:(415)669-1702

Circa 1906. Guests rave about the outdoor breakfasts served in the garden or on the deck. Situated on the edge of a coastal village, Hotel Inverness, near Tomales Bay, is surrounded by the Point Reyes National Seashore. The garden lawn accommodates picnics, lounging or croquet. Boasting one of the best birdwatching areas in the west, the inn has a park-like setting where one can relax and admire the surrounding wooded area. This great natural area reminds many of Yosemite National Park.

Innkeeper(s): Susan & Tom Simms. $125-195. MC, VISA, AX, PC, TC. TAC5. 5 rooms with PB. Breakfast included in rates. Type of meal: Cont plus. Beds: Q. Fax and croquet on premises. Hiking, birdwatching, horseback riding, kayaking, parks and water sports nearby.

Ten Inverness Way

10 Inverness Way, PO Box 63
Inverness, CA 94937-0063
(415)669-1648 Fax:(415)669-7403
E-mail: inn@teninvernessway.com
Web: www.teninvernessway.com

Circa 1904. Shingled in redwood, this handsome bed & breakfast features a sunny library with many good books, and close access to a wonderful hiking area. After an afternoon of hiking, guests can enjoy a soak in the garden hot tub. Inverness is located on Tomales Bay, offering close access to nearby beaches at Point Reyes National Seashore. The Golden Gate Bridge is 45 minutes from the inn.

Innkeeper(s): Teri Mowery. $145-180. MC, VISA, PC, TC. 5 rooms with PB. Breakfast and afternoon tea included in rates. Types of meals: Full bkfst and early coffee/tea. Beds: Q. Fax, spa and library on premises. Antiquing, fishing, parks and water sports nearby.

"Everything we could have wanted for our comfort was anticipated by our hosts. Great hot tub. Lovely rooms and common areas."

Jackson   G6

Wedgewood Inn

11941 Narcissus Rd
Jackson, CA 95642-9600
(209)296-4300 (800)933-4393 Fax:(209)296-4301

Circa 1987. Located in the heart of Sierra gold country on a secluded, five acres, this Victorian replica is crammed full of sentimental family heirlooms and antiques. Each room has

been designed with careful attention to detail. A baby grand piano rests in the parlor. The carriage house is a separate cottage with its own private entrance. It boasts four generations of family heirlooms, a carved canopy bed, a wood-burning stove and a two-person Jacuzzi tub. The innkeepers' 1921 Model-T, "Henry," is located in its own special showroom. Gourmet breakfasts are served on bone china and include specialties such as cheese-filled blintzes, fruit and baked goods. Breakfast is available in selected guest rooms by request. There is a gift shop and Thomas Kincade Gallery on the premises.

Innkeeper(s): Vic & Jeannine Beltz. $110-175. MC, VISA, AX, DS, PC, TC. TAC10. 6 rooms with PB and 1 suite. Breakfast included in rates. Types of meals: Full gourmet bkfst and early coffee/tea. Snacks/refreshments available. Beds: Q. Turndown service, ceiling fan and jacuzzi in room. Air conditioning. Fax, copier, croquet, hammocks and horseshoes on premises. Antiquing, fishing, golf, live theater, shopping, downhill skiing and cross-country skiing nearby.

Jamestown   H7

1859 Historic National Hotel, A Country Inn

18183 Main St, PO Box 502
Jamestown, CA 95327
(209)984-3446 (800)894-3446 Fax:(209)984-5620

Circa 1859. Located between Yosemite National Park and Lake Tahoe, this is one of the 10 oldest continuously operating hotels in California. In the Gold Country, the inn maintains its original redwood bar where thousands of dollars in gold dust were once spent. Electricity and plumbing were added for the first time when the inn was restored. Original furnishings, Gold Rush period antiques, as well as brass beds, lace curtains and quilts are among the guest room appointments. A soaking room is an additional amenity, although all rooms have their own private baths. A bountiful continental breakfast is complimentary. Be sure and arrange for romantic dining at the inn's gourmet restaurant, considered to be one of the finest in the Mother Lode. Order a favorite liquor or espresso from the saloon or try the area's wine tasting. Favorite diversions include gold panning, live theatre and antiquing.

Historic Interest: Railtown 1897 State Historic Park, located in Jamestown, is a few blocks from the hotel.

Innkeeper(s): Stephen Willey. $80-120. MC, VISA, AX, DC, CB, DS, PC, TC. TAC10. 9 rooms with PB and 1 conference room. Breakfast included in rates. Types of meals: Cont plus and early coffee/tea. Gourmet dinner, snacks/refreshments, picnic lunch, gourmet lunch, banquet service and catering service available. Restaurant on premises. Beds: QT. Cable TV in room. Air conditioning. VCR and fax on premises. Weddings, small meetings, family reunions and seminars hosted. Spanish spoken. Antiquing, fishing, live theater, parks, downhill skiing, cross-country skiing and water sports nearby.

Pets allowed: By arrangement - credit card or cash deposit required.

Publicity: *Bon Appetit, California Magazine, Focus, San Francisco Magazine, Gourmet, Sunset.*

Royal Hotel

18239 Main St
Jamestown, CA 95327-0219
(209)984-5271 Fax:(209)984-1675

Circa 1922. Guests can experience a bit of the Old West at the Royal Hotel, which was built in the early '20s to provide luxurious lodging for travelers. The hotel originally had a ballroom and restaurant, and for those who preferred to ignore Prohibition, there was a secret "back bar." Rooms are decorated in Victorian style with turn-of-the-century antiques. In addition to the guest rooms, there are two suites and a honeymoon  cottage. Jamestown is California's second oldest gold mining town and has been the site of more than 150 movies and television shows. Jamestown offers shops, antique stores, restaurants and gold mining attractions. The innkeepers can arrange for steam train rides, whitewater rafting and golf packages.
Innkeeper(s): Richard & Cora Riddell. $55-100. MC, VISA. 19 rooms, 17 with PB, 2 suites, 3 cottages and 1 conference room. Breakfast included in rates. Types of meals: Cont plus and early coffee/tea. Beds: QT. Ceiling fan in room. Air conditioning. Fax, copier, library and Jamestown Visitor Center on premises. Small meetings and seminars hosted. Antiquing, fishing, steam Train Rides, live theater, parks, shopping, downhill skiing and water sports nearby.

Joshua Tree   O13

Joshua Tree Inn

61259 29 Palms Hwy, PO Box 340
Joshua Tree, CA 92252-0340
(760)366-1188 (800)366-1444 Fax:(760)366-3805

Circa 1940. The hacienda-style inn was once a '50s motel. It now offers Victorian-style rooms with king-size beds. Antiques and Old West memorabilia add to the  decor. Throughout the inn, local artists display their creations. The inn is one mile from the gateway to the 467,000-acre Joshua Tree National Park.
Innkeeper(s): Dr. Daniel & Evelyn Shirbroun. $85-155. MC, VISA, AX, DC, CB, DS, TC. TAC10. 10 rooms with PB, 2 suites and 1 conference room. MAP. Types of meals: Cont and early coffee/tea. Afternoon tea available. Beds: KQDT. Cable TV, phone and ceiling fan in room. Air conditioning. VCR, fax, copier and swimming on premises. Weddings, small meetings, family reunions and seminars hosted. Antiquing, golf, Joshua Tree National Park, live theater, parks, shopping and tennis nearby.
Pets allowed: In designated rooms.
Publicity: *Los Angeles Times, Press Enterprise.*
"Quiet, clean and charming."

Julian   P12

Butterfield B&B

2284 Sunset Dr
Julian, CA 92036
(760)765-2179 (800)379-4262 Fax:(760)765-1229
E-mail: butterfield@abac.com
Web: butterfieldbandb.com

Circa 1935. Reserve the French Suite here and not only will you have a fireplace, private entrance and sitting area, but you will have the option of having breakfast served in a romantic French antique bed. Located on three acres at the edge of town, the hillside Butterfield B&B also boasts a private cottage, Rose Bud. The inn's breakfast is served in the garden gazebo in the summer and offers specialities such as eggs Benedict and peach and basil crepes. In cool weather, breakfast is served fireside. The innkeepers are able to arrange a private candlelight dinner or a horse-drawn-carriage ride for your special celebrations.
Innkeeper(s): Ed Glass. $115-160. MC, VISA, AX, PC. TAC10. 5 rooms with PB, 2 with FP and 1 cottage. Breakfast and snacks/refreshments included in rates. AP. Types of meals: Full gourmet bkfst and early coffee/tea. Gourmet dinner, catered breakfast and room service available. Beds: QD. Cable TV and ceiling fan in room. Library on premises. Antiquing, fishing, golf, live theater, parks, shopping and sporting events nearby.

Julian Gold Rush Hotel

2032 Main St, PO Box 1856
Julian, CA 92036-1856
(760)765-0201 (800)734-5854

Circa 1897. The dream of a former slave and his wife lives today in this sole surviving hotel in Southern California's "Mother Lode of Gold Mining." This Victorian charmer is listed in the National Register of Historic Places and is a designated State of California Point of Historic Interest (#SDI-  09). Guests enjoy the feeling of a visit to Grandma's and a tradition of genteel hospitality.
Historic Interest: Entire town site is a State Historic Landmark.
Innkeeper(s): Steve & Gig Ballinger. $72-175. MC, VISA, AX, PC, TC. TAC10. 15 rooms with PB, 1 suite, 2 cottages and 1 conference room. Breakfast and afternoon tea included in rates. Type of meal: Full bkfst. Beds: QDT. Weddings, small meetings and seminars hosted. Antiquing, fishing, live theater and parks nearby.
Publicity: *San Diego Union, PSA.*

"Any thoughts you have about the 20th century will leave you when you walk into the lobby of this grand hotel— Westways Magazine."

Orchard Hill Country Inn

2502 Washington St, PO Box 425
Julian, CA 92036-0425
(760)765-1700 (800)716-7242
E-mail: information@orchardhill.com
Web: www.orchardhill.com

This Craftsman-style inn is a perfect country getaway for those seeking solace from the city lights. There are four, 1920s-style cottages, and a new lodge built as a companion. Expansive, individually appointed cottage rooms offer amenities such as fireplaces, whirlpool tubs, hand-knitted afghans and down comforters all surrounded by warm, country decor. Gourmet coffee, tea and cocoa also are provided in each cottage room, as are refrigerators. Guests can enjoy a breakfast of fruits, muffins and a special egg dish in the dining room. Wine and hors d'oeuvres are provided each afternoon. Dinner is served on selected evenings. The expansive grounds boast a variety of gardens highlighting native plants and flowers.

Historic Interest: Orchard Hill is located in the heart of a state historic district, and the innkeepers offer a comprehensive visitors' guide of the Julian area, including maps and a historic walking tour route.

Innkeeper(s): Darrell & Pat Straube. $160-265. MC, VISA, AX, PC, TC. TAC10. 22 rooms with PB, 11 with FP and 1 conference room. Breakfast and snacks/refreshments included in rates. Types of meals: Full bkfst and early coffee/tea. Gourmet dinner, picnic lunch, banquet service and catering service available. Beds: KQ. Cable TV, ceiling fan, VCR, whirlpool tub and wet bar in room. Air conditioning. Fax, copier and pet boarding off-site on premises. Handicap access. Small meetings and seminars hosted. Antiquing, fishing, music/art festivals, hiking, horse trails, hiking trails, live theater, parks and shopping nearby.

"The quality of the rooms, service and food were beyond our expectations."

La Jolla
Q11

The Bed & Breakfast Inn at La Jolla

7753 Draper Ave
La Jolla, CA 92037
(858)456-2066 (800)582-2466 Fax:(858)456-1510
E-mail: bed+breakfast@innlajolla.com
Web: www.innlajolla.com

Circa 1913. This historic gem truly is a treasure, surrounded by the coastal beauty of La Jolla. The home was designed by George Kautz and was built in the Cubist style. John Philip Sousa and his family lived in the house for several years during the 1920s. The guest rooms and suites offer beautiful furnishings and romantic décor. The Holiday room includes a massive four-poster, canopy bed, hardwood floors topped with Oriental rugs and a fireplace. Other rooms include amenities such as clawfoot tubs and fireplaces; some rooms offer an ocean view. The gourmet breakfasts are a treat, rivaled only by the setting. Guests partake of their morning meal either on a secluded patio or in the garden. Californians have long enjoyed the splendor of La Jolla, a charming village with a spectacular coastline. Guests can walk to the many unique shops or take a stroll along the beach and enjoy an unforgettable sunset. A short drive out of La Jolla will take guests to the myriad of sites in San Diego. After a day exploring the area, guests return to the inn and enjoy a sampling of wine and cheese.

Historic Interest: Bishop's School (next door), Old Town (5 miles), Balboa Park (5 miles).

Innkeeper(s): Ron Shanks. $129-329. MC, VISA, AX, PC, TC. TAC10. 15 rooms with PB, 4 with FP, 2 suites and 1 conference room. Breakfast and snacks/refreshments included in rates. Type of meal: Early coffee/tea. Picnic lunch, catering service and catered breakfast available. Beds: KQT. Cable TV, phone, turndown service, ceiling fan and VCR in room. Central air. Fax, bicycles, library, beach chairs, towels and picnic lunches can be ordered on premises. Weddings, small meetings, family reunions and seminars hosted. Spanish spoken. Amusement parks, antiquing, art galleries, beaches, bicycling, canoeing/kayaking, fishing, golf, hiking, live theater, museums, parks, shopping, sporting events, tennis and water sports nearby.

Prospect Park Inn

1110 Prospect St
La Jolla, CA 92037-4533
(858)454-0133 (800)433-1609 Fax:(858)454-2056

Circa 1946. Although this is a newer property, built in 1946, the hotel is located within walking distance to many wonderful shops, restaurants and sites in beautiful La Jolla, an upscale suburb of San Diego. Guests enjoy stunning ocean views from some rooms. The decor is done in a modern and pleasing hotel style. Made-to-order continental breakfasts are served on the sun deck, which faces the Pacific and La Jolla Cove. San Diego

is just minutes away, but guests can easily spend a whole day enjoying this seaside village.

Innkeeper(s): John Heichman. $120-375. MC, VISA, AX, DC, CB, DS, TC. TAC10. 22 rooms with PB and 2 suites. Breakfast and afternoon tea included in rates. Type of meal: Cont. Beds: KQT. Cable TV and phone in room. Air conditioning. Fax, copier, bicycles, library and sun deck on premises. Weddings, small meetings, family reunions and seminars hosted. Spanish, German, Russian and Arabic spoken. Amusement parks, fishing, golf, live theater, parks, shopping, sporting events, tennis and water sports nearby.

Lake Tahoe/Soda Springs
F7

Royal Gorge's Rainbow Lodge

9411 Hillside Dr PO Box 1100
Lake Tahoe/Soda Springs, CA 95728
(530)426-3871 (800)500-3871 Fax:(530)426-9221

Circa 1930. Located in the Sierras by a bend of the Yuba River, this old mountain lodge is a nostalgic, picturesque getaway spot. The lodge was built using local granite and hand-hewn timber. A mountain decor permeates the 32 guest rooms.

There are two dining rooms, featuring fine Californian and French cuisine. The Engadine Cafe offers breakfast, lunch, dinner and Sunday brunch. The cocktail lounge, which offers a bar menu throughout the day and into the evening, is decorated with a variety of photographs documenting the area's history. Chairs and tables have been set up for those who wish to relax and enjoy the river view. The lodge is adjacent to the Royal Gorge Ski Area, which is the largest cross-country ski area in North America. Summer activities include hiking, mountain biking and fishing.

Innkeeper(s): Trudi Baer. $79-139. MC, VISA, TC. 32 rooms, 10 with PB, 2 suites and 1 conference room. Breakfast included in rates. Type of meal: Full gourmet bkfst. Gourmet dinner, gourmet lunch and banquet service available. Restaurant on premises. Beds: QDT. Fax on premises. Weddings, small meetings, family reunions and seminars hosted. Antiquing, fishing, parks, shopping, downhill skiing, cross-country skiing, sporting events and water sports nearby.

Long Beach
O10

Kennebec Corner B&B

2305 E 2nd St
Long Beach, CA 90803-5126
(562)439-2705 Fax:(310)518-0616
E-mail: kennebec@earthlink.net
Web: bbhost.com/kennebeccorner

Circa 1912. This California Craftsman-style home offers a large four-room suite with a sitting room, office, fireplace, bathroom with a double sunken tub and a bedroom with a one-of-a-kind, four-poster king-size bed. There is an outdoor spa available in the home's courtyard. The innkeepers deliver the morning paper and a tray with coffee or tea to your door an hour prior to breakfast. On weekdays, a healthy California or continental breakfast is served, and on weekends, guests enjoy a full,

gourmet meal. The home is located in Bluff Park, a local historic district two blocks from the beach.

Innkeeper(s): Michael & Marty Gunhus. $125-150. MC, VISA, AX, PC, TC. TAC20. 1 suites. Breakfast included in rates. Types of meals: Full gourmet bkfst, cont plus and early coffee/tea. Picnic lunch available. Beds: K. Cable TV, phone and VCR in room. Fax, spa, bicycles and library on premises. Antiquing, fishing, live theater, parks, shopping, sporting events and water sports nearby.

Lord Mayor's B&B Inn

435 Cedar Ave
Long Beach, CA 90802-2245
(562)436-0324 Fax:(562)436-0324
E-mail: innkeepers@lordmayors.com
Web: www.lordmayors.com

Circa 1904. The first mayor of Long Beach lived in this beautifully restored turn-of-the-century home. Granite pillars flank the veranda of this historical landmark. Rooms are full of ambience and antiques, and all five rooms have access to porches or sun decks. One room features a hand-carved, oak Hawaiian bed, another boasts an Eastlake bed. In the evenings, guest are served tea, sherry and homemade fare. The inn, located in a redevelopment area, is within walking distance of the convention center, a mall, the beach and performing arts theaters.

Historic Interest: Queen Mary (three-fourth mile), Port of Long Beach (half mile).
Innkeeper(s): Laura & Reuben Brasser. $85-125. MC, VISA, AX, DC, CB, DS, PC, TC. TAC10. 12 rooms, 10 with PB, 1 cottage and 1 conference room. Breakfast and snacks/refreshments included in rates. Types of meals: Full bkfst and early coffee/tea. Beds: QDT. VCR, fax and library on premises. Weddings, small meetings, family reunions and seminars hosted. Danish and Dutch spoken. Antiquing, art galleries, beaches, bicycling, golf, live theater, museums and parks nearby.

"Your hospitality and beautiful room were respites for the spirit and body after our long trip."

The Turret House Victorian B&B

556 Chestnut Ave
Long Beach, CA 90802-2213
(562)983-9812 (888)488-7798 Fax:(562)437-4082
E-mail: innkeepers@turrethouse.com
Web: www.turrethouse.com

Circa 1906. This Queen Anne Victorian does, of course, display a turret as one of its delightful architectural features. The home, located in a Long Beach historic district, remained in the same family until it was purchased by the current owners. The decor is elegant and romantic. Fine linens top the beds and the wallpapers and furnishings are all coordinated with similar prints and colors. Each room has a clawfoot tub, and bubble bath is provided for a relaxing soak. The breakfasts are an imaginative gourmet treat. Guests might partake of a menu with a granola parfait, followed by cranberry scones and spinach parasol pie. There are two Victorian parlors to enjoy, and a proper afternoon tea is served with succulent treats such as a mocha cheesecake or rich peanut butter pie. Long Beach offers plenty of shops and restaurants, and the city is well situated for those enjoying the many attractions in Southern California.

Historic Interest: Queen Mary (half mile), Civil War Drum Barracks (7 miles), waterfront amusement park.

Innkeeper(s): Marsha Franks. $100-135. MC, VISA, AX, DS, PC, TC. TAC2510. 5 rooms with PB. Breakfast and afternoon tea included in rates. AP. Types of meals: Full gourmet bkfst and early coffee/tea. Beds: KQT. Turndown service, ceiling fan, table and chairs and balcony in room. Air conditioning. VCR, fax and piano on premises. Weddings, small meetings, family reunions and seminars hosted. Amusement parks, antiquing, art galleries, beaches, bicycling, canoeing/kayaking, fishing, golf, hiking, horseback riding, aquarium, Queen Mary, live theater, museums, parks, shopping, sporting events, tennis, water sports and wineries nearby.

Mariposa   I8

Meadow Creek Ranch B&B Inn

2669 Triangle Rd
Mariposa, CA 95338-9737
(209)966-3843

Circa 1858. This Wells Fargo stagecoach stop is now a rambling farmhouse framed by a black walnut tree, old-fashioned climbing roses and an old water wheel. A cozy country cottage in back is called the "Chicken Coop," but is decorated with a clawfoot tub and antiques.

Innkeeper(s): Willie & Diana Wilcoxen. $95. MC, VISA, AX, DS, PC, TC. TAC10. 2 rooms with PB. Breakfast included in rates. Types of meals: Full gourmet bkfst and early coffee/tea. Beds: QT. Ceiling fan, swamp Coolers, tea and coffee in each unit and private patio in room. Air conditioning. Library and old water wheel on premises. Spanish spoken. Antiquing, fishing, golf, Yosemite National Park, parks, shopping, cross-country skiing, tennis and water sports nearby.

"A wonderful spot to begin a trip through the Gold Country or into Yosemite."

Mendocino   F2

Joshua Grindle Inn

PO Box 647
Mendocino, CA 95460-0647
(707)937-4143 (800)474-6353
E-mail: stay@joshgrin.com
Web: www.joshgrin.com

Circa 1879. The town banker, Joshua Grindle, built this New England-style home on two acres. The decor is light and airy, with Early American antiques, clocks and quilts. In addition to lodging in the house, there are rooms in the water tower and in an adjacent cottage. Six of the guest rooms have fireplaces. Some have views over the town to the ocean.

Innkeeper(s): Arlene & Jim Moorehead. $110-225. MC, VISA, TC. TAC10. 10 rooms with PB, 6 with FP. Breakfast and snacks/refreshments included in rates. Type of meal: Full gourmet bkfst. Beds: KQT. Fishing, live theater, parks and shopping nearby.

"We are basking in the memories of our stay. We loved every moment."

MacCallum House Inn

45020 Albion St
Mendocino, CA 95460
(707)937-0289 (800)609-0492

Circa 1882. Built by William H. Kelley for his newly wed daughter, Daisy MacCallum, the MacCallum House Inn is a splendid example of New England architecture in the Victorian village of Mendocino. Besides the main house, accommodations include the barn, carriage house, greenhouse, gazebo and water tower rooms.

Innkeeper(s): Melanie & Joe Reding. $100-190. MC, VISA, DS. 19 rooms, 7 with PB. Type of meal: Cont. Beds: KQT. Handicap access.

Mendocino Hotel

PO Box 587
Mendocino, CA 95460-0587
(707)937-0511 (800)548-0513 Fax:(707)937-0513

Circa 1878. In the heart of Mendocino on Main Street, the Mendocino Hotel originally was established as a temperance hotel for lumbermen. An Old West facade was added. The historic Heeser House, home of Mendocino's first settler, was

annexed by the hotel along with its acre of gardens. Many of the guest rooms and suites boast tall, four-poster and canopy beds or fireplaces and coastal views. The hotel has several dining rooms and is a member of the National Trust Historic Hotels of America.

Innkeeper(s): Cynthia Reinhart. $85-275. MC, VISA, AX. 51 rooms, 37 with PB, 20 with FP, 6 suites and 1 conference room. Type of meal: Cont. Gourmet dinner, lunch and room service available. Restaurant on premises. Beds: KQDT. Copier on premises. Antiquing, fishing, live theater and water sports nearby.

"The hotel itself is magnificent, but more importantly, your staff is truly incredible."

Sea Rock B&B Inn

11101 Lansing St
Mendocino, CA 95460
(707)937-0926 (800)906-0926
E-mail: searock@mcn.org
Web: www.searock.com

Circa 1930. Enjoy sea breezes and ocean vistas at this inn, which rests on a bluff looking out to the Pacific. Most of the accommodations include a wood-burning Franklin fireplace and featherbed. Four guest rooms are available in the Stratton House, and each affords an ocean view. There are six cottages on the grounds, most offering a sea view. The innkeepers also offer deluxe accommodations in four special suites. Each has an ocean view, wood-burning fireplace, private entrance and a deck. The grounds, which now feature gardens, were the site of an 1870s brewery. The inn is less than half a mile from Mendocino.

Innkeeper(s): Susie & Andy Plocher. $85-259. MC, VISA, AX, DS, PC, TC. 14 rooms with PB, 13 with FP, 8 suites and 6 cottages. Breakfast included in rates. Type of meal: Cont plus. Beds: KQ. Cable TV, phone and VCR in room. Antiquing, fishing, golf, live theater, parks, shopping, tennis and water sports nearby.

Publicity: *California Visitors Review.*

Whitegate Inn

499 Howard St
Mendocino, CA 95460
(707)937-4892 (800)531-7282 Fax:(707)937-1131
E-mail: staff@whitegateinn.com
Web: www.whitegateinn.com

Circa 1883. When it was first built, the local newspaper called Whitegate Inn "one of the most elegant and best appointed residences in town." Its bay windows, steep gabled roof, redwood siding and fish-scale shingles are stunning examples of Victorian architecture. The house's original wallpaper and candelabras adorn the double parlors. There, an antique 1827 piano, at one time part of Alexander Graham Bell's collection, and inlaid pocket doors take you back to a more gracious time. French and Victorian antique furnishings and fresh flowers add to the inn's elegant hospitality and old world charm. The gourmet breakfasts are artfully presented in the inn's sunlit dining room. The inn is just a block from the ocean, galleries, restaurants and the center of town.

Historic Interest: Mendocino Headlands State Park surrounds the village, which was once the property of the original lumber mill.

Innkeeper(s): Carol & George Bechtloff. $129-249. MC, VISA, AX, DC, DS, PC, TC. TAC10. 6 rooms with PB, 6 with FP, 1 suite, 1 cottage and 1 conference room. Breakfast, afternoon tea and snacks/refreshments included in rates. Types of meals: Full gourmet bkfst and early coffee/tea. Catering service available. Beds: KQT. Cable TV, phone, welcome basket and evening sherry in room. Fax and copier on premises. Weddings, small meetings, family reunions and seminars hosted. Italian and Spanish spoken. Antiquing, fishing, golf, whale watching, live theater, parks, shopping, tennis and water sports nearby.

Merced   I7

Rambling Rose

436 W 20th St
Merced, CA 95340-3714
(209)723-4084

Circa 1897. Built by the founder of the Merced Lumber Company, this Victorian predates the town's incorporation. Furnishings include family pieces, as well as unique items the

innkeeper found at markets. Lace curtains and antiques decorate the bedchambers, which feature names such as the Blue Heaven and Wedding Heritage Room. One bathroom is decorated in a nostalgic theme using copies of local newspapers from the 1930s as wallpaper. Homemade breakfasts include items such as buttermilk pancakes, French toast, fresh fruit and freshly baked rolls. The home is within walking distance to many of the town's attractions, including museums, a zoo, shops and restaurants. Gold Rush towns and Yosemite National Park are within two hours of the home.

Historic Interest: Yosemite.

Innkeeper(s): Corina Brazil. $85-125. MC, VISA. TAC10. 4 rooms, 1 with PB. Breakfast included in rates. Types of meals: Full bkfst and cont. Beds: DT. Cable TV and ceiling fan in room. Central air. Portuguese spoken. Art galleries, live theater, museums, parks, shopping, downhill skiing, cross-country skiing and wineries nearby.

Mill Valley   H4

Mountain Home Inn

810 Panoramic Hwy
Mill Valley, CA 94941-1765
(415)381-9000 Fax:(415)381-3615

Circa 1912. At one time the only way to get to Mountain
Home was by taking the train up Mount Tamalpais. With 22
trestles and 281 curves, it was called "the crookedest railroad
in the world." Now accessible by auto, the trip still provides a
spectacular view of San Francisco Bay. Each guest room has a
view of the mountain, valley or bay.

Innkeeper(s): Lynn Saggese. $143-269. MC, VISA, AX, PC, TC. TAC10. 10
rooms with PB, 5 with FP and 1 conference room. Breakfast included in rates.
Type of meal: Full bkfst. Gourmet dinner and lunch available. Beds: KQ.
Phone and TV upon request in room. Fax and copier on premises. Weddings,
small meetings and family reunions hosted. Parks and shopping nearby.

Publicity: *San Francisco Examiner, California.*

*"A luxurious retreat. Echoes the grand style and rustic feeling of
national park lodges."* — Ben Davidson, Travel & Leisure.

Monrovia   O10

Chez Noel

210 W Colorado Blvd
Monrovia, CA 91016
(626)256-6622 (877)256-6622

Circa 1886. It's rare to find 19th-century homes in the Los
Angeles area, so Chez Noel is a rare find. The Eastlake Victorian
was built by a Civil War captain. The home is decorated in an
eclectic style and features artwork created by the innkeepers.
Healthy, gourmet breakfasts include items such as whole-grain
French toast, homemade muffins and fresh fruit. Chez Noel is
located in Old Town Monrovia. Pasadena is five minutes away,
and most popular local attractions are less than 40 minutes
from the inn, including Disneyland and Knott's Berry Farm.

Innkeeper(s): Scott & Cammie Noel. $100-140. MC, VISA, PC. 3 rooms with
PB. Breakfast included in rates. Types of meals: Full gourmet bkfst and early
coffee/tea. Snacks/refreshments and picnic lunch available. Beds: KQT. Air
conditioning. VCR, fax, bicycles and library on premises. Amusement parks,
antiquing, golf, old town Monrovia, Pasadena nearby,

Disneyland 30 minutes, live theater, parks, shopping, downhill skiing and
sporting events nearby.

Montara   I4

The Goose & Turrets B&B

835 George St, PO Box 937
Montara, CA 94037-0937
(650)728-5451 Fax:(650)728-0141
E-mail: rhmgt@montara.com
Web: www.montara.com/Goose.html

Circa 1908. In the peaceful setting of horse ranches and
strawflower farms, this Italian villa features beautiful gardens
surrounded by a 20-foot-high cypress hedge. The gardens
include an orchard, vegetable garden, herb garden, rose garden,
fountains, a hammock, swing and plenty of spots to enjoy the
surroundings. The large dining and living room areas are filled
with art and collectibles. Classical music plays during afternoon
tea. Among its many previous uses, the Goose & Turrets once
served as Montara's first post office, the town hall and a country club for Spanish-American War veterans.

Historic Interest: The historic district of Half Moon Bay is eight miles away.
Pescadero and a historic mansion and gardens are about 15 miles away.

Innkeeper(s): Raymond & Emily Hoche-Mong. $110-150. MC, VISA, AX, DC,
DS, PC, TC. TAC10. 5 rooms with PB, 3 with FP. Breakfast and afternoon
tea included in rates. Beds: KQDT. Turndown service and towel warmer in
room. Library, bocce ball court and piano on premises. French spoken.
Antiquing, fishing, golf, nature reserves, whale watching, aero sightseeing,
golf, birding, hiking, horseback riding, biking, parks and water sports nearby.

Publicity: *San Jose Mercury News, Half Moon Bay Review, Peninsula Times
Tribune, San Mateo Times, Los Angeles Times, Tri-Valley Herald, Contra
Costa Times.*

*"You have truly made an art of breakfast and tea-time conversation.
We will be back."*

Monterey   J5

The Jabberwock

598 Laine St
Monterey, CA 93940-1312
(831)372-4777 (888)428-7253 Fax:(831)655-2946
Web: www.jabberwockinn.com

Circa 1911. Set in a half-acre of gardens, this Craftsman-style
inn provides a fabulous view of Monterey Bay with its famous
barking seals. When you're ready to settle in for the evening,

The Jabberwock

you'll find huge Victorian
beds complete with lace-
edged sheets and goose-
down comforters. One room
includes a Jacuzzi tub. In the
late afternoon, hors d'oeuvres
and aperitifs are served in an
enclosed sun porch. After
dinner, guests are tucked into
bed with homemade chocolate chip cookies and milk. To help
guests avoid long lines, the innkeepers have tickets available for
the popular and nearby Monterey Bay Aquarium.

Historic Interest: Historic adobes and Cannery Row are within walking distance of The Jabberwock.

Innkeeper(s): Joan & John Kiliany. $110-210. MC, VISA. 7 rooms, 5 with
PB, 3 with FP. Types of meals: Full gourmet bkfst and early coffee/tea. Beds:
KQ. One room with Jacuzzi in room. Fax and copier on premises. Weddings,
small meetings and family reunions hosted. Antiquing, fishing, restaurants,
live theater, parks, shopping and water sports nearby.

Publicity: *Sunset, Travel & Leisure, Sacramento Bee, San Francisco
Examiner, Los Angeles Times, Country Inns, San Francisco Chronicle,
Diablo, Elmer Dill's KABC-Los Angeles TV.*

*"Words are not enough to describe the ease and tranquility of the
atmosphere of the home, rooms, owners and staff at the
Jabberwock."*

Mount Shasta　　B5

Mount Shasta Ranch B&B

1008 W.A. Barr Rd
Mount Shasta, CA 96067-9465
(530)926-3870 Fax:(530)926-6882

Circa 1923. This large two-story ranch house offers a full view of Mt. Shasta from its 60-foot-long redwood porch. Spaciousness abounds from the 1,500-square-foot living room with a massive rock fireplace to the large suites with private bathrooms that include large tubs and roomy showers. A full country breakfast may offer cream cheese-stuffed French toast or fresh, wild blackberry crepes. Just minutes away, Lake Siskiyou boasts superb fishing, sailing, swimming, and 18 hole golf course with public tennis courts.

Historic Interest: Built in 1923 by HD "Curley" Brown as a thoroughbred horse ranch.

Innkeeper(s): Bill & Mary Larsen. $50-95. MC, VISA, AX, DS, PC, TC. 9 rooms, 4 with PB, 1 cottage and 1 conference room. Breakfast included in rates. Types of meals: Full bkfst and early coffee/tea. Afternoon tea available. Beds: Q. Cable TV and ceiling fan in room. Air conditioning. VCR, fax, copier, spa and library on premises. Small meetings, family reunions and seminars hosted. Antiquing, fishing, parks, shopping, downhill skiing, cross-country skiing and water sports nearby.

Pets Allowed.

Murphys　　H7

Dunbar House, 1880

271 Jones St
Murphys, CA 95247-1375
(209)728-2897 (800)692-6006 Fax:(209)728-1451
E-mail: innkeep@dunbarhouse.com
Web: www.dunbarhouse.com

Circa 1880. A picket fence frames this Italianate home, built by Willis Dunbar for his bride. The porch, lined with rocking chairs, is the perfect place to take in the scenery of century-old gardens decorated by fountains, birdhouses and swings. A collection of antiques, family heirlooms and comfortable furnishings fill the interior. The two-room garden suite includes a bed dressed with fine linens and a down comforter and a two-person Jacuzzi spa. Guests can enjoy the morning fare in the dining room, garden or opt for breakfast in their room.

Historic Interest: Columbia State Park (10 miles), Big Trees State Park (14 miles).

Innkeeper(s): Bob & Barbara Costa. $135-190. MC, VISA, AX, PC, TC. TAC10. 4 rooms with PB, 4 with FP and 2 suites. Breakfast and afternoon tea included in rates. Types of meals: Full gourmet bkfst and early coffee/tea. Room service available. Beds: KQ. Cable TV, phone, turndown service, ceiling fan and VCR in room. Air conditioning. Fax, copier and library on premises. Antiquing, fishing, live theater, parks, shopping, downhill skiing, cross-country skiing and water sports nearby.

Publicity: Los Angeles Times, Gourmet, Victorian Homes, Country Inns, Travel & Leisure.

"Your beautiful gardens and gracious hospitality combine for a super bed & breakfast."

Trade Carriage House

230 Big Trees Rd/600 Algiers St
Murphys, CA 95247
(209)728-3909 (800)800-3408 Fax:(209)728-2527

Circa 1930. This little cottage is surrounded by a white picket fence. The structure was built in Stockton and was later moved 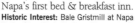 to Murphys, a historic California town. There are two bedrooms, furnished with antiques and wicker pieces. A second cottage three doors down offers a deck overlooking the treetops. There is no meal service, but the cottages have kitchens. Shops, restaurants and other local sites are within walking distance.

Innkeeper(s): Cynthia Trade. $125. PC, TC. TAC10. 2 cottages. Beds: QD. Cable TV and phone in room. Air conditioning. Antiquing, fishing, golf, major area for wineries, live theater, parks, shopping, downhill skiing, cross-country skiing, tennis and water sports nearby.

Napa　　H4

1801 Inn

1801 First St
Napa, CA 94581
(707)224-3739 (800)518-0146 Fax:(707)224-3932
E-mail: the1801inn@aol.com
Web: www.napavalley.com/lodging/inns/1801/index.html

Circa 1903. The innkeepers at this Queen Anne Victorian have created a setting perfect for romance.  The guest rooms feature Victorian decor, Oriental rugs top the hardwood floors, and beds are dressed with fine linens and soft comforters. Each guest bathroom has a large soaking tub, and each bedchamber has a fireplace. The turn-of-the-century inn is located in Old Town Napa and is close to the multitude of wineries in the valley, as well as antique shops and restaurants.

Innkeeper(s): Linda & Chris Craiker. $135-229. MC, VISA, DS, TC. TAC10. 5 rooms with PB, 5 with FP. Breakfast and snacks/refreshments included in rates. Meal: Full gourmet bkfst. Beds: K. Ceiling fan in room. Air conditioning. VCR and fax on premises. Spanish spoken. Antiquing, fishing, golf, ballooning, hiking, horseback riding, live theater, parks, shopping, tennis and water sports nearby.

Publicity: Sacramento Bee.

Beazley House

1910 1st St
Napa, CA 94559-2351
(707)257-1649 (800)559-1649 Fax:(707)257-1518
E-mail: innkeeper@beazleyhouse.com
Web: www.beazleyhouse.com

Circa 1902. Nestled in green lawns and gardens, this graceful shingled mansion is frosted with white trim on its bays and balustrades. Stained-glass windows and polished-wood floors set the atmosphere in the parlor.  There are six rooms in the main house, and the carriage house features five more, many with fireplaces and whirlpool tubs. The venerable Beazley House was Napa's first bed & breakfast inn.

Historic Interest: Bale Gristmill at Napa

Bothe State Park, Beringer Vineyards, Chas Kreug Winery, Old Town Napa.

Innkeeper(s): Carol Beazley, Jim Beazley, Scott Beazley, Lorna T. $115-250. MC, VISA, AX, PC. 11 rooms with PB. Breakfast included in rates. Meal: Full bkfst. Beds: KQDT. Phone, ceiling fan and fireplaces in room. Central air. Fax & library on premises. Handicap access. Weddings and small meetings hosted. Spanish & French spoken. Amusement parks, antiquing, art galleries, bicycling, fishing, golf, hiking, horseback riding, museums, parks, shopping, tennis and wineries nearby.

"There's a sense of peace & tranquility that hovers over this house, sprinkling magical dream dust & kindness."

Belle Epoque

1386 Calistoga Ave
Napa, CA 94559-2552
(707)257-2161 (800)238-8070 Fax:(707)226-6314
E-mail: innkeeper@labelleepoque.com
Web: labelleepoque.com

Circa 1893. This Queen Anne Victorian has a wine cellar and tasting room where guests can casually sip Napa Valley wines. The inn, which is one of the most unique architectural structures

found in the wine country, is located in the heart of Napa's Calistoga Historic District. Beautiful original stained-glass windows include a window from an old church. One guest room  offers a whirlpool tub. A selection of fine restaurants and shops are within easy walking distance, as well as the riverfront, city parks and the Wine Train Depot. The train, which serves all meals, takes you just beyond St. Helena and back.

Innkeeper(s): Georgia Jump. $159-229. MC, VISA, AX, DS, PC, TC. TAC10. 6 rooms with PB, 3 with FP, 1 suite and 1 conference room. Breakfast and snacks/refreshments included in rates. Types of meals: Full gourmet bkfst and early coffee/tea. Beds: KQT. Cable TV, phone, ceiling fan, VCR and one with whirlpool in room. Air conditioning. Fax, copier and spa on premises. Weddings, small meetings, family reunions and seminars hosted. Amusement parks, antiquing, golf, live theater, parks, shopping, sporting events and tennis nearby.

"At first I was a bit leery, how can a B&B get consistent rave reviews? After staying here two nights, I am now a believer!"

Blue Violet Mansion

443 Brown St
Napa, CA 94559-3349
(707)253-2583 (800)959-2583 Fax:(707)257-8205
E-mail: bviolet@napanet.net
Web: www.bluevioletmansion.com

Circa 1886. English lampposts, a Victorian gazebo, and a rose garden welcome guests to this blue and white Queen Anne Victorian. Listed in the National Register, the house originally was built for a tannery executive. There are three-story

bays, and from the balconies guests often view hot air balloons in the early morning. Rooms are available with two-person spas and fireplaces. A full breakfast is served in the dining room. In the  evenings, desserts are presented and elegant dinners are served in the grand salon. Nearby is the wine train and restaurants. The Official Hotel Guide gave the Blue Violet Mansion a gold award in 1996, voting it "Best Bed & Breakfast in North America."

Historic Interest: Napa County Landmarks prestigious Award of Merit for historical restoration 1993.

Innkeeper(s): Kathy & Bob Morris. $169-319. MC, VISA, AX, DC, DS, PC, TC. TAC10. 14 rooms with PB, 12 with FP, 3 suites and 3 conference rooms. Breakfast and snacks/refreshments included in rates. Type of meal: Full bkfst. Gourmet dinner, picnic lunch, banquet service, catering service and room service available. Restaurant on premises. Beds: KQ. Phone, turndown service, ceiling fan, balcony and in room massage in room. Air conditioning. VCR, fax, copier, spa, swimming and massage on premises. Handicap access. Weddings, small meetings, family reunions and seminars hosted. Amusement parks, antiquing, fishing, live theater, parks, shopping and water sports nearby.

The Candlelight Inn

1045 Easum Dr
Napa, CA 94558-5524
(707)257-3717 Fax:(707)257-3762

Circa 1929. This graceful English Tudor-style house is situated on an acre of lawns and gardens a few blocks from the center of town. Hardwood floors shine under the light of the fireplace in the parlor. Each suite features a two-person marble fireplace and two-person marble Jacuzzi inside the room, and the Candlelight Suite boasts a canopy bed and private sauna. The inn's breakfast room features French doors and windows overlooking the garden. Breakfast is served by candlelight.

Innkeeper(s): Johanna & Wolfgang Brox. $125-245. MC, VISA, AX, DS. 10 rooms with PB, 6 with FP and 6 suites. Breakfast, afternoon tea and snacks/refreshments included in rates. Type of meal: Full gourmet bkfst. Beds: Q. Cable TV, phone and jacuzzi's in room. Air conditioning. Fax, copier and swimming on premises. Small meetings and family reunions hosted. German and French spoken. Antiquing, golf, winetasting, restaurants, wineries, parks and shopping nearby.

"We still haven't stopped talking about the great food, wonderful accommodations and gracious hospitality."

Churchill Manor

485 Brown St
Napa, CA 94559-3349
(707)253-7733 Fax:(707)253-8836

Circa 1889. Listed in the National Register of Historic Places, each room of this stately Napa Valley manor is individually decorated with fine European antiques. Five rooms have fireplaces, and the original bath tiles and fireplaces in Edward's Room and Rose's Room are trimmed with 24-karat gold. Guests are treated to delicious breakfasts, and freshly baked cookies and refreshments in the after-  noons. In the evening, there is a complimentary two-hour wine and cheese reception. The breakfast buffet offers an abundant selection of fresh fruits, fresh-baked croissants and muffins, gourmet omelets and French toast made-to-order as each guest arrives. The innkeepers add Victorian flavor by keeping tandem bicycles and a croquet set on hand for their guests. Napa Wine Train and balloon ride packages are available to make any vacation memorable.

Historic Interest: Churchill Manor, which is listed in the National Register, is located in the National Register Historic District of Old Town Napa.

Innkeeper(s): Joanna Guidotti & Brian Jensen. $95-205. MC, VISA, DS, PC, TC. TAC10. 10 rooms with PB, 5 with FP and 3 conference rooms. Breakfast included in rates. Catering service available. Beds: KQ. Phone in room. Air conditioning. VCR, fax, copier, bicycles, library, grand piano, croquet and limited handicap access on premises. Handicap access. Weddings, small meetings, family reunions and seminars hosted. Spanish spoken. Amusement parks, antiquing, fishing, wineries, mud baths, galleries, live theater, parks, shopping and water sports nearby.

Publicity: *Napa County Record, Food & Beverage Journal, ABC-KGO TV, San Francisco Bay Guardian.*

"Retaining the ambiance of the 1890s yet providing comfort for the 1990s."

Hennessey House-Napa's 1889 Queen Anne Victorian B&B

1727 Main St
Napa, CA 94559-1844
(707)226-3774 Fax:(707)226-2975
E-mail: inn@hennesseyhouse.com
Web: www.hennesseyhouse.com

Circa 1889. This gracious Victorian was once home to Dr. Edwin Hennessey, a Napa County physician. Pristinely renovated, the inn features stained-glass windows and a curving wraparound porch. A handsome hand-painted, stamped-tin ceiling graces the dining room. All rooms are furnished in antiques. The four guest rooms in the carriage house boast whirlpool baths, fireplaces or patios. There is a sauna and a garden fountain.

Historic Interest: Historic Old Town Napa.

Innkeeper(s): Alex & Gilda Feit. $105-250. MC, VISA, AX, DS. TAC10. 10 rooms with PB, 5 with FP. Breakfast included in rates. Type of meal: Full bkfst. Beds: KQT. Ceiling fan in room. Air conditioning. Fax, spa and sauna on premises. Weddings, small meetings, family reunions and seminars hosted. Antiquing, wine train packages and shopping nearby.

Publicity: *AM-PM Magazine.*

"This is a great place to relax."

La Residence Country Inn

4066 Saint Helena Hwy
Napa, CA 94558-1635
(707)253-0337 Fax:(707)253-0382

Circa 1870. This inn offers luxurious accommodations for those exploring the enchanting Napa Valley wine country. The uniquely decorated rooms in the French-style farmhouse or Gothic Revival Mansion are spacious and well-appointed, with fine antiques and designer fabrics. Many rooms also feature fireplaces, patios or balconies. Guests will be impressed with the lovely gardens and pool area at the inn, not to mention the discreet but attentive service. Be sure to inquire about excursions into the winery-rich valley.

Innkeeper(s): David Jackson, Craig Claussen. $195-350. MC, VISA, AX, DC, PC, TC. TAC10. 20 rooms with PB, 16 with FP, 5 suites and 1 conference room. Breakfast and snacks/refreshments included in rates. Types of meals: Full bkfst and early coffee/tea. Banquet service, catering service and room service available. Beds: Q. Phone and heated pool in room. Air conditioning. Fax, copier, spa, swimming and child care on premises. Handicap access. Weddings, small meetings, family reunions and seminars hosted. French, Dutch, German and Spanish spoken. Antiquing, fishing, golf, wineries, ballooning, biking, glyder riding, live theater, parks, shopping and tennis nearby.

Publicity: *Travel & Leisure.*

Old World Inn

1301 Jefferson St
Napa, CA 94559-2412
(707)257-0112 (800)966-6624 Fax:(707)257-0118

Circa 1906. The decor in this exquisite bed & breakfast is second to none. In 1981, Macy's sought out the inn to showcase a new line of fabrics inspired by Scandinavian artist Carl Larrson. Each romantic room is adorned in bright, welcoming colors and includes special features such as canopy beds and clawfoot tubs. The Garden Room boasts three skylights, and the Anne Room is a must for honeymoons and romantic retreats. The walls and ceilings are painted in a warm peach and blue, bows

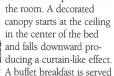

are stenciled around the perimeter of the room. A decorated canopy starts at the ceiling in the center of the bed and falls downward producing a curtain-like effect. A buffet breakfast is served each morning and a delicious afternoon tea and wine and cheese social will curb your appetite until dinner. After sampling one of Napa's gourmet eateries, return to the inn where a selection of desserts await you.

Innkeeper(s): Sam Van Hoeve. $135-225. MC, VISA, AX, DS, PC, TC. TAC10. 10 rooms with PB, 6 with FP, 1 suite and 1 cottage. Breakfast, afternoon tea and snacks/refreshments included in rates. Types of meals: Full gourmet bkfst and early coffee/tea. Beds: KQT. Cable TV, phone, ceiling fan and VCR in room. Air conditioning. Fax and spa on premises. French and Dutch spoken. Antiquing, fishing, golf, live theater, parks, shopping, sporting events and tennis nearby.

Publicity: *Napa Valley Traveller.*

"Excellent is an understatement. We'll return."

Inn on Randolph

411 Randolph St
Napa, CA 94559-3374
(707)257-2886 (800)670-6886 Fax:(707)257-8756
E-mail: randolph@i-cafe.net
Web: www.virtualcities.com/ca/randolph.htm

Circa 1860. Located in Napa's historic district, this shuttered Gothic Revival is a city landmark and one of the oldest homes in the valley. Common rooms feature antique Victorian furnishings, hardwood floors and a sweeping spindled staircase. A hand-painted flower mural, white wicker and sleigh bed are just a few of the romantic touches featured in the five guest rooms located in the original house. Besides privacy, the Randolph and Laurel cottages offer two suites decorated in antiques, fireplaces and whirlpool tubs for two. The Arbor Cottage overlooks a semi-private stone patio and is complete with a fireplace, kitchenette, two-person walk-in shower and whirlpool tub for two. Breakfast begins with freshly ground coffee, tea and juice, followed by peach and strawberry French toast or Mexican quiche served with fresh salsa and jalapeno cheese bread. Wine tasting, shopping, bicycling and golf are nearby.

Innkeeper(s): Deborah Coffee. $129-259. MC, VISA, AX, DS. TAC10. 5 rooms with PB, 7 with FP and 3 cottages. Breakfast and snacks/refreshments included in rates. Types of meals: Full bkfst and early coffee/tea. Beds: KQT. Phone, turndown service, ceiling fan, robes, cottages have TV and VCR and CD player and 8 rooms with whirlpool tubs in room. Air conditioning. Fax and library on premises. Antiquing, golf, live theater, parks, shopping and tennis nearby.

"You reinforced our reason for staying in lovely bed & breakfasts."

Stahlecker House B&B Country Inn & Garden

1042 Easum Dr
Napa, CA 94558-5525
(707)257-1588 (800)799-1588 Fax:(707)224-7429
E-mail: stahlbnb@aol.com
Web: www.stahleckerhouse.com

Circa 1949. This country inn is situated on the banks of tree-lined Napa Creek. The acre and a half of grounds feature rose and orchard gardens, fountains and manicured lawns. Guests often relax on the sun deck. There is an antique refrigerator stocked with soft drinks and lemonade. Full, gourmet breakfasts

are served by candlelight in the glass-wrapped dining room that overlooks the gardens. In the evenings, coffee, tea and freshly made chocolate chip cookies are served. The Napa Wine Train station is five minutes away. Wineries, restaurants, antique shops, bike paths and hiking all are nearby.

Innkeeper(s): Ron & Ethel Stahlecker. $135-185. MC, VISA, AX, DS, TC. TAC10. 4 rooms with PB, 4 with FP and 1 suite. Breakfast and snacks/refreshments included in rates. Types of meals: Full gourmet bkfst and early coffee/tea. Afternoon tea available. Beds: QT. TV, phone, turndown service and couple spa/couple shower in room. Air conditioning. Library and ping pong and croquet on premises. Antiquing, fishing, golf, hiking, hot air balloons, live theater, parks, shopping, tennis and wineries nearby.

"Friendly hosts and beautiful gardens."

Napa Valley   H4

Tall Timbers Chalets

1012 Darms Ln
Napa Valley, CA 94558
(707)252-7810 Fax:(707)252-1055

Circa 1930. Flowers decorate the exterior of these little cottages, painted white with dark and light green trim. The chalets were built between 1930 and 1940, and the grounds were the site of several movies during the 1930s. Each cottage includes a bedroom, bathroom, sitting room and kitchen. The sitting rooms include a sofa bed, so the cottages can accommodate four guests comfortably. Dozens of wineries, shops and restaurants are nearby.

Innkeeper(s): Mary Sandmann-Montes. $65-150. MC, VISA, AX, PC, TC. TAC10. 8 cottages with PB. Breakfast included in rates. Type of meal: Cont plus. Beds: Q. Cable TV in room. Air conditioning. Fax on premises. Weddings, small meetings, family reunions and seminars hosted. Antiquing, golf, vineyard and winery tours and parks nearby.

Nevada City   F6

Deer Creek Inn

116 Nevada St
Nevada City, CA 95959
(530)265-0363 (800)655-0363 Fax:(530)265-0980

Circa 1860. A prominent local citizen who served as postmaster, as well as holding several other important city and county posts built this Queen Anne Victorian. The inn boasts many original features, including an abundance of stained glass, which frames many of the windows. Guest rooms and common areas are decorated with period antiques. Beds are topped with down comforters, and some rooms include a canopy bed or clawfoot tub. Each room is named for one of the women who have owned the house throughout the year. Breakfasts, served on a veranda overlooking Deer Creek, include several courses, beginning with a fruit dish such as poached pears in apricot nectar. This is followed by an egg dish, perhaps a mushroom and spinach strata accompanied by honey maple sausage and potatoes. Finally, guests are treated to a special entrée. One delectable example is orange pecan French toast topped with hot orange-maple syrup. During California's gold rush, hundreds of pounds of gold were discovered in Deer Creek, which runs

behind the inn's one-acre property. This local gold rush was the catalyst that created Nevada City, a quaint historic town that offers shops, walking tours, carriage rides, art galleries and museums. Two state parks represent the area's mining history, and there are plenty of outdoor activities, as well.

Historic Interest: Deer Creek, Empire State Mine (3 miles), longest covered bridge at Bridgeport (9 miles), restored Colfax Narrow Gauge Railroad(3 miles).

Innkeeper(s): Chuck & Elaine Mataroni. $100-155. MC, VISA, AX, PC, TC. TAC10. 5 rooms with PB and 1 conference room. Breakfast and snacks/refreshments included in rates. Types of meals: Full bkfst and early coffee/tea. Beds: KQ. Ceiling fan and roman tub in room. Central air. VCR and fax on premises. Family reunions hosted. Antiquing, art galleries, beaches, bicycling, canoeing/kayaking, fishing, golf, hiking, horseback riding, live theater, museums, parks, shopping, cross-country skiing, tennis, water sports and wineries nearby.

Emma Nevada House

528 E Broad St
Nevada City, CA 95959-2213
(530)265-4415 (800)916-3662 Fax:(530)265-4416

Circa 1856. The childhood home of 19th-century opera star Emma Nevada now serves as an attractive Queen Anne Victorian inn. English roses line the white picket fence in front, and the forest-like back garden has a small stream with benches. The Empress' Chamber is the most romantic room with ivory Italian linens atop a French antique bed, a bay window and a massive French armoire. Some rooms have  whirlpool baths. Guests enjoy relaxing in the hexagonal sunroom and on the inn's wraparound porches. Empire Mine State Historic Park is nearby.

Historic Interest: Malakoff Diggins (20 miles), Nevada City Historical District (3 blocks).

Innkeeper(s): Ruth Ann Riese. $100-155. MC, VISA, AX, DC, PC, TC. TAC10. 6 rooms with PB, 2 with FP. Breakfast and afternoon tea included in rates. Types of meals: Full bkfst and early coffee/tea. Beds: Q. Clawfoot tub in room. Air conditioning. Fax and library on premises. Weddings and small meetings hosted. Antiquing, fishing, live theater, parks, shopping, downhill skiing and water sports nearby.

Publicity: *Country Inns, Los Angeles Times, San Jose Mercury News, Sacramento Bee, Karen Browns.*

"A delightful experience: such airiness and hospitality in the midst of so much history. We were fascinated by the detail and the faithfulness of the restoration. This house is a quiet solace for city-weary travelers. There's a grace here."

Grandmere's Inn

449 Broad St
Nevada City, CA 95959-2430
(530)265-4660

Circa 1856. Aaron Sargent, U.S. Congressman, senator and author of the women's suffrage bill, was the first owner of this white Colonial Revival house. He and his wife often received Susan B. Anthony here. Shaker pine furnishings and white wooden shutters predominate the spacious interior design. Lavish creature comforts include six pillows on the four-poster beds. Huge country breakfasts may include onion-caraway quiche, cornbread and the inn's trademark, Grandmere's French Toast. A half acre of terraced gardens cascade behind the inn to the block below.

$110-170. MC, VISA, AX, PC, TC. TAC10. 6 rooms with PB. Type of meal: Full bkfst. Beds: Q. TV and phone in room. Weddings hosted. Antiquing, fishing, restaurants, live theater and shopping nearby.

The Parsonage B&B

427 Broad St
Nevada City, CA 95959-2407
(530)265-9478 Fax:(530)265-8147

Circa 1865. Guests in search of California history would do well to stop in Nevada City and at the Parsonage. The Gold Rush town is a registered National Monument, and the home is one of the older homes in the state, dating to the 1860s. Innkeeper Deborah Dane's family has been in California since Gold Rush days, and the home features many heirlooms. Although used to house Methodist ministers for 80 years, the home was in a quite ungodly state by the time Deborah found it. She painstakingly restored the gem and filled it with beautiful antiques and delightful, elegant decor. Special furnishings, knickknacks and artwork are located throughout, including an amazing carved mahogany bed the Dane family brought along the Oregon Trail. In addition to her flair for restoration and decorating, Deborah is a dietitian and Cordon Bleu graduate, so be prepared for a gourmet breakfast that's as healthy as it is delicious.

Innkeeper(s): Deborah Dane. $70-135. MC, VISA, PC, TC. TAC10. 6 rooms with PB, 1 with FP, 1 cottage and 1 conference room. Breakfast included in rates. Types of meals: Full bkfst, cont plus and early coffee/tea. Restaurant on premises. Beds: QT. Cable TV and ceiling fan in room. Air conditioning. Fax, copier and library on premises. Weddings, small meetings, family reunions and seminars hosted. Antiquing, fishing, golf, live theater, shopping, downhill skiing, cross-country skiing and water sports nearby.

Nice   F4

Featherbed Railroad Company B&B

2870 Lakeshore Blvd, PO Box 4016
Nice, CA 95464
(707)274-4434 (800)966-6322
E-mail: rooms@featherbedrailroad.com
Web: featherbedrailroad.com

Circa 1940. Located on five acres on Clear Lake, this unusual inn features guest rooms in nine luxuriously renovated, painted and papered cabooses. Each has its own featherbed and private bath, most have Jacuzzi tubs for two. The Southern Pacific cabooses have a bay window alcove, while those from the Santa Fe feature small cupolas.

Innkeeper(s): Lorraine Bassignani. $90-140. MC, VISA, AX, DS. 9 rooms with PB. Breakfast included in rates. Type of meal: Full bkfst. Beds: QDT. Cable TV and VCR in room. Spa on premises.

Nipomo   M7

The Kaleidoscope Inn

130 E Dana St
Nipomo, CA 93444-1297
(805)929-5444 Fax:(805)929-5440
E-mail: kaleidoscope@pronet.net
Web: sites.netscape.net/kaleidoscopeinn/homepage

Circa 1887. The sunlight that streams through the stained-glass windows of this charming Victorian creates a kaleidoscope effect and thus the name. The inn is surrounded by one acre of gardens. Each romantic guest room is decorated with antiques, and the library offers a fireplace. The parlor includes an 1886 Steinway upright piano. Fresh flowers add a special touch.

Breakfast is served either in the dining room or in the gardens. L.A. Times readers voted the inn as one of the best lodging spots for under $100 per night.

Historic Interest: Built and lived in by the founding family of Nipomo, the Dana Family.

Innkeeper(s): Edward & Carol De Leon. $95. MC, VISA, AX, DS. TAC10. 3 rooms with PB and 1 conference room. Breakfast included in rates. Types of meals: Full gourmet bkfst and early coffee/tea. Beds: KQ. Turndown service and ceiling fan in room. VCR and library on premises. Weddings, small meetings and family reunions hosted. Antiquing, fishing, live theater, parks, shopping and water sports nearby.

"Beautiful room, chocolates, fresh flowers, peaceful night's rest, great breakfast."

Nipton   L14

Hotel Nipton

HC 1, Box 357, 107355 Nipton Rd
Nipton, CA 92364-9735
(760)856-2335

Circa 1904. This Southwestern-style adobe hotel with its wide verandas once housed gold miners and Clara Bow, wife of movie star Rex Bell. It is decorated in period furnishings and historic photos of the area. A 1920s rock and cactus garden blooms, and an outdoor spa provides the perfect setting for watching a flaming sunset over Ivanpah Valley, the New York Mountains and Castle Peaks. Later, a magnificent star-studded sky appears undimmed by city lights.

Historic Interest: Gold mining town started in 1885.

Innkeeper(s): Gerald & Roxanne Freeman. $55. MC, VISA, DS. TAC7. 4 rooms. Breakfast included in rates. Types of meals: Cont and early coffee/tea. Beds: DT. Air conditioning. Fax, library and Jacuzzi on premises. Weddings, small meetings, family reunions and seminars hosted. Amusement parks, fishing, golf, golf and stables, live theater, parks, shopping, sporting events and water sports nearby.

Publicity: *National Geographic Traveler, Town & Country, U.S. News & World Report.*

"Warm, friendly, unpretentious, genuine. The hotel's historical significance is well-researched and verified."

Orland   E5

Inn at Shallow Creek Farm

4712 County Rd DD
Orland, CA 95963
(530)865-4093 (800)865-4093

Circa 1900. This vine-covered farmhouse was once the center of a well-known orchard and sheep ranch. The old barn, adjacent to the farmhouse, was a livery stop. The citrus orchard, now restored, blooms with 165 trees. Apples, pears, peaches, apricots, persimmons, walnuts, figs, and pomegranates are also grown here. Guests can meander about and examine the Polish crested chickens, silver guinea fowl, Muscovy ducks, and African geese. The old caretaker's house is now a four-room guest cottage. Hundreds of narcissus grow along the creek that flows through the property.

Innkeeper(s): Mary & Kurt Glaeseman. $60-85. MC, VISA, PC. 4 rooms, 2 with PB and 1 suite. Breakfast included in rates. Types of meals: Cont plus and early coffee/tea. Beds: QT. TV, phone and ceiling fan in room. Air conditioning. Library on premises. French, German and Spanish spoken. Antiquing, fishing, birding, live theater and parks nearby.

Publicity: *Adventure Road, Orland Press Register, Focus, Chico Enterprise Record, Minneapolis Star.*

"Now that we've discovered your country oasis, we hope to return as soon as possible."

Pacific Grove   J5

Gatehouse Inn

225 Central Ave
Pacific Grove, CA 93950-3017
(408)649-8436 (800)753-1881 Fax:(408)648-8044

Circa 1884. This Italianate Victorian seaside inn is just a block from the Monterey Bay. The inn is decorated with Victorian and 20th-century antiques and touches of Art Deco. Guest rooms feature fireplaces, clawfoot tubs and down comforters. Some rooms have ocean views. The dining room boasts opulent Bradbury & Bradbury Victorian wallpapers as do some of the guest rooms. Afternoon hors d'oeuvres, wine and tea are served. The refrigerator is stocked for snacking.

Innkeeper(s): Lois Deford. $110-195. MC, VISA, AX, DS, PC, TC. TAC10. 9 rooms with PB, 5 with FP. Breakfast, afternoon tea and snacks/refreshments included in rates. Beds: KQT. Phone and turndown service in room. Fax and copier on premises. Weddings and family reunions hosted. Antiquing, fishing, live theater, parks, shopping and water sports nearby.

Publicity: *San Francisco Chronicle, Monterey Herald, Time, Newsweek, Inland Empire, Bon Appetit.*

"Thank you for spoiling us."

Grand View Inn

557 Ocean View Blvd
Pacific Grove, CA 93950-2653
(831)372-4341
Web: www.7gables-grandview.com

Circa 1910. Overlooking Lover's Point beach on the edge of Monterey Bay, this site was chosen by noted marine biologist Dr. Julia Platt to build this Edwardian-style home. As the first mayor of Pacific Grove, she was also one of those responsible for preserving the landmark beach and park for future generations. Most of the 10 guest rooms offer unsurpassed ocean views and are elegantly appointed with authentic and reproduction antiques. Guests will delight in strolling the gardens surrounding the inn or venturing outdoors to walk along the seashore. A full breakfast and afternoon tea are served in the ocean-view dining room.

Historic Interest: The world-famous 17-Mile Drive along the ocean to Pebble Beach and Carmel, Cannery Row and Monterey Bay made famous by John Steinbeck. Old Fisherman's Wharf is also located nearby.

Innkeeper(s): Susan & Ed Flatley. $165-285. MC, VISA, PC, TC. TAC10. 10 rooms with PB. Breakfast and afternoon tea included in rates. Types of meals: Full bkfst and early coffee/tea. Beds: Q. Turndown service in room. Handicap access. Antiquing, fishing, golf, live theater, parks, shopping, tennis and water sports nearby.

Martine Inn

255 Ocean View Blvd
Pacific Grove, CA 93950
(831)373-3388 (800)852-5588 Fax:(831)373-3896

Circa 1890. This turn-of-the-century oceanfront manor sits atop a jagged cliff overlooking the coastline of Monterey Bay.

Bedrooms are furnished with antiques, and each room contains a fresh rose and a silver Victorian bridal basket filled with fresh fruit. Thirteen rooms also boast fireplaces. Some of the museum-quality antiques were exhibited in the 1893 Chicago World's Fair. Other bedroom sets include furniture that belonged to Edith Head, and there is an 1860 Chippendale Revival four-poster bed with a canopy and side curtains. Innkeeper Don Martine has a collection of old MGs, four on display for guests. Twilight wine and hors d'oeuvres are served, and Godiva mints accompany evening turndown service. The inn is a beautiful spot for romantic getaways and weddings.

Historic Interest: Pacific Grove Historic Walking Tour.

Innkeeper(s): Don Martine. $165-300. MC, VISA, AX, DS, PC, TC. TAC10. 23 rooms with PB, 11 with FP, 3 suites and 6 conference rooms. Breakfast included in rates. Types of meals: Full bkfst and early coffee/tea. Picnic lunch available. Beds: KQD. Phone and turndown service in room. Fax, copier, spa, library and wine & hors d'oeuvres on premises. Handicap access. Weddings, small meetings, family reunions and seminars hosted. Antiquing, fishing, Monterey Bay Aquarium, Cannery Row, live theater, parks, shopping, sporting events and water sports nearby.

"Wonderful, can't wait to return."

Old St. Angela Inn

321 Central Ave
Pacific Grove, CA 93950-2934
(831)372-3246 (800)748-6306 Fax:(831)372-8560

Circa 1910. This Cape-style inn once served as a rectory then a convent. Guest rooms are decorated with period antiques. Three rooms include a fireplace, and two offer a cast-iron stove. Six rooms have a whirlpool tub. Breakfasts are served in a glass solarium. The ocean is a block away and it's just a short walk to the aquarium or fisherman's wharf.

Innkeeper(s): Lewis Shaefer & Susan Kuslis. $110-195. MC, VISA, DS, PC, TC. TAC10. 9 rooms with PB. Breakfast, afternoon tea and snacks/refreshments included in rates. Types of meals: Full gourmet bkfst and early coffee/tea. Beds: KQT. Phone in room. Fax and spa on premises. Small meetings and family reunions hosted. Antiquing, fishing, live theater, parks, shopping and water sports nearby.

"Outstanding inn and outstanding hospitality."

Seven Gables Inn

555 Ocean View Blvd
Pacific Grove, CA 93950-2653
(831)372-4341
Web: www.7gables-grandview.com

Circa 1886. At the turn of the century, Lucie Chase, a wealthy widow and civic leader from the East Coast, embellished this Victorian with gables and verandas, taking full advantage of its spectacular setting on Monterey Bay. All guest rooms feature ocean views, and there are elegant antiques, intricate Persian carpets, chandeliers and beveled-glass armoires throughout. A full breakfast is served in a dining room that features an ocean view. Sea otters, harbor seals and whales often can be seen from the inn.

Innkeeper(s): The Flatley Family. $165-375. MC, VISA, PC, TC. TAC10. 14 rooms with PB. Breakfast and afternoon tea included in rates. Types of meals: Full bkfst and early coffee/tea. Gourmet dinner and picnic lunch available. Beds: Q. Turndown service in room. Antiquing, fishing, golf, live theater, parks, shopping and water sports nearby.

"Our stay was everything your brochure said it would be, and more."

Palm Springs 012

Casa Cody Country Inn

175 S Cahuilla Rd
Palm Springs, CA 92262-6331
(760)320-9346 (800)231-2639 Fax:(760)325-8610

Circa 1920. Casa Cody, built by a relative of Wild Bill Cody
and situated in the heart of Palm Springs, is the town's oldest
continuously operating inn. The San Jacinto Mountains provide
a scenic background for the
tree-shaded spa, the pink and
purple bougainvillea and the
blue waters of the inn's two
swimming pools. Each suite
has a small kitchen and fea-

tures red and turquoise Southwestern decor. Several have
wood-burning fireplaces. There are Mexican pavers, French
doors and private patios. The area offers many activities,
including museums, a heritage center, boutiques, a botanical
garden, horseback riding and golf.

Historic Interest: Village Heritage Center, Village Theater and numerous historic estates within blocks; Mooten Botanic Gardens and Indian Canyons
within minutes.

Innkeeper(s): Elissa Goforth. $79-299. MC, VISA, AX, DC, CB, DS, PC, TC.
TAC10. 23 rooms, 24 with PB, 10 with FP, 8 suites and 2 cottages. Breakfast
included in rates. Type of meal: Cont plus. Beds: KQT. Cable TV, phone and
ceiling fan in room. Air conditioning. Fax, copier, spa, swimming and library on
premises. Weddings, small meetings, family reunions and seminars hosted.
French, Dutch and limited German & Spanish spoken. Antiquing, hiking,
horseback riding, tennis, golf, ballooning, polo and live theater nearby.

Pets Allowed.

Publicity: *New York Times, Washington Post, Los Angeles Times, San
Diego Union Tribune, Seattle Times, Portland Oregonian, Los Angeles, San
Diego Magazine, Pacific Northwest Magazine, Sunset, Westways, Alaska
Airlines Magazine.*

"Outstanding ambiance, friendly relaxed atmosphere."

Villa Royale Inn

1620 Indian Tr
Palm Springs, CA 92264
(760)327-2314 (800)245-2314 Fax:(760)322-3794

Circa 1940. Rich European decor and furnishings create the
ambiance of a secluded Mediterranean inn at this Palm Springs
retreat. Rooms are charming and romantic, decorated with
European antiques. Some rooms
have wooden beams and tile
floors. In many rooms, French
doors lead out to a private patio.
Seventeen rooms include a fireplace, and seven have their own
spa. Two dozen rooms include a
kitchen. The suites and rooms

are secluded on more than three acres. Paths meander through
the gardens. There are two pools and a spa on the premises.
Europa, the inn's acclaimed restaurant, serves continental specialties for dinner and a casual pool-side lunch.

Innkeeper(s): Ann Aguno. $77-325. MC, VISA, AX, DC, DS, TC. TAC10. 31
rooms with PB, 17 with FP and 11 suites. Breakfast included in rates. Type
of meal: Full bkfst. Gourmet dinner, banquet service, catering service and
room service available. Restaurant on premises. Beds: KQT. Cable TV, phone,
some rooms with kitchens and in room. Air conditioning. Fax, spa, swimming,
19 rooms w/pvt patio and spa in 7 rooms on premises. Weddings,
small meetings and family reunions hosted. Amusement parks, antiquing,
golf, hiking, horseback riding, live theater, parks, shopping and tennis nearby.

The Willows Historic Palm Springs Inn

412 W Tahquitz Canyon Way
Palm Springs, CA 92262
(760)320-0771 (800)966-9597 Fax:(760)320-0780
E-mail: innkeeper@thewillowspalmsprings.com
Web: www.thewillowspalmsprings.com

Circa 1927. This beautiful Italianate Mediterranean estate was
once the abode of Marion Davies, mistress of William Randolf
Hearst. Carole Lombard and Clark Gable stayed here as part of
"the world's longest honeymoon," and Albert Einstein was also
a guest. The building's architecture
includes the construction of a second shell inside the exterior to provide a natural cooling effect with
the air pocket created. Mahogany
beams, hardwood floors, a grand
piano and a carved fireplace accen-

tuate the Great Hall. It's difficult to
choose a room, but for your first trip you might try the Rock
Room with a shower flowing onto a protruding piece of San
Jacinto Mountain and a double tub built into a rock. The
Marion Davies Room offers fine antiques, a balcony with view,
and a fireplace. Its bath has a stone floor, silver chandelier, a
chaise lounge and double tub as well as a shower with a private
garden view. The arches of the inn's veranda are set off with
long drapes and there are frescoed ceilings and views out over
the pool. Guests enjoy wine and hors d'oeuvres in the evening,
sometimes with live music, and in the morning, a full gourmet
breakfast is served within view of a hillside waterfall. Cross the
street to Le Vallauris, an excellent French restaurant, or walk to
several historical sites.

Historic Interest: Desert Museum (1 block), Historic Adobe & Museum (3
blocks), Palm Springs Aerial Tran (5 miles).

Innkeeper(s): Connie Stevens/Gordon Leake. $175-500. MC, VISA, AX, DC,
CB, DS, PC, TC. TAC10. 8 rooms with PB, 4 with FP and 1 conference
room. Breakfast and snacks/refreshments included in rates. MAP. Types of
meals: Full gourmet bkfst and early coffee/tea. Room service available. Beds:
KQ. Cable TV, phone, turndown service and VCR in room. Central air. Fax,
copier, spa and swimming on premises. Weddings, small meetings and family
reunions hosted. Spanish spoken. Antiquing, bicycling, golf, hiking, horseback
riding, live theater, museums, parks, shopping and tennis nearby.

Palo Alto I5

The Victorian on Lytton

555 Lytton Ave
Palo Alto, CA 94301-1538
(650)322-8555 Fax:(650)322-7141

Circa 1896. This Queen Anne home was built for Hannah
Clapp, a descendant of Massachusetts Bay colonist Roger Clapp.
The house has been graciously restored, and each guest room
features its own sitting area. Most rooms boast a canopy or four-
poster bed. Stanford University is within walking distance.

Innkeeper(s): Susan & Maxwell Hall. $147-250. MC, VISA, AX. 10 rooms with
PB, 1 with FP. Breakfast and snacks/refreshments included in rates. EP. Types of
meals: Cont plus and early coffee/tea. Beds: KQ. Cable TV, phone and modem
line in room. Air conditioning. Fax and computer modem jacks on premises.
Handicap access. Antiquing, parks, shopping and sporting events nearby.

Publicity: *USA Today.*

"A beautiful inn! My favorite."

Petaluma   H4

Cavanagh Inn

10 Keller St
Petaluma, CA 94952-2939
(707)765-4657 (888)765-4658 Fax:(707)769-0466

Circa 1902. Embrace turn-of-the-century California at this picturesque Georgian Revival manor. The garden is filled with beautiful flowers, plants and fruit trees. Innkeeper Jeanne Farris is an award-winning chef and prepares the mouthwatering breakfasts. The innkeepers also serve wine at 5:30 p.m. The parlor and library, which boasts heart-of-redwood paneled walls, is an ideal place to relax. Cavanagh Inn is located at the edge of Petaluma's historic district, and close to shops and the riverfront. Petaluma is 32 miles north of the Golden Gate.

Innkeeper(s): Ray & Jeanne Farris. $85-130. MC, VISA, AX, PC. TAC10. 7 rooms, 5 with PB and 1 conference room. Breakfast included in rates. Meal: Full gourmet bkfst. Beds: KQDT. Turndown service and electric blankets in room. VCR, fax and library on premises. Small meetings, family reunions and seminars hosted. Spanish spoken. Antiquing, live theater, parks and shopping nearby.
Publicity: *Argus-Courier, Arizona Daily Star, Travel Today, L.A. Times.*

"This is our first B&B. . .sort of like learning to drive with a Rolls-Royce!"

Placerville   G6

Chichester-McKee House B&B

800 Spring St
Placerville, CA 95667-4424
(530)626-1882 (800)831-4008
E-mail: inn@innercite.com
Web: www.innercite.com/~inn/

Circa 1892. This fanciful Victorian home, with all its gables, gingerbread and fretwork draws the breath of many a passerby. The house is full of places to explore and admire, including the parlor, library and conservatory. Guest rooms are filled with family treasures and antiques, and the home features fireplaces and stained glass. Breakfast at the inn includes freshly baked goods and delicious entrees. Evening refreshments are a treat, and the special blends of morning coffee will wake your spirit. Ask the innkeepers about the discovery of a gold mine beneath the dining room floor and for advice on adventures in the Placerville and Sierra Foothills area.

Historic Interest: Marshall State Historic Gold Discovery Park, Gold Bug Park Mine, Apple Hill.
Innkeeper(s): Doreen & Bill Thornhill. $80-125. MC, VISA, AX, DS, PC, TC. TAC10. 4 rooms. Breakfast and snacks/refreshments included in rates. Meals: Full gourmet bkfst and early coffee/tea. Beds: QT. VCR and library on premises. Small meetings and family reunions hosted. Antiquing, fishing, wineries, live theater, parks, shopping, downhill skiing, cross-country skiing & water sports nearby.
Publicity: *Hi Sierra, Mount Democrat.*

Quincy   E6

The Feather Bed

542 Jackson St PO Box 3200
Quincy, CA 95971-9412
(530)283-0102 (800)696-8624

Circa 1893. Englishman Edward Huskinson built this Queen Anne house shortly after he began his mining and real estate ventures. Ask for the secluded cottage with its own deck and clawfoot tub. Other rooms in the main house overlook downtown Quincy or the mountains. Check out a bicycle to explore the countryside.

Historic Interest: County Historic Designation.
Innkeeper(s): Bob & Jan Janowski. $80-130. MC, VISA, AX, DC, DS, PC, TC. TAC10. 7 rooms with PB, 4 with FP, 1 suite, 2 cottages and 1 conference room. Breakfast and snacks/refreshments included in rates. Types of meals: Full gourmet bkfst and early coffee/tea. Beds: QT. TV, phone, ceiling fan and radio in room. Air conditioning. VCR, fax, copier, bicycles, library and TVs upon request on premises. Handicap access. Small meetings hosted. Antiquing, fishing, live theater, parks, shopping, cross-country skiing and water sports nearby.
Publicity: *Focus, Reno Gazette, San Francisco Chronicle, Country Accents, Sunset.*

"After living and traveling in Europe where innkeepers are famous, we have found The Feather Bed to be one of the most charming in the U.S. and Europe!"

Red Bluff   D5

Faulkner House

1029 Jefferson St
Red Bluff, CA 96080-2725
(530)529-0520 (800)549-6171 Fax:(530)527-4970
E-mail: faulknerbb@snowcrest.net
Web: www.snowcrest.net/faulknerbb

Circa 1890. This Queen Anne Victorian stands on a quiet, tree-lined street in the Victorian town of Red Bluff. Furnished in antiques, the house has original stained-glass windows, ornate molding, and eight-foot pocket doors separating the front and back parlors. The Tower Room is a cozy spot or choose the Rose Room with its brocade fainting couch and queen bed.

Historic Interest: Ide Adobe (1 mile), Kelly Griggs Museum (one-half mile).
Innkeeper(s): Harvey & Mary Klingler. $65-90. MC, VISA, AX. 4 rooms with PB. Breakfast included in rates. Type of meal: Full bkfst. Beds: QD. Antiquing, fishing, parks and cross-country skiing nearby.
Publicity: *Red Bluff Daily News.*

"Enjoyed our stay at your beautiful home."

Sacramento   G6

Amber House

1315 22nd St
Sacramento, CA 95816-5717
(916)444-8085 (800)755-6526 Fax:(916)552-6529
E-mail: innkeeper@amberhouse.com
Web: www.amberhouse.com

Circa 1905. These three historic homes on the city's Historic Preservation Register are in a neighborhood of fine historic homes eight blocks from the capitol. Each room is named for a famous poet, artist or composer and features stained glass, English antiques, and amenities such as bath robes and fresh flowers. Ask about the Van Gogh Room where you can soak in the heart-shaped Jacuzzi tub-for-two or enjoy one of the rooms with marble baths and Jacuzzi tubs in either the adjacent 1913 Mediterranean mansion or the 1895 Colonial Revival. A gourmet breakfast can be served in your room or in the dining room at a time you request.

Historic Interest: California State Capitol, State

Railroad Museum, Crocker Art Museum, Governor's Mansion, Old Sacramento State Historic Park (all within 8 to 22 blocks).

$139-269. MC, VISA, AX, DC, CB, DS, PC, TC. TAC10. 14 rooms with PB, 3 with FP and 1 conference room. Breakfast included in rates. Types of meals: Full gourmet bkfst and early coffee/tea. Beds: KQ. Cable TV, phone, turndown service and VCR in room. Air conditioning. Fax, bicycles, library and voice mail on premises. Weddings, small meetings and seminars hosted. Antiquing, fishing, live theater, parks, shopping, downhill skiing, cross-country skiing and water sports nearby.

Publicity: *Travel & Leisure, Village Crier.*

"Your cordial hospitality, the relaxing atmosphere and delicious breakfast made our brief business/pleasure trip so much more enjoyable."

Saint Helena   G4

Deer Run Inn

PO Box 311 3995 Spring Mountain Rd
Saint Helena, CA 94574-0311
(707)963-3794 (800)843-3408 Fax:(707)963-9026

Circa 1929. This secluded mountain home is located on four forested acres just up the road from the house used for the television show "Falcon Crest." A fir-tree-shaded deck provides a quiet spot for breakfast while watching birds and deer pass by. Your host, Tom, was born on Spring Mountain and knows the winery area well. There is a watercolorist in residence.

Historic Interest: Robert Louis Stevenson Museum & Library (5 miles), Old Faithful Geyser (12 miles), Petrified Forest (15 miles).

Innkeeper(s): Tom & Carol Wilson. $140-195. MC, VISA, AX, PC, TC. TAC10. 4 rooms with PB, 3 with FP, 1 suite and 1 cottage. Breakfast included in rates. Types of meals: Full gourmet bkfst and early coffee/tea. Beds: KQ. Ceiling fan in room. Air conditioning. Fax, copier and swimming on premises. Amusement parks, antiquing, fishing, museums, golf, spas, art galleries, live theater, parks, shopping, sporting events and water sports nearby.

Publicity: *Forbes, Chicago Tribune, Napa Record.*

"The perfect honeymoon spot! We loved it!"

Ink House

1575 Saint Helena Hwy S
Saint Helena, CA 94574-9775
(707)963-3890

Circa 1884. Theron H. Ink, owner of thousands of acres in Marin, Napa and Sonoma counties, was an investor in livestock, wineries and mining. He built his Italianate Victorian with a glass-walled observatory on top, and from this room, visitors can enjoy 360-degree views of the Napa Valley and surrounding vineyards. Listed in the National Register, the Ink House is an elegant, spacious retreat of a time gone by.

Innkeeper(s): Diane DeFilipi. $99-200. MC, VISA, PC, TC. TAC10. 7 rooms, 5 with PB. Breakfast included in rates. Type of meal: Full gourmet bkfst. Beds: Q. Air conditioning. VCR, bicycles, library, pool table, observatory, picnic table, historic barn and gardens on premises. Weddings and family reunions hosted. Italian spoken. Antiquing, fishing, golf, spas, horseback riding, hot air balloon rides, parks, shopping, tennis and water sports nearby.

"Your hospitality made us feel so much at home. This is a place and a time we will long remember."

San Andreas   H7

Robin's Nest

PO Box 1408
San Andreas, CA 95249-1408
(209)754-1076 (888)214-9202 Fax:(209)754-3975

Circa 1895. Expect to be pampered from the moment you walk through the door at this three-story Queen Anne Victorian. Guests are made to feel at home, and treated to an

elegant, gourmet breakfast. The late 19th-century gem includes many fine architectural features, including eight-foot round windows, 12-foot ceilings on the first floor and gabled ceilings with roof windows on the second floor. Antiques decorate the

guest rooms, with pieces such as a four-poster, step-up bed. One bathroom includes an original seven-foot bathtub. The grounds boast century-old fruit trees, grapevines, a brick well, windmill and the more modern addition of a hot spa.

Historic Interest: Three large caverns are within 30 minutes of the home.

Innkeeper(s): Karen & Bill Konietzny. $75-125. 9 rooms, 7 with PB. Breakfast included in rates. Type of meal: Full bkfst. Gourmet dinner available. Beds: KQDT. Antiquing, fishing, live theater, downhill skiing, cross-country skiing and water sports nearby.

Publicity: *Stockton Record, In Flight, Westways.*

"An excellent job of making guests feel at home."

San Diego   Q12

The Cottage

3829 Albatross St
San Diego, CA 92103-3017
(619)299-1564
E-mail: cemerick@adnc.com
Web: www.sandiegobandb.com/cottage

Circa 1913. The furnishings in this homestead-style inn are an eclectic mix originating from 1880 to 1940. The Garden Room with private entrance is part of the innkeepers' home and is adjacent to the patio. The Cottage is a small house with Victorian decor, a wood burning stove, oak pump organ and fully equipped kitchen. Sages, mints, lavenders,

verbenas and 30 more herbs can be found in the unique garden. Guests will find a quiet retreat in the heart of the city.

Innkeeper(s): Robert & Carol Emerick. $65-125. MC, VISA, AX, DS. 2 rooms. Type of meal: Cont. Beds: K. TV and phone in room.

"The two pictures taken in your garden are wonderful momentos of the restful, restorative time I spent at your B&B."

Heritage Park Inn

2470 Heritage Park Row
San Diego, CA 92110-2803
(619)299-6832 (800)995-2470 Fax:(619)299-9465
E-mail: innkeeper@heritageparkinn.com
Web: www.heritageparkinn.com

Circa 1889. Situated on a seven-acre Victorian park in the heart of Old Town, this inn is two of seven preserved classic structures. The main house offers a variety of beautifully appointed guest rooms, decked in traditional Victorian furnishings and decor. The opulent Manor Suite includes two bedrooms, a Jacuzzi tub and sitting room. Several rooms offer ocean views, and guest also can see the nightly fireworks show at nearby Sea World. A collection of classic movies is available, and a different movie is shown each night in the inn's parlor. Guests are treated to a light afternoon tea, and breakfast is served on fine china on candlelit tables. The home is within walking distance to the many sites, shops and restaurants in the historic Old Town.

Innkeeper(s): Nancy & Charles Helsper. $100-235. MC, VISA, TC. TAC10. 12 rooms with PB, 1 suite and 1 conference room. Breakfast and afternoon tea included in rates. MAP. Types of meals: Full gourmet bkfst and early coffee/tea. Gourmet dinner, picnic lunch and catering service available. Beds: KQT. Phone, turndown service and ceiling fan in room. VCR, fax and copier on premises. Small meetings, family reunions and seminars hosted. Antiquing, fishing, San Diego Zoo, Tijuana, live theater, parks, shopping, sporting events and water sports nearby.

"A beautiful step back in time. Peaceful and gracious."

San Francisco   H4

The Amsterdam Hotel

749 Taylor St
San Francisco, CA 94108-3897
(415)673-3277 (800)637-3444 Fax:(415)673-0453
E-mail: info@amsterdamhotel.com
Web: www.amsterdamhotel.com

Circa 1909. This brick Victorian has the feel of a small European hotel. All San Francisco attractions are easily reached from the inn's downtown location. The cable cars are two blocks away and Union Square is three blocks away. Guests staying on business as well as pleasure are accommodated with clean spacious rooms, direct-dial phone and a fax machine on premises.

Innkeeper(s): Harry Hainf. $89-99. MC, VISA, AX, TC. TAC10. 34 rooms with PB. Breakfast included in rates. Types of meals: Cont and early coffee/tea. Beds: KQD. Cable TV and phone in room. VCR, fax, copier and sauna on premises. Amusement parks, antiquing, Nob Hill, Union Square, Chinatown, live theater, parks and shopping nearby.

Archbishop's Mansion

1000 Fulton St (at Steiner)
San Francisco, CA 94117-1608
(415)563-7872 (800)543-5820 Fax:(415)885-3193

Circa 1904. This French Empire-style manor was built for the Archbishop of San Francisco. It is designated as a San Francisco historic landmark. The grand stairway features redwood paneling, Corinthian columns and a stained-glass dome. The parlor has a hand-painted ceiling. Each of the guest rooms is named for an opera. Rooms have antiques, Victorian window treatments and embroidered linens. Continental breakfast is served in the dining room, and guests also are treated to a complimentary wine and cheese reception each night.

Innkeeper(s): Sondra Lender. $189-419. MC, VISA, AX, DC. TAC10. 15 rooms with PB, 11 with FP and 5 suites. Breakfast included in rates. Type of meal: Cont. Beds: KQ. Cable TV, phone, turndown service and VCR in room. Fax and copier on premises. Weddings and small meetings hosted. Parks nearby.

Publicity: *Travel-Holiday, Travel & Leisure.*

"The ultimate, romantic honeymoon spot."

Art Center/Wamsley Gallery/B&B

1902 Filbert St
San Francisco, CA 94123-3504
(415)567-1526

Circa 1857. The Art Center Bed & Breakfast was built during the Louisiana movement to San Francisco at the time of the Gold Rush. It was the only permanent structure on the path

between the Presidio and Yerba Buena village. There are five guest suites here, convenient to much of San Francisco. The building is next to what was reputedly Washer Woman's Cove, a freshwater lagoon at the foot of Laguna Street that served as the village laundry.

Historic Interest: Muir Woods, Giant Redwoods & Sausalito, Wine Country - Napa & Sonoma.

Innkeeper(s): George & Helvi Wamsley. $105-145. MC, VISA, AX. 5 rooms with PB, 3 with FP and 1 suite. Breakfast included in rates. Types of meals: Cont and early coffee/tea. Beds: Q. TV and ceiling fan in room. Library and kitchen on premises. Small meetings, family reunions and seminars hosted. Finnish spoken. Art galleries, fishing, golf, Golden Gate Bridge, Fisherman's Wharf, Marina Green, Palace of Fine Arts, live theater, museums, parks, shopping, sporting events, tennis and water sports nearby.

"This must be our 12th to 15th visit and it's just as good as ever."

Golden Gate Hotel

775 Bush St
San Francisco, CA 94108-3402
(415)392-3702 (800)835-1118 Fax:(415)392-6202

Circa 1913. News travels far when there's a bargain. Half of the guests visiting this four-story Edwardian hotel at the foot of Nob Hill are from abroad. Great bay windows on each floor provide many of the rooms with gracious spaces at humble prices. An original bird cage elevator kept in working order floats between floors. Antiques, fresh flowers, and afternoon tea further add to the atmosphere. Union Square is two-and-a-half blocks from the hotel.

Innkeeper(s): John & Renate Kenaston. $72-115. MC, VISA, AX, DC, TC. TAC10. 25 rooms, 14 with PB. Breakfast and afternoon tea included in rates. Type of meal: Cont. Beds: QDT. Cable TV and phone in room. Fax on premises. French, German and Spanish spoken. Antiquing, restaurants and live theater nearby.

Publicity: *Los Angeles Times, Melbourne Sun (Australia), Sunday Oregonian, Globe & Mail.*

"Stayed here by chance, will return by choice!"

The No Name Victorian B&B

847 Fillmore St
San Francisco, CA 94117-1703
(415)899-0060 Fax:(415)899-9923
E-mail: bbsf@linex.com
Web: www.bbsf.com/noname.html

Circa 1890. Located in the historic district of Alamo Square, this Second Empire Victorian sits close to the Civic Center, Opera House, Davies Symphony Hall and Union Square. An 1830s wedding bed from mainland China adorns the honeymoon room. The massive hand-carved bed is believed to bring good spirits and luck to the couple who spend their wedding night there. Chinese antiques, a wood-burning fireplace, a city view and Chinese robes also are included. There's a family accommodation with a private entrance, full kitchen and a crib.

Innkeeper(s): Eva Strakova. $69-125. MC, VISA, AX, PC, TC. TAC10. 5 rooms, 3 with PB, 4 with FP and 1 suite. Breakfast included in rates. Types of meals: Full bkfst and early coffee/tea. Beds: QT. Spa and child care on premises. Weddings and family reunions hosted. Live theater, parks, shopping and sporting events nearby.

Pensione International

875 Post St
San Francisco, CA 94109-6012
(415)775-3344 Fax:(415)775-3320
Web: www.travelassist.com/reg/ca123s.html

Circa 1906. Located in an early 20th-century Victorian, Pensione International offers guests comfortably and reasonably priced accommodations in a historic setting. The hotel includes 50 rooms, 35 of which include shared bath facilities. The 15 deluxe rooms include a private bath. The hotel is decorated with contemporary art, and each room is different. Continental breakfast is served every day except Thursdays. Pensione International is located in San Francisco's Union Square area, close to cable cars, restaurants, shops and the civic center.
Historic Interest: Fisherman's wharf (2 miles).
Innkeeper(s): Christian Kiyabu. $60-105. MC, VISA, AX. TAC10. 50 rooms, 15 with PB. Type of meal: Cont. Beds: D. Fax on premises. Spanish spoken. Art galleries, beaches, Union Square, Moscone Center, live theater, museums and shopping nearby.

Stanyan Park Hotel

750 Stanyan St
San Francisco, CA 94117-2725
(415)751-1000 Fax:(415)668-5454

Circa 1904. Many of the guest rooms of this restored Victorian inn overlook Golden Gate Park. The turret suites and bay suites are popular, and all suites include kitchens. Museums, horseback riding and biking are available in the park, as well as the Japanese Tea Garden. Guests enjoy an expanded continental breakfast and evening tea service.
Innkeeper(s): John Brocklehurst. $115-300. MC, VISA, AX, DC, CB, DS, TC. TAC10. 36 rooms with PB and 6 suites.
Type of meal: Cont plus. Beds: QT. Cable TV, phone and suites have kitchens in room. Fax, copier and bicycles on premises. Handicap access. Live theater, parks, shopping and sporting events nearby.
Publicity: *Metropolitan Home, New York Times, Sunset Magazine.*

Victorian Inn on The Park

301 Lyon St
San Francisco, CA 94117-2108
(415)931-1830 (800)435-1967 Fax:(415)931-1830
E-mail: vicinn@aol.com
Web: www.citysearch.com/sfo/victorianinn

Circa 1897. This grand three-story Queen Anne inn, built by William Curlett, has an open belvedere turret with a teahouse roof and Victorian railings. Silk-screened wallpapers, created especially for the inn, are accentuated by intricate mahogany and redwood paneling. The opulent Belvedere Suite features French doors opening to a Roman tub for two. Overlooking Golden Gate Park, the inn is 10 minutes from downtown.
Innkeeper(s): Lisa & William Benau. $139-179. MC, VISA, AX, DC, CB, DS, PC, TC. TAC10. 12 rooms with PB, 3 with FP and 2 suites. Breakfast included in rates. Types of meals: Cont plus and early coffee/tea. Beds: QT. Phone and balcony in room. Fax, library, child care and refrigerator on premises. Small meetings and family reunions hosted. Russian and Spanish spoken. Antiquing, museums, live theater, parks and sporting events nearby.

Publicity: *Insider, Country Inns, Good Housekeeping, New York Times, Good Morning America, Country Inns USA, Great Country Inns of America.*

"The excitement you have about your building comes from the care you have taken in restoring and maintaining your historic structure."

Washington Square Inn

1660 Stockton St
San Francisco, CA 94133-3316
(415)981-4220 (800)388-0220 Fax:(415)397-7242

Circa 1978. Situated one block from Telegraph Hill in the area of North Beach and the Italian district, the inn is just opposite Washington Square. Decorated by designer and owner Sandra Norwitt, the appointments include a mixture of French and English antiques and upholstered window seats, canopied beds, writing desks and comfortable reading chairs. This is a non-smoking hotel.
Innkeeper(s): David Norwitt. $125-210. MC, VISA, AX, DC, CB, DS, PC, TC. TAC10. 15 rooms with PB. Breakfast and afternoon tea included in rates. Type of meal: Cont plus. Beds: KQDT. Cable TV, phone and turndown service in room. VCR and copier on premises. Handicap access. Weddings and family reunions hosted. Amusement parks, antiquing, hiking. Boating. Dancing, live theater, parks, shopping, sporting events and tennis nearby.

Santa Barbara   N8

Blue Dolphin Inn

420 W Montecito St
Santa Barbara, CA 93101-3879
(805)965-2333 (877)722-3657 Fax:(805)962-4907
E-mail: info@sbbluedolphininn.com
Web: www.sbbluedolphininn.com

Circa 1920. It's a short walk to the beach and harbor from this Victorian inn, which offers accommodations in the main house and adjacent carriage house. Guest rooms are decorated in period style with antiques. Brass beds, tapestry pillows, and fluffy comforters add a romantic touch. Several rooms include fireplaces, Jacuzzi tubs or private balconies.
Historic Interest: The Trussei Whinchester Adobe and Fernald House.
Innkeeper(s): Pete Chiarenza, Edward Skolak. $98-225. MC, VISA, AX, PC, TC. TAC10. 9 rooms, 7 with PB and 2 suites. Breakfast and afternoon tea included in rates. Types of meals: Full gourmet bkfst and veg bkfst. Beds: KQT. Cable TV, phone and VCR in room. Air conditioning. Fax, copier and library on premises. Small meetings and family reunions hosted. French and Spanish spoken. Antiquing, art galleries, beaches, bicycling, golf, hiking, horseback riding, roller skating, live theater, museums, parks, water sports and wineries nearby.

Cheshire Cat Inn & Cottages

36 W Valerio St
Santa Barbara, CA 93101-2524
(805)569-1610 Fax:(805)682-1876
E-mail: cheshire@cheshirecat.com
Web: www.cheshirecat.com

Circa 1894. The Eberle family built two graceful houses side by side, one a Queen Anne, the other a Colonial Revival. President McKinley was entertained here on a visit to Santa

Barbara. There is a pagoda-like porch, a square and a curved bay, rose gardens, grassy lawns and a gazebo. Laura Ashley wallpapers and furnishings are featured. Outside, guests will enjoy English flower gardens, an outdoor Jacuzzi, a new deck with sitting areas and fountains.

Historic Interest: Santa Barbara Beautiful Award.

Innkeeper(s): Christine Dunstan. $140-350. MC, VISA, PC, TC. 17 rooms with PB, 7 suites and 1 conference room. Breakfast included in rates. Type of meal: Full bkfst. Room service available. Beds: KQT. Cable TV, phone, ceiling fan and in some rooms in room. Spa on premises. Small meetings, family reunions and seminars hosted. Amusement parks, antiquing, fishing, live theater, shopping, sporting events and water sports nearby.

"Romantic and quaint."

Glenborough Inn

1327 Bath St
Santa Barbara, CA 93101-3630
(805)966-0589 (800)962-0589 Fax:(805)564-8610
E-mail: info@glenborough.com
Web: www.glenboroughinn.com

Circa 1885. The Victorian and California Craftsman-style homes that comprise the Glenborough are located in the theatre and arts district. Antiques, rich wood trim and elegant fireplace suites with canopy beds are offered. Some rooms also have mini refrigerators or whirlpools tubs. There's always plenty of hospitality and an invitation to try the secluded garden hot tub. Homemade breakfasts, served in the privacy of your room, have been written up in Bon Appetit and Chocolatier. Bedtime cookies and beverages are served, as well. It's a three-block walk to restaurants, shops and the shuttle to the beach.

Historic Interest: Walking distance to historic downtown Santa Barbara, Mission Santa Barbara (1 1/4 mile).

Innkeeper(s): Michael & Steve. $100-420. MC, VISA, AX, DC, CB, PC, TC. TAC10. 13 rooms with PB, 12 with FP, 6 suites and 1 cottage. Breakfast included in rates. Types of meals: Full bkfst and cont. Beds: KQD. Phone, ceiling fan, coffee maker, robes and some A/C and mini fridge in room. Fax and spa on premises. Spanish spoken. Antiquing, fishing, live theater, parks, shopping, sporting events and water sports nearby.

Publicity: *Houston Post, Los Angeles Times, Pasadena Choice.*

"Only gracious service is offered at the Glenborough Inn."

The Old Yacht Club Inn

431 Corona Del Mar
Santa Barbara, CA 93103-3601
(805)962-1277 (800)676-1676 Fax:(805)962-3989

Circa 1912. This California Craftsman house was the home of the Santa Barbara Yacht Club during the Roaring '20s. It was opened as Santa Barbara's first B&B and has become renowned for its gourmet food and superb hospitality. Dinner is offered to guests on Saturday nights. Innkeeper Nancy Donaldson is the author of The Old Yacht Club Inn Cookbook.

Innkeeper(s): Nancy Donaldson. $110-195. MC, VISA, AX, DS, PC, TC. 12 rooms with PB and 1 conference room. Breakfast included in rates. Types of meals: Full gourmet bkfst and early coffee/tea. Gourmet dinner available. Beds: KQ. TV and phone in room. Fax, copier and bicycles on premises. Small meetings and seminars hosted. Antiquing, fishing, live theater, shopping, sporting events and water sports nearby.

Publicity: *Los Angeles, Valley.*

"Donaldson is one of Santa Barbara's better-kept culinary secrets."

The Parsonage

1600 Olive Street
Santa Barbara, CA 93101-1115
(805)962-9336 (800)775-0352

Circa 1892. Built for the Trinity Episcopal Church, The Parsonage is one of Santa Barbara's most notable Queen Anne  Victorian structures. Each room is elegantly decorated in fine antiques and furnishings distinctive to the period. It is nestled between downtown Santa Barbara and the foothills in a quiet residential, upper eastside neighborhood. The inn has ocean and mountain views and is within walking distance of the Santa Barbara Mission, shops, theater and restaurants.

Innkeeper(s): Kim Curran-Moore. $130-305. MC, VISA, AX, DC, DS. TAC10. 6 rooms with PB, 2 with FP and 1 suite. Breakfast and afternoon tea included in rates. Type of meal: Full bkfst. Beds: KQ. Fax on premises. Antiquing, fishing, live theater and water sports nearby.

"Bravo! You have created a beautiful treasure here in Santa Barbara."

Secret Garden Inn and Cottages

1908 Bath St
Santa Barbara, CA 93101-2813
(805)687-2300 (800)676-1622 Fax:(805)687-4576
E-mail: garden@secretgarden.com
Web: secretgarden.com

Circa 1908. The main house and adjacent cottages surround the gardens and are decorated in American and English-Country style. The Hummingbird is a large cottage guest room with a queen-size white iron bed and a private deck with a hot tub for your exclusive use. The three suites have private outdoor hot tubs. Wine and light hors d'oeuvres are served in the late afternoon, and hot apple cider is served each evening.

Innkeeper(s): Jack Greenwald, Christine Dunstan. $115-225. MC, VISA, AX, PC, TC. TAC10. 11 rooms with PB, 1 with FP, 3 suites and 4 cottages. Breakfast, afternoon tea and snacks/refreshments included in rates. Types of meals: Full bkfst and early coffee/tea. Beds: KQ. TV in room. Fax and copier on premises. Small meetings, family reunions and seminars hosted. Antiquing, fishing, live theater, shopping and water sports nearby.

Publicity: *Los Angeles Times, Santa Barbara, Independant.*

"A romantic little getaway retreat that neither of us will be able to forget. It was far from what we expected to find."

Simpson House Inn

121 E Arrellaga
Santa Barbara, CA 93108
(805)963-7067 (800)676-1280 Fax:(805)564-4811
E-mail: reservations@simpsonhouseinn.com
Web: www.simpsonhouseinn.com

Circa 1874. The Simpson House is currently the only bed and breakfast in North America holding a Five Diamond award from AAA. If you were one of the Simpson family's first visitors, you would have arrived in Santa Barbara by stagecoach or by ship. The railroad was not completed for another 14 years. A stately Italianate Victorian house, the inn, a historic landmark, is situated on an acre of English gardens hidden behind a 20-foot-tall eugenia hedge. In the evenings, guests are treated to a sampling of local wines, as well as a lavish Mediterranean hors d'oeuvre buffet. The evening turndown service includes delectable chocolate truffles. The innkeepers can arrange for in-room European spa treatments, and guests can workout at a nearby private health club. Guests also receive complimentary passes for the Santa Barbara trolley.

Historic Interest: Santa Barbara Mission, Presidio, El Paseo all within 1 mile.

Innkeeper(s): Linda & Glyn Davies, Dixie Adair Budke(General Man. $195-450. MC, VISA, AX, DS. 14 rooms with PB, 7 with FP, 5 suites and 1 conference room. Breakfast, afternoon tea and snacks/refreshments included in rates. Gourmet dinner available. Beds: KQ. Fax, copier and bicycles on premises. Handicap access. Antiquing, fishing, live theater and water sports nearby.

Publicity: *Country Inns, Santa Barbara, LA Magazine, Avenues.*

"Perfectly restored and impeccably furnished. Your hospitality is warm and heartfelt and the food is delectable. Whoever said that 'the journey is better than the destination' couldn't have known about the Simpson House."

Tiffany Inn

1323 De La Vina St
Santa Barbara, CA 93101-3120
(805)963-2283

Circa 1898. This Victorian house features a steep front gable and balcony accentuating the entrance. Colonial diamond-paned bay windows and a front veranda welcome guests to an antique-filled inn. The honeymoon Suite is a favorite with its secluded garden entrance, canopied bed, jacuzzi tub and fireplace. The Penthouse occupies the entire third floor and includes a living room with a fireplace, a terrace offering ocean views and a Jacuzzi tub. Other rooms are just as interesting, with antique toy collections, floral chintzes and Victorian beds. Fine restaurants and shops are within walking distance.

Innkeeper(s): Carol & Larry Mac Donald. $125-250. MC, VISA, AX. 7 rooms with PB, 5 with FP. Type of meal: Full bkfst. Beds: Q. Phone and Jacuzzi tub in three rooms in room.

"We have stayed at a number of B&Bs, but this is the best. We especially liked the wonderful breakfasts on the porch overlooking the garden."

The Upham Hotel & Garden Cottages

1404 De La Vina St
Santa Barbara, CA 93101-3027
(805)962-0058 (800)727-0876 Fax:(805)963-2825

Circa 1871. Antiques and period furnishings decorate each of the inn's guest rooms and suites. The inn is the oldest continuously operating hostelry in Southern California. Situated on an acre of gardens in the center of downtown, it's within easy walking distance of restaurants, shops, art galleries and museums. The staff is happy to assist guests in discovering Santa Barbara's varied attractions. Garden cottage units feature porches or secluded patios and several have gas fireplaces.

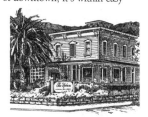

Innkeeper(s): Jan Martin Winn. $140-385. MC, VISA, AX, DC, DS, TC. TAC10. 50 rooms with PB, 8 with FP, 4 suites, 3 cottages and 3 conference rooms. Breakfast included in rates. Types of meals: Cont plus and early coffee/tea. Snacks/refreshments available. Beds: KQD. Cable TV, phone and ceiling fan in room. Fax and copier on premises. Weddings, small meetings, family reunions and seminars hosted. Antiquing, golf, live theater, parks, shopping and water sports nearby.

Publicity: *Los Angeles Times, Santa Barbara, Westways, Santa Barbara News-Press, Avenues.*

"Your hotel is truly a charm. Between the cozy gardens and the exquisitely comfortable appointments, The Upham is charm itself."

Santa Barbara (Carpinteria)

Prufrock's Garden Inn By The Beach

600 Linden Ave
Santa Barbara (Carpinteria), CA 93013-2040
(805)566-9696 Fax:(805)566-9404

Circa 1904. A white fence surrounds this California-style cottage, located on a palm-lined small-town main street. The home is one block from a beautiful oceanfront state park, said by some to be the "Best Beach in the West." The inn has been honored by a number of awards, including the L.A. Times "Reader's Favorite" and the Santa Barbara Independent's "Most Romantic Getaway." You can understand all this when you note the Jacuzzis, fireplaces and private sitting areas. Relax on the porch or stroll through the lush gardens. Guests will enjoy the inviting aroma of the inn's busy kitchen, a source for sunset hors d'oeuvres and beach picnics. The innkeeper offers romance and historic themed packages.

Historic Interest: The Old Mission and historic county courthouse are about 12 minutes away in Santa Barbara. Other nearby historic attractions include adobes and a state historic park.

Innkeeper(s): Judy & Jim Halvorsen. $110-230. MC, VISA, DS. 7 rooms, 5 with PB. Breakfast, afternoon tea and snacks/refreshments included in rates. Types of meals: Full bkfst, cont and early coffee/tea. Beds: Q. Turndown service, sitting area and daybeds in room. VCR, bicycles and gardens on premises. Small meetings, family reunions and seminars hosted. Antiquing, beaches, bicycling, fishing, hiking, tidepools, live theater, parks, shopping, sporting events and wineries nearby.

Santa Cruz

Chateau Victorian

118 1st St
Santa Cruz, CA 95060-5402
(831)458-9458

This plum-colored Victorian is within a block of the waterfront and offers seven guest rooms. The romantic Bay Side Room is a favorite of guests, as it offers a marble fireplace and a clawfoot tub with an overhead shower. Breakfasts, including a variety of tempting fruits and pastries, can be enjoyed on the patio, dining room or on the secluded side deck. After a day of exploring Santa Cruz and its surroundings, evening refreshments are a perfect touch. The inn is within

walking distance to downtown, the wharf, a variety of restaurants, the Boardwalk Amusement Park and the beach.

Innkeeper(s): Alice June. $115-145. MC, VISA, PC. 7 rooms with PB and 1 cottage. Breakfast included in rates. Type of meal: Cont plus. Beds: Q. Cottage has 2 fireplaces in room. Small meetings hosted. Amusement parks, antiquing, fishing, live theater, parks, shopping and water sports nearby.

Publicity: *Times Tribune, Santa Cruz Sentinel, Good Times.*

"Certainly enjoyed our most recent stay and have appreciated all of our visits."

Santa Monica
010

Channel Road Inn

219 W Channel Rd
Santa Monica, CA 90402-1105
(310)459-1920 Fax:(310)454-9920

Circa 1910. This shingle-clad building is a variation of the Colonial Revival Period, one of the few remaining in Los Angeles. The abandoned home was saved from the city's wrecking crew by owner Susan Zolla, with the encouragement of the local historical society. The rooms feature canopy beds, fine linens, custom mattresses and private porches. Chile Cheese Puffs served with salsa are a popular breakfast speciality. The Pacific Ocean is one block away, and guests often enjoy borrowing the inn's bicycles to pedal along the 30-mile coastal bike path. In the evening, the inn's spectacular cliffside spa is popular.

Innkeeper(s): Heather Suskin. $145-295. MC, VISA, AX, PC, TC. TAC10. 12 rooms with PB, 2 with FP and 2 suites. Breakfast, afternoon tea and snacks/refreshments included in rates. Types of meals: Full bkfst and early coffee/tea. Room service available. Beds: KQT. Cable TV, phone, ceiling fan and VCR in room. Fax, copier, spa and bicycles on premises. Handicap access. Antiquing, fishing, beach, bike path, Paul Getty Museum, live theater, parks, shopping, sporting events and water sports nearby.

Publicity: Los Angeles Magazine, New York Times, Brides, Country Inns.

"One of the most romantic hotels in Los Angeles."

Santa Rosa
G4

The Gables Inn

4257 Petaluma Hill Rd
Santa Rosa, CA 95404-9796
(707)585-7777 (800)422-5376 Fax:(707)584-5634
E-mail: innkeeper@thegablesinn.com
Web: www.thegablesinn.com

Circa 1877. Fifteen gables accentuate this striking Gothic Revival house with a French influence. Situated on three-and-a-half acres in the center of Sonoma Wine Country, the inn has 12-foot ceilings, a winding staircase with ornately carved balustrades and three marble fireplaces. The Brookside Suite overlooks Taylor Creek and is decorated in an Edwardian theme. Other rooms feature views of the sequoias, meadows and the barn. The surrounding Sonoma Wine Country offers more than 150 wineries and vineyards, as well as the Pacific coast and California Redwoods Park.

Innkeeper(s): Michael & Judy Ogne. $135-225. MC, VISA, AX, DS. TAC10. 8 rooms with PB, 4 with FP, 1 suite and 1 cottage. Breakfast and afternoon tea included in rates. Types of meals: Full gourmet bkfst and early coffee/tea. Beds: KQT. Handicap access. Redwood forest and wineries nearby.

"You all have a warmth about you that makes it home here."

Pygmalion House B&B Inn

331 Orange St
Santa Rosa, CA 95401-6226
(707)526-3407 Fax:(707)526-3407

Circa 1880. This historic Victorian, which has been restored to its 19th-century grandeur, is just a few blocks from Santa Rosa's Old Town, "Railroad Square" and many antique shops,

cafes, coffeehouses and restaurants. The home is filled with a unique mix of antiques, many of which belonged to famed, Gypsy Rose Lee. Each of the Victorian guest rooms includes a bath with a clawfoot tub. Five different varieties of coffee are blended each morning for the breakfast service, which includes homemade entrees, freshly baked breads and fresh fruit.

Innkeeper(s): Caroline Berry. $89-109. MC, VISA, PC, TC. 6 rooms with PB. Breakfast and snacks/refreshments included in rates. Type of meal: Full bkfst. Beds: KQDT. Cable TV in room. Air conditioning. Fax, copier, library, mall and Railroad Square on premises. Antiquing, fishing, golf, live theater, parks, shopping and wineries nearby.

Seal Beach
010

The Seal Beach Inn & Gardens

212 5th St
Seal Beach, CA 90740-6115
(562)493-2416 (800)443-3292 Fax:(562)799-0483
E-mail: hideaway@sealbeachinn.com
Web: www.sealbeachinn.com

Circa 1923. This historic Southern California inn has lush gardens and the look of an oceanside estate. It's a short walk to the Seal Beach pier, shops and restaurants. Major attractions in Orange County and the Los Angeles area are within short driving distances. Business travelers can plan meetings in rooms where 24 people can sit comfortably. The inn has a Mediterranean villa ambience, and no two rooms are alike.

Historic Interest: The Bower Museum and Queen Mary are nearby historic attractions, and the inn is within an hour from most of Los Angeles' historic sites. Rancho Los Alamitos, a five-acre historic preserve of an original 1520s Spanish land grant, is just three miles from the inn and includes on its grounds the oldest house in the L.A. area.

Innkeeper(s): Marjorie B. & Harty Schmaehl. $165-225. MC, VISA, AX, DC, CB, DS, TC. 23 rooms with PB, 10 with FP and 11 suites. Breakfast, afternoon tea and snacks/refreshments included in rates. AP. Types of meals: Full bkfst and early coffee/tea. Beds: KQ. Phone, turndown service, some have A/C, CD in room. Fax and copier on premises. Weddings, small meetings, family reunions and seminars hosted. Amusement parks, antiquing, fishing, golf, fine restaurants, live theater, parks, shopping, sporting events and water sports nearby.

Publicity: Brides, Country Inns, Glamour, Country, Long Beach Press Telegram, Orange County Register, Los Angeles Times, Country Living, Sunset.

"The closest thing to Europe since I left there. Delights the senses and restores the soul."

Sequoia
K9

Plantation B&B

33038 Sierra Hwy 198
Sequoia, CA 93244-1700
(559)597-2555 (800)240-1466 Fax:(559)597-2551
E-mail: relax@plantationbnb.com
Web: www.plantationbnb.com

Circa 1908. The history of orange production is deeply entwined in the roots of California, and this home is located on what once was an orange plantation. The original 1908 house burned in the 1960s, but the current home was built on its foundation. In keeping with the home's

plantation past, the innkeepers decorated the bed and breakfast with a "Gone With the Wind" theme. The comfortable, country guest rooms sport names such as the Scarlett O'Hara, the Belle Watling, and of course, the Rhett Butler. A hot tub is located in the orchard, and there also is a heated swimming pool.

Innkeeper(s): Scott & Marie Munger. $69-159. MC, VISA, AX, DC, DS, PC, TC. TAC10. 8 rooms, 6 with PB, 2 with FP and 2 suites. Breakfast and snacks/refreshments included in rates. Types of meals: Full gourmet bkfst and early coffee/tea. Beds: KQD. Cable TV, ceiling fan and VCR in room. Air conditioning. Fax, spa and swimming on premises. Small meetings and family reunions hosted. Antiquing, fishing, golf, parks, shopping, cross-country skiing, sporting events and water sports nearby.

Publicity: *Exeter Sun, Kaweah Commonwealth, Los Angeles Times, Fresno Bee, Visalia Delta Times.*

"Scarlett O'Hara would be proud to live on this lovely plantation."

Smith River
A2

White Rose Mansion Inn

149 S Fred Haight Dr
Smith River, CA 95567
(707)487-9260

Circa 1869. Drive through the security gate and up the hill, and you'll feel you are coming home to your own country estate. Built in the style of an Italiante Victorian with large double bay windows, this gra-

cious three-story house is located on more than four acres with fruit and nut trees, a creek, gazebo and green lawns. The Swan Room boasts a king-size canopy bed, a whirlpool for two and antiques original to the Haight family who once lived here. The Country Cottage Room, recommended for families with children, offers a kitchen, sitting room and bedroom with a four-poster canopy bed. The inn is located in the Smith River Valley, minutes from the ocean, Smith River, and Redwood National Park.

Innkeeper(s): Candy Gallo. $89-185. MC, VISA, DS, PC. 7 rooms with PB, 1 suite and 1 cottage. Breakfast included in rates. Types of meals: Cont plus and early coffee/tea. Beds: KQDT. Turndown service and whirlpool tubs for two in room. Fax, copier, swimming and fruit & berry picking on premises. Weddings, small meetings, family reunions and seminars hosted. Antiquing, fishing, golf, live theater, parks, shopping and water sports nearby.

"The Swan Suite at the White Rose Inn is a wonderful honeymoon suite. Great scenery, great service, plenty of pampering and R&R. Just the perfect way to start our new life together."

Sonoma
H4

Sonoma Hotel

110 W Spain St
Sonoma, CA 95476-5696
(707)996-2996 (800)468-6016 Fax:(707)996-7014
Web: www.sonomahotel.com

Circa 1879. Originally built as a two-story adobe, a third story was added in the '20s. Today, the first floor now boasts an award-winning restaurant with a Four-Star rating featuring "new American" cuisine with a touch of French influence. The inn's guest rooms offer French-country furnishings from Harvest Home Stores, which is located on the square. Guests can order the same bed or chair that they enjoy in their room and have it delivered to their home. In Room 30, Maya Angelou wrote "Gather Together in My Name." A short walk away from the tree-lined plaza are several wineries.

Historic Interest: Mission San Francisco Solano, Bear Flag Revolt, Casa Grande Indian Servants Quarters (all within walking distance).

Innkeeper(s): Timothy Farfan & Craig Miller. $95-235. MC, VISA, AX, DC, TC. TAC5. 16 rooms with PB. Breakfast included in rates. Types of meals: Cont and early coffee/tea. Gourmet dinner and gourmet lunch available. Restaurant on premises. Beds: QDT. Fax and copier on premises. Weddings and family reunions hosted. Antiquing, live theater, parks and shopping nearby.

"Great food and service! I was so pleased to see such a warm and lovable place."

Trojan Horse Inn

19455 Sonoma Hwy
Sonoma, CA 95476-6416
(707)996-2430 (800)899-1925 Fax:(707)996-9185

Circa 1887. This Victorian home rests on one acre on the banks of Sonoma Creek. Recently restored, the pristine interior offers antiques and a romantic country decor. The Bridal Veil Room has a canopied bed, wood-burning stove and windows overlooking a magnolia tree, while a private Jacuzzi tub is a popular feature in the Grape Arbor Room. Bicycles, an additional outdoor Jacuzzi, flower gardens and grand old bay and spruce trees add to the experience.

Innkeeper(s): Joe & Sandy Miccio. $135-165. MC, VISA, AX. 6 rooms with PB, 1 with FP and 1 conference room. Types of meals: Full bkfst and early coffee/tea. Beds: Q. Ceiling fan in room. Air conditioning. Spa and bicycles on premises. Handicap access. Small meetings and family reunions hosted. Antiquing, live theater and shopping nearby.

"We came for one night and stayed for four."

Victorian Garden Inn

316 E Napa St
Sonoma, CA 95476-6723
(707)996-5339 (800)543-5339 Fax:(707)996-1689

Circa 1870. Authentic Victorian gardens cover more than an acre of grounds surrounding this Greek Revival farmhouse. Pathways wind around to secret gardens, and guests can walk to world-famous wineries and historical sites. All rooms are decorated with the romantic flair of the innkeeper, an interior designer. Ask to stay in the renovated water tower. Enjoy a therapeutic spa in the gardens.

Historic Interest: Northernmost mission in California chain; home of General M.G. Vallejo; historic Sonoma Plaza, site of 1846 "Bear Flag Rebellion" (establishment of California Republic); Sonoma Barracks - all within 4 blocks.

Innkeeper(s): Donna Lewis. $99-185. MC, VISA, AX, DC, PC, TC. TAC10. 4 rooms, 3 with PB, 1 with FP, 1 suite and 1 conference room. Types of meals: Cont plus, veg bkfst and early coffee/tea. Snacks/refreshments and room service available. Beds: QDT. Phone, ceiling fan and fireplaces some rooms in room. Air conditioning. Spa, swimming, sauna, library and beautiful gardens on premises. Antiquing, therapeutic spa, beautiful gardens, restaurants, live theater and wineries nearby.

"I'll be back! So romantic, this place is for lovers! What a perfect spot for a honeymoon! Great! Wonderful! Fabulous! We could not have asked for anything more."

Sonora   H7

Bradford Place Inn & Gardens

56 Bradford Ave
Sonora, CA 95370
(209)532-6303
E-mail: innkeeper@bradfordplaceinn.com
Web: bradfordplaceinn.com

Circa 1889. Located in the foothills of the Sierra Nevada and in the center of town, this is a two-story Queen Anne-style house with white picket fence, gabled red roof and wraparound veranda. It was originally constructed for a Wells Fargo agent. A well on the property was one of the area's three original water sources for the gold rush camp that developed here in the 1850s. In addition to the usual amenities, Bradford Place also offers in-room satellite television, phones with data ports as well as cookies and a garden filled with flowers. Breakfast may feature a gourmet entree or the inn's specialty, "Mother Lode Skillet," a serving of eggs, potatoes and sourdough pancakes. Guests have the option of being served in the parlor before the fireplace, on the veranda, or in their room. The historic county courthouse is next door, and guests can walk to cafes, antique stores, bookstores and shops. Nearby is Columbia (three miles) Jamestown and Murphys, and there are giant sequoias and caverns to explore. Other activities include gold panning, river rafting, trout fishing, horseback riding, sleigh rides or carriage rides.
Historic Interest: 1850's gold rush camp, Colubia State Historic Park-3 miles, Railtown State Park-3 miles, Tuolemne County Courthouse-1 block.
Innkeeper(s): Dottie Musser, Elizabeth McQueen, John Eisemara. $85-160. MC, VISA, AX, PC, TC. TAC10. 4 rooms, 3 with PB, 1 with FP, 1 suite and 1 conference room. Breakfast, afternoon tea and snacks/refreshments included in rates. Types of meals: Cont plus, country bkfst and veg bkfst. Beds: Q. TV, phone, turndown service, ceiling fan, VCR, satellite TV and microwave in room. Central air. Fax, parking, ice machine, microwave and refrigerator on premises. Small meetings and seminars hosted. Antiquing, art galleries, canoeing/kayaking, fishing, golf, hiking, horseback riding, horse drawn carriage rides, rafting, caverns, redwoods, steam train rides, county fairgrounds, live theater, museums, parks, shopping, downhill skiing, cross-country skiing, sporting events, tennis, water sports and wineries nearby.

Lavender Hill B&B

683 S Barretta St
Sonora, CA 95370-5132
(209)532-9024 (800)446-1333

Circa 1900. In the historic Gold Rush town of Sonora is this Queen Anne Victorian inn. Its four guest rooms include the Lavender Room, which has a mini-suite with desk, sitting area

and clawfoot tub and shower. After a busy day fishing, biking, river rafting or exploring nearby Yosemite National Park, guests may relax in the antique-filled parlor or the sitting room. Admiring the inn's gardens from the wraparound porch is also a favorite activity. Be sure to ask about dinner theater packages.
Innkeeper(s): Charlie & Jean Marinelli. $79-99. MC, VISA, AX, PC, TC. TAC10. 4 rooms with PB and 1 suite. Breakfast included in rates. Types of meals: Full bkfst and early coffee/tea. Beds: KQ. Ceiling fan in room. Air conditioning. Library on premises. Weddings, small meetings and family reunions hosted. Italian spoken. Antiquing, fishing, golf, live theater, parks, shopping, downhill skiing, cross-country skiing and water sports nearby.

Soquel   J5

Blue Spruce Inn

2815 S Main St
Soquel, CA 95073-2412
(831)464-1137 (800)559-1137 Fax:(831)475-0608

Circa 1875. Near the north coast of Monterey Bay, this old farmhouse has been freshly renovated and refitted with luxurious touches. The Seascape is a favorite room with its private entrance, wicker furnishings and bow-shaped Jacuzzi for two.  The Carriage House offers skylights above the bed, while a heart decor dominates Two Hearts. Local art, Amish quilts and featherbeds are featured throughout. Brunch enchiladas are the inn's speciality. Santa Cruz is four miles away.
Historic Interest: Redwood Forests (5 miles), Santa Cruz Mission (4 miles), Carmel Mission (30 miles), Monterey (20 miles).
Innkeeper(s): Patricia & Tom O'Brien. $85-175. MC, VISA, AX, PC, TC. TAC10. 6 rooms with PB, 5 with FP and 1 conference room. Breakfast included in rates. Types of meals: Full bkfst and early coffee/tea. Beds: KQ. Cable TV, phone, turndown service and VCR in room. Fax and library on premises. Small meetings and seminars hosted. Spanish spoken. Amusement parks, antiquing, fishing, live theater, parks, shopping and water sports nearby.
Publicity: *Village View.*

"You offer such graciousness to your guests and a true sense of welcome."

South Pasadena   O10

The Artists' Inn B&B

1038 Magnolia St
South Pasadena, CA 91030-2518
(626)799-5668 (888)799-5668 Fax:(626)799-3678
E-mail: artistsinn@artistsinns.com
Web: www.artistsinns.com

Circa 1895. A poultry farm once surrounded this turn-of-the-century home. Today, the streets are lined with trees and a variety of beautiful homes. Interior designer Janet Marangi restored the historic ambiance of the cheery, yellow home and cottage, filling them with antiques and original artwork. Each of the guest rooms captures a different artistic style. Soft, soothing colors enrich the

Impressionist room, which includes a clawfoot tub and antique brass bed. The 18th Century English room is filled with pieces by Gainsborough, Reynolds and Constable and includes a romantic canopied bed. Fireplaces and Jacuzzis are offered in the inn's five newest cottage suites. There are plenty of helpful amenities, including hair dryers, toiletries and desks in each room. The innkeeper creates a breakfast menu with freshly made breads, homemade granola, fruit and a special entree. The home is just a few blocks from South Pasadena's many shops, boutiques, cafes and restaurants.

Historic Interest: The historic Mission West district is a short distance from the inn. The Norton Simon Museum of Art, Old Town Pasadena, Mission San Gabriel and the Huntington Library are other nearby historic attractions.

Innkeeper(s): Janet Marangi. $110-205. MC, VISA, AX, PC, TC. TAC10. 9 rooms with PB and 4 suites. Breakfast and afternoon tea included in rates. Types of meals: Full gourmet bkfst, cont plus, cont and early coffee/tea. Picnic lunch and catered breakfast available. Beds: KQDT. Ceiling fan, fresh flowers, TV, Jacuzzi's and fireplace in room. Air conditioning. Fax and library on premises. Weddings, small meetings and family reunions hosted. Amusement parks, antiquing, live theater, parks, shopping and sporting events nearby.

Publicity: *Pasadena Star News, San Marino Tribune, Stanford, Pasadena Weekly, South Pasadena Review, Recommended by Elmer Dills, Travel & Leisure, New York Times.*

Sutter Creek   G6

Foxes In Sutter Creek

77 Main St, PO Box 159
Sutter Creek, CA 95685
(209)267-5882 (800)987-3344 Fax:(209)267-0712
E-mail: foxes@cdepot.net
Web: www.foxesinn.com

Circa 1857. This Greek Revival home is known for its elegant furnishings. There are canopied beds and handsome armoires, all brought together by the innkeeper's collection of foxes featured in old prints, pillows, plates and even wallpaper. The Fox Den is a favorite upstairs guest room with a private library and wood-burning fireplace. Cooked-to-order breakfasts are presented on silver service and delivered to each. Guests choose the menu, as well as the breakfast time.

Innkeeper(s): Pete & Min Fox. $125-195. MC, VISA, DS, PC, TC. TAC10. 7 rooms with PB, 5 with FP. Type of meal: Full bkfst. Beds: Q. Cable TV and VCR in room.

"Foxes is without a doubt the most charming B&B anywhere."

Grey Gables B&B Inn

161 Hanford St, PO Box 1687
Sutter Creek, CA 95685-1687
(209)267-1039 (800)473-9422 Fax:(209)267-0998

Circa 1897. The innkeepers of this Victorian home offer poetic accommodations both in the delightful decor and by the names of their guest rooms. The Keats, Bronte and Tennyson rooms afford garden views, while the Byron and Browning rooms include clawfoot tubs. The Victorian Suite, which

encompasses the top floor, affords views of the garden, as well as a historic churchyard. All of the guest rooms boast fireplaces. Stroll down brick pathways through the terraced garden or relax in the parlor. A proper English tea is served with cakes and scones. Hors d'oeuvres and libations are served in the evenings.

Historic Interest: Property was once owned by Patrick Riordan, Archbishop of San Francisco.

Innkeeper(s): Roger & Susan Garlick. $100-150. MC, VISA, DS, PC, TC. TAC10. 8 rooms with PB, 8 with FP. Breakfast, afternoon tea and snacks/refreshments included in rates. Types of meals: Full gourmet bkfst and early coffee/tea. Beds: KQT. Ceiling fan in room. Air conditioning. Fax and copier on premises. Handicap access. Antiquing, fishing, live theater, parks, shopping, downhill skiing, cross-country skiing, water sports and wineries nearby.

Sutter Creek Inn

PO Box 385
Sutter Creek, CA 95685-0385
(209)267-5606 Fax:(209)267-9287

Circa 1859. Nestled among fruit trees, many of the guest rooms open onto latticed enclaves or trellised grapevines. Columbine and lilacs are part of the lawn and garden's charm. As depicted in Thomas Kinkade's painting of the inn called "The Village Inn", guests can relax in chaise lounges or in the hammocks. Many rooms offer private patios, fireplace, swinging beds and tubs for two. Country breakfasts are served family style in the dining room. The area offers a variety of activities, including wineries, golfing, gold panning and historical sites. Massage and handwriting analysis is available by appointment.

Innkeeper(s): Jane Way. $65-175. MC, VISA. 18 rooms with PB. Breakfast included in rates. Type of meal: Full bkfst. Beds: QDT. Antiquing, fishing, cross-country skiing, theater and watersports nearby.

Publicity: *Fun Times, Motorland, Country Inns.*

"Very pleasant, excellent breakfast, good company."

Truckee   F7

Richardson House

10154 High St
Truckee, CA 96161-0110
(530)587-5388 (888)229-0365 Fax:(530)587-0927
E-mail: innkeeper@richardsonhouse.com
Web: www.richardsonhouse.com

Circa 1887. Guests enjoy views of the rugged Sierra Nevadas and the charm of a historic Old West town while at Richardson House. The historic Victorian bears the name of the prominent lumber baron who built it, Warren Richardson. Each guest room is individually appointed with timely antiques and accessories and the elegant touch of fresh flowers, fine linens, feather beds and down comforters. Some rooms offer views of the Sierra Mountains, while others have views of gardens. The gingerbread-adorned gazebo is the highlight of the Victorian gardens, a perfect setting for a memorable wedding. Meandering paths lead visitors past a cascading waterfall, native aspens, a contemplation bench and a sundial. Inside, the parlor is set up for relaxation with a player piano, television, VCR and stereo. The innkeepers also provide a well-stocked, 24-hour refreshment center, and freshly baked cookies are another treat.

Innkeeper(s): Lesley & Joel Friedman. $100-200. MC, VISA, AX, DS, PC, TC. TAC15. 8 rooms, 6 with PB. Breakfast included in rates. Types of meals: Full gourmet bkfst and early coffee/tea. Catering service available. Beds: KQDT. Air conditioning. VCR, fax, copier, morning paper and books on tape on premises. Handicap access. Weddings, small meetings and family reunions hosted. Fishing, golf, hiking, parks, shopping, skiing and water sports nearby.

Ukiah F3

Vichy Hot Springs Resort & Inn

2605 Vichy Springs Rd
Ukiah, CA 95482-3507
(707)462-9515 Fax:(707)462-9516
E-mail: vichy@vichysprings.com
Web: www.vichysprings.com

Circa 1854. This famous spa, now a California State Historical Landmark (#980), once attracted guests Jack London, Mark Twain, Robert Louis Stevenson, Ulysses Grant and Teddy Roosevelt. Eighteen rooms and four cottages have been renovated for bed & breakfast, while the 1860s naturally warm and carbonated mineral baths remain unchanged. A hot spa and historic, Olympic-size pool await your arrival. A magical waterfall is a 30-minute walk along a year-round stream.

Historic Interest: Sun House Museum California Historic Landmark (4 miles west), Tallest trees in the world-Montgomery Woods (18 miles west, Redwoods).

Innkeeper(s): Gilbert & Marjorie Ashoff. $99-225. MC, VISA, AX, DC, CB, DS, PC, TC. TAC10. 22 rooms with PB, 4 with FP, 4 cottages and 1 conference room. Breakfast included in rates. Type of meal: Full bkfst. Catering service available. Beds: QT. Phone in room. Air conditioning. Fax, copier, spa, swimming, massages and facials on premises. Handicap access. Family reunions and seminars hosted. Spanish spoken. Antiquing, fishing, redwood parks, live theater, parks, water sports and wineries nearby.

Ventura N8

Bella Maggiore Inn

67 S California St
Ventura, CA 93001-2801
(805)652-0277

Circa 1925. Albert C. Martin, the architect of the former Grauman's Chinese Theater, designed and built this Spanish Colonial Revival-style hotel. Located three blocks from the beach, it is noted for its richly-carved caste-stone entrance and frieze. An Italian chandelier and a grand piano dominate the parlor. Rooms surround a courtyard with a fountain. Miles of coastal bike paths are nearby, as well as restaurants and antique shops.

Innkeeper(s): Thomas Wood. $75-150. MC, VISA, AX, DC, DS. 24 rooms with PB, 6 with FP and 1 conference room. Type of meal: Full bkfst. Beds: KQD. Fax, copier and spa on premises. Handicap access.

Publicity: *Ventura County & Coast Reporter, Sunset.*

"Very friendly and attentive without being overly attentive."

La Mer European B&B

411 Poli St
Ventura, CA 93001-2614
(805)643-3600 Fax:(805)653-7329
Web: www.lamerbnb.com

Circa 1890. This three-story Cape Cod Victorian overlooks the heart of historic San Buenaventura and the spectacular California coastline. Each room is decorated to capture the feeling of a specific European country. French, German, Austrian, Norwegian and English-style accommodations are available. Gisela, your hostess, is a native of Siegerland, Germany. Midweek specials include romantic candlelight dinners, ther-

apeutic massages and a mineral spa in the country. Horse-drawn antique carriage rides and island cruises are also available.

Historic Interest: The old Mission, Archaeological Dig County Museum and many historical homes, within one-half block.

Innkeeper(s): Gisela & Mike Baida. $95-185. MC, VISA, AX. TAC10. 5 rooms, 1 with FP. Breakfast included in rates. Type of meal: Full bkfst. Beds: KQ. TV, ceiling fan and historic radio in room. Fax on premises. Antiquing, fishing, golf, parks, tennis and water sports nearby.

Publicity: *Los Angeles Times, California Bride, Los Angeles Magazine, Westways, The Tribune, Daily News.*

"Where to begin? The exquisite surroundings, the scrumptious meals, the warm feeling from your generous hospitality! What an unforgettable weekend in your heavenly home."

Visalia K8

Ben Maddox House B&B

601 N Encina St
Visalia, CA 93291-3603
(559)739-0721 (800)401-9800 Fax:(559)625-0420

Circa 1876. Just 40 minutes away from Sequoia National Park sits this late 19th-century home, constructed completely of gorgeous Sequoia redwood. The parlor, dining room and bedrooms remain in their original state. The house has been tastefully furnished with antiques from the late 1800s to the early 20th century. Breakfast menu choices include fresh fruit, a selection of homemade breads, eggs and meat. The meal is served either in the historic dining room or on the deck, and it is complemented by flowers, antique china and goldware. The half-acre of grounds includes gardens, a finch aviary, pool and century-old trees.

Historic Interest: Sequoia/King's Canyon National Parks (40 minutes), Tulare Co. Museum (10 minutes), Historical District Walking Tour.

Innkeeper(s): Diane & Al Muro. $75-95. MC, VISA, AX, DS. 4 rooms with PB. Breakfast included in rates. Types of meals: Full bkfst and early coffee/tea. Beds: KQ. Cable TV and phone in room. Air conditioning. Swimming on premises. Antiquing, fishing, Sequoia National Park, live theater, parks, shopping, cross-country skiing, sporting events and water sports nearby.

Spalding House

631 N Encina St
Visalia, CA 93291-3603
(559)739-7877 Fax:(559)625-0902

Circa 1901. This Colonial Revival home, built by a wealthy lumberman, has been restored and decorated with antiques and reproductions. The elegant interior includes polished wood floors topped with Oriental rugs and rich wallcoverings. The music room features a 1923 Steinway player grand piano. The library, which boasts some of the home's rich woodwork, includes shelves filled with books. Breakfasts include fresh fruit, yogurt, muffins and entrees such as a cheese blintz, apple crepe or French toast. The home is near downtown Visalia, as well as Sequoia National Park.

Innkeeper(s): Wayne & Peggy Davidson. $85. MC, VISA, AX, DS, PC. TAC10. 3 suites. Breakfast included in rates. AP. Type of meal: Full gourmet bkfst. Beds: QD. Ceiling fan in room. Air conditioning. Fax, copier and library on premises. Antiquing, fishing, golf, Sequoia National Park, live theater, parks, shopping, downhill skiing, cross-country skiing, tennis and water sports nearby.

Westport E3

DeHaven Valley Farm

39247 N Highway 1
Westport, CA 95488-8712
(707)961-1660 Fax:(707)961-1677
E-mail: info@dehaven-valley-farm.com
Web: www.dehaven-valley-farm.com

Circa 1875. This farmhouse was built by Alexander Gordon, a prosperous sawmill owner and cattle rancher. A double-tiered porch wraps around the front and side of the house and extends across the wing, offering vistas of the ocean and the inn's 20 acres of meadows, woodland and coastal hills. A hilltop hot tub provides a panoramic view of the valley. Guest rooms are in the main house and in cottages. The DeHaven Cottage features cabbage rose prints, a Franklin stove and a king-size bed. Dinner is served when at least six make reservations. There are farm animals, picnic areas, walking trails and a secluded beach.

Innkeeper(s): Christa Stapp. $85-140. MC, VISA, PC. TAC10. 8 rooms, 6 with PB, 5 with FP, 2 suites and 3 cottages. Breakfast included in rates. Type of meal: Full bkfst. Gourmet dinner available. Beds: KQT. Phone in room. VCR, spa, walking trails, picnic areas, decks, balcony w/ocean view and farm animals on premises. Weddings, small meetings, family reunions and seminars hosted. German spoken. Antiquing, art galleries, beaches, bicycling, canoeing/kayaking, fishing, hiking, horseback riding, live theater, parks, shopping, tennis, water sports and wineries nearby.

"We've talked about it so much that convoys of Southern California folks might be heading your way this very minute!"

Howard Creek Ranch

40501 N Hwy One, PO Box 121
Westport, CA 95488
(707)964-6725 Fax:(707)964-1603
Web: www.howardcreekranch.com

Circa 1871. First settled as a land grant of thousands of acres, Howard Creek Ranch is now a 40-acre farm with sweeping views of the Pacific Ocean, sandy beaches and rolling mountains. A 75-foot bridge spans a creek that flows past barns and outbuildings to the beach 200 yards away. The farmhouse is surrounded by green lawns, an award-winning flower garden, and grazing cows, horses and llama. This rustic rural location offers antiques, a hot tub, sauna and heated pool. A traditional ranch breakfast is served each morning.

Innkeeper(s): Charles & Sally Grigg. $75-160. MC, VISA, AX. 11 rooms, 9 with PB, 5 with FP, 3 suites and 3 cottages. Breakfast included in rates. Types of meals: Full bkfst and early coffee/tea. Beds: KQD. Ceiling fan in room. Fax, spa, swimming, sauna, library and massages on premises. German and Spanish spoken. Antiquing, beaches, fishing, hiking, horseback riding, farm animals, live theater, parks and shopping nearby. Pets allowed: By prior arrangement.

"This is one of the most romantic places on the planet."

Yuba City F5

Harkey House B&B

212 C St
Yuba City, CA 95991-5014
(530)674-1942 Fax:(530)674-1840

Circa 1875. An essence of romance fills this Victorian Gothic house set in a historic neighborhood. Every inch of the home has been given a special touch, from the knickknacks and photos in the sitting room to the quilts and furnishings in the guest quarters. The Harkey Suite features a poster bed with a down comforter and extras such as an adjoining library room and a gas stove. Full breakfasts of muffins, fresh fruit, juice and freshly ground coffee are served in a glass-paned dining room or on the patio.

Historic Interest: Located in the oldest part of Yuba City.

Innkeeper(s): Bob & Lee Jones. $80-100. MC, VISA, AX, DS, PC, TC. TAC10. 4 rooms with PB, 2 with FP, 1 suite and 1 conference room. Breakfast included in rates. Types of meals: Full bkfst and early coffee/tea. Beds: Q. Cable TV, phone, turndown service and ceiling fan in room. Air conditioning. VCR, spa and library on premises. Weddings, small meetings and family reunions hosted. Antiquing, fishing, live theater, parks, shopping and water sports nearby.

Publicity: *Country Magazine.*

"This place is simply marvelous...the most comfortable bed in travel."

Colorado

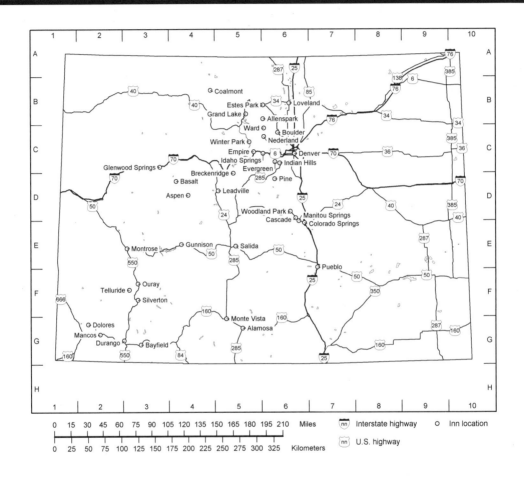

0 15 30 45 60 75 90 105 120 135 150 165 180 195 210   Miles

0 25 50 75 100 125 150 175 200 225 250 275 300 325   Kilometers

⬭ Interstate highway   ○ Inn location

⬭ U.S. highway

Alamosa   G5

Cottonwood Inn & Gallery: A B&B Inn

123 San Juan Ave
Alamosa, CO 81101-2547
(719)589-3882 (800)955-2623 Fax:(719)589-6437
E-mail: julie@cottonwoodinn.com
Web: www.cottonwoodinn.com.

Circa 1912. This refurbished Colorado bungalow is filled with antiques and paintings by local artists.
The Stickley dining room set once belonged to Billy Adams, a Colorado governor in the 1920s. Blue-corn blueberry pancakes, banana crepes with Mexican chocolate are the inn's specialties. A favorite day trip is riding the Cumbres-Toltec Scenic Railroad over the La Magna Pass, site of an Indiana Jones movie.

Innkeeper(s): Julie Mordecai. $56-125. MC, VISA, AX, DS, PC, TC. TAC10. 5 rooms, 3 with PB and 4 suites. Breakfast and afternoon tea included in rates. Types of meals: Full gourmet bkfst and veg bkfst. Gourmet dinner available. Beds: KQD. Cable TV and phone in room. Fax, library and child care on premises. Small meetings, family reunions and seminars hosted. Spanish spoken. Antiquing, art galleries, bicycling, fishing, golf, hiking, horseback riding, live theater, museums, parks, shopping, cross-country skiing, sporting events and tennis nearby.

Pets allowed: In two suites with guests present.

"My husband wants to come over every morning for blueberry pancakes and strawberry rhubarb sauce."

Allenspark   B6

Allenspark Lodge

PO Box 247, 184 Main St
Allenspark, CO 80510-0247
(303)747-2552 Fax:(303)747-2552

Circa 1933. Since its opening in the 1930s, this lodge has welcomed visitors with a combination of beautiful scenery and hospitality. The lodge was constructed out of Ponderosa pine, and its rustic interior

still maintains exposed log walls and a fireplace of native stone. Rooms are comfortable and each has its own unique atmosphere. Three rooms include antique clawfoot tubs. There is plenty to do in the area, no matter the season. Skiing, snowshoeing, hiking, backpacking, horseback riding and birdwatching are among the options.

Innkeeper(s): Bill & Juanita Martin. $65-135. MC, VISA, AX, DS, PC, TC. TAC10. 13 rooms, 5 with PB, 1 with FP and 1 conference room. Breakfast included in rates. Type of meal: Full bkfst. Beds: QDT. Ceiling fan in room. Fax, spa, library, ping pong, pool table and snack bar on premises. Weddings, small meetings, family reunions and seminars hosted. Antiquing, fishing, golf, horseback riding, horseback riding, extensive hiking, cross-country trails, live theater, parks, shopping, downhill skiing, cross-country skiing, tennis and water sports nearby.

Aspen   D4

Hotel Lenado

128 E Main St
Aspen, CO 81611-1731
(970)925-6246 (800)321-3457 Fax:(970)920-4478

Circa 1892. This Victorian bed & breakfast boasts a variety of carefully selected woods featured in its interiors such as cherry, pine, willow and birch. Sofas upholstered in red plaid invite guests to linger in the parlor and enjoy the massive fireplace. Each guest room offers carved applewood beds or four-poster hickory beds. Additional amenities you can choose are wood burning stoves and whirlpool tubs. In the evening, try the rooftop hot tub and watch the stars and moon shine on Aspen Mountain or try the sundeck tub. Breakfast is hearty and may include eggs Benedict, Belgian waffles or cinnamon French toast to name a few of the entrees. Markham's Bar is the spot for a glass of wine or lemonade and complimentary hors d'oeuvres.

Innkeeper(s): Susan Keating. $110-500. MC, VISA, AX, DC. 20 rooms, 14 with PB and 6 suites. Breakfast included in rates. Types of meals: Full gourmet bkfst, veg bkfst and early coffee/tea. Gourmet dinner, banquet service, catering service and room service available. Restaurant on premises. Beds: KQT. Cable TV, phone, turndown service, ceiling fan, jets in tubs and heated towel racks in room. Fax, spa, swimming and sauna on premises. Weddings, small meetings and family reunions hosted. Spanish spoken. Antiquing, art galleries, bicycling, canoeing/kayaking, fishing, golf, hiking, horseback riding, live theater, museums, parks, shopping, downhill skiing, cross-country skiing and tennis nearby.

Pets allowed: In rooms with private entrance.

Basalt   D4

Shenandoah Inn

600 Frying Pan Rd
Basalt, CO 81621
(970)927-4991 (800)804-5520 Fax:(970)927-4990

Circa 1897. Once a commune, this inn on the banks of the Frying Pan River has been restored into a peaceful country inn. The innkeepers completed an amazing restoration of the house, which was

very dilapidated when they discovered the property. In addition to restoring the 1960-era main house, they brought back to life a century-old log cabin. Innkeepers Bob and Terri Ziets can tell an array of fascinating stories about the former occupants, as well as their own exhaustive work. The idyllic setting includes decks for relaxing and a riverside hot tub. On a chilly day, enjoy a hot drink in front of the 16-foot rock fireplace in the living room. Rooms are decorated with antiques, and beds are topped with down quilts. The historic cabin is especially well suited to honeymooners in search of privacy or families, as it sleeps up to six guests. Breakfasts are a treat. Peach-stuffed French toast is a possibility, accompanied by gourmet coffee and a fruit appetizer. Everything is homemade, from the freshly baked breads to the preserves and apple butter. Refreshments are served daily.

Innkeeper(s): Bob & Terri Ziets. $88-165. MC, VISA, AX, PC, TC. TAC10. 4 rooms with PB and 1 cabin. Breakfast included in rates. Types of meals: Full bkfst and early coffee/tea. Beds: KQT. Turndown service, robes, fresh flowers and candy in room. VCR, fax, spa and library on premises. Weddings, small meetings and family reunions hosted. French and Spanish spoken. Antiquing, fishing, golf, horseback, kayak, rafting, live theater, parks, shopping, downhill skiing, cross-country skiing, tennis and water sports nearby.

Bayfield   G3

Wit's End Guest Ranch

254 Country Rd 500
Bayfield, CO 81122
(970)884-4113 (800)236-9483 Fax:(970)884-3261

Circa 1870. When the owners of this Adirondack-style guest ranch bill their place as "luxury at the edge of the wilderness," it isn't just a snappy slogan, it's true. If a half million acres of wilderness and stunning views of snow capped mountain peaks don't entice you, the historic lodge's interior should. Picture polished exposed beams and wood paneled or log walls, a mix of Victorian and country French furnishings and just enough antlers to create that rustic, lodge atmosphere. Each guest room includes a stone fireplace. There is also an assortment of cabins to consider, some more than a century old. The cabins include a living room, stone fireplace, kitchen and a private porch or deck. There is a full-service, fine-dining restaurant and a tavern often hosting live musical groups from nearby Durango. There's also little shortage of things to do here. Guided wilderness hikes, fly fishing in ponds, rivers and lakes, hayrides, mountain biking, dogsled rides, snowshoeing, sleigh rides and watersports are just a few of the possibilities. Horseback and trail riding, of course, are a major part of the fun. The ranch offers a full children's program with many interesting activities. As is typical of dude ranches, rates are quoted for weekly visits.

Innkeeper(s): Jim & Lynn Custer. $4043-4824. MC, VISA, AX, DS, PC, TC. TAC10. 4 rooms and 35 cottages. Breakfast, dinner, snacks/refreshments and picnic lunch included in rates. AP. Types of meals: Full gourmet bkfst and cont plus. Gourmet lunch, banquet service, catering service, catered breakfast and room service available. Restaurant on premises. Beds: Q. Phone, turndown service, VCR and luxury furniture and decor in room. Fax, copier, spa, swimming, stables, bicycles, tennis, library, full children's program, riding and tours on premises. Handicap access. Weddings, small meetings, family reunions and seminars hosted. Spanish, French, Italian and German spoken. Antiquing, fishing, snow mobiling, jeep tours, live theater, parks, shopping, downhill skiing, cross-country skiing, sporting events and water sports nearby.

Boulder   C6

Briar Rose B&B

2151 Arapahoe Ave
Boulder, CO 80302-6601
(303)442-3007 Fax:(303)786-8440

Circa 1896. Known locally as the McConnell House, this English-style brick house is situated in a neighborhood originally comprised of bankers, attorneys, miners and carpenters. The

inn recently was selected as "Best Bed and Breakfast Inn" in Boulder County by the readers of the Boulder Weekly. Fresh flowers, handmade feather comforters and turndown service with chocolates are among the inn's offerings.

Historic Interest: Historic Boulder offers walking tours of the town, including tours of four historic districts and a cemetery.

Innkeeper(s): Bob & Margaret Weisenbach. $99-189. MC, VISA, AX, DC, PC, TC. TAC10. 9 rooms with PB, 2 with FP. Breakfast and afternoon tea included in rates. Types of meals: Cont plus and early coffee/tea. Beds: QDT. TV, phone, turndown service, ceiling fan and modem attach in room. Air conditioning. Fax and copier on premises. Weddings, small meetings and family reunions hosted. Spanish and American Sign Language spoken. Antiquing, fishing, many summer festivals, hiking, biking, live theater, parks, shopping, downhill skiing, cross-country skiing and sporting events nearby.

Breckenridge   D5

The Evans House B&B

102 S French St, PO Box 387
Breckenridge, CO 80424
(970)453-5509

Circa 1886. A view of the famed Breckenridge ski slopes is visible from the windows of this former miner's home. The historic shed houses an eight-person hot tub. A cornucopia of activities are available to guests who have a love for the outdoors, including rafting, boating and an alpine slide. A ski shuttle is available at the front door, and there is on site parking. This 150-year-old mining town offers many interesting shops and restaurants. In the heart of a historic district with 120 circa 1860-1890 buildings and three museums, tours are available.

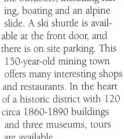

Historic Interest: The area is full of abandoned gold mines now open for tours. The Carter Museum was the foundation of the Denver Museum of Natural History, and is now open for tours.

Innkeeper(s): Pete & Georgette Contos. $63-140. PC, TC. 4 rooms with PB and 2 suites. Breakfast and afternoon tea included in rates. Type of meal: Full bkfst. Beds: KQT. TV, phone and ski and bike storage on premises in room. VCR on premises. Greek and French spoken. Amusement parks, antiquing, fishing, hiking, hiking, mountain biking, music festivals, mining, historical car tours, snowmobiling, sleigh rides, ice skating, live theater, parks, shopping, downhill skiing, cross-country skiing, sporting events and water sports nearby.

Publicity: *Denver Post.*

"Very clean, outstanding hospitality."

Bed & Breakfasts on North Main Street

303 N Main St
Breckenridge, CO 80424
(970)453-2975 (800)795-2975

Circa 1880. Within the Breckenridge National Historic District, the Williams House and exceptionally private Victorian Cottage have been meticulously restored to offer visitors period antiques in a romantic setting. The main house has two parlors with manteled fireplaces. Ask for the deluxe room and enjoy mountain views, fireplace, large whirlpool and TV. The cottage offers three rooms, a fireplace, private parlor, kitchenette, double shower, whirlpool for two, TV, VCR and stereo. Or consider a room in the new post and beam country-style "Barn Above

the River" with fireplaces, double showers and decks with mountain and river views. Complimentary afternoon refreshments are served each day. A candlelight breakfast, often morning burritos with stir-fried potatoes, is served in the dining room. The inn was featured on the Travel Channel's Romantic Inns of America series and Home and Garden Television, "If Walls Could Talk."

Innkeeper(s): Fred Kinat & Diane Jaynes. $85-245. MC, VISA, AX, PC. TAC10. 11 rooms with PB, 6 with FP and 1 cottage. Breakfast included in rates. Types of meals: Full bkfst and early coffee/tea. Beds: KQT. Cable TV, phone, ceiling fan and VCR in room. Spa and library on premises. Antiquing, bicycling, fishing, golf, hiking, snowmobiling, ice skating, music festivals, bike/rollerblade path, hiking, historic tours, live theater, shopping, downhill skiing, cross-country skiing, tennis and water sports nearby.

Publicity: Denver Post, Rocky Mountain News, Summit Daily News, Los Angeles Times.

The Walker House

103 S French St, PO Box 5107
Breckenridge, CO 80424-0509
(970)453-2426

Circa 1875. This three-story log home with Victorian accents is located in a beautiful ski town with a historic past as a mining community. The upstairs rooms have spectacular views of the ski runs, sunsets and a magically lit town at night. While having breakfast in the dining room the sun streams through a stained-glass door. The innkeepers supply flowers and treats to honeymooners and romantic souls.

Historic Interest: A historical walking tour will take guests past a variety of interesting sites.

Innkeeper(s): Sue Ellen Strong. $89-115. MC, VISA. 2 rooms, 1 with PB and 1 suite. Breakfast and afternoon tea included in rates. Type of meal: Early coffee/tea. Snacks/refreshments and catering service available. Beds: KQT. Extra Toiletries in room. Snacks and Tea & Coffee on premises. Antiquing, live theater, shopping, downhill skiing and cross-country skiing nearby.

The Wellington Inn

200 North Main St
Breckenridge, CO 80424
(970)453-9464 (800)655-7557 Fax:(970)453-0149
E-mail: Innkeeper@TheWellingtonInn.com
Web: thewellingtoninn.com

Circa 1979. This Victorian country inn offers not only gracious architecture but also a plethora of luxury amenities. Popular for weddings and anniversaries, guest rooms are decorated with a pristine touch. They offer deluxe baths with whirlpools as well as showers, TV and thick down comforters. Some rooms have window seats, mountain views chandeliers and four-poster beds. Comfortable parlors with fireplaces are inviting after exploring the nearby shops, coming back on the ski bus shuttle, or after cycling excursions. In the morning, guests enjoy a gourmet breakfast, which may include eggs Benedict Florentine, parfaits and home-baked breads. Be sure to reserve at least one night's dinner by candlelight in the inn's romantic

restaurant. Beef Wellington is a specialty, but there is a generous menu with other choices, just be sure to ask for the chocolate bread pudding served with Creme Anglaise for desert.

Innkeeper(s): Lynn Crowell. $139-249. MC, VISA, AX, DS, TC. 44 rooms, 4 with PB. Types of meals: Full gourmet bkfst, cont and veg bkfst. Gourmet dinner, snacks/refreshments and banquet service available. Restaurant on premises. Beds: Q. Cable TV and VCR in room. Weddings hosted. Art galleries, bicycling, canoeing/kayaking, fishing, golf, hiking, horseback riding, live theater, parks, shopping, downhill skiing and cross-country skiing nearby.

Cascade   D6

Eastholme In The Rockies

PO Box 98, 4445 Haggerman Ave
Cascade, CO 80809
(719)684-9901 (800)672-9901

Circa 1885. Although Cascade is only six miles from Colorado Springs, guests will feel as though they are staying in a secluded mountain getaway at this Victorian inn, in the National Register. An affluent New Yorker built the historic hotel, which accommodates the many guests traveling the Ute Pass. The most recent innkeeper, Terry Thompson, redecorated the inn and added double Jacuzzi tubs and fireplaces in the two cottages. The decor is Victorian, but rooms are uncluttered and airy. Several rooms are furnished with antiques original to the hotel. Three different homemade breads and entrees such as frittatas with herbed potatoes are served during breakfast service.

Innkeeper(s): Terry Thompson. $69-140. MC, VISA, AX, DS, PC, TC. TAC10. 8 rooms, 6 with PB, 2 with FP, 2 suites, 2 cottages and 1 conference room. Breakfast and snacks/refreshments included in rates. Types of meals: Full gourmet bkfst, veg bkfst and early coffee/tea. Catering service available. Beds: QDT. Cable TV, ceiling fan, VCR and guest kitchen on second floor in room. Library and jacuzzi tubs in cottages on premises. Weddings, small meetings, family reunions and seminars hosted. Antiquing, art galleries, bicycling, canoeing/kayaking, fishing, golf, hiking, horseback riding, climbing, rafting, live theater, museums, parks, shopping, downhill skiing, cross-country skiing, sporting events, tennis, water sports and wineries nearby.

Coalmont   B4

Shamrock Ranch

4363 Rd 11
Coalmont, CO 80430
(970)723-8413

Circa 1934. At an elevation of 8,800 feet and below the crest of the Continental Divide, the ranch is adjacent to thousands of acres of wilderness in the Routt National Forest. Overlooking the secluded cattle country of North Park, Colo., the lodge is built of native spruce logs and provides comfortable accommodations for 10 guests. The innkeeper likes to provide a personalized touch and secluded atmosphere for your family or small group and offers both a full breakfast and gourmet dinners included in nightly rates. Guests may enjoy outstanding fly-fishing and a variety of hiking trails.

Innkeeper(s): Cindy Wilson. $180. 2 suites. Type of meal: Full bkfst. Gourmet dinner available. VCR, fly fishing and wildlife on premises. Small meetings and family reunions hosted.

Colorado Springs   E6

Hearthstone Inn

506 N Cascade Ave
Colorado Springs, CO 80903-3308
(719)473-4413 (800)521-1885

Circa 1885. This elegant Queen Anne is actually two houses joined by an old carriage house. It has been restored as a period showplace with six working fireplaces, carved oak staircases and  magnificent antiques throughout. A lush lawn, suitable for croquet, surrounds the house, and flower beds match the Victorian colors of the exterior.

Innkeeper(s): David & Nancy Oxenhandler. $90-170. MC, VISA, AX, DS. 23 rooms with PB, 3 with FP and 1 conference room. Type of meal: Full gourmet bkfst. Beds: KQDT.

"We try to get away and come to the Hearthstone at least twice a year because people really care about you!"

Holden House-1902 B&B Inn

1102 W Pikes Peak Ave
Colorado Springs, CO 80904-4347
(719)471-3980 (888)565-3980 Fax:(719)471-4740
E-mail: mail@holdenhouse.com
Web: www.holdenhouse.com

Circa 1902. Built by the widow of a prosperous rancher and businessman, this Victorian inn has rooms named after the many Colorado towns in which the Holdens owned mining interests. The main house, adjacent carriage  house and Victorian house next door include the Cripple Creek, Aspen, Silverton, Goldfield and Independence suites. The inn's suites boast fireplaces and oversized tubs for two. Guests can relax in the living room with fireplace, front parlor with TV, or veranda with mountain views. There are friendly cats in residence.

Historic Interest: Miramont Castle, McAllister House, Glen Eyrie Castle, The Pioneer's Museum, the Broadmoor Hotel & Carriage House Museum, Cliff Dwellings Museum, Pikes Peak, and Garden of the Gods Park are among the area's many historic attractions.

Innkeeper(s): Sallie & Welling Clark. $125-140. MC, VISA, AX, DC, CB, DS, TC. TAC10. 5 suites, 5 with FP. Breakfast included in rates. Types of meals: Full bkfst and early coffee/tea. Afternoon tea available. Beds: Q. TV, phone, turndown service, ceiling fan and tubs for two in room. Air conditioning. VCR, fax, copier and modem hookups in rooms on premises. Seminars hosted. Antiquing, fishing, hiking, biking, horseback riding, live theater, parks, shopping and sporting events nearby.

Publicity: *Denver Post, Rocky Mountain News, Victorian Homes, Pikes Peak Journal, Glamour.*

"Your love of this house and nostalgia makes a very delightful experience."

Room at the Inn B&B

618 N Nevada Ave
Colorado Springs, CO 80903-1006
(719)442-1896 (800)579-4621 Fax:(719)442-6802
E-mail: roomatinn@pcisys.net
Web: www.roomattheinn.com

Circa 1896. A Colorado pioneer built this Queen Anne Victorian, a delightful mix of turret, gables and gingerbread trim. While restoring their century-old Victorian, the innkeepers discovered several hand-painted murals had once decorated the interior. Original fireplace mantels and a collection of antiques add to the nostalgic ambiance. Fresh flowers, turndown service and a bountiful breakfast are just a few of the amenities. Several rooms include a fireplace or double whirlpool tub.

Innkeeper(s): Chick & Jan McCormick. $90-150. MC, VISA, AX, DC, CB, DS, PC, TC. TAC10. 7 rooms with PB, 3 with FP, 2 suites, 1 cottage and 1 conference room. Breakfast, afternoon tea and snacks/refreshments included in rates. Types of meals: Full bkfst, cont and early coffee/tea. Beds: Q. Phone, turndown service, clocks and whirlpool tubs in room. Air conditioning. VCR, fax, copier, spa and hot tub on premises. Handicap access. Small meetings, family reunions and seminars hosted. Antiquing, fishing, museums, Fine Arts center, live theater, parks, shopping and sporting events nearby.

"Staying at your Bed & Breakfast was indeed a "second honeymoon" and rare treat for us. Your kindness, graciousness, and professionalism made our stay at the Room at the Inn the highlight of our trip to Colorado."

Denver   C6

The Adagio Bed & Breakfast

1430 Race Street
Denver, CO 80206
(303)370-6911 (800)533-3241 Fax:(303)377-5968
E-mail: cremmins@sni.net
Web: www.sni.net/adagio

Circa 1892. Two themes mingle at this historic Victorian, the innkeepers' love of music and a sense of relaxation. The restored home maintains original hardwood floors, wainscoting and its grand staircase. The richly appointed parlor includes one of the original fireplaces, traditional furnishings and a guitar and grand piano. Rooms are named for famous composers and decorated with a comfortable and often romantic mix of contemporary and antique furnishings. Each bedchamber is different. The Copland Suite includes an in-room, two-person tub and a sitting room with fireplace. The Brahms Suite also includes a two-person tub and the décor features an exposed brick wall. The

Holst Suite includes a unique ceiling mural with images of a nighttime sky and full moon. Other rooms include an indoor fountain or a king-size iron bed. Adagio is near to many popular city attractions, including the home of "Unsinkable" Molly Brown, the Buffalo Bill grave site, Denver's Capitol building and much more.

Historic Interest: Molly Brown House (1 mile), Buffalo Bill's Grave (15 miles).
Innkeeper(s): Jim & Amy Cremmins. $95-170. MC, VISA, AX, DS, TC. TAC5. 5 rooms with PB, 2 with FP and 1 conference room. Breakfast and snacks/refreshments included in rates. Types of meals: Full bkfst and veg bkfst. Beds: KQT. Cable TV, phone, ceiling fan, VCR and robes in room. Air conditioning. Fax, copier, spa and library on premises. Weddings, small meetings and family reunions hosted. Amusement parks, antiquing, art galleries, bicycling, golf, hiking, horseback riding, live theater, museums, parks, shopping, sporting events and tennis nearby.

Castle Marne - A Luxury Urban Inn

1572 Race St
Denver, CO 80206-1308
(303)331-0621 (800)926-2763 Fax:(303)331-0623
E-mail: diane@castlemarne.com
Web: www.castlemarne.com

Circa 1889. This 6,000-square-foot fantasy was designed by William Lang and is in the National Register. It is constructed of hand-hewn rhyolite stone. Inside, polished oak, cherry and black ash woodwork enhance the ornate fireplaces, peri-

od antiques and opulent Victorian decor. For special occasions ask for the Presidential Suite with its tower sitting room, king-size tester bed, whirlpool tub in the solarium and private balcony.

Historic Interest: Downtown Historic District (7 minutes), State Capitol (2 minutes), Byers-Evans Museum (5 minutes), Molly Brown House Museum (3 minutes), State Historical Society (4 minutes), Four Mile House (20 minutes).
Innkeeper(s): The Peiker Family. $90-235. MC, VISA, AX, DC, CB, DS. 9 rooms with PB, 2 suites and 1 conference room. Breakfast and afternoon tea included in rates. Type of meal: Full bkfst. Gourmet dinner available. Beds: KQDT. Double hot tubs and private balconies in room. Fax and copier on premises. Antiquing, fishing, live theater, downhill skiing, cross-country skiing and water sports nearby.
Publicity: *Denver Post, Innsider, Rocky Mountain News, Los Angeles Times, New York Times, Denver Business Journal, Country Inns, Brides, U.S. Air.*

"The beauty, service, friendliness, delicious breakfasts - everything was so extraordinary! We'll be back many times."

Haus Berlin B&B

1651 Emerson St
Denver, CO 80218-1411
(303)837-9527 (800)659-0253 Fax:(303)837-9527
E-mail: haus.berlin@worldnet.att.net
Web: www.hausberlinbandb.com

Circa 1892. This brick Victorian townhouse is a delightful place from which to enjoy Denver. The inn is listed in the National Register of Historic Places and located in a neighborhood filled with charming architecture. The cozy guest rooms are well-appointed and feature beds dressed in fine linens and topped with down comforters. The suite is the most luxurious, and it offers a view of downtown Denver, which is a 10-minute

walk from Haus Berlin. The breakfast menu varies, one morning it might be eggs Benedict, the next day could bring a traditional European breakfast with freshly baked rolls, scones with lemon curd and imported hams and cheeses.

Innkeeper(s): Christiana & Dennis Brown. $100-140. MC, VISA, AX, DC, DS, PC, TC. TAC10. 4 rooms with PB and 1 suite. Breakfast included in rates. Types of meals: Full gourmet bkfst and early coffee/tea. Beds: KQ. Cable TV, phone, ceiling fan, fresh flowers and hair dryers in room. Air conditioning. VCR and fax on premises. German spoken. Amusement parks, antiquing, fishing, golf, live theater, parks, shopping, downhill skiing, cross-country skiing, sporting events, tennis and water sports nearby.
Publicity: *Denver Post, Life on Capital Hill.*

Merritt House Bed & Breakfast Inn

941 E 17th Ave
Denver, CO 80218-1407
(303)861-5230 (877)861-5230 Fax:(303)861-9009

Circa 1889. Colorado Senator Elmer Merritt was this home's first resident, and through the years the home found use as a boarding house, office building, apartment house and the

Denver office for the United Steel Workers of America. The innkeepers, however, refurbished the Queen Anne Victorian back to the glorious state it

was in when the Merritt family called it home. Beautiful elements such as the carved wood paneling and leaded-glass windows have either been restored or authentic reproductions have been added. A mix of turn-of-the-century Victorian furnishings completes the look. Each guest room, as the innkeepers say, features modern amenities such as Mr. Bell's latest invention, Mr. Edison's electric filament lighting and a private water closet. Some of the "private water closets" include a whirlpool tub. Breakfast is a splendid affair, as guests choose their own combination of treats from a wide menu that includes omelets, pancakes, savory meats and more. Downtown Denver, the state capitol and the U.S. mint all are close by.

Innkeeper(s): Cathy Kuykendall. $90-150. MC, VISA, AX, DC, DS, PC, TC. TAC10. 10 rooms with PB. Breakfast included in rates. Type of meal: Full bkfst. Restaurant on premises. Beds: Q. Cable TV, phone and Jacuzzis in room. Air conditioning. Fax and copier on premises. Amusement parks, antiquing, convention center, cultural activities, live theater, parks, shopping and sporting events nearby.

The Oxford Hotel

1600 17th St
Denver, CO 80202-1204
(303)628-5400 (800)228-5838 Fax:(303)628-5408
E-mail: oxfordhot@aol.com
Web: www.theoxfordhotel.com

Circa 1891. The Oxford Hotel, Denver's oldest operating hotel, was designed by Colorado's leading architect. The hotel is listed in the National Register. The morning paper is delivered to each individually decorated guest room, and complimentary coffee and shoe shine services are available. Guests also enjoy limousine service, round-the-clock room service, turndown service and privileges at the adjacent Oxford Club, a fitness center with a spa and salon.

Historic Interest: The Oxford Hotel is located in the downtown historic district and affords close access to an art museum and many other historic Denver sites.

Innkeeper(s): Jane Hugo. $129-395. MC, VISA, AX, DC, DS. 80 rooms and 1 suite. Types of meals: Full bkfst, cont plus and cont. Dinner, lunch, catering service and room service available. Restaurant on premises. Beds: QD. Antiques in room. Spa, salon and health club on premises. Antiquing nearby.

"Your staff, from the maids to the front desk, is wonderful. The Hotel has great character and you are doing things right."

Dolores   G2

Rio Grande Southern Hotel

101 S 5th St, PO Box 516
Dolores, CO 81323-0516
(303)882-7527 (800)258-0434

Circa 1893. Located in the town square, the turn-of-the-century decorated inn has been in continuous use as a hostelry for more than 100 years. Having also served as a railroad hotel, the inn is located at 7,000 feet elevation at the base of the San Juan Mountains and close to the arid desert. This results in an exceptionally diverse environment. Arid and alpine vegetation and wildlife are found in the regions surrounding the Dolores River Valley.

Innkeeper(s): Fred & Cathy Green. $45-140. MC, VISA, DS. 7 rooms, 2 with PB and 1 suite. Breakfast included in rates. Types of meals: Full bkfst and early coffee/tea. Picnic lunch, lunch and banquet service available. Restaurant on premises. Beds: QDT. Turndown service in room. VCR on premises. Weddings, small meetings, family reunions and seminars hosted. Antiquing, fishing, shopping, downhill skiing, cross-country skiing and water sports nearby.

Durango   G3

Leland House B&B Suites

721 East Second Ave
Durango, CO 81301-5403
(970)385-1920 (800)664-1920 Fax:(970)385-1967

Circa 1927. The rooms in this Craftsman-style brick building are named after historic figures associated with this former apartment house and Durango's early industrial growth. The

decor features unique cowboy and period antiques designed for both comfort and fun. Gourmet breakfasts include inn specialties of homemade granola, cranberry scones, and a variety of entrees like Southwest burritos and multi-grain waffles. Located in the historic district downtown, guests can take walking tours, enjoy specialty shops, restaurants, galleries and museums nearby.

Innkeeper(s): Kirk & Diane Komick. $99-300. MC, VISA, AX, DS, PC, TC. TAC10. 10 rooms with PB and 6 suites. Breakfast and afternoon tea included in rates. Type of meal: Full gourmet bkfst. Picnic lunch and catering service available. Restaurant on premises. Beds: QD. Cable TV, phone and ceiling fan in room. Air conditioning. VCR, fax and copier on premises. Weddings, small meetings, family reunions and seminars hosted. Spanish spoken. Antiquing, fishing, live theater, parks, shopping, downhill skiing, cross-country skiing and water sports nearby.

"It is great! Charming and warm, friendly staff and superb food. Marvelous historic photo collection."

The Rochester Hotel

721 East Second Ave
Durango, CO 81301-5403
(970)385-1920 (800)664-1920 Fax:(970)385-1967
E-mail: leland@rochesterhotel.com
Web: www.rochesterhotel.com

Circa 1892. This Federal-style inn's decor is inspired by many Western movies filmed in and around the town. The building is an authentically restored late-Victorian hotel with the charm

and luxury of the Old West, completely furnished in antiques from the period. The inn is situated on a beautifully landscaped setting that features a flower-filled courtyard, and is located just one block from historic Main Avenue downtown. The inn is close to all major attractions, museums, galleries, shops, restaurants, and outdoor activities.

Historic Interest: Listed in National Register of Historic Places.

Innkeeper(s): Kirk & Diane Komick. $125-229. MC, VISA, AX, DS, PC, TC. TAC10. 15 rooms with PB, 2 suites and 2 conference rooms. Breakfast included in rates. Type of meal: Full gourmet bkfst. Afternoon tea, picnic lunch and catering service available. Beds: KQ. Cable TV, phone and ceiling fan in room. Air conditioning. VCR, fax and copier on premises. Handicap access. Weddings, small meetings, family reunions and seminars hosted. Spanish spoken. Antiquing, fishing, Mesa Verde National Park, live theater, parks, shopping, downhill skiing, cross-country skiing and water sports nearby.

Pets allowed: Small pets, prior permission needed.

Publicity: Conde Nast Traveler.

"In a word — exceptional! Far exceeded expectations in every way."

Strater Hotel

699 Main Ave
Durango, CO 81301-5423
(970)247-4431 (800)247-4431 Fax:(970)259-2208
E-mail: rod@frontier.net
Web: www.strater.com

Circa 1877. This ornate, Victorian hotel is an impressive site, built with red brick and adonred in white trim. The hotel is stunning, inside and out, with rooms boasting fine furnishings and Old West Victorian decor. A stay at this inn is truly a step back in time. The hotel was built just a few years after Durango's founding during the Gold Rush days. For more than a century, guests have enjoyed hospitality at the Strater. The Diamond Belle Saloon, an Old West bar, is a wonderful place to relax and enjoy a drink. The waitresses and bartenders are decked out in authentic costumes. The hotel's Victorian restaurant serves fine cuisine in a picturesque setting with stained glass and ornate, carved walls. Guests can enjoy turn-of-the-century plays at the hotel's Diamond Circle Theatre. The hotel is located two blocks from the narrow gauge railroad depot.

Innkeeper(s): Rod Barker. $99-235. MC, VISA, AX, DC, CB, DS, PC, TC. TAC10. 93 rooms with PB and 6 conference rooms. Breakfast included in rates. AP. Type of meal: Full bkfst. Dinner, picnic lunch, lunch, banquet service, catering service and room service available. Beds: KQT. Cable TV, phone and turndown service in room. Air conditioning. VCR, fax and copier on premises. Handicap access. Weddings, small meetings, family reunions and seminars hosted. Limited French and limited Spanish spoken. Antiquing, bicycling, fishing, live theater, parks, shopping, downhill skiing, cross-country skiing, sporting events and water sports nearby.

Eldora   C6

Goldminer Hotel

601 Klondyke Ave
Eldora, CO 80466-9542
(303)258-7770 (800)422-4629 Fax:(303)258-3850

Circa 1897. This turn-of-the-century National Register hotel is
a highlight in the Eldora National Historic District. Suites and
rooms are decorated with period
antiques. The inn provides
packages that include guided
jeep, horseback, hiking
and fishing tours in the
summer and back-country
ski tours in the winter.

Historic Interest: The surrounding historic district offers many
interesting homes and sites. The
Goldminer Hotel was dedicated
as a Boulder County landmark
in 1996.

Innkeeper(s): Scott Bruntjen. $89-229. MC, VISA, AX, DS, TC. 7 rooms, 5
with PB, 1 with FP, 1 suite, 1 cottage and 1 conference room. Breakfast
included in rates. Types of meals: Full bkfst and early coffee/tea. Beds: KD.
TV in room. VCR, fax, copier, spa, library and cross country skis on premises.
Weddings, small meetings, family reunions and seminars hosted. Antiquing,
fishing, parks, shopping, downhill skiing, cross-country skiing and sporting
events nearby.

Pets allowed: Cottage only.

Empire   C5

Mad Creek B&B

PO Box 404
Empire, CO 80438-0404
(303)569-2003

Circa 1881. This mountain town cottage has just the right
combination of Victorian decor with lace, flowers, antiques and
gingerbread trim on the facade. Unique touches include door
frames of old mineshaft wood, kerosene lamps, Eastlake
antiques and complimentary cross-country ski gear and mountain bikes. Relax in front of the rock fireplace while watching a
movie, peruse the library filled with local lore, or plan your
next adventure with Colorado guides and maps. Empire, which
was once a mining town, is conveniently located within 15 to
45 minutes of at least six major ski areas.

Innkeeper(s): Myrna & Tonya Payne. $55-85. MC, VISA, TC. 3 rooms, 1 with
PB. Breakfast, afternoon tea and snacks/refreshments included in rates.
Types of meals: Full bkfst and early coffee/tea. Beds: KD. Ceiling fan, toiletries and down comforters in room. VCR, bicycles and complimentary ski
gear & shoes on premises. Weddings and family reunions hosted. Antiquing,
fishing, horseback riding, gambling, parks, shopping, downhill skiing, cross-
country skiing and water sports nearby.

The Peck House

PO Box 428
Empire, CO 80438-0428
(303)569-9870 Fax:(303)569-2743
E-mail: info@thepeckhouse.com
Web: www.thepeckhouse.com

Circa 1862. Built as a residence for gold mine owner James
Peck, this is the oldest hotel still in operation in Colorado.
Many pieces of original furniture brought here by ox cart

remain in the inn,
including a red antique
fainting couch and wal-
nut headboards. Rooms
such as Mountain View
provide magnificent
views of the eastern
slope of the Rockies,
and a panoramic view
of Empire Valley can be seen from the old front porch.

Historic Interest: The Hamill House Museum, Georgetown Loop Narrow Guage
Railroad, Hotel de Paris Museum, Silver Plume National Historic District.

Innkeeper(s): Gary & Sally St. Clair. $45-85. MC, VISA, AX, DC, CB, DS, PC,
TC. TAC10. 11 rooms, 9 with PB and 1 suite. Breakfast included in rates.
Type of meal: Cont. Gourmet dinner available. Restaurant on premises. Beds:
DT. Fax, spa and library on premises. Small meetings and seminars hosted.
French spoken. Antiquing, art galleries, bicycling, fishing, hiking, horseback
riding, museums, parks, shopping, downhill skiing, cross-country skiing and
tennis nearby.

Publicity: American West, Rocky Mountain News, Denver Post, Colorado Homes.

Estes Park   B6

Anniversary Inn

1060 Mary's Lake Rd
Estes Park, CO 80517
(970)586-6200

Circa 1890. High in the Colorado Rockies, at 7,600 feet, this
authentic log home is surrounded by spectacular views. There
are two acres with a pond and river nearby. An exposed-log living room is dominat-
ed by a massive moss-
rock fireplace. The
guest rooms boast
stenciled walls and
other country accents.
The full breakfasts are
served on a glass-

enclosed wraparound porch. The inn specializes in honeymoons and anniversaries and features a honeymoon cottage.

Innkeeper(s): Harry & Norma Menke. $95-160. MC, VISA, AX, DS, PC, TC.
TAC10. 4 rooms with PB, 1 with FP and 1 cottage. Breakfast included in
rates. Types of meals: Full bkfst and early coffee/tea. Beds: Q. TV and jetter
tubs in room. VCR and library on premises. Fishing, golf, hiking, backpacking, snowshoeing, golfing, Rocky Mountain National Park, live theater, shopping and cross-country skiing nearby.

Publicity: Denver Post, Columbus Dispatch, Rocky Mountain News.

"The splendor and majesty of the Rockies is matched only by the
warmth and hospitality you showed us during our stay."

Evergreen   C6

Bears Inn B&B

27425 Spruce Lane
Evergreen, CO 80439
(303)670-1205 (800)863-1205 Fax:(303)670-8542
E-mail: inquire@bearsinn.com
Web: www.bearsinn.com

Circa 1924. Since the 1920s, this historic lodge has welcomed
guests drawn to its stunning views and tradition of hospitality.
Originally, the lodge served as a summer resort, but today
guests are welcome throughout the year. The rustic interior

boasts exposed logs and hardwood floors. Antiques and claw-foot tubs add a nostalgic elegance. Each room features a different theme. The Colorado is perfect for the outdoorsy guest, decorated with snowshoes and fly-fishing tackle. Native American fabrics decorate the Dakota room. It's not unusual to encounter stuffed bears, as well as the innkeepers' friendly golden retrievers during your stay. Breakfasts begin with fresh fruit and homemade fruit bread and are followed by entrees such as a strata, omelettes or Belgian waffles served with bacon, sausage or ham. Ask about the innkeepers' monthly murder-mystery events. Evergreen offers a myriad of outdoor activities, including biking, fishing, ice skating, hiking and cross-country

skiing. Gold Mine tours and museums are other attractions, and guests also have the option of driving into Denver, 35 minutes away.

Historic Interest: Georgetown Loop RR (30 miles), Blackhawk/Central City (20 miles), Hiwan museum (4 miles).

Innkeeper(s): Darrell & Chris Jenkins. $100-160. MC, VISA, AX, PC, TC. TAC10. 11 rooms with PB, 1 suite and 1 conference room. Breakfast and snacks/refreshments included in rates. Types of meals: Full bkfst, country bkfst and veg bkfst. Afternoon tea available. Beds: KQ. Cable TV, phone and VCR in room. Fax, copier, spa and library on premises. Small meetings, family reunions and seminars hosted. Amusement parks, antiquing, art galleries, bicycling, canoeing/kayaking, fishing, golf, hiking, horseback riding, museums, parks and shopping nearby.

Gunnison   E4

Mary Lawrence Inn

601 N Taylor St
Gunnison, CO 81230-2241
(970)641-3343 Fax:(970)641-6719

Circa 1885. A local entrepreneur and saloon owner built this Italianate home in the late 19th century, but the innkeepers named their home in honor of Mary Lawrence, a later resident.

Lawrence, a teacher and administrator for the local schools, used the building as a boarding house. The innkeepers have created an inviting interior with touches such as patchwork quilts, antique furnishings and stenciled walls. The innkeepers serve a variety of treats each morning for breakfast, and keep the cookie jars full. The inn offers convenient access to the area's bounty of outdoor activities.

Historic Interest: In the hills near Gunnison are several mining ghost towns. A local museum is open during the summer months. Self-guided tours of the historic buildings are available. The Crested Butte historic district is 30 miles away.

Innkeeper(s): Doug & Beth Parker. $69-109. MC, VISA. TAC10. 7 rooms with PB and 3 suites. Breakfast included in rates. Types of meals: Full gourmet bkfst and early coffee/tea. Beds: KQT. VCR, fax, copier, spa, tennis and library on premises. Family reunions hosted. Fishing, live theater, parks, shopping, downhill skiing, cross-country skiing and water sports nearby.

"You two are so gracious to make our stay a bit of 'heaven' in the snow."

Idaho Springs   C6

Miners Pick B&B

1639 Colorado Blve, Box 3156
Idaho Springs, CO 80452
(303)567-2975 (800)567-2975 Fax:(303)567-2975
E-mail: minerspik@bewellnet.com
Web: www.coloradovacation.com/bed/miners

Circa 1895. This historic home was built during the area's heyday as a mining Mecca. Each guest room is different. The Quarry room features Southwestern-style décor. The Placer room is country in style. The Prospector includes a queen bed and day bed, accommodating up to three guests. Beds are topped with down comforters, and fresh flowers brighten each room. Breakfasts include fresh orange juice, homemade breads and an entrée such as a quiche accompanied by sausage, fresh fruit and mint from the garden. Gold was discovered just a half-mile away from the home, and gold mine tours are available in the area. Guests also can take a trip along the Narrow Gauge Railroad or visit the natural hot springs. Ski areas are within 30 minutes to an hour and a half of the home.

Historic Interest: Gold mine tours, Georgetown Narrow Guage Railroad (12 miles).

Innkeeper(s): Deb & Ty Davies. $95-120. MC, VISA, DS, PC, TC. TAC10. 3 rooms with PB. Breakfast included in rates. Type of meal: Veg bkfst. Beds: Q. Ceiling fan in room. Air conditioning. VCR, fax, cable TV and refrigerator on premises. Antiquing, art galleries, bicycling, canoeing/kayaking, fishing, hiking, horseback riding, opera house, rafting, Narrow Guage Railroad, gold mine tours, museums, shopping, downhill skiing and cross-country skiing nearby.

Indian Hills   C6

Mountain View B&B

4754 Picutis Rd
Indian Hills, CO 80454
(303)697-6896 (800)690-0434 Fax:(303)697-6896
E-mail: mtnviewbandb@juno.com
Web: www.fourcorners.com/co/inns/mtnview.html

Circa 1920. Two-and-a-half acres surround this mountain home, which was built as a writer's retreat. In the mid-1950s, the home served as a lodge. The innkeepers hail from Great Britain and Germany and have decorated the home in European style. In addition to rooms in the main house, there is a cottage decorated in Southwestern style. Breakfasts include items such as homemade coffeecake accompanied with a savory egg casserole entrée. The bed & breakfast is a half-hour from downtown Denver.

Innkeeper(s): Graham & Ortrud Richardson. $80-165. MC, VISA, AX, DC, PC, TC. TAC10. 4 rooms with PB, 1 suite and 1 cottage. Breakfast, afternoon tea and snacks/refreshments included in rates. Types of meals: Full bkfst, veg bkfst and early coffee/tea. Beds: Q. Cable TV, turndown service and VCR in room. Fax and CD player in cabin on premises. German spoken. Antiquing, bicycling, parks, shopping and cross-country skiing nearby.

Leadville   D5

The Apple Blossom Inn Victorian B&B

120 W 4th St
Leadville, CO 80461-3630
(719)486-2141 (800)982-9279 Fax:(719)486-0994

Circa 1879. Originally the home of Leadville banker Absalom Hunter, who lived here with his wife Estelle until 1918, the inn offers a glimpse into the good life of the late 19th century.

Brass lights, beautiful crystal, fireplaces with Florentine tile, beveled mirrors, maple and mahogany inlaid floors, and stained-glass windows, including one in a front window that gives The Apple Blossom Inn its name, are evidence to Hunter's prosperity. Innkeeper Maggie Senn invites guests to raid her cookie jar, which can include fudge brownies and chocolate chip cookies.

Innkeeper(s): Maggie Senn. $89-128. MC, VISA, AX, DC, DS, PC, TC. TAC10. 5 rooms with PB, 1 with FP and 3 suites. Breakfast and afternoon tea included in rates. MAP. Types of meals: Full gourmet bkfst, cont plus, cont and early coffee/tea. Catered breakfast available. Beds: KQDT. Turndown service in room. Air conditioning. Fax, bicycles, library and child care on premises. Handicap access. Weddings, small meetings and family reunions hosted. Antiquing, fishing, golf, live theater, parks, shopping, downhill skiing, cross-country skiing, tennis and water sports nearby.

Publicity: *Rocky Mountain News, Denver Post.*

"You have done a really superb job of creating of a beautiful place to welcome strangers...your warm welcome makes it feel like home!"

Historic Delaware Hotel

700 Harrison Ave
Leadville, CO 80461-3562
(719)486-1418 (800)748-2004 Fax:(719)486-2214

Circa 1886. Often referred to as the Crown Jewel of Leadville, this hotel has served as an architectural cornerstone of the town's National Historic District. The interior has an elegant

Victorian lobby, which includes period antiques, crystal chandeliers, brass fixtures and oak paneling that reflects Leadville's Boom Days. Adding to the atmosphere are lace curtains, heirloom quilts and bedspreads in the guest rooms.

Innkeeper(s): Susan & Scott Brackett. $70-125. MC, VISA, AX, DC, DS. 36 rooms with PB, 4 suites and 1 conference room. Type of meal: Full bkfst. Restaurant on premises. Beds: QDT. Fax and copier on premises. Antiquing, fishing, museums, downhill skiing and cross-country skiing nearby.

The Ice Palace Inn Bed & Breakfast

813 Spruce St
Leadville, CO 80461-3555
(719)486-8272 (800)754-2840 Fax:(719)486-0345
E-mail: ipalace@sni.net
Web: icepalaceinn.com

Circa 1899. Innkeeper Kami Kolakowski was born in this historic Colorado town, and it was her dream to one day return and run a bed & breakfast. Now with husband Giles, she has created a restful retreat out of this turn-of-the-century home built with lumber from the famed Leadville Ice Palace. Giles and Kami have filled the home with antiques and pieces of history from the Ice Palace and the town. Guests are treated to a mouth-watering gourmet breakfast with treats such as stuffed French toast or German apple pancakes. After a day enjoying Leadville, come back and enjoy a soak in the hot tub.

Historic Interest: The Baby Doe Tabor Museum, National Mining Hall of Fame, Tabor Opera House and Healy House are among Leadville's historic

attractions, and all are near the Ice Palace Inn.

Innkeeper(s): Giles & Kami Kolakowski. $79-139. MC, VISA, AX, DS, PC, TC. TAC10. 8 rooms with PB, 5 with FP. Breakfast, afternoon tea and snacks/refreshments included in rates. Types of meals: Full gourmet bkfst and early coffee/tea. Catering service and room service available. Beds: KQDT. TV, turndown service, ceiling fan and VCR in room. Spa, library and hot tub on premises. Weddings, small meetings, family reunions and seminars hosted. Antiquing, fishing, live theater, parks, shopping, downhill skiing, cross-country skiing and water sports nearby.

Loveland   B6

The Lovelander B&B Inn

217 W 4th St
Loveland, CO 80537-5524
(970)699-0798 (800)459-6694 Fax:(970)699-0797

Circa 1902. Prepare to be pampered at the Lovelander. Chocolate turndown service, fresh flowers, whirlpool tubs and bubble bath are just a few of the idyllic touches. Guest rooms are appointed in an uncluttered and romantic Victorian style. Four rooms include either a fireplace or whirlpool tub. Enjoy the gentle sounds of a waterfall in the garden or sit back and relax on the wraparound porch. If weather permits, specialties such as pumpkin apple waffles topped with caramel pecan sauce can be enjoyed on the veranda or in the garden. The inn's memorable cuisine has been featured on the TV shows "Inn Country USA" and "Inn Country Chefs." In addition to the more romantic amenities, there is a fax and copier available, a concierge and tour planning service, and conference facilities, which are located across the street.

Innkeeper(s): Lauren & Gary Smith. $102-150. MC, VISA, AX, DS, PC, TC. TAC10. 11 rooms with PB, 1 with FP and 1 conference room. Breakfast included in rates. Types of meals: Full gourmet bkfst and early coffee/tea. Picnic lunch available. Beds: KQDT. Phone and turndown service in room. Air conditioning. Fax, copier and library on premises. Weddings, small meetings, family reunions and seminars hosted. Antiquing, parks, shopping and cross-country skiing nearby.

Manitou Springs   E6

Red Crags B&B Inn

302 El Paso Blvd
Manitou Springs, CO 80829-2308
(719)685-1920 (800)721-2248 Fax:(719)685-1073
E-mail: info@redcrags.com
Web: www.redcrags.com

Circa 1870. Well-known in this part of Colorado, this unique, four-story Victorian mansion sits on a bluff with a combination of views that includes Pikes Peak, Manitou Valley, Garden of the Gods and the city of Colorado Springs. There are antiques throughout the house. The formal dining room features a rare cherrywood Eastlake fireplace. Two of the suites include double whirlpool tubs. Outside,

guests can walk through beautifully landscaped gardens or enjoy a private picnic area with a barbecue pit and a spectacular view. Wine is served in the evenings.

Innkeeper(s): Howard & Lynda Lerner. $80-180. MC, VISA, AX, DS, PC, TC. TAC10. 8 rooms with PB, 7 with FP and 5 suites. Breakfast, afternoon tea and snacks/refreshments included in rates. Types of meals: Full bkfst and early coffee/tea. Beds: K. Phone, two jetted tubs for two, clock, feather beds and in room. Fax, copier, spa and TV available upon request on premises. Weddings, small meetings, family reunions and seminars hosted. Antiquing, fishing, golf, Pikes Peak, Olympic Training Center, live theater, parks, shopping, cross-country skiing, sporting events and tennis nearby.

"What a beautiful, historical and well-preserved home - exceptional hospitality and comfort. What wonderful people! Highly recommended!"

Two Sisters Inn-A Bed and Breakfast

10 Otoe Pl
Manitou Springs, CO 80829-2014
(719)685-9684
Web: www.twosisinn.com

Circa 1919. Originally built by two sisters as the Sunburst boarding house, this award-winning Victorian inn, now celebrating its 10th anniversary, includes a honeymoon cottage in the back garden. A beautiful stained-glass door, hardwood floors, a stone fireplace in the parlor and a library are among the inn's features. Nestled at the base of Pikes Peak, it is one block from the center of the historic district and close to mineral springs, art galleries, shops, restaurants and the beginning of the historic Manitou Springs Walking Tour. Guests come back to the inn for the fine cuisine and the camaraderie with the caring and fun-loving innkeepers.

Historic Interest: Pikes Peak, Garden of the Gods, Pikes Peak Cog Railway.

Innkeeper(s): Wendy Goldstein & Sharon Smith. $69-110. MC, VISA, DS. 5 rooms, 4 with PB. Breakfast included in rates. Type of meal: Full gourmet bkfst. Beds: D. Antiquing, bicycling, hiking and shopping nearby.

Montrose   E3

The Uncompahgre Lodge B&B

21049 Uncompahgre Rd
Montrose, CO 81401-8750
(970)240-4000 (800)318-8127 Fax:(970)249-5124
E-mail: rhelm@gwe.net
Web: www.uncbb.com

Circa 1914. Once the local schoolhouse, this modified prairie-style brick building boasts a penthouse and small bell tower. The inn's tall windows provide views of the surrounding mountains and country setting. Some of the guest rooms allow for as many as six people, with two queen beds and one king-size bed, making it comfortable for families with children. The French Country Room offers a two-person Jacuzzi with mirror, a king bed, CD music, candles and an electric log fireplace popular in both winter and summer because it crackles, flickers and smells like pine but does not generate heat. The great room, formerly the old auditorium and stage area, is the location for breakfast.

Innkeeper(s): Barbara & Richard Helm. $55-95. MC, VISA, AX, DC, CB, DS, PC, TC. TAC10. 7 rooms with PB and 1 conference room. Breakfast and afternoon tea included in rates. Types of meals: Full bkfst and early coffee/tea. Beds: KQ. Cable TV, ceiling fan and VCR in room. Fax, copier, spa and library on premises. Handicap access. Weddings, small meetings, family reunions and seminars hosted. Spanish spoken. Antiquing, fishing, golf, live theater, parks, shopping, downhill skiing, cross-country skiing, tennis and water sports nearby.

Pets Allowed.

Ouray   F3

St. Elmo Hotel

426 Main St, PO Box 667
Ouray, CO 81427-0667
(970)325-4951 Fax:(970)325-0348
E-mail: steh@rmi.net
Web: www.stelmohotel.com

Circa 1898. The inn was built by Kitty Heit, with views of the amphitheater, Twin Peaks and Mt. Abrams, and it has operated as a hotel for most of its life. Rosewood sofas and chairs covered in red and green velvet, and a player piano furnish the parlor. The Bon Ton Restaurant occupies the stone-walled basement, and it's only a short walk to the hot springs.

Historic Interest: The Town of Ouray is a National Historical District.

Innkeeper(s): Dan & Sandy Lingenfelter. $65-110. MC, VISA, AX, DS. 9 rooms with PB and 2 suites. Breakfast included in rates. Gourmet dinner and catering service available. Restaurant on premises. Beds: KQ. TV in room. Spa and sauna on premises. Antiquing, fishing, downhill skiing, cross-country skiing and water sports nearby.

Publicity: *Colorado Homes & Lifestyles.*

"So full of character and so homely, it is truly delightful. The scenery in this area is breathtaking."

Pine   D6

Meadow Creek B&B Inn

13438 Hwy 285
Pine, CO 80470
(303)838-4167

Circa 1929. This marvelous stone structure, shrouded by pines and aspens, was built as a summer home for Italian Prince Balthasar Gialma Odescalchi, a descendant of rulers of the Holy Roman Empire. Enjoy views of the surrounding mountains as you breath in Colorado's cool, clean air. The lush 35-acre grounds include the main house, barns, a smoke house and a cabin. Although Meadow Creek has been home to royalty, it had been vacant for some time when the current innkeepers found and restored their little treasure. Their restoration efforts have created a truly memorable inn. Rooms are filled with country charm, gracious furnishings and little extras such as teddy bears, flowers, beautiful quilts and lacy curtains. Grandma's Attic, a secluded loft bedroom, offers a sitting area and views at tree-top level. The Colorado Sun Suite offers the modern amenities of a bar, microwave, coffee pot and refrigerator, combined with the romantic amenities of a private sitting room and a Jacuzzi underneath a skylight, perfect for stargazing. Some rooms boast fireplaces, and all guests are pampered with stocked cookie jars and refreshments available throughout the day.

A luscious full breakfast with unique entrees, home-baked breads and other treats is served each morning.

Historic Interest: The main house and surrounding structures are listed in the Colorado Historical Register. Meadow Creek is just an hour out of Denver, which offers many historic attractions.

Innkeeper(s): Pat & Dennis Carnahan. $95-180. MC, VISA. 7 rooms with PB and 3 suites. Breakfast and snacks/refreshments included in rates. Types of meals: Full bkfst and early coffee/tea. Beds: KQ. Jacuzzis in room. Weddings, small meetings, family reunions and seminars hosted. Antiquing, bicycling, fishing, hiking, horseback riding. Golf. Hiking, shopping and cross-country skiing nearby.

Pueblo E7

The Baxter Inn

325 W 15th St
Pueblo, CO 81003
(719)542-7002 Fax:(719)583-1560
E-mail: baxtrinn@rmi.net
Web: www.puebloonline.com/baxterinn

Circa 1893. The Victorian era lives on at this historic inn, listed in the National Register. Fine furnishings and period antiques decorate the rooms. Intricately carved fireplace mantels and a grand main staircase add to the period ambiance. Guest rooms have been designed with romance in mind; some include a whirlpool tub for two. The Charles Kretschmer Room, named to honor the home's builder, includes a fireplace, damask wallcoverings, a four-poster bed and a bath with a whirlpool tub set among stained glass. The inn is named for the home's most notable resident, a pioneer businessman, rancher and politician. A three-course, gourmet breakfast is served each morning, beginning with a special "wake-up" course that is set up on a sideboard outside the guest rooms. The final two courses, a fresh fruit dish and a savory egg dish, are served in the formal dining room.

Historic Interest: Rosemount Museum.

Innkeeper(s): Dave & Lois Jones. $75-120. MC, VISA, AX, DC, PC, TC. TAC10. 5 rooms with PB, 1 with FP, 1 suite and 1 conference room. Breakfast included in rates. Types of meals: Full gourmet bkfst, veg bkfst and early coffee/tea. Afternoon tea, snacks/refreshments and picnic lunch available. Beds: Q. Cable TV, phone, turndown service and robes in room. Central air. Fax, copier, library and music room baby grand piano on premises. Weddings, small meetings, family reunions and seminars hosted. Antiquing, art galleries, bicycling, canoeing/kayaking, golf, hiking, horseback riding, museums, parks, cross-country skiing, tennis and water sports nearby.

Salida E5

River Run Inn

8495 Co Rd 160
Salida, CO 81201
(719)539-3818 (800)385-6925

Circa 1892. This gracious brick home, a National Register building, is located on the banks of the Arkansas River, three miles from town. It was once the poor farm, for folks down on their luck who were willing to work in exchange for food and lodging. The house has been renovated to reflect a country-eclectic style and has seven guest rooms, most enhanced by mountain views. The location is ideal for anglers,

rafters, hikers, bikers and skiers. A 13-bed, third floor is great for groups. A full country breakfast, afternoon cookies and refreshments, and evening brandy and sherry are offered daily.

Innkeeper(s): Virginia Nemmers. $60-150. MC, VISA, AX, PC, TC. TAC10. 7 rooms, 3 with PB. Breakfast included in rates. Types of meals: Full bkfst and early coffee/tea. Dinner and picnic lunch available. Beds: KQT. VCR, library, fishing and lawn games on premises. Weddings, small meetings, family reunions and seminars hosted. Antiquing, fishing, golf, art galleries, winery, hiking, snowshoeing, live theater, shopping, downhill skiing, cross-country skiing, tennis and water sports nearby.

Publicity: *Men's Journal, Post, Colorado Springs Gazette.*

"So glad we found a B&B with such character and a great owner as well."

Thomas House

307 E 1st St
Salida, CO 81201-2801
(719)539-7104 (888)228-1410
E-mail: office@thomashouse.com
Web: www.thomashouse.com

Circa 1888. This home was built as a boarding house to help accommodate the thousands of railroad workers and travelers who passed through Salida. Today, the home still serves as a restful place for weary travelers drawn to the Colorado wilderness.

The inn is decorated with antiques, collectibles and contemporary furnishings. Each guest room is named for a mountain. The Mt. Princeton suite includes a bedroom, private bath with an antique clawfoot tub and a separate sitting area. The innkeepers keep reading materials on hand, and there is an outdoor hot tub as well. Breakfasts are continental, yet hearty, with a variety of freshly baked breads and muffins, yogurt, granola, cheese and fruit.

Innkeeper(s): Tammy & Steve Office. $55-100. MC, VISA, AX, DS, PC, TC. TAC10. 6 rooms with PB, 1 suite and 1 cottage. Breakfast included in rates. Types of meals: Cont and early coffee/tea. Beds: KQT. Ceiling fan and kitchenette in suite in room. Spa, library and shared kitchen on premises. Small meetings and family reunions hosted. Antiquing, fishing, art galleries, live theater, parks, shopping, downhill skiing, cross-country skiing and water sports nearby.

The Tudor Rose B&B

6720 County Rd 104
Salida, CO 81201
(719)539-2002 (800)379-0889 Fax:(719)530-0345
E-mail: tudorose@amigo.net
Web: www.thetudorose.com

Circa 1979. Thirty-seven acres of woods surround this secluded bed & breakfast, which offers views of the surrounding hills and mountains. Rooms are spacious and comfortably furnished. The Henry Tudor Suite includes an oversize Jacuzzi hot tub. Feather beds and fluffy robes are some of the amenities. Gourmet breakfasts include items such as seasoned eggs on puff pastry topped with a rich bearnaise sauce. Guests who bring their own horses can board them, and then enjoy a trek around the expansive property. The surrounding area offers an abundance of outdoor activities, such as hiking, mountain biking, river rafting and more.

Innkeeper(s): Jon & Terre Terrell. $60-145. MC, VISA, DS. TAC10. 6 rooms with PB and 2 suites. Breakfast and snacks/refreshments included in rates. Types of meals: Full gourmet bkfst and early coffee/tea. Afternoon tea and catered breakfast available. Beds: KQ. Cable TV and phone in room. VCR, fax, spa, stables and library on premises. Weddings, small meetings and family reunions hosted. Antiquing, fishing, golf, hiking, rafting, four wheeling, live theater, parks, shopping, downhill skiing, cross-country skiing, tennis and water sports nearby.

Silverton   F3

The Wyman Hotel & Inn

1371 Greene St
Silverton, CO 81433
(970)387-5372 (800)609-7845 Fax:(970)387-5745

Circa 1902. Silverton, a Victorian-era mining town in the heart of the San Juan Mountains, is the location for this National Register inn. The historic building still maintains an original tin ceiling and an elevator. However, the elevator is now housed in one of the guest rooms, surrounding a Jacuzzi tub. Other unique features include a stone carving of a mule created by the hotel's builder. The mule is displayed on the roof. One-of-a-kind antiques provide the furnishing for all of the rooms. Aside from the historic ambiance, the innkeepers offer plenty of amenities. Rooms include a TV and VCR, and there are hundreds of movies guests can choose, all free of charge. A gourmet breakfast is served, typically featuring seasonal fruit, freshly baked muffins, breads, cereals, special egg dishes and Silverton Spuds, potatoes baked with onions, peppers, tomatoes and cheese. Tea and homemade cookies are served every afternoon.

Innkeeper(s): Lorraine Lewis. $95-175. MC, VISA, AX, DS, TC. TAC10. 17 rooms, 18 with PB and 2 suites. Breakfast and afternoon tea included in rates. Types of meals: Full gourmet bkfst and early coffee/tea. Picnic lunch available. Beds: KQ. Cable TV, phone, ceiling fan, VCR, whirlpool tubs, video collection and in room. Fax, copier and library on premises. Weddings, small meetings and family reunions hosted. Antiquing, bicycling, fishing, hiking, hiking, horseback riding, folk festival, jeeping to ghost towns, live theater, parks, shopping and water sports nearby.

Telluride   F3

Johnstone Inn

PO Box 546
Telluride, CO 81435-0546
(970)728-3316 (800)752-1901
E-mail: bschiff@rmi.com
Web: www.johnstoneinn.com

Circa 1891. This Victorian boarding house is located on Telluride's main street, in view of the San Juan Mountain ski slopes. Guest rooms all have new bathrooms with marble floors and showers. Brass beds are painted with pink and white flowers and topped with fluffy comforters. Laundry use is available. Ski lifts are a short walk away.

Innkeeper(s): Bill Schiffbauer. $80-135. MC, VISA, AX, DS. 8 rooms with PB. Type of meal: Full bkfst. Beds: Q. Spa on premises.

"Cannot say enough good things, had a great time."

Ward   C6

Gold Lake Mountain Resort & Spa

3371 Gold Lake Rd
Ward, CO 80481-9602
(303)459-3544 (800)450-3544 Fax:(303)459-9080
E-mail: goldlake@goldlake.com
Web: www.goldlake.com

Circa 1922. Surrounded by National Forest and overlooking the Continental Divide, this resort was originally a summer camp for girls. There are 18 log cabins, all furnished tastefully with period antiques and local art and featuring romantic, artistically designed baths. There are extra-plush down comforters and gas stoves. Accommodations include such imaginative names as Paco's, Zen Den, Victoria's, Eve's Escape, Lefthand & Niwot's and Haiku. Birdland, as an example, features log beds, mission-period antiques, a collection of music memorabilia and a large marble bathtub with a handsome copper surround. A variety of pampering spa treatments are available. The inn's four-course candlelight gourmet dining was voted "Best of Denver" in Westwords and features hearty "Mountain Spa Cuisine" with wild game, fish or vegetarian options. Although there are more than 95 acres to explore, the favorite spot is soaking in the hot pools overlooking Gold Lake. Hiking, canoeing, sailing, kayaking, fly fishing, cycling and skiing are popular, as well.

Historic Interest: Enos Mills Cabin(founder of Rocky Mtn National Par,)-30 miles, Nederland Mining Museum-15 miles, St. Malos Chapel (site of Pope visit).

Innkeeper(s): Jill Fleming. $150-495. MC, VISA, PC. 18 rooms, 9 with PB, 18 with FP, 8 suites. 1 guest house and 1 conference room. Breakfast and afternoon tea included in rates. Type of meal: Cont plus. Gourmet dinner, lunch and banquet service available. Restaurant on premises. Ceiling fan in room. Fax, spa, sauna and stables on premises. Weddings and small meetings hosted. Bicycling, canoeing/kayaking, fishing, hiking, horseback riding, boating, spa services, downhill skiing and cross-country skiing nearby.

Woodland Park   D6

Pikes Peak Paradise

236 Pinecrest Rd
Woodland Park, CO 80863
(719)687-6656 (800)728-8282 Fax:(719)687-9008

Circa 1987. This three-story Georgian Colonial with stately white columns rises unexpectedly from the wooded hills west of Colorado Springs. The south wall of the house has large windows to enhance its splendid views of Pikes Peak. A glass door opens from each guest suite onto a private deck or patio with the same riveting view. Eggs Benedict and baked French apple toast are some of the favorites offered for breakfast.

Innkeeper(s): Rayne & Bart Reese. $175-220. MC, VISA, AX, DS, PC, TC. TAC10. 5 suites, 4 with FP. Breakfast included in rates. Type of meal: Full bkfst. Beds: KQ. Ceiling fan and deluxe suites have TV/VCR in room. VCR, fax and spa on premises. Handicap access. Weddings and family reunions hosted. Amusement parks, antiquing, bicycling, fishing, golf, hiking, horseback riding, gambling, live theater, parks, shopping, cross-country skiing, sporting events and water sports nearby.

Pets allowed: Small pets with prior approval.

Connecticut

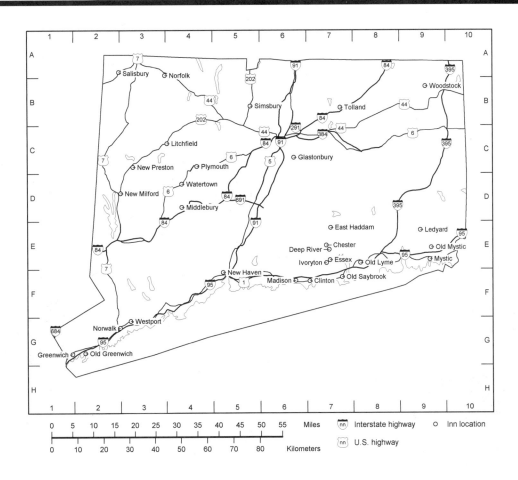

	Miles
0 5 10 15 20 25 30 35 40 45 50 55	
0 10 20 30 40 50 60 70 80	Kilometers

(nn) Interstate highway   ○ Inn location

(nn) U.S. highway

Chester E7

The Inn at Chester

318 W Main St
Chester, CT 06412-1026
(860)526-9541 (800)949-7829 Fax:(860)526-4387
E-mail: innkeeper@innatchester.com
Web: www.innatchester.com

Circa 1778. More than 200 years ago, Jeremiah Parmelee built a clapboard farmhouse along a winding road named the Killingworth Turnpike. The Parmelee Homestead stands as a reflection of the past and is an inspiration for the Inn at Chester. Each of the rooms is individually appointed with Eldred Wheeler Reproductions. The Lincoln Suite has a sitting room with a fireplace. Enjoy lively conversation or live music while imbibing your favorite drink at the inn's tavern, Dunk's Landing. Outside Dunk's Landing, a 30-foot fireplace soars into the rafters. Fine dining is offered in the inn's post-and-beam restaurant.

Innkeeper(s): Leonard Lieberman. $105-215. MC, VISA, AX, DS. 42 rooms with PB, 2 with FP, 1 suite and 3 conference rooms. Breakfast included in rates. Type of meal: Cont plus. Gourmet dinner, lunch and banquet service available. Restaurant on premises. Beds: KQDT. Cable TV and phone in room. Air conditioning. VCR, fax, copier, sauna, bicycles, tennis, library and pet boarding on premises. Handicap access. Weddings, small meetings, family reunions and seminars hosted. Antiquing, fishing, golf, live theater, parks, shopping, downhill skiing, cross-country skiing and water sports nearby.

Pets Allowed.

Clinton F7

Captain Dibbell House

21 Commerce St
Clinton, CT 06413-2054
(860)669-1646 (888)889-6882 Fax:(860)669-2300

Circa 1866. Built by a sea captain, this graceful Victorian house is only two blocks from the harbor where innkeeper Ellis Adams used to sail his own vessel. A ledger of household accounts dating from the 1800s is on display, and there are fresh flowers in each guest room.

Historic Interest: Gillette Castle (20 miles), Stanton House (one-half mile), Essex Steam Train (10 minutes), Yale University (30 miles).

Innkeeper(s): Helen & Ellis Adams. $79-109. MC, VISA, PC, TC. TAC10. 4 rooms with PB. Breakfast included in rates. Type of meal: Full bkfst. Beds: KQT. Turndown service, ceiling fan and bathrobes in room. Air conditioning. Bicycles on premises. Antiquing, fishing, live theater, parks, shopping and water sports nearby.

Publicity: Clinton Recorder, New Haven Register, Hartford Courant.

"This was our first experience with B&Bs and frankly, we didn't know what to expect. It was GREAT!"

Deep River E7

Riverwind

209 Main St
Deep River, CT 06417-2022
(860)526-2014

Circa 1790. Chosen "most romantic inn in Connecticut" by Discerning Traveler Newsletter, this inn features a wraparound gingerbread porch filled with gleaming white wicker furniture. A happy, informal country decor includes antiques from Barbara's Virginia home. There are fireplaces everywhere, including a 12-foot cooking fireplace in the keeping room.

Innkeeper(s): Barbara Barlow & Bob Bucknall. $95-175. MC, VISA. 8 rooms with PB. Breakfast included in rates. Meal: Full bkfst. Gourmet dinner available. Beds: QD. Weddings hosted. Antiquing, hiking trails and live theater nearby.

Publicity: Hartford Courant, Country Living, Country Inns, Country Decorating, New York, Travel & Leisure, New York Times, Boston Globe, Los Angeles Times.

"Warm, hospitality, a quiet homey atmosphere, comfortable bed, well thought-out and delightful appointments, delicious light hot biscuits — a great find!"

East Haddam E7

Bishopsgate Inn

7 Norwich Rd
East Haddam, CT 06423-0290
(860)873-1677 Fax:(860)873-3898

Circa 1818. This Colonial house is furnished with period antiques, and each floor of the inn has a sitting area where guests often relax with a good book. Four of the guest rooms include a fireplace and the suite has a sauna. The innkeepers serve a hearty breakfast, and for an additional charge, they can prepare picnic lunches and five-course dinners. Although secluded on two acres, the inn is a short walk to the Goodspeed Opera House and shopping.

Innkeeper(s): Kagel Family. $100-150. MC, VISA, PC. 6 rooms with PB, 4 with FP and 1 suite. Breakfast and afternoon tea included in rates. MAP. Types of meals: Full bkfst and early coffee/tea. Gourmet dinner, snacks/refreshments, picnic lunch and lunch and room service available. Beds: KQD. Sauna in room. Air conditioning. Small meetings and family reunions hosted. Antiquing, fishing, live theater, parks, shopping, downhill skiing, cross-country skiing and water sports nearby.

Publicity: Discerning Traveler, Adventure Road, Manhattan Cooperator.

". . . Attention to detail, ambiance and amenities . . . Bishopsgate is truly outstanding."

Essex E7

Griswold Inn

36 Main St
Essex, CT 06426-1132
(860)767-1776 Fax:(860)767-0481

Circa 1776. The main building of the colonial Griswold Inn is said to be the first three-story frame structure built in Connecticut. The Tap Room, just behind the inn, has been called the most handsome barroom in America. The inn is famous for its fine New England fare as well as its English Hunt Breakfast, originally served at the request of the British after they invaded the harbor at Essex during the war of 1812. Ask for a quiet room at the back of the inn unless you'd enjoy a Fife & Drum corps marching by under your window on Main Street.

Historic Interest: Important historic houses line many of the lanes of Essex. Changing exhibits of early river valley life can be seen at the Connecticut River Museum. Mystic Seaport and Gillette's Castle are also on the "must see" list.

Innkeeper(s): Douglas & Joan Paul. $90-195. MC, VISA, AX, TC. 31 rooms with PB, 8 with FP and 1 conference room. Type of meal: Cont. Dinner and lunch available. Beds: KQDT. TV in room. Air conditioning. Fax and copier on premises. Weddings, small meetings and family reunions hosted. Antiquing, art galleries, hiking, bicycling, steam train and boating, historic homes, live theater and shopping nearby.

Pets allowed: certain rooms with advance notice.

"A man in search of the best inn in New England has a candidate in the quiet, unchanged town of Essex, Connecticut." — Country Journal

Glastonbury C6

Butternut Farm
1654 Main St
Glastonbury, CT 06033-2962
(860)633-7197 Fax:(860)659-1758

Circa 1720. This Colonial house sits on two acres of landscaped grounds amid trees and herb gardens. Prize-winning goats, pigeons, chickens, ducks, and pigs are housed in the old barn on the property. Eighteenth-century Connecticut antiques are placed throughout the inn, enhancing the natural beauty of the pumpkin-pine floors and eight brick fireplaces.

Innkeeper(s): Don Reid. $79-99. AX, PC, TC. 4 rooms with PB, 3 with FP and 2 suites. Breakfast included in rates. Type of meal: Full bkfst. Beds: DT. Phone and VCR in room. Air conditioning. Fax on premises. Family reunions hosted. Antiquing, fishing, live theater, parks, shopping, downhill skiing, cross-country skiing and sporting events nearby.

Greenwich G1

Cos Cob Inn
50 River Rd
Greenwich, CT 06807
(203)661-5845 Fax:(203)661-2054
E-mail: innkeeper@coscobinn.com
Web: www.coscobinn.com

Circa 1870. Located in the Cos Cob section of Greenwich, this three-story, Federal-style inn offers 14 individually decorated guest rooms. Each elegant bed chamber is special. The Wedding Room is spacious, and with its bay window and four-poster bed, a perfect choice for a romantic getaway. Suites include sitting areas and Jacuzzis. For business travelers, the innkeepers have provided data ports and voice mail in each guest room. Many rooms offer a river view. Restaurants, museums, shops and outdoor activities are all nearby.

Innkeeper(s): Rick & Cindy Kral. $59-189. MC, VISA, AX, DC, PC. 14 rooms with PB, 1 with FP and 4 suites. Breakfast and snacks/refreshments included in rates. Type of meal: Cont. Beds: KQ. Cable TV, phone, ceiling fan, VCR, hair dryer and irons & ironing boards in room. Air conditioning. Fax and copier on premises. Small meetings and family reunions hosted. Antiquing, fishing, golf, live theater, parks, shopping and tennis nearby.

Ivoryton E7

The Copper Beech Inn
46 Main St
Ivoryton, CT 06442-1004
(860)767-0330 (888)809-2056
Web: www.copperbeechinn.com

Circa 1887. The Copper Beech Inn was once the home of ivory importer A.W. Comstock, one of the early owners of the Comstock Cheney Company, which produced ivory combs and keyboards. The village took its name from the ivory trade centered here. An enormous copper beech tree shades the property. Each room in the renovated Carriage House boasts a whirlpool bath and French doors opening onto a deck. The wine list and French-country cuisine at the inn's restaurant have received numerous accolades.

Historic Interest: Connecticut River Museum (4 miles), Goodspeed Opera House (15 miles), Ivoryton Playhouse (one-half mile), Mystic Seaport (25 miles).

Innkeeper(s): Eldon & Sally Senner. $123-202. MC, VISA, AX, DC, CB, PC, TC. 13 rooms with PB and 1 conference room. Breakfast included in rates. Type of meal: Cont plus. Gourmet dinner and banquet service available. Restaurant on premises. Beds: KQDT. Cable TV in room. Air conditioning. Library on premises. Handicap access. Weddings, small meetings and seminars hosted. Limited Spanish and Portuguese spoken. Antiquing, fishing, live theater, parks, shopping and water sports nearby.

Publicity: *Los Angeles Times, Bon Appetit, Connecticut, Travel & Leisure, Discerning Traveler.*

"The grounds are beautiful ... just breathtaking ... accommodations are wonderful."

Ledyard E9

Applewood Farms Inn
528 Colonel Ledyard Hwy
Ledyard, CT 06339-1649
(860)536-2022 Fax:(860)536-6015

Circa 1826. Five generations of the Gallup family worked this farm near Mystic. The classic center-chimney Colonial, furnished with antiques and early-American pieces, is situated on 33 acres of fields and meadows. Stone fences meander through the property and many of the original outbuildings remain. It is in the National Register, cited as one of the best surviving examples of a 19th-century farm in Connecticut.

Innkeeper(s): Frankie & Tom Betz. $105-170. MC, VISA, AX, PC, TC. TAC10.

4 rooms with PB, 4 with FP and 1 suite. Breakfast included in rates. Types of meals: Full bkfst and early coffee/tea. Beds: KDT. TV and turndown service in room. Air conditioning. VCR, fax, copier, spa, pitch & putt golf green and hot tub spa on premises. Weddings, small meetings and family reunions hosted. Amusement parks, antiquing, fishing, putting green, Indian casinos, live theater, parks, shopping, cross-country skiing, sporting events and water sports nearby.

Pets allowed: call for policy.

Publicity: *Country, New Woman, Travel Host, New York Post, Getaways Magazine.*

"This bed & breakfast is a real discovery."

Litchfield   C4

Abel Darling B&B

PO Box 1502, 102 West St
Litchfield, CT 06759
(860)567-0384 Fax:(860)567-2638

Circa 1782. The spacious guest rooms in this 1782 colonial home offer a light romantic feel and comfortable beds. Breakfast is served in the sunny dining room and includes home-baked breads and muffins. This bed and breakfast is in the heart of the historic district, and nearby is the village green, hosting many restaurants and boutique shops, and the Litchfield countryside.
Innkeeper(s): Colleen Murphy. $85-125. PC, TC. 2 rooms with PB. Breakfast included in rates. Types of meals: Cont plus and cont. Beds: QD. Table and chairs in room. VCR, fax, copier, bicycles and library on premises. Family reunions hosted. Antiquing, fishing, golf, live theater, parks, shopping, downhill skiing, cross-country skiing and tennis nearby.

Madison   F6

Tidewater Inn

949 Boston Post Rd
Madison, CT 06443-3236
(203)245-8457

Circa 1880. Long ago, this 19th-century home was no doubt a welcome site to travelers needing a rest after a bumpy stage-coach ride. Although its days as a stagecoach stop have long since past, the inn is still a welcoming place for those needing a romantic getaway. The rooms are elegantly appointed with items such as four-poster or canopy beds, Oriental rugs and fine furnishings. The inn's sitting area is a cozy place to relax, with its fireplace and exposed beams. The one-and-a-half-acre grounds include an English garden. The inn is within walking distance to many of Madison's sites, and beaches are just a mile away.
Innkeeper(s): Jean Foy & Rich Evans. $80-170. MC, VISA, AX, PC, TC. 9 rooms with PB, 2 with FP. Breakfast included in rates. Types of meals: Full bkfst, cont and early coffee/tea. Beds: KQDT. Cable TV and one with Jacuzzi in room. Air conditioning. Antiquing, fishing, live theater, parks, shopping and water sports nearby.

Middlebury   D4

Tucker Hill Inn

96 Tucker Hill Rd
Middlebury, CT 06762-2511
(203)758-8334 Fax:(203)598-0652

Circa 1923. There's a cut-out heart in the gate that opens to this handsome three-story estate framed by an old stone wall. The spacious Colonial-style house is shaded by tall trees. Guests enjoy a parlor with fireplace and an inviting for-

mal dining room. Guest rooms are furnished with a flourish of English country or romantic Victorian decor.
Innkeeper(s): Susan & Richard Cebelenski. $85-125. MC, VISA, AX, PC, TC. TAC10. 4 rooms, 2 with PB. Breakfast included in rates. Types of meals: Full bkfst and early coffee/tea. Afternoon tea available. Beds: QT. Cable TV, ceiling fan and VCR in room. Air conditioning. Fax on premises. Small meetings and family reunions hosted. Amusement parks, antiquing, golf, lake, live theater, parks, shopping, cross-country skiing and tennis nearby.

Publicity: *Star, Waterbury American Republican, Voices.*

"Thanks for a special visit. Your kindness never went unnoticed."

Mystic   E9

Adams House

382 Cow Hill Rd
Mystic, CT 06355-1408
(860)572-9551 Fax:(860)572-9552

Circa 1749. A little over a mile from the village, this old colonial house has a walk-in fireplace in the dining room. A separate cottage suite features its own sauna and wet bar.
Historic Interest: Fort Griswold, Fort Trumbull, Mystic Seaport Museum.
Innkeeper(s): Mary Lou & Gregory B. Peck. $85-175. MC, VISA, PC, TC. 6 rooms with PB, 1 with FP and 1 guest house. Breakfast and afternoon tea included in rates. Types of meals: Full bkfst, country bkfst, veg bkfst and early coffee/tea. Beds: QT. Cable TV and phone in room. Air conditioning. Fax, sauna in guest house and living room with fireplace on premises. Family reunions hosted. Antiquing, art galleries, beaches, bicycling, canoeing/kayaking, fishing, golf, horseback riding, Mystic Aquarium, live theater, museums, parks, shopping, water sports and wineries nearby.

"Beautiful, peaceful home away from home."

Harbour Inn & Cottage

15 Edgemont St
Mystic, CT 06355-2853
(860)572-9253

Circa 1898. Known as Charley's Place after its innkeeper, this New England inn located on the Mystic River is comfortably decorated with cedar paneling and hardwood floors throughout. A large stone fireplace and piano are featured in the common room. There is a gazebo, six-person hot tub, picnic area and boat dock on the grounds. The inn is minutes from the Olde Mystic Village, Factory Outlet Stores and casinos.
Innkeeper(s): Charles Lecouras, Jr. $55-250. TC. TAC10. 6 rooms with PB, 1 with FP and 1 cottage. Beds: D. Cable TV in room. Air conditioning. Spa, picnic area, gazebo and boat dock on premises. Weddings, small meetings and family reunions hosted. Greek spoken. Antiquing, fishing, golf, museums, nautilus submarine, aquarium, casino, live theater, parks, shopping, tennis and water sports nearby.

New Haven
F5

Three Chimneys Inn at Yale University

1201 Chapel St
New Haven, CT 06511-4701
(203)789-1201 (800)443-1554 Fax:(203)776-7363

Circa 1870. Three Chimneys is an elegant, historic mansion located a mere block from Yale University and is near to the Yale Center for British Art and the Yale Art Museum. The inn is located in a historic, restored section of New Haven, and shops, boutiques, night clubs, theater and fine restaurants all are just minutes away. The Georgian and Federal decor includes fine furnishings such as a four-poster or canopy bed, Edwardian bed drapes, Oriental rugs and Chippendale desks. Each room includes modern amenities such as color TVs and telephones with dataports.

$170. MC, VISA, AX, DS, PC, TC. TAC10. 10 rooms with PB, 2 with FP and 2 conference rooms. Breakfast included in rates. Type of meal: Full bkfst. Catering service available. Beds: KQ. Cable TV and phone in room. Air conditioning. Fax, copier and private on-site parking on premises. Small meetings and seminars hosted. Dining, museums, live theater, parks, shopping and sporting events nearby.

New Milford
D3

Heritage Inn

34 Bridge St
New Milford, CT 06776-3530
(860)354-8883

Circa 1870. Once a warehouse for locally grown tobacco, the inn is located directly across from the restored train depot and adjacent to small community stores. The front porch is graced with wooden chairs. A turn-of-the-century decor features blue and white floral carpeting, swag curtains and framed prints. Suites are available. In the morning, a full breakfast features French toast, pancakes and omelets.

Innkeeper(s): Lou Sproviero & Ray Barton. $75-100. MC, VISA, AX, DS. 20 rooms with PB. Type of meal: Full bkfst. Fax on premises.

Homestead Inn

5 Elm St
New Milford, CT 06776-2995
(860)354-4080
Web: www.homesteadct.com

Circa 1853. Built by the first of three generations of John Prime Treadwells, the inn was established 80 years later. Victorian architecture includes high ceilings, spacious rooms and large verandas. There is a small motel adjacent to the inn.

Innkeeper(s): Rolf & Peggy Hammer. $85-108. MC, VISA, AX, DC, DS. 14 rooms with PB. Type of meal: Cont plus. Beds: KQDT. Cable TV and phone in room. Air conditioning. Publicity: *Litchfield County Times, ABC Home Show, Food & Wine.*

"One of the homiest inns in the U.S.A. with most hospitable hosts. A rare bargain to boot."

New Preston
C3

Boulders Inn

East Shore Rd, Rt 45
New Preston, CT 06777
(860)868-0541 (800)55-BOULDERS Fax:(860)868-1925

Circa 1895. Views of Lake Waramaug and its wooded shores can be seen from the living room and most of the guest rooms and cottages of this country inn. The terrace is open in the summer for cocktails, dinner and sunsets over the lake. Antique furnishings, a basement game room, and a beach house with a hanging wicker swing are all part of Boulders Inn. There is a private beach with boats, and bicycles are available.

Innkeeper(s): Kees & Ulla Adema. $225-395. MC, VISA, AX, PC, TC. TAC10. 17 rooms with PB, 11 with FP, 2 suites, 8 cottages and 1 conference room. Breakfast, afternoon tea and dinner included in rates. MAP. Types of meals: Full gourmet bkfst and early coffee/tea. Room service available. Restaurant on premises. Beds: KQ. TV, phone, turndown service and ceiling fan in room. Air conditioning. VCR, fax, copier, swimming, bicycles and library on premises. Handicap access. Weddings, small meetings, family reunions and seminars hosted. Dutch, German, French and Spanish spoken. Antiquing, fishing, golf, live theater, parks, shopping, downhill skiing, cross-country skiing, tennis and water sports nearby.

Norfolk
A3

Manor House

69 Maple Ave
Norfolk, CT 06058-0447
(860)542-5690 Fax:(860)542-5690
E-mail: tremblay@esslink.com
Web: www.manorhouse-norfolk.com

Circa 1898. Charles Spofford, designer of London's subway, built this home with many gables, exquisite cherry paneling and grand staircase. There are Moorish arches and Tiffany windows. Guests can enjoy hot-mulled cider after a sleigh ride, hay ride, or horse and carriage drive along the country lanes nearby. The inn was named by "Discerning Traveler" as Connecticut's most romantic hideaway.

Historic Interest: Norfolk is a historic community with many historic homes; the Yale Chamber Music Festival is held at one such historic estate. Litchfield County has many museums and historic homes to tour.

Innkeeper(s): Hank & Diane Tremblay. $100-250. MC, VISA, AX, DS, PC, TC. TAC10. 9 rooms with PB, 4 with FP, 1 suite and 1 conference room. Breakfast and afternoon tea included in rates. Types of meals: Full gourmet bkfst and early coffee/tea. Catering service, catered breakfast and room service available. Beds: KQDT. Ceiling fan in room. Fax and library on premises. Weddings, small meetings, family reunions and seminars hosted. French spoken. Antiquing, fishing, live theater, parks, shopping, downhill skiing, cross-country skiing, sporting events and water sports nearby.

Publicity: *Boston Globe, Philadelphia Inquirer, Innsider, Rhode Island Monthly, Gourmet, National Geographic Traveler, Good Housekeeping, New York Times.*

"Queen Victoria, eat your heart out."

Norwalk　　　　　　　　　　　　　G2

Silvermine Tavern

194 Perry Ave
Norwalk, CT 06850-1123
(203)847-4558 Fax:(203)847-9171

Circa 1790. The Silvermine consists of the
Old Mill, the Country Store, the Coach
House and the Tavern itself. Primitive paintings and furnishings, as well as family heirlooms, decorate the inn. Guest rooms and
dining rooms overlook the Old Mill, the
waterfall and swans gliding across the
millpond. Some guest rooms offer items

such as canopy bed or private decks. In the
summer, guests can dine al fresco and gaze at the mill pond.
Historic Interest: Lockwood Matthews Mansion (10 miles).

Innkeeper(s): Frank Whitman, Jr. $99-135. MC, VISA, AX, DC, CB, PC, TC.
TAC10. 10 rooms with PB and 1 suite. Breakfast included in rates. Type of
meal: Cont. Dinner, lunch and banquet service available. Restaurant on
premises. Beds: DT. Some canopied beds in room. Air conditioning. VCR, fax,
copier and handicap access to restaurant on premises. Weddings, small
meetings, family reunions and seminars hosted. Antiquing, fishing, parks and
shopping nearby.

Old Greenwich　　　　　　　　　　G2

Harbor House Inn

165 Shore Rd
Old Greenwich, CT 06870-2120
(203)637-0145 Fax:(203)698-0943

Circa 1890. This turn-of-the-century inn is decorated with
unique, Old World flair. Guest rooms feature poster beds and
sturdy, comfortable furnishings. Each room includes a mini
refrigerator and a coffee maker, and there are laundry facilities

on the premises. Business trav-
elers will appreciate the availability of a fax machine and
copier, and the inn offers a
conference room. Restaurants
and shops are nearby, and the
inn is 45 minutes by train
from New York City.

Innkeeper(s): Rosemarie Stuttig & Dawn Browne. $109-275. MC, VISA, AX,
TC. TAC10. 23 rooms and 1 conference room. Breakfast included in rates.
Type of meal: Cont. Beds: QDT. Cable TV, phone and VCR in room. Air conditioning. Fax, copier and bicycles on premises. Weddings, small meetings and
family reunions hosted. Antiquing, beaches, fishing, live theater, parks and
shopping nearby.

Old Lyme　　　　　　　　　　　　E8

Bee and Thistle Inn

100 Lyme St
Old Lyme, CT 06371-1426
(860)434-1667 (800)622-4946 Fax:(860)434-3402
E-mail: info@beeandthistleinn.com
Web: www.beeandthistle.com

Circa 1756. This stately inn is situated along the banks of the
Lieutenant River. There are five and one-half acres of trees, lawns
and a sunken English garden. The inn is furnished with

Chippendale antiques and reproductions. A guitar duo plays in
the parlor on Friday, and a harpist performs on Saturday
evenings. Bee and Thistle was voted the most romantic inn in
the state, the most romantic dinner spot, and for having the best
restaurant in the state by readers of "Connecticut Magazine."

Innkeeper(s): Bob, Penny, Lori and Jeff Nelson. $79-210. MC, VISA, DC, DS,
PC, TC. TAC10. 11 rooms with PB, 1 with FP and 1 cottage. EP. Type of
meal: Full gourmet bkfst. Afternoon tea, gourmet dinner and lunch available.
Restaurant on premises. Beds: QDT. Phone and ceiling fan in room. Air con-
ditioning. Weddings, small meetings and family reunions hosted. Antiquing,
art galleries, fishing, live theater, museums, parks and shopping nearby.
Publicity: *Countryside, Country Living, Money, New York, U.S. Air, New York
Times, Country Traveler.*

Old Mystic　　　　　　　　　　　　E9

Red Brook Inn

PO Box 237
Old Mystic, CT 06372-0237
(860)572-0349

Circa 1740. If there was no other reason to visit Mystic, a
charming town brimming with activities, the Red Brook Inn
would be reason enough. The Crary Homestead features three
unique rooms with working fire-
places, while the Haley Tavern
offers seven guest rooms, some
with canopy beds and
fireplaces.Two have whirlpool
tubs. Innkeeper Ruth Keyes has
beautiful antiques decorating her
inn. Guests are sure to enjoy her

wonderful country breakfasts. A special winter dinner takes
three days to complete and she prepares it over an open hearth.
In addition to a full breakfast, afternoon and evening beverages
are provided. The aquarium, Mystic Seaport Museum, a cider
mill, casinos and many shops are only minutes away.
Historic Interest: Mystic Seaport Museum.

Innkeeper(s): Ruth Keyes. $189. MC, VISA, AX, DS, PC, TC. 10 rooms with
PB, 7 with FP and 3 conference rooms. Breakfast included in rates. Type of
meal: Full bkfst. Beds: QDT. Whirlpool tub in room. VCR, library, terrace and
parlors on premises. Small meetings, family reunions and seminars hosted.
Amusement parks, antiquing, fishing, museums, casino, live theater, parks,
shopping, sporting events and water sports nearby.

Publicity: *Travel & Leisure, Yankee, New York, Country Decorating,
Philadelphia Inquirer, National Geographic Traveler, Discerning Traveler.*

*"The staff is wonderful. You made us feel at home. Thank you for
your hospitality."*

Old Saybrook　　　　　　　　　　　F7

Deacon Timothy Pratt House B&B

325 Main St
Old Saybrook, CT 06475
(860)395-1229 Fax:(860)395-4748

Circa 1746. Built prior to the Revolutionary
War, the Pratt House is an out-
standing example of center
chimney Colonial-style architecture. The slate blue
National Register inn
includes many original features, including six working

fireplaces, hand-hewn beams and wide board floors. A beehive oven and built-in corner cupboard also are original to the house. Four-poster beds, Oriental rugs and period furnishings create an elegant New England country inn ambiance. One guest room includes a whirlpool tub. Breakfasts are multi-course and include items such as homemade muffins or scones, a fresh fruit plate and entrees such as heart-shaped blueberry pancakes or eggs Benedict. The morning fare is served by candlelight on a table set with fine china, crystal and silver. After breakfasts, guests have many choices. There are a variety of historic house museums to visit, including the William Hart house, which is across the street. In addition, there is a century-old ice cream parlor, galleries and antique shops to enjoy. Beaches, state park and river cruises are other options.

Innkeeper(s): Shelley Nobile. $95-190. MC, VISA, AX, PC, TC. TAC8. 3 rooms with PB, 3 with FP, 1 suite and 1 conference room. Breakfast, afternoon tea and snacks/refreshments included in rates. Types of meals: Full bkfst and cont. Beds: QT. Cable TV, phone, turndown service and VCR in room. Air conditioning. Fax, library, guest refrigerator with complimentary soft drinks and massage therapy on premises. Weddings, small meetings, family reunions and seminars hosted. Antiquing, art galleries, beaches, bicycling, canoeing/kayaking, fishing, golf, hiking, casino, playhouses, tennis and wineries nearby.

Plymouth Village C4

Shelton House B&B

663 Main St (Rt 6)
Plymouth Village, CT 06782
(860)283-4616 Fax:(860)283-4616

Circa 1825. This home's most famous resident was a carriage maker whose wares were sold as far away as Chicago. The Greek Revival is listed in the National Register and was a stop on the town's bicentennial homes tour. Antiques and reproductions decorate the interior. Beds are topped with fine quality linens and soft, fluffy comforters. There are three tranquil acres of grounds, shaded by trees. After breakfast, guests can take a trip to historic Litchfield, which is just 12 miles down the road. Antique shops, restaurants, skiing and other activities are all nearby.

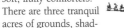

Innkeeper(s): Pat & Bill Doherty. $75-95. PC, TC. 4 rooms, 2 with PB. Breakfast and afternoon tea included in rates. Type of meal: Full bkfst. Beds: QDT. Robes, window fans and alarm clocks in room. Air conditioning. Fax, pineapple fountain and perrenial gardens on premises. Amusement parks, antiquing, fishing, golf, soaring center, live theater, museums, parks, shopping and cross-country skiing nearby.

"Accommodations were excellent. Breakfast was great. I was pampered and I loved it."

Salisbury A2

Under Mountain Inn

482 Under Mountain Rd
Salisbury, CT 06068-1104
(860)435-0242 Fax:(860)435-2379

Circa 1732. Situated on three acres, this was originally the home of iron magnate Jonathan Scoville. A thorned locust tree, believed to be the oldest in Connecticut, shades the inn.

Under Mountain Inn
Salisbury, Connecticut

Paneling that now adorns the pub was discovered hidden between the pub and attic floorboards. The boards were probably placed there in violation of a Colonial law requiring all wide lumber to be given to the king of England. British-born Peter Higginson was happy to reclaim it in the name of the Crown.

Historic Interest: Several Blast Furnaces (6-10 miles), The Salisbury Cannon Museum (5 1/2 miles), Holley-Williams House (5 1/2 miles), Colonel Ashley House (7 miles).

Innkeeper(s): Peter & Marged Higginson. $170-215. TAC10. 7 rooms with PB. Breakfast, afternoon tea and dinner included in rates. Restaurant on premises. Beds: KQD. Air conditioning. VCR and fax on premises. Weddings and small meetings hosted. Music nearby.

Publicity: *Travel & Leisure, Country Inns, Yankee, Connecticut, Country Accents.*

"You're terrific!"

Simsbury B5

Simsbury 1820 House

731 Hopmeadow St
Simsbury, CT 06070-2238
(860)658-7658 (800)879-1820 Fax:(860)651-0724

Circa 1820. This graciously restored country manor was originally home to the son of an American Revolutionary War hero. In the heart of the scenic Farmington Valley, it was also home to generations of distinguished American families, including Gifford Pinchot, father of the American Conservation Movement. The rooms are decorated with fabrics, wall hangings and reproductions reminiscent of the 18th and 19th centuries. Charming antiques grace meandering nooks and crannies. Over-stuffed chairs and comfortable beds, including many four-posters, invite complete relaxation.

Historic Interest: Hillstead Museum (6 miles), Stanley Whitman House (7 miles), Mark Twain House (12 miles), Massocoh Plantation (one-half mile).

Innkeeper(s): Diane Ropiak. $135-195. MC, VISA, AX, DC, DS. 32 rooms with PB, 3 suites and 4 conference rooms. Breakfast included in rates. Type of meal: Cont. Dinner, banquet service and room service available. Restaurant on premises. Beds: KQ. Cable TV, phone, VCR and hair dryers in room. Air conditioning. Weddings, small meetings, family reunions and seminars hosted. Amusement parks, antiquing, fishing, live theater, shopping, downhill skiing, cross-country skiing, sporting events and water sports nearby.

Tolland B7

Tolland Inn

63 Tolland Green, PO Box 717
Tolland, CT 06084-0717
(860)872-0800 (877)465-0800 Fax:(860)870-7958

Circa 1790. This late 18th-century Colonial offers seven guest rooms, two with sitting rooms. A first-floor room and second-floor suite each offer both a hot tub and fireplace. All rooms have private baths, air conditioning and phones. The inn is decorated in antiques and hand-built furniture throughout. Susan was raised in Nantucket and is a third-generation innkeeper, while Stephen is a designer and builder of fine furniture. Guests are invited to enjoy breakfast and afternoon tea, fireside in cool weather. The inn is convenient to UCONN, Old Sturbridge Village, Brimfield Antique Shows, Caprilands.

Innkeeper(s): Susan & Stephen Beeching. $75-150. MC, VISA, AX, DC, CB, DS, PC, TC. TAC10. 7 rooms with PB, 3 with FP, 2 suites and 1 conference room. Breakfast and afternoon tea included in rates. Types of meals: Full gourmet bkfst and early coffee/tea. Beds: KQDT. Phone in room. VCR, fax, spa and library on premises. Small meetings, family reunions and seminars hosted. Antiquing, fishing, live theater, parks, shopping, cross-country skiing and sporting events nearby.

Publicity: *Journal Inquirer, Hartford Courant, Tolland County Times.*

Watertown   D4

Addington's B&B

1002 Middlebury Rd
Watertown, CT 06795-3025
(860)274-2647 (877)250-9711

Circa 1840. Addington's is a beautifully preserved Italianate home, once part of a 19th-century dairy farm. Guests can relax on the porch swing or take in the view from the widow's walk. The interior is decorated in country style accented by quilts, dolls

and collectibles, many of which are made by the innkeeper and available for purchase. One guest room includes a Jacuzzi tub. The B&B is close to a multitude of antique shops, as well as outdoor activities.

Historic Interest: Litchfield Country (5 miles), antique shops.

Innkeeper(s): Jan Lynn & Eric Addington. $80-125. MC, VISA, PC, TC. 3 rooms, 1 with PB. Breakfast and snacks/refreshments included in rates. Types of meals: Full bkfst, cont plus, cont, veg bkfst and early coffee/tea. Beds: KQ. Cable TV and VCR in room. Library on premises. Amusement parks, antiquing, art galleries, beaches, canoeing/kayaking, fishing, golf, hiking, horseback riding, museums, parks, shopping, downhill skiing, cross-country skiing, sporting events, tennis and water sports nearby.

Westport   G3

The Inn at National Hall

2 Post Rd W
Westport, CT 06880-4203
(203)221-1351 (800)628-4255 Fax:(203)221-0276
Web: www.innatnationalhall.com

Circa 1873. This exquisite inn is consistently named as one of the nation's best, and it is quite deserving of its four-star and five-diamond rating. The inn is situated on the Saugatuck River and guests can meander by the water on the boardwalk. The renovation of this National Register gem cost upwards of $15 million, and the result is evident. Rooms are masterfully

appointed with the finest fabrics and furnishings. The Acorn Room is a stunning example. Walls are painted a deep red hue, and guests slumber atop a massive canopy bed enveloped in luxurious yellow fabrics. The conference room is filled with regal touches. Guests can enjoy a European-style continental breakfast in the Drawing Room. There are ample amenities, valet and room service. Gourmet dinners can be enjoyed at the inn's restaurant. Westport's posh boutiques, art galleries and antique shops are a stone's throw away.

Innkeeper(s): Steve Schapiro. $200-625. MC, VISA, AX, DC, TC. TAC10. 8 rooms with PB, 1 with FP, 7 suites and 1 conference room. Breakfast included in rates. Types of meals: Cont plus and early coffee/tea. Gourmet dinner, lunch and room service available. Restaurant on premises. Beds: KQT. Cable TV, phone, turndown service and VCR in room. Air conditioning. Fax and copier on premises. Weddings, small meetings, family reunions and seminars hosted. Antiquing, beaches, live theater, parks, shopping and tennis nearby.

Publicity: *Architectural Digest, Country Inns.*

Woodstock   B9

Elias Child House B&B

50 Perrin Rd
Woodstock, CT 06281
(860)974-9836 (877)974-9836
E-mail: tfelice@compuserve.com
Web: www.eliaschildhouse.com

Circa 1700. Nine fireplaces warm this heritage three-story colonial home, referred to as "the mansion house" by early settlers. There are two cooking fireplaces, both walk-in size and a bee-hive oven. Original floors, twelve-over-twelve windows and paneling remain. A bountiful breakfast is served fireside in the dining room and a screened porch and a patio provide nesting spots for reading and

relaxing. The inn's grounds are spacious and offer a pool and hammocks. Woodland walks on the 47 acres and antiquing are popular activities.

Innkeeper(s): Anthony Felice, Jr. & MaryBeth Gorke-Felice. $95-120. MC, VISA, DS, PC, TC. TAC10. 3 rooms with PB and 1 suite. Breakfast included in rates. Types of meals: Full bkfst and early coffee/tea. Beds: QDT. Turndown service in room. VCR, fax, copier, swimming and bicycles on premises. Small meetings and family reunions hosted. Cooking demonstrations and cross-country skiing nearby.

Pets allowed: Small dogs with cage.

Publicity: *Journal Inquirer, Forbes, Hartford Courant, Yankee Traveler, Connecticut Magazine.*

"Comfortable rooms and delightful country ambiance."

Delaware

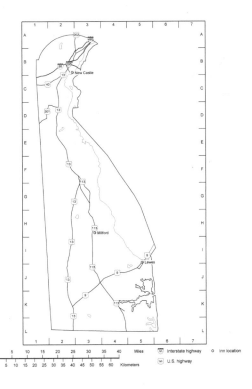

Lewes   I5

The Bay Moon B&B

128 Kings Hwy
Lewes, DE 19958-1418
(302)644-1802 (800)917-2307 Fax:(302)644-1802

Circa 1887. The exterior of this three-story, cedar Victorian features a front veranda shrouded by the flowers and foliage that also decorate the front walk. The custom-made, hand-crafted beds in the guest rooms are topped with feather pillows and down comforters. A champagne turndown service is available, and wine is served each evening. The innkeeper offers plenty of ameni-

ties. Beach supplies and a heated outdoor shower are helpful for guests who want to enjoy the ocean.

Historic Interest: Bay Moon is located in historic Lewes, Del., the first town in the first state. A wildlife sanctuary and Cape Henlopen State Park, with its four miles of preserved beaches, are nearby.

Innkeeper(s): Pamela Rizzo. $95-150. MC, VISA, PC, TC. 4 rooms with PB and 1 suite. Breakfast included in rates. EP. Types of meals: Full bkfst and early coffee/tea. Snacks/refreshments available. Beds: KQ. Cable TV, ceiling fan and VCR in room. Central air. Fax, spa, library and outdoor Jacuzzi on premises. Weddings, small meetings and family reunions hosted. Antiquing, fishing, beach, live theater, parks, shopping, sporting events and water sports nearby.

Kings Inn

151 Kings Hwy
Lewes, DE 19958-1459
(302)645-6438

Circa 1888. This nine-bedroom Victorian features high ceilings, stained-glass windows and hardwood floors. The decor is eclectic. A Jacuzzi tub for two, backyard wisteria arbor,  enclosed porch and bicycles are offerings. Breakfast is served in the sunroom and usually includes freshly baked items such as cranberry nut bread or cinnamon scones. Lewes dates from 1631 and offers an interesting collection of historic houses and churches. The Cape May Ferry is here, as well as deep sea charters. One of the largest outlet malls in the United States is nearby.

Innkeeper(s): Patricia & Leon Rockett. $65-85. MC, VISA, DS, PC, TC. TAC10. 5 rooms, 3 with PB. Breakfast included in rates. Type of meal: Early coffee/tea. Beds: KQDT. Ceiling fan in room. Air conditioning. VCR, spa, sauna, bicycles, tennis, library, pet boarding, pool table and Compac on premises. Small meetings hosted. German, Spanish and French spoken. Amusement parks, antiquing, fishing, golf, live theater, parks, shopping, sporting events, tennis and water sports nearby.

Pets Allowed.

Wild Swan Inn

525 Kings Hwy
Lewes, DE 19958-1421
(302)645-8550 Fax:(302)645-8550

Circa 1900. This Queen Anne Victorian is a whimsical sight, painted in pink with white, green and burgundy trim. The interior is dotted with antiques and dressed in Victorian style. A full, gourmet breakfast and freshly ground coffee are served each morning. The innkeepers have placed many musical treasures in their inn, including an early Edison phonograph and a Victrola. Michael often serenades guests on a 1912 player piano during breakfast. Lewes, which was founded in 1631, is

the first town in the first state. Wild Swan is within walking distance of downtown where several fine restaurants await you. Nearby Cape Henlopen State Park offers hiking and water-sports, and the surrounding countryside is ideal for cycling and other outdoor activities. Listed in the National Trust for Historic Preservation, the inn was 3rd place winner in Jones Dairy Farm National Cooking Contest for B&B Inns.

Innkeeper(s): Michael & Hope Tyler. $85-150. PC, TC. 3 rooms with PB. Breakfast and snacks/refreshments included in rates. Types of meals: Full gourmet bkfst and early coffee/tea. Beds: Q. Turndown service in room. Air conditioning. Swimming, bicycles, library, player piano, Edison & Victrola phonographs and music entertainment on premises. Antiquing, fishing, birding, bicycling, museums, live theater, parks, shopping and water sports nearby.

"The house is beautiful with lovely detailed pieces. Mike and Hope are gracious hosts. You'll sleep like a baby and wake up to a scrumptious breakfast and a great concert!"

Milford   H3

The Towers B&B

101 NW Front St
Milford, DE 19963-1022
(302)422-3814 (800)366-3814
E-mail: mispillion@exon.com
Web: www.mispillion.com

Circa 1783. Once a simple colonial house, this ornate Steamboat Gothic fantasy features every imaginable Victorian architectural detail, all added in 1891. There are 10 distinct styles of gingerbread as well as towers, turrets, gables, porches and bays. Inside, chestnut and cherry woodwork, window seats and stained-glass windows are complemented with American and French antiques. The back garden boasts a gazebo porch and swimming pool. Ask for the splendid Tower Room or Rapunzel Suite.

Historic Interest: Historic districts in Milford, town of Lewes, Dickinson Plantation, historic city of Dover.

Innkeeper(s): Daniel & Rhonda Bond. $95-135. MC, VISA, AX. TAC15. 6 rooms with PB and 2 suites. Breakfast included in rates. Beds: QD. TV and ceiling fan in room. Air conditioning. Swimming on premises. Russian spoken. Antiquing, fishing, live theater, parks, shopping and water sports nearby.

Publicity: *Washington Post, Baltimore Sun, Washingtonian, Mid-Atlantic Country.*

"I felt as if I were inside a beautiful Victorian Christmas card, surrounded by all the things Christmas should be."

New Castle   B2

Armitage Inn

2 The Strand
New Castle, DE 19720-4826
(302)328-6618 Fax:(302)324-1163

Circa 1732. The major portion of this historic home was constructed in the early 1730s, but the back wing may have been constructed in the 17th century. For centuries, the Armitage has been a place of elegance, and its current state as a country inn is no exception. Deluxe bed linens, fluffy towels, canopy beds and whirlpool tubs are just a few of the romantic amenities guests might find in their quarters. Gourmet coffee and teas accompany the breakfasts of fruit, cereal, yogurt, homemade baked goods and a special entree.

Innkeeper(s): Stephen & Rina Marks. $105-150. MC, VISA, AX, DS. TAC10. 5 rooms with PB, 3 with FP. Breakfast included in rates. Type of meal: Full gourmet bkfst. Beds: KQ. Cable TV, phone, ceiling fan, whirlpool bath in two rooms and hair dryer in room. Air conditioning. Fax, copier, library, riverwalk, Battery Park and summer concerts on premises. Amusement parks, antiquing, fishing, tennis, live theater, parks and shopping nearby.

"I could not have dreamed of a lovelier place to wake up on Christmas morning."

Terry House B&B

130 Delaware St
New Castle, DE 19720-4814
(302)322-2505 Fax:(302)328-1987

Circa 1860. In the center of the historic area, the Terry House is a three-and-a-half-story brick Federal townhouse with long double verandas, overlooking a half acre of beautifully landscaped back gardens that slope down to Battery Park which fronts on the Delaware River. Inside the inn, frieze work, ornately carved woodwork and red pine floors are elegantly set off with Oriental rugs, period antiques and paintings. Guest rooms look out to the park or onto Market Square and the Court House. Breakfast casseroles, breads and fruit

are served in the dining room. New Castle was surveyed by Peter Stuyvesant in 1651 and William Penn landed here in 1682. Museums and gardens are abundant and include Longwood Gardens, Winterthur Museum, Brandywine River Museum, and Nemour Mansion and Gardens.

Innkeeper(s): Greg & Margaret Bell, Evelyn Weston. $90-98. MC, VISA, AX, DS, PC, TC. 4 rooms with PB. Breakfast included in rates. Type of meal: Cont plus. Beds: Q. Cable TV and phone in room. Air conditioning. Fax on premises. Weddings and small meetings hosted. Antiquing, golf, Longwood Gardens, Winterthier, parks, sporting events and tennis nearby.

Florida

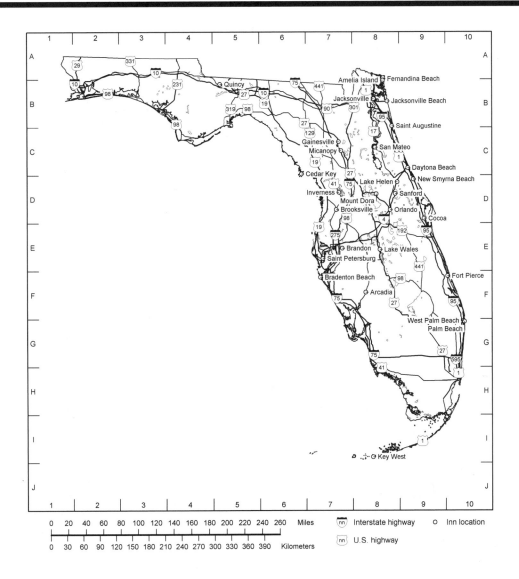

1	2	3	4	5	6	7	8	9	10	

0 20 40 60 80 100 120 140 160 180 200 220 240 260   Miles

0 30 60 90 120 150 180 210 240 270 300 330 360 390   Kilometers

nn Interstate highway   ○ Inn location

nn U.S. highway

83

Amelia Island   B8

1857 Florida House Inn

PO Box 688, 22 S 3rd St
Amelia Island, FL 32034-4207
(904)261-3300 (800)258-3301 Fax:(904)277-3831
E-mail: innkeepers@floridahouseinn.com
Web: www.floridahouseinn.com

Circa 1857. Located in the heart of a 50-block historic National Register area, the Florida House Inn is thought to be the oldest continuously operating tourist hotel in Florida. Recently renovated, the inn features a small pub, guest parlor, library and a New Orleans-style courtyard in which guests may enjoy the shade of 200-year-old oaks. Rooms are decorated with country pine and oak antiques, cheerful handmade rugs and quilts, and 10 rooms offer fireplaces and Jacuzzi tubs. The Carnegies, Rockefellers and Ulysses S. Grant have been guests.

Innkeeper(s): Bob & Karen Warner. $70-170. MC, VISA, AX. 15 rooms with PB, 10 with FP, 1 suite and 1 conference room. Breakfast included in rates. Types of meals: Full bkfst and early coffee/tea. Dinner, picnic lunch, lunch and catering service available. Restaurant on premises. Beds: KQT. Cable TV, phone, ceiling fan and 10 Jacuzzi tubs in room. Air conditioning. Fax and copier on premises. Handicap access. Small meetings, family reunions and seminars hosted. Antiquing, fishing, live theater and sporting events nearby.

Amelia Island Williams House

103 S 9th St
Amelia Island, FL 32034-3616
(904)277-2328 (800)414-9257 Fax:(904)321-1325
E-mail: topinn@aol.com
Web: www.williamshouse.com

Circa 1856. It's not this grand Antebellum mansion's first owner, but its second for whom the house is named. Marcellus Williams and his wife, a great-great-granddaughter of the King of Spain, are its most esteemed residents. Among their many influential guests, the two once hosted Jefferson Davis, and, ironically, the first owners used part of the home for the Underground Railroad. It will be hard for guests to believe that the home was anything but opulent. The innkeepers painstakingly restored the home and the result is fabulous. Antiques from nine different countries decorate the home. The guest rooms are romantic; the gourmet breakfast served on the finest china; and the lush, fragrant grounds are shaded by a 500-year-old oak tree. The innkeepers also have restored the historic home next door, which was used as an infirmary during the Civil War. Four of the guest rooms are housed here, complete with clawfoot or Jacuzzi tubs.

Innkeeper(s): Dick Flitz & Chris Carter. $145-225. MC, VISA, PC. TAC10. 8 rooms with PB, 5 with FP and 2 suites. Breakfast and afternoon tea included in rates. Type of meal: Full gourmet bkfst. Beds: KT. Cable TV, phone, turndown service, ceiling fan, VCR and daily maid service in room. Air conditioning. Fax, copier, bicycles and video Library on premises. Handicap access. Family reunions hosted. Antiquing, fishing, golf, zoo, live theater, parks, shopping, sporting events, tennis and water sports nearby.

Bailey House

28 S 7th St
Amelia Island, FL 32034-3960
(904)261-5390 (800)251-5390 Fax:(904)321-0103
E-mail: bailey@net-magic.net
Web: www.bailey-house.com

Circa 1895. This elegant Queen Anne Victorian was a wedding present that steamship agent Effingham W. Bailey gave to his bride. He shocked the locals by spending the enormous sum of $10,000 to build the house with all its towers, turrets, gables and verandas. The parlor and dining room open to a fireplace in a reception hall with the inscription "Hearth Hall - Welcome All." A spirit of hospitality has reigned in this home from its beginning.

Historic Interest: The historic seaport is within walking distance, Fort Clinch (2 miles).

Innkeeper(s): Tom & Jenny Bishop. $105-175. MC, VISA, AX, PC. TAC10. 10 rooms with PB, 7 with FP. Breakfast included in rates. AP. Types of meals: Full bkfst and early coffee/tea. Beds: KQDT. Cable TV, phone and ceiling fan in room. Air conditioning. Fax, copier and bicycles on premises. Small meetings hosted. Antiquing, fishing, golf, history museum, live theater, parks, shopping, sporting events, tennis and water sports nearby.

"Well, here we are back at Mickey Mouse land. I think we prefer the lovely Bailey House!"

Elizabeth Pointe Lodge

98 S Fletcher Ave
Amelia Island, FL 32034-2216
(904)277-4851 (800)772-3359 Fax:(904)277-6500

Circa 1991. Situated directly on the ocean, this newly constructed inn is in an 1890s Nantucket shingle-style design. Guest rooms feature king-size beds and oversized tubs. Several rooms have private whirlpools.

Lemonade is served on the porch, which is filled with rockers for viewing the sea and its treasures of pelicans, dolphins and sea birds. Touring bikes, beach equipment and airport pickup are available.

Innkeeper(s): David & Susan Caples. $150-245. MC, VISA, AX, DS. 25 rooms with PB, 2 suites and 1 conference room. Breakfast included in rates. Picnic lunch, lunch, catering service and room service available. Beds: KQ. Cable TV, phone, newspaper and flowers in room. Air conditioning. Fax and copier on premises. Small meetings, family reunions and seminars hosted. Antiquing, fishing, live theater, shopping and water sports nearby.

"The innkeeper's labor of love is evident in every detail. Outstanding. Superb accommodations and service."

The Fairbanks House

227 S 7th St
Amelia Island, FL 32034
(904)277-0500 (888)891-9939 Fax:(904)277-3103
E-mail: fairbanks@net-magic.net
Web: www.fairbankshouse.com

Circa 1885. The living and dining room fireplace tiles of this Italianate-style mansion bring to life scenes from Shakespeare's works and "Aesop's Fables." Other features include polished

hardwood floors, intricately carved moldings and eight other fireplaces that grace spacious rooms. Each of the guest rooms is furnished with a four-poster or canopied king, queen or twin bed, Jacuzzi and clawfoot tubs or showers. Guests can step outside to enjoy an inviting courtyard, swimming pool and gardens bursting with roses, palms and magnolias. The Fairbanks was named one of the "Top 10 Luxury Inns In America" by Country Inns Magazine.

Innkeeper(s): Bill & Theresa Hamilton. $150-250. MC, VISA, AX, DS. TAC10. 12 rooms with PB, 9 with FP, 3 suites and 3 cottages. Breakfast included in rates. Type of meal: Full gourmet bkfst. Beds: KQT. Cable TV, phone, ceiling fan, hair dryer and ironing board in room. Air conditioning. Swimming, bicycles, beach towels and beach chairs on premises. Antiquing, beaches, fishing, golf, restaurants, live theater, parks, shopping, sporting events, tennis and water sports nearby.

Walnford Inn

102 S 7th St
Amelia Island, FL 32034-3923
(904)277-4941 (800)277-6660 Fax:(904)277-4646

Circa 1904. Two Victorian homes comprise the inn, situated behind a handsome white picket fence and one block from downtown Centre Street. A library and several porches are favorite guest respites. Guest rooms include features such as whirlpool tubs, private balconies, antique bedsteads and Oriental carpets. The innkeepers offer bicycles and can arrange for special activities such as a carriage ride through the historic district or horseback riding on the beach.

Innkeeper(s): Linda & Bob Waln. $75-145. MC, VISA, AX, DS, PC, TC. TAC10. 9 rooms. Breakfast included in rates. Type of meal: Full bkfst. Afternoon tea available. Beds: KQD. Cable TV, phone and ceiling fan in room. Air conditioning. Fax and copier on premises. Handicap access. Weddings, small meetings and family reunions hosted. Antiquing, fishing, golf, live theater, parks, tennis and water sports nearby.

Arcadia F8

Historic Parker House

427 W Hickory St
Arcadia, FL 34266-3703
(863)494-2499 (800)969-2499

Circa 1895. Period antiques, including a wonderful clock collection, grace the interior of this turn-of-the-century home, which was built by a local cattle baron. Along with two charming rooms and a bright, "yellow" suite, innkeepers Shelly and Bob Baumann added the spacious Blue Room, which offers a

white iron and brass bed and clawfoot bathtub. An expanded continental breakfast with pastries, fresh fruits, cereals, muffins and a variety of beverages is offered each morning, and afternoon teas can be prepared on request.

Historic Interest: The home, which is listed in the National Register, is within walking distance of historic downtown Arcadia with more than 350 buildings also listed on the register.

Innkeeper(s): Bob & Shelly Baumann. $69-85. MC, VISA, AX, TC. 4 rooms, 2 with PB, 2 with FP and 1 conference room. Breakfast and afternoon tea included in rates. Types of meals: Cont plus and early coffee/tea. Room service available. Beds: QDT. Cable TV, phone and ceiling fan in room. Air conditioning. Small meetings and family reunions hosted. Antiquing, fishing, historical sites, parks, shopping and water sports nearby.

Publicity: *Tampa Tribune, Desoto Sun Herald, Florida Travel & Life, Miami Herald (Palm Beach Edition), WINK-TV News.*

"Everything was first class and very comfortable."

Sandusky Manor B&B & Victorian Tea Room

606 E Oak St
Arcadia, FL 34266-4630
(941)494-7338 (800)348-5057

Circa 1913. This bungalow is named for its first resident, Carl Sandusky. The interior is comfortable and eclectic. There are collectibles, photographs, quilts, lanterns and old clocks throughout. Breakfasts with freshly baked biscuits, sweet rolls, fruit and egg dishes are served in the dining room or on the front porch. In the evenings, the innkeepers serve coffee, tea and dessert. Antique shops in historic downtown Arcadia, swamp buggy tours, golf and horseback riding are among the area attractions.

Innkeeper(s): Wayne & Judy Haligus. $65-75. MC, VISA, AX, DC, DS, TC. 4 rooms, 3 with PB. Breakfast and snacks/refreshments included in rates. AP. Types of meals: Full bkfst and early coffee/tea. Dinner, picnic lunch and lunch available. Beds: KQDT. Ceiling fan and VCR in room. Air conditioning. Small garden w/benches & table for our guests on premises. Weddings, small meetings and family reunions hosted. Antiquing, fishing, golf, canoeing and shopping nearby.

"The southern hospitality you provided was to die for!"

Brandon E7

Behind The Fence B&B Inn

1400 Viola Dr at Countryside
Brandon, FL 33511-7327
(813)685-8201 (800)448-2672

Circa 1976. Experience the charm of New England on Florida's west coast at this secluded country inn surrounded by tall pines and oaks. Although the frame of the home was built in the mid-1970s, the innkeepers searched Hillsborough County for 19th-century and turn-of-the-century artifacts, including old stairs, doors, windows, a pantry and the back porch. Guests can stay either in the main house or in a two-bedroom cottage. All rooms are filled with antique Amish-county furniture. The innkeepers serve fresh popcorn on cool nights in front of the fireplace. Breakfast includes fresh fruit, cereals, juices, coffees and delicious Amish sweet rolls.

Historic Interest: The inn is a short distance from historic Ybor City, known as Tampa's second city.

Innkeeper(s): Larry & Carolyn Yoss. $59-79. PC, TC. TAC7. 5 rooms, 3 with PB, 1 suite, 1 cottage and 1 conference room. Breakfast, afternoon tea and snacks/refreshments included in rates. Types of meals: Cont plus and early coffee/tea. Beds: DT. Cable TV, phone and VCR in room. Air conditioning. Swimming on premises. Small meetings and seminars hosted. Amusement parks, antiquing, fishing, river canoeing, horseback riding, night bicycle rides (groups), live theater, parks, shopping, sporting events and water sports nearby.

Publicity: *Brandon News, Travel Host, Country Living.*

"One of the best kept secrets in all of Tampa! Thanks again!"

Brooksville D7

Verona House

201 S Main St
Brooksville, FL 34601-3337
(352)796-4001 (800)355-6717 Fax:(352)799-0612

Circa 1925. In the 1920s, the Verona was one of several styles of homes available to buyers through the Sears-Roebuck catalog. This inn arrived by train along with an instruction book. Obviously, its builder follow the directions, and now guests enjoy this charming Dutch Colonial. There are four rooms inside the house, and the innkeepers also offer a cottage with a kitchen and covered deck. Antique shopping and many outdoor activities are all nearby.

Innkeeper(s): Bob & Jan Boyd. $55-80. MC, VISA, AX, DS, PC, TC. TAC10. 4 rooms with PB and 1 cottage. Breakfast and afternoon tea included in rates. Types of meals: Full bkfst, cont plus, cont and early coffee/tea. Room service available. Beds: QT. Ceiling fan in room. Air conditioning. VCR, fax, copier and spa on premises. Handicap access. Weddings, small meetings and family reunions hosted. Antiquing, fishing, golf, live theater, parks, shopping, tennis and water sports nearby.

Cedar Key C6

Island Hotel

2nd & B St
Cedar Key, FL 32625
(352)543-5111 (800)432-4640
E-mail: info@islandhotel-cedarkey.com
Web: www.islandhotel-cedarkey.com

Circa 1859. The history of Island Hotel begins at about the same time as the history of Cedar Key. Constructed from seashell tabby with oak supports, the hotel and its walls have withstood wind

and weather for a century and a half. Owners and innkeepers Dawn and Tony Cousins have worked to restore the home's traditional charm. Some rooms boast views of the Gulf or Back Bayou. All rooms include access to the inn's balcony, an ideal spot for relaxation. A casual, gourmet seafood restaurant is located on the premises, promising a delightful array of local catch, and Neptune Bar, also at the inn, is open to guests and locals.

Historic Interest: 1859 building has original murals dating from 1915 and 1948.

Innkeeper(s): Dawn & Tony Cousins. $75-110. MC, VISA, DS, TC. 13 rooms with PB. Breakfast included in rates. Type of meal: Full gourmet bkfst. Restaurant on premises. Beds: QD. Air conditioning. Weddings, small meetings, family reunions and seminars hosted. Antiquing, fishing, parks, sporting events and water sports nearby.

86

Cocoa D9

Indian River House

3113 Indian River Dr
Cocoa, FL 32922-6501
(321)631-5660 Fax:(321)631-5268

Circa 1900. Built at the turn of the 20th century, this historic home offers four comfortable guest rooms. The home is casually decorated, and a few antiques have been placed among the furnishings. The home is located along the Intracoastal Waterway, and guests only have to walk a few feet to reach the inn's dock where they can fish or just enjoy the scenery. Breakfasts include items

such as freshly baked biscuits, fresh fruit, eggs Benedict or perhaps French toast. In the late afternoons, wine, cheese and iced tea is served on the patio, which features a cistern original to the house. The home offers close access to many attractions, including the sites of Orlando, the Daytona Speedway, canoeing, kayaking and biking. Space shuttle launches can be seen from the front porch.

Historic Interest: Historic Cocoa Village (3 miles).

$85-90. MC, VISA, AX, PC, TC. 4 rooms with PB, 2 with FP. Breakfast included in rates. AP. Types of meals: Full bkfst and veg bkfst. Beds: KQ. Central air. VCR, fax, copier, bicycles and library on premises. Antiquing, art galleries, beaches, bicycling, canoeing/kayaking, fishing, horseback riding, live theater, museums, parks, shopping, tennis and water sports nearby.

Daytona Beach C9

Coquina Inn B&B

544 S Palmetto Ave
Daytona Beach, FL 32114-4924
(904)254-4969 (800)805-7533

Circa 1912. Located in the Daytona Beach Historic District, this handsome house boasts an exterior of coquina rock blended from shells, arched windows, and a picket porch on the second floor. The Jasmine Room is accentuated with a seven-foot canopy bed draped in a delicate netting. French leather chairs, a fireplace and a Victorian tub are featured. The Hibiscus Room is decorated with wicker furnishings, and includes French doors that lead to a private balcony.

Historic Interest: Sugar Mill Gardens (5 miles), Gamble House (8 miles), Tomoka State Park & Museum (14 miles).

Innkeeper(s): Ann Christoffersen & Dennis Haight. $80-110. MC, VISA, AX. 4 rooms with PB, 1 with FP. Breakfast included in rates. Type of meal: Full gourmet bkfst. Beds: QD. TV and ceiling fan in room. Air conditioning. Bicycles on premises. Antiquing, fishing, live theater, shopping, sporting events and water sports nearby.

Publicity: *Florida Sports, Sun Sentinel, Southern Living, Miami Herald.*

"Better than chocolate. A little bit of heaven on earth."

The Villa

801 N Peninsula Dr
Daytona Beach, FL 32118-3724
(904)248-2020 Fax:(904)248-2020

Circa 1926. This Spanish Revival manor is listed in the National Register of Historic Places and is located within walking distance of the beach. The acre-and-a-half grounds are tropical, highlighted by soaring palm trees. The interior boasts many original elements, as well as stenciled ceilings and artwork. Rooms, with names such as the Queen Isabella and Christopher Columbus, honor the state's history of Spanish exploration. Within an hour of Daytona Beach, guests can reach Orlando, St. Augustine and Cape Canaveral or stay and explore Daytona, which offers plenty of shopping and restaurants, as well as the ocean.

Innkeeper(s): Jim Camp. $100-250. MC, VISA, AX, TC. 4 rooms with PB. Breakfast included in rates. AP. Types of meals: Cont plus and early coffee/tea. Beds: KQ. Cable TV and ceiling fan in room. Air conditioning. VCR, fax, copier, spa and swimming on premises. Weddings, small meetings and family reunions hosted. Antiquing, fishing, golf, live theater, parks, shopping, sporting events, tennis and water sports nearby.

Fernandina Beach   A8

The 1735 House and Amelia Island Lodging Systems

584 S Fletcher Ave
Fernandina Beach, FL 32034-2226
(904)261-4148 (800)872-8531 Fax:(904)261-9200
E-mail: frontdesk@1735house-bb.com
Web: www.1735house-bb.com

Circa 1938. Perched at the edge of the Atlantic, the inn is just 15 steps across the sand to the ocean (any closer and it would be below the tide line). All rooms in this New England clapboard-style inn are actually suites. Antiques, wicker and rattan add to the decor and comfort. The sixth suite is a lighthouse on the beach. Breakfast is delivered to your suite in a wicker picnic basket. The innkeepers can help you arrange day fishing, horseback riding along the white sandy beaches, or restaurant reservations.

Historic Interest: Fernandina Beach, downtown historical block and harbor (1 mile).

Innkeeper(s): William & Paul Auld. $105-170. MC, VISA, DS, PC, TC. 6 suites. Breakfast included in rates. Type of meal: Cont. Snacks/refreshments available. Beds: QD. Cable TV, turndown service and ceiling fan in room. Central air. Fax, copier and swimming on premises. Antiquing, art galleries, beaches, bicycling, canoeing/kayaking, fishing, golf, hiking, horseback riding, museums, parks, shopping, tennis and water sports nearby.

"It was a delightful surprise to find a typical old New England Nautical inn in Florida with the charm of Cape Cod and warm ocean breezes and waves lapping at the door."

Greyfield Inn

PO Box 900
Fernandina Beach, FL 32035
(904)261-6408 Fax:(904)321-0666

Circa 1900. This elegant four-story mansion was built by the Thomas Carnegies on the barrier island of Cumberland Island. Guests seeking seclusion have the advantage of 1,300 private acres on an island most of which has been designated as a National Seashore. Only 300 persons a day are allowed to visit, a stipulation of the National Park Service. The mansion affords elegant dining opportunities and picnics are available. There's an honor bar in the old gun room, and guests enjoy mingling fireside in the living and dining room or out on the swing on the tree shaded porch. Expansive views of the Intracoastal Waterway may be seen from the inn's balcony. All guest rooms are furnished in family antiques and traditional pieces including four-poster beds, high boys and lounge chairs. Enjoy one of the inn's bicycles and tour the island to view wild horses, deer, an occasional bobcat, armadillos and a variety of birds. Hiking in the marshes, beach combing and clam digging are favored activities. Plan on making phone calls before arriving on the island since only a radio phone is available.

Innkeeper(s): Zachary Zoul, Brycea Merrill. $275-450. MC, VISA, DS, PC, TC. 17 rooms, 9 with PB, 5 suites and 2 cottages. Breakfast, afternoon tea, dinner, snacks/refreshments and picnic lunch included in rates. MAP. Types of meals: Full gourmet bkfst and early coffee/tea. Catered breakfast available. Restaurant on premises. Beds: KQDT. Turndown service and ceiling fan in room. Central air. Fax, copier, swimming, bicycles and library on premises. Weddings, small meetings, family reunions and seminars hosted. Beaches, bicycling, canoeing/kayaking, fishing, hiking, museums, parks and water sports nearby.

Gainesville   C7

Magnolia Plantation

309 SE 7th St
Gainesville, FL 32601-6831
(352)375-6653 Fax:(352)338-0303

Circa 1885. This restored French Second Empire Victorian is in the National Register. Magnolia trees surround the house. Five guest rooms are filled with family heirlooms. All bathrooms feature clawfoot tubs and candles. Guests may enjoy the gardens, reflecting pond with waterfalls and gazebo. Bicycles are also available. Evening wine and snacks are included. The inn is two miles from the University of Florida.

Innkeeper(s): Joe & Cindy Montalto. $85-150. MC, VISA, AX. TAC10. 5 rooms with PB, 5 with FP and 2 cottages. Breakfast and afternoon tea included in rates. AP. Type of meal: Full bkfst. Beds: Q. TV, turndown service and ceiling fan in room. Air conditioning. VCR, fax, bicycles and library on premises. Antiquing, live theater, parks, shopping and sporting events nearby.

"This has been a charming, once-in-a-lifetime experience."

Sweetwater Branch Inn B&B

625 E University Ave
Gainesville, FL 32601-5449
(352)373-6760 (800)595-7760 Fax:(352)371-3771
E-mail: reservations@sweetwaterinn.com
Web: www.sweetwaterinn.com

Circa 1885. Seven fountains highlight the handsome gardens of this Queen Anne Victorian, listed in the National Register. Next to the University of Florida, the inn offers a spacious banquet hall, attractive parlor and dining room and finely appointed guest rooms. Poached pears with English custard and Sweetwater Crepes are specialties of the inn. The gazebo and the inn's grounds attract special events such as weddings. The nearby historic district offers dining, theater and music.

Innkeeper(s): Cornelia Holbrook. $67-150. MC, VISA, AX, PC. TAC10. 15 rooms, 7 with PB, 7 with FP, 4 suites, 2 cottages and 3 conference rooms. Breakfast included in rates. AP. Types of meals: Full gourmet bkfst and early coffee/tea. Afternoon tea, gourmet dinner, gourmet lunch, banquet service, catering service, catered breakfast and room service available. Beds: KQDT. Cable TV, phone, turndown service and ceiling fan in room. Air conditioning. Fax, bicycles and library on premises. Handicap access. Weddings and small meetings hosted. Spanish, Italian and French spoken. Antiquing, fishing, golf, live theater, parks and sporting events nearby.

"You have met every need we could possibly have. It has been a wonderful stay."

Holmes Beach F7

Harrington House Beachfront B&B Inn

5626 Gulf Dr N
Holmes Beach, FL 34217-1666
(941)778-5444 (888)828-5566 Fax:(941)778-0527

Circa 1925. A mere 40 feet from the water, this gracious home, set among pine trees and palms, is comprised of a main house and two beach houses. Constructed of 14-inch-thick coquina blocks, the house features a living room with a 20-foot-high beamed ceiling, fireplace, '20s wallpaper and French doors. Many of the guest rooms have four-poster beds, antique wicker furnishings and French doors opening onto a deck that

overlooks the swimming pool and Gulf of Mexico. Some offer Jacuzzi-type tubs and fireplaces. Kayaks are available for dolphin watching.

Innkeeper(s): Jo & Frank Davis. $129-239. MC, VISA. 16 rooms with PB. Breakfast included in rates. Type of meal: Full bkfst. Beds: KQDT. TV, phone, ceiling fan and VCR in room. Air conditioning. Handicap access. Weddings, small meetings, family reunions and seminars hosted. Amusement parks, antiquing, fishing, live theater, shopping, sporting events and water sports nearby.

"Elegant house and hospitality."

Inverness D7

The Lake House B&B

8604 E Gospel Island Rd
Inverness, FL 34450
(352)344-3586 Fax:(352)344-3586

Circa 1930. The Lake House was built as a fishing lodge, and with its location on Big Lake Henderson, offers picturesque views of woodland and water. Guests usually arrange to be fin-

ished with daytime adventures in time to return to the inn for sunset views over the lake. A library and a huge stone fireplace are additional gathering places. Guest rooms are

furnished in a French Country decor. Miles of paved pathways entice roller skaters and cyclers to Withlacoochee State Trail nearby. There are many lakes to choose from for fishing, waterskiing and boating.

Innkeeper(s): Caroline & Blake Jenkins. $70-100. MC, VISA, PC, TC. TAC10. 5 rooms with PB. Breakfast included in rates. Type of meal: Cont plus. Beds: KQDT. Cable TV and ceiling fan in room. Central air. VCR and library on premises. Weddings and family reunions hosted. Amusement parks, antiquing, bicycling, canoeing/kayaking, fishing, golf, hiking, horseback riding, museums, parks, shopping, tennis and water sports nearby.

Pets allowed: small animals.

Jacksonville B8

House on Cherry St

1844 Cherry St
Jacksonville, FL 32205-8702
(904)384-1999 Fax:(904)384-5013

Circa 1909. Seasonal blooms fill the pots that line the circular entry stairs to this Federal-style house on tree-lined Cherry Street. It was moved in two pieces to its present site on St. Johns River in the historic Riverside area. Traditionally decorated rooms include antiques, collections of hand-carved decoy ducks and old clocks that chime and tick. Most rooms overlook the river. A canoe and kayak are available for guest use. Your host is a guidance counselor and tennis official.

Innkeeper(s): Carol Anderson. $85-105. MC, VISA, AX, PC, TC. TAC10. 4 suites. Breakfast and snacks/refreshments included in rates. Type of meal: Cont. Beds: QT. Cable TV, phone, ceiling fan, some refrigerators and flowers in room. Air conditioning. VCR, fax, copier, fishing, canoeing and kayaking on premises. Small meetings, family reunions and seminars hosted. Antiquing, fishing, canoe/kayaking on premises, live theater, parks, shopping, sporting events and water sports nearby.

Key West I8

Blue Parrot Inn

916 Elizabeth St
Key West, FL 33040-6406
(305)296-0033 (800)231-2473
Web: www.blueparrotinn.com

Circa 1884. This Bahamian-style inn is decorated in a pleasing, tropical style. The grounds are lush and peaceful. Continental-plus breakfasts of fresh fruit, bagels, muffins and quiche are served poolside. There is plenty of space around the pool to relax and tan. The inn is located in a historic neighborhood and is near shops and restaurants. The ocean is just a few blocks away.

Innkeeper(s): Larry Rhinard & Frank Yaccino. $70-170. MC, VISA, AX, DC, CB, DS, TC. TAC10. 10 rooms with PB. Breakfast included in rates. Type of meal: Cont. Beds: KQDT. Cable TV, phone and ceiling fan in room. Air conditioning. Fax, copier, swimming and bicycles on premises. Handicap access. Weddings, small meetings and family reunions hosted. Antiquing, fishing, live theater, parks, shopping and water sports nearby.

Center Court-Historic Inn & Cottages

916 Center St
Key West, FL 33040
(305)296-9292 (800)797-8787 Fax:(305)294-4104
E-mail: centerct@aol.com
Web: www.centercourtkw.com

Circa 1873. The main house at Center Court was built by a ship's captain around 1873. Three circa 1880 cottages also are located on the property, and all four buildings are listed in the National Register. In all, guests can choose from four rooms in the main guest house and 14 private cottages. The decor is contemporary with a tropical flair. The cottages include a full or efficiency kitchen, and most have private decks or verandas and spas; one has a private pool. Several cottages can accommodate four to eight guests. There are two pools, several Jacuzzis and an exercise area for guest use.

Innkeeper(s): Naomi R. Van Steelandt. $88-338. MC, VISA, AX, DS, PC, TC. TAC10. 6 rooms with PB and 12 cottages. Breakfast included in rates. Type of meal: Cont plus. Beds: KQD. TV, phone, ceiling fan, hair dryer and exercise pavilion in room. Air conditioning. VCR, fax, copier, spa, exercise pavilion and swimming pool on premises. Weddings, small meetings and family reunions hosted. Antiquing, fishing, golf, one half block off famous Duval Street, live theater, parks, shopping and water sports nearby.

Pets allowed: In cottages, $10 pet fee per night.

Publicity: *Town & Country, Florida Keys.*

Conch House Heritage Inn

625 Truman Ave
Key West, FL 33040-3233
(305)293-0020 (800)207-5806 Fax:(305)293-8447

Circa 1889. This restored Victorian inn is located in a historic Key West neighborhood and is listed in the National Register. In 1895, the home was purchased by Lance and Herminia Lester, and it has remained in the family ever since. The inn is surrounded by a picturesque white picket fence. The interior is light, airy and elegant. Walls are painted in bright colors and the home has a spacious, uncluttered feel. Rooms are appointed with elegant antiques. The continental-plus breakfast includes locally made Cuban bread.

Innkeeper(s): W. Sam Holland Jr. $88-188. MC, VISA, AX, DS, PC, TC. TAC10. 6 rooms with PB, 1 with FP. Breakfast included in rates. Type of meal: Cont plus. Beds: KQD. Cable TV, phone and ceiling fan in room. Air conditioning. Fax, copier, swimming and bicycles on premises. Handicap access. Spanish spoken. Antiquing, fishing, golf, live theater, parks, shopping, tennis and water sports nearby.

The Curry Mansion Inn

511 Caroline St
Key West, FL 33040-6604
(305)294-5349 (800)253-3466 Fax:(305)294-4093
E-mail: frontdesk@currymansion.com
Web: www.currymansion.com

Circa 1892. This three-story white Victorian was billed as the most elaborate home on Caroline Street when it was built in 1867 by Florida's first millionaire. The inn still contains original features such as bookcases, chandeliers and fireplaces, as well as an abundance of antiques. The innkeepers use the inn to display some of their beautiful collectibles, including a fami-

ly Limoges service for 120. Guests enjoy Key West's mild weather while enjoying a European-style breakfast. Piano music serenades guests at a nightly "cocktail" party with hors d'oeuvres and a full open bar.

Innkeeper(s): Albert & Edith Amsterdam. $140-275. MC, VISA, AX, DC, CB, DS, PC, TC. 28 rooms with PB and 10 suites. Breakfast and snacks/refreshments included in rates. Type of meal: Full gourmet bkfst. Beds: KQ. Cable TV, phone and ceiling fan in room. Air conditioning. VCR, fax, copier, spa, swimming, bicycles and library on premises. Handicap access. Weddings, small meetings, family reunions and seminars hosted. Antiquing, swimming, boating, fishing, live theater, shopping and water sports nearby.

Pets allowed: under 20 pounds.

Publicity: *Mariner Outboards SLAM, New York Times, Southern Living, Colonial Homes.*

"Everything was so tastefully tended to. We truly felt like 'Royalty'. We certainly will not consider returning to Key West unless we are able to book accommodations at the Curry Mansion."

Cypress House

601 Caroline St
Key West, FL 33040-6674
(305)294-6969 (800)525-2488 Fax:(305)296-1174
E-mail: cypresskw@aol.com
Web: www.cypresshousekw.com

Circa 1888. There's much to see and do in popular Key West, and Cypress House is an ideal place for those visiting the area. The National Register inn was built by one of Key West's first settlers, and it still maintains many original features. Guest rooms are airy and spacious, decorated in a variety of styles. A continental breakfast with muffins, bagels, fresh fruit and more is served daily. A cocktail hour also is included in the rates. The inn is just a block from Duval Street, which offers shops, galleries, eateries and plenty of nightlife.

Innkeeper(s): Dave Taylor. $99-275. MC, VISA, AX, DS, TC. TAC10. 14 rooms, 8 with PB and 1 suite. Breakfast included in rates. Type of meal: Cont plus. Beds: KQD. Cable TV, phone and ceiling fan in room. Air conditioning. Swimming on premises. Weddings, small meetings, family reunions and seminars hosted. Antiquing, fishing, live theater, parks, shopping and water sports nearby.

Douglas House

419 Amelia St
Key West, FL 33040-3120
(305)294-5269 (800)833-0372 Fax:(305)292-7665
Web: www.douglashouse.com

Circa 1896. This 19th-century Victorian was built during Key West's heyday of cigar production. Rooms are decorated in a contemporary tropical style. Suites with kitchens are available. The grounds include two swimming pools and a Jacuzzi. The home is three blocks from the ocean and beaches, and located right off popular Duval Street.

Innkeeper(s): Robert Marrero. $88-208. MC, VISA, AX. TAC10. 16 rooms. Breakfast and afternoon tea included in rates. Types of meals: Cont plus, cont and early coffee/tea. Beds: KQD. Cable TV, phone and ceiling fan in room. Air conditioning. Fax, copier, spa and swimming on premises. Weddings hosted. Antiquing, fishing, golf, live theater, parks, shopping, tennis and water sports nearby.

Pets Allowed.

Eaton Manor Guest House

1024 Eaton St
Key West, FL 33040-6925
(305)294-9870 (800)305-9870 Fax:(305)294-1544

Circa 1896. Nestled in a Key West historic district, Eaton Manor Guest House is just minutes from local attractions, as well as the Lands End Marina. The home features a tropical fish theme. Rooms are decorated with wicker furnishings and beds are topped with fish bedspreads, fish sheets and towels with fish motifs. Fish lamps also add to the whimsy. The front office boasts a massive saltwater aquarium and the exterior has a hand-painted mural of an underwater reef. Breakfasts include items such as homemade blueberry or chocolate chip muffins, Belgian waffles, fresh fruit and freshly brewed coffee.

Historic Interest: In the heart of old town historic district.

Innkeeper(s): Delaine, Jim & Carine Lowry. $49-249. MC, VISA, AX, DS. 23 rooms, 19 with PB. Breakfast included in rates. Type of meal: Cont. Beds: KQDT. Cable TV. Copier and spa on premises. Weddings, small meetings, family reunions and seminars hosted. French, German and Spanish spoken. Antiquing, beaches, bicycling, canoeing/kayaking, fishing, golf, harbor walk, Duval Street, live theater, shopping and water sports nearby.

Pets allowed: In two rooms only.

Eden House

1015 Fleming St
Key West, FL 33040-6962
(305)296-6868 (800)533-5397 Fax:(305)294-1221

Circa 1924. This Art Deco hotel was once a hot spot for writers, intellectuals and European travelers. Innkeeper Mike Eden improved the home, adding a 10-person Jacuzzi, decks, gazebos, an elevated sun deck, waterfalls and hammocks. Ceiling fans and wicker furniture complete the tropical atmosphere found in each room. The home was the site for the Goldie Hawn movie, "Criss Cross." Guests are served cold

refreshments upon arrival, and there is a complimentary happy hour. Caribe Soul is the inn's restaurant, offering Caribbean cuisine with specialities such as stir-fried cabbage, sweet potatoes, collard greens and crab cakes. Poolside breakfasts, although not included in the room price, offer cinnamon coffee and a variety of entrees. Smoking allowed outside only.

Innkeeper(s): Mike Eden. $55-275. MC, VISA, AX, TC. 42 rooms, 26 with PB and 6 suites. EP. Restaurant on premises. Beds: QDT. Ceiling fan in room. Air conditioning. Fax, swimming, bicycles and jacuzzi on premises. Fishing, shopping and water sports nearby.

Publicity: *Chicago Tribune, Woman's Day, Southern Living, Miami Herald.*

Heron House

512 Simonton St
Key West, FL 33040-6832
(800)294-1644 Fax:(305)294-5692
Web: www.heronhouse.com

Circa 1856. Orchid gardens in a rain forest-style landscape is an inviting aspect of Heron House, one of the oldest homes remaining in Key West. With its Conch architecture, the inn

showcases many beautiful features, including hand-crafted wood walls, marble baths, stained-glass transoms and Chicago brick patios. Rated four diamonds by AAA, there are many other amenities such as private decks and balconies and French doors. Suites with wet bars and sitting areas also are available. Duval Street is one block away, and guests can walk to restaurants and beaches or rent a bicycle or motor scooter.

Innkeeper(s): Fred Geibelt. $119-329. MC, VISA, AX, DC, CB. 23 rooms. Breakfast included in rates. Type of meal: Cont plus. Beds: KQD. Phone in room.

Paradise Inn

819 Simonton St
Key West, FL 33040-7445
(305)293-8007 (800)888-9648 Fax:(305)293-0807

Circa 1995. Although this inn was constructed recently, its Bahamian architecture is reminiscent of Key West's early days. Rooms are open and spacious, decorated with elegant, contemporary furnishings, such as king-size sleigh beds. Jacuzzi tubs and a bar with a refrigerator are a few of the in-room amenities. There is a fountain-fed pool, Jacuzzi and koi pond on the premises, too. In addition to the modern accommodations, guests also may stay in one of the historic cigar-makers' cottages. The cottages are ideal for families, and each has two bedrooms and two bathrooms. The inn is located in the Key West historic district and is close to the many shops, restaurants and nightclubs on Duval Street.

Innkeeper(s): Shel Segel. $175-545. MC, VISA, AX, DC, CB, DS, TC. TAC10. 18 rooms with PB, 15 suites and 3 cottages. Breakfast included in rates. Type of meal: Cont. Beds: K. Cable TV, phone, ceiling fan, robes and capes in room. Air conditioning. VCR, fax, copier, spa and swimming on premises. Handicap access. Weddings, small meetings, family reunions and seminars hosted. Spanish, Portuguese and Czech spoken. Antiquing, fishing, golf, live theater, parks, shopping, tennis and water sports nearby.

Publicity: *New York Times, Key West Citizen, New Mobility, Travel & Leisure, Conde Nast, Country Inns.*

"Your fresh rooms and lovely grounds are truly paradise."

The Popular House, Key West B&B

415 William St
Key West, FL 33040-6853
(305)296-7274 (800)438-6155 Fax:(305)293-0306
E-mail: relax@keywestbandb.com
Web: www.keywestbandb.com

Circa 1890. This pink and white Victorian sits elegantly behind a white picket fence. It was constructed by shipbuilders with sturdy heart-pine walls and 13-foot ceilings. With two stories of porches, the inn is located in the center of the Historic District.

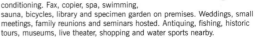

Innkeeper(s): Jody Carlson. $59-265. MC, VISA, AX, DC, DS, PC, TC. TAC10. 8 rooms, 4 with PB and 1 suite. Breakfast included in rates. Type of meals: Cont plus and early coffee/tea. Beds: KQDT. Ceiling fan in room. Air conditioning. Fax, copier, spa, swimming, sauna, bicycles, library and specimen garden on premises. Weddings, small meetings, family reunions and seminars hosted. Antiquing, fishing, historic tours, museums, live theater, shopping and water sports nearby.

"The essence of charming."

Lake Helen   D8

Clauser's B&B

201 E Kicklighter Rd
Lake Helen, FL 32744-3514
(904)228-0310 (800)220-0310 Fax:(904)228-2337
E-mail: clauserinn@totcon.com
Web: www.clauserinn.com

Circa 1890. This three-story, turn-of-the-century vernacular Victorian inn is surrounded by a variety of trees in a quiet, country setting. The inn is listed in the national, state and local historic registers, and offers eight
guest rooms, all with private
bath. Each room features a different type of country decor,
such as Americana, English and
prairie. Guests enjoy hot tubbing
in the Victorian gazebo or relaxing on the inn's porches, which

feature rockers, a swing and cozy wicker furniture. Borrow a bike to take a closer look at the historic district. Stetson University, fine dining and several state parks are nearby.

Innkeeper(s): Tom & Marge Clauser, Janet Watson. $95-140. MC, VISA, AX, DS, PC, TC. TAC10. 8 rooms with PB, 1 with FP. Breakfast and snacks/refreshments included in rates. Types of meals: Full bkfst and early coffee/tea. Beds: KQ. Phone, ceiling fan and private screened porch in room. Air conditioning. VCR, fax, copier, spa, bicycles, library and nature trail through forest on premises. Handicap access. Small meetings, family reunions and seminars hosted. Amusement parks, antiquing, fishing, atlantic beaches, live theater, parks, sporting events and water sports nearby.

Lake Wales   E8

Chalet Suzanne Country Inn & Restaurant

3800 Chalet Suzanne Dr
Lake Wales, FL 33853-7060
(863)676-6011 (800)433-6011 Fax:(863)676-1814
E-mail: info@chaletsuzanne.com
Web: www.chaletsuzanne.com

Circa 1924. Situated on 70 acres adjacent to Lake Suzanne, this country inn's architecture includes gabled roofs, balconies, spires and steeples. The superb restaurant has a glowing reputation and offers a
six-course candlelight
dinner. Places of
interest on the property include the
Swiss Room, Wine
Dungeon, Gift

Boutique, Autograph Garden, Chapel Antiques, Ceramic Salon, Airstrip and the Soup Cannery. The inn has been transformed into a village of cottages and miniature chateaux, one connected to the other seemingly with no particular order.

Historic Interest: This wonderful inn is located in a National Historic District.

Innkeeper(s): Vita Hinshaw & Family. $129-229. MC, VISA, AX, DC, CB, DS, PC, TC. TAC10. 30 rooms with PB. Breakfast included in rates. Meal: Full bkfst. Gourmet dinner, lunch and room service available. Beds: KDT. Cable TV, phone and ceiling fan in room. Air conditioning. VCR, fax, copier, swimming and library on premises. Handicap access. Weddings, small meetings, family reunions and seminars hosted. German spoken. Amusement parks, antiquing, fishing, golf, live theater, parks, shopping, sporting events, tennis and water sports nearby.

Publicity: Southern Living, Country Inns, National Geographic Traveler. Uncle Ben's 1992 award.

"I now know why everyone always says, 'Wow!' when they come up from dinner. Please don't change a thing."

Micanopy   C7

Herlong Mansion

402 NE Cholokka Blvd
Micanopy, FL 32667
(800)437-5664 Fax:(352)466-3322

Circa 1845. This mid-Victorian mansion features four two-story carved-wood Roman Corinthian columns on its veranda. The mansion is surrounded by a garden with statuesque old oak and
pecan trees. Herlong Mansion
features leaded-glass windows, mahogany inlaid oak
floors, 12-foot ceilings and
floor-to-ceiling windows in
the dining room. Guest
rooms have fireplaces and are
furnished with antiques.

Historic Interest: St. Augustine is about one and one-half hours from the mansion. The Marjorie Kennan Rawlings Home is eight miles away. Micanopy is the oldest inland town in Florida, and has been the site for several movies.

Innkeeper(s): H.C. (Sonny) Howard, Jr. $70-175. MC, VISA, PC, TC. TAC10. 12 rooms with PB, 6 with FP, 4 suites, 2 cottages and 1 conference room. Breakfast and snacks/refreshments included in rates. Types of meals: Full gourmet bkfst and early coffee/tea. Banquet service and catering service available. Beds: KQD. TV and ceiling fan in room. Air conditioning. VCR, fax, copier and bicycles on premises. Handicap access. Weddings, small meetings, family reunions and seminars hosted. Antiquing, fishing, golf, Marjorie Kennan Rawlings House, live theater, parks, shopping, sporting events, tennis and water sports nearby.

Mount Dora   D8

Darst Victorian Manor

495 Old Hwy 441
Mount Dora, FL 32757
(352)383-4050 Fax:(352)383-7653
E-mail: darstb&b@mpinet.net

Circa 1995. Although this home is of recent construction, it is an outstanding example of Victorian architecture. The exterior boasts a turret, wraparound veranda and gingerbread trim. The interior is decorated in
Victorian style. The
warm, inviting Queen
Victoria Suite is done
in deep shades of
crimson and includes
a four-poster bed,

hardwood floors, a fireplace with a beautifully carved mantel and a spacious sitting area. Other rooms are equally romantic with Victorian furnishings, canopy beds and fresh flowers. Gourmet breakfasts include treats such as spinach strata accompanied by potato pancakes, freshly baked biscuits, homemade preserves and fresh fruit. Downtown Mount Dora is only two blocks away.

Innkeeper(s): Nanci & Jim Darst. $125-220. MC, VISA, AX, DS, PC, TC. TAC10. 6 rooms with PB, 2 with FP and 2 suites. Types of meals: Full gourmet bkfst and early coffee/tea. Afternoon tea and snacks/refreshments available. Beds: KQDT. Turndown service and ceiling fan in room. Central air. VCR, fax, copier, spa and library on premises. Weddings and family reunions hosted. Antiquing, art galleries, canoeing/kayaking, fishing, golf, hiking, horseback riding, live theater, parks, shopping, tennis, water sports and wineries nearby.

Magnolia Inn

347 E 3rd Ave
Mount Dora, FL 32757-5654
(352)735-3800 (800)776-2112 Fax:(352)735-0258
E-mail: magnolia@cde.com
Web: magnolia.cde.com

Circa 1926. This Mediterranean-style inn in Central Florida offers elegant accommodations to its guests, who will experience the Florida Boom furnishings of the 1920s. Guests will enjoy the convenience of early coffee or tea before sitting down to the inn's full breakfasts. Guests can take a soak in the inn's spa, relax in the hammock by the garden wall or swing beneath the magnolias of this one-acre estate. Lake Griffin State Recreational Area and Wekiwa Springs State Park are within easy driving distance. Just an hour from Disneyworld and the other Orlando major attractions, Mount Dora is the antique capital of Central Florida. Known as the Festival City, it is also recommended by Money magazine as the best retirement location in Florida. It's also the site of Renninger's Winter Antique Extravaganzas. Romantic carriage rides and historic trolley tours of the downtown, two blocks from the inn, are available.

Innkeeper(s): Dave & Betty Cook. $135-185. MC, VISA, AX, PC, TC. 5 rooms with PB. Breakfast included in rates. Types of meals: Full bkfst and early coffee/tea. Beds: KQ. Ceiling fan in room. Air conditioning. VCR, fax, copier and spa on premises. Antiquing, fishing, live theater, parks, shopping and water sports nearby.

Publicity: *Mount Dora Topic.*

New Smyrna Beach D9

Night Swan Intracoastal B&B

512 S Riverside Dr
New Smyrna Beach, FL 32168-7345
(904)423-4940 (800)465-4261 Fax:(904)427-2814
E-mail: nightswanb@aol.com
Web: www.nightswan.com

Circa 1906. From the 140-foot dock at this waterside bed & breakfast, guests can gaze at stars, watch as ships pass or perhaps catch site of dolphins. The turn-of-the-century home is decorated with period furnishings, including an antique baby grand piano, which guests are invited to use. Several guest rooms afford views of the Indian River, which is part of the Atlantic Intracoastal Waterway. Seven rooms include a whirlpool tub. The innkeepers have created several special packages, featuring catered gourmet dinners, boat tours or romantic baskets with chocolate, wine and flowers.

Innkeeper(s): Martha & Chuck Nighswonger. $80-150. MC, VISA, AX, DS, PC, TC. TAC10. 15 rooms with PB, 4 suites and 1 conference room. Breakfast and snacks/refreshments included in rates. Types of meals: Full bkfst and early coffee/tea. Catering service available. Beds: KQ. Cable TV, phone, ceiling fan and 7 whirlpool tubs in room. Air conditioning. Fax and library on premises. Weddings, small meetings, family reunions and seminars hosted. Antiquing, fishing, live theater, parks, shopping and water sports nearby.

Orlando D8

Meadow Marsh B&B

940 Tildenville School Rd
Orlando, FL 34787
(407)656-2064 (888)656-2064
Web: www.bbonline.com/fl/meadowmarsh/

Circa 1877. Meadow Marsh is located on 12 tranquil acres just 14 miles west of downtown Orlando. One of the town's settlers built the Victorian manor, which is highlighted by verandas on the first and second stories. The home remained in the original family until the 1980s. The current owners, John and Cavelle

Pawlack, had the home placed in the National Register. The Pawlacks have made some pleasant additions to their historic home, including adding whirlpool tubs in three of the five available rooms. A three-course breakfast is served promptly at 8:30 a.m. in the glassed sunporch. Snacks are always available in the pantry for Meadow Marsh guests. Cavelle moved her gift shop and tea room to Meadow Marsh and serves luncheons by reservation Wednesday through Saturday.

Innkeeper(s): Cavelle & John Pawlack. $95-199. MC, VISA, TC. TAC6. 5 rooms with PB, 1 with FP, 2 suites and 1 cottage. Breakfast included in rates. Dinner, picnic lunch, lunch and catering service available. Beds: QD. Ceiling fan in room. Air conditioning. VCR, fax, copier, library and piano on premises. Amusement parks, antiquing, live theater, parks, sporting events and water sports nearby.

"What a beautiful home with such warm, gracious Southern hospitality."

Palm Beach G10

Plaza Inn

215 Brazilian Ave
Palm Beach, FL 33480-4682
(561)832-8666 (800)233-2632 Fax:(561)835-8776
E-mail: plazainn@aol.com
Web: www.plazainnpalmbeach.com

Circa 1940. Located just one block from the beach, Plaza Inn is a European-style boutique hotel with old-world charm. Antiques grace the lobby, which features gilded ceilings adorned with Austrian chandeliers. Among the interesting antiques are the Louis XIV front desk and a baby grand piano. Guest rooms are individually decorated with French, Italian and Traditional beds. The inn features the Stray Fox Pub, twice-a-week entertainment and a Charleston-style courtyard where guests can relax.

Innkeeper(s): Ajit Asrani. $105-255. MC, VISA, AX. 47 rooms with PB and 2 suites. Breakfast included in rates. Type of meal: Full bkfst. Beds: KQDT. Cable TV, phone and ceiling fan in room. Air conditioning. VCR, copier, spa, swimming and jacuzzi on premises. Weddings, small meetings and family reunions hosted. French and Spanish spoken. Antiquing, fishing, golf, art galleries, museums, live theater, parks, sporting events, tennis and water sports nearby.

Pets allowed: Small.

Quincy   B5

Allison House Inn

215 N Madison St
Quincy, FL 32351
(850)875-2511 (888)904-2511 Fax:(850)875-2511

Circa 1843. Crepe myrtle, azaleas, camellias and roses dot the acre of grounds that welcomes guests to the Allison House. A local historic landmark located in the 36-block historic district, the inn is in a Georgian, English-country style with shutters and an entrance portico. It was built for General Allison, who became Governor of Florida. There are two parlors, and all the rooms are appointed with English antiques. Homemade biscotti is always available for snacking and for breakfast, English muffins and freshly baked breads are offered. Walk around the district and spot the 51 historic homes and buildings. Nearby dining opportunities include the historic Nicholson Farmhouse Restaurant.

Innkeeper(s): Stuart & Eileen Johnson. $80-95. MC, VISA, AX, DS, PC, TC. TAC10. 5 rooms with PB. AP. Type of meal: Cont plus. Beds: KQD. Cable TV and ceiling fan in room. Central air. Fax and bicycles on premises. Handicap access. Family reunions hosted. Antiquing, art galleries, bicycling, golf, horseback riding, live theater, sporting events and tennis nearby.

Pets Allowed.

McFarlin House B&B Inn

305 E King St
Quincy, FL 32351
(850)875-2526 Fax:(850)627-4703
E-mail: inquiries@mcfarlinhouse.com
Web: mcfarlinhouse.com

Circa 1895. Tobacco farmer John McFarlin built this Queen Anne Victorian, notable for its left-handed turret and grand, wraparound porch. The home, which is listed in the National Register, boasts original woodwork, hand-carved mantels, Italian tile work and stained glass. Romantic guest rooms are decorated with Victorian furnishings, and each is unique. The Southern Grace includes a fireplace and whirlpool tub for two. In the King's View, the double whirlpool tub is set in front of bay windows. The Pink Magnolia Room is located in the home's turret. The Ribbons and Roses Room includes a six-foot-long clawfoot tub, a fireplace and a canopy bed draped in netting. Breakfast begins with two different baked goods, followed by a main course, perhaps an omelet or quiche. McFarlin House is located in a Quincy historic district, just a short drive from Florida's capital city, Tallahassee.

Historic Interest: B&B within 30 block historic district.

Innkeeper(s): Richard & Tina Fauble. $75-175. MC, VISA, AX, DC, DS, PC, TC. 9 rooms with PB. Breakfast and snacks/refreshments included in rates. Type of meal: Full bkfst. Beds: KQD. Cable TV, phone, ceiling fan and VCR in room. Central air. Fax and spa on premises. Weddings, small meetings, family reunions and seminars hosted. Antiquing, art galleries, fishing, golf, museums and sporting events nearby.

Saint Augustine   B8

Carriage Way B&B

70 Cuna St
Saint Augustine, FL 32084-3684
(904)829-2467 (800)908-9832 Fax:(904)826-1461
E-mail: bjohnson@aug.com
Web: www.carriageway.com

Circa 1883. A two-story veranda dominates the facade of this Victorian. Painted creamy white with blue trim, the house is located in the heart of the historic district. It's within a three-block walk to restaurants and shops and the Intracoastal Waterway. Guest rooms reflect the charm of a light Victorian touch, with brass canopy and four-poster beds. Many furnishings have been in the house for 60 years. The "Cottage" offers two guest rooms, a comfortable living/dining room and a kitchenette. A full gourmet breakfast is provided in the morning.

Innkeeper(s): Bill & Diane Johnson. $69-175. MC, VISA, AX, DS, TC. 11 rooms with PB, 1 with FP. Breakfast and snacks/refreshments included in rates. Types of meals: Full bkfst and early coffee/tea. Dinner and picnic lunch available. Beds: KQD. Phone and ceiling fan in room. Air conditioning. Fax, copier and bicycles on premises. Weddings, small meetings and family reunions hosted. Amusement parks, antiquing, fishing, live theater, parks, shopping, sporting events and water sports nearby.

Casa De La Paz Bayfront B&B

22 Avenida Menendez
Saint Augustine, FL 32084-3644
(904)829-2915 (800)929-2915
E-mail: delapaz@aug.com
Web: www.casadelapaz.com

Circa 1915. Overlooking Matanzas Bay, Casa de la Paz was built after the devastating 1914 fire leveled much of the old city. An ornate stucco Mediterranean Revival house, it features clay barrel tile roofing, bracketed eaves, verandas and a lush walled courtyard. The home is listed in the National Register of Historic Places. Guest rooms offer ceiling fans, central air, hardwood floors, antiques, a decanter of sherry, chocolates and complimentary snacks.

Historic Interest: Fountain of Youth, Castillo de San Marcos, Lightner Museum, Flagler College (walking distance).

Innkeeper(s): Bob & Donna Marriott. $120-225. MC, VISA, DS, PC, TC. 6 rooms with PB, 1 with FP. Breakfast included in rates. Types of meals: Full bkfst and early coffee/tea. Beds: KQ. Cable TV, phone and ceiling fan in room. Air conditioning. Antiquing, fishing, live theater, parks, shopping, sporting events and water sports nearby.

"We will always recommend your beautifully restored, elegant home."

Casa De Solana, B&B Inn

21 Aviles St
Saint Augustine, FL 32084-4441
(904)824-3555 Fax:(904)824-3316

Circa 1763. Spanish military leader Don Manuel Solana built this home in the early European settlement, and Spanish records show that a Solana child was the first European child born in

America. The thick coquina-shell walls (limestone formed of broken shells and corals cemented together), high ceilings with dark, hand-hewn beams and polished hand-pegged floors are part of the distinctive flavor of this period. Two Minorican fireplaces are in the house. A Southern breakfast is served at an elegant 10-foot-long mahogany table.

Innkeeper(s): Faye' Lang-McMurry. $125-175. MC, VISA, AX, DS, PC. 4 suites, 2 with FP. Breakfast included in rates. AP. Type of meal: Full bkfst. Beds: KQD. Cable TV and phone in room. Air conditioning. Amusement parks, antiquing, fishing, golf, live theater, parks, shopping, tennis and water sports nearby.

Publicity: *House Beautiful, Palm Beach Post, Innsider, North Florida Living, Jacksonville Today, PM Magazine.*

Castle Garden B&B

15 Shenandoah St
Saint Augustine, FL 32084-2817
(904)829-3839
E-mail: castleg@aug.com
Web: www.castlegarden.com

Circa 1860. This newly-restored Moorish Revival-style inn was the carriage house to Warden Castle. Among the seven guest rooms are three bridal rooms with in-room Jacuzzi tubs and sunken bedrooms with cathe-

dral ceilings. The innkeepers offer packages including carriage rides, picnic lunches, gift baskets and other enticing possibilities. Guests enjoy a homemade full, country breakfast each morning.

Historic Interest: Castle Warden next door, Fort Mantanza's (200 yards to south), Alligator Farm, Saint Augustine Lighthouse (nearby).

Innkeeper(s): Bruce & Kimmy Kloeckner. $79-155. MC, VISA, AX, DS. 7 rooms with PB and 3 suites. Breakfast included in rates. Types of meals: Full bkfst and early coffee/tea. Picnic lunch available. Beds: KQT. Ceiling fan and TV in some rooms in room. Air conditioning. Common sitting room with cable on premises. Antiquing, fishing, golf, ballooning nearby, live theater, shopping, tennis and water sports nearby.

Cedar House Inn Victorian B&B

79 Cedar St
Saint Augustine, FL 32084-4311
(904)829-0079 (800)233-2746 Fax:(904)825-0916
E-mail: russ@aug.com
Web: www.cedarhouseinn.com

Circa 1893. A player piano entertains guests in the parlor of this restored Victorian, which offers plenty of relaxing possibilities. Enjoy refreshments on the veranda or simply curl up with a good book in the library. Innkeepers Russ and Nina Thomas have preserved the home's luxurious heart-of-pine floors and 10-foot ceilings. They highlighted this architectural treasure with period furnishings and reproductions. Guests rooms are decked in Victorian decor and boast either clawfoot or Jacuzzi tubs.

The innkeepers also offer an outdoor Jacuzzi spa. Elegant breakfasts are served either in the dining room or on the veranda. Guests may borrow bicycles perfect for exploring historic Saint Augustine or nearby beaches.

Innkeeper(s): Russ & Nina Thomas. $89-155. MC, VISA, AX, DS, PC, TC. TAC10. 6 rooms with PB, 3 with FP, 1 suite and 1 conference room. Breakfast and snacks/refreshments included in rates. Types of meals: Full gourmet bkfst and early coffee/tea. Dinner and picnic lunch available. Beds: Q. Ceiling fan in room. Air conditioning. Fax, spa and bicycles on premises. Weddings, small meetings, family reunions and seminars hosted. Antiquing, fishing, historic sites and museums, live theater, parks, shopping and water sports nearby.

"What a special 'home' to spend our honeymoon! Everything was terrific! We feel this is our place now and will be regular guests here! Thank you!"

Kenwood Inn

38 Marine St
Saint Augustine, FL 32084-4439
(904)824-2116 (800)824-8151 Fax:(904)824-1689

Circa 1865. Originally built as a summer home, the Kenwood Inn has taken in guests for more than 100 years. Early records show that it was advertised as a private boarding house as early as 1886. Rooms are decorated in periods ranging from the simple Shaker decor to more formal colonial and Victorian styles.

Historic Interest: Lightner Museum, Oldest House Museum, Bridge of Lions (walking distance).

Innkeeper(s): Mark & Kerrianne Constant. $85-185. MC, VISA, DS, PC, TC. 14 rooms with PB and 4 suites. Breakfast included in rates. Type of meal: Cont. Beds: KQD. TV and ceiling fan in room. Air conditioning. Fax and swimming on premises. Antiquing, fishing, live theater, shopping and water sports nearby.

"It's one of my favorite spots for a few days of relaxation and recuperation."

Inn on Charlotte Street

52 Charlotte St
Saint Augustine, FL 32084-3647
(904)829-3819 Fax:(904)810-2134
Web: www.innoncharlotte.com

Circa 1914. Majestic palms accentuate the exterior of this brick home, adorned by a sweeping second-story veranda. The inn is located among many historic gems within Saint Augustine's historic district. Innkeeper Vanessa Noel has been an innkeeper for more than 30 years, hosting guests in Maine and New Hampshire. Now she has brought her considerable talents to Saint Augustine, a perfect vacation spot for history buffs. Noel has decorated the inn with antiques, over-stuffed sofas and

wicker. Some rooms include a Jacuzzi tub, fireplace or private veranda. The inn is within walking distance to many shops and restaurants, as well as the Castillo de San Marcos. Golf, sailing and fishing are other popular local activities.

Historic Interest: Castillo De San Marcos, Cathedral, Bridge of Lions, all within a three minute walk.

Innkeeper(s): Vanessa Noel. $75-150. MC, VISA, AX, PC, TC. TAC10. 6 rooms with PB, 2 with FP and 1 suite. Breakfast and afternoon tea included in rates. Types of meals: Full bkfst, country bkfst, veg bkfst and early coffee/tea. Picnic lunch available. Beds: KQ. Cable TV, ceiling fan and VCR in room. Central air. Fax, copier and library on premises. Weddings, small meetings, family reunions and seminars hosted. Antiquing, art galleries, beaches, bicycling, canoeing/kayaking, fishing, golf, hiking, oldest city in the U.S, live theater, museums, parks, shopping, sporting events, tennis, water sports and wineries nearby.

St. Francis Inn

279 Saint George St
Saint Augustine, FL 32084-5031
(904)824-6068 (800)824-6062 Fax:(904)810-5525
E-mail: innceasd@aug.com
Web: www.stfrancisinn.com

Circa 1791. Long noted for its hospitality, the St. Francis Inn is nearly the oldest house in town. A classic example of Old World architecture, it was built by Gaspar Garcia, who received a Spanish grant to the plot of land. Coquina was the main building material. A buffet breakfast is served. Some rooms have whirlpool tubs and fireplaces. The city of Saint Augustine was founded in 1565.

Historic Interest: The nation's oldest house (free admission for guests at the St. Francis Inn), Saint Augustine Antigua.

Innkeeper(s): Joe Finnegan. $79-189. MC, VISA, AX, PC. TAC10. 14 rooms, 8 with PB, 4 with FP, 6 suites, 1 cottage and 2 conference rooms. Breakfast included in rates. Type of meal: Full bkfst. Beds: KQDT. Cable TV, phone, ceiling fan and whirlpool tubs in room. Air conditioning. Fax, copier, swimming, bicycles and whirlpool tubs on premises. Weddings, small meetings, family reunions and seminars hosted. American Sign Language spoken. Antiquing, fishing, parks, shopping, sporting events and water sports nearby.

Publicity: *Orlando Sentinel.*

"We have stayed at many nice hotels but nothing like this. We are really enjoying it."

Victorian House B&B

11 Cadiz St
Saint Augustine, FL 32084-4431
(904)824-5214 (877)703-0432

Circa 1897. Enjoy the historic ambiance of Saint Augustine at this turn-of-the-century Victorian, decorated to reflect the grandeur of that genteel era. The heart-of-pine floors are topped with hand-hooked rugs, stenciling highlights the walls, and the innkeepers have filled the guest rooms with canopy beds and period furnishings. The full breakfast includes homemade granola, fresh fruit, hot entree and a variety of freshly made breads.

Innkeeper(s): Ken & Marcia Cerotzke. $100-135. MC, VISA, AX, TC. 8 rooms with PB and 2 suites. Breakfast included in rates. Type of meal: Full bkfst. Beds: KQDT. Ceiling fan and refrigerator in room. Air conditioning. Antiquing, fine restaurants, live theater, parks and shopping nearby.

Westcott House Inn on the Bay

146 Avenida Menendez
Saint Augustine, FL 32084-5049
(904)824-4301 Fax:(904)824-4301

Circa 1890. Dr. John Westcott, a man notable for his part in building the St. John Railroad and linking the Intracoastal Waterway from St. John's River to Miami, built this stunning vernacular Victorian. The elegant inn overlooks Matanzas bay,

affording guests an enchanting view both inside and out. The interior is filled with Victorian furnishings, from marble-topped tables to white iron beds. The inn is located in St. Augustine's historic district, and plenty of historic sites, restaurants and shops are within walking distance.

Innkeeper(s): Janice & Robert Graubard. $95-225. MC, VISA, AX, DS, TC. 9 rooms with PB, 4 with FP. Breakfast included in rates. Type of meal: Cont. Beds: KQ. Cable TV, turndown service and ceiling fan in room. Air conditioning. Antiquing, fishing, golf, marina and shopping nearby.

Saint Pete Beach   E7

Island's End

1 Pass A Grille Way
Saint Pete Beach, FL 33706-4326
(727)360-5023 Fax:(727)367-7890

Circa 1950. This collection of cottages is truly at the edge of the beach, where the Gulf of Mexico and Intracoastal Waterway merge. Guests enjoy beach access and can walk along a boardwalk and through a gazebo to reach water and a fishing dock. The six cottages are comfortable, with contemporary decor. Each comes with a full kitchen. A few cottages date back half a century. Unit A is the largest of the accom-

modations, offering three bedrooms, a water view and a private pool. Continental breakfast is provided three times each week.

Innkeeper(s): Jone & Millard Gamble. $70-185. MC, VISA, PC, TC. 6 cottages with PB. Breakfast included in rates. Beds: KQT. Cable TV, phone, ceiling fan, VCR and fully equipped kitchens in room. Air conditioning. Fax, copier, gas grill, fishing pier and gazebo on premises. Lithuanian and Latvian spoken. Amusement parks, antiquing, fishing, golf, live theater, parks, shopping, sporting events, tennis and water sports nearby.

Publicity: *Vanity Fair, Travel Holiday.*

Saint Petersburg   E7

Bayboro House B&B on Old Tampa Bay

1719 Beach Dr SE
Saint Petersburg, FL 33701-5917
(877)823-4955 Fax:(877)823-4955
Web: www.bayborohousebandb.com

Circa 1907. Victorian decor and beautiful antique furnishings fill the Bayboro House, a charming turn-of-the-century manor. The veranda is set up for relaxation with a variety of rockers, swings, wicker chairs and chaise lounges. Breakfasts, served in the formal dining room, feature what every Florida breakfast should, freshly squeezed juices and in-season fruits. Before heading out to one of Saint Petersburg's many restaurants, relax and sip a glass of wine in the parlor.

Historic Interest: The Bayboro House is only minutes from six museums and downtown Saint Petersburg.

Innkeeper(s): Sandy & Dave Kelly. $125-195. MC, VISA, AX, PC, TC. 5 rooms with PB and 2 suites. Breakfast included in rates. Type of meal: Cont plus. Beds: KQD. Ceiling fan and VCR in room. Air conditioning. Fax, spa and swimming on premises. Amusement parks, antiquing, fishing, live theater, parks, shopping, sporting events and water sports nearby.

"It was well worth the price, a long weekend that I'll never forget. It was everything that you advertised it to be and so much more. Thanks so much."

Bay Gables B&B, Garden & Tea Room

136 4th Ave NE
Saint Petersburg, FL 33701
(727)822-8855 (800)822-8803 Fax:(727)824-7223
E-mail: solomio@msn.com
Web: tampabay.citysearch.com/E/V/TPAFL/0003/76/75/

Circa 1910. Bay Gables is a historic Key West-style inn, located just a half block from the waterfront and minutes from shops, museums and restaurants. The décor is influenced by the Victorian style, with flowery comforters and wallcoverings. The Wedgewood, Bristol and Covington rooms each include a private bath with a clawfoot tub. The Windsor Rose includes a clawfoot tub and a view of Tampa Bay. The suites each include a bedroom with a queen or king bed and a sitting room with a day bed, as well as a kitchenette and private bath. The spacious Camelot Suite includes a canopy bed and whirlpool tub. The inn is surrounded by an acre of grounds, and weddings often are held in the garden.
Historic Interest: Ft. DeSoto (20 miles).
Innkeeper(s): David Lee. $85-150. MC, VISA, AX, DS, TC. TAC10. 9 rooms, 5 with PB and 4 suites. Breakfast and snacks/refreshments included in rates. Types of meals: Cont plus, cont and early coffee/tea. Beds: Q. Cable TV, phone and ceiling fan in room. Air conditioning. Fax and copier on premises. Handicap access. Weddings hosted. Antiquing, art galleries, beaches, bicycling, fishing, golf, live theater, museums, parks, shopping, sporting events, tennis and water sports nearby.

Sanford   D8

The Higgins House

420 S Oak Ave
Sanford, FL 32771-1826
(407)324-9238 (800)584-0014 Fax:(407)324-5060

Circa 1894. This inviting blue Queen Anne-style home features cross gables with patterned wood shingles, bay windows and a charming round window on the second floor. Pine floors, paddle fans and a piano in the parlor, which guests are encouraged to play, create Victorian ambiance. The second-story balcony affords views not only of a charming park and Sanford's oldest church, but of Space Shuttle launches from nearby Cape Canaveral. The Queen Anne room looks out over a Victorian box garden, while the Wicker Room features a bay window sitting area. The Country Victorian room  boasts a 19th-century brass bed. Guests also can opt to stay in Cochran's Cottage, which features two bedrooms and baths, a living room, kitchen and porch. Nature lovers will enjoy close access to Blue Spring State Park, Ocala National Forest, Lake Monroe and the Cape Canaveral National Seashore. And of course, Walt Disney World, Sea World and Universal Studios aren't far away.
Historic Interest: Historic downtown Sanford offers a variety of early Cracker and Victorian architecture and many book stores, antique shops, cafes and art galleries. Twenty-two buildings in the district are listed in the National Register.
Innkeeper(s): Walter & Roberta Padgett. $85-165. MC, VISA, AX, DS, PC, TC. TAC10. 3 rooms and 1 cottage. Breakfast and snacks/refreshments included in rates. Types of meals: Cont plus and early coffee/tea. Picnic lunch available. Beds: QD. Turndown service and ceiling fan in room. Air condition-

ing. VCR, spa and bicycles on premises. Small meetings and seminars hosted. Antiquing, fishing, parks, shopping and water sports nearby.
Publicity: *Southern Living, Sanford Herald, Connecticut Traveler, LifeTimes, Orlando Sentinel, Southern Accents, Country Inns, Florida Living.*

"The Higgins House is warm and friendly, filled with such pleasant sounds, and if you love beauty and nature, you're certain to enjoy the grounds."

San Mateo   C8

Ferncourt B&B

150 Central Ave, PO Box 758
San Mateo, FL 32187-0758
(904)329-9755

Circa 1889. This Victorian "painted lady," is one of the few remaining relics from San Mateo's heyday in the early 1900s. Teddy Roosevelt once visited the elegant home. The current owners have restored the Victorian atmosphere with rooms decorated with bright, floral prints and gracious furnishings. Awake to the smells of brewing coffee and the sound of a rooster crowing before settling down to a full gourmet breakfast. Historic Saint Augustine is a quick, 25-mile drive.
Innkeeper(s): Jack & Dee Morgan. $55-85. MC, VISA, PC, TC. TAC10. 6 rooms, 5 with PB. Breakfast included in rates. Types of meals: Full gourmet bkfst and early coffee/tea. Beds: KQD. Ceiling fan in room. Air conditioning. Bicycles and library on premises. Handicap access. Small meetings and family reunions hosted. Antiquing, fishing, golf, live theater, parks and shopping nearby.

"First class operation! A beautiful house with an impressive history and restoration. Great company and fine food."

West Palm Beach   G10

Royal Palm House

3215 Spruce Ave
West Palm Beach, FL 33407-5153
(561)863-9836 (800)655-3196 Fax:(561)848-7350

Circa 1925. Located in the Northwood Historic District in West Palm Beach, this Twenties Florida house has a front lawn dotted with palm trees. There's a large deck, a morning room and Florida Room. A cottage is available in addition to the three guest rooms. Outside, enjoy the pool and garden with citrus trees. Visit Jupiter Lighthouse, Lion Country Safari, Palm Beach Polo, the zoo, Norton Museum, the Water Park or Palm Beach Kennel Club. Shop along Worth Avenue, stroll along the Intracoastal Waterway or try scuba diving, antiquing or golf. Key West is five hours away, Orlando three hours away and Miami one hour.
Historic Interest: Flageler Museum-2 miles, Old Northwood Historic District.
Innkeeper(s): Betty & Bob Faub. $65-155. MC, VISA, AX, DC, CB, DS, PC, TC. TAC10. 5 rooms with PB, 1 suite and 1 cottage. Breakfast and snacks/refreshments included in rates. Types of meals: Full bkfst, country bkfst and early coffee/tea. Beds: KQ. Cable TV, phone, ceiling fan and jacuzzi in room. Central air. VCR, fax, copier, swimming, library, cD Player and piano guest refrigerator on premises. Weddings, small meetings, family reunions and seminars hosted. Amusement parks, antiquing, art galleries, beaches, bicycling, canoeing/kayaking, fishing, golf, hiking, horseback riding, live theater, museums, parks, shopping, sporting events and tennis nearby.

Georgia

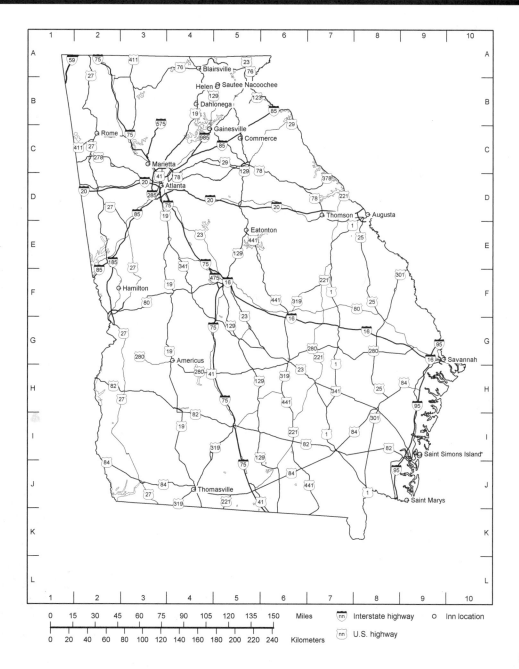

0 15 30 45 60 75 90 105 120 135 150 Miles

0 20 40 60 80 100 120 140 160 180 200 220 240 Kilometers

Interstate highway   o Inn location

U.S. highway

97

Americus
G4

1906 Pathway Inn B&B

501 S Lee St
Americus, GA 31709-3919
(912)928-2078 (800)889-1466 Fax:(912)928-2078

Circa 1906. This turn-of-the-century inn is located along the Andersonville Trail and not far from the city of Andersonville, a Civil War village with a museum. Located between Andersonville and Plains, the home of former President Jimmy Carter, where you may attend and hear him teach Sunday school. The gracious, wraparound porch is a perfect spot for relaxation. The innkeepers plan the morning meal to accommodate their guests' schedules, serving up a candle-lit breakfast with freshly baked breads using silver, crystal and china. The guest rooms offer romantic amenities such as whirlpools and snug down comforters. Two of the rooms are named in honor of Jimmy and Rosalynn Carter. Late afternoons are reserved for wine and refreshments. Several restaurants are within walking distance.

Innkeeper(s): Angela & Chuck Nolan. $75-125. MC, VISA, AX, DS, PC, TC. TAC10. 5 rooms with PB, 2 with FP. Breakfast included in rates. Types of meals: Full gourmet bkfst and early coffee/tea. Snacks/refreshments and room service available. Beds: KQ. Cable TV, phone, turndown service, ceiling fan, VCR and whirlpool tubs in room. Air conditioning. Fax and copier on premises. Small meetings hosted. Antiquing, federal historic sites, live theater and parks nearby.

Pets allowed: With prior approval.

Atlanta
D3

Ansley Inn

253 15th St NE
Atlanta, GA 30309-3512
(404)872-9000 (800)446-5416 Fax:(404)892-2318
E-mail: ansleyinn@mindspring.com
Web: www.ansleyinn.com

Circa 1907. This handsome English Tudor-style home is located on one acre in a neighborhood of stately homes, near Peachtree and Piedmont. Guest rooms offer four-poster beds and Jacuzzi tubs, and some have fireplaces and ceiling fans. A full, Southern breakfast is served and includes eggs, potatoes, bacon, homemade biscuits and fresh fruit. Guests can walk to the Atlanta Botanical Gardens, Symphony Hall and High Museum of Art.

Innkeeper(s): Alan Thompson & Morris Levy. $99-159. MC, VISA, AX. TAC10. 22 rooms with PB, 3 with FP and 1 conference room. Breakfast and snacks/refreshments included in rates. Type of meal: Full bkfst. Beds: QD. Cable TV and phone in room. Fax, copier, jacuzzi tubs, hair dryers, ironing boards and makeup mirrors on premises. Amusement parks, antiquing, golf, live theater, museums, parks, shopping, sporting events and tennis nearby.

Publicity: Country Inns.

Beverly Hills Inn

65 Sheridan Dr NE
Atlanta, GA 30305-3121
(404)233-8520 (800)331-8520 Fax:(404)233-8659
E-mail: info@beverlyhillsinn.com
Web: www.beverlyhillsinn.com

Circa 1929. Period furniture and polished-wood floors decorate this inn located in the Buckhead neighborhood. There are private balconies, kitchens and a library with a collection of

newspapers and books. The governor's mansion, Neiman-Marcus, Saks and Lord & Taylor are five minutes away.

Innkeeper(s): Mit Amin. $99-160. MC, VISA, AX, DC, DS, PC, TC. TAC10. 18 suites. Breakfast included in rates. Type of meal: Cont plus. Beds: QD. Cable TV and phone in room. Air conditioning. Health club on premises. Small meetings and family reunions hosted. French, Italian and Spanish spoken. Antiquing, parks and shopping nearby.

Pets allowed: With kennels/cages.

Publicity: Country Inns, Southern Living, Time.

"Our only regret is that we had so little time. Next stay we will plan to be here longer."

Gaslight Inn B&B

1001 St Charles Ave NE
Atlanta, GA 30306-4221
(404)875-1001 Fax:(404)876-1001
E-mail: innkeeper@gaslightinn.com
Web: www.gaslightinn.com

Circa 1913. Flickering gas lanterns outside, original gas lighting inside and six working fireplaces add to the unique quality of this inn. Beautifully appointed guest rooms offer individual decor. The Ivy Cottage is a romantic bungalow with a living room and kitchen. The regal English Suite boasts a four-poster bed covered in rich blue hues and a private deck. The Rose Room features a fireplace and four-poster bed covered with lace. Located in the Virginia Highlands neighborhood, the inn is approximately five minutes from downtown and is served by Atlanta's public transportation system.

Innkeeper(s): Jim Moss. $95-195. MC, VISA, AX, DC, DS, PC, TC. TAC10. 7 rooms with PB, 3 with FP, 3 suites, 2 cottages and 1 conference room. Breakfast included in rates. Types of meals: Cont plus and early coffee/tea. Beds: KQ. Cable TV, phone, ceiling fan and VCR in room. Air conditioning. Fax, copier, spa, sauna and library on premises. Handicap access. Weddings, small meetings, family reunions and seminars hosted. Amusement parks, antiquing, live theater, parks, shopping and sporting events nearby.

Publicity: Travel Channel.

"Best B&B I've ever stayed in."

King-Keith House B&B

889 Edgewood Ave NE
Atlanta, GA 30307
(404)688-7330 (800)728-3879 Fax:(404)584-0730

Circa 1890. This beautifully restored and preserved Queen Anne Victorian features many wonderful elements, including a whimsical chimney that vividly declares "1890," the year the home was built. Inside, the hardwood floors and intricate woodwork glisten. Walls are painted in deep, rich hues and antiques fill the rooms. Marble-topped tables and delicate love seats decorate the parlor. Each guest room is special, and beds are topped with luxury linens. One room is lit by a colorful stained-glass window, another features a Victorian dollhouse. The opulent home is located in an Atlanta historic district listed in the National Register. It's just two blocks from the subway station. Innkeeper(s): Jan & Windell Keith. $80-175. MC, VISA, AX, DS, PC, TC. TAC10. 3 rooms with PB, 1 suite and 1 cottage. Breakfast included in rates. Types of meals: Full gourmet bkfst and early coffee/tea. Beds: KQDT. Cable TV, phone, ceiling fan, hair dryer and cottage with Jacuzzi and fireplace in room. Air conditioning. Fax and gift shop on premises. Weddings, small meetings, family reunions and seminars hosted. Amusement parks, antiquing, golf, live theater, parks, shopping, sporting events and tennis nearby.

Augusta   D8

The Azalea Inn

312-334 Greene St
Augusta, GA 30901
(706)724-3454 Fax:(706)724-3454
E-mail: azalea@theazaleainn.com
Web: www.theazaleainn.com

Circa 1895. Three tastefully restored Victorian homes comprise the Azalea Inn, located in the Olde Town Historic District. Elegantly furnished suites with 11-foot ceilings also offer fireplaces and large Jacuzzi tubs. Breakfast is delivered to your room in a basket. The inn is within walking distance to the Riverwalk on the Savannah River, fine restaurants, museums, antique shops and unique boutiques.

$79-150. MC, VISA, AX, PC, TC. TAC10. 21 rooms with PB, 13 with FP, 4 suites and 1 conference room. Meal: Cont plus. Beds: KQ. Cable TV, phone, ceiling fan and jacuzzi tubs in room. Air conditioning. Fax on premises. Handicap access. Small meetings & family reunions hosted. Antiquing, fishing, golf, historic sites, live theater, parks, shopping, sporting events, tennis & water sports nearby.
"Third time and loved it!"

Blairsville   A4

Misty Mountain Inn & Cottages

4376 Misty Mountain Ln
Blairsville, GA 30512-5604
(706)745-4786 (888)647-8966 Fax:(706)781-1002

Circa 1890. This Victorian farmhouse is situated on a four-acre compound and also features six mountain-side cottages located in the woods surrounding the inn. There are four spacious guest rooms in the main house, all appointed with private baths and fireplaces. All are decorated in country antiques with hand-crafted accessories, quilts and green plants. Two cottages boast antique beds and Jacuzzi tubs. The bedroom cottages have lofts and can comfortably sleep more than two people, while offering separate bedrooms, living rooms and eat-in kitchens. Flea markets, festivals, antique shops and arts and crafts are located nearby.

Historic Interest: Close to Lake Winfield Scott, Lake Nottely, Lake Chatuge, Young Harris College, Georgia Mountain Fair, Vogel State Park and the Appalachian Trail.
$55-85. MC, VISA, TC. TAC10. 4 rooms with PB, 10 with FP and 6 cottages. Breakfast included in rates. Types of meals: Full bkfst, cont plus, cont and early coffee/tea. Beds: QT. Ceiling fan and fireplace & private balcony in room. Air conditioning. Fax and copier on premises. Handicap access. Weddings, small meetings and family reunions hosted. Antiquing, fishing, golf, parks, shopping and water sports nearby.
Pets allowed: in cottages.

Commerce   C5

Magnolia Inn

206 Cherry St
Commerce, GA 30529-2414
(706)335-7257

Circa 1909. This cozy Queen Anne Victorian features a wrap-around porch and elegant front entry. With its six fireplaces, 12-foot-high ceilings and hardwood floors, the home is the ideal setting for the inn's tea parties for little girls offered for special occasions. (The innkeekper provides appropriate dress-up clothes from the attic, and sometimes the big girls get involved, too.) Antiques, collectibles and a rose garden with a Dogwood tree enhance the inn's natural charm. Ask about Valentine specials available year round. Just one block away is Main Street and the historic downtown.

Historic Interest: A short drive from North Georgia Mountains, University of Georgia, outlet malls and the racetrack.
Innkeeper(s): Annette & Jerry Potter. $60-75. MC, VISA, PC. TAC10. 4 rooms, 3 with PB, 1 with FP and 1 conference room. Breakfast and snacks/refreshments included in rates. Types of meals: Full gourmet bkfst and early coffee/tea. Picnic lunch, banquet service, catering service and room service available. Beds: QDT. Cable TV and turndown service in room. Air conditioning. Child care on premises. Weddings, small meetings, family reunions and seminars hosted. Amusement parks, antiquing, fishing, golf, outlet malls, live theater, parks, shopping, sporting events and tennis nearby.

Dahlonega   B4

Worley Homestead Inn

168 Main St W
Dahlonega, GA 30533-1005
(706)864-7002

Circa 1845. Two blocks from the historic town square is this beautiful old Colonial Revival inn. Several guest rooms are equipped with fireplaces, adding to the romantic atmosphere and Victorian ambiance. All the rooms have private baths, and feature antique beds. A popular spot for honeymooners and couples celebrating anniversaries, Dahlonega is close to the lures of the Chattahoochee National Forest.

Innkeeper(s): Bill, Francis & Christine. $85-95. MC, VISA. 7 rooms. Breakfast and snacks/refreshments included in rates. Types of meals: Full bkfst and early coffee/tea. Cable TV in room. Air conditioning. Weddings and small meetings hosted. Antiquing and shopping nearby.

Eatonton   E5

The Crockett House

671 Madison Rd
Eatonton, GA 31024-7830
(706)485-2248

Circa 1895. Century-old pecan, oak, pine and magnolia trees shade this alluring Victorian. The sweeping veranda is lined with rockers and wicker for those who wish to relax and enjoy a gentle Georgia breeze. Guests are welcomed with refreshment, and treated to a gourmet, candlelight breakfast. Rooms are decorated with antiques, and exude an old-fashioned, Southern ambiance. The bed & breakfast is located on the historic Antebellum Trail, which stretches from Athens to Macon, and the inn is about midway between both towns. Atlanta is about an hour and 15 minutes away; Augusta is an hour-and-a-half drive.

Innkeeper(s): Christa & Peter Crockett. $85-95. MC, VISA, PC, TC. TAC15. 6 rooms with PB, 4 with FP. Breakfast included in rates. Types of meals: Full gourmet bkfst and early coffee/tea. Afternoon tea available. Beds: KQD. Cable TV and ceiling fan in room. Air conditioning. Antiquing, fishing, live theater, parks, shopping, sporting events and water sports nearby.

Gainesville   C4

Dunlap House

635 Green St N W
Gainesville, GA 30501-3319
(770)536-0200 (800)276-2935 Fax:(770)503-7857
E-mail: dunlaphouse@mindspring.com
Web: www.dunlaphouse.com

Circa 1910. Located on Gainesville's historic Green Street, this inn offers 10 uniquely decorated guest rooms, all featuring period furnishings. Custom-built king or queen beds and remote-controlled cable TV are found in all of the rooms, several of which have romantic fireplaces. Guests may help themselves to coffee, tea and light refreshments in the inn's common area. Breakfast may be enjoyed in guests' rooms or on the picturesque veranda, with its comfortable wicker furniture. Road Atlanta, Mall of Georgia, Lake Lanier, Brenall University, Riverside Academy and the Quinlan Art Center are nearby.

Innkeeper(s): David & Karen Peters. $85-155. MC, VISA, AX, TC. 10 rooms with PB, 2 with FP. Breakfast included in rates. Types of meals: Full bkfst and early coffee/tea. Beds: KQ. Cable TV, phone, laptop computer and phone hook-up in room. Air conditioning. Copier on premises. Handicap access. Weddings, small meetings and family reunions hosted. Antiquing, fishing, golf, Road Atlanta Racing, Lake Lanier, live theater, parks, shopping and water sports nearby.

Hamilton   F2

Magnolia Hall B&B

127 Barnes Mill Rd
Hamilton, GA 31811
(706)628-4566

Circa 1890. Fancy fretwork decorates the wide veranda of this two-story Victorian settled in an acre of magnolias and century-old hollies, near the courthouse. Heart-pine floors, tall ceilings, antiques, a grand piano and china, crystal and silver service for breakfast, set the mood for a gracious inn stay. One of the house specialties is Baked Georgia Croissant with fresh peaches and toasted almonds. It's five miles to Callaway Gardens and 20 miles to Warm Springs.

Innkeeper(s): Dale & Kendrick Smith. $95-115. PC. TAC10. 5 rooms with PB, 1 with FP and 2 suites. Breakfast and snacks/refreshments included in rates. Types of meals: Full gourmet bkfst and early coffee/tea. Beds: QT. Cable TV, turndown service, VCR and refreshments in rooms in room. Air conditioning. Rockers and porch swing on premises. Handicap access. Amusement parks, antiquing, fishing, golf, Wild Animal Park, FDR Home, live theater, parks, shopping, sporting events, tennis and water sports nearby.

Little St. Simons Island   I9

The Lodge on Little St. Simons Island

PO Box 21078
Little St. Simons Island, GA 31522-0578
(912)638-7472 (888)733-5774 Fax:(912)634-1811

Once a part of the Butler Plantation, Little St. Simons Island was purchased at the turn of the century by the Berolzheimer family. Deer roam freely and birds soar over 10,000 acres of pristine

forests, fresh water ponds, isolated beaches and marshland. There are more than 220 species of birds, and guests can enjoy horseback riding on miles of private trails. There are seven miles of isolated beach to enjoy, as well as boating, canoeing, fishing, birdwatching, swimming and naturalist programs. All activities are included in the rates. The Hunting Lodge, filled with books and memorabilia, is the gathering spot for the island. To ensure solitude and privacy, the innkeepers allow only 30 overnight guests at a time. Full-Island rates, ranging from $4,400 to $6,200 are available. Breakfast, lunch and dinner, served family style, are included in the rates. The lodge also offers extras such as barge cruises, oyster roasts, beach picnics and crab boils.

Historic Interest: Fort Frederica National Monument (neighboring Island), Fort George (13 miles), Jekyll Island Club and historic district homes of turn-of-the-century millionaires (Jekyll Island).

Innkeeper(s): Maureen Ahern. $325-900. MC, VISA, AX, PC. TAC10. 13 rooms with PB, 1 suite and 3 conference rooms. Breakfast and dinner included in rates. AP. Types of meals: Full bkfst and early coffee/tea. Beds: KQT. Ceiling fan and coffee maker in room. Air conditioning. Fax, copier, swimming, stables, bicycles, boats, interpretive guides and fishing on premises. Weddings, small meetings, family reunions and seminars hosted. On-site fishing nearby.

"The staff is unequaled anywhere."

Marietta   C3

Whitlock Inn

57 Whitlock Ave
Marietta, GA 30064-2343
(770)428-1495 Fax:(770)919-9620

Circa 1900. This cherished Victorian has been restored and is located in a National Register Historic District, one block from the Marietta Square. Amenities even the Ritz doesn't provide are in every room, and you can rock on the front verandas. An afternoon snack also is served. There is a ballroom grandly suitable for weddings and business meetings.

Historic Interest: Kennesaw Mountain Battlefield & Civil War National Park (3 miles), numerous historic homes, several from Civil War era (within 6 blocks).

Innkeeper(s): Alexis Edwards. $100-145. MC, VISA, AX, DS. TAC10. 5 rooms with PB and 3 conference rooms. Breakfast included in rates. Type of meal: Cont plus. Beds: KQT. Cable TV, phone and ceiling fan in room. Air conditioning. Fax and copier on premises. Weddings, small meetings, family reunions and seminars hosted. Amusement parks, antiquing, live theater, parks, shopping and sporting events nearby.

Publicity: *Marietta Daily Journal.*

"This is the most beautiful inn in Georgia and I've seen nearly all of them."

Rome
C2

Claremont House B&B

906 E Second Ave
Rome, GA 30161
(706)291-0900 (800)254-4797 Fax:(706)232-9865
E-mail: clarinrome@aol.com
Web: www.bbonline.com/ga/claremont

Circa 1882. Colonel Hamilton Yancey, a prominent cotton farmer, built this grand Victorian mansion. The beautifully restored home boasts many original features, including 11 fireplaces, 14-foot ceilings, intricate crown molding and fine woodwork throughout. Six varieties of woods were used in the home's creation, including walnut and chestnut parquet floors and built-in bookcases and china cabinets that extend from floor to ceiling. One particularly notable item is a massive antique safe built into the home's stairwell. Each of the guest rooms includes a fireplace, and most include a clawfoot tub. Guests can relax on one of the porches and enjoy the scent of magnolias and the melodic ring of a distant train. Gourmet breakfasts are served by candlelight and include fresh fruit, homemade breads and a daily entrée. The home, located in a Rome historic district, is about an hour from both Atlanta and Chattanooga.

Historic Interest: Chieftain Museum (3.5 miles), Martha Berry House & Berry College (4 miles), clock tower (1 mile).

Innkeeper(s): George & Gwen Kastanias. $85-125. MC, VISA, AX, PC, TC. 5 rooms with PB, 5 with FP and 1 cottage. Breakfast included in rates. Beds: KQD. TV, phone and ceiling fan in room. Central air. Fax and YMCA facilities available on premises. Weddings, small meetings and family reunions hosted. Antiquing, bicycling, fishing, golf, hiking, live theater, museums, parks and shopping nearby.

"The smell of magnolias, the gentle rustle of wind in the leaves, the feel of solid oak, pine and chestnut boards underfoot and the taste of wonderful Southern cooking, these are some of the memories which we shall take with us back home."

Saint Marys
J9

Goodbread House

209 Osborne St
Saint Marys, GA 31558-8415
(912)882-7490 (888)236-6482

Circa 1870. In the heart of Saint Marys Historic District, this Victorian inn rests behind a white picket fence, a three-minute walk from the Cumberland Island Ferry. There are five antique-filled guest rooms, three with fireplaces. Visitors will enjoy the original wood trim, high

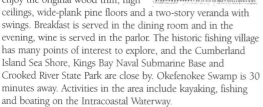

ceilings, wide-plank pine floors and a two-story veranda with swings. Breakfast is served in the dining room and in the evening, wine is served in the parlor. The historic fishing village has many points of interest to explore, and the Cumberland Island Sea Shore, Kings Bay Naval Submarine Base and Crooked River State Park are close by. Okefenokee Swamp is 30 minutes away. Activities in the area include kayaking, fishing and boating on the Intracoastal Waterway.

Historic Interest: Okefenokee Swamp Park (30 miles), Amelia Island (20 miles), Jacksonville (30 miles), Saint Simons (30 miles).

Innkeeper(s): Michele Becnel. $65-85. 5 rooms with PB. Breakfast included in rates. Type of meal: Full bkfst. Picnic lunch available. Beds: KQT. TV, phone and ceiling fan in room. Air conditioning. Weddings, small meetings and family reunions hosted. Antiquing nearby.
Publicity: *Seabreeze.*

Sautee
B5

The Stovall House

1526 Hwy 255 N
Sautee, GA 30571
(706)878-3355

Circa 1837. This house, built by Moses Harshaw and restored in 1983 by Ham Schwartz, has received two state awards for its restoration. The handsome farmhouse has an extensive wrap-around porch providing vistas of 26 acres of cow pastures and mountains. High ceilings, polished walnut woodwork and decorative stenciling provide a pleasant backdrop for the inn's collection of  antiques. Victorian bathroom fixtures include pull-chain toilets and pedestal sinks. The inn has its own restaurant.

Historic Interest: Sautee Nacoochee Arts and Community Center (1 mile), Museum of Indian and local history, Stovall Covered Bridge (1 mile).

Innkeeper(s): Ham Schwartz. $72-84. MC, VISA, AX, PC, TC. 5 rooms with PB. Breakfast included in rates. Type of meal: Cont. Dinner and catering service available. Restaurant on premises. Beds: KQDT. Ceiling fan in room. Air conditioning. Library on premises. Weddings, small meetings and family reunions hosted. Amusement parks, antiquing, fishing, live theater, parks, shopping and water sports nearby.

"Great to be home again. Very nostalgic and hospitable."

Savannah
G9

Broughton Street Bed & Breakfast

511 E Broughton St
Savannah, GA 31401-3501
(912)232-6633 Fax:(912)232-6633

Circa 1883. This historic Victorian townhouse offers five guest rooms. Each is decorated with Victorian furnishings, antiques and contemporary artwork. One room includes a Jacuzzi tub and a fireplace. In the afternoons, the innkeepers serve hors d'oeuvres to their guests. Breakfasts feature such items as quiche, homemade Amish bread and fresh fruit.

Innkeeper(s): Tonya & JP Saleeby. $125-225. MC, VISA, AX, DS, PC, TC. TAC10. 5 rooms, 3 with PB, 2 with FP. Breakfast, afternoon tea and snacks/refreshments included in rates. Type of meal: Full bkfst. Beds: KQ. Cable TV, phone, turndown service, ceiling fan and VCR in room. Air conditioning. Fax, copier, bicycles and library on premises. Weddings hosted. Antiquing, fishing, golf, live theater, parks, shopping, sporting events, tennis and water sports nearby.

"Our stay was so romantic, we're rejuvenated and ready to take on the world!"

Eliza Thompson House

5 W Jones St
Savannah, GA 31401-4503
(912)236-3620 (800)348-9378 Fax:(912)238-1920
E-mail: elizath@aol.com
Web: www.elizathompsonhouse.com

Circa 1847. Spared General Sherman's wrath during the Civil War, this elegantly restored Federalist-style mansion built by Eliza Thompson is one of Savannah's oldest operating inns. Set on a brick-paved street in the heart of the historic district, this architectural landmark built around a magnificent courtyard consists of 25 spacious guest rooms, all featuring gleaming heart-pine floors and period antiques. Many of the rooms offer fireplaces. Richly brewed coffee, freshly baked croissants, pastries and homemade muffins along with fresh seasonal fruits and cereals are offered each morning. Guests can explore the historic downtown just a few minutes away by foot.

Innkeeper(s): Carol Day. $99-225. MC, VISA, PC, TC. TAC10. 25 rooms with PB, 12 with FP. Breakfast, afternoon tea and snacks/refreshments included in rates. Types of meals: Full bkfst and early coffee/tea. Beds: KQD. Cable TV, phone, turndown service and ceiling fan in room. Fax on premises. Weddings, small meetings and seminars hosted. Antiquing, fishing, golf, live theater, parks and shopping nearby.

Forsyth Park Inn

102 W Hall St
Savannah, GA 31401-5519
(912)233-6800

Circa 1893. This graceful yellow and white three-story Victorian features bay windows and a large veranda overlooking

Forsyth Park. Sixteen-foot ceilings, polished parquet floors of oak and maple, and a handsome oak stairway provide an elegant background for the guest rooms. There are several whirlpool tubs, marble baths, four-poster beds, fireplaces and there is a walled garden courtyard.

Historic Interest: Located in the heart of historic district, overlooking the largest park in the District Two Historic Forts. A lighthouse and beach are nearby.

Innkeeper(s): Hal & Virginia Sullivan. $145-225. MC, VISA, AX, DS, PC, TC. 10 rooms with PB, 8 with FP and 1 cottage. Breakfast included in rates. Type of meal: Cont. Beds: KQT. Air conditioning. French spoken. Antiquing, fishing, live theater, parks, shopping and water sports nearby.

Publicity: *Savannah Morning News, Land's End Catalog, United Airlines, Vis-A-Vis, Learning Channel.*

"Breathtaking, exceeded my wildest dreams."

Kehoe House

123 Habersham St
Savannah, GA 31401-3820
(912)232-1020 (800)820-1020 Fax:(912)231-1587

Circa 1892. A wealthy Irish businessman built this Renaissance Revival manor. The interior has been impeccably restored and decorated in Victorian style with antiques, reproductions and original artwork. In honor of the original owner, the individually decorated guest rooms are named for a county in Ireland. Each day begins with a gourmet,

Southern-style breakfast. Fresh fruit, freshly squeezed orange juice and home-baked breads accompany such entrees as eggs Savannah, bacon, grits and potatoes. The staff is always happy to assist guests and can direct you to fine restaurants, shops and attractions in the Savannah area. This inn has received both a four-diamond rating from AAA and four stars from Mobil.

Innkeeper(s): Martha Geiger. $195-270. MC, VISA, AX, DC, CB, DS, TC. TAC10. 15 rooms with PB, 2 suites and 2 conference rooms. Breakfast and snacks/refreshments included in rates. Types of meals: Full gourmet bkfst and early coffee/tea. Afternoon tea, picnic lunch and lunch available. Beds: KQT. Cable TV, phone, turndown service and ceiling fan in room. Air conditioning. Fax and copier on premises. Handicap access. Small meetings hosted. Antiquing, fishing, live theater, parks, shopping and water sports nearby.

The President's Quarters Inn and Guesthouse

225 E President St
Savannah, GA 31401-3806
(912)233-1600 (800)233-1776 Fax:(912)238-0849
E-mail: info @presidentsquarters.com
Web: www.presidentsquarters.com

Circa 1855. In the heart of Savannah's Historic District, The President's Quarters is comprised of Federal-style townhouses constructed by the W.W. Gordon estate and in 1870 Robert E. Lee paid a call here. Nineteen presidents are thought to have visited Savannah and the rooms at the inn today offer suitable accommodations for such dignitaries. Antique period furnishings, working fireplaces, four-poster rice beds, canopy or high carved beds are featured, and the suites boast additional amenities such as balconies, hand-painted ceilings and loft bedrooms. Special services include a complimentary fruit basket and a chilled bottle of wine, afternoon hors d'oeuvres, nightly turndown service with cordials and local sweets and 24-hour concierge service. Breakfast is served in your room or in the courtyard. River Street is three blocks away.

Innkeeper(s): Stacy Stephens/ Hank Smalling. $137-225. MC, VISA, DC, DS, PC, TC. 19 rooms with PB, 19 with FP and 8 suites. Type of meal: Cont plus. Snacks/refreshments available. Beds: KQD. Turndown service in room. Fax, copier and telephones with data ports on premises. Handicap access. Publicity: *Country Inns, Southern Homes.*

"President's Quarters was truly a home away from home." - Karl Malden.

RSVP Savannah B&B Reservation Service

611 E 56th St
Savannah, GA 31405
(912)232-7787 (800)729-7787 Fax:(912)353-8060

Circa 1848. This is a reservation service that offers several historic accommodations for travelers, including more than 30 inns and guest houses. The traveler seeking history and beauty, from South Carolina's Low Country to Georgia's Sea Islands can simply choose the area he wishes to visit and describe his needs to the service. Choices include private homes or villas on the water.

Areas include Savannah, Tybee, St. Simons Islands, Macon, Darien and Brunswick in Georgia; Beaufort and Charleston in South Carolina; and St. Augustine, Florida.

Innkeeper(s): Sonja Lazzaro. MC, VISA, AX, PC. 250 rooms with PB. Meals: Full bkfst, cont plus, cont and early coffee/tea. Afternoon tea, dinner, snacks/refreshments and catering service available. Beds: KQDT. Cable TV, phone and VCR in room. Central air. Fax and pet boarding on premises. Handicap access. Pets allowed: In some Inns.

Thomasville J4

Melhana, the Grand Plantation

301 Showboat Ln
Thomasville, GA 31792
(912)226-2290 (888)920-3030 Fax:(912)226-4585
E-mail: info@melhana.com
Web: www.melhana.com

Circa 1820. More than 50 acres surround the historic Melhana Plantation comprised of 30 buildings including the manor, The Hibernia Cottage and a village. There are 30 buildings, all in the National Register. Traditional décor includes furnishings and amenities such as king- and queen-size four-poster beds, desks, paintings, puffy down comforters and pretty duvets. Some accommodations offer marble Jacuzzis and veranda entrances. Most include views of expansive green lawns, the Avenue of Magnolias, camellia gardens, the sunken garden or the plantation's pasture land. The inn's elegantly appointed restaurant has received acclaims from prestigious critics for its Southern cuisine, enhanced by herbs garnered from private kitchen gardens. To fully enjoy the plantation, consider arranging for horseback riding, quail hunting or a carriage ride, but be sure to allow time to linger on the veranda or to enjoy the indoor swimming pool, theater and fitness center.

$250-650. MC, VISA, AX, DS, PC, TC. TAC10. 26 rooms with PB, 7 with FP, 14 suites, 2 cottages and 3 conference rooms. Afternoon tea included in rates. Types of meals: Full bkfst, cont plus, cont, country bkfst, veg bkfst and early coffee/tea. Gourmet dinner, snacks/refreshments, picnic lunch, gourmet lunch, banquet service, catering service, catered breakfast and room service available. Restaurant on premises. Beds: KQ. Cable TV, phone, turndown service and VCR in room. Central air. Fax, copier, spa, stables and library on premises. Weddings, small meetings and seminars hosted. Amusement parks, antiquing, art galleries, beaches, bicycling, fishing, golf, horseback riding, live theater, museums, parks, shopping, sporting events, tennis and water sports nearby.

Serendipity Cottage

339 E Jefferson St
Thomasville, GA 31792-5108
(912)226-8111 (800)383-7377 Fax:(912)226-2656
E-mail: goodnite@rose.net
Web: www.bbhost.com/serendipity

Circa 1906. A wealthy Northerner hand picked the lumber used to build this Four Square house for his family. The home still maintains its original oak pocket doors and leaded-glass

windows. The decor in guest rooms ranges from Victorian with antiques to rooms decorated with wicker furnishings. Breakfasts are hearty and made from scratch, including freshly baked breads and homemade jams. The home is located in a neighborhood of historic houses, and guests can take a walking or driving tour of the town's many historic sites.

Innkeeper(s): Kathy & Ed Middleton. $85-110. MC, VISA, AX, DS, PC, TC. TAC10. 4 rooms with PB, 2 with FP. Breakfast included in rates. Types of meals: Full bkfst, cont and early coffee/tea. Beds: QD. Cable TV, phone, turndown service, ceiling fan, VCR and complimentary sherry in room. Air conditioning. Bicycles on premises. Antiquing, fishing, plantation tours, live theater, parks, shopping and sporting events nearby.

"Thank you for the wonderful weekend at Serendipity Cottage. The house is absolutely stunning and the food delicious."

Thomson D7

1810 West Inn

254 N Seymour Dr
Thomson, GA 30824-7209
(706)595-3156 (800)515-1810

Circa 1810. Restoration expert and now innkeeper Virginia White refurbished this plantation farmhouse as well as the several turn-of-the-century tenant houses that adjoin the main property. Virginia had the historic houses moved to the 11-acre farm and has restored them into quaint country dwellings. Peacocks and other farm creatures mingle on the grounds, which are dotted with magnolias and lush gardens. The

Whites' "continental" morning fare is more akin to a hearty country breakfast, with items such as individual quiches, freshly baked biscuits and fresh fruit. Virginia was born in Thomson and has named each of the richly decorated guest quarters after her local ancestors. Rooms offer cozy fireplaces, shiny pine paneled walls, antique beds and handmade Native American rugs. The country kitchen is stocked with snacks and guests are welcome to peruse the cupboards for a cup of tea or a small treat. The grounds offer a jogging trail, and guests are allowed privileges at a nearby golf and tennis club, but the inn offers.

Historic Interest: Nearby Wrightsborough, one of Georgia's first communities, includes the historic Rock House, which was built in 1785. Other historic attractions in the area include the site of a Quaker settlement and part of the Bartram Trail.

Innkeeper(s): Virginia White. $55-105. MC, VISA, AX. 10 rooms with PB and 3 suites. Meals: Cont plus and early coffee/tea. Picnic lunch and catering service available. Beds: QDT. Antiquing, fishing, golf. Hiking. Boating & shopping nearby.

Four Chimneys B&B

2316 Wire Rd SE
Thomson, GA 30824-7326
(706)597-0220

Circa 1800. The architecture of the Four Chimneys is referred to as Plantation Plain and was built by Quakers. All the wood in the house is heart pine, including floors, walls and ceilings. Four-poster beds and working fireplaces tastefully accentuate the home's authentic simplicity. The innkeeper is a master gardener with a specialty in herb gardens, and there are herb and heirloom flower gardens scattered about the three acres of grounds. The back yard is a certified wildlife habitat. Fresh herbs often enhance entrees presented at breakfast, and the innkeepers

serve seasonally, peaches, blueberries or strawberries with cream. Although many visitors to the inn find it difficult to venture past the wide front veranda with its enticing rockers and porch swing, the area offers antiquing, equestrian events, golf and fox hunting. November's "Blessings of the Hounds" is the start of the hunting season, which continues through March.

Innkeeper(s): Maggie & Ralph Zieger. $45-75. MC, VISA, PC, TC. 3 rooms, 2 with PB, 3 with FP and 1 suite. Breakfast included in rates. Type of meal: Full bkfst. Afternoon tea and picnic lunch available. Beds: QD. TV and ceiling fan in room. Central air. VCR and library on premises. German spoken. Antiquing, art galleries, fishing, golf, historic sites, live theater, museums, parks, shopping and sporting events nearby.

Hawaii

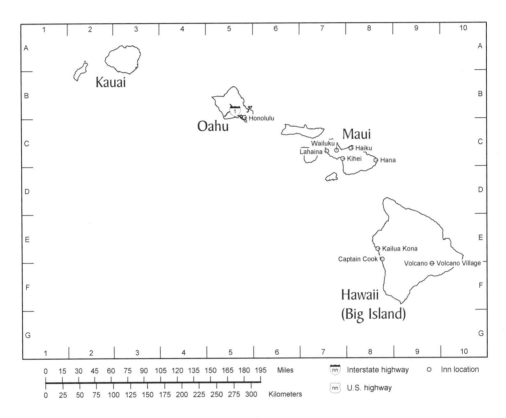

	1	2	3	4	5	6	7	8	9	10	

Kauai

Oahu ○ Honolulu

Maui

Wailuku ○ Haiku
Lahaina ○ ○ Kihei ○ Hana

Hawaii
(Big Island)

○ Kailua Kona
Captain Cook ○ Volcano ⊖ ○ Volcano Village

0 15 30 45 60 75 90 105 120 135 150 165 180 195 Miles
0 25 50 75 100 125 150 175 200 225 250 275 300 Kilometers

(nn) Interstate highway   ○ Inn location

(nn) U.S. highway

Hawaii (Big Island)

Volcano   F9

Hale Ohia Cottages

PO Box 758
Volcano, HI 96785-0758
(808)967-7986 (800)455-3803 Fax:(808)967-8610

Circa 1931. These country cottages, nestled in the quaint
Volcano Village area, are surrounded by Hawaiian gardens and
lush forest. You can stroll the serene property on paths made of
lava rock and enjoy the many orchids and native plants. The gardens are some of the finest in Volcano. Volcano National Park is
only one mile from the cottage.
Historic Interest: The home is a historic estate, built by locals, and preserv-

ing Hawaii's heritage. Volcano Village itself has more than 150 historic
homes or buildings. The historic town of Hilo is 23 miles away.

Innkeeper(s): Michael Tuttle. $85-125. MC, VISA, DC, CB, DS, PC, TC.
TAC10. 2 rooms with PB, 2 with FP, 1 suite, 3 cottages and 1 conference
room. Breakfast included in rates. Type of meal: Cont. Beds: QDT. VCR, fax,
copier and spa on premises. Handicap access. Weddings, small meetings,
family reunions and seminars hosted. Antiquing, fishing, live theater, parks,
shopping and water sports nearby.

Publicity: *National Geographic Traveler,
New York Times, Hawaii Bride, Pacific
Connection, Travel & Leisure.*

*"The hospitality and accommoda-
tions couldn't have been better. A
beautiful cottage in a peaceful,
tropical garden."*

Kilauea Lodge

PO Box 116
Volcano, HI 96785-0116
(808)967-7366 Fax:(808)967-7367
E-mail: stay@kilauealodge.com
Web: www.kilauealodge.com

Circa 1938. Guests are pampered at this gorgeous tropical paradise, only a mile from the entrance to Volcanoes National Park. Fluffy towels, towel warmers, robes, cozy, comfortable beds and rich decor create a feeling of warmth and romance in

each of the guest rooms. Fresh flowers and original art add to the majesty of the lodge. The wonderful, gourmet meals are served in front of the lodge's historic Fireplace of Friendship, which is decked with all sorts of artifacts. The innkeepers offer truly memorable meals, praised by such publications as Bon Appetit and Gourmet Magazine. The inn has an interesting history. Built as a YMCA, it later was used during World War II as offices and a military bivouac.

Historic Interest: Historical Hilo Town is 26 miles away and the Volcano Art Center and the original Volcano House, built in the 1890s, are only two miles away.

Innkeeper(s): Lorna & Albert Jeyte. $110-150. MC, VISA, PC, TC. 14 rooms, 11 with PB, 8 with FP, 3 cottages and 1 conference room. Breakfast included in rates. Types of meals: Full bkfst and country bkfst. Dinner and room service available. Restaurant on premises. Beds: KQT. Heaters and heated towel warmers in room. VCR, fax, copier, library and gazebo on premises. Handicap access. Weddings, small meetings, family reunions and seminars hosted. German and Spanish spoken. Antiquing, art galleries, beaches, bicycling, golf, hiking, horseback riding, volcano viewing, live theater, museums, parks, shopping and wineries nearby.

"Your rooms were outstanding both for cleanliness and decor. As to the dinner we had, it was superb, and as far as I'm concerned the best four-course dinner I have ever eaten."

Volcano Village   F9

The Chalet Kilauea Collection

Box 998, Wright Rd
Volcano Village, HI 96785
(808)967-7786 (800)937-7786 Fax:(808)967-8660
E-mail: reservations@volcano-hawaii.com
Web: www.volcano-hawaii.com

Circa 1945. This collection of lodging accommodations includes deluxe boutique inns, modest lodges, and spacious vacation homes. There are five inns and lodges and five vacation homes. The main inn, the Inn at Volcano, has six rooms, each with a special theme. The rooms sport names such as the Out of Africa, Treehouse or

Oriental Jade. The Bridal and Treehouse suites include Jacuzzi tubs. Inn guests are treated to a three-course, gourmet breakfast served by candlelight, as well as afternoon tea. There's an outdoor Jacuzzi for soaking.

Innkeeper(s): Lisha & Brian Crawford. $45-395. MC, VISA, AX, DC, DS, PC. TAC10. 40 rooms and 1 conference room. Breakfast included in rates. Types of meals: Full gourmet bkfst, cont plus, cont, veg bkfst and early coffee/tea. Afternoon tea and catering service available. Beds: KQT. Cable TV, phone, turndown service and VCR in room. Fax, copier, spa and library on premises. Weddings, small meetings, family reunions and seminars hosted. French, Dutch and German spoken. Antiquing, art galleries, beaches, bicycling, canoeing/kayaking, fishing, golf, hiking, horseback riding, lava viewing, live theater, museums, shopping, sporting events, tennis, water sports and wineries nearby.

"Your attention to detail is what makes Chalet Kilauea special to all who stay here. Everything from the mints on the bed to the tea service set you apart from other establishments. Thank you for the enjoyable and relaxing atmosphere."

Maui

Haiku   C8

Haikuleana B&B Inn, Plantation Style

555 Haiku Rd (formerly 69 Haiku Rd)
Haiku, HI 96708-5884
(808)575-2890 Fax:(808)575-9177

Circa 1850. A true plantation house, the Haikuleana sits in the midst of pineapple fields and Norfolk pine trees. With high ceilings and a tropical decor, the inn has all of the flavor of Hawaiian country life. The porch looks out over exotic gardens. Beaches and waterfalls are nearby.

Innkeeper(s): Ralph H. & Jeanne Elizabeth Blum.
$100-150. PC, TC. TAC10. 4 rooms, 3 with PB. Breakfast included in rates. Types of meals: Full gourmet bkfst and early coffee/tea. Picnic lunch available. Beds: KQT. TV, phone and ceiling fan in room. VCR, fax, copier, spa, library and croquet on premises. Weddings, small meetings, family reunions and seminars hosted. Russian, French, Italian, German and Spanish spoken. Antiquing, fishing, live theater, parks, shopping and water sports nearby.

Publicity: *Honolulu Advertiser, Maui News, Los Angeles Times, Portland Oregonian.*

"Great, great, extra great! Maui is paradise thanks to your daily guidance, directions and helpful hints."

Lahaina   C7

The Lahaina Inn

127 Lahainaluna Rd
Lahaina, Maui, HI 96761-1502
(808)661-0577 (800)669-3444 Fax:(808)667-9480

Circa 1938. After a fire in 1963, the inn was rebuilt in a frontier storefront style. Renovated in 1984 by Rick Ralston, founder of Crazy Shirts, the inn has been appointed in furnishings chosen from Ralston's warehouse of 12,000 antiques. Each of the stunning guest rooms boasts balconies with views of the harbor or mountains. The 12 rooms feature individual decor with coordinating bed covers and linens, Oriental rugs, antique beds made from iron, brass or wood, and ceiling fans. An antique sideboard outside the guest rooms is stocked each morning with steaming Kona coffee. The inn's restaurant, David Paul's Lahaina Grill, features a variety of gourmet fare and was named "Maui's Best Restaurant" four years in a row by Honolulu Magazine.

Historic Interest: A walking tour of this charming Hawaiian town includes such sites as the Baldwin House, Government Market, a courthouse, fort and canal. The Hauola Stone, a stop of the tour, was believed to have been used by Hawaiians as a healing place.

Innkeeper(s): Melinda A Mower. $99-169. MC, VISA, AX, DS, PC, TC. TAC10. 9 rooms and 3 suites. Breakfast included in rates. Types of meals: Cont and early coffee/tea. Restaurant on premises. Beds: KQDT. Phone and ceiling fan in room. Air conditioning. Fax, copier and internet access on premises. Antiquing, beaches, golf, harbor activities, shopping and tennis nearby.

"Outstanding lodging and service. Ahhh! Paradise. Fantastic. Excellent. Exquisite."

Wailuku   C7

Old Wailuku Inn

2199 Kahookele St
Wailuku, HI 96796-2130
(808)244-5897 (800)305-4899 Fax:(808)242-9600
E-mail: mauibandb@aol.com
Web: www.mauiinn.com

Circa 1924. Not everything wonderful in Hawaii is located along its impressive shoreline. A case in point is this restored plantation-style home located in Wailuku's historic district and away from the crowded tourist spots. Wailuku is where the people of Maui live and offers shopping, dining and cultural events. The home maintains many original features, including floors made of eucalyptus and a unique elliptical shower. The innkeepers, both of whom are born-and-raised islanders, have been in the hotel and restaurant businesses for more than 30 years, and their expertise is evident. The décor is imaginative and romantic with an eclectic mix of styles that all seem to fit together perfectly. The Hawaiian influence is predominant; each guest room is named after a flower. The Ilima Room is done in a creamy shade of yellow. The bed is topped with a quilt featuring its namesake flower, and the room also includes a spacious whirlpool tub. Several guest rooms afford mountain views. The half-acre grounds are decorated with palms, and guests can enjoy the setting on the inn's wicker-filled porch. The innkeepers serve breakfast on the enclosed porch with a view of Mt. Haleakala, and the menu might include the following: a fresh papaya filled with mango and garnished with straw-berries, a Portuguese version of the beignet, and a spinach, tofu and mushroom tart. The inn's central location offers close access to most Maui attractions, including Kahului Airport. The innkeepers offer many amenities for business travelers, including modem jacks, phones with voice mail and fax service.

Historic Interest: Bailey House (half a mile), Alexander House (half a mile), courthouse (2 blocks), Union church (1 block(, Historic Wailuku Town(half a mile), Halekii and Piihana Kalani Heiau (1 mile).

Innkeeper(s): Janice & Thomas Fairbanks. $120-180. MC, VISA, AX, DC, CB, DS, PC, TC. TAC10. 7 rooms with PB. Breakfast and snacks/refreshments included in rates. Type of meal: Veg bkfst. Catered breakfast available. Beds: KQT. Cable TV, phone, turndown service, ceiling fan and VCR in room. Central air. Fax, copier and library on premises. Weddings and family reunions hosted. German and Spanish spoken. Antiquing, art galleries, beaches, bicycling, canoeing/kayaking, fishing, golf, hiking, horseback riding, live theater, museums, parks, shopping, sporting events, tennis, water sports and wineries nearby.

Oahu

Honolulu   B5

The Manoa Valley Inn

2001 Vancouver Dr
Honolulu, HI 96822-2451
(808)947-6019 Fax:(808)946-6168
E-mail: manoavalleyin@aloha.net
Web: www.aloha.net/~wery/

Circa 1915. This exquisite home offers the best of two worlds, a beautiful, country home that is also surrounded by a tropical paradise. Each restored room features lavish decor with ornate beds, ceiling fans and period furniture. Little amenities such as the his and her robes create a romantic touch. Breakfasts with kona coffee, juices, fresh fruits and baked goods are served. The inn's common rooms offer unique touches such as a nickelodeon and antique Victrola. The Manoa Valley is a perfect location to enjoy Hawaii and is only blocks away from the University of Hawaii.

Historic Interest: The Honolulu Art Academy, founded by an early missionary, features a unique architectural mix of Polynesian design and missionary style. The Iolani Place was built by King David Kalakaua and was the home of Hawaiian royalty until the demise of the monarchy in 1893.

Innkeeper(s): Theresa Wery. $99-190. MC, VISA, TC. TAC10. 8 rooms, 3 with PB, 1 suite and 1 cottage. Breakfast included in rates. Type of meal: Cont. Beds: KQD. TV, phone, ceiling fan and daily maid service in room. Fax, copier, billiard room, Port wine on coffee table in living room & upstairs sitting room and iron on premises. Weddings and small meetings hosted. Museums and art museums nearby.

"A wonderful place!! Stepping back to a time of luxury!"

Idaho

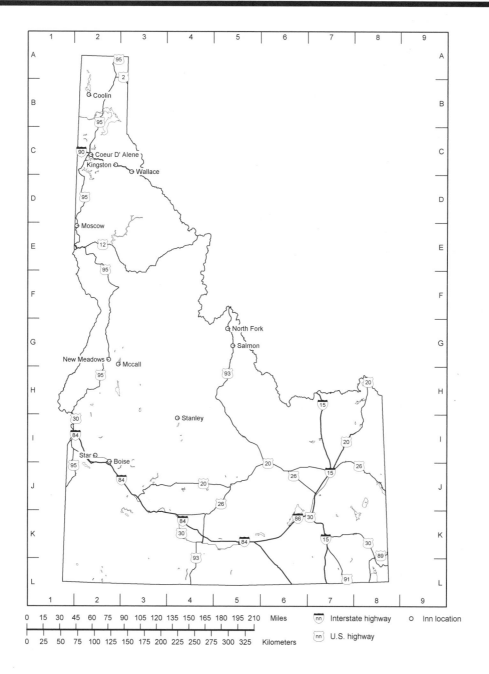

A 1 2 3 4 5 6 7 8 9 A

95
2
Coolin
B B
95
90 Coeur D' Alene
Kingston
Wallace
C C
95
D D
Moscow
E 12 E
95
F F
North Fork
G Salmon G
New Meadows Mccall
95
93
H 20 H
15
30
84 Stanley 20
I Star 20 I
95 Boise 20 26 15 26
J 84 20 J
26 15
86 30
K 84 84 30 K
30 15 30
84 89
93
L 91 L

1 2 3 4 5 6 7 8 9

0 15 30 45 60 75 90 105 120 135 150 165 180 195 210   Miles   🔲 nn Interstate highway   ○ Inn location

0   25   50   75   100 125 150 175 200 225 250 275 300 325   Kilometers   🛡 nn U.S. highway

Boise I2

Idaho Heritage Inn

109 W Idaho St
Boise, ID 83702-6122
(208)342-8066 Fax:(208)343-2325

Circa 1904. This Colonial Revival home, set back on a tree-lined street near downtown, was once the home of Senator Frank Church and is in  the National Register. Because of its location in the historic Warm Springs district, geothermal water is used for heating and bathing. Period furnishings and wall coverings are found throughout. Bicycles are available for enjoying the nearby greenbelt, which winds along the Boise River.

Innkeeper(s): Phyllis Lupher. $60-105. MC, VISA, AX, DS, PC, TC. TAC10. 6 rooms with PB, 3 suites and 1 cottage. Breakfast included in rates. Types of meals: Full gourmet bkfst and early coffee/tea. Beds: Q. TV and phone in room. Air conditioning. VCR, fax and bicycles on premises. Small meetings and seminars hosted. Antiquing, fishing, golf, parks, shopping, downhill skiing, cross-country skiing, sporting events, tennis and water sports nearby.

"Thanks so much for the hospitality and warmth."

Coeur d'Alene C2

Gregory's McFarland House

601 E Foster Ave
Coeur d'Alene, ID 83814
(208)667-1232 (800)335-1232

Circa 1905. This yellow and white three-story historic home, shaded by tall trees, offers a wraparound porch with swaying swing, a deck and summerhouse, overlooking green lawns and gardens. English chintz, Oriental rugs and antiques are found throughout. A three-course gourmet breakfast is offered in the glass conservatory, next to the scenic deck. The inn has a resident minister and professional photographer, so it is popular for weddings and for renewing marriage vows. Water skiing, fishing, bird watching, skiing and digging for garnets are favorite activities. Coeur d'Alene Lake, within walking distance, is considered one of the most beautiful lakes in the world. Spokane is 30 minutes away and the international airport 45 minutes.

Innkeeper(s): Winifred, Carol & Stephen Gregory. $90-175. MC, VISA, DS, PC, TC. TAC10. 5 rooms with PB, 4 suites and 1 conference room. Breakfast included in rates. Type of meal: Full gourmet bkfst. Beds: KQ. Turndown service, ceiling fan and bath robes in room. Air conditioning. VCR and central air conditioning on premises. Weddings, small meetings, family reunions and seminars hosted. Amusement parks, antiquing, fishing, golf, live theater, parks, shopping, downhill skiing, cross-country skiing, sporting events, tennis and water sports nearby.

The Roosevelt Inn

105 E Wallace Ave
Coeur d'Alene, ID 83814-2947
(208)765-5200 (800)290-3358 Fax:(208)664-4142
E-mail: info@therooseveltinn.com
Web: www.therooseveltinn.com

Circa 1905. This turn-of-the-century, red brick home was named for President Roosevelt and is the oldest schoolhouse in

town. Roosevelt translates to Rosefield in Dutch, and the innkeepers have created a rosy theme for the inn. The Bell Tower Suite and the Honeymoon Suite are the favorite room requests, but all rooms offer Victorian antiques and some have lake views. Coeur d'Alene has been recognized by National Geographic Magazine as one of the five most beautiful lakes in the world. The area offers the world's longest floating boardwalk and Tubb's Hill Nature Park. A variety of shops and restaurants are within a five minute stroll from the inn. The natural surroundings offer mountain biking, boating, skiing and hiking.

Innkeeper(s): John & Tina Hough. $80-249. MC, VISA, AX, DS. TAC10. 15 rooms, 10 with PB, 3 with FP, 5 suites and 2 conference rooms. Breakfast and snacks/refreshments included in rates. Types of meals: Full gourmet bkfst, veg bkfst and early coffee/tea. Afternoon tea available. Beds: Q. Cable TV, turndown service and VCR in room. Central air. Fax, copier, spa, sauna, library, rose greeting in room and exercise room on premises. Handicap access. Weddings, small meetings, family reunions and seminars hosted. Amusement parks, antiquing, art galleries, beaches, bicycling, canoeing/kayaking, fishing, golf, hiking, horseback riding, live theater, museums, parks, shopping, downhill skiing, cross-country skiing, sporting events, tennis, water sports and wineries nearby.

Pets allowed: house pets only in two rooms, $125 deposit.

Coolin B2

Old Northern Inn

PO Box 177, 220 Bayview
Coolin, ID 83821-0177
(208)443-2426 Fax:(208)443-3856

Circa 1890. This historic inn was built to serve guests riding the Great Northern rail line. Today, travelers come to enjoy trout-filled Priest Lake and all its offerings. The inn is located on the lake shore, and guests enjoy use of a small marina and private beach. There is also a volleyball court, but guests are welcome to simply sit and relax on the spacious deck. The natural surroundings are full of wildlife, and it's not unusual to see deer, caribou and even a moose. The hotel itself is a two-story log and shingle structure, quite at home among the tall cedars. The interior is warm and inviting. There is a common area with a stone fireplace and country furnishings, as well as a view of mountains and the lake. Rooms are decorated with turn-of-the-century antiques, and the suites include a small sitting room. Huckleberry pancakes have been a staple at the inn's breakfast table since the 19th century. In the afternoons, wine, cheese and fruit are served.

$85-130. MC, VISA, PC, TC. TAC10. 6 rooms with PB and 2 suites. Breakfast included in rates. Types of meals: Full bkfst and early coffee/tea. Beds: Q. Fax, copier and swimming on premises. Handicap access. Small meetings and family reunions hosted. Antiquing, fishing, golf, shopping, tennis and water sports nearby.

Publicity: *Seattle Times.*

Kingston C2

Kingston 5 Ranch B&B

42297 Silver Valley Rd
Kingston, ID 83839-0130
(208)682-4862 (800)254-1852 Fax:(208)682-9445
E-mail: k5ranch@nidlink.com
Web: www.nidlink.com/~k5ranch

Circa 1930. With the Coeur d'Alene Mountains as its backdrop, this red roofed farmhouse has been renovated with French door and wraparound decks to make the most of its

sweeping mountain views and pastoral setting. Innkeepers Walt and Pat Gentry have graced the guest rooms with lace, down comforters, cozy chairs and romantic touches such as four-poster beds. The suites offer outdoor spas on private decks with mountain views, fireplaces, and baths with whirlpool tubs. The innkeeper is a recipient of several national awards for her recipes. Specialties include Kingston Benedict and stuffed French Toast topped with fresh huckleberry sauce along with freshly baked, prize winning lemon huckleberry muffins. Enjoy activities such as touring two historic gold mines, the Kellogg Gondola, boating or dinner cruises on Lake Coeur d'Alene, skiing,, hiking, fishing, bird watching and driving excursions where you may encounter elk, deer, eagles and other wildlife. Often guests find the greatest pleasure to be watching the horses grazing in the pasture or volunteering to pick fresh strawberries, raspberries or loganberries to top an evening desert of vanilla ice cream.

Historic Interest: The Historic Cataldo Mansion, the oldest building in Idaho, is just five minutes away. Wallace, a town listed on the historic register, is 20 minutes from the farmhouse.

Innkeeper(s): Walter & Pat Gentry. $100-125. MC, VISA, TC. TAC10. 2 suites, 2 with FP. Breakfast included in rates. Types of meals: Full bkfst and early coffee/tea. Beds: Q. Digital clocks, fireplaces, Jacuzzi tub and central heat in room. Air conditioning. VCR, fax, copier, spa, stables, bicycles and kennel one mile off site on premises. Small meetings hosted. Amusement parks, antiquing, fishing, horseback riding, canoeing, mountain biking, live theater, parks, shopping, downhill skiing, cross-country skiing and water sports nearby.

McCall   G2

Northwest Passage

201 Rio Vista, PO Box 4208
McCall, ID 83638-8208
(208)634-5349 (800)597-6658 Fax:(208)634-4977

Circa 1938. This mountain country inn rests on five acres and offers six guest rooms, two of them suites. Guests enjoy the inn's two sitting rooms, fireplace and full breakfasts. There are horse corrals on the premises, and most pets can be accommodated when arrangements are made in advance. The inn is furnished in country decor and provides easy access to a myriad of recreational opportunities found in the area. Payette Lake is just a short distance from the inn, and the Brundage Mountain Ski Area and Ponderosa State Park are nearby.

Historic Interest: Inn built in 1938 to house the cast of the movie "Northwest Passage".

Innkeeper(s): Steve & Barbara Schott. $65-85. MC, VISA, AX, DS. 6 rooms, 5 with PB, 1 with FP, 2 suites and 1 conference room. Breakfast included in rates. Type of meal: Full bkfst. VCR, fax, television and horse corrals on premises. Weddings, small meetings, family reunions and seminars hosted. Antiquing, fishing, live theater, shopping, downhill skiing and cross-country skiing nearby.

New Meadows   G2

Hartland Inn

211 Norris Hwy 95
New Meadows, ID 83654-0215
(208)347-2114 Fax:(208)347-2535

Circa 1911. This handsome, three-story house was built by the president of the PIN Railroad. The mansion's pleasant interiors include a sunny sitting room and a formal dining room.

Guest rooms offer polished wood floors and ceiling fans, and some include period antiques. Breakfast includes strata, muffins and fruit smoothies. Enjoy the area's mountains, forests, rivers, lakes and scenic drives. The Little Salmon River is three blocks away.

Innkeeper(s): Stephen & JoBeth Mehen. $78-102. MC, VISA, AX, DS, TC. TAC10. 3 rooms, 1 with PB. Breakfast included in rates. Types of meals: Full bkfst and early coffee/tea. Beds: QD. Ceiling fan in room. VCR, fax, copier, spa and library on premises. Small meetings hosted. Antiquing, fishing, golf, parks, downhill skiing, cross-country skiing and water sports nearby.

Salmon   G5

Greyhouse Inn B&B

HC 61, Box 16
Salmon, ID 83467
(208)756-3968 (800)348-8097
E-mail: osgoodd@dmi.net
Web: www.greyhouseinn.com

Circa 1894. The scenery at Greyhouse is nothing short of wondrous. In the winter, when mountains are capped in white and the evergreens are shrouded in snow, this Victorian appears as a safe haven from the chilly weather. In the summer, the rocky peaks are a contrast to the whimsical house, which looks like something out of an Old West town. The historic home is known around town as the old maternity hospital, but there is nothing medicinal about it now. The rooms are Victorian in style with antique furnishings. The parlor features deep red walls and carpeting, floral overstuffed sofas and a dressmaker's model garbed in a black Victorian gown. Outdoor enthusiasts will find no shortage of activities, from facing the rapids in nearby Salmon River to fishing to horseback riding. The town of Salmon is just 12 miles away.

Innkeeper(s): David & Sharon Osgood. $65-80. MC, VISA, DS, PC, TC. TAC10. 4 rooms, 2 with PB. Breakfast included in rates. Types of meals: Full bkfst and early coffee/tea. Afternoon tea, gourmet dinner and snacks/refreshments available. Beds: KQDT. Room fans in room. VCR, bicycles, library and pet boarding on premises. Weddings, small meetings and family reunions hosted. Antiquing, fishing, golf, float trips, hot springs, horseback riding, hiking, mountain biking, parks, shopping, downhill skiing, cross-country skiing and water sports nearby.

Pets allowed: We have a kennel.

"To come around the corner and find the Greyhouse, as we did, restores my faith! Such a miracle. We had a magical evening here, and we plan to return to stay for a few days. Thanks so much for your kindness and hospitality. We love Idaho!"

Stanley   I4

Idaho Rocky Mountain Ranch

HC 64 Box 9934
Stanley, ID 83278-9602
(208)774-3544 Fax:(208)774-3477

Circa 1930. This thousand-acre ranch is situated at the 6,600-foot level in the Sawtooth Valley. The lodge dining room and spacious front porch overlook the Salmon River, which runs through the property, and beyond to the spectacular ragged

ridges of the Sawtooth Mountains. Near the edge of the river, the inn has a swimming pool completely fed by a natural hot springs. Rustic accommodations in lodgepole pine cabins feature handmade log, hickory and cane furniture and fieldstone fireplaces. The lodge is listed in the National Register of Historic Places.

Historic Interest: Ghost towns of Vienna, Boulder, Bonanza and Custer (within 50 miles), Stanley Historical Museum (10 miles), Yankee Fork Dredge/Museum (30 miles).

Innkeeper(s): Bill Leavell & Sandra Beckwith. $145-240. MC, VISA, DS, PC, TC. 21 rooms with PB, 17 with FP and 9 cottages. Breakfast and dinner included in rates. MAP. Type of meal: Full bkfst. Picnic lunch available. Beds: QT. Fax, copier, swimming, stables, bicycles, library, fishing pond, hiking trails and ski touring on premises. Spanish spoken. Bicycling, fishing, hiking, horseback riding, whitewater rafting, rock climbing, parks, downhill skiing, cross-country skiing and water sports nearby.

"We had such a great time! The kids loved it! Can't you adopt us so we can stay longer?."

Star   I2

The Maples B&B

PO Box 1
Star, ID 83669
(877)286-7419

Circa 1888. This prim little farmhouse is shaded by maple trees and rests behind a picket fence. Early American furnishings with quilts, wallpapers and wainscoting are featured. The

morning meal is served family style, and made-to-order breakfasts are available for guests with special diets. (Or ask for the Sunday Brunch with scrambled eggs, shrimp and mushrooms with melted cheeses served atop an English muffin.) The homeowners are retired schoolteachers who raised their children in the home. Ask Don about his special fishing spots and for advice on the area's white-water rafting opportunities.

Historic Interest: Oregon trail (1/2 mile), massacre site (8 mile), State Capitol (16 miles), ghost town (15 miles), Old Fort Boise (25 miles), Idaho Historical Museum (16 miles).

Innkeeper(s): Mary & Don Wertman. $60-125. MC, VISA, PC, TC. TAC10. 4 rooms with PB and 1 suite. Breakfast and snacks/refreshments included in rates. Types of meals: Full gourmet bkfst, country bkfst and veg bkfst. Picnic lunch available. Beds: KQDT. Cable TV, phone, turndown service, ceiling fan, VCR and quilts in room. Central air. Library, patio, sunroom and large yard on premises. Weddings, small meetings and family reunions hosted. Antiquing, art galleries, beaches, bicycling, canoeing/kayaking, fishing, golf, hiking, horseback riding, live theater, museums, parks, shopping, downhill skiing, cross-country skiing, sporting events, tennis, water sports and wineries nearby.

Wallace   C3

The Beale House

107 Cedar St
Wallace, ID 83873-2115
(208)752-7151 (888)752-7151

Circa 1904. This attractive, three-story Colonial Revival home is listed in the National Register, as is the town of Wallace. Original parquet wood floor, antiques and memorabilia combine to lend an authentic aura of the past. Each of the five guest rooms offers a unique feature, such as a fireplace, balcony or wall of windows. The innkeepers are well versed in their home's history and guests are welcome to look over a photographic record of the house and its former owners. A backyard hot tub provides views of the mountains and creek. Guests can enjoy birdwatching on the property. Recreational activities abound in the vicinity, famous for its silver mines. There are also museums nearby.

Historic Interest: Town of Wallace, Cataldo Mission.

Innkeeper(s): Jim & Linda See. $85-125. PC, TC. TAC10. 5 rooms, 1 with PB, 1 with FP and 1 suite. Breakfast included in rates. Types of meals: Full bkfst, cont and early coffee/tea. Beds: QDT. Turndown service in room. VCR, spa and library on premises. Weddings hosted. Antiquing, bicycling, fishing, golf, hiking, museums, bird watching, live theater, parks, shopping, downhill skiing, cross-country skiing and water sports nearby.

Illinois

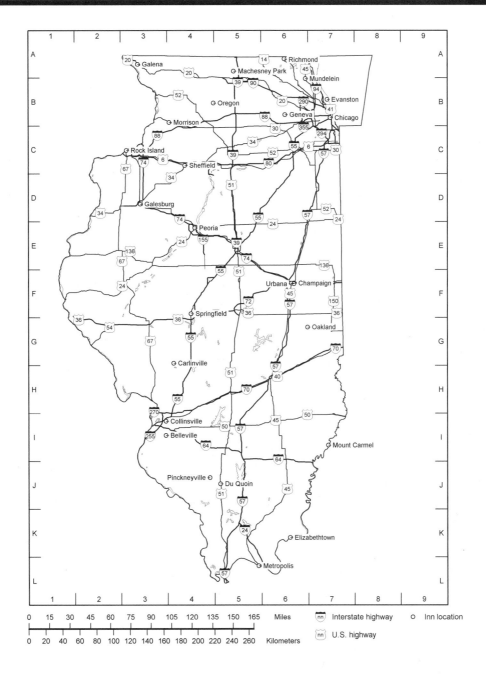

1	2	3	4	5	6	7	8	9

Galena, Machesney Park, Richmond, Mundelein, Evanston, Oregon, Geneva, Chicago, Morrison, Rock Island, Sheffield, Galesburg, Peoria, Urbana, Champaign, Springfield, Oakland, Carlinville, Collinsville, Belleville, Mount Carmel, Pinckneyville, Du Quoin, Elizabethtown, Metropolis

0 15 30 45 60 75 90 105 120 135 150 165   Miles

0 20 40 60 80 100 120 140 160 180 200 220 240 260   Kilometers

Interstate highway   o Inn location

U.S. highway

Belleville   I3

Swans Court B&B
421 Court St
Belleville, IL 62220-1201
(618)233-0779 (800)840-1058 Fax:(618)277-3150

Circa 1883. This home, designated by the Department of the Interior as a certified historic structure, was once home to David Baer, known as the "mule king of the world." Baer sold

more than 10,000 mules each year to British troops in World War I and to American troops in World War II. The home is furnished almost entirely in antiques. Innkeeper Monty Dixon searched high and low to fill her B&B with authentic pieces, creating a nostalgic ambiance. The library offers a selection of books, games and puzzles for guests to enjoy. The home is located in a historic neighborhood, within walking distance to shops and restaurants. Belleville is convenient to St. Louis, and there are casinos, historic sites, a racetrack and a state park nearby.

Innkeeper(s): Ms. Monty Dixon. $65-90. MC, VISA, AX, DS, PC, TC. TAC10. 4 rooms, 2 with PB, 2 with FP. Breakfast and snacks/refreshments included in rates. Type of meal: Full bkfst. Beds: QD. Phone, ceiling fan and folding tables upon request in room. Air conditioning. VCR and library on premises. Handicap access. Weddings, small meetings, family reunions and seminars hosted. Spanish spoken. Antiquing, golf, live theater, shopping, sporting events and tennis nearby.

"We feel like we have made a new friend. We appreciated all of the nice little touches, such as the fresh flowers."

Victory Inn
712 S Jackson St
Belleville, IL 62220-2672
(618)277-1538 (888)277-8586 Fax:(618)277-1576
E-mail: jo@victoryinn.com
Web: www.victoryinn.com

Circa 1877. Carefully chosen period reproductions and decor create the Victorian ambiance at Victory Inn, a historic home just minutes from downtown Belleville. Two rooms share a

bath, but can be combined as a suite. Two rooms include a Jacuzzi tub. Breakfasts include several different types of homemade breads and fresh fruit. Belleville offers shops, restaurants and two historic house museums. St. Louis is a short drive away.

Innkeeper(s): Jo & Tom Brannon. $60-115. MC, VISA, AX, PC, TC. TAC10. 2 rooms with PB and 1 suite. Breakfast included in rates. Types of meals: Cont plus and early coffee/tea. Beds: Q. Phone, turndown service and two Jacuzzi's in room. Air conditioning. VCR and fax on premises. Antiquing, fishing, golf, live theater, parks, shopping and sporting events nearby.

Carlinville   G4

Victoria Tyme Inn
511 E First South St
Carlinville, IL 62626-1827
(217)854-8689 Fax:(217)854-5122

Circa 1857. This National Register home actually is comprised of two historic homes, one was built in the 1850s and the other home in 1876. The structures eventually were joined

together. Noted author Mary Hunter Austin was born in the home. The inn's spacious suite is named for her, and it includes a whirlpool tub. The decor is an understated Victorian with antiques, and two rooms display pressed tin ceilings. The verandas offer rocking chairs for those who wish to relax, and the half-acre grounds are decorated with gardens. In the morning, the innkeeper's signature waffles or perhaps a rich, stuffed French toast are accompanied by homemade jams and marmalade, fresh fruit and muffins straight from the oven. Carlinville boasts the country's largest collection of Sears catalog homes, as well as shops, antiquing and festivals throughout the year. The town is midway between Springfield, Ill., and St. Louis.

Innkeeper(s): Jeff & Jodie Padgett. $69-135. MC, VISA, DS, PC, TC. 4 rooms with PB and 1 suite. Types of meals: Full gourmet bkfst and early coffee/tea. Beds: Q. Turndown service, ceiling fan and home baked goodies in room. Air conditioning. VCR, fax and library on premises. French and Spanish spoken. Antiquing, fishing, golf, parks and shopping nearby.

"The warmth, beauty and charm of this beautiful home is certainly reflected through both of you."

Champaign   F6

Golds B&B
2065 County Road 525 E
Champaign, IL 61821-9521
(217)586-4345

Circa 1874. Visitors to the University of Illinois area may enjoy a restful experience at this inn, west of town in a peaceful farmhouse setting. Antique country furniture collected by the innkeepers over the past 25 years is showcased in the inn and is beautifully offset by early American stenciling on its walls. An apple tree and garden are on the grounds, and seasonal items are sometimes used as breakfast fare.

Innkeeper(s): Rita & Bob Gold. $45-50. PC, TC. TAC10. 3 rooms, 1 with PB. Breakfast included in rates. Types of meals: Cont plus and early coffee/tea. Beds: QT. Air conditioning. VCR on premises. Antiquing, fishing, live theater, parks, shopping, cross-country skiing, sporting events and water sports nearby.

Publicity: *News Gazette.*

Chicago B7

House Of Two Urns

1239 N Greenview Ave
Chicago, IL 60622-3318
(312)810-2466 (800)835-9303 Fax:(773)235-1410

Circa 1912. This historic townhouse offers guests a unique experience in the Windy City. The house is built in late Victorian style, and innkeeper Kapra Fleming has decorated the B&B in an eclectic style with antiques and family heirlooms. Kapra has included many thoughtful amenities, such as robes, hair dryers, slippers and an alarm clock. Rooms are inviting and tastefully furnished. The spacious loft suite includes a queen and full bed, as well as a private bath. The continental-plus breakfasts include items such as French toast with almonds and bananas or chocolate chip scones. The home is located in the Wicker Park section of Chicago, less than three miles from downtown and six miles from McCormick Center.

Innkeeper(s): Kapra Fleming. $69-160. MC, VISA, AX, DS, TC. TAC10. 4 rooms and 1 suite. Breakfast included in rates. Types of meals: Cont plus and early coffee/tea. Beds: QD. Cable TV, phone, ceiling fan, VCR and hair dryer in room. Fax on premises. Family reunions hosted. German, Spanish and French spoken. Antiquing, live theater, parks, shopping, sporting events and water sports nearby.

Collinsville I3

Maggie's B&B

2102 N Keebler Ave
Collinsville, IL 62234-4713
(618)344-8283

Circa 1900. A rustic two-acre wooded area surrounds this friendly Victorian inn, once a boarding house. Rooms with 14-foot ceilings are furnished with exquisite antiques and art objects collected on worldwide travels. Downtown St. Louis, the Gateway Arch and the Mississippi riverfront are just 10 minutes away.

Historic Interest: Cahokia Indian Mounds (3 miles), Gateway Arch (15 miles).

Innkeeper(s): Maggie Leyda. $40-85. PC, TC. 5 rooms, 3 with PB, 2 with FP and 1 conference room. Breakfast included in rates. Types of meals: Full bkfst and early coffee/tea. Beds: QDT. Cable TV, turndown service, ceiling fan and VCR in room. Air conditioning. Spa and library on premises. Handicap access. Weddings, small meetings and family reunions hosted. Amusement parks, antiquing, fishing, live theater, parks, shopping and sporting events nearby.

"We enjoyed a delightful stay. You've thought of everything. What fun!"

Du Quoin J5

Francie's B&B

104 S Line St
Du Quoin, IL 62832-2344
(618)542-6686
E-mail: bbinn@midwest.net
Web: www.midwest.net/bbinn

Circa 1908. This solid three-story home on three acres served as an orphanage for 39 years. The inside is decorated with a Victorian flair, and the rooms feature extravagant touches such as puffy comforters, as well as writing desks and lounge chairs. The Ciara room has a brass and iron bed, while the Desiree room boasts white wicker furniture and a view of the front grounds. The Van Arsdale Suite has a four-poster bed, antique wardrobe and clawfoot tub. Breakfasts are served in bed, on the balcony or in the Tea Room, which seats 60 and is an ideal location for a wedding reception or business function. There's a wide veranda that stretches across the front of the inn. Southern Illinois University and Shawnee National Forest is nearby.

Innkeeper(s): Cathy & Benny Trowbridge. $60-85. MC, VISA, AX, DS, PC. 4 rooms with PB. Type of meal: Full bkfst. Beds: KQT. TV and phone in room. Shopping nearby.

Elizabethtown K6

River Rose Inn B&B

1 Main St PO Box 78
Elizabethtown, IL 62931-0078
(618)287-8811 Fax:(618)287-8853

Circa 1914. Large, shade trees veil the front of this Greek Gothic home, nestled along the banks of the Ohio River. From the grand front entrance, guests look out to polished woodwork and a staircase leading to shelves of books. Rooms are cheerful and nostalgic, decorated with antiques. Each guest room offers something special. One has a four-poster bed, another offers a fireplace. The Scarlet Room has its own balcony and whirlpool tub, and the Rose Room has a private patio with a swing. The Magnolia Cottage is ideal for honeymooners and includes a whirlpool tub for two, fireplace and a deck that overlooks the river. Breakfasts are served in the dining room where guests can enjoy the water views.

Innkeeper(s): Don & Elisabeth Phillips. $59-96. MC, VISA, PC, TC. 5 rooms with PB, 2 with FP and 1 cottage. Breakfast included in rates. Types of meals: Full gourmet bkfst and early coffee/tea. Beds: QT. Cable TV, ceiling fan and VCR in room. Air conditioning. Fax, copier, spa, swimming and library on premises. French and German spoken. Amusement parks, antiquing, fishing, golf, hiking, biking, parks, shopping and water sports nearby.

Evanston B7

The Homestead

1625 Hinman Ave
Evanston, IL 60201-6021
(847)475-3300 Fax:(847)570-8100

Circa 1927. This hotel, the only lodging in Evanston's Lakeshore Historic District, was built by a local architect and his Colonial structure is very much unchanged from its beginnings in the 1920s. Several rooms offer views of Lake Michigan, which is just two blocks away. Northwestern University also is just a

two-block walk from the hotel. The inn's much-renown restaurant, Trio, serves specialties such as grilled pheasant with pine nut bread pudding or perhaps roasted Maine sea scallops served with a black truffle and parmesan risotto.

Innkeeper(s): David Reynolds. $95-190. MC, VISA, AX, DC, DS, PC, TC. 35 rooms, 1 suite and 1 conference room. Breakfast included in rates. Type of meal: Cont. Gourmet dinner available. Restaurant on premises. Beds: QDT. Cable TV and phone in room. Air conditioning. Fax, copier and library on premises. Small meetings and seminars hosted. Live theater, parks, sporting events, tennis and water sports nearby.

Margarita European Inn

1566 Oak Ave
Evanston, IL 60201-4298
(847)869-2273 Fax:(847)869-2353

Circa 1927. This stately inn, once the proper home to young area working women, has a proud tradition in the city's history. The Georgian architecture is complemented by an impressive interior, featuring arched French doors, vintage period molding and a large parlor with floor-to-ceiling windows. Near the lakefront and Northwestern University, it also boasts a library, large-screen TV room and VaPenisero, a restaurant serving regional Italian specialties. Guests often enjoy renting a bike and exploring the area's many attractions, including 24 nearby art galleries.

Innkeeper(s): Barbara & Tim Gorham. $75-145. MC, VISA, AX, DC, TC. 44 rooms, 21 with PB and 1 conference room. Breakfast included in rates. Types of meals: Cont and early coffee/tea. Restaurant on premises. Beds: KQDT. Phone and ceiling fan in room. Weddings, small meetings, family reunions and seminars hosted. Antiquing, live theater, shopping and sporting events nearby.

Galena   A3

DeSoto House Hotel

230 S Main St
Galena, IL 61036-2274
(815)777-0090 (800)343-6562

Circa 1855. Abraham Lincoln, Theodore Roosevelt and Mark Twain are among the DeSoto's famous guests. An original winding staircase still graces the lobby, and a ballroom with floor-to-ceiling windows is used for banquets. The renovated hotel, which is listed in the National Register, features comfortable rooms. There are a variety of dining options. The Courtyard, located in a four-story, sun-lit atrium serves breakfast and lunch. The Generals' Restaurant, named to honor Galena's nine Civil War generals, is open for dinner. The hotel also includes Green Street Tavern, which serves more casual fare.

Innkeeper(s): Daniel Kelley. $89-195. MC, VISA, AX, DS. 55 rooms with PB, 2 with FP and 7 conference rooms. Restaurant on premises. Beds: KD. Fax and copier on premises. Handicap access.

Farmers' Guest House

334 Spring St
Galena, IL 61036-2128
(815)777-3456 Fax:(815)777-3514

Circa 1867. This two-story brick commercial building was built as a bakery and served as a store and hotel, as well. Rows of arched, multi-paned windows add charm to the exterior. The rooms are decorated with antiques, lace curtains and floral wallpapers. The accommodations include seven rooms with queen-size beds, one room with a double bed, the two-room Master Suite and the two-room Queen Suite. There's a bar, featured in the movie "Field of Dreams." A hot tub is offered in the backyard. The inn also has a cabin in the woods available for rent.

Innkeeper(s): Tom & Pam Cummings. $79-150. MC, VISA, AX, DS, PC. TAC10. 9 rooms with PB and 1 cottage. Breakfast included in rates. Type of meal: Early coffee/tea. Picnic lunch available. Beds: KQD. Cable TV and phone in room. Air conditioning. Fax and spa on premises. Small meetings, family reunions and seminars hosted. Antiquing, fishing, golf, live theater, parks, shopping, downhill skiing, cross-country skiing, sporting events and tennis nearby.

"Neat old place, fantastic breakfasts."

Park Avenue Guest House

208 Park Ave
Galena, IL 61036-2306
(815)777-1075

Circa 1893. A short walk from Grant Park sits this attractive Queen Anne Victorian with turret and wraparound porch. Gardens and a gazebo add to this peaceful neighborhood charm, as does the original woodwork throughout. The Helen Room features a gas fireplace, TV, tub and shower, while Miriam Room's brass bed highlights a cheerful floral decor and a fireplace. The Anna Suite also has a fireplace and boasts a comfortable sitting room in the inn's turret area and the Lucille Room is tastefully furnished in mauve, gray and white tones. The holiday decorations, including twelve Christmas trees, are not to be missed.

Innkeeper(s): Sharon & John Fallbacher. $95-125. MC, VISA, DS, PC, TC. 4 rooms with PB, 3 with FP and 1 suite. Snacks/refreshments included in rates. Types of meals: Full bkfst and early coffee/tea. Beds: QT. Cable TV and ceiling fan in room. Air conditioning. VCR on premises. Weddings, small meetings and family reunions hosted. Antiquing, fishing, casino, riverboat, live theater, shopping, downhill skiing and cross-country skiing nearby.

Galesburg   D3

Seacord House

624 N Cherry St
Galesburg, IL 61401-2731
(309)342-4107

Circa 1891. A former county sheriff and businessman built this Eastlake-style Victorian, which is located in the town's historic district. The home was named for its builder, Wilkens Seacord, a prominent local man whose family is mentioned in Carl Sandburg's autobiography. In keeping with the house's historical prominence, the innkeepers have tried to maintain its turn-of-the-century charm. Victorian wallpapers, lacy curtains and a collection of family antiques grace the guest rooms and living areas. The bedrooms, however, fea-ture the modern amenity of waterbeds. For those celebrating romantic occasions, the innkeepers provide heart-shaped muffins along with regular morning fare.

Historic Interest: Built in 1894, house has natural woodwork on first floor and working pocket doors.

Innkeeper(s): Gwen and Lyle. $48. MC, VISA, DS. 3 rooms. Breakfast included in rates. Type of meal: Cont plus. Fax on premises.

Geneva   B6

The Oscar Swan Country Inn

1800 W State St
Geneva, IL 60134-1002
(630)232-0173

Circa 1902. This turn-of-the-century Colonial Revival house rests on seven acres of trees and lawns. Its 6,000 square feet are filled with homey touches. There is a historic barn on the

property and a gazebo on the front lawn. A pillared breezeway connects the round garage to the house. The stone pool is round, as well. Nina is a retired home economics teacher and Hans speaks German and was a professor of business administration at Indiana University.

Innkeeper(s): Nina Heymann. $88-150. MC, VISA, AX. 8 rooms, 4 with PB and 3 conference rooms. Breakfast included in rates. Type of meal: Full bkfst. Lunch and catering service available. Beds: KQD. Phone and VCR in room. Air conditioning. Weddings, small meetings, family reunions and seminars hosted. Antiquing, live theater, shopping and cross-country skiing nearby.

Publicity: *Chicago Tribune, Windmill News.*

"Thank you for making our wedding such a beautiful memory. The accommodations were wonderful, the food excellent."

Metropolis   L5

Isle of View B&B

205 Metropolis St
Metropolis, IL 62960-2213
(618)524-5838 (800)566-7491
E-mail: kimoff@hcis.net
Web: www.bbonline.com/il/isleofview

Circa 1889. Metropolis, billed as the "home of Superman," is not a bustling concrete city, but a quaint, country town tucked along the Ohio River. The Isle of View, a stunning Italianate manor, is just a short walk from shops, restaurants and the Players Riverboat Casino. All the guest rooms are appointed in

Victorian design with antiques. The Master Suite was originally the home's library and includes a unique coal-burning fireplace, canopy bed and two-person whirlpool tub.

Innkeeper(s): Kim & Gerald Offenburger. $65-125. MC, VISA, AX, DC, CB, DS, TC. 5 rooms with PB. Breakfast included in rates. Types of meals: Full gourmet bkfst and early coffee/tea. Beds: KQD. Cable TV, phone and ceiling fan in room. Air conditioning. Small meetings and family reunions hosted. Antiquing, fishing, riverboat casino, live theater, parks, shopping and water sports nearby.

Pets allowed: please ask.

"You may never want to leave."

Morrison   B4

Hillendale B&B

600 W Lincolnway
Morrison, IL 61270-2058
(815)772-3454 Fax:(815)772-7023
E-mail: hillend@clinton.net
Web: www.hillend.com

Circa 1891. Guests at Hillendale don't simply spend the night in the quaint town of Morrison, Ill., they spend the night in France, Italy, Hawaii or Africa. Each of the guests rooms in this Tudor manor reflects a different theme from around the world. Travelers and innkeepers Barb and Mike Winandy cleverly decorated each of the guest quarters. The Kimarrin room reflects Mayan culture with photographs of antiquities. The Outback, a private cottage, boasts a fireplace and whirlpool spa for two along with Australian decor. The Failte room includes a rococo Victorian antique high-back bed, fireplace and Irish-themed decor. And these are just a few of the possibilities. Barb creates wonderful  breakfasts full of muffins, breads and special entrees. Stroll the two-acre grounds and you will encounter a three-tier water pond, which sits in front of a teahouse, built by the original owner after a trip to Japan. One of the tiers houses Japanese Koi and another a water garden. The area has riverboat gambling and plenty of outdoor activities.

Innkeeper(s): Barb & Mike Winandy. $60-160. MC, VISA, AX, DS, TC. 10 rooms with PB. Breakfast included in rates. Type of meal: Full bkfst. Beds: KQT. Cable TV, phone, ceiling fan, VCR and selected amenities in select rooms only in room. Air conditioning. Fax, copier, pool table and fitness room on premises. Small meetings hosted. Antiquing, fishing, gambling, live theater, parks and cross-country skiing nearby.

"We've never been any place else that made us feel so catered to and comfortable. Thank you for allowing us to stay in your beautiful home. We feel very privileged."

Mount Carmel   I7

The Poor Farm B&B

Poor Farm Rd
Mount Carmel, IL 62863-9803
(618)262-4663 (800)646-3276 Fax:(618)236-4618
E-mail: poorfarm@midwest.net
Web: www.travelassist.com/reg/il102s.html

Circa 1915. This uniquely named inn served as a home for the homeless for more than a century. Today, the stately Federal-style structure hosts travelers and visitors to this area of Southeastern Illinois, offering a "gracious glimpse of yesteryear." An antique player piano and a selection of 4,200 in-room movies are available for guests' enjoyment. There are bicycles for those wishing to explore the grounds. The Poor Farm B&B sits adjacent to a recreational park with a well-stocked lake and is within walking distance of an 18-hole golf course and driving range. Riverboat gambling is 45 minutes away in Evansville, Ind.

Historic Interest: Historic New Harmony, Indiana (40 Minutes).

Innkeeper(s): Liz & John Stelzer. $45-85. MC, VISA, AX, DS, PC, TC. TAC10. 5 rooms with PB, 2 with FP, 2 suites and 2 conference rooms. Breakfast included in rates. Types of meals: Full bkfst and early coffee/tea. Afternoon tea, dinner, snacks/refreshments, lunch, banquet service and catering service available. Restaurant on premises. Beds: QDT. Phone, turndown service, ceiling fan and VCR in room. Air conditioning. Fax, copier, bicycles and library on premises. Handicap access. Weddings, small meetings, family reunions and seminars hosted. Amusement parks, antiquing, fishing, live theater, parks, shopping, cross-country skiing, sporting events and water sports nearby.

Pets allowed: None inside-outside enclosure.

Mundelein   B6

Round-Robin Guesthouse

231 Maple Ave
Mundelein, IL 60060
(847)566-7664 (800)301-7664 Fax:(847)566-4021
E-mail: rndrobin@aol.com
Web: www.roundrobininn.com

Circa 1907. Escape from the big city at this peaceful bed & breakfast, located just 38 miles from Chicago. Guests can relax on the porch swing or take a stroll into town and browse for antiques. Candlelight decorates the welcoming interior. Each guest room has a different theme. The Stars & Stripes Forever room honors President Lincoln and includes Civil War decorations. Other rooms include canopy, four-poster or brass beds. The suites can accommodate more than two guests, for an additional charge. Breakfasts include items such as quiche, banana bread and fresh fruit. As guests enjoy the morning meal, innkeeper Laura Loffredo serenades guests with piano music. Museums, gardens, the Long Grove Historical Village and Six Flags are among the area's attractions.

Historic Interest: Long Grove Historic Village (5 miles).

Innkeeper(s): Laura Loffredo. $50-140. MC, VISA, AX, PC, TC. TAC20. 6 rooms, 2 with PB, 1 with FP, 2 suites and 1 conference room. Types of meals: Full bkfst, veg bkfst and early coffee/tea. Afternoon tea and snacks/refreshments available. Beds: KQDT. Cable TV, phone and ceiling fan in room. Central air. VCR and fax on premises. Weddings, small meetings, family reunions and seminars hosted. Amusement parks, antiquing, beaches, bicycling, golf, horseback riding, live theater, museums and shopping nearby.

Oakland   G6

Inn on The Square

3 Montgomery
Oakland, IL 61943
(217)346-2289 Fax:(217)346-2005

Circa 1878. This inn features hand-carved beams and braided rugs on wide pine flooring. The Tea Room has oak tables, fresh flowers and a hand-laid brick fireplace. Guests may wander in the forest behind the inn or relax in the library with a book or jigsaw puzzle. Guest rooms have oak poster beds and hand-made quilts. The Pine Room boasts an heirloom bed with a  carved headboard. In addition to guest rooms, the inn houses shops selling ladies apparel, gifts and antiques. The Amish communities of Arthur and Arcola are 14 miles away.

Innkeeper(s): Linda & Gary Miller. $55-65. MC, VISA, PC, TC. 3 rooms with PB, 1 with FP and 1 conference room. Breakfast included in rates. Types of meals: Full bkfst and early coffee/tea. Picnic lunch, lunch and banquet service available. Restaurant on premises. Beds: D. TV, ceiling fan and homemade cookies in room. Air conditioning. VCR and library on premises. Weddings, small meetings, family reunions and seminars hosted. Antiquing, golf, Amish community, forest preserve, Lincoln sites, boating, live theater, parks, shopping, sporting events, tennis and water sports nearby.

Publicity: *Amish Country News, PM, Midwest Living, Country Living.*

Oregon   B4

Patchwork Inn

122 N 3rd St
Oregon, IL 61061
(815)732-4113 Fax:(815)732-6557
E-mail: patchworkinn@essex1.com
Web: www.essex1.com/people/patchworkinn

Circa 1845. Would you like to sleep where Abraham Lincoln once stayed? This historic inn actually can boast of Mr. Lincoln having "slept here." The Patchwork Inn is the sort you can imagine as providing a speaking platform as well from its two-level veranda across the front façade. Guest rooms feature access to the veranda, and there are high-ceilings and beds with handmade quilts, the theme of the inn. Guests are pampered at breakfast with a choice of service in your room, the parlor, sun room or on the front porch. A walk away is the river, dam and tree-lined streets filled with historic houses. Guests often enjoy canoeing on Rock River, picnicking in one of the three state parks or visiting Ronald Reagan's homestead in Dixon.

Historic Interest: Black Hawk Statue-1 mile, John Deere Historic Site-6 miles, Ronald Regan boyhood home-15 miles.

Innkeeper(s): Michael & Jean McNamara & Ron Bry. $75-115. MC, VISA, DS, PC, TC. 10 rooms with PB and 1 conference room. Breakfast and snacks/refreshments included in rates. Type of meal: Cont. Banquet service and catering service available. Beds: DT. Cable TV, phone and whirlpools (two rooms) in room. Air conditioning. Fax, copier, library and whirlpool tubs on premises. Family reunions and seminars hosted. Antiquing, art galleries, bicycling, canoeing/kayaking, fishing, golf, hiking, horseback riding, live theater, museums, parks, shopping and cross-country skiing nearby.

Pinehill B&B

400 Mix St
Oregon, IL 61061-1113
(815)732-2067

Circa 1874. This Italianate country villa is listed in the National Register. Ornate touches include guest rooms with Italian marble fireplaces and French silk-screened mural wallpaper. Outside, guests may enjoy porches, swings and century-old pine trees. Seasonal events include daily chocolate tea parties featuring the inn's own exotic homemade fudge collection.
Historic Interest: The historic Ogle County Courthouse is just a few blocks from the home.
Innkeeper(s): Susan Koppes. $110-225. MC, VISA, PC, TC. TAC10. 5 rooms with PB, 3 with FP. Breakfast and afternoon tea included in rates. Types of meals: Full gourmet bkfst and early coffee/tea. Beds: KQD. Turndown service in room. Air conditioning. Weddings, small meetings, family reunions and seminars hosted. Antiquing, parks, shopping, sporting events and water sports nearby.

Publicity: *Fox Valley Living, Victorian Sampler, Freeport Journal.*

"We enjoyed our stay at Pine Hill, your gracious hospitality and the peacefulness. Our thanks to you for a delightful stay. We may have to come again, if just to get some fudge."

Peoria (Mossville) D4

Old Church House Inn

1416 E Mossville Rd
Peoria (Mossville), IL 61552
(309)579-2300

Circa 1869. Guests will find this restored Colonial a true sanctuary. The inn once served as a country church, but now entices guests with promises of relaxation and hospitality. Each of the guest rooms offers something unique, such as an 1860s carved bedstead, featherbeds, handmade quilts and lacy curtains. Afternoon tea can be enjoyed by a crackling fire or among the garden's menagerie of flowers.
Innkeeper(s): Dean & Holly Ramseyer. $75-115. MC, VISA, DS. 2 rooms, 1 with PB. Breakfast included in rates. Types of meals: Cont plus and early coffee/tea. Gourmet dinner, picnic lunch and room service available. Beds: Q. Turndown service in room. Air conditioning. Weddings and small meetings hosted. Antiquing, fishing, live theater, shopping, cross-country skiing, sporting events and water sports nearby.

Publicity: *Chillicothe Bulletin, Journal Star.*

"Your hospitality, thoughtfulness, the cleanliness, beauty, I should just say everything was the best."

Pinckneyville J4

Oxbow B&B

3967 State Rt 13/127
Pinckneyville, IL 62274
(618)357-9839 (800)929-6888
E-mail: oxbowbb@midwest.net
Web: www.bbonline.com/il/oxbow/

Circa 1929. Several of the guest rooms at this unique brick veneer farmhouse feature beds designed and built by innkeeper Al Doughty, who among his other trades has been a rural veterinarian, Civil War historian and coal miner. His wife, innkeeper Peggy Doughty, raises prize Arabian horses, some of which have gone on to reach Top Ten Championships. Each of the antique-filled guest rooms features names from the Civil War. The Shiloh room boasts a seven-foot headboard, marble-top dresser and quaint wash stand with a pitcher and mirror, while the Pilot Knob room features a four-poster, canopy bed made from aged barn timbers. There's is a large parking area at the B&B.
Historic Interest: Oxbow B&B is near several historic sites, including Fort Kaskaskia, St. Mary River Covered Bridge, Charter Oak Schoolhouse, Pierre Menard Home, The Old Slave House and Fort De Chartes. The Perry County Historical Jail is only one mile from the home.
Innkeeper(s): Al & Peggy Doughty. $50-65. MC, VISA. 5 rooms with PB and 1 suite. Breakfast included in rates. Type of meal: Full bkfst. Beds: Q. Spa, swimming, library, exercise equipment and pool table on premises. Antiquing, fishing and water sports nearby.

Richmond A6

Gazebo House B&B

10314 East St
Richmond, IL 60071
(815)678-2505

Circa 1893. This intimate, homestay B&B is located in a charming "Painted Lady," whimsically painted and set on a fragrant five acres with gardens and trees. The well-designed interior has a hint of the Victorian era, with a few flowery touches, but mostly elegant and understated decor. One room offers a brass bed and a unique rocking horse, the other has a four-poster bed. The Richmond room also has a whirlpool tub. Guests can relax on the veranda, stroll the scenic grounds or relax with a good book. The innkeepers have more than 1,000 volumes on bookshelves around the home.
Innkeeper(s): Sandy & Jeff Heaney. $89-109. MC, VISA, DS, PC. TAC5. 2 rooms with PB, 1 with FP. Breakfast included in rates. Type of meal: Cont plus. Beds: Q. Cable TV and ceiling fan in room. Air conditioning. VCR, fax, spa, library, grand piano, fishing, croquet, hiking path, gazebos and carousel horses on premises. Antiquing, fishing, golf, horseback riding, snowmobile trails, nature watching, live theater, parks, shopping, downhill skiing, cross-country skiing, tennis and water sports nearby.

"The quiet and calm atmosphere was just what I needed!"

Rock Island C3

Victorian Inn

702 20th St
Rock Island, IL 61201-2638
(309)788-7068 (800)728-7068 Fax:(309)788-7086

Circa 1876. Built as a wedding present for the daughter of a Rock Island liquor baron, the inn's striking features include illuminated stained-glass tower windows. Other examples of the Victorian decor are the living room's beveled-plate-glass French doors and the dining room's Flemish Oak ceiling beams and paneling, crowned by turn-of-the-century tapestries. Standing within sight of three other buildings listed in the National Register, the inn's wooded grounds are home to many songbirds from the area. A glassed-in Florida porch is perfect for relaxing during any season and a patio table in the gardens is a great place to enjoy a glass of pink lemonade on warm evenings.

Innkeeper(s): David & Barbara Parker. $65-125. MC, VISA, AX, PC, TC. 6 rooms with PB, 2 with FP. Breakfast included in rates. Types of meals: Full gourmet bkfst and early coffee/tea. Afternoon tea and snacks/refreshments available. Beds: KQDT. Ceiling fan in room. Air conditioning. Fax, copier and library on premises. Small meetings, family reunions and seminars hosted. Antiquing, fishing, live theater, parks, cross-country skiing, sporting events and water sports nearby.

Sheffield   C4

Chestnut Street Inn

301 E Chestnut St
Sheffield, IL 61361
(815)454-2419 (800)537-1304
E-mail: gail@chestnut-inn.com
Web: www.chestnut-inn.com

Circa 1854. Originally built in Italianate style, this mid-19th-century reborn Colonial Revival is the dream-come-true for innkeeper Gail Bruntjen. She spent more than 15 years searching for just the right country home to open a bed & breakfast. With its gracious architectural character and well-organized interior spaces, the Chestnut Street Inn fit the bill. Classic French doors open to a wide foyer with gleaming chandeliers and a floating spindle staircase. Sophisticated chintz fabrics and authentic antiques highlight each room. The four guest rooms offer down comforters, four-poster beds and private baths. Guests will be delighted by the gourmet selections offered every morning such as broccoli mushroom quiche, homemade breads and fresh fruit, all exquisitely presented by candlelight on fine China and crystal. Afternoon tea and evening snacks are served in the public rooms. Antiquing, shops, golf and fishing are located nearby.

Innkeeper(s): Gail Bruntjen. $75-150. MC, VISA, PC, TC. TAC10. 4 rooms with PB, 1 with FP, 1 suite and 1 conference room. Breakfast, afternoon tea and snacks/refreshments included in rates. Types of meals: Full bkfst and early coffee/tea. Beds: KQT. Cable TV, turndown service and VCR in room. Air conditioning. Library on premises. Weddings and small meetings hosted. Antiquing, fishing, golf, parks and shopping nearby.

Publicity: *The Illinois Review, Illinois Country Living.*

"Without a doubt, the best B&B I've ever been to."

Springfield   F4

The Inn on Edwards B&B

810 E Edwards St
Springfield, IL 62703
(217)528-0420

Circa 1865. The cheerful blue Italianate Victorian displays many original features, from its curving walnut staircase, fine woodwork and fireplace mantel with faux marbling. The home was appointed by a local interior design firm, and rooms feature antiques. The home is adjacent to the Lincoln Home National Historic Site, which includes Abraham Lincoln's family home and several blocks of historic Springfield.

Innkeeper(s): Charles Kirchner. $65-75. MC, VISA, PC. TAC10. 4 rooms with PB. Breakfast included in rates. Type of meal: Full bkfst. Beds: QT. Cable TV and ceiling fan in room. Air conditioning. Amusement parks, antiquing, fishing, golf, muni Opera, State Fair, Lincoln sites, live theater, parks, shopping, sporting events, tennis and water sports nearby.
Publicity: *State Journal Register.*

Urbana   F6

Lindley House

312 W Green St
Urbana, IL 61801-3222
(217)384-4800 Fax:(217)384-8280
E-mail: lindley@shout.net
Web: www.shout.net/~lindley

Circa 1895. Designed by architect Rudolph Zachariah Gill from the University of Illinois for Dr. Austin Lindley, a prominent physician, this classic Queen Anne Victorian displays many of the whimsical architectural details popular during this era. The facade features imposing gables, an octagonal turret and a curved porch. Gleaming parquet floors in the four public rooms, a magnificent oak gingerbread staircase, beveled- and stained-glass windows are all part of the interior Victorian detailing. All second-floor queen guest rooms are decorated in antiques, while the spacious king attic suite offers a sitting area and private bath. There is also a carriage house. Fresh fruit, homemade breads and Columbian coffee are offered in the morning. Lindley House is located close to restaurants, parks, sports activities and the University of Illinois.

Innkeeper(s): Carolyn Baxley. $75-150. MC, VISA, PC, TC. 5 rooms, 2 with PB, 1 suite and 1 cottage. Breakfast included in rates. Type of meal: Cont plus. Beds: KQ. Cable TV, phone, ceiling fan and VCR in room. Air conditioning. Internet Access on premises. Weddings, small meetings and family reunions hosted.

Indiana

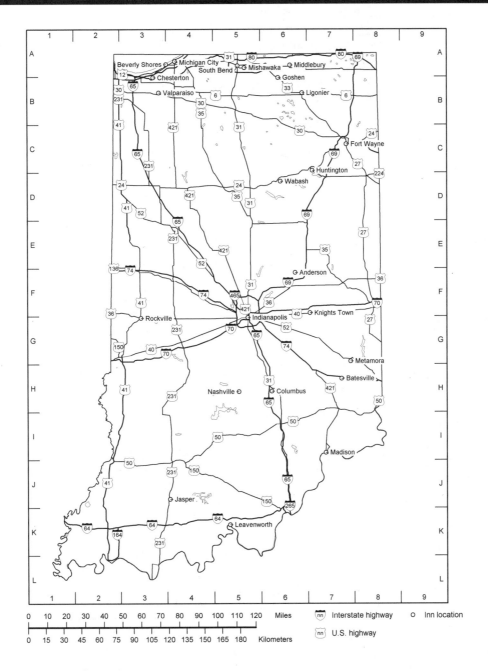

0   10   20   30   40   50   60   70   80   90   100   110   120   Miles

0   15   30   45   60   75   90   105   120   135   150   165   180   Kilometers

(nn) Interstate highway   o   Inn location

(nn) U.S. highway

Anderson
F6

Plum Retreat B&B

926 Historical W Eighth St
Anderson, IN 46016
(765)649-7586 Fax:(765)649-9928

Circa 1892. This Queen Anne Victorian, so named because of its light purple hue, is surrounded by a wrought-iron fence, roses and foliage. The front
doors, fashioned out of a
rich wood, feature an intricate glass pattern. The
veranda offers wicker furnishings so guests can enjoy
the scenery and relax. The
three guest rooms include
antiques such as a high-
back walnut bed. The home
was built by the vice presi-

dent of a local loan association, and at one time the grounds included a racetrack. Antique shops, museums, horse racing and wilderness areas are nearby.

$70-120. PC. 3 rooms, 1 with PB, 1 with FP, 1 suite and 2 conference rooms. Breakfast, afternoon tea and snacks/refreshments included in rates. Types of meals: Full bkfst and early coffee/tea. Beds: QD. Central air. VCR and library on premises. Weddings, small meetings, family reunions and seminars hosted. Antiquing, golf, live theater, parks, shopping, sporting events and tennis nearby.

"This house was a life long dream of my wife, we both fell in love with it. We appreciate you letting us have this most wonderful experience in your home."

Batesville
H7

Sherman House Restaurant & Inn

35 S Main St
Batesville, IN 47006-1278
(812)934-2407 (800)445-4939

Circa 1852. This hotel has been in business for more than 147 years. During this century it acquired a Tudor facade. The inn's restaurant is the focal point of town, with business meetings and frequent banquets in the Chalet Room. Antique shopping and nearby covered bridges are also a highlight of this quaint town.

Innkeeper(s): Joe Shook. $44-66. MC, VISA, AX, DC. 23 rooms with PB and 3 conference rooms. Types of meals: Full bkfst and early coffee/tea. Dinner and lunch available. Beds: KQD. Phone in room.

Chesterton
B3

The Gray Goose

350 Indian Boundary Rd
Chesterton, IN 46304-1511
(219)926-5781 (800)521-5127 Fax:(219)926-4845
E-mail: graygoose@niia.net
Web: www.graygooseinn.com

Circa 1939. Situated on 100 wooded acres, just under one hour from Chicago, this English country inn overlooks a private lake. Guests can see Canadian geese and ducks on the lake and surrounding area. Rooms are decorated in 18th-century

English, Shaker and
French-country styles.
Some of the rooms fea-
ture fireplaces, Jacuzzi
and poster beds.
Complimentary
snacks, soft drinks,
coffee and tea are available throughout the day. Strains of Mozart or Handel add to the ambiance.

Historic Interest: The Dunes State and National Lakeshore is less than three miles from the inn.

Innkeeper(s): Tim Wilk & Chuck Ramsey. $80-165. MC, VISA, AX, DS, PC, TC. 8 rooms with PB, 3 with FP, 3 suites and 1 conference room. Breakfast, afternoon tea and snacks/refreshments included in rates. Types of meals: Full gourmet bkfst and early coffee/tea. Beds: KQ. TV, phone, ceiling fan, VCR and one room with fireplace and Jacuzzi in room. Air conditioning. Fax, copier and library on premises. Weddings, small meetings, family reunions and seminars hosted. Antiquing, fishing, live theater, parks, shopping, downhill skiing, cross-country skiing, sporting events and water sports nearby.

"Extremely gracious! A repeat stay for us because it is such a wonderful place to stay."

Columbus
H6

The Columbus Inn

445 5th St
Columbus, IN 47201-6206
(812)378-4289 Fax:(812)378-4289

Circa 1895. Dances, basketball games and poultry shows once convened in the auditorium of the old Columbus City Hall during its years as the focal point of town. The original terra-cotta floors, enormous brass chandeliers and hand-carved oak woodwork now welcome overnight guests. Lavishly decorated rooms feature reproduction antiques such as cherry sleigh beds. Twelve-foot-high windows and 21-foot ceilings grace the Charles Sparrell Suite with its separate sleeping level.

Historic Interest: In the National Register.

$90. MC, VISA, AX, DC, CB, DS, PC, TC. 34 rooms with PB, 5 suites and 3 conference rooms. Breakfast included in rates. Types of meals: Full gourmet bkfst and early coffee/tea. Afternoon tea, gourmet dinner, banquet service and catering service available. Beds: QD. Cable TV and phone in room. Air conditioning. VCR, fax and copier on premises. Handicap access. Weddings, small meetings, family reunions and seminars hosted. Amusement parks, antiquing, fishing, live theater, parks, shopping, downhill skiing, sporting events and water sports nearby.

"A delicious and beautifully served breakfast was the crowning glory of our stay."

Fort Wayne
C7

The Carole Lombard House B&B

704 Rockhill St
Fort Wayne, IN 46802-5918
(219)426-9896 (888)426-9896

Circa 1895. Jane Alice Peters, a.k.a. Carole Lombard, spent her first six years in this turn-of-the-century home located in Ft. Wayne's historic West-Central neighborhood. The innkeepers named two guest rooms in honor of Lombard and her second husband, Clark Gable. Each of these rooms features memorabilia from the Gable-Lombard romance. A video library with a collection of classic movies is available, including many of Lombard's films. The innkeepers provide bicycles for exploring

Fort Wayne and also provide information for a self-guided architectural tour of the historic area.

Historic Interest: On Oct. 6, 1908, Jane Alice Peters was born in the handsome house at the foot of Rockhill Street. The world knew her as Carole Lombard.

Innkeeper(s): Bev Fiandt. $55-85. MC, VISA, DS, PC, TC. TAC5. 4 rooms with PB. Breakfast included in rates. Types of meals: Full bkfst and early coffee/tea. Beds: KQDT. Cable TV and phone in room. Air conditioning. VCR and bicycles on premises. Small meetings hosted. Antiquing, live theater, parks and sporting events nearby.

Publicity: *Michigan Living.*

"The elegance and ambience are most appreciated."

Goshen   B6

Indian Creek B&B

20300 CR 18
Goshen, IN 46528
(219)875-6606 Fax:(219)875-3968

Circa 1993. This Victorian was built recently, but offers a nostalgic charm reminiscent of its historic architectural style. The comfortable bed rooms are decorated with family antiques, and each room is named after one of the innkeepers' grandchildren. The home is located in Amish country, and antique stores, the Shipshewana Flea Market and Notre Dame are nearby.

Innkeeper(s): Herman & Shirley Hochstetler. $69-79. MC, VISA, AX, DS, PC, TC. 1 suites. Breakfast included in rates. Type of meal: Full bkfst. Beds: QDT. Cable TV, phone, turndown service and ceiling fan in room. Air conditioning. VCR, fax, copier and library on premises. Handicap access. Small meetings and seminars hosted. Antiquing, fishing, Shipshewana flea market, live theater, parks, shopping, cross-country skiing, sporting events and water sports nearby.

Prairie Manor B&B

66398 US Hwy 33
Goshen, IN 46526-9482
(219)642-4761 (800)791-3952 Fax:(219)642-4762

Circa 1925. Local craftsman created this elegant English-style country manor home. The home's original features have remained unchanged, including the original window seats, arched doorways and a winding staircase. The inn's 12 acres include a swimming pool and play area for children. Breakfasts include items such  as crepes filled with fresh strawberries and bananas topped with a yogurt-whipped cream sauce or baked eggs with fresh herbs and three cheeses. Homemade breads, such as raspberry cream cheese coffeecake, also are served.

Historic Interest: Goshen Historic District (5 miles), Bonneyville Mill (15 miles).

Innkeeper(s): Jean & Hesston Lauver. $65-95. MC, VISA, DS, PC, TC. 3 rooms with PB, 1 suite and 2 conference rooms. Breakfast and snacks/refreshments included in rates. Types of meals: Full bkfst, veg bkfst and early coffee/tea. Beds: QT. Cable TV and ceiling fan in room. Air conditioning. VCR, fax, swimming, stables and library on premises. Weddings, small meetings, family reunions and seminars hosted. Antiquing, art galleries, bicycling, canoeing/kayaking, fishing, golf, hiking, live theater, museums, parks, shopping, cross-country skiing, sporting events and tennis nearby.

Pets allowed: only in barn.

Huntington   C7

Purviance House

326 S Jefferson St
Huntington, IN 46750-3327
(219)356-4218

Circa 1859. This Italianate-Greek Revival house is listed in the National Register of Historic Places. The inn features a winding cherry staircase, parquet floors, original interior shutters, tile fireplaces, ornate ceiling designs, antiques and period reproductions. The gold parlor offers well-stocked bookshelves.

Historic Interest: Forks of the Wabash Historic Park is three miles away, and the Dan Quayle Center also is nearby.

Innkeeper(s): Bob & Jean Gernand. $45-65. MC, VISA, DS, TC. TAC5. 5 rooms, 2 with PB, 2 with FP and 2 conference rooms. Breakfast and snacks/refreshments included in rates. Types of meals: Full bkfst and early coffee/tea. Banquet service and room service available. Beds: QDT. Ceiling fan, rocker/recliners and books in room. Air conditioning. Library on premises. Weddings, small meetings, family reunions and seminars hosted. Antiquing, fishing, parks, shopping and water sports nearby.

"A completely delightful experience!"

Indianapolis   G5

Speedway B&B

1829 Cunningham Dr
Indianapolis, IN 46224-5338
(317)487-6531 (800)975-3412 Fax:(317)481-1825
E-mail: speedwaybb@msn.com
Web: www.bbchannel.com:8010/bbc/p600351.asp

Circa 1906. This two-story white columned inn reflects a plantation-style architecture. The inn is situated on an acre of lawn and trees. The bed & breakfast has a homey decor that includes a wood-paneled common room and elegantly furnished guest rooms. Breakfast includes items such as homemade coffee cake and Danish or sausage and egg casserole. Nearby attractions include President Harrison's home, the Hall of Fame Museum and the largest city park in the nation, Eagle Creek Park.

Innkeeper(s): Pauline Grothe. $65-125. PC, TC. 5 rooms with PB. Breakfast included in rates. Type of meal: Full bkfst. Beds: KQD. Cable TV and phone in room. Air conditioning. VCR, fax and bicycles on premises. Weddings, small meetings, family reunions and seminars hosted. Antiquing, fishing, golf, live theater, parks, shopping, cross-country skiing, sporting events, tennis and water sports nearby.

"It is people like you who have given B&Bs such a good reputation."

The Tranquil Cherub

2164 N Capitol Ave
Indianapolis, IN 46202-1251
(317)923-9036 Fax:(317)923-8676
E-mail: innkeeper@tranquilcherub.com
Web: www.tranquilcherub.com

Circa 1905. Visitors to the bustling Indianapolis area will appreciate the quiet elegance of the Tranquil Cherub, a Greek Revival home. The morning routine begins with freshly brewed

coffee and juice served prior to breakfast, which is eaten in the oak-paneled dining room or on a back deck overlooking a pond. Guests may choose from the blue and white Victorian Room, with its antique wicker furniture and lace curtains, or the Gatsby Room, highlighted by its Art Deco-era four-poster cannonball bed. The jade-green and navy Rogers Room features stained glass and an oak bedroom set that originated in an old Chicago hotel.

Innkeeper(s): Thom & Barb Feit. $65-90. MC, VISA, AX, PC, TC. TAC10. 4 rooms with PB and 1 suite. Breakfast and snacks/refreshments included in rates. Types of meals: Full bkfst and early coffee/tea. Beds: KQ. Ceiling fan in room. Air conditioning. VCR, fax and library on premises. Small meetings, family reunions and seminars hosted. Antiquing, golf, live theater, parks, shopping, sporting events, tennis and water sports nearby.

Publicity: *Indianapolis Star.*

Jasper   J4

Powers Inn B&B

325 W 6th St
Jasper, IN 47546-2719
(812)482-3018

Circa 1880. This B&B's location was meant for hospitality. A local attorney built this Second Empire Victorian on this spot, but it once was the site of a local log cabin inn. The innkeepers painstakingly restored their Victorian, which included rebuilding the foundation. They managed to save many original elements along the way. The rooms are elegant, decorated with antiques and reproductions. Antique dressers house the bathroom sinks, and one bathroom includes an original clawfoot tub.

Innkeeper(s): Alice & Larry "Joe" Garland. $60. MC, VISA, PC. 3 rooms with PB. Breakfast included in rates. Type of meal: Full bkfst. Beds: DT. Air conditioning. VCR on premises. Amusement parks, antiquing, fishing, golf, live theater, parks, shopping, downhill skiing, tennis and water sports nearby.

Publicity: *Chicago Tribune, Dubois County Daily Herald.*

"Warm, cozy and very friendly!"

Knightstown   F7

Old Hoosier House

7601 S Greensboro Pike
Knightstown, IN 46148-9613
(765)345-2969 (800)775-5315

Circa 1840. The Old Hoosier House was owned by the Elisha Scovell family, who were friends of President Martin Van Buren, and the president stayed overnight in the home. Features of the Victorian house include tall, arched windows and a gabled entrance. Rooms are decorated with antiques and lace curtains. Hearty Hoosier breakfasts include such specialties as a breakfast pizza of egg, sausage and cheese, and Melt-Away Puff Pancakes. The inn's eight acres are wooded, and the deck overlooks a pond on the fourth hole of the adjacent golf course.

Historic Interest: Wilbur Wright Memorial and birthplace (20 miles), Metamora restored canal village (40 miles), Noblesville Transportation Museum (25 miles), James Whitcomb Riley birthplace & museum (10 miles).

Innkeeper(s): Jean & Tom Lewis. $60-70. PC. TAC10. 4 rooms with PB, 1 with FP and 1 suite. Breakfast, afternoon tea and snacks/refreshments included in rates. Types of meals: Full bkfst and early coffee/tea. Beds: KQT. Phone and ceiling fan in room. Air conditioning. VCR and library on premises. Handicap access. Weddings, small meetings and family reunions hosted. Antiquing, fishing, live theater, parks, shopping and sporting events nearby.

"We had such a wonderful time at your house. Very many thanks."

Leavenworth   K5

The Leavenworth Inn

930 West State Road 62
Leavenworth, IN 47137
(812)739-2120 (888)739-2120 Fax:(812)739-2012
E-mail: theinn@theremc.com
Web: www.leavenworthinn.com

Circa 1800. Gardens highlight the exterior of Leavenworth Inn, and the six-acre grounds afford views of the Ohio River. The inn was once part of Forest Grove Farm, and guests would visit the farmhouse to enjoy fresh milk, homegrown vegetables and wine produced on the grounds. Today, guests can relax and enjoy the view on a porch swing, curl up with a book in front of the fireplace in the library or select a classic movie and pop it into the VCR. The grounds are perfect for a game of croquet or horseshoes, and guests can borrow bicycles from the innkeepers and take a tour of the town. Leavenworth offers craft shops, galleries and antique shops. Other unique attractions include trips to the Wyandotte Cave, Marengo Cave or Squire Boone Cavern.

Historic Interest: Lincoln Boyhood Memorial (45 miles), Corydon Capitol State Historic Site (15 miles).

Innkeeper(s): Bert Collins. $65-95. MC, VISA, AX, DS, TC. 10 rooms with PB, 1 with FP, 1 suite and 1 conference room. Breakfast included in rates. Type of meal: Early coffee/tea. Beds: KQT. Cable TV, phone and VCR in room. Central air. Fax, bicycles, tennis and library on premises. Weddings, small meetings, family reunions and seminars hosted. Amusement parks, antiquing, bicycling, canoeing/kayaking, fishing, golf, hiking, horseback riding, live theater, museums, parks, shopping, downhill skiing, sporting events, tennis, water sports and wineries nearby.

Ligonier   B6

Solomon Mier Manor

508 S Cavin St
Ligonier, IN 46767-1802
(219)894-3668
E-mail: solomon@ligtel.com

Circa 1899. This turn-of-the-century Queen Anne-Italianate manor boasts hand-painted ceilings, intricate woodwork and stained-glass windows. The ornate, carved staircase is especially appealing. Antiques fill the guest rooms and common areas. The National Register home originally was home to Solomon Mier, one of the area's first Jewish residents who came to the Ligonier area in search of religious tolerance. Guests will find many antique stores in the area, as well as the Shipshewana Flea Market.

Innkeeper(s): Ron & Doris Blue. $70. MC, VISA, PC, TC. 4 rooms with PB. Breakfast, afternoon tea and snacks/refreshments included in rates. Types of meals: Full bkfst and early coffee/tea. Beds: KQD. Phone and ceiling fan in room. Air conditioning. VCR and library on premises. Small meetings, family reunions and seminars hosted. Antiquing, fishing, golf, parks, shopping, sporting events and tennis nearby.

"Complete and beautiful experience."

Madison I7

Schussler House B&B

514 Jefferson St
Madison, IN 47250
(812)273-2068 (800)392-1931

Circa 1849. This Federal-style home was built by a local doctor who used it as both house and office. The three guest rooms include antiques and reproductions. The innkeepers pamper guests with a delectable full breakfast, served by candlelight. Madison, a picturesque Ohio River town surrounded by rolling hills, has more than 100 blocks listed in the National Register and designated a National Trust Historic District. The B&B is within walking distance to many shops and sites, and the river is just five blocks away.

Innkeeper(s): Judy & Bill Gilbert. $90-120. MC, VISA, DS, PC, TC. TAC10. 3 rooms with PB. Breakfast and snacks/refreshments included in rates. Types of meals: Full bkfst and early coffee/tea. Beds: QT. Turndown service in room. Air conditioning. Refrigerator on premises. Small meetings and family reunions hosted. Antiquing, fishing, golf, parks, shopping and tennis nearby.

Publicity: *Update, Cincinnati Magazine, The Downtowner.*

"Five star all the way!"

Metamora G7

The Thorpe House Country Inn

19049 Clayborne St, PO Box 36
Metamora, IN 47030
(765)647-5425 (888)427-7932

Circa 1840. The steam engine still brings passenger cars and the gristmill still grinds cornmeal in historic Metamora. The Thorpe House is located one block from the canal. Rooms feature original pine and poplar floors, antiques, stenciling and country accessories. Enjoy a hearty breakfast selected from the inn's restaurant menu. (Popular items include home-  made biscuits, egg dishes and sourdough pecan rolls.) Walk through the village to explore more than 100 shops.

Historic Interest: Indian mounds, historic Brookville, Laurel, and "village of spires" Oldenburg are within 10 minutes. Historic Connersville and Batesville are within one-half hour.

Innkeeper(s): Mike & Jean Owens. $70-125. MC, VISA, AX, DS, PC, TC. TAC10. 5 rooms with PB and 1 suite. Breakfast and snacks/refreshments included in rates. Types of meals: Full bkfst and early coffee/tea. Picnic lunch, lunch and catering service available. Restaurant on premises. Beds: KDT. Air conditioning. Gift shops/pottery studio on premises. Small meetings and family reunions hosted. Amusement parks, antiquing, fishing, golf, parks, shopping, tennis and water sports nearby.

Pets allowed: by prior arrangement.

Publicity: *Cincinnati Enquirer, Chicago Sun-Times, Midwest Living.*

"Thanks to all of you for your kindness and hospitality during our stay."

Michigan City A4

Brickstone B&B

215 W 6th St
Michigan City, IN 46360
(219)878-1819

Circa 1880. Originally the parsonage of the First Congregational Church, the Brickstone offers a Great Room with fireplace and a wicker-filled screened porch. There are four guest rooms, each decorated in a style reflecting one of the four seasons. All feature fresh flowers and double or single Jacuzzi tubs. A breakfast buffet is provided in the morning and afterward you can walk or take a bicycle to the marina, beach or zoo. Guests often enjoy walking across to the Prime Outlet Center.

Innkeeper(s): Jim & Sidney Hoover. $80-140. MC, VISA, PC. 4 rooms with PB. Breakfast included in rates. Types of meals: Full gourmet bkfst and early coffee/tea. Beds: QT. Ceiling fan in room. VCR, fax and library on premises. Weddings hosted. Antiquing, fishing, golf, live theater, parks, shopping and water sports nearby.

Pets allowed: House trained.

The Hutchinson Mansion Inn

220 W 10th St
Michigan City, IN 46360-3516
(219)879-1700

Circa 1875. Built by a lumber baron in 1875, this grand, red-brick mansion features examples of Queen Anne, Classic Revival and Italianate design. The mansion boasts 11 stained-glass pan-  els and the front parlor still has its original plaster friezes, ceiling medallion and a marble fireplace. The dining room's oak-paneled walls include a secret panel. The library is stocked with interesting books and games, and classical compositions and Victorian parlor music are piped in. The second floor offers a host of places perfect for relaxation, including a small game room, mini library and a sun porch. Rooms are filled with antiques and unusual pieces such as the Tower Suite's octagon, Gothic-style bed. The carriage house suites include a sitting room, refrigerator and either a whirlpool or large, soaking tub.

Historic Interest: The mansion is nestled in Michigan City's historic district and a short distance from other gracious homes. The Barker Mansion, a house museum, is only three blocks away. A lighthouse museum is less than a mile from the inn. Bailly Homestead and Chellberg Farm, a turn-of-the-century Swedish farm, are 15 minutes away.

Innkeeper(s): Ben & Mary DuVal. $68-140. MC, VISA, AX. 10 rooms with PB and 5 suites. Breakfast included in rates. Beds: QD. Antiquing, fishing, national Lakeshore, stables, shopping, hiking, live theater, shopping and cross-country skiing nearby.

Publicity: *Midwest Living, Midwest Motorist, Heritage Country, Indianapolis Star, Michigan Living, South Bend Tribune, Chicago Tribune.*

"Beautiful, romantic inn, exceptional hospitality, your breakfasts were fabulous."

Middlebury   A6

Tiffany Powell's Bed & Breakfast

523 South Main Street
Middlebury, IN 46540-9004
(219)825-5951

Circa 1914. The porch of this B&B is a favorite spot for guests
to sit and watch Amish buggies pass by, especially on Saturday
nights. The inn features leaded and beveled glass and original
oak floors and woodwork. Guest rooms reflect a fresh country
decor with bright handmade quilts sewn by Judy's grandmother. Known locally and acknowledged nationally on the Oprah
show for her hospitality, the innkeeper offers a full breakfast.
Amish Sausage Casserole is a speciality of the house and is
served in the dining room. Shipshewana is seven minutes away,
and Amish markets and craft shops are nearby.

Innkeeper(s): Judy Powell. $50-80. PC, TC. 5 rooms, 3 with PB, 1 with FP.
Breakfast, afternoon tea and snacks/refreshments included in rates. Types of
meals: Full bkfst, cont plus and early coffee/tea. Beds: QDT. Cable TV, turndown service and ceiling fan in room. Air conditioning. VCR and bicycles on
premises. Small meetings and seminars hosted. Antiquing, fishing, golf, live
theater, parks, shopping, cross-country skiing, sporting events, tennis and
water sports nearby.

Mishawaka   A5

The Beiger Mansion Inn

317 Lincoln Way E
Mishawaka, IN 46544-2012
(219)256-0365 (800)437-0131 Fax:(219)259-2622
E-mail: beiger@michiana.org
Web: business.michiana.org/beiger/

Circa 1903. This Neoclassical limestone mansion was built to
satisfy Susie Beiger's wish to copy a friend's Newport,
R.I. estate. Palatial rooms that
were once a gathering
place for local society
now welcome guests
who seek gracious
accommodations.
Notre Dame, St.
Mary's and Indiana
University in South Bend are nearby.

Innkeeper(s): Ron Montandon. $80-95. MC, VISA, AX, DC, CB, DS, PC, TC.
TAC10. 6 rooms with PB and 1 suite. Breakfast included in rates. Type of
meal: Full bkfst. Gourmet dinner, banquet service and catering service available. Restaurant on premises. Beds: Q. Cable TV and phone in room. Air
conditioning. VCR, fax and copier on premises. Weddings, small meetings,
family reunions and seminars hosted. Antiquing, fishing, golf, live theater,
parks, sporting events and tennis nearby.
Publicity: *Tribune.*

"Can't wait until we return to Mishawaka to stay with you again!"

Nashville   H5

Allison House

90 S Jefferson St
Nashville, IN 47448
(812)988-0814

Circa 1883. This inviting yellow home was restored to include
cozy, comfortable furnishings in a relaxed atmosphere. A full

breakfast begins a day of browsing
through the village's hundreds of shops and famed
arts and crafts colony.
Indiana's largest state park
is less than two miles from
Allison House.

Historic Interest: T.C. Steele's
studio and home is nine miles
away. Architectural tours are
available in Columbus, 17 miles away.

Innkeeper(s): Tammy Galm. $95. PC, TC. 5 rooms with PB. Breakfast includ-
ed in rates. Type of meal: Early coffee/tea. Beds: QDT. VCR and library on
premises. Weddings, small meetings, family reunions and seminars hosted.
Antiquing, fishing, golf, live theater, parks, downhill skiing, cross-country skiing, sporting events and tennis nearby.

Rockville   G3

Billie Creek Inn

RR 2, Box 27, Billie Creek Village
Rockville, IN 47872
(765)569-3430 Fax:(765)569-3582

Circa 1996. Although this inn was built recently, it rests on
the outskirts of historic Billie Creek Village. The village is a
non-profit, turn-of-the-century living museum, complete with
30 historic buildings and three covered bridges. Guests can
explore an 1830s cabin, a farmstead, a general store and much
more to experience how Americans lived in the 19th century.
The innkeepers take part in the history, dressing in period cos-
tume. The inn is decorated in a comfortable, country style. The
nine suites include the added amenity of a two-person
whirlpool tub. All inn guests receive complimentary admission
to Billie Creek Village. Coffee and continental breakfast fare are
available around the clock. Special packages include canoeing
and bike tours, Civil War Days and covered bridge festivals.

Innkeeper(s): Carol Gum & Doug Weisheit. $49-99. MC, VISA, AX, DS, PC,
TC. TAC10. 31 rooms with PB, 9 suites and 2 conference rooms. Breakfast
included in rates. Type of meal: Cont. Catering service available. Beds: KD.
Cable TV and phone in room. Air conditioning. VCR, fax, copier, swimming,
stables, pet boarding, historical village, general store, player piano concerts
nightly, ATM and crafts on premises. Handicap access. Weddings, small
meetings, family reunions and seminars hosted. Antiquing, fishing, golf, Ivey
Tech, St Mary's, Rose Hulman, Indiana State, live theater, parks, shopping,
sporting events, tennis and water sports nearby.
Pets allowed: Home to Scott Pet Hotel.

Knoll Inn

317 W High St
Rockville, IN 47872
(765)569-6345 (888)569-6345 Fax:(765)569-3445

Circa 1842. This inn, of Greek Revival and Italianate influence,
is situated on one acre of gardens in the historic district.
Renovated recently, it offers suites with whirlpool tubs and
romantic decor. Farmer's Strada is a favored dish for breakfast,
which also includes freshly baked breads and muffins, homemade preserves and fresh fruit such as strawberries and peaches in season. The area offers 32 covered bridges for exploring.

Innkeeper(s): Mark & Sharon Nolin. $85-110. MC, VISA, PC, TC. TAC10. 3
suites and 1 conference room. Breakfast included in rates. Types of meals: Full
bkfst, cont plus, cont and early coffee/tea. Beds: Q. Cable TV, ceiling fan, VCR,
two suites with whirlpool spas and in room. Air conditioning. Spa on premises.
Weddings and family reunions hosted. Antiquing, fishing, golf, covered bridges,
parks, shopping, sporting events, tennis and water sports nearby.

Suits Us B&B

514 N College St
Rockville, IN 47872-1511
(765)569-5660 (888)478-4878

Circa 1883. Sixty miles west of Indianapolis is this stately Colonial Revival inn, where Woodrow Wilson, Annie Oakley and James Witcomb Riley were once guests of the Strause Family. The inn offers video library and bicycles. There are 32 covered bridges to visit in the small, surrounding county. Turkey Run State Park is nearby. The Ernie Pyle State Historic Site, Raccoon State Recreation Area and four golf courses are within easy driving distance.

Historic Interest: There are 32 covered bridges in the area.

Innkeeper(s): Andy & Lianna Willhite. $55-125. TC. 4 rooms with PB and 1 suite. Breakfast included in rates. Types of meals: Full bkfst and early coffee/tea. Beds: KQD. Cable TV, ceiling fan and VCR in room. Air conditioning. Bicycles, movie library and exercise room on premises. Antiquing, fishing, golf, parks, shopping and water sports nearby.

Publicity: *Touring America, Traces Historic Magazine.*

South Bend   A5

English Rose Inn

116 S Taylor St
South Bend, IN 46601
(219)289-2114 Fax:(219)287-1311
E-mail: englishroseinn@cyberlink.com

Circa 1892. A stunning Queen Anne Victorian, the English Rose is indeed adorned in a fanciful light pink hue. A prominent local doctor built the turn-of-the-20th-century home. The innkeeper has filled the inn with antiques and period-style decorations. The inviting guest rooms include quilt-topped beds with coordinating linens and special touches, such as a delicate tea set. Guests can enjoy the multi-course breakfast in the privacy of their room. The inn is close to Notre Dame, as well as historic sites such as Tippecanoe Place and the Copshalom Home.

Historic Interest: Tippecanoe Place, Copshalom Home.

Innkeeper(s): Barry & Susan Kessler. $65-115. MC, VISA, PC, TC. 5 rooms with PB. Breakfast and snacks/refreshments included in rates. Type of meal: Full bkfst. Beds: QDT. Cable TV in room. Central air. VCR, fax and library on premises. Small meetings, family reunions and seminars hosted. Sign spoken. Antiquing, art galleries, canoeing/kayaking, fishing, golf, hiking, live theater, museums, parks, shopping, sporting events, tennis and wineries nearby.

Oliver Inn

630 W Washington St
South Bend, IN 46601-1444
(219)232-4545 (888)697-4466 Fax:(219)288-9788
E-mail: oliver@michiana.org
Web: www.lodging-south-bend.com

Circa 1886. This stately Queen Anne Victorian sits amid 30 towering maples and was once home to Josephine Oliver Ford, daughter of James Oliver, of chilled plow fame. Located in South Bend's historic district, this inn offers a comfortable library and nine inviting guest rooms, some with built-in fireplaces or double Jacuzzis. The inn is within walking distance of downtown and is next door to the Tippecanoe Restaurant in the Studebaker Mansion.

Innkeeper(s): Richard & Venera Monahan. $95-225. MC, VISA, AX, DS, PC, TC. 9 rooms, 7 with PB, 2 with FP, 3 suites and 1 conference room. Breakfast and snacks/refreshments included in rates. Types of meals: Full bkfst and early coffee/tea. Beds: KQ. Cable TV, phone and ceiling fan in room. Air conditioning. Fax and baby Grand with computer disk system on premises. Handicap access. Weddings, small meetings, family reunions and seminars hosted. Antiquing, fishing, museums, live theater, parks, shopping, cross-country skiing, sporting events and water sports nearby.

Valparaiso   B3

The Inn at Aberdeen

3158 South SR 2
Valparaiso, IN 46385
(219)465-3753 Fax:(219)465-9227

Circa 1890. An old stone wall borders this inn, once a dairy farm, horse farm and then hunting lodge. Recently renovated and expanded, this Victorian farmhouse is on more than an acre. An elegant getaway, there's a solarium, library, dining room and parlor for relaxing. The inn offers traditional Queen Anne furnishings in the guest rooms. The Timberlake Suites include fireplaces, two-person Jacuzzi tubs and balconies. The Aberdeen Suite includes a living room and fireplace, while the Alloway Suite offers a kitchenette. A conference center on the property is popular for executive meetings and special events, and there is a picturesque gazebo overlooking the inn's beautifully landscaped lawns and English gardens. Golf packages and mystery weekends have received enthusiastic response from guests. There is a golf course adjacent to the inn.

Innkeeper(s): Bill Simon. $94-160. MC, VISA, AX, DC, CB, DS, TC. 11 suites, 9 with FP and 1 conference room. Breakfast and snacks/refreshments included in rates. Types of meals: Full gourmet bkfst and early coffee/tea. Beds: KQ. Cable TV, phone, ceiling fan and VCR in room. Air conditioning. Fax, copier, swimming, bicycles, tennis, library, snack bar and gazebo on premises. Handicap access. Weddings, small meetings, family reunions and seminars hosted. Antiquing, fishing, golf, live theater, parks, shopping, downhill skiing, cross-country skiing, sporting events, tennis and water sports nearby.

"Every time we have the good fortune to spend an evening here, it is like a perfect fairy tale, transforming us into King and Queen."

Wabash   D6

Lamp-Post Inn B&B

261 W Hill St
Wabash, IN 46992
(219)563-3094

Circa 1896. Built in Romanesque style, this home features many original features, including handsome oak woodwork. The home is comfortably decorated and includes antiques. The Pink Room, which has a private bath, also has a turret window and four-poster bed. One of the shared bathrooms has a clawfoot tub. Belgian waffles, topped with fruit, are a specialty of the house.

Innkeeper(s): Janet L. Conner. $50-70. PC, TC. 4 rooms, 1 with PB. Breakfast included in rates. Types of meals: Full bkfst and early coffee/tea. Beds: QDT. Cable TV, phone, turndown service and ceiling fan in room. Air conditioning. VCR and piano on premises. Small meetings hosted. Antiquing, fishing, golf, live theater, parks, shopping, sporting events, tennis and water sports nearby.

Iowa

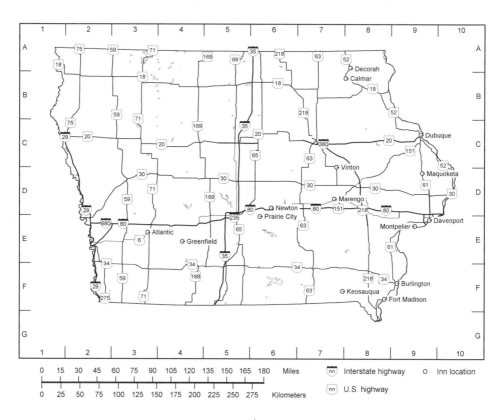

	1	2	3	4	5	6	7	8	9	10
A								Decorah / Calmar		
B										
C							Dubuque		Maquoketa	
D							Marengo			
E	Atlantic / Greenfield					Newton / Prairie City	Montpelier / Davenport			
F						Keosauqua	Burlington / Fort Madison			
G										

Miles: 0 15 30 45 60 75 90 105 120 135 150 165 180

Kilometers: 0 25 50 75 100 125 150 175 200 225 250 275

(nn) Interstate highway   o Inn location
(nn) U.S. highway

Atlantic   E3

Chestnut Charm B&B

1409 Chestnut St
Atlantic, IA 50022-2547
(712)243-5652

Circa 1898. Victorian architecture and an enchanting interior
await you at this richly appointed bed & breakfast. The interior
boasts natural hardwood floors, stained-glass windows and original wallcoverings that were hand painted by a Depression-era
artist. Outside, guests will find a courtyard with a fountain, gazebo, Victorian-style street lamps and two acres of lush grounds.
The accommodations include five elegant guest rooms and four
suites in a romantic carriage house. The carriage house suites
include king-size beds, double whirlpool tubs, clawfoot tubs and
pedestal sinks. One includes a balcony, another has a window

seat. One suite includes a heart-shaped Jacuzzi. The scent of
freshly ground coffee brewing serves as a pleasant wake-up call
and is soon followed with a delicious, homemade full breakfast.

Historic Interest: Explore the bevy of historical day trips, including the historic bridges of Madison County. A Danish Windmill and museum, Pellett
Memorial Gardens and plenty of antiquing are also within driving distance.

Innkeeper(s): Barbara Stensvad. $70-250. MC, VISA, PC. TAC10. 9 rooms with
PB, 7 with FP and 6 suites. Breakfast included in rates. Type of meal: Full
gourmet bkfst. Gourmet dinner available. Beds: KQD. TV and whirlpool tubs and
in-room saunas in room. Air conditioning. Library,
gazebo and fountained patio and gardens on premises. Antiquing, fishing, historical
sites, parks and shopping nearby.

Publicity: *Atlantic News
Telegraph, Midwest Living, Iowan,
Iowa Lady, Home & Away, Omaha
World Herald.*

*"We truly had a wonderful
weekend. Your hospitality was
unsurpassed!"*

Burlington
F9

Mississippi Manor

809 N 4th St
Burlington, IA 52601-5008
(319)753-2218
E-mail: fhdjd@aol.com

Circa 1877. Located just two blocks from the Mississippi River in the National Landmark District, this Italianate Victorian manor house was built by a lumber baron who incorporated European craftsmanship into the fine architectural detailing.

Inside, the inn is elegantly decorated and includes four guest rooms with private baths. Two spacious suites offer wood burning fireplaces. A continental breakfast is included in the rates. The inn is close to downtown and the Mississippi River.

Innkeeper(s): Francesca Harris. $75. MC, VISA, PC. 4 rooms with PB, 2 with FP. Breakfast included in rates. Meal: Cont plus. Beds: QT. Cable TV, phone and ceiling fan in room. Air conditioning. VCR on premises. Weddings, small meetings, family reunions and seminars hosted. Antiquing, fishing, golf, magnificent park system and arboretum, parks, shopping, tennis and water sports nearby.

Schramm House B&B

616 Columbia St
Burlington, IA 52601
(800)683-7117 Fax:(319)754-0373

Circa 1866. "Colossal" would be an excellent word to describe this Queen Anne Victorian. The home is an impressive site in this Burlington historic district. The exterior is brick on the first story with clapboard on the second, and a third-story tower is one of the architectural highlights. Inside, the parquet floors and

woodwork have been restored to their 19th-century grandeur. The home was built just after the Civil War by a local department store owner. Additions were made in the 1880s. Eventually, the home was converted into apartments, so the innkeepers took on quite a task refurbishing the place back to its original state. The Victorian is decorated with the innkeepers collection of antiques. One particularly appealing guest room includes an exposed brick wall and tin ceiling. Breakfast might begin with a baked pear topped with toasted almonds and a raspberry sauce. From there, freshly baked muffins arrive, followed by an entree, perhaps a frittata or French toast. All courses are served with fine china and crystal. The home is just six blocks from the Mississippi, and don't pass up a walk down the historic Snake Alley.

Innkeeper(s): Sandy & Bruce Morrison. $85-125. MC, VISA, AX, DS, PC, TC. TAC10. 4 rooms with PB. Breakfast included in rates. Types of meals: Full bkfst and early coffee/tea. Beds: Q. Turndown service, ceiling fan, robes and hair dryers in room. VCR, fax and library on premises. Weddings and small meetings hosted. Antiquing, fishing, golf, parks, shopping and tennis nearby.
Publicity: Hawk Eye.

Calmar
B8

Calmar Guesthouse

103 W North St
Calmar, IA 52132-7605
(319)562-3851

Circa 1890. This beautifully restored Victorian home was built by John B. Kay, a lawyer and poet. Stained-glass windows, carved moldings, an oak-and-walnut staircase and gleaming woodwork highlight the gracious interior. A grandfather clock ticks in the living room. In the foyer, a friendship yellow rose is incorporated into the stained-glass window pane. Breakfast is served in the formal dining room. The Laura Ingalls Wilder Museum is nearby in Burr Oak. The Bily Brothers Clock Museum, Smallest Church, Luther College and Norwegian Museum are located nearby.

Historic Interest: The Norwegian Museum is 10 minutes away. The Smallest Church, Bily Brothers Clocks Museum and Luther College are nearby.

Innkeeper(s): Lucille Kruse. $45-50. MC, VISA, PC, TC. 5 rooms, 1 with PB. Breakfast included in rates. Types of meals: Full bkfst and early coffee/tea. Beds: Q. Cable TV in room. Air conditioning. VCR, bicycles and library on premises. Small meetings hosted. Antiquing, fishing, live theater, parks, shopping, downhill skiing, cross-country skiing, sporting events and water sports nearby.

Publicity: Iowa Farmer Today, Calmar Courier, Minneapolis Star-Tribune, Home and Away, Iowan.

"What a delight it was to stay here. No one could have made our stay more welcome or enjoyable."

Davenport
E9

Fulton's Landing Guest House

1206 E River Dr
Davenport, IA 52803-5742
(319)322-4069 Fax:(319)322-8186
Web: www.fultonslanding.com

Circa 1871. Enjoy views of the Mississippi River from the porches of this stone, Italianate home, which is listed in the National Register. The guest rooms are decorated with antiques, including ceiling fans. After enjoying the morning meal, guests have a variety of activities to choose. Riverboat gambling, shopping and downtown Davenport all are nearby.

Innkeeper(s): Pat & Bill Schmidt. $60-125. MC, VISA, AX. 5 rooms with PB and 1 suite. Breakfast included in rates. Type of meal: Full gourmet bkfst. Beds: Q. Cable TV, phone and ceiling fan in room. Air conditioning. Fax, copier and bicycles on premises. Antiquing, fishing, live theater, parks, shopping, cross-country skiing, sporting events and water sports nearby.

"I have never felt more pampered and cared for staying away from home."

Decorah
A8

Elmhurst Cottage

3618 - 258th Ave
Decorah, IA 52101
(319)735-5310 (888)413-5600

Circa 1885. Located on 80 acres, this family cottage provides simple accommodations in a peaceful farm setting. Outdoor activities such as volleyball, horseshoes, tetherball and badminton are available on the property. Area attractions include the Laura Ingalls-Wilder Museum, Norwegian-American Museum, local caves and Amish community tours and shops. Innkeeper(s): Opal Underbakke. $28-65. MC, VISA, DS, PC. 9 rooms, 1 with PB, 1 suite and 1 cottage. Breakfast included in rates. Types of meals: Full bkfst and early coffee/tea. Afternoon tea, dinner, snacks/refreshments, picnic lunch, lunch, catering service and room service available. Beds: KQDT. Alarm clock and wall clock in room. Air conditioning. VCR on premises. Handicap access. Weddings, small meetings, family reunions and seminars hosted. Antiquing, canoeing/kayaking, fishing, golf, live theater, parks, shopping, downhill skiing, sporting events and water sports nearby.

Pets allowed: deposit required, restricted areas.

Dubuque
C9

The Hancock House

1105 Grove Ter
Dubuque, IA 52001-4644
(319)557-8989 Fax:(319)583-0813
Web: www.thehancockhouse.com

Circa 1891. Victorian splendor can be found at The Hancock House, one of Dubuque's most striking examples of Queen Anne architecture. Rooms feature period furnishings and offer views of the Mississippi River states of Iowa, Illinois and Wisconsin. The Hancock House, listed in the National Register, boasts several unique features, including a fireplace judged blue-ribbon best at the 1893 World's Fair in Chicago. Guests can enjoy the porch swings, wicker furniture and spectacular views from the wraparound front porch.

Innkeeper(s): Chuck & Susan Huntley. $80-175. MC, VISA, AX, DS, PC, TC. TAC10. 9 rooms with PB, 3 with FP, 4 suites and 1 cottage. Breakfast included in rates. Types of meals: Full bkfst and early coffee/tea. Beds: Q. Cable TV and feather mattress in room. Air conditioning. Fax, copier and gift shop on premises. Small meetings, family reunions and seminars hosted. Antiquing, fishing, golf, riverboat casino, live theater, parks, shopping, downhill skiing, cross-country skiing, sporting events, tennis and water sports nearby.

The Mandolin Inn

199 Loras Blvd
Dubuque, IA 52001-4857
(319)556-0069 (800)524-7996 Fax:(319)556-0587
E-mail: innkeeper@mandolininn.com
Web: www.mandolininn.com

Circa 1908. This three-story brick Edwardian with Queen Anne wraparound veranda boasts a mosaic-tiled porch floor. Inside are in-laid mahogany and rosewood floors, bay windows and a turret that starts in the parlor and ascends to the second-floor Holly Marie Room, decorated in a wedding motif. This room features a seven-piece French Walnut bedroom suite and a crystal chandelier. A gourmet breakfast is served in the dining room with a fantasy forest mural from the turn-of-the-century. There is an herb garden outside the kitchen. A church is across the street and riverboat gambling is 12 blocks away.

Innkeeper(s): Amy Boynton. $75-135. MC, VISA, AX, DS, PC, TC. 7 rooms, 5 with PB and 2 conference rooms. Breakfast included in rates. Types of meals: Full gourmet bkfst and early coffee/tea. Beds: KQ. Cable TV in room. Central air. Fax on premises. Weddings, small meetings, family reunions and seminars hosted. Antiquing, live theater, parks, shopping, downhill skiing, cross-country skiing, sporting events and water sports nearby.

"From the moment we entered the Mandolin, we felt at home. I know we'll be back."

The Richards House

1492 Locust St
Dubuque, IA 52001-4714
(319)557-1492

Circa 1883. Owner David Stuart estimates that it will take several years to remove the concrete-based brown paint applied by a bridge painter in the '60s to cover the 7,000-square-foot, Stick-style Victorian house. The interior, however, only needed a tad of polish. The varnished cherry and bird's-eye maple woodwork is set aglow under electrified gaslights. Ninety stained-glass windows, eight pocket doors with stained glass and a magnificent entryway reward those who pass through.

Historic Interest: Five historic districts are in Dubuque.
Innkeeper(s): Michelle A. Delaney. $40-95. MC, VISA, AX, DC, CB, DS, TC. 6 rooms, 3 with PB, 5 with FP, 1 suite and 1 conference room. Breakfast included in rates. Types of meals: Full bkfst and early coffee/tea. Afternoon tea and snacks/refreshments available. Beds: Q. Cable TV, phone, VCR and vCR in room. Fax on premises. Weddings, small meetings and family reunions hosted. Antiquing, fishing, live theater, parks, shopping, downhill skiing, cross-country skiing and water sports nearby.

Pets Allowed.

Publicity: *Collectors Journal, Telegraph Herald.*

"Although the guide at the door had warned us that the interior was incredible, we were still flabbergasted when we stepped into the foyer of this house."

Fort Madison   F8

Kingsley Inn

707 Avenue H (Hwy 61)
Fort Madison, IA 52627
(319)372-7074 (800)441-2327 Fax:(319)372-7096
E-mail: kingsley@interl.net
Web: www.kingsleyinn.com

Circa 1858. Overlooking the Mississippi River, this century-old inn is located in downtown Fort Madison. Though furnished with antiques, all 14 rooms offer modern amenities and private baths (some with whirlpools) as well as river views. A two-bedroom, two-bath suite also is available. The suite includes a living room, dining area, kitchen and a whirlpool tub in one bathroom. A riverboat casino and a variety of shops  are within a few blocks of the inn. There is a restaurant, Alphas on the Riverfront, and a gift shop on the premises.

Historic Interest: A museum and historic fort are nearby. Historic Nauvoo, Ill., known as the "Williamsburg of the Midwest," is only 11 miles from the inn.

Innkeeper(s): Alida Willis. $65-115. MC, VISA, AX, DC, DS. 14 rooms with PB, 1 suite and 1 conference room. Breakfast included in rates. Types of meals: Cont plus and early coffee/tea. Restaurant on premises. Beds: KQD. Cable TV and phone in room. Air conditioning. Fax on premises. Handicap access. Weddings, small meetings, family reunions and seminars hosted. Antiquing, fishing, casino and shopping nearby.

Greenfield   E4

The Brass Lantern

2446 State Hwy 92
Greenfield, IA 50849-9757
(515)743-2031 (888)743-2031 Fax:(515)343-7500
E-mail: info@brasslantern.com
Web: www.brasslantern.com

Circa 1918. Located on 20 acres, just minutes from the famous bridges of Madison County, this B&B is highlighted by an indoor pool complex with a curving 40-foot pool. Spacious, luxuriously appointed guest rooms overlook the  pool and rolling countryside and share the use of a fully furnished kitchenette. A hearty breakfast is served next door in the formal dining room of the antique-filled 1918 farm house.

Historic Interest: The antique aircraft museum, the Warren Opera House and the original Mormon Trail are located nearby.

Innkeeper(s): Terry & Margie Moore. $100-195. PC, TC. 3 rooms, 2 with PB. Breakfast included in rates. Types of meals: Full bkfst and early coffee/tea. Snacks/refreshments available. Beds: Q. Cable TV and phone in room. Air conditioning. Fax and copier on premises. Antiquing, fishing, golf, hunting and shopping nearby.

Pets allowed: with prior approval.

"Iowa is a beautiful place and The Brass Lantern is its crown jewel!"

Keosauqua   F7

Mason House Inn of Bentonsport

RR 2, Box 237
Keosauqua, IA 52565
(319)592-3133 (800)592-3133

Circa 1846. A Murphy-style copper bathtub folds down out of the wall at this unusual inn built by Mormon craftsmen, who stayed in Bentonsport for one year on their trek to Utah. More than half of the furniture is original to the home, including a nine-foot walnut headboard and a nine-foot mirror. This is the only  operating pre-Civil War steamboat inn in Iowa. Guests can imagine the days when steamboats made their way up and down the Des Moines River, while taking in the scenery. A full breakfast is served, but if guests crave a mid-day snack, each room is equipped with its own stocked cookie jar.

Innkeeper(s): William McDermet III. $64-79. MC, VISA. 9 rooms with PB and 1 conference room. Breakfast included in rates. Types of meals: Full bkfst and early coffee/tea. Beds: KQD. Cookie jar filled in room. Air conditioning. Handicap access. Weddings, small meetings, family reunions and seminars hosted. Antiquing, shopping and cross-country skiing nearby.

"The attention to detail was fantastic, food was wonderful and the setting was fascinating."

Maquoketa   D9

Squiers Manor B&B

418 W Pleasant St
Maquoketa, IA 52060-2847
(319)652-6961
E-mail: banowetz@caves.net
Web: www.squiersmanor.com

Circa 1882. Innkeepers Virl and Kathy Banowetz are ace antique dealers, who along with owning one of the Midwest's largest antique shops, have refurbished this elegant, Queen Anne Victorian. The inn is furnished with period antiques that are beyond compare. Guest rooms boast museum-quality pieces such as a Victorian brass bed with lace curtain wings and inlaid mother-of-pearl or an antique mahogany bed with carved birds and flowers. Six guest rooms include whirlpool tubs, and one includes a unique Swiss shower. The innkeepers restored the home's original woodwork, shuttered-windows, fireplaces, gas and electric chandeliers and stained- and engraved-glass windows back to their former glory. They also recently renovated the mansion's attic ballroom into two luxurious suites. The Loft, which is made up of three levels, features pine and wicker furnishings, a sitting room and gas-burning wood stove. On the second level, there is a large Jacuzzi, on the third, an antique queen-size bed. The huge Ballroom Suite boasts 24-foot ceilings, oak and pine antiques, gas-burning wood stove and a Jacuzzi snuggled beside a dormer window. Suite guests enjoy breakfast delivered to their rooms. Other guests feast on an array of mouth-watering treats, such as home-baked breads, seafood quiche and fresh fruits. Evening desserts are served by candlelight.

Historic Interest: The area has 70 sites listed in the National Register.

Innkeeper(s): Virl & Kathy Banowetz. $80-195. MC, VISA, AX. 8 rooms with PB and 3 suites. Breakfast included in rates. Type of meal: Full gourmet bkfst. Beds: KQT. Small meetings hosted. Antiquing, fishing, parks, shopping, downhill skiing, cross-country skiing and water sports nearby.

Publicity: Des Moines Register Datebook, Daily Herald.

"We couldn't have asked for a more perfect place to spend our honeymoon. The service was excellent and so was the food! It was an exciting experience that we will never forget!"

Montpelier   E9

Varners' Caboose

204 E 2nd, Box 10
Montpelier, IA 52759
(319)381-3652

Circa 1956. Located halfway between Davenport and Muscatine, this original Rock Island Lines caboose rests on its own track behind the Varners' home, the former Montpelier Depot. The caboose is decorated in simple, country style. The innkeepers prepare a full breakfast and deliver it to their guests. Llamas, ducks and geese are available for petting.

Innkeeper(s): Bob & Nancy Varner. $60. PC. 1 rooms with PB. Breakfast included in rates. Type of meal: Full bkfst. Beds: QT. Cable TV, VCR, small kitchen and microwave in room. Air conditioning. Fishing and parks nearby. Pets Allowed.

Newton   D6

La Corsette Maison Inn

629 1st Ave E
Newton, IA 50208-3305
(515)792-6833 Fax:(515)792-6597

Circa 1909. This unusual Mission-style building has an arts-and-crafts interior. All the woodwork is of quarter-sawn oak, and the dining room furniture was designed by Limbert.
Stained and beveled
glass is found
throughout. French
bedchambers feature
reproduction and
antique furnishings.
One of the suites

includes a fireplace and double whirlpool tub. The inn's restaurant has received four-and-one-half stars from the Des Moines Register's Grumpy Gourmet. The mansion also has three working wood-burning fireplaces.

Historic Interest: Jasper County Courthouse (7 blocks), Saint Stevens Episcopal Church (3 blocks).

Innkeeper(s): Kay Owen. $70-190. MC, VISA, AX. 7 rooms with PB, 3 with FP and 2 suites. Breakfast included in rates. AP. Type of meal: Full bkfst. Gourmet dinner and picnic lunch available. Restaurant on premises. Beds: KQD. Fax on premises. Antiquing, fishing, downhill skiing and cross-country skiing nearby.

Pets allowed: by prior arrangements.

"We shall return. You and your house are an inspiration."

Prairie City   E6

The Country Connection B&B

9737 West 93rd St S
Prairie City, IA 50579
(515)994-2023

Circa 1910. This sixth generation Four Square home is on three acres. Much of the home's original walnut woodwork remains, and there are many original furnishings, as well. Grandma's Room has a walnut wardrobe and is accessorized with antique linens, a pair of high button shoes, a sleigh and handmade dolls. Coming to this homestay is very much as if you were staying at Grandma's house, complete with cookie jar, home-canned fruit, home-baked breads, sourdough pancakes and turkey or sausage. In honor of your adulthood, Grandma pulls out beautiful pieces of antique china and lights candles for you at breakfast. Children of all ages are welcome. (Ask Grandpa about making some home made ice cream before you go to bed.) There's a train room in the house or enjoy the lawn swing. Nearby are the Walnut Creek Wildlife Refuge, Lake Red Rock, Pella Tulip Time, Trainland USA and many antique stores.

Historic Interest: Pella (15 miles), Historic Valley Junction (25 miles), Newton Museum.

Innkeeper(s): Alice Foreman. $50-60. MC, VISA, PC, TC. 2 rooms. Breakfast and snacks/refreshments included in rates. AP. Type of meal: Country bkfst. Beds: Q. TV and ceiling fan in room. Central air. VCR and library on premises. Amusement parks, antiquing, art galleries, bicycling, hiking, new Smithsonian wildlife refuge, live theater, museums, parks, shopping, sporting events, tennis and water sports nearby.

Vinton   C7

Lion & The Lamb B&B

913 2nd Ave
Vinton, IA 52349-1729
(319)472-5086 (888)390-5262 Fax:(319)472-5086

Circa 1892. This Queen Anne Victorian, a true "Painted Lady," boasts a stunning exterior with intricate chimneys, gingerbread trim, gables and turrets. The home still maintains its original pocket doors and parquet flooring, and antiques add to the nostalgic flavor. One room boasts a 150-year-old bedroom set. Breakfasts, as any meal in such fine a house should, are served on china. Succulent French toast topped with powdered sugar and a rich strawberry sauce is a specialty. In the evenings, desserts are served.

Innkeeper(s): Richard & Rachel Waterbury. $65-95. MC, VISA, AX, DS, PC, TC. TAC10. 4 rooms, 2 with PB, 2 with FP. Breakfast included in rates. Types of meals: Full bkfst and early coffee/tea. Beds: KQ. TV and ceiling fan in room. Air conditioning. VCR, fax and bicycles on premises. Weddings, small meetings, family reunions and seminars hosted. Antiquing, fishing, golf, live theater, parks, shopping, cross-country skiing, tennis and water sports nearby.

Publicity: Cedar Valley Times, Waterloo Courier, Cedar Rapids Gazette.

"It is a magical place!"

Kansas

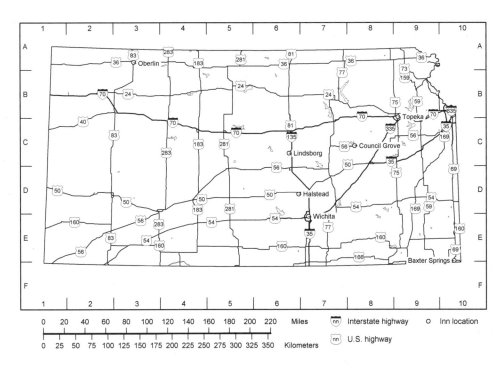

Scale:
0 20 40 60 80 100 120 140 160 180 200 220 Miles

0 25 50 75 100 125 150 175 200 225 250 275 300 325 350 Kilometers

[nn] Interstate highway   o Inn location

[nn] U.S. highway

Baxter Springs   E10

Little Brick Inn

1101 Military Ave
Baxter Springs, KS 66713
(316)856-5646 (877)223-3466 Fax:(316)856-5646
E-mail: rls2525@aol.com

Circa 1860. Fashioned entirely of brick, this historic building
conjures up images of the Old West. In fact, this inn once served
as the Baxter Bank building and was robbed by Jesse James in
1876. The restored inn includes its original hardwood floors and
transoms above the doors. Rooms are decorated with antiques.

There is a kitchen avail-
able for guest use. Guests
are treated to a full, country breakfast in an
upstairs dining room.
Lunch and dinner also
are available in the inn's
restaurant. The inn rests

on historic Route 66, which offers many interesting attractions
along its path. Baxter Springs is Kansas' first cow town.

Historic Interest: Ft. Blair, Quantrail's Raid, 1st cow town in KS.

Innkeeper(s): Richard & Amy Sanell. $40-100. MC, VISA, AX, DS, PC, TC.
TAC10. 7 rooms with PB, 3 suites and 2 conference rooms. Breakfast
included in rates. AP. Types of meals: Full bkfst, country bkfst and early cof-
fee/tea. Banquet service and catering service available. Restaurant on
premises. Beds: KQD. Cable TV, ceiling fan, microwave, tea and popcorn in
room. Central air. Library on premises. Weddings, small meetings, family
reunions and seminars hosted. Antiquing, canoeing/kayaking, fishing, golf
and shopping nearby.

Pets Allowed.

Council Grove   C8

The Cottage House Hotel

25 N Neosho St
Council Grove, KS 66846-1633
(316)767-6828 (800)727-7903

Circa 1898. The inn is located in Council Grove, the rendezvous
point on the Santa Fe Trail. The building grew from a boarding
house to an elegant home before it became the hotel of a local

banker. The home's original section dates to 1872, and the home was built in stages until 1898. Listed in the National Register of Historic Places, the inn has been completely renovated and is a beautiful example of Victorian architecture in a prairie town. There is a honeymoon cottage on the premises, as well.

Historic Interest: National Register.

Innkeeper(s): Connie Essington. $60-140. MC, VISA, AX, DC, DS. 26 rooms with PB, 1 cottage and 2 conference rooms. Type of meal: Cont. Beds: KQD. Whirlpool tubs in room. Spa and sauna on premises. Handicap access. Fishing, golf and riverwalk nearby.

"A walk back into Kansas history; preserved charm and friendliness."

Lindsborg   C6

Swedish Country Inn

112 W Lincoln St
Lindsborg, KS 67456-2319
(785)227-2985 (800)231-0266

Circa 1904. Founded in the 1860s by Swedish immigrants, the town of Lindsborg is still known as "Little Sweden," maintaining its heritage through a variety of cultural events, festivals, galleries, shops and restaurants. The Swedish Country Inn adds to the town's ethnic flavor. All the furnishings have been imported from Sweden. Bright, airy rooms feature pine furnishings, handmade quilts and hand-painted cupboards. A Swedish-style buffet breakfast is served each morning, with items such as meatballs, lingonberries, herring, knackebread, fruit, cheese, cold meats and fresh baked goods. The Christmas season is an especially festive time to visit this inn and picturesque small town.

Innkeeper(s): Becky Anderson. $50-80. MC, VISA, AX, DS, PC, TC. 19 rooms with PB and 2 suites. Breakfast, afternoon tea and snacks/refreshments included in rates. Types of meals: Full gourmet bkfst and early coffee/tea. Beds: QD. Cable TV, phone and sauna in room. Air conditioning. Sauna and bicycles on premises. Weddings, small meetings, family reunions and seminars hosted. Antiquing, parks and shopping nearby.

Oberlin   A3

The Landmark Inn at The Historic Bank of Oberlin

189 S Penn
Oberlin, KS 67749
(785)475-2340 (888)639-0003 Fax:(785)475-2869

Circa 1886. In 1886, this inn served as the Bank of Oberlin, one of the town's most impressive architectural sites. The bank lasted only a few years, though, and went through a number of uses, from county courthouse to the telephone company. Today, it serves as both inn and a historic landmark, a reminder of the past with rooms decorated Victorian style with antiques. One room includes a fireplace; another has a whirlpool tub. In addition to the inviting rooms, there is a restaurant serving dinner specialties such as buttermilk pecan chicken and roasted beef with simmered mushrooms. The inn is listed in the National Register.

Innkeeper(s): Gary Anderson.
$59-99. MC, VISA, AX, DS,

PC, TC. 7 rooms with PB, 1 with FP, 1 suite and 2 conference rooms. Breakfast included in rates. Types of meals: Full gourmet bkfst and early coffee/tea. Afternoon tea, gourmet dinner, snacks/refreshments, gourmet lunch, catering service and room service available. Restaurant on premises. Beds: QD. Cable TV, phone, ceiling fan and VCR in room. Air conditioning. Fax, sauna, bicycles and library on premises. Handicap access. Weddings, small meetings, family reunions and seminars hosted. Antiquing, golf, parks, shopping and tennis nearby.

Topeka   B9

Brickyard Barn Inn

4020 NW 25th St
Topeka, KS 66618
(785)235-0057 Fax:(785)234-0924
E-mail: umoo2me@cjnetworks.com
Web: www.cjnetworks.com/~umoo2me

Circa 1927. Designed by novice architectural students at Kansas State University, this bed & breakfast was built for use as a dairy barn. Each of the guest rooms is comfortable and casually furnished with antiques. Modem hookups are available for the business traveler. Breakfast specialties include Brickyard Barn Inn Swiss Quiche Pie and a fresh fruit salad topped with raspberry sauce. The inn is 10 miles from the state capitol building. Other nearby points of interest include casinos and the historic Menninger site.

Historic Interest: Topeka Capital Bldg (10 miles), Menninger Site (10 miles), Civil War battle sites (30 miles).

Innkeeper(s): Scott & Truanna Nickel. $65-95. MC, VISA, PC. TAC10. 3 rooms with PB and 2 conference rooms. Breakfast and snacks/refreshments included in rates. Types of meals: Full gourmet bkfst, veg bkfst and early coffee/tea. Gourmet dinner, picnic lunch, gourmet lunch, banquet service, catering service, catered breakfast and room service available. Beds: Q. Ceiling fan in room. Central air. VCR, fax, swimming and reception facility on premises. Weddings, small meetings, family reunions and seminars hosted. Amusement parks, antiquing, art galleries, fishing, golf, hiking, horseback riding, casinos, live theater, museums, parks, shopping, sporting events, tennis, water sports and wineries nearby.

Wichita   E7

Inn at the Park

3751 E Douglas Ave
Wichita, KS 67218-1002
(316)652-0500 (800)258-1951 Fax:(316)652-0610
E-mail: iap@innatthepark.com
Web: www.innatthepark.com

Circa 1910. This popular three-story brick mansion offers many special touches, including unique furnishings in each of its 12 guest rooms, three of which are suites. All of the rooms feature fireplaces. The inn's convenient location makes it ideal for business travelers or those interested in exploring Wichita at length. The inn's parkside setting provides additional opportunities for relaxation or recreation. Ask for information about shops and restaurants in Wichita's Old Town.

Innkeeper(s): Judy Hess and/or Jan Lightner. $89-164. MC, VISA, AX, DS. 12 rooms with PB, 8 with FP, 3 suites and 1 conference room. Breakfast included in rates. Types of meals: Cont plus and early coffee/tea. Catering service available. Beds: KQ. Cable TV, phone, turndown service and VCR in room. Air conditioning. Fax, copier and spa on premises. Antiquing, adjacent to conference facility, live theater and shopping nearby.

Publicity: *Wichita Business Journal.*

"This is truly a distinctive hotel. Your attention to detail is surpassed only by your devotion to excellent service."

The Castle Inn Riverside

1155 N River Blvd
Wichita, KS 67203
(316)263-9300
E-mail: lcastle@gte.net
Web: www.castleinnriverside.com

Circa 1886. This luxurious inn is a stunning example of Richardsonian Romanesque architecture. The home includes 14 guest rooms, each individually appointed. Twelve of the guest rooms include a fireplace, and six include a double whirlpool tub. Guests are pampered with a gourmet breakfast, and later in the day, with a sampling of wine, cheeses, light hors d'oeuvres, gourmet coffees and teas and homemade desserts. The inn offers many amenities for its business travelers, including rooms equipped with TVs, VCRs, telephones and dataports. The inn is just a few minutes from downtown Wichita.

Historic Interest: The area offers several historic attractions, including nearby Old Town, a Native American center and several museums.

Innkeeper(s): Terry & Paula Lowry. $125-295. MC, VISA, DC, CB, DS, PC, TC. TAC10. 14 rooms with PB, 12 with FP, 1 suite and 1 conference room. Breakfast included in rates. Type of meal: Full gourmet bkfst. Snacks/refreshments available. Beds: KQ. TV, phone and VCR in room. Air conditioning. Fax and copier on premises. Handicap access. Weddings, small meetings, family reunions and seminars hosted. Antiquing, fishing, live theater, parks, shopping, sporting events and water sports nearby.

Kentucky

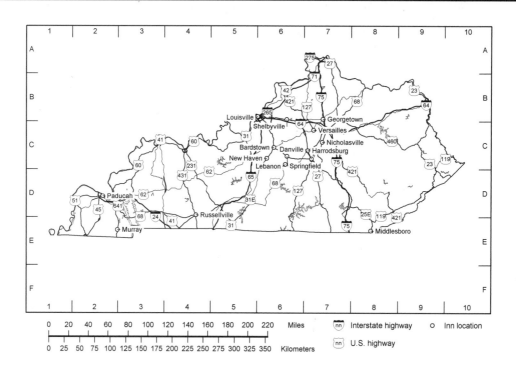

	1	2	3	4	5	6	7	8	9	10

0 20 40 60 80 100 120 140 160 180 200 220 Miles

0 25 50 75 100 125 150 175 200 225 250 275 300 325 350 Kilometers

(nn) Interstate highway   O Inn location

(nn) U.S. highway

Bardstown   C6

Jailer's Inn

111 W Stephen Foster Ave
Bardstown, KY 40004-1415
(502)348-5551 (800)948-5551 Fax:(502)349-1837

Circa 1819. As the innkeepers say, guests can come and "do time" at this inn, which was used as a jail as late as 1987. However, today, accommodations are bit less restrictive. Each of the elegant guest rooms is individually appointed. From the Victorian Room to the Garden Room, each captures a different theme. Two guest rooms include a double Jacuzzi tub. Only one guest room resembles a jail cell, it contains two bunks, as well as the more luxurious addition of a waterbed. In the summer, the full breakfasts are served in a

courtyard. The inn is located in the heart of historic Bardstown.
Historic Interest: Tours of "My Old Kentucky Home," conducted by guides in antebellum costumes, are a popular attraction. Lincoln's birthplace and boyhood home and the oldest cathedral west of Alleghany are nearby, as is the Getz Museum of Whiskey History.

Innkeeper(s): Paul McCoy. $65-105. MC, VISA, AX, DS, PC, TC. TAC10. 6 rooms with PB. Breakfast included in rates. Types of meals: Full bkfst and early coffee/tea. Beds: KQD. Cable TV, turndown service and ceiling fan in room. Air conditioning. VCR on premises. Weddings, small meetings and family reunions hosted. Antiquing, live theater, parks and shopping nearby.

"Wonderful experience! A very special B&B."

The Mansion Bed & Breakfast

1003 N 3rd St
Bardstown, KY 40004-2616
(502)348-2586 (800)399-2586 Fax:(502)349-6098

Circa 1851. The Confederate flag was raised for the first time in Kentucky on this property. The beautifully crafted Greek Revival mansion is in the National Register of Historic Places. Period antiques and hand-crocheted bedspreads, dust ruffles and shams are featured in the guest rooms. There are more than three acres of tall trees and gardens. The Courthouse in historic Bardstown is nine blocks away.

Innkeeper(s): Joseph & Charmaine Downs. $95-140. AX, DS, PC. 7 rooms with PB and 1 conference room. Breakfast included in rates. Type of meal: Cont plus. Gourmet dinner available. Beds: KD. Ceiling fan in room. Air conditioning. VCR on premises. Small meetings and seminars hosted. Antiquing, fishing, live theater and shopping nearby.

Danville   C7

Randolph House

463 W Lexington Ave
Danville, KY 40422-1455
(606)236-9594

Circa 1860. This Georgian-style inn is situated on a half-acre in the heart of the historic district in this quiet college town. Decorated in period antiques, the inn is inviting, and guests may browse the shelves in the library or relax in the afternoon on the front porch. Guest rooms feature antiques, private baths, telephones and TVs. A gourmet breakfast is served in the cozy dining room or in guest rooms by request. Dinner is available by prior reservation. Randolph House is close to shopping, town center, theater, colleges and antiques.

Innkeeper(s): Georgie Heizer. $75-85. MC, VISA, AX, PC, TC. TAC10. 3 rooms with PB. Breakfast included in rates. Type of meal: Full gourmet bkfst. Gourmet dinner available. Beds: QT. Cable TV, phone, ceiling fan, VCR and coffee pot in room. Air conditioning. Library on premises. Antiquing, live theater, parks and sporting events nearby.

Pets allowed: only with prior arrangements.

Georgetown   B7

Pineapple Inn

645 S Broadway St
Georgetown, KY 40324-1135
(502)868-5453

Circa 1876. White gingerbread trim decorates the yellow Victorian Pineapple Inn, highlighting its gables, large front porch, dentil trim and bay window. In the Kentucky Historic Register and the Bluegrass historic list, the house provides a cheerful welcome to guests visiting Kentucky's antique center. Polished antiques throughout, a country French dining room and handsome wallcoverings make the interiors pristine and inviting. A full Kentucky breakfast is served.

Innkeeper(s): Muriel & Les. $65-95. MC, VISA. 4 rooms with PB. Breakfast included in rates. Type of meal: Full bkfst. Gourmet dinner available. Beds: QD. Antiquing and fishing nearby.

Publicity: *Country Extra.*

"Your hospitality was wonderful. The food was fantastic."

Harrodsburg   C7

Bauer Haus

362 N College
Harrodsburg, KY 40330-1116
(606)734-6289 (877)734-6289
Web: www.bbonline.com/ky/bauer

Circa 1880. This Queen Anne Victorian, sans gingerbread, features a wicker-filled front porch, complete with swing. In the National Register, it was built on one of the first outlots in Harrodsburg. The town is Kentucky's oldest settlement, estab-

lished in 1774. Inside the parlor, archways adorn the mantel and date back to the early 19th century. Upstairs, the spacious guest rooms are furnished in a traditional decor with antiques. Coffee or tea is served to your room a half hour before the breakfast seating. Lower-fat dishes and fresh fruit are complemented with low-fat, made-from-scratch breakfast cakes or muffins.

Innkeeper(s): Dick & Marian Bauer. $60-110. MC, VISA, AX. 4 rooms, 2 with PB, 3 with FP. Breakfast and snacks/refreshments included in rates. Types of meals: Full bkfst and early coffee/tea. Beds: QDT. Air conditioning. VCR on premises. Small meetings, family reunions and seminars hosted. Antiquing, fishing, golf, historic sites, live theater and water sports nearby.

Baxter House

1677 Lexington Rd
Harrodsburg, KY 40330-9283
(606)734-4877 (888)809-4457

Circa 1913. Located in an area of bucolic sheep and horse farms, this American Four Square house rests on seven acres. Pleasantly decorated the inn offers three guest rooms including The Navy Room which is more of a suite and features cherry furniture including a four-poster rice bed, and The Charleston Room which offers a wood-burning fireplace. Breakfast menus include fruit, home baked breads and egg dishes. The innkeepers have worked in careers, which include interior design, painting and teaching school. Nearby activities and attractions include Shaker Village, the Perryville Civil War Battlefiled, Old Fort Harrod State Park, Daniel Boone Cave and the Kentucky Horse Park.

Innkeeper(s): Dennis Kirk, Gay Lynn Garadner. $69-99. MC, VISA, AX, DS, DC, PC, TC. 3 rooms with PB, 3 with FP. 1 conference room. Breakfast and snacks/refreshments included in rates. Types of meals: Full gourmet bkfst, vegetarian bkfst, early coffee/tea, snacks/refreshments. Beds: Q. Air conditioning. Ceiling fans, reading lamps, refrigerator, snack bar, central air, clock radio, coffee maker, phone, turndown service in room. TV, VCR, phone, copy machine, computers, bicycles, fireplace, library, parlor games on premises. Small meetings, family reunions, weddings and seminars hosted. Antiquing, biking, fishing, golf, live theater, parks, shopping, sporting events, tennis and water sports nearby.

Canaan Land Farm B&B

700 Canaan Land Rd
Harrodsburg, KY 40330-9220
(606)734-3984 (888)734-3984

Circa 1795. This National Register farmhouse, one of the oldest brick houses in Kentucky, is appointed with antiques, quilts and featherbeds. Your host is a shepherd/attorney and your hostess is a large flock of sheep, goats and other assorted barnyard animals graze the pastures at this working farm. In 1995, the innkeepers reconstructed an 1815, historic log house on the grounds. The log house includes three guest rooms and two working fireplaces.

Historic Interest: In 1992, Canaan Land Farm was named a Kentucky historic farm. Nearby Shakertown, a restored Shaker village, features daily craft demonstrations, riverboat rides and tours.

Innkeeper(s): Theo & Fred Bee. $75-125. PC, TC. 7 rooms with PB, 2 with FP. Breakfast included in rates. Types of meals: Full bkfst and early coffee/tea. Beds: DT. VCR, spa and swimming on premises. Weddings, family reunions and seminars hosted. Antiquing, fishing, golf, horseback riding, parks, shopping and water sports nearby.

Publicity: *Danville Advocate, Lexington Herald Leader.*

"You truly have a gift for genuine hospitality."

Shaker Village of Pleasant Hill

3501 Lexington Rd
Harrodsburg, KY 40330-9218
(606)734-5411 (800)734-5611 Fax:(606)734-5411

Circa 1809. A living history museum, this 19th-century Shaker village is set atop a pleasant meadow and includes 2,800 acres of farmland. Guest rooms are in 15 of the 33 restored buildings where Shakers once lived. Guest rooms are furnished with Shaker reproductions and hand-woven rugs.
The entire village is a National
Historic Landmark. Costumed inter-
preters work at 19th-century
crafts and describe Shaker culture and craft. A dining room in
the village serves bountiful
Kentucky fare and Shaker
recipes and the Summer
Kitchen is available for lunch from May through October.

Innkeeper(s): James Thomas. $66-190. MC, VISA, TC. TAC10. 81 rooms with PB, 8 suites, 2 cottages and 4 conference rooms. MAP. Types of meals: Full bkfst and cont. Dinner and lunch available. Beds: DT. Cable TV and phone in room. Air conditioning. VCR, fax and copier on premises. Small meetings, family reunions and seminars hosted. Antiquing, fishing, golf, hiking, historic sites, state park, live theater, parks and shopping nearby.

Lebanon   C6

Myrtledene B&B

370 N Spalding Ave
Lebanon, KY 40033-1557
(502)692-2223 (800)391-1721

Circa 1833. Once a Confederate general's headquarters at one point during the Civil War, this pink brick inn, located at a bend in the road, has greeted visitors entering Lebanon for more than 150 years. When General John Hunt Morgan returned in 1863 to destroy the town, the white flag hoisted to signal a truce was flown at
Myrtledene. A country
breakfast usually features
ham and biscuits as well
as the innkeepers' specialty, peaches and cream
French toast.

Historic Interest: Headquarters of confederate General John Hunt Morgan. Morgan rode his mare up to front hall stairs.

Innkeeper(s): James F. Spragens. $75. MC, VISA, PC, TC. TAC10. 4 rooms, 2 with PB, 1 with FP and 1 conference room. Breakfast included in rates. Types of meals: Full gourmet bkfst and early coffee/tea. Afternoon tea available. Beds: DT. Turndown service and bourbon chocolates in room. Air conditioning. VCR and library on premises. Weddings, small meetings, family reunions and seminars hosted. Antiquing, fishing, live theater, parks, shopping and water sports nearby.

"Our night in the Cabbage Rose Room was an experience of another time, another culture. Your skill in preparing and presenting break-fast was equally elegant! We'll be back!"

Louisville   B6

Inn at The Park

1332 S 4th St
Louisville, KY 40208-2314
(502)637-6930 (800)700-7275 Fax:(502)637-2796
E-mail: innatpark@aol.com
Web: www.bbonline.com/ky/innatpark

Circa 1886. An impressive sweeping staircase is one of many highlights at this handsome Richardsonian Romanesque inn, in the historic district of Old Louisville.

Guests also will appreciate the hardwood floors, 14-foot ceilings and
stone balconies on the second and
third floors. The seven guest rooms
offer a variety of amenities and a view
of Central Park.

Innkeeper(s): John & Sandra Mullins. $89-179. MC, VISA, AX, PC, TC. TAC10. 7 rooms with PB, 5 with FP and 3 suites. Breakfast included in rates. Types of meals: Full bkfst and early coffee/tea. Beds: KQ. Cable TV, phone and ceiling fan in room. Air conditioning. VCR and fax on premises. German spoken. Amusement parks, antiquing, churchill Downs, live theater, parks, shopping and sporting events nearby.

Old Louisville Inn

1359 S 3rd St
Louisville, KY 40208-2378
(502)635-1574 Fax:(502)637-5892

Circa 1901. This 12,000-square-foot, three-story Beaux Arts inn boasts massive ornately carved mahogany columns in the lobby. Rooms are filled with antiques gathered from local auctions and shops, and three
rooms have whirlpool
tubs. The third-floor
Celebration Suite, with its
whirlpool bath, fireplace
and king-size canopy bed,
offers perfect honeymoon
accommodations. The

morning meal, including the inn's famous popovers, is served in the breakfast room, courtyard or in the guest rooms. The inn's location, in the heart of Louisville's Victorian district, makes sightseeing inviting.

Historic Interest: Churchill Downs (2 miles), Kentucky Derby Museum (2 miles).

Innkeeper(s): Marianne Lesher. $75-195. MC, VISA, AX, DC, DS, PC, TC. 10 rooms with PB, 2 with FP, 2 suites and 2 conference rooms. Breakfast included in rates. MAP. Types of meals: Full gourmet bkfst and early coffee/tea. Beds: KQDT. Air conditioning. VCR, fax, copier and library on premises. Small meetings, family reunions and seminars hosted. Amusement parks, antiquing, golf, live theater, parks, shopping, sporting events and tennis nearby.

Pets allowed: upon approval.

"My most enjoyable, relaxed business trip!"

The Inn at Woodhaven

401 S Hubbard Lane
Louisville, KY 40207-4074
(502)895-1011 (888)895-1011
E-mail: woodhavenb@aol.com
Web: www.bbonline.com/ky/woodhaven/

Circa 1853. This Gothic Revival, painted in a cheerful shade of yellow, is still much the same as it was in the 1850s, when it served as the home on a prominent local farm. The rooms still feature the outstanding carved woodwork, crisscross window designs, winding staircases, decorative mantels and hardwood floors. Guest quarters are tastefully appointed with antiques, suitable for their 12-foot, nine-inch tall ceilings.

Complimentary coffee and tea stations are provided in each room. There are several common areas in the Main House, and guests also take advantage of the inn's porches. Rose Cottage is octagon shaped and features a 25-foot vaulted ceiling, a king bed, fireplace, sitting area, double whirlpool, steam shower and wraparound porch. The National Register home is close to all of Louisville's attractions.

Innkeeper(s): Marsha Burton. $75-175. MC, VISA, AX. 8 rooms with PB, 3 with FP, 2 suites and 1 cottage. Breakfast included in rates. Type of meal: Full gourmet bkfst. Gourmet dinner and picnic lunch available. Beds: KQDT. Cable TV, phone, ceiling fan, coffee, tea and hot chocolate facility in room. Air conditioning. Fax, copier, library and three rooms with double whirlpools on premises. Handicap access. Weddings, small meetings, family reunions and seminars hosted. Amusement parks, antiquing, golf, live theater, parks, shopping, sporting events, tennis and water sports nearby.

Publicity: *Courier Journal.*

Middlesborough   D6

The Ridge Runner B&B

208 Arthur Hts
Middlesborough, KY 40965-1728
(606)248-4299

Circa 1890. Bachelor buttons, lilacs and wildflowers line the white picket fence framing this 20-room brick Victorian mansion. Guests enjoy relaxing in its turn-of-the-century library and parlor filled with Victorian antiques. Ask for the President's Room and you'll enjoy the best view of the Cumberland

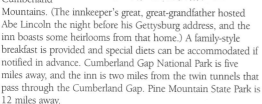

Mountains. (The innkeeper's great, great-grandfather hosted Abe Lincoln the night before his Gettysburg address, and the inn boasts some heirlooms from that home.) A family-style breakfast is provided and special diets can be accommodated if notified in advance. Cumberland Gap National Park is five miles away, and the inn is two miles from the twin tunnels that pass through the Cumberland Gap. Pine Mountain State Park is 12 miles away.

Historic Interest: Restoration of a P-38 fighter plane, Abraham Lincoln artifacts and museum.

Innkeeper(s): Susan Richards & Irma Gall. $65-75. PC. 4 rooms, 2 with PB. Breakfast and snacks/refreshments included in rates. Type of meal: Early coffee/tea. Beds: DT. Turndown service and ceiling fan in room. Small meetings and family reunions hosted. Antiquing, parks and shopping nearby.

Publicity: *Lexington Herald Leader, Blue Ridge Country, Indianapolis Star, Daily News, Courier Journal, Country Inn.*

Murray   E2

The Diuguid House B&B

603 Main St
Murray, KY 42071-2034
(502)753-5470 (888)261-3028

Circa 1895. This Victorian house features eight-foot-wide hallways and a golden oak staircase with stained-glass window.

There is a sitting area adjoining the portico. Guest rooms are generous in size.

Historic Interest: Listed in the National Register.

Innkeeper(s): Karen & George Chapman. $40. MC, VISA, DC, PC, TC. 3 rooms. Breakfast included in rates. Types of meals: Full bkfst and early coffee/tea.

Beds: QT. TV, phone and turndown service in room. Air conditioning. Weddings, small meetings and family reunions hosted. Antiquing, fishing, live theater, parks and water sports nearby.

Pets allowed: Advance approval.

Publicity: *Murray State News.*

"We enjoyed our visit in your beautiful home, and your hospitality was outstanding."

New Haven   C6

The Sherwood Inn

138 S Main St
New Haven, KY 40051
(502)549-3386 Fax:(502)549-5822

Circa 1914. Since 1875, the Johnson family has owned the Sherwood Inn. A week after the original building burned in 1913, construction for the current building began. In the National Register, the inn catered to passengers of the nearby L & N (Louisville and Nashville) Railroad. Antiques and reproductions complement some of the inn's original furnishings. The restaurant is open for dinner Wednesday through Saturday. The inn's slogan, first advertised in 1875 remains, "first class table and good accommodations."

Historic Interest: Kentucky Railway Museum (next door), Trappist Monastery (3 miles), Abraham Lincoln Museum (11 miles).

Innkeeper(s): Cecilia Johnson. $45-65. MC, VISA, DS. 5 rooms, 3 with PB. Breakfast included in rates. Type of meal: Full bkfst. Restaurant on premises. Beds: D. Ceiling fan in room. Air conditioning. Small meetings, family reunions and seminars hosted. Shopping nearby.

"A memorable stop."

Nicholasville C7

Sandusky House & O'Neal Log Cabin B&B

1626 Delaney Ferry Rd
Nicholasville, KY 40356-8729
(606)223-4730

Circa 1855. This Greek Revival inn rests in the tree-lined
countryside, surrounded by horse farms and other small farms.
Its tranquil setting offers a perfect getaway from busy nearby
Lexington. The inn, which is listed
on Kentucky's state register, boasts
six porches, seven fireplaces and
impressive brick columns. The
three guest rooms feature desks,
private baths and turndown service. There is a small garden with
benches and a table for guests to use and enjoy. The innkeepers also offer lodging in a two-bedroom, 180-year-old log cabin.
Although historic, the National Register cabin includes modern
amenities such as a full kitchen and whirlpool tub. Area attractions include Asbury College, Keeneland Race Course, the
Mary Todd Lincoln House and the University of Kentucky.
Innkeeper(s): Jim & Linda Humphrey. $79-120. MC, VISA, PC. 3 rooms with
PB and 1 cabin. Breakfast included in rates. Types of meals: Full bkfst and
early coffee/tea. Beds: D. Cable TV and local TV in room. Air conditioning.
VCR and bicycles on premises. Weddings hosted. Antiquing, golf, parks,
shopping and sporting events nearby.
Publicity: *Lexington Herald-Leader, Country Inns.*

Russellville D4

The Log House

2139 Franklin Rd
Russellville, KY 42276-9410
(502)726-8483 Fax:(502)726-4610

Circa 1976. This ideal log cabin retreat was built from hand-
hewn logs from old cabins and barns in the area. Rooms are full
of quilts, early American furnishings and folk art from around the
world. The log walls and hardwood floors create an unparalleled
atmosphere of country warmth. An impressive kitchen is decorated with an old-fashioned stove and brick floor. The innkeepers
create hand-woven garments and hand-spun items in an adjacent
studio. Nashville and Opryland are about an hour's drive, and
the local area boasts a number of antique shops.
Innkeeper(s): Mike & Sam Hossom. $95. MC, VISA, PC, TC. 4 rooms with PB, 2
with FP. Breakfast included in rates. Meal: Full gourmet bkfst. Beds: QDT. Air conditioning. VCR, fax, copier, spa & library on premises. Amusement parks, antiquing,
fishing, live theater, parks, shopping, sporting events & water sports nearby.

Shelbyville B6

The Wallace House

613 Washington St
Shelbyville, KY 40065-1131
(502)633-2006

Circa 1804. This Federal-style house, midway between Louisville
and Frankfort, is listed in the National Register of Historic Places.
Its four well-appointed guest suites all feature kitchenettes.
Historic Interest: Kentucky Horse Park (50 miles), Shakertown (50 miles),
Churchill Downs Derby Museum (30 miles).
Innkeeper(s): Evelyn Laurent. $65-85. MC, VISA, AX. 4 suites. Type of meal:
Cont plus. Beds: Q. Cable TV in room. Air conditioning. Antiquing, fishing,
live theater and shopping nearby.

Springfield C6

Maple Hill Manor

2941 Perryville Rd
Springfield, KY 40069-9611
(606)336-3075 (800)886-7546

Circa 1851. This brick Revival home with Italianate detail is a
Kentucky Landmark home and is listed in the National Register
of Historic Places. It features 13-1/2-foot ceilings, 10-foot
doors, nine-foot windows, a cherry spiral staircase, stenciling in
the foyer, a large parlor, period fur-
nishings and a dining room with
a fireplace. The library has floor-
to-ceiling mahogany bookcases
and the Honeymoon Room
features a canopy bed and
Jacuzzi. A large patio area is
set among old maple trees.
Historic Interest: Bardstown (20 miles), Danville (23 miles), Perryville
Battlefield (15 miles).
Innkeeper(s): Kathleen Carroll. $50-90. MC, VISA, PC, TC. 7 rooms with PB
and 1 conference room. Breakfast included in rates. Types of meals: Full
bkfst and early coffee/tea. Snacks/refreshments available. Beds: QDT. Phone,
ceiling fan, jacuzzi and honeymoon room in room. Air conditioning. VCR on
premises. Weddings, small meetings, family reunions and seminars hosted.
Antiquing, fishing, murder Mystery, live theater and shopping nearby.

"Thank you again for your friendly and comfortable hospitality."

Versailles C7

1823 Historic Rose Hill Inn

233 Rose Hill
Versailles, KY 40383-1223
(606)873-5957 (800)307-0460
E-mail: innkeepers@rosehillinn.com
Web: www.rosehillinn.com

Circa 1823. Both Confederate and Union troops used this
manor during the Civil War. The home maintains many elegant
features, including original woodwork, 14-foot ceilings and
floors fashioned from timber on the property. The decor is
comfortable, yet elegant. One
guest bath includes a clawfoot bathtub, another
includes a double marble
Jacuzzi. The innkeepers
restored the home's sum-
mer kitchen into a private
cottage, which now includes a pri-
vate porch, kitchen and two queen/double beds. Three generations of the Amberg family live and work here, including friendly dogs. The mother/daughter innkeepers serve a hearty, full
breakfast, and the cookie jar is always filled with homemade
treats. Among the sites are a Shaker Village, antique shops,
horse farms, Keeneland Race Track and a wildlife sanctuary.
Innkeeper(s): Sharon Amberg & Marianne Amberg. $85-125. MC, VISA, AX,
DS, TC. TAC10. 4 rooms with PB, 1 suite and 1 cottage. Breakfast included
in rates. Types of meals: Full bkfst and early coffee/tea. Beds: KQDT. Cable
TV, phone, turndown service and ceiling fan in room. Air conditioning. VCR,
bicycles and library on premises. Small meetings and family reunions hosted.
Antiquing, fishing, golf, horse farm tours, Kentucky Horse Park, Shaker
Village, parks, shopping and sporting events nearby.
Pets allowed: In cottage with prior approval.

Louisiana

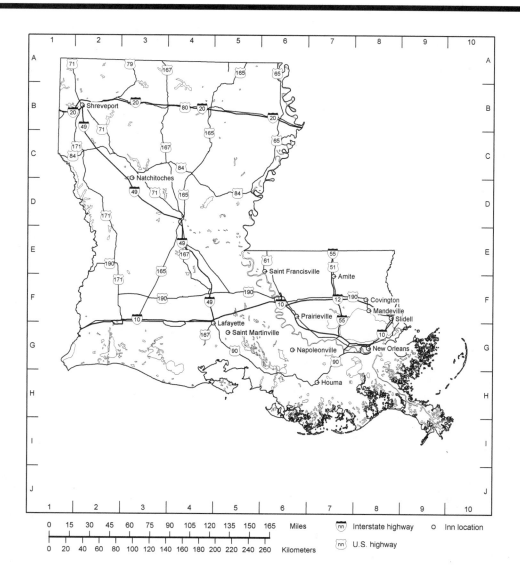

0 15 30 45 60 75 90 105 120 135 150 165 Miles

0 20 40 60 80 100 120 140 160 180 200 220 240 260 Kilometers

Interstate highway   ○ Inn location

U.S. highway

Amite   F7

Elliott House

801 N Duncan Ave
Amite, LA 70422-2222
(504)748-8553 (800)747-8553

Circa 1908. Innkeeper Flora Elliott Landwehr's grandfather, a State Court of Appeals judge, built this Neoclassical home. Flora and husband Joseph painstakingly restored the inheri-

tance, which had deteriorated and was shrouded in overgrown brush. Now, the old pine floors shine and rooms feature Victorian antiques. Two bedchambers have a fire-

place. In the mornings, homemade granola, fresh fruit and Louisiana coffee accompany entrees such as eggs Benedict. Guests can spend the day relaxing at the inn and enjoying the five acres. The area offers plenty of outdoor activities, and New Orleans is an hour away.

Innkeeper(s): Joseph and Flora Landwehr. $75-125. MC, VISA, PC, TC. TAC10. 4 rooms, 3 with PB, 2 with FP, 1 suite and 1 conference room. Breakfast and afternoon tea included in rates. Types of meals: Full gourmet bkfst and early coffee/tea. Beds: KD. Ceiling fan in room. Air conditioning. Bicycles and library on premises. Small meetings, family reunions and seminars hosted. Antiquing, golf, historic sites, wildlife parks, swamp tours, parks, shopping and water sports nearby.

"What you are doing and the type of people you are, give folks a memory, not just a place to stay."

Houma   H7

Maison des Anges

508 Academy St
Houma, LA 70360
(504)873-7662 Fax:(504)580-3117

Circa 1902. J.C. Cunningham, a prominent local resident, built this turn-of-the-20th-century home, which includes both Victorian and Acadian influences. Cunningham was a green gro-

cer, lumberman and later served as a city marshall. The bed & breakfast's name translates to "House of the Angels." Guest rooms and common areas include many original features, and the three guest bathrooms all have antique clawfoot tubs. Trees shade the

grounds that include a courtyard with fountains. Several historic plantations are within a few miles of the home, as well as parks, a wetlands center, antique shops and restaurants. Guest can arrange to take a swamp tour, fishing trip or a walking tour of historic downtown Houma. Houma also holds one of the state's largest Mardi Gras celebrations, second only to New Orleans.

Historic Interest: Ellendale Plantation (8 miles), Magnolia Plantation (3 miles), Ardoyne Plantation, St. Francis de Sales Cathedral (.2 miles).

Innkeeper(s): Magnus LeBlanc/Ray Cheramie. $45-145. MC, VISA, AX, DS,

PC, TC. 4 rooms, 2 with PB, 1 suite and 1 conference room. Breakfast included in rates. Type of meal: Full bkfst. Beds: QDT. Cable TV, phone, turn-down service, ceiling fan and VCR in room. Central air. Fax and pet boarding on premises. Weddings, small meetings, family reunions and seminars hosted. French spoken. Antiquing, art galleries, fishing, plantations, Swamp tours, live theater, museums, parks, shopping and water sports nearby.
Pets Allowed.

Lafayette   G4

La Maison De Campagne, Lafayette

825 Kidder Rd
Lafayette, LA 70520-9119
(318)896-6529 (800)895-0235 Fax:(318)896-1494

Circa 1871. Built by a successful plantation owner, this turn-of-the-century Victorian has once again found a new life with innkeepers Fred and Joeann McLemore. The McLemores turned what was an almost dilapidated old home into a welcoming B&B, surrounded by nine acres of manicured lawns dotted with flowers and trees. The home is filled with antiques and treasures Joeann collected during Fred's three decades of military service, which took them around the world. Fine Victorian pieces are accented by lace and Oriental rugs. The innkeepers offer accommodations in the main house, or for longer stays, in an adjacent sharecropper's cottage. The cottage includes kitchen and laundry facilities. Joeann prepares gourmet Cajun-style breakfasts. Several different homemade breads or pastries accompany meal items such as banana-strawberry soup, sweet potato biscuits, spicy Cajun egg souffles or a potato and sausage quiche. Many of the recipes served are featured in Joeann's new cookbook, "Lache Pas La Patate," (Don't Drop the Potato).

Innkeeper(s): Joeann & Fred McLemore. $110-145. MC, VISA, DS, PC, TC. TAC10. 4 rooms with PB and 1 cottage. Breakfast included in rates. AP. Types of meals: Full gourmet bkfst and early coffee/tea. Snacks/refreshments available. Beds: KQ. Turndown service and ceiling fan in room. Air conditioning. Fax, copier and swimming on premises. Small meetings hosted. Cajun French spoken. Antiquing, fishing, swamp tours, live theater, parks, shopping, sporting events and water sports nearby.

Mandeville   F8

Cozy Corner Guest House

736 Lafayette St
Mandeville, LA 70448
(504)626-9189

Circa 1889. Sections of this historic house date back more than a century. The guesthouse includes two comfortable bedrooms, each with a private bath and eclectic furnishings. Upon arrival, guests are treated to refreshments, and in the mornings, an English-style breakfast is served. The home is five blocks from Mandeville Lake, and 30 minutes from downtown New Orleans. Borrow a bicycle from the innkeepers and enjoy the 31-mile bike path that runs through the area.

Innkeeper(s): Barbara & Chris Clark. $85-95. MC, VISA, PC, TC. 2 rooms with PB. Breakfast included in rates. Types of meals: Full bkfst, cont, country bkfst and veg bkfst. Afternoon tea and snacks/refreshments available. Beds: KQ. Cable TV, phone and ceiling fan in room. Central air. VCR, swimming and bicycles on premises. Antiquing, beaches, bicycling, canoeing/kayaking, fishing, golf, hiking, live theater, shopping and wineries nearby.

"Your warm home and generous hospitality makes us eager to return."

Napoleonville
G6

Madewood Plantation House

4250 Highway 308
Napoleonville, LA 70390-8737
(504)369-7151 (800)375-7151 Fax:(504)369-9848
E-mail: madewoodpl@aol.com
Web: www.madewood.com

Circa 1846. Six massive ionic columns support the central portico of this striking Greek Revival mansion, a National Historic Landmark. Framed by live oaks and ancient magnolias, Madewood, on 20 acres, across from Bayou Lafourche. It was designed by Henry Howard, a noted architect from Cork, Ireland. There are elegant double parlors, a ballroom, library, music room and dining room where regional specialties are served by candlelight.
Historic Interest: Swamp tours, other plantations (one-half hour).
Innkeeper(s): Keith Marshall. $225. MC, VISA, AX, DS. 8 rooms with PB, 1 with FP, 2 suites and 1 conference room. Breakfast and dinner included in rates. MAP. Type of meal: Full bkfst. Beds: QDT. Copier on premises.

"We have stayed in many hotels, other plantations and English manor houses, and Madewood has surpassed them all in charm, hospitality and food."

Natchitoches
C3

Fleur De Lis B&B

336 Second St
Natchitoches, LA 71457
(318)352-6621 (800)489-6621

Circa 1903. A prosperous lumberman built this Victorian so that his children could attend a nearby college. The home is located in a National Historic Landmark District, and it features original woodwork and a pressed-tin roof. The guest rooms are decorated with period antiques. A full breakfast is served, perhaps French toast or Southern fare, such as ham and freshly made biscuits.

Innkeeper(s): Tom & Harriette Palmer. $65-100. MC, VISA, AX, DS. TAC10. 5 rooms with PB. Breakfast included in rates. Types of meals: Full gourmet bkfst and early coffee/tea. Beds: KQ. Ceiling fan in room. Air conditioning. VCR on premises. Small meetings and family reunions hosted. Antiquing, fishing, golf, plantation, Fort St. Jean Baptiste, parks, shopping, sporting events and tennis nearby.

"Each time I come, I feel more and more at home. It is a gift you have given me."

New Orleans
G8

A Creole House Hotel

1013 Saint Ann St
New Orleans, LA 70116-3012
(504)524-8076 (800)535-7858 Fax:(504)581-3277

Circa 1883. The many sites of the French Quarter surround this historic hotel, which was once home to a Voodoo queen. The guest rooms and suites are elegant and decorated in period style. Guided tours, including an evening nightclub tour, stop at the hotel daily. Guests can walk to fine restaurants and boutiques, and Bourbon Street is just two blocks away.
Innkeeper(s): Brent Kovach. $49-189. MC, VISA, AX, DS, TC. TAC10. 27 rooms. Breakfast included in rates. Type of meal: Cont. Beds: KQ. Cable TV, phone and ceiling fan in room. Air conditioning. Fax and copier on premises. Antiquing, fishing, golf, live theater, parks and sporting events nearby.

A Villa B&B-New Orleans, L.L.C.

3336 Gentilly Blvd
New Orleans, LA 70122-4954
(504)945-4253 (800)973-1020

Circa 1939. Close to the French Quarter and the Mississippi River, this Spanish Colonial Revival home offers a unique blend of privacy and romance. The innkeepers' two great-great-great-grandfathers fought the battle of New Orleans. Rooms feature oak floors and are decorated with antiques and original art. Guest rooms all have ceiling fans, refrigerators, and there are breakfast nooks to enjoy the fresh pastry, juice and coffee that is served in your room. Guests will delight in walking or jogging beneath the beautiful oak trees that populate the area. Free parking is available on the premises.

Innkeeper(s): Ann & Walter Hingle. $69-125. MC, VISA, TC. TAC10. 2 rooms with PB. Breakfast included in rates. Type of meal: Cont. Beds: KQD. Cable TV, ceiling fan and breakfast nooks in room. Air conditioning. Portico & courtyards on premises. Antiquing, fishing, golf, steamboats, museums, zoo, aquarium, live theater, parks, shopping, sporting events, tennis and water sports nearby.

"Thank you so much for a great room and great service. What a perfect romantic getaway."

Bonne Chance B&B

621 Opelousas Ave
New Orleans, LA 70114
(504)367-0798 Fax:(504)368-4643
Web: www.bonne-chance.com

Circa 1890. This recently renovated two-story Eastlake Victorian boasts balconies and a porch with fretwork and columns painted pastel blue and cream. Antique furnishings and Oriental rugs are found throughout, and fully furnished apartments with kitchens are available. There are gardens and a fountain. A free five-minute ferry boat ride takes you to the French Quarter.
Innkeeper(s): Dolores Watson. $85-175. MC, VISA, AX, PC. TAC10. 3 suites. Breakfast included in rates. Type of meal: Cont plus. Beds: Q. Cable TV, phone, ceiling fan and three apartments with fully equipped kitchens in room. Air conditioning. VCR, fax, copier and library on premises. French spoken. Amusement parks, antiquing, fishing, golf, French Quarter, live theater, parks, shopping, sporting events and tennis nearby.
Publicity: *New Orleans.*

Bougainvillea House

841 Bourbon St
New Orleans, LA 70116-3106
(504)525-3983 Fax:(504)283-7777

Circa 1822. Originally built by a plantation owner, and located directly in the French Quarter, this French Townhouse served as a hospital during the Civil War. The Riverboat Suite faces the courtyard and has French doors that open onto a balcony. It offers a living room and full kitchen. The inn is furnished with Victorian antiques and traditional pieces. The courtyard and patio are behind private locked gates. Bourbon Street is one block away, while Royal Street and its restaurants and museums is two blocks away. Guests can walk to Antoines for dinner.

Innkeeper(s): Flo Cairo. $90-250. VISA, AX. TAC10. 3 suites. Beds: KQD. Cable TV, phone and ceiling fan in room. Air conditioning. Fax on premises. Antiquing, golf, live theater, parks, shopping and sporting events nearby.

"We love your home and always enjoy our visits here so much!"

Chateau du Louisiane

1216 Louisiana Ave
New Orleans, LA 70115
(504)269-2600 (800)734-0137 Fax:(504)269-2603
E-mail: chateau@neworleans.com
Web: www.chateaulouisiane.com

Circa 1885. Built in Greek Revival style, Chateau du Louisiane is located on the edge of New Orleans' famous Garden District. The home, along with the myriad of other historic homes and buildings, is listed in the National Register of Historic Places. Period furnishings decorate the guest rooms, suites and common areas. Each guest room is named after someone famous in Louisiana history, such as Louis Armstrong. The chateau is one mile from the French Quarter, and the St. Charles streetcar stops just three blocks away.

Historic Interest: In Garden District, French Quarter (1 mile), St. Charles Streetcar (3 blocks).

Innkeeper(s): Jeff O'Hara. $79-159. MC, VISA, AX, DS, TC. TAC10. 5 rooms with PB, 2 suites and 2 conference rooms. Breakfast and snacks/refreshments included in rates. Types of meals: Cont plus and early coffee/tea. Cable TV, phone and ceiling fan in room. Central air. Fax, copier, bicycles and library on premises. Weddings, small meetings, family reunions and seminars hosted. Antiquing, art galleries, bicycling, fishing, golf, live theater, museums, parks, shopping, sporting events, tennis and water sports nearby.

Cornstalk Hotel

915 Royal St
New Orleans, LA 70116-2701
(504)523-1515

Circa 1805. This home belonged to Judge Francois Xavier-Martin, the author of the first history of Louisiana and Louisiana's first State Supreme Court Chief Justice. Andrew Jackson stayed here and another guest, Harriet Beecher Stowe, wrote Uncle Tom's Cabin after viewing the nearby slave markets. The

Civil War followed the widely read publication. Surrounding the inn is a 150-year-old wrought-iron cornstalk fence. Stained-glass windows, Oriental rugs, fireplaces and antiques grace the property. Breakfast and the morning newspaper can be served in your room or set up on the balcony, porch or patio.

Innkeeper(s): Debi & David Spencer. $75-185. MC, VISA, AX. 14 rooms with PB, 8 with FP. Beds: KQDT.

Publicity: *London Sunday Times.*

Essem's House New Orleans 1st B&B

3660 Gentilly Blvd
New Orleans, LA 70122-4910
(504)947-3401 Fax:(504)838-0140
E-mail: info@neworleansbandb.com
Web: www.neworleansbandb.com

Circa 1930. A grassy lawn sets off this two-story brick Mediterranean-style house located on a tree-lined street. There's a steep gabled roof and red tile. A solarium and parlor with fireplace are inviting spots. The innkeeper has offered bed and breakfast to New Orleans visitors for more than 20 years. Art Deco and traditional decor is featured in the guest rooms and there are some antiques.

Innkeeper(s): Sarah-Margaret Brown. $60-85. MC, VISA, AX, DS, TC. 3 rooms, 2 with PB, 1 suite and 1 cottage. Breakfast included in rates. Type of meal: Cont plus. Beds: KDT. Ceiling fan and guest Common Room in room. Air conditioning. VCR and fax on premises. Family reunions hosted. Amusement parks, antiquing, fishing, golf, live theater, parks, shopping, sporting events and tennis nearby.

Pets allowed: With restrictions.

Fairchild House

1518 Prytania St
New Orleans, LA 70130-4416
(504)524-0154 (800)256-8096 Fax:(504)568-0063
E-mail: fairchildhou@earthlink.net
Web: www.fairchildhouse.com

Circa 1841. Situated in the oak-lined Lower Garden District of New Orleans, this Greek Revival home was built by architect L.H. Pilie. The house and its guest houses maintain a Victorian ambiance with elegantly appointed guest rooms. Wine and cheese is served upon guests' arrival. Afternoon tea can be served upon request. The bed & breakfast, which is on the Mardi Gras parade route, is 17 blocks from the French Quarter and eight blocks from the convention center. Streetcars are just one block away, as are many local attractions, including paddleboat cruises, Canal Place and Riverwalk shopping, an aquarium, zoo, the Charles Avenue mansions and Tulane and Loyola universities.

Innkeeper(s): Rita Olmo & Beatriz Aprigliano-Ziegler. $75-145. MC, VISA, AX, TC. 14 rooms with PB and 1 suite. Breakfast included in rates. Type of meal: Cont plus. Beds: KQDT. Phone in room. Air conditioning. Fax and copier on premises. Weddings and family reunions hosted. Antiquing, live theater and shopping nearby.

"Accommodations were great; staff was great...Hope to see ya'll soon!"

The Frenchmen Hotel

417 Frenchmen
New Orleans, LA 70116-2003
(504)948-2166 (800)831-1781 Fax:(504)948-2258

Circa 1897. The Mississippi River is just a few blocks away from this historic hotel, located in New Orleans' famed French Quarter. The trolley stops less than a block away, whisking you to museums, shops, gourmet restaurants and many unique attractions. The elegant guest rooms boast period furnishings, and each room has been individually decorated. The inn's lush courtyard includes a pool and Jacuzzi. A concierge service is available around the clock, and the staff can help you plan tours and other activities.

Innkeeper(s): Brent Kovach. $59-175. MC, VISA, AX, DS, TC. TAC10. 28 rooms. Breakfast included in rates. Type of meal: Cont. Beds: QD. Cable TV, phone and ceiling fan in room. Air conditioning. Fax, copier, swimming and jacuzzi on premises. Antiquing, fishing, golf, live theater, parks, shopping and sporting events nearby.

The House on Bayou Road

2275 Bayou Rd
New Orleans, LA 70119-2666
(504)945-0992 (800)882-2968 Fax:(504)945-0993

Circa 1798. Romantic guest rooms, gourmet cuisine and two-acre grounds dotted with ponds, herb and flower gardens await guests at this Creole Plantation home. The home was built as

the main house to an indigo plantation just prior to the turn of the 19th century. The lush surroundings are a distraction from city life, yet this restful inn is just a few blocks from

the French Quarter. The guest quarters are appointed with fine linens and elegant furnishings. Breakfast is a don't-miss, three-course event. The innkeeper is co-director of a New Orleans cooking school. Guests with a flair for the gourmet might consider signing up for the school's popular Grand or Mini classes, which include tuition and lodging.

Innkeeper(s): Cynthia Reeves. $125-295. MC, VISA, AX, TC. TAC10. 8 rooms with PB, 2 with FP, 3 suites and 2 cottages. Breakfast included in rates. Type of meal: Full gourmet bkfst. Beds: KQT. Cable TV, phone, turndown service, ceiling fan and mini Bars in room. Air conditioning. VCR, fax, copier, spa and swimming on premises. Weddings and small meetings hosted. Spanish and French spoken. Antiquing, fishing, live theater and parks nearby.

Publicity: *Southern Living, Travel & Leisure.*

"Once again our stay was delightful. I can't imagine coming to New Orleans without staying here."

Lafitte Guest House

1003 Bourbon St
New Orleans, LA 70116-2707
(504)581-2678 (800)331-7971 Fax:(504)581-2677
E-mail: lafitte@travelbase.com
Web: www.lafitteguesthouse.com

Circa 1849. This elegant French manor house has been meticulously restored. The house is filled with fine antiques and paintings collected from around the world. Located in the heart of the French Quarter, the inn is near world-famous restaurants, museums, antique shops and rows of Creole and Spanish cottages. Between 5:30 p.m. and 7 p.m., there is a wine and cheese social hour.

Historic Interest: Historic New Orleans Collection, Keyes House, Beauregard House, Gallier House (few blocks away), famous Jackson Square and Saint Louis Cathedral (4 blocks), French Market (3 blocks).

Innkeeper(s): Edward G. Dore & Andrew J. Crocchiolo. $109-189. MC, VISA, AX, DC, DS, TC. 14 rooms with PB, 7 with FP and 2 suites. Breakfast included in rates. Type of meal: Cont plus. Beds: KQ. TV, phone and ceiling fan in room. Air conditioning. Fax and copier on premises. Amusement parks, antiquing, fishing, live theater, parks, shopping, sporting events and water sports nearby.

Publicity: *Glamour, Antique Monthly, McCall's, Dixie, Country Living.*

"This old building offers the finest lodgings we have found in the city." — McCall's Magazine

Lamothe House

621 Esplanade Ave
New Orleans, LA 70116-2018
(504)947-1161 (800)367-5858 Fax:(504)943-6536

Circa 1830. A carriageway that formerly cut through the center of many French Quarter buildings was enclosed at the Lamothe House in 1866, and it is now the foyer. Splendid Victorian furnishings enhance moldings, high ceilings and hand-turned mahogany stairway railings. Gilded opulence goes unchecked in the Mallard and Lafayette suites. Registration takes place in the second-story salon above the courtyard.

Historic Interest: National Register.

Innkeeper(s): Carol Chauppette. $75-250. MC, VISA, AX, PC, TC. TAC10. 20 rooms with PB, 1 with FP, 9 suites, 2 cottages and 1 conference room. Breakfast included in rates. Type of meal: Cont plus. Afternoon tea available. Beds: QDT. Cable TV, phone, turndown service and ceiling fan in room. Air conditioning. VCR, fax, copier, swimming, child care and free parking on premises. Weddings, small meetings and family reunions hosted. Amusement parks, antiquing, fishing, French Quarter, live theater, parks, shopping and sporting events nearby.

Publicity: *Houston Post, Travel & Leisure.*

Maison Esplanade

1244 Esplanade Ave
New Orleans, LA 70116-1978
(504)523-8080 (800)892-5529 Fax:(504)527-0040
E-mail: maison@neworleans.com
Web: www.maisonesplanade.com

Circa 1846. Experience the splendor of New Orleans at this Greek Revival mansion, which is located within walking distance of the French Quarter. Polished wood floors, ceiling fans and 13-foot ceilings highlight this historic district home, which is furnished with antiques and replicas. Bedchambers honor New Orleans' jazz tradition, bearing names such as the Louis Armstrong Suite or Count Basie Room. Cable TV, individual climate control and telephones with dataports and voice mail are among the modern amenities. Continental breakfasts, featuring cereals, bagels, fresh fruit, New Orleans-style chicory coffee, teas and other beverages, are provided each morning. The hosts are full of information about the myriad of tours available in the city, including tours of the French Quarter, plantation homes, historic homes or the city itself. Be sure to ask about the vampire, ghost and swamp tours.

Innkeeper(s): Jarret Marshall. $79-189. MC, VISA, AX, DS, TC. 10 rooms with PB and 2 suites. Breakfast included in rates. Type of meal: Cont. Beds: Q. Phone and ceiling fan in room. Air conditioning. Fax on premises. Antiquing, art galleries, French Quarter, aquarium, casino, concert venue, gourmet dining, lake, live music, movie theater, Superdome, Convention Center, zoo, live theater, museums and shopping nearby.

Pets allowed: in some rooms.

"I had a marvelous visit to New Orleans and your delightful hospitality and friendship made it even more special."

The Melrose Mansion

937 Esplanade Ave
New Orleans, LA 70116-1942
(504)944-2255 Fax:(504)945-1794

Circa 1884. It's little wonder why this dramatic Italianate Victorian has been named a top accommodation. Aside from its gracious exterior, the interior has been carefully restored and filled with the finest of furnishings. Antique-filled guest rooms offer amenities such as down pillows, private patios, fresh flowers, whirlpool tubs and bathrooms stocked with fine soaps. Despite the elegance, guests are encouraged to relax and enjoy the New Orleans' tradition of hospitality. The National Register home is located in the French Quarter.

Innkeeper(s): The Torres Family. $225-425. MC, VISA, AX, DS, PC, TC. TAC10. 10 rooms with PB and 5 suites. Breakfast included in rates. Meals: Full gourmet bkfst and early coffee/tea. Beds: KQT. Cable TV, phone, ceiling fan and whirlpool tubs in suites in room. Air conditioning. Fax, copier and swimming on premises. Antiquing, fishing, live theater, parks, shopping and sporting events nearby.

The Prytania Park Hotel

1525 Prytania St
New Orleans, LA 70130-4448
(504)524-0427 (800)862-1984 Fax:(504)522-2977
E-mail: prytaniapk@aol.com
Web: www.prytaniaparkhotel.com

Circa 1850. Prytania Park consists of a historic Greek Revival building and a restored Queen Anne Victorian, located in a National Historic Landmark District. The Greek Revival building includes rooms decorated with Victorian reproductions, some include fireplaces. A newer section, with 12 Queen Anne-style suites, includes rooms with modern amenities such as refrigerators, microwaves and contemporary decor. The hotel's historic Victorian mansion is listed in the National Register and maintains original features such as 14-foot ceilings, hardwood floors and intricate fireplace mantels. Several rooms include balconies overlooking Prytania Street. Amenities include shuttle service to the French Quarter and nearby Convention Center.

Innkeeper(s): Edward Halpern. $99-229. MC, VISA, AX, DC, CB, DS, PC, TC. TAC10. 74 rooms with PB and 18 suites. Breakfast included in rates. Type of meal: Cont plus. Lunch available. Beds: KQDT. Cable TV, phone, ceiling fan and microwaves in room. Air conditioning. Fax and copier on premises. Small meetings and family reunions hosted. Spanish spoken. Antiquing, parks, shopping and sporting events nearby.

"A little jewel—Baton Rouge Advocate."

St. Peter Guest House Hotel

1005 Saint Peter St
New Orleans, LA 70116-3014
(504)524-9232 (800)535-7815 Fax:(504)523-5198

Circa 1800. The St. Peter House, which is ideally situated in the middle of the French Quarter, offers a delightful glance at New Orleans French heritage and 18th-century charm. From the lush courtyards to the gracious balconies, guests will enjoy the view of the busy quarter. Rooms are individually appointed, some with period antiques.

Innkeeper(s): Brent Kovach. $49-225. MC, VISA, AX, DS, PC, TC. TAC10. 28 rooms with PB and 11 suites. Breakfast included in rates. Meal: Cont plus. Beds: KQDT. Cable TV, phone and ceiling fan in room. Air conditioning. Fax on premises. Amusement parks, antiquing, fishing, live theater, parks and shopping nearby.

Sully Mansion - Garden District

2631 Prytania St
New Orleans, LA 70130-5944
(504)891-0457 Fax:(504)899-7237
Web: www.sullymansion.com

Circa 1890. This handsome Queen Anne Victorian, designed by its namesake, Thomas Sully, maintains many original features common to the architecture. A wide veranda, stained glass, heart-of-pine floors and a grand staircase are among the notable items. Rooms are decorated in a comfortable mix of antiques and more modern pieces. Sully Mansion is the only inn located in the heart of New Orleans' Garden District.

Innkeeper(s): Maralee Prigmore. $125-225. MC, VISA, AX, DS, PC, TC. TAC10. 7 rooms with PB. Breakfast included in rates. Meal: Cont plus. Beds: KQT. Phone in room. Air conditioning. Fax on premises. Antiquing and parks nearby.

"I truly enjoyed my stay at Sully Mansion—the room was wonderful, the pastries memorable."

Sun Oak Museum and Guest House

2020 Burgundy St
New Orleans, LA 70116-1606
(504)945-0322 Fax:(504)945-0322

Circa 1836. This historic home was restored to its former glory as an early 19th-century manor by innkeeper Eugene Cizek. Cizek heads the preservation program at Tulane University and has won awards for historic preservation. His expertise has turned a dilapidated home into a beautiful showplace. Rooms feature a variety of French, Creole, Acadian and mid-French Louisiana antiques, Oriental rugs, ceiling fans, fine fabrics and beautiful light fixtures. Behind the home lie lush, landscaped patios, gardens and the Sun Oak tree.

Historic Interest: The edge of the French Quarter is five minutes from the historic Sun Oak, and the inn itself is located in a local and national historic district.

Innkeeper(s): Eugene D. Cizek & Lloyd L. Sensat, Jr. $75-150. PC, TC. TAC10. 2 rooms with PB. Breakfast included in rates. Meal: Cont. Beds: D. Cable TV, phone and ceiling fan in room. Air conditioning. Library on premises. Weddings, small meetings, family reunions and seminars hosted. Some Spanish spoken. Amusement parks, antiquing, fishing, golf, cafes, restaurants, night clubs, live theater, parks, shopping, sporting events, tennis and water sports nearby.

Publicity: Colonial Homes, Better Homes & Gardens, Traditional Home, Old House Interiors, Classic New Orleans, New Orleans Elegance and Decadence.

"From A-Z we loved our visit to Sun Oak. The house is so warm and charming."

Wisteria Inn

2127 Esplanada Ave
New Orleans, LA 70119
(504)943-8418 (888)246-4183 Fax:(504)558-0319
E-mail: nowisteria@aol.com
Web: www.wisteriainn.com

Circa 1800. A French Canadian landowner purchased the land that surrounds Wisteria Inn in the early 1700s. The inn, built in Edwardian style, has accommodated guests for a century. Antiques grace the guest rooms and common areas. Each guest room has been appointed individually in authentic, period style. The grounds feature a pond, as well as wisteria, peach, pecan, pear and banana trees. The inn is located in the historic Esplanade Ridge District of New Orleans. The French Quarter, Riverwalk and many other popular attractions are just a few minutes away.

Innkeeper(s): Zennette Austin. $75-125. AX. TAC10. 6 rooms, 4 with PB. Breakfast included in rates. Type of meal: Cont. Beds: KQDT. Cable TV in room. Air conditioning.

Ramsay/Covington   F8

Mill Bank Farms

75654 River Rd
Ramsay/Covington, LA 70435-7635
(504)892-1606

Circa 1832. This home was built to house offices for a lumber mill. After all but one tree had been cut down, the innkeeper's father purchased the house in 1915 and transformed the place

into a farm. There are two bed-chambers, and guests have run of the living and dining rooms. Beds are topped with quilts, and robes and fresh flowers appear in each guest room. Before breakfast is presented, guests can relax on the

porch with coffee or perhaps a mimosa. Guests also have the option of enjoying coffee or tea in bed. The morning meal is always fabulous since the innkeeper studied at the famed Cordon Bleu school. The 70-acre grounds offer birdwatching, swimming and fishing. New Orleans is just 40 minutes away.

Innkeeper(s): Mrs. Katie Planche Friedrichs. $100-125. MC, VISA, AX, DS, PC, TC. TAC10. 2 rooms with PB. Breakfast and afternoon tea included in rates. Types of meals: Full gourmet bkfst, cont plus and early coffee/tea. Beds: D. Cable TV, phone, turndown service and ceiling fan in room. Air conditioning. Swimming, bicycles, library, wake up call, coffee served in bed, night cap cream sherry and fresh flowers on premises. Some French and Spanish spoken. Antiquing, fishing, golf, live theater, parks, shopping, sporting events and water sports nearby.

Pets allowed: If house broken and de-fleaed.

Saint Francisville   E6

Myrtles Plantation

PO Box 1100, US Hwy 61N
Saint Francisville, LA 70775
(225)635-6277

Circa 1796. Sitting high on the rolling hills of St. Francisville, the Myrtles Plantation is elegantly appointed with many original pieces of artwork and furniture. Its entrance hall features a 17th Century French chandelier of Baccarat crystal and hand-painted and etched stained glass that is original to the mansion. Matching twin parlors have chandeliers, Carrara marble mantles and French gilded mirrors. The innkeepers claim that Myrtles is listed as one of America's most haunted house.

Innkeeper(s): Teeta & John Moss. $95-195. MC, VISA, AX. 10 rooms with PB. Types of meals: Full gourmet bkfst and cont. Beds: QD.

Saint Martinville   G5

The Old Castillo Hotel

PO Box 172
Saint Martinville, LA 70582-0172
(318)394-4010 (800)621-3017 Fax:(318)394-7983

Circa 1825. Ionic columns and a second-story veranda grace the exterior of this Greek Revival home, which was used originally as an inn. From the turn of the century until the mid 1980s, the home served as a Catholic girls' school. Today, the home once again serves travelers, both as hotel and restaurant. Guest rooms are furnished with antiques and reproductions. The restaurant

serves up Bayou favorites such as fried alligator, catfish, crawfish, frog legs, as well as other seafood and steak specialties.

Innkeeper(s): Peggy Hulin. $50-80. MC, VISA, AX, DS. TAC10. 5 rooms with PB and 1 conference room. Breakfast included in rates. Types of meals: Full bkfst, cont plus, cont and early coffee/tea. Dinner and lunch available. Restaurant on premises. Beds: QD. Air conditioning. Fax on premises. Small meetings, family reunions and seminars hosted. French spoken. Amusement parks, antiquing, fishing, live theater, parks, shopping, sporting events and water sports nearby.

Shreveport   B2

2439 Fairfield, A Bed & Breakfast

2439 Fairfield Ave
Shreveport, LA 71104-2986
(318)424-2424 Fax:(318)424-3658

Circa 1905. This turn-of-the-century Victorian mansion is located in the Highland historical district. The home is surrounded by English gardens, and guests can take in this view on their own private balcony, complete with rocking chairs and porch swings. English antiques and Amish quilts fill the guest rooms, which feature special extras such as Waverly linens, feather beds and down pillows and comforters. Each bath includes a whirlpool tub. The morning room is a cheerful place for a full English breakfast.

Innkeeper(s): Jimmy & Vicki Harris. $125-200. MC, VISA, AX, DC. 4 rooms with PB. Types of meals: Full bkfst and early coffee/tea. Beds: KQ. Cable TV, phone, turndown service, ceiling fan, VCR and whirlpool baths in room. Air conditioning. Fax and copier on premises. Amusement parks, antiquing, horse racing, live theater, shopping and sporting events nearby.

Slidell   F8

Salmen-Fritchie House B&B

127 Cleveland Ave
Slidell, LA 70458-3919
(504)643-1405 (800)235-4168 Fax:(504)643-2251
E-mail: sfritbb@salmen-fritchie.com
Web: www.salmen-fritchie.com

Circa 1895. At one time, most of the residents in Slidell worked for the owner of this Victorian home at his lumber and brickworks business. Eventually, the home passed on to innkeeper Homer Fritchie's grandmother and then to him. He and his wife, Sharon, spent hundreds of thousands of dollars restoring the place and transforming it into a

B&B. The home is decorated with period antiques, including family heirlooms from both the Salmen and Fritchie families. Guests are offered two different breakfast options, one might be a Belgian waffle topped with fresh strawberries and cream or perhaps a Creole omelet. New Orleans is a half-hour away.

Innkeeper(s): Homer & Sharon Fritchie. $85-150. MC, VISA, AX, DS, PC, TC. TAC10. 6 rooms with PB, 3 with FP, 3 suites, 1 cottage and 1 conference room. Breakfast and afternoon tea included in rates. Types of meals: Full bkfst and early coffee/tea. Beds: QDT. Cable TV, phone and ceiling fan in room. Air conditioning. Fax and library on premises. Small meetings, family reunions and seminars hosted. Antiquing, fishing, golf, live theater, parks, shopping and tennis nearby.

"Never again shall I sit down to breakfast without wishing I were in the Salmen-Fritchie House."

Maine

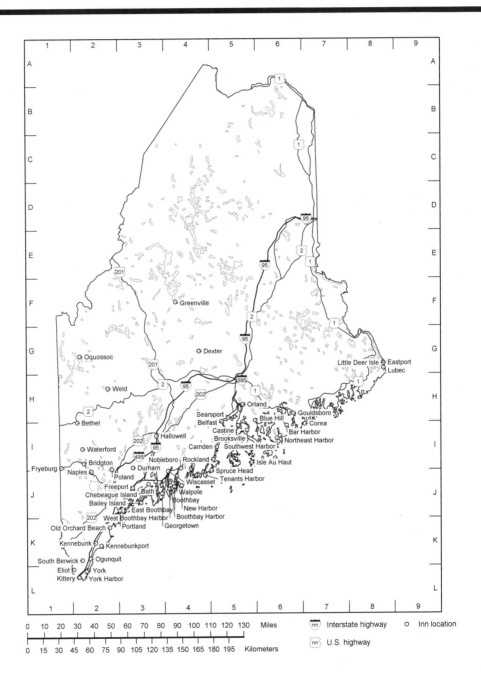

1 2 3 4 5 6 7 8 9

A

B

C

D

E

1

F Greenville

G Oquossoc   Dexter   Little Deer Isle   Eastport
                                                Lubec
201
Weld   95   201   95   2   1
Bethel   2   202   Orland   Gouldsboro
                    Hallowell   Searsport   Blue Hill   Corea
Waterford   202   Castine   Belfast   Bar Harbor
Bridgton   495   Nobleboro   Camden   Brooksville   Northeast Harbor
Fryeburg   Naples   Durham   Rockland   Southwest Harbor
         Poland   Spruce Head   Isle Au Haut
    Freeport   Wiscasset   Tenants Harbor
Chebeague Island   Bath   Walpole
Bailey Island   202   Boothbay
         West Boothbay Harbor   East Boothbay   New Harbor
Old Orchard Beach   Portland   Boothbay Harbor
         Kennebunk   Georgetown
South Berwick   Ogunquit
Eliot   York
Kittery   York Harbor

0 10 20 30 40 50 60 70 80 90 100 110 120 130   Miles

0 15 30 45 60 75 90 105 120 135 150 165 180 195   Kilometers

nn Interstate highway   o Inn location

nn U.S. highway

146

Augusta (Hallowell)   13

Maple Hill Farm B&B Inn

RR 1 Box 1145, Outlet Rd
Augusta (Hallowell), ME 04347
(207)622-2708 (800)622-2708 Fax:(207)622-0655

Circa 1890. Visitors to Maine's capitol city have the option of staying at this nearby inn, a peaceful farm setting adjacent to a 550-acre state wildlife management area that is available for canoeing, fishing, hiking and hunting. This Victorian Shingle-style inn was once a stagecoach stop and dairy farm. The inn's suite includes a double whirlpool tub. The inn, with its 130-acre

grounds, easily accommodates conferences, parties and receptions. Guests are welcome to visit the many farm animals. Cobbossee Lake is a five-minute drive from the inn. The center portion of Hallowell is listed as a National Historic District and offers antique shops and restaurants.

Historic Interest: State capitol building, state museum, archives, & Fort Western (5 miles).

Innkeeper(s): Scott Cowger. $50-125. MC, VISA, AX, DC, CB, DS, PC, TC. 7 rooms, 4 with PB, 1 suite and 1 conference room. Breakfast and afternoon tea included in rates. Types of meals: Full bkfst and early coffee/tea. Snacks/refreshments, picnic lunch, banquet service and catering service available. Beds: QD. TV and phone in room. VCR and whirlpool tub on premises. Handicap access. Weddings, small meetings, family reunions and seminars hosted. Antiquing, live theater, shopping, cross-country skiing and water sports nearby.

"You add many thoughtful touches to your service that set your B&B apart from others, and really make a difference. Best of Maine, hands down!" (Maine Times)."

Bailey Island   J3

Captain York House B&B

Rt 24, PO Box 298
Bailey Island, ME 04003
(207)833-6224
E-mail: athorn7286@aol.com
Web: www.iwws.com/captainyork

Circa 1906. Bailey Island is the quaint fisherman's village of stories, poems and movies. Guests cross the world's only cribstone bridge to reach the island, where beautiful sunsets and dinners of fresh Maine lobster are the norm. This shingled, turn-of-the-century, Mansard-style B&B was the home of a famous Maine sea captain, Charles York. Now a homestay-style bed & breakfast, the

innkeepers have restored the home to its former glory, filling it with many antiques. Guests at Captain York's enjoy water views from all the guest rooms. Wild Maine blueberries often find a significant place on the breakfast menu.

Innkeeper(s): Alan & Jean Thornton. $68-100. MC, VISA, PC, TC. TAC10. 5 rooms with PB. Breakfast included in rates. Type of meal: Full bkfst. Beds: QT. VCR on premises. Weddings, small meetings, family reunions and seminars hosted. Antiquing, McMilan Museum, Maine Maritime Museum, live theater, parks, shopping, sporting events and water sports nearby.

"Bailey Island turned out to be the hidden treasure of our trip and we hope to return for your great hospitality again."

Bar Harbor   I6

Bar Harbor Tides B&B

119 West St
Bar Harbor, ME 04609-1430
(207)288-4968

Circa 1887. As innkeeper Joe Losquadro might explain, The Tides has endurance. The gracious Victorian survived a 10-day firestorm that destroyed more than 17,000 acres and 60 of Mt. Desert Island's grand summer homes. The Tides still stands as testament to local resilience. Each of the suites offers something special. The Master Suite includes an ocean view, a four-poster, king-size bed and working fire-place. The Ocean Suite, also with a king bed, boasts water views from every window,

including the bath. The suite includes a parlor with cable TV, bedroom with a working fireplace and balcony. Guests in the Captain's Suite with a new king-sized iron bed, enjoy a bubble bath in a clawfoot tub and the view of the historic, tree-lined West Street as well as the bay. Joe has been an innkeeper on the island for more than seven years and is full of local information and plenty of ideas for vacationers.

Historic Interest: Acadia National Park, the first national park established east of the Mississippi River, is nearby and includes the Abbe Museum, with its vast collection of Native American artifacts. The Islesford Museum on Little Cranberry Island offers many maritime exhibits. The Bar Harbor Historical Museum provides documents and photographs from Bar Harbor's heyday as grand resort for the country's wealthiest citizens.

Innkeeper(s): Joe & Judy Losquadro. $150-295. MC, VISA, TC. 4 rooms with PB, 2 with FP and 3 suites. Breakfast included in rates. AP. Types of meals: Full bkfst and early coffee/tea. Beds: KQ. Cable TV and ceiling fan in room. Refrigerator on premises. Antiquing, live theater, parks, shopping, cross-country skiing and water sports nearby.

"Your hospitality made us feel very welcome. Thank you once again."

Bayview Inn

111 Eden St
Bar Harbor, ME 04609-1105
(207)288-5861 (800)356-3585 Fax:(207)288-3173
E-mail: reservations@barharbor.com
Web: www.barharbor.com/bayview

Circa 1930. This inn's location is stunning, set just yards off Frenchman Bay with mountains and woods as a backdrop. The six-room Georgian inn was built by George McMurty, who was one of Theodore Roosevelt's Rough Riders. McMurty was awarded the Medal of Honor for his service during World War I. Among his influential friends and guests was Winston Churchill. Four of the rooms offer ocean views, and two include a fireplace. Elegant accommodations also are available in an adjacent hotel and townhomes, so for a historic experience, be sure to ask for rooms in the 1930s inn.

Innkeeper(s): Trish Nolan. $75-275. MC, VISA, AX, DC, CB, PC, TC. TAC10. 6 rooms with PB, 2 with FP, 1 suite and 3 conference rooms. Breakfast included in rates. Type of meal: Cont plus. Beds: KQD. Cable TV, phone and turndown service in room. Air conditioning. Fax, copier, swimming, tennis and library on premises. Small meetings, family reunions and seminars hosted. Antiquing, fishing, golf, live theater, parks, shopping, tennis and water sports nearby.

Castlemaine Inn

39 Holland Ave
Bar Harbor, ME 04609-1433
(207)288-4563 (800)338-4563 Fax:(207)288-4525

Circa 1886. This Queen Anne charmer was once the summer home to the Austro-Hungarian ambassador to the United States. Rooms are decorated in a light, comfortable Victorian style. Two guest rooms include a whirlpool tub and most include a private balcony or deck and a fireplace. In the mornings, a generous breakfast buffet is presented, with freshly baked scones, muffins, breads and coffee cake, as well as bagels, cream cheese, fresh fruit, cereals and a variety of beverages.

Innkeeper(s): Terence O'Connell & Norah O'Brien. $50-195. MC, VISA, PC, TC. 15 rooms with PB, 11 with FP and 5 suites. Breakfast included in rates. Type of meal: Cont plus. Beds: KQ. Cable TV and VCR in room. Air conditioning. Fax and copier on premises. Antiquing, fishing, golf, live theater, parks, shopping, tennis and water sports nearby.

Publicity: *Country Inns.*

"This year we celebrate our tenth anniversary in our relationship with Castlemaine."

Graycote Inn

40 Holland Ave
Bar Harbor, ME 04609-1432
(207)288-3044 Fax:(207)288-2719
E-mail: innkeepers@graycoteinn.com
Web: www.graycoteinn.com

Circa 1881. This Victorian inn was built by the first rector of St. Saviour's Episcopal Church. Some of the guest rooms have fireplaces, while others have sun rooms or balconies. A full, hot breakfast is served on a glass-enclosed porch with tables set for two or four. Afternoon refreshments also are served. The inn is located on a one-acre lot with lawns, large trees, flower gardens, a croquet court and hammocks.

Guests can also relax on the veranda, which is furnished with wicker. The innkeepers are happy to make activity and dining recommendations. Guests can walk to restaurants, and Acadia National Park is nearby.

Historic Interest: Acadia National Park is less than two miles from the inn.

Innkeeper(s): Pat & Roger Samuel. $65-159. MC, VISA, DS, PC, TC. 12 rooms with PB, 3 with FP. Breakfast included in rates. Type of meal: Full bkfst. Beds: KQ. Ceiling fans in some rooms and a/c in some rooms in room. Small meetings and seminars hosted. Antiquing, music theatre, Acadia National Park, walk to excellent restaurant, live theater, parks, shopping, cross-country skiing and water sports nearby.

Hearthside Bed & Breakfast

7 High St
Bar Harbor, ME 04609-1816
(207)288-4533
E-mail: bnbinns@hearthsideinn.com
Web: www.hearthsideinn.com

Circa 1907. Originally built for a doctor, this three-story shingled house sits on a quiet street in town. Guests enjoy four working fireplaces and a porch. Three rooms include a whirlpool bath. The parlor includes a library and fireplace. Acadia National Park is five minutes away.

Innkeeper(s): Susan & Barry Schwartz. $95-140. MC, VISA, DS, PC, TC. 9 rooms with PB, 3 with FP. Breakfast and afternoon tea included in rates. Type of meal: Full bkfst. Beds: Q. Ceiling fan and whirlpool baths in room. Air conditioning. Bicycling, canoeing/kayaking, golf, hiking, cross-country skiing and water sports nearby.

Publicity: *Philadelphia Jewish Exponent.*

"I have only one word to describe this place, 'Wow!' My wife and I are astonished at the splendor, the warmth of your care and the beauty of the surroundings."

The Kedge

112 West St
Bar Harbor, ME 04609-1429
(207)288-5180 (800)597-8306

Circa 1870. Originally, this bed & breakfast was located at the edge of the harbor and served as a social club for gentlemen. In the 1880s, it was moved to its current location on West Street. The home rests on a portion of the street that is listed in the National Register of Historic Places. The interior is Victorian in style, and flowered wallpapers brighten the rooms. One room has a whirlpool tub. The veranda is filled with hunter green wicker furnishings for those who wish to relax. For breakfast, innkeeper Margaret Roberts serves items such as baked peaches with Maine blueberries followed by gingerbread pancakes topped with marmalade syrup.

$60-170. MC, VISA, AX, PC, TC. 3 rooms with PB, 2 with FP. Breakfast included in rates. Types of meals: Full bkfst and early coffee/tea. Beds: KQ. Cable TV in room. Family reunions hosted. Antiquing, golf, museums, oceanarium, concerts, movies, ocean activities, Acadia National Park, live theater, parks, shopping, cross-country skiing, tennis and water sports nearby.

Manor House Inn

106 West St
Bar Harbor, ME 04609-1856
(207)288-3759 (800)437-0088 Fax:(207)288-2974

Circa 1887. Colonel James Foster built this 22-room Victorian mansion, now in the National Register. It is an example of the tradition of gracious summer living for which Bar Harbor was and is famous. In addition to the main house, there are several charming cottages situated in the extensive gardens on the property.

Innkeeper(s): Mac Noyes. $60-185. MC, VISA. TAC10. 14 rooms, 7 with
PB, 6 with FP and 7 suites. Breakfast and afternoon tea included in rates.
Types of meals: Full bkfst and early coffee/tea. Beds: KQT. TV, ceiling fan and
fireplaces some rooms in room. Fax and copier on premises. Weddings, small
meetings, family reunions and seminars hosted. Antiquing, fishing, national
park, parks, shopping and water sports nearby.

*"Wonderful honeymoon spot! Wonderful inn, elegant, delicious break-
fasts, terrific innkeepers. We loved it all! It's our fourth time here and
it's wonderful as always."*

The Maples Inn

16 Roberts Ave
Bar Harbor, ME 04609-1820
(207)288-3443 Fax:(207)288-0356
E-mail: maplesinn@acadia.net
Web: www.maplesinn.com

Circa 1903. This Victorian "summer cottage" once served
wealthy summer visitors to Mt. Desert Island. Located on a
quiet residential street, away from Bar Harbor traffic, it has
been tastefully restored and filled
with Victorian furnishings. The
inn is within walking distance
of shops, boutiques and
restaurants. Acadia
National Park is five minutes away. Hiking, kayak-
ing and cycling are among
the nearby activities.

Innkeeper(s): Tom & Sue Palumbo.
$60-150. MC, VISA, DS, PC, TC. 6
rooms with PB, 1 with FP and 1 suite. Breakfast and afternoon tea included
in rates. Types of meals: Full gourmet bkfst and early coffee/tea. Beds: Q. Fax
and library on premises. Weddings, small meetings, family reunions and seminars hosted. Antiquing, fishing, live theater, parks, shopping, cross-country
skiing, sporting events and water sports nearby.

*"What a wonderful place this is. Warm, comfortable, friendly, terrific
breakfasts, great tips for adventure around the island. I could go on
and on."*

Mira Monte Inn & Suites

69 Mount Desert St
Bar Harbor, ME 04609-1327
(207)288-4263 (800)553-5109 Fax:(207)288-3115
E-mail: mburns@acadia.net
Web: www.miramonte.com

Circa 1864. A gracious 18-room Victorian mansion, the Mira
Monte has been newly renovated in the style of early Bar
Harbor. It features period furnishings, pleasant common rooms,
a library and wraparound porches. Situated on estate grounds,
there are sweeping lawns, paved terraces and many gardens.
The inn was one of the earliest of Bar Harbor's famous summer
cottages. The two-room suites each feature canopy beds, two-
person whirlpools, a parlor with a sleeper sofa, fireplace and
kitchenette unit. The two-bedroom suite includes a full
kitchen, dining area and parlor. The suites boast private decks
with views of the gardens.

Historic Interest: Acadia National Park is nearby. Many estates are still visible by water tours around the island.

Innkeeper(s): Marian Burns. $145-215. MC, VISA, AX, DC, DS, TC. TAC10.
16 rooms with PB, 14 with FP and 3 suites. Breakfast and afternoon tea
included in rates. Types of meals: Full bkfst and early coffee/tea. Beds: KQT.
Cable TV, phone and VCR in room. Air conditioning. Fax and library on

premises. Handicap access. Small meetings hosted. Antiquing, fishing,
Acadia National Park, live theater, parks and shopping nearby.
Publicity: *Los Angeles Times.*

*"On our third year at your wonderful inn in beautiful Bar Harbor. I
think I enjoy it more each year. A perfect place to stay in a perfect
environment."*

Town Motel & Moseley Cottage Inn

12 Atlantic Ave
Bar Harbor, ME 04609-1704
(207)288-5548 (800)458-8644 Fax:(207)288-9406
E-mail: paluga@acadia.net
Web: www.mainesunshine.com/townmotl

Circa 1894. Although the innkeepers do offer simple, comfortable accommodations in their nine-room motel, they also offer
a more historic experience in a late 19th-century Queen Anne
Victorian. Bar Harbor has been a popular
vacation spot for well over a century.
This spacious house was built
as a "cottage" for a wealthy
family who spent their
summers on Maine's
scenic coast. The
rooms are decorated
with period furnish-
ings, Oriental rugs, lacy curtains and flowery wallpapers. Each
of eight rooms in the historic home has been decorated individually. Guests at the historic inn are treated to a continental-
plus breakfast. Guests can walk to many attractions, and everything, from the harbor to Acadia National Park, is nearby.

Innkeeper(s): Joe & Paulette. $95-155. MC, VISA, AX, DS, PC, TC. TAC10.
17 rooms with PB, 4 with FP. Breakfast included in rates. Types of meals:
Cont plus and early coffee/tea. Beds: QDT. Cable TV and ceiling fan in room.
Air conditioning. VCR, fax and copier on premises. Small meetings and family
reunions hosted. Antiquing, fishing, golf, live theater, parks, shopping, tennis
and water sports nearby.

Bath   *J3*

Benjamin F. Packard House

45 Pearl St
Bath, ME 04530-2746
(207)443-6069 (800)516-4578
E-mail: packardhouse@clinic.net
Web: www.mainecoast.com/packardhouse/

Circa 1790. Shipbuilder Benjamin F. Packard purchased this handsome home in 1870. The inn
reflects the Victorian influence so prominent in
Bath's busiest shipbuilding years. The
Packard family, who lived in the
house for five generations, left many
family mementos. Period furnishings, authentic colors and shipbuilding memorabilia all reflect
Bath's romantic past. The mighty
Kennebec River is just a block
away. A full breakfast is served daily.

Historic Interest: The inn is situated in a historic district, and nearby historic
Front Street offers many antique stores and other commercial business in historic buildings. Maine Maritime Museum, 10-acre site on original shipyard (1
mile), Front Street (one-half mile); forts and lighthouses at Mouth of
Kennebee River (12 miles south).

Innkeeper(s): Debby & Bill Hayden. $75-100. MC, VISA, AX, DC, DS, PC, TC. 3 rooms with PB and 1 suite. Breakfast included in rates. Type of meal: Full bkfst. Beds: KQT. Library on premises. Antiquing, golf, live theater, parks, shopping and water sports nearby.

Publicity: *Times Record, Maine Sunday Telegram, Coastal Journal.*

"Thanks for being wonderful hosts."

The Donnell House Inn B&B

251 High St
Bath, ME 04530
(207)443-5324 (888)595-1664

Circa 1860. From the cupola atop the roof of this Italianate home, guests may enjoy a moonlit view of the Kennebec River. The inn's exterior is elegantly painted in gray with white on the columns and trim. Inside are hardwood floors and antiques, set against cheerful wall colors and white woodwork. There are two front parlors, one a sunny yellow and white, and the other with marble fireplace, Oriental rug and a rose-patterned wallpaper. Guest bedrooms offer four-poster beds, and some have fireplaces. One room boasts a Roman tub. A three-course breakfast is served on Blue Willow china in the formal dining room.

Innkeeper(s): Kenneth & Rachel Parlin. $100-160. PC, TC. 4 rooms with PB, 2 with FP and 1 suite. Breakfast and afternoon tea included in rates. Types of meals: Full bkfst, cont plus and early coffee/tea. Picnic lunch available. Beds: Q. Cable TV, one with a fireplace and Roman tub whirlpool and floor fans in room. Air conditioning. Piano room and background stereo music on premises. Seminars hosted. Antiquing, art galleries, beaches, bicycling, canoeing/kayaking, fishing, golf, hiking, maine Maritime Museum, live theater, museums, parks, shopping, cross-country skiing and tennis nearby.

"Your beautiful home offered the space and energy we all needed."

Fairhaven Inn

118 N Bath Rd
Bath, ME 04530
(207)443-4391 (888)443-4391 Fax:(207)443-6412
E-mail: fairhvn@gwi.net
Web: www.mainecoast.com/fairhaveninn

Circa 1790. With its view of the Kennebec River, this site was so attractive that Pembleton Edgecomb built his Colonial house where a log cabin had previously stood. His descendants occupied it for the next 125 years. Antiques and country furniture fill the inn. Meadows and lawns, and woods of hemlock, birch and pine cover the inn's 16 acres.

Innkeeper(s): Susie & Dave Reed. $80-120. MC, VISA, DS, PC, TC. TAC10. 8 rooms, 6 with PB, 1 suite, 1 cottage and 1 conference room. Breakfast included in rates. Types of meals: Full bkfst and early coffee/tea. Beds: KQT. Fax and library on premises. Small meetings and family reunions hosted. Antiquing, live theater, parks, shopping, cross-country skiing, sporting events and water sports nearby.

"The Fairhaven is now marked in our book with a red star, definitely a place to remember and visit again."

The Galen C. Moses House

1009 Washington St
Bath, ME 04530-2759
(207)442-8771 (888)442-8771 Fax:(207)443-6861
E-mail: galenmoses@clinic.net
Web: www.galenmoses.com

Circa 1874. This Victorian mansion is filled with beautiful architectural items, including stained-glass windows, wood-carved and marble fireplaces and a grand staircase. The innkeepers have filled the library, a study, morning room and the parlor with antiques. A corner fireplace warms the dining room, which overlooks the lawns and gardens. Tea is presented in the formal drawing room.

Historic Interest: Maine Maritime Museum, Ford Popham, weekly historic house tours, Bath Iron Works (boat launchings).

Innkeeper(s): James Haught, Larry Kieft. $79-129. MC, VISA, PC, TC. 4 rooms with PB. Breakfast and afternoon tea included in rates. Types of meals: Full gourmet bkfst and cont. Beds: QDT. Turndown service in room. VCR and library on premises. Family reunions and seminars hosted. Antiquing, fishing, beaches, live theater, parks, shopping, cross-country skiing and water sports nearby.

"For our first try at B&B lodgings, we've probably started at the top, and nothing else will ever measure up to this. Wonderful food, wonderful home, grounds and wonderful hosts!"

Pleasant Cove B&B

73 George Wright Rd
Bath, ME 04579
(207)442-0045 (800)949-2982 Fax:(207)442-0045
E-mail: innkeeper@pleasantcovebb.com
Web: www.pleasantcovebb.com

Circa 1850. A brochure from the early 1900s assured guests at this historic Colonial that "even on the hottest days there is a cooling breeze from the bay," and the inn is "an ideal home . . . for those who need only a quiet place to rest." A century later, these words still ring true. Pleasant Cove offers three comfortable bedrooms decorated with a mix of antiques and contemporary furnishings. Guests can walk down to the cove and water, and watch as bald eagles and blue heron soar through the sky.

Innkeeper(s): Birgit Koschwitz/Reinhard Zeiler. Call for rates. 3 rooms, 1 with PB. Beds: Q. Phone in room.

"Pleasant Cove is more than pleasant. It is superb! Will stay again when in Maine."

Belfast H5

The Jeweled Turret Inn

40 Pearl St
Belfast, ME 04915-1907
(207)338-2304 (800)696-2304

Circa 1898. This grand Victorian is named for the staircase that winds up the turret, lighted by stained- and leaded-glass panels and jewel-like embellishments. It was built for attorney James Harriman. Dark pine beams adorn the ceiling of the den,  and the fireplace is constructed of bark and rocks from every state in the Union. Elegant antiques furnish the guest rooms. Guests can relax in one of the inn's four parlors, which are furnished with period antiques, wallpapers, lace and boast fireplaces. Some rooms have a ceiling fan. The verandas feature wicker and iron bistro sets and views of the historic district. The inn is within walking distance of the town and its shops, restaurants and the harbor.

Historic Interest: The home, which is listed in the National Register, is near many historic homes. Walking tours are available.

Innkeeper(s): Cathy & Carl Heffentrager. $85-135. MC, VISA, PC, TC. TAC10. 7 rooms with PB, 1 with FP. Breakfast and afternoon tea included in rates. Types of meals: Full gourmet bkfst and early coffee/tea. Beds: QDT. TV and one room with whirlpool tub in room. Small meetings and family reunions hosted. Antiquing, fishing, live theater, shopping, downhill skiing, cross-country skiing and water sports nearby.

"The ambiance was so romantic that we felt like we were on our honeymoon."

The Thomas Pitcher House B&B

19 Franklin St
Belfast, ME 04915-1105
(207)338-6454 (888)338-6454
E-mail: tpitcher@acadia.net
Web: www.thomaspitcherhouse.com

Circa 1873. This richly appointed home was considered state-of-the-art back in 1873, for it was one of only a few homes offering central heat and hot or cold running water. Today, innkeepers have added plenty of modern amenities, but kept the ambiance of the Victorian era. Some vanities include original walnut and marble, while another bathroom includes tin ceilings and a step-down bath. Some rooms have cozy reading areas. Guests enjoy a full breakfast each morning with menus that feature specialties such as Maine blueberry buttermilk pancakes or a French toast puff made with homemade raisin bread.

Historic Interest: A short walk from the Thomas Pitcher House will take you into the center of historic Belfast, which includes a variety of shops and galleries and the harbor. Walking tours through historic tree-lined streets are available and nearby Seasport offers plenty of antiquing. The Penobscot Marine Museum is 10 miles away, Fort Knox and Montpelier are easy day trips, as is the Owl's Head Transportation Museum.

Innkeeper(s): Fran & Ron Kresge. $75-95. MC, VISA, PC, TC. TAC10. 4 rooms with PB. Breakfast included in rates. Types of meals: Full gourmet bkfst and early coffee/tea. Beds: QDT. Clocks, portable fans and reading bays/areas in room. VCR, library, porch with rockers and deck with wicker furniture on premises. German and limited French spoken. Antiquing, fishing, museums, historic sites, lighthouses, live theater, parks, shopping, downhill skiing, cross-country skiing and water sports nearby.

Publicity: *Boston Herald, Jackson Clarion-Ledger, Toronto Sunday Sun, Bride's, Knoxville News-Sentinel, Saturday Evening Post, Allentown Morning Call, Waldo Independent, Victorian Homes.*

"A home away from home."

Bethel   I2

Chapman Inn

PO Box 1067
Bethel, ME 04217-1067
(207)824-2657 (877)359-1498

Circa 1865. As one of the town's oldest buildings, this Federal-style inn has been a store, a tavern and a boarding house known as "The Howard." It was the home of William Rogers Chapman, composer, conductor and founder of the Rubenstein Club and the Metropolitan Musical Society, in addition to the

Maine Music Festival. The inn is a convenient place to begin a walking tour of Bethel's historic district.

Innkeeper(s): Sandra & Fred. $25-105. MC, VISA, AX, DS, PC, TC. 10 rooms with PB and 2 suites. Breakfast included in rates. Types of meals: Full bkfst and early coffee/tea. Afternoon tea and catering service available. TV and phone in room. Air conditioning. VCR, fax and sauna on premises. Weddings, small meetings, family reunions and seminars hosted. Antiquing, fishing, golf, live theater, parks, shopping, downhill skiing, cross-country skiing, tennis and water sports nearby.
Pets Allowed.

L'Auberge Country Inn

Mill Hill Rd, PO Box 21
Bethel, ME 04217-0021
(207)824-2774 (800)760-2774 Fax:(207)824-0806

Circa 1870. In the foothills of the White Mountains, surrounded by five acres of gardens and woods, this former carriage house was converted to a guest house in the 1920s. Among its seven guest rooms are two spacious suites. The Theater Suite offers a four-poster queen bed and dressing room. The Family Suite can accommodate up to six guests. Mount Abrahms and Sunday River ski areas are just minutes away.

Innkeeper(s): Tom Rideout. $65-125. MC, VISA, AX, DS. 6 rooms, 2 suites and 1 conference room. Breakfast included in rates. Types of meals: Full bkfst and early coffee/tea. Gourmet dinner, banquet service and catering service available. VCR and child care on premises. Weddings, small meetings, family reunions and seminars hosted. Antiquing, shopping, downhill skiing and cross-country skiing nearby.

Blue Hill   H5

Captain Isaac Merrill Inn

1 Union St
Blue Hill, ME 04614
(207)374-2555 Fax:(207)374-2555
E-mail: imi@midmail.com
Web: www.captainmerrillinn.com

Circa 1830. Built in the Federal style, this home was constructed for a sea captain. After several decades, another sea captain, Isaac Merrill, purchased the home. The Merrill family lived in the home for more than 70 years, selling it in the 1940s. Eventually Captain Merrill's great-granddaughter purchased the home, restored it, and opened it for bed & breakfast guests. The guest rooms and common areas are decorated in period style with antiques, some of which are family pieces. Bedchambers feature four-poster beds, and two include a fireplace. Guests are pampered with a gourmet breakfast, and the inn also has a café that serves dinner. A dinner menu might include a starter of shrimp scampi on a bed of greens, followed by seafood chowder or Caesar salad. For the entrée, guests might select duck breast in maple port sauce. The inn is within walking distance to antique shops, art galleries and restaurants. Bar Harbor and Acadia National Park are within a 45-minute drive. Hiking, biking and kayaking are other popular local activities.

Historic Interest: Parson Fisher House-2 miles, Blue Hill Historical Society.
Innkeeper(s): Dan & Jane Hemmerly-Brown. $65-125. MC, VISA, AX, DC, DS, PC, TC. TAC10. 6 rooms, 5 with PB, 3 with FP, 1 suite and 1 conference room. Breakfast included in rates. Types of meals: Full gourmet bkfst, cont, veg bkfst and early coffee/tea. Afternoon tea, gourmet dinner, snacks/refreshments, gourmet lunch, banquet service and catered breakfast available. Restaurant on premises. Beds: QDT. VCR, library and modem hook-up on premises. Small meetings, family reunions and seminars hosted. Amusement parks, antiquing, art galleries, beaches, bicycling, canoeing/kayaking, fishing, golf, hiking, horseback riding, live theater, parks, shopping, cross-country skiing, tennis, water sports and wineries nearby.

Boothbay J4

Hodgdon Island Inn

PO Box 492, Barter Island Rd
Boothbay, ME 04571
(207)633-7474
E-mail: info@hodgonislandinn.com
Web: www.hodgdonislandinn.com

Circa 1796. This early 19th-century Victorian still boasts many original features, including molding and windows. Antiques and wicker furnishings decorate the guest rooms. There is a heated swimming pool available to summer guests. The historic inn is minutes from downtown Boothbay Harbor.

$95-125. MC, VISA, DS, PC, TC. 6 rooms with PB. Breakfast included in rates. Types of meals: Full gourmet bkfst and early coffee/tea. Afternoon tea available. Beds: KQT. Ceiling fan in room. VCR and swimming on premises. Small meetings and family reunions hosted. Antiquing, fishing, golf, lobster bake on island cruise, live theater, parks, shopping and tennis nearby.

Boothbay Harbor J4

1830 Admiral's Quarters Inn

71 Commercial St
Boothbay Harbor, ME 04538-1827
(207)633-2474 Fax:(207)633-5904
E-mail: loon@admiralsquartersinn.com
Web: www.admiralsquartersinn.com

Circa 1830. Set on a rise looking out to the sea, this recently renovated sea captain's house commands a splendid harbor view. The inn is decorated with white wicker and antiques. Each room features
French doors or
sliding glass doors
that open to a pri-
vate deck or terrace
to take advantage of
the water view. Most
accommodations
are two-room suites.

A new solarium overlooks the harbor and is the inviting location for a hearty New England breakfast served buffet style. In the afternoons, guests can enjoy refreshments in front of the fire or as they watch lobster boats glide through the harbor. Guests may walk a short distance to shops and harbor activities.

Historic Interest: Maine Maritime Museum, St. Patricks Roman Catholic Church (35 minutes).

Innkeeper(s): Les & Deb Hallstrom. $85-155. MC, VISA, DS, PC, TC. 6 rooms with PB and 4 suites. Breakfast, afternoon tea and snacks/refreshments included in rates. Types of meals: Full bkfst, country bkfst, veg bkfst and early coffee/tea. Beds: KQT. Cable TV, phone, ceiling fan and toiletries in room. Fax, copier, library and glider swing on premises. Weddings, small meetings, family reunions and seminars hosted. Antiquing, art galleries, beaches, bicycling, canoeing/kayaking, fishing, golf, hiking, horseback riding, boat trips, pottery shops, live theater, museums, parks, shopping, downhill skiing, cross-country skiing, sporting events, tennis and water sports nearby.

"If you're looking to put down stakes in the heart of Boothbay Harbor, the Admiral's Quarters Inn provides an eagle's eye view on land and at sea —Yankee Traveler."

Harbour Towne Inn on The Waterfront

71 Townsend Ave
Boothbay Harbor, ME 04538-1158
(207)633-4300 (800)722-4240 Fax:(207)633-4300
E-mail: mainco@gwi.net
Web: www.acadia.net/harbourtowneinn

Circa 1880. This Victorian inn's well-known trademark boasts that it is "the finest B&B on the waterfront." Most of the inn's 12 rooms offer an outside deck and the Penthouse has an outstanding view of the
harbor from its pri-
vate deck. Breakfast is
served in the inn's
Sunroom, and guests
also may relax in the
parlor, which has a
miniature antique
library and a beauti-
ful antique fireplace.

A conference area is available for meetings. The inn's meticulous grounds include flower gardens and well-kept shrubs and trees. It's an easy walk to the village and its art galleries, restaurants, shops and boat trips. Special off-season packages are available. Ft. William Henry and the Fisherman's Memorial are nearby.

Historic Interest: Boothbay Region Historical Building (3 blocks), lighthouses (5 to 50 minutes).

Innkeeper(s): George Thomas & family. $59-249. MC, VISA, AX, DS, PC, TC. TAC10. 12 rooms with PB and 1 conference room. Breakfast included in rates. Type of meal: Cont plus. Beds: KQDT. Cable TV and phone in room. Fax and copier on premises. Handicap access. Weddings, small meetings, family reunions and seminars hosted. Antiquing, fishing, boatings, live theater, parks, shopping, downhill skiing, cross-country skiing and water sports nearby.

Newagen Seaside Inn

PO Box 29, Rt 27
Boothbay Harbor, ME 04576
(207)633-5242 (800)654-5242 Fax:(207)633-5242
E-mail: seaside@wiscasset.net
Web: www.newagenseasideinn.com

Circa 1903. Europeans have inhabited Cape Newagen since the 1620s, and a fort built on this property was destroyed in a skirmish with Native Americans. Rachel Carson sought refuge at this seaside inn, and it is here that her final resting place is located. The peaceful scenery includes vistas of islands and lighthouses, and guests can enjoy the view from an oceanside gazebo. There are both freshwater and saltwater swimming pools, nature trails, tennis courts and a mile of rocky shoreline to enjoy. Some rooms offer private decks, and each is decorated in traditional style. The innkeepers also offer three cottages. Maine Lobster is a specialty at the inn's restaurant.

Innkeeper(s): Heidi & Peter Larsen. $85-200. MC, VISA, PC, TC. TAC10. 26 rooms with PB, 3 suites, 3 cottages and 1 conference room. Breakfast included in rates. EP. Types of meals: Full bkfst and early coffee/tea. Gourmet dinner, picnic lunch and banquet service available. Restaurant on premises. Beds: KQT. VCR, fax, copier, swimming, tennis, library, lawn games, nature trails, rowboats, dock and tide pools on premises. Handicap access. Weddings, small meetings, family reunions and seminars hosted. Antiquing, fishing, golf, whale watching, live theater, parks, shopping, tennis and water sports nearby.

Publicity: *Down East, Yankee, New England Travel.*

Bridgton 12

Noble House

PO Box 180
Bridgton, ME 04009-0180
(207)647-3733 Fax:(207)647-3733

Circa 1903. Located on Highland Lake, this inn is tucked among three acres of old oaks and a grove of pine trees, providing an estate-like view from all guest rooms. The elegant parlor contains a library, grand piano and hearth. Bed chambers are furnished with antiques, wicker and quilts. Three rooms have whirlpool tubs, and family suites are available. A hammock placed at the water's edge provides a view of the lake and Mt. Washington. The inn's lake frontage also allows for canoeing at sunset and swimming. Restaurants are nearby.

Historic Interest: Shaker Village (30 minutes), Willowbrook, a restored 19th-century village (45 minutes), Narramissic, unspoiled early 19th-century rural farm homestead (15 minutes), Songo River Queen, replica of the Mississippi River Stern paddle wheelers (15 minutes).

Innkeeper(s): Jane Starets. $78-130. MC, VISA, AX. 9 rooms, 6 with PB and 3 suites. Breakfast included in rates. Type of meal: Full bkfst. Beds: QDT. TV and three rooms have whirlpool tubs in room. Antiquing, fishing, live theater, downhill skiing, cross-country skiing and water sports nearby.

Publicity: *Bridgton News.*

"It's my favorite inn."

Tarry-A-While Resort

Box A, Highland Ridge Rd
Bridgton, ME 04009
(207)647-2522 Fax:(207)647-5512
E-mail: tarryayl@megalink.net
Web: www.tarryawhile.com

Circa 1897. Tarry-A-While offers a variety of comfortable accommodations, including a Victorian inn and cottages. There is also a social hall. The resort is located on a 25-acre hillside and there are plenty of outdoor activities. Tennis and boating are included in the rates, and sailing or waterskiing is available. An 18-hole golf course is a walk away. The inn's dining

room, which overlooks Highland Lake and Pleasant Mountain, serves "new American" cuisine as you gaze at the sunset.

Innkeeper(s): Marc & Nancy Stretch. $60-135. MC, VISA, PC, TC. 27 rooms, 22 with PB. Breakfast included in rates. Type of meal: Cont. Beds: KQDT. Air conditioning. Bicycles, tennis, golf course, canoes and rowboats on premises. Weddings, small meetings and family reunions hosted. Antiquing, boats, live theater, shopping and tennis nearby.

"Thanks for sharing this magical place with us! What a wonderful experience."

Brooksville 15

Oakland House and Shore Oaks Seaside Inn

Herrick Rd, RR 1 Box 400
Brooksville, ME 04617
(207)359-8521 (800)359-7352
E-mail: jim@oaklandhouse.com
Web: www.oaklandhouse.com

Circa 1907. Guests at this seaside getaway enjoy the best of Maine, from the half-mile of private ocean front to the miles of hiking trails. Your host, a fourth-generation innkeeper, is a descendant of John Billings, who received the property's original land grant from King George of England in the 18th century. The land has remained in the family since that time. Fifteen cottages comprise the resort as well

as Shore Oaks Seaside Inn, a bed and breakfast. In the summer a restaurant is open in the old farmhouse offering fine dining with five courses. Built in 1907, the inn is an excellent example of Arts and Crafts style. Original oak furnishings and period decor enhance the 10 guest rooms, which are decorated in shades of soft green. The living room has a large stone fireplace, original wicker and oak furnishings, huge multi-paned windows and offers a panoramic view of Penobscot Bay. Breakfasts for B&B guests are served in Shore Oaks year round. Guests staying in the cottages are offered a breakfast buffet in the farmhouse in season. Some cottages are nestled along the shoreline of the 50-acre property. Many of the cottages include amenities such as kitchenettes and living rooms with fireplaces, and most boast panoramic views. Each cottage is unique; a few are more than 100 years old and some have five bedrooms. During the high season, breakfast and dinner are included in the rates.

Historic Interest: The Brooksville area was a trading post of the Puritans of Plymouth in the early 1600s and was taken by the French in 1635, then captured by the Dutch and later abandoned. Fort George was the largest fort built by the British during the Revolutionary War. In the waters off nearby Castine, America suffered its greatest naval disaster until Pearl Harbor.

Innkeeper(s): Jim & Sally Littlefield. $89-209. MC, VISA, PC, TC. TAC10. 10 rooms, 7 with PB, 15 with FP, 15 cottages and 2 conference rooms. Breakfast and dinner included in rates. MAP. Types of meals: Full bkfst, cont plus, cont and early coffee/tea. Picnic lunch and catering service available. Beds: QDT. VCR, fax, copier, swimming and library on premises. Weddings, small meetings, family reunions and seminars hosted. Antiquing, fishing, concerts, musical events, parks, shopping, cross-country skiing and water sports nearby.

Pets allowed: $12/dog/day, in some cottages only.

"We have dreamt of visiting Maine for quite some time. Our visit here at Shore Oaks and the beautiful countryside surpassed our dreams. We will be back to enjoy it again."

Camden 15

Abigail's B&B By The Sea

8 High St
Camden, ME 04843-1611
(207)236-2501 (800)292-2501 Fax:(207)230-0657
E-mail: abigails@midcoast.com
Web: www.midcoast.com/~abigails

Circa 1847. This Federal home was the former residence of
Maine senator E.K. Smart. Each guest room is decorated with
poster beds, antiques, quilts, fireplaces and Jacuzzis. English
chintzes and wicker
abound. Enjoy break-
fast in bed or share it
with other guests in
the sunny dining
room. Everything from
French toast, scones
and fresh fruit to souf-
fles and quiche high-
light the meal. An
afternoon tea is served

in the parlor, which boasts two fireplaces. Unique shops, galleries, restaurants and musical festivals and craft fairs are but a
few ways to enjoy this harbor-side town.

Innkeeper(s): Donna & Ed Misner. $95-175. MC, VISA. 4 rooms with PB.
Breakfast and afternoon tea included in rates. Type of meal: Full bkfst.
Gourmet dinner available. Beds: QT. Air conditioning. Antiquing, fishing, golf,
live theater, downhill skiing, cross-country skiing and water sports nearby.

A Little Dream

66 High St
Camden, ME 04843-1768
(207)236-8742

Circa 1888. This Victorian was built as a guest cottage on an
estate that is the home to Norumberg Castle, a vast manor
built by the inventor of the dual teletype, J.B. Stearns. The
rooms are wonderfully romantic, displaying a divine English-
country ambiance.
One room features a
pencil-post bed deco-
rated with dried flow-
ers. Another boasts a
cozy sitting area with a
fireplace. Whimsical
touches include a col-

lection of teddy bears and antique toys. Views of the bay and
islands add to the romance. Breakfasts are artfully displayed on
fine china. Edible flowers decorate plates with items such as an
apple-brie omelet or lemon-ricotta pancakes with a raspberry
sauce. Guests, if they can tear themselves away from the inn,
are sure to leave rejuvenated.

Innkeeper(s): JoAnna Ball & Bill Fontana. $95-225. MC, VISA, AX, PC, TC. 7
rooms with PB, 2 with FP and 2 suites. Breakfast and afternoon tea included
in rates. Types of meals: Full gourmet bkfst and early coffee/tea. Beds: KQ.
Cable TV, phone, turndown service and VCR in room. Air conditioning.
Library on premises. French, German and Italian spoken. Antiquing, fishing,
golf, live theater, parks, shopping, downhill skiing, cross-country skiing, tennis and water sports nearby.

Publicity: *Country Inns, Glamour, Yankee Magazine, Country Living.*

Blackberry Inn

82 Elm St
Camden, ME 04843-1907
(207)236-6060 (800)388-6000
E-mail: blkberry@midcoast.com
Web: www.blackberryinn.com

Circa 1860. Blackberry Inn is a true Painted Lady. The exterior
of the elaborate Italianate Victorian-style home is highlighted by
contrasting shades of Blackberry Purple outlining its bays and
friezes. The interiors are lavished with elaborate plaster ceiling
designs, polished parquet floors, finely crafted fireplace mantels
and original tin ceilings. Guest rooms are decorated in authentic Victorian period style, but include modern amenities. Two
rooms offer whirlpool tubs and private garden entrances.
Several also include a fireplace. The inn is within walking distance to shops, the harbor and restaurants.

Innkeeper(s): Jim & Cindy Ostrowski. $80-175. MC, VISA, DS, PC. 10 rooms
with PB, 5 with FP. Type of meal: Full gourmet bkfst. Beds: KQDT. Some
have whirlpools in room.

"Charming. An authentic reflection of a grander time."

The Camden Windward House B&B

6 High St
Camden, ME 04843-1611
(207)236-9656 Fax:(207)230-0433
E-mail: bnb@windwardhouse.com
Web: www.windwardhouse.com

Circa 1854. Each guest room at this Greek Revival home has
been individually decorated and sports names such as the
Carriage Room, Trisha Romance Room or Brass Room. The
Mount Battie room
offers a mountain
view and a skylight,
so guests can stargaze
as they relax on a
queen-size bed. The
rooms include
antiques and roman-
tic amenities such as
candles and fine

linens. The innkeepers further pamper guests with a hearty
breakfast featuring a variety of juices, freshly ground coffee and
teas and a choice of items such as featherbed eggs, pancakes,
French toast or Belgian waffles topped with fresh Maine blueberries. After the morning meal, guests are sure to enjoy a day
exploring Camden, noted as the village where "the mountains
meet the sea." The inn is open year-round.

Innkeeper(s): Del & Charlotte Lawrence. $90-195. MC, VISA, AX, PC, TC.
TAC10. 8 rooms with PB, 3 with FP. Breakfast and afternoon tea included in
rates. Types of meals: Full gourmet bkfst and early coffee/tea. Beds: Q. Phone
and ceiling fan in room. Central air. Fax, copier and library on premises. Small
meetings hosted. Antiquing, fishing, windjammer cruises, hiking, live theater,
parks, shopping, downhill skiing, cross-country skiing and water sports nearby.

Captain Swift Inn

72 Elm St
Camden, ME 04843-1907
(207)236-8113 (800)251-0865 Fax:(207)230-0464

Circa 1810. This inviting Federal-style home remains much as it
did in the 19th century, including the original 12-over-12 windows and a beehive oven. The innkeepers have worked diligently

to preserve the historic flavor, and the home's original five fireplaces, handsome wide pine floors, restored moldings and exposed beams add to the warm and cozy interior. Guest rooms are filled with period antiques and reproductions

and offer down pillows, handmade quilts and comfortable beds. The only addition to the home was a new section, which includes the innkeeper's quarters, a kitchen and a guest room entirely accessible for guests with wheelchairs. A gourmet, three-course breakfast includes items that sound decadent, but are truly low in fat and cholesterol, such as an apple pancake souffle.

Innkeeper(s): Tom & Kathy Filip. $95-125. MC, VISA, PC, TC. TAC10. 4 rooms with PB. Breakfast and afternoon tea included in rates. Types of meals: Full gourmet bkfst and early coffee/tea. Beds: QT. Table and chairs in room. Air conditioning. VCR, fax, copier and library on premises. Handicap access. Small meetings and family reunions hosted. Antiquing, fishing, golf, schooners, lighthouses, museums, live theater, parks, shopping, downhill skiing, cross-country skiing, tennis and water sports nearby.

"We came intending to stay for one night and ended up staying for five. . .need we say more!"

Castleview By The Sea

59 High St
Camden, ME 04843-1733
(207)236-2344 (800)272-8439

Circa 1856. This classic American cape house is the only B&B located on the waterside of the ocean view section of Camden's flowered historic district. Guest rooms feature wide pine floors, beamed ceilings, stained glass and balconies. The inn reflects the owner's world-wide travel in its eclectic decorating. Guests can literally enjoy views of the ocean right from their bed. Rooms offer cable TV and air conditioning.

Innkeeper(s): Bill Butler. $75-175. MC, VISA, PC. TAC10. 3 rooms with PB. Breakfast included in rates. Types of meals: Full bkfst and cont plus. Beds: KQ. Cable TV, phone, ceiling fan and VCR in room. Air conditioning. Library on premises. Family reunions hosted. Antiquing, fishing, live theater, museums, parks, shopping, downhill skiing, cross-country skiing, tennis and water sports nearby.

"Wonderful food, wonderful view, wonderful host."

The Elms B&B

84 Elm St
Camden, ME 04843-1907
(207)236-6250 (800)755-3567 Fax:(207)236-7330
E-mail: theelms@midcoast.com
Web: www.midcoast.com/~theelms/

Circa 1806. Captain Calvin Curtis built this Colonial a few minutes' stroll from the picturesque harbor. Candlelight shimmers year round from the inn's windows. A sitting room, library and parlor are open for guests. Tastefully appointed bed chambers scattered with antiques are available in both the main house and the carriage house. A cottage garden can

be seen beside the carriage house. A lighthouse theme permeates the decor, and there is a wide selection of lighthouse books, collectibles and artwork.

Historic Interest: Guests can take a boat tour and view Camden's Curtis Island lighthouse and others, which have been in operation since the early 19th century. There are a variety of lighthouses and maritime museums within an hour to an hour and a half of Camden, including active lighthouses that date back to the 1820s.

Innkeeper(s): Ted & Jo Panayotoff. $75-105. MC, VISA, PC, TC. 6 rooms with PB, 1 with FP. Breakfast and afternoon tea included in rates. Types of meals: Full bkfst and early coffee/tea. Beds: QT. Phone in room. Handicap access. Antiquing, windjammer trips, lighthouses, museums, sailing, hiking, live theater, parks, shopping, downhill skiing and cross-country skiing nearby.

"If something is worth doing, it's worth doing first class, and your place is definitely first class."

Hartstone Inn

41 Elm St
Camden, ME 04843-1910
(207)236-4259 (800)788-4823
E-mail: info@hartstoneinn.com
Web: www.hartstoneinn.com

Circa 1835. This historic home was transformed into a Victorian at the turn-of-the-century with the addition of large bay windows and a mansard roof. The inn is located in the heart of the village of Camden and is within walking distance of the harbor. Romantic guest rooms offer amenities such as fireplaces, lace canopy beds, designer linens, fresh robes, candlelight, flowers and chocolate truffles. The innkeepers careers were in luxury hotels and Michael was awarded Caribbean Chef of the Year. He prepares the inn's gourmet breakfasts which may include Maine Lobster and Asparagus Quiche or perhaps, Atlantic Smoked Salmon Benedict. Dinners are also available and all meals are presented elegantly on fine china and crystal.

Innkeeper(s): Mary Jo & Michael Salmon. $100-150. MC, VISA, PC, TC. TAC10. 10 rooms with PB, 2 with FP and 2 suites. Breakfast included in rates. Type of meal: Full gourmet bkfst. Afternoon tea and gourmet dinner available. Beds: KQ. TV, phone, refrigerators and Cable TV in two rooms in room. Library and game room on premises. Weddings, small meetings and family reunions hosted. Antiquing, fishing, live theater, parks, shopping, downhill skiing, cross-country skiing and water sports nearby.

"When can I move in?"

Hawthorn Inn

9 High St
Camden, ME 04843-1610
(207)236-8842 Fax:(207)236-6181
E-mail: hawthorn@midcoast.com
Web: www.camdeninn.com

Circa 1894. This handsome yellow and white turreted Victorian sits on an acre and a half of sloping lawns with a view of the harbor. The interior boasts a grand, three-story staircase and original stained-glass windows. The inn has 10 rooms all with private baths. The carriage house rooms offer harbor views, private decks, double Jacuzzi tubs and fireplaces. Breakfasts with fresh fruit, coffeecakes and egg dishes are served by fireside, or during warm weather, guests are invited to eat on the deck overlooking the harbor.

Historic Interest: Downtown Camden features many shops, galleries and restaurants nestled around its beautiful harbor.

Innkeeper(s): Nicholas & Patricia Wharton. $100-205. MC, VISA, AX, PC, TC. TAC10. 10 rooms with PB, 3 with FP. Breakfast included in rates. Types of meals: Full bkfst and early coffee/tea. Beds: QDT. Phone and TV and VCR in some rooms in room. Fax on premises. Small meetings hosted. Antiquing, bicycling, hiking, sailing, ocean kayaking, island hopping, shopping, downhill skiing and cross-country skiing nearby.

Publicity: *Glamour, Country Inns, Outside, Yankee, Down East, Cleveland Plain Dealer, Minneapolis Tribune.*

"The outstanding location, excellent rates and marvelous innkeepers make this one of the B&Bs we will be frequenting for years to come."

The Maine Stay Inn

22 High St
Camden, ME 04843-1735
(207)236-9636
E-mail: innkeeper@mainestay.com
Web: www.mainestay.com

Circa 1802. The innkeepers of this treasured colonial, that is one of the oldest of the 66 houses which comprise the High Street Historic District, take great pleasure in making guests feel at home. One of the trio of innkeepers is known for his down-east stories told in a heavy down-east accent. Antiques from the 17th, 18th and 19th centuries adorn the rooms. The center of the village and the Camden Harbor are a short five-minute walk away.

Historic Interest: The Camden Opera House, historic mill and manufacturing buildings, and the First Congregational Church are among the area's historic sites.

Innkeeper(s): Peter & Donny Smith & Diana Robson. $100-145. MC, VISA, AX. 8 rooms with PB, 4 with FP. Breakfast included in rates. Beds: QT. TV in room.

Publicity: *Miami Herald, Lewiston Sun-Journal, Country Inns, Glamour, Country Living, Rand McNally's Best B&Bs, Discerning Traveler, Bazaar, Boston Globe, Down East Magazine.*

"We've traveled the East Coast from Martha's Vineyard to Bar Harbor and this is the only place we know we must return to."

Swan House B&B

49 Mountain St
Camden, ME 04843-1635
(207)236-8275 (800)207-8275 Fax:(207)236-0906
E-mail: hikeinn@swanhouse.com
Web: www.swanhouse.com

Circa 1870. Nestled on just under an acre of wooded grounds at the foot of Mt. Battie, this Victorian is a welcoming site inside and out. Antique-filled guest rooms are comfortable, each named

for a different variety of swan. Four of the rooms offer private entrances. The Lohengrin Suite is a spacious room with its own sitting area, while the Trumpeter Room offers a private deck. Hearty breakfasts include country-style fare, fruit, homemade granola and special pastry of the day. The village of Camden and the surrounding area offer plenty of activities, and the innkeepers are happy to point guests in an interesting direction.

Innkeeper(s): Lyn & Ken Kohl. $75-145. MC, VISA, PC, TC. 6 rooms with PB and 1 suite. Breakfast included in rates. Types of meals: Full bkfst and early coffee/tea. Afternoon tea available. Beds: QD. Phone in room. Fax, gazebo and mountain hiking trails on premises. Small meetings and family reunions hosted. Antiquing, fishing, mountain hiking trails, live theater, parks, shopping, downhill skiing, cross-country skiing and water sports nearby.

"We loved our stay at the Swan House and our breakfast there was by far the most excellent breakfast we have ever had."

Castine   I5

The Castine Harbor Lodge

PO Box 215
Castine, ME 04421-0215
(207)326-4335
E-mail: chl@acadia.net
Web: www.castinemaine.com

Circa 1893. Relax on the expansive harbor-side verandas of this Edwardian mansion and soak up the ocean views while you enjoy the sounds of waves crashing on the shore. Guest quarters boast ocean views, and the innkeepers also offer a waterfront cottage. The delicious, homemade breakfasts are a treat. A variety of outdoor activities and antique shopping are available nearby.

Historic Interest: Castine, which has been claimed as the property of four countries, is home to the Maine Maritime Academy. The academy includes old British barracks and the school keeps a training ship anchored at the town dock.

Innkeeper(s): Paul & Sara Brouillard. $65-125. MC, VISA, DC, DS, PC, TC. 9 rooms, 7 with PB and 1 cottage. Breakfast included in rates. Type of meal: Cont plus. Beds: KQDT. Swimming and library on premises. Weddings, small meetings and family reunions hosted. Antiquing, fishing, golf, parks and tennis nearby.

Pets allowed: Well-behaved, leash $10 charge.

Publicity: *Conde Nast Travel, Yankee, Boats & Harbors.*

Chebeague Island   J3

Chebeague Island Inn

South Rd, PO Box 492
Chebeague Island, ME 04017
(207)846-5155

Circa 1925. This three-story inn overlooks rolling lawns and Casco Bay. The wraparound porch is a popular place to rock and immerse yourself in the view. A huge stone fireplace dominates the great room. The inn caters to weddings and lunch and dinner can be taken on the inn's porch. Bicycles are available and a scenic golf course is adjacent to the inn. White sandy beaches abound.

Innkeeper(s): Bowden Family. $74-150. MC, VISA, AX, DC, CB, DS. 21 rooms, 15 with PB and 6 conference rooms. Types of meals: Full gourmet bkfst and cont plus. Beds: DT.

Corea 17

The Black Duck Inn on Corea Harbor

PO Box 39 Crowley Island Rd
Corea, ME 04624-0039
(207)963-2689 Fax:(207)963-7495

Circa 1890. Two of the guest rooms at this turn-of-the-century farmhouse boast harbor views, while another offers a wooded scene out its windows. The innkeepers have decorated the home in an eclectic mix of old and new with antiques and contemporary pieces. There are two waterfront cottages for those who prefer more privacy. The full, gourmet breakfasts include house specialties, such as "eggs Black Duck" or items such as orange glazed French toast, blintzes or perhaps eggs Benedict.

Innkeeper(s): Barry Canner & Bob Travers. $75-155. MC, VISA, DS, PC, TC. TAC10. 6 rooms, 2 with PB, 1 suite, 2 cottages and 2 cabins. Breakfast included in rates. Types of meals: Full gourmet bkfst and early coffee/tea. Beds: QDT. VCR, fax, copier and library on premises. Small meetings hosted. Danish and French spoken. Antiquing, fishing, golf, parks, shopping, cross-country skiing and water sports nearby.

Publicity: *Boston Globe, Miami.*

"Never could we have known how warmly received we would all four feel and how really restored we would be by the end of the week."

Damariscotta Mills 14

Mill Pond Inn

50 Main St
Damariscotta Mills, ME 04555
(207)563-8014

Circa 1780. The one acre of grounds surrounding this 18th-century home are packed with scenery. A pond with a waterfall flows into the adjacent Damariscotta Lake and trees offer plenty of shade. Rooms are decorated in a whimsical country style and they have pond views and fresh flowers. Breakfasts are served in a room that overlooks the pond and grounds. Innkeeper Bobby Whear is a registered Maine guide, and the innkeepers offer private fishing trips. Complimentary canoeing and biking are available.

Innkeeper(s): Bobby & Sherry Whear. $90. 6 rooms with PB, 3 with FP and 1 suite. Breakfast and afternoon tea included in rates. Types of meals: Full bkfst and early coffee/tea. Beds: KQT. VCR, bicycles, private fishing trips available with Registered Maine Guide and canoes on premises. Weddings, small meetings, family reunions and seminars hosted. Antiquing, fishing, bird watching, live theater, parks, shopping, downhill skiing, cross-country skiing, sporting events and water sports nearby.

Dexter G4

Brewster Inn of Dexter, Maine

37 Zions Hill Rd
Dexter, ME 04930-1122
(207)924-3130 Fax:(207)924-9768
E-mail: brewster@nconline.net
Web: www.bbonline.com/me/brewsterinn

Circa 1934. Located on two acres with rose and perennial gardens, this handsome Colonial Revival-style house was built by architect John Calvin Stevens for Governor Ralph Brewster. It is in the National Register. Some guest rooms offer fireplaces, window seats, original tile bathrooms and views of the gardens. One

has a whirlpool tub for two. Furnishings include antiques and reproductions. A breakfast buffet includes hot entrees such as quiche, gingerbread pancakes or stuffed apples.

Innkeeper(s): Ivy & Michael Brooks. $59-89. MC, VISA, PC, TC. TAC10. 7 rooms with PB, 2 with FP and 2 suites. Breakfast and snacks/refreshments included in rates. MAP. Types of meals: Full bkfst and early coffee/tea. Dinner, picnic lunch, gourmet lunch and catering service available. Beds: KQDT. Cable TV, phone and books in room. Air conditioning. VCR, fax, copier, tennis and library on premises. Handicap access. Weddings, small meetings, family reunions and seminars hosted. Antiquing, fishing, golf, parks, shopping, cross-country skiing, tennis and water sports nearby.

Publicity: *Bangor Daily News, People, Places & Plants.*

Durham 13

The Bagley House

1290 Royalsborough Rd
Durham, ME 04222-5225
(207)865-6566 (800)765-1772 Fax:(207)353-5878
E-mail: bglyhse@aol.com
Web: members.aol.com/bedandbrk/bagley

Circa 1772. Six acres of fields and woods surround the Bagley House. Once an inn, a store and a schoolhouse, it is the oldest house in town. Guest rooms are decorated with colonial furnishings and hand-sewn Maine quilts. For breakfast, guests gather in the country kitchen in front of a huge brick fireplace and beehive oven.

Historic Interest: Bowdoin College, Maritime Museum and Old Sea Captain Homes.

Innkeeper(s): Suzanne O'Connor & Susan Backhouse. $70-135. MC, VISA, AX, DS, PC, TC. 8 rooms with PB, 4 with FP and 2 conference rooms. Breakfast and afternoon tea included in rates. Type of meals: Full bkfst and early coffee/tea. Snacks/refreshments and picnic lunch available. Beds: QDT. Fax and blueberry picking on premises. Small meetings and family reunions hosted. Antiquing, live theater, shopping, downhill skiing, cross-country skiing & sporting events nearby.

Publicity: *Los Angeles Times, New England Getaways, Lewiston Sun, Springfield Register.*

"I had the good fortune to stumble on the Bagley House. The rooms are well-appointed and the innkeepers are charming."

East Boothbay J4

Five Gables Inn

PO Box 335 Murray Hill Road
East Boothbay, ME 04544
(207)633-4551 (800)451-5048
E-mail: info@fivegablesinn.com
Web: www.fivegablesinn.com

Circa 1887. One could hardly conjure up a more perfect setting than this Maine inn's location, just yards from Linekin Bay with wooded hills as a backdrop. For more than a century, guests have come here to enjoy the Maine summer. The porch offers a hammock and rockers, as well as a pleasing view. Guest rooms offer bay views, and five include a fireplace. Breakfasts offer a wide assortment of items, a menu might include puff pancakes, grilled tomatoes, ham, freshly baked scones, fruit and home-made granola. The inn is open from mid-May to October.

Innkeeper(s): Mike & De Kennedy. $100-175. MC, VISA, TC. TAC10. 16 rooms with PB, 5 with FP. Breakfast and afternoon tea included in rates. Types of meals: Full gourmet bkfst and early coffee/tea. Beds: KQT. Phone in room. Library on premises. Antiquing, fishing, golf, whale watching, windjammers, live theater, parks, shopping, tennis and water sports nearby.

Publicity: *Calendar, Atlanta Journal-Constitution, Down East Magazine, Yankee Traveler.*

Ocean Point Inn

Shore Rd
East Boothbay, ME 04544
(207)633-4200 (800)552-5554
E-mail: opi@oceanpointinn.com
Web: www.oceanpointinn.com

Circa 1898. Ocean Point Inn is comprised of a white clapboard main house, lodge, cottages, apartments and motel units located on three oceanfront acres. There are gardens and a

lovely road along
the bay where
guests watch lob-
stermen, seals and
passing windjam-
mers. Four light-
houses may be

viewed among the nearby islands. Boothbay Harbor is six miles away, but right at hand is the pier and the inn's restaurant with a view of the ocean. In addition to lobster dishes and crab cakes, the specialty of the house is fresh Maine salmon poached in Court Boullion served with dill sauce. Select from a wide choice of activities such as swimming, fishing and hiking, or simply settle into the Adirondack chairs and watch the soothing sea. Guests can rent motor boats or kayaks in Boothbay Harbor.

Innkeeper(s): Beth & Dave Dudley. $99-160. MC, VISA, AX, DS, TC. 61 rooms with PB, 3 with FP, 10 suites and 7 cottages. EP. Type of meal: Full bkfst. Dinner available. Beds: KQDT. Cable TV and phone in room. Air conditioning. Swimming and outdoor heated pool. Family reunions hosted. Antiquing, fishing, golf, live theater, parks, shopping, tennis and water sports nearby.

Eastport   G8

The Milliken House

29 Washington St
Eastport, ME 04631-1324
(207)853-2955

Circa 1846. This inn is
filled with beautiful furnishings and knickknacks,
much of which belonged
to the home's first owner,
Benjamin Milliken.
Ornately carved, marble-
topped pieces and period
decor take guests back in
time to the Victorian Era.

Milliken maintained a wharf on Eastport's waterfront from which he serviced the tall trading ships that used the harbor as a port of entry to the United States. An afternoon glass of port or sherry and chocolate turn-down service are among the amenities. Breakfasts are a gourmet treat, served in the dining room with its carved, antique furnishings.

Historic Interest: The waterfront historic district is just two blocks away as is the Barracks Historical Museum.

Innkeeper(s): Joyce Weber. $50-65. MC, VISA, AX, PC, TC. 5 rooms with PB and 1 conference room. Breakfast included in rates. Type of meal: Full bkfst. Beds: QT. TV and phone in room.

"A lovely trip back in history to a more gracious time."

Todd House

Todd's Head
Eastport, ME 04631
(207)853-2328

Circa 1775. Todd House is a typical full-Cape-style house with a huge center chimney. In 1801, Eastern Lodge No. 7 of the Masonic Order was chartered here. It became temporary barracks when Todd's Head was fortified. Guests may use barbecue facilities overlooking Passamaquoddy Bay. Children and well-behaved pets are welcome.

Innkeeper(s): Ruth McInnis. $45-80. MC, VISA. 6 rooms, 2 with PB, 3 with FP and 2 suites. Breakfast included in rates. Type of meal: Cont plus. Beds: QDT. Handicap access. Fishing and live theater nearby.

Pets Allowed.

"Your house and hospitality were real memory makers of our vacation."

Weston House

26 Boynton St
Eastport, ME 04631-1305
(207)853-2907 (800)853-2907 Fax:(207)853-0981

Circa 1810. Jonathan Weston, an 1802 Harvard graduate, built this Federal-style house on a hill overlooking Passamaquoddy Bay. John Audubon stayed here as a guest of the Westons while

awaiting passage to
Labrador in 1833.
Each guest room is
furnished with
antiques and Oriental
rugs. The Weston and
Audubon rooms boast
views of the bay and
gardens. Breakfast
menus vary, including

such delectables as heavenly pancakes with hot apricot syrup or freshly baked muffins and coddled eggs. Seasonal brunches are served on weekends and holidays. The area is full of outdoor activities, including whale watching. Nearby Saint Andrews-by-the-Sea offers plenty of shops and restaurants.

Historic Interest: Nearby historic attractions include Campobello Island, where Franklin D. Roosevelt spent his summers. King's Landing, a restored Loyalist settlement dating back to 1780, is two hours away.

Innkeeper(s): Jett & John Peterson. $50-75. PC, TC. 5 rooms, 1 with FP and 1 suite. Breakfast and afternoon tea included in rates. Type of meal: Full gourmet bkfst. Picnic lunch and catering service available. Beds: KQDT. Weddings, small meetings and family reunions hosted. Fishing, whale watching, nature, tennis, live theater and shopping nearby.

Publicity: *Down East, Los Angeles Times, Boston Globe, Boston Magazine, New York Times.*

"All parts of ourselves have been nourished."

Eliot   L2

High Meadows B&B

Rt 101
Eliot, ME 03903
(207)439-0590 Fax:(207)439-6343

Circa 1740. A ship's captain built this house, now filled with remembrances of colonial days. At one point, it was raised and a floor added underneath, so the upstairs is older than the downstairs. It is conveniently located to factory outlets in Kittery, Maine, and great dining and historic museums in Portsmouth, N.H.

Innkeeper(s): Elaine & Ray. $80-90. MC, VISA, AX, PC, TC. 4 rooms with PB. Breakfast and afternoon tea included in rates. Types of meals: Full bkfst and early coffee/tea. Beds: QDT. Weddings, small meetings and family reunions hosted. Antiquing, fishing, shopping and water sports nearby.

"High Meadows was the highlight of our trip."

Freeport   J3

Captain Briggs House B&B

8 Maple Ave
Freeport, ME 04032-1315
(207)865-1868 (800)217-2477

Circa 1853. This mid-19th-century home's most notable resident was John A. Briggs, a shipbuilder whose ancestors arrived in America via the Mayflower. There are six comfortable guest rooms, offering beds topped with quilts and country decor. A full breakfast prepares guests for a day of outlet shopping in Freeport. The famous L.L. Bean factory store and about a hun-

dred more outlets are just minutes away. Harbor cruises, fishing, seal watching, hiking and just enjoying the scenery in this coastal town are other options.

Innkeeper(s): Frank Family. $67-110. MC, VISA, PC, TC. 6 rooms with PB. Breakfast included in rates. Type of meal: Full bkfst. Beds: KQDT. Phone in room. Air conditioning. VCR on premises. Small meetings and family reunions hosted. Antiquing, fishing, golf, I.L. Bean Headquarters, seal watching, harbor cruises, live theater, parks, shopping, downhill skiing, cross-country skiing, sporting events, tennis and water sports nearby.

Captain Josiah Mitchell House B&B

188 Main St
Freeport, ME 04032-1407
(207)865-3289

Circa 1789. Captain Josiah Mitchell was commander of the clipper ship "Hornet." In 1866, en route from New York to San Francisco it caught fire, burned and was lost. The passengers and crew survived in three longboats, drifting for 45 days. When the boats finally drifted into one of the South Pacific Islands, Samuel Clemens was there, befriended the Captain and wrote his first story, under the name of Mark Twain and about the captain. The diary of Captain Mitchell parallels episodes of "Mutiny on the Bounty." Flower gardens and a porch swing on the veranda now welcome guests to Freeport and Captain Mitchell's House.

Historic Interest: Henry Wadsworth Longfellow house (13 miles), Admiral

McMillan, polar explorer with Perry, Bowdoin College (7 miles) and Freeport.

Innkeeper(s): Alan & Loretta Bradley. $78-95. MC, VISA, PC, TC. TAC10. 7 rooms with PB. Breakfast included in rates. Meal: Full bkfst. Beds: QDT. Ceiling fan in room. Air conditioning. Amusement parks, antiquing, fishing, I.L. Bean, live theater, parks, shopping, skiing and sporting events nearby.

"Your wonderful stories brought us all together. You have created a special place that nurtures and brings happiness and love. This has been a dream!"

Kendall Tavern B&B

213 Main St
Freeport, ME 04032-1411
(207)865-1338 (800)341-9572

Circa 1800. Kendall Tavern is a welcoming farmhouse painted in a cheerful, creamy yellow hue with white trim. The interior is appointed in an elegant New England country style. Each of the parlors has a fireplace. One parlor includes an upright piano and is a perfect place to curl up with a book, the other has a television and VCR. Breakfasts are creative and plentiful. The morning meal might start off with poached pears topped with a French vanilla yogurt sauce and accompanied by blueberry muffins. From there, guests enjoy a broccoli and mushroom quiche, grilled ham and home fries. Another menu might include baked apples stuffed with cranberries, cream cheese raspberry coffeecake, blueberry pancakes, scrambled eggs and crisp bacon. Whatever the menu, the breakfast is always a perfect start to a day of shopping in outlet stores, hiking, sailing or cross-country skiing, all of which are nearby.

$70-120. MC, VISA, AX, DS, TC. 7 rooms with PB. Breakfast included in rates. Type of meal: Full gourmet bkfst. Beds: QT. VCR, fax, copier and spa on premises. Small meetings hosted. Antiquing, fishing, live theater, parks, shopping, cross-country skiing and water sports nearby.

Maple Hill B&B

18 Maple Ave
Freeport, ME 04032-1315
(207)865-3730 (800)667-0478 Fax:(207)865-9859
E-mail: mplhll@aol.com
Web: www.web-knowledge.com/maplehill

Circa 1831. Maple Hill is comprised of a Greek Revival farmhouse and attached barn located on two tree-shaded acres of lawns and gardens. Furnished with antiques, the inn is in an

amazing location two blocks from L. L. Bean. A family suite is offered (the innkeepers have raised six children and enjoy hosting families). Queen-size guest rooms are also available, and a romantic atmosphere is provided at the inn with its fireplace, candlelight, flowers and music. Hearty breakfasts are served in the morning, featuring fruit compotes, French toast, waffles, blueberry muffins or biscuits.

Innkeeper(s): Lloyd H Lawarence & Susie Vietor. $97-166. MC, VISA, AX, DS, PC, TC. 3 rooms with PB, 1 suite and 1 conference room. Types of meals: Full bkfst, country bkfst, veg bkfst and early coffee/tea. Afternoon tea and snacks/refreshments available. Beds: KQT. Cable TV and VCR in room. Air conditioning. Fax, copier, bicycles, library and child care available on premises. Weddings, small meetings, family reunions and seminars hosted. Antiquing, art galleries, beaches, bicycling, canoeing/kayaking, fishing, golf, hiking, horseback riding, live theater, museums, parks, shopping, cross-country skiing, sporting events, tennis and water sports nearby.

Pets Allowed.

Fryeburg   I1

Admiral Peary House

9 Elm St
Fryeburg, ME 04037-1114
(207)935-3365 (800)237-8080 Fax:(207)935-3365

Circa 1865. Robert E. Peary, the American explorer who discovered the North Pole, once lived in this mid-19th-century home. Each of the guest rooms is named to honor Peary's memory. The North Pole room includes a scenic mountain view and a king-size brass bed. The Admiral's Quarters include a four-poster bed. Breakfasts are served on tables in the country kitchen and dining room and include such entrees as stuffed French toast, wild blueberry pancakes or the signature dish, Admiral Peary Penguin Pie, a savory combination of cheese, herbs and eggs. In addition to the cozy rooms and hearty breakfasts, the innkeepers offer a variety of amenities. There is a clay tennis court, an outdoor spa, billiard table and, in the winter months, guests can rent or buy snowshoes and traverse the innkeeper's acres of marked snowshoe trails. Guests also can canoe the Saco River, climb to the top of the world's largest boulder, discover covered bridges or visit historic sites.

Historic Interest: Mt. Washington (25 miles), Hemlock Covered Bridge (5 miles), Farm Museum-Fryeburg Fair (1 mile), Shaker Village (30 miles).

Innkeeper(s): Ed & Nancy Greenberg. $80-138. MC, VISA, AX, PC, TC. TAC10. 6 rooms with PB. Breakfast included in rates. Types of meals: Full bkfst, country bkfst, veg bkfst and early coffee/tea. Snacks/refreshments available. Beds: KQT. Air conditioning. VCR, fax, spa, bicycles, tennis, library, wet bar w/complimentary beverages, billiards and snowshoe trail and rentals on premises. Small meetings and seminars hosted. French spoken. Antiquing, beaches, bicycling, canoeing/kayaking, fishing, golf, hiking, horseback riding, snowshoeing, snowmobiling, live theater, museums, parks, shopping, downhill skiing, cross-country skiing, tennis and water sports nearby.

Gouldsboro   H6

Sunset House

Rt 186, HCR 60
Gouldsboro, ME 04607
(207)963-7156 (800)233-7156 Fax:(207)963-5859
E-mail: lodging@sunsethousebnb.com
Web: www.sunsethousebnb.com

Circa 1898. This coastal country farm inn is situated near Acadia National Park. Naturalists can observe rare birds and other wildlife in an unspoiled setting. Seven spacious bedrooms are spread over three floors. Four of the bedrooms have ocean views; a fifth overlooks a freshwater pond behind the house.

During winter, guests can ice skate on the pond, while in summer it is used for swimming. The innkeepers have a resident cat and poodle, and they also raise goats.

Guests enjoy a full country breakfast cooked by Carl, who has been an executive chef for more than 20 years.

Innkeeper(s): Kathy & Carl Johnson. $79-99. MC, VISA, AX, DS, PC, TC. 7 rooms, 4 with PB. Breakfast included in rates. Types of meals: Full bkfst and early coffee/tea. Beds: KQT. Turndown service in room. VCR, fax and copier on premises. Weddings and family reunions hosted. German spoken. Antiquing, fishing, golf, parks, shopping, cross-country skiing, tennis and water sports nearby.

Greenville   F4

The Lodge at Moosehead Lake

Upon Lily Bay Rd, Box 1167
Greenville, ME 04441
(207)695-4400 Fax:(207)695-2281
E-mail: innkeeper@lodgeatmooseheadlake.com
Web: www.lodgeatmooseheadlake.com

Circa 1916. Westerly views of the lake can be enjoyed from four of the five lodge rooms, all of the suites and the living and dining rooms of this inn. Each of the lodge rooms ha hand-carved, four-poster beds with dual-control electric blankets and fireplaces. At the end of the day, relax in a Jacuzzi tub found in each private bath. In 1997, the adjacent carriage house was transformed into three luxurious suites that offer a total retreat. Each of the suites features the above as well as river-stone whirlpool baths, sunken living rooms and private decks and gardens. The Katahdin Suite has a fireplace in the bathroom. The Allegash and Baxter Suites feature queen-size beds that are suspended from the ceiling to gently rock visitors to sleep.

Innkeeper(s): Roger Cauchi. $175-395. MC, VISA, DS. 8 rooms with PB. Breakfast included in rates. Type of meal: Full bkfst. Beds: Q. Cable TV, turndown service and VCR in room. Guest pantry on premises. Small meetings and seminars hosted. Canoeing/kayaking, fishing, golf, hiking, horseback riding, downhill skiing, cross-country skiing and water sports nearby.

Isle Au Haut   I5

The Keeper's House

PO Box 26
Isle Au Haut, ME 04645-0026
(207)367-2261
Web: www.keepershouse.com

Circa 1907. Designed and built by the U.S. Lighthouse Service, the handsome 48-foot-high Robinson Point Light guided vessels into this once-bustling island fishing village. Guests arrive on the mailboat. Innkeeper Judi Burke, whose father was a keeper at the Highland Lighthouse on Cape Cod, provides picnic lunches so guests may explore the scenic island trails. Dinner is served in the keeper's dining room.

The lighthouse is adjacent to the most remote section of Acadia National Park. It's not uncommon to hear the cry of an osprey, see deer approach the inn, or watch seals and porpoises cavorting off the point. Guest rooms are comfortable and serene, with stunning views of the island's ragged shore line, forests and Duck Harbor.

Historic Interest: Acadia National Park, adjacent 18th-century one-room school house, church & town hall (1-mile walk away).

Innkeeper(s): Jeff & Judi Burke. $257-294. PC, TC. 5 rooms and 1 cottage.

Breakfast, dinner and picnic lunch included in rates. Types of meals: Full gourmet bkfst and early coffee/tea. Beds: D. Wood stove in room. Swimming, bicycles and library on premises. Weddings, small meetings, family reunions and seminars hosted. Spanish spoken. Parks and shopping nearby.

Publicity: *New York Times, USA Today, Los Angeles Times, Ladies Home Journal, Christian Science Monitor, Down East, New York Woman, Philadelphia Inquirer, McCalls, Country, Men's Journal, Travel & Leisure.*

"Simply one of the unique places on Earth."

Kennebunk   K2

Arundel Meadows Inn

PO Box 1129
Kennebunk, ME 04043-1129
(207)985-3770

Circa 1827. This expansive farmhouse features seven bedrooms, each with their own sitting areas. Three rooms boast fireplaces. A gourmet breakfast is prepared by innkeeper Mark Bachelder, who

studied under Madeleine Kamman, a popular chef on PBS. Mark's freshly baked delicacies also are served during afternoon

teas. Antiques and paintings by innkeeper Murray Yaeger decorate the house. Nearby Kennebunkport provides excellent shopping at factory outlets, antique galleries and a variety of restaurants.

Historic Interest: Rachel Carson Reserve and Laud Holm Farm (5 miles), Brick Stone Museum (2 miles), Kennebunkport Historical Society (Nott House, etc.), tours of homes and Historical Landmarks (5 miles), Strawberry Bank Restorations (18 miles south).

Innkeeper(s): Mark Bachelder & Murray Yaeger. $75-175. 7 rooms with PB, 3 with FP and 2 suites. Breakfast and afternoon tea included in rates. Type of meal: Full bkfst. Beds: KQDT. TV in room. Antiquing, live theater and water sports nearby.

Publicity: *York County Coast Star.*

"The room was beautiful. Breakfast wonderful."

The Kennebunk Inn

45 Main St
Kennebunk, ME 04043-1888
(207)985-3351 Fax:(207)985-8865

Circa 1799. Built at the turn of the 19th century, Kennebunk Inn has been serving guests since the 1920s. The rooms and suites feature a variety of decor; guests might discover a clawfoot tub or four-poster bed. Games and a selection of books are available for guests, as well as televisions. For a special treat, make dinner reservations at the inn's restaurant, which serves a seasonally changing menu with fresh local seafood and produce. Guests can choose from filet mignon wrapped in puff pastry and topped with Brie cheese or perhaps pan-seared scallops and basil ravioli with a pink peppercorn and white wine cream sauce. Portland Press heralded the inn's restaurant with four stars.

Innkeeper(s): Kristen & John Martin. $55-155. MC, VISA, AX, DS, PC, TC. TAC10. 27 rooms with PB, 1 with FP, 5 suites and 1 conference room. Breakfast included in rates. MAP. Types of meals: Cont plus, cont and early coffee/tea. Dinner and banquet service available. Restaurant on premises. Beds: KQDT. Cable TV, phone and VCR in room. Air conditioning. Fax, copier, library, pet boarding and on-line access on premises. Handicap access. Weddings, small meetings, family reunions and seminars hosted. French spoken. Amusement parks, antiquing, fishing, golf, live theater, parks, shopping, cross-country skiing, sporting events, tennis and water sports nearby.

Pets allowed: One dog per room.

Kennebunk Beach   K2

The Ocean View

171 Beach Ave
Kennebunk Beach, ME 04043-2524
(207)967-2750
E-mail: arena@theoceanview.com
Web: www.theoceanview.com

Circa 1900. This brightly painted Victorian is literally just steps to the beach. Nine oceanfront guest rooms are located either in the turn-of-the-century Victorian or in the Ocean View Too, a wing of the main house with four suites. Hand-painted furniture and colorful fabrics decorate the whimsical, eclectic guest rooms. Breakfast is served in an oceanfront breakfast room. Specialties, which are served on colorful china, include baked pears with yogurt, honey and slivered almonds, followed by Belgian waffles topped with seasonal fresh fruit and a dollop creme fraiche. Suite guests also can opt to enjoy breakfast in bed. The village of Kennebunkport is just one mile away.

Historic Interest: National Register Historic Walk.

Innkeeper(s): Carole & Bob Arena. $130-295. MC, VISA, AX, DS, TC. 9 rooms with PB and 5 suites. Breakfast and afternoon tea included in rates. Types of meals: Full gourmet bkfst and early coffee/tea. Beds: KQT. TV, phone, ceiling fan, VCR and luxurious robes in room. Fax, library and fireplaced living room on premises. French spoken. Antiquing, fishing, beach, ocean, live theater, parks, shopping, sporting events and water sports nearby.

Publicity: *Boston Magazine, New York Times Syndicated, Entree, Elegance.*

Kennebunkport   K2

Captain Fairfield Inn

8 Pleasant St
Kennebunkport, ME 04046-2690
(207)967-4454 (800)322-1928 Fax:(207)967-8537
E-mail: jrw@captainfairfield.com
Web: www.captainfairfield.com

Circa 1813. Located in the historic district and only steps to the Village Green and Harbor, this sea captain's mansion features period furnishings in the guest rooms. There are fireplaces, four-poster and canopy beds, down comforters and fresh garden flowers. Breakfast is served next to an open-hearth fireplace in the gathering room.

Innkeeper(s): Janet & Rick Wolf. $110-250. MC, VISA, AX, DC, DS. 9 rooms with PB, 4 with FP and 1 conference room. Types of meals: Full gourmet bkfst and early coffee/tea. Afternoon tea and snacks/refreshments available. Beds: QT. Air conditioning. Small meetings, family reunions and seminars hosted. Antiquing, fishing, live theater, shopping and cross-country skiing nearby.

"How can one improve upon perfection? Stay the course."

Captain Jefferds Inn

PO Box 691, 5 Pearl St
Kennebunkport, ME 04046-0691
(207)967-2311 (800)839-6844 Fax:(207)967-0721
E-mail: captjeff@captainjefferdsinn.com
Web: www.captainjefferdsinn.com

Circa 1804. This Federal-style home was given as a wedding gift from a father to his daughter and new son-in-law. It was constructed the same year Thomas Jefferson was re-elected to

the presidency. Each guest room is different. Several offer two-person whirlpools, eight have a fireplace. Canopy, four-poster and sleigh beds are among the furnishings. In the afternoons, tea is served in the garden room. The breakfasts feature gourmet fare and are served by candlelight. The inn is located in a local historic district, just minutes from shops and restaurants.

Innkeeper(s): Pat & Dick Bartholomew. $135-285. MC, VISA, AX, PC, TC. TAC10. 16 rooms with PB, 8 with FP and 5 suites. Breakfast and afternoon tea included in rates. Types of meals: Full gourmet bkfst, cont and early coffee/tea. Beds: KQDT. Air conditioning. VCR, fax and library on premises. Weddings, small meetings and family reunions hosted. Antiquing, fishing, golf, whale watching, parks, shopping, downhill skiing, cross-country skiing and water sports nearby.

Pets allowed: Dogs with prior approval.

The Captain Lord Mansion

Corner Pleasant & Green, PO Box 800
Kennebunkport, ME 04046
(207)967-3141 Fax:(207)967-3172
E-mail: captain@biddeford.com
Web: www.captainlord.com

Circa 1812. In the National Register, the Captain Lord Mansion was built during the War of 1812 and is one of the finest examples of Federal architecture on the coast of Maine.

The home rests at the edge of the village green within view of the Kennebunk River and within walking distance of the town's many historic sites. The romantically appointed guest

rooms include roomy four-poster beds, gas fireplaces and heated marble and tile floors in the bathrooms. Some rooms include a double Jacuzzi tub. Guests are further pampered with fresh flowers, a full breakfast and afternoon treats.

Innkeeper(s): Bev Davis & Rick Litchfield. $99-399. MC, VISA, DS. TAC7. 16 rooms with PB, 15 with FP and 2 conference rooms. Breakfast included in rates. Types of meals: Full bkfst and early coffee/tea. Afternoon tea available. Beds: KQ. Phone in room. Air conditioning. Fax, copier and library on premises. Small meetings, family reunions and seminars hosted. Antiquing, fishing, live theater, shopping and cross-country skiing nearby.

"A showcase of elegant architecture. Meticulously clean and splendidly appointed. It's a shame to have to leave."

Captains Hideaway

12 Pleasant St
Kennebunkport, ME 04046-2746
(207)967-5711 Fax:(207)967-3843
E-mail: hideaway@cybertours.com
Web: www.captainshideaway.com

Circa 1800. Each of the two guest rooms at this bed & breakfast has been decorated with romance in mind. The Captain's Room features a massive four-poster canopy bed dressed with luxurious linens. The room is further decorated with a Victorian fainting couch that rests at the foot of the bed and a fireplace warms the bedchamber. In addition to this, the spacious bathroom includes a two-person whirlpool tub and another fireplace. The Garden Room is another option, decorated with light lilac floral wallpaper, a lace canopy bed and iron furnishings. This room also includes a whirlpool tub. The innkeepers create a customized breakfast for their guests that might include muffins, croissants, scones and an entrée of waffles, French toast or eggs and bacon.

Historic Interest: Nott House.

Innkeeper(s): Susan Jackson & Judith Hughes-Boulet. $179-279. MC, VISA, PC, TC. 2 rooms with PB, 2 with FP. Breakfast, afternoon tea and snacks/refreshments included in rates. Types of meals: Full gourmet bkfst, cont plus, cont, country bkfst, veg bkfst and early coffee/tea. Beds: KQ. Cable TV, phone, VCR and jacuzzi in room. Air conditioning. Fax on premises. Weddings hosted. Amusement parks, antiquing, art galleries, beaches, bicycling, canoeing/kayaking, fishing, golf, hiking, horseback riding, live theater, museums, parks, shopping, downhill skiing, cross-country skiing, sporting events, tennis and water sports nearby.

Crosstrees

6 South St, PO Box 1333
Kennebunkport, ME 04046-1333
(207)967-2780 (800)564-1527 Fax:(207)967-2610
E-mail: info@crosstrees.com
Web: www.crosstrees.com

Circa 1818. Located in Maine's largest historic district, this Federal-style house was built by Daniel Walker, a descendant of an original Kennebunkport family. Later, Maine artist and archi-

tect Abbot Graves purchased the property and named it "Crosstrees" for its maple trees. The inn features New England antiques and brilliant flower gardens in view of the formal dining

room in spring and summer. A full breakfast is provided. Art galleries, beaches, antiquing and golf are nearby.

Historic Interest: Built by one of the first four families in Kennebunkport.

Innkeeper(s): Dennis Rafferty & Keith Henley. $100-215. MC, VISA, PC, TC. 4 rooms with PB, 3 with FP. Breakfast included in rates. Types of meals: Full bkfst and early coffee/tea. Beds: KQ. Suite with Jacuzzi in room. Weddings, small meetings and family reunions hosted. Antiquing, fishing, ocean, live theater and shopping nearby.

"Absolutely gorgeous inn. You two were wonderful to us. What a great place to relax."

The Inn at Harbor Head

41 Pier Rd
Kennebunkport, ME 04046
(207)967-5564 Fax:(207)967-1294
E-mail: info@harborhead.com
Web: www.harborhead.com

Circa 1890. This shingled saltwater farmhouse is located directly on the water in historic Cape Porpoise — a fishing village where lobstermen have worked for generations. Sounds of sea gulls and bell buoys blend with the foghorn from the lighthouse nearby. There are outstanding views of the harbor, ocean and islands.

Guest rooms feature antiques, paddle fans and down comforters. A gourmet breakfast is served in the Oriental dining room amid collections of silver and crystal.

Innkeeper(s): Eve & Dick Roesler. $130-315. MC, VISA, PC, TC. 4 rooms with PB, 2 with FP and 2 suites. Breakfast included in rates. Types of meals: Full gourmet bkfst and early coffee/tea. Beds: KQ. Turndown service, ceiling fan, phone on request and seating area in room. Air conditioning. Fax, swimming and library on premises. Weddings, small meetings, family reunions and seminars hosted. Amusement parks, antiquing, fishing, live theater, shopping, cross-country skiing and water sports nearby.

Publicity: *Boston Globe, Country Inns, Los Angeles Times, Morning Sentinel.*

"Your lovely home is our image of what a New England B&B should be. Unbelievably perfect! So glad we found you."

Kennebunkport Inn

One Dock Sq
Kennebunkport, ME 04046
(207)967-2621 (800)248-2621 Fax:(207)967-3705

Circa 1899. The Kennebunkport Inn offers a wonderful combination of elegance and relaxation. The main lounge is furnished with velvet loveseats and chintz sofas. Guest rooms are decorated with mahogany queen-size beds, wing chairs and Queen Anne writing desks. Innkeeper Martha Griffin is a gradu-  ate of Paris' prestigious La Varenne Ecole de Cuisine and London's Elizabeth Pomeroy Cooking School. Her culinary creations are unforgettable and award-winning. Maine lobster is a dinner staple, but save room for dessert. The inn also includes a fire-lit lounge with a piano bar.

Historic Interest: Nott House.

Innkeeper(s): Rick & Martha Griffin. $89-289. MC, VISA, AX, PC, TC. TAC10. 34 rooms with PB, 3 with FP and 1 suite. MAP, AP, EP. Type of meal: Full bkfst. Gourmet dinner available. Beds: KQDT. Cable TV, phone, telephone, clock radio and desks in some rooms in room. Air conditioning. Fax, copier and swimming on premises. Small meetings hosted. Amusement parks, antiquing, fishing, live theater, shopping, cross-country skiing and water sports nearby.

"From check-in, to check-out, from breakfast through dinner, we were treated like royalty."

Maine Stay Inn & Cottages

PO Box 500-A
Kennebunkport, ME 04046-6174
(207)967-2117 Fax:(207)967-8757
E-mail: innkeeper@mainestayinn.com
Web: www.mainestayinn.com

Circa 1860. In the National Register, this is a square-block Italianate contoured in a low hip-roof design. Later additions reflecting the Queen Anne period include a suspended spiral staircase, crystal windows, ornately carved mantels and moldings, bay windows and porches. A sea captain built the handsome cupola that became a favorite spot for making taffy. In the '20s, the cupola was a place from which to spot offshore rum-  runners. Guests enjoy afternoon tea with stories of the Maine Stay's heritage. Two suites and one room in the main building and five of the cottage rooms have working fireplaces.

Innkeeper(s): Carol & Lindsay Copeland. $105-250. MC, VISA, AX, PC, TC. 17 rooms with PB, 9 with FP, 4 suites and 10 cottages. Breakfast and afternoon tea included in rates. Types of meals: Full bkfst and early coffee/tea. Beds: KQDT. Cable TV and four rooms with whirlpool tubs in room. Air conditioning. Fax, copier and child care on premises. Amusement parks, antiquing, fishing, whale watching, live theater, shopping, cross-country skiing and water sports nearby.

"We have traveled the East Coast from Martha's Vineyard to Bar Harbor, and this is the only place we know we must return to."

The Inn on South Street

PO Box 478A
Kennebunkport, ME 04046-1778
(207)967-5151 (800)963-5151
E-mail: innkeeper@innonsouthst.com
Web: www.innonsouthst.com

Circa 1806. This early 19th-century Greek Revival manor is within walking distance of Kennebunkport's many shops, restaurants and the ocean. A unique "Good Morning" staircase will be one of the first items guests will notice upon entering the inn. Richly appointed rooms are full of beautiful furnishings, lovely window dressings and pine plank floors. Guests will enjoy such amenities as telephones, fireplaces and fresh flowers in the guest rooms. Breakfasts are a treat, served up in the second-floor country kitchen with views of the river and ocean or, if weather permits, in the garden. The morning meal features special dishes with herbs from the inn's herb garden.

Historic Interest: Kennebunkport boasts many two- and three-story wooden Federal-style dwellings, which date back to the early 19th century. Cape Arundel, one mile away, features the work of John Calvin Stevens, a noted 19th-century architect. Among the roomy summer cottages he created was the home of former President Bush.

Innkeeper(s): Jacques & Eva Downs. $105-245. MC, VISA. 3 rooms with PB, 1 with FP and 1 suite. Breakfast and afternoon tea included in rates.

Types of meals: Full gourmet bkfst and early coffee/tea. Beds: QT. Phone in room. German, Spanish and Russian spoken. Antiquing, fishing, live theater, parks and water sports nearby.

"Superb hospitality. We were delighted by the atmosphere and your thoughtfulness."

Kittery   L2

Enchanted Nights B&B

29 Wentworth St, Rt 103
Kittery, ME 03904-1720
(207)439-1489
E-mail: info@enchanted-nights-bandb.com
Web: www.enchanted-nights-bandb.com

Circa 1890. The innkeepers bill this unique inn as a "Victorian fantasy for the romantic at heart." Each of the guest rooms is unique, from the spacious rooms with double

whirlpool tubs to the cozy turret room. A whimsical combination of country French and Victorian decor permeates the interior. Wrought-iron beds and hand-painted furnishings add to the ambiance. Breakfasts, often with a vegetarian theme, are served with gourmet coffee in the morning room on antique floral china.

Historic Interest: There are museums, forts, churches, historic homes and buildings all within five miles in Portsmouth, NH and Kittery.

Innkeeper(s): Nancy Bogerberger & Peter Lamandia. $47-222. MC, VISA, AX, DS, PC, TC. 6 rooms with PB. Breakfast included in rates. Type of meal: Full gourmet bkfst. Beds: QD. Cable TV, ceiling fan, VCR and 2 rooms handicap access in room. Air conditioning. Refrigerator on premises. Handicap access. Weddings, small meetings, family reunions and seminars hosted. Antiquing, outlet shopping, historic homes, whale watching, museums harbor cruises, live theater and parks nearby.

"The atmosphere was great. Your breakfast was elegant. The breakfast room made us feel we had gone back in time. All in all it was a very enjoyable stay."

Little Deer Isle   G8

Eggemoggin Inn

RFD Box 324
Little Deer Isle, ME 04650
(207)348-2540

Circa 1906. This old Maine inn, with wide wraparound porch, was once a private estate. Located at the end of a 300-yard dirt road, the inn features modest accommodations, most with twin beds. However, the location is superb, sitting on a secluded point overlooking the ocean. Run since 1964 as a tourist house, there is an extra charge for the continental and full breakfast.

Innkeeper(s): Barbara Broadhead-Allen. $90-125125. 10 rooms, 1 with PB, 2 with FP. Types of meals: Full bkfst and cont. Phone in room.

Lubec   G8

Peacock House

27 Summer St
Lubec, ME 04652-1134
(207)733-2403

Circa 1860. Built by a sea captain from Bedford, England, the inn is nestled in the country's most northeastern town. Six generations of the Peacock family have lived here, hosting some prominent people. Guests included Margaret Chase Smith, several governors, Donald McMillen (Arctic explorer), Sen. Edmund Muskie and members of the Roosevelt family and their staff. The house originally was constructed as a Victorian with later updates making it more of a mixture of Federal and Greek Revival architectural styles. The Bay of Fundy is two blocks away. The Peacock House is the county's only three-diamond rated B&B.

Historic Interest: The island home of Franklin Delano Roosevelt is a nearby historic attraction.

Innkeeper(s): Chet & Veda Childs. $60-80. MC, VISA. 5 rooms with PB and 3 suites. Breakfast and afternoon tea included in rates. Type of meal: Full bkfst. Beds: KQT. Fax on premises. Handicap access. Antiquing nearby.

"A perfect B&B — great beds, fantastic breakfast and a hospitable family."

Naples   J2

Inn at Long Lake

Lake House Rd, PO Box 806
Naples, ME 04055
(207)693-6226 (800)437-0328
E-mail: innatll@megalink.net
Web: www.innatlonglake.com

Circa 1906. Reopened in 1988, the inn housed the overflow guests from the Lake House resort about 90 years ago. Guests traveled to the resort via the Oxford-Cumberland Canal, and each room is named for a historic canal boat. The cozy rooms offer fluffy comforters and a warm, country decor in a romantic atmosphere. Warm up

in front of a crackling fire in the great room, or enjoy a cool Long Lake breeze on the veranda while watching horses in nearby pastures. The setting is ideal for housing guests for weddings or reunions.

Historic Interest: Songo Locks, Shaker Museum, Jones Glass Museum.

Innkeeper(s): Maynard & Irene Hincks. $49-158. MC, VISA, DS, PC, TC. TAC10. 16 rooms with PB, 2 suites and 1 conference room. Breakfast included in rates. Types of meals: Cont plus and early coffee/tea. Beds: QDT. TV in room. Air conditioning. Library on premises. Weddings, family reunions and seminars hosted. Spanish and French spoken. Antiquing, fishing, biking, hiking, parks, shopping, downhill skiing, cross-country skiing and water sports nearby.

"Convenient location, tastefully done and the prettiest inn I've ever stayed in."

Lamb's Mill Inn

RR 1, Box 676, Lambs Mill Rd
Naples, ME 04055
(207)693-6253

Circa 1800. This cheery, yellow farmhouse offers six guest rooms, each filled with comfortable furnishings. Guests are pampered with down comforters, a hot tub and 20 peaceful acres of woods, fields and perennial gardens. Fresh vegetable

frittata with items picked from the garden and raspberry Belgian waffles are among the breakfast entrees. Evening snacks are served as well. The home is close to cross-country and alpine skiing, golf, tennis, parasailing, shopping, restaurants and antiquing.

Innkeeper(s): Laurel Tinkham & Sandy Long. $85-120. MC, VISA, PC, TC. TAC10. 6 rooms with PB. Breakfast, afternoon tea and snacks/refreshments included in rates. Types of meals: Full gourmet bkfst and early coffee/tea. Beds: KQ. Cable TV and turndown service in room. Air conditioning. VCR, spa, library and outside stone barbeque pit on premises. Weddings and family reunions hosted. Antiquing, fishing, live theater, parks, shopping, downhill skiing, cross-country skiing and water sports nearby.

"We really enjoyed our week in your lovely home."

New Harbor   J4

Gosnold Arms

146 State Route 32
New Harbor, ME 04554
(207)677-3727 Fax:(207)677-2662
Web: www.gosnold.com

Circa 1840. Located on the historic Pemaquid peninsula, the Gosnold Arms includes a remodeled, saltwater farmhouse situated on a rise above the harbor. There are several cottages and many accommodations with views. A cozy lounge offers two large stone fireplaces and a glassed-in dining porch overlooking the water.

Historic Interest: Pemaquid archaeological dig at Pemaquid Beach; Pemaquid Lighthouse and Fisherman's Museum (1 mile), Summer boat to Monhegan Island from New Harbor (1 hour ride).

Innkeeper(s): The Phinney Family. $89-154. MC, VISA, PC, TC. 25 rooms with PB and 14 cottages. Breakfast included in rates. Type of meal: Full bkfst. Beds: QDT. Antiquing, fishing and live theater nearby.

Publicity: *New York, Down East.*

Northeast Harbor   I6

Asticou Inn

PO Box 337, Rt 3/198
Northeast Harbor, ME 04662
(207)276-3344 (800)258-3373 Fax:(207)276-3373

Circa 1883. Offering splendid vistas of the mountains and the blue waters of Northeast Harbor, this treasured old inn is one of Mount Desert Island's two remaining luxury Victorian hotels. In the National Register, the gray-shingled and gabled

inn was rebuilt after a fire in 1899. Asticou is the name of a chief of the Penobscot Native American tribe who lived in the area in 1613 when Champlain first came. Guest rooms are decorated with summer furniture, wicker and antiques. Across the road is the Asticou Azealea Gardens, dazzling in spring but inviting in all seasons. The inn offers a game room, TV room, lobby, bar, deck and covered porch. The dining room boasts a large menu, which includes lamb, filet mignon, salmon and Maine lobster.

Innkeeper(s): Joseph J. Joy. $120-349. MC, VISA, PC, TC. TAC10. 47 rooms with PB, 10 with FP, 13 suites and 2 conference rooms. Breakfast and dinner included in rates. MAP. Types of meals: Full gourmet bkfst and early coffee/tea. Afternoon tea, picnic lunch, banquet service, catering service and room service available. Restaurant on premises. Beds: KQDT. Phone and turndown service in room. VCR, fax, copier, swimming, tennis, library and child care on premises. Weddings, small meetings, family reunions and seminars hosted. Antiquing, fishing, golf, parks, shopping, tennis and water sports nearby.

Publicity: *Down East.*

Ogunquit   K2

Chestnut Tree Inn

PO Box 2201
Ogunquit, ME 03907-2201
(207)646-4529 (800)362-0757

Circa 1870. Gable roofs peak out from the top of this Victorian inn, which has greeted guests for more than a century. A smattering of antiques and Victorian decor creates a 19th-century

atmosphere. Guests can relax on the porch or head out for a stroll on Marginal Way, a mile-long path set along Maine's scenic coastline. The beach, shops, Ogunquit Playhouse and a variety of restaurants are just a few minutes down the road.

Innkeeper(s): Cynthia Diana & Ronald St. Laurent. $35-125. MC, VISA, AX, TC. TAC10. 22 rooms, 15 with PB and 1 suite. Type of meal: Cont plus. Beds: QDT. Cable TV and phone in room. Air conditioning. Family reunions hosted. French spoken. Amusement parks, antiquing, fishing, live theater, parks, shopping, downhill skiing, cross-country skiing, sporting events and water sports nearby.

"Your inn was absolutely beautiful and peaceful. Your kindness will not be forgotten."

Hartwell House Inn & Conference Center

118 Shore Rd, PO Box 393
Ogunquit, ME 03907-0393
(207)646-7210 (800)235-8883
E-mail: hartwell@cybertours.com
Web: www.hartwellhouseinn.com

Circa 1921. Hartwell House offers suites and guest rooms furnished with distinctive early American and English antiques. Many rooms are available with French doors opening to private balconies overlooking sculpted flower gardens. Guests are treated to both a full, gourmet breakfast and afternoon tea. Seasonal dining packages are available. Restaurants, beaches, hiking and outlet shopping is nearby.

Innkeeper(s): Christopher & Tracey Anderson. $90-190. MC, VISA, AX, DS,

TC. 16 rooms with PB, 3 suites and 4 conference rooms. Type of meal: Full gourmet bkfst. Afternoon tea and catering service available. Beds: QT. TV and ceiling fan in room. Air conditioning. Fax on premises. Weddings hosted. Antiquing, fishing, restaurants, outlet and boutique shopping, beaches, live theater, parks, shopping, cross-country skiing, sporting events and water sports nearby.

Publicity: *Innsider.*

"This engaging country inn will be reserved for my special clients."

Rockmere Lodge

40 Stearns Rd
Ogunquit, ME 03907
(207)646-2985 Fax:(207)646-6947

Circa 1899. Offering an outstanding view of the Atlantic from its site on Marginal Way (the town's oceanside path), this shingle-style Victorian is enhanced by gardens, fountains and a wraparound veranda filled with white wicker. The inn is furnished with period antiques and Victorian collectibles. Every room except one enjoys an ocean view. Walk to galleries, boutiques and fine restaurants. Ten miles south is Kittery, a center for factory outlets.

Innkeeper(s): Andy Antoniuk & Bob Brown. $75-175. MC, VISA, AX, DS, TC. 8 rooms with PB. Type of meal: Cont plus. Beds: QD. Cable TV in room. VCR, fax and library on premises. Antiquing, fishing, golf, live theater, parks, shopping, cross-country skiing, sporting events and water sports nearby.

Yardarm Village Inn

142 Shore Rd, PO Box 773
Ogunquit, ME 03907-0773
(207)646-7006 (888)927-3276 Fax:(207)646-9034

Circa 1874. This three-story white inn is decorated with black shutters and features a wide covered front veranda lined with wicker rocking chairs for those who wish to enjoy the ocean view. Guest rooms are done in a Colonial-country style with comfortable furnishings. For an additional charge, the innkeepers will provide a light, continental breakfast. The innkeepers also offer two cottages. The inn houses a wine and cheese shop.

Innkeeper(s): L.C. & P.C. Drury. $69-99. PC, TC. 8 rooms with PB, 3 suites and 2 cottages. Beds: KQDT. Cable TV in room. Air conditioning. Fax and copier on premises. Small meetings and family reunions hosted. Amusement parks, fishing, golf, live theater, parks, shopping, tennis and water sports nearby.

Old Orchard Beach K2

Atlantic Birches Inn

20 Portland Ave Rt 98
Old Orchard Beach, ME 04064-2212
(207)934-5295 (888)934-5295
E-mail: info@atlanticbirches.com
Web: www.atlanticbirches.com

Circa 1903. The front porch of this Shingle-style Victorian and 1920s bungalow are shaded by white birch trees. Badminton and croquet are set up on the lawn. The houses are a place

for relaxation and enjoyment, uncluttered, simple havens filled with comfortable furnishings. The guest rooms are decorated with a few antiques and pastel wallcoverings. Maine's coast offers an endless amount of activities, from boating to whale watching. It is a five-minute walk to the beach and the pier.

Innkeeper(s): Dan & Cyndi Bolduc. $85-109. MC, VISA, AX, DS, TC. TAC10. 10 rooms with PB. Breakfast included in rates. EP. Type of meal: Cont plus. Beds: KQDT. Ceiling fan in room. Air conditioning. VCR, copier, swimming and library on premises. Small meetings and family reunions hosted. French spoken. Amusement parks, antiquing, fishing, parks, shopping, sporting events and water sports nearby.

"Your home and family are just delightful! What a treat to stay in such a warm & loving home."

Oquossoc G2

Oquossoc's Own B&B

Rangeley Ave, PO Box 27
Oquossoc, ME 04964-0027
(207)864-5584

Circa 1903. The recreation-rich mountains of Western Maine are home to this Victorian inn, which offers five guest rooms and easy access to local outdoor attractions. The inn's living room offers a cozy spot for guests to read or watch TV. Basketball and tennis courts are nearby, and a grocery store and post office are within easy walking distance of the inn. Innkeeper Joanne Conner Koob is well-known in the area for her catering skills. The Saddleback Mountain Ski Area, elevation 4,116 feet, is nearby. Three popular restaurants and the marina cove are within walking distance.

Innkeeper(s): Joanne Conner Koob. $65. 5 rooms. Types of meals: Full bkfst and early coffee/tea. Picnic lunch and catering service available. VCR on premises. Small meetings and family reunions hosted. Antiquing, shopping, downhill skiing and cross-country skiing nearby.

Poland I2

Wolf Cove Inn

5 Jordan Shore Dr
Poland, ME 04274-7111
(207)998-4976 Fax:(207)998-7049
E-mail: wolfcove@exploremaine.com
Web: www.wolfcoveinn.com

Circa 1910. The pristine lakeside setting of this inn calms the spirit of the busiest city slicker, and there are more than two acres of grounds with perennial gardens, giant pine trees and an herb garden. The inn offers a variety of rooms, most with lake or garden views, period furnishings and queen or king beds. Request a third-floor room for a fireplace and whirlpool tub. The Calla Lily Suite includes a sitting area as well as a tub overlooking Tripp Lake. The Magnolia Room is the largest guest room and has views of Tripp Lake. The inn's favorite guest space is the flagstone terrace overlooking the water. Breakfast offerings are provided in the glassed-in porch (also a great spot to watch the sunset).

Historic Interest: All Souls Chapel, The Maine Stark building, Paris Hill.
Innkeeper(s): Rose Aikman. $70-250. MC, VISA, AX, PC, TC. 10 rooms, 4 with PB. Breakfast and snacks/refreshments included in rates. Types of meals: Full bkfst and early coffee/tea. Beds: KQT. Air conditioning. VCR, fax, spa and swimming on premises. Weddings, small meetings, family reunions and seminars hosted. Antiquing, beaches, bicycling, canoeing/kayaking, golf, hiking, horseback riding, shopping, downhill skiing and cross-country skiing nearby.

Portland   J3

Inn At St John

939 Congress St
Portland, ME 04102-3031
(207)773-6481 (800)636-9127 Fax:(207)756-7629
E-mail: info@innatstjohn
Web: www.innatstjohn.com

Circa 1897. Tucked on a city street, this Victorian inn is conveniently located near many Portland sites, including museums, restaurants and shops. The guest rooms feature antiques and traditional furnishings, and hardwood floors are topped with Oriental rugs. Pictures showcasing Portland's railroad history are on display. The inn is European in style, and some rooms have a shared bath. Children are welcome, and those younger than 12 can stay for free.

Innkeeper(s): Paul Hood. $36-146. MC, VISA, AX, DC, CB, DS, PC, TC. TAC15. 40 rooms, 26 with PB. Breakfast included in rates. Types of meals: Cont plus and early coffee/tea. Beds: KQDT. Cable TV and phone in room. Air conditioning. Fax, copier, library, child care, bicycle storage and free parking on premises. Weddings and family reunions hosted. Amusement parks, antiquing, fishing, golf, historic district, live theater, parks, shopping, cross-country skiing, sporting events, tennis and water sports nearby.

Pets allowed: Not to be left unattended in guest room.

Publicity: *Down East, Portland Press Herald.*

"We were surprised at how much charm there is tucked in to this building."

West End Inn

146 Pine St
Portland, ME 04102-3541
(207)772-1377 (800)338-1377

Circa 1871. Located in Portland's Western Promenade Historic District, this Georgian-style inn is one of many Victorian-era homes found there. Rooms are decorated with four-poster, canopy beds. The inn's
full, New England-style
breakfasts include such
items as blueberry
pancakes, sausage,
eggs and fruit. The
menu changes daily
and guests may opt for
lighter fare. An afternoon tea also is served

and provides a perfect opportunity to relax after an activity-filled day. The inn also offers facilities for meetings, reunions and wedding receptions. The Museum of Art and the University of South Maine are nearby.

Innkeeper(s): John Leonard and Kelly Gillespie. $99-189. MC, VISA, AX, PC. TAC10. 6 rooms with PB. Breakfast included in rates. Type of meal: Full bkfst. Beds: KQT. Cable TV, phone and ceiling fan in room. Bicycles and library on premises. Small meetings hosted. Antiquing, fishing, live theater, parks, shopping, downhill skiing, cross-country skiing, sporting events and water sports nearby.

Rockland   I5

Lakeshore Inn Bed & Breakfast

184 Lakeview Dr (Rt 17)
Rockland, ME 04841-5705
(207)594-4209 Fax:(207)596-6407
E-mail: lakshore@midcoast.com
Web: www.midcoast.com/~lakshore

Circa 1767. Surrounded by a 200-year-old apple orchard, hemlock and pine trees, this recently renovated farmhouse is one of the most historic buildings in the area. Providing pleasant vistas, the inn's green lawns slope down toward the lake. It was built

by one of the 23 children of Isaiah Tolman. Each of the guest rooms offer a view of Lake Chickawaukie, and two have decks. Guests are invited to enjoy the outdoor Jacuzzi hot tub spa or come indoors to sit by one of the cozy fireplaces. Breakfast includes entrees such as feta omelets and Belgian waffles.

Innkeeper(s): Joseph McCluskey & Paula Nicols. $120-135. MC, VISA, AX, PC, TC. TAC10. 4 rooms with PB. Breakfast included in rates. Types of meals: Full gourmet bkfst and early coffee/tea. Beds: Q. Phone, fluffy robes, hair dryers, soaps, chocolates and theme baskets are available by prior arrangement in room. Air conditioning. VCR, fax, copier, library and massage therapist and relfexologist on call by prior arrangement on premises. Weddings, small meetings and family reunions hosted. Greek spoken. Antiquing, fishing, golf, shopping and water sports nearby.

Publicity: *Bangor Daily News.*

Searsport   H5

Brass Lantern Inn

81 W Main St
Searsport, ME 04974-3501
(207)548-0150 (800)691-0150

Circa 1850. This Victorian inn is nestled at the edge of the woods on a rise overlooking Penobscot Bay. Showcased throughout the inn are many collectibles, antiques and family heirlooms, as well as artifacts from innkeeper Maggie Zieg's home in
England and
two-year stay in
Ethiopia. Enjoy
breakfast by candlelight in the
dining room
with its ornate
tin ceiling,
where you'll

feast on Maine blueberry pancakes and other sumptuous treats. Centrally located between Camden and Bar Harbor, Searsport is known as the antique capital of Maine. There are many local attractions, including the Penobscot Marine Museum, fine shops and restaurants, as well as a public boat facility.

Historic Interest: Fort Knox (8 miles).

Innkeeper(s): Maggie & Dick Zieg. $75-95. MC, VISA, DS, PC, TC. TAC5. 5 rooms with PB. Breakfast included in rates. Meals: Full bkfst and early coffee/tea. Beds: QDT. Library on premises. Small meetings and family reunions hosted. Antiquing, fishing, live theater, parks, shopping and cross-country skiing nearby.

Publicity: *Country Living, Republication Journal, Travel Today, Down East, Saturday Evening Post,* AAA Car & Travel.

"Very elegant surrounding, cozy atmosphere. We felt really spoiled. It was my daughter's first stay at a B&B and she's still praising the blueberry pancakes. Everything was just perfect!"

Searsport (Waldo County)   H5

Watchtide...B&B by the Sea

190 W Main St, US Rt 1
Searsport (Waldo County), ME 04974-3514
(207)548-6575 (800)698-6575
E-mail: stay@watchtide.com
Web: www.watchtide.com

Circa 1795. Originally built for a sea captain, this is a New England salt-water cape house. It was once owned by General Henry Knox, first Secretary of War. There are nearly four seaside acres of lawns and gardens, as well as a bird sanctuary and spectacular views of Penobscot Bay. Four individually decorated

rooms are available, all with private baths and one with a double Jacuzzi. The innkeeper's motto, "we love to spoil our guests," is apparent in the morning in the four-course gourmet breakfast served on the 60-foot-long wicker furnished sun porch, which overlooks the inn's bird sanctuary and the bay. Angels to Antiques is a shop on the premises with the resident artist. (Special guest discounts are offered.) Walk to the beach at Moosepoint State Park, or enjoy the area's lighthouses, sea sports, theater, or golf, boating and fishing.

Historic Interest: Penobscot Marine Museum, Acadia National Park (nearby).

Innkeeper(s): Nancy-Linn Nellis & Jack Elliott. $75-145. MC, VISA, DS, PC, TC. TAC15. 4 rooms with PB. Breakfast and snacks/refreshments included in rates. Types of meals: Full gourmet bkfst and early coffee/tea. Beds: KDT. Turndown service in room. Library on premises. Limited French spoken. Antiquing, fishing, lighthouses, live theater, parks, shopping, sporting events and water sports nearby.

South Berwick   K2

Academy Street Inn

15 Academy St
South Berwick, ME 03908-1506
(207)384-5633

Circa 1903. Built at the turn of the 20th-century, Academy Street Inn features an elegant mix of Colonial and Victorian architecture. The home was built by a prominent local lawyer and remained in his family until the 1950s. From there, it became a restaurant, then faculty housing for a local private

school. It was restored and opened as a bed & breakfast inn in the mid-1980s. The home is decorated in period style with antiques and Oriental rugs. The huge, screened-in porch offers a wonderful spot for conversation and relaxation. Guests

begin the day with a gourmet breakfast featuring unique recipes. The morning fare might include a starter of homemade Granny Smith apple soup and an entrée of spinach and mushroom egg bake with sweet potato relish and New England sausage. The area offers many historical attractions, and beaches, outlet shops and the University of New Hampshire also are nearby.

Historic Interest: Strawbery Bank (14 miles), Fort Foster (15 miles), Fort McClary (13 miles), Old York Village (12 miles).

Innkeeper(s): Paul & Lee Fopeano. $65-75. MC, VISA, AX, DS, PC, TC. 5 rooms with PB and 1 conference room. Breakfast and afternoon tea included in rates. Types of meals: Full bkfst, veg bkfst and early coffee/tea. Banquet service available. Beds: QDT. Ceiling fan in room. Weddings, small meetings, family reunions and seminars hosted. Amusement parks, antiquing, art galleries, beaches, bicycling, canoeing/kayaking, fishing, golf, hiking, horseback riding, live theater, museums, parks, shopping, downhill skiing, cross-country skiing, sporting events, tennis, water sports and wineries nearby.

Southwest Harbor   I6

Harbour Cottage Inn

9 Dirigo
Southwest Harbor, ME 04679-0258
(207)244-5738 Fax:(207)244-7003

Circa 1870. Originally known as the Island House cottage, this historic inn served as an annex for a summer hotel. Eventually, it turned into a boarding house and was used as apartments. Now more than a century old, the inn has returned to its original purpose, accommodating the many guests who flock to Maine's idyllic seashore. Some guest rooms offer a harbor view, and room sizes range from a cozy little room with a whirlpool tub to rooms with king-size canopy beds and sitting areas. Clawfoot or whirlpool tubs are available in many rooms. For breakfast, guests enjoy items such as homemade granola and freshly baked muffins or breads with an entree of perhaps blueberry pancakes or eggs Benedict. Bar Harbor and Acadia National Park are about 20 minutes away, and museums, lighthouses, restaurants and shops are nearby.

Innkeeper(s): Glenda & Mike Sekulich. $70-145. MC, VISA, AX, DS, PC, TC. TAC5. 8 rooms, 7 with PB and 1 suite. Breakfast included in rates. Meals: Full bkfst, cont plus, cont and early coffee/tea. Snacks/refreshments available. Beds: KQDT. Ceiling fan, TV in suite and hair dryers in room. VCR on premises. Small meetings and family reunions hosted. Antiquing, fishing, golf, live theater, parks, shopping, cross-country skiing, tennis and water sports nearby.

The Island House

121 Clark Point Rd
Southwest Harbor, ME 04679
(207)244-5180

Circa 1850. The first guests arrived at Deacon Clark's door as early as 1832. When steamboat service from Boston began in the 1850s, the Island House became a popular summer hotel. Among the guests was Ralph Waldo Emerson. In 1912, the hotel was taken down and rebuilt as two separate homes using much of the woodwork from the original building.

Innkeeper(s): Ann and Charles Bradford. $50-165. MC, VISA. 5 rooms with PB and 2 suites. Breakfast and afternoon tea included in rates. Types of meals: Full bkfst and early coffee/tea. Beds: KQDT. TV in room. VCR, library, efficiency apartment has refrigerator; radio, TV and stove clock on premises. Small meetings and family reunions hosted. Amusement parks, antiquing, fishing, golf, sailing, whale watching, live theater, parks, shopping, cross-country skiing and tennis nearby.

"Island House is a delight from the moment one enters the door! We loved the thoughtful extras. You've made our vacation very special!"

The Lambs Ear Inn

60 Clark Point Rd, PO Box 30
Southwest Harbor, ME 04679-0030
(207)244-9828 Fax:(207)244-9924

Circa 1857. This stately colonial inn was built by Captain Mayo, one of the town's earliest settlers. Guests can view lobster boats, sailing ships and all the other activities of Southwest Harbor. The harbor is surrounded by Acadia National Park with its pristine pine forests, lakes and mountains. Breakfasts at the inn are known to be as artistic as they are excellent.

Innkeeper(s): Elizabeth Hoke. $85-165. MC, VISA, PC, TC. 6 rooms, 8 with PB, 2 with FP and 1 suite. Breakfast and afternoon tea included in rates. Meals: Full gourmet bkfst and early coffee/tea. Beds: QDT. Cable TV in room. Amusement parks, antiquing, fishing, live theater, parks, shopping, cross-country skiing and water sports nearby.

"The food is delicious, the presentation is beautiful."

Lindenwood Inn

PO Box 1328
Southwest Harbor, ME 04679-1328
(207)244-5335

Circa 1906. Sea Captain Mills named his home "The Lindens" after stately linden trees in the front lawn. Elegantly refurbished, this historic house features many items collected from the new innkeeper's world travels. The rooms have sun-drenched balconies overlooking the harbor and its sailboats and lobster boats. A hearty full breakfast is served in the dining room with a roaring fireplace in the winter. The inn has a heated, in-ground swimming pool and a spa. From the inn you may take a tree-lined path down to the wharf.

Innkeeper(s): Esther Cavagnaro. $75-245. MC, VISA, DS. 18 rooms with PB and 5 suites. Breakfast included in rates. Types of meals: Full bkfst and early coffee/tea. Beds: QDT. Cable TV, phone and ceiling fan in room. Spa, swimming, bicycles and child care on premises. Weddings, small meetings, family reunions and seminars hosted. Amusement parks, antiquing, fishing, shopping, cross-country skiing and water sports nearby.

Publicity: *McCall's.*

"We had a lovely stay at your inn. Breakfast, room and hospitality were all first-rate. You made us feel like a special friend instead of a paying guest."

Spruce Head   J5

Craignair Inn

533 Clark Island Rd
Spruce Head, ME 04859
(207)594-7644 (800)320-9997 Fax:(207)596-7124

Circa 1930. Craignair originally was built to house stonecutters working in nearby granite quarries. Overlooking the docks of the Clark Island Quarry, where granite schooners once were loaded, this roomy, three-story inn is tastefully decorated with local antiques. A bountiful continental breakfast is served in the inn's dining room which offers scenic ocean and coastline views.

Historic Interest: General Knox (Washington's Secretary of War) Mansion, called Montpelier (8 miles).

Innkeeper(s): Steve & Neva Joseph. $83-120. MC, VISA, PC, TC. TAC10. 24 rooms, 8 with PB. Breakfast included in rates. Type of meal: Cont plus. Gourmet dinner, banquet service and catering service available. Restaurant on premises. Beds: KDT. Phone and fax and copier on premises. Weddings, small meetings, family reunions and seminars hosted. Antiquing, fishing, live theater, parks, shopping, downhill skiing, cross-country skiing and water sports nearby.

Pets Allowed.

Publicity: *Boston Globe, Free Press, Tribune.*

"A coastal oasis of fine food and outstanding service with colonial maritime ambiance!"

Tenants Harbor   J4

East Wind Inn

Mechanic St, PO Box 149
Tenants Harbor, ME 04860-0149
(207)372-6366 (800)241-8439 Fax:(207)372-6320
E-mail: info@eastwindinn.com
Web: www.eastwindinn.com

Circa 1860. This seaside inn affords vistas of the nearby harbor and islands. The inn is comprised of a former sail loft, a captain's house, the Meeting House and adjacent Wheeler Cottage, all restored. Rooms and suites are decorated with antiques. Breakfast is served in the dining room overlooking the harbor, also the location of evening dining by candlelight. Guests can relax on one of the wraparound porches and enjoy gentle sea breezes coming in over manicured lawns and bright flower beds, or stroll around 350 feet of waterfront. For a special treat, board the historic Friendship Sloop Surprise, which departs three times daily from the inn's private dock.

Innkeeper(s): Tim Watts & Joy Taylor. $96-275. MC, VISA, AX, DS, PC, TC. TAC10. 26 rooms, 12 with PB, 3 suites, 4 cottages and 1 conference room. Breakfast included in rates. Type of meal: Full bkfst. Dinner and banquet service available. Beds: KQDT. Phone in room. VCR, fax, copier, library and grand piano on premises. Weddings, small meetings, family reunions and seminars hosted. Antiquing, fishing, golf, museums, Farnsworth and Owls Head transportation, sailing, island trips, tennis and water sports nearby.

Pets allowed: By arrangement.

Walpole   J4

Brannon-Bunker Inn

349 S St Rt 129
Walpole, ME 04573
(207)563-5941 (800)563-9225

Circa 1820. This Cape-style house has been a home to many generations of Maine residents, one of whom was captain of a ship that sailed to the Arctic. During the '20s, the barn served as a dance hall. Later, it was converted into comfortable guest rooms. Victorian and American antiques are featured, and there are collections of military and political memorabilia.

Innkeeper(s): Joe & Jeanne Hovance. $60-75. MC, VISA, AX, PC, TC. TAC10. 8 rooms, 5 with PB and 1 suite. Breakfast included in rates. Type of meal: Cont plus. Beds: QDT. TV in room. VCR, library and child care on premises. Handicap access. Weddings, small meetings and family reunions hosted. Antiquing, fishing, golf, live theater, parks, shopping, cross-country skiing, tennis and water sports nearby.

"Wonderful beds, your gracious hospitality and the very best muffins anywhere made our stay a memorable one."

Waterford   I2

Kedarburn Inn

Rt 35 Box 61
Waterford, ME 04088
(207)583-6182 Fax:(207)583-6424

Circa 1858. The innkeepers of this Victorian establishment invite guests to try a taste of olde English hospitality and cuisine at their inn, nestled in the foothills of the White

Mountains in Western Maine. Located in a historic village, the inn sits beside the flowing Kedar Brook, which runs to the shores of Lake Keoka. Each of the spacious rooms is decorated with handmade quilts and dried flowers. Explore the inn's shop and you'll discover a variety of quilts and crafts, all made by innkeeper Margaret Gibson. Ask about special quilting weekends. With prior reservation, the innkeepers will prepare an English afternoon tea.

Innkeeper(s): Margaret & Derek Gibson. $71-125. MC, VISA, AX, DS, PC, TC. 7 rooms, 5 with PB, 1 suite and 1 conference room. Breakfast included in rates. Types of meals: Full bkfst and early coffee/tea. Afternoon tea, dinner, snacks/refreshments, banquet service, catering service and room service available. Restaurant on premises. Beds: KQDT. Air conditioning. VCR, fax and PC computer on premises. Weddings, small meetings, family reunions and seminars hosted. Antiquing, fishing, live theater, shopping, downhill skiing, cross-country skiing and water sports nearby.

Publicity: *Maine Times.*

Weld   H2

Kawanhee Inn Lakeside Lodge

Rt 142 Webb Lk
Weld, ME 04285
(207)585-2000

Circa 1929. This rustic lodge offers outstanding views of Webb Lake and the surrounding mountains (Tumbledown, Big

Jackson, Mt. Blue and Bald Mt.). Four-foot logs are often thrown on the fire in the massive fieldstone fireplace. Both cabins and lodge rooms are available, and if you reserve ahead you may be able to stay in one at the water's edge. Gold panning on the Swift River, enjoying the sandy beach, moose watching, viewing Angel Falls and Smalls Falls and hiking are favorite activities.

Innkeeper(s): Martha Strunk & Sturges Butler. $65-165. MC, VISA. TAC15. 9 rooms, 5 with PB, 1 suite and 12 cabins. EP. Types of meals: Cont and early coffee/tea. Dinner, picnic lunch and banquet service available. Restaurant on premises. Beds: QDT. Canoe and kayak rentals on premises. Weddings, small meetings, family reunions and seminars hosted. Antiquing, fishing, gold panning, hiking, sandy beach, parks, shopping and tennis nearby.

Pets allowed: Some cabins, not the Inn.

Publicity: *1997 & 1998 Editor Pick Yankee Magazine Travel Guide.*

"It was just great, relaxed and fun!"

West Boothbay Harbor   J4

Lawnmeer Inn

PO Box 505
West Boothbay Harbor, ME 04575-0505
(800)633-7645
E-mail: cooncat@lawnmeerinn.com
Web: www.lawnmeerinn.com

Circa 1899. This pleasant inn sits by the shoreline, providing a picturesque oceanfront setting. Located on a small, wooded island, it is accessed by a lift bridge. Family-oriented rooms are clean and homey, and there is a private honeymoon cottage in the Smoke House. The dining room is waterside and serves continental cuisine with an emphasis on seafood. Boothbay Harbor is two miles away.

Innkeeper(s): Lee & Jim Metzger. $90-195. MC, VISA. TAC10. 32 rooms with PB, 1 suite and 1 cottage. Types of meals: Full bkfst and early coffee/tea. Gourmet dinner and banquet service available. Restaurant on premises. Beds: KQD. Weddings, small meetings and family reunions hosted. Antiquing, fishing, live theater, shopping and water sports nearby.

Pets allowed: Small pets-one per room.

Publicity: *Los Angeles Times, Getaways for Gourmets.*

"Your hospitality was warm and gracious and the food delectable."

Wiscasset   J4

The Squire Tarbox Inn

Box 1181 Westport Island
Wiscasset, ME 04578-3501
(207)882-7693 Fax:(207)882-7107
E-mail: squiretarbox@ime.net
Web: squiretarboxinn.com

Circa 1763. Meadows, stone walls and woods surround this country inn. Squire Tarbox built this rambling farmhouse around a building originally constructed in 1763. Today, the rooms are

warm and comfortable in the inn and in the remodeled hayloft. The innkeepers raise Nubian goats, all photogenic, that have become part of the entertainment (milking and goat cheese). A house-party atmosphere pervades the inn. Beaches, harbors and lobster shacks are some of the nearby visitor hot spots.

Historic Interest: Maritime Museum, old forts, lighthouses, sea captain's homes, abundant antique shops, fishing museums, windjammers, beaches, lobster shacks, etc. (30 minutes). World's finest Music Box Museum.

Innkeeper(s): Bill & Karen Mitman. $90-179. MC, VISA, AX, DS, PC, TC. TAC10. 11 rooms with PB, 4 with FP. Breakfast included in rates. Types of meals: Full bkfst and early coffee/tea. Afternoon tea and gourmet dinner available. Restaurant on premises. Beds: KQDT. Air conditioning. Bicycles, library, row boat and farm animals on premises. Antiquing, fishing, beaches, lobster shacks, museums, harbors, live theater, parks and shopping nearby.

Publicity: *Washington Post, New York Times, Yankee, Bon Appetit.*

"Your hospitality was warm, friendly, well-managed and quite genuine. That's a rarity, and it's just the kind we feel best with."

York L2

Dockside Guest Quarters

PO Box 205
York, ME 03909-0205
(207)363-2868 (800)270-1977 Fax:(207)363-1977
E-mail: info@docksidegq.com
Web: www.docksidegq.com

Circa 1900. This small resort provides a panoramic view of the Atlantic Ocean and harbor activities. Guest rooms are located in the classic, large New England home, which is the Maine House, and modern multi-unit cottages. Most rooms have private balconies or porches with unobstructed views of the water. Some suites have fireplaces. The resort is available for weddings. The on-premise restaurant is bi-level with floor to ceiling windows, affording each table a view of the harbor. Child-care services are available.

Historic Interest: The York Historic District offers several interesting sites.

Innkeeper(s): Lusty Family. $80-190. MC, VISA, DS, PC. TAC10. 21 rooms, 2 with FP, 6 suites and 1 conference room. Types of meals: Cont plus and early coffee/tea. Afternoon tea and lunch available. Restaurant on premises. Beds: KQDT. Cable TV in room. Fax, bicycles, library, child care and complete wedding facilities on premises. Weddings, small meetings and family reunions hosted. French spoken. Amusement parks, antiquing, fishing, live theater, parks, shopping, cross-country skiing and water sports nearby.

"We've been back many years. It's a paradise for us, the scenery, location, maintenance, living quarters."

York Harbor L2

Bell Buoy B&B

570 York St
York Harbor, ME 03911
(207)363-7264

Circa 1884. Just a short walk to The Harbor, this Victorian inn is located in prestigious York Harbor. Stroll the Marginal Way along the ocean shore or catch the scenic trolley that stops across the street and takes travelers to points of interest, while providing a narrative about the town. After a day of enjoying the area, check out one of the many outstanding restaurants in the area, some within walking distance. Breakfasts can be relished in the family dining room or on the porch.

Innkeeper(s): Wes & Kathie Cook. $70-95. PC. TAC10. 4 rooms with PB and 1 suite. Breakfast included in rates. Types of meals: Full bkfst and early coffee/tea. Beds: KQT. Cable TV, turndown service and ceiling fan in room. VCR on premises. Amusement parks, antiquing, fishing, live theater, parks, shopping and water sports nearby.

York Harbor Inn

PO Box 573, Rt 1A
York Harbor, ME 03911-0573
(207)363-5119 (800)343-3869 Fax:(207)363-7151
E-mail: garyinkeep@aol.com
Web: www.yorkharborinn.com

Circa 1800. The core building of the York Harbor Inn is a small log cabin constructed on the Isles of Shoals. Moved and reassembled at this dramatic location overlooking the entrance to York Harbor, the cabin is now a gathering room with a handsome stone fireplace. There is an English-style pub in the cellar, a large ballroom and five meeting rooms. The dining room and many guest rooms overlook the ocean. Several guest rooms have ocean view decks, working fireplaces and Jacuzzi spas. One three-room suite is available.

Historic Interest: Old York Historical Society Museum buildings (1.5 miles), Strawberry Banke Colonial Village Museum (6 miles).

Innkeeper(s): Joseph & Garry Dominguez. $89-239. MC, VISA, AX, DC, CB, PC, TC. 33 rooms with PB, 4 with FP, 1 suite and 4 conference rooms. Breakfast included in rates. MAP. Types of meals: Cont plus, cont and early coffee/tea. Gourmet dinner, lunch, banquet service, catering service and room service available. Restaurant on premises. Beds: KQD. Cable TV, phone and iron & ironing board in room. Air conditioning. VCR, fax, copier, spa, swimming and child care on premises. Weddings, small meetings, family reunions and seminars hosted. Amusement parks, antiquing, fishing, beach, museums, outlet mall, live theater, parks, shopping, cross-country skiing and water sports nearby.

"It's hard to decide where to stay when you're paging through a book of country inns. This time we chose well."

Maryland

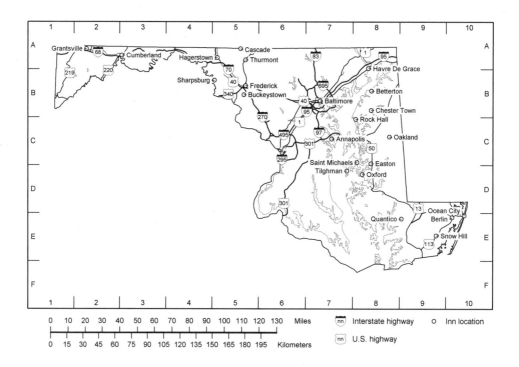

Scale:
0 10 20 30 40 50 60 70 80 90 100 110 120 130 Miles
0 15 30 45 60 75 90 105 120 135 150 165 180 195 Kilometers

Interstate highway   O   Inn location
U.S. highway

Annapolis C7

Gibson's Lodgings

110 Prince George St
Annapolis, MD 21401-1704
(410)268-5555

Circa 1786. This Georgian house in the heart of the Annapolis Historic District was built on the site of the Old Courthouse, circa 1680. Two historic houses make up the inn, and there was a new house built in 1988. All the rooms, old and new, are furnished with antiques. Only a few yards away is the City Dock Harbor and within two blocks is the Naval Academy visitor's gate.

Historic Interest: U.S. Naval Academy, Chesapeake Bay.

Innkeeper(s): Beverly H Snyder. $79-139. MC, VISA, AX, TC. 21 rooms, 9 with PB, 2 suites and 1 conference room. Breakfast included in rates. Type of meal: QDT. Air conditioning. Parking on premises. Handicap access. Small meetings and seminars hosted. Antiquing, fishing, live theater, parks, shopping, sporting events and water sports nearby.

"We had a delightful stay! We enjoyed the proximity to the waterfront, the fun atmosphere and the friendly people."

Jonas Green House B&B

124 Charles St
Annapolis, MD 21401-2621
(410)263-5892 Fax:(410)263-5895
E-mail: jghouse@erols.com
Web: www.bbhost.com/jghouse

Circa 1690. For those seeking a truly historic vacation, Jonas Green House is a perfect starting place. The kitchen building of this historic home was completed in the 1690s and still houses the original cooking fireplace and an original crane. From this point, more was added until its completion sometime in the 1740s. Much of the home's original floors, wainscoting, fireplace and a corner cabinet with original glass has survived through the years. The home is named for one of innkeeper Randy Brown's relatives, who was a colonial patriot and printer. Jonas Green brought his bride to Annapolis and in 1738 settled at the  home where the current innkeeper's family has resided ever since. Restoration of the home uncovered many interesting artifacts, which guests are sure to enjoy. Traditional furnishings fill the home, adding to its historic flavor. The innkeepers have kept the decor simple and authentic.

Historic Interest: The National Landmark home rests in the middle of a historic district. The Colonial Capitol Building is three blocks north and all of Annapolis' historic structures and the U.S. Naval Academy are within five or six blocks of the inn.

Innkeeper(s): Randy & Dede Brown. $100-135. MC, VISA, AX, DS, PC, TC. 3 rooms, 1 with PB, 2 with FP. Breakfast included in rates. Type of meal: Full bkfst. Beds: KQDT. Central air. Fax and copier on premises. Small meetings hosted. Danish spoken. Antiquing, fishing, live theater, parks, shopping, sporting events and water sports nearby.

Pets allowed: Stay with owner in room.

Publicity: *Annapolitan, Capital, Washington Post, National Geographic Traveler, New York Times.*

"Thank you for your hospitality in a wonderful house so full of personal and American history."

Baltimore B7

Abacrombie Badger B&B

58 W Biddle St
Baltimore, MD 21201-5534
(410)244-7227 Fax:(410)244-8415
E-mail: abadger722@aol.com
Web: www.badger-inn.com

Circa 1890. This five-story row house was once the home to Colonel Biddle of the Union Army. The home includes a dozen guest rooms with English appointments. Guests can relax in the first-floor parlor and enjoy dinner at La Tesso Tana, also located in the inn. The Meyerhoff Symphony Hall is across the street from the B&B, which is located in Baltimore's cultural center. Antique shops and an opera house are just a few blocks away, as is the streetcar line, which will take guests to the convention center, stadiums and other attractions.

Historic Interest: Basilica of the Assumption 1st Catholic Cathedral in US (half mile).

Innkeeper(s): Paul Bragaw. $110-150. MC, VISA, AX, DC, DS, PC, TC. TAC8. 12 rooms with PB. Breakfast included in rates. Type of meal: Cont plus. Restaurant on premises. Beds: Q. Cable TV and phone in room. Central air. Fax, copier, library and parking off street on premises. French, German and Dutch spoken. Antiquing, art galleries, canoeing/kayaking, golf, live theater, museums, parks, shopping and sporting events nearby.

Gramercy Mansion

1400 Greenspring Valley Rd, Box 119
Baltimore, MD 21153-0119
(410)486-2405 (800)553-3404 Fax:(410)486-1765
Web: www.gramercymansion.com

Circa 1902. This English Tudor mansion was built as a wedding present for the daughter of Alexander Cassatt, president of Pennsylvania Railroad and brother to Mary Cassatt, famous impressionist. A mother and daughter team runs the B&B. There is a music room, library and parlors, all decorated with antiques and Oriental rugs. Most of the guest rooms have fireplaces  and a few have whirlpool baths. There are commercial herb gardens, an orchard, a stream and flower gardens. The house was featured as the Decorator Showhouse to benefit the Baltimore Symphony. The inn is known for its delectable breakfasts.

Innkeeper(s): Cristin Kline, Anne Pomykala. $90-275. MC, VISA, AX, DC, DS, PC, TC. 12 rooms, 7 with PB, 4 with FP, 1 suite and 4 conference rooms. Breakfast included in rates. Types of meals: Full bkfst, veg bkfst and coffee/tea. Beds: KD. TV, phone, turndown service and VCR in room. Air conditioning. Fax, copier, swimming, tennis and library on premises. Weddings, small meetings, family reunions and seminars hosted. Antiquing, art galleries, bicycling, canoeing/kayaking, fishing, golf, hiking, horseback riding, live theater, parks, shopping, sporting events, tennis, water sports and wineries nearby.

"The hospitality, atmosphere, food, etc. were top-notch."

Mr. Mole B&B

1601 Bolton St
Baltimore, MD 21217-4317
(410)728-1179 Fax:(410)728-3379

Circa 1869. Set on a quiet, up-scale street in the historic Bolton Hill neighborhood, this beautifully restored brick town house, named after the fastidious character in The Wind in the Willows, is a combination of whimsical romantic ambiance and old Baltimore society. Throughout the house, 18th- and 19th-century antiques enhance wainscoting, painted draped ivy and 14-foot ceilings. Each guest room and suite features a different theme. The Garden Suite, blooming with sunny floral prints and plaid, offers a bright, third-floor sun room, sitting room and a spacious private bath. The Explorer Suite features sophisticated leopard-print fabrics and a zebra-skin rug. The only Mobil four-star B&B in Maryland, the inn is located six blocks from the Meyerhoff Symphony Hall, the Lyric Opera House, the Metro and the beginning of Baltimore's Antique Row.

Historic Interest: On historic Bolton Hill. Located close to Johns Hopkins University and the University of Baltimore. Downtown Baltimore, the Inner Harbor and Fells Point are five minutes away by car, Metro or trolley.
Innkeeper(s): Paul Bragaw & Collin Clarke. $105-155. MC, VISA, AX, DC, DS, PC, TC. TAC8. 5 rooms with PB, 4 with FP and 2 suites. Breakfast included in rates. Type of meal: Cont plus. Beds: Q. Phone and turndown service in room. Air conditioning. Fax and library on premises. Antiquing, golf, live theater, parks, shopping and sporting events nearby.

Berlin   E10

Atlantic Hotel Inn & Restaurant

2 N Main St
Berlin, MD 21811-1043
(410)641-3589 (800)814-7672 Fax:(410)641-4928

Circa 1895. The exterior of this stunning Victorian hotel is a red brick wonder, decked with ornate trim. The hotel was built by Horace and Ginny Harmonson, and it was Ginny who ran the hotel until passing it on to her daughter. Through the years, the inn has had a succession of owners, the current of which refurbished the hotel back to its 19th-century glory. Rich fabrics cover the period antiques, which are set on polished wood floors and Oriental rugs. Bedchambers are awash in color with lacy touches and canopy or poster beds. The hotel has established a grand culinary tradition, carried on today by chef Larry Wilgus, a graduate of the Baltimore International Culinary College. Subtle lighting, linen tablecloths and soft decor create a romantic environment in the hotel dining room, where guests can choose from a variety of seasonal cuisine.
Innkeeper(s): Gary Weber. $65-165. MC, VISA, AX, TC. 17 rooms with PB, 1 suite and 1 conference room. Breakfast included in rates. Type of meal: Full bkfst. Gourmet dinner, lunch and banquet service available. Restaurant on premises. Beds: QD. Cable TV, phone and turndown service in room. Air conditioning. Weddings, small meetings, family reunions and seminars hosted. Amusement parks, antiquing, fishing, golf, national Seashore, parks and water sports nearby.

Merry Sherwood Plantation

8909 Worcester Hwy
Berlin, MD 21811-3016
(410)641-2112 (800)660-0358 Fax:(410)641-9528
E-mail: info@merrysherwood.com
Web: www.merrysherwood.com

Circa 1859. This magnificent pre-Civil War mansion is a tribute to Southern plantation architecture. The inn features antique period furniture, hand-woven, Victorian era rugs and a square grand piano. The ballroom, now a parlor for guests, boasts twin fireplaces and pier mirrors. (Ask to see the hidden cupboards behind the fireside bookcases in the library.) Nineteen acres of grounds

are beautifully landscaped and feature azaleas, boxwoods and 125 varieties of trees.

Innkeeper(s): Kirk Burbage. $95-175. MC, VISA. 8 rooms, 6 with PB, 4 with FP and 1 suite. Breakfast included in rates. Type of meal: Full gourmet bkfst. Afternoon tea and gourmet dinner available. Beds: QD. Air conditioning. Weddings, small meetings, family reunions and seminars hosted. Amusement parks, antiquing, fishing, shopping and water sports nearby.
Publicity: *Washington Post, Baltimore Sun, Southern Living.*

"Pure elegance and privacy at its finest."

Betterton   B8

Lantern Inn

115 Ericsson Ave, PO Box 29
Betterton, MD 21610-9746
(410)348-5809 (800)499-7265 Fax:(410)348-2323

Circa 1904. Framed by a picket fence and a wide two-story front porch, this four-story country inn is located one block from the nettle-free public beach on Chesapeake Bay. Comfortable rooms are furnished with antiques and handmade quilts. The surrounding area is well-known for its wildlife preserves. Antique shops and restaurants are nearby. Kent County offers plenty of cycling possibilities, and there are detailed maps available at the inn for trips that start at the inn and go for 10 to 90 miles. Tennis courts are two blocks away.

Historic Interest: Historic Chestertown (12 miles), Chesapeake Bay (1 block).
Innkeeper(s): Ray & Sandi Sparks. $75-90. MC, VISA, AX. 13 rooms, 4 with PB. Breakfast included in rates. Type of meal: Cont plus. Beds: KQDT. VCR on premises. Antiquing, fishing, horseback riding and sporting clays nearby.
Publicity: *Richland Times-Dispatch, North Carolina Outdoorsman, Washingtonian, Mid-Atlantic Country.*

Buckeystown   B5

The Inn at Buckeystown

3521 Buckeystown Pike Gen Del
Buckeystown, MD 21717
(301)874-5755 (800)272-1190 Fax:(301)831-1355

Circa 1897. Gables, bay windows and a wraparound porch are features of this grand Victorian mansion located on two-and-a-half acres of lawns and gardens (and an ancient cemetery). The inn features a polished staircase, antiques and elegantly decorated guest rooms. Ask for the Deja Vu Suite, which boasts a working fireplace and oak decor. A gourmet dinner is served each Friday, Saturday and holiday. The inn also hosts weddings, rehearsals and retreats. The village of Buckeystown is in the National Register.

Historic Interest: Frederick, Barbara Fritchie and Francis Scott Key grave sites (4 miles), National Battle of the Monocacy Civil War Battlefield Park (3 miles), Camp David (15 miles).
Innkeeper(s): Janet Wells. $90-225. MC, VISA, AX, DS, PC, TC. TAC10. 7 rooms, 5 with PB. Breakfast and snacks/refreshments included in rates. MAP.

Types of meals: Full gourmet bkfst, country bkfst, veg bkfst and early coffee/tea. Dinner and catering service available. Restaurant on premises. Beds: QD. Cable TV in room. Air conditioning. VCR and fax on premises. Weddings, small meetings, family reunions and seminars hosted. Antiquing, art galleries, bicycling, canoeing/kayaking, fishing, golf, live theater, museums, parks, shopping, downhill skiing, sporting events and wineries nearby.
Publicity: *Mid-Atlantic, Innsider, The Washingtonian, Washington Post, Baltimore Sun.*

"The courtesy of you and your staff were the glue that bound the whole experience together."

Catoctin Inn and Conference Center

3613 Buckeystown Pike
Buckeystown, MD 21717
(301)874-5555 (800)730-5550 Fax:(301)874-2026
E-mail: catoctin@fred.net
Web: www.catoctininn.com

Circa 1780. The inn's four acres of dogwood, magnolias, maples and sweeping lawns overlook the village and the Catoctin Mountains range. Some special features of the inn

include a library with marble fireplaces and a handsome wraparound veranda. A Victorian carriage house marks the site for weddings, showers and receptions for up to 150 guests. Fifteen of the guest rooms include a fireplace and a whirlpool tub. Nearby villages to visit include Harper's Ferry, Antietam and New Market. Buckeystown's Monocacy River provides canoeing and fishing.

Innkeeper(s): Terry & Sarah MacGillivray. $85-150. MC, VISA, AX, DS, PC. 20 rooms with PB, 15 with FP, 8 suites, 3 cottages & 3 conference rooms. Breakfast included in rates. Meal: Full bkfst. Afternoon tea and catering service available. Restaurant on premises. Beds: KQ. Cable TV, phone, turndown service and VCR in room. Air conditioning. Weddings, small meetings, family reunions and seminars hosted. Antiquing, fishing, hiking, biking, Appalachian Trail, Harper's Ferry, Sugarloaf Mountain, swimming, boating, Civil War history nearby, live theater, shopping, downhill skiing, cross-country skiing & sporting events nearby.

Cascade   A5

Bluebird on the Mountain

14700 Eyler Ave
Cascade, MD 21719-1938
(301)241-4161 (800)362-9526

Circa 1900. In the mountain village of Cascade, this gracious shuttered Georgian manor is situated on two acres of trees and wildflowers. Three suites have double whirlpool tubs. There is an outdoor hot tub as well. The Rose Garden Room and Mt. Magnolia suites have fireplaces and porches overlooking the

back garden. The inn is appointed with antiques, lace and white linens, and white wicker. On Sundays, a full breakfast is served. Cascade is located in between Frederick, Md., and Gettysburg, Pa.

Innkeeper(s): Eda Smith-Eley. $105-125. MC, VISA, PC. TAC10. 5 rooms with PB, 2 with FP and 2 suites. Breakfast included in rates. Types of meals: Full bkfst, cont plus and early coffee/tea. Room service available. Beds: KQT. Cable TV, turndown service, ceiling fan and VCR in room. Air conditioning. Spa on premises. Small meetings, family reunions and seminars hosted. Antiquing, fishing, hiking, live theater, parks, shopping, downhill skiing, sporting events and water sports nearby.

"A wonderful balance of luxury and at-home comfort."

Chestertown   B8

Great Oak Manor

10568 Cliff Rd
Chestertown, MD 21620-4115
(410)778-5943 (800)504-3098 Fax:(410)778-5943
E-mail: innkeeper@greatoak.com
Web: www.greatoak.com

Circa 1938. This elegant Georgian mansion anchors vast lawns at the end of a long driveway. Situated directly on the Chesapeake

Bay, it is a serene and picturesque country estate. A library with fireplace, den and formal parlors are available to guests. With its grand circular stairway, bayside gazebo, private beach and nearby marina,

the Manor is a remarkable setting for events such as weddings and reunions. Chestertown is eight miles away.

Innkeeper(s): Don & Dianne Cantor. $76-175. MC, VISA, PC, TC. TAC10. 11 rooms with PB, 5 with FP, 1 suite and 2 conference rooms. Breakfast included in rates. Types of meals: Full bkfst and early coffee/tea. Beds: KT. Phone, some VCRs and refrigerator (in suite) in room. Air conditioning. VCR, fax, copier, bicycles, library and computer ready-two rooms on premises. Weddings, small meetings, family reunions and seminars hosted. Antiquing, fishing, golf, tennis, kayaking, Historic Washington College, live theater and shopping nearby.

"The charming setting, professional service and personal warmth we experienced at Great Oak will long be a pleasant memory. Thanks for everything!"

The Inn at Mitchell House

8796 Maryland Pkwy
Chestertown, MD 21620-4209
(410)778-6500

Circa 1743. This pristine 18th-century manor house sits as a jewel on 12 acres overlooking Stoneybrook Pond. The guest rooms and the inn's several parlors are preserved and appointed in an authentic Colonial mood, heightened by handsome polished wide-board floors. Eastern Neck Island National Wildlife Refuge, Chesapeake Farms, St. Michaels, Annapolis and nearby Chestertown are all delightful to explore. The Inn at Mitchell House is a popular setting for romantic weddings and small corporate meetings.

Innkeeper(s): Tracy & Jim Stone. $90-110. MC, VISA, PC, TC. 6 rooms, 5 with PB, 4 with FP. Breakfast included in rates. Types of meals: Full bkfst and early coffee/tea. Gourmet dinner available. Beds: KQD. Turndown service in room. Air conditioning. VCR on premises. Weddings, small meetings, family reunions and seminars hosted. Antiquing, fishing, live theater, shopping, sporting events and water sports nearby.

Cumberland   A3

The Inn at Walnut Bottom

120 Greene St
Cumberland, MD 21502-2934
(301)777-0003 (800)286-9718 Fax:(301)777-8288
E-mail: iwb@iwbinfo.com
Web: www.iwbinfo.com

Circa 1820. Two historic houses comprise the Inn at Walnut Bottom: the 1815 Federal-style Cowden House and the 1890

Queen Anne Victorian-style Dent House, both located on Cumberland's oldest street. Antiques and reproduction furnishings decorate the parlors, guest rooms and family suites. A full breakfast and afternoon refreshment hour are offered, and there's a restaurant on the premises as well as a boutique featuring work by local artisans. Ask to borrow one of the inn's bicycles for exploring the C&O Canal Towpath.

Innkeeper(s): Grant M. Irvin & Kirsten O. Hansen. $79-190. MC, VISA, AX, DS, PC, TC. 12 rooms, 8 with PB and 2 suites. Breakfast included in rates. MAP. Types of meals: Full bkfst, cont and early coffee/tea. Gourmet dinner and room service available. Restaurant on premises. Beds: KQDT. Cable TV, phone, ceiling fan, hair dryers and iron in room. Air conditioning. Fax, copier and bicycles on premises. Weddings, small meetings, family reunions and seminars hosted. Danish, German and French spoken. Antiquing, bicycling, fishing, live theater, parks, downhill skiing and cross-country skiing nearby.

Deep Creek Lake   C8

Haley Farm B&B and Retreat Center

16766 Garrett Hwy
Deep Creek Lake, MD 21550-4036
(301)387-9050 (888)231-3276 Fax:(301)387-9050
E-mail: kam@haleyfarm.com
Web: www.haleyfarm.com

Circa 1920. This farmhouse is surrounded by 65 acres of rolling hills and farmland in the mountains of Western Maryland. Inside, the innkeepers have added many elegant touches, transforming the home into a gracious retreat with Chinese carpets, tapestries and European furnishings. There are three luxury suites, which include a heart-shaped Jacuzzi, king-size bed, kitchenette and sitting room with a fireplace. In addition, there are two smaller suites and six deluxe rooms. Croquet and badminton are set up on the grounds. Other popular activities are fishing in the trout pond, soaking in the hot tub, stretching out in the hammock or taking a picnic to the gazebo. The innkeepers can create special romantic packages with flowers and champagne, massages and even horseback riding. A variety of retreats and workshops are offered with subjects ranging from conflict resolution and negotiating strategies to yoga. The farm is three hours from Washington, D.C., and minutes from Deep Creek Lake, five state parks and the WISP ski and golf resort.

Innkeeper(s): Wayne & Kam Gillespie. $100-210. MC, VISA, AX, DS, PC, TC. 11 rooms with PB, 5 with FP and 6 suites. Breakfast included in rates. Type of meal: Full bkfst. Beds: KQ. Ceiling fan in room. Air conditioning. VCR, spa, bicycles, library and trout pond on premises. Weddings, small meetings, family reunions and seminars hosted. German, limited French and limited Spanish spoken. Antiquing, fishing, white water rafting, parks, shopping, downhill skiing, cross-country skiing and water sports nearby.

"A beautiful setting for a quiet, romantic escape."

Easton   C8

The Bishop's House B&B

214 Goldsborough St
Easton, MD 21601
(410)820-7290 (800)223-7290 Fax:(410)820-7290

Circa 1880. The innkeepers of this in-town Victorian lovingly restored it in 1988. The three-and-a-half-story clapboard and gabled roof home includes three spacious first-floor rooms with 14-foot-high ceilings and generously sized second- and third-

floor guest rooms. With its period-style furnishings, working fireplaces and whirlpool tubs, the inn offers its guests both romance and the ambiance of the Victorian era. A hot breakfast is served every morning. Located in Easton's Historic District, it is within three blocks of boutiques, antique shops, restaurants and historic sites. The inn provides off-street parking.

Historic Interest: Within 10 miles of historic Oxford and St. Michaels.

Innkeeper(s): John & Diane Ippolito. Call for rates. Breakfast included in rates. Type of meal: Early coffee/tea.

Fredericksburg   B5

Spring Bank, A B&B Inn

7945 Worman's Mill Rd
Fredericksburg, MD 21701
(301)694-0440 (800)400-4667
E-mail: rcomp@aol.com
Web: www.bbonline.com/md/springbank

Circa 1880. Both Gothic Revival and Italianate architectural details are featured in this National Register brick Victorian. High ceilings accommodate 10-foot arched windows. The original interior shutters remain. The parlor has a marbleized slate fireplace, and there is original hand-stenciling and a plaster fresco in the Billiards Room. Victorian furnishings and Oriental rugs have been collected from the family's antique shop. Black birch, pine, maple and poplar trees dot the inn's 10 acres.

Innkeeper(s): Ray Compton. $80-95. MC, VISA, AX, DS, PC, TC. TAC7. 5 rooms, 1 with PB. Breakfast included in rates. Type of meal: Cont plus. Beds: D. Air conditioning. VCR and library on premises. Antiquing, fishing and live theater nearby.

Grantsville   A2

Walnut Ridge Bed & Breakfast

92 Main St, PO Box 368
Grantsville, MD 21536
(301)895-4248 (888)419-2568 Fax:(301)895-4248
E-mail: walnutridge@usa.net
Web: www.walnutridge.net

Circa 1864. A grove of walnut trees and a wood-fired hot tub next to a vegetable garden are the unique offerings of this historic farmhouse B&B. The living room is decorated with Amish items and there are country pieces throughout. The accommodations offered include a family suite with full kitchen. The inn's cabin in the woods has its own clawfoot tub, stone fireplace, deck and queen bed. The innkeeper's husband is a local Mennonite minister.

Innkeeper(s): Tim & Candy Fetterly. $75-125. MC, VISA, PC, TC. TAC5. 4 rooms with PB, 1 suite and 1 cabin. Breakfast included in rates. Types of meals: Full bkfst and early coffee/tea. Beds: QD. Cable TV and ceiling fan in room. VCR and fax on premises. Weddings, small meetings and family reunions hosted. Antiquing, fishing, golf, parks, shopping, downhill skiing, cross-country skiing, sporting events, tennis and water sports nearby.

Pets allowed: in suite and cabin.

Publicity: *Washington Post, Lancaster Farming.*

"Best nights' sleep I've had this summer"."

Hagerstown   A5

Beaver Creek House B&B

20432 Beaver Creek Rd
Hagerstown, MD 21740-1514
(301)797-4764 Fax:(301)797-4978

Circa 1905. History buffs enjoy this turn-of-the-century inn located minutes away from Antietam and Harpers Ferry National Historical Parks. The surrounding villages house antique shops and some hold weekend auctions. The inn features a courtyard with a fountain and a country garden. Innkeepers Don and Shirley Day furnished the home with family antiques and memorabilia. Guests can sip complimentary sherry in the elegant parlor or just relax on the porch and take in the view of South Mountain.

Historic Interest: Antietam National Battlefield (12 miles), Gettysburg (34 miles), Fort Frederick (16 miles), Appalachian Trail (4 miles).

Innkeeper(s): Donald & Shirley Day. $75-95. MC, VISA, AX, PC, TC. TAC10. 5 rooms with PB and 1 conference room. Breakfast included in rates. Type of meal: Full gourmet bkfst. Beds: DT. Ceiling fan in room. Air conditioning. Copier on premises. Small meetings, family reunions and seminars hosted. Amusement parks, antiquing, fishing, live theater, parks, shopping, downhill skiing, cross-country skiing, sporting events and water sports nearby.

Publicity: *Baltimore Sun, Hagerstown Journal, Herald Mail, Washington Post, Frederick.*

"Thanks so much for your hospitality. You're wonderful hosts and breakfast was delicious as usual. Don't change a thing."

Havre de Grace   A8

Currier House

800 S Market St
Havre de Grace, MD 21078
(410)939-7886 (800)827-2889 Fax:(410)939-6145
E-mail: janec@currier-bb.com
Web: www.currier-bb.com

Circa 1790. The Susquehanna River flows into the Chesapeake Bay within view of the Currier House. A wraparound porch welcomes guests to this Victorian home. Family heirlooms and artifacts are incorporated into the inn's decor, which also reflects the area's historical appeal to waterfowl hunters. In season, a regional favorite is served, "Watermen's Breakfast," which offers sautéed oysters and Maryland stewed tomatoes. The innkeeper is a direct descendant of Matthew Currier, who lived in the home in 1861 when he operated the ferry. The innkeeper will add much enrichment to your experience of the historic home and the area. Be sure to check out the lighthouse, a tenth of a mile away.

Historic Interest: Concord Point Lighthouse, John O'Neil House (1/10 of a mile), Stepping Stone Farm (3 miles).

Innkeeper(s): Jane & Paul Belbot. $85-115. MC, VISA, AX, DS, PC, TC. TAC10. 4 rooms with PB. Breakfast and snacks/refreshments included in rates. Type of meal: Full bkfst. Beds: Q. TV and VCR in room. Central air. Library on premises. Antiquing, art galleries, bicycling, canoeing/kayaking, fishing, golf, hiking, horseback riding, live theater, museums, parks, shopping, water sports and wineries nearby.

"My whole "bride's" party showed up on your doorstep. You opened your home to us, with a smile."

Ocean City   E10

An Inn on the Ocean

1001 Atlantic Avenue
Ocean City, MD 21842
(410)289-8894 (877)226-6223 Fax:(410)289-8215
E-mail: innonoc@aol.com
Web: www.InnOnTheOcean.com

Circa 1920. From the wraparound porch of this inn, guests can watch birds soar and ocean waters crash upon the rocks. The inn includes six elegant guest rooms, each individually decorated with rich fabrics and designer linens. The Hunt and Tapestry rooms each boast an ocean view. The Oceana Suite includes a private balcony that looks out to the sea. The Veranda Room has its own oceanfront porch. Most rooms include a Jacuzzi tub. The continental-plus breakfasts include homemade breads, fruit and special egg dishes, such as a frittata. The inn is oceanfront, so guests need only walk a few steps to enjoy the beach and nearby boardwalk. Golfing, outlet stores, fishing, water sports, antique shops and harness racing are other local attractions.

Historic Interest: Snow Hill(15 miles), Berlin (10 miles).

Innkeeper(s): The Barrett's. $125-275. MC, VISA, AX, DS, TC. 6 rooms with PB and 1 conference room. Breakfast and snacks/refreshments included in rates. Types of meals: Cont plus, cont and early coffee/tea. Gourmet dinner and catering service available. Beds: KQ. Cable TV, ceiling fan, VCR, jacuzzi and bathrobes in room. Air conditioning. Fax, copier, bicycles, beach chairs, umbrellas and health club passes on premises. Weddings, small meetings, family reunions and seminars hosted. Amusement parks, antiquing, art galleries, beaches, bicycling, canoeing/kayaking, fishing, golf, hiking, horseback riding, live theater, museums, parks, shopping, sporting events, tennis, water sports and wineries nearby.

Atlantic House B&B

501 N Baltimore Ave
Ocean City, MD 21842-3926
(410)289-2333 Fax:(410)289-2430
E-mail: ocbnb@atlantichouse.com
Web: www.atlantichouse.com

Circa 1923. From the front porch of this bed & breakfast, guests can partake in ocean and boardwalk views. The rooms are decorated in antique oak and wicker, complementing a relaxing beach stay. The morning's abundant breakfast buffet includes such items as freshly baked muffins and cakes, fruit, egg casseroles, cereals and yogurt. In the afternoons, light refreshments also are served. The inn, nestled in the original Ocean City, is a short walk to the beach, boardwalk and entertainment, but many guests enjoy cycling the scenic trail to Assateague Island. Privileges at a local health club are available.

Innkeeper(s): Paul & Debi Cook. $55-225. MC, VISA, AX, DS, TC. TAC10. 11 rooms, 7 with PB and 1 suite. Breakfast, afternoon tea and snacks/refreshments included in rates. Types of meals: Full bkfst and early coffee/tea. Beds: QD. Cable TV and ceiling fan in room. Air conditioning. Weddings, small meetings and family reunions hosted. Amusement parks, antiquing, fishing, golf, boardwalk, harness racing, spa and swimming across town, bird watching, biking, live theater, parks, shopping, sporting events and water sports nearby.

Oxford
D8

The Robert Morris Inn

314 N Morris St PO Box 70
Oxford, MD 21654
(410)226-5111 Fax:(410)226-5744
Web: www.robertmorrisinn.com

Circa 1710. Once the home of Robert Morris Sr., a representative of an English trading company, the house was constructed by ship carpenters with wooden-pegged paneling, ship's nails and hand-hewn beams. Bricks brought to Oxford as ballast in trading ships were used to build the fireplaces. Robert Morris Jr., a partner in a Philadelphia law firm, used his entire savings to help finance the Continental Army. He signed the Declaration of Independence, Articles of Confederation and United States Constitution. James A. Michener, author of "Chesapeake," rated the inn's crab cakes as his favorite.
Historic Interest: Talbot Historic Society (15 minutes), Chesapeake Maritime Museum (25 minutes).
Innkeeper(s): Jay Gibson. $100-240. MC, VISA, AX, PC. TAC10. 35 rooms with PB, 2 cottages and 1 conference room. EP. Restaurant on premises. Beds: KQDT. Air conditioning. Fax, copier & library on premises. Handicap access. Small meetings & seminars hosted. Antiquing, fishing, live theater, parks & shopping nearby.
Publicity: *Southern Accents, The Evening Sun, Maryland, Mid-Atlantic Country, Bon Appetite.*

"Impressed! Unbelievable!"

Quantico
E9

Whitehaven B&B

23844 River St #48
Quantico, MD 21856-2506
(410)873-3320 (888)205-5921 Fax:(410)873-2162
E-mail: whavnbb@dmv.com
Web: www.whitehaven.com

Circa 1850. Two historic properties comprise this bed & breakfast. The Charles Leatherbury House, which dates to 1886, includes two guest rooms, decorated in country Victorian style. The two rooms share a bath, perfect for couples traveling together. Book both rooms and you'll enjoy the utmost of privacy in a historic setting. The Otis Lloyd House, constructed prior to the Civil War, includes three guest rooms, each with a private bath. Guests at both houses enjoy a full breakfast, including farm-fresh eggs and homemade baked goods. Whitehaven guests enjoy privileges at the nearby Green Hill Yacht and Country Club. The village of Whitehaven, originally chartered in 1685, includes 22 buildings listed in the National Register.
Historic Interest: Pemberton Hall (12 miles).
Innkeeper(s): Maryen, Carlton & Mark Herrett. $75-100. MC, VISA, AX, DS, PC, TC. 5 rooms, 3 with PB. Breakfast and snacks/refreshments included in rates. Types of meals: Full bkfst, veg bkfst and early coffee/tea. Beds: KQ. VCR, fax, copier, library and refrigerators on premises. Weddings and family reunions hosted. Antiquing, art galleries, beaches, bicycling, canoeing/kayaking, fishing, golf, museums, parks and water sports nearby.

Rock Hall
C8

Moonlight Bay Marina & Inn

6002 Lawton Ave
Rock Hall, MD 21661-1369
(410)639-2660 Fax:(410)639-7739

Circa 1850. Moonlight Bay offers an ideal setting, right at the edge of the Chesapeake Bay. The pre-Civil War home includes a veranda lined with wicker furnishings and a swing, and the grounds boast a gazebo. Five rooms are located in the main inn, and several offer outstanding bay views. The West Wing includes five bay-front rooms, all with a whirlpool bath. Guests are pampered in Victorian style with a full breakfast and afternoon tea. Guests can rent boats, fish, golf or take a nature walk at one of two local wildlife preserves. Other local attractions include auctions and antique shops.
Innkeeper(s): Robert & Dorothy Santangelo. $98-134. MC, VISA, DS, PC, TC. 10 rooms with PB and 2 conference rooms. Breakfast and afternoon tea included in rates. Types of meals: Full bkfst and early coffee/tea. Beds: KQT. Ceiling fan and whirlpool tub in room. Air conditioning. VCR, fax and bicycles on premises. Handicap access. Weddings, small meetings, family reunions and seminars hosted. Antiquing, fishing, golf, live theater, shopping and tennis nearby.
Publicity: *Washingtonian, Washington Post.*

Saint Michaels
C8

Kemp House Inn

412 Talbot St, PO Box 638
Saint Michaels, MD 21663-0638
(410)745-2243

Circa 1807. This two-story Georgian house was built by Colonel Joseph Kemp, a shipwright and one of the town forefathers. The inn is appointed in period furnishings accentuated by candlelight. Guest rooms include patchwork quilts, a collection of four-poster rope beds and old-fashioned nightshirts. There are several working fireplaces. Robert E. Lee is said to have been a guest.
Historic Interest: Listed in the National Register.
Innkeeper(s): Diane M. Cooper. $80-120. MC, VISA, DS. 8 rooms, 6 with PB, 4 with FP. Breakfast included in rates. Meals: Cont and early coffee/tea. Beds: QDT. Air conditioning. Antiquing, fishing, shopping and water sports nearby.
Pets Allowed.
Publicity: *Gourmet, Philadelphia.*

"It was wonderful. We've stayed in many B&Bs, and this was one of the nicest!"

Parsonage Inn

210 N Talbot St
Saint Michaels, MD 21663-2102
(410)745-5519 (800)394-5519
E-mail: parsinn@dmv.com
Web: www.parsonage-inn.com

Circa 1883. A striking Victorian steeple rises next to the wide bay of this brick residence, once the home of Henry Clay Dodson, state senator, pharmacist and brickyard owner. The house features brick detail in a variety of patterns and inlays, perhaps a design statement for brick customers. Porches are decorated with filigree and spindled columns. Laura Ashley linens, late Victorian furnishings, fireplaces and decks add to the creature comforts. Six bikes await guests who wish to ride to Tilghman Island or to the ferry that goes to Oxford. Gourmet breakfast is served in the dining room.
Historic Interest: Maritime Museum & Historic Boats (2 blocks), Town of Oxford (10 miles), Town of Easton (9 miles).
Innkeeper(s): Jane & Walt Johnson. $100-185. MC, VISA, PC, TC. TAC10. 8 rooms with PB, 3 with FP. Breakfast included in rates. Meal: Full gourmet bkfst. Beds: KQD. Ceiling fan & TV (two rooms) in room. Air conditioning. Bicycles on premises. Handicap access. Small meetings & family reunions hosted. Antiquing, fishing, Chesapeake Bay Maritime Museum, shopping and water sports nearby.
Publicity: *Wilmington, Delaware News Journal, Philadelphia Inquirer.*

"Striking, extensively renovated."

Wades Point Inn on The Bay

PO Box 7, Wades Point Rd, McDaniel
Saint Michaels, MD 21663
(410)745-2500 (888)923-3466

Circa 1819. This waterfront estate is located on 120 acres and was named for Zachary Wade, who received the land grant in 1657. Thomas Kemp, a notable ship builder, built the house in 1819. The Kemp families' burial

grounds are adjacent to the inn's mile-long walking trail. The trail passes the farm's crops and culti-vated flowers and ponds. Deer, rab-bit, fox, raccoons, bald eagles, blue heron, swans and osprey are often seen. There is a fishing pier. All rooms afford a water view. Rooms are available in the his-toric main house and in an adjoining building with balconies and screened porches overlooking the Chesapeake Bay.

Innkeeper(s): Betsy & John Feiler. $110-230. MC, VISA, TC. 24 rooms, 17 with PB, 1 suite and 1 conference room. Breakfast included in rates. AP. Types of meals: Cont plus and early coffee/tea. Beds: QDT. Ceiling fan and kitchenettes in room. Air conditioning. Fax, copier and library on premises. Handicap access. Small meetings, family reunions and seminars hosted. Antiquing, fishing, golf, live theater, parks, shopping, sporting events, tennis and water sports nearby.

Publicity: *Maryland Magazine, Travel & Leisure, Chesapeake Bay Magazine, Washingtonian, Mid-Atlantic Country.*

Sharpsburg   B5

The Inn at Antietam

220 E Main St, PO Box 119
Sharpsburg, MD 21782-0119
(301)432-6601 (877)835-6011

Circa 1908. Eight acres of meadows surround this gracious Victorian framed by English walnut trees. A columned veranda provides a view of the countryside, the town with its old stone churches, and the Blue Ridge Mountains. Gleaming floors accentuate romantically designed Victorian guest rooms. An invit-

ing smokehouse features beamed ceilings, a wide brick fireplace and handsome upholstered chairs.

Innkeeper(s): Bob LeBlanc & Charles Van Metre. $110-175. MC, VISA, AX. 5 suites, 1 with FP. EP. Type of meal: Full bkfst. Beds: Q. Penthouse suite in room. Library and solarium on premises. Parks nearby.

"A romantic setting and a most enjoyable experience."

Snow Hill   E9

River House Inn

201 E Market St
Snow Hill, MD 21863-2000
(410)632-2722 Fax:(410)632-2866
E-mail: innkeeper@riverhouseinn.com
Web: www.riverhouseinn.com

Circa 1860. This picturesque Gothic Revival house rests on the banks of the Pocomoke River and boasts its own dock. Its two acres roll down to the river over long tree-studded lawns. Lawn furniture and a hammock add to the invitation to relax as do the inn's porches. Some guest rooms feature faux marble fireplaces.

The 17th-century village of Snow Hill boasts old brick sidewalks and historic homes. Canoes can be rented two doors from the inn or you may wish to take a river cruise on the innkeeper's pontoon boat.

Innkeeper(s): Larry & Susanne Knudsen. $100-195. MC, VISA, AX, DS, TC. TAC10. 10 rooms, 8 with PB, 8 with FP, 3 suites and 2 cottages. Breakfast and snacks/refreshments included in rates. Types of meals: Full bkfst and early coffee/tea. Beds: KQT. Ceiling fan in room. Air conditioning. VCR, fax, copier, bicycles, library and child care on premises. Handicap access. Weddings, small meetings and family reunions hosted. Amusement parks, antiquing, fishing, boating, canoeing, beaches, shopping and water sports nearby.

Pets allowed: pets considered.

Publicity: *Daily Times, Washington Times, Washingtonian, Washington Post.*

Thurmont   A5

Cozy Country Inn

103 Frederick Rd
Thurmont, MD 21788-1813
(301)271-4301 Fax:(301)271-4301
E-mail: cozyville@aol.com
Web: www.cozyvillage.com

Circa 1929. This Country Victorian-style inn has evolved into a unique destination point for travelers throughout the years. The six-acre compound includes the inn, a restaurant with seating capacity for 700 and a craft and antique village. Still operated by the founding family, the Cozy features lodging that should please a variety of travelers. Many of the rooms are themed after past presidents. Memorabilia from nearby Camp David, past presidents and political dignitaries are displayed throughout.

Innkeeper(s): Jerry & Becky Freeze. $44-150. MC, VISA, AX, DS, TC. 21 rooms with PB, 5 with FP, 4 suites, 5 cottages and 5 conference rooms. Breakfast included in rates. EP. Types of meals: Full bkfst and cont. Gourmet dinner, picnic lunch, lunch, banquet service, catering service and room service available. Restaurant on premises. Beds: KQD. Cable TV, phone, VCR, robes, wet bars, hair dryers, towel warmers and in room. Air conditioning. Fax, copier and spa on premises. Handicap access. Weddings, small meetings, family reunions and seminars hosted. Antiquing, fishing, golf, craft shop, parks, shopping, downhill skiing, cross-country skiing, sporting events and tennis nearby.

Tilghman   D7

Black Walnut Point Inn

Black Walnut Rd, PO Box 308
Tilghman, MD 21671
(410)886-2452 Fax:(410)886-2053
E-mail: mward@shore.intercom.net
Web: www.tilghmanisland.com/blackwalnut

Circa 1843. Located on 57 beautiful acres set aside as a wildlife sanctuary, this handsome Colonial Revival manor com-mands waterfront views from its private peninsula location. Charter fishing and island river cruises can be arranged by the innkeepers. From its bayside hammock to its nature walk, swimming pool and lighted tennis court, the inn provides an amazingly private getaway. Accommodations are in the main house as well as the Riverside Cottage. The Cove Cottage has its own kitchen and screened porch facing the river.

Innkeeper(s): Tom & Brenda Ward. $120-175. MC, VISA, PC, TC. 7 rooms with PB, 2 cottages and 1 conference room. Breakfast included in rates. Meals: Cont plus and early coffee/tea. Beds: Q. Air conditioning. Fax, copier, spa, swimming, bicycles, tennis and library on premises. Small meetings, family reunions and seminars hosted. Antiquing, fishing, parks, shopping and water sports nearby.

Massachusetts

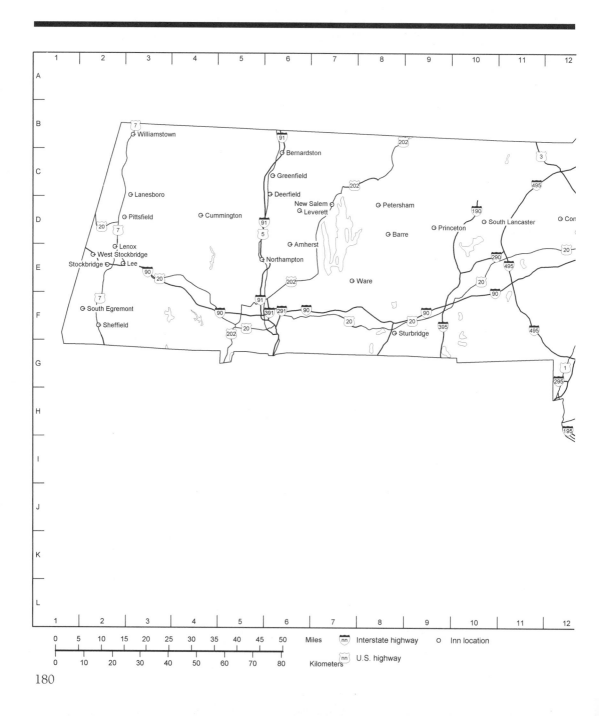

Williamstown

Bernardston

Greenfield

Lanesboro

Deerfield

New Salem

Petersham

Cummington

Leverett

Pittsfield

South Lancaster

Con

Barre

Princeton

Lenox

Amherst

West Stockbridge

Northampton

Stockbridge

Lee

Ware

South Egremont

Sturbridge

Sheffield

Miles

Interstate highway

Inn location

Kilometers

U.S. highway

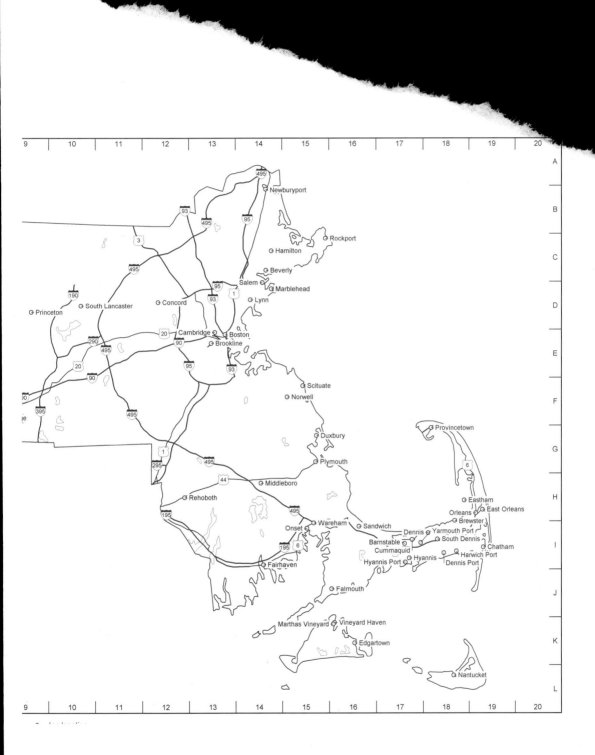

...n with guest rooms that feature period repro-
...allpapers, pedestal sinks, carved golden oak and

brass beds, painted wooden floors and plenty of antiques. Among its many other treasures include Eastlake fireplace mantels. Unforgettable breakfasts include specialties such as Eggs Benedict or French toast stuffed with rich cream cheese. Afternoon tea is a treat, and the inn offers plenty of examples of poetry from Emily Dickinson, whose home is just across the street from the inn.

Historic Interest: Aside from the Dickinson home, the area offers many museums and the inn is within walking distance of Amherst College, Hampshire College and the University of Massachusetts. Emily Dickinson Homestead (less than one-fourth mile), historic Deerfield (15 miles north), Norman Rockwell Museum and Tanglewood (less that 1 hour away).

Innkeeper(s): Alan & Ann Zieminski. $55-135. MC, VISA, DS, PC, TC. 7 rooms with PB. Breakfast, afternoon tea and snacks/refreshments included in rates. Types of meals: Full bkfst and early coffee/tea. Beds: QDT. Phone, ceiling fan and down comforters & pillows in room. Air conditioning. Fax, copier and library on premises. Small meetings and seminars hosted. Amusement parks, antiquing, fishing, golf, live theater, parks, shopping, downhill skiing, cross-country skiing, sporting events, tennis and water sports nearby.

Publicity: *New York Times, Boston Magazine, Bon Appetit, Yankee Travel, Victorian Homes.*

"Our room and adjoining bath were spotlessly clean, charming, and quiet, with good lighting. Our meals were delicious and appetizing, and the casual, family-like atmosphere encouraged discussions among the guests."

Barnstable 117

Beechwood Inn

2839 Main St, Rt 6A
Barnstable, MA 02630-1017
(508)362-6618 (800)609-6618 Fax:(508)362-0298
E-mail: info@beechwoodinn.com
Web: www.beechwoodinn.com

Circa 1853. Beechwood is a beautifully restored Queen Anne Victorian offering period furnishings, some rooms with fireplaces or ocean views. Its warmth and elegance make it a favorite hideaway for couples looking for a peaceful and romantic return to the Victorian era. The inn is named for rare old beech trees that shade the veranda.

Historic Interest: Plymouth Rock (30 minutes), Kennedy Compound and JFK Monument (10 minutes), Oldest library in USA (walking distance).

Innkeeper(s): Debbie & Ken Traugot. $95-175. MC, VISA, AX, DS, PC,

---

...noon tea included
...Beds: KQD. Fans, wine
... Fax, copier and bicycles on
...ecings and family reunions hosted. French spoken.
... cities, whale watching, bird watching, horseback rid-
...er, parks, shopping, sporting events and water sports nearby.

Publicity: *National Trust Calendar, New England Weekends, Rhode Island Monthly, Cape Cod Life, Boston Magazine.*

"Your inn is pristine in every detail. We concluded that the innkeepers, who are most hospitable, are the best part of Beechwood."

Honeysuckle Hill B&B

591 Old Kings Hwy, Rt 6A
Barnstable, MA 02668
(508)362-8418 (800)441-8418 Fax:(508)362-8386

Circa 1810. This Queen Anne Victorian, which is listed in the National Register, is set on a picturesque acre with gardens. The interior is decorated with antiques and white wicker furnishings. The hearty breakfasts include items such as Captain's Eggs, homemade granola, fresh fruit and cranberry-orange muffins. Nearby are the dunes of Sandy Neck Beach. Hyannis is 10 minutes away.

Historic Interest: Plimouth Plantation, Hyannisport, Sandwich Village, Plymouth Rock and Mayflower II.

Innkeeper(s): Bill & Mary Kilburn. $100-150. MC, VISA, AX, DS, PC, TC. 5 rooms, 4 with PB. Breakfast included in rates. Types of meals: Full bkfst and early coffee/tea. Snacks/refreshments available. Beds: QD. TV, ceiling fan, feather beds, fresh flowers and terry cloth robes in room. Air conditioning. Library, beach towels, chairs and umbrellas, guest refrigerator, fish pond, porch and gardens on premises. Antiquing, fishing, golf, beach, ferries, whale watching, live theater and shopping nearby.

"The charm, beauty, service and warmth shown to guests are impressive, but the food overwhelms. Breakfasts were divine!—Judy Kaplan, St. Louis Journal."

Barnstable, Cape Cod 117

Ashley Manor Inn

3660 Olde Kings Hwy PO Box 856
Barnstable, Cape Cod, MA 02630
(508)362-8044 (888)535-2246
E-mail: ashleymn@capecod.net
Web: www.capecod.net/ashleymn

Circa 1699. This manor house has lived through a succession of expansions, the first addition built in 1750. The final effect is wonderful and mysterious. The inn, thought to be a hiding place for Tories during the Revolutionary War, features huge open-hearth fireplace with beehive oven and a secret passageway connecting the upstairs and downstairs suites. The inn is reminiscent of a gracious English country house and is filled with Oriental rugs and antiques. Each of the guest rooms boasts fireplaces, and four have large whirlpool baths. Two acres of manicured lawns include a regulation-size tennis court. Nature-lovers will enjoy the landscape, dotted with cherry and apple trees. The romantic gazebo is the perfect location to view the fountain garden. A full gourmet breakfast is served on the brick terrace or fireside in the formal dining room.

Historic Interest: Nantucket and Martha's Vineyard, Chatham, the National Seashore and Provincetown on the Cape.

Innkeeper(s): Donald Bain. $135-195. MC, VISA, DS, PC, TC. TAC10. 6 rooms with PB, 5 with FP and 4 suites. Breakfast included in rates. Type of meal: Full gourmet bkfst. Beds: KQ. Flowers, chocolates and beverages & snacks in room. Air conditioning. Bicycles, tennis, library and whirlpool baths in three rooms on premises. French spoken. Antiquing, fishing, golf, tennis, restaurants, historic sites, live theater, parks and water sports nearby.

Publicity: *Chicago Tribune, Boston Globe, Bon Appetit, Tennis, New York Times, Pittsburgh Press, Gourmet, GBH, Newsday.*

"This is absolutely perfect! So many very special, lovely touches."

The Lamb & Lion

2504 Main St, Rt 6A, PO Box 511
Barnstable, MA 02630
(508)362-6823 (800)909-6923 Fax:(508)362-0227

Circa 1740. This rambling collection of Cape-style buildings sits on four acres overlooking the Old King's highway. Newly decorated, the inn offers a feeling of casual elegance. The Innkeeper's Pride is a romantic suite with sunken tub, fireplace, kitchenette and a deck overlooking a garden and woods. The Barn-stable is one of the original buildings and now offers three sleeping areas, a living and dining area and French doors to a private patio. A large central courtyard houses a generous sized pool and hot tub spa.

Innkeeper(s): Alice Pitcher. $115-165. MC, VISA, PC, TC. 10 rooms with PB, 2 with FP, 2 suites, 2 cottages and 1 conference room. Breakfast included in rates. Type of meal: Cont plus. Catering service available. Beds: KQDT. Cable TV and phone in room. Air conditioning. VCR and swimming on premises. Weddings, small meetings, family reunions and seminars hosted. Antiquing, fishing, golf, whale watching, live theater, parks, shopping, tennis and water sports nearby.

Barre D8

Stevens Farm B&B

Old Coldbrk Rd
Barre, MA 01005
(978)355-2227 Fax:(978)355-2234

Circa 1789. Guests enjoy an old-fashioned country experience at Stevens Farm. The 18th-century farmhouse has been in the innkeepers' family for nine generations since 1789. Guests can take tours of the 350-acre working farm, enjoy a swimming pool or just relax and enjoy the view from the gazebo. During the winter months, guests can cross-country ski on the property or ice skate on the pond. Colorful, handmade Afghans and comfortable antiques decorate the bedchambers. The parlor features Victorian furnishings,

an upright piano and a tin ceiling. The innkeeper once worked as a cook and professional baker and prepares the savory full breakfasts. Dinner, featuring items such as Yankee pot roast, homemade bread and cranberry walnut pie, can be arranged.

Historic Interest: Quark Walker slave grave, first all girls school, Sturbridge Village, Rocking Stone Park.

Innkeeper(s): Richard & Irene Stevens. $55-85. MC, VISA, AX, DC, DS, PC, TC. 5 rooms, 1 with PB and 1 conference room. Breakfast and afternoon tea included in rates. AP. Types of meals: Full bkfst, cont plus, cont and early coffee/tea. Snacks/refreshments, picnic lunch and room service available. Beds: DT. Window fans in room. Weddings, small meetings, family reunions and seminars hosted. Antiquing, art galleries, bicycling, canoeing/kayaking, fishing, golf, hiking, horseback riding, live theater, museums, shopping, downhill skiing, cross-country skiing, tennis and wineries nearby.

Bernardston C6

Falls River Inn

1 Brattleboro Rd
Bernardston, MA 01337-9532
(413)648-9904 Fax:(413)648-0538

Circa 1905. Guests have been welcomed to this site since the late 18th century. The first inn burned down in the 1800s, and the current Federal-style Victorian inn was built in its place. Guests will find various styles of antiques in their comfortable, country rooms, three of which include a fireplace. During the week, a continental breakfast is served, and on weekends, guests are treated to a full breakfast. The inn's restaurant is open

Wednesday through Sunday, and features everything from chicken pot pie to pepper shrimp served on a bed of angel hair pasta and surrounded by an orange cream sauce. Don't forget to try the restaurant's signature "Vampire Chasers."

Innkeeper(s): Kerber Family. $55-93. MC, VISA, AX, DS, PC, TC. TAC10. 7 rooms with PB, 5 with FP. Breakfast included in rates. Type of meal: Country bkfst. Dinner, lunch and banquet service available. Restaurant on premises. Beds: KQDT. Ceiling fan in room. Weddings, small meetings, family reunions and seminars hosted. Antiquing, bicycling, fishing, golf, hiking, live theater, parks, shopping, cross-country skiing, sporting events, tennis and water sports nearby.

"The food was excellent, the rooms charming and clean, the whole atmosphere so relaxing."

Beverly C14

Beverly Farms B&B

28 Hart St
Beverly, MA 01915
(978)922-6074

Circa 1839. This colonial home is appropriately appointed in colonial furnishings, stenciling, fireplaces with painted mantels, many-paned windows and polished pine floors. Indian shutters and antique latches and hardware increase the authenticity of the inn. Guest rooms offer

American antiques, handmade quilts and Oriental rugs. A buffet breakfast of fresh fruit, coffee, juice, cereal and sweet bread is served in the dining room. The House of Seven Gables is five miles away.

Historic Interest: House of Seven Gables (5 miles), Peabody Essex Museum.
Innkeeper(s): Steve & Peg Powers. $90-135. PC, TC. 3 rooms, 2 with PB. Type of meal: Cont plus. Beds: KDT. Turndown service in room. Air conditioning. Weddings hosted. Antiquing, art galleries, canoeing/kayaking, fishing, golf, horseback riding and private beach nearby.

Bunny's B&B

17 Kernwood Hgts
Beverly, MA 01915
(978)922-2392 Fax:(978)922-2392

Circa 1940. This Dutch Colonial inn is located on a scenic route along the state's northeastern coast. One room features a decorative fireplace and a handmade Oriental rug. Breakfasts in the formal dining room always feature homemade muffins and the innkeepers will make every effort to meet special dietary needs if notified in advance.

Innkeeper(s): Bunny & Joe Stacey. $65-95. PC, TC. 4 rooms, 2 with PB. Breakfast included in rates. Type of meal: Cont plus. Beds: QDT. TV on premises. Weddings, small meetings, family reunions and seminars hosted. Antiquing, historic sites, live theater, parks and shopping nearby.

Boston   E13

B&B Reservations

Greater Boston Branch
Boston, MA 02460
(617)964-1606 (800)832-2632 Fax:(617)332-8572
E-mail: info@bbreserve.com
Web: www.bbreserve.com

For a wide selection of unique lodging experiences in and around Boston or on Cape Cod this reservation service can help you find a guest room in a private home in an upscale historic neighborhood, an unhosted city apartment, a cottage or perhaps a vacation house. Choose the area you want and indulge your fantasy. Water view? Water front? Cobblestone street? Since 1985 this reservation service has been collecting listings in locations such as Boston's Back Bay, Beacon Hill as well as areas such as Brookline, Concord, Chestnut Hill, Lexington, Arlington and Cambridge. Additional listings in Cape Cod and Massachusetts North Shore can also be found.
$70-175. MC, VISA, AX. Types of meals: Full gourmet bkfst, cont and country bkfst. Beds: KQDT. TV, jacuzzi, fireplace and pool in room. Air conditioning. Beaches, whale watching, boat cruises, Island ferries, restaurants, live theater and shopping nearby.

Host Homes of Boston

PO Box 117-Waban Branch
Boston, MA 02468-0001
(617)244-1308

Circa 1864. One of the many fine homes available through this reservation service includes a stately townhouse on Commonwealth Avenue in Boston's chic Back Bay, less than one block away from the Boston Common and a short walk to Copley Square. Host Homes offers a variety of vacation possibilities throughout the Boston area and its suburbs. Country and coastal locations also are available.

Historic Interest: Boston and its surrounding areas are full of historic sites. Each of the accommodations is near something unique.

Innkeeper(s): Marcia Whittington. $75-175. MC, VISA, AX, PC. Breakfast included in rates. Type of meal: Cont plus. Beds: KQDT. Antiquing, historic sites, museums, whale watching, live theater, shopping and sporting events nearby.

Publicity: *Changing Times, USA Today, What's Doing in Boston, BBC Holiday, Marie Claire.*

"Very special. I have never stayed at such an excellent, elegant B&B. Our hosts were delightful, the place, magnificent!"

Oasis Guest House

22 Edgerly Rd
Boston, MA 02115-3007
(617)267-2262 Fax:(617)267-1920
E-mail: oasisgh@tiac.net
Web: www.oasisgh.com

Circa 1885. Located in the Back Bay area of Boston, this historic row house offers an excellent location from which to enjoy the city. More than one half of the guest rooms include a private bath, and all are comfortably furnished with antiques and contemporary pieces. The home still maintains some of its Victorian features, including a grand fireplace in one of the common areas. Continental fare is available in the mornings.

Innkeeper(s): Joe Haley. $72-119. MC, VISA, AX. TAC12. 16 rooms, 10 with PB. Breakfast and snacks/refreshments included in rates. Meal: Cont. Beds: QDT. Cable TV & phone in room. Air conditioning. Fax & copier on premises. Antiquing, museums, live theater, parks, shopping, sporting events & tennis nearby.

Brewster   H18

Candleberry Inn

1882 Main St
Brewster, MA 02631-1827
(508)896-3300 (800)573-4769 Fax:(508)896-4016
E-mail: candle@cape.com
Web: www.candleberryinn.com

Circa 1750. The two-acre grounds of this 250-year-old inn feature gardens complete with lawn swings. Wainscoting is dominant in the guest rooms, which feature Oriental rugs on top of pine-planked floors. Antiques and family heirlooms decorate the inn. Three rooms include working fireplaces and one has a Jacuzzi. A full, gourmet breakfast is served in the dining room, which is also the inn's oldest room. The beach is less than a mile away, and Brewster offers many shops and restaurants.

Innkeeper(s): Gini & David Donnelly. $80-165. MC, VISA, AX, DS, PC, TC. 9 rooms with PB, 3 with FP and 2 suites. Breakfast included in rates. Meal: Full gourmet bkfst. Beds: KQDT. Robes and hair dryers in room. Air conditioning. Fax and copier on premises. Family reunions hosted. Antiquing, fishing, golf, bike and nature trails, live theater, parks, shopping, tennis and water sports nearby.

Publicity: *Brewster Oracle, New York Times.*

"Wonderful, relaxing time, don't want to leave."

Old Manse Inn

1861 Main St PO Box 745
Brewster, MA 02631-0745
(508)896-3149
E-mail: oldmanse@cape.com
Web: www.oldmanseinn.com

Circa 1800. This completely renovated sea captain's house is tucked behind tall trees and has a gracious mansard roof. It was built by Captain Winslow F. Lewis Knowles and served as a link in the Underground Railroad during the Civil War.

Innkeeper(s): David & Suzanne Plum. $105-125. MC, VISA, AX, DS. 8 rooms with PB. Type of meal: Full bkfst. Gourmet dinner available. Restaurant on premises. Beds: QDT. Cable TV and phone in room. Air conditioning. Weddings, small meetings and family reunions hosted. Antiquing, fishing, live theater and shopping nearby.

Publicity: *Travel & Leisure, Boston Herald, Boston Globe.*

"Our stays at the Old Manse Inn have always been delightful. The innkeepers are gracious, the decor charming and the dining room has a character all its own."

Old Sea Pines Inn

2553 Main St, PO Box 1026
Brewster, MA 02631-1959
(508)896-6114 Fax:(508)896-7387
E-mail: seapines@c4.net
Web: www.oldseapinesinn.com

Circa 1900. This turn-of-the-century mansion on three-and-one-half acres of lawns and trees was formerly the Sea Pines School of Charm and Personality for Young Women, established in 1907. Recently renovated, the inn displays elegant wallpapers and a grand sweeping stairway. It is located near beaches and bike paths, as well as village shops and restaurants.

Historic Interest: Local Historic Registry.

Innkeeper(s): Michele & Stephen Rowan. $65-125. MC, VISA, AX, DC, DS. 23 rooms, 14 with PB, 3 with FP, 2 suites and 1 conference room. Breakfast and afternoon tea included in rates. Types of meals: Full bkfst and early coffee/tea. Snacks/refreshments, picnic lunch, banquet service, catering service and room service available. Beds: QDT. Cable TV and phone in room. Air conditioning. Handicap access. Weddings, small meetings, family reunions and seminars hosted. Antiquing, fishing, dinner theatre in summer, live theater, shopping and water sports nearby.

Publicity: *New York Times, Cape Cod Oracle, For Women First, Home Office, Entrepreneur, Boston Magazine.*

"The loving care applied by Steve, Michele and staff is deeply appreciated."

Pepper House Inn

2062 Main St (Rt 6A)
Brewster, MA 02631
(508)896-4389 Fax:(508)896-5012

Circa 1793. This handsome two-story, red Federal-style home has the typical five-window facade with a fanlight over the centered door. A sea captain's house now in the National Register, it has been handsomely restored. Guest rooms offer four-poster beds, antiques, reproductions, original wide pine floors, wallpapers, chandeliers and colonial fireplaces. An outdoor deck with market umbrellas is a favored spot in good weather for breakfast. Located near the center of the village, the inn is convenient to the historic district, galleries, antique shops and craft studios. Bike trails and beaches are a short walk or drive away.

Innkeeper(s): Bill & Cheri Metters. $89-139. MC, VISA, AX. 4 rooms with PB, 4 with FP. Breakfast and snacks/refreshments included in rates. Types of meals: Full gourmet bkfst and early coffee/tea. Beds: Q. Cable TV in room. Air conditioning. Fax on premises. Antiquing, fishing, golf, bike trail, museums, beaches, live theater, parks, shopping, tennis and water sports nearby.

"We weren't quite sure if we were B&B compatible, but after this most hospitable five days, we are hooked!"

Ruddy Turnstone B&B

463 Main St
Brewster, MA 02631-1049
(508)385-9871 (800)654-1995

Circa 1810. This restored antique-filled farmhouse affords ocean views. Guests opt for rooms in the main house or in the restored carriage house, which was brought to the property

from Nantucket. Each guest room offers something special. The Bayview Suite includes a fireplace and boasts ocean views. Both carriage house rooms includes canopy beds and period furniture. In 1998, the bed & breakfast was named as the best B&B on the Lower Cape by Cape Cod Life Magazine. Guests to this Cape Cod retreat can relax and enjoy views of the marsh and the bay or stroll to shops, museums and restaurants.

Innkeeper(s): Gordon & Sally Swanson. $90-165. MC, VISA, AX, PC, TC. TAC10. 5 rooms with PB, 1 with FP, 2 suites and 2 conference rooms. Breakfast included in rates. Types of meals: Full bkfst and early coffee/tea. Beds: Q. Turndown service in room. Air conditioning. Weddings, small meetings, family reunions and seminars hosted. Antiquing, beaches, fishing, golf, galleries, whale watching, live theater, parks, shopping and tennis nearby.

Publicity: *National Geographic Traveler, Victoria, Cape Cod Life Magazine.*

"Here lies the true New England, warm, comfortable and welcoming."

Brookline   E13

The Bertram Inn

92 Sewall Ave
Brookline, MA 02146-5327
(617)566-2234 (800)295-3822 Fax:(617)277-1887

Circa 1907. Antiques and authenticity are the rule at this turn-of-the-century Gothic Revival inn, found on a peaceful, tree-lined street two miles from central Boston. The Bertram Inn

features old-English stylings and Victorian decor. Guests can enjoy breakfast or afternoon tea by the fire in the common room or, if weather permits, on the front porch overlooking the garden. Boston College, Boston University, Fenway Park and the F.L. Olmstead National Historic Site all are nearby. Shops and restaurants are within walking distance, and the Boston area's many attractions are nearby. Parking is included in the rates.

Historic Interest: Faneuil Hall and the Freedom Trail (10 minutes).

Innkeeper(s): Bryan Austin. $84-219. MC, VISA, AX, TC. TAC10. 14 rooms with PB, 2 with FP and 4 suites. Breakfast included in rates. Type of meal: Cont plus. Afternoon tea available. Beds: KQDT. Cable TV, phone and hair dryer in room. Air conditioning. Fax on premises. German, French, Spanish and Italian spoken. Sporting events nearby.

Pets Allowed.

"The Bertram Inn is a gem, and you may be sure I will highly recommend it to anyone coming this way. So pleased to have discovered you!"

Cambridge E13

Harding House

288 Harvard St
Cambridge, MA 02139
(617)876-2888 Fax:(617)497-0953

Circa 1867. Located in the mid-Cambridge area, this historic Victorian is within walking distance to Harvard Square, and guests can hop on the Red Line and head into Boston. The

guest rooms feature a comfortable decor and amenities include fax service and in-room hair dryers. A continental buffet is set up in the breakfast room. The owners also operate Irving House at Harvard.

Innkeeper(s): Rachael Solem. $80-180. MC, VISA, AX, DC, PC, TC. TAC10. 14 rooms with PB. Breakfast included in rates. Type of meal: Cont plus. Beds: QT. TV and phone in room. Air conditioning. Fax and limited parking on premises. Antiquing, historic tours, restaurants, shopping and sporting events nearby.

Irving House at Harvard

24 Irving Street
Cambridge, MA 02138-3007
(617)547-4600 (877)547-4600 Fax:(617)576-2814
E-mail: reserve@irvinghouse.com
Web: www.irvinghouse.com

Circa 1893. Irving House is located in a historic, turn-of-the-century Colonial Revival and has been receiving guests since the 1940s. The simple, comfortable rooms feature a modern hotel decor, and more than half include a private bath. In the

mornings, a continental buffet with fruit, pastries and cereals is set up for guests to enjoy. Harvard Square is just minutes away, and guests can walk to the Red Line stop that goes into Boston.

Innkeeper(s): Patsy Yike. $75-200. MC, VISA, AX, DS, TC. TAC10. 44 rooms, 27 with PB and 1 conference room. Breakfast included in rates. Type of meal: Cont plus. Beds: QDT. Phone and TV (some rooms) in room. Air conditioning. Fax and library on premises. Handicap access. Antiquing, bookstores, history, live theater, shopping and sporting events nearby.

The Mary Prentiss Inn

6 Prentiss St
Cambridge, MA 02140-2212
(617)661-2929 Fax:(617)661-5989
E-mail: njfandetti.com
Web: www.maryprentissinn.com

Circa 1843. Only a half-mile from Harvard Square, this restored Greek Revival Inn features ionic fluted columns and Doric trim. During summer months, guests are treated to breakfast under umbrella-covered tables on the outdoor deck, while wintertime guests enjoy their morning fare in front of a roaring fire in the parlor room. Several of the unique guest rooms feature kitchenettes, three suites include a working fireplace. The inn is winner of the 1995 Massachusetts Historic Commission Preservation Award.

Historic Interest: Cambridge offers no shortage of activities, including the Cambridge Common where George Washington took command of the Continental Army, and the church where he and wife, Martha, worshiped. Historic battlefields and Walden Pond are only a short drive away.

Innkeeper(s): Jennifer & Nicholas Fandetti. $99-229. MC, VISA, AX, PC, TC. TAC10. 20 rooms with PB, 3 with FP and 5 suites. Breakfast and afternoon tea included in rates. Type of meal: Full bkfst. Catering service available. Beds: QT. Cable TV, phone and ceiling fan in room. Air conditioning. Fax on premises. Handicap access. Weddings and family reunions hosted. Antiquing, golf, live theater, parks, shopping, sporting events, tennis and water sports nearby.

Publicity: *Cambridge Chronicle, Travel & Leisure, Discerning Traveler, Cambridge Current.*

"We thank you for the special privilege of staying at such a magnificent inn. We had a wonderful time, and you helped to make it so."

Cape Cod, Harwich Port I18

Augustus Snow House

528 Main St
Cape Cod, Harwich Port, MA 02646-1842
(508)430-0528 (800)320-0528 Fax:(508)432-6638

Circa 1901. This gracious, Queen Anne Victorian is a turn-of-the-century gem, complete with a wide, wraparound veranda, gabled windows and a distinctive turret. Victorian wallpapers,

stained glass and rich woodwork complement the interior, which is appropriately decorated in period style. Each of the romantic guest quarters offers something special. One room has a canopy bed

and all rooms have fireplaces, while another includes a relaxing clawfoot tub. Three rooms have Jacuzzi tubs. The beds are dressed in fine linens. As is the Victorian way, afternoon refreshments are served each day. The breakfasts include delectables, such as banana chip muffins, baked pears in raspberry cream sauce or, possibly, baked French toast with layers of homemade cinnamon bread, bacon and cheese.

Innkeeper(s): Joyce & Steve Roth. $105-180. MC, VISA, AX, DS, PC, TC. 5 rooms with PB, 5 with FP. Breakfast included in rates. Types of meals: Full gourmet bkfst and early coffee/tea. Beds: KQ. Cable TV, phone, ceiling fan and fireplace one room in room. Air conditioning. Fax, copier and bicycles rented nearby on premises. Weddings, small meetings and family reunions hosted. Antiquing, fishing, golf, private beach, restaurants, bike trails, parks, shopping and water sports nearby.

Chatham   119

The Azubah Atwood Inn

177 Cross St
Chatham, MA 02633
(508)945-7075 (888)265-6220 Fax:(508)945-0714

Circa 1789. A sea captain built this 18th-century home, and additions were made to the home in 1838. The innkeepers live on the premises of the historic home, which boasts one of the few cupolas in the community. Guests can enjoy the peaceful grounds from the porch or, perhaps, from a bench tucked in the side yard.

Innkeeper(s): William & Audrey Gray. $159. MC, VISA, AX, PC, TC. TAC10. 3 rooms with PB, 1 with FP. Breakfast and afternoon tea included in rates. Types of meals: Full bkfst and early coffee/tea. Beds: Q. Cable TV and phone in room. Air conditioning. Fax and library on premises. Antiquing, fishing, golf, live theater, parks, shopping, tennis and water sports nearby.

Carriage House Inn

407 Old Harbor Rd
Chatham, MA 02633-2322
(508)945-4688 (800)355-8868 Fax:(508)945-8909

Circa 1890. This Colonial Revival inn is an easy find as it is located adjacent to Chatham's tallest flagpole. Antiques and family pieces decorate the interior. Chintzes and floral prints permeate the six guest rooms, and the three carriage house rooms each include a fireplace and an entrance to an outside sitting area. Breakfast items such as fresh fruit,

juices, pancakes, French toast, eggs Benedict and quiche can be enjoyed either in the dining room or on the sun porch. Guests can walk to Chatham's Main Street and to shops and galleries, or just relax and enjoy the grounds, which include gardens. Beach towels are furnished for trips to the shore, just a quarter mile away.

Historic Interest: Cape Cod National Seashore (20 minutes).

Innkeeper(s): Patty & Dennis O'Neill. $95-180. MC, VISA, AX, DS, PC, TC. TAC10. 6 rooms with PB, 3 with FP. Breakfast and snacks/refreshments included in rates. Types of meals: Full bkfst and early coffee/tea. Beds: Q. Ceiling fan in room. Air conditioning. VCR and fax on premises. Antiquing, fishing, hiking, live theater, parks, shopping and water sports nearby.

"This might well have been our best B&B experience ever. It was the hosts who made it so memorable."

The Cranberry Inn of Chatham

359 Main St
Chatham, MA 02633-2425
(508)945-9232 (800)332-4667 Fax:(508)945-3769

Circa 1830. Continuously operating for over 150 years, this inn originally was called the Traveler's Lodge, then the Monomoyic after a local Indian tribe. A cranberry bog adjacent to the property inspired the current name. Recently restored, the inn is located in the heart of the historic district. It's within walking distance of the lighthouse, beaches, shops and restaurants. Guest rooms feature four-poster beds, wide-planked floors and coordinated fabrics. Antique and reproduction furnishings throughout.

Innkeeper(s): Kay & Bill DeFord Chef: Will DeFord. $100-260. MC, VISA, AX, PC, TC. 18 rooms with PB, 8 with FP and 2 suites. Breakfast and afternoon tea included in rates. Type of meal: Full gourmet bkfst. Beds: QDT. Private balconies and wet bars and fireplaces in some rooms in room. Fully licensed tavern on premises. Antiquing, art galleries, bicycling, fishing, golf, live theater, parks and sporting events nearby.

Cyrus Kent House

63 Cross St
Chatham, MA 02633-2207
(508)945-9104 (800)338-5368 Fax:(508)945-9104

Circa 1877. A former sea captain's home, the Cyrus Kent House was built in the Greek Revival style. The award-winning restoration retained many original features such as wide pine floorboards, ceiling rosettes, and marble fireplaces. Although furnished with antiques and reproductions, all modern amenities are available. Most bedrooms have four-poster beds. Suites feature sitting rooms with fireplaces. Chatham's historic district is a short stroll away.

Innkeeper(s): Sharon Mitchell-Swan. $85-250. MC, VISA. 10 rooms with PB. Breakfast and afternoon tea included in rates. Types of meals: Cont plus and early coffee/tea. Beds: QD. Cable TV and phone in room. Fax on premises. Weddings, small meetings, family reunions and seminars hosted. Antiquing, fishing, shopping and water sports nearby.

Moses Nickerson House

364 Old Harbor Rd
Chatham, MA 02633-2374
(508)945-5859 (800)628-6972

Circa 1839. This historic, rambling sea captain's house, built in 1839, features wide pine floors, many fireplaces and colorful gardens. Unforgettably charming, the inn is decorated with antique furnishings and Oriental rugs, retaining the character of by-gone days. Each of the rooms offers its own distinctive decor. Breakfast is served in a glass-enclosed dining area that radiates morning sunlight. The inn provides an ambiance of simple elegance.

Innkeeper(s): Linda & George Watts. $95-189. MC, VISA, AX, DS. 7 rooms with PB, 3 with FP. Type of meal: Full bkfst. Beds: Q. TV and phone in room. Air conditioning.

"The attention to detail in unsurpassed."

Old Harbor Inn

22 Old Harbor Rd
Chatham, MA 02633-2315
(508)945-4434 (800)942-4434 Fax:(508)945-7665

Circa 1932. This pristine New England bed & breakfast was once the home of "Doc" Keene, a popular physician in the area. A meticulous renovation has created an elegant, beautiful-

ly appointed inn offering antique furnishings, designer linens and lavish amenities in an English country decor. A buffet breakfast, featuring Judy's homemade muffins, is served in the sunroom or on the deck. The beaches, boutiques and galleries are a walk away and there is an old grist mill, the Chatham Lighthouse, and a railroad museum. Band concerts are offered Friday nights in the summer at Kate Gould Park.

Historic Interest: The Whit Tileston Band Stand Gazebo in Kate Gould Park (one-half mile), The Nickerson Family Genealogical Research Center (2 miles), The Training Field of the Colonial Militia, Old Burial Grounds, Atwood House Museum.

Innkeeper(s): Judy & Ray Braz. $99-239. MC, VISA, PC, TC. TAC10. 8 rooms with PB, 2 with FP and 1 conference room. Breakfast included in rates. Types of meals: Cont plus and early coffee/tea. Afternoon tea available. Beds: KQT. Ceiling fan, toiletries and Welcome Package in room. Air conditioning. Concierge and gift shop on premises. Small meetings hosted. Antiquing, fishing, beaches, art festivals, concerts, golf, tennis, live theater, parks, shopping and water sports nearby.

Port Fortune Inn

201 Main St
Chatham, MA 02633-2423
(508)945-0792 (800)750-0792

Circa 1910. The fronts of these charming Cape Cod buildings are decorated with colorful flowers and plants. The interiors of each of the inn's two historic buildings is elegant and inviting

with traditional furnishings, and most of the guest rooms are decorated with four-poster beds. The breakfast room and some of the guest rooms have ocean views. The grounds include perennial gardens and a patio set up with furniture for those who wish to relax and catch a few sea breezes. The inn is featured on the walking tour through the historic Old Village, which is Chatham's oldest neighborhood. Port Fortune Inn is a short walk away from beaches and the historic Chatham Lighthouse.

Innkeeper(s): Mike & Renee Kahl. $90-190. MC, VISA, AX. TAC10. 14 rooms with PB. Breakfast included in rates. Types of meals: Cont plus and early coffee/tea. Beds: Q. Phone in room. Air conditioning. Fax, copier, library and beach towels and chairs on premises. Amusement parks, antiquing, fishing, golf, whale watching, live theater, parks, shopping, tennis and water sports nearby.

"Excellent. The entire experience was wonderful as usual."

Concord D12

Colonel Roger Brown House

1694 Main St
Concord, MA 01742-2831
(978)369-9119 (800)292-1369 Fax:(978)369-1305

Circa 1775. This house was the home of Minuteman Roger Brown, who fought the British at the Old North Bridge. The frame for this center-chimney Colonial was being raised on April 19, 1775, the day the battle took place. Some parts of the

house were built as early as 1708. The adjacent Damon Mill houses a fitness club available to guests. Both buildings are in the National Register. Among the many nearby historic sites are Thoreau's Walden Pond, the Concord Museum, the Alcott House, Old North Bridge, Lexington, the National Heritage Museum, Lowell Mills and much more.

Historic Interest: Thoreau's Walden Pond, Concord Museum, Alcott House, Wayside, Old Manse, Old North Bridge (all 3 miles), Lexington, National Heritage Museum (11 miles), Lowell Mills and national historic district (15 miles).

Innkeeper(s): Lauri Berlied. $80-115. MC, VISA, AX, PC, TC. TAC10. 5 rooms with PB and 1 suite. Breakfast and afternoon tea included in rates. Type of meal: Cont plus. Beds: QDT. Cable TV, phone, color TV and refrigerator upon request in room. Air conditioning. Fax, copier, spa, swimming, sauna, library and data port on premises. Family reunions and seminars hosted. Antiquing, fishing, live theater, parks, shopping, downhill skiing, cross-country skiing and water sports nearby.

"The Colonel Roger Brown House makes coming to Concord even more of a treat! Many thanks for your warm hospitality."

Hawthorne Inn

462 Lexington Rd
Concord, MA 01742-3729
(978)369-5610 Fax:(978)287-4949
E-mail: hawthorneinn@concordmass.com
Web: www.concordmass.com

Circa 1870. The Hawthorne Inn is situated on land that once belonged to Ralph Waldo Emerson, the Alcotts and Nathaniel Hawthorne. It was here that Bronson Alcott planted his fruit trees, made pathways to the Mill Brook, and erected his Bath House. Hawthorne purchased the land and repaired a path leading to his home with trees planted on either side. Two of these trees still stand. Across the road is Hawthorne's House, The Wayside. Next to it is the Alcott's Orchard House and Grapevine Cottage where the Concord grape was developed. Nearby is Sleepy Hollow Cemetery where Emerson, the Alcotts, the Thoreaus and Hawthorne were laid to rest.

Historic Interest: Old North Bridge and Walden Pond are just a few minutes away.

Innkeeper(s): Marilyn Mudry & Gregory Burch. $140-215. MC, VISA, AX,

DS, PC, TC. TAC10. 7 rooms with PB. Breakfast and afternoon tea included in rates. Type of meal: Cont plus. Beds: QDT. Air conditioning. Fax, library and piano on premises. Weddings, small meetings and family reunions hosted. Antiquing, fishing, authors homes, parks, shopping and cross-country skiing nearby.

Publicity: *New York Times, Boston Globe, Yankee.*

"Surely there couldn't be a better or more valuable location for a comfortable, old-fashioned country inn."

Cummaquid — I17

The Acworth Inn

4352 Old Kings Hwy, PO Box 256
Cummaquid, MA 02637
(508)362-3330 (800)362-6363

Circa 1860. This inn, located on the Olde Kings Highway on the north side of Cape Cod, offers a strategic midway point for those exploring the area. The historic Cape-style farmhouse features five guest rooms, including a luxury suite. Hand-painted, restored furniture adds charm to the inn's interior. Guests select from the Cummaquid, Chatham, Yarmouth Port,  Barnstable and Orleans rooms, all named for Cape Cod villages. Visitors will find the shore just a half-mile from the inn.

Historic Interest: Sturgis Library (2 miles away in Barnstable), Old Colonial Courthouse. Route 6A is part of America's largest historic district.

Innkeeper(s): Cheryl & Jack Ferrell. $95-185. MC, VISA, AX, DS, PC, TC. TAC10. 5 rooms with PB, 2 with FP. Breakfast and afternoon tea included in rates. Types of meals: Full bkfst and early coffee/tea. Beds: QT. Turndown service in room. Library and newspaper on premises. German spoken. Antiquing, fishing, museum, live theater, parks, shopping and water sports nearby.

"...great accommodations, food, tour guiding, local flavor, etc...We will be back."

Cummington — D4

Cumworth Farm

472 W Cummington Rd
Cummington, MA 01026-9603
(413)634-5529

Circa 1780. Fresh raspberries and blueberries are harvested each season at this 200-year-old working farm. Innkeeper Ed McColgan produces 250 gallons of maple syrup each year in the farm's sugar house, and cattle and sheep also are raised. The farm house itself is decorated in colonial furnishings. Cummington has a special fair each August and nearby Worthington holds a balloon festival in the fall. Other local attractions include the Hill Gallery, which offers a variety of pottery and paintings by local artists.

Innkeeper(s): Edward McColgan. $75. PC. 6 rooms, 1 with FP. Breakfast included in rates. Type of meal: Full bkfst. Beds: DT. Ceiling fan in room. Copier and spa on premises. Weddings, small meetings and family reunions hosted. Amusement parks, antiquing, fishing, golf, live theater, parks, shopping, cross-country skiing, sporting events, tennis and water sports nearby.

Deerfield — C6

Deerfield Inn

81 Old Main St
Deerfield, MA 01342-0305
(413)774-5587 (800)926-3865 Fax:(413)775-7221
E-mail: innkeeper@deerfieldinn.com
Web: www.deerfieldinn.com

Circa 1884. The village of Deerfield was settled in 1670. Farmers in the area still unearth bones and ax and arrow heads from French/Indian massacre of 1704. Now, 50 beautifully restored 18th- and 19th-century homes line the mile-long main street, considered by many to be the loveliest street in New England. Fourteen of these hous-  es are museums of Pioneer Valley decorative arts and are open year-round to the public. The Memorial Hall Museum, open from May to November, is the oldest museum in New England and full of local antiquities. The inn is situated at the center of this peaceful village, and for those who wish to truly experience New England's past, this is the place. The village has been designated a National Historic Landmark.

Innkeeper(s): Jane & Karl Sabo. $146-241. MC, VISA, AX. 23 rooms with PB and 1 conference room. Breakfast and afternoon tea included in rates. Type of meal: Full bkfst. Dinner and lunch available. Restaurant on premises. Beds: T. TV in room. Fax and copier on premises. Handicap access. Antiquing, fishing, live theater and cross-country skiing nearby.

"We've stayed at many New England inns, but the Deerfield Inn ranks among the best."

Dennis — I18

Isaiah Hall B&B Inn

152 Whig St, PO Box 1007
Dennis, MA 02638
(508)385-9928 (800)736-0160 Fax:(508)385-5879
E-mail: info@isaiahhallinn.com
Web: www.isaiahhallinn.com

Circa 1857. Adjacent to the Cape's oldest cranberry bog is this Greek Revival farmhouse built by Isaiah Hall, a cooper. His grandfather was the first cultivator of cranberries in America and Isaiah designed and patented the original barrel for shipping cranberries. In 1948,  Dorothy Gripp, an artist, established the inn. Many examples of her artwork remain.

Historic Interest: Cape Playhouse (one-third mile), Old Kings Highway (one-third mile), Old Salt Works (2 miles).

Innkeeper(s): Marie Brophy. $97-163. MC, VISA, AX, TC. 9 rooms, 10 with PB, 1 with FP and 1 suite. Breakfast included in rates. Types of meals: Cont plus and early coffee/tea. Beds: KQDT. Cable TV and phone in room. Air conditioning. Fax on premises. Antiquing, fishing, golf, whale watching, bike paths, live theater, parks, shopping and water sports nearby.

Publicity: *Cape Cod Life, New York Times, Golf, National Geographic Traveler.*

"Your place is so lovely and relaxing."

Dennisport

I18

Rose Petal B&B

152 Sea St PO Box 974
Dennisport, MA 02639-2404
(508)398-8470

Circa 1872. This Cape Cod-style home was built for Almond Wixon, whose seafaring family was among the original settlers of Dennisport. In 1918, Wixon was lost at sea with all on board. The Wixon homestead was completely restored in

1986. Surrounded by a white picket fence and attractively landscaped yard, the Rose Petal is situated in the heart of Cape Cod, a short walk from the beach. Home-baked pastries highlight a full breakfast in the dining room.

Historic Interest: JFK Museum, family compound (10 miles).

Innkeeper(s): Gayle & Dan Kelly. $59-98. MC, VISA, AX. TAC10. 3 rooms, 2 with PB. Breakfast included in rates. Types of meals: Full gourmet bkfst and early coffee/tea. Beds: QT. Air conditioning. Family reunions hosted. Some French spoken. Antiquing, fishing, whale watching, live theater, parks, shopping and water sports nearby.

"Perfect. Every detail was appreciated."

Dennis (South)

I18

Captain Nickerson Inn

333 Main St
Dennis (South), MA 02660-3643
(508)398-5966 (800)282-1619

Circa 1828. This Queen Anne Victorian inn is located in the mid-Cape area. Guests can relax on the front porch with white wicker rockers and tables. The guest rooms are decorated with period four-poster

or white iron queen beds and hand-woven or Oriental-style rugs. The dining room has a fireplace and a stained-glass picture window. The Cape Cod bike Rail Trail, which is more than 20 miles long, is less than a mile away.

Historic Interest: Jericho House is one mile away, while Scargo Tower is a five-mile drive.

Innkeeper(s): Pat & Dave York. $82-135. MC, VISA, DS, PC. TAC10. 5 rooms with PB and 1 suite. Breakfast included in rates. Type of meal: Full bkfst. Beds: QDT. Ceiling fan and terry robes in room. Air conditioning. VCR, fax and bicycles on premises. Small meetings and family reunions hosted. Antiquing, fishing, beaches, historic sites, museums, bike trails, live theater, parks, shopping and water sports nearby.

"Your inn is great!"

Duxbury

G15

The Winsor House Inn

390 Washington St
Duxbury, MA 02332-4552
(781)934-0991 Fax:(781)934-5955

Circa 1803. A visit to this inn is much like a visit back in time to Colonial days. The early 19th-century home was built by a prominent sea captain and merchant, Nathaniel Winsor, as a wedding gift for his

daughter, Nancy. With an eye for the authentic, the innkeepers have restored parts of the inn to look much the way it might have when the young bride and groom took up residence. Rooms are decorated with Colonial furnishings, canopied beds, fresh flowers and three rooms have fireplaces. The Carriage House offers seasonal lunch fare and year-round dinner. Guests may enjoy a drink at the inn's English-style pub. For a romantic dinner, try the inn's Dining Room, which serves everything from roasted venison with a juniper berry and mushroom crust to herb-seared salmon with plum tomato saffron vinaigrette.

Historic Interest: Plimouth Plantation, Mayflower and Plymouth Rock, 15 minutes away. Twenty miles to Cape Cod.

Innkeeper(s): Mr & Mrs David M O'Connell. $130-210. MC, VISA, AX, DS, PC, TC. 4 rooms with PB, 3 with FP and 2 suites. Breakfast included in rates. Type of meal: Full bkfst. Gourmet dinner, picnic lunch, banquet service and catering service available. Restaurant on premises. Beds: QT. Fax and copier on premises. Small meetings and family reunions hosted. Antiquing, fishing, Plymouth, shopping, cross-country skiing and water sports nearby.

Eastham

H18

Penny House Inn

4885 County Rd, PO Box 238
Eastham, MA 02651
(508)255-6632 (800)554-1751 Fax:(508)255-4893
E-mail: pennyhouse@aol.com
Web: pennyhouseinn.com

Circa 1690. Captain Isaiah Horton built this house with a shipbuilder's bow roof. Traditional wide-planked floors and 200-year-old beams buttress the ceiling of the public room. The Captain's Quarters, the largest guest room with its own fireplace, bears the motto: Coil up your ropes and anchor here, Til better weather doth appear.

Innkeeper(s): Margaret Keith. $125-190. MC, VISA, AX, DS, PC, TC. TAC10. 11 rooms with PB, 3 with FP and 1 conference room. Breakfast and afternoon tea included in rates. Types of meals: Full bkfst and early coffee/tea. Beds: KQDT. Ceiling fan and fireplaces (some rooms) in room. Air conditioning. VCR, fax, copier and library on premises. Weddings, small meetings, family reunions and seminars hosted. Antiquing, fishing, live theater, parks, shopping and water sports nearby.

Publicity: *Cape Cod Life, Cape Codder.*

"Enjoyed my stay tremendously. My mouth waters thinking of your delicious breakfast."

The Whalewalk Inn

220 Bridge Rd
Eastham, MA 02642-3261
(508)255-0617 Fax:(508)240-0017
E-mail: whalewak@capecod.net
Web: www.whalewalkinn.com

Circa 1830. Three acres of meadow and lawn surround the Whalewalk, originally a whaling captain's house. An old picket fence frames the elegant house and there is a widow's walk. In addition to the main house, suites are available in a separate guest house, a renovated barn, a carriage house and a salt-box cottage. Common rooms boast 19th-century antiques from

England, France and Denmark, and guest rooms boast antique low-post beds, country furnishings and lovely

linens. Start off the day with a delectable full breakfast including crepes, waffles or Grand Marnier French toast. The inn is within walking distance of Cape Cod's bayside beaches and the Cape Cod Rail Trail, a 27-mile bike path.

Historic Interest: Cape Cod National Seashore is 10 minutes away, as is First Encounter Beach. Pilgrim Monument Provincetown is a 30-minute drive.

Innkeeper(s): Carolyn & Richard Smith. $155-275. MC, VISA, AX, PC, TC. TAC10. 16 rooms with PB, 13 with FP and 5 suites. Breakfast and snacks/refreshments included in rates. Types of meals: Full gourmet bkfst and early coffee/tea. Beds: KQT. Air conditioning. Fax, copier, bicycles and library on premises. Small meetings, family reunions and seminars hosted. Antiquing, fishing, live theater, shopping and water sports nearby.

"Your hospitality will long be remembered."

East Orleans   H19

The Nauset House Inn

143 Beach Rd, PO Box 774
East Orleans, MA 02643
(508)255-2195 Fax:(508)240-6276

Circa 1810. Located a 1/2 mile from Nauset Beach, this inn is a renovated farmhouse set on three acres, which include an old apple orchard. A Victorian conservatory was purchased from a Connecticut estate and reassembled here, then filled with wicker furnishings, Cape flowers and stained glass. Hand-stenciling,

handmade quilts, antiques and more bouquets of flowers decorate the rooms. The breakfast room

features a fireplace, brick floor and beamed ceiling. Breakfast includes treats such as ginger pancakes or waffles with fresh strawberries. Wine and cranberry juice are served in the evenings.

Innkeeper(s): Al & Diane Johnson, John & Cindy Vessella. $75-135. MC, VISA, DS, PC, TC. 14 rooms, 8 with PB and 1 cottage. Breakfast and snacks/refreshments included in rates. Types of meals: Full bkfst and early coffee/tea. Afternoon tea available. Beds: KQDT. Terry robes for shared bath guests in room. Antiquing, fishing, biking, tennis, ocean, golf, live theater, parks, shopping, sporting events and water sports nearby.

"The inn provided a quiet, serene, comforting atmosphere."

The Parsonage Inn

202 Main St, PO Box 1501
East Orleans, MA 02643
(508)255-8217 (888)422-8217 Fax:(508)255-8216

Circa 1770. Originally a parsonage, this Cape-style home is now a romantic inn nestled in the village of East Orleans and only a mile and a half from Nauset Beach. Rooms are decorated with antiques, quilts, Laura Ashley fabrics and stenciling, and they include the original pine floors and low ceilings. Freshly baked breakfasts are served either in the dining

room or on the brick patio. The innkeepers keep a selection of menus from local restaurants on hand and serve appetizers and refreshments each evening while guest peruse their dining choices. The Parsonage is the perfect location to enjoy nature, with the national seashore, Nickerson State Park and whale-watching opportunities available to guests.

Historic Interest: Cape Cod offers plenty of historic homes and sites.

Innkeeper(s): Ian & Elizabeth Browne. $100-135. MC, VISA, AX. TAC10. 8 rooms with PB and 2 suites. Breakfast included in rates. Beds: QDT. Phone, ceiling fan and TV (some rooms) in room. Air conditioning. Fax, refrigerator in parlor and piano on premises. Antiquing, restaurants, live theater, shopping and water sports nearby.

"Your hospitality was as wonderful as your home. Your home was as beautiful as Cape Cod. Thank you!"

Ship's Knees Inn

186 Beach Rd, PO Box 756
East Orleans, MA 02643
(508)255-1312 Fax:(508)240-1351
Web: capecodtravel.com/shipskneesinn

Circa 1820. This 175-year-old restored sea captain's home is a three-minute walk to the ocean. Rooms are decorated in a nautical style with antiques. Several rooms feature authentic ship's knees, hand-painted trunks, old clipper ship models and four-

poster beds. Some rooms boast ocean views and the Master Suite has a working fireplace. The inn offers swimming and tennis facilities on the grounds. About three miles away, the innkeepers also offer a one-bedroom efficiency apartment and two heated cottages on the Cove. Head into town or spend the day basking in the beauty of Nauset Beach with its picturesque sand dunes.

Innkeeper(s): Jean & Ken Pitchford. $55-135. MC, VISA. 19 rooms with PB, 3 with FP. Breakfast included in rates. Type of meal: Cont. Beds: KQDT. Weddings, small meetings and family reunions hosted. Amusement parks, antiquing, fishing, live theater, parks, shopping and water sports nearby.

Publicity: *Boston Globe.*

"Warm, homey and very friendly atmosphere. Very impressed with the beamed ceilings."

Edgartown   K16

The Arbor

222 Upper Main St, PO Box 1228
Edgartown, MA 02539
(508)627-8137

Circa 1880. Originally built on the adjoining island of
Chappaquiddick, this house was moved over to Edgartown on
a barge at the turn of the century. Located on the bicycle path,
it is within walking distance from downtown and the harbor.

Guests may relax in
the hammock, have
tea on the porch, or
walk the unspoiled
island beaches of
Martha's Vineyard.
Historic Interest: Methodist
Camp Meeting Ground.

Innkeeper(s): Peggy Hall. $125-175. MC, VISA, PC, TC. TAC10. 10 rooms,
8 with PB. Breakfast and afternoon tea included in rates. Type of meal: Cont.
Beds: QD. Air conditioning. Guest refrigerator on premises. Antiquing, fishing,
biking, live theater, shopping and water sports nearby.

Publicity: *Herald News, Yankee Traveler.*

*"Thank you so much for your wonderful hospitality! You are a superb
hostess. If I ever decide to do my own B&B, your example would be
my guide."*

Colonial Inn of Martha's Vineyard

38 N Water St, PO Box 68
Edgartown, MA 02539-0068
(508)627-4711 (800)627-4701 Fax:(508)627-5904
Web: www.colonialinnmvy.com

Circa 1911. This impressive Colonial structure has served as
an inn since opening its doors in 1911. Somerset Maugham
and Howard Hughes were among the regulars at the inn.
Guests at Colonial Inn can sit back and relax on a porch lined
with rockers as they gaze at the harbor and enjoy refreshing sea
breezes. Flowers, an atrium and courtyards decorate the
grounds. The inn has a full-service restaurant and seven boutiques on the premises. Some guest rooms boast harbor views,
and all are decorated in an elegant country style. The inn is
located in the heart of the town's historic district.

Innkeeper(s): Linda Malcouronne. $100-350. MC, VISA, AX, PC, TC. TAC10.
44 rooms with PB, 5 suites and 3 conference rooms. Breakfast included in
rates. Type of meal: Cont plus. Dinner and lunch available. Restaurant on
premises. Beds: QD. Cable TV, phone, VCRs, refrigerators in some rooms,
HBO and Cinemax in room. Air conditioning. Fax and library on premises.
Handicap access. Small meetings and seminars hosted. Portuguese and
Spanish spoken. Antiquing, fishing, art galleries, concerts, swimming, cycling,
golf, tennis, live theater, parks, shopping and water sports nearby.

*"The Colonial Inn is fortunate to have people like Linda, Darlene,
Evelyn, Veronica and Chris to represent its honor and image."*

The Kelley House

PO Box 37
Edgartown, MA 02539-0037
(508)627-7900 (800)225-6005 Fax:(508)627-8142
Web: www.kelley-house.com

Circa 1742. Located in the heart of both downtown Edgartown
and the historic district, this is one of the island's oldest inns.
Over the years, four additional buildings have been added, all
maintaining the inn's colonial style. It has recently been extensively restored and refurbished. Rooms include many modern
amenities, such as television, radio and iron with ironing board.
There is a heated swimming pool. Private parking is another
plus. The inn is open from May through October.

Innkeeper(s): Taran Guilliksen. $110-675. MC, VISA, AX. 53 rooms.
Breakfast included in rates. EP. Type of meal: Cont. TV and irons and ironing
boards in room. Air conditioning. Swimming and private parking on premises.
"News from America" pub on site nearby.

Shiretown Inn on the Island of Martha's Vineyard

44 North Water St
Edgartown, MA 02539-0921
(508)627-3353 (800)541-0090 Fax:(508)627-8478

Circa 1795. Listed in the National Register of Historic Places,
Shiretown Inn is located in a historic district of whaling captain
homes on Martha's Vineyard, the famed island seven miles off
the coast of Massachusetts. Ask to stay in one of the inn's two
1795 houses where you can choose a traditionally furnished
guest room with a variety of amenities such as a canopy bed
and an Oriental rug. More modest rooms are available in the
Carriage Houses, and there is a cottage with kitchen and living
room that is particularly popular for families with small children. The inn's restaurant offers indoor dining or seating on a
garden terrace. There's also a pub. Walk one block to the
Chappaquiddick Ferry and the harbor. (Make reservations in
advance if you plan to bring your car, as there is limited space
on the ferry.) Shops, galleries, restaurants and beaches are nearby. Cycling, golf, windsurfing, sailing, tennis and horseback riding are also close.

Innkeeper(s): Gene Strimling. $89-449. MC, VISA, DS. TAC10. 39 rooms
with PB, 5 suites and 1 cottage. Breakfast included in rates. Type
of meal: Cont. Restaurant on premises. Beds: KQDT. Cable TV and phone in
room. Air conditioning. Fax on premises. Weddings, small meetings, family
reunions and seminars hosted. Antiquing, fishing, golf, parks, shopping, tennis and water sports nearby.

Fairhaven   I14

Edgewater B&B

2 Oxford St
Fairhaven, MA 02719-3310
(508)997-5512
E-mail: kprof@aol.com
Web: www.rixsan.com/edgewater

Circa 1760. On the historic Moby Dick Trail, Edgewater over-
looks the harbor from the grassy slopes of the Acushnet River.
The inn is in the charming, rambling, eclectic-style of the area.
Its lawns and porches provide water views. Across the harbor in
New Bedford, is Herman Melville's "dearest place in all New
England." There, visitors immerse themselves in the history
and lore of whaling. Near the B&B is the Gothic Revival-style
Unitarian Church with stained glass by Tiffany.

Innkeeper(s): Kathy Reed. $75-110. MC, VISA, AX, DS. 6 rooms with PB, 2
with FP. Type of meal: Cont plus. Beds: KQDT. Cable TV in room.

Publicity: *Standard Times, Fairhaven Advocate.*

Falmouth   *J16*

Captain Tom Lawrence House

75 Locust St
Falmouth, MA 02540-2658
(508)540-1445 (800)266-8139 Fax:(508)457-1790
E-mail: captntom@gateway.net
Web: www.sunsol.com/captaintom/

Circa 1861. After completing five whaling trips around the world, each four years in length, Captain Lawrence retired at 40 and built this house. There is a Steinway piano here now and elegantly furnished
guest rooms, some with
canopied beds. There
also is a furnished apartment available that sleeps
four. The house is near
the beach, bikeway, fer-
ries and bus station.
Freshly ground organic
grain is used to make

Belgian waffles with warm strawberry sauce, crepes Gisela and pancakes. German is spoken here. The home is listed in the National Register.

Historic Interest: Hyannisport (Kennedy compound) (20 miles), birthplace of Kathryn Lee Bates who wrote "America the Beautiful" (in Falmouth).

Innkeeper(s): Barbara Sabo-Feller. $95-200. MC, VISA, PC, TC. 6 rooms with PB and 1 cottage. Breakfast included in rates. Type of meal: Full bkfst. Gourmet dinner available. Beds: KQT. Cable TV and ceiling fan in room. Air conditioning. Mini fridge on premises. Family reunions hosted. Antiquing, fishing, live theater, parks, shopping and water sports nearby.

"This is our first B&B experience. Better than some of the so-called 4-star hotels!! We loved it here."

Gladstone Inn

219 Grand Ave
Falmouth, MA 02540-3780
(508)548-9851 Fax:(508)548-9851
Web: www.sunsol.com/gladstoneinn

Circa 1880. A soft, ever-present ocean breeze ensures a sound night's sleep at this oceanfront inn offering Cape Cod charm and homeyness. Wake up to a more than ample buffet breakfast on the enclosed porch over-
looking the ocean. Guests
can use the inn's bicycles
for a ride on the Shining
Sea Bike Path. After a
day at the beach or a
game of golf or ten-
nis, enjoy the back-
yard area with its

barbecue and picnic table. An enclosed shower and rest room adjoining the inn lets guests leave their room upon check-out but still take in one last swim.

Innkeeper(s): James & Gayle Carroll. Call for rates. VCR on premises. Antiquing, live theater and shopping nearby.

Hewins House B&B

Village Green
Falmouth, MA 02540
(508)457-4363

Circa 1820. Built by a wealthy merchant and sea captain, this handsomely restored Federal-style home overlooks Falmouth's Historic Village Green and is a short walk to the Woods Hole Ferry to Martha's Vineyard. Both the house and the green are in the National Register. The inn's back porch overlooks formal gardens. Inside is a new country kitchen. Although all the guest rooms are decorated attractively, ask for the room with the four poster canopy bed and French armoire for a truly romantic setting. Breakfast is served in the formal dining room.

Innkeeper(s): Virginia Price. $100-115. MC, VISA, AX, DS, PC, TC. TAC10. 3 rooms with PB, 2 with FP. Breakfast included in rates. Type of meal: Full bkfst. Beds: QDT. Phone in room. Air conditioning. VCR, copier and porch and gardens on premises. Antiquing, fishing, golf, Martha's Vineyard, live theater, parks, shopping, sporting events, tennis and water sports nearby.

Mostly Hall B&B Inn

27 Main St
Falmouth, MA 02540-2652
(508)548-3786 (800)682-0565 Fax:(508)457-1572
E-mail: mostlyhl@cape.com
Web: www.mostlyhall.com

Circa 1849. Albert Nye built this Southern plantation house with wide verandas and a cupola to observe shipping in Vineyard Sound. It was a wedding gift for his New Orleans bride. Because of the seemingly endless halls on every floor
(some 30 feet long), it was
whimsically called Mostly
Hall. The inn recently was
placed in the National
Register. All rooms have
queen-size canopy beds.
Bicycles are available for guest
use, and the inn is near the
bicycle path to Woods Hole
and Martha's Vineyard ferries.

Historic Interest: The birthplace of Kathryn Lee Bates, author of "America the Beautiful," is across the street. Plymouth and Plimoth Plantation is 35 miles, and the Kennedy Museum and Monument in Hyannisport is 23 miles.

Innkeeper(s): Caroline & Jim Lloyd. $105-150. MC, VISA, AX, DS, PC, TC. 6 rooms with PB. Breakfast and afternoon tea included in rates. Types of meals: Full gourmet bkfst and early coffee/tea. Beds: Q. Ceiling fan and two comfortable reading chairs in room. Central air. VCR, fax, bicycles, library and gazebo on premises. German spoken. Antiquing, art galleries, beaches, Martha's Vineyard ferries, restaurants, island ferries, nature trails, restaurants, live theater and shopping nearby.

"Of all the inns we stayed at during our trip, we enjoyed Mostly Hall the most. Imagine, Southern hospitality on Cape Cod!"

The Inn at One Main Street

1 Main St
Falmouth, MA 02540-2652
(508)540-7469 (888)281-6246

Circa 1892. In the historic district, where the road to Woods Hole begins, is this shingled Victorian with two-story turret, an open front porch and gardens framed by a white picket fence. It first became a tourist house back in the '50s. Cape Cod cranber-ry pecan waffles and gingerbread pancakes with whipped cream are favorite specialties. Within walking distance, you'll find the

Shining Sea Bike Path, beaches, summer theater, tennis, ferry shuttle and bus station. The innkeepers are available to offer their expertise on the area.

Innkeeper(s): Jeanne Dahl & Ilona Cleveland. $80-150. MC, VISA, AX, DS, PC, TC. 6 rooms with PB. Breakfast included in rates. Type of meal: Full bkfst. Beds: QT. Ceiling fan in room. Air conditioning. Antiquing, bike path, ferries to islands, Woods Hole Oceanographic Institute, live theater, shopping and water sports nearby.

"The art of hospitality in a delightful atmosphere, well worth traveling 3,000 miles for."

Palmer House Inn

81 Palmer Ave
Falmouth, MA 02540-2857
(508)548-1230 (800)472-2632 Fax:(508)540-1878
E-mail: innkeepers@palmerhouseinn.com
Web: www.palmerhouseinn.com

Circa 1901. Just off the village green in Falmouth's historic district, sits this turn-of-the-century Victorian and its adjacent guest house. The polished woodwork, stained-glass windows and collection of antiques tie the home to a romantic, bygone era. Some guest rooms have fireplaces and whirlpool tubs. Innkeeper Joanne Baker prepares an opulent feast for the morning meal, which is served in traditional Victorian style, by candlelight on tables set with fine china and crystal. Creamed eggs in puff pastry and chocolate-stuffed French toast are two of the reasons why the cuisine has been featured in Gourmet and Bon Appetit. Joanne also offers heart-healthy fare for those monitoring their fat and cholesterol. Afternoon refreshments quell those before-dinner hunger pangs.

Innkeeper(s): Ken & Joanne Baker. $79-199. MC, VISA, AX, DC, CB, DS, PC, TC. TAC10. 16 rooms with PB and 1 suite. Breakfast and snacks/refreshments included in rates. Types of meals: Full gourmet bkfst and early coffee/tea. Beds: KQDT. TV, phone, turndown service and ceiling fan in room. Air conditioning. Fax, copier and bicycles on premises. Handicap access. Small meetings, family reunions and seminars hosted. Antiquing, fishing, live theater, parks, shopping and water sports nearby.

Publicity: *Country Inns, Gourmet, Runners World, Yankee Traveler, Bon Appetit.*

Village Green Inn

40 Main St
Falmouth, MA 02540-2667
(508)548-5621 (800)237-1119 Fax:(508)457-5051

Circa 1804. The inn, listed in the National Register, originally was built in the Federal style for Braddock Dimmick, son of Revolutionary War General Joseph Dimmick. Later, "cranberry king" John Crocker moved the house onto a granite slab foundation, remodeling it in the Victorian style. There are

inlaid floors, large porches and gingerbread trim.

Historic Interest: Plimoth Plantation and Heritage Plantation are nearby.

Innkeeper(s): Diane & Don Crosby. $85-165. MC, VISA, AX, PC, TC. TAC10. 5 rooms with PB, 2 with FP and 1 suite. Breakfast and afternoon tea included in rates. Types of meals: Full gourmet bkfst and early coffee/tea. Snacks/refreshments available. Beds: Q. Cable TV, phone, ceiling fan and hair dryers in room. Air conditioning. Bicycles on premises. Small meetings and family reunions hosted. Antiquing, fishing, golf, whale watching, live theater, parks, shopping and water sports nearby.

"Tasteful, comfortable and the quintessential New England flavor ... You have turned us on to the B&B style of travel and we now have a standard to measure our future choices by."

Falmouth Heights   J16

Grafton Inn

261 Grand Ave S
Falmouth Heights, MA 02540-3784
(508)540-8688 (800)642-4069 Fax:(508)540-1861
E-mail: alamkid@aol.com
Web: www.graftoninn.com

Circa 1870. If you want to enjoy grand ocean views while staying at an inn in Cape Cod, this is the place. Oceanfront and within walking distance to the ferries, the inn is an ideal place to hop on board a ferry and spend a day on Nantucket Island or Martha's Vineyard and return that evening to relax and watch the moon over the ocean from your bedroom window. Snacks of wine and cheese are served in the afternoon. The inn is often seen on television and ESPN because of its unique location at the final leg of the Falmouth Road Race.

Historic Interest: Plimoth Plantation (30 miles), Heritage Plantation (15 miles), Bourne Farm (6 miles).

Innkeeper(s): Liz & Rudy Cvitan. $95-189. MC, VISA, AX, TC. TAC10. 11 rooms with PB. Breakfast included in rates. Type of meal: Full gourmet bkfst. Beds: KQDT. Cable TV, ceiling fan, bathrobes and makeup mirrors in room. Air conditioning. Fax, swimming, library and sand chairs on premises. Small meetings hosted. Antiquing, fishing, live theater, parks, shopping and water sports nearby.

Publicity: *Enterprise, At Your Leisure, Cape Cod Life, Cape Cod Times, Cape Cod Travel Guide.*

"You have certainly created a lovely inn for those of us who wish to escape the city and relax in luxury."

The Moorings Lodge

207 Grand Ave
Falmouth Heights, MA 02540-3742
(508)540-2370 (800)398-4007 Fax:(508)457-6074

Circa 1905. Captain Frank Spencer was a clever man. He built this wood-shingled Victorian, but first made sure that his ocean view would always be unobstructed. Spencer convinced the town to purchase the beach directly across the street from his home. Guests can relax and enjoy a view of Martha's Vineyard and Vineyard Sound from the

inn's glassed-in front porch. Rooms are comfortable and some can accommodate more than two guests. Start off the day with a Vineyard view and breakfasts of homemade granola, freshly baked breads and entrees such as quiche, souffles or Belgium waffles topped with strawberries. The inn is open from May 15 through Columbus Day.

Innkeeper(s): Ernie & Shirley Benard. $95-150. MC, VISA, PC, TC. 8 rooms with PB. TV in room. Bicycling, fishing, golf, ferry to Martha's Vineyard and tennis nearby.

Greenfield
C6

The Brandt House

29 Highland Ave
Greenfield, MA 01301-3605
(413)774-3329 (800)235-3329 Fax:(413)772-2908

Circa 1890. Three-and-a-half-acre lawns surround this impressive three-story Colonial Revival house, situated hilltop. The library and poolroom are popular for lounging, but the favorite gathering areas are the sunroom and the covered north porch. Ask for the aqua and white room with the fireplace, but all the rooms are pleasing. A full breakfast often includes homemade scones and is sometimes available on  the slate patio in view of the expansive lawns and beautiful gardens. There is a clay tennis court and nature trails, and in winter, lighted ice skating at a nearby pond. Historic Deerfield and Yankee Candle Company are within five minutes.

Historic Interest: Poet's Seat Tower & Historic Homes (walking distance), Shelburne Falls & the Bridge of Flowers (15 minutes).

Innkeeper(s): Phoebe Compton. $105-195. MC, VISA, AX, DS, TC. TAC10. 9 rooms, 7 with PB, 2 with FP, 1 suite and 1 conference room. Breakfast included in rates. Types of meals: Full bkfst, cont plus and early coffee/tea. Gourmet lunch available. Beds: KQT. Cable TV, phone, ceiling fan, fireplaces in two rooms and microwave in room. Air conditioning. VCR, fax, copier, tennis and library on premises. Weddings, small meetings, family reunions and seminars hosted. Antiquing, fishing, Old Deerfield, Lunt Silver, live theater, parks, shopping, downhill skiing, cross-country skiing, sporting events and water sports nearby.

Pets allowed: Call for approval.

The Hitchcock House B&B

15 Congress St
Greenfield, MA 01301-3503
(413)774-7452

Circa 1881. F.C. Currier, a renowned Springfield architect, designed this three-story Victorian gem. Guests can enjoy its pristine appearance, which includes a tower, gables with gingerbread and brackets, a bay and an abundance of porches. The interior is tastefully decorated with period furniture and country quilts. Tall shade trees dot the grounds along with gardens and a croquet court. The town of Greenfield, a scenic 10-minute walk away, was formerly part of historic Deerfield. Deerfield itself is three miles away.

Innkeeper(s): Betty Gott. $85-110. PC, TC. 5 rooms, 2 with PB. MAP. Type of meal: Cont plus. Hiking nearby.

Hamilton
C14

Miles River Country Inn

823 Bay Rd, Box 149
Hamilton, MA 01936
(978)468-7206 Fax:(978)468-3999

Circa 1789. This rambling colonial inn sits on more than 30 acres of magnificent curving lawns bordered by trees and formal gardens that lead to the Miles River. There are meadows, woodlands and wetlands surrounding the property and available for exploring. The river flows through the property, which is a haven for a wide variety of wildlife. Many of the inn's 12 fireplaces are in the guest rooms. Family heirloom antiques compliment the interior.

Historic Interest: Ipswich, which features the nation's largest collection of homes built prior to 1800, is one of the area's many historic attractions. Salem, home to the House of Seven Gables, is another interesting destination.

Innkeeper(s): Gretel & Peter Clark. $80-210. MC, VISA, AX, PC, TC. 8 rooms, 6 with PB, 4 with FP, 1 suite and 2 conference rooms. Breakfast and afternoon tea included in rates. Types of meals: Full bkfst and early coffee/tea. Beds: QDT. Fans and clocks in room. VCR, fax, copier, bicycles, library, walking trails and gardens on premises. Weddings, small meetings, family reunions and seminars hosted. Spanish and French spoken. Antiquing, fishing, world class horse events, live theater, parks, shopping, downhill skiing, cross-country skiing, sporting events and water sports nearby.

Hyannis
I17

Mansfield House

70 Gosnold St
Hyannis, MA 02601-4827
(508)771-9455 Fax:(508)775-8813

Circa 1899. Mansfield House, a turn-of-the-century farmhouse, was built to serve as a private beach cottage. Each guest room is different, and all feature names that seem to fit with Cape Cod setting. The Cranberry Bog includes a sliding door that leads to a small deck. The Blueberry Patch includes a unique half-oval window, as well as maple and wicker furnishings. The Sand  Dunes is a cozy retreat with the private bath located nearby in the hallway, and for this reason, bathrobes are provided. The final room selection is Bayberry Brambles, which features flowery wallpaper and cathedral ceilings. Breakfasts include a buffet set up with beverages, freshly baked breads, fruit and cereals. Every day a new main entre is presented, and the innkeepers are happy to accommodate dietary needs.

Innkeeper(s): Donald M. Patrell. $80-95. MC, VISA, AX, PC, TC. TAC10. 4 rooms with PB. Breakfast included in rates. Type of meal: Full bkfst. Beds: KQT. Cable TV, ceiling fan and VCR in room. Fax on premises. Small meetings and family reunions hosted. Fishing, golf, live theater, parks, shopping, tennis and water sports nearby.

The Inn on Sea Street

358 Sea St
Hyannis, MA 02601-4509
(508)775-8030 Fax:(508)771-0878
E-mail: innonsea@capecod.net
Web: www.capecod.net/innonsea

Circa 1849. This white Victorian inn is comprised of two homes, both are listed in the town's register of historic buildings. Guest rooms are decorated with four-poster canopy beds. Its charm includes Colonial portraits, Persian carpets and a grand curved staircase. Breakfast is served on the sun porch or elegant dining room on tables set with sterling silver, china, crystal  and fresh flowers from the garden. A log book in the living room is open for guests to rate local restaurants and get opinions before going out on the town.

Historic Interest: Kennedy Library & Compound is less than one mile from the home.

Innkeeper(s): Sylvia & Fred LaSelva. $85-135. MC, VISA, AX, DS. 9 rooms, 7 with PB and 1 cottage. Breakfast included in rates. Type of meal: Full bkfst. Beds: QDT. Cable TV, phone, umbrellas, floor fans and clocks in room. Air conditioning. Small meetings and family reunions hosted. Antiquing, fishing, live theater, shopping and water sports nearby.

Publicity: *Journal.*

"A lot of people really don't know how much they are missing, until they visit you."

Hyannis Port   I17

The Simmons Homestead Inn

288 Scudder Ave
Hyannis Port, MA 02647
(508)778-4999 (800)637-1649 Fax:(508)790-1342
E-mail: simmonsinn@aol.com
Web: www.capecodtravel.com/simmonsinn

Circa 1805. This former sea captain's home features period decor and includes huge needlepoint displays and lifelike ceramic and papier-mache animals that give the inn a country feel. Some rooms boast canopy beds, and each is individually decorated. Traditional full breakfasts are served in the formal dining room. Evening wine helps guests relax after a day of touring the Cape. There is a billiard room on the premises.

Innkeeper(s): Bill Putman. $120-200. MC, VISA, AX, DS, PC, TC. TAC10. 14 rooms with PB, 2 with FP and 1 suite. Breakfast included in rates. Types of meals: Full bkfst and early coffee/tea. Beds: KQT. Ceiling fan in room. VCR, fax, copier, bicycles, library, pet boarding, child care, billiard room and modem hook-up on premises. Weddings, small meetings and family reunions hosted. Antiquing, fishing, golf, live theater, parks, shopping, tennis and water sports nearby.

Pets Allowed.

"I want to say that part of what makes Cape Cod special for us is the inn. It embodies much of what is wonderful at the Cape. By Sunday, I was completely rested, relaxed, renewed, and restored."

Lanesboro   C3

Bascom Lodge

PO Box 1800
Lanesboro, MA 01237-1800
(413)443-0011 Fax:(413)442-9010

Circa 1933. Operated by the Appalachian Mountain Club, this historic lodge was constructed in the '30s by the CCC using native stone and timber. It commands 100-mile Berkshire vistas from its location on the summit of Mount Greylock, the highest mountain in southern New England. The lodge is at the center of the 12,000-acre Mount Greylock State Reservation, known for its 50 miles of trails. Although the rooms are simple with private bed- and bunk-rooms, travelers find the lodge a comfortable place to rest and enjoy the views. The library/sitting room offers historical and educational displays, and there's a trading post stocked with maps, trail guides, hiking items and a snack bar.

Innkeeper(s): Glenn Oswald. Call for rates. Type of meal: Full bkfst. Dinner, snacks/refreshments and picnic lunch available. Weddings, small meetings and family reunions hosted. Antiquing, live theater and shopping nearby.

Lee   E2

Applegate

279 W Park St
Lee, MA 01238-1718
(413)243-4451 (800)691-9012
E-mail: lenandgloria@applegateinn.com
Web: www.applegateinn.com

Circa 1920. This romantic bed & breakfast is an ideal accommodation for those visiting the Berkshires. Well-dressed, four-poster beds rest atop polished wood floors. Gracious furnishings, Oriental rugs and soft lighting add to the ambiance. Two guest rooms offer fireplaces, and several offer views of woods or gardens. Fresh flowers, brandy and Godiva chocolates are just a few extras that await guests. In the early evening, wine and cheese is served. Breakfasts are served by candlelight, with crystal stemware and antique china. The innkeepers offer several special getaway packages, such as a wine-tasting and dinner weekends. Golf and tennis facilities are located across the street.

Historic Interest: Norman Rockwell Museum is nearby.

Innkeeper(s): Len & Gloria Friedman. $95-230. MC, VISA, PC, TC. 6 rooms with PB, 2 with FP and 1 cottage. Breakfast included in rates. Type of meal: Cont plus. Beds: KQD. Steam shower, flowers and brandy and chocolates in room. Air conditioning. VCR, fax, copier, swimming, bicycles, library, CD player, baby grand piano and screened porch overlooking gardens on premises. Weddings, small meetings, family reunions and seminars hosted. Antiquing, Norman Rockwell museum, Tanglewood concerts, Jacobs Pillow, live theater, parks, shopping, downhill skiing, cross-country skiing and water sports nearby.

Devonfield

85 Stockbridge Rd
Lee, MA 01238-9308
(413)243-3298 (800)664-0880 Fax:(413)243-1360

Circa 1800. The original section of this Federal inn was built by a Revolutionary War soldier. Guest rooms are spacious with charming furniture and patterned wallcoverings. Three of the rooms feature fireplaces. The one-bedroom cottage has both a fireplace and an efficiency kitchen. Guests are treated to a full breakfast. One need not wander far from the grounds to find something to do. The innkeepers offer a tennis court, swimming pool and bicycles for guests, and a nine-hole golf course is just across the way. Inside, guests can relax in the living room with its fireplace and library or in the television room. The area is full of boutiques, antique shops and galleries to explore, as well as hiking, fishing and skiing. Tanglewood, summer home of the Boston Symphony, is close by.

Historic Interest: Among the many historic sites offered in this part of Massachusetts are the Norman Rockwell Museum and the Hancock Shaker Village. There's no shortage of historic homes to visit.

Innkeeper(s): Sally & Ben Schenck. $80-275. MC, VISA, AX, DS, PC, TC. TAC10. 10 rooms with PB, 4 with FP, 4 suites and 1 cottage. Beds: KQT. Cable in some rooms. Air conditioning. Fax, copier, swimming, bicycles, tennis and library on premises.

"A special thank you for your warm and kind hospitality. We feel as though this is our home away from home."

The Parsonage on The Green

20 Park Pl
Lee, MA 01238-1618
(413)243-4364
E-mail: parsonage@berkshire.net
Web: www.bbhost.com/parsonageonthegreen

Circa 1851. As the former parsonage to the first Congregational Church (known as having the highest wooden steeple in the country), this white colonial inn is tucked behind a white picket fence on a quiet side of the village common. The boughs of an old apple tree shade a pleasant wicker-filled side veranda. Family heirlooms, 18th-century American antiques and Oriental rugs are set against polished maple and

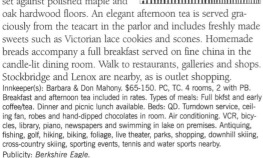

oak hardwood floors. An elegant afternoon tea is served graciously from the teacart in the parlor and includes freshly made sweets such as Victorian lace cookies and scones. Homemade breads accompany a full breakfast served on fine china in the candle-lit dining room. Walk to restaurants, galleries and shops. Stockbridge and Lenox are nearby, as is outlet shopping.

Innkeeper(s): Barbara & Don Mahony. $65-150. PC, TC. 4 rooms, 2 with PB. Breakfast and afternoon tea included in rates. Types of meals: Full bkfst and early coffee/tea. Dinner and picnic lunch available. Beds: QD. Turndown service, ceiling fan, robes and hand-dipped chocolates in room. Air conditioning. VCR, bicycles, library, piano, newspapers and swimming in lake on premises. Antiquing, fishing, golf, hiking, biking, foliage, live theater, parks, shopping, downhill skiing, cross-country skiing, sporting events, tennis and water sports nearby.

Publicity: *Berkshire Eagle.*

"Our dream came true, the perfect romantic getaway."

Lenox   E2

Birchwood Inn

7 Hubbard St, Box 2020
Lenox, MA 01240-4604
(413)637-2600 (800)524-1646 Fax:(413)637-4604
E-mail: innkeeper@birchwood-inn.com
Web: www.birchwood-inn.com

Circa 1767. This inn, which is the only privately owned Lenox building listed in the National Register, is situated on a hilltop and overlooks the village. The gardens and lawns are surrounded by old New England stone fences. Guests can enjoy the wood-burning fireplaces and large library. Full country breakfasts include items such as Sunrise Souffle', waffles and home-baked muffins.

Historic Interest: Edith Wharton's home is two miles away, while Herman Melville's home is three miles from the inn. The Norman Rockwell Museum is about four miles away.

Innkeeper(s): Ellen Gutman Chenaux. $60-250. MC, VISA, AX, DS, PC, TC. 12 rooms, 10 with PB, 3 with FP and 1 conference room. Breakfast and afternoon tea included in rates. Types of meals: Full bkfst and early coffee/tea. Beds: KQDT. Cable TV, phone and ceiling fan in room. Air conditioning. VCR, fax, copier and library on premises. Weddings, small meetings, family reunions and seminars hosted. Antiquing, fishing, golf, live theater, parks, shopping, downhill skiing, cross-country skiing and water sports nearby.

Publicity: *Country Inns, Country Living.*

"Inn-credible! Inn-viting! Inn-spiring! Inn-comparable! Our ultimate getaway. Wonderful ambiance, great food and the finest hosts we ever met. We have been going to the Birchwood Inn for more than 15 years and each time we enjoy it even more."

Blantyre

16 Blantyre Rd, PO Box 995
Lenox, MA 01240-0995
(413)637-3556 Fax:(413)637-4282
E-mail: hide@blantyre.com
Web: www.blantyre.com

Circa 1902. Situated on manicured lawns near Tanglewood, this Tudor manor is entered through a massive portico. Grandly-sized rooms include the Great Hall and an elegantly paneled dining room. Breakfast is graciously served in the conservatory. Formal grounds offer four tennis courts, two championship croquet courts, a pool and carriage house.

Historic Interest: Hancock Shaker Village (10 miles), Norman Rockwell Museum (7 miles), Chesterwood (7 miles).

Innkeeper(s): Roderick Anderson, Managing Director. $270-700. MC, VISA, AX, DC, PC, TC. TAC10. 23 rooms with PB, 7 with FP, 10 suites, 2 cottages and 1 conference room. Types of meals: Full gourmet bkfst and cont. Gourmet dinner, picnic lunch, lunch, banquet service and room service available. Restaurant on premises. Beds: KQD. Cable TV, phone, turndown service, hair dryer, robes and fruit and cheese tray on arrival in room. Air conditioning. VCR, fax, copier, swimming, sauna, tennis, croquet and walking trails on premises. Handicap access. Weddings, small meetings, family reunions and seminars hosted. French spoken. Antiquing, fishing, golf, many cultural events, Tanglewood, live theater, shopping, tennis and water sports nearby.

Publicity: *Hideaway Report, Country Inns, Conde Nast Traveler, Zagat, Victoria Magazine, Discovery Channel-Great Country Inns.*

"There was not a single aspect of our stay with you that was not worked out to total perfection."

Brook Farm Inn

15 Hawthorne St
Lenox, MA 01240-2404
(413)637-3013 (800)285-7638 Fax:(413)637-4751
E-mail: innkeeper@brookfarm.com
Web: www.brookfarm.com

Circa 1870. Brook Farm Inn is named after the original Brook Farm, a literary commune that sought to combine thinker and worker through a society of intelligent, cultivated members. In keeping with that theme, this gracious Victorian inn offers poetry and writing seminars and has a 650-volume poetry library. Canopy beds, Mozart and a swimming pool tend to the spirit.

Historic Interest: Home of Edith Wharton (the Mount), home of Herman Melville (Arrowhead), home of Daniel Chester French, Lincoln Memorial (Chesterwood).

Innkeeper(s): Joe & Anne Miller. $90-205. MC, VISA, DS, PC, TC. 12 rooms with PB, 6 with FP. Breakfast and afternoon tea included in rates. Types of meals: Full bkfst and early coffee/tea. Beds: KQT. Phone, ceiling fan, fluffy towels and toiletries in room. Air conditioning. Fax, copier, swimming, butler's pantry, round-the-clock coffee and tea on premises. Family reunions hosted. Antiquing, fishing, Tanglewood, live theater, parks, shopping, downhill skiing, cross-country skiing, sporting events and water sports nearby.

"We've been traveling all our lives and never have we felt more at home."

The Gables Inn

81 Walker St, Rt 183
Lenox, MA 01240-2719
(413)637-3416 (800)382-9401

Circa 1885. At one time, this was the home of Pulitzer Prize-winning novelist, Edith Wharton. The Queen Anne-style Berkshire cottage features a handsome eight-sided library and Mrs. Wharton's own four-poster bed. An unusual indoor swimming pool with spa is available in warm weather.

Innkeeper(s): Mary & Frank Newton. $80-225. MC, VISA, DS, PC, TC. 17 rooms with PB, 15 with FP and 4 suites.
Breakfast included in rates. Beds: Q. Cable TV and VCR in room. Air conditioning. Fax, swimming and tennis on premises. Family reunions hosted. Antiquing, fishing, live theater, parks, shopping, downhill skiing, cross-country skiing, sporting events and water sports nearby.

"You made us feel like old friends and that good feeling enhanced our pleasure. In essence, it was the best part of our trip."

Garden Gables Inn

PO Box 52
Lenox, MA 01240-0052
(413)637-0193 Fax:(413)637-4554

Circa 1780. Several distinctive gables adorn this home set on five wooded acres. Deer occasionally wander into the garden to help themselves to fallen apples. Breakfast is served in the dining room, which overlooks tall maples, flower gardens and fruit trees. The swimming pool was the first built in the county and is still the

longest. Guests will find many special amenities including in-room phones, fireplaces and whirlpool tubs. There is a Baby Grand Piano in the living room.

Innkeeper(s): Mario & Lynn Mekinda. $80-250. MC, VISA, AX, DS, PC, TC. 18 rooms with PB, 8 with FP, 2 suites and 4 cottages. Breakfast and afternoon tea included in rates. Types of meals: Full bkfst and early coffee/tea. Beds: KQT. Cable TV, phone, hair dryers and canopy beds in room. Air conditioning. VCR, fax and swimming on premises. Weddings, small meetings, family reunions and seminars hosted. French and German spoken. Antiquing, fishing, Tanglewood Music Festival, live theater, parks, shopping, downhill skiing, cross-country skiing and water sports nearby.

Publicity: *National Geographic Traveler, Berkshire Eagle, Los Angeles Times, Long Island News.*

"Charming and thoughtful hospitality. You restored a portion of my sanity and I'm very grateful—Miami Herald."

The Kemble Inn

2 Kemble St
Lenox, MA 01240-2813
(413)637-4113 (800)353-4113
Web: www.kembleinn.com

Circa 1881. Named for a famous 19th-century actress, Fanny Kemble, this three-story Georgian-style inn boasts an incredible view of the mountains in the Berkshires. The inn's 15 elegant guest rooms are named for American authors, including Nathaniel Hawthorne, Henry Wadsworth Longfellow, Herman Melville, Mark Twain and Edith Wharton. The impressive Fanny Kemble Room, which features mountain views, includes two fireplaces, a Jacuzzi tub and a king-size, four-poster bed. The inn is within minutes of five major ski areas, and Tanglewood is less than two miles away.

Historic Interest: Norman Rockwell Museum, Edith Wharton Restoration.

Innkeeper(s): J. Richard & Linda Reardon. $85-295. MC, VISA, DS, TC. 15 rooms with PB, 6 with FP. Breakfast included in rates. Type of meal: Cont. Cable TV and phone in room. Air conditioning. Refrigerator for guest use on premises. Handicap access. Antiquing, fishing, live theater, parks, shopping, downhill skiing, cross-country skiing and water sports nearby.

"Kemble Inn was a showcase B&B - just what we had hoped for."

Lilac Inn

PO Box 2294, 33 Main St
Lenox, MA 01240-5294
(413)637-2172 Fax:(413)637-2172
E-mail: aliceatlilacinn@msn.com
Web: www.berkshireweb.com/lilacinn

Circa 1836. Aptly named for a flower, this Italian Revival inn features guest rooms that appear much like a garden. Flowery prints, wicker and antique furnishings and views of Lilac Park from the two porches enhance this cheerful atmosphere. Guests are treated to afternoon refreshments, with a proper mix of savory and sweet tidbits. Breakfasts are bountiful and delicious, yet surprisingly healthy with low-fat, vegetarian versions of treats such as banana nut bread, French toast and vegetable quiche. The library is stocked with books, and the living room, which has a fireplace, is a good place to curl up and relax. The

innkeeper also offers a one-bedroom apartment with a kitchen.
Innkeeper(s): Alice Maleski. $100-225. PC. 6 rooms with PB, 1 with FP.
Breakfast and afternoon tea included in rates. Types of meals: Full gourmet
bkfst and early coffee/tea. Beds: KQT. Turndown service and ceiling fan in
room. VCR, fax, copier and library on premises. Handicap access. Weddings,
small meetings, family reunions and seminars hosted. French and Lithuanian
spoken. Antiquing, fishing, golf, outlet shops, live theater, parks, shopping,
downhill skiing, cross-country skiing and water sports nearby.

*"We are really looking forward to shamelessly overindulging in
your breakfasts, and being carried away by the music, the time
and the place."*

Rookwood Inn

11 Old Stockbridge Rd, PO Box 1717
Lenox, MA 01240-1717
(413)637-9750 (800)223-9750
E-mail: stay@rookwoodinn.com
Web: www.rookwoodinn.com

Circa 1885. This turn-of-the-century Queen Anne Victorian
inn offers 20 elegant guest rooms, including suites. Among the
amenities in the air-conditioned guest rooms are antiques and
fireplaces. The public
rooms and halls are
decorated with the
innkeepers' collection
of antique handbags
and Wallace Nutting
prints. The day begins
with a bountiful heart-
healthy breakfast, pre-

pared by innkeeper Steve Lindner-Lesser. The beautiful
Berkshires are famous for cultural and recreational opportunities, and guests can walk to shops and restaurants. Tanglewood
is one mile away.
Innkeeper(s): Amy & Stephen Lindner-Lesser. $85-295. MC, VISA, AX, DC,
DS, PC, TC. TAC10. 20 rooms, 21 with PB, 8 with FP, 2 suites and 2 conference rooms. Breakfast and snacks/refreshments included in rates. Type of
meal: Full bkfst. Beds: KQT. Phone and ceiling fan in room. Air conditioning.
Handicap access. Weddings, small meetings, family reunions and seminars
hosted. Antiquing, fishing, golf, live theater, parks, shopping, downhill skiing,
cross-country skiing, tennis and water sports nearby.
Publicity: *New York Times, Boston Globe, London Times.*

*"Of all the inns I've visited, Rookwood, by far, was the most comfort-
able, with personable, friendly and obliging innkeepers, excellent
breakfasts and cozy atmosphere."*

Seven Hills Country Inn & Restaurant

40 Plunkett St
Lenox, MA 01240-2795
(413)637-0060 (800)869-6518 Fax:(413)637-3651
E-mail: 7hills@berkshire.net
Web: www.sevenhillsinn.com

Circa 1911. Descendants of those who sailed on the
Mayflower built this rambling, Tudor-style mansion. The inn's
27 acres of terraced lawns and stunning gardens often serve as
the site for weddings, receptions and meetings. The grounds
include two tennis courts and a swimming pool. Guest rooms
are elegantly appointed with antiques, and the mansion still
maintains its hand-carved fireplaces and leaded glass windows.
In addition to the original elements, some rooms contain the
modern amenity of a jet tub. The inn's chef, whose cuisine has
been featured in Gourmet magazine, prepares creative, conti-

nental specialties. Seven Hills offers close access to many attrac-
tions in the Berkshires.
Innkeeper(s): Patricia & Jim Eder. $85-295. MC, VISA, AX, DC, CB, DS, PC,
TC. TAC10. 52 rooms with PB, 5 with FP, 2 suites and 4 conference rooms.
Breakfast included in rates. MAP, EP. Types of meals: Full bkfst and cont plus.
Dinner available. Beds: KQD. Cable TV and phone in room. Air conditioning.
VCR, fax, copier, swimming, tennis and library on premises. Handicap
access. Weddings, small meetings, family reunions and seminars hosted.
Spanish and French spoken. Antiquing, fishing, live theater, museums, parks,
shopping, downhill skiing, cross-country skiing and water sports nearby.
Pets allowed: Sometimes.

Summer Hill Farm

950 East St
Lenox, MA 01240-2205
(413)442-2059 (800)442-2059 Fax:(413)448-6106
E-mail: innkeeper@summerhillfarm.com
Web: www.summerhillfarm.com

Circa 1796. Situated on a scenic 19 acres, this Colonial home
was once part of a 300-acre farm deeded to the Steven family
just after the French & Indian War. Several rooms include fireplaces or brass beds.
The Loft and
Mountain View
rooms both offer
superb views. The
Cottage, an old hay
barn, includes a bed-
room as well as sit-
ting, dining and
cooking areas. Fresh
fruit, homemade gra-

nola, and home-baked bread accompany the morning's special
breakfast entree. After a hearty breakfast, guests should have no
trouble finding something to do. Arts and sports activities are
nearby, as are museums, Hancock Shaker Village, antique
shops, Tanglewood, theatres and many other cultural attractions. The innkeepers also have a three-bedroom, two-bath
farmhouse on the property. The farmhouse is self-contained
and can be rented by the week or month.
Historic Interest: Herman Melville's "Arrowhead" (1 mile), Edith Wharton's
"The Mount" (6 miles).
Innkeeper(s): Sonya & Michael Wessel. $70-200. MC, VISA, AX, PC, TC.
TAC10. 8 rooms with PB, 3 with FP and 2 cottages. Breakfast included in
rates. Type of meal: Full bkfst. Beds: KQDT. Cable TV, refrigerator (two
rooms) and ceiling fan (one room) in room. Central air. VCR on premises.
Family reunions hosted. Amusement parks, antiquing, art galleries, beaches,
bicycling, canoeing/kayaking, fishing, golf, hiking, horseback riding, live theater, museums, parks, shopping, downhill skiing, cross-country skiing, tennis,
water sports and wineries nearby.

"You and your home are wonderfully charming."

The Village Inn

16 Church St
Lenox, MA 01240
(413)637-0020 (800)253-0917 Fax:(413)637-9756
E-mail: villinn@ugernet.net
Web: www.villageinn-lenox.com

Circa 1771. Four years after the Whitlocks built this Federal-
style house, they converted it and two adjoining buildings for
lodging. Since 1775, it has operated as an inn. Now, there are
luxurious amenities available including rooms with four-poster
canopy beds, fireplaces, VCRs and Jacuzzi tubs. Stenciled walls,

Oriental rugs, maple floors and country antiques and reproductions furnish the inn. Rates include a continental breakfast but a full breakfast may also be arranged for in the inn's restaurant. Be sure to try afternoon tea and enjoy the freshly baked scones served with real clotted cream.

Historic Interest: The Mount (1 mile), Arrowhead (3 miles), Hancock Shaker Village (10 miles).. Hancock Shaker Village-5 miles, Edith Wharton home-1 mile, Herman Melville home-2 miles, Norman Rockwell Museum-5 miles.

Innkeeper(s): Clifford Rudisill & Ray Wilson. $50-255. MC, VISA, AX, DC, CB, DS, TC. TAC10. 32 rooms with PB, 6 with FP, 1 suite and 2 conference rooms. Breakfast included in rates. EP. Types of meals: Full gourmet bkfst, cont plus, cont and early coffee/tea. Afternoon tea and gourmet dinner available. Restaurant on premises. Beds: KQDT. Cable TV, phone, VCR, hair dryers, magnifying mirror, VCR library and some rooms with Jacuzzi tubs in room. Air conditioning. Fax and library on premises. Handicap access. Weddings, small meetings, family reunions and seminars hosted. Spanish, French, German and Italian spoken. Amusement parks, antiquing, art galleries, beaches, bicycling, canoeing/kayaking, fishing, golf, hiking, Tanglewood summer festival, live theater, museums, parks, shopping, downhill skiing, cross-country skiing, sporting events, tennis, water sports and wineries nearby.

"Kathy and I stayed at your beautiful inn in early October. It was the highlight of our trip to New England."

Walker House

64 Walker St
Lenox, MA 01240-2718
(413)637-1271 (800)235-3098 Fax:(413)637-2387
E-mail: phoudek@vgernet.net
Web: www.walkerhouse.com

Circa 1804. This beautiful Federal-style house sits in the center of the village on three acres of graceful woods and restored gardens. Guest rooms have fireplaces and private baths. Each is

named for a favorite composer such as Beethoven, Mozart or Handel. The innkeepers' musical backgrounds include associations with the San Francisco Opera, the New York City Opera, and the Los Angeles Philharmonic. Walker House concerts are scheduled from time to time. The innkeepers offer film and opera screenings nightly on a twelve-foot screen. With prior approval, some pets may be allowed.

Historic Interest: Tanglewood and The Mount are both nearby attractions.

Innkeeper(s): Peggy & Richard Houdek. $80-210. PC. 8 rooms with PB, 5 with FP and 1 conference room. Breakfast and afternoon tea included in rates. Types of meals: Cont plus and early coffee/tea. Beds: QDT. TV in room. Air conditioning. VCR, fax, copier, library, theatre with internet access and 100 inch screen on premises. Handicap access. Weddings, small meetings and family reunions hosted. French and Spanish spoken. Antiquing, fishing, music, live theater, parks, shopping, downhill skiing, cross-country skiing and water sports nearby.

Pets allowed: With prior approval.

"We had a grand time staying with fellow music and opera lovers! Breakfasts were lovely."

Whistler's Inn

5 Greenwood St
Lenox, MA 01240-2029
(413)637-0975 Fax:(413)637-2190
E-mail: rmears3246@aol.com
Web: www.whistlersinnlenox.com

Circa 1820. Whistler's Inn is an English Tudor home surrounded by seven acres of woodlands and gardens. Inside, elegance is abundant. In the impressive Louis XVI music room, you'll find a Steinway piano, chandeliers and gilt palace furniture. There is an English library with chintz-covered sofas, paintings and etchings, hundreds of volumes of books and a fireplace of black marble. Here, guests have sher-

ry or tea and perhaps engage in conversation with their well-traveled hosts, both authors. A baronial dining room features Baroque candelabrums, chinoiserie and a huge marble and limestone fireplace.

Innkeeper(s): Richard & Joan Mears. $80-275. MC, VISA, AX, DS, PC, TC. TAC10. 14 rooms with PB, 2 with FP and 3 conference rooms. Breakfast included in rates. Type of meal: Full bkfst. Afternoon tea available. Beds: KQDT. Phone and ceiling fan in room. Air conditioning. Fax, copier and library on premises. Small meetings, family reunions and seminars hosted. Antiquing, live theater, museums, parks, shopping, downhill skiing, cross-country skiing and water sports nearby.

Leverett   D6

Hannah Dudley House Inn

114 Dudleyville Rd
Leverett, MA 01054-9713

Circa 1797. Each season brings with it a new reason to visit this 18th-century Colonial, which is named for a member of the first family to inhabit this home. In autumn, the home's 66 acres explode in color. In winter, snow-capped pines add to the festive atmosphere, and guests snuggle up in front of a roaring fire. Two guest rooms include fireplaces, and the house offers four others. The guest room refrigerators are always stocked with drinks. At certain times of the year, dinner specials are available. During warm months, guests enjoy use of a swimming pool. Stroll the grounds and you'll find plenty of wildlife, including two ponds inhabited by beavers, ducks, goldfish, trout, turtles and bullfrogs. During the winter months, the pond transforms into the inn's skating rink.

Innkeeper(s): Erni & Daryl Johnson. $155-175. MC, VISA, PC, TC. 4 rooms, 2 with PB, 2 with FP. Breakfast and snacks/refreshments included in rates. MAP. Types of meals: Full bkfst and early coffee/tea. Beds: Q. Turndown service in room. Air conditioning. Swimming, library, hiking trails, recreation area and fishing on premises. Antiquing, fishing, golf, live theater, parks, shopping, downhill skiing, cross-country skiing, sporting events and tennis nearby.

Publicity: Boston Globe, New York Times, Daily Hampshire Gazette.

Lynn D14

Diamond District Inn

142 Ocean St
Lynn, MA 01902-2007
(781)599-4470 (800)666-3076 Fax:(781)595-2200
E-mail: diamonddistrict@msn.com
Web: www.diamonddistrictinn.com

Circa 1911. This Georgian house was built for shoe manufacturer P.J. Harney-Lynn. Many of the original fixtures remain, and the inn is suitably furnished with Oriental rugs and antiques. The parlor

features a collection of antique musical instruments. There are several views of the ocean from the house, but the veranda is the most popular spot for sea gazing. There is a heated outdoor spa for guest rooms and two romantic suites feature fireplaces, whirlpool tubs, ocean view and deck. Candlelight breakfast is served in the dining room or on the porch. Fresh fruits, homemade breads and hot coffee, tea or cider start off the meal, followed by a special entree. The beach is just steps away, and guests can walk to the promenade and restaurants.

Historic Interest: The Lynn Museum, Mary Baker Eddy home, the founder of Christian Science, Grand Army of the Republic meeting hall and museum are within walking distance. Located eight miles north of Boston.

Innkeeper(s): Sandra & Jerry Caron. $120-250. MC, VISA, AX, DC, CB, DS, PC, TC. TAC10. 11 rooms, 7 with PB, 2 suites and 1 conference room. Breakfast included in rates. Type of meal: Full bkfst. Beds: KQDT. Cable TV, phone and ceiling fan in room. Air conditioning. Fax, copier, spa and voice mail and modem on premises. Antiquing, fishing, North Shore & Salem, cross-country skiing and water sports nearby.

"The room was spectacular and breakfast was served beautifully. Bed and breakfast were both outstanding! Thanks so much for your hospitality."

Marblehead D14

Harborside House B&B

23 Gregory St
Marblehead, MA 01945-3241
(781)631-1032

Circa 1840. Enjoy the Colonial charm of this home, which overlooks Marblehead Harbor on Boston's historic North Shore. Rooms are decorated with antiques and period wallpaper. A third-story sundeck offers excellent views. A generous continental breakfast of home-baked breads, muffins and fresh fruit is served each morning in the well-decorated dining room or on the open porch. The village of Marblehead provides many shops and restaurants. Boston and Logan airport are 30 minutes away.

Historic Interest: Lee Mansion (1768), King Hooper Mansion (1745) and St. Michael's Church (1714).

Innkeeper(s): Susan Livingston. $70-90. PC, TC. TAC10. 2 rooms. Breakfast, afternoon tea and snacks/refreshments included in rates. Type of meal: Cont plus. Beds: DT. Bathrobes in room. Bicycles on premises. Antiquing, parks, shopping and water sports nearby.

Publicity: *Marblehead Reporter.*

"Harborside Inn is restful, charming, with a beautiful view of the water. I wish we didn't have to leave."

The Nesting Place B&B

16 Village St
Marblehead, MA 01945-2213
(781)631-6655

Circa 1890. Conveniently located one-half hour away from Boston and Cape Ann, this turn-of-the-century house located in a quiet neighborhood offers as much privacy as you require. Full breakfasts are served and include home baked breads and muffins and fresh fruit. Discover the world of the early clipper ships as you walk the narrow winding streets and the beaches of Marblehead's renowned harbor, only minutes away. There's a relaxing hot tub to top off a day of browsing through art galleries, antique shops and quaint boutiques. Massages and facials also are available off premises.

Innkeeper(s): Louise Hirshberg. $65-75. MC, VISA, PC, TC. 2 rooms. Breakfast included in rates. Types of meals: Cont plus and early coffee/tea. Beds: KQT. VCR and spa on premises. Antiquing, fishing, live theater, parks, shopping, cross-country skiing, sporting events and water sports nearby.

Martha's Vineyard K16

Captain Dexter House of Edgartown

35 Pease's Point Way, Box 2798
Martha's Vineyard, MA 02539
(508)627-7289 Fax:(508)627-3328
Web: www.mvy.com/captdexter

Circa 1843. Located just three blocks from Edgartown's harbor and historic district, this black-shuttered sea merchant's house has a graceful lawn and terraced flower gardens. A gentle Colonial atmosphere is enhanced by original wooden beams, exposed floorboards, working fireplaces, old-fashioned dormers and a collection of period antiques. Luxurious canopy beds are featured, and some rooms include fireplaces.

Historic Interest: The marine biology laboratories at Woods Hole (45 minutes by ferry).

Innkeeper(s): Birdie. $85-250. MC, VISA, AX, PC, TC. TAC10. 11 rooms with PB, 3 with FP. Breakfast included in rates. Type of meal: Cont plus. Afternoon tea available. Beds: QD. TV and ceiling fan in room. Air conditioning. Fax on premises. Weddings, small meetings, family reunions and seminars hosted. Antiquing, fishing, live theater, parks and water sports nearby.

"Since we were on our honeymoon, we were hoping for a quiet, relaxing stay, and the Captain Dexter House was perfect!"

Captain Dexter House of Vineyard Haven

92 Main St, PO Box 2457
Martha's Vineyard, MA 02568
(508)693-6564 Fax:(508)693-8448
Web: www.mvy.com/captdexter

Circa 1840. Captain Dexter House was the home of sea captain Rodulphus Dexter. Authentic 18th-century antiques and reproductions are among the inn's appointments. There are Count Rumford fireplaces and hand-stenciled walls in several rooms. Located on a street of historic homes, the inn is a short stroll to the beach, town and harbor. The innkeepers offer an evening aperitif and in the summer, lemonade is served.

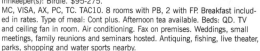

Historic Interest: Marine Biology Laboratories at Woods Hole (45 minutes by ferry). Many of the buildings in this quaint Martha's Vineyard locale are historic.

Innkeeper(s): Birdie. $95-275. MC, VISA, AX, PC, TC. TAC10. 8 rooms with PB, 2 with FP. Breakfast included in rates. Type of meal: Cont plus. Afternoon tea available. Beds: QD. TV and ceiling fan in room. Air conditioning. Fax on premises. Weddings, small meetings, family reunions and seminars hosted. Antiquing, fishing, live theater, parks, shopping and water sports nearby.

"The house is sensational. Your hospitality was all one could expect. You've made us permanent bed & breakfast fans."

Thorncroft Inn

460 Main St, PO Box 1022
Martha's Vineyard, MA 02568-1022
(508)693-3333 (800)332-1236 Fax:(508)693-5419
E-mail: innkeeper@thorncroft.com
Web: www.thorncroft.com

Circa 1918. The Thorncroft Estate is a classic craftsman bungalow with a dominant roof and neo-colonial details. It was built by Chicago grain merchant John Herbert Ware as the guest house of a large oceanfront estate. Most guest rooms include working fireplaces and canopied beds. Some also boast

two-person whirlpool tubs or private 300-gallon hot tubs. The inn is situated in three buildings on three-and-one-half acres of lawns and woodlands. In its naturally romantic setting, the Thorncroft provides the perfect ambiance for honeymooners, anniversaries and special couples' getaways. Full breakfasts and afternoon teas are served in the dining rooms, but guests can opt for a continental breakfast served in their room.

Innkeeper(s): Karl & Lynn Buder. $225-475. MC, VISA, AX, DC, CB, DS. 14 rooms with PB, 10 with FP and 1 cottage. Breakfast and afternoon tea included in rates. Type of meal: Full bkfst. Room service available. Beds: KQD. TV in room. Fax and copier on premises. Antiquing, fishing, live theater and water sports nearby.

Publicity: *Cape Cod Life, Glamour, Travel & Leisure, Great Country Inns on the Learning Channel.*

"It's the type of place where we find ourselves falling in love all over again."

Middleboro   H14

On Cranberry Pond B&B

43 Fuller St
Middleboro, MA 02346-1706
(508)946-0768 Fax:(508)947-8221

Circa 1989. Nestled in the historic "cranberry capital of the world," this modern farmhouse rests on a working berry bog by the shores of its namesake tarn. There are two miles of trails

to meander, and during berry picking season, guests can watch as buckets of the fruit are collected. Rooms are comfortable and well appointed. The Master Suite includes a working fireplace. A 93-foot deck overlooks the cranberry bog. Innkeeper Jeannine LaBossiere creates breakfasts which begin with fresh coffee, muffins, cookies and scones.

Innkeeper(s): Jeannine LaBossiere & Tim Dombrowski. $75-140. MC, VISA, AX, DC, CB, PC, TC. TAC10. 5 rooms, 3 with PB, 2 with FP, 2 suites and 1 conference room. Breakfast and snacks/refreshments included in rates. Types of meals: Full gourmet bkfst and early coffee/tea. Afternoon tea and banquet service available. Beds: QD. Cable TV, phone, turndown service, ceiling fan and VCR in room. Air conditioning. Fax, copier, stables, bicycles and library on premises. Weddings, small meetings, family reunions and seminars hosted. Amusement parks, antiquing, fishing, live theater, parks, shopping, downhill skiing and water sports nearby.

"Your dedication to making your guests comfortable is above and beyond. You are tops in your field."

Nantucket   L18

Corner House

49 Center St, PO Box 1828
Nantucket, MA 02554-1828
(508)228-1530
E-mail: cornerhs@nantucket.net
Web: www.cornerhousenantucket.com

Circa 1790. The Corner House is a charming 18th-century village inn. Architectural details such as the original pine floors, paneling and fireplaces have been preserved. A screened porch overlooks the English perennial garden, where guests often take afternoon tea. All of the romantically appointed bedchambers feature canopy or four-poster beds. Three rooms are adorned with non-working fireplaces, some have refrigerators.

Innkeeper(s): John & Sandy Knox-Johnston. $65-205. MC, VISA, AX, TC. 15 rooms with PB and 2 suites. Breakfast and afternoon tea included in rates. AP. Type of meal: Cont plus. Beds: QDT. Cable TV in room. Air conditioning. Fax, library, beach towels, bike rack and concierge services on premises. Limited French and German spoken. Antiquing, fishing, golf, art galleries, whaling museum, sportfishing, live theater, tennis and water sports nearby.

"Thank you so much for the care, atmosphere, cleanliness and peace you provided for us this week."

Jared Coffin House

29 Broad St
Nantucket, MA 02554-3502
(508)228-2400

Circa 1845. Jared Coffin was one of the island's most successful ship owners and the first to build a three-story mansion. The house's brick walls and slate roof resisted the Great Fire of 1846 and, in 1847, it was purchased by the Nantucket Steamship Company for use as a hotel. Additions were made and a century later, the Nantucket Historical Trust purchased and restored the house. Today, the inn consists of five historic houses and a 1964 building. The oldest is the Swain House.

Innkeeper(s): John J. Cowden, Jr. $100-250. MC, VISA, AX, DC. 60 rooms with PB and 3 conference rooms. Type of meal: Full bkfst. Dinner and lunch available. Restaurant on premises. Beds: QDT. Fax and copier on premises.

"The dining was superb, the atmosphere was gracious and the rooms were charming and spotless."

Pineapple Inn

10 Hussey St
Nantucket, MA 02554-3612
(508)228-9992 Fax:(508)325-6051
E-mail: email@pineappleinn.com
Web: www.pineappleinn.com

Circa 1838. Built for a prominent whaling ship captain, this classic colonial has been restored and refurnished to inspire the gracious and elegant standard of a time in history that most of us only read about in books. Reproduction and authentic 19th-century antiques, artwork and Oriental rugs are featured throughout the inn. Luxurious goose down comforters and Ralph Lauren linens top beautiful handmade, four-poster canopy beds in most of the 12 guest rooms. The innkeepers, seasoned restaurateurs, offer guests a delightful combination of steaming cappuccinos, freshly squeezed orange juice, a fresh fruit plate and a selection of pastries served restaurant-style in the formal dining room or on the bricked garden patio.

Innkeeper(s): Caroline & Bob Taylor. $110-295. MC, VISA, AX, PC, TC. 12 rooms with PB, 3 with FP and 1 conference room. Breakfast included in rates. Types of meals: Cont plus, cont and early coffee/tea. Beds: KQ. Cable TV and phone in room. Air conditioning. Fax and copier on premises. Weddings, small meetings, family reunions and seminars hosted. Antiquing, fishing, golf, historic homes, whaling museum, live theater, shopping, tennis and water sports nearby.

"Our time here was more than just a lovely room. The patio breakfast was heavenly... and you always took time to chat and make us feel welcome. The essence of elegance—the most modern comforts and the charm of an old whaling Captain's house."

Stumble Inne

109 Orange Street
Nantucket, MA 02554-3947
(508)228-4482 Fax:(508)228-4752

Circa 1704. This Nantucket Island inn is appointed with fine antiques and period reproductions. Rooms feature wide pine floors, antique beds and ceiling fans. At the back of the inn's hydrangea-filled gardens, there is a two-bedroom cottage that can accommodate up to four people. The cottage also includes a bathroom, kitchen, living room and a private deck. The inn was voted "Best B&B" by Cape Cod Life.

Historic Interest: Nantucket Historical Association Exhibits (one-half mile).

Innkeeper(s): Jeanne & George Todor. $75-250. MC, VISA, AX, TC. 6 rooms with PB and 1 suite. Breakfast included in rates. Types of meals: Cont plus and early coffee/tea. Beds: Q. Cable TV, ceiling fan and VCR in room. Air conditioning. Fax on premises. Small meetings, family reunions and seminars hosted. Antiquing, fishing, restaurants, live theater, shopping and water sports nearby.

"A relaxing, comfortable week with gracious hosts. Thanks for your Southern hospitality in the Northeast."

The White House

48 Center St
Nantucket, MA 02554-3664
(508)228-4677

Circa 1800. For more than 40 years a favorite hostelry of visitors to Nantucket, The White House is situated ideally in the heart of the historic district and a short walk to the beach and ferry terminal. The first floor houses an antique shop. Guests stay in rooms on the second floor or a housekeeping apartment. Afternoon wine and cheese is served in the garden.

Innkeeper(s): Nina Hellman. $75-130. MC, VISA, AX. 3 rooms with PB and 1 suite. Breakfast included in rates. Type of meal: Cont. Beds: Q. Phone in room. Antiquing, fishing, museums, fine restaurants, live theater, shopping and water sports nearby.

The Woodbox Inn

29 Fair St
Nantucket, MA 02554-3798
(508)228-0587
E-mail: woodbox@nantucket.net
Web: www.woodboxinn.com

Circa 1709. In the heart of the historic district, the Woodbox Inn was built in 1709 by Captain George Bunker. Guest rooms are decorated with antiques and reproductions and some have canopy beds. The six suites offer sitting rooms and fireplaces. Walk to Main Street and enjoy fine boutiques and art galleries. Other activities include biking, tennis, golf, whale watching and sandy beaches for sunning. The inn's award-winning gourmet dining room features an

early American atmosphere with low-beamed ceilings and pine-paneled walls. (Meals are not included in room rates.).

Innkeeper(s): Dexter Tutein. $175-285. PC, TC. 9 rooms with PB, 6 with FP and 6 suites. Type of meal: Full bkfst. Gourmet dinner available. Restaurant on premises. Beds: KQDT. Weddings, small meetings and family reunions hosted. French, German and Spanish spoken. Antiquing, fishing, live theater, parks, shopping, tennis and water sports nearby.

Newburyport B14

Clark Currier Inn

45 Green St
Newburyport, MA 01950-2646
(978)465-8363 (800)360-6582

Circa 1803. Once the home of shipbuilder Thomas March Clark, this three-story Federal-style inn provides gracious accommodations to visitors in the Northeast Massachusetts area. Visitors will enjoy the inn's details added by Samuel McEntire, one of the nation's most celebrated home builders and woodcarvers. Breakfast is served in the dining room or garden room, with an afternoon tea offered in the garden room. The inn's grounds also boast a picturesque garden and gazebo. Parker River National Wildlife Refuge and Maudslay State Park are nearby, as well as Plum Island beaches.

Historic Interest: The Cushing House Museum, Firehouse Center, Custom House Museum and Market Square are within walking distance. Lowell's Boat Shop, a museum across the river, houses the Amesbury dory and highlights more than 200 years of boat building.

Innkeeper(s): Mary & Bob Nolan. $95-155. MC, VISA, AX, DS. 8 rooms with PB. Breakfast and afternoon tea included in rates. Meal: Cont. Beds: QDT. Phone in room. Air conditioning. Library on premises. Weddings, small meetings, family reunions and seminars hosted. Amusement parks, antiquing, fishing, live theater, parks, shopping, cross-country skiing and water sports nearby.

"We had a lovely stay in your B&B! We appreciated your hospitality!"

Windsor House

38 Federal St
Newburyport, MA 01950-2820
(978)462-3778 (888)873-5296 Fax:(978)465-3443

Circa 1786. This brick Federal-style mansion was designed as a combination home and ship's chandlery (an outfitter and broker for cargo). The Merchant Suite was once the sales room and features a 14-foot ceiling with hand-hewn, beveled beams.

The Bridal Suite was once the master suite. The newest suite, England's Rose, is a tribute to Princess Diana. The English innkeepers serve a hearty English-country breakfast and an English tea in the afternoon.

Historic Interest: William Lloyd Garrison birthplace (across the street), Newburyport Custom's House and Caleb Cushing House (walking distance).

Innkeeper(s): Judith & John Harris. $110-145. MC, VISA, AX, DS, PC, TC. TAC10. 4 rooms with PB. Breakfast and afternoon tea included in rates. Type of meal: Full bkfst. Beds: KQD. TV, phone, ceiling fan, fans/Alarm clocks and tea and coffee facilities in room. Air conditioning. VCR, fax and copier on premises. Small meetings and seminars hosted. Antiquing, fishing, golf, bird watching, wildlife refuge, live theater, parks, shopping, cross-country skiing, tennis and water sports nearby.

Pets allowed: Special arrangement.

"You will find what you look for and be met by the unexpected too. A good time!"

Northhampton   E5

Lupine House

185 North Main St
Northhampton, MA 01060
(413)586-9766 (800)890-9766

Circa 1872. This Colonial offers a comfortable setting for those enjoying a New England getaway. Rooms are simply furnished with antiques adding to the ambiance. Light, continental-plus fare is served in the mornings, including homemade granola, fresh fruit, cereals, breads and muffins. The B&B is a short drive from downtown Northampton and many area schools, including Amherst, Smith, Hampshire and Mount Holyoke colleges and the University of Massachusetts.

Historic Interest: Old Deerfield is just a few minutes drive away.

Innkeeper(s): Evelyn & Gil Billings. $70. MC, VISA, PC, TC. 3 rooms with PB. Breakfast included in rates. Types of meals: Cont plus and early coffee/tea. Beds: QDT. Turndown service in room. Library on premises. Antiquing, fishing, golf, biking, museums, live theater, parks, shopping, downhill skiing, cross-country skiing, sporting events and tennis nearby.
Publicity: *Daily Hampshire Gazette.*

"You certainly provide 'the extra mile' of hospitality and service. Thank you."

North New Salem   D7

Bullard Farm B&B

89 Elm St
North New Salem, MA 01355-9502
(978)544-6959 Fax:(978)544-6959

Circa 1793. This inn's four guest rooms are found in a farmhouse containing six working fireplaces. The farm has been in the family of the innkeeper's mother since 1864, and guests

are welcome to hike the inn's grounds, observing its history as a lumber mill and tannery. The inn features many original pieces used in its country-style decor. Full breakfasts may include banana sour cream coffee cake. Winter visitors may enjoy a sleigh ride or cross-country skiing on the inn's 300 acres. Quabbin Reservoir is a one-mile drive from the inn.

Innkeeper(s): Janet F. Kraft. $70-95. MC, VISA, PC. 4 rooms, 2 with FP and 2 conference rooms. Breakfast included in rates. Type of meal: Full bkfst. Beds: QDT. Phone in room. Air conditioning. VCR and fax on premises. Small meetings, family reunions and seminars hosted. Antiquing, fishing, hiking, swimming, shopping, downhill skiing, cross-country skiing and sporting events nearby.

Norwell   F15

1810 House B&B

147 Old Oaken Bucket Rd
Norwell, MA 02061-1320
(781)659-1810 (888)833-1810
E-mail: tuttle1810@aol.com
Web: 1810house.com

Circa 1810. Exposed beams, original to this early 19th-century house, add a rustic touch to the 1810 House. Guest rooms are simply furnished in a traditional country decor. One includes a canopy bed and another offers an antique spool bed. Savory New England breakfasts with fresh fruit, yogurt, muffins, egg dishes, sausage, bacon and ham are served in the fireside dining room or on the screened-in porch. Guests can take a tour of the village via the innkeeper's restored 1915 Model T. The 1810 house is located midway between Plymouth and Boston.

Innkeeper(s): Susanne & Harold Tuttle. $75-95. PC, TC. TAC10. 3 rooms, 2 with PB and 1 suite. Breakfast included in rates. Types of meals: Full bkfst and early coffee/tea. Beds: QT. Turndown service and ceiling fan in room. Air conditioning. VCR and copier on premises. Antiquing, fishing, live theater, shopping and water sports nearby.

"We will remember the warmth of your welcome and hospitality."

Onset   I15

Onset Pointe Inn

9 Eagle Way, PO Box 1450
Onset, MA 02558-1450
(508)295-8100 (800)356-6738 Fax:(508)295-5241

Circa 1880. This restored Victorian mansion is surrounded by the ocean on Point Independence. Its casually elegant decor is enhanced by sea views, sunlight, bright colors and florals. Spacious verandas, an enclosed circular sun porch and a bayside gazebo are available to guests. Accommodations are divided among the main house and two additional buildings. An all-you-can-eat hearty continental breakfast is available in the waterfront dining room. The Onset Pointe Inn received the National Trust first prize for preservation in its B&B category.

Innkeeper(s): Peter Della Monica & Barry Eisenberg. $55-235. MC, VISA, AX, DS, TC. 14 rooms with PB and 6 suites. Breakfast included in rates. Beds: QDT. Phone in room. Fax, copier, swimming and meeting room on premises. Weddings, small meetings, family reunions and seminars hosted. Antiquing, fishing, historical sites, live theater, parks, shopping and water sports nearby.

"We've found the B&B we've been looking for!"

Orleans H19

The Farmhouse at Nauset Beach

163 Beach Rd
Orleans, MA 02653-2732
(508)255-6654

Circa 1870. Feel the intimacy of Orleans and capture the flavor of Cape Cod at this quiet country inn resting in a seashore setting. Rooms in this Greek Revival-style inn are comfortably furnished to depict their 19th-century past. Some rooms offer ocean views, and one includes a decorated fireplace. Nauset Beach is a short walk

away. Spend a day charter fishing in Cape Cod Bay or the Atlantic. To make your stay complete, your itinerary can include antiquing, shopping, exploring quiet country lanes or a day at the beach. The inn offers gift certificates and is open year-round.

Innkeeper(s): Dorothy Standish. $52-110. MC, VISA, PC, TC. 8 rooms with PB, 1 with FP. Breakfast included in rates. Type of meal: Cont plus. Beds: KQD. Ceiling fan in some rooms in room. Bike rack on premises. Family reunions hosted. Antiquing, fishing, horseback riding, windsurfing, bike trails, live theater, shopping and water sports nearby.

Petersham D8

Winterwood at Petersham

19 N Main St
Petersham, MA 01366-9500
(978)724-8885

Circa 1842. The town of Petersham is often referred to as a museum of Greek Revival architecture. One of the grand houses facing the common is Winterwood. It boasts fireplaces in almost every room. Private dining is available for groups of up to 70 people. The inn is listed in the National Register.

Innkeeper(s): Jean & Robert Day. $90.
MC, VISA, AX, DS. 6 rooms with PB, 5 with FP and 1 conference room. Type of meal: Cont plus. Beds: QT. Weddings, small meetings, family reunions and seminars hosted. Antiquing, downhill skiing and cross-country skiing nearby.

"Between your physical facilities and Jean's cooking, our return to normal has been made even more difficult. Your hospitality was just a fantastic extra to our total experience."

Pittsfield D2

Olde White Horse Inn

378 South St
Pittsfield, MA 01201-6804
(413)442-2512

Circa 1902. Innkeeping runs in the family at the Olde White Horse, which features an elegant Colonial exterior set on an acre of manicured lawn. The current innkeeper's grandparents also were innkeepers, and two rooms are named in honor of them. The Colonial theme continues into the home and to its eight guest rooms, decorated with antiques and beds topped with cozy comforters. The innkeepers' daughters also pitch in and help run the inn; the oldest prepares the breakfasts. The morning meal includes such items as quiche, pancakes, homemade muffins or breads and fresh fruit.

Innkeeper(s): Joe & Linda Kalisz. $95-180. MC, VISA, AX, DC, CB, DS, TC. 8 rooms with PB. Breakfast included in rates. Types of meals: Full bkfst and early coffee/tea. Snacks/refreshments available. Beds: QD. TV, phone and turndown service in room. Air conditioning. Fax and copier on premises. Weddings, small meetings and family reunions hosted. Antiquing, fishing, live theater, parks, shopping, downhill skiing, cross-country skiing, sporting events and water sports nearby.

Plymouth G15

Plymouth Bay Manor Bed & Breakfast

259 Court St Rte 3A
Plymouth, MA 02360
(508)830-0426 (800)492-1828 Fax:(508)747-3382
E-mail: info@plymouthbaymanor.com
Web: www.plymouthbaymanor.com

Circa 1904. Views of Plymouth Bay and a lighthouse can be seen from this shingled, Colonial Revival home. Each guest room has been decorated with romance in mind. Beds are topped with fine linens and flowery comforters. Fresh flowers brighten each room. The Master's Chamber includes a four-poster bed and a fireplace. The Delft Suite includes a fireplace and a clawfoot tub. The Garden Suite is a vision of English country, lightened by a bay window. All three rooms offer an ocean view. Breakfast includes items such as fresh fruit, muffins and Belgian waffles. The home is within walking distance to Plymouth Rock, Plimoth Plantation, the Mayflower II, museums and antique shops.

Historic Interest: Historic Plymouth-1/2 miles, Plymouth Rock, Mayflower-1/2 mile, Plantation.

Innkeeper(s): Larry & Cindi Hamlin. $85-125. MC, VISA, PC, TC. 3 rooms with PB, 2 with FP and 1 conference room. Breakfast included in rates. Types of meals: Full bkfst and early coffee/tea. Beds: KQT. Turndown service in room. Central air. VCR, fax, library and beach on premises. Small meetings hosted. Antiquing, art galleries, beaches, bicycling, canoeing/kayaking, fishing, golf, hiking, horseback riding, live theater, museums, parks, shopping, tennis, water sports and wineries nearby.

Princeton D9

Fernside B&B

PO Box 303, 162 Mountain Rd
Princeton, MA 01541-0303
(978)464-2741 (800)545-2741 Fax:(978)464-2065

Circa 1835. Originally built by Capt. Benjamin Harrington, this elegant Federal mansion was transformed in 1870 into a tavern and boarding house for Harvard professors and students. In

1890, the home changed owners and served as a vacation house for working women for more than 100 years. In 1994, the Morrisons transformed it once again and meticulously restored it. Situated on the eastern slope of Mount Wachusett, the inn is nestled on seven acres with breathtaking sunrise views. Designed for entertaining, there are eight cozy fireplaces, numerous sitting rooms and a variety of porches. The common rooms as well as the guest rooms are elegantly decorated with antiques and period reproductions and Oriental rugs. A home-cooked breakfast includes fresh fruit, pastries and a variety of entrees.

Innkeeper(s): Jocelyn & Richard Morrison. $115-165. MC, VISA, AX, PC, TC. TAC10. 6 rooms with PB, 4 with FP, 2 suites and 1 conference room. Breakfast included in rates. Types of meals: Full gourmet bkfst and early coffee/tea. Afternoon tea available. Beds: QT. Phone and turndown service in room. Fax and copier on premises. Handicap access. Weddings, small meetings, family reunions and seminars hosted. Antiquing, golf, parks, shopping, downhill skiing, cross-country skiing and tennis nearby.

"You cannot help but feel at ease the moment you walk into the inn."

Provincetown G18

Land's End Inn

22 Commercial St
Provincetown, MA 02657-1910
(508)487-0706 (800)276-7088

Circa 1904. Built originally as a summer bungalow for Charles Higgins, a Boston merchant, Lands End commands a panoramic view of Provincetown and Cape Cod Bay. It still houses part

of the Higgins' collection of Oriental wood carvings and stained glass. While David Schoolman was the inn's owner, he enhanced it by decorating with an eclectic array of wonderful antiques. Amid luxuriant gardens, the inn successfully retains an air of quiet and relaxation.

Innkeeper(s): Anthony Arakelian. $87-285. MC, VISA, PC, TC. 16 rooms with PB. Breakfast included in rates. Types of meals: Cont and early coffee/tea. Beds: QD. Ceiling fan in room. Refrigerator in breakfast room and view of Cape Cod Bay on premises. Weddings, small meetings, family reunions and seminars hosted. Antiquing, fishing, live theater, parks, shopping and water sports nearby.

Publicity: *Travel Magazine, Cape Cod Review, Cape Cod Life.*

Watership Inn

7 Winthrop St
Provincetown, MA 02657-2116
(508)487-0094 (800)330-9413

Circa 1820. This stately manor was built as a home port for a Provincetown sea captain. During the past 10 years, it has been renovated and the original beamed ceilings and polished plank

floors provide a background for the inn's antiques and simple decor. Guests enjoy the inn's sun decks and large yard, which offers volleyball and croquet sets.

Historic Interest: Landing site of the Pilgrims, The Provincetown Heritage Museum, Pilgrim Monument and Museum (within walking distance).

Innkeeper(s): Richard Conley. $36-200. MC, VISA, AX, DS. 15 rooms with PB. Breakfast included in rates. Type of meal: Cont plus. Beds: QDT. Cable TV in room. Antiquing and parks nearby.

"We found your hospitality and charming inn perfect for our brief yet wonderful escape from Boston."

Rehoboth H12

Gilbert's Tree Farm B&B

30 Spring St
Rehoboth, MA 02769-2408
(508)252-6416

Circa 1835. This country farmhouse sits on 17 acres of woodland that includes an award-winning tree farm. Cross-country skiing, hiking, and pony-cart rides are found right outside the door. If they choose to,

guests can even help with the farm chores, caring for horses and gardening. A swimming pool is open during summer. Three antique-filled bedrooms share a second-floor sitting room.

There is a first-floor room with a working fireplace and private bath. The nearby town of Rehoboth is 350 years old.

Historic Interest: Battleship Massachusetts (8 miles), Museum of Lizzie Borden artifacts (8 miles), Carpenter Museum (4 miles), Plimouth Plantation (1 hour), Newport mansions (45 minutes).

Innkeeper(s): Jeanne Gilbert. $60-80. PC, TC. TAC10. 4 rooms. Breakfast, afternoon tea and snacks/refreshments included in rates. Types of meals: Full bkfst and early coffee/tea. Beds: KDT. Fireplace in one room. VCR, copier, swimming, stables, bicycles, library, pet boarding and horse boarding only on premises. Antiquing, fishing, live theater, parks, shopping, cross-country skiing, sporting events and water sports nearby.

"This place has become my second home. Thank you for the family atmosphere of relaxation, fun, spontaneity and natural surroundings."

Perryville Inn

157 Perryville Rd
Rehoboth, MA 02769-1922
(508)252-9239 (800)439-9239 Fax:(508)252-9054
E-mail: pvinn@hotmail.com
Web: www.perryvilleinn.com

Circa 1820. The Perryville Inn was a dairy farm for more than 140 years. During that time, in 1897, the original two-story colonial was remodeled into a handsome three-story Victorian, now in the National Register.

(The house was raised and an additional floor added underneath.) The pasture is now a public golf course, but the icehouse remains. There are old stone walls, a mill pond, trout stream and wooded paths. Inside the inn, cozy rooms are decorated with comfortable antiques.

Innkeeper(s): Tom & Betsy Charnecki. $75-105. MC, VISA, AX, DS, PC, TC. 4 rooms with PB, 1 suite and 1 conference room. Breakfast included in rates. Type of meal: Cont plus. Beds: KQDT. Phone in room. Air conditioning. Bicycles on premises. Antiquing, fishing and cross-country skiing nearby.

"The family voted the Perryville the best place we stayed on our entire trip, without hesitation!"

Rockport   C15

Addison Choate Inn

49 Broadway
Rockport, MA 01966-1527
(978)546-7543 (800)245-7543 Fax:(978)546-7638

Circa 1851. Antiques and reproductions decorate the interior of this mid-19th-century home. The guest rooms feature antique and wicker furnishings, artwork and polished, pine floors. Freshly ground coffee, homemade baked breads, fruit and cereals are served each morning in the inn's dining room, which still contains the original fireplace with a beehive oven. If weather permits, breakfasts are served on the inn's wraparound porch, offering a view of the garden. Shops, restaurants and art galleries all are nearby.

Innkeeper(s): Knox Johnson. $95-145. MC, VISA, DS, PC, TC. TAC10. 8 rooms with PB. Breakfast and afternoon tea included in rates. Types of meals: Cont plus and early coffee/tea. Beds: KQT. Television, telephones and refrigerators in room. Air conditioning. VCR, fax, copier and swimming on premises. Antiquing, fishing, golf, live theater, parks, shopping, tennis and water sports nearby.

"Our stay was a delight!"

The Inn on Cove Hill

37 Mount Pleasant St
Rockport, MA 01966-1727
(978)546-2701 (888)546-2701
Web: www.cape-ann.com/covehill

Circa 1791. Pirate gold found at Gully Point paid for this Federal-style house. A white picket fence and granite walkway welcome guests. Inside, an exquisitely crafted spiral staircase, random-width, pumpkin-pine floors and hand-forged hinges display the original artisan's handiwork. Furnishings include family heirlooms, four-poster canopy beds, and paintings by area artists. Muffin Du Jour is baked fresh each day by John. Bicycles can be rented, and you can enjoy whale watching, fishing the local waters, or simply exploring the antique shops and village streets.

Historic Interest: For historic sites, Gloucester is just five miles away, offering tours of Beauport, a historic 1907 home and the Hammond Castle Museum.

Innkeeper(s): John & Marjorie Pratt. $51-125. MC, VISA, PC, TC. 11 rooms, 9 with PB. Breakfast included in rates. Types of meals: Cont and early coffee/tea. Beds: QDT. Air conditioning. Antiquing, fishing, live theater and parks nearby.

Emerson Inn By The Sea

Phillips Ave
Rockport, MA 01966
(798)546-6321 (800)964-5550 Fax:(798)546-7043
E-mail: info@emersoninnbythesea.com
Web: www.emersoninnbythesea.com

Circa 1840. This Greek Revival inn's namesake once called the place, "thy proper summer home." As it is the oldest continuously operated inn on Cape Ann, decades of travelers agree with his sentiment. The guest rooms are comfortable, yet tastefully furnished, and some boast ocean views. The grounds include a heated, saltwater swimming pool as well as a sauna and whirlpool. Breakfast is included in rates. Guests also can enjoy dinner at the inn's dining room, an area added to the 19th-century inn in 1912.

Innkeeper(s): Bruce & Michele Coates. $95-195. MC, VISA, DS, TC. TAC10. 36 rooms with PB, 3 suites and 3 conference rooms. EP. Types of meals: Full bkfst, cont plus, cont and early coffee/tea. Gourmet dinner available. Restaurant on premises. Beds: KQDT. Phone in room. Air conditioning. VCR, fax, copier, spa, swimming and sauna on premises. Weddings, small meetings, family reunions and seminars hosted. Antiquing, fishing, whale watches, live theater, parks and water sports nearby.

"We were very impressed with every aspect of the Emerson Inn."

Rocky Shores Inn

Eden Rd
Rockport, MA 01966
(978)546-2823 (800)348-4003
Web: www.rockportusa.com/rockyshores

Circa 1905. This grand country mansion was built on wooded land selected to provide maximum views of Thacher Island and the open sea. There are seven unique fireplaces, handsome woodwork, and a graceful stairway. Guest quarters feature wicker or period antiques. Guest cottages, nestled among the trees, include kitchens and are ideal for families. Lawns flow from the mansion down to the picturesque shoreline, and the front porch affords a view of the ocean.

Historic Interest: The home is located on the historic north shore of Boston.

Innkeeper(s): Renate & Gunter Kostka. $90-135. MC, VISA, AX. 11 suites, 7 with FP. Breakfast included in rates. Types of meals: Cont plus and cont. Beds: QDT. Antiquing, fishing, live theater and water sports nearby.

Publicity: *Yankee, Get Away Guide.*

"Fabulous! You and your inn are a five-star rating as far as we are concerned."

Sally Webster Inn

34 Mount Pleasant St
Rockport, MA 01966-1713
(978)546-9251 (877)546-9251

Circa 1832. William Choate left this pre-Civil War home to be divided by his nine children. Sally Choate Webster, the ninth child, was to receive several first-floor rooms and the attic chamber, but ended up owning the entire home. Innkeepers

Rick and Carolyn Steere have filled the gracious home with antiques and period reproductions, which complement the original pumpkin pine floors, antique door moldings and six fireplaces. Shops, restaurants, the beach and the rocky coast are all within three blocks of the inn. Whale watching, kayaking, antique shops, music festivals, island tours and museums are among the myriad of nearby attractions. In addition to these, Salem is just 15 miles away, and Boston is a 35-mile drive.

Innkeeper(s): Rick & Carolyn Steere. $70-94. MC, VISA, PC, TC. 8 rooms with PB. Breakfast included in rates. Type of meal: Cont plus. Beds: KQDT. TV and guest phone available in room. Air conditioning.

"All that a bed and breakfast should be."

Seacrest Manor

99 Marmion Way
Rockport, MA 01966-1927
(978)546-2211
Web: www.rockportusa.com/seacrestmanor/

Circa 1911. After more than two decades of serving guests, the innkeepers at this estate inn have achieved "ace" status, welcoming travelers with well-polished hospitality. Their inn was

once summer home to a prominent Boston restaurateur and looks out to the sea. The two-and-a half acres include gardens to stroll through, and inside there is a well-

stocked library. Fresh flowers are placed in each guest room, and some rooms are further enhanced with decorative fireplaces. Various types of berry pancakes, Irish oatmeal topped with dates, corn fritters and French toast are just a few of the items that might be found on the morning table. The inn is located across the street from the nine-acre John Kieran Nature Reserve. This is a non-smoking inn.

Innkeeper(s): Leighton Saville & Dwight MacCormack, Jr. $102-148. PC, TC. 8 rooms, 6 with PB. Breakfast and afternoon tea included in rates. Types of meals: Full gourmet bkfst and early coffee/tea. Beds: KQDT. Cable TV and turndown service in room. Bicycles, library and prize winning gardens on premises. French spoken. Antiquing, fishing, tours, whale watching, bicycling, sailing, music festival, art galleries, live theater, parks, shopping and water sports nearby.

"We'll always have many fond memories."

Tuck Inn B&B

17 High St
Rockport, MA 01966-1644
(978)546-7260 (800)789-7260
E-mail: tuckinn@shore.net
Web: www.rockportusa.com/tuckinn/

Circa 1790. Two recent renovations have served to make this charming Colonial inn all the more enticing. Period antiques and paintings by local artists are featured throughout the spacious inn. A favorite gathering spot is the living room with its fireplace, wide pine floors, tasteful furnishings and a piano available for guest use. Buffet breakfasts feature homemade breads, muffins, cakes and scones, granola accompanied by fresh fruit and yogurt. Guests may take a

dip in the swimming pool or at local beaches. Within easy walking distance are the many art galleries, restaurants and shops of Bearskin Neck. A nearby train station offers convenient access to Boston.

Historic Interest: The inn is 10 minutes from Gloucester. Other historic towns, such as Salem, Boston, Lexington and Concord, are within an hour's drive of the inn.

Innkeeper(s): Liz & Scott Wood. $59-129. MC, VISA, PC, TC. 11 rooms with PB and 1 suite. Breakfast included in rates. Types of meals: Cont plus and early coffee/tea. Beds: KQDT. Cable TV in room. Air conditioning. VCR, swimming, bicycles and library on premises. Antiquing, fishing, live theater, parks, shopping, cross-country skiing, sporting events and water sports nearby.

Publicity: *Fall River Herald News, North Shore News, Cape Ann Weekly, San Francisco Chronicle.*

"Wonderful people, lovely scenery, and great food, all good for the soul! Your hospitality and service was wonderful and we look forward to returning very soon!"

Yankee Clipper Inn

PO Box 2399
Rockport, MA 01966-3399
(508)546-3407 (800)545-3699 Fax:(508)546-9730

Circa 1840. This white clapboard oceanfront mansion features sweeping views of the sea and the rocky shoreline. Gleaming mahogany woodwork and fireplaces combined with fine antiques create an old-fashioned, elegant ambiance in the main building. Some accommodations offer canopy beds and balconies. The Bulfinch House, a Greek Revival building housing extra guest rooms, is situated away from the water uphill from the main inn. A heated salt water pool is in view of the ocean.

Historic Interest: Town of Salem - House of Seven Gables, etc. (one-half hour), Concord, Lexington - Revolutionary War sites (one hour). Rockport and Gloucester founded in 1600s.

Innkeeper(s): Robert & Barbara Ellis. $120-289. MC, VISA, AX, DS, PC, TC. TAC10. 26 rooms with PB, 6 suites, 1 cottage and 1 conference room. Breakfast included in rates. MAP. Types of meals: Full gourmet bkfst and cont plus. Gourmet dinner and room service available. Restaurant on premises. Beds: KQDT. TV, phone, cable TV, VCRs some rooms, hair dryers and jet tubs in room. Air conditioning. VCR, fax, copier, swimming and library on premises. Weddings, small meetings, family reunions and seminars hosted. German spoken. Antiquing, fishing, whale watching, live theater, parks, shopping and water sports nearby.

Publicity: *Gloucester Daily Times, Los Angeles Times, North Shore Life, Country Living, Discerning Traveler, Country Inns, Travel Holidays, Great Country Inns TV Show.*

"The rooms were comfortable, the views breathtaking from most rooms, and the breakfasts delicious, with prompt and courteous service."

Salem D14

Amelia Payson House

16 Winter St
Salem, MA 01970-3807
(978)744-8304

Circa 1845. This elegantly restored two-story house features four white columns and is a prime example of Greek Revival architecture. Period antiques and wallpapers decorate the guest rooms and the formal dining room. Located in the heart of the Salem Historic District, it is a short walk to shops, museums, Pickering Wharf and waterfront restaurants. Train service to Boston is four blocks away. This is a non-smoking establishment.

Historic Interest: House of Seven Gables (2 blocks), Peabody Museum (1 block), Witch Museum (1 block), Maritime Historic Site (2 blocks).

Innkeeper(s): Ada & Donald Roberts. $75-130. MC, VISA, AX. 4 rooms with PB. Breakfast included in rates. Type of meal: Cont plus. Beds: QT. Antiquing and water sports nearby.

"Your hospitality has been a part of my wonderful experience."

Coach House Inn

284 Lafayette St
Salem, MA 01970-5462
(978)744-4092 (800)688-8689 Fax:(978)745-8031

Circa 1879. Captain Augustus Emmerton, one of the last Salem natives to earn his living from maritime commerce, built this stately home. Emmerton's house is an imposing example of Second Empire architecture and situated just two blocks from the harbor in a Salem historic district. Guest rooms are cheerful and romantic, furnished with antiques, four-poster beds and Oriental rugs. The House of Seven Gables and the Salem Witch Museum are nearby. Boston is just a short drive away.

$80-135. MC, VISA, AX, DS. 11 rooms, 9 with PB, 7 with FP. Type of meal: Cont. Beds: DT.

Publicity: *The North Shore, Gourmet.*

The Salem Inn

7 Summer St
Salem, MA 01970-3315
(978)741-0680 (800)446-2995 Fax:(978)744-8924
E-mail: saleminn@earthlink.net
Web: www.saleminnma.com

Circa 1834. Located in the heart of one of America's oldest cities, the inn's 39 individually decorated guest rooms feature an array of amenities such as antiques, Jacuzzi baths, fireplaces and canopy beds. Luxury suites, as well as comfortable and spacious two-bedroom family suites with kitchenettes, are available. A complimentary continental breakfast is offered. Nearby are other fine restaurants, shops, museums, Pickering Wharf and whale watching boats for cruises.

Historic Interest: Located 18 miles from Boston, the inn is the perfect base to explore nearby Concord and Lexington, as well as the coastal towns of Rockport and Gloucester. Historic Salem is home to the Salem Witch Museum, the Peabody Essex Museum, the House of Seven Gables, Salem Maritime National Historic Site, Pickering Wharf and whale watching cruises.

Innkeeper(s): Richard & Diane Pabich. $129-290. MC, VISA, AX, DC, CB,

DS, TC. TAC10. 39 rooms with PB, 18 with FP and 11 suites. Breakfast included in rates. Types of meals: Cont and early coffee/tea. Gourmet dinner available. Beds: KQT. Cable TV and phone in room. Air conditioning. Fax on premises. Weddings and small meetings hosted. Antiquing, fishing, live theater, parks, shopping, sporting events and water sports nearby. Pets Allowed.

Suzannah Flint House

98 Essex St
Salem, MA 01970-5225
(978)744-5281 (800)893-9973
Web: www.salemweb.com/biz/suzannahflint

Circa 1808. Adjacent to Salem Common and the historic district, this fine example of a Federal-style home is completely restored both inside and out. Antiques, Oriental rugs and original hardwood floors add to the inn's natural charm. The inn's original 1808 fireplaces, featured in each room, although not operating, add to the inn's architectural character. Muffins, croissants, bagels and fresh fruit  are the morning fare. The home is one block from the visitor's center and close to the Maritime Historic Site, Peabody Essex Museum, the Salem Witch Museum, House of Seven Gables and whale-watching cruises. Guests can walk to the train and head out for a day exploring Boston.

Innkeeper(s): Scott Eklind. $60-110. MC, VISA, AX, DS, PC, TC. 3 rooms with PB. Breakfast included in rates. Meal: Cont plus. Beds: Q. Cable TV, VCR and writing tables in room. Air conditioning. Antiquing, fishing, golf, museums and historic sites, live theater, parks, shopping, sporting events and tennis nearby.
Publicity: *Washington Post.*

Sandwich I16

Captain Ezra Nye House

152 Main St
Sandwich, MA 02563-2232
(508)888-6142 (800)388-2278 Fax:(508)833-2897
E-mail: captnye@aol.com
Web: www.captainezranyehouse.com

Circa 1829. Captain Ezra Nye built this house after a record-shattering Halifax to Boston run, and the stately Federal-style house reflects the opulence and romance of the clipper ship era. Hand-stenciled walls and museum-quality antiques decorate the interior. Within walking distance are the Doll Museum, the Glass Museum, restaurants, shops, the famous Heritage Plantation, the beach and marina.

Innkeeper(s): Elaine & Harry Dickson. $85-110. MC, VISA, AX, DS, PC, TC. TAC10. 6 rooms with PB, 1 with FP and 1 suite. Breakfast included in rates. Types of meals: Full gourmet bkfst and early coffee/tea. Beds: KQ. VCR, fax and library on premises. Small meetings and family reunions hosted. Spanish spoken. Antiquing, fishing, museums, plantation, bike trails, tennis, live theater, parks, shopping and water sports nearby.
Publicity: *Glamour, Innsider, Cape Cod Life, Toronto Life, Yankee.*

"The prettiest room and most beautiful home we have been to. We had a wonderful time."

The Dan'l Webster Inn

149 Main St
Sandwich, MA 02563-2231
(508)888-3622

Circa 1692. Originally built as a parsonage in the late 17th century, the inn offers the essence of Colonial charm and elegance. Each of the 54 guest rooms is individually appointed with period furnishings. Many rooms offer canopy and four-

poster beds, working fireplaces and whirlpool tubs. Guests are invited to enjoy their meals by the fireside, in the sun room or moon-lit conservatory. The inn is recognized for its outstanding service and innovative cuisine. Eight new rooms offer spectacular amenities such as heated tile baths.

Innkeeper(s): Steve Catania. $103-285. MC, VISA, AX, DC, CB, DS. 54 rooms with PB, 15 with FP and 2 conference rooms. MAP, EP. Types of meals: Full gourmet bkfst and cont plus. Dinner and lunch available. Restaurant on premises. Beds: KQDT. 15 rooms have whirlpool tubs in room. Fax, copier and swimming pool on premises. Handicap access. Fishing, golf and tennis nearby.

"Excellent accommodations and great food."

The Dunbar House

1 Water St
Sandwich, MA 02563-2303
(508)833-2485 Fax:(508)833-4713

Circa 1741. This Colonial house overlooks Shawme Pond in the charming setting of Cape Cod's oldest town. The three guest rooms are appointed in Colonial style, and all boast a view of the pond. The Ennerdale room has a four-poster bed. Each morning, guests are pampered with a homemade breakfast, and guests receive a voucher for afternoon tea served in the innkeeper's English tea shop. The inn is within walking distance to many historic sites and the beach.

Innkeeper(s): Nancy Iribarren & David Bell. $80-100. MC, VISA, PC, TC. TAC10. 3 rooms with PB, 3 with FP. Breakfast included in rates. Types of meals: Full gourmet bkfst and early coffee/tea. Afternoon tea and lunch available. Restaurant on premises. Beds: KQT. Fans in room. VCR, fax, copier, bicycles, library and canoe on premises. Weddings, small meetings, family reunions and seminars hosted. Limited Spanish spoken. Antiquing, fishing, museums, Heritage Plantation, live theater, parks, shopping and water sports nearby.

Spring Garden Inn

578 Rt 6A, PO Box 867
Sandwich, MA 02537
(508)888-0710 (800)303-1751 Fax:(508)833-2849
E-mail: springg@capecod.net
Web: www.springgarden.com

Circa 1940. Nestled on 11 rural acres, this shingled Cape Cod cottage offers guests panoramic views of the Great Sandwich Salt Marsh, the Tidal Scorton River and the New England country side. Surrounded by a 1,000-acre wildlife sanctuary, the inn is located along one of America's 10 most scenic highways. Each of the 11 spacious rooms is equipped with two double

beds, refrigerators and a sundeck or patio. A freshly-baked continental breakfast is offered in the morning. The beach, fine dining, shopping and golf are nearby.

Innkeeper(s): Steve & Betty Kauffman. $72-104. MC, VISA, DS, TC. 11 rooms with PB and 3 suites. Breakfast included in rates. Type of meal: Cont. Beds: D. Cable TV and phone in room. Air conditioning. Fax, swimming and grills on premises. Handicap access. Family reunions hosted. Antiquing, fishing, golf, museums, air rides, birding, live theater, parks, shopping, tennis and water sports nearby.

The Summer House

158 Main St
Sandwich, MA 02563-2232
(508)888-4991 (800)241-3609
E-mail: sumhouse@capecod.net
Web: www.capecod.net/summerhouse

Circa 1835. The Summer House is a handsome Greek Revival in a setting of historic homes and public buildings. (Hiram Dillaway, one of the owners, was a famous mold maker for the Boston & Sandwich Glass Company.) The house is fully restored and decorated with antiques and hand-stitched quilts. Four of the guest rooms have fireplaces. The breakfast room and parlor have black marble fireplaces.  The sunporch overlooks an old-fashioned perennial garden, antique rose bushes, and a 70-year-old rhododendron hedge. The inn is open year-round.

Historic Interest: Sandwich Glass Museum (1 block), Thornton Burgess Museum (1 block), Heritage Plantation Museum (1 mile).

Innkeeper(s): Erik Suby & Phyllis Burg. $65-105. MC, VISA, AX, DS, PC, TC. 5 rooms with PB, 4 with FP. Breakfast and afternoon tea included in rates. Types of meals: Full gourmet bkfst and early coffee/tea. Beds: KQT. Window fan in room. Library, lawn & gardens and sunroom on premises. Weddings, small meetings and family reunions hosted. Antiquing, fishing, live theater, parks, shopping, cross-country skiing and water sports nearby.

"An absolutely gorgeous house and a super breakfast. I wish I could've stayed longer! Came for one night, stayed for three! Marvelous welcome."

Sandwich (Cape Cod)   I16

Isaiah Jones Homestead

165 Main St
Sandwich (Cape Cod), MA 02563-2283
(508)888-9115 (800)526-1625

Circa 1849. This fully restored Victorian homestead is situated on Main Street in the village. Eleven-foot ceilings and two bay windows are features of the Gathering Room. Guest rooms contain antique Victorian bedsteads such as the half-canopy bed of burled birch in the Deming Jarves Room, where there is an oversized whirlpool tub and a fireplace. Candlelight breakfasts are highlighted with the house speciality, freshly baked cornbread, inspired by nearby Sandwich Grist Mill.

Innkeeper(s): Jan & Doug Klapper. $85-155. MC, VISA, AX, DS, PC, TC. TAC10. 5 rooms with PB, 3 with FP. Breakfast and afternoon tea included in rates. Types of meals: Full bkfst and early coffee/tea. Snacks/refreshments available. Beds: Q. Three fireplaces and two oversize Jacuzzi tubs in room. Weddings, small meetings, family reunions and seminars hosted. Antiquing, beaches, fishing, live theater, parks, shopping and water sports nearby.

"Excellent! The room was a delight, the food wonderful, the hospitality warm & friendly. One of the few times the reality exceeded the expectation."

Scituate   F15

Allen House

18 Allen Pl
Scituate, MA 02066-1302
(781)545-8221 Fax:(781)545-8221
E-mail: allenhousebnb@att.net
Web: allenhousebnb.com

Circa 1905. Originally a prosperous merchant's home, the Allen House was converted into a bed & breakfast by English owners Iain and Christine Gilmour. Christine, also a caterer, likes to embellish her breakfasts with flowers and herbs. English afternoon tea, classical music and two resident cats provide a cozy, civilized ambiance. Some guest rooms have views of

Scituate (pronounced "Situate") harbor, where the famous New England lobsters are landed. The town was established more than 350 years ago.

Innkeeper(s): Christine & Iain Gilmour. $69-199. MC, VISA, AX, DS, PC, TC. TAC10. 6 rooms with PB and 1 conference room. Breakfast included in rates. Type of meal: Early coffee/tea. Gourmet dinner available. Beds: KQD. Turndown service in room. Fax on premises. Handicap access. Small meetings and family reunions hosted. Some French & German spoken. Antiquing, fishing, charter boats and historical sites nearby.

"Everything one could possibly wish for is provided here.. a wonderful weekend."

Sheffield   F2

Ivanhoe Country House

254 S Undermountain Rd
Sheffield, MA 01257-9639
(413)229-2143

Circa 1780. Vast reaches of manicured lawns provide the setting for this country house on 25 acres, adjacent to the Appalachian Trail. The Chestnut Room is a popular gathering area with its fireplace, library and games. Antiques and comfortable country furnishings are found throughout the inn. Breakfast is brought to each guest bedroom. Well-behaved pets are welcome, though requirements are stringent.

Historic Interest: Hancock Shaker Village, Norman Rockwell Museum and the Colonial Ashley House are all nearby.

Innkeeper(s): Carole & Dick Maghery. $75-125. 9 rooms with PB. Breakfast included in rates. Type of meal: Cont. Beds: DT. TV in room. Air conditioning. Family reunions hosted. Antiquing, fishing, swimming pool, live theater, shopping, downhill skiing and cross-country skiing nearby.

Pets Allowed.

"Everything was terrific, especially the blueberry muffins."

Staveleigh House

59 Main St, PO 608
Sheffield, MA 01257-9701
(413)229-2129

Circa 1821. The Reverend Bradford, minister of Old Parish Congregational Church, the oldest church in the Berkshires, built this home for his family. Afternoon tea is served and the inn is especially favored for its four-course breakfasts and gracious hospitality. Located next to the town green, the house is in a historic district in the midst of several fine antique shops. It is also near Tanglewood, skiing and all Berkshire attractions.

Innkeeper(s): Dorothy Marosy & Marion Whitman. $80-105. PC, TC. 5 rooms, 2 with PB. Breakfast and afternoon tea included in rates. Types of meals: Full bkfst and early coffee/tea. Beds: KQDT. Turndown service and ceiling fan in room. Handicap access. Weddings, small meetings, family reunions and seminars hosted. Antiquing, fishing, art galleries, live theater, parks, shopping, downhill skiing, cross-country skiing and water sports nearby.

"Our annual needlework workshops are so much fun, we have a waiting list to join our group."

South Egremont   F2

Egremont Inn

Old Sheffield Rd
South Egremont, MA 01258
(413)528-2111 (800)859-1780 Fax:(413)528-3284

Circa 1780. This three-story inn, listed in the National Register, was once a stagecoach stop. Guest rooms are furnished with country antiques. Dinner is available Wednesday through Sunday in the elegant dining room, and there is also a tavern. Five fireplaces adorn the common rooms. A wraparound porch, tennis courts and a swimming pool are on the premises.

Historic Interest: Minutes from the site of Shays Rebellion, formerly a mustering-in location and hospital during the Revolutionary War.

Innkeeper(s): Karen & Steven Waller. $80-170. MC, VISA, AX, DS, PC, TC. TAC10. 19 rooms with PB, 1 suite and 1 conference room. Breakfast included in rates. MAP. Types of meals: Full bkfst and cont. Dinner available. Restaurant on premises. Beds: KQDT. Phone in room. Air conditioning. VCR, swimming and tennis on premises. Weddings, small meetings, family reunions and seminars hosted. Antiquing, fishing, live theater, parks, shopping, downhill skiing, cross-country skiing and sporting events nearby.

"All the beauty of the Berkshires without the hassle, the quintessential country inn."

Weathervane Inn

Rt 23, Main St
South Egremont, MA 01258
(413)528-9580 (800)528-9580 Fax:(413)528-1713

Circa 1785. The original post-and-beam New England farmhouse with its beehive oven was added on to throughout its history. It has been restored to combine today's modern amenities with the charm of the inn's historic past. The inn's historic architectural features include broad plank floors, tree trunk supports and granite columns. A full breakfast is offered every morning.

Historic Interest: Norman Rockwell Museum, Berkshire Museum, The Clark Museum and Hoosac Railroad Tunnel built during the Civil War are all nearby.

Innkeeper(s): Maxine & Jeffrey Lone. $115-245. MC, VISA, AX. 8 rooms with PB and 2 suites. Breakfast included in rates. Type of meal: Full bkfst. Beds: KQD. Limited Handicap Access on premises. Antiquing, fishing, golf, live theater, downhill skiing, cross-country skiing and water sports nearby.

South Lancaster · D10

College Town Inn

PO Box 876, Rt 110
South Lancaster, MA 01561
(978)368-7000 (800)369-2717 Fax:(978)365-5426

Circa 1940. This bed and breakfast offers a country location, and guests may choose a room with a private patio or balcony from which to enjoy it. Rooms are furnished with contemporary pieces. In summer,  a full breakfast is provided on the patio. Families may prefer the accommodation that has its own kitchen. Nearby are Revolutionary War battlefields, Concord and Longfellow's Wayside Inn.

Innkeeper(s): Jack & Charlotte Creighton. $55-95. MC, VISA, AX, DS, PC, TC. 4 rooms with PB, 1 suite and 1 conference room. Breakfast included in rates. Type of meal: Full bkfst. Beds: KQDT. Cable TV and phone in room. Air conditioning. Fax and copier on premises. Small meetings and family reunions hosted. Antiquing, fishing, golf, downhill skiing and cross-country skiing nearby.

Stockbridge · E2

Arbor Rose B&B

8 Yale Hill, Box 114
Stockbridge, MA 01262
(413)298-4744
E-mail: innkeeper@arborrose.com
Web: www.arborrose.com

Circa 1810. This New England farmhouse overlooks an 1800s mill, pond and gardens with the mountains as a backdrop. During the winter months, guests often relax in front of the wood stove in the inn's cozy front parlor. Four-poster beds, antiques and rural-themed paintings decorate the rooms. The inn's 19th-century mill now houses guests. The mill was one of five in the vicinity and was still in operation as late as the 1930s. The Berkshire Theatre, open for the  summer season, is across the street. The Norman Rockwell Museum, Tanglewood Music Festival, ski areas and antique, outlet and specialty shops are all within a seven-mile radius.

Historic Interest: Mission House, the first mission set up for the Stockbridge Indians, and the historic Main Street of Stockbridge are among the nearby historic sites.

Innkeeper(s): Christina Alsop. $85-175. MC, VISA, AX, PC, TC. TAC10. 6 rooms with PB and 1 conference room. Breakfast included in rates. Types of meals: Full gourmet bkfst and early coffee/tea. Beds: KQT. Ceiling fan and TVs in some rooms in room. Air conditioning. Weddings, small meetings, family reunions and seminars hosted. Antiquing, cultural arts, music, dance, live theater, parks, shopping, downhill skiing and cross-country skiing nearby.

Publicity: *Yankee Traveler.*

"If houses really do exude the spirit of events and feelings stored from their history, it explains why a visitor feels warmth and joy from the first turn up the driveway."

The Red Lion Inn

Main St
Stockbridge, MA 01262
(413)298-5545 Fax:(413)298-5130

Circa 1773. The venerable white clapboard Red Lion Inn has been continuously operated as a tavern and inn since its inception. The originator, Silas Pepoon, is said to have initiated a rally to protest the use of British goods. This meeting resulted in a letter said to have been the first Declaration of Independence. A vital part of the area's history, the inn is the last of the 18th-century Berkshire hotels still in operation. The collection of fine antique furnishings, colonial pewter and Staffordshire china found in the inn's parlor was gathered in the late 19th century by proprietor Mrs. Charles Plumb. The inn is part of the Norman Rockwell "Mainstreet Stockbridge" painting. Traditional decor extends to the comfortable guest rooms and some have four-poster and canopy beds, fireplaces, antique vanities and desks. The inn is home to four restaurants. Rocking on the long front porch is a favored activity, and one wonders if former visitors such as presidents Cleveland, McKinley, Theodore Roosevelt, Coolidge and Franklin Roosevelt enjoyed the privilege. Regional cuisine is the specialty of the inn's restaurants.

Innkeeper(s): Brooks Bradbury. $87-165. MC, VISA, AX, DC, CB, DS, PC, TC. TAC10. 110 rooms, 87 with PB, 23 suites, 7 cottages and 4 conference rooms. EP. Types of meals: Full bkfst, cont plus, cont and early coffee/tea. Gourmet dinner, picnic lunch, lunch, banquet service and room service available. Restaurant on premises. Beds: KQDT. Cable TV, phone and turndown service in room. VCR, fax, copier, swimming and library on premises. Handicap access. Weddings, small meetings, family reunions and seminars hosted. Antiquing, fishing, golf, live theater, shopping, downhill skiing, cross-country skiing and tennis nearby.

Publicity: *Country Folk Art, The Age, USA Today.*

"My family and I travel quite a bit and your facility and employees top them all."

Roeder House B&B

Rt 183
Stockbridge, MA 01262
(413)298-4015 Fax:(413)298-3413
E-mail: innkeeper@roederhouse
Web: www.roederhouse.com

Circa 1856. Shaded by tall trees, this Federal-style farmhouse sits on a knoll overlooking four acres of grounds that include carefully tended perennial beds, an old carriage barn and green lawns. Decorated in a country-cottage style, there is a library and sitting room with fireplace and a screened porch. Four-poster canopy beds are features of the guest rooms that are furnished with Federal antiques. Breakfast specialties include blueberry muffins, malted waffles and pure maple syrup. In cool weather, hot cider is offered before the fire. The home is a half-mile from the Rockwell Museum and close to ski lifts.

Innkeeper(s): Diane & Vernon Reuss. $145-320. MC, VISA, AX, DS, PC, TC. TAC10. 7 rooms with PB. Breakfast included in rates. Types of meals: Full bkfst and early coffee/tea. Beds: QT. Ceiling fan in room. Air conditioning. VCR, fax, copier and swimming on premises. Small meetings and family reunions hosted. Antiquing, upscale outlets, shopping, downhill skiing and cross-country skiing nearby.

"A wonderful experience, please adopt me."

The Inn at Stockbridge

PO Box 618
Stockbridge, MA 01262-0618
(413)298-3337 Fax:(413)298-3406

Circa 1906. Giant maples shade the drive leading to this Southern-style Georgian Colonial with its impressive pillared entrance. Located on 12 acres, the grounds include a reflecting pool, a fountain, meadows and woodland as well as wide vistas of the rolling hillsides. The guest rooms feature antiques and handsome 18th-century reproductions. Breakfast is graciously presented with fine china, silver and linens.

Innkeeper(s): Alice & Len Schiller. $115-275. MC, VISA, AX, DS. TAC10. 12 rooms with PB, 4 with FP, 4 suites and 1 conference room. Breakfast and snacks/refreshments included in rates. Types of meals: Full gourmet bkfst and early coffee/tea. Beds: KQDT. Cable TV, phone, ceiling fan, VCR, sherry and three Jacuzzi's in room. Air conditioning. Fax, copier and swimming on premises. Handicap access. Weddings, small meetings, family reunions and seminars hosted. Antiquing, golf, live theater, parks, shopping, downhill skiing, cross-country skiing, tennis and water sports nearby.

Publicity: *Vogue, New York, New York Daily News, Country Inns Northeast, Arts & Antiques.*

"Classy & comfortable."

Stockbridge (South Lee)   E2

Historic Merrell Inn

1565 Pleasant St, Rt 102
Stockbridge (South Lee), MA 01260
(413)243-1794 (800)243-1794 Fax:(413)243-2669
E-mail: info@merrell-inn-com
Web: www.merrell-inn.com

Circa 1794. This elegant stagecoach inn was carefully preserved under supervision of the Society for the Preservation of New England Antiquities. Architectural drawings of Merrell Inn have been preserved by the Library of Congress. Eight fireplaces in the inn include two with original beehive and warming ovens. An antique circular birdcage bar serves as a check-in desk. Comfortable rooms feature canopy and four-poster beds with Hepplewhite and Sheraton-style antiques. The Riverview Suite is tucked on the back wing of the building and has a private porch which overlooks the Housatonic River.

Historic Interest: Hancock Shaker Village and the Norman Rockwell Museum are all nearby.

Innkeeper(s): Charles & Faith Reynolds. $75-225. MC, VISA. 9 rooms with PB, 3 with FP. Breakfast included in rates. Type of meal: Full bkfst. Beds: KQDT. Phone and fireplaces (some rooms) in room. Fax on premises. Family reunions and seminars hosted. Antiquing, fishing, tanglewood Music Festival, Norman Rockwell Museum, live theater, parks, shop-

ping and cross-country skiing nearby.

Publicity: *Americana, Country Living, New York Times, Boston Globe, Country Accents, Travel Holiday, USA Today.*

"We couldn't have chosen a more delightful place to stay in the Berkshires. Everything was wonderful. We especially loved the grounds and the gazebo by the river."

Sturbridge   F8

Commonwealth Cottage

11 Summit Ave
Sturbridge, MA 01566-1225
(508)347-7708

Circa 1873. This 16-room Queen Anne Victorian house, on an acre near the Quinebaug River, is just a few minutes from Old Sturbridge Village. Both the dining room and parlor have fireplaces. The Baroque theme of the Sal Raciti room makes it one of the guest favorites and it features a queen mahogany bed. Breakfast may be offered on the gazebo porch or in the formal dining room. It includes a variety of homemade specialties, such as freshly baked breads and cakes.

Historic Interest: Old Sturbridge Village is approximately 1-1/2 miles away.

Innkeeper(s): Robert & Wiebke Gilbert. $85-145. PC, TC. 3 rooms with PB. Types of meals: Full bkfst and early coffee/tea. Snacks/refreshments available. Beds: QDT. Ceiling fan in room. Library on premises. Weddings and family reunions hosted. German spoken. Antiquing, fishing, museum, live theater, parks, shopping and water sports nearby.

"Your home is so warm and welcoming we feel as though we've stepped back in time. Our stay here has helped to make the wedding experience extra special!"

Publick House Historic Inn & Country Motor Lodge

PO Box 187, On The Common Rte 131
Sturbridge, MA 01566-0187
(800)PUB-LICK Fax:(508)347-5073
E-mail: info@publickhouse.com
Web: www.publickhouse.com

Circa 1771. This property includes four lodging facilities, two restaurants, 12 meeting rooms and 60 acres of countryside. Many special events take place throughout the year, including a New England Lobster Bake, a Beer and Wine Maker's Dinner, Harvest Weekend, Yankee Winter Weekends and Murder-Mystery Weekends. All the rooms in the main building are decorated with period furnishings.

Innkeeper(s): Albert Cournoyer. $75-160. MC, VISA, AX, DC, CB, PC, TC. TAC10. 15 rooms with PB and 2 suites. Types of meals: Full gourmet bkfst, cont plus, cont and early coffee/tea. Afternoon tea, gourmet dinner, snacks/refreshments, picnic lunch, gourmet lunch, banquet service, catering service and room service available. Restaurant on premises. Beds: KQDT. Cable TV, phone and TVs available on request in room. Air conditioning. VCR, fax and swimming on premises. Handicap access. Weddings, small meetings, family reunions and seminars hosted. Spanish and French spoken. Antiquing, fishing, live theater, parks, shopping, cross-country skiing and sporting events nearby.

Sturbridge Country Inn

PO Box 60, 530 Main St
Sturbridge, MA 01566-0060
(508)347-5503 Fax:(508)347-5319

Circa 1840. Shaded by an old silver maple, this classic Greek
Revival house boasts a two-story columned entrance. The

attached carriage house now serves as the lobby and displays
the original post-and-beam construction and exposed rafters.
All guest rooms have individual fireplaces and whirlpool tubs.
They are appointed gracefully in reproduction colonial furnishings, including queen-size, four-posters. A patio and gazebo are
favorite summertime retreats.
Innkeeper(s): Patricia Affenito. $59-159. MC, VISA, AX, DS, PC, TC. TAC10.
9 rooms with PB, 9 with FP, 1 suite and 1 conference room. Breakfast
included in rates. Types of meals: Cont and early coffee/tea. Room service
available. Restaurant on premises. Beds: KQ. Cable TV, phone, ceiling fan
and VCR in room. Air conditioning. Fax, copier and spa on premises.
Weddings, small meetings, family reunions and seminars hosted. Spanish
spoken. Antiquing, fishing, old Sturbridge Village, live theater, parks, shopping, downhill skiing, cross-country skiing and water sports nearby.
Publicity: *Southbridge Evening News, Worcester Telegram & Gazette.*

"Best lodging I've ever seen."

Vineyard Haven   K16

The Crocker House Inn

12 Crocker Ave, PO Box 1658
Vineyard Haven, MA 02568
(508)693-1151 (800)772-0206 Fax:(508)693-1123
E-mail: crockerinn@aol.com
Web: www.crockerhouseinn.com

Circa 1900. Enjoy all that Martha's Vineyard has to offer at
this historic inn, which has close access to beaches, restaurants, galleries, museums, shops and a winery. Guest rooms
offer amenities such as fireplaces, Jacuzzi's, water views or private porches. The front porch is lined with rockers, a perfect
spot for relaxation with a splendid harbor view. The innkeepers
provide a continental breakfast to get guests started before
heading out and enjoying the island. The inn is within walking
distance to the ferry service.
Innkeeper(s): Jeff & Jynell Kristal. $115-385. MC, VISA, AX, PC, TC. 8
rooms with PB. Breakfast included in rates. Type of meal: Cont. Beds: KQDT.
VCR in room. Air conditioning. Fax and pullout sofa's on premises. Weddings,
small meetings and family reunions hosted. Antiquing, fishing, golf, parks,
shopping, tennis and water sports nearby.

Wareham   I15

Mulberry B&B

257 High St
Wareham, MA 02571-1407
(508)295-0684 Fax:(508)291-2909

Circa 1847. This former blacksmith's house is in the historic
district of town and has been featured on the local garden club
house tour. Frances, a former school teacher, has decorated the
guest rooms in a country style with antiques. A deck, shaded
by a tall mulberry tree, looks out to the back garden.
Historic Interest: Plymouth (18 miles), New Bedford Whaling Capitol (17
miles), Provincetown/Eastham, where Pilgrims first landed (70 miles).
Innkeeper(s): Frances Murphy. $50-75. MC, VISA, AX, DS, PC, TC. TAC10.
3 rooms. Breakfast included in rates. Type of meal: Full bkfst. Afternoon
tea available. Beds: KDT. TV and turndown service
in room. Air conditioning. VCR on
premises. Antiquing, fishing, whale
watching, live theater, parks,
shopping, cross-country skiing,
sporting events and water
sports nearby.

*"Our room was
pleasant and I
loved the cranber-
ry satin sheets."*

Ware   E7

The Wildwood Inn

121 Church St
Ware, MA 01082-1203
(413)967-7798 (800)860-8098

Circa 1880. This yellow Victorian has a wraparound porch and
a beveled-glass front door. American primitive antiques include
a collection of New England cradles and heirloom quilts, a sad-
dlemaker's bench and a spin-
ning wheel. The inn's two
acres are dotted with maple,
chestnut and apple trees.
Through the woods, you'll
find a river.
Historic Interest: Old Sturbridge
Village (15 miles), Old Deerfield (30
miles), Amherst College (15 miles).
Innkeeper(s): Fraidell Fenster & Richard
Watson. $50-90. MC, VISA, AX, DC, DS, PC, TC. TAC10. 9 rooms, 7 with PB,
1 suite and 2 conference rooms. Breakfast and afternoon tea included in rates.
Types of meals: Full gourmet bkfst and early coffee/tea. Banquet service and
catering service available. Beds: KQDT. Turndown service in room. Air conditioning. Bicycles and library on premises. Handicap access. Weddings, small
meetings, family reunions and seminars hosted. Amusement parks, antiquing,
fishing, horseback riding, hiking, canoeing, kayaking, live theater, parks, shopping, downhill skiing, cross-country skiing and sporting events nearby.

*"Excellent accommodations, not only in rooms, but in the kind and
thoughtful way you treat your guests. We'll be back!"*

West Stockbridge E2

Card Lake Inn

PO Box 38
West Stockbridge, MA 01266-0038
(413)232-0272 Fax:(413)232-0294
E-mail: innkeeper@cardlakeinn.com
Web: www.cardlakeinn.com

Circa 1880. Located in the center of town, this Colonial Revival inn features a popular local restaurant on the premises. Norman Rockwell is said to have frequented its tavern. Stroll around historic West Stockbridge then enjoy the inn's deck cafe with its flower boxes and view of the sculpture garden of an art gallery across the street. Original lighting, hardwood floors and antiques are features of the inn. Chesterwood and Tanglewood are within easy driving distance.

Historic Interest: The Norman Rockwell Museum is approximately two miles away.

Innkeeper(s): Ed & Lisa Robbins. $100-150. MC, VISA, AX, DS. 8 rooms. Breakfast included in rates. Types of meals: Cont and early coffee/tea. Restaurant on premises. Beds: KQ. Ceiling fan in room. Air conditioning. VCR on premises. Weddings, small meetings, family reunions and seminars hosted. Amusement parks, antiquing, shopping and sporting events nearby.

Williamsville Inn

Rt 41
West Stockbridge, MA 01266
(413)274-6118 Fax:(413)274-3539

Circa 1797. At the foot of Tom Ball Mountain is this Federal-style inn, formerly the Tom Ball farm. Some guest rooms feature fireplaces or wood stoves. The inn's grounds sport gardens, a swimming pool and tennis court. Guests often enjoy relaxing in a swing that hangs from an ancient elm. Chesterwood, Mission House, The Norman Rockwell Museum and Tanglewood are within easy driving distance.

Innkeeper(s): Gail & Kathleen Ryan. $120-185. MC, VISA, AX, PC, TC. TAC10. 16 rooms with PB, 2 with FP, 1 suite and 1 conference room. Breakfast included in rates. Types of meals: Full bkfst and early coffee/tea. Gourmet dinner, picnic lunch, banquet service and room service available. Restaurant on premises. Beds: KQDT. Air conditioning. Fax, copier, swimming and tennis on premises. Weddings, small meetings, family reunions and seminars hosted. Antiquing, fishing, golf, live theater, parks, shopping, downhill skiing, cross-country skiing and tennis nearby.

Pets allowed: By special arrangement, subject to availability.

Publicity: *Boston Globe, Bon Appetit, Genre, Ladies Home Journal.*

Williamstown B3

Steep Acres Farm

520 White Oaks Rd
Williamstown, MA 01267-2227
(413)458-3774

Circa 1900. Built at the turn of the century, Steep Acres was constructed as a chicken farm. The hilltop home, secluded on 50 peaceful acres, offers a view of the Berkshire Hills and the Green Mountains in Vermont. Guests are free to enjoy canoe-ing, fishing or swimming in the 1.5-acre pond. The interior is decorated in country style with antiques. Breakfast includes homemade maple syrup and honey.

$50-85. PC, TC. 4 rooms, 1 with PB. Breakfast and afternoon tea included in rates. Types of meals: Full gourmet bkfst and early coffee/tea. Ceiling fan in room. Swimming on premises. Weddings and family reunions hosted. Antiquing, fishing, golf, live theater, parks, shopping, downhill skiing, cross-country skiing, sporting events and tennis nearby.

Yarmouth Port I17

Olde Captain's Inn on The Cape

101 Main St Rt 6A
Yarmouth Port, MA 02675-1709
(508)362-4496 (888)407-7161
E-mail: general@oldecaptainsinn.com
Web: www.oldecaptainsinn.com

Circa 1812. Located in the historic district and on Captain's Mile, this house is in the National Register. It is decorated in a traditional style, with coordinated wallpapers and carpets, and there are two suites that include kitchens and living rooms. Apple trees, blackberries and raspberries grow on the acre of grounds and often contribute to the breakfast menus. There is a summer veranda overlooking the property. Good restaurants are within walking distance.

Historic Interest: Plymouth Rock and Plantation (30 miles).

Innkeeper(s): Sven Tilly. $60-120. 3 rooms, 1 with PB and 2 suites. Breakfast included in rates. Type of meal: Cont plus. Beds: QD. Cable TV in room. Antiquing, fishing, live theater, shopping, sporting events and water sports nearby.

One Centre Street Inn

1 Center St
Yarmouth Port, MA 02675-1342
(508)362-8910 (888)407-1653 Fax:(508)362-0195

Circa 1824. A rustic cookstove warms the dining room where such items as freshly baked scones, homemade granola and orange French toast topped with a strawberry-Grand Marnier sauce get the morning off to a perfect start. This National Register inn was used as a church parsonage when it was built in the 1820s. Four-poster or brass beds decorated the guest rooms, appointed in a mix of styles, from Queen Anne to Colonial.

Innkeeper(s): Karen Iannello. $95-145. MC, VISA, DS, PC, TC. TAC10. 6 rooms, 4 with PB, 1 with FP. Breakfast included in rates. Type of meal: Full gourmet bkfst. Beds: QDT. Cable TV in one room. Bicycles on premises. Small meetings and family reunions hosted. Antiquing, fishing, live theater, parks, shopping and water sports nearby.

Michigan

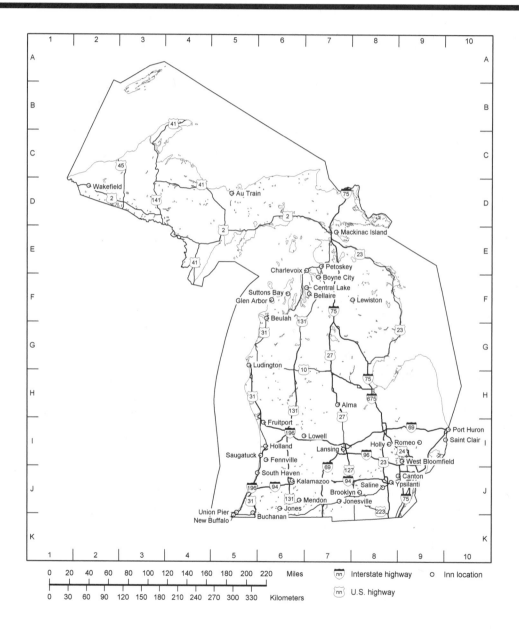

Miles

| 0 | 20 | 40 | 60 | 80 | 100 | 120 | 140 | 160 | 180 | 200 | 220 | Miles |

| 0 | 30 | 60 | 90 | 120 | 150 | 180 | 210 | 240 | 270 | 300 | 330 | Kilometers |

Interstate highway   ○ Inn location

U.S. highway

Alma   H7

Saravilla

633 N State St
Alma, MI 48801-1640
(517)463-4078
E-mail: ljdarrow@saravilla.com
Web: www.saravilla.com

Circa 1894. This 11,000-square-foot Dutch Colonial home with its Queen Anne influences was built as a magnificent wedding gift for lumber baron Ammi W. Wright's only surviving child, Sara. Wright spared no expense building this mansion for his daughter, and the innkeepers have spared nothing in restoring the home to its former prominence. The foyer and dining room boast imported English oak woodwork. The foyer's hand-painted canvas wallcoverings and the ballroom's embossed wallpaper come from France. The home still features original leaded-glass windows, built-in bookcases, window seats and light fixtures. In 1993, the innkeepers added a sunroom with a hot tub that overlooks a formal garden. The full, formal breakfast includes such treats as homemade granola, freshly made coffeecakes, breads, muffins and a mix of entrees.

Historic Interest: Alma is within three hours of almost every portion of Michigan's lower peninsula and plenty of historic sites.

Innkeeper(s): Linda and Jon Darrow. $75-125. MC, VISA, DS, PC, TC. 7 rooms with PB, 3 with FP. Breakfast and afternoon tea included in rates. Type of meal: Full bkfst. Room service available. Beds: KQT. Whirlpool tub in room. Antiquing, fishing, canoeing, live theater and cross-country skiing nearby.

Publicity: *Morning Sun, Saginaw News, Sault Sunday.*

"I suggest we stay longer next time. We are looking forward to that visit."

Bellaire   F7

Bellaire Bed & Breakfast

212 Park St
Bellaire, MI 49615-9595
(231)533-6077 (800)545-0780

Circa 1879. Maple trees line the drive to this American Gothic home. Relax on the porch swing, or enjoy the warmth of a crackling fire in the English-style library. The fresh, family-style continental-plus breakfast is a treat. A nearby park offers swim-

ming, tennis, basketball, shuffleboard and a playground. Browse through the downtown shops or hunt for antiques. Guests can take in 18 rounds at "The Legend" at Shanty Creek golf course, and in winter, enjoy skiing.

Innkeeper(s): David Schulz & Jim Walker. $70-100. MC, VISA, DS. 5 rooms, 3 with PB. Type of meal: Cont plus. Afternoon tea available. Beds: QD.

Grand Victorian B&B Inn

402 N Bridge St
Bellaire, MI 49615-9591
(616)533-6111 (800)336-3860 Fax:(616)533-8197

Circa 1895. It's hard to believe that anything but joy has ever been associated with this beautiful Queen Anne Victorian inn, but its original owner, who built it in anticipation of his

upcoming nuptials, left town broken-hearted when his wedding plans fell through. The eye-pleasing inn, with its gables, square corner towers, bays and overhangs, is listed in the National Register of Historic Places. There is much to do in this popular area of Northern Michigan, with its famous nearby skiing and

fishing spots, but the inn's impressive interior may entice guests to stay on the premises. Guest rooms are well-appointed with period antiques and lavish touches. Visitors may borrow a bicycle built for two for a relaxing tour of town.

Innkeeper(s): Steve & Glenda Shaffer. $100-130. MC, VISA. 4 rooms with PB. Breakfast and afternoon tea included in rates. Types of meals: Full bkfst and early coffee/tea. Picnic lunch available. Beds: QD. Air conditioning. VCR on premises. Weddings, small meetings, family reunions and seminars hosted. Antiquing, fishing, shopping, downhill skiing, cross-country skiing and water sports nearby.

Publicity: *Featured on Nabisco Crackers/Cookies Boxes Promotion, Midwest Living, Country Inns.*

"We certainly enjoyed our visit to the Grand Victorian. It has been our pleasure to stay in B&Bs in several countries, but never one more beautiful and almost never with such genial hosts."

Beulah   F6

Brookside Inn

115 US Hwy 31
Beulah, MI 49617-9701
(231)882-9688 Fax:(231)882-4600
E-mail: brookside@brooksideinn.com
Web: www.brooksideinn.com

Circa 1939. Antiques and country furnishings decorate the interior of Brookside Inn, located near Crystal Lake. King-size canopy waterbeds, Polynesian spas and wood-burning stoves

are just a few of the romantic amenities. The inn also boasts a 100,000-bottle wine cellar. Both breakfast and dinner are included in the rates, and guests may dine on the outdoor deck or by the fireplace. The inn's seven-acre grounds include a bridge to an herb and flower garden. Private sauna, steam bath and tanning bed are available in your room.

Innkeeper(s): Pam & Kirk Lorenz. $215-275. MC, VISA, AX, DC, CB, DS, PC, TC. TAC10. 20 rooms with PB, 20 with FP, 3 cabins and 3 conference rooms. Breakfast and dinner included in rates. MAP. Types of meals: Full gourmet bkfst and early coffee/tea. Snacks/refreshments, picnic lunch, gourmet lunch, banquet service and catering service available. Restaurant on premises. Beds: K. Cable TV, ceiling fan, VCR, sauna steam and tanning bed also available in room. Air conditioning. Fax, copier, spa and sauna on premises. Handicap access. Weddings, small meetings, family reunions and seminars hosted. German spoken. Fishing, golf, snowmobiling, ice fishing, hot air balloons, live theater, parks, downhill skiing, sporting events, tennis and water sports nearby.

Publicity: *Detroit Free Press.*

"Michigan's romantic retreat...works a spell. - Rick Sylvain, Detroit Free Press."

Brooklyn
J8

Dewey Lake Manor

11811 Laird Rd
Brooklyn, MI 49230-9035
(517)467-7122
Web: www.getaway2smi.com/dewey

Circa 1868. This Italianate house overlooks Dewey Lake and is situated on 18 acres in the Irish Hills. The house is furnished in a country Victorian style with antiques. An enclosed porch is a favorite spot to relax and take in the views of the lake while having breakfast. Favorite  pastimes include lakeside bonfires in the summertime and ice skating or cross-country skiing in the winter. Canoe and paddleboats are available to guests.

Historic Interest: The Great Saulk Trail (2 miles from U.S. 12), Walker Tavern, a stagecoach stop on the trail (2 miles), Saint Joseph Catholic Shrine (5 miles).

Innkeeper(s): Barb & Joe Phillips. $55-125. MC, VISA, AX. 5 rooms with PB, 5 with FP and 1 conference room. Breakfast included in rates. Types of meals: Full bkfst and early coffee/tea. Snacks/refreshments and picnic lunch available. Beds: QDT. Cable TV, phone, ceiling fan and one room has Jacuzzi in room. Air conditioning. VCR on premises. Weddings, small meetings and family reunions hosted. Antiquing, fishing, golf, live theater, shopping, cross-country skiing, sporting events and water sports nearby.

Publicity: *Ann Arbor News.*

"I came back and brought my friends. It was wonderful."

Buchanan
J5

The Primrose Path B&B

413 E Front St
Buchanan, MI 49107-1442
(616)695-6321 Fax:(616)695-6591

Circa 1905. Both Tudor and Arts & Crafts influences are present in the design of this turn-of-the-century home. The interior boasts leaded-glass windows and a beautifully designed built-in china cabinet that is the centerpiece of the dining room. The five guest rooms feature romantic touches such as lacy curtains, decorated hats, antique wedding photos or a brass bed decorated with roses. Breakfast includes such delectable items as stuffed French toast topped with fresh blueberries or, perhaps, a flavorful quiche. The home is a short drive from South Bend, home of the University of Notre Dame. Shops, restaurants, wineries, antiquing, lakeshore beaches and outdoor activities also are nearby.

Innkeeper(s): Kathy Barnett. $60-135. MC, VISA, PC. TAC5. 5 rooms, 3 with PB. Breakfast included in rates. Types of meals: Full bkfst and early coffee/tea. Beds: QD. Cable TV in room. Air conditioning. VCR and fax on premises. Antiquing, fishing, golf, live theater, parks, shopping, cross-country skiing, sporting events and water sports nearby.

Canton
J9

Willow Brook Inn

44255 Warren Rd
Canton, MI 48187-2147
(734)454-0019 (888)454-1919

Circa 1929. Willow Brook winds its way through the backyard of this aptly named inn, situated on a lush, wooded acre. Innkeepers Bernadette and Michael Van Lenten filled their home with oak and pine country antiques and beds covered with soft quilts. They also added special toys and keepsakes from their own childhood to add a homey touch. After a peaceful rest, guests are invited to partake in the morning meal either in the "Teddy Bear" dining room, in the privacy of their rooms or on the deck. Breakfasts consist of luscious treats such as homemade breads, scones topped with devon cream and a choice of entree.

Historic Interest: The Henry Ford Museum and historic Greenfield Village are just 20 minutes away.

Innkeeper(s): Bernadette & Michael Van Lenten. $95-125. MC, VISA, AX. TAC10. 3 suites. Breakfast and snacks/refreshments included in rates. Types of meals: Full gourmet bkfst and early coffee/tea. Afternoon tea, dinner, picnic lunch and catering service available. Beds: KQDT. Cable TV, phone, turndown service, ceiling fan, VCR and non-cable TV (in suite) in room. Air conditioning. Fax, copier, bicycles and pet boarding on premises. Small meetings and family reunions hosted. French spoken. Antiquing, henry Ford Museum, zoo, live theater, parks, shopping, cross-country skiing, sporting events and water sports nearby.

Pets allowed: Not permitted in bedrooms.

"We've stayed in B&Bs in Europe, Australia and New Zealand, and we put yours at the top of the list for luxury, friendly care and delicious food (especially the scones). We're glad we found you. Thanks."

Central Lake
F7

Bridgewalk B&B

2287 S Main, PO Box 399
Central Lake, MI 49622-0399
(616)544-8122

Circa 1895. Secluded on a wooded acre, this three-story Victorian is accessible by crossing a foot bridge over a stream. Guest rooms are simply decorated with Victorian touches, floral prints and fresh flowers. The Garden Suite includes a clawfoot tub. Much of the home's Victorian elements have been restored, including pocket doors and the polished woodwork. Breakfasts begin with such items as a cold fruit soup, freshly baked muffins or scones accompanied with homemade jams and butters. A main dish, perhaps apple-sausage blossoms, tops off the meal.

Innkeeper(s): Janet & Tom Meteer. $85-95. MC, VISA, PC, TC. TAC10. 5 rooms with PB and 1 suite. Breakfast included in rates. Types of meals: Full bkfst and early coffee/tea. Beds: KQT. Ceiling fan in room. Small meetings hosted. Antiquing, fishing, golf, gourmet restaurants, parks, shopping, downhill skiing and cross-country skiing nearby.

Charlevoix E7

The Inn at Grey Gables

306 Belvedere Ave
Charlevoix, MI 49720-1413
(616)547-2251 (800)280-4667 Fax:(616)547-1944

Circa 1887. Guests at this attractive two-story inn are just a short walk from a public beach. Visitors have their choice of seven rooms, including two suites. The Pine Suite features a kitchen and private entrance, perfect for honeymooners or for those enjoying a longer-than-usual stay. All of the rooms offer private baths and most have queen beds.
Guests may opt to relax and enjoy the beautiful surroundings or take advantage of the many recreational activities available in the Charlevoix area, including Fisherman's Island State Park.

Innkeeper(s): Gary & Kay Anderson. $110-135. MC, VISA, PC, TC. 7 rooms, 5 with PB and 2 suites. Breakfast included in rates. Type of meal: Full bkfst. Beds: KQT. Ceiling fan in room. VCR and fax on premises. Small meetings and family reunions hosted. Antiquing, fishing, parks, shopping, downhill skiing, cross-country skiing and water sports nearby.

Fennville I6

The Kingsley House

626 W Main St
Fennville, MI 49408-9442
(616)561-6425 Fax:(616)561-2593
E-mail: garyking@accn.org
Web: www.kingsleyhouse.com

Circa 1886. Construction of this Queen Anne Victorian, with a three-story turret, was paid for in silver bricks by the Kingsley family. Mr. Kingsley is noted for having introduced the apple tree to the area. In recognition of him, guest rooms are named Dutchess, Golden Delicious, Granny Smith, McIntosh and Jonathan. The Northern Spy, complete with hot tub, is nestled in the third-floor suite. A winding oak staircase leads to the antique-filled guest chambers. Family heirlooms and other period pieces add to the inn's elegance.

Historic Interest: Historic Saugatuck and Holland just minutes away.

Innkeeper(s): Gary & Kari King. $80-165. MC, VISA, AX, DS, PC, TC. TAC10. 8 rooms with PB, 4 with FP and 3 suites. Breakfast and snacks/refreshments included in rates. Types of meals: Full bkfst, cont plus and early coffee/tea. Afternoon tea and picnic lunch available. Beds: KQD. Cable TV and ceiling fan in room. Air conditioning. VCR, fax, copier, bicycles and library on premises. Small meetings and seminars hosted. Antiquing, fishing, golf, live theater, parks, shopping, downhill skiing, cross-country skiing, tennis and water sports nearby.

Publicity: *Insider, Battle Creek Enquirer, Fennville Herald, Commercial Record, Glamour, Country, Country Victorian Decorating Ideas, National Geographic Traveler.*

"It was truly enjoyable. You have a lovely home and a gracious way of entertaining."

Spruce Cutters Cottage B&B

6670 126th Ave
Fennville, MI 49408-8541
(616)543-4285 (800)493-5888 Fax:(616)543-4285

Circa 1920. The six-acre grounds at this bed & breakfast include acres of spruce trees, and the property is surrounded by a Christmas tree farm. In addition to the spruce trees, the grounds are decorated with gardens and shaded by maple trees, fitted with hammocks and swings. The cozy ranch home was built in the 1920s and features an eclectic mix of antiques and other comfortable furnishings. The innkeeper provides a hearty country breakfast each morning with items such as Finnish pancakes, baked apple cinnamon French toast or perhaps potato pancakes. The home is minutes from downtown Saugatuck and the shores of Lake Michigan. Other attractions include a variety of golf courses, a historic steamship, biking, cross-country skiing, galleries, shopping and a winery.

Historic Interest: Pier Cove (2.5 miles), SS Keewatin (2 miles), Mt. Baldhead (2.5 miles).

Innkeeper(s): Michael A Morey. $80-155. MC, VISA, DS, PC, TC. 3 rooms, 2 with PB and 1 suite. Breakfast included in rates. Types of meals: Full bkfst and early coffee/tea. Beds: QD. TV, turndown service, ceiling fan, VCR and jacuzzi in suite in room. Central air. Fax and bicycles on premises. Antiquing, art galleries, beaches, bicycling, canoeing/kayaking, fishing, golf, hiking, horseback riding, u-Pick fruit, live theater, museums, parks, shopping, downhill skiing, cross-country skiing, water sports and wineries nearby.

Pets Allowed.

Fruitport I6

Village Park B&B

60 W Park St
Fruitport, MI 49415-9668
(616)865-6289 (800)469-1118

Circa 1873. Located in the midst of Western Michigan's Tri-Cities area, this inn's small-town village location offers comfort and relaxation to those busy partaking of the many nearby activities. This country classic farmhouse-style inn overlooks Spring Lake and a park where guests may picnic, play tennis, use a pedestrian/bike path and boat launch. There also is a hot tub and exercise room on the premises. The inn offers six guest rooms, all with private bath. A library is just across the street. P.J. Hoffmaster State Park, the Gillette Nature Sand Dune Center are nearby.

Innkeeper(s): John and Linda Hewett. $60-90. MC, VISA, DS, PC, TC. TAC10. 6 rooms with PB. Breakfast included in rates. Types of meals: Full bkfst, cont plus, cont and early coffee/tea. Beds: KQDT. Cable TV in room. Air conditioning. VCR, fax, sauna, bicycles, exercise room, hot tub and two-person kayak on premises. Small meetings and family reunions hosted. Amusement parks, antiquing, fishing, museums, nature centre, live theater, parks, shopping, cross-country skiing and water sports nearby.

Glen Arbor F6

The Sylvan Inn

PO Box 648,6680 Western (M-109)
Glen Arbor, MI 49636-0309
(231)334-4333

Circa 1885. During restoration, innkeepers Jenny and Bill Olson worked diligently to maintain their 19th-century farmhouse's historic flavor. The older portion of the inn is furnished

with antiques, and guest rooms feature brass or iron beds dressed with fine linens and down comforters. In the newer "Great House," there are six additional guest rooms with more contemporary decor and furnishings. There are plenty of things to see and do in the Glen Arbor area, including winery tours, activities at Lake Michigan, hiking, skiing, golf and more.

Innkeeper(s): Jenny & Bill Olson. $65-130. MC, VISA, PC, TC. TAC10. 14 rooms, 7 with PB and 1 suite. Breakfast included in rates. Types of meals: Cont plus and early coffee/tea. Beds: QT. Cable TV, phone and ceiling fan in room. Spa and sauna on premises. Handicap access. Weddings and family reunions hosted. Antiquing, fishing, live theater, parks, shopping, downhill skiing, cross-country skiing and water sports nearby.

"Your wonderful service and luxurious accommodations helped to make our wedding a very memorable occasion."

White Gull Inn

PO Box 351, 5926 SW Manitou Trl
Glen Arbor, MI 49636-9702
(616)334-4486 (888)334-4496 Fax:(616)334-3546

Circa 1900. One of Michigan's most scenic areas is home to the White Gull Inn. With the Sleeping Bear Dunes and alluring Glen Lake just minutes away, visitors will find no shortage of

sightseeing or recreational activities during a stay here. The inn's farmhouse setting, country decor and five comfortable guest rooms offer a relaxing haven no matter what the season. Lake Michigan is a block away, and guests also will enjoy the area's fine dining and shopping opportunities.

Innkeeper(s): Bill & Dotti Thompson. $60-75. MC, VISA, AX, DS, PC. 5 rooms, 1 with FP. Breakfast included in rates. Type of meal: Cont plus. Beds: QDT. Cable TV in room. Air conditioning. Fax on premises. Weddings and family reunions hosted. Antiquing, fishing, golf, parks, shopping, downhill skiing, cross-country skiing, tennis and water sports nearby.

Holland I6

Dutch Colonial Inn

560 Central Ave
Holland, MI 49423-4846
(616)396-3664 Fax:(616)396-0461
E-mail: dutchcolonialinn@juno.com
Web: www.bbonline.com/mi/dutch

Circa 1928. Romantic rooms at this Dutch-inspired home include the Tulip Suite with a Battenberg lace coverlet, fireplace and whirlpool tub for two. Another choice is the Jenny Lind suite with a king bed, raspberry and creme decor and a whirlpool tub for two. A few prized family heirlooms from the Netherlands are featured.

Historic Interest: The Cappon House Museum (5 minutes).

Innkeeper(s): Bob & Pat Elenbaas. $60-150. MC, VISA, AX, DS, PC. 4 rooms with PB and 3 suites. Breakfast included in rates. Types of meals: Full bkfst and early coffee/tea. Beds: KQ. Cable TV and phone in room. Air conditioning. VCR and fax on premises. Antiquing, fishing, parks, shopping, cross-country skiing and water sports nearby.

Publicity: *Shoreline Living, Country Folk Art.*

"Thank you again for your generous hospitality, Dutch cleanliness and excellent breakfasts."

Holly I8

Holly Crossing B&B

304 S Saginaw St
Holly, MI 48442-1614
(248)634-7075 (800)556-2262 Fax:(248)634-4481
E-mail: hollybb@tir.com
Web: hollybandb.com

Circa 1900. A unique wraparound veranda fashioned from stones decorates the exterior of this Queen Anne Victorian, which is surrounded by a white picket fence. The interior maintains original fireplace mantels and woodwork. Rooms are Victorian in style and comfortable, offering romantic items such as lacy curtains, silk flowers or perhaps even a double whirlpool tub. The spacious honeymoon suite offers a whirlpool tub, fireplace and a private balcony. All guests enjoy a delicious full breakfast, but guests in the whirlpool rooms have the meal delivered to their door. Holly is a historic railroad village, and the inn is conveniently located within walking distance of shops and restaurants. Battle Alley, a quaint street filled with restored 19th-century buildings, offers many shops and is a popular local attraction. Holly is within 45 minutes of Detroit.

Innkeeper(s): Carl & Nicole Cooper. $50-159. MC, VISA, AX, DS, PC, TC. TAC10. 5 rooms with PB, 3 with FP and 1 suite. Breakfast included in rates. Type of meal: Full bkfst. Room service available. Beds: QD. Phone and ceiling fan in room. Air conditioning. Fax, copier and library on premises. Antiquing, golf, live theater, parks, shopping, downhill skiing and cross-country skiing nearby.

"What a charming Bed & Breakfast! The Oak Room was delightful. My husband and I enjoyed the old world charm mixed in with the modern necessities. This is the nicest B&B we have stayed in thus far."

Jonesville J7

Horse & Carriage B&B

7020 Brown Rd
Jonesville, MI 49250-9720
(517)849-2732 Fax:(517)849-2732

Circa 1898. Enjoy a peaceful old-fashioned day on the farm. Milk a cow, gather eggs and cuddle baby chicks. In the winter, families are treated to a horse-drawn sleigh ride at this 18th-century home, which is surrounded by a 700-acre cattle farm. In the warmer months, horse-drawn carriage rides pass down an old country lane past Buck Lake. The innkeeper's family has lived on the property for more than 150 years. The home itself was built as a one-room schoolhouse. A mix of cottage and Mission furnishings decorate the interior. The Rainbow Room, a perfect place for children, offers twin beds and a playroom. Guests are treated to hearty breakfasts made with farm-fresh eggs, fresh fruits and vegetables served on the porch or fireside.

Innkeeper(s): Keith Brown & family. $85-100. PC. 3 rooms, 1 with PB. Breakfast and snacks/refreshments included in rates. Types of meals: Full gourmet bkfst, cont plus, cont and early coffee/tea. Beds: QT. Phone and the inn is air-conditioned in room. Fax, copier, milk a cow, pet lambs, gather eggs and horse/carriage rides on premises. Small meetings and family reunions hosted. Portuguese spoken. Antiquing, fishing, Jackson Space Ctr, Speedway, Country Fair, live theater, parks, shopping, cross-country skiing, sporting events and water sports nearby.

Munro House B&B

202 Maumee St
Jonesville, MI 49250-1247
(517)849-9292 (800)320-3792

Circa 1840. Ten fireplaces and two Franklin stoves are found in the rooms of the historic Munro House built by George C. Munro, a Civil War brigadier general. The Greek Revival struc-

ture, Hillsdale County's first brick house, also served as a safe haven for slaves on the Underground Railroad with a secret room that still exists. Many guests enjoy selecting a book or a movie to spend a quiet evening in front of the fireplace in their room or to enjoy with friends in the library. Seven guest rooms include a fireplace, and two rooms have a whirlpool tub. Breakfast is enjoyed overlooking the inn's gardens and before an open-hearth fireplace in the 1830's kitchen. Hillsdale College is just five miles away.

Innkeeper(s): Mike & Lori Venturini. $80-150. MC, VISA. 7 rooms with PB, 5 with FP. Breakfast included in rates. Type of meal: Full bkfst. Snacks/refreshments available. Cable TV, phone, VCR and two rooms with Jacuzzi's in room. Air conditioning. Weddings, small meetings, family reunions and seminars hosted. Antiquing, bicycling, canoeing/kayaking, golf, horseback riding, massage therapy, reflexology, live theater, shopping, cross-country skiing and sporting events nearby.

"What a delightful stay. Beautiful house, wonderful history and a delightful hostess. Felt like we knew her forever. We will tell all our friends."

Kalamazoo J6

Hall House

106 Thompson St
Kalamazoo, MI 49006-4537
(616)343-2500 (888)761-2525 Fax:(616)343-1374
E-mail: hofferth@hallhouse.com
Web: www.hallhouse.com

Circa 1923. In a National Historic District, this Georgian Colonial Revival-style house was constructed by builder H.L. Vander Horst as his private residence. Special features include

polished mahogany woodwork and marble stairs. The living room boasts a domed ceiling, while the library is graced with a hand-painted mural. Other special features of the house include an early intercom system. The inn is located on the edge of Kalamazoo College campus. Western Michigan University and downtown are a few minutes away.

Innkeeper(s): Jerry & Joanne Hofferth. $75-140. MC, VISA, AX, PC, TC. 6 rooms with PB, 2 with FP and 2 suites. Breakfast included in rates. Types of meals: Full bkfst and cont plus. Beds: KQDT. Cable TV, phone, VCR and one Jacuzzi in room. Air conditioning. Antiquing, golf, live theater and shopping nearby.

"A step into the grace, charm and elegance of the 19th century but with all the amenities of the 20th century right at hand."

Lansing I7

Ask Me House

1027 Seymour Ave
Lansing, MI 48906-4836
(517)484-3127 (800)275-6341 Fax:(517)484-4193
E-mail: mekiener@aol.com
Web: www.askmehouse.com

Circa 1911. This early 20th-century home still includes its original hardwood floors and pocket doors. A hand-painted mural was added to the dining room in the 1940s. Guests can enjoy the unique art during the breakfasts, which are served on antique Limoges china and Depression glass. The home is near a variety of museums, theaters, a historical village and Michigan State University.

Innkeeper(s): Mary Elaine Kiener & Alex Kruzel. $65. MC, VISA, PC, TC. TAC10. 2 rooms. Breakfast included in rates. Types of meals: Full gourmet bkfst and early coffee/tea. Beds: DT. Ceiling fan in room. VCR and fax on premises. Weddings and small meetings hosted. Polish spoken. Antiquing, live theater, parks and sporting events nearby.

Lowell 16

McGee Homestead B&B

2534 Alden Nash NE
Lowell, MI 49331
(616)897-8142
E-mail: mcgeebb@iserv.net
Web: www.iserv.net/~mcgeebb

Circa 1880. Just 18 miles from Grand Rapids, travelers will find the McGee Homestead B&B, an Italianate farmhouse with four antique-filled guest rooms. Surrounded by orchards, it is one of the largest farmhous-

es in the area. Breakfasts feature the inn's own fresh eggs. Guests may golf at an adjacent course or enjoy nearby fishing and boating. Lowell is home to Michigan's largest antique mall, and many historic covered bridges are found in the surrounding countryside. Travelers who remain on the farm may relax in a hammock or visit a barnful of petting animals.

Innkeeper(s): Bill & Ardie Barber. $42-62. MC, VISA, AX, DS, PC, TC. 4 rooms with PB and 1 conference room. Breakfast, afternoon tea and snacks/refreshments included in rates. Types of meals: Full bkfst and early coffee/tea. Beds: KDT. TV and ceiling fan in room. Air conditioning. VCR and library on premises. Small meetings hosted. Antiquing, fishing, parks, shopping, downhill skiing and cross-country skiing nearby.

Ludington G5

Lamplighter B&B

602 E Ludington Ave
Ludington, MI 49431-2223
(231)843-9792 (800)301-9792 Fax:(231)845-6070

Circa 1895. This Queen Anne home offers convenient access to Lake Michigan's beaches, the Badger car ferry to Wisconsin and Ludington State Park. A collection of European antiques, original paintings and lithographs deco-

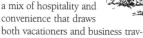

rate the inn. The home's centerpiece, a golden oak curved staircase, leads guests up to their rooms. Two rooms feature whirlpool tubs, one a fireplace. The innkeepers have created a mix of hospitality and convenience that draws both vacationers and business travelers. A full, gourmet breakfast is served each morning. Freddy, the inn's resident cocker spaniel, is always available for a tour of the area. The innkeepers are fluent in German.

Innkeeper(s): Judy & Heinz Bertram. $100-135. MC, VISA, AX, DS, PC, TC. TAC10. 5 rooms with PB, 1 with FP. Breakfast included in rates. Types of meals: Full gourmet bkfst and early coffee/tea. Beds: Q. Cable TV, phone, turndown service and whirlpool for two in room. Air conditioning. VCR, fax, copier and gazebo and terrace on premises. Amusement parks, antiquing, fishing, golf, parks, shopping, cross-country skiing, tennis and water sports nearby.

"For my husband's first bed and breakfast experience, it couldn't have been better."

The Inn at Ludington

701 E Ludington Ave
Ludington, MI 49431-2224
(231)845-7055 (800)845-9170
Web: www.inn-ludington.com

Circa 1890. This Queen Anne Victorian was built during the heyday of Ludington's lumber era by a local pharmacist and doctor. The innkeepers stress relaxation at the inn despite its elegant exterior with its three-story turret. The rooms are filled with comfortable, vintage furnishings. Guests can snuggle up with a book in front of a warming fireplace or enjoy a soak in a claw-foot tub. A hearty, buffet-style breakfast is served

each morning. The innkeepers take great pride in their cuisine and are always happy to share some of their award-winning recipes with guests. After a day of beachcombing, antiquing, cross-country skiing or perhaps a bike ride, guests return to the inn to find a chocolate atop their pillow. Don't forget to ask about the innkeepers' murder-mystery weekends.

Innkeeper(s): Diane & David Nemitz. $75-100. MC, VISA, AX, PC, TC. TAC10. 6 rooms with PB, 2 with FP and 1 suite. Breakfast included in rates. Types of meals: Full bkfst and early coffee/tea. Beds: QD. Cable TV, turndown service and ceiling fan in room. Air conditioning. Fax, copier and library on premises. Weddings, small meetings and seminars hosted. Amusement parks, antiquing, fishing, live theater, parks, shopping, downhill skiing, cross-country skiing and water sports nearby.

"Loved the room and everything else about the house."

Schoenberger House

409 E Ludington Ave
Ludington, MI 49431
(231)843-4435 Fax:(231)843-4435

Circa 1903. The carved white columns of this elegant brick Greek Revival mansion rise two stories to a beautifully designed pediment. A wide balcony with balustrades overlooks the front garden. Inside, a variety of finely crafted woodwork is highlighted throughout the mansion starting with the white oak entrance hall. There's a black walnut library, a cherry living room, American sycamore dining room and mahogany music room. Original chandeliers and five fireplaces are complemented with antique and reproduction furnishings and contemporary art. An abundant, expanded continental breakfast is served. Ludington and this part of the Lake Michigan shoreline offer beautiful uncrowded beaches.

Historic Interest: Mason County Courthouse (1 block), Big Sable Point Lighthouse (8.5 miles), White Pine Village (3 miles).

Innkeeper(s): Marlene Schoenberger. $120-195. MC, VISA, AX, PC, TC. 6 rooms, 5 with PB and 1 suite. Breakfast included in rates. Types of meals: Cont plus and early coffee/tea. Beds: KQD. Fax, copier and library on premises. Small meetings and seminars hosted. Antiquing, beaches, bicycling, canoeing/kayaking, fishing, golf, hiking, horseback riding, live theater, parks, shopping and cross-country skiing nearby.

Mackinac Island · E7

Cloghaun

PO Box 1540
Mackinac Island, MI 49757-0203
(906)847-3885 (888)442-5929

Circa 1884. Pronounced "Clah hann," the inn's name is Gaelic for "stoney ground" in reference to Mackinac Island's beaches. Built spacious enough to house Thomas and Bridgett Donnelly's large Irish family, this handsome Victorian home is owned and operated by their great grandson James Bond. The inn's gracious exterior boasts a front porch and upper balcony where guests enjoy watching the horse-drawn carriages pass by. Guest rooms are furnished in period antiques. Kelton Library is a welcoming retreat for reading or watching videos. Afternoon tea is served. The inn's location on Market Street affords easy access to parks, restaurants, ferries and shops.

Innkeeper(s): Marti & Paul Carey. $90-140. PC. 11 rooms, 9 with PB. Breakfast included in rates. Type of meal: Cont plus. Beds: KQD. VCR and library on premises. Weddings, small meetings, family reunions and seminars hosted. Restaurants and ferry lines, parks and shopping nearby.

Publicity: *Country Inns.*

Metivier Inn

Market St, PO Box 285
Mackinac Island, MI 49757-0285
(906)847-6234 (888)695-6562

Circa 1877. The Metivier Inn is in the downtown historic district where horse-drawn carriages and bicyclists preside in the absence of motorized vehicles. French and English decor is found throughout the turreted Victorian home. Guests can relax in the living room before the fire or out on the wicker-filled porch.

Innkeeper(s): George & Angela Leonard. $115-275. MC, VISA, AX, DS, PC. 21 rooms with PB, 1 suite and 1 conference room. Breakfast included in rates. Type of meal: Cont plus. Beds: KQ. VCR, fax, copier and child care on premises. Handicap access. Small meetings, family reunions and seminars hosted. Bicycling, golf, shopping and tennis nearby.

Publicity: *Travel & Leisure, Michigan Living, Detroit News, New York Times, Chicago Tribune.*

Mendon · J6

The Mendon Country Inn

PO Box 98
Mendon, MI 49072-9502
(616)496-8132 (800)304-3366 Fax:(616)496-8403
E-mail: wildwoodinns@voyager.net
Web: www.rivercountry.com/mci

Circa 1873. This two-story stagecoach inn was constructed with St. Joseph River clay bricks fired on the property. There are eight-foot windows, high ceilings and a walnut staircase. Country antiques are accentuated with woven rugs, collectibles and bright quilts. There are nine antique-filled guest rooms and nine suites which include a fireplace and Jacuzzi tub. Depending on the season, guests may also borrow a tandem bike or arrange for a canoe trip. Special events are featured throughout the year. The inn's Golden Getaway package includes lodging, a dinner for two and special activity, which might be golfing, a river canoe trip, skiing or perhaps a relaxing massage. A rural Amish community and Shipshewana are nearby.

Historic Interest: National Register.

Innkeeper(s): Dick & Dolly Buerkle. $69-169. MC, VISA, AX, DS, PC, TC. TAC10. 18 rooms with PB, 14 with FP, 9 suites, 2 cottages and 1 conference room. Breakfast included in rates. Types of meals: Full bkfst and early coffee/tea. Beds: QD. TV, ceiling fan and most rooms with fireplaces in room. Air conditioning. Fax, sauna, bicycles, library and canoeing on premises. Handicap access. Family reunions and seminars hosted. Antiquing, canoeing/kayaking, fishing, shopping, downhill skiing and cross-country skiing nearby.

"A great experience. Good food and great hosts. Thank you."

New Buffalo · K5

Sans Souci Euro Inn

19265 S Lakeside Rd
New Buffalo, MI 49117-9276
(616)756-3141 Fax:(616)756-5511

Circa 1940. Fifty acres of wildflower meadows and tall pine trees surround Lake Sans Souci (French for "without a care"). The inn's European decor is a crisp contemporary style featuring king-size beds. Rather than simply rooms, honeymoon suites, family homes and fisherman's cottages are available. For a family or two couples, for example, the Dutch House offers two bedrooms, a whirlpool, sunken den and kitchen. Outdoor weddings, reunions and meetings are popular here. Chicago is 70 miles away.

Innkeeper(s): The Siewert Family. $110-195. MC, VISA, AX, DS, PC, TC. 9 rooms with PB, 2 suites, 2 cottages and 2 guest houses. Beds: K. Whirlpool on premises.

"A little piece of heaven."

Petoskey (Bay View) · E7

Terrace Inn

1549 Glendale
Petoskey (Bay View), MI 49770
(231)347-2410 (800)530-9898 Fax:(231)347-2407
E-mail: info@theterraceinn.com
Web: theterraceinn.com

Circa 1911. This late Victorian inn is located on what began as a Chautauqua summer resort, surrounded by more than 400 Victorian cottages. Terrace Inn was built in 1911, and most of

its furnishings are original to the property. Guests will enjoy stunning views of Lake Michigan and Little Traverse Bay, and they can enjoy the shore at the private Bay View beach. In keeping with the surrounding homes, the guest rooms are decorated in a romantic-country cottage style. To take guests back in time, there are no televisions or telephones in the rooms. This historic resort town offers many attractions, from swimming and watersports to hiking to summer theater. During the summer season, the inn's restaurant and outdoor veranda are great spots for dinner.

Innkeeper(s): Tom & Denise Erhart. $49-105. MC, VISA, AX. TAC10. 43 rooms with PB and 2 conference rooms. Breakfast included in rates. Type of meal: Cont plus. Dinner, picnic lunch and banquet service available. Restaurant on premises. Beds: QDT. Air conditioning. VCR, fax, copier, swimming, bicycles, tennis and cross-country skiing on premises. Handicap access. Weddings, small meetings and family reunions hosted. Antiquing, fishing, golf, Chautauqua, live theater, parks, shopping, downhill skiing, cross-country skiing, tennis and water sports nearby.

Publicity: *Oakland Press & Observer Eccentric, Michigan Magazine.*

Port Huron   I10

Victorian Inn

1229 7th St
Port Huron, MI 48060-5303
(810)984-1437

Circa 1896. This finely renovated Queen Anne Victorian house has both an inn and restaurant. Gleaming carved-oak woodwork, leaded-glass windows and fireplaces in almost every room reflect the home's gracious air. Authentic wallpapers and

draperies provide a background for carefully selected antiques. At the three-star, AAA-rated Pierpont's Pub & Wine Cellar, Victorian-inspired menus include such entrees as rack-o-lamb, filets, fish and seafood, all served on antique china.

Innkeeper(s): Marv & Sue Burke. $65-135. MC, VISA, AX, DC, CB, DS, PC, TC. 4 rooms, 2 with PB, 2 with FP and 1 suite. Breakfast included in rates. Restaurant on premises. Beds: QDT. Pub on premises. Weddings and small meetings hosted. Antiquing, fishing, live theater, parks, shopping, cross-country skiing and water sports nearby.

Publicity: *Detroit Free Press.*

"In all of my trips, business or pleasure, I have never experienced such a warm and courteous staff."

Romeo   I9

Hess Manor B&B

186 S Main St
Romeo, MI 48065-5128
(810)752-4726 Fax:(810)752-6456

Circa 1854. This pre-Civil War home is located in a town listed in the National Register. The inn boasts a fireplace and Victorian decor. The innkeepers also renovated the inn's 110-year-old carriage house into an antique and gift shop. At night, guests are encouraged to enjoy the inn's complimentary soda pop and wine while viewing a wide selection free movies. For

stargazers, there is a wonderful outdoor Jacuzzi. Much of Romeo's historic sites are within walking distance of Hess Manor, including galleries, antique shops, bookstores and restaurants. Frontier Town, a collection of Old West-style buildings, is a popular attraction.

Innkeeper(s): Thom & Kelly Stephens. $69-80. MC, VISA, AX, PC. TAC15. 4 rooms, 2 with PB. Breakfast included in rates. Type of meal: Full gourmet bkfst. Beds: Q. Air conditioning. VCR, copier, free video, free beverages and Jacuzzi under stars on premises. Small meetings hosted. Antiquing, fishing, golf, horseback riding, live theater, parks, shopping and water sports nearby.

Saint Clair   I10

William Hopkins Manor

613 N Riverside Ave
Saint Clair, MI 48079-5417
(810)329-0188 Fax:(810)329-6239

Circa 1876. This three-story Second Empire Victorian, encompasses 10,000 square feet and comes complete with tower, slate mansard roof, dormers, porches and an elaborate wrought iron fence. Its riverfront location across the street from the St. Clair River affords the pastime of watching freighters and barges pass by. Guest rooms feature reproductions and antiques, and some rooms have fireplaces. A billiard room and two parlors are available for relaxing. Breakfast is served family style in the dining room. The Historic St. Clair Inn, a five-minute walk away, offers an interesting dining option.

Innkeeper(s): Sharon Llewellyn/Terry Mazzarese. $80-100. MC, VISA, PC. 5 rooms, 1 with PB, 1 with FP. Breakfast included in rates. Types of meals: Full bkfst, veg bkfst and early coffee/tea. Beds: QD. Air conditioning. CD players on premises. Small meetings, family reunions hosted. Antiquing, art galleries, beaches, canoeing/kayaking, fishing, golf, horseback riding, live theater, museums, parks, shopping and water sports nearby.

Saline   J8

The Homestead B&B

9279 Macon Rd
Saline, MI 48176-9305
(734)429-9625

Circa 1851. The Homestead is a two-story brick farmhouse situated on 50 acres of fields, woods and river. The house has 15-inch-thick walls and is furnished with Victorian antiques and family heirlooms. This was a favorite camping spot for Native Americans while they salted their fish, and many arrowheads have been found on the farm. Activities include long walks through meadows of wildflowers and cross-country skiing in season. It is 40 minutes from Detroit and Toledo and 10 minutes from Ann Arbor.

Innkeeper(s): Shirley Grossman. $65-70. MC, VISA, AX, DS, PC, TC. 5 rooms and 1 conference room. Breakfast and snacks/refreshments included in rates. Types of meals: Full bkfst and early coffee/tea. Beds: DT. TV in room. Air conditioning. VCR on premises. Small meetings, family reunions and seminars hosted. Antiquing, parks, shopping, cross-country skiing and sporting events nearby.

"We're spoiled now and wouldn't want to stay elsewhere! No motel offers deer at dusk and dawn!"

Saugatuck 16

Bayside Inn

618 Water St Box 186
Saugatuck, MI 49453
(616)857-4321 Fax:(616)857-1870
Web: www.bbonline.com/mi/bayside

Circa 1926. Located on the edge of the Kalamazoo River and across from the nature observation tower, this downtown inn was once a boathouse. The common room now has a fireplace and view of the water. Each guest room has its own deck. The inn is near several restaurants, shops and beaches. Fishing for salmon, perch and trout is popular.

Innkeeper(s): Kathy Wilson. $65-235. MC, VISA, AX, DS. 10 rooms with PB, 4 with FP, 4 suites and 1 conference room. Breakfast included in rates. Type of meal: Cont plus. Beds: KQD. Cable TV, phone and VCR in room. Air conditioning. Fax, copier and spa on premises. Weddings, small meetings, family reunions and seminars hosted. Antiquing, fishing, live theater, shopping, cross-country skiing and water sports nearby.

"Our stay was wonderful, more pleasant than anticipated, we were so pleased. As for breakfast, it gets our A 1 rating."

J. Paules' Fenn Inn

2254 S 58th St
Saugatuck, MI 49408
(616)561-2836 Fax:(616)561-2836

Circa 1900. Located 18 miles from Holland and minutes from Saugatuck, this friendly three-story historic home features white pillars at the front and baskets and planters brimming with spring and summer flowers. Oak pillars are repeated on the main floor and oak floors and an oak staircase is featured. The breakfast room has its own fireplace and there's a sun deck on the second floor. In the summer, the inn's gourmet breakfast is served in the sunroom off the kitchen. Festivals held locally include the Holland Tulip Festival, Blueberry Festival and the Fennville Goose Festival. Hiking, golfing, cycling, fishing, and both downhill and cross-country skiing are popular activities.

Innkeeper(s): Paulette Clouse. $70-135. MC, VISA, DS, PC. 5 rooms. Breakfast included in rates. Type of meal: Full bkfst. Beds: QDT. Ceiling fan in room. Air conditioning. VCR, fax, copier and bicycles on premises. Handicap access. Amusement parks, antiquing, fishing, golf, live theater, parks, shopping, downhill skiing, cross-country skiing, tennis and water sports nearby.

Pets allowed: $10 fee per pet per day.

"Your house is gorgeous and we really enjoyed spending time with you."

The Park House

888 Holland St
Saugatuck, MI 49453-9607
(616)857-4535 (800)321-4535 Fax:(616)857-1065
E-mail: parkhouse@softhouse.com
Web: www.bbonline.com/mi/parkhouse

Circa 1857. This Greek Revival-style home is the oldest residence in Saugatuck and was constructed for the first mayor. Susan B. Anthony was a guest here for two

weeks in the 1870s, and the local Women's Christian Temperance League was established in the parlor. A country theme pervades the inn, with antiques, old woodwork and pine floors. A cottage with a hot tub and a river-front guest house are also available.

Historic Interest: Listed in the National Register.

Innkeeper(s): Lynda & Joe Petty, Dan Osborn. $70-225. MC, VISA, AX, DS, PC, TC. TAC10. 8 rooms with PB, 6 with FP, 3 suites and 4 cottages. Breakfast included in rates. Types of meals: Full bkfst and early coffee/tea. Beds: KQT. Cable TV, phone and VCR in room. Air conditioning. Fax and copier on premises. Handicap access. Small meetings, family reunions and seminars hosted. Antiquing, fishing, live theater, parks, shopping, cross-country skiing and water sports nearby.

"Thanks again for your kindness and hospitality during our weekend."

Twin Gables Inn

PO Box 1150, 900 Lake St
Saugatuck, MI 49453-1150
(616)857-4346 (800)231-2185
E-mail: relax@twingablesinn.com
Web: www.twingablesinn.com

Circa 1865. Twin Gables, a state historic site, overlooks Kalamazoo Lake. The interior features comfortable guest rooms, furnished with antiques. Some rooms include a fireplace. After a day of cross-country skiing, golfing or just exploring the area, enjoy a soak in the indoor hot tub. There is also a heated outdoor pool. This inn is the only remaining original mill left in the area, a reminder of the busy lumbering days of Saugatuck's past. Among its other uses, the home has served as a brewery icehouse, a tannery and a boat building factory. The inn is within walking distance to the many shops in Saugatuck and is a good base for those hoping to take in the variety of outdoor activities.

Historic Interest: Saugatuck has its own historical museum and a retired Victorian cruise liner is docked nearby. Guided tours are available.

Innkeeper(s): Bob Lawrence & Susan Schwaderer. $75-150. MC, VISA, AX, DS. 14 rooms with PB and 3 cottages. Breakfast included in rates. Type of meal: Full bkfst. Beds: KQDT. Air conditioning. VCR, fax, spa, swimming and bicycles on premises. Handicap access. Weddings, small meetings, family reunions and seminars hosted. Antiquing, beaches, fishing, golf, live theater, parks, shopping, cross-country skiing, tennis, water sports and wineries nearby.

Twin Oaks Inn

PO Box 867, 227 Griffith St
Saugatuck, MI 49453-0867
(616)857-1600

Circa 1860. This large Queen Anne Victorian inn was a boarding house for lumbermen at the turn of the century. Now an old-English-style inn, it offers a variety of lodging choices, including a room with its own Jacuzzi and a cozy cottage, which boasts a fireplace and an outdoor hot tub. There are many diversions at Twin Oaks, including a collection of videotaped movies numbering more than 700. Guests may borrow bicycles or play horseshoes on the inn's grounds.

Innkeeper(s): Jerry & Nancy Horney. $75-125. MC, VISA, DS, TC. 7 rooms with PB and 1 conference room. Types of meals: Full bkfst and early coffee/tea. Snacks/refreshments available. Beds: KQ. Cable TV and VCR in room. Air conditioning. Weddings, small meetings and family reunions hosted. Antiquing, fishing, live theater, parks, shopping, cross-country skiing and water sports nearby.

Publicity: *Home & Away, Cleveland Plain Dealer, South Bend Tribune, Shape, AAA Magazine.*

Saugatuck (Douglas)　I6

Sherwood Forest B&B

938 Center St
Saugatuck (Douglas), MI 49453
(616)857-1246 (800)838-1246 Fax:(616)857-1996

Circa 1902. As the name suggests, this gracious Victorian is surrounded by woods. A large wraparound porch, gables, and leaded-glass windows add to the appeal. There are hardwood floors and each guest room features antiques, wing chairs and queen-

size beds. Two suites offer a Jacuzzi and fireplace. Another room boasts a gas fireplace and a unique hand-painted mural that transforms the room into a canopied tree-top loft. A breakfast of delicious coffees or teas and homemade treats can be enjoyed either in the dining room or on the porch. The outdoor heated pool features a hand-painted mural of a sunken Greek ship embedded in a coral reef and surrounded by schools of fish. The eastern shore of Lake Michigan is only a half block away.

Innkeeper(s): Keith & Sue Charak. $95-165. MC, VISA, DC, DS, PC, TC. TAC10. 5 rooms with PB, 3 with FP, 2 suites and 1 cottage. Breakfast included in rates. Types of meals: Full gourmet bkfst, cont plus and early coffee/tea. Afternoon tea, gourmet dinner and catering service available. Beds: Q. Ceiling fan in room. Air conditioning. VCR, fax, swimming and bicycles on premises. Weddings, small meetings, family reunions and seminars hosted. Antiquing, fishing, golf, boat charters, golf, hiking, horseback riding, live theater, parks, shopping, cross-country skiing, sporting events, tennis and water sports nearby.

"We enjoyed our weekend in the forest, the atmosphere was perfect, and your suggestions on where to eat and how to get around was very appreciated. Thanks for remembering our anniversary."

South Haven　J5

Carriage House At The Harbor

118 Woodman St
South Haven, MI 49090-1471
(616)639-2161

Circa 1897. Carriage House is comprised of two restored Victorian homes with two separate locations: Carriage House at the Park and Carriage House at the Harbor. Both accommodations feature individually decorated rooms with fireplaces and private baths. Many of the rooms also offer whirlpool tubs for two, fireplaces and decks or balconies with splendid harbor and marina views. Breakfast specialties

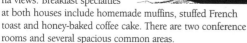

at both houses include homemade muffins, stuffed French toast and honey-baked coffee cake. There are two conference rooms and several spacious common areas.

Historic Interest: One block from Lake Michigan. The inn is walking distance to the downtown.

Innkeeper(s): Jay & Joyce Yelton. $95-185. MC, VISA, AX, DS. 11 rooms with PB and 1 conference room. Breakfast included in rates. Types of meals: Full bkfst and country bkfst. Beds: KQ. Cable TV, phone, ceiling fan and VCR in room. Central air. Fax and copier on premises. Handicap access.

Publicity: *Midwest Living, Detroit Free Press, Kalamazoo Gazette, Great Lakes Getaway.*

"Everything was wonderful from the time we walked in the front door to the time we (sadly) left."

The Seymour House

1248 Blue Star Hwy
South Haven, MI 49090-9696
(616)227-3918 Fax:(616)227-3010
E-mail: seymour@cybersol.com
Web: www.seymourhouse.com

Circa 1862. Less than half a mile from the shores of Lake Michigan, this pre-Civil War, Italianate-style home rests upon 11 acres of grounds, complete with nature trails. Each of the guest rooms is named for a state significant in the innkeepers' lives. The Arizona Room, popular with honeymooners, includes a double Jacuzzi tub. Poached pears with raspberry sauce, butter-

milk blueberry pancakes and locally made sausages are a few of the items that might appear on the breakfast menu. The inn is midway between Saugatuck and South Haven, which offer plenty of activities. Beaches, Kal-Haven Trail, shopping, horseback riding and winery tours are among the fun destination choices.

Innkeeper(s): Tom & Gwen Paton. $85-145. MC, VISA, PC, TC. TAC10. 5 rooms with PB, 2 with FP and 1 cabin. Breakfast and afternoon tea included in rates. Types of meals: Full gourmet bkfst and early coffee/tea. Beds: KQD. Cable TV, ceiling fan, VCR and jacuzzi in room. Air conditioning. Fax, copier, swimming and library on premises. Antiquing, fishing, golf, live theater, parks, shopping, downhill skiing, cross-country skiing and water sports nearby.

Publicity: *Country, Michigan Living.*

"As one who comes from the land that invented B&Bs, I hope to say that this is a truly superb example."

Yelton Manor Bed & Breakfast

140 N Shore Dr
South Haven, MI 49090-1135
(616)637-5220
E-mail: elaine@yeltonmanor.com
Web: www.yeltonmanor.com

Circa 1872. Sunsets over Lake Michigan, award-winning gardens and gourmet breakfasts are just a sampling of what guests will partake of at this restored Victorian. There are 11 guest rooms from which to choose, each named for a flower. The anniversary and honeymoon suites offer lakeside views. Several rooms include a Jacuzzi tub. Each of the guest rooms includes a TV and VCR, and there is a large video library to peruse. Bountiful breakfasts include items such as blueberry pancakes or a homemade egg strata with salsa. Yelton Manor guests also enjoy evening hors d'oeuvres, and don't forget to sample one of the inn's signature chocolate chip cookies. During the Christmas season, a tree is placed in every room, and more than 15,000 lights decorate the inn. The innkeepers also offer six additional

rooms in the new Manor Guest House, a Victorian home built in 1993. Those staying at the guest house enjoy a continental breakfast delivered to their room door.

Innkeeper(s): Elaine Herbert & Robert Kripaitis. $95-240. MC, VISA, AX. 17 rooms with PB, 7 with FP and 1 conference room. Type of meal: Full bkfst. Beds: KQ. Cable TV, phone, VCR, gardens, books and music in room. Library on premises.

Publicity: *Great Lakes Getaway, Adventure Roads, Chicago Tribune, New York Times, Hour Detroit, Chicago Sun Times, Country Living.*

"The Yelton Manor is a lovely place to unwind and enjoy the special amenities provided by the very friendly staff. We appreciate all your hard work and will definitely plan to be back! Thank You!"

Suttons Bay   F6

Open Windows

PO Box 698, 613 St Marys Ave
Suttons Bay, MI 49682-0698
(231)271-4300 (800)520-3722

Circa 1893. The bay is just two blocks away for guests staying at this bed & breakfast, and those opting for the home's Rose Garden Room enjoy the water view from their quarters. The home's half-acre of grounds is dotted with flower gardens. Adirondack-style chairs, created by the innkeeper, line the front porch. Guests may borrow snowshoes in winter or use the home's grill and picnic table during the warmer months.

Locally produced fresh fruits, entrees such as spinach and cheese crepes and homemade breads are among the breakfast fare, which is often served in a room with bay views.

Innkeeper(s): Don & Norma Blumenschine. $95-135. PC, TC. TAC10. 3 rooms with PB. Breakfast and snacks/refreshments included in rates. Types of meals: Full gourmet bkfst and early coffee/tea. Picnic lunch available. Beds: KQT. Ceiling fan in room. Air conditioning. VCR, bicycles, library, snowshoes, grill, picnic table and refrigerator on premises. Weddings, small meetings, family reunions and seminars hosted. Antiquing, fishing, Sleeping Bear Dunes, live theater, parks, shopping, downhill skiing, cross-country skiing and water sports nearby.

Union Pier   J5

The Inn at Union Pier

9708 Berrien
Union Pier, MI 49129-0222
(616)469-4700 Fax:(616)469-4720
Web: www.innatunionpier.com

Circa 1920. Set on a shady acre across a country road from Lake Michigan, this inn features unique Swedish ceramic wood-burning fireplaces, a hot tub and sauna, a veranda ringing the house and a large common room with comfortable overstuffed furniture and a grand piano. Rooms offer such amenities as private balconies and porches, whirlpools, views of the English garden and furniture dating from the early 1900s. Breakfast includes fresh fruit and homemade jams made of fruit from surrounding farms.

Innkeeper(s): Joyce & Mark Pitts. $135-205. MC, VISA, DS, PC, TC. 16 rooms with PB, 12 with FP, 2 suites and 1 conference room. Breakfast and snacks/refreshments included in rates. Types of meals: Full gourmet bkfst, cont and early coffee/tea. Catering service available. Beds: KQT. TV, phone and ceiling fan in room. Air conditioning. VCR, fax, copier, spa, swimming, sauna, bicycles and library on premises. Handicap access. Weddings, small meetings, family reunions and seminars hosted. Antiquing, wine tasting, gallery hopping, hiking, biking, galleries, wineries, parks, cross-country ski-

ing, sporting events and water sports nearby.

Publicity: *Chicago Tribune, Chicago, Midwest Living, Chicago Sun Times, Country Living, Romantic-Inns-The Travel Channel, Travel & Leisure.*

"The food, the atmosphere, the accommodations, and of course, the entire staff made this the most relaxing weekend ever."

West Bloomfield   I9

Wren's Nest

7405 W Maple Rd
West Bloomfield, MI 48322-2710
(248)624-6874 Fax:(248)624-9869
Web: www.bbonline.com/mi/wrensnest/

Circa 1840. Tulips and a plethora of perennial and annual flower beds accent the professionally landscaped grounds surrounding this farmhouse adjacent to a woodland, in a country setting. Numerous birdhouses, creations of the innkeeper, are scattered around the property, and the innkeeper has planted more than 60 varieties of heirloom tomatoes in a heritage vegetable garden. Ask for the cozy canopy room for a comfortable bed and floral wallpaper. A large breakfast is served in the dining room. The innkeeper raised all five of her children here and welcomes families.

Innkeeper(s): Irene Scheel. $85-95. PC, TC. TAC10. 6 rooms, 2 with PB. Breakfast, afternoon tea and snacks/refreshments included in rates. Types of meals: Full bkfst and early coffee/tea. Room service available. Beds: KDT. Cable TV, phone and turndown service in room. Air conditioning. VCR, fax, copier and baby Grand Piano on premises. Weddings, small meetings and family reunions hosted. Antiquing, fishing, golf, live theater, parks, shopping, downhill skiing, cross-country skiing, sporting events and tennis nearby.

Publicity: *Detroit News, Midwest Living, Japanese Free Press.*

Ypsilanti   J8

Parish House Inn

103 S Huron St
Ypsilanti, MI 48197-5421
(734)480-4800 (800)480-4866 Fax:(734)480-7472
E-mail: parishinn@aol.com
Web: bbhost.com/parish

Circa 1893. This Queen Anne Victorian was named in honor of its service as a parsonage for the First Congregational Church. The home remained a parsonage for more than 50 years after its construction and then served as a church office and Sunday school building. It was moved to its present site in Ypsilanti's historic district in the late 1980s. The rooms are individually decorated with Victorian-style wallpapers and antiques. One guest room includes a two-person Jacuzzi tub. Those in search of a late-night snack need only venture into the kitchen to find drinks and the cookie jar. For special occasions, the innkeepers can arrange trays with flowers, non-alcoholic champagne, chocolates, fruit or cheese. The terrace overlooks the Huron River.

Innkeeper(s): Mrs. Chris Mason. $89-129. MC, VISA, AX, DS, PC, TC. TAC10. 9 rooms with PB, 2 with FP and 1 conference room. Breakfast and snacks/refreshments included in rates. Types of meals: Full gourmet bkfst, cont and early coffee/tea. Afternoon tea, picnic lunch and catering service available. Beds: QDT. Cable TV, phone, ceiling fan and VCR in room. Air conditioning. Fax and library on premises. Handicap access. Small meetings, family reunions and seminars hosted. Amusement parks, antiquing, fishing, live theater, parks, shopping, cross-country skiing, sporting events and water sports nearby.

Minnesota

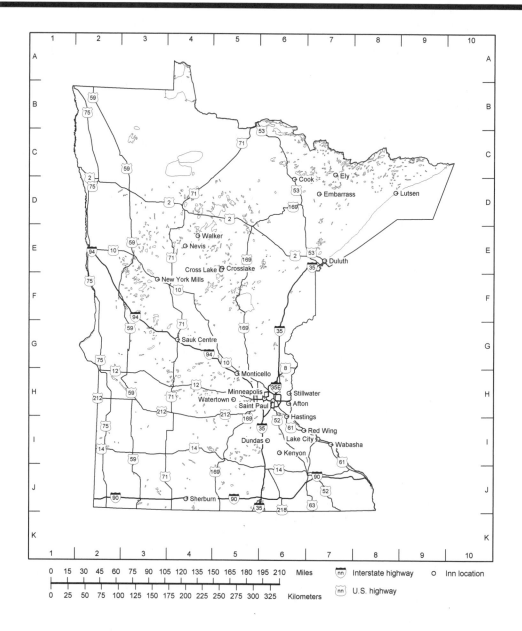

	Miles
0 15 30 45 60 75 90 105 120 135 150 165 180 195 210	Miles
0 25 50 75 100 125 150 175 200 225 250 275 300 325	Kilometers

(nn) Interstate highway   o Inn location

(nn) U.S. highway

Afton H6

The Historic Afton House Inn

3291 S, St. Croix Tr
Afton, MN 55001
(651)436-8883 (877)436-8883 Fax:(651)436-6859
E-mail: info@aftonhouseinn.com
Web: www.aftonhouseinn.com

Circa 1867. Located on two acres of waterfront on the St. Croix River, this historic inn reflects an old New England-style architecture. Guest rooms offer Jacuzzi tubs, fireplaces, waterfront balconies and are decorated with American country antiques. A restaurant on the premises provides candlelight dining in the

Wheel Room. (Ask for cherries jubilee, or any flaming dessert - a house specialty.) Or you might prefer to dine aboard the Grand Duchess, a ship that will accommodate 300 for weddings and corporate getaways. The Afton Princess is a smaller cruiser, also available for river cruises.

Historic Interest: Old Lumber Mill (1/4 mile), Boyles Creek, site of first settlers of Minnesota.

Innkeeper(s): Gordy & Kathy Jarvis. $60-140. MC, VISA, AX, DS, PC. 15 rooms. Breakfast included in rates. Types of meals: Cont plus and cont. Gourmet dinner, banquet service, catering service and room service available. Restaurant on premises. Beds: KQD. TV, phone, VCR and gas fireplaces in room. Air conditioning. Fax, copier and spa on premises. Handicap access. Weddings, small meetings, family reunions and seminars hosted. Antiquing, art galleries, beaches, bicycling, canoeing/kayaking, fishing, golf, hiking, horseback riding, parks, shopping, downhill skiing, cross-country skiing, sporting events and water sports nearby.

Cook D6

Ludlow's Island Lodge

8166 Ludlow Dr
Cook, MN 55723
(218)666-5407 (877)583-5697 Fax:(218)666-2488

Circa 1939. A collection of 18 rustic cabins is nestled on two shores of the lake and a private island. They range in style and size and are from one to five bedrooms. All have fireplaces, kitchens and outdoor decks. All cabins have multiple baths and are equipped with tubs and showers. This resort is very private with many activities on the property that are free of charge including tennis, racquetball, canoeing and sailboating. A 24-hour convenience grocery store is also on premises. Children may enjoy watching movies that are shown every evening in the lodge, and there are daily activities that focus on the surrounding environment.

Innkeeper(s): Mark & Sally Ludlow. $165-370. MC, VISA, AX, PC. TAC10. 56 rooms. Catering service available. Beds: KQDT. Cable TV, ceiling fan, VCR and kitchen in room. Fax, copier, swimming, sauna, tennis, library and child care on premises. Weddings, small meetings, family reunions and seminars hosted. Fishing, golf, shopping, tennis and water sports nearby.

Crosslake E5

Birch Hill Inne Bed & Breakfast

PO Box 468
Crosslake, MN 56442
(218)692-4857
E-mail: stay@birchhillinne.com
Web: birchhillinne.com

Circa 1926. An immense screened-in front porch highlights the exterior of this historic home, which offers five individually decorated guest rooms. Each bedchamber contains something unique. The Garden room includes a private sunroom. The Norway Pine Room includes an unusual twig headboard and a double Jacuzzi tub. The inn affords views of Ox Lake, and guests can canoe across the lake in search of hiking trails and a picnic area. The canoes, paddleboats and snowshoes all are available for guests at the inn.

Innkeeper(s): Deanna Engen, Heidi Engen. $72-80. MC, VISA, AX, PC. 5 rooms with PB. Breakfast included in rates. Types of meals: Cont plus and early coffee/tea. Beds: QD. Cable TV and 2 rooms with double Jacuzzi's in room. Air conditioning. VCR, swimming, bicycles and snow shoes on premises. Handicap access. Small meetings hosted. Amusement parks, antiquing, fishing, golf, near Paul Bunyan bike trail, parks, shopping, downhill skiing, cross-country skiing, tennis and water sports nearby.

Duluth E7

The Cotton Mansion

2309 East 1st St
Duluth, MN 55812
(218)724-6405 (800)228-1997 Fax:(218)728-0952
Web: www.visitduluth.com/cotton

Circa 1908. Four blocks from Lake Superior in the historic East Side, this 16,000 square-foot, three-story Italian Renaissance mansion was once the home of John D. Rockefeller's mining industry attorney, Joseph Bell Cotton. Its grand entrance, beautiful solarium, library and elegant parlor with carved alabaster fireplace and beamed ceiling invite you to a refined inn experience. Guest suites are generous in size and offer fireplaces, whirlpools, overstuffed lounge chairs and sofas, Oriental rugs and antique furnishings. The inn's signature candlelit breakfast is provided on fine china, crystal and silver in the mansion dining room which boasts an original dining set created for the mansion and an original tapestry. Eggs Benedict, sourdough waffles and fresh berries are among the inn's offerings. Wine and cheese are served in the evening. The inn offers a uniquely gracious setting for small weddings and corporate gatherings.

Historic Interest: Historic Congdon Estate.

Innkeeper(s): Ken & Kimberly Aparicio. $110-215. MC, VISA, AX, DS, PC, TC. TAC10. 5 rooms with PB, 4 with FP and 3 suites. Type of meal: Early coffee/tea. Picnic lunch available. Beds: Q. Fireplace and whirlpool suites in room. Library on premises. Family reunions hosted. Antiquing, bicycling, canoeing/kayaking, fishing, golf, hiking, horseback riding, live theater, museums, parks, shopping, downhill skiing, cross-country skiing, tennis and water sports nearby.

The Firelight Inn on Oregon Creek

2211 East Third St
Duluth, MN 55812
(218)724-0272 (888)724-0273 Fax:(218)724-0304

Circa 1910. This three-story red brick mansion boasts eleven fireplaces built of a variety of materials including marble, granite and copper. A massive glassed-in porch overlooks the inn's creek, which flows to Lake Superior a few blocks away. In addition to a gas fireplace, four suites offer a Jacuzzi tub and a brass, canopy or four-poster bed. The inn features beautifully preserved woodwork, a carved staircase and polished wood floors. There's a baby grand piano in the living room. Breakfast is brought to your room, and it is usually eaten fireside. Specialties include dishes such as stuffed strawberry French toast, bacon, fruit and lemon pecan bread.

Historic Interest: Gooseberry Falls (40 miles), Split Rock Lighthouse (55 miles).
Innkeeper(s): Jim & Joy Fischer. $129-229. MC, VISA, AX, DS, PC. 6 rooms with PB, 6 with FP. Breakfast and snacks/refreshments included in rates. Types of meals: Full bkfst and early coffee/tea. Picnic lunch available. Beds: KQ. Cable TV, ceiling fan and VCR in room. Fax and copier on premises. Weddings, small meetings, family reunions and seminars hosted. Antiquing, art galleries, beaches, bicycling, canoeing/kayaking, fishing, golf, hiking, museums, parks, shopping, downhill skiing, cross-country skiing and sporting events nearby.

Manor on the Creek Country Inn/ Bed & Breakfast

2215 E 2nd St
Duluth, MN 55812-1864
(218)728-3189 (800)428-3189 Fax:(218)724-3915
E-mail: manor@cpinternet.com
Web: www.visitduluth.com/manor

Circa 1907. This exquisite mansion is one of Duluth's five largest homes. As you enter this cherished home, you will first be taken by its remarkable woodwork. The home's architects, the team of Bray and Nystrom, were originally influenced by Louis Sullivan and Frank Lloyd Wright. The interior design is magnificent, and the innkeepers complement its beauty by filling the home with period furnishings. The suites include whirlpool tubs and fireplaces, and guests will find fresh flowers and candies in their rooms. The inn's grounds also are noteworthy, two acres set along Oregon Creek overlooking woods and a ravine. The gourmet breakfasts include such items as dilled scones topped with grilled tomatoes, poached eggs and a tarragon bechamel sauce, homemade chorizo and roasted baby red potatoes. Special event dining is available as well.

Innkeeper(s): Ken, Mona, Casey Knutson. $98-229. MC, VISA, DS, PC, TC. TAC8. 8 rooms with PB, 2 with FP, 4 suites, 1 cottage and 2 conference rooms. Breakfast included in rates. Types of meals: Full gourmet bkfst, cont and early coffee/tea. Picnic lunch and banquet service available. Beds: KQ. Phone, ceiling fan, porch, balconies, cable TV and VCRs (some rooms) in room. Air conditioning. VCR, fax and special event dining on premises. Weddings, small meetings, family reunions and seminars hosted. Antiquing, fishing, golf, live theater, parks, shopping, downhill skiing, cross-country skiing, sporting events, tennis and water sports nearby.

Pets allowed: Not allowed alone in rooms, must be leashed, must be good with people, $10 a night charge, damage deposit.

Publicity: *MN Monthly, Rochester Press, St Paul Pioneer Press.*

Dundas   I6

Martin Oaks B&B

107 First St, PO Box 207
Dundas, MN 55019-0207
(507)645-4644

Circa 1869. The rich blue exterior and rail fence at this prairie Victorian conjure up nostalgic images of yesteryear. The home is listed in the National Register. Antiques, flowers, featherbeds, down comforters and candles add to the homey, cozy feel. Multi-course breakfasts of fresh fruit, home-baked breads and special entrees are served on china. Guests return in the evenings to find not just the usual chocolate turndown service, but rather a rich, fudge brownie or other special treat decoratively arranged on a plate atop a fluffy pillow. Bubble bath and soft robes are just a few of the many extras guests enjoy. The innkeepers can arrange teas or gourmet dinners.

Innkeeper(s): Marie & Frank Gery. $60-85. MC, VISA, PC, TC. 2 rooms. Breakfast, afternoon tea and snacks/refreshments included in rates. MAP. Types of meals: Full gourmet bkfst and early coffee/tea. Beds: DT. Turndown service and ceiling fan in room. Air conditioning. Library on premises. Small meetings, family reunions and seminars hosted. French spoken. Amusement parks, antiquing, fishing, live theater, parks, shopping, downhill skiing, cross-country skiing, sporting events and water sports nearby.

"It's been wonderful living in fantasy land for a few days. Thanks for the enchantment."

Ely   C7

Burntside Lodge

2755 Burntside Lodge Rd
Ely, MN 55731-8402
(218)365-3894

Circa 1913. "Staying here is like taking a vacation 80 years ago," states innkeeper Lou LaMontagne. Families have come here for more than 80 years to enjoy the waterfront and woodside setting. The lodge and its cabins are in the National Register and much of the original hand-carved furnishings remain from the jazz age. Guests can choose from lodging in rustic cabins that date back to the 1920s, and there also are elegant, renovated cabins that include up to three bedrooms. Fishing, listening to the cry of the loon and boating around the lake's 125 islands are popular activities. Breakfast and dinner are available in the waterside dining room, and there is a lounge, espresso bar and gift shop. The lodge is open from mid-May through September.

Innkeeper(s): Lou & Lonnie LaMontagne. $90-230. MC, VISA, AX, DS. 24 cottages, 1 with FP. EP. Types of meals: Full bkfst and early coffee/tea. Dinner available. Beds: KQDT. Fax, copier, swimming, sauna and library on premises. Small meetings hosted. Antiquing, fishing, parks, shopping and water sports nearby.

Publicity: *Midwest Living, Gourmet Magazine.*

"Unforgettable."

Embarrass
D7

Finnish Heritage Homestead

4776 Waisanen Rd
Embarrass, MN 55732-8347
(218)984-3318 (800)863-6545

Circa 1901. This turn-of-the-century, Finnish-American log house offers outdoor recreation and family-style full breakfasts to visitors, who receive many personal touches, such as

bathrobes and slipper socks. Guests also may utilize the inn's relaxing Finnish sauna and enjoy badminton, boccie ball, croquet and horseshoes on the spacious grounds. There are flower and berry gardens, and a gazebo and gift shop are on the premises. Be sure to inquire about the availability of picnic lunches to take along on excursions to nearby historic and mining sites.

Innkeeper(s): Elaine Braginton & Buzz Schultz. $69. MC, VISA. 4 rooms. Breakfast included in rates. Types of meals: Full bkfst and early coffee/tea. Beds: QT. Turndown service and ceiling fan in room. VCR, gazebo, horseshoe, badminton and wood fired sauna on premises. Weddings and family reunions hosted. Antiquing, fishing, international Wolf Center, historic tours, snowmobiling, parks, shopping and downhill skiing nearby.

Kenyon
I6

Grandfather's Woods

3640 450th St
Kenyon, MN 55946-3626
(507)789-6414

Circa 1860. This 440-acre working farm boasts a handsome two-story Scandinavian clapboard home, and off in the woods, the original log cabin built six generations ago by the Langemo family. Abraham Lincoln personally endorsed the original homestead document displayed in the house. Old photos include one of Grandfather Jorgen next to a tiny tree in 1861. The same tree has

grown to giant proportions and now shades the entire house. An antique rocking chair, now in the parlor, is seen in an ancient photo of Great-grandmother Karen. The Solarium, one of the bedrooms, has a brass bed and wicker furni-

ture, and it looks out over the fishpond and garden to the fields and woods along the river. There are 65 acres of wooded trails on the property. Guests enjoy the farm's horses and sheep, and in springtime, the young lamb. The inn offers hay and sleigh rides, cross-country skiing, croquet, a large flower garden and a nine-hole golf course across from the hay field. A fancy farm breakfast may include homemade caramel rolls and oven eggs. It is halfway between Minneapolis/St. Paul and Rochester, Minn.

Innkeeper(s): Judy & George Langemo. $70-120. PC. 3 rooms, 2 with PB, 1 with FP and 1 suite. Breakfast and snacks/refreshments included in rates. Types of meals: Full bkfst, cont and early coffee/tea. Dinner, picnic lunch and lunch available. Beds: QDT. Ceiling fan in room. VCR, stables, bicycles, library and skiis on premises. Small meetings and family reunions hosted. Antiquing, fishing, golf, sleigh/hay rides, live theater, parks, shopping, downhill skiing, cross-country skiing, sporting events and water sports nearby.

Publicity: Rochester Post-Bulletin, Republican Eagle-Red Wing, Life & Leisure.

Lake City
I7

The Victorian B&B

620 S High St
Lake City, MN 55041-1757
(651)345-2167 (888)345-2167

Circa 1896. This Victorian stick-style was built by a wealthy local banker and landowner. Fine, carved woodwork and stained-glass windows are among the home's architectural features. All offer views of Lake Pepin. Antique furnishings deco-

rate the interior. The innkeepers are adding a guest house with two guest rooms. Lake Pepin's riverwalk is across the street from the B&B. Area attractions include skiing, shopping and hiking.

Innkeeper(s): Bernard & Ione Link. $75-150. PC. TAC10. 5 rooms with PB, 2 with FP. Breakfast and snacks/refreshments included in rates. Type of meal: Full bkfst. Beds: KQ. Ceiling fan in room. Air conditioning. VCR on premises. Antiquing, fishing, golf, parks, shopping, downhill skiing, cross-country skiing, tennis and water sports nearby.

"You've attended to every detail to make sure our stay was perfect. We'd come back in a heartbeat!"

Lutsen
D8

Lindgren's B&B on Lake Superior

5552 County Rd 35, PO Box 56
Lutsen, MN 55612-0056
(218)663-7450

Circa 1926. This '20s log home is in the Superior National Forest on the north shore of Lake Superior. The inn features massive stone fireplaces, a baby grand piano, wildlife decor and

a Finnish-style sauna. The living room has tongue-and-groove, Western knotty cedar wood paneling and seven-foot windows offering a view of the lake. The innkeeper's

homemade jams, freshly baked breads and entrees such as French Toast topped with homemade chokecherry syrup, eggs Benedict or Danish pancakes get the day off to a pleasant start. In addition to horseshoes and a bonfire pit, guests can gaze at the lake on a swinging love seat.

Innkeeper(s): Shirley Lindgren. $90-135. MC, VISA, PC. TAC10. 4 rooms with PB, 1 with FP. Breakfast included in rates. Types of meals: Full bkfst and early coffee/tea. Afternoon tea, snacks/refreshments and picnic lunch available. Beds: KDT. One room with two-person whirlpool in room. VCR, sauna, library, CD player, volleyball, horseshoes and piano on premises. Antiquing, bicycling, fishing, golf, hiking, horseback riding, fall colors, kayaking snowmobiling, canoeing, state parks nearby, live theater, parks, shopping, downhill skiing, cross-country skiing, tennis and water sports nearby.

Publicity: Brainerd Daily Dispatch, Duluth News-Tribune, Tempo, Midwest Living, Minnesota Monthly, Lake Superior, Country, Minneapolis-St. Paul.

Minneapolis   H6

Nan's B&B

2304 Fremont Ave S
Minneapolis, MN 55405-2645
(612)377-5118

Circa 1895. Guests at Nan's enjoy close access to downtown Minneapolis, including the Guthrie Theatre, shopping and restaurants. The Lake of the Isles with its scenic walking paths is just four blocks away, and a bus stop is just down the street. The late Victorian home is furnished with antiques and decorated in a country Victorian style. The innkeepers are happy to help guests plan their day-to-day activities.

Innkeeper(s): Nan & Jim Zosel. $50-60. MC, VISA, AX, DC, PC, TC. 3 rooms. Breakfast included in rates. Type of meal: Full bkfst. Beds: QD. Air conditioning. Antiquing, fishing, lakes, walking, biking, live theater, shopping, cross-country skiing and water sports nearby.

"I had a wonderful stay in Minneapolis, mostly due to the comfort and tranquility of Nan's B&B."

Monticello   H5

The Rand House

One Old Territorial Rd
Monticello, MN 55362
(612)295-6037 Fax:(612)295-6037

Circa 1884. Located in the Monticello Historic District on more than three secluded acres, this three-story Queen Anne country Victorian is in the National Register of Historic Places as one of the last remaining country estates of its kind in the region. The

grounds boast extensive gardens, wooded walking paths, a pond and fountains. There is a library and drawing room, and the winter parlor features

arched windows and a stone fireplace. A favorite guest room is The Turret with its clawfoot tub, tiled fireplace and an octagonal sitting area with views of the grounds and the city. Breakfast is served in the solarium, wraparound porch or in the dining room with linen, china, silver, flowers and candlelight. Specialties at breakfast include items such as fruit plate, freshly baked scones and a frittata or quiche with sausage. The inn is 40 minutes from downtown Minneapolis. The innkeepers won a state award for outstanding historic preservation.

Innkeeper(s): Duffy & Merrill Busch. $95-145. MC, VISA, AX, PC. TAC10. 4 rooms with PB, 3 with FP and 1 suite. Breakfast included in rates. Types of meals: Full gourmet bkfst, cont plus and early coffee/tea. Beds: KQ. Phone and turndown service in room. Central air. Fax and library on premises. Family reunions hosted. Antiquing, fishing, golf, outlet malls, live theater, parks, shopping, cross-country skiing, sporting events, tennis and water sports nearby.

"We're glad we discovered the Rand House and are looking forward to visiting again."

Nevis   E4

The Park Street Inn

106 Park St
Nevis, MN 56467-9704
(218)652-4500 (800)797-1778

Circa 1912. This late Victorian home was built by one of Minnesota's many Norwegian immigrants, a prominent businessman. He picked an ideal spot for the home, which overlooks Lake Belle Taine and sits across from a town park. The suite includes an all-season porch and a double whirlpool tub. The Grotto Room, a new addition, offers an oversize whirlpool and a waterfall. Oak lamposts light the foyer, and the front parlor is highlighted by a Mission oak fireplace.

Homemade fare such as waffles, pancakes, savory meats, egg dishes and French toast are served during the inn's daily country breakfast. Bicyclists will appreciate the close access to the Heartland Bike Trail, just half a block away.

Innkeeper(s): Irene & Len Hall. $70-125. MC, VISA, PC, TC. TAC10. 4 rooms with PB and 1 suite. Breakfast included in rates. MAP. Types of meals: Full bkfst and early coffee/tea. Picnic lunch available. Beds: KQD. VCR, spa, bicycles and library on premises. Small meetings and family reunions hosted. Amusement parks, antiquing, fishing, golf, parks, shopping, cross-country skiing and water sports nearby.

Pets allowed: By arrangement only.

"Our favorite respite in the Heartland, where the pace is slow, hospitality is great and food is wonderful."

New York Mills   F3

Whistle Stop Inn B&B

RR 1 Box 85
New York Mills, MN 56567-9704
(218)385-2223 (800)328-6315

Circa 1903. A choo-choo theme permeates the atmosphere at this signature Victorian home. Antiques and railroad memorabilia decorate guest rooms with names such as Great Northern or Burlington Northern. The Northern Pacific room includes a bath with a clawfoot tub. For something unusual, try a night in the beautifully restored 19th-century Pullman dining car. It is paneled in mahogany and features floral carpeting and

white curtains as well as a double whirlpool, TV, VCR and refrigerator. A caboose offers a queen-size Murphy bed and whirlpool. Freshly baked breads and seasonal fruit accompany the mouth-watering, homemade breakfasts.

Innkeeper(s): Roger & Jann Lee. $49-125. MC, VISA, AX, DS, PC. TAC10. 5 rooms with PB, 1 suite, 1 cottage and 1 conference room. Breakfast included in rates. Types of meals: Full bkfst, cont and early coffee/tea. Afternoon tea available. Beds: QD. Cable TV, phone, ceiling fan and microwave in room. Bicycles on premises. Weddings, small meetings, family reunions and seminars hosted. Antiquing, fishing, golf, snowmobiling trails & cultural center, parks, shopping, cross-country skiing and tennis nearby.

Red Wing
I6

The Candlelight Inn

818 W 3rd St
Red Wing, MN 55066-2205
(800)254-9194
E-mail: www.candlerw@rconnect.com
Web: www.candlelightinn-redwing.com

Circa 1877. Listed in the Minnesota historic register, this modified Queen Anne Victorian was built by a prominent Red Wing businessman. The interior woodwork of Candlelight Inn is an impressive sight. Butternut, cherry, oak and walnut combine throughout the house to create the rich parquet floors and stunning grand staircase. A crackling fire in the library welcomes guests and its leather furnishings and wide selection of books make this a great location for relaxation. The wraparound-screened porch offers comfortable wicker furnishings. Each of the guest rooms includes a fireplace, and three rooms also feature a whirlpool tub. Homemade scones, fresh peaches with custard sauce and wild rice quiche are some of the gourmet breakfast dishes. The Mississippi River town of Red Wing features many historic homes and buildings, as well as shops, restaurants and the restored Sheldon Theater. Hiking and biking trails are nearby, as well as Treasure Island Casino.
Historic Interest: River towns.

Innkeeper(s): Lynette and Zig Gudrais. $89-169. MC, VISA, AX, DS, PC, TC. 5 rooms with PB, 5 with FP. Breakfast and snacks/refreshments included in rates. Types of meals: Full bkfst, cont and early coffee/tea. Picnic lunch available. Beds: Q. Air conditioning. Library on premises. Small meetings hosted. Antiquing, bicycling, golf, hiking, live theater, museums, parks, shopping, downhill skiing, cross-country skiing, water sports and wineries nearby.

Saint Paul
H6

The Garden Gate B&B

925 Goodrich Ave
Saint Paul, MN 55105-3127
(612)227-8430 (800)967-2703 Fax:(612)225-9791

Circa 1907. One of the most striking of the city's Victoria Crossing neighborhood homes is this recently redecorated Prairie-style Victorian. The large duplex features guest rooms named Gladiolus, Rose and Delphinium, and the rooms are as lovely as they sound. A short stroll takes Garden Gate visitors to historic Summit Avenue and the shops, boutiques and restaurants on nearby Grand Avenue.

Historic Interest: St. Paul's Cathedral is one-and-one-half miles away, Governor's Mansion is two blocks away and the State Capitol is 2 miles away.

Innkeeper(s): Miles & Mary Conway. $55-75. MC, VISA, AX, DS, PC, TC. 4 rooms. Breakfast included in rates. Type of meal: Cont plus. Beds: QT. Massage available in room. Air conditioning. Swimming, tennis & yoga, restaurants, live theater, parks, shopping and cross-country skiing nearby.

"I couldn't have felt more at home!"

Sauk Centre
G4

Palmer House Hotel

228 Main St
Sauk Centre, MN 56378
(630)352-3431 (888)222-3431 Fax:(320)352-5602

Circa 1901. Stained-glass windows, antique furnishings and paneled ceilings are among the features of this hotel, located on the old main street of town. There is a pub with a fireplace and a pianist plays the baby grand in the lobby. Some rooms offer Jacuzzis. The inn's restaurant offers homemade soups, prime rib, salads and breads in a setting with white table cloths and candles.

$59. MC, VISA, AX, DC, CB, DS, PC, TC. 22 rooms with PB, 8 suites and 1 conference room. Breakfast included in rates. AP. Types of meals: Full bkfst and cont. Lunch available. Restaurant on premises. Beds: QDT. Cable TV and phone in room. Air conditioning. VCR, fax, copier and library on premises. Handicap access. Small meetings and family reunions hosted. Antiquing, fishing, golf, parks, shopping, cross-country skiing, tennis and water sports nearby.

Sherburn
J4

Four Columns Inn

668 140th St
Sherburn, MN 56171-9732
(507)764-8861

Circa 1884. This Greek Revival home rests on a 320-acre working farm, with 10 acres of flowers, trees and lawns surrounded by wrought iron and wood fences. The four guest

rooms are decorated with antiques. Rooms are further adorned with wicker, Tiffany lamps, stained-glass windows and decorative fireplaces. Guests can relax in the redwood hot tub or take a look at the greenhouse filled with flowers. For those celebrating a special occasion, try the Bridal Suite, which offers a rooftop deck with a view of the peaceful countryside. Hearty breakfasts are served either in the formal dining room, on the balcony, in the greenhouse, Victorian gazebo or perhaps in front of a crackling fire in the kitchen. There are music rooms with a player piano, phonographs, an antique pump organ and a jukebox. The inn is located two miles north of I-90 in between Chicago and the Black Hills. The inn also is close to Iowa's Lake Okoboji. Ask about the romantic getaway package.
Historic Interest: Lake Okoboji.

Innkeeper(s): Norman & Pennie Kittleson. $65-75. PC, TC. TAC10. 4 rooms with PB. Breakfast and afternoon tea included in rates. Types of meals: Full gourmet bkfst and early coffee/tea. Snacks/refreshments available. Beds: KQ. Phone, ceiling fan, balcony, widows walk and musical instruments in room. Air conditioning. Gazebo and deck on premises. Weddings, small meetings and family reunions hosted. Amusement parks, antiquing, fishing, Queen Excursion Boat, live theater, parks, shopping, downhill skiing, cross-country skiing and water sports nearby.

"I think I'm in heaven. This has been so enjoyable."

Stillwater H6

James A. Mulvey Residence Inn

622 W Churchill
Stillwater, MN 55082
(651)430-8008 (800)820-8008
E-mail: truettldem@aol.com
Web: www.jamesmulveyinn.com

Circa 1878. A charming river town is home to this Italianate-style inn, just a short distance from the Twin Cities, but far from the metro area in atmosphere. Visitors select from seven guest rooms, many decorated Victorian style. The three suites have Southwest, Art Deco or Country French themes, and there are double Jacuzzi tubs and fire-

places. The inn, just nine blocks from the St. Croix River, is a popular stop for couples celebrating anniversaries. Guests enjoy early coffee or tea service that precedes the full breakfasts. A handsome great room in the vine-covered Carriage House invites relaxation. Antiquing, fishing and skiing are nearby, and there are many picnic spots in the area.

Innkeeper(s): Truett & Jill Lawson. $99-199. MC, VISA, PC, TC. 7 rooms with PB, 7 with FP and 3 suites. Breakfast and afternoon tea included in rates. Types of meals: Full gourmet bkfst and early coffee/tea. Beds: QD. Seven double whirlpool Jacuzzi tubs in room. Air conditioning. Bicycles on premises. Small meetings and family reunions hosted. Antiquing, fishing, 30 minutes from Mall of America, live theater, parks, shopping, downhill skiing, cross-country skiing and water sports nearby.

Rivertown Inn

306 Olive St W
Stillwater, MN 55082-4932
(651)430-2955 (800)562-3632 Fax:(651)430-0034
E-mail: rivertown@rivertowninn.com
Web: www.rivertowninn.com

Circa 1882. This three-story Victorian, built by lumbermill owner John O'Brien, is the town's first bed & breakfast. Framed by an iron fence, the home has a wraparound veranda.

Each guest room has been deco-rated with care, but we suggest the honeymoon suite or Patricia's Room with its giant whirlpool and white iron bed. A burl-wood buffet in the din-ing room is laden each morning with home-baked breads and cakes. The St. Croix River is a short walk away.

Innkeeper(s): Chuck & Judy Dougherty. $89-169. MC, VISA, AX, DC, DS, PC, TC. TAC10. 8 rooms with PB, 5 with FP and 3 suites. Breakfast and snacks/refreshments included in rates. Types of meals: Full gourmet bkfst and early coffee/tea. Afternoon tea, catering service and room service available. Beds: QD. Ceiling fan and double whirlpool tubs in room. Air conditioning. Fax and copier on premises. Small meetings hosted. Amusement parks, antiquing, fishing, golf, live theater, parks, shopping, downhill skiing, cross-country skiing, sporting events, tennis and water sports nearby.

Publicity: *Country Magazine, Minneapolis Star Tribune, Pioneer Press.*

Wabasha I7

The Anderson House

333 Main St, PO Box 270
Wabasha, MN 55981-0262
(651)565-4524 (800)535-5467
E-mail: info@theandersonhouse.com
Web: theandersonhouse.com

Circa 1856. Said to be Minnesota's oldest continuously operat-ing hotel, the inn has been filled with high-back beds, marble-topped dressers and antiques. A filled cookie jar sits at the front desk, and guests can choose an actual kitty (complete with litter box and cat food) to spend the night in their rooms. Breakfast is extra, but the giant cinnamon rolls and omelets with red flannel hash are worth it. There's no charge for the warming brick if your feet are cold.

$50-145. MC, VISA, AX, DS, PC, TC. 51 rooms with PB. Restaurant on premises. Beds: QD. TV in room. Fax and copier on premises. Weddings, small meetings and seminars hosted. Fishing, golf, house boat rental, snow-mobiling, eagle watching, downhill skiing and cross-country skiing nearby.

Mississippi

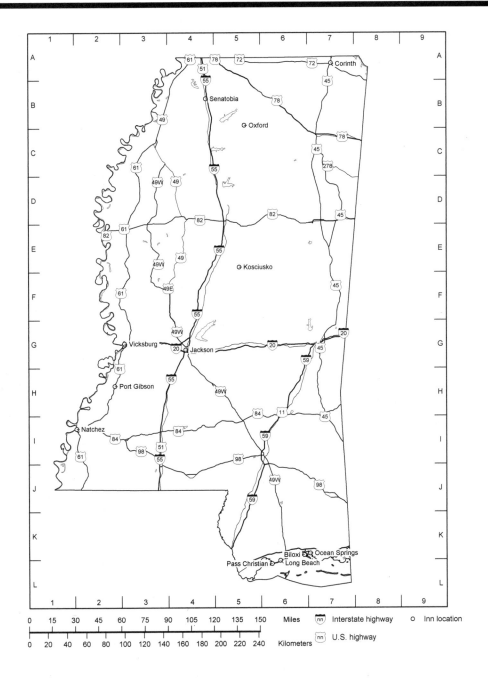

	1	2	3	4	5	6	7	8	9

A — 61, 78, 72, 72, Corinth, 51, 45, 55

B — Senatobia, 78, 49, Oxford, 78

C — 45, 61, 278, 49W, 49, 55

D — 82, 82, 61, 45

E — 82, 49W, 49, 55, Kosciusko, 45

F — 61, 49E, 55, 45

G — 49W, 20, 20, 20, Vicksburg, 20, Jackson, 45, 59

H — 61, 55, Port Gibson, 49W, 84, 11, 45

I — Natchez, 84, 84, 59, 98, 51, 98

J — 61, 55, 49W, 98, 59

K — Biloxi, Ocean Springs, Pass Christian, Long Beach

| | 0 | 15 | 30 | 45 | 60 | 75 | 90 | 105 | 120 | 135 | 150 | Miles |
| | 0 | 20 | 40 | 60 | 80 | 100 | 120 | 140 | 160 | 180 | 200 | 220 | 240 | Kilometers |

nn — Interstate highway   o — Inn location

nn — U.S. highway

Biloxi
K6

Green Oaks

580 Beach Blvd
Biloxi, MS 39530
(228)436-6257 (800)436-6257 Fax:(228)436-6225

Circa 1826. The romantic guest rooms are a highlight of any stay at Green Oaks, a restored antebellum plantation home overlooking the Gulf of Mexico. Built in the 1820s, Green Oaks is the oldest remaining beachfront home on the Gulf Coast. Antique beds add drama to the guest rooms. Rooms feature special touches such as a fireplace, clawfoot tub, exposed brick walls or a chandelier original to the home. There are three rooms available in the guest cottage, as well. Guests are treated to a gourmet breakfast. One specialty of the house is eggs Diaz, which includes grits topped with a poached egg, lump crabmeat and hollandaise sauce. Green Oaks is located in a Biloxi historic district, minutes from shops and restaurants. The innkeepers can help plan dinner reservations or treks to local casinos.

Historic Interest: Church of the Redeemer-2 miles, Beauvior.

Innkeeper(s): Lydia Pena & Jennifer Diaz. $125-155. MC, VISA, AX, DS, TC. TAC10. 8 rooms with PB, 1 with FP and 1 suite. Breakfast and afternoon tea included in rates. Type of meal: Early coffee/tea. Beds: QD. Cable TV, phone, turndown service and ceiling fan in room. Air conditioning. Fax on premises. Small meetings hosted. Antiquing, art galleries, beaches, fishing, golf, live theater, museums, parks and water sports nearby.

Old Santini House B&B

964 Beach Blvd
Biloxi, MS 39530-3740
(228)436-4078 (800)686-1146 Fax:(228)436-4078

Circa 1837. This pre-Civil War home is named not for its first resident, but for the residents that lived there for the longest time. The Santini family lived in this historic home for more

than a century. Each room is decorated with a different theme. One room features a Western motif, one is African in style and the third is decorated with an Oriental flair. In addition to the guest rooms in the main house, the innkeepers also offer a private honeymoon cottage with a Jacuzzi tub, wet bar and king-size bed. A full, Southern-style breakfast is served in the formal dining room on a table set with fine china, sterling silver and crystal. Among the nearby attractions is Jefferson Davis' home, Beauvoir. Charter boats, sunset cruises, walking tours, a lighthouse, NASA and outlet shops are other options.

Historic Interest: Biloxi Lighthouse (4 miles), Jeff Davis' last home (5 miles).

Innkeeper(s): James A & Patricia S Dunay. $80-175. MC, VISA, AX, DS, TC. TAC5. 4 rooms, 3 with PB, 1 with FP, 1 cottage and 1 conference room. Breakfast and afternoon tea included in rates. Types of meals: Full bkfst and early coffee/tea. Beds: KD. Cable TV, phone and turndown service in room. Air conditioning. Spa, bicycles and BBQ grills and picnic area on premises. Weddings, small meetings and family reunions hosted. Amusement parks, antiquing, art galleries, beaches, bicycling, canoeing/kayaking, fishing, golf, live theater, museums, parks, shopping, sporting events and water sports nearby.

Corinth
A7

The Generals' Quarters B&B Inn

924 Fillmore St
Corinth, MS 38834-4125
(601)286-3325 Fax:(601)287-8188

Circa 1872. History buffs will enjoy this inn, located 22 miles from Shiloh National Military Park and in the historic district of Corinth, a Civil War village. Visitors to this Queen Anne Victorian, with its quiet, tree-lined lot, enjoy a full breakfast and grounds decorated with a pond and flowers. Three guest rooms and two suites are available. Fort Robinette and Corinth National

Cemetery are nearby. The inn is within walking distance to shops, museums, historic sites, restaurants and more.

Innkeeper(s): Charlotte Brandt & Luke Doehner. $75-100. MC, VISA, DS, TC. 5 rooms with PB, 4 with FP, 2 suites and 1 conference room. Breakfast and snacks/refreshments included in rates. Types of meals: Full gourmet bkfst and early coffee/tea. Dinner, picnic lunch, gourmet lunch, banquet service, catering service and room service available. Restaurant on premises. Beds: KQDT. Cable TV, phone, turndown service, ceiling fan, VCR and room service in room. Air conditioning. Fax, bicycles and private dining on premises. Handicap access. Weddings, small meetings, family reunions and seminars hosted. Antiquing, fishing, historical tours, hiking and biking trails, live theater, parks, shopping and water sports nearby.

"Ranks with the best, five stars. You have thought of many comforts."

Bed & Breakfast at Robbins Nest

1523 E Shiloh Rd
Corinth, MS 38834-3632
(662)286-3109 Fax:(662)286-0018

Circa 1869. This gracious columned plantation-style mansion rests on four acres of grounds with tall oaks and a pink, red and white hedge of dogwood. Azaleas bloom on the inn's grounds in spring. A walnut staircase and pine floors are among the features of the house. The formal dining room or the back porch is the setting for hearty Southern breakfasts. Afternoon refreshments also are included in the rates.

Innkeeper(s): Anne & Tony Whyte. $80-90. MC, VISA, PC, TC. 3 rooms with PB and 1 suite. Breakfast and snacks/refreshments included in rates. Type of meal: Full gourmet bkfst. Beds: QDT. Cable TV, phone, turndown service and ceiling fan in room. Air conditioning. VCR on premises. Weddings and small meetings hosted. Antiquing, fishing, golf, live theater, parks, shopping, tennis and water sports nearby.

"We felt like we were visiting a favorite cousin."

Jackson   G4

Fairview Inn

734 Fairview St
Jackson, MS 39202-1624
(601)948-3429 (888)948-1908 Fax:(601)948-1203
E-mail: fairview@fairviewinn
Web: www.fairviewinn.com

Circa 1908. There's little question why this magnificent
Colonial Revival mansion has been chosen as one of the United
States' premiere inns. Designed by an associate of Frank Lloyd
Wright, the home boasts unforgettable polished hardwood
floors, a beautiful marble floor, fine furnishings and
tasteful decor. The
innkeepers, Carol and
William Simmons,
pamper guests with a
plentiful cook-to-order
breakfast, fresh flowers
and have hosted many a wedding reception and party. History
buffs will appreciate William's knowledge of Mississippi's past.
There are helpful business amenities here, including in-room
dataports. The inn has been hailed for its hospitality and cuisine
by Country Inns magazine and the James Beard Foundation.

Historic Interest: The home, one of few of its kind remaining in Jackson, is
listed in the National Register. The Old Capitol Museum is just over a mile
from Fairview. Historic Manship House is only half a mile, and an art museum and agriculture and forestry museum are two miles away.

Innkeeper(s): Carol & William Simmons. $115-165. MC, VISA, AX, DS, PC,
TC. TAC10. 8 rooms with PB, 5 suites and 4 conference rooms. Breakfast
included in rates. EP. Types of meals: Full gourmet bkfst, cont and early cof-
fee/tea. Gourmet dinner, snacks/refreshments, gourmet lunch, banquet service
and catering service available. Beds: KQ. Cable TV, phone and turndown service in room. Air conditioning. VCR, fax, copier, library, voice mail and dataports on premises. Handicap access. Weddings, small meetings, family
reunions and seminars hosted. French spoken. Antiquing, live theater, parks,
shopping, sporting events and tennis nearby.

"Elegant and comfortable."

Millsaps-Buie House

628 N State St
Jackson, MS 39202-3303
(601)352-0221 (800)784-0221 Fax:(601)352-0221
E-mail: info@millsapsbuiehouse.com
Web: millsapsbuiehouse.com

Circa 1888. Major Millsaps, founder of Millsaps College, built
this stately mansion more than 100 years ago. Today the house
remains in the family. A handsome, columned entrance, bays
and gables are features of
the house decorated by
Berle Smith, designer for
Mississippi's governor's
mansion. The parlor features
a grand piano. The guest
rooms are appointed in
antiques and canopied beds.

Historic Interest: Listed in the National Register.

Innkeeper(s): Judy Fenter, Vicki Harrell & Harriet Brewer. $100-170. MC, VISA,
AX, DC, DS. 11 rooms with PB and 1 conference room. Type of meal: Full bkfst.
Beds: KQ. Cable TV and turndown service in room. Fax, copier and off-street
parking on premises. Handicap access. Fitness center and live theater nearby.

Publicity: *New York Times, Jackson Clarion Ledger, Mississippi Magazine,
Travel & Leisure.*

Kosciusko   E5

The Redbud Inn

121 N Wells St
Kosciusko, MS 39090-3647
(601)289-5086 (800)379-5086 Fax:(601)289-5086

Circa 1884. Kosciusko, the birthplace of Oprah Winfrey, is
also home to this striking Queen Anne Victorian inn, which
boasts a long and distinguished history as a traveler's haven.
Beautiful woodwork and
an impressive square
staircase highlight the
inn's interior, and its
architectural details have
made it a well-known
local landmark. Five
guest rooms are available,
all filled with antiques.
An antique shop/tea
room is on the premises.

Innkeeper(s): Maggie Garrett & Ruth Aldridge. $70-100. MC, VISA, AX, DS,
PC, TC. TAC10. 5 rooms, 4 with PB, 1 suite and 1 conference room.
Breakfast and afternoon tea included in rates. Types of meals: Full bkfst and
early coffee/tea. Gourmet dinner, gourmet lunch, banquet service and catering
service available. Restaurant on premises. Beds: QT. Cable TV, phone, turndown service, ceiling fan and clock in room. Air conditioning. Fax on premises. Handicap access. Weddings, small meetings and family reunions hosted.
French spoken. Antiquing, parks and sporting events nearby.

Long Beach   L6

Red Creek Inn, Vineyard & Racing Stable

7416 Red Creek Rd
Long Beach, MS 39560-8804
(228)452-3080 (800)729-9670 Fax:(228)452-4450
E-mail: info@redcreekinn.com
Web: redcreekinn.com

Circa 1899. This inn was built in the raised French cottage-
style by a retired Italian sea captain, who wished to entice his
bride to move from her parents' home in New Orleans. There
are two swings on the 64-
foot front porch and one
swing that hangs from a 300-
year-old oak tree. Magnolias
and ancient live oaks, some
registered with the Live Oak
Society of the Louisiana
Garden Club, dot 11 acres.
The inn features a parlor, six fireplaces, ceiling fans and
antiques, including a Victorian organ, wooden radios and a
Victrola. The inn's suite includes a Jacuzzi tub.

Historic Interest: The inn is near Beauvoir, Jefferson Davis' last home.

Innkeeper(s): Karl &. $49-134. PC. TAC10. 6 rooms, 5 with PB, 1 with FP,
1 suite and 1 conference room. Breakfast included in rates. Types of meals:
Cont plus and early coffee/tea. Beds: QDT. TV in room. Air conditioning. VCR,
fax, copier and library on premises. Weddings, small meetings, family
reunions and seminars hosted. Spanish spoken. Amusement parks, antiquing,
fishing, golf, casinos, live theater, parks, shopping and water sports nearby.

Publicity: *Jackson Daily News, Innviews, TV Channel 13, Mississippi ETV,
Men's Journal, The Bridal Directory.*

*"We loved waking up here on these misty spring mornings. The Old
South is here."*

Natchez   *12*

The Briars Inn & Garden

PO Box 1245
Natchez, MS 39121-1245
(601)446-9654 (800)634-1818 Fax:(601)445-6037
E-mail: thebriarsinn@bkbank.com
Web: www.thebriarsinn.com

Circa 1814. Set on 19 wooded and landscaped acres overlooking the Mississippi River, the Briars is most noted for having been the family home of Varina Howell where she married Jefferson

Davis in 1845. One can only imagine the romance evoked from the simple ceremony in the parlor in front of the carved wood Adam-style mantel. Everything about this elegant and sophisticated Southern Planter-style home brings to life glorious traditions of the Old South, from the 48-foot drawing room with its twin staircases, five Palladian arches and gallery to the lush gardens with more than 1,000 azaleas and camellias. The current owners are interior designers, which is evident in their fine use of fabrics, wall coverings, tastefully appointed guest rooms decorated in period antiques, Oriental rugs and selected art. A gourmet breakfast is served each morning.

Innkeeper(s): R E Canon-Newton Wilds. $145-160. MC, VISA, AX, PC, TC. TAC10. 16 rooms with PB, 6 with FP, 3 suites, 1 cottage and 1 conference room. Breakfast included in rates. Types of meals: Full gourmet bkfst and early coffee/tea. Beds: KQT. Cable TV, phone, turndown service and ceiling fan in room. Central air. Fax, copier and swimming on premises. Handicap access. Family reunions hosted. Antiquing, bicycling, fishing, golf, hiking, museums, parks, shopping, tennis and wineries nearby.

"We so enjoyed the splendor of your beautiful gardens. Breakfast was superb and the service outstanding! Thanks!"

Dunleith

84 Homochitto St
Natchez, MS 39120-3996
(601)446-8500 (800)433-2445

Circa 1856. This Greek Revival plantation house is listed as a National Historic Landmark. During the Civil War, the Davis family raised thoroughbred horses here, and the story goes that when they heard Union officers were coming to take their horses, they hid their favorites in the cellar under the dining room. The officers ate dinner and heard nothing so the horses were saved. Rare French Zuber mural wallpaper decorates the dining room.

Innkeeper(s): Nancy Gibbs. $95-140. MC, VISA, DS, TC. 11 rooms with PB, 11 with FP and 1 conference room. Breakfast included in rates. Type of meal: Full bkfst. Beds: QDT. Cable TV and phone in room. Air conditioning. Antiquing nearby.

Publicity: *Southern Accents, Unique Homes, Good Housekeeping, Country Inns.*

"The accommodations at the mansion were wonderful. Southern hospitality is indeed charming and memorable!"

Linden

1 Linden Pl
Natchez, MS 39120-4077
(601)445-5472 (800)254-6336 Fax:(601)442-7548

Circa 1800. Mrs. Jane Gustine-Connor purchased this elegant white Federal plantation home in 1849, and it has remained in her family for six generations. Nestled on seven wooded acres, the inn boasts one of the finest collections of Federal antique furnishings in the South. The stately dining room contains an original Hepplewhite banquet table, set with many pieces of family coin silver and heirloom china. Three Havell editions of John James Audubon's bird prints are displayed on the walls. Throughout the years, the inn has served as a respite for famous Mississippi statesmen, including the wife of Senator Percy Quinn. Each of the seven guest rooms features canopy beds and authentic Federal antiques. A full Southern breakfast is included in the rates. The Linden is on the Spring and Fall Pilgrimages.

Historic Interest: The inn is in the National Register.

Innkeeper(s): Jeanette Feltus. $90-120. PC, TC. TAC10. 7 rooms with PB. Breakfast included in rates. Types of meals: Full gourmet bkfst and early coffee/tea. Beds: KQDT. Ceiling fan in room. Air conditioning. Fax, copier, library and TV on back gallery on premises. Handicap access. Antiquing, fishing, golf, live theater, parks, shopping, tennis and water sports nearby.

Monmouth Plantation

36 Melrose Ave
Natchez, MS 39120-4005
(601)442-5852 (800)828-4531 Fax:(604)446-7762
E-mail: luxury@monmouthplantation.com
Web: www.monmouthplantation.com

Circa 1818. Monmouth was the home of General Quitman who became acting Governor of Mexico, Governor of Mississippi, and a U.S. Congressman. In the National Historic Landmark, the inn features antique four-poster and canopy beds, turndown service and an evening cocktail hour. Guests Jefferson Davis and Henry Clay enjoyed the same acres of gardens, pond and walking paths available today. Elegant, five-course Southern dinners are served in the beautifully appointed dining room and parlors.

Innkeeper(s): Ron & Lani Riches. $155-375. MC, VISA, AX, DC, CB, DS, PC, TC. 31 rooms with PB, 18 with FP, 16 suites, 6 cottages and 1 conference room. Breakfast included in rates. Types of meals: Full bkfst and early coffee/tea. Dinner available. Restaurant on premises. Beds: KQDT. Cable TV and turndown service in room. Air conditioning. Fax and copier on premises. Weddings, small meetings, family reunions and seminars hosted. French and German spoken. Antiquing and shopping nearby.

"The best historical inn we have stayed at anywhere."

Oakland Plantation

1124 Lower Woodville Rd
Natchez, MS 39120-8132
(601)445-5101 (800)824-0355 Fax:(601)442-5182

Circa 1785. Andrew Jackson courted his future wife, Rachel Robards, at this gracious 18th-century home. This working cattle plantation includes nature trails and a game preserve, fishing ponds, a tennis court and canoeing. Rooms are filled with antiques, and the innkeepers provide guests with a tour of the main home and plantation. They also will arrange tours of Natchez.

Historic Interest: The historic mansions of Natchez are all within 10 miles of the inn.

Innkeeper(s): Jean & Andy Peabody. $70-80. MC, VISA, AX, TC. TAC10. 3 rooms, 2 with PB, 3 with FP and 1 conference room. Breakfast included in rates. AP. Type of meal: Full bkfst. Beds: KT. Air conditioning. Tennis on premises. Small meetings hosted. Antiquing, fishing, touring Natchez Mansions, live theater, parks and water sports nearby.

"Best kept secret in Natchez! Just great!"

Ocean Springs   K7

Shadowlawn B&B

112 A Shearwater Dr
Ocean Springs, MS 39564
(228)875-6945 Fax:(228)875-6595

Circa 1907. A canopy of trees shades the long drive that leads up to Shadowlawn. The home rests on the edge of the Mississippi Sound. Innkeeper Nancy Wilson's grandparents once owned this turn-of-the-century home. A screened-in porch affords a view of the grounds and water and offers a great place to relax. Antiques and traditional furnishings decorate the home's interior. The full breakfasts often include Southern items such as grits and homemade biscuits.

Innkeeper(s): Bill & Nancy Wilson. $100-125. MC, VISA, PC, TC. TAC10. 4 rooms with PB and 1 conference room. Breakfast and afternoon tea included in rates. Types of meals: Full bkfst and early coffee/tea. Picnic lunch available. Beds: QT. Cable TV, ceiling fan and VCR in room. Air conditioning. Fax, copier and library on premises. Weddings, small meetings, family reunions and seminars hosted. Antiquing, fishing, golf, gambling casinos, live theater, parks, shopping, sporting events, tennis and water sports nearby.

Oxford   B5

Oliver-Britt House

512 Van Buren Ave
Oxford, MS 38655-3838
(601)234-8043

Circa 1905. White columns and a picturesque veranda highlight the exterior of this Greek Revival inn shaded by trees. English country comfort is the emphasis in the interior, which includes a collection of antiques. On weekends, guests are treated to a Southern-style breakfast with all the trimmings. A travel service is located on the premises.

Innkeeper(s): Glynn Oliver & Mary Ann Britt. $55-75. MC, VISA, AX, DS, TC. 5 rooms with PB. Breakfast included in rates. Meals: Full bkfst and early coffee/tea. Banquet service and catering service available. Beds: KQ. Cable TV and ceiling fan in room. Air conditioning. Weddings, small meetings, family reunions and seminars hosted. Antiquing, parks, shopping and sporting events nearby. Pets Allowed.

Pass Christian   L6

Inn At The Pass

125 E Scenic Dr
Pass Christian, MS 39571-4415
(228)452-0333 (800)217-2588 Fax:(228)452-0449
E-mail: innatpas@aol.com
Web: www.innatthepass.com

Circa 1885. Listed in the National Register, this Victorian is adorned by a veranda where guests can relax and catch a tranquil breeze wafting off the Mississippi Gulf Coast. Five of the rooms are located in the main house, but there is also a secluded cot-

tage out back. The décor is Victorian in style, but the rooms include modern amenities such as in-room coffee makers, CD players and televisions with VCRs. On the weekends, a full, Southern-style breakfast is served. A beach resort town for more than a century, Pass Christian and its surrounding area offers a variety of activities, including water sports, fishing and casinos.

Historic Interest: Beauvoir (Jefferson Davis' home).

Innkeeper(s): Phyllis Hines & Mimi Smith. $85-115. MC, VISA, AX, DS, PC, TC. TAC10. 6 rooms, 5 with PB, 3 with FP and 1 cottage. Breakfast included in rates. Types of meals: Full bkfst, cont plus, veg bkfst and early coffee/tea. Beds: QDT. Cable TV, phone, ceiling fan and VCR in room. Central air. Fax, copier, spa and bicycles on premises. Weddings, small meetings, family reunions and seminars hosted. Amusement parks, antiquing, art galleries, beaches, bicycling, fishing, golf, hiking, horseback riding, live theater, museums, parks, shopping, sporting events, tennis and water sports nearby.

Port Gibson   H2

Oak Square Plantation

1207 Church St
Port Gibson, MS 39150-2609
(601)437-4350 (800)729-0240 Fax:(601)437-5768

Circa 1850. Six 22-foot-tall fluted Corinthian columns support the front gallery of this 30-room Greek Revival plantation. The owners furnished the mansion with 18th- and 19th-century Mississippi heirloom antiques and the guest rooms offer beautiful canopy beds. The parlor holds a carved rosewood Victorian suite, original family documents and a collection of Civil War memorabilia. A hearty southern breakfast is served. Enormous oaks and magnolia trees grace the grounds and the innkeeper offers tours of the mansion. The inn holds a four-diamond award.

Historic Interest: Listed in the National Register.

Innkeeper(s): Ms. William D. Lum. $95-125. MC, VISA, AX, DS, PC, TC. 10 rooms with PB. Breakfast included in rates. Type of meal: Full bkfst. Beds: QT. Cable TV, phone and turndown service in room. Air conditioning. VCR and fax on premises. State park, Civil War battlefields and museum nearby.

Senatobia   B4

Spahn House B&B

401 College St
Senatobia, MS 38668-2128
(601)562-9853 (800)400-9853 Fax:(601)562-8160
E-mail: spahn@gmi.net
Web: www.spahnhouse.com

Circa 1904. Originally built by a cotton and cattle baron, this 5,000-square-foot Neoclassical house sits on two acres and is listed in the National Register. Professionally decorated, it features fine antiques and luxuriously furnished rooms with elegant bed linens and Jacuzzi tubs. Private candlelight dinners are available by advance request. Breakfasts feature gourmet cuisine as the inn also manages a full-time catering business. (Guests sometimes are invited to sample food in

the kitchen before it makes its way to local parties and events.) Memphis is 30 minutes north.

Historic Interest: Elvis Presley's Graceland, Sun Studio, Clarksdale's Delta Blues Museum.

Innkeeper(s): Daughn & Joe Spahn. $65-150. MC, VISA, AX, DS, PC, TC. TAC10. 4 rooms with PB and 5 conference rooms. Breakfast included in rates. Type of meal: Full bkfst. Catering service available. Beds: Q. Cable TV, phone, ceiling fan and abundant toiletries in room. Air conditioning. VCR, fax, library and full catering staff/floral supply on premises. Weddings, small meetings, family reunions and seminars hosted. Limited French, German and Spanish spoken. Amusement parks, antiquing, fishing, hiking, wetlands, live theater, parks, shopping, sporting events and water sports nearby.

"I hope everyone gets to experience that type of Southern hospitality just once in their lifetime."

Vicksburg   G3

Anchuca

1010 First East St
Vicksburg, MS 39180-2513
(601)661-0111 (888)686-0111

Circa 1832. This early Greek Revival mansion rises resplendently above the brick-paved streets of Vicksburg. It houses magnificent period antiques and artifacts. Confederate President Jefferson Davis once addressed the townspeople from the balcony while his brother was living in the home after the Civil War. The turn-of-the-century guest cottage has been transformed into an enchanting hideaway and rooms in the mansion are appointed with formal decor and four-poster beds. A swimming pool and Jacuzzi are modern amenities.

Historic Interest: Vicksburg National Military Park (10 minutes), Old Courthouse Museum (2 blocks), Cairo Museum (one-half mile).

$80-140. MC, VISA, PC. 7 rooms with PB. Breakfast included in rates. Type of meal: Full bkfst. Beds: QD. Cable TV and turndown service in room. Air conditioning. Swimming and library on premises. Small meetings, family reunions and seminars hosted. Antiquing, fishing, golf, parks, shopping, sporting events and tennis nearby.

"The 'Southern Hospitality' will not be forgotten. The best Southern breakfast in town."

Annabelle

501 Speed St
Vicksburg, MS 39180-4065
(601)638-2000 (800)791-2000 Fax:(601)636-5054
E-mail: annabelle@vicksburg.com
Web: www.annabellebnb.com

Circa 1868. From the outside, Annabelle looks like a friendly mix of Victorian and Italianate architecture set on an unassuming lawn of magnolias and pecan trees. It is the gracious interior and hospitality that has earned this bed & breakfast consistently high ratings. Walls are painted in deep, rich hues, highlighting the polished wood floors, Oriental rugs and beautiful antiques. Some of the furnishings are family  heirlooms, and some rooms include a whirlpool tub. Innkeepers George and Carolyn Mayer spent many years in the restaurant business and offer delicious Southern fare during the morning meal. Carolyn hails from New Orleans and George, a native of

Moravia, speaks German, Portuguese and some Spanish.

Historic Interest: Antebellum homes and civil war history sites.

Innkeeper(s): Carolyn & George Mayer. $90-150. MC, VISA, AX, DC, CB, DS, PC, TC. TAC10. 8 rooms with PB, 2 with FP, 1 suite and 1 cottage. Breakfast and afternoon tea included in rates. Types of meals: Full gourmet bkfst and early coffee/tea. Beds: KQ. Cable TV, phone and turndown service in room. Air conditioning. Fax, swimming and library on premises. Family reunions hosted. German and Portuguese spoken. Amusement parks, antiquing, fishing, civil war historic sites, casinos, antebellum homes, live theater, parks, shopping and water sports nearby.

Pets allowed: Small.

"You have a beautiful home. The history and decor really give the place flavor."

Cedar Grove Mansion Inn

2200 Oak St
Vicksburg, MS 39180-4008
(601)636-1000 (800)862-1300 Fax:(601)634-6126

Circa 1840. It's easy to relive "Gone With the Wind" at this grand antebellum estate built by John Klein as a wedding present for his bride. Visitors sip mint juleps and watch gas chandeliers flicker in the finely appointed parlors. Many rooms contain their original furnishings. Although Cedar Grove survived the Civil War, a Union cannonball is still lodged in the parlor wall. There is a magnificent view of the Mississippi from the terrace and front gallery. Four acres of gardens include fountains and gazebos. There is a bar, and the inn's restaurant opens each evening at 6 p.m, except on Mondays.

Historic Interest: National Military Park (5 miles) and museums.

$95-185. MC, VISA, AX, DS, TC. TAC10. 29 rooms with PB, 3 with FP, 11 suites, 8 cottages and 4 conference rooms. Breakfast included in rates. Type of meal: Full bkfst. Gourmet dinner, banquet service and room service available. Restaurant on premises. Beds: KQDT. Cable TV, phone and turndown service in room. Air conditioning. Fax, copier, swimming, bicycles, tennis and library on premises. Handicap access. Weddings, small meetings and family reunions hosted. Amusement parks, antiquing, fishing, casino river boat gaming, live theater, parks, shopping and water sports nearby.

"Love at first sight would be the best way to describe my feelings for your home and the staff."

Stained Glass Manor - Oak Hall

2430 Drummond St
Vicksburg, MS 39180-4114
(601)638-8893 Fax:(601)636-3055

Circa 1902. Billed by the innkeepers as "Vicksburg's historic Vick inn," this restored, Mission-style manor boasts 40 stained-glass windows, original woodwork and light fixtures. Period furnishings create a Victorian flavor. George Washington Maher, who employed a young draftsman named Frank Lloyd Wright, probably designed the home, which was built from 1902 to 1908. Lewis J. Millet did the art for 36 of the stained-glass panels. The home's first owner, Fannie Vick Willis Johnson, was a descendent of the first Vick in Vicksburg. All but one guest room has a fireplace, and all are richly appointed with antiques, reproductions and Oriental rugs. "New Orleans" breakfasts begin with cafe au lait, freshly baked bread, Quiche Lorraine and other treats.

Innkeeper(s): Bill & Shirley Smollen. $85-185. MC, VISA, DS, TC. TAC10. 6 rooms, 4 with PB, 5 with FP, 1 suite, 1 cottage and 3 conference rooms. Breakfast included in rates. Meals: Full gourmet bkfst and early coffee/tea. Beds: KQDT. Cable TV in room. Air conditioning. VCR, fax & library on premises. Weddings, small meetings, family reunions and seminars hosted. Antiquing, fishing, home tours, historic sites, live theater, parks, shopping & water sports nearby.

Pets allowed: If kept under control.

Missouri

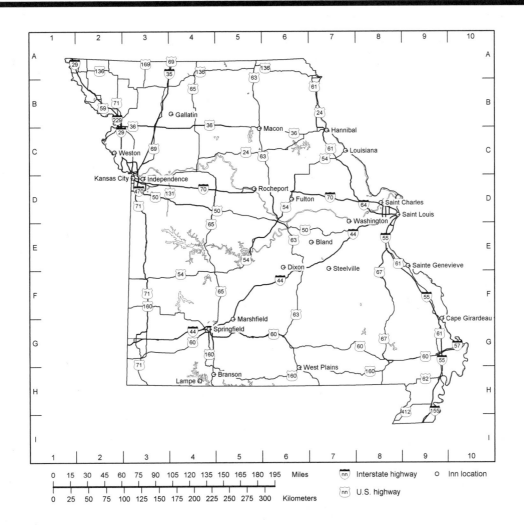

Scale:
Miles: 0 15 30 45 60 75 90 105 120 135 150 165 180 195
Kilometers: 0 25 50 75 100 125 150 175 200 225 250 275 300

Interstate highway
U.S. highway
Inn location

Bland E7

Caverly Farm & Orchard B&B

100 Cedar Ridge Rd
Bland, MO 65014
(573)646-3732 Fax:(573)646-5274

Circa 1850. Built prior to the Civil War, this farmhouse has been renovated completely. The innkeepers preserved many original features, and to keep the home authentic, they used original as accents within the home.

Guest rooms are decorated in Colonial style and include family antiques. Take a stroll around the inn's 50-plus acres, and you'll find woods, a pond, a variety of birds and perhaps a deer or two. Breakfasts include items such as farm-fresh cheesy eggs with chives, Canadian bacon, fresh fruit and homemade breads served with homemade preserves and jams. The home is within an hour's drive of antique shops, craft stores, farm auctions, wineries and the state capital, Jefferson City. Hermann, a historic town about 45 miles away, is an interesting place to visit, especially during its famous Oktoberfest.
Historic Interest: State Capital (43 miles), Wineries, Several 1850-1900 stone farmhouses.
Innkeeper(s): David & Nancy Caverly. $45-50. PC, TC. 3 rooms with PB. Breakfast included in rates. Types of meals: Full bkfst, country bkfst, veg bkfst and early coffee/tea. Beds: QDT. Ceiling fan in room. Central air. VCR and library on premises. Antiquing, canoeing/kayaking, fishing, golf, hiking, shopping and wineries nearby.

Branson H4

Branson Historic Hotel B&B Inn

214 W Main St
Branson, MO 65616-2724
(417)335-6104

Circa 1903. A picket fence frames the Branson Hotel, a Four Square style Victorian and a Branson Historic Landmark. Adirondack chairs fill the fieldstone veranda and the front balcony, affording guests the pleasure of visiting and enjoying the view. As Branson's oldest commercial structure,

important gatherings here played a significant part in the history of Branson, and the novel "Shepherd of the Hills" was written here. Because the innkeepers are Branson natives, they can let you in on all the local lore and their favorite scenic places. A harvest table in the glass-enclosed dining room is laden with hearty breakfast offerings including strata, potatoes, corn muffins or apple-walnut muffins.
Historic Interest: Lake Taneycomo and historic downtown Branson.
Innkeeper(s): Opal Kelly & Teri Murguia. $75-105. MC, VISA, AX, TC. TAC10. 8 rooms with PB. Breakfast, afternoon tea and snacks/refreshments included in rates. Type of meal: Early coffee/tea. Beds: KQ. Cable TV, phone, turndown service, ceiling fan and robes in room. Central air. Guest refrigerator on premises. Family reunions hosted. Antiquing, art galleries, bicycling, canoeing/kayaking, fishing, golf, hiking, horseback riding, live theater, parks, shopping, water sports and wineries nearby.

Branson House

120 North 4th St
Branson, MO 65616
(417)334-0959

Circa 1923. A landscape architect for the Missouri state park system, A. L. Drumeller, built this stone and wood home, surrounding it with fieldstone walls, country flower gardens and orchards. Exposed-beam ceilings, built-in glass cabinets and pine woodwork add to the inn's English country decor. From its hillside location, the veranda overlooks the town and bluffs of Lake Taneycomo. Sherry is served in the late afternoon.
Innkeeper(s): Sylvia Voyce. $65-90. 6 rooms with PB. Type of meal: Full bkfst. Beds: KQDT. TV in room.

Cape Girardeau G9

Bellevue B&B

312 Bellevue St
Cape Girardeau, MO 63701-7233
(573)335-3302 (800)768-6822 Fax:(573)335-6204

Circa 1891. Within three blocks of Mississippi River front Park, this Queen Anne Victorian with gables and bay windows is in the local historic register. The house is painted deep hunter green with taupe and cranberry trim, emphasizing the historic craftsmanship of its gables, bay windows, balustrades, cornices and stained glass windows. A glider and two wicker rocking chairs sit on the front porch. Inside, the original woodwork remains as well as several sets of original pocket doors and fireplaces. Ask for the Parkridge Room where a six-foot high antique headboard is the focal point or for the Shea Lorraine or Dearborn rooms, both with large whirlpool tubs. There's a fireplace on the patio for evening get-togethers. SEMO University is nearby.
Innkeeper(s): Marsha Toll. $70-105. MC, VISA, AX, DS, PC, TC. TAC10. 4 rooms with PB. Breakfast included in rates. AP. Type of meal: Full bkfst. Beds: Q. Cable TV, ceiling fan, whirlpool and phones in some rooms in room. Air conditioning. Weddings, small meetings and family reunions hosted.

Fulton D6

Romancing The Past Victorian B&B

830 Court St
Fulton, MO 65251
(573)592-1996 Fax:(573)592-1999

Circa 1867. A porch wraps around this pristine Victorian home and offers white wicker furnishings. There's a hammock and hot tub in the garden. Finely crafted and restored fretwork, brackets and bay windows decorate the exterior. Polished woodwork, a gracious staircase and parquet floors are highlighted with well-chosen Victorian antiques. The Renaissance Suite boasts a fainting couch and carved walnut canopy bed, a sitting room and a large bath decorated in the Neoclassical style.

Innkeeper(s): Jim & ReNee Yeager. $80-150. MC, VISA, AX, DS, PC, TC. 3 rooms with PB, 3 with FP, 1 suite and 1 conference room. Breakfast, afternoon tea and snacks/refreshments included in rates. Types of meals: Full

gourmet bkfst, cont and early coffee/tea. Picnic lunch and room service available. Beds: Q. Phone, turndown service, ceiling fan and clock in room. VCR, fax, copier, spa, bicycles and library on premises. Weddings, small meetings, family reunions and seminars hosted. Antiquing, fishing, golf, UMC, bike trails, live theater, parks, shopping, sporting events and tennis nearby.

Pets allowed: pets are not allowed inside the inn.

Gallatin   B4

Ray Home B&B

212 W Van Buren
Gallatin, MO 64640
(660)663-3874 (800)301-stay Fax:(660)663-3473

Circa 1896. The Ray Home is quite simply a masterpiece, from its extravagant Queen Anne design to its painstaking restoration. The Victorian mansion includes half-dozen fireplaces, an intri-

cately carved staircase and a fanciful turret. The century-old home is named for its original owners and is listed in the National Register. There are three guest rooms, two of which share a bath. The rooms are decorated in Victorian style with plenty of interesting

memorabilia to admire, some of which belonged to the Ray family. Among the noteworthy bedchambers is a room with floral wallcoverings, deep hunter carpeting, a quilt-topped Eastlake bed and a red velvet Victorian loveseat. Breakfasts are served by candlelight, and entrees include stuffed French toast with berry sauce or perhaps a quiche with country ham or bacon. Gallatin offers many interesting attractions, including a historic, Octagon-shaped jail, a bank robbed by the James Gang, and a historic Mormon shrine. Jamesport, which includes Missouri's largest Amish settlement, is nearby and offers many antique stores.

Historic Interest: Rotary Jail (3 blocks), Dauriss County Courthouse (1 block).
Innkeeper(s): Bill & Jane Due. $75-85. MC, VISA, AX, DS, PC, TC. 3 rooms, 1 with PB, 2 with FP. Breakfast and snacks/refreshments included in rates. Type of meal: Early coffee/tea. Beds: QD. Cable TV and VCR in room. Central air. Fax, copier, bicycles and library on premises. Weddings, small meetings and family reunions hosted. Antiquing, fishing, golf, hiking, horseback riding, museums, parks and shopping nearby.

Hannibal   C7

Fifth Street Mansion B&B

213 S 5th St
Hannibal, MO 63401-4421
(573)221-0445 (800)874-5661 Fax:(573)221-3335
E-mail: 5thstbb@nemonet.com
Web: www.hanmo.com/fifthstreetmansion

Circa 1858. This 20-room Italianate house listed in the National Register displays extended eaves and heavy brackets, tall windows and decorated lintels. A cupola affords a view of the town. Mark Twain was invited to dinner here by the Garth family and joined Laura Frazer (his Becky Thatcher) for the evening. An enormous stained-glass window lights

the stairwell. The library features a stained-glass window with the family crest and is paneled with hand-grained walnut.

Innkeeper(s): Donalene & Mike Andreotti. $65-110. MC, VISA, AX, DS, TC. 7 rooms with PB and 1 conference room. Breakfast included in rates. Type of meal: Full bkfst. Beds: Q. TV and phone in room. Air conditioning. VCR and fax on premises. Weddings, small meetings, family reunions and seminars hosted. Antiquing, fishing and shopping nearby.

"We thoroughly enjoyed our visit. Terrific food and hospitality!"

Garth Woodside Mansion

11069 New London Rd
Hannibal, MO 63401-9644
(573)221-2789 (888)427-8409
E-mail: garth@nemonet.com
Web: www.hannibal-missouri.com

Circa 1871. This Italian Renaissance mansion is set on 39 acres of meadow and woodland. Original Victorian antiques fill the house. An unusual flying staircase with no visible means of support vaults three stories. Best of all, is the Samuel Clemens Room where Mark Twain slept. Afternoon beverages are served, and there are nightshirts tucked away in your room.

Historic Interest: Mark Twain Boyhood Home (3 miles), a rare inland lighthouse, lit by the President (3 miles).
Innkeeper(s): Julie & John Rolsen. $83-150. MC, VISA. 8 rooms with PB, 4 with FP. Breakfast and afternoon tea included in rates. Types of meals: Full gourmet bkfst and early coffee/tea. Beds: QD. Turndown service in room. Air conditioning. Small meetings hosted. Amusement parks, antiquing, fishing, live theater and parks nearby.

Publicity: *Country Inns, Chicago Sun-Times, Glamour, Victorian Homes, Midwest Living, Innsider, Country Living, Conde Nast Traveler, Bon Appetit.*

"So beautiful and romantic and relaxing, we forgot we were here to work—Jeannie and Bob Ransom, Innsider."

Independence   D3

Serendipity B&B

116 S Pleasant St
Independence, MO 64050
(816)833-4719 (800)203-4299 Fax:(816)833-4719
Web: www.bbhost.com/serendipitybb

Circa 1887. This three-story brick home offers guests a memorable Victorian experience. Antique furnishings and period appointments create an authentic period ambiance. Victorian children's books and toys, antique pictures, china figurines and a collection of antique colored glassware add to the home's charm. Stereoscopes and music boxes are other special touches. A full breakfast is served by candlelight in the formal dining room. Outside gardens include arbors, Victorian gazing balls, birdhouses, birdbaths, a hammock, swing and fountain. If time and weather permit, guests may request a ride in an antique car and tour of the house.

Innkeeper(s): Susan & Doug Walter. $30-95. MC, VISA, DS, TC. TAC10. 6 rooms with PB and 3 suites. Type of meal: Full bkfst. Beds: KQD. Air conditioning. VCR, fax and copier on premises. Amusement parks, antiquing, fishing, golf, historic sites, live theater, parks, shopping, sporting events, tennis and water sports nearby.

Pets Allowed.

"It was so special to spend time with you and to share your lovely home."

Woodstock Inn B&B

1212 W Lexington Ave
Independence, MO 64050-3524
(816)833-2233 (800)276-5202 Fax:(816)461-7226
E-mail: woodstock@independence-missouri.com
Web: www.independence-missouri.com

Circa 1900. This home, originally built as a doll and quilt factory, is in the perfect location for sightseeing in historic Independence. Visit the home of Harry S Truman or the Truman Library and Museum. The Old Jail Museum is another popular attraction. A large country breakfast is served each morning featuring malted Belgian waffles and an additional entree. Independence is less than 30 minutes from Kansas City, where you may spend the day browsing through the shops at Country Club Plaza or Halls' Crown Center.

Innkeeper(s): Todd & Patricia Justice. $69-189. MC, VISA, AX, DS, PC, TC. TAC10. 11 rooms with PB and 2 suites. Breakfast included in rates. Types of meals: Full bkfst and early coffee/tea. Beds: KQDT. Cable TV, phone, turndown service, VCR and fireplaces in room. Air conditioning. Fax on premises. Handicap access. Weddings, small meetings, family reunions and seminars hosted. Spanish spoken. Amusement parks, antiquing, art galleries, fishing, golf, live theater, museums, parks, shopping and sporting events nearby.

"Pleasant, accommodating people, a facility of good character."

Kansas City   D3

The Inn on Crescent Lake

1261 Saint Louis Ave
Kansas City, MO 64024
(816)630-6745 Fax:(816)630-9326

Circa 1915. This three-story, Georgian-style house rests on 22 acres. The inn is just a half-hour drive from downtown Kansas City and the airport. Guest rooms all have private baths, and guests can choose to have either a whirlpool or clawfoot tub. Both innkeepers graduated from the French Culinary Institute in New York City; guests are encouraged to book a dinner reservation at the inn's formal dining room. The lush grounds offer two ponds, paddle boats, a bass boat and fishing rods.

Innkeeper(s): Bruce & Anne Libowitz. $125-175. MC, VISA. 8 rooms with PB and 2 suites. Breakfast included in rates. Type of meal: Full bkfst. Dinner available. Beds: KQT. Cable TV, phone and ceiling fan in room. Air conditioning. Copier on premises. Weddings hosted. Antiquing, fishing, parks and shopping nearby.

The Doanleigh Inn

217 E 37th St
Kansas City, MO 64111-1473
(816)753-2667 Fax:(816)531-5185

Circa 1907. This three-story Georgian inn overlooks Hyde Park and is a perfect spot to enjoy the best of Kansas City. American and European antiques grace the guest rooms. Jacuzzis, fireplaces and decks are among the amenities. A gourmet breakfast is served each morning, and in the evenings, wine and cheese are served.

Innkeeper(s): Terry Maturo & Cynthia Brogdon. $90-160. MC, VISA, AX, DS,

PC, TC. 5 rooms with PB, 2 with FP, 1 suite and 1 conference room. Breakfast and snacks/refreshments included in rates. Types of meals: Full gourmet bkfst and early coffee/tea. Beds: KQ. Cable TV, phone, turndown service, VCR, robes, afternoon cookies, fireplace and deck in room. Air conditioning. Fax, copier, evening wine and cheese and complimentary snack bar on premises. Weddings, small meetings, family reunions and seminars hosted. Antiquing, live theater, parks, shopping, sporting events and water sports nearby.

Southmoreland on The Plaza

116 E 46th St
Kansas City, MO 64112-1702
(816)531-7979 Fax:(816)531-2407

Circa 1913. Located just two blocks off the illustrious Country Club Plaza, this four-star inn blends classic New England B&B ambience with small hotel amenities. Paired glass doors flank the foyer and original stair designs and fireplaces have been restored. Each of the inn's twelve guest rooms include private baths, and each has something special. Eight guest rooms include treetop decks. Fireplaces and Jacuzzi tubs are other possibilities. Guests staying in the carriage house enjoy a Jacuzzi, fireplace and deck. In the afternoon, guests are pampered with wine and hors d'oeuvres. Guests are invited to enjoy privileges at a Plaza athletic club. Explore the elegant shops that line the Plaza or visit Crown Center, an elaborate enclosed area featuring specialty shops and gourmet restaurants. The inn is a four-block walk from the Nelson-Atkins Museum of Art.

Innkeeper(s): Nancy Miller Reichle & Mark Reichle. $125-225. MC, VISA, AX, PC, TC. 12 rooms with PB, 3 with FP and 2 conference rooms. Breakfast included in rates. Types of meals: Full gourmet bkfst. Beds: KQ. Phone and TV in room. Air conditioning. Computers, fax, copier and VCR on premises. Small meetings hosted. Handicap access. Antiquing, live theater, parks, riverwalk, museums, tennis, swimming, jogging trail, shopping and sporting events nearby.

Kirkwood   D8

Fissy's Place

500 N Kirkwood Rd
Kirkwood, MO 63122-3914
(314)821-4494

Circa 1939. The innkeeper's past is just about as interesting as the history of this bed & breakfast. A former Miss Missouri, the innkeeper has acted in movies with the likes of Burt Reynolds and Robert Redford, and pictures of many movie stars decorate the home's interior. A trained interior designer, she also shares this talent in the cheerfully decorated guest rooms. Historic downtown Kirkwood is within walking distance to the home, which also offers close access to St. Louis.

Innkeeper(s): Fay Haas. $69-76. MC, VISA, PC, TC. TAC10. 3 rooms with PB and 1 conference room. Breakfast and snacks/refreshments included in rates. Types of meals: Full bkfst, cont plus and early coffee/tea. Catering service available. Beds: QDT. Cable TV, phone, turndown service, ceiling fan and VCR in room. Air conditioning. Copier on premises. Handicap access. Small meetings, family reunions and seminars hosted. Antiquing, many fine restaurants, live theater, parks, shopping and sporting events nearby.

Lampe
H4

Grandpa's Farm B&B

HC 3, PO Box 476
Lampe, MO 65681-0476
(417)779-5106 (800)280-5106
E-mail: keithpat@inter-line.net
Web: www.grandpasfarmandb.com

Circa 1891. This limestone farmhouse in the heart of the Ozarks offers guests a chance to experience country life in a relaxed farm setting. Midway between Silver Dollar City and Eureka Springs, Ark., and close to Branson, the inn boasts several lodging options, including a duplex with suites and a honeymoon suite. The innkeepers are known for their substantial country breakfast and say guests enjoy comparing how long the meal lasts before they eat again. Although the inn's 116 acres are not farmed extensively, domesticated farm animals are on the premises.

Innkeeper(s): Keith & Pat Lamb. $65-95. MC, VISA, DS, PC, TC. TAC15. 4 suites. Breakfast included in rates. Type of meal: Full bkfst. Beds: KQ. Ceiling fan in room. Air conditioning. VCR, fax, spa and RCA satellite dish with 32-inch TV screen on premises. Handicap access. Small meetings, family reunions and seminars hosted. Amusement parks, antiquing, fishing, country western shows, Passion Plays in Branson, live theater, parks, shopping and water sports nearby.

Louisiana
C7

Serando's House

918 Georgia St, PO Box 205
Louisiana, MO 63353-1812
(573)754-4067 (800)754-4067

Circa 1876. Southerners traveling up the Mississippi River discovered this lush area in the early 19th century, founded it and

named their little town Louisiana. The town still features many of the earliest structures in the downtown historic district. Serando's House still showcases much of its original woodwork and stained glass. The two guest rooms are comfortably furnished, and one includes a balcony. Guests select their breakfast from a variety of menu items.

Innkeeper(s): Jeannie Serandos. $65-85. MC, VISA, AX, DS, PC, TC. TAC5. 2 rooms, 1 with PB. Breakfast included in rates. Types of meals: Full bkfst and early coffee/tea. Dinner, picnic lunch and lunch available. Beds: Q. Cable TV, ceiling fan and VCR in room. Air conditioning. Spa on premises. Small meetings hosted. Antiquing, fishing, parks, shopping and water sports nearby.
Publicity: *Discover Mid-America.*

Macon
C5

St. Agnes Hall B&B

502 Jackson St
Macon, MO 63552-1717
(660)385-2774 Fax:(660)385-4436

Circa 1846. This two-and-a-half story brick home boasts a rather unique history. As a stop along the Underground Railroad, it served as a "safe-house" for many slaves seeking

freedom in the North. During the Civil War, it was used as Union headquarters. Eventually in the 1880s, the home was converted into a boarding house and day school for young women. In 1895, the home was renovated and used as a private residence. It was the boyhood home of U.S. Sen. James Preston Kem. Antiques and collectibles decorate the interior, all surrounded by Victorian decor.

Innkeeper(s): Scott & Carol Phillips. $68-98. MC, VISA, AX, TC. 4 rooms with PB, 2 with FP and 1 suite. Breakfast included in rates. Types of meals: Full bkfst and early coffee/tea. Beds: KQ. Cable TV and ceiling fan in room. Air conditioning. VCR, fax and copier on premises. Weddings, small meetings, family reunions and seminars hosted. Antiquing, fishing, golf, swimming, fine dining, parks, shopping and water sports nearby.

Marshfield
G5

The Dickey House B&B, Ltd.

331 S Clay St
Marshfield, MO 65706-2114
(417)468-3000 Fax:(417)859-2775

Circa 1913. This Greek Revival mansion is framed by ancient oak trees and boasts eight massive two-story Ionic columns. Burled woodwork, beveled glass and polished hardwood floors accentuate the gracious rooms.

Interior columns soar in the parlor, creating a suitably elegant setting for the innkeeper's outstanding collection of antiques. A queen-size canopy bed, fireplace and sunporch are featured in the Heritage Room.

Some rooms offer amenities such as Jacuzzi tubs and a fireplace. All rooms include cable TV and a VCR. The innkeepers also offer a sun room with a hot tub.

Innkeeper(s): Larry & Michaelene Stevens. $65-145. MC, VISA, AX, DS, PC, TC. TAC10. 7 rooms, 6 with PB, 3 suites and 1 cottage. Breakfast included in rates. Type of meal: Full gourmet bkfst. Beds: KQD. Cable TV, phone, ceiling fan, double Jacuzzi in two rooms and new sun room with therapeutic hot tub in room. Air conditioning. Fax, copier and library on premises. Handicap access. Weddings, small meetings, family reunions and seminars hosted.

Rocheport
D5

School House B&B Inn

504 Third St
Rocheport, MO 65279
(573)698-2022

Circa 1914. This three-story brick building was once a schoolhouse. Now luxuriously appointed as a country inn, it features 13-foot-high ceilings, small print wallpapers and a bridal suite with Victorian furnishings and a private spa. Rooms feature names such as The Spelling Bee and The Schoolmarm. The basement houses an antique bookshop, The

Bookseller. Nearby is a winery and a trail along the river providing many scenic miles for cyclists and hikers.

Historic Interest: Historic Katy Trail (2 blocks), Missouri River (4 blocks), local museum (4 blocks), Rocheport, has 80 buildings in the National Register.

Innkeeper(s): Vicki Ott & Penny Province. $85-175. MC, VISA, DS. TAC10. 10 rooms with PB, 1 suite and 1 conference room. Breakfast and snacks/refreshments included in rates. Types of meals: Full bkfst, cont plus, cont and early coffee/tea. Afternoon tea available. Beds: KQDT. TV, phone and ceiling fan in room. Air conditioning. VCR, bicycles and library on premises. Small meetings and family reunions hosted. Antiquing, fishing, hiking, bicycling, live theater, parks, shopping and sporting events nearby.

Publicity: *Midwest Motorist, Successful Farming, Hallmark Greeting Cards, Romance of Country Inns, Southern Living, New York Times.*

"We are still talking about our great weekend in Rocheport. Thanks for the hospitality, the beautiful room and delicious breakfasts, they were really great."

Saint Charles   D8

Boone's Lick Trail Inn

1000 South Main St
Saint Charles, MO 63301-3514
(636)947-7000

Circa 1840. This Federal-style brick and limestone house, overlooks the wide Missouri River and Katy Trail. Situated in an old river settlement with its brick street and green spaces, the inn is at the start of the Boone's Lick Trail. V'Anne's delicate lemon biscuits, fresh fruit and hot entrees are served amid regional antiques and Paul's working duck decoy collection. Because of its setting and decor, travelers have remarked at how close the inn resembles a European inn.

Historic Interest: Goldenrod Showboat (one-fourth mile), Missouri First State Capitol (one-half mile), Daniel Boone Homestead (25 miles), Gateway Arch (20 minutes), Jefferson Memorial Courthouse.

Innkeeper(s): V'Anne & Paul Mydler. $85-175. MC, VISA, AX, DC, CB, DS, PC, TC. 5 rooms with PB and 1 suite. Breakfast included in rates. Types of meals: Full bkfst and cont plus. Beds: QT. TV and phone in room. Antiquing, golf, historic district, museums, wineries, casino, birding, biking, restaurants, swimming, hiking and shopping nearby.

Sainte Genevieve   E9

The Southern Hotel

146 S 3rd St
Sainte Genevieve, MO 63670-1667
(573)883-3493 (800)275-1412 Fax:(573)883-9612
E-mail: mike@southernhotelbb.com
Web: southernhotelbb.com

Circa 1790. This Federal building is the largest and oldest brick home west of the Mississippi. It features a long front porch, large parlors and a spacious dining room. Highlights of the guest rooms include a rosewood tester bed, a unique iron bed, several hand-painted headboards and a delicately carved Victorian bed. The clawfoot tubs are hand-painted. Guests are invited to add their names to a quilt-in-progress,

which is set out in the parlor. Guests also can browse through the Summer Kitchen Gift Shop, located by the gardens.

Innkeeper(s): Mike & Barbara Hankins. $70-128. MC, VISA, DS, PC, TC. 8 rooms with PB, 4 with FP and 1 conference room. Breakfast included in rates. Types of meals: Full gourmet bkfst and early coffee/tea. Restaurant on premises. Beds: KQD. Ceiling fan in room. Air conditioning. Bicycles on premises. Small meetings, family reunions and seminars hosted. Antiquing, parks and shopping nearby.

"I can't imagine ever staying in a motel again! It was so nice to be greeted by someone who expected us. We felt right at home."

Inn St. Gemme Beauvais

78 N Main St
Sainte Genevieve, MO 63670-1336
(573)883-5744 (800)818-5744 Fax:(573)883-3899

Circa 1848. This three-story, Federal-style inn is an impressive site on Ste. Genevieve's Main Street. The town is one of the oldest west of the Mississippi River, and the St. Gemme Beauvais is the oldest operating Missouri bed & breakfast. The rooms are nicely appointed in period style, but there are modern amenities here, too. The Jacuzzi tubs in some guest rooms are one relaxing example. There is an outdoor hot tub, as well. The romantic carriage house includes a king-size bed, double Jacuzzi tub and a fireplace. Guests are pampered with all sorts of cuisine, including full breakfasts and tea time in the afternoons, wine, hors d'oeuvres and refreshments are served early evenings.

Innkeeper(s): Janet Joggerst. $89-179. MC, VISA, DS, PC, TC. 9 rooms with PB, 1 with FP, 6 suites and 1 conference room. Breakfast, afternoon tea and snacks/refreshments included in rates. Type of meal: Full gourmet bkfst. Beds: KQD. Cable TV and ceiling fan in room. Air conditioning. VCR, fax, copier, spa and bicycles on premises. Weddings, small meetings, family reunions and seminars hosted. Antiquing, historic area, parks and shopping nearby.

Saint Louis   D8

Lafayette House

2156 Lafayette Ave
Saint Louis, MO 63104-2543
(314)772-4429 (800)641-8965 Fax:(314)664-2156

Circa 1876. Lafayette House encompasses two historic homes, built by Captain James Eads, the designer and builder of the first trestle bridge to cross the Mississippi. Eads built the homes as wedding gifts for his two daughters. Each home is Victorian in style, and each is decorated with antiques.

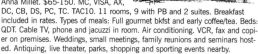

Innkeeper(s): Nancy Hammersmith, Anna Millet. $65-150. MC, VISA, AX, DC, CB, DS, PC, TC. TAC10. 11 rooms, 9 with PB and 2 suites. Breakfast included in rates. Types of meals: Full gourmet bkfst and early coffee/tea. Beds: QDT. Cable TV, phone and jacuzzi in room. Air conditioning. VCR, fax and copier on premises. Weddings, small meetings, family reunions and seminars hosted. Antiquing, live theater, parks, shopping and sporting events nearby.

"We had a wonderful stay at your house and enjoyed the furnishings, delicious breakfasts and friendly pets."

Napoleon's Retreat

1815 Lafayette Ave
Saint Louis, MO 63104
(314)772-6979 (800)700-9980 Fax:(314)772-7675

Circa 1880. This three-story, French-style Second Empire Victorian townhouse is located in Lafayette Square, a National Historic District that offers the largest collection of French

Second Empire Victorians in the country. Pocket doors, twelve-foot ceilings, pine floors, artworks, collectibles and period antiques are features of the inn. Ask for the green room for beautifully draped windows and an elegant decor. The innkeeper offers Napoleon French Toast, quiche or Belgian waffles along with fruit and other freshly baked breads for breakfast. The inn is a mile and a half from the convention center and close to historic Soulard Market, the Missouri Botanical Gardens, the zoo, St. Louis Cathedral and Fox Theater.

Historic Interest: Jefferson National Expansion Memorial Arch (1-1/2 miles). Innkeeper(s): Jeff Archuleta/Michael Lance. $80-125. MC, VISA, AX, DC, DS, PC, TC. TAC10. 5 rooms, 4 with PB, 1 with FP and 1 suite. Breakfast and snacks/refreshments included in rates. Types of meals: Full gourmet bkfst and early coffee/tea. Beds: Q. Cable TV, phone and ceiling fan in room. Central air. Fax and copier on premises. Amusement parks, antiquing, art galleries, fishing, golf, hiking, horseback riding, live theater, museums, parks, shopping, sporting events and wineries nearby.

The Winter House

3522 Arsenal St
Saint Louis, MO 63118-2004
(314)664-4399
E-mail: kmwinter@swbell.net
Web: www.thewinterhouse.com

Circa 1897. Original brass hardware, three fireplaces and a turret provide ambiance at this turn-of-the-century brick Victorian. Embossed French paneling adds elegance. The suite features a balcony, and the bedroom has a pressed-tin ceiling. The Rose Room is decorated with its name-sake flower and a king-size bed. The home is ideally located three miles from the downtown area. Exotic restaurants are within walking distance. Breakfast is served on antique Wedgewood china and includes hand-squeezed orange juice, gourmet coffees, teas and a full breakfast. With special reservations, guests can enjoy breakfast accompanied by professional piano music.

Historic Interest: Tower Grove Park (one-half block), Missouri Botanical Garden (1 mile).
Innkeeper(s): Kendall Winter. $85-115. MC, VISA, AX, DC, CB, DS, PC, TC. TAC10. 3 rooms with PB and 1 suite. Breakfast included in rates. Type of meal: Full bkfst. Beds: KQD. Ceiling fan in room. Air conditioning. Live piano music w/breakfast on premises. Amusement parks, antiquing, museums, live theater, parks, shopping and sporting events nearby.
Publicity: *Innsider, St. Louis Post Dispatch.*

"A delightful house with spotless, beautifully appointed rooms, charming hosts. Highly recommended."

Springfield   G4

Virginia Rose B&B

317 E Glenwood St
Springfield, MO 65807-3543
(417)883-0693

Circa 1906. Three generations of the Botts family lived in this home before it was sold to the current innkeepers, Virginia and Jackie Buck. The grounds still include the rustic red barn. Comfortable, country rooms are named after Buck family members and feature beds covered with quilts. The innkeepers also offer a two-bedroom suite, the Rambling Rose, which is decorated in a sportsman theme in honor of the nearby Bass Pro. Hearty breakfasts are served in the dining room, and the innkeepers will

provide low-fat fare on request.

Historic Interest: Wild Bill Hickock shot Dave Tutt on the public square in Springfield, which is about two miles from the inn. Wilson's Creek National Battlefield is about eight miles away. Other Springfield attractions include Springfield National Cemetery, The Frisco Railroad Museum and the History Museum for Springfield and Greene County.
Innkeeper(s): Jackie & Virginia Buck. $50-90. MC, VISA, AX, DS, PC, TC. TAC10. 5 rooms, 3 with PB and 1 suite. Breakfast included in rates. Meals: Full bkfst and early coffee/tea. Snacks/refreshments and picnic lunch available. Beds: QD. Phone and turndown service in room. Air conditioning. VCR and fax on premises. Family reunions and seminars hosted. Amusement parks, antiquing, fishing, live theater, parks, shopping, sporting events and water sports nearby.
Publicity: *Auctions & Antiques, Springfield Business Journal, Today's Women Journal.*

"The accommodations are wonderful and the hospitality couldn't be warmer."

Walnut Street Inn

900 E Walnut St
Springfield, MO 65806-2603
(417)864-6346 (800)593-6346 Fax:(417)864-6184

Circa 1894. This three-story Queen Anne gabled house has cast-iron Corinthian columns and a veranda. Polished wood floors and antiques are featured throughout. Upstairs you'll find the gathering room with a fireplace. Ask for the McCann guest room with two bay windows, or one of the four rooms with a hot tub. A full breakfast is served, including items such as peach-stuffed French toast.

Historic Interest: Springfield History Museum (3 blocks), Laura Ingalls Wilder Museum (40 minutes), Wilson's Creek National Battlefield (20 minutes), General Sweeney's Civil War Museum (20 minutes).
Innkeeper(s): Gary & Paula Blankenship. $69-159. MC, VISA, AX, DC, DS, PC, TC. 12 rooms with PB, 8 with FP and 1 suite. Breakfast included in rates. Types of meals: Full gourmet bkfst and early coffee/tea. Afternoon tea available. Beds: QD. Cable TV, phone, turndown service, ceiling fan, VCR and coffeemakers and beverage bars in room. Air conditioning. Fax and copier on premises. Handicap access. Amusement parks, antiquing, fishing, live theater, parks, shopping, sporting events and water sports nearby.
Publicity: *Southern Living, Women's World, Midwest Living, Victoria, Country Inns, Innsider, Glamour, Midwest Motorist, Missouri, Saint Louis Post, Kansas City Star, USA Today.*

"Rest assured your establishment's qualities are unmatched and through your commitment to excellence you have won a life-long client."

Steelville   E7

Frisco Street B&B

305 Frisco St, PO Box 1219
Steelville, MO 65565
(573)775-4247 (888)229-4247
E-mail: friscomone@juno.com

Circa 1871. This Victorian farmhouse is painted baby blue and pink and features a wraparound porch. Breakfast is often served in the gazebo part of the porch. The parlor with armoire, fireplace, floral wallpaper and antique paintings has a Victorian flavor. Ask for the English Rose Garden Suite and you'll have a room with country decor, a canopy bed and a Jacuzzi for two. Upstairs guest rooms all have private balconies. Nearby attractions include three Ozark rivers, Meramec Spring Park, a winery, shops and a country music show.

Innkeeper(s): Sandy Berrier. $68-118. MC, VISA, AX, DS. TAC10. 4 rooms with PB and 1 suite. Breakfast and snacks/refreshments included in rates. Types of meals: Full gourmet bkfst and early coffee/tea. Picnic lunch available. Beds: Q. Cable TV, phone and ceiling fan in room. Air conditioning. Weddings, small meetings, family reunions and seminars hosted. Antiquing, fishing, golf, horseback riding, live theater, parks, shopping, water sports and wineries nearby.

"We felt so pampered and special here."

Washington D7

Schwegmann House

438 W Front St
Washington, MO 63090-2103
(636)239-5025 (800)949-2262
E-mail: cathy@schwegmannhouse.com
Web: www.schwegmannhouse.com

Circa 1861. John F. Schwegmann, a native of Germany, built a flour mill on the Missouri riverfront. This stately three-story home was built not only for the miller and his family, but also to provide extra lodging for overnight customers who traveled long hours to the town. Today, weary travelers enjoy the formal

gardens and warm atmosphere of this restful home. Patios overlook the river, and the gracious rooms are decorated with antiques and handmade quilts. The new Miller Suite boasts a tub for two and

breakfast can be delivered to their door. Guests enjoy full breakfasts complete with house specialties such as German apple pancakes or a three-cheese strata accompanied with homemade breads, meat, juice and fresh fruit. There are 11 wineries nearby, or guests can visit one of the historic districts, many galleries, historic sites, antique shops, excellent restaurants and riverfront park located nearby.

Historic Interest: The home is part of the historic downtown Washington area and full of homes and buildings to admire. Daniel Boone's home is 20 miles away. Old Bethel Church and Anna Belle Chapel are short drives. The house is 10 blocks from the Washington Historical Museum.

Innkeeper(s): Catherine & Bill Nagel. $85-150. MC, VISA, AX, PC, TC. TAC10. 9 rooms with PB and 1 suite. Breakfast and snacks/refreshments included in rates. Types of meals: Full gourmet bkfst and early coffee/tea. Beds: QD. Phone and ceiling fan in room. Air conditioning. Small meetings, family reunions and seminars hosted. Antiquing, Missouri River Wine Country and Katy Bike Trail nearby.

Publicity: *St. Louis Post-Dispatch, West County Journal, Midwest Living, Country Inns, Midwest Motorist, Ozark.*

"Like Grandma's house many years ago."

Weston C2

The Hatchery House

618 Short St
Weston, MO 64098-1228
(816)640-5700 (888)640-4051
E-mail: hatcherybb@earthlink.net
Web: home.earthlink.net/~hatcherybb/

Circa 1845. This brick Federal home, built prior to the Civil War, was constructed by one of Weston's mayors. It derives its unusual name from its years serving as a boarding house. It seems that many young couples started their families in the house, and the townspeople began calling it the "hatchery," because of the hatching of babies. The inn is still family orient-

ed, and there are antique dolls, toys and books for children to enjoy. Breakfasts include fanciful items such as homemade chocolate chip muffins baked in heart-shaped tins. Entrees include specialty items such as French toast

almondine. Local wines are served in the early evenings. Weston offers a variety of antique shops, wineries, a brewery, and an orchard. Fort Leavenworth and the Snow Creek Ski Resort are other attractions. Kansas City is an easy drive to the south.

Historic Interest: McCormick's Distillery (1 mile), Pirtle's Winery (2 blocks), The Downtown Weston (1 block).

Innkeeper(s): Bill & Anne Lane. $90-125. MC, VISA, PC, TC. 4 rooms, 3 with PB, 4 with FP and 1 suite. Breakfast and afternoon tea included in rates. Types of meals: Full gourmet bkfst, cont plus, veg bkfst and early coffee/tea. Picnic lunch available. Beds: QT. Cable TV, phone and ceiling fan in room. Central air. Handicap access. Weddings and small meetings hosted. Amusement parks, antiquing, art galleries, bicycling, hiking, festivals, orchards, farms, museums, parks, shopping, downhill skiing and wineries nearby.

West Plains H6

Pinebrook Lodge B&B

791 State Route T
West Plains, MO 65775
(417)257-7769 (888)892-7699

Circa 1924. Pinebrook Lodge originally served as a health resort for wealthy guests, including presidents and a few more notorious guests. Today, guests still flock here, drawn by the secluded Ozark setting and the hospitality. Each of the inviting guest rooms is unique and decorated with antiques or reproductions. The sitting room is stocked with snacks, and breakfasts include entrees such as cheese-stuffed crepes with strawberry-rhubarb sauce. The lodge's ground encompasses 100 acres, which includes a four-acre lake where guests can enjoy catch-and-release fishing. The surrounding Ozarks offer a multitude of attractions, including float, canoe and kayak excursions, hunting,

fishing, wilderness trails and several historic mills.

Historic Interest: Mills & Springs (30 miles).

Innkeeper(s): Alice-Jean & Robert Eckhart. $60-85. PC. TAC10. 7 rooms, 5 with PB. Breakfast and snacks/refreshments included in rates. Type of meal: Full gourmet bkfst. Beds: KQDT. Turndown service and ceiling fan in room. VCR, library, fishing and hiking on premises. Weddings, small meetings, family reunions and seminars hosted. Antiquing, art galleries, canoeing/kayaking, fishing, golf, hiking, live theater, museums, parks, shopping, sporting events and tennis nearby.

"Thank you for providing the opportunity to relax and enjoy peacefulness."

Montana

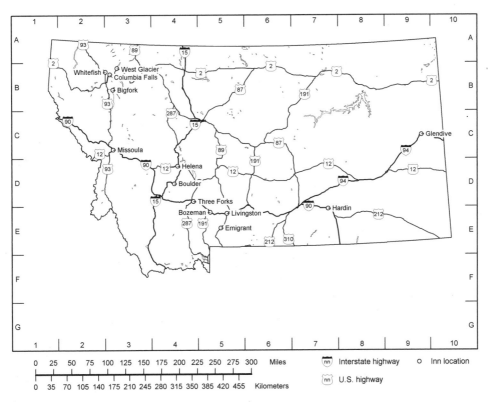

Legend:
- ☐ nn Interstate highway
- ☐ nn U.S. highway
- ○ Inn location

Scale:
Miles: 0 25 50 75 100 125 150 175 200 225 250 275 300
Kilometers: 0 35 70 105 140 175 210 245 280 315 350 385 420 455

Boulder   E7

Boulder Hot Springs B&B

PO Box 930
Boulder, MT 59632-0930
(406)225-4339 Fax:(406)225-4345

Circa 1888. This Spanish-style hotel with its peaked Moorish gables and red roofline is under restoration. In the National Register, the 33 rooms in the east wing, the pool and bathhouse have been renovated. Forty springs are on the inn's 274 acres. There are hotel rooms as well as B&B rooms, which offer antiques and original paintings. A comfortable lobby with wood stove provides a variety of games. Breakfast is generous with omelets and

sausage or French toast and pancakes. Enjoy the geothermal baths or hike along Deerlodge National Forest. An abundant wildlife includes bear, deer, fox, antelope and moose. Some guests enjoy exploring the area's radon mines which are nearby.

$45-90. MC, VISA, PC. 33 rooms, 15 with PB and 2 conference rooms. Breakfast included in rates. Meal: Full bkfst. Beds: DT. Fax, copier, spa, swimming and sauna on premises. Handicap access. Weddings, small meetings, family reunions & seminars hosted. Fishing, shopping & cross-country skiing nearby.

Bozeman   E5

Gallatin Gateway Inn

Hwy 191
Bozeman, MT 09715
(406)763-4672
E-mail: gatewayinn@gallatingatewayinn.com
Web: www.gallatingatewayinn.com

Circa 1927. Just outside of Bozeman, and 75 miles north of Yellowstone National Park, lies one of the grand railroad hotels of the Rocky Mountains West. Stunningly restored, the original hand-hewn beams, palatial windows and mahogany woodwork still grace the common rooms. The inn is located in the heart of Yellowstone Country amid spectacular scenery, hiking and fly-fishing opportunities. The inn has its own casting pond, outdoor swimming pool and outdoor Jacuzzi. The rooms are comfortable and well appointed, and a continental breakfast is served every morning. The inn's historic dining room offers fine dining and more casual fare is found in the Baggage Room Pub.

Innkeeper(s): Martha Riley. $60-145. MC, VISA, AX, DS. 35 rooms and 1 conference room. Type of meal: Cont. Dinner available. Beds: KQT. TV and radios in room. Spa on premises.

Publicity: *Travel & Leisure, Conde Naste Traveler, Bon Appetite, Country Living, House & Garden, Diversions, Bon Appetit, Historic Gourmet, Travel Holiday, Adventure West.*

Lehrkind Mansion

719 N Wallace Ave
Bozeman, MT 59715-3063
(406)585-6932 (800)992-6932
E-mail: lehrkindmansion@imt.net
Web: www.bozemanbedandbreakfast.com

Circa 1897. Peaked gables, gingerbread trim and a captivating corner tower are among the fanciful architectural elements found in this Queen Anne Victorian. Inside, original woodwork and leaded- and stained-glass windows join period antiques and elegant decor. The home is located in Bozeman's Historic Brewery District, one of only five brewery districts listed in the National Register. The home's first owner built it next to his brewery. In the afternoons, enjoy refreshments in the parlor as you listen to melodies from an antique music box. Excellent local skiing is a short drive away at Bridger Bowl and Big Sky ski resorts. Bozeman's charming historic downtown area offers a variety of shops and restaurants. Yellowstone National Park is an hour and a half away.

Innkeeper(s): Jon Gerster & Christopher Nixon. $78-158. MC, VISA, AX, DS, PC, TC. TAC10. 5 rooms, 3 with PB, 1 suite and 1 conference room. Breakfast and afternoon tea included in rates. Types of meals: Full gourmet bkfst, veg bkfst and early coffee/tea. Beds: QD. Turndown service in room. Spa, library and refrigerator on premises. Small meetings hosted. German spoken. Antiquing, art galleries, bicycling, canoeing/kayaking, fishing, golf, hiking, horseback riding, live theater, museums, parks, shopping, downhill skiing, cross-country skiing and sporting events nearby.

"The entire mansion is beautiful and each room so nicely decorated. The breakfast was excellent!"

Silver Forest Inn

15325 Bridger Canyon Rd
Bozeman, MT 59715-8278
(406)586-1882 (800)835-5970 Fax:(406)582-0492
E-mail: jackson@silverforestinn.com
Web: www.silverforestinn.com

Circa 1932. This historic log home was originally built as a summer artist colony and school of drama. It later served as a hunting lodge. The unusual turret, stone and massive pine log construction makes for a unique accommodation and the secluded setting adds to the experience. Ask to stay in the Turret Room for an expansive view overlooking Bridger Mountains. It boasts a queen-size log bed. (The bath is shared.) A family suite is offered for families with children. Breakfast specialties include vanilla and almond French toast, scrambled eggs and maple sausage. The

innkeepers work in the local ski and hospitality industry.

Innkeeper(s): Chris & Ashley Jackson. $75-250. MC, VISA, AX, PC. TAC10. 6 rooms, 4 with PB. Breakfast and snacks/refreshments included in rates. Types of meals: Full gourmet bkfst and early coffee/tea. Picnic lunch and catering service available. Beds: QT. VCR, fax, spa and pet boarding on premises. Weddings, small meetings, family reunions and seminars hosted. Antiquing, bicycling, canoeing/kayaking, fishing, golf, hiking, horseback riding, museums, parks, shopping, downhill skiing and cross-country skiing nearby.

Pets allowed: negotiable.

"I love the way they make the beds here, just the right way. I've long admired log places and this one is a gem!"

Torch & Toes B&B

309 S 3rd Ave
Bozeman, MT 59715-4636
(406)586-7285 (800)446-2138

Circa 1906. This Colonial Revival home, three blocks from the center of town, boasts an old-fashioned front porch with porch swing and a carriage house. Antique furnishings in the dining room feature a Victrola and a pillared and carved oak fireplace. Ron is a retired professor of architecture at nearby Montana State University and Judy is a weaver.

Innkeeper(s): Ron & Judy Hess. $80-90. MC, VISA, PC, TC. TAC10. 4 rooms with PB. Breakfast included in rates. Type of meal: Full gourmet bkfst. Beds: KQT. VCR on premises. Small meetings, family reunions and seminars hosted. Antiquing, fishing, live theater, parks, shopping, downhill skiing, cross-country skiing, sporting events and water sports nearby.

Publicity: *Bozeman Chronicle, San Francisco Peninsula Parent, Northwest.*

"Thanks for your warm hospitality."

Voss Inn

319 S Willson Ave
Bozeman, MT 59715-4632
(406)587-0982 Fax:(406)585-2964

Circa 1883. The Voss Inn is a restored two-story house with a large front porch and a Victorian parlor. Old-fashioned furnishings include an upright piano and chandelier. Two of the inn's six rooms include air conditioning. A full breakfast is served, with freshly baked rolls kept in a unique warmer that's built into an ornate 1880s radiator.

Historic Interest: Little Big Horn (Custer battle site, 18 miles), Virginia City and Nevada City (60 miles), Madison Buffalo Jump (30 miles).

Innkeeper(s): Bruce & Frankee Muller. $90-110. MC, VISA, AX, PC, TC. TAC7. 6 rooms with PB. Breakfast and afternoon tea included in rates. Type of meal: Full gourmet bkfst. Picnic lunch available. Beds: KQ. Phone in room. Fax on premises. Weddings, small meetings and family reunions hosted. Spanish and some Dutch spoken. Antiquing, fishing, golf, hunting, hiking, biking, parks, shopping, cross-country skiing, downhill skiing and water sports nearby.

"First class all the way."

Columbia Falls   B3

Bad Rock Country B&B

480 Bad Rock Dr
Columbia Falls, MT 59912-9213
(406)892-2829 (800)422-3666 Fax:(406)892-2930

This inn features four guest rooms in two newly constructed log buildings that are lavish versions of an old settler's home.

Hand-hewn square logs with dove-tail corners were fashioned to create the buildings, using the original building techniques of Montana settlers 150 years ago. The main house is furnished in Old West antiques, while the log building features hand-made lodge-pole pine furniture. Grizzly Big Bite, an egg casserole served on jalapeno biscuits, and Montana Potato Pie or Sundance eggs are specialties created by Sue. The inn is a great place to stay while visiting Glacier National Park.

Innkeeper(s): Jon & Sue Alper. $120-169. MC, VISA, AX, DC, CB, DS, PC, TC. TAC10. 7 rooms with PB, 4 with FP. Breakfast included in rates. Type of meal: Full gourmet bkfst. Beds: KQT. Phone, turndown service, ceiling fan and fireplaces in four rooms and satellite TV in room. Air conditioning. VCR, fax, copier and spa on premises. Antiquing, fishing, golf, glacier National Park, live theater, parks, shopping, skiing, tennis and water sports nearby.

Publicity: *Country Inns.*

Glendive   C9

The Hostetler House B&B

113 N Douglas St
Glendive, MT 59330-1619
(406)377-4505 (800)965-8456 Fax:(406)377-8456

Circa 1912. Casual country decor mixed with handmade and heirloom furnishings are highlights at this Prairie School home. The inn features many comforting touches, such as a romantic hot tub and gazebo, enclosed sun porch and sitting room filled with books. The two guest rooms share a bath, and are furnished by Dea, an interior decorator. The full breakfasts may be enjoyed on Grandma's china in the dining room or on the sun porch. The Yellowstone River is one block from the inn, and downtown shopping is two blocks away. Makoshika State Park, home of numerous fossil finds, is nearby.

Historic Interest: Guests are invited to tour Glendive's historic district on the innkeeper's tandem mountain bike.

Innkeeper(s): Craig & Dea Hostetler. $50. PC, TC. TAC10. 2 rooms. Breakfast included in rates. Types of meals: Full gourmet bkfst and early coffee/tea. Beds: DT. Ceiling fan in room. Air conditioning. VCR, fax, spa, bicycles, library and secretarial service on premises. Small meetings hosted. German spoken. Antiquing, fishing, fossil and agate hunting, live theater, parks, shopping, cross-country skiing, sporting events and water sports nearby.

Publicity: *Ranger Review.*

"Warmth and loving care are evident throughout your exquisite home. Your attention to small details is uplifting. Thank you for a restful sojourn."

Hardin   E7

Kendrick House Inn, B&B

206 N Custer Ave
Hardin, MT 59034-1917
(406)665-3035

Circa 1915. Originally a boarding house, this bed & breakfast also served as a local hospital and private apartments before falling into disrepair. Innkeepers Steve and Marcie Smith restored the historic gem, transforming it into a Victorian B&B. The decor includes period furnishings, many restored by Marcie. Oriental rugs and chandeliers add to the Victorian elegance, and guests will find a vast array of books. Each guest room includes a pedestal sink and shares a bath with a claw-

foot tub. The innkeepers serve a hearty, Montana-style breakfast. Loosely translated, this means "big" with fresh fruit, savory breakfast meats, made-to-order eggs and French toast. Little Bighorn Battlefield National Monument is nearby.

Innkeeper(s): Steve & Marcianna Smith. $65-85. MC, VISA, PC, TC. TAC10. 5 rooms. Beds: D. Air conditioning. VCR and library on premises.

Helena   D4

Appleton Inn B&B

1999 Euclid Avenue
Helena, MT 59601-1908
(406)449-7492 (800)956-1999 Fax:(406)449-1261

Circa 1890. Montana's first resident dentist called this Victorian his home. It remained in his family until the 1970s when it was transformed into apartments. Fortunately, the innkeepers bought and restored the home, bringing back the original beauty. The innkeepers have their own furniture-making company and have created many of the pieces that decorate the guest rooms. Rooms range from the spacious Master Suite, with its oak, four-poster bed and bath with a clawfoot tub, to the quaint and cozy Attic Playroom. The inn is a convenient place to enjoy the Helena area, and there are mountain bikes on hand for those who wish to explore.

Historic Interest: West Mansion District, Montana Historic Society Museum and the state capitol building all are nearby historic sites.

Innkeeper(s): Tom Woodall & Cheryl Boid. $78-150. MC, VISA, AX, DS, PC, TC. TAC10. 5 rooms with PB and 1 suite. Breakfast included in rates. AP. Beds: Q. Cable TV and phone in room. Air conditioning. VCR, fax, copier, bicycles and guest pass to athletic pass on premises. Small meetings, family reunions and seminars hosted. Antiquing, fishing, national forest, live theater, parks, shopping, downhill skiing, cross-country skiing, sporting events and water sports nearby.

Pets allowed: Need prior approval.

"Cheryl and Tom have provided a perfect place to call home away from home. The surroundings are delightful - the rooms, the plants, the grounds - and the breakfast very tasty. And they provide lots of helpful information to help you enjoy touring the area. A truly delightful B&B."

The Sanders - Helena's Bed & Breakfast

328 N Ewing St
Helena, MT 59601-4050
(406)442-3309 Fax:(406)443-2361
E-mail: thefolks@sandersbb.com
Web: www.sandersbb.com

Circa 1875. This historic inn is filled with elegantly carved furnishings, paintings and collections that are original to the house. Wilbur Sanders, an attorney and a Montana senator, built his house near the Governor's Mansion, in the heart of Helena. The three-story house features a front and side porch, and balconies and bay windows that provide views of the mountains and downtown Helena. In addition to the rich interior and hospitality, guests are pampered with gourmet breakfasts that might include items such as an orange souffle, sourdough or huckleberry pancakes, French toast with sauteed fruit or savory frittatas. The main dish is accompanied by fresh fruit, juice, freshly ground organically grown coffee and an assortment of homemade muffins, coffee cakes or breads.

Historic Interest: Montana State Historical Museum, Cathedral of St. Helena, Reeders Alley & Capital.

Innkeeper(s): Bobbi Uecker & Rock Ringling. $85-105. MC, VISA, AX, DC, DS, PC, TC. 7 rooms with PB and 2 conference rooms. Breakfast included in rates. Types of meals: Full gourmet bkfst and early coffee/tea. Afternoon tea, catering service and room service available. Beds: Q. Cable TV, phone, turndown service, ceiling fan, TV, fireplace, hair dryer and computer hook-up in room. Air conditioning. VCR, fax, copier, library, porch with garden, smoke-free, off street parking, cookies, fruit, sherry and data port on premises. Weddings, small meetings, family reunions and seminars hosted. Antiquing, fishing, galleries, state capitol, historic museum, Governor's mansion, museums, Helena's Cathedral, live theater, parks, shopping, skiing, sporting events and water sports nearby.

Livingston   E5

The River Inn on The Yellowstone

4950 Hwy 89 S
Livingston, MT 59047
(406)222-2429
E-mail: riverinn@wtp.net
Web: www.wtp.net/go/riverinn

Circa 1895. Crisp, airy rooms decorated with a Southwestern flavor are just part of the reason why this 100-year-old farmhouse is an ideal getaway. There are five acres to meander, including more than 500 feet of riverfront, and close access to a multitude of outdoor activities. Two rooms have decks boasting views of the river, and the third offers a canyon view.

Guests also can stay in Calamity Jane's, a rustic riverside cabin. For an unusual twist, summer guests can opt for Spangler's Wagon and experience life as it was on the range. This is a true, turn-of-the-century sheepherders' wagon and includes a double bed and wood stove. The innkeepers guide a variety of interesting hikes, bike and canoe trips in the summer and fall. The inn is close to many outdoor activities. Don't forget to check out Livingston, just a few miles away. The historic town has been used in several movies and maintains an authentic Old West spirit. The inn is 50 miles from Yellowstone National Park.

Historic Interest: Yellowstone National Park is located nearby.

Innkeeper(s): Dee Dee VanZyl & Ursula Neese. $40-90. MC, VISA. TAC10. 3 rooms with PB and 1 cottage. Breakfast included in rates. Meals: Full gourmet bkfst and early coffee/tea. Picnic lunch available. Beds: QDT. Table & chairs, private deck and hot tub/Jacuzzi in room. VCR, bicycles, wood stove, fire pit, horse boarding, horseshoes, fishing, BBQ & birdwatching on premises. Weddings, small meetings, family reunions & seminars hosted. Limited Spanish spoken. Antiquing, fishing, museum of the Rockies, historical museum, art galleries, music, live theater, parks, shopping, skiing, sporting events & water sports nearby.

Pets allowed: Horses. Dogs permitted in the cabin and wagon only. Other, by arrangement.

Missoula   C3

Goldsmith's B&B Inn

809 E Front St
Missoula, MT 59802-4704
(406)721-6732 Fax:(406)543-0095
E-mail: dickgsmith@aol.com
Web: www.goldsmithsinn.com

Circa 1911. Missoula, made famous for its "A River Runs Through It" connection, is the site of this Four-Square-style inn

originally the home of the president of the University of Montana, Clyde Duniway. It would be difficult for the inn to offer a better view of the Clark Fork River, the waterway is just a few feet from the home's front door. Guest quarters are a mixture of turn-of-the-century country and romantic whimsy with bright flowery patterns and quilts dressing the sleigh, pewter, porcelain or wicker beds. Several rooms boast river views. There is a full-service restaurant in an adjoining building, and guests are treated to a memorable full breakfast. Omelets and ice cream batter pancakes are famed specialties of the house. The restaurant features Italian specialties and deep-dish Chicago-style pizza, and guests can enjoy the fare on an outdoor patio overlooking the river.

Innkeeper(s): Dick & Jeana Goldsmith. $69-119. MC, VISA, TC. TAC10. 7 rooms with PB, 2 with FP and 4 suites. Breakfast included in rates. Types of meals: Full bkfst and early coffee/tea. Dinner available. Restaurant on premises. Beds: QD. Cable TV, phone and ceiling fan in room. Air conditioning. Library on premises. Small meetings, family reunions and seminars hosted. Fishing, walking distance to University of Montana, live theater, parks, shopping, downhill skiing, cross-country skiing and sporting events nearby.

Three Forks   D4

Sacajawea Hotel Restaurant & Bar

PO Box 648
Three Forks, MT 59752-0648
(406)285-6515 (800)821-7326
E-mail: sac3forks@aol.com
Web: www.sacajaweahotel.com

Circa 1910. Rocking chairs fill the wide front porch of this National Register hotel. Named after the famous guide who led Lewis and Clark through the Three Forks area, the hotel was founded by John Quincy Adams. The 30,000-square-foot building was renovated in 1991 by its former owners. Current owner, Paul Tripp, also has given the historic gem a facelift, adding a tavern area and refurbishing the lobby and dining room. The hotel also includes the restored Railroad Depot across the street, often the site of parties, receptions and conferences. The hotel's dining choices include a casual setting with an emphasis on steak and seafood specialties. Golf, fishing, canoeing, horseback riding, hiking and hunting for deer, elk and pheasants are all nearby. It's two hours to Yellowstone National Park.

Innkeeper(s): Paul Tripp. $60-105. MC, VISA, AX, DS, TC. 30 rooms with PB, 1 suite and 3 conference rooms. Breakfast included in rates. Types of meals: Full bkfst, cont plus, cont and early coffee/tea. Gourmet dinner, picnic lunch, lunch and banquet service available. Restaurant on premises. Beds: KQDT. Phone in room. VCR, fax, copier, bicycles and outside patio/lawn on premises. Handicap access. Weddings, small meetings, family reunions and seminars hosted. Antiquing, fishing, parks, cross-country skiing, sporting events and water sports nearby.

Pets Allowed.

"You should be commended for the time, resources, and energy you put into this worthy landmark in our fine valley."

Nebraska

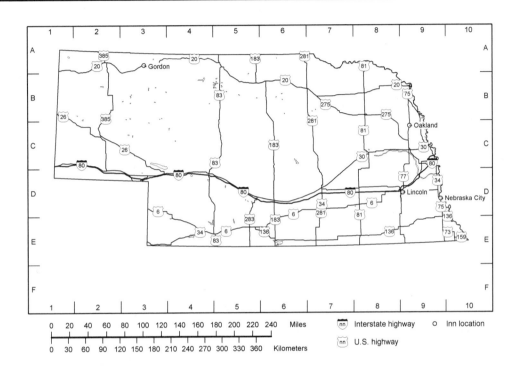

0 20 40 60 80 100 120 140 160 180 200 220 240 Miles
0 30 60 90 120 150 180 210 240 270 300 330 360 Kilometers

(nn) Interstate highway ○ Inn location
(nn) U.S. highway

Gordon

A3

Meadow View Ranch B&B Bunkhouse

HC 91 Box 29
Gordon, NE 69343-9111
(308)282-0679

Circa 1920. For an added charge, guests at this working ranch can take the saddle horses for a ride across the 5,000-acre grounds. The unpretentious guest quarters at Meadow View originally served as a bunkhouse for ranch hands. The simple guest rooms feature country decor and comfortable antiques. Innkeepers Clyde and Billie Lefler serve up a full country breakfast and can arrange cookouts.

Historic Interest: The Gordon area

is full of historic attractions within a half-hour drive, including Old-Time Cowboy's Museum and Mari Sandoz Museum. The Fur Trade Museum and Red Cloud Indian National Art Show are about an hour from the ranch.

Innkeeper(s): Clyde & Billie Lefler. $45-75. 4 rooms with PB. Breakfast included in rates. Type of meal: Full bkfst. Beds: QT. Antiquing and fishing nearby. Pets Allowed.

Lincoln

D9

The Atwood House B&B

740 S 17th St
Lincoln, NE 68508-3708
(402)438-4567 (800)884-6554 Fax:(402)477-8314

Circa 1894. Located two blocks from the state capitol, this 7,000-square-foot mansion, in the Neoclassical Georgian Revival style, features four massive columns. Interior columns are repeated throughout such as on the dressing room vanity, on the staircase and on the parlor fireplace. Classically appointed, the parlor and entranceway set an elegant yet inviting tone. Guest suites are large and feature spacious sitting rooms, fire-

253

places, massive bedsteads and Oriental carpets. The 800-square-foot bridal suite consists of three rooms, and it includes a fireplace, a carved walnut bed and a large whirlpool tub set off by columns. Breakfast is served on bone china with Waterford crystal and sterling flatware.

Innkeeper(s): Ruth & Larry Stoll. $78-165. MC, VISA, AX, DS, PC, TC. 3 suites, 1 with FP and 1 conference room. Breakfast and snacks/refreshments included in rates. Types of meals: Full gourmet bkfst and early coffee/tea. Beds: KQ. Cable TV, phone, turndown service, VCR and whirlpool in room. Air conditioning. Fax, copier and library on premises. Weddings and small meetings hosted. Antiquing, fishing, golf, live theater, parks, shopping, cross-country skiing, sporting events, tennis and water sports nearby.

Publicity: *Lincoln Journal Star.*

"Such a delightful B&B! It is such a nice change in my travels."

Nebraska City   D9

Whispering Pines

21st St & 6th Ave
Nebraska City, NE 68410-9802
(402)873-5850
E-mail: wppines@navix.net
Web: www.bbonline.com/ne/whispering/

Circa 1892. An easy getaway from Kansas City, Lincoln or Omaha, Nebraska City's Whispering Pines offers visitors a relaxing alternative from big-city life. Fresh flowers in each bedroom greet guests at this two-story brick Italianate, furnished with Victorian and country decor. Situated on more than six acres of trees, flowers and ponds, the inn is a birdwatcher's delight. Breakfast is served formally in the dining room, or guests may opt to eat on the deck with its view of the garden and pines. The inn is within easy walking distance to Arbor Lodge, home of the founder of Arbor Day.

Historic Interest: Nebraska City is the home of Arbor Day. Guests can take a short walk from the B&B and tour Arbor Lodge, a 52-room mansion owned by J. Sterling Morton, founder of Arbor Day. The mansion is located on a 64-acre state park. Wildwood Historic Home, built in 1869, also is open for tours. There also are several museums in town, as well.

Innkeeper(s): W.B. Smulling. $55-75. MC, VISA, DS. 5 rooms, 2 with PB. Breakfast included in rates. Type of meal: Full gourmet bkfst.

Oakland   C9

Benson B&B

402 N Oakland Ave
Oakland, NE 68045-1135
(402)685-6051

Circa 1905. This inn is on the second floor of the Benson Building, a sturdy, turreted brick structure built of walls nearly 12 inches thick. Decorated throughout in mauve, blue and cream, the Benson B&B features three comfortable guest rooms, and a restful, small-town atmosphere. Guests may visit the Swedish Heritage Center and a nearby city park. An 18-hole golf course is a five-minute drive away. The bed & breakfast features a small gift shop, as well as a collection of soft drink memorabilia. Be sure to ask about the Troll Stroll.

Innkeeper(s): Stan & Norma Anderson. $53-60. DS, PC, TC. TAC10. 3 rooms. Breakfast and snacks/refreshments included in rates. Types of meals: Full bkfst and early coffee/tea. Beds: QD. Toiletries in room. VCR, spa and library on premises. Small meetings and family reunions hosted. Antiquing, parks, shopping and sporting events nearby.

Nevada

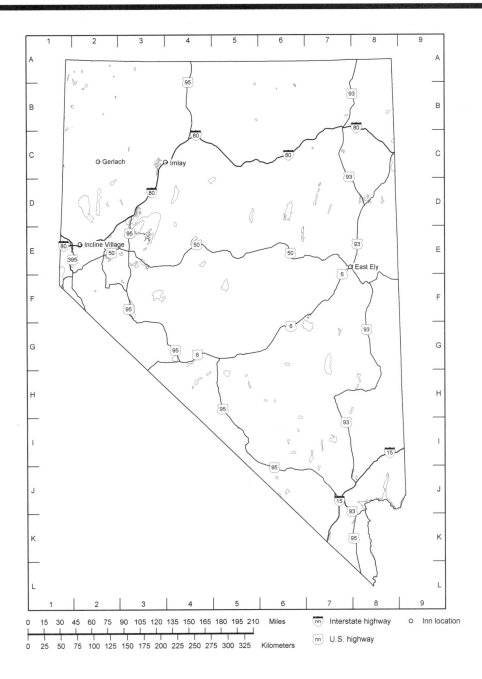

		Miles
0 15 30 45 60 75 90 105 120 135 150 165 180 195 210		

		Kilometers
0 25 50 75 100 125 150 175 200 225 250 275 300 325		

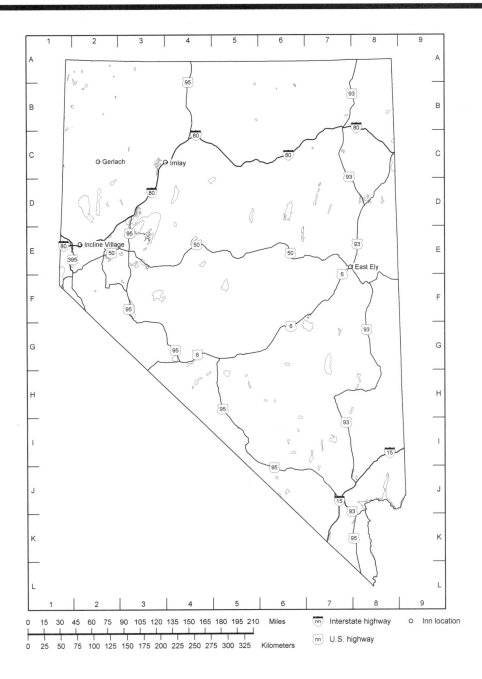 Interstate highway   O   Inn location

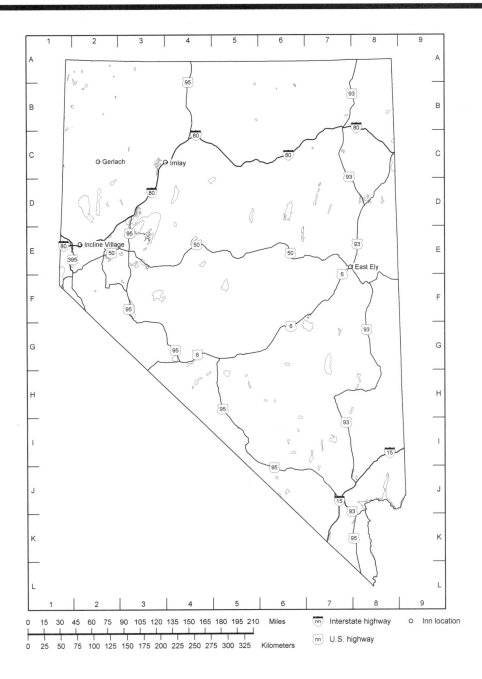 U.S. highway

Ely   E7

Steptoe Valley Inn

220 E 11th St, PO Box 150100
Ely, NV 89315-0100
(775)289-8687

Circa 1907. Originally a grocery store at the turn of the century, this inn has been lovingly reconstructed and resembles a fancy, Old West-style store. The interior is decorated in Victorian country-cottage style. Five uniquely decorated guest rooms are named for local pioneers. The rooms also have views of the inn's scenic surroundings, and three of them feature queen beds. A nearby railroad museum offers train rides and Great Basin National Park is 70 miles away. This inn is open from June to October.

Historic Interest: Nevada Northern Railway Museum (one-half block), Ward Charcoal Ovens (12 miles), Liberty Copper Pit (3 miles).

Innkeeper(s): Jane & Norman Lindley. $84-95. MC, VISA, AX, PC, TC. TAC10. 5 rooms with PB and 1 conference room. Breakfast and snacks/refreshments included in rates. Type of meal: Full bkfst. Beds: QT. Cable TV, phone and ceiling fan in room. Air conditioning. VCR, library, jeep rental, gazebo and croquet on premises. Weddings, small meetings and family reunions hosted. Spanish spoken. Fishing, weekend train rides, four-wheel drive trails, garnet hunting, hiking, casinos and parks nearby.

Publicity: Las Vegas Review Journal, Great Getaways, Yellow Brick Road.

"Everything was so clean and first-rate."

Gerlach   C2

Soldier Meadows Guest Ranch & Lodge

Soldier Meadows Rd
Gerlach, NV 89412
(530)233-4881 Fax:(530)233-1183

Circa 1865. Once known as Fort McGarry, this historic working ranch once housed the troops who were assigned to protect pioneers traveling the Applegate-Lassen Trail from the Paiute Indians of the area. The Estill family now runs cattle on the land. Green meadows and willow trees frame the ranch house and the bunkhouse. Stone stables erected by the U. S. Army are still in use, as well as the original Officers' Quarters. There are two natural hot springs for swimming. Wildlife is abundant in the area, including wild mustangs, mule deer and antelope. Guests may opt to work the range with the ranch's cowhands and enjoy trail riding, hunting, fishing or hiking. Some like to mine for opals at the adjacent opal mine, while others organize a camping experience at one of the two sheep camps in the aspen and mahogany forests of the foothills. For the complete experience, join the crew in the cookhouse early for breakfast or later for lunch. A ranch supper is offered in the evening where, after a day or two, you may find yourself spinning a yarn of your own about the Old West.

Historic Interest: Applegate-Lassen Trail-7 miles, High Rock Canyon-12 miles.

Innkeeper(s): Bruce & Kathy Lanning. $40-120. MC, VISA, PC, TC. 10 rooms, 2 suites and 1 conference room. Breakfast, dinner, snacks/refreshments and picnic lunch included in rates. AP. Types of meals: Full bkfst and early coffee/tea. Lunch available. Beds: QT. Natural hot springs on premises. Small meetings and family reunions hosted. Bicycling, canoeing/kayaking, hiking, horseback riding and historic Pioneer Trails nearby.

Pets Allowed.

Unionville   D4

Old Pioneer Garden Country Inn

2805 Unionville Rd
Unionville, NV 89418-8204
(702)538-7585

Circa 1861. Once a bustling silver mining town, Unionville now has only a handful of citizens, and Old Pioneer Garden Guest Ranch is just down the road from town. Accommodations are in a renovated blacksmith's house, a farmhouse and across the meadow in the Hadley House. Guests can settle down in front of a fire in the inn's library. A Swedish-style gazebo rests beside a bubbling stream, and there are orchards, grape arbors, vegetable gardens, sheep and goats. A country supper is available. The innkeepers can accommodate visiting horses in their barn and corrals.

Innkeeper(s): Mitzi & Lew Jones. $75-85. 12 rooms, 4 with PB, 1 with FP, 1 suite and 1 conference room. Breakfast included in rates. Types of meals: Full gourmet bkfst and early coffee/tea. Dinner, picnic lunch, gourmet lunch, banquet service and catering service available. Beds: D. Library and tournament size pool table on premises. Handicap access. Antiquing and fishing nearby.

"An array of charm that warms the heart and delights the soul."

New Hampshire

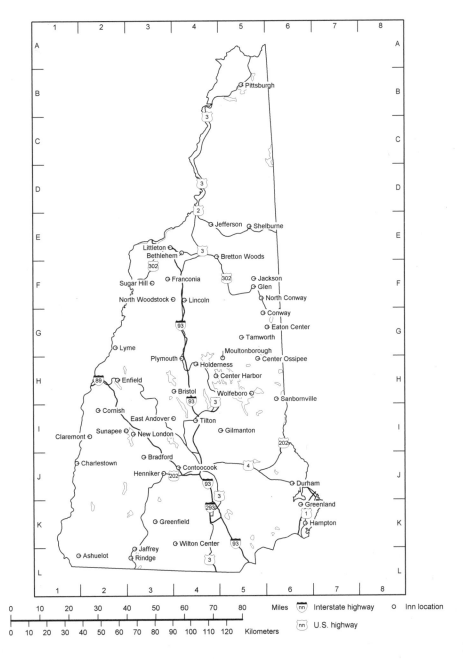

1	2	3	4	5	6	7	8	

A

B   Pittsburgh

3

C

D

3

2

E   Jefferson   Shelburne

Littleton
Bethlehem   3   Bretton Woods
302

F   Sugar Hill   Franconia   302   Jackson
Glen
North Woodstock   Lincoln   North Conway
Conway

G   93   Eaton Center
Tamworth
Lyme   Moultonborough
Plymouth   Center Ossipee
Holderness

H   89   Enfield   Center Harbor
Bristol   Wolfeboro
93   3   Sanbornville

I   Cornish   Tilton
East Andover   Gilmanton
Claremont   Sunapee   New London   202

J   Charlestown   Bradford   4
Henniker   Contoocook   Durham
202   93
3   Greenland
293   1

K   Greenfield   Hampton

Ashuelot   Jaffrey   Wilton Center   93
Rindge   3

L

1	2	3	4	5	6	7	8	

0   10   20   30   40   50   60   70   80   Miles   Interstate highway   o Inn location

0   10   20   30   40   50   60   70   80   90   100   110   120   Kilometers   U.S. highway

257

Ashuelot
L1

Crestwood

400 Scofield Mountain Rd
Ashuelot, NH 03441-2600
(603)239-6393
E-mail: info@crestwd.com
Web: www.crestwd.com

Circa 1895. Guests at Crestwood choose from several different accommodations, all of which are decorated in the height of elegance. The most romantic spot is the private Pavilion, a two-bedroom luxury accommodation that also includes a living-dining room with two marble fireplaces, a vast Jacuzzi tub and a gourmet kitchen. The Rectory, another lavish option, can serve as a private accommodation for two or can be used to serve families or small groups. It includes three full baths, fireplaces, a private balcony, and the Rectory is handicap accessible. Breakfasts are delivered right to your room, as are afternoon snacks. The innkeepers also offer catering service, including kosher foods for bar mitzvahs or weddings. The 200-acre grounds include manicured areas with formal gardens and plenty of countryside with a 100-mile view. Guests can walk along wooded paths enjoying the colors of wildflowers and the mountain views. There is a picturesque and historic little chapel, and, not surprisingly, weddings often are held here by candlelight.
$250-500. MC, VISA, AX, DS, TC. TAC5. 5 rooms, 3 with FP, 1 suite and 2 cottages. Breakfast and afternoon tea included in rates. Type of meal: Full gourmet bkfst. Dinner, gourmet lunch, banquet service, catering service and room service available. Beds: KQT. Cable TV, phone, turndown service, ceiling fan and VCR in room. Air conditioning. Fax, copier, spa, sauna, bicycles, library and child care on premises. Weddings, small meetings, family reunions and seminars hosted. French and Spanish spoken. Antiquing, fishing, golf, live theater, shopping, downhill skiing, cross-country skiing, tennis and water sports nearby.
Pets allowed: With interview.

Bethlehem
E4

The Mulburn Inn

2370 Main St, Rt 302
Bethlehem, NH 03574
(603)869-3389 (800)457-9440 Fax:(603)869-5633

Circa 1908. This English Tudor mansion was once the summer estate of the Woolworth family. The home was built by notable architect Sylvanius D. Morgan, whose inspired design includes many intricate details. The home's romantic ambiance entices a multitude of visitors, and it is within these idyllic walls that Cary Grant and Barbara Hutton enjoyed their honeymoon. Today, guests also have use of a hot tub.

Historic Interest: Crawford Notch State Park, Franconia Notch State Park, Heritage, Mount Washington.
Innkeeper(s): Christina Ferraro & Alecia Loveless. $70-100. MC, VISA, AX, PC, TC. TAC10. 7 rooms with PB. Breakfast and afternoon tea included in rates. Types of meals: Full bkfst and early coffee/tea. Beds: KQDT. TV in room. VCR, fax and library on premises. Weddings and small meetings hosted. Amusement parks, antiquing, fishing, golf, parks, shopping, downhill skiing, cross-country skiing and tennis nearby.
Publicity: The Record, Yankee, Boston Globe.

"You have put a lot of thought, charm, beauty and warmth into the inn. Your breakfasts were oh, so delicious!!"

Bradford
J3

Candlelite Inn

5 Greenhouse Ln
Bradford, NH 03221-3505
(603)938-5571 (888)812-5571

Circa 1897. Nestled on three acres of countryside in the valley of the Lake Sunapee region, this Victorian inn has all of the grace and charm of an era gone by. The inn offers a gazebo porch perfect for sipping lemonade on a summer day. On winter days, keep warm by the parlor's fireplace, while relaxing with a good book. Enjoy a three-course gourmet breakfast, including dessert, in the sun room overlooking the pond. Country roads invite fall strolls, cross-country skiing and snowshoeing.

Historic Interest: Close to the John Hay.
Innkeeper(s): Les & Marilyn Gordon. $70-95. MC, VISA, AX, DS. 6 rooms with PB. Breakfast included in rates. Types of meals: Full bkfst and early coffee/tea. Snacks/refreshments available. Beds: Q. Antiquing, live theater, shopping, downhill skiing, cross-country skiing and sporting events nearby.

Mountain Lake Inn

2871 Rt 114, PO Box 443
Bradford, NH 03221
(603)938-2136 (800)662-6005
E-mail: rfoor@conknet.com
Web: mountainlakeinn.amtg.com

Circa 1760. Originally built as an inn, this white colonial house overlooks Lake Massasecum and is situated on 167 acres, including eight acres of lakefront. Four rooms are in the main house, while the remaining accommodations are in the wing. Breakfast is served in the dining room with a different entree each morning as well as fruit and baked goods. The inn's private sandy beach on Lake Massasecum offers sunning, swimming and fishing, but guests often prefer to take out the canoe and rowboat. Ice skating and snowmobiling on the lake is a popular activity in winter, and there's a snowmobile trail through the property that connects the Bradford and Henniker trails. In summer, enjoy the inn's picnic area and barbecue by the beach, or better yet, take a picnic basket to the waterfall 50 yards from the inn. Mount Sunapee and Pat's Peak ski resorts are nearby.

Innkeeper(s): Bob & Tracy Foor. $85. MC, VISA, AX, DS. 10 rooms. Types of meals: Full bkfst and full gourmet bkfst. Beds: King, Queen, double and twin.. Antiquing, canoeing/kayaking, fishing, golf, hiking, snowmobiling, snowshoeing and downhill skiing nearby.
Publicity: Country Inns, Boston Globe, Star Ledger.

Bretton Woods E4

Bretton Arms Country Inn

Route 302
Bretton Woods, NH 03575
(603)278-1000 (800)258-0330 Fax:(603)278-8838
E-mail: info@mtwashington.com
Web: www.mtwashington.com

Circa 1896. This magnificent Victorian was once a private home and later served as lodging at the prestigious Mount Washington Resort. The inn eventually closed, but it now has been completely restored and reopened. The guest rooms and suites are appointed in Victorian style. The inn has been designated a National Historic Landmark. Guests enjoy use of all that the Mount Washington Resort has to offer, including 2,600 scenic acres. There are a dozen tennis courts, two golf courses, swimming pools, cross-country and alpine ski trails and a Jacuzzi and sauna. Sleigh and carriage rides can be arranged, or guests can simply stroll through the beautifully maintained gardens. Guests can enjoy a gourmet dinner in the inn's impressive dining room. Nightly entertainment is provided mid-May through mid-October and late November through early April at the resort's Cave Lounge, an intimate setting reminiscent of an old speakeasy.

Innkeeper(s): Eleanor Imrie. $89-209. MC, VISA, AX, DS, PC. TAC10. 34 rooms with PB and 3 suites. EP. Type of meal: Full bkfst. Gourmet dinner available. Restaurant on premises. Beds: Q. Cable TV and phone in room. VCR, fax, copier, swimming, sauna, stables, bicycles, tennis, library, child care, downhill skiing and cross country skiing and golf on premises. Handicap access. Weddings, small meetings, family reunions and seminars hosted. Bicycling, fishing, golf, hiking, live theater, parks, shopping, downhill skiing and tennis nearby.

Center Harbor H4

Red Hill Inn

RR 1 Box 99M
Center Harbor, NH 03226-9603
(603)279-7001 (800)573-3445 Fax:(603)279-7003

Circa 1904. The mansion was once the centerpiece of a 1,000-acre estate. It was called "keewaydin" for the strong north wind that blows across Sunset Hill. When the Depression was over, the inn was sold. New owners included European royalty escaping from Nazi Germany. Now the mansion is a restored

country inn with spectacular views of the area's lakes and mountains. From your room you can see a panoramic view of the mountains. Eighteen of the rooms boast wood burning fireplaces, and 10 rooms have private whirlpool baths.

Historic Interest: The White Mountains are a 45-minute drive from the inn.

Innkeeper(s): Don Leavitt & Rick Miller. $105-175. MC, VISA, AX, DC, DS. TAC15. 26 rooms with PB, 18 with FP. Breakfast included in rates. EP. Type of meal: Full bkfst. Gourmet dinner and lunch available. Restaurant on premises. Beds: KQDT. Phone in room. VCR, copier and swimming on premises. Weddings, small meetings, family reunions and seminars hosted. Amusement parks, antiquing, fishing, live theater, shopping, downhill skiing, cross-country skiing and water sports nearby.

Publicity: *New England Getaways, Yankee, Yankee Traveler, Boston, New Hampshire Profiles, Country Living.*

"Our stay was very enjoyable."

Center Ossipee H5

Hitching Post Village Inn

Grant Hill Rd
Center Ossipee, NH 03814
(603)539-3360 (800)482-POST

Circa 1830. All the rooms of this historic inn are spacious and comfortable and overlook the main street, yard or garden. Two second-story rooms offer views of the white steeple of the First Congregational Church and the ever-changing colors of Ossipee Mountains. The canopy room boasts an antique four-poster queen canopy, while the Rose Room features a vintage dental cabinet filled with antique dolls. Items such as homemade sticky buns, stuffed French toast with apples and walnuts, potato pie or chocolate chip pancakes are served for breakfast, often by the innkeeper's children donned with hats and aprons. This is one of the few inns in the area that welcome families with children, so there's plenty of thought given to their entertainment. They can play ping pong in the barn, climb Michael's Fort, a two-story playhouse, cross the street for basketball or the ice cream shop, or go down the road to pick apples. Other activities include canoeing, fishing, swimming and skiing.

Innkeeper(s): Michael & Jessica Drakely. $50-67. MC, VISA, AX, DS, PC, TC. 9 rooms, 1 with PB and 1 conference room. Breakfast and afternoon tea included in rates. Types of meals: Country bkfst and early coffee/tea. Beds: KQDT. VCR on premises. Weddings and family reunions hosted. Amusement parks, antiquing, beaches, bicycling, canoeing/kayaking, fishing, golf, hiking, horseback riding, live theater, parks, shopping, downhill skiing, cross-country skiing, tennis, water sports and wineries nearby.

Pets Allowed.

Charlestown J1

Maple Hedge B&B

355 Main St, PO Box 638
Charlestown, NH 03603
(603)826-5237 (800)962-9539 Fax:(603)826-5237
E-mail: debrine@fmis.net
Web: www.maplehedge.com

Circa 1820. This elegantly restored home is set among acres of lawn and 200-year-old maple trees. The bed & breakfast boasts five distinctive bedrooms. The Beale Room is named for the innkeeper's grandparents from Buffalo; her grandma's high button shoes and Larkin products are displayed. The Butterfly Suite is filled with white wicker and Victorian butterfly trays. The rooms are furnished in antiques and beds are topped with freshly ironed linens. A delectable three-course breakfast is served includes fresh fruit, homemade muffins or scones and a special hot entree. Evening refreshments include California

wine with New Hampshire cheese. Guests can go antiquing, attend country auctions or visit historic sites. There are many outdoor activities, as well. The innkeeper keeps brochures and tourist information on hand.

Historic Interest: Located within the longest National Historic District in the state, Fort Number Four (1 mile), Saint Gauden's National Historic Site (20 minutes), and Dartmouth College (35 minutes).

Innkeeper(s): Joan & Dick DeBrine. $90-105. MC, VISA, PC. TAC10. 5 rooms with PB, 1 suite and 1 conference room. Breakfast and afternoon tea included in rates. Types of meals: Full gourmet bkfst and early coffee/tea. Snacks/refreshments available. Beds: QT. Turndown service in room. Central air. VCR, fax, copier, library and life safety system on premises. Small meetings, family reunions and seminars hosted. Antiquing, fishing, golf, live theater, parks, shopping, downhill skiing, cross-country skiing, sporting events, tennis and water sports nearby.

"The highlight of my two weeks in New England. A breakfast worth jumping out of bed for."

Claremont I2

Goddard Mansion B&B

25 Hillstead Rd
Claremont, NH 03743-3317
(603)543-0603 (800)736-0603 Fax:(603)543-0001
E-mail: deb@goddardmansion.com
Web: www.goddardmansion.com

Circa 1905. This English-style manor house and adjacent garden tea house is surrounded by seven acres of lawns and gardens. Each of the guest rooms is decorated in a different style. One features French Country decor, another sports a Victorian look. The living

room with its fireplace, window seats and baby grand piano is a perfect place to relax. Homemade breakfasts, made using natural ingredients and fresh produce, include items such as souffles, pancakes, freshly baked muffins and fruit. The hearty meals are served in the wood paneled dining room highlighted by an antique Wurlitzer jukebox.

Innkeeper(s): Debbie Albee. $75-125. MC, VISA, AX, DS, PC, TC. 10 rooms, 3 with PB, 1 suite and 2 conference rooms. Breakfast included in rates. Types of meals: Full gourmet bkfst and cont plus. Beds: KQDT. TV, phone, turndown service, some desks and refrigerator (in hall) in room. Air conditioning. VCR, fax, bicycles, library and child care available on premises. Weddings, small meetings, family reunions and seminars hosted. Antiquing, fishing, live theater, parks, shopping, downhill skiing and cross-country skiing nearby.

"A perfect romantic getaway spot."

Conway G5

The Darby Field Inn

Bald Hill, RR1 Box 450
Conway, NH 03818-9801
(603)447-2181 (800)426-4147 Fax:(603)447-5726
E-mail: marc@darbyfield.com
Web: www.darbyfield.com

Circa 1826. This rambling, blue clapboard farmhouse has a huge fieldstone fireplace, stone patio and outstanding views of the Mt. Washington Valley and the Presidential Mountains. For many years, it was

called the Bald Hill Grand View Lodge, but was renamed to honor the first man to climb Mt. Washington, Darby

Field. Modified American Plan rates are $175 to $270 per couple. For those wanting bed & breakfast only, rates range from $130 to $230 per couple.

Innkeeper(s): Marc & Maria Donaldson. $110-250. MC, VISA, PC, TC. 13 rooms with PB and 2 suites. Gourmet dinner available. Beds: KQDT. TV, ceiling fan, VCR and fireplace and Jacuzzi available in room. Air conditioning. Cross-country skiing on premises. Weddings, small meetings, family reunions and seminars hosted. Amusement parks, antiquing, live theater, shopping, downhill skiing and cross-country skiing nearby.

Cornish I2

Chase House B&B Inn

Rt 12A, RR 2 Box 909
Cornish, NH 03745
(603)675-5391 (800)401-9455 Fax:(603)675-5010
Web: www.chasehouse.com

Circa 1776. Cornish's first English settler, Dudley Chase, built this Federal house noted for its fine architecture. In 1845, it was moved to accommodate the Sullivan County Railroad. Designated a National Historic Landmark, it was the birthplace of Salmon Chase, Governor of Ohio, Secretary of the Treasury for President Lincoln and Chief Justice of the Supreme Court. The Chase Manhattan Bank was named after him.

Historic Interest: Saint Gauden's Historic Site (5 minutes), Fort Number Four (30 minutes), American Precision Museum (5 minutes), Dartmouth College (30 minutes).

Innkeeper(s): Barbara Lewis & Ted Doyle. $105-150. MC, VISA. 8 rooms with PB and 3 suites. Breakfast included in rates. Type of meal: Full bkfst. Beds: KQDT. TV in room. Antiquing, hiking and canoeing nearby, downhill skiing and cross-country skiing nearby.

Publicity: *Hartford Courant, The Philadelphia Inquirer, USA Today.*

Durham J6

The Pines Guest House

47 Dover Rd, Rt 108
Durham, NH 03824
(603)868-3361
E-mail: coescorner@aol
Web: newenglandinns.com/inns/pines

Circa 1870. This rambling Victorian manor is surrounded by 15 acres of countryside, including a pond. The home has remained in the same family for five generations, and many of the furnishings are family pieces. The screened-in porches are set up with wicker furniture for those who wish to relax. Three of the guest rooms include a fireplace. Breakfasts are served in a dining room decorated with period furniture. Tables are set with antique china and silver. The University of New Hampshire is a half-mile from the home.

Innkeeper(s): Roger & Mary Margaret Jaques. $55-95. MC, VISA, AX, PC, TC. TAC10. 5 rooms, 3 with PB, 3 with FP and 1 suite. Breakfast included in rates. Types of meals: Cont plus and early coffee/tea. Beds: QDT. Cable TV, phone and VCR in room. Air conditioning. Library and screened porch with wicker in season; family room/art gallery for reading on premises. French spoken. Antiquing, fishing, live theater, parks, shopping, cross-country skiing, sporting events and water sports nearby.

"What a beautiful setting with these towering pines."

Three Chimneys Inn

17 Newmarket Rd
Durham, NH 03824
(603)868-7800 (888)399-9777 Fax:(603)868-2964
E-mail: chimneys3@threechimneysinn.com
Web: www.threechimneysinn.com

Circa 1649. Valentine Hill, a 17th-century entrepreneur, was responsible for building this inn. Not surprisingly, the 1649 inn is listed in the National Register. After passing from owner to owner, the historic gem fell into disrepair, but fortunately has been restored to its former state. Most of the rooms include a fireplace or wood-burning stove. Although the inn is among the nation's most historic buildings, there are modern amenities to be found, including Jacuzzi tubs, dataports and fax services. If all the history isn't enough, the inn affords views of Oyster River and Little Bay. A traditional menu, featuring local items, is offered at the inn's restaurant.

Innkeeper(s): Ron & Jane Peterson. $169 and up. MC, VISA, AX, DS, TC. TAC10. 23 rooms with PB, 17 with FP and 2 conference rooms. Breakfast and afternoon tea included in rates. Types of meals: Full gourmet bkfst and afternoon coffee/tea. Gourmet dinner, snacks/refreshments, gourmet lunch, banquet service and room service available. Restaurant on premises. Beds: KQ. Cable TV, phone, turndown service, data port and Jacuzzi in room. Air conditioning. Fax and copier on premises. Handicap access. Weddings, small meetings, family reunions and seminars hosted. Amusement parks, antiquing, fishing, golf, museums, historic home tours, live theater, parks, shopping, cross-country skiing, sporting events, tennis and water sports nearby.

East Andover   I4

Highland Lake Inn B&B

32 Maple St, PO Box 164
East Andover, NH 03231-0164
(603)735-6426 Fax:(603)735-5355

Circa 1767. This early Colonial-Victorian inn overlooks three mountains, and all the rooms have views of either the lake or the mountains. Many guest rooms feature handmade quilts and

some have four-poster beds. Guests may relax with a book from the inn's library in front of the sitting room fireplace or walk the seven-acre grounds and enjoy old apple and maple trees, as well as the shoreline of the lake. Adjacent to a 21-acre nature conservancy, there are scenic trails and a stream to explore. Highland Lake is stocked with bass and also has trout. Fresh fruit salads, hot entrees, and homemade breads are featured at breakfast.

Historic Interest: Two Shaker Villages, old one-room school house.

Innkeeper(s): Mary Petras. $85-125. MC, VISA, AX. 10 rooms with PB. Breakfast included in rates. Type of meal: Full bkfst. Beds: KQT. Ceiling fan in room. VCR on premises. Weddings, small meetings, family reunions and seminars hosted. Amusement parks, antiquing, fishing, live theater, shopping, downhill skiing, cross-country skiing, sporting events and water sports nearby.

Publicity: *Andover Beacon.*

Eaton Center   G6

Rockhouse Mountain Farm Inn

PO Box 90
Eaton Center, NH 03832-0090
(603)447-2880

Circa 1900. This handsome old house is framed by maple trees on 450 acres of forests, streams, fields and wildflowers.

Milking cows, pigs, geese, peacocks and llamas provide entertainment for city youngsters of all ages. Three generations of the Edges have operated this inn and some guests have been coming since 1946, the year it opened. A 250-year-old barn bulges at times with new-mown hay, and there is a nearby beach with swimming and boating for the exclusive use of guests.

Innkeeper(s): Johnny & Alana Edge. $56-64. PC, TC. 18 rooms, 8 with PB, 1 with FP and 2 cottages. Breakfast and dinner included in rates. MAP. Type of meal: Full bkfst. Beds: DT. TV in room. Swimming, library and farm animals on premises. Handicap access. Small meetings and family reunions hosted. French spoken. Antiquing, fishing, golf, live theater, parks, shopping, tennis and water sports nearby.

Publicity: *New York Times, Family Circle, Woman's Day, Boston Globe, Country Vacations.*

"We have seen many lovely places, but Rockhouse remains the real high spot, the one to which we most want to return."

Enfield   H2

Mary Keane House

Box 5 Lower Shaker Village, Rt 4 A
Enfield, NH 03748
(603)632-4241 (888)239-2153
E-mail: mary.keane.house@valley.net
Web: www.tneorg.com/marykeane/

Circa 1930. This lakeside Queen Anne Victorian is pristinely restored and painted mauve with gray and white trim. It adjoins a chapel, all encircled with a white picket fence. Views from the porches and balconies include the inn's flower beds, Lake Mascoma and 1,200 acres of woodland and meadow. A handsome drawing room with antiques and fireplace, mahogany paneling, stained and beveled glass, and a gracious front staircase are featured. Mini frittatas with salsa, rhubarb coffee cake and hot oatmeal scones are among the items offered on the inn's bountiful table. Walk to the Shaker Museum, herb gardens, Shaker Village and the Dana Robes Woodcraftsmen Workshop where Shaker furniture is fashioned.

Innkeeper(s): Sharon & David Carr. $89-139. MC, VISA, AX, TC. TAC10. 5 rooms with PB and 3 suites. Breakfast included in rates. AP. Types of meals: Full gourmet bkfst and early coffee/tea. Beds: KQDT. Cable TV in room. VCR, copier, swimming and library on premises. Weddings, small meetings and family reunions hosted. Antiquing, fishing, golf, live theater, shopping, downhill skiing, cross-country skiing, sporting events, tennis and water sports nearby.

Pets allowed: If well behaved.

Franconia   F3

The Inn at Forest Hills

Rt 142, PO Box 783
Franconia, NH 03580
(603)823-9550 (800)280-9550 Fax:(603)823-8701
E-mail: ahi@innfhills.com
Web: www.innatforesthills.com

Circa 1890. This Tudor-style inn in the White Mountains offers a solarium, a living room with fireplace and a large common room

with fireplace and cathedral ceilings. Breakfast is served with a quiet background of classical music in the dining room, where in the winter there's a blazing fireplace, and in summer the French doors open to the scenery. Guest rooms feature a casual country decor with quilts, flowered wall coverings and some four-poster beds. Cross-country ski for free on the inn's property and at the local touring center. Downhill facilities are found at Bretton Woods, Cannon or Loon Mountain. Nearby Franconia Notch Park and the White Mountains feature trails designed for cycling and hiking. Innkeepers are justices of the peace, and will do weddings or a renewal of vows.

Historic Interest: Mount Washington Hotel (20 minutes), Franconia Notch State Park (5 minutes), Robert Frost Museum (10 minutes).

Innkeeper(s): Gordon & Joanne Haym. $95-165. MC, VISA, PC, TC. 7 rooms with PB. Breakfast included in rates. Type of meal: Full bkfst. Gourmet dinner and snacks/refreshments available. Beds: KQ. VCR, fax, tennis and library on premises. Weddings, small meetings, family reunions and seminars hosted. Antiquing, fishing, golf, parks, shopping, downhill skiing, cross-country skiing and water sports nearby.

"What a delightful inn! I loved the casual country elegance of your B&B and can understand why you are so popular with brides and grooms."

Franconia Inn

1300 Easton Rd
Franconia, NH 03580-4921
(603)823-5542 (800)473-5299 Fax:(603)823-8078

Circa 1934. Beautifully situated on 117 acres below the White Mountain's famous Franconia Notch, this white clapboard inn is three stories high. An oak-paneled library, parlor, rathskeller lounge and two verandas offer relaxing retreats. The inn's rooms are simply decorated in a pleasing style and there is a special honeymoon suite with private Jacuzzi. Bach, classic wines and an elegant American cuisine are featured in the inn's unpretentious dining room. There's no shortage of activity here. The inn offers four clay tennis courts, horseback riding, a heated swimming pool, croquet, fishing, cross-country ski trails and glider rides among its outdoor amenities.

Innkeeper(s): Alec Morris. $103-188. MC, VISA, AX. 34 rooms, 29 with PB, 3 with FP, 4 suites and 1 conference room. Breakfast included in rates. MAP, EP. Types of meals: Full gourmet bkfst and early coffee/tea. Gourmet dinner, picnic lunch and catering service available. Restaurant on premises. Beds: KQDT. VCR, copier, spa, swimming, bicycles, tennis, child care, sleighs and ice skating on premises. Weddings, small meetings, family reunions and seminars hosted. Amusement parks, antiquing, fishing, live theater, parks, shopping, downhill skiing, cross-country skiing and sporting events nearby.

Publicity: *Philadelphia Inquirer, Boston Globe, Travel & Leisure, Powder.*

"The piece de resistance of the Franconia Notch is the Franconia Inn."—Philadelphia Inquirer

Gilmanton I5

The Historic Temperance Tavern

PO Box 369
Gilmanton, NH 03237-0369
(603)267-7349 Fax:(603)267-7503

Circa 1793. This historic Colonial inn has been welcoming visitors for more than 200 years, and it acquired its name during a temperance movement in the early 19th century. The inn offers five guest rooms, including one suite, all of which feature private baths and turndown service. The rooms all boast furnishings that reflect an authentic Federal decor. Visitors enjoy the inn's many fireplaces, its common rooms and fine food. Guests often schedule outings to Gunstock Mountain Ski Resort, Loudon Raceway and Shaker Village.

Innkeeper(s): Beverly Nametz. $75-125. MC, VISA, TC. 6 rooms, 5 with PB, 2 with FP, 1 suite and 1 conference room. Breakfast included in rates. MAP. Types of meals: Full gourmet bkfst and early coffee/tea. Gourmet dinner, picnic lunch, gourmet lunch and catering service available. Beds: T. VCR, fax, copier and pet boarding on premises. Weddings, small meetings, family reunions and seminars hosted. Amusement parks, antiquing, fishing, parks, shopping, downhill skiing, cross-country skiing, sporting events and water sports nearby. Pets Allowed.

Glen F5

Bernerhof Inn

Rt 302, PO Box 240
Glen, NH 03838-0240
(603)383-9132 (800)548-8007 Fax:(603)383-0809
E-mail: stay@bernerhofinn.com
Web: www.bernerhofinn.com

Circa 1880. Built in the late 19th century for travelers passing through the Crawford Notch, in the fifties this historic inn was renamed Bernerhof Inn by its proprietors, the Zumsteins, who brought fame to their inn by providing guests with fine accommodations, musical entertainment and cuisine reflecting their Swiss heritage. Today's innkeepers are proud to continue to feature some of the original Swiss recipes (such as Emince de Veau Zurichoise, the national dish of Switzerland), as part of their award-winning menu. Guest rooms are decorated with antiques, and many include two-person Jacuzzi tubs. One offers a fireplace. Novice chefs will enjoy the "Taste of the Mountains Cooking School," where they can pick up many tricks of the trade from chef.... The inn's location in the foothills of the White Mountains provides easy access to a variety of outdoor activities including skiing, alpine slides and summer water slides at Attitash Bear Peak. In addition to the historic inn, the innkeepers also offer The Red Apple Inn, a motel-style property. Both properties are non-smoking.

Innkeeper(s): Sharon Wroblewski. $75-150. MC, VISA, AX, DS, PC, TC. 9 rooms with PB and 2 suites. Breakfast included in rates. MAP. Types of meals: Full bkfst and early coffee/tea. Gourmet dinner, picnic lunch, catering service and room service available. Restaurant on premises. Beds: KQ. Cable TV, phone, ceiling fan and VCR in room. Air conditioning. Fax, copier and sauna on premises. Weddings, small meetings and family reunions hosted. Amusement parks, antiquing, bicycling, fishing, golf, hiking, rock climbing, ice climbing, snow shoeing, live theater, parks, shopping, downhill skiing and cross-country skiing nearby.

"When people want to treat themselves, this is where they come."

Greenfield   K3

The Greenfield Inn

Forest Rd at Rts 31N & 136
Greenfield, NH 03047
(603)547-6327 (800)678-4144 Fax:(603)547-2418

Circa 1817. In the 1850s this inn was purchased by Henry
Dunklee, innkeeper of the old Mayfield Inn across the street.
When there was an overflow of guests at his tavern, Mr.
Dunklee accommodated them here. This totally renovated
Victorian mansion features veranda views of Crotched, Temple
and Monadnock Mountains. There is a conference room with a
lovely mountain view. The gracious innkeepers and comfortable
interiors have been enjoyed by many well-traveled guests,
including Dolores and Bob Hope.

Historic Interest: The inn is located near the historic town graveyard and the
first town hall in New Hampshire.

Innkeeper(s): Barbara & Vic Mangini. $49-139. MC, VISA, AX, PC, TC.
TAC10. 13 rooms, 10 with PB, 2 suites, 1 cottage and 1 conference room.
Breakfast included in rates. Type of meal: Full bkfst. Beds: KQDT. Phone,
ceiling fan and VCR in room. Air conditioning. Fax, copier, spa, library,
jacuzzis and whirlpool tubs on premises. Small meetings, family reunions and
seminars hosted. Antiquing, fishing, no-tax shopping, live theater, parks,
shopping, downhill skiing, cross-country skiing and water sports nearby.

Publicity: *Manchester Union Leader, Insider.*

"I'm coming back for more of this New Hampshire therapy."—
Bob Hope.

Greenland   K6

Captain Folsom Inn

Rt 151, PO Box 396
Greenland, NH 03840-0396
(603)436-2662

Circa 1758. George Washington is said to have stopped at this
former tavern along the Boston to Portland stage coach route,
where he gave a speech on the front lawn. Located on six
acres, the inn was an active
American Revolution site and
one of the most prominent
inns in the state. A three-
story federal building, it still
has the original kitchen fireplaces with brick ovens. The
innkeeper has taught open

hearth cooking classes and has a collection of old colonial
recipes. In the tavern at the back of the inn, guests can experience the atmosphere and life of colonial times. Guest rooms
feature canopy beds, antiques and reproductions. There are
wraparound porches on the back of the house on two levels.

Innkeeper(s): Faith & Bob McTigue. $45-85. MC, VISA, AX, DS, PC, TC. 6
rooms, 2 with PB, 6 with FP. Breakfast and afternoon tea included in rates.
Types of meals: Full bkfst and early coffee/tea. Beds: QT. Air conditioning.
VCR, swimming, child care and Nordic Track machine on premises.
Weddings, small meetings, family reunions and seminars hosted. Antiquing,
fishing, golf, beaches, sailing, hiking, bicycling, live theater, downhill skiing
and water sports nearby.

Pets allowed: Size.

Publicity: *Lifestyles, Salmon Falls Stoneware.*

Hampton   K6

The Oceanside Inn

365 Ocean Blvd
Hampton, NH 03842-3633
(603)926-3542 Fax:(603)926-3549

Circa 1900. This two-story hotel with upper veranda is located
directly across the street from the ocean and adjacent to the
Oceanside Mall. Elegant interiors include a pillared living
room/library with fire-
place, comfortable sit-
ting areas, Oriental
rugs and paintings. A
sample guest room,
the Patriot Gove
Room, has two dou-
ble beds, wicker

chairs and views of the ocean. Other rooms, such as the Moses
Leavitt Room, offer a canopy bed. A continental-plus breakfast
is available, and there is nightly turndown service. Beach
chairs and towels are offered for enjoying the sandy beaches.

Innkeeper(s): Skip & Debbie Windemiller. $125-145. MC, VISA, AX, DS, TC.
TAC5. 10 rooms with PB and 1 cottage. Breakfast included in rates. Type of
meal: Cont plus. Beds: KQDT. Phone and turndown service in room. Air conditioning. VCR, fax, copier and library on premises. Amusement parks,
antiquing, golf, live theater, shopping, tennis and water sports nearby.

Henniker   J3

Colby Hill Inn

3 The Oaks, PO Box 779
Henniker, NH 03242-0779
(603)428-3281 (800)531-0330 Fax:(603)428-9218
E-mail: info@colbyhillinn.com
Web: www.colbyhillinn.com

Circa 1797. This 18th-century Colonial and its surrounding
five acres is a classic example of an old New England Farm.
There are still old barns on the grounds, as well as a restored
carriage house. Stroll the
grounds with friendly inn
dog Delilah and you'll
also find gardens, a swimming pool and a pic-
turesque gazebo. Antiques
fill the guest rooms, each
of which is individually

appointed in an elegant, traditional style. Four rooms have
working fireplaces. Guests and others can enjoy a romantic dinner by candlelight at the inn's dining room. Specialties of the
house include items such as baked brie with toasted almonds,
poached salmon in a mustard cream sauce and rich desserts,
including maple walnut pie. Dinner is served every night.

Innkeeper(s): Ellie & John Day, Laurel Day Mack. $85-185. MC, VISA, AX,
DC, CB, DS, PC, TC. TAC10. 16 rooms with PB, 4 with FP and 1 conference
room. Breakfast included in rates. Types of meals: Full gourmet bkfst and
early coffee/tea. Gourmet dinner, snacks/refreshments, banquet service and
room service available. Restaurant on premises. Beds: KQDT. Phone and data
port in room. Air conditioning. VCR, fax, copier, swimming and skating on
premises. Weddings, small meetings, family reunions and seminars hosted.
Antiquing, fishing, Canterbury Shaker village, parks, downhill skiing and
cross-country skiing nearby.

Holderness H4

The Inn on Golden Pond

Rt 3, PO Box 680
Holderness, NH 03245
(603)968-7269
E-mail: innongp@lr.net
Web: www.innongoldenpond.com

Circa 1879. Framed by meandering stone walls and split-rail fences more than 100 years old, this inn is situated on 50 acres of woodlands. Most rooms over-look picturesque countryside and nearby is Squam Lake, setting for the film "On Golden Pond." An inviting, 60-foot screened porch provides a place to relax during the summer.

Innkeeper(s): Bill & Bonnie Webb. $85-140. MC, VISA, AX, DS. TAC10. 7 rooms with PB and 1 suite. Breakfast included in rates. Types of meals: Full bkfst and early coffee/tea. Beds: KQT. Turndown service in room. Antiquing, fishing, live theater, shopping, downhill skiing, cross-country skiing, sporting events and water sports nearby.

Publicity: *Boston Globe, Baltimore Sun, Los Angeles Times.*

"Another sweet flower added to my bouquet of life."

Hopkinton J4

The Country Porch B&B

281 Moran Rd
Hopkinton, NH 03229
(603)746-6391 Fax:(603)746-6391

Circa 1978. This farmhouse does in fact sport a wraparound covered porch where guests are often found relaxing and enjoying the peaceful 15-acre grounds. The home was built in the late 1970s, but it is a replica of an 18th-century Colonial. There

are three guest rooms, decorated in Colonial style. One room has a fireplace, another includes a canopy bed. Whatever the season, guests will find something to do in the Hopkinton area. Guests can visit a restored Shaker Village, shop for antiques, fish, pick berries, ski and much more.

Innkeeper(s): Tom & Wendy Solomon. $60-80. MC, VISA, PC, TC. TAC10. 3 rooms with PB, 1 with FP and 1 conference room. Breakfast included in rates. Types of meals: Full bkfst and early coffee/tea. Beds: KT. Ceiling fan in room. VCR, fax, copier and swimming on premises. Weddings, small meetings, family reunions and seminars hosted. Antiquing, fishing, golf, live theater, parks, shopping, downhill skiing, cross-country skiing, sporting events, tennis and water sports nearby.

"A highlight of our trip and will be forever a treasured memory."

Jackson F5

Carter Notch Inn

Carter Notch Rd, Box 269
Jackson, NH 03846
(603)383-9630 (800)794-9434
Web: carternotchinn.com

Circa 1900. This turn-of-the-century home rests on a wooded acre, offering views of the surrounding mountains, Eagle Mt.

Golf Course and the Wildcat River. Guest rooms are charming, some have painted wood floors, throw rugs, quilts and wicker or oak furnishings. The innkeepers latest addition is "The Treehouse," which features suites with two-person Jacuzzi tubs, private decks and fireplaces. Breakfast is a treat; be sure to ask for Jim's Grand Marnier French toast. Cross-country ski trails begin right out the front door, as does golfing. Hiking and other outdoor activities abound in the area. After a day touring the area, return to the inn for a relaxing soak in the outdoor hot tub or sit on the wraparound front porch and enjoy the view.

Innkeeper(s): Jim & Lynda Dunwell. $59-159. MC, VISA, AX, DS, PC, TC. TAC10. 7 rooms, 6 with PB and 1 suite. Breakfast and afternoon tea included in rates. Types of meals: Full gourmet bkfst and early coffee/tea. Beds: KQD. Air conditioning. VCR, fax, spa, swimming and tennis on premises. Weddings, small meetings, family reunions and seminars hosted. Antiquing, fishing, golf, live theater, parks, downhill skiing, cross-country skiing, tennis and water sports nearby.

Dana Place Inn

Rt 16, Pinkham Notch Rd
Jackson, NH 03846
(603)383-6822 (800)537-9276 Fax:(603)383-6022
E-mail: dpi@ncia.net
Web: www.danaplace.com

Circa 1860. The original owners received this Colonial farm-house as a wedding present. The warm, cozy atmosphere of the inn is surpassed only by the spectacular mountain views. During autumn, the fall leaves explode with color, and guests can enjoy the surroundings while taking a hike or bike ride through the area. The beautiful Ellis River is the perfect place for an afternoon of fly-fishing or a picnic. After a scrumptious country breakfast, winter guests can step out the door and into skis for a day of cross-country skiing.

Historic Interest: Mount Washington Auto Road (5 miles), 1860s Coq. Railroad (30 miles).

Innkeeper(s): The Levine Family. $95-225. MC, VISA, AX, DC, CB, DS, PC, TC. TAC10. 35 rooms with PB. Breakfast and afternoon tea included in rates. Type of meal: Full bkfst. Gourmet dinner, picnic lunch, banquet service and room service available. Restaurant on premises. Beds: KQDT. VCR, fax, copier, spa, swimming, tennis, library and hiking on premises. Weddings, small meetings, family reunions and seminars hosted. Amusement parks, antiquing, fishing, golf, White Mountain attractions, live theater, parks, shopping, downhill skiing, cross-country skiing and water sports nearby.

Pets allowed: Exterior rooms.

Publicity: *Travel & Leisure, Inn Spots, Bon Appetit, Country Journal.*

"We had such a delightful time at Dana Place Inn. We will recommend you to everyone."

Ellis River House

Rt 16, Box 656
Jackson, NH 03846
(603)383-9339 (800)233-8309 Fax:(603)383-4142
E-mail: innkeeper@erhinn.com
Web: www.erhinn.com

Circa 1893. Andrew Harriman built this farmhouse, as well as the village town hall and three-room schoolhouse where the innkeepers' children attended school. Classic antiques and Laura Ashley prints decorate the guest rooms and riverfront

"honeymoon" cottage, and each window reveals views of magnificent mountains, the vineyard or spectacular Ellis River. In 1993, the innkeepers added 18 rooms, 11 of which feature fireplaces and six offer two-person Jacuzzis. They also added three suites, a heated, outdoor pool, an indoor Jacuzzi and a sauna.

Historic Interest: The White Mountains School of Art is nearby. Artists such as Albert Bierstadt and Benjamin Champney were among the many to attend this school.

Innkeeper(s): Barry & Barbara Lubao. $89-289. MC, VISA, AX, DC, CB, DS, PC, TC. TAC5. 18 rooms with PB, 11 with FP, 3 suites, 1 cottage and 1 conference room. Breakfast included in rates. MAP. Types of meals: Full bkfst and early coffee/tea. Afternoon tea, dinner and picnic lunch available. Beds: KQDT. Cable TV and phone in room. Air conditioning. Fax, spa, swimming and sauna on premises. Handicap access. Weddings, small meetings, family reunions and seminars hosted. Polish spoken. Amusement parks, antiquing, fishing, live theater, parks, shopping, downhill skiing, cross-country skiing, sporting events and water sports nearby.

"We have stayed at many B&Bs all over the world and are in agreement that the beauty and hospitality of Ellis River House is that of a world-class bed & breakfast."

The Inn at Jackson

PO Box 807, Main St at Thornhill Rd
Jackson, NH 03846
(603)383-4321 (800)289-8600 Fax:(603)383-4085
E-mail: innjack@ncia.net
Web: www.innatjackson.com

Circa 1902. Architect Stanford White designed this inn for the Baldwin family of New York (of piano fame) and served as their summer residence. The inn offers a grand foyer, spacious guest

rooms, some with TV and air conditioning, private baths, hardwood floors, fireplaces and an outdoor hot tub Jacuzzi. A full breakfast is served in our sunporch overlooking the mountains.

Historic Interest: Mount Washington (15 minutes) and Cog Railway (45 minutes).
Innkeeper(s): Lori Tradewell. $86-195. MC, VISA, AX, DC, CB, DS, PC, TC. TAC10. 14 rooms with PB, 6 with FP. Breakfast included in rates. Type of meal: Full bkfst. Beds: KQT. TV in room. Air conditioning. VCR, fax, spa and library on premises. Fishing, live theater, parks, shopping, downhill skiing and cross-country skiing nearby.

"We had a terrific time and found the inn warm and cozy and most of all relaxing."

Nestlenook Farm Resort

Dinsmore Rd
Jackson, NH 03846
(603)383-9443 (800)659-9443 Fax:(603)383-4515
E-mail: nestlenk@ncia.net
Web: www.luxurymountaingetaways.com

Circa 1790. This 200-year-old Victorian is decorated with white gingerbread trim on windows, balustrades and porches. Each guest room has its own Jacuzzi and antique furnishings. In the dining room is a handsome Victorian bird cage complete

with exotic finches. The Murdoch Suite boasts a double Jacuzzi, original art and views of the inn's 65 acres of grounds. Sleigh rides and mountain bikes are available.

Innkeeper(s): Robert Cyr. $125-320. MC, VISA, DS. TAC10. 7 rooms with PB, 1 with FP. Breakfast included in rates. Type of meal: Full bkfst. Snacks/refreshments available. Beds: KQ. Phone in room. Fax, copier, swimming, bicycles, recreation room with stereo, VCR and surround sound and pool table on premises. Antiquing, fishing, hiking, live theater, parks, shopping, downhill skiing, cross-country skiing and water sports nearby.
Publicity: *Ski, Friends, Manage Quebec, Discerning Traveler.*

Jaffrey   L3

The Benjamin Prescott Inn

Rt 124 E, 433 Turnpike Rd
Jaffrey, NH 03452
(603)532-6637 Fax:(603)532-6637

Circa 1853. Colonel Prescott arrived on foot in Jaffrey in 1775 with an ax in his hand and a bag of beans on his back. The family built

this classic Greek Revival many years later. Now, candles light the windows, seen from the stonewall-lined lane adjacent to the inn. Each room bears the name of a Prescott family member and is furnished with antiques.

Innkeeper(s): Jan & Barry Miller. $75-150. MC, VISA, AX, PC, TC. TAC10. 10 rooms with PB, 3 suites and 1 conference room. Breakfast included in rates. EP. Type of meal: Full bkfst. Beds: KQDT. Phone and ceiling fan in room. VCR, fax and library on premises. Weddings, small meetings, family reunions and seminars hosted. Antiquing, fishing, national Shrine, live theater, parks, shopping, downhill skiing, cross-country skiing, sporting events and water sports nearby.

"The coffee and breakfasts were delicious and the hospitality overwhelming."

Jefferson   E4

Applebrook B&B

Rt 115A, PO Box 178
Jefferson, NH 03583-0178
(603)586-7713 (800)545-6504

Circa 1797. Panoramic views surround this large Victorian farmhouse nestled in the middle of New Hampshire's White Mountains. Guests can awake to the smell of freshly baked muffins made with locally picked berries. A comfortable, fire-lit sitting room boasts stained glass, a goldfish pool and a beautiful view of Mt.

Washington. The innkeeper's newest room, Nellie's Nook, includes a king-size bed and a balcony with views of the mountains and a two-person spa. Test your golfing skills at the nearby 18-hole championship course, or spend the day antique hunting. A trout stream and spring-fed rock pool are nearby. Wintertime guests can ice skate or race through the powder at nearby ski resorts or by way of snowmobile, finish off the day with a moonlight toboggan ride. After a full day, guests can enjoy a soak in the hot tub under the stars, where they might see shooting stars or the Northern Lights.

Historic Interest: The area boasts several covered bridges within 10 miles of the bed & breakfast. The Cog Railroad is 15 miles away, while the Jefferson Historical Museum is only one mile from the inn.

Innkeeper(s): Sandra Conley & Martin Kelly. $50-90. MC, VISA, PC, TC. TAC10. 14 rooms, 7 with PB and 1 conference room. Breakfast included in rates. Types of meals: Full bkfst and early coffee/tea. Beds: KQDT. Ceiling fan in room. Spa and library on premises. Weddings, small meetings, family reunions and seminars hosted. Amusement parks, antiquing, fishing, live theater, parks, shopping, downhill skiing, cross-country skiing and water sports nearby.

Pets allowed: Two rooms kept pet-free; $6.00/night per pet-half of which is donated to Lancaster Humane Society.

"We came for a night and stayed for a week."

Lincoln   F4

Red Sleigh Inn

PO Box 562
Lincoln, NH 03251-0562
(603)745-8517

Circa 1900. This house was built by J. E. Henry, owner of the Lincoln Paper Mill, a huge lumber business and dairy farm. The foundation was constructed of stones taken from the Pemigawasset River. Loretta's blueberry muffins are a guest favorite.

Innkeeper(s): Bill & Loretta Deppe. $55-85. MC, VISA, TC. 6 rooms, 2 with PB. Breakfast included in rates. Type of meal: Full bkfst. Beds: KQ. TV in room. VCR on premises. Weddings and family reunions hosted. Amusement parks, antiquing, fishing, live theater, parks, shopping, downhill skiing, cross-country skiing, sporting events and water sports nearby.

Publicity: *Newsday, Ski, Skiing.*

"Your ears must be ringing because we haven't stopped talking about the Red Sleigh Inn and its wonderful, caring owners."

Littleton   E3

Thayers Inn

136 Main St
Littleton, NH 03561-4014
(603)444-6469 Fax:(800)634-8179
E-mail: don@thayersinn.com
Web: www.thayersinn.com

Circa 1843. Ulysses Grant is said to have spoken from the inn's balcony in 1869. In those days, fresh firewood and candles were delivered to guest rooms each day as well as a personal thunder-jug. The handsome facade features four 30-foot, hand-carved pillars and a cupola with views of the surrounding mountains.

Innkeeper(s): Don & Carolyn Lambert. $50-100. MC, VISA, AX, DC, CB, DS. 41 rooms, 38 with PB and 6 suites. AP. Dinner and lunch available. Beds: KQDT. Fax and copier on premises. Antiquing, fishing, live theater, downhill skiing, cross-country skiing and water sports nearby.

Publicity: *Business Life, Vacationer, Bon Appetit, Yankee.*

"This Thanksgiving, Russ and I spent a lot of time thinking about the things that are most important to us. It seemed appropriate that we should write to thank you for your warm hospitality as innkeepers."

Lyme   G2

Alden Country Inn

Route 10, On The Common
Lyme, NH 03768
(603)795-2222
E-mail: info@aldencountryinn.com
Web: www.aldencountryinn.com

Circa 1809. This handsome country inn, standing at the village common, first became a stagecoach stop in the 1830s. It has recently been restored and is decorated in a traditional style with antiques. A full breakfast is served and the inn's restaurant offers New England cookery. Guests staying on Saturday night will especially enjoy the next morning's Sunday brunch, included in the rates. Townsfolk mingle with guests on the porch or in the inn's tavern and restaurant.

Innkeeper(s): Mickey Dowd. $105-165. MC, VISA, AX, DC, DS. 15 rooms with PB, 3 with FP. MAP. Type of meal: Full bkfst. Restaurant on premises. Beds: KQ. Phone and tV upon request in room.

Moultonborough   H5

Olde Orchard Inn

RR 1 Box 256, Lee Rd & Lees Mill
Moultonborough, NH 03254-9502
(603)476-5004 (800)598-5845 Fax:(603)476-5419

Circa 1790. This farmhouse rests next to a mountain brook and pond in the midst of an apple orchard. Nine guest rooms are available, all with private baths. Three rooms have a Jacuzzi tub. After enjoying a large country breakfast, guests may borrow a bicycle for a ride to Lake Winnipesaukee, just a mile away. The inn is within an hour's drive of five downhill skiing areas, and guests also may cross-country ski nearby. The Castle in the Clouds and the Audubon Loon Center are nearby.

Innkeeper(s): Jim & Mary Senner. $75-140. MC, VISA, PC, TC. TAC10. 9 rooms with PB, 3 with FP. Breakfast included in rates. Type of meal: Full bkfst. Beds: QDT. Air conditioning. VCR, fax, child care and sauna on premises. Small meetings, family reunions and seminars hosted. Antiquing, fishing, live theater, parks, shopping, downhill skiing, cross-country skiing and water sports nearby.

Pets allowed: In kennel or barn.

Newfound Lake   H4

The Inn on Newfound Lake

1030 Mayhew Tpke
Newfound Lake, NH 03222-5108
(603)744-9111 (800)745-7990 Fax:(603)744-3894

Circa 1840. This inn was the mid-way stop on the stage coach route from Boston to Montreal and formerly was known as the Pasquaney Inn. A full veranda overlooks the lake with its spectacular sunsets. Located in the foothills of the White Mountains, the inn is situated on more than seven acres of New Hampshire countryside.

Historic Interest: Cantebury, an authentic Shaker village, is just 20 minutes away. Daniel Webster's birthplace and the state capital are about a half-hour drive from the inn.
Innkeeper(s): Phelps C. Boyce II. $75-295. MC, VISA, AX, DS. 31 rooms, 23 with PB and 2 suites. Breakfast included in rates. MAP, AP. Type of meal: Cont. Dinner available. Beds: QT. Antiquing, fishing, downhill skiing, cross-country skiing and water sports nearby.

"The rooms were quaint and cozy with just the right personal touches, and always immaculate. The bed and pillows were so comfortable, it was better than sleeping at home! The inn itself is magnificent, elegance never felt so warm and homey."

New London   13

The Inn at Pleasant Lake

125 Pleasant St, PO Box 1030
New London, NH 03257-1030
(603)526-6271 (800)626-4907 Fax:(603)526-4111
E-mail: bmackenz@kear.tds.net
Web: www.innatpleasantlake.com

Circa 1790. In its early days, this inn served as a farmhouse. By the late 1870s, it was serving guests as a summer resort. Its tradition of hospitality continues today with relaxing guest

rooms, which offer lake or wood views. The five-acre grounds face Pleasant Lake, which has a private beach. Guests may enjoy the lake on their own rowboat or canoe, but the innkeepers will lend theirs if requested. Meander over wooded trails or take a stroll around New London. Innkeeper and Culinary Institute of America graduate Brian MacKenzie prepares the inn's five-course, prix fixe dinners.

Innkeeper(s): Linda & Brian MacKenzie. $110-165. MC, VISA, DS, PC, TC. TAC10. 11 rooms with PB and 3 suites. Breakfast and afternoon tea included in rates. Types of meals: Full bkfst and cont plus. Dinner and banquet service available. Beds: KQD. Copier, swimming and exercise room on premises. Weddings, small meetings and family reunions hosted. Antiquing, fishing, golf, hiking, biking, live theater, shopping, downhill skiing, cross-country skiing, sporting events and tennis nearby.

"What a perfect setting for our first ever visit to New England."

North Conway   F5

The 1785 Inn

3582 White Mountain Hwy
North Conway, NH 03860-1785
(603)356-9025 (800)421-1785 Fax:(603)356-6081
E-mail: the1785inn@aol.com
Web: www.the1785inn.com

Circa 1785. The main section of this center-chimney house was built by Captain Elijah Dinsmore of the New Hampshire Rangers. He was granted the land for service in the American Revolution. Original hand-hewn beams, corner posts, fireplaces, and a brick oven are still visible and operating. The inn is located at the historical marker popularized by the White

Mountain School of Art in the 19th century.

Historic Interest: Mount Washington.
Innkeeper(s): Becky & Charles Mallar. $69-239. MC, VISA, AX, DC, CB, DS, PC, TC. TAC10. 17 rooms, 12 with PB, 1 suite and 2 conference rooms. Breakfast included in rates. Types of meals: Full gourmet bkfst and early coffee/tea. Gourmet dinner, snacks/refreshments, banquet service and room service available. Restaurant on premises. Beds: KQD. Air conditioning. VCR, fax, copier, swimming, library and child care on premises. Weddings, small meetings, family reunions and seminars hosted. French spoken. Amusement parks, antiquing, fishing, hiking, walking, gardens, nature trails, rock climbing, ice climbing, live theater, parks, shopping, downhill skiing, cross-country skiing and water sports nearby.

Publicity: *Valley Visitor, Bon Appetit, Ski, Travel Holiday, Connecticut, Country.*

"Occasionally in our lifetimes is a moment so unexpectedly perfect that we use it as our measure for our unforgettable moments. We just had such an experience at The 1785 Inn."

Cabernet Inn

Rt 16, Box 489
North Conway, NH 03860
(603)356-4704 (800)866-4704 Fax:(603)356-5399
E-mail: info@cabernetinn.com
Web: www.cabernetinn.com

Circa 1842. Built prior to the Civil War, this historic home features a deep burgundy exterior highlighted by hunter green shutters and trim. Window boxes filled with flowers add a

touch more color. The one-acre grounds are shaded by trees and colored by a variety of flowers. More than half of the guest rooms include a fireplace, and

some have double whirlpool tubs. In the afternoons, homemade treats are served, and in the mornings, guests enjoy a full country breakfast with items such as eggs, French toast, pancakes, bacon, sausages and fresh seasonal fruits.

Historic Interest: Mt. Washington Auto Road, Cog Railway (18 miles).
Innkeeper(s): Debbie & Rich Howard. $95-199. MC, VISA, AX, DS, PC, TC. TAC10. 11 rooms with PB, 6 with FP. Breakfast and afternoon tea included in rates. Types of meals: Full bkfst, country bkfst and early coffee/tea. Beds: Q. Ceiling fan and antiques in room. Air conditioning. VCR and fax on premises. Small meetings, family reunions and seminars hosted. Antiquing, art galleries, bicycling, canoeing/kayaking, fishing, golf, hiking, horseback riding, live theater, parks, shopping, downhill skiing and cross-country skiing nearby.

Old Red Inn & Cottages

PO Box 467
North Conway, NH 03860-0467
(603)356-2642 (800)338-1356 Fax:(603)356-6626

Circa 1810. Guests can opt to stay in an early 19th-century home or in one of a collection of cottages at this country inn. The rooms are decorated with handmade quilts and stenciling dots the walls. Several rooms include four-poster or canopy beds. One of the two-bedroom cottages includes a kitchenette, and both feature a screened porch. A hearty, country meal accompanied by freshly baked breads, muffins and homemade preserves starts off the day. The inn is near many of the town's shops, restaurants and outlets.

Innkeeper(s): Dick & Terry Potochniak. $59-165. MC, VISA, AX, DS, PC. 17

rooms, 15 with PB, 1 suite and 10 cottages. Breakfast included in rates. Types of meals: Full bkfst and early coffee/tea. Beds: QDT. Cable TV in room. Air conditioning. Fax, copier and swimming on premises. Weddings, small meetings, family reunions and seminars hosted. Amusement parks, antiquing, fishing, golf, live theater, parks, shopping, downhill skiing, cross-country skiing, sporting events, tennis and water sports nearby.

Wyatt House Country Inn

PO Box 777
North Conway, NH 03860-0777
(603)356-7977 (800)527-7978
E-mail: wyatthouse@webtv.net
Web: www.wyatthouse.com

Circa 1880. This rambling Victorian is surrounded by acres of manicured grounds and trees on the banks of the Saco River. The mountain view, double Jacuzzi suite is an inspiration for romance. Rooms are decorated with antiques in Country Victorian style, and guests are pampered with in-room sherry, canopy beds and views of the river and mountains. The delightful, multi-course breakfasts are served on fine English Wedgwood and lace. Everything is fresh and homemade, including granola, muffins and squeezed orange juice. Apple cobbler with vanilla ice cream, cheese souffles, shirred eggs, spinach and Vermont cheese quiche, chocolate chip pancakes and New England breakfast pie are among the memorable treats.

Innkeeper(s): Arlene & Bill Strickland. $50-189. MC, VISA, AX, DS, PC, TC. TAC10. 7 rooms, 5 with PB and 5 suites. Breakfast and afternoon tea included in rates. Types of meals: Full gourmet bkfst and early coffee/tea. Room service available. Beds: QDT. Cable TV, ceiling fan and clock in room. Air conditioning. Swimming, bicycles, library and two person Jacuzzi on premises. Small meetings and family reunions hosted. Antiquing, fishing, ice climbing, hiking, live theater, parks, shopping, downhill skiing, cross-country skiing, sporting events and water sports nearby.

North Woodstock   F4

Wilderness Inn B&B

Rfd 1, Box 69, Rts 3 & 112
North Woodstock, NH 03262-9710
(603)745-3890 (800)200-9453
E-mail: wildernessinn@juno.com
Web: www.musar.com/wildernessinn/

Circa 1912. Surrounded by the White Mountain National Forest, this charming shingled home offers a picturesque getaway for every season. Guest rooms are furnished with antiques and Oriental rugs, and the innkeepers also offer family suites and a private cottage with a fireplace, Jacuzzi and a view of Lost River. Breakfast is a delightful affair with choices ranging from fresh muffins to brie cheese omelets, French toast topped with homemade apple syrup, crepes or specialty pancakes. For the children, the innkeepers create teddy bear pancakes or French toast. If you have room, an afternoon tea also is prepared.

Innkeeper(s): Michael & Rosanna Yarnell. $50-135. MC, VISA, AX, PC, TC. 7 rooms with PB and 1 cottage. Breakfast included in rates. MAP. Type of meal: Full gourmet bkfst. Beds: QDT. TV in room.

"The stay at your inn, attempting and completing the 3D jig-jaw puzzle, combined with those unforgettable breakfasts, and your combined friendliness, makes the Wilderness Inn a place for special memories."

Pittsburgh   B5

The Glen

First Connecticut Lake, 77 The Glen Rd
Pittsburgh, NH 03592
(603)538-6500 (800)445-GLEN Fax:(603)538-7121

Circa 1900. This mountain lodge is located on the 45th parallel, midway between the equator and the North Pole. More than 160 acres surround the lodge, offering a bounty of activities. Guests can fish in a lake stocked with trout and salmon, or they can fish at the river, which offers rainbow and brown trout. The surrounding area also provides opportunities for hunters. Birdwatchers can enjoy gazing at dozens of different species. The Glen provides stunning views of the mountains and First Connecticut Lake, as well as the vast expanse of forestland. The interior of the lodge features natural wood paneling and hardwood floors; rooms are decorated in a comfortable lodge style. In addition to the lodge rooms and suite, there are 10 cabins. Breakfast, lunch and dinner are included in the rates. The hosts have been welcoming guests for nearly 40 years.

Innkeeper(s): Betty Falton. Call for rates. 24 rooms, 5 with PB, 1 suite and 10 cabins. Beds: QDT. Fishing nearby.

Plymouth   H4

Colonel Spencer Inn

RR 1, Box 206
Plymouth, NH 03264
(603)536-3438

Circa 1764. This pre-Revolutionary Colonial boasts Indian shutters, gleaming plank floors and a secret hiding place. Joseph Spencer, one of the home's early owners, fought at Bunker Hill and with General Washington. Within view of the river and the mountains, the inn is now a cozy retreat with warm Colonial decor. A suite with a kitchen is also available.

Innkeeper(s): Carolyn & Alan Hill. $45-65. PC, TC. TAC10. 7 rooms with PB and 1 suite. Breakfast and snacks/refreshments included in rates. Type of meal: Full bkfst. Beds: D. Fans in room. Small meetings and family reunions hosted. Antiquing, fishing, water parks, live theater, parks, shopping, downhill skiing, cross-country skiing, sporting events and water sports nearby.

"You have something very special here, and we very much enjoyed a little piece of it!"

Rindge   L3

Cathedral House B&B

63 Cathedral Entrance
Rindge, NH 03461
(603)899-6790

Circa 1850. This pre-Civil War, Colonial-style farmhouse is surrounded by 450 acres with meadows, a fishing pond, nature trails and scenic vistas. The five, comfortable bedrooms have been decorated in Colonial style, with artwork and fresh flowers in season. Rooms offer views of mountains and Emerson

Pond. A hearty country breakfast is served. The bed & breakfast is located on the grounds of the Cathedral of the Pines, a non-denominational place of worship, which offers solitude in natural surroundings. The grounds originally were selected by a young pilot and his wife as a location for their home upon his return from World War II. The pilot was killed in the line of duty, and his parents created the Cathedral of the Pines in his memory and others who served. The site has been recognized by the U.S. Congress as a national memorial.

Innkeeper(s): Donald & Shirley Mahoney. $45-125. MC, VISA, PC. 5 rooms. Breakfast included in rates. Type of meal: Full bkfst. Beds: QDT. Library on premises. Antiquing, fishing, live theater, parks, shopping, downhill skiing, cross-country skiing, sporting events and water sports nearby.

"Thank you for making our wedding day such a success and for making our family feel so welcome."

Woodbound Inn

Woodbound Rd
Rindge, NH 03461
(603)532-8341 (800)688-7770 Fax:(603)532-8341
E-mail: woodbound@aol.com
Web: www.nhweb.com/woodbound/index.html

Circa 1819. Vacationers have enjoyed the Woodbound Inn since its opening as a year-round resort in 1892. The main inn actually was built in 1819, and this portion offers 19 guest rooms, all appointed with classic-style furnishings. The innkeepers offer more modern accommodations in the Edgewood Building, and there are eleven cabins available. The one- and two-bedroom cabins rest along the shore of Lake Contoocook. The inn's 162

acres include a private beach, fishing, hiking, nature trails, tennis courts, a volleyball court, a game room and a golf course. There is a full service restaurant, a cocktail lounge and banquet facilities on premises. If for some reason one would want to venture away from the inn, the region is full of activities, including ski areas, more golf courses and Mount Monadnock.

Innkeeper(s): Kohlmorgen Family. $79-135. MC, VISA, AX, PC. TAC10. 45 rooms, 40 with PB, 11 cabins and 5 conference rooms. Breakfast included in rates. EP. Type of meal: Full bkfst. Dinner, lunch, banquet service and catering service available. Restaurant on premises. Beds: QDT. Phone and cabins are lakefront with fireplaces in room. Air conditioning. VCR, copier, swimming, tennis and library on premises. Handicap access. Weddings, small meetings, family reunions and seminars hosted. Amusement parks, antiquing, fishing, live theater, parks, shopping, downhill skiing, cross-country skiing and water sports nearby.

Pets allowed: In cabins only.

Shelburne   E5

Wildberry Inn B&B

592 State Rt 2
Shelburne, NH 03581
(603)466-5049
E-mail: rec@moose.ncia.net
Web: www.northernwhitemountains.com/wildberry

Circa 1877. This colonial salt-box home is located on seven acres in the White Mountains National Forest with the Appalachian Trail passing through part of the property. Rooms

are decorated in a fresh country style with quilts and Priscilla curtains. There's a separate suite in the "barn" with fireplace, upstairs bedroom and a downstairs living room with views of the pond, waterfall and garden from its many windows. In

winter, snowshoeing, cross-country skiing and snowmobiling are popular activities. In summer and fall, guests enjoy canoeing and fishing or simply hiking along the property to enjoy the golden oaks, birches, and red and orange maple foliage. Breakfast usually features freshly picked berries in season, homemade breads and dishes to accommodate a lavish pouring of local maple syrup.

Historic Interest: Northern New Hampshire Heritage Park (8 miles).

Innkeeper(s): Bob & Jackie Corrigan. $65-125. MC, PC, TC. 3 rooms with PB, 1 with FP and 1 cottage. Breakfast and afternoon tea included in rates. Types of meals: Full gourmet bkfst and country bkfst. Beds: QDT. TV and VCR in room. Air conditioning. Swimming on premises. Weddings and family reunions hosted. Antiquing, bicycling, canoeing/kayaking, fishing, golf, hiking, horseback riding, parks, shopping, downhill skiing and cross-country skiing nearby.

Sugar Hill   F3

Foxglove, A Country Inn

Rt 117 at Lovers Ln
Sugar Hill, NH 03585
(603)823-8840 Fax:(603)823-5755

Circa 1898. Three acres, dotted with trees, gardens, fountains and a spring-fed pond, surround Foxglove. The turn-of-the-century home originally served as a summer house for an heiress. Upscale French-country decor permeates the six guest rooms, which include designer linens and fine furnishings. Guests can relax and enjoy the peaceful surroundings on a hammock for two.
Gourmet breakfasts are served on the sun porch, the posh setting includes antique china, crystal and fine linens. A menu might include a vegetable frittata with fresh herbs,

sliced tomato and fresh asparagus dressed in a light vinaigrette and sunflower whole wheat toast. The innkeepers also will prepare gourmet candlelight dinners by request. Skiing, biking, fishing and outlet shopping are among the nearby attractions.

Innkeeper(s): Janet & Walter Boyd. $85-165. MC, VISA, PC. TAC10. 6 rooms with PB, 1 with FP. Breakfast included in rates. Types of meals: Full gourmet bkfst and early coffee/tea. Afternoon tea, gourmet dinner and picnic lunch available. Beds: KQDT. Turndown service in room. VCR, fax, copier, bicycles, tennis, library and CD Player on premises. Weddings, small meetings, family reunions and seminars hosted. Antiquing, fishing, golf, live theater, parks, shopping, downhill skiing, cross-country skiing, tennis and water sports nearby.

Publicity: *New Hampshire Magazine, Yankee Traveler.*

"We were extremely fortunate to be able to stay in a home that sparkles from the obvious attention given to all aspects of housekeeping."

Sunset Hill House

Sunset Hill Rd
Sugar Hill, NH 03585
(603)823-5522 (800)786-4455 Fax:(603)823-5738
E-mail: sunsethill@landmarknet.net
Web: www.sunsethill.com

Circa 1882. This Second Empire Victorian has views of two mountain ranges. Three parlors, all with cozy fireplaces, are favorite gathering spots. The inn's lush grounds offer many opportunities for recreation or relaxing, and guests often enjoy special events here, such as the Fields of Lupine Festival. The Cannon Mountain Ski Area and Franconia Notch State Park are nearby, and there is 30 kilometers of cross-country ski trails at the inn. Be sure to inquire about golf and ski packages.

Historic Interest: Robert Frost Cottage (1 mile), site of first ski school (one-half mile), Sugar Hill Historic Museum (one-half mile).

Innkeeper(s): Michael & Tricia Coyle. $90-225. MC, VISA, AX, DS, TC. 30 rooms with PB, 5 suites and 1 conference room. Breakfast included in rates. MAP. Types of meals: Full bkfst and early coffee/tea. Dinner, picnic lunch, lunch, banquet service and catering service available. Restaurant on premises. Beds: KQDT. Suites with fireplaces and/or whirlpools and ceiling fans (many rooms) in room. Fax on premises. Weddings, small meetings, family reunions and seminars hosted. Antiquing, fishing, golf course, live theater, parks, shopping, downhill skiing, cross-country skiing and water sports nearby.

"I have visited numerous inns and innkeepers in my 10 years as a travel writer, but have to admit that few have impressed me as much as yours and you did."

Sunapee   I2

The Inn at Sunapee

PO Box 336
Sunapee, NH 03782-0336
(603)763-4444 (800)327-2466 Fax:(603)763-9456

Circa 1875. Formerly part of a dairy farm, this spacious farmhouse inn also is home to a restaurant. The innkeepers, who spent nearly 30 years in the Far East and Southeast Asia, have blended that inter-national flavor into the traditional antique furnishings and New England menu items. The inn offers three sitting rooms, an impressive fieldstone fireplace, a library, swimming and tennis. The family-oriented inn also hosts meetings, reunions and weddings. Mt. Sunapee State Park and ski area are nearby.

Innkeeper(s): Ted & Susan Harriman. $60-110. MC, VISA, AX, DS, PC, TC. 16 rooms with PB and 1 conference room. MAP, EP. Type of meal: Full bkfst. Restaurant on premises. Weddings, small meetings, family reunions and seminars hosted. Antiquing, fishing, live theater, shopping, downhill skiing and cross-country skiing nearby.

Tamworth   G5

Tamworth Inn

PO Box 189
Tamworth, NH 03886-0189
(603)323-7721 (800)642-7352 Fax:(603)323-2026
E-mail: inn@tamworth.com
Web: www.tamworth.com

Circa 1833. Thoroughbred horses frolic in the pasture that borders the inn's three acres. Originally a stagecoach stop, Tamworth Inn is furnished with many antiques and handmade  quilts. There's a sparkling trout stream adjacent to the property and across the street is the Barnstormer's Theater, one of the country's oldest summer stock theaters. The library has a cozy fireplace.

Historic Interest: Grover Cleveland's summer home (2 miles), Chinook Kennels.

Innkeeper(s): Bob & Virginia Schrader. $100-180. MC, VISA. 15 rooms with PB, 1 with FP, 5 suites and 1 conference room. Breakfast included in rates. EP. Type of meal: Full gourmet bkfst. Gourmet dinner, picnic lunch and catering service available. Restaurant on premises. Beds: KQDT. Small meetings hosted. Antiquing, fishing, live theater, downhill skiing and cross-country skiing nearby.

Pets Allowed.

"It was great spending the day touring and returning to the quiet village of Tamworth and your wonderful inn."

Tilton   I4

Tilton Manor

40 Chestnut St
Tilton, NH 03276-5546
(603)286-3457 Fax:(603)286-3308

Circa 1884. This turn-of-the-century Folk Victorian inn is just two blocks from downtown Tilton. The inn's comfortable guest rooms are furnished with antiques and sport handmade afghans. Guests are treated to a hearty country breakfast featuring freshly baked muffins, and dinner is available with advance reservations. Visitors enjoy relaxing in the sitting room, where they may play games, read or watch TV after a busy day exploring the historic area. Gunstock is nearby and the Daniel Webster Birthplace and Shaker Village are within easy driving distance. Shoppers will enjoy Tilton's latest addition — an outlet center.

Historic Interest: Historic Concord is just 15 minutes from the manor.

Innkeeper(s): Chip & Diane. $70-80. MC, VISA, AX, DS, PC, TC. 4 rooms, 2 with PB, 1 with FP and 1 suite. Breakfast included in rates. Type of meal: Full bkfst. Gourmet dinner available. Beds: KDT. Library and child care on premises. Weddings, small meetings and family reunions hosted. Antiquing, fishing, outlet mall, shopping, downhill skiing, cross-country skiing and water sports nearby.

Pets allowed: Small pets with responsible owners.

Wakefield
H6

Wakefield Inn

2723 Wakefield Rd
Wakefield, NH 03872-4374
(603)522-8272 (800)245-0841

Circa 1804. Early travelers pulled up to the front door of the Wakefield Inn by stagecoach, and while they disembarked, their luggage was handed up to the second floor. It was brought in through the door, which is still visible over the porch roof. A spiral stair-case, ruffled cur-tains, wallpapers and a wraparound porch  all create the roman-tic ambiance of days gone by. In the living room, an original three-sided fireplace casts a warm glow on guests as it did more than 190 years ago.

Historic Interest: New Hampshire Farm Museum, Museum of Childhood.
Innkeeper(s): Harry & Lou Sisson. $50-80. MC, VISA, PC, TC. 7 rooms with PB. Breakfast included in rates. Types of meals: Full bkfst and early coffee/tea. Beds: QDT. TV and ceiling fan in room. VCR on premises. Antiquing, fishing, golf, shopping and cross-country skiing nearby.

"Comfortable accommodations, excellent food and exquisite decor highlighted by your quilts."

Wilton Center
K4

Stepping Stones B&B

Bennington Battle Tr
Wilton Center, NH 03086
(603)654-9048 (888)654-9048 Fax:(603)654-6821

Circa 1790. Decks and terraces overlook the enormous gardens of this Greek Revival house, listed in the local historic register. Guest rooms feature white-washed pine, cherry or Shaker-style country pieces accented with botanical prints, handwoven throws, rugs, pillows and fresh flowers. Poached eggs on asparagus with hollandaise sauce, blueberry Belgian waffles and jumbo apple muffins with streusel topping are guests' favorite breakfast choices. The innkeeper is both a garden designer and weaver, and there is a handweaving studio on the premises.

Innkeeper(s): D. Ann Carlsmith. $60-65. PC, TC. 3 rooms with PB. Breakfast included in rates. Types of meals: Full bkfst and early coffee/tea. Afternoon tea available. Beds: QDT. Library on premises. Weddings and family reunions hosted. Antiquing, hiking, handweaving studio on premises, chamber music, live theater, parks, downhill skiing and cross-country skiing nearby.

Pets allowed: If well-behaved.

"A very relaxing and beautiful getaway. The color and fragrance of the gardens is stunning."

Wolfeboro
H5

Tuc' Me Inn B&B

118 N Main St, PO Box 657, Rt 109 N
Wolfeboro, NH 03894-0657
(603)569-5702

This 1850 Federal Colonial-style house features a music room, parlor and screen porches. Chocolate chip or strawberry pan-cakes are often presented for breakfast in the dining room or Victorian Garden Room. The inn is a short walk to the quaint village of Wolfeboro and the shores of Lake Winnipesaukee.

Innkeeper(s): Terrille Foutz. $75-95. MC, VISA, PC, TC. 7 rooms, 3 with PB. Breakfast included in rates. Types of meals: Full bkfst and early coffee/tea. Afternoon tea available. Beds: QT. TV in room. VCR and air conditioning and ceiling fans on premises. Weddings, small meetings, family reunions and seminars hosted. Antiquing, fishing, live theater, shopping, downhill skiing and cross-country skiing nearby.

Publicity: *Granite State News, Wolfeboro Times.*

New Jersey

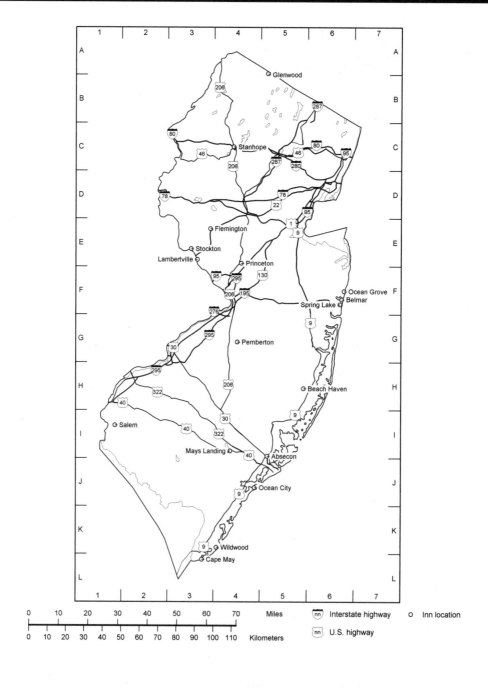

A
B
C
D
E
F
G
H
I
J
K
L

1 2 3 4 5 6 7

Glenwood
206
287
80
Stanhope
46 46 80 95
206 287 280
78 78
22
95
1
Flemington 9
Stockton
Lambertville Princeton
130
95 295
206 195
276
295
30 Pemberton
295
322
208
40 Beach Haven
30 9
Salem
40 322
Mays Landing 40 Absecon
9 Ocean City
Ocean Grove
Belmar
Spring Lake
9

9 Wildwood
Cape May

0 10 20 30 40 50 60 70 Miles
0 10 20 30 40 50 60 70 80 90 100 110 Kilometers

nn Interstate highway   ○ Inn location
nn U.S. highway

Absecon Highlands   I5

White Manor Inn

739 S 2nd Ave
Absecon Highlands, NJ 08201-9542
(609)748-3996 Fax:(609)652-0073

Circa 1932. This quiet country inn was built by the innkeeper's father and includes unique touches throughout, many created by innkeeper Howard Bensel himself, who became a master craftsman from his father's teachings and renovated the home extensively.

Beautiful flowers and
plants adorn both the
lush grounds and the
interior of the home.
Everything is comfort-
able and cozy at this
charming B&B, a relax-
ing contrast to the glitz
of nearby Atlantic City.

Historic Interest: A short drive will take guests to a number of historic sites, including the Towne of Smithville, Atlantic City Boardwalk, Renault Winery, Wharton State Forest, the Somers Mansion, and Margate, home of Lucy the Elephant, a National Historic Landmark.

Innkeeper(s): Anna Mae & Howard R. Bensel Jr. $65-105. PC, TC. 7 rooms, 5 with PB, 1 suite and 1 conference room. Breakfast and snacks/refreshments included in rates. Types of meals: Cont plus, cont and early coffee/tea. Beds: QDT. Ceiling fan in room. Air conditioning. VCR on premises. Small meetings, family reunions and seminars hosted. Amusement parks, antiquing, fishing, golf, bird watching, casinos, live theater, parks, shopping, sporting events and water sports nearby.

"We felt more like relatives than total strangers. By far the most clean inn that I have seen — spotless!"

Beach Haven   H5

Amber Street Inn

118 Amber St
Beach Haven, NJ 08008-1744
(609)492-1611

Circa 1885. Located on Long Beach Island, just six miles off the New Jersey Coast, this historic inn was one of Beach Haven's earliest homes. The Victorian rests within the town's historic district across from Bicentennial Park. Rooms are decorated in an eclectic Victorian style with refurbished antiques. Breakfasts are continental-plus and served buffet style with fresh fruit, granola, muffins, homemade tea breads and, perhaps, baked eggs. The beach is a short walk away, and the innkeepers provide beach passes and chairs.

Innkeeper(s): Joan & Michael Fitzsimmons. $110-175. PC, TC. 6 rooms with PB and 1 suite. Breakfast included in rates. Types of meals: Cont plus and early coffee/tea. Afternoon refreshments available. Beds: KQ. Phone and ceiling fan in room. Air conditioning. Fax, bicycles, library, english garden and porch rockers on premises. Weddings and small meetings hosted. Spanish spoken. Beaches, antiquing, fishing, golf, live theater, parks, shopping, tennis and water sports nearby.

Belmar   F6

The Inn at The Shore

301 4th Ave
Belmar, NJ 07719-2104
(732)681-3762 Fax:(732)280-1914

Circa 1880. This country Victorian actually is near two different shores. Both the ocean and Silver Lake are within easy walking distance of the inn. From the inn's wraparound porch, guests can view swans on the lake. The innkeepers decorated their Victorian home in period style. The inn's patio is set up for barbecues.

Innkeeper(s): Rosemary & Tom Volker. $80-130. MC, VISA, AX. 12 rooms, 3 with PB and 1 conference room. Breakfast included in rates. Type of meal: Full bkfst. Cable TV and phone in room. Air conditioning. VCR, bicycles, aquarium, guest pantry with refrigerator, microwave and patio with gas grill on premises. Weddings, small meetings, family reunions and seminars hosted. Amusement parks, antiquing, fishing, live theater, parks, shopping, sporting events and water sports nearby.

"You both have created a warm, cozy and comfortable refuge for us weary travelers."

Cape May   L3

The Inn at 22 Jackson

22 Jackson St
Cape May, NJ 08204-1465
(609)884-2226 (800)452-8177 Fax:(609)884-2226

Circa 1899. The gingerbread on this Queen Anne Victorian is painted purple, white and navy. The inn boasts a three-story tower. Suites are outfitted with wet bars, refrigerators and microwaves, as well as cable TV and private baths. The inn is decorated in a light, bright eclectic style with furnishings ranging from 1860 Victorian antiques, pieces from the '30s and antique toy and game collections. The inn's four porches are popular for rocking and having breakfast.

Innkeeper(s): Barbara & Chip Masemore. Call for rates. 5 suites. Cable TV, ceiling fan and VCR in room. Air conditioning. Weddings, small meetings, family reunions and seminars hosted. Antiquing, live theater and shopping nearby.

The Abbey Bed & Breakfast

34 Gurney St at Columbia Ave
Cape May, NJ 08204
(609)884-4506 Fax:(609)884-2379

Circa 1869. This historic inn consists of two buildings, one a Gothic Revival villa with a 60-foot tower, Gothic arched windows and shaded verandas. Furnishings include floor-to-ceiling mirrors, ornate gas chandeliers, marble-topped dressers and beds of carved walnut, wrought iron and brass. The cottage adjacent to the villa is a classic Second Empire-style cottage with a mansard roof. A full breakfast is served in the dining room in spring and fall and on the veranda in the summer. Late afternoon refreshments and tea are served each day at 5 p.m. The beautiful inn is featured in the town's Grand Christmas Tour, and public tours and tea are offered three times a week in season.

Innkeeper(s): Jay & Marianne Schatz. $100-275. MC, VISA, DS, TC. 14 rooms with PB, 2 suites and 2 conference rooms. Breakfast and afternoon tea included in rates. Type of meal: Full bkfst. Beds: KQD. Some air conditioning and ceiling fans and desks in room. Beach chairs and on and off site parking on premises. Small meetings and seminars hosted. Antiquing, fishing, birding, live theater, parks, shopping and water sports nearby.

Publicity: *Richmond Times-Dispatch, New York Times, Glamour, Philadelphia Inquirer, National Geographic Traveler. Smithsonian.*

"Staying with you folks really makes the difference between a 'nice' vacation and a great one!"

Angel of The Sea

5 Trenton Ave
Cape May, NJ 08204-2735
(609)884-3369 (800)848-3369 Fax:(609)884-3331
Web: www.angelofthesea.com

Circa 1850. This recently renovated Victorian mansion features a mansard roof, a tower and views of the ocean from almost every room. A double-tiered, ocean-front

veranda stretches across the house. Each room is uniquely furnished and some boast handsome antique beds. Afternoon tea is offered as well as wine and cheese. Complimentary bicycles, beach tags, chairs, umbrellas and towels are available.

Innkeeper(s): Greg & Lorie Whissell. $95-285. MC, VISA, AX, PC. 27 rooms with PB. Breakfast and afternoon tea included in rates. Types of meals: Full gourmet bkfst and early coffee/tea. Catered breakfast available. Beds: KQD. Cable TV and turndown service in room. Air conditioning. Bicycles on premises. Weddings and family reunions hosted. Art galleries, beaches, bicycling, canoeing/kayaking, fishing, golf, hiking, horseback riding, live theater, museums, shopping, tennis, water sports and wineries nearby.

"We've travelled bed and breakfasts for years and this is by far the best."

Barnard-Good House

238 Perry St
Cape May, NJ 08204-1447
(609)884-5381

Circa 1865. The Barnard-Good House is a Second Empire Victorian with a mansard roof and original shingles. A wraparound veranda adds to the charm of this lavender, blue and tan cottage along with the original picket fence and a concrete-formed flower garden. The inn was selected by New Jersey Magazine as the No. 1 spot for breakfast in New Jersey, and breakfasts are a special, four-course, gourmet feast.

Innkeeper(s): Nan & Tom Hawkins. $100-175. MC, VISA, PC. 5 rooms with PB and 2 suites. Breakfast included in rates. Type of meal: Full gourmet bkfst. Beds: KQD. Ceiling fan and alarm clocks in room. Air conditioning. Antiquing, fishing, live theater, parks, shopping and water sports nearby.

"Even the cozy bed can't hold you down when the smell of Nan's breakfast makes its way upstairs."

Brass Bed Inn

719 Columbia Ave
Cape May, NJ 08204-2307
(609)884-2302 Fax:(609)884-2296

Circa 1872. Nineteenth-century brass beds and antiques original to this three-story Carpenter Gothic Victorian give the Brass Bed Inn a particular uniqueness in its Historic District setting.

Oriental carpets, vintage wallpapers and the old-fashioned wraparound veranda filled with rockers make it easy to envision the home's original life as a private seaside retreat.

Guests enjoy watching the horses and carriages pass by or occasionally stop while an engagement ring or proposal is offered to a surprised beloved. Full stick-to-your-ribs breakfasts are served hearthside in the morning and include freshly baked cakes, scones or pineapple bread pudding, all made from scratch. Butterfly bushes, lilies, roses and baby's breath fill the garden. Most surprising is the unusual color of the hydrangeas — red — due to the iron in the hairpin lace fence that has encircled the home all these years. The water is one block away.

Historic Interest: C.M. Lighthouse (1 mile), Sunset Beach (3 miles), U.S. Coast Guard Academy (1 mile).

Innkeeper(s): Marilyn & Tony Codario. $100-170. MC, VISA, PC, TC. 9 rooms, 7 with PB. Breakfast and afternoon tea included in rates. Type of meal: Early coffee/tea. Beds: KQDT. Ceiling fan in room. Air conditioning. Fax and library on premises. Weddings, small meetings and family reunions hosted. Antiquing, art galleries, beaches, bicycling, canoeing/kayaking, fishing, golf, horseback riding, tours of B&B's, wonderful restaurants, live theater, parks, shopping, tennis and water sports nearby.

Captain Mey's B&B Inn

202 Ocean St
Cape May, NJ 08204-2322
(609)884-7793 (800)981-3702
Web: www.captainmeys.com

Circa 1890. Named after Dutch explorer Capt. Cornelius J. Mey, who named the area, the inn displays its Dutch heritage with table-top Persian rugs, Delft china and imported Dutch lace curtains. The dining room features chestnut and oak

Eastlake paneling and a fireplace. One guest room has a double whirlpool tub, another includes a brass-footed, Victorian whirlpool tub. Some guest rooms include both a queen and a single bed. A hearty breakfast is served by candlelight or on the wraparound veranda in the summertime. The ferry and lighthouse are nearby.

Historic Interest: Cold Spring Village and the Cape May Lighthouse are five minutes away. Lewes, Del., is one hour by ferry.

Innkeeper(s): George & Kathleen Blinn. $85-225. MC, VISA, AX, PC, TC. TAC10. 7 rooms with PB and 1 suite. Breakfast and afternoon tea included in rates. Type of meal: Full bkfst. Beds: QT. Ceiling fan and Jacuzzi (some rooms) in room. Air conditioning. Small meetings and family reunions hosted. Amusement parks, antiquing, fishing, bicycling, bird watching, lighthouse, ferry, live theater, parks, shopping and water sports nearby.

"The innkeepers pamper you so much you wish you could stay forever."

The Carroll Villa B&B

19 Jackson St
Cape May, NJ 08204-1417
(609)884-9619 Fax:(609)884-0264
E-mail: mbatter@cybernet.net
Web: www.carrollvilla.com

Circa 1882. This Victorian hotel is located one-half block from the ocean on the oldest street in the historic district of Cape May. Breakfast at the Villa is a memorable event, featuring dishes acclaimed by the New York Times and Frommer's. Homemade fruit breads, Italian omelets and Crab Eggs Benedict are a few specialties. Meals are served in the Mad Batter Restaurant on a European veranda, a secluded garden terrace or in the sky-lit Victorian dining room. The restaurant serves breakfast, lunch and dinner daily. The decor of this inn is decidedly Victorian with period antiques and wallpapers.

Innkeeper(s): Mark Kulkowitz & Pamela Ann Huber. $75-180. MC, VISA, AX, DS, PC. TAC10. 22 rooms with PB and 2 conference rooms. Breakfast included in rates. Type of meal: Full bkfst. Dinner, lunch, banquet service and catering service available. Beds: QD. Phone, ceiling fan and TV and VCR (some rooms) in room. Air conditioning. VCR, fax and copier on premises. Weddings, small meetings, family reunions and seminars hosted. Amusement parks, antiquing, fishing, live theater, parks and shopping nearby.

Publicity: Atlantic City Press, Asbury Press, Frommer's, New York Times, Washington Post.

"Mr. Kulkowitz is a superb host. He strives to accommodate the diverse needs of guests."

The Chalfonte Hotel

301 Howard St, PO Box 475
Cape May, NJ 08204-0475
(609)884-8409 Fax:(609)884-4588
E-mail: chalfontnj@aol.com
Web: www.chalfonte.com

Circa 1876. This 108-room hotel was built by Civil War hero Colonel Henry Sawyer. The hotel features wraparound porches, simply appointed rooms with marble-topped dressers and other original antiques. The fare in the Magnolia Room is Southern-style with fresh fish daily and vegetarian options. Children of all ages are welcome, and there is a supervised children's dining room for guests aged six and under. Much of the hotel's restoration and preservation is accomplished by dedicated volunteers who have adopted the hotel as their own. Painting workshops, Elderhostel educational programs, weekly events and entertainment, group retreats, weddings and family reunions are offered. An early continental breakfast is provided to those guests who may be heading out to go birdwatching, cycling, walking or any of the area's many activities.

Historic Interest: Cold Springs Village (4 miles).

Innkeeper(s): Anne LeDuc & Judy Bartella. $90-210. MC, VISA, AX, PC. TAC10. 70 rooms, 10 with PB, 2 cottages and 2 conference rooms. Breakfast and dinner included in rates. MAP. Types of meals: Full bkfst and early coffee/tea. Restaurant on premises. Beds: KQDT. TV and ceiling fan in room. VCR, fax and copier on premises. Weddings, small meetings, family reunions and seminars hosted. Amusement parks, antiquing, fishing, golf, nature trails, whale watching, birding, live theater, parks, shopping, sporting events, tennis and water sports nearby.

Publicity: Travel & Leisure, Washingtonian, Philadelphia Inquirer, New York Times, Country Inns, Richmond Times, Mid-Atlantic Country, Star and Wave, Virginian Pilot & Ledger-Star, USA Today, Washington Post, Dallas Morning News, National Public Radio, PBS, South Jersey Weddings.

"We love the relaxed and genteel atmosphere, the feeling of having stepped into another time is delightful."

Cliveden B&B Inn & Cottage

709 Columbia Ave
Cape May, NJ 08204-2307
(609)884-4516 (800)884-2420

Circa 1884. This three-story Victorian boasts gingerbread trim on the gables and the front porch. The spacious wraparound porch is furnished with white antique wicker and is shaded by cranberry colored awnings. There are sitting areas and ceiling fans in the air-conditioned rooms. The inn is two blocks from the beach and a short stroll from the Victorian shopping area with its fine restaurants and shops. A full breakfast is served buffet-style. Guests enjoy taking breakfast on the veranda most of the time. There is a two-bedroom Victorian cottage popular for families with children.

Innkeeper(s): Susan & Al DeRosa. $100-160. PC. 10 rooms with PB, 1 with FP and 1 cottage. Breakfast and afternoon tea included in rates. Type of meal: Full gourmet bkfst. Beds: QD. Ceiling fan in room. Air conditioning. Library on premises. Weddings, small meetings, family reunions and seminars hosted. Antiquing, fishing, golf, live theater, parks, shopping and water sports nearby.

Dormer House

800 Columbia Ave
Cape May, NJ 08204-2310
(609)884-7446 (800)884-5052
Web: www.dormerhouse.com

Circa 1899. This three-story Colonial Revival estate is three blocks from the ocean and the historic walking mall. The inviting wraparound porch, with its red drapes and striped awnings, is often enjoyed as the site for afternoon tea. Originally built by marble-dealer John Jacoby, the inn retains much of the original marble and furniture.

Innkeeper(s): Lucille & Dennis Doherty. $80-210. MC, VISA, AX, DS, PC, TC. 9 rooms, 2 suites and 1 cottage. Breakfast and afternoon tea included in rates. Type of meal: Full bkfst. Beds: Q. Cable TV, ceiling fan and some with jacuzzi tubs in room. Air conditioning. Bicycles, beach chairs and and outside showers on premises. Amusement parks, antiquing, fishing, live theater, parks, shopping and water sports nearby.

Publicity: Cape May Star & Wave.

The Duke of Windsor Inn

817 Washington St
Cape May, NJ 08204-1651
(609)884-1355 (800)826-8973
E-mail: innkeeper@dukeofwindsorinn.com
Web: www.dukeofwindsorinn.com

Circa 1896. This Queen Anne Victorian was built by Delaware River boat pilot Harry Hazelhurst and his wife, Florence. They were both six feet tall, so the house was built with large open rooms and doorways, and extra-wide stairs. The inn has a carved, natural oak open staircase with stained-glass windows at top and bottom. Five antique chandeliers grace the dining room. There are beach tags and parking available on premises.

Historic Interest: National Register.

Innkeeper(s): Patricia Joyce. $85-200. MC, VISA, PC, TC. 10 rooms with PB. Breakfast and afternoon tea included in rates. Types of meals: Full bkfst and early coffee/tea. Beds: QDT. Ceiling fan in room. Air conditioning. Off-street parking, outside hot and cold shower and refrigerator available for guest use on premises. Antiquing, fishing, live theater, parks, shopping and water sports nearby.

"Breakfast at 9:00 am and tea at 4:00 pm were delicious and relaxing. We can't wait to come back."

Fairthorne B&B

111 Ocean St
Cape May, NJ 08204-2319
(609)884-8791 (800)438-8742 Fax:(609)884-1902
E-mail: wehfair@aol.com
Web: www.fairthorne.com

Circa 1892. Antiques abound in this three-story Colonial Revival. Lace curtains and a light color scheme complete the charming decor. There is a new, yet historic addition to the B&B. The innkeepers now offer guest quarters (with fireplaces) in The Fairthorne Cottage, a restored 1880s building adjacent to the inn. The signature breakfasts include special daily entrees along with an assortment of

home-baked breads and muffins. A light afternoon tea also is served with refreshments. The proximity to the beach will be much appreciated by guests, and the innkeepers offer the use of beach towels, bicycles and sand chairs. The nearby historic district is full of fun shops and restaurants.

Innkeeper(s): Diane & Ed Hutchinson. $160-230. MC, VISA, AX, DS, TC. 10 rooms and 1 suite. Breakfast and afternoon tea included in rates. Types of meals: Full bkfst and early coffee/tea. Beds: KQ. Ceiling fan in room. Air conditioning. Fax on premises. Antiquing, fishing, historic lighthouse & Victorian architectural tours, live theater, parks, shopping and water sports nearby.

"I feel as if I have come to stay with a dear old friend who has spared no expense to provide me with all that my heart can desire! ... I will savor the memory of your hospitality for years to come. Thanks so much."

Gingerbread House

28 Gurney St
Cape May, NJ 08204
(609)884-0211
E-mail: frede@bellatlantic.net
Web: gingerbreadinn.com

Circa 1869. The Gingerbread is one of eight original Stockton Row Cottages, summer retreats built for families from Philadelphia and Virginia. It is a half-block from the ocean and breezes waft over the wicker-filled porch. The inn is listed in the National Register. It has been meticulously restored and decorated

with period antiques and a fine collection of paintings. The inn's woodwork is especially notable, guests enter through handmade teak double doors.

Historic Interest: Historic tours are available.

Innkeeper(s): Fred & Joan Echevarria. $90-260. MC, VISA, PC, TC. 6 rooms, 3 with PB and 1 suite. Breakfast and afternoon tea included in rates. Type of meal: Full bkfst. Beds: QD. Air conditioning. Small meetings and family reunions hosted. Antiquing, fishing, birding. Victorian homes, live theater, parks, shopping and water sports nearby.

Publicity: *Philadelphia Inquirer, New Jersey Monthly, Atlantic City Press Newspaper.*

"The elegance, charm and authenticity of historic Cape May, but more than that, it appeals to us as `home'."

The Henry Sawyer Inn

722 Columbia Ave
Cape May, NJ 08204-2332
(609)884-5667 (800)449-5667 Fax:(609)884-9406

Circa 1877. This fully restored, three-story peach Victorian home boasts a gingerbread embellished veranda, brick-colored shutters and brown trim. Inside, the parlor features Victorian antiques, a marble fireplace, polished wood floors, an Oriental rug, formal wallcoverings, a crystal chandelier and fresh flowers. Guest rooms have been decorated with careful attention to a romantic and fresh Victorian theme, as well. One room includes a whirlpool tub, one includes a private porch, and another a fireplace.

Innkeeper(s): Mary & Barbara Morris. $85-195. MC, VISA, AX, DC, DS, PC, TC. TAC5. 5 rooms with PB, 1 with FP and 2 suites. Breakfast and afternoon tea included in rates. Types of meals: Full bkfst and early coffee/tea. Beds: KQT. Cable TV, ceiling fan, whirlpool and private porch in room. Air conditioning. VCR, fax and parking on premises. Weddings, small meetings, family reunions and seminars hosted. Antiquing, fishing, golf, carriage, Victorian trolley, live theater, parks, shopping, tennis and water sports nearby.

Mainstay Inn

635 Columbia Ave
Cape May, NJ 08204-2305
(609)884-8690

Circa 1872. This was once the elegant and exclusive Jackson's Clubhouse popular with gamblers. Many of the guest rooms and the grand parlor look much as they did in the 1870s. Fourteen-foot-high ceilings, elaborate chandeliers, a sweeping veranda and a cupola add to the atmosphere. Tom and Sue Carroll received

the American Historic Inns award in 1988 for their preservation efforts, and have been making unforgettable memories for guests for decades. A writer for Conde Nast Traveler once wrote, "architecturally, no inn, anywhere, quite matches the Mainstay."

Historic Interest: Cape May Lighthouse & State Park Museum (2 miles).

Innkeeper(s): Tom & Sue Carroll. $95-295. PC, TC. 16 rooms with PB, 4 with FP and 7 suites. Breakfast and afternoon tea included in rates. Types of meals: Full bkfst, cont plus and early coffee/tea. Beds: KQD. Phone and ceiling fan in room. Air conditioning. Library on premises. Handicap access. Small meetings and seminars hosted. Amusement parks, antiquing, fishing, historic attractions, tennis, golf, birding, biking, hiking, live theater, parks, shopping, sporting events and water sports nearby.

"By far the most lavishly and faithfully restored guesthouse...run by two arch-preservationists—Travel & Leisure."

The Mason Cottage

625 Columbia Ave
Cape May, NJ 08204-2305
(609)884-3358 (800)716-2766

Circa 1871. Since 1946, this elegant seaside inn has been open to guests. The curved-mansard, wood-shingle roof was built by local shipyard carpenters. Much of the original furniture remains in the house, and it has endured both hurricanes and the 1878 Cape May fire. Two of the inn's suites include a fireplace and whirlpool tub.

Historic Interest: The inn is listed in the New Jersey Historic Register.

Innkeeper(s): Dave & Joan Mason. $95-285. MC, VISA, AX, TC. 9 rooms with PB, 2 with FP, 4 suites and 1 conference room. Breakfast and afternoon tea included in rates. Type of meal: Full bkfst. Beds: QD. Ceiling fan and two with whirlpool tubs in room. Air conditioning. Weddings, small meetings, family reunions and seminars hosted. Antiquing, fishing, live theater, parks, shopping and water sports nearby.

"We relaxed and enjoyed ourselves. You have a beautiful and elegant inn, and serve great breakfasts. We will be back on our next trip to Cape May."

The Inn on Ocean

25 Ocean St
Cape May, NJ 08204-2411
(609)884-7070 (800)304-4477 Fax:(609)884-1384
E-mail: innocean@bellatlantic.net
Web: www.theinnonocean.com

Circa 1880. A strawberry pink roof adorned with a crown of wrought iron is accentuated with bright green, white and yellow accents at this Second Empire Victorian. The interior is done in an elegant Victorian style. The inn boasts the only Victorian billiard room in Cape May.

Innkeeper(s): Jack & Katha Davis. $129-259. MC, VISA, AX, DC, CB, DS, TC. TAC10. 4 rooms with PB, 1 with FP and 1 suite. Breakfast and afternoon tea included in rates. Type of meal: Full bkfst. Beds: KQ. Cable TV and ceiling fan in room. Air conditioning. Antiquing, fishing, tennis, golf, live theater, parks, shopping and water sports nearby.

"A wonderful and beautiful experience. Great comfort, great breakfast and great hospitality."

Poor Richard's Inn

17 Jackson St
Cape May, NJ 08204-1417
(609)884-3536

Circa 1882. The unusual design of this Second-Empire house has been accentuated with five colors of paint. Arched gingerbread porches tie together the distinctive bays of the house's facade. The combination of exterior friezes, balustrades and fretwork has earned the inn an individual listing in the National Register. Some rooms sport an eclectic country Victorian decor with patchwork quilts and pine furniture, while others tend toward a more traditional turn-of-the-century ambiance. An apartment suite is available.

Innkeeper(s): Richard Samuelson. $59-143. MC, VISA. 10 rooms with PB

and 1 suite. Breakfast included in rates. EP. Types of meals: Cont plus and early coffee/tea. Beds: QDT. Cable TV in room. Air conditioning. Copier on premises. Small meetings and family reunions hosted. Amusement parks, antiquing, fishing, ocean beach, live theater, parks and water sports nearby.

"Hold our spot on the porch. We'll be back before you know it."

The Primrose B&B

1102 Lafayette St
Cape May, NJ 08204-1722
(609)884-8288 (800)606-8288 Fax:(609)884-2358

Circa 1850. The Primrose is an adorable country Victorian painted in shades of rose with gingerbread trim. The grounds are dotted with gardens, and a view of historic homes can be seen from the inn's front porch, which includes wicker and white iron furnishings. The interior is decorated in country Victorian style, featuring five cozy guest rooms, each one individually decorated. The rates include both afternoon refreshments, as well as a gourmet breakfast with entrees such as baked oatmeal, stuffed French toast or a unique blueberry lasagna, as well as muffins and fresh fruit. Cape May boasts dozens and dozens of historic Victorian homes, as well as shops, restaurants and the beach. The innkeepers provide both bicycles and beach tags for their guests.

Historic Interest: Emlen Physick Estate (1 block), lighthouse (2 miles), over 600 Victorian homes.

Innkeeper(s): Sally & Bart Denithorne. $85-200. MC, VISA, PC, TC. 5 rooms. Breakfast and afternoon tea included in rates. Type of meal: Early coffee/tea. Beds: KQD. Ceiling fan and hair dryer in room. Air conditioning. VCR and bicycles on premises. Handicap access. Antiquing, art galleries, beaches, bicycling, canoeing/kayaking, fishing, golf, hiking, live theater, museums, parks, shopping, tennis, water sports and wineries nearby.

Queen's Hotel

601 Columbia Ave
Cape May, NJ 08204-2305
(609)884-1613
Web: www.queenshotel.com

Circa 1876. This charming Victorian hotel is located just a block from the beach in the center of Cape May's historic district. Period decor graces the luxurious guest rooms. The feeling is both romantic and historic. Many of the rooms and suites offer double whirlpool tubs and glass-enclosed marble showers. Other amenities include hair dryers, TV, heated towel bar, air conditioning, coffee makers and mini refrigerators. Some have private balconies and ocean views. As this is a hotel, meals are not included in the rates; however, a multitude of restaurants and cafes are within walking distance or you can ask for the continental breakfast basket for a small charge. The hotel's staff includes professional concierge service. Shops are one block away. There are bicycles on the premises to explore the town and scenic water views.

Innkeeper(s): Dane & Joan Wells. $75-260. MC, VISA, PC. 11 rooms, 9 with PB, 1 with FP and 2 suites. Beds: QD. Cable TV, phone, ceiling fan, hair dryer, coffeemaker and heated towel bar in room. Air conditioning. Bicycles on premises. Weddings, small meetings and family reunions hosted. Amusement parks, antiquing, bicycling, fishing, golf, historic tours, live theater, parks and water sports nearby.

Publicity: *Philadelphia Inquirer.*

The Queen Victoria

102 Ocean St
Cape May, NJ 08204-2320
(609)884-8702
E-mail: qvinn@bellatlantic.net
Web: www.queenvictoria.com

Circa 1881. This nationally acclaimed inn, a block from the ocean and shops in the historic district, is comprised of two beautiful Victorian homes, restored and furnished with

antiques. "Victorian Homes" magazine featured 23 color photographs of The Queen Victoria, because of its décor and luxury amenities. Guest rooms offer handmade quilts, antiques, air conditioning, mini-refrigerators and all have

private baths. Some luxury suites include handsome fireplaces and whirlpool tubs. Afternoon tea is enjoyed while rocking on the porch in summer or before a warm fireplace in winter. Breakfast is hearty buffet style and the inn has its own cookbook. The innkeepers keep a fleet of complimentary bicycles available for guests and there are beach chairs and beach towels as well. The inn is open all year with special Christmas festivities and winter packages.

Innkeeper(s): Dane & Joan Wells. $90-290. MC, VISA, PC. 15 rooms with PB, 4 suites and 2 cottages. Breakfast and afternoon tea included in rates. Types of meals: Full bkfst and early coffee/tea. Beds: QD. Phones and TVs (some rooms) in room. Air conditioning. Bicycles on premises. Small meetings hosted. Amusement parks, antiquing, golf, historic tours, parks, ocean swimming and water sports nearby.

Sea Holly B&B Inn

815 Stockton Ave
Cape May, NJ 08204-2446
(609)884-6294 Fax:(609)884-8215
E-mail: seaholly@bellatlantic.com
Web: www.seahollyinn.com

Circa 1875. The home-baked cuisine at this three-story Gothic cottage is an absolute delight. Innkeepers Patti and Walt Melnick, frequent inngoers themselves, have incorporated their

own guest expectations into Sea Holly. The aroma of Patti's special chocolate chip cookies entice guests to search for the dining room. The home is decorated with *circa 1875* authentic Renaissance Revival and Eastlake antique pieces. Some rooms boast ocean views. The inn is a wonderful place for a special occasion, and honeymooners or those celebrating an anniversary receive complimentary champagne. In addition to the romantic amenities, the innkeeper provides practical extras such as hair dryers, irons and ironing boards in each room or suite. All rooms and suites include a television. Winter guests should be sure to ask about the inn's midweek winter specials.

Innkeeper(s): Patti & Walt Melnick. $80-200. MC, VISA, AX, TC. 8 rooms with PB and 2 suites. Breakfast and afternoon tea included in rates. Types of meals: Full bkfst and early coffee/tea. Beds: KQ. Ceiling fan, iron & ironing board and cable TV (some rooms) in room. Air conditioning. Fax on premises. Weddings and family reunions hosted. Amusement parks, antiquing, fishing, live theater, parks, shopping and water sports nearby.

Seventh Sister Guesthouse

10 Jackson St
Cape May, NJ 08204-1418
(609)884-2280 Fax:(609)898-9899

Circa 1888. Most of the Seventh Sister's guest rooms have ocean views. The inn is listed in the National Register. The artist/architect innkeepers have original art collections on dis-

play. Wicker and original antique furnishings fill the rooms. Guests can relax in front of a warm fire in the living room. The home's three floors are joined by a spectacular central circular staircase. The center of town is a one-block walk, and the beach is just 100 feet away.

Historic Interest: Coldspring Village (7 miles).

Innkeeper(s): Bob & JoAnne Echevarria-Myers. $75-175. MC, VISA, AX, PC. 6 rooms, 1 with PB. EP. Beds: QD. Air conditioning. Fax and refrigerator on premises. French, Spanish and German spoken. Amusement parks, antiquing, fishing, golf, live theater, parks, shopping, tennis and water sports nearby.

White Dove Cottage

619 Hughes St
Cape May, NJ 08204-2317
(609)884-0613 (800)321-3683

Circa 1866. The beautiful octagonal slate on the Mansard roof of this Second Empire house is just one of the inn's many handsome details. Bright sunny rooms are furnished in American and

European antiques, period wallpapers, paintings, prints and handmade quilts. Rooms with fireplaces or Jacuzzi tub are available. Breakfast is served to the soft music of an antique music

box and boasts heirloom crystal, fine china and lace. Located on a quiet, gas-lit street, the inn is two blocks from the beach, restaurants and shops. Ask about mystery weekends and the inn's Honeymoon and Romantic Escape packages.

Innkeeper(s): Frank & Sue Smith. $90-225. 4 rooms with PB and 2 suites. Breakfast and afternoon tea included in rates. Types of meals: Full gourmet bkfst and early coffee/tea. Beds: KQD. Two suites with fireplace and Jacuzzi in room. Antiquing, fishing, live theater, shopping and water sports nearby.

The Wooden Rabbit

609 Hughes St
Cape May, NJ 08204-2317
(609)884-7293

Circa 1838. Robert E. Lee brought his wife to stay at this sea captain's house to ease her arthritis. The house was also part of the Underground Railroad. The inn is decorated throughout with antiques and collectibles. In keeping with the name, the innkeeper's serve the full breakfasts on blue and white Dedham pottery that features the traditional rabbit pattern. In the warmer months, guests enjoy afternoon tea in the garden room. During the cooler seasons, guests can relax and enjoy refreshments by one of the inn's fireplace.

Innkeeper(s): Nancy & Dave McGonigle. $80-200. MC, VISA. 4 rooms with PB and 2 suites. Breakfast and afternoon tea included in rates. Meal: Full bkfst. Beds: KQ. Cable TV and sofa beds for extra guests in room. Air conditioning. Amusement parks, antiquing, fishing, beaches, live theater and shopping nearby.

"As 20 year veterans of B&Bs we are very impressed. We'll be back!"

Woodleigh House

808 Washington St
Cape May, NJ 08204-1652
(609)884-7123 (800)399-7123

Circa 1866. Rocking chairs line the veranda of this former sea captain's home. It's natural cedar siding is highlighted with burgundy and creme trim. Period antiques are featured. The dining room, for instance, boasts a carved antique sideboard from Brussels, an  Oriental carpet and an original chandelier. Guest rooms offer romantic seven-foot-high carved antique headboards and marble-top dressers.
Popular breakfast dishes are Banana Blinni (a French toast made from banana bread) and breakfast casseroles featuring herbs and home grown tomatoes from the garden. Afternoon tea is hot or cold depending upon the season and may feature Heath-nut crunch cookies or other home made goodies. The innkeepers are developing a secret garden with butterfly bushes and a wisteria arbor to add to the inn's inviting outdoor spaces.

Innkeeper(s): Joe & Joanne Tornambe. $95-185. MC, VISA. 4 rooms with PB and 1 suite. Breakfast and afternoon tea included in rates. Type of meal: Full bkfst. Beds: QT. TV in room. Air conditioning. Antiquing, beaches, fishing, live theater, shopping, tennis and water sports nearby.

"Clean and comfortable, delicious breakfast, charming hosts."

Flemington   E3

Jerica Hill B&B Inn

96 Broad St
Flemington, NJ 08822-1604
(908)782-8234 (888)650-88499 Fax:(908)237-0587

Circa 1901. There are plenty of places to relax at this bed & breakfast. The living room beckons with a fireplace, deep, comfortable furniture, a TV and bookcases full of interesting vol-umes. The screened porch is decorated with flowering plants and wicker furnishings. Guest rooms are bright and airy with ceiling fans, bay windows, flowers and other amenities. A bountiful country breakfast is served in the dining room or during warm, sunny mornings on the porch.
The innkeeper has several romantic packages available to guests. His "Country Winery Tour" package includes a wine tour, tastings and a wicker basket filled with a country picnic and wine tasting glasses.

Innkeeper(s): Gene Refalvy. $85-125. MC, VISA, AX, PC, TC. TAC10. 5 rooms with PB. Breakfast and snacks/refreshments included in rates. Types of meals: Full bkfst and early coffee/tea. Picnic lunch available. Beds: KQD. Phone in room. Air conditioning. Fax and copier on premises. Small meetings, family reunions and seminars hosted. Antiquing, fishing, live theater, parks, shopping, downhill skiing, cross-country skiing, sporting events and water sports nearby.

"If you've been searching for an inn that's homey and unpretentious - then I've found the place for you: Jerica Hill."

Glenwood   A5

Apple Valley Inn

967 County Rt, 517
Glenwood, NJ 07418
(973)764-3735 Fax:(973)764-1050

Circa 1804. This three-story Colonial farmhouse is set on three acres with its own apple orchard and in-ground pool. A brook running next to the house is a great trout-fishing spot. The innkeeper is an avid antique collector and guest rooms (named after varieties of apples) include American antiques. Try the Red Delicious room. Across the street is a popular pick-your-own-fruit farm. Check with the innkeeper to find when the strawberries, peaches, cherries and apples are ripe so you can gather your favorites. Mountain Creek, ski slopes and the Appalachian Trail are five minutes away.

Innkeeper(s): Mitzi & John Durham. $80-120. MC, VISA, DS, PC, TC. TAC10. 7 rooms, 2 with PB. Breakfast and afternoon tea included in rates. Types of meals: Full bkfst and early coffee/tea. Picnic lunch available. Beds: DT. Ceiling fan in room. Air conditioning. VCR, fax, copier, swimming, bicycles and library on premises. Weddings, small meetings, family reunions and seminars hosted. Amusement parks, antiquing, fishing, hiking, Appalachian Trail, live theater, parks, shopping, downhill skiing, cross-country skiing and sporting events nearby.

Publicity: *Cleveland Plain Dealer, Appalachian Trail News, New Jersey Herald, Country Living.*

Lambertville   E3

Chimney Hill Farm Estate
& The Ol'Barn Inn

207 Goat Hill Rd
Lambertville, NJ 08530
(609)397-1516 Fax:(609)397-9353
E-mail: chbb@erols.com
Web: www.chimneyhillinn.com

Circa 1820. Chimney Hill, in the hills above the riverside town of Lambertville, is a grand display of stonework, designed with both Federal and Greek Revival-style architecture. The inn's sunroom is particularly appealing, with its stone walls, fireplaces and French windows looking out to eight acres of gardens and fields. All eight of the guest rooms in the estate farmhouse include fireplaces, and some have canopied beds. The Ol' Barn has four suites with fireplaces, Jacuzzis, steam rooms, guest pantries, spiral staircases and loft bedrooms. The innkeepers offer adventure, romance and special interest packages for their guests, and the inn is also popular for corporate retreats. There are plenty of seasonal activities nearby, from kayaking to skiing. New Hope is the neighboring town and offers many charming restaurants and shops, as well.

Innkeeper(s): Terry Ann & Richard Anderson. $95-289. MC, VISA, AX, PC, TC. TAC10. 12 rooms with PB, 8 with FP and 2 conference rooms. Breakfast and snacks/refreshments included in rates. MAP, AP. Types of meals: Full

bkfst, cont plus and early coffee/tea. Catering service available. Beds: KQD. Phone in room. Air conditioning. Copier, library and butler pantry with snacks on premises. Weddings, small meetings, family reunions and seminars hosted. Antiquing, fishing, live theater, parks, shopping, downhill skiing, cross-country skiing, sporting events and water sports nearby.

"We would be hard pressed to find a more perfect setting to begin our married life together."

York Street House

42 York St
Lambertville, NJ 08530-2024
(609)397-3007 (888)398-3199 Fax:(609)397-9677
E-mail: yorksthse@aol.com
Web: www.yorkstreethouse.com

Circa 1909. Built by early industrialist George Massey as a 25th wedding anniversary present for his wife, the gracious manor house is situated on three quarters of an acre in the heart of the Lambertville's historical district. A winding three-story staircase leads to five well-appointed guest rooms decorated with period furnishings. The public rooms are warmed by Mercer Tile fireplaces, original Waterford Crystal chandeliers and a baby grand piano. Breakfast is served in the dining room with its built-in leaded-glass china and large oak servers, looking out over the lawn and sitting porch. Art galleries, antique shops, bookstores and restaurants are all within walking distance from the inn. Lambertville is nestled along the scenic Delaware River and Raritan Canal. Horseback riding, mule-drawn barges and carriage rides are just some of the activities available. A short walk across the Delaware River Bridge brings you to New Hope, Penn., with its many quaint shops.

Innkeeper(s): Nancy Ferguson & Beth Wetterskog. $95-189. MC, VISA, AX, DS, PC, TC. TAC5. 5 rooms with PB. Breakfast included in rates. Types of meals: Full gourmet bkfst and early coffee/tea. Picnic lunch available. Beds: KQ. Cable TV, ceiling fan and fireplaces in room. Air conditioning. VCR and fax on premises. Small meetings hosted. Antiquing, fishing, live theater, parks and shopping nearby.

Mays Landing   I4

Abbott House

6056 Main St
Mays Landing, NJ 08330-1852
(609)625-4400
E-mail: theabbotthouse@email.msn.com
Web: bbianj.com/abbott

Circa 1865. Guests at this Victorian-style mansion can relax on the bluff overlooking the Great Egg Harbor River, read on the second-floor veranda with its intricate fretwork or take afternoon tea in the belvedere (cupola) with spectacular views of historic Mays Landing. The inn is within walking distance to Lake Lenape and its various summer attractions. Each room is individually decorated with antiques, wicker, handmade quilts and other special touches. The Victorian Parlor is a place for games, reading and conversation. Refreshments can be enjoyed on one of the many porches and verandas.

Innkeeper(s): Linda Maslanko, Cathy Foschia. $89-119. MC, VISA, AX, DS. 3 rooms and 1 suite. Breakfast included in rates. Type of meal: Full bkfst. Turndown service in room. Air conditioning. Small meetings and family reunions hosted. Antiquing and shopping nearby.

North Wildwood   K4

Candlelight Inn

2310 Central Ave
North Wildwood, NJ 08260-5944
(609)522-6200 (800)992-2632 Fax:(609)522-6125
E-mail: info@candlelight-inn.com
Web: www.candlelight-inn.com

Circa 1905. Candlelight Inn offers nearly ten guest rooms in a restored Queen Anne Victorian. The home is decorated with an assortment of period pieces. Among its antiques are a Victorian sofa dating to 1855 and an 1890 Eastlake piano. Breakfasts begin with a fresh fruit course, followed by homemade breads and a daily entrée, such as waffles, pancakes or a specialty egg dish. Candlelight Inn is about eight miles from the historic towns of Cape May and Cold Spring Village.

Historic Interest: Cape May (8 miles), Cold Spring Village (7 miles).
Innkeeper(s): Bill & Nancy Moncrief. $110-200. MC, VISA, AX, DS, TC. TAC12. 10 rooms with PB, 2 with FP and 3 suites. Breakfast and afternoon tea included in rates. Types of meals: Full bkfst and early coffee/tea. Snacks/refreshments available. Beds: KQDT. Cable TV, ceiling fan, jacuzzi and fireplace in room. Central air. Fax, copier and spa on premises. Weddings, small meetings, family reunions and seminars hosted. German spoken. Amusement parks, antiquing, art galleries, beaches, bicycling, fishing, golf, live theater, museums, parks, shopping, tennis, water sports and wineries nearby.

Ocean City   J4

Barnagate B&B

637 Wesley Ave
Ocean City, NJ 08226-3855
(609)391-9366 Fax:(609)399-5048

Circa 1896. Three-and-a-half blocks from the ocean, the Barnagate B&B offers Victorian-style guest rooms with paddle fans and country quilts. The top floor of the four-story inn features a private sitting room. Guests enjoy fresh fruit and homemade breads at breakfast.

Innkeeper(s): Lois & Frank Barna. $85-160. MC, VISA, AX, PC. TAC10. 5 rooms, 1 with PB and 1 suite. Breakfast included in rates. Types of meals: Cont plus and early coffee/tea. Beds: QDT. TV and ceiling fan in room. Air conditioning. VCR, fax and library on premises. Small meetings and family reunions hosted. Amusement parks, antiquing, fishing, golf, live theater, parks, shopping, tennis and water sports nearby.

Ebbie Guest House

820 E 6th St
Ocean City, NJ 08226-3837
(609)399-4744

Circa 1920. This family owned and operated seashore house includes both rooms and apartments. There is a two-bedroom apartment with a living area and kitchen, as well as an efficiency apartment and a studio. Both of the smaller apartments include a kitchen. Guest quarters and common areas are decorated in a comfortable, relaxed-country style. The home is a half block from the beach and boardwalk.

Innkeeper(s): Dave & Liz Warrington. $75-100. TC. 7 rooms, 5 with PB. Type of meal: Cont. Beds: DT. Cable TV in room. Air conditioning. Large screen TV on premises. Family reunions hosted. Amusement parks, beaches, fishing, golf, boardwalk, recreational parks, parks, shopping, sporting events, tennis and water sports nearby.

New Brighton Inn

519 5th St
Ocean City, NJ 08226-3940
(609)399-2829 Fax:(609)398-7786
E-mail: dhand@bellatlantic.net
Web: www.newbrighton.com

Circa 1880. Ocean City was founded as a Christian retreat in the 19th century, and the builder of this home was instrumental in the town's founding. The home is a stunning example of Queen Anne architecture, featuring a tower, wraparound veranda and an arbor-covered terrace. The innkeepers provide guests with beach passes and bicycles, and it is a four-block walk to the beach and boardwalk.

Innkeeper(s): Daniel & Donna Hand. $105-155. MC, VISA, AX, DC, DS, PC, TC. 6 rooms with PB, 2 suites and 1 cottage. Breakfast included in rates. Types of meals: Cont plus and early coffee/tea. Beds: Q. Cable TV, ceiling fan, VCR and one with a two-person Jacuzzi in room. Air conditioning. Fax, copier, bicycles and library on premises. Weddings and family reunions hosted. Amusement parks, antiquing, fishing, golf, parks, shopping, tennis and water sports nearby.

Northwood Inn B&B

401 Wesley Ave
Ocean City, NJ 08226-3961
(609)399-6071 Fax:(609)398-5553
E-mail: info@northwoodinn.com
Web: www.northwoodinn.com

Circa 1894. This gracious three-story Queen Anne Victorian with Colonial Victorian touches has been restored by the innkeeper, who is a wooden boat builder and custom-home builder. There are gleaming plank floors, a sweeping staircase, a billiard room and a stocked library. The two-room Tower Suite in the turret is a favorite, offering a luxurious bath with a double Jacuzzi tub and over-sized shower. The Magnolia Room is another popular choice with its taupe-colored walls, lace curtains and double Jacuzzi. There is a rooftop, four-person spa where guests can relax and enjoy the sunset. The inn is within walking distance of the beach, boardwalk, shops and restaurants. The innkeepers offer bicycles and beach tags to their guests.

Historic Interest: Cape May (30 miles).

Innkeeper(s): Marj & John Loeper. $80-150. MC, VISA, AX, PC. 8 rooms with PB and 2 suites. Types of meals: Full bkfst and cont plus. Beds: QT. One suite with Jacuzzi in room. Air conditioning. VCR, fax, spa and library on premises. Weddings and small meetings hosted. Amusement parks, antiquing, fishing, casino/Atlantic City, live theater, parks, shopping and water sports nearby.

Publicity: *Philadelphia Magazine.*

"In all our years of staying at B&Bs - still our favorite. Comfortable, relaxing, wonderful breakfasts, and hosts who couldn't be more welcoming. In season, off season, or whenever a break is needed, we head for the Northwood to renew!"

Scarborough Inn

720 Ocean Ave
Ocean City, NJ 08226-3787
(609)399-1558 (800)258-1558 Fax:(609)399-4472
E-mail: cgbruno@earthlink.net
Web: www.scarboroughinn.com

Circa 1895. Painted in wedgewood, rose and soft cream, the Scarborough Inn is a familiar Victorian landmark in this seaside resort. Family-owned and operated, the inn is filled with the innkeepers' artwork collection and intriguing mementos.

Breakfast is served in an elegant dining room or on the wraparound porch. Afternoon refreshments also are served. The beach and boardwalk are a short stroll from the inn.

Historic Interest: Wheaten Village (1 hour), Cold Spring Village (40 minutes), Leemings Run Gardens (30 minutes), Atlantic City (20 minutes).

Innkeeper(s): Gus & Carol Bruno. $90-180. MC, VISA, AX, DS, TC. TAC10. 18 rooms with PB and 5 suites. Breakfast included in rates. Type of meal: Early coffee/tea. Afternoon tea and catering service available. Beds: KQDT. Cable TV, phone and alarm clocks in room. Air conditioning. VCR, fax and library on premises. Small meetings and family reunions hosted. Italian spoken. Amusement parks, antiquing, fishing, golf, birding, casinos, cultural and historical sites, live theater, parks, shopping, sporting events and water sports nearby.

Serendipity B&B

712 E 9th St
Ocean City, NJ 08226-3554
(609)399-1554 (800)842-8544 Fax:(609)399-1527

Circa 1912. The beach and boardwalk are less than half a block from this renovated inn. Healthy full breakfasts are served, and the innkeepers offer dinners by reservation with a mix of interesting, vegetarian items. In the summer, breakfasts are served on a vine-shaded veranda. The guest rooms are decorated in pastels with wicker pieces.

Innkeeper(s): Clara & Bill Plowfield. $80-159. MC, VISA, AX, DS, PC, TC. TAC10. 6 rooms, 4 with PB. Breakfast and snacks/refreshments included in rates. Type of meal: Full bkfst. Dinner available. Beds: KQDT. Cable TV, ceiling fan, bathrobes and bottled water in room. Air conditioning. Library and dressing rooms with showers & beach towels on premises. Amusement parks, antiquing, fishing, ocean beach and boardwalk, live theater, parks, shopping and water sports nearby.

"Serendipity is such a gift. For me it's a little like being adopted during vacation time by a caring sister and brother. Your home is a home away from home. You make it so."

Ocean Grove   F6

The Cordova

26 Webb Ave
Ocean Grove, NJ 07756-1334
(732)774-3084 Fax:(212)207-4720

Circa 1885. This century-old Victorian community was founded as a Methodist retreat. Ocean-bathing and cars were not allowed on Sunday until a few years ago. There are no souvenir

shops along the white sandy beach and wooden boardwalk. The inn has hosted Presidents Wilson, Cleveland and Roosevelt, who were also speakers at the Great Auditorium with its 7,000 seats. Guests have use of the kitchen, lounge, picnic and barbecue areas, thus making this a popular place for family reunions, retreats, showers and weddings. Ask about the inn's murder-mystery and tai chi weekends, as well as other special events. Three suites and two cottage apartments also are available. The Cordova was chosen by New Jersey Magazine as one of the seven best places on the Jersey Shore. For information during the winter season, call (212) 751-9577.

Historic Interest: The home is listed in the National Register. Ocean Grove, a charming Victorian town, also is listed in the National Register.

Innkeeper(s): Doris Chernik, Steve & Rosie Manchester. $46-150. PC. TAC10. 15 rooms, 7 with PB, 3 suites and 2 cottages. Breakfast included in rates. Type of meal: Cont plus. Beds: KQDT. TV in room. VCR, bicycles, tennis and library on premises. Antiquing, fishing, music concerts, garden tours, dances, shopping and tennis nearby.

"Warm, helpful and inviting, homey and lived-in atmosphere."

The Manchester Inn B&B and Secret Garden Restaurant

25 Ocean Pathway
Ocean Grove, NJ 07756-1645
(732)775-0616
E-mail: thenjinn@aol.com
Web: www.themanchesterinn.com

Circa 1880. Enjoy cool ocean breezes while you lounge on the front porch of this quaint Victorian, which is featured in the town's annual Victorian Holiday House Tour each December.

The full-service restaurant has bright, flowery decor and offers plenty of choices for breakfast, lunch and dinner. Ocean Grove is an ideal spot to bask in the Victorian tradition. The beach is only one block and the inn looks out onto Ocean Parkway, one of Ocean Grove's finest streets. The town itself offers many festivals throughout the year, plus a variety of interesting shops to explore.

Historic Interest: The Great Auditorium is the pride of Ocean Grove. Built in 1894, it seats more than 6,000 people, and its speakers and visitors have included presidents Grant, Garfield, McKinley, Teddy Roosevelt, Taft, Wilson and Nixon. Surrounding the auditorium is the Tent Community, where descendants of the founding families spend their summers.

Innkeeper(s): Margaret & Clark Cate. $55-400. MC, VISA, AX, DS. 42 rooms, 20 with PB. Breakfast included in rates. Type of meal: Cont. Dinner, picnic lunch, lunch and catering service available. Restaurant on premises. Beds: KQDT. Antiquing, fishing and water sports nearby.

Pemberton Boro — G4

Isaac Hilliard House

31 Hanover St
Pemberton Boro, NJ 08068
(609)894-0756 (800)371-0756

Circa 1750. A wrought-iron fence sets off this two-story green and white Victorian. The inn is filled with antique collections and books. There's an antique bridal gown in the suite, which includes a remote-controlled gas fireplace, sitting room with TV and VCR, and private bathroom with a garden tub. Walk two minutes to the canoe rental, then paddle along the Rancocas River. The Grist Mill Village Antiques is within walking distance, and several other antique shops and fine restaurants are close by.

Historic Interest: Trenton, N.J., battlefield and buildings (25 minutes), Washington Crossing State Park (40 minutes), Ye Olde Lock Up Building (5-minute walk).

Innkeeper(s): Phyllis Davis & Gene R. O'Brien. $65-140. MC, VISA, AX, DS, PC, TC. 4 rooms with PB and 1 suite. Breakfast included in rates. Types of meals: Full bkfst and veg bkfst. Beds: Q. Turndown service, ceiling fan, gas fireplace with remote control in one suite and hair dryer in room. Air conditioning. Swimming and refrigerator on premises. Weddings and small meetings hosted. Amusement parks, antiquing, fishing, newly dedicated Pemberton Rail Trail with visitor center, live theater, parks and water sports nearby.

"Every little detail was made so kind and warm. For even a short time, we both felt as if we traveled abroad. Your home is kept gorgeous and so tasteful."

Princeton — E4

Red Maple Farm

211 Raymond Rd
Princeton, NJ 08540
(732)329-3821

Circa 1740. Located four miles from Princeton University and shaded by towering trees, this Colonial home rests on more than two acres of flower beds, fruit trees and berry bushes.

There's a stone smokehouse built in 1740 and an old barn. The house is in the National Register, and Hessian soldiers were quartered here. It was also part of the Underground Railroad. Guest rooms are decorated comfortably, and one offers a working fireplace, pine armoire and brass bed. The innkeeper, a former noted chef, nurtures a vegetable garden that provides fresh produce for the inn's breakfast (shirred eggs, frittatas and buckwheat pancakes are some of the specialities).

Innkeeper(s): Roberta & Lindsey Churchill. $65-85. MC, VISA, AX, PC, TC. 3 rooms with PB, 1 with FP. Breakfast included in rates. Type of meal: Full gourmet bkfst. Beds: QT. Air conditioning. VCR, fax, copier, swimming, bicycles, library and barn smokehouse on premises. Some French spoken. Antiquing, fishing, golf, live theater, parks, shopping, cross-country skiing, sporting events and tennis nearby.

"Thank you for making an overnight stop so completely relaxing. A great start to a much-needed vacation!"

Salem
I1

Brown's Historic Home B&B

41-43 Market St
Salem, NJ 08079
(856)935-8595 Fax:(856)935-8595

Circa 1738. Brown's Historic Home originally was built as a Colonial house. Around 1845, the house was modernized to the Victorian era. The inn is furnished with antiques and heirlooms, including a handmade chess set and quilt. The fireplaces are made of King of Prussia marble. The backyard garden features a lily pond, wildflowers and a waterfall. There is a ferry nearby offering transport to Delaware. On Saturdays, guests can enjoy performances at the Cowtown Rodeo, eight miles away.

Historic Interest: Fort Mott State Park is four miles away.

Innkeeper(s): William & Margaret Brown. $55-100. MC, VISA, AX, DS, TC. 4 rooms, 2 with PB, 1 with FP. Breakfast included in rates. Types of meals: Full bkfst and early coffee/tea. Beds: DT. Cable TV, phone and ceiling fan in room. Air conditioning. Fax on premises. Small meetings and family reunions hosted. Antiquing, fishing, hunting, bird watching, live theater, parks, shopping and water sports nearby.

Pets allowed: Kennel nearby.

"Down-home-on-the-farm breakfasts with great hospitality."

Spring Lake
F6

Ashling Cottage

106 Sussex Ave
Spring Lake, NJ 07762-1248
(732)449-3553 (888)274-5464
E-mail: ashling@lonekeep.com
Web: www.bbianj.com/ashling

Circa 1877. Surrounded by shady sycamores on a quiet residential street, this three-story Victorian residence features a mansard-and-gambrel roof with hooded gambrel dormers. One of the two porches has a square, pyramid-roofed pavilion, which has been glass-enclosed and screened. Guests can watch the sun rise over the ocean one block away or set over Spring Lake. A full buffet breakfast can

be enjoyed in the plant- and wicker-filled pavilion.

Historic Interest: Allaire State Park (5 miles).

Innkeeper(s): Jack Stewart. $99-184. PC, TC. 10 rooms, 8 with PB. Breakfast and afternoon tea included in rates. Types of meals: Full bkfst and early coffee/tea. Beds: Q. Ceiling fan and clock in room. Air conditioning. VCR, bicycles and library on premises. Weddings, small meetings, family reunions and seminars hosted. Limited German spoken. Amusement parks, antiquing, fishing, race tracks, live theater, parks, shopping, sporting events and water sports nearby.

Publicity: *New York Times, New Jersey Monthly, Town & Country, Country Living, New York, Harrods of London.*

La Maison

404 Jersey Ave
Spring Lake, NJ 07762-1437
(908)449-0969 (800)276-2088 Fax:(908)449-4860

Circa 1870. A French Victorian with a wide wraparound veranda, this historic inn is located four blocks from the water. The French influence is repeated in romantic furnishings such as French beds, Jacuzzis, French-country and Louis Philippe pieces. At breakfast, creme brule French toast is often served. A cottage is popular in summer for families with children. The inn is also affiliated with a top health club facility in the area.

Innkeeper(s): Julianne Corrigan. $125-325. MC, VISA, AX, DS, PC, TC. TAC10. 8 rooms with PB, 2 suites and 1 cottage. Breakfast included in rates. Types of meals: Full gourmet bkfst and early coffee/tea. Beds: QT. Cable TV, phone and happy hour in room. Air conditioning. Fax, bicycles, handicap access/cottage, beach badges and towels and chairs on premises. Weddings, small meetings, family reunions and seminars hosted. Antiquing, fishing, live theater, parks, shopping and water sports nearby.

The Normandy Inn

21 Tuttle Ave
Spring Lake, NJ 07762-1533
(732)449-7172 (800)449-1888 Fax:(732)449-1070
E-mail: normandy@bellatlantic.com
Web: www.normandyinn.com

Circa 1888. The house was moved onto the present site around 1910. Normandy Inn combines both Italianate and Queen Anne features, and the gracious home is listed in the National Register. The home rises up four stories with a notable circular window gracing the front exterior. The innkeepers have kept the historic home as authentic as possible. The interior is filled with a remarkable selection

of period pieces, including a stunning, museum quality four-poster bed that graces one of the guest rooms. The Victorian antiques are accentuated by Victorian colors documented and researched by Roger Moss. Lavish country breakfasts are served on little lace-covered tables set with fine china and silver. In the afternoons, homemade treats are accompanied with a selection of teas, coffees and other refreshments. Spring Lake is a gem, an idyllic hamlet of historic homes along the Jersey shore.

Historic Interest: Allaire State Park (5 miles).

Innkeeper(s): Jeri & Mike Robertson. $106-320. MC, VISA, AX, DC, CB, DS, PC, TC. TAC10. 19 rooms with PB, 6 with FP, 2 suites and 2 conference rooms. Breakfast and snacks/refreshments included in rates. Types of meals: Full bkfst, country bkfst and early coffee/tea. Afternoon tea available. Beds: KQDT. Cable TV, phone and VCR in room. Air conditioning. Fax, copier and bicycles on premises. Small meetings and seminars hosted. Amusement parks, antiquing, art galleries, beaches, pool passes, bicycling, fishing, golf, horseback riding, live theater, parks, shopping, tennis and water sports nearby.

"The cozy and delicious accommodations of your inn were beyond expectations."

Victoria House

214 Monmouth Ave
Spring Lake, NJ 07762-1127
(732)974-1882 Fax:(732)974-2132
E-mail: www.victoriahousebb@postoffice.worldnet.att.net
Web: www.victoriahouse.net

Circa 1882. Queen Victoria surely would have enjoyed a trip to this bed & breakfast, as well as to Spring Lake, a pleasant village on the Jersey Shore. Each of the guest rooms is individually decorated with pieces such as an antique Eastlake armoire and wicker or brass beds. Several bathrooms include clawfoot tubs. The beach is within walking distance, and the innkeepers provide beach passes for their guests. Shops and restaurants are nearby as well.

Innkeeper(s): Louise & Robert Goodall. $115-225. MC, VISA, AX, DS, PC, TC. TAC10. 8 rooms. Breakfast included in rates. Type of meal: Full bkfst. Beds: KQ. Ceiling fan one room and whirlpool/shower in room. Air conditioning. Fax and bicycles on premises. Small meetings and seminars hosted. Antiquing, fishing, Monmouth, Rutgers college/university campus, live theater, parks, shopping (local crafts), sporting events and water sports nearby.

"A very charming stay. We enjoyed your hospitality."

Stanhope   C4

Whistling Swan Inn

110 Main St
Stanhope, NJ 07874-2632
(973)347-6369 Fax:(973)347-3391
E-mail: wswan@worldnet.att.net
Web: www.whistlingswaninn.com

Circa 1905. This Queen Anne Victorian has a limestone wraparound veranda and a tall, steep-roofed turret. Family antiques fill the rooms and highlight the polished ornate woodwork, pocket doors and winding staircase. It is a little more than a mile from Waterloo Village and the International Trade Center.

Historic Interest: Waterloo Village (3 miles), Washington's Headquarters & Jockey Hollow (12 miles), Sterling Hill Mine (15 miles).

Innkeeper(s): Joe Mulay & Paula Williams. $95-150. MC, VISA, AX, DC, DS, PC, TC. 10 rooms with PB, 1 suite and 1 conference room. Breakfast included in rates. Type of meal: Full bkfst. Beds: Q. Cable TV, phone, ceiling fan, VCR, iron and hair dryer in room. Air conditioning. Fax, copier, bicycles, tubs for two and Victorian garden on premises. Seminars hosted. Antiquing, fishing, golf, hiking, boating, live theater, parks, shopping, sporting events and water sports nearby.

Publicity: *Sunday Herald, New York Times, New Jersey Monthly, Mid-Atlantic Country, Star Ledger, Daily Record, Philadelphia, Country, Chicago Sun Times.*

"Thank you for your outstanding hospitality. We had a delightful time while we were with you and will not hesitate to recommend the inn to our listening audience, friends and anyone else who will listen!" — Joel H. Klein, Travel Editor, WOAI AM.

Stockton   E3

The Stockton Inn

1 Main St, PO Box C
Stockton, NJ 08559-0318
(609)397-1250

Circa 1710. The Stockton Inn, known as Colligan's, has operated as an inn since 1796. It received national prominence when Richard Rogers & Lorenz Hart included reference to it in a song from musical comedy — "There is a small hotel with a wishing well." (The Broadway show was "On Your Toes.") Band leader Paul Whiteman later signed off his radio and television shows announcing he was going to dinner at "Ma Colligan's." Guest rooms are scattered throughout the inn's four buildings and feature fireplaces, balconies or canopy beds. The restaurant serves innovative American/Continental cuisine and there is a full service bar.

Historic Interest: Washington's Crossing State Park (one-half hour drive), Mercer Museum (American Artifacts-Tools) (one-half hour).

Innkeeper(s): Jack Boehlert. $60-165. MC, VISA, AX, DS. 11 rooms with PB, 8 with FP, 8 suites and 1 conference room. Breakfast included in rates. Type of meal: Cont. Gourmet dinner, lunch and catering service available. Restaurant on premises. Beds: QDT. Phone in room. Fishing and live theater nearby.

"My well-traveled parents say this is their favorite restaurant."

New Mexico

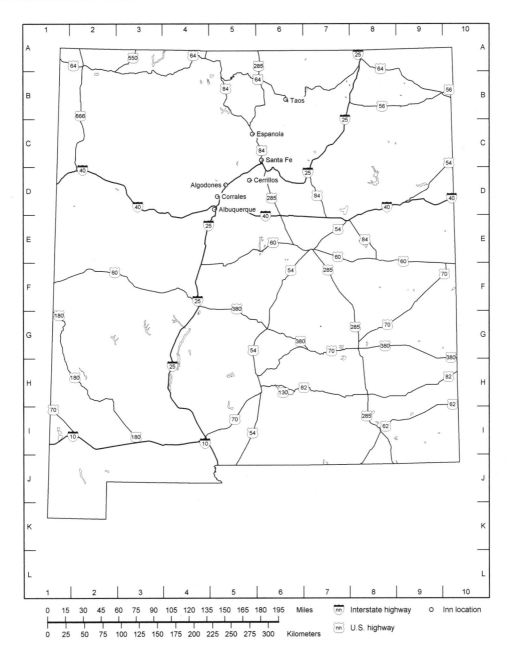

Albuquerque D5

Brittania & W.E. Mauger Estate B&B

701 Roma Ave NW
Albuquerque, NM 87102-2038
(505)242-8755 (800)719-9189 Fax:(505)842-8835
E-mail: maugerbb@aol.com
Web: www.maugerbb.com

Circa 1897. This former boarding house is now an elegantly restored Victorian in the National Register. Linda Ronstadt and Martin Sheen have been among some of the inn's notable guests. Guest rooms include amenities such as refrigerators, phones with voice mail, coffee makers, a basket with snacks, and beds topped with down comforters. The inn is located four blocks from the convention center and business district, and it is less than one mile from Old Town.

Historic Interest: Albuquerque is full of unique museums, featuring topics from Native American culture to the atomic age.

Innkeeper(s): Mark Brown & Keith Lewis. $89-179. MC, VISA, AX. 8 rooms with PB and 1 conference room. Breakfast included in rates. Types of meals: Full bkfst and early coffee/tea. Gourmet dinner and snacks/refreshments available. Beds: KQDT. TV, phone, ceiling fan, coffee maker, iron and hair dryer in room. Air conditioning. VCR, organ and laser disc player on premises. Small meetings and family reunions hosted. Amusement parks, antiquing, live theater and shopping nearby.
Publicity: *Albuquerque Journal, Phoenix Home and Garden, Albuquerque Monthly, National Geographic Traveler, New Mexico Business Week, Golf Digest, Great Estates.*

"Because of your hospitality, kindness and warmth, we will always compare the quality of our experience by the W.E. Mauger Estate."

Casa Del Granjero & El Rancho Guest House

414 C De Baca Ln NW
Albuquerque, NM 87114-1600
(505)897-4144 (800)701-4144 Fax:(505)897-9788

Circa 1890. Innkeepers Victoria and Butch Farmer, who appropriately named their home Casa del Granjero, or "the farmer's house," have designed their bed & breakfast to reflect Southwestern style with a hint of old Spanish flair. The adobe's guest rooms all include a rustic, kiva fireplace. Cuarto Allegre is the largest suite in the main house, and it includes a canopy bed covered in lace and French doors that open onto a small porch. Cuarto del Rey affords a mountain view and includes Mexican furnishings and handmade quilts. Cuarto de Flores also has quilts, Mexican tile and French doors leading to a private porch. The innkeepers have a hot tub open for guest use in a special garden area. The innkeepers also have restored a historic adobe ranch house across the road. The accommodations here include three suites and a guest room with a double bed. A kitchen, common area and wood-burning stove also are located in this house. A variety of baked goods, New Mexican-style recipes and fresh fruit are served each morning in the dining room or on the portal. Several recipes have been featured in a cookbook.
Innkeeper(s): Victoria Farmer. $79-149. MC, VISA. 7 rooms with PB and 5 suites. Breakfast included in rates. Type of meal: Full bkfst. Gourmet dinner, picnic lunch, catering service and room service available. Beds: KQT. Antiquing, fishing, live theater, downhill skiing, cross-country skiing and water sports nearby.

"Wonderful place, wonderful people. Thanks so much."

Hacienda Antigua B&B

6708 Tierra Dr NW
Albuquerque, NM 87107-6025
(505)345-5399 (800)201-2986 Fax:(505)345-3855

Circa 1780. In the more than 200 years since this Spanish Colonial-style hacienda was constructed, the current innkeepers are only the fourth owners. Once a stagecoach stop on the El Camino Real, it also served as a cantina and mercantile store. It was built by Don Pablo Yrisarri, who was sent by the King of Spain to search the area for gold. The home is elegant, yet maintains a rustic, Spanish charm with exposed beams, walls up to 30 inches thick, brick floors and adobe fireplaces. Along with a sitting room and kiva fireplace, the Don Pablo Suite includes a "ducking door" that leads onto the courtyard. Other rooms have clawfoot tubs, antique iron beds or a private patio. The cuisine is notable and one of the inn's recipes appeared in Culinary Trends magazine. Guests might sample a green chile souffle along with bread pudding and fresh fruit. The inn has been featured on the TV series "Great Country Inns."
Innkeeper(s): Ann Dunlap & Melinda Moffitt. $95-159. MC, VISA, AX, DS, PC, TC. TAC10. 5 rooms with PB, 5 with FP and 1 suite. Breakfast included in rates. Types of meals: Full bkfst and early coffee/tea. Beds: KQT. Phone and ceiling fan in room. Air conditioning. VCR, fax, spa and swimming on premises. Small meetings, family reunions and seminars hosted. Spanish and Italian spoken. Amusement parks, antiquing, fishing, golf, hiking, biking, balloon fiesta, live theater, parks, shopping, downhill skiing, cross-country skiing, sporting events and tennis nearby.

Espanola C5

Casa del Rio

PO Box 92
Espanola, NM 87532-0092
(505)753-2035 (800)920-1495

Circa 1988. These authentic, replica adobe guest houses are filled with local handmade crafts, rugs, bed coverings and furniture. Bathrooms boast handmade Mexican tile, and rooms are

decorated in traditional New Mexico style. The guest houses also boast kiva fireplaces. The patio windows afford a view of cliffs above the Rio Chama, which is just a short walk from the home. Casa del Rio is near many attractions, including Indian pueblos, the many museums of Ghost Ranch, galleries and an abundance of outdoor activities. The adobe is halfway between both Taos and Santa Fe.
Innkeeper(s): Eileen Sopanen-Vigil. $100-125. MC, VISA. 4 rooms. Breakfast included in rates. Type of meal: Full bkfst. Beds: KQT. Bicycling, fishing, hiking, shopping and sporting events nearby.

Madrid D5

Java Junction

2855 State Highway 14 N
Madrid, NM 87010
(505)438-2772

Circa 1916. So named because its first story contains a shop featuring specialty coffees, lattes and cappuccinos, as well as a variety of packaged Southwestern foods and gifts, this Victorian offers a spacious suite on its second story. The suite is decorated in Victorian style with antiques and includes a variety of amenities, such as a clock radio, coffee maker, TV and refrigerator. Guests enjoy a continental breakfast with some of the Junction's signature coffee drinks, as well as a stuffed croissant or homemade muffin. Madrid, once a railroad-company and coal-mining town, is located about 40 minutes in between Santa Fe and Albuquerque.

Innkeeper(s): Linda Dunnill. $65. MC, VISA, TC. 1 suites. Breakfast included in rates. Types of meals: Cont plus and cont. Restaurant on premises. Beds: Q. TV in room. Air conditioning. Art galleries, horseback riding, live theater, museums, parks and shopping nearby.

Pets allowed: Must get approval before registering.

Santa Fe   C6

Alexander's Inn

529 E Palace Ave
Santa Fe, NM 87501-2200
(505)986-1431 (888)321-5123 Fax:(505)982-8572
E-mail: alexandinn@aol.com
Web: www.collectorsguide.com/alexandinn

Circa 1903. Twin gables and a massive front porch are prominent features of this Craftsman-style brick and wood inn. French and American country decor, stained-glass windows and

a selection of antiques create a light Victorian touch. The inn also features beautiful gardens of roses and lilacs. The exquisite Southwest adobe casitas are a favorite for families and romantic getaways. Breakfast is often served in the backyard garden. Home-baked treats are offered to guests in the afternoon.

Historic Interest: Puye Cliffs, Bandalier and Pecos National Monument all are within one hour from the inn.

Innkeeper(s): Carolyn Lee. $80-160. MC, VISA, DS, PC, TC. TAC10. 7 rooms with PB, 5 with FP, 1 suite and 3 cottages. Breakfast and afternoon tea included in rates. EP. Types of meals: Full gourmet bkfst, cont plus and early coffee/tea. Beds: KQT. Cable TV, phone and VCR in room. Fax, spa, library and child care on premises. Weddings and family reunions hosted. French spoken. Antiquing, fishing, museums, Pueblos, live theater, parks, shopping, downhill skiing, cross-country skiing and water sports nearby.

Pets allowed: Well behaved.

"Thanks to the kindness and thoughtfulness of the staff, our three days in Santa Fe were magical."

Casa De La Cuma B&B

105 Paseo De La Cuma
Santa Fe, NM 87501-1213
(505)983-1717 (888)366-1717 Fax:(505)983-2241
E-mail: casacuma@swcp.com
Web: www.casacuma.com/bb

Circa 1940. Offering a warm and serene atmosphere, Casa De La Cuma B&B has three unique rooms and a suite decorated with Navajo textiles, original artwork and Southwestern-period

furniture. Guests enjoy breakfast on the glassed-in porch or simply relaxing on the shaded patio. During cooler weather, the fireplace in the living room is the gathering spot. The inn features views of the Sangre De Cristo Mountains and is within walking distance of the Plaza.

Historic Interest: The inn is located on the same hill as the original cross which honors Spanish priests killed during the 1680 pueblo revolt.

Innkeeper(s): Dona Hufton. $70-145. MC, VISA, PC, TC. TAC10. 4 rooms. Breakfast and snacks/refreshments included in rates. Type of meal: Cont plus. Afternoon tea available. Beds: KQT. Cable TV, phone and ceiling fan in room. Air conditioning. Antiquing, museums, hiking, rafting, parks and downhill skiing nearby.

Publicity: *Denver Post.*

Dunshee's

986 Acequia Madre
Santa Fe, NM 87501-2819
(505)982-0988
E-mail: sdunshee@aol.com
Web: www.bbhost.com/dunshee

Circa 1930. Where better could one experience Santa Fe's rich history than in an authentic adobe casita or a restored adobe home? Innkeeper Susan Dunshee offers accommodations in both. Guests can stay in the adobe home's spacious suite or rent the casita by the day, week or month. The casita offers two bedrooms, a kitchen, a living room warmed by a rustic, Kiva fireplace and a private patio. The antique-filled rooms are decorated in a warm, Santa Fe style, and bedrooms sport a more country look. Guests who opt for the bed & breakfast suite are treated to Southwestern breakfasts with items such as a green chile souffle. The refrigerator at the casita is stocked with treats for the guests' breakfast.

Innkeeper(s): Susan Dunshee. $125. MC, VISA, PC, TC. 3 rooms, 2 with PB, 3 with FP, 1 suite and 1 cottage. Breakfast included in rates. Types of meals: Full gourmet bkfst, cont plus and early coffee/tea. Beds: QD. Cable TV, phone, fresh flowers and homemade cookies in room. Library on premises. Weddings, small meetings and family reunions hosted. Antiquing, opera, Indian pueblos, live theater, parks, shopping, downhill skiing and cross-country skiing nearby.

El Farolito B&B Inn

514 Galisteo St
Santa Fe, NM 87501
(505)988-1631 (888)634-8782 Fax:(505)988-4589
E-mail: innkeeper@farolito.com
Web: www.farolito.com

Circa 1920. El Farolito's seven guest rooms or casitas are spread among four adobe buildings, some of which date back to the 1920s. The beamed ceilings, tile or brick floors and kiva fireplaces enhance the Southwestern decor. The bed & breakfast is located within Santa Fe's historic district, and a 10-minute walk will take you to the famous plaza. Other sites, the Capitol building, shops and restaurants are even closer.

Innkeeper(s): Walt Wyss & Wayne Mainus. $95-155. MC, VISA, AX, DS, TC. TAC10. 7 rooms with PB. Breakfast included in rates. EP. Type of meal: Cont plus. Beds: QD. Cable TV and phone in room. Air conditioning. Fax, copier and refrigerators and coffee service on premises. Small meetings, family reunions and seminars hosted. Antiquing, fishing, golf, live theater, parks, shopping, downhill skiing, cross-country skiing and sporting events nearby.

Publicity: *Winner of "Best small property of the year" awarded in 1999 by the New Mexico Hotel & Motel Association.*

El Paradero

220 W Manhattan Ave
Santa Fe, NM 87501-2622
(505)988-1177
E-mail: elpara@trail.com
Web: www.elparadero.com

Circa 1820. This was originally a two-bedroom Spanish farmhouse that doubled in size to a Territorial style in 1860, was remodeled as a Victorian in 1912, and became a Pueblo Revival in 1920. All styles are present and provide a walk through many years of history.

Historic Interest: Indian Ruins, Pueblos.

Innkeeper(s): Ouida MacGregor & Thomas Allen. $65-140. MC, VISA. TAC10. 14 rooms, 12 with PB, 7 with FP, 2 suites and 1 conference room. Breakfast and afternoon tea included in rates. Types of meals: Full gourmet bkfst and early coffee/tea. Beds: QT. Phone, fireplace, cable TV and refrigerator (some rooms) in room. Air conditioning. Fishing, pueblos, opera, mountains, live theater, shopping and cross-country skiing nearby.

Pets allowed: Only by pre-arrangement and only in certain rooms.

"I'd like to LIVE here."

Four Kachinas Inn

512 Webber St
Santa Fe, NM 87501-4454
(505)982-2550 (800)397-2564 Fax:(505)989-1323
E-mail: info@fourkachinas.com
Web: www.fourkachinas.com

Circa 1910. This inn is built in the pitched-tin roof style around a private courtyard. Rooms are decorated with Southwestern art and crafts, including Navajo rugs, Hopi Kachina dolls, Saltillo tile floors and handmade wooden furniture. Three bedrooms have individual garden patios, while a fourth looks out at the Sangre de Cristo Mountains. Two additional rooms are located in the cottage, which was built in 1910. Breakfast, delivered to the rooms, features the inn's award-winning baked goods.

Historic Interest: Santa Fe Plaza (4 1/2 blocks).

Innkeeper(s): Walt Wyss & Wayne Manus. $70-149. MC, VISA, DS. 6 rooms with PB. Breakfast and afternoon tea included in rates. Type of meal: Cont plus. Gourmet dinner available. Beds: KQT. Handicap access. Antiquing, fishing, live theater, downhill skiing and cross-country skiing nearby.

"We found the room to be quiet and comfortable and your hospitality to be very gracious. We also really enjoyed breakfast, especially the yogurt!"

The Galisteo Inn

9 La Vega, HC75 Box 4
Santa Fe, NM 87450
(505)466-4000 Fax:(505)466-4008

Circa 1740. In the historic Spanish village of Galisteo, this adobe hacienda is surrounded by giant cottonwoods. The inn features a comfortable Southwestern decor, a library and eight fireplaces. Located on eight acres, there is a duck pond and a creek (the Galisteo River) forms the boundary of the property.

Sophisticated cuisine includes dishes such as lobster ravioli with curry oil or chile-rubbed venison with roasted baby vegetables and chive corn cakes. Hazelnut chocolate mousse cake is one of the mouthwatering desserts.

Historic Interest: Santa Fe (23 miles), petroglyphs (8 miles).

Innkeeper(s): Joanna Kaufman & Wayne Aarniokoski. $115-190. MC, VISA, DS, PC, TC. TAC10. 12 rooms, 9 with PB, 5 with FP. Breakfast included in rates. Type of meal: Full bkfst. Gourmet dinner and picnic lunch available. Beds: KQDT. TV and ceiling fan in room. Fax, copier, spa, swimming, sauna, stables, bicycles and library on premises. Handicap access. Weddings, small meetings, family reunions and seminars hosted. Live theater, shopping, downhill skiing and cross-country skiing nearby.

Pets allowed: Horses only.

"Ahhh, what peace and perfection. Thank you so very much for this magic time in a magic space."

Grant Corner Inn

122 Grant Ave
Santa Fe, NM 87501-2031
(505)983-6678 (800)964-9003 Fax:(505)983-1526

Circa 1905. Judge Robinson and his family lived here for 30 years and many couples were married in the parlor. Still a romantic setting, the inn is secluded by a garden with willow trees, and there is a white picket fence. Rooms are appointed with antique furnishings and the personal art collections of the innkeeper.

Historic Interest: Bandelier and Pecos National Monuments, Indian Pueblos.

Innkeeper(s): Louise Stewart. $90-170. MC, VISA. 10 rooms with PB, 1 with FP. Breakfast included in rates. Type of meal: Full gourmet bkfst. Gourmet dinner, catering service and room service available. Beds: KQT. Copier on premises. Handicap access. Antiquing, fishing, live theater, downhill skiing and cross-country skiing nearby.

"The very best of everything — comfort, hospitality, food and T.L.C."

Inn on the Paseo

630 Paseo De Peralta
Santa Fe, NM 87501-1957
(505)984-8200 (800)457-9045 Fax:(505)989-3979
E-mail: erthsf@aol.com
Web: www.innonthepaseo.com

Circa 1992. Santa Fe is a city with many interesting lodging choices, and the Inn on the Paseo is an elegant example. It was created from two historic homes and the result is an exterior that appears as a New Mexican farmhouse with a pitched roof. Inside, sparkling guest rooms are decorated in contemporary, Southwest style. Beds are dressed with handmade quilts and down comforters. The suite, which boasts a fireplace and four-poster bed, is ideal for honeymooners. Fresh fruits, still-warm-from-the-oven muffins, coffeecake and other treats fill the daily continental breakfast buffet. The inn is located just three blocks from historic Santa Fe Plaza.

Innkeeper(s): John & Lissa Hastings. $65-155. MC, VISA, AX, DC, PC, TC. TAC10. 18 rooms with PB, 1 with FP and 1 suite. Breakfast and afternoon tea included in rates. Types of meals: Cont plus and early coffee/tea. Beds: KQT. Cable TV, phone and ceiling fan in room. Air conditioning. Fax and library on premises. Handicap access. Spanish and French spoken. Antiquing, fishing, opera, chamber music, Indian pueblos, parks, shopping, downhill skiing and cross-country skiing nearby.

The Madeleine
(formerly The Preston House)

106 Faithway St
Santa Fe, NM 87501
(505)982-3465 (888)877-7622 Fax:(505)982-8572
E-mail: alexandinn@aol.com
Web: www.madeleineinn.com

Circa 1886. This gracious 19th-century home is the only authentic example of Queen Anne architecture in Santa Fe. This home displays a wonderful Victorian atmosphere with period furnishings, quaint wallpapers and beds covered with down quilts. Afternoon tea is a must, as Carolyn serves up a mouth-watering array of cakes, pies, cookies and tarts. The Madeleine, which is located in downtown Santa Fe, is within walking distance of the Plaza.

Innkeeper(s): Cindy Carano. $80-165. MC, VISA, DS, PC, TC. 8 rooms, 6 with PB, 4 with FP, 2 cottages and 1 conference room. Breakfast and afternoon tea included in rates. Types of meals: Full bkfst and early coffee/tea. Beds: KQDT. Cable TV, phone and ceiling fan in room. Fax and copier on premises. Weddings, small meetings, family reunions and seminars hosted. Spanish spoken. Antiquing, fishing, live theater, parks, shopping, downhill skiing and cross-country skiing nearby.

Pets Allowed.

"We were extremely pleased — glad we found you. We shall return."

Inn of The Turquoise Bear B&B

342 E Buena Vista St
Santa Fe, NM 87501-4423
(505)983-0798 (800)396-4104 Fax:(505)988-4225
E-mail: bluebear@roadrunner.com
Web: www.turquoisebear.com

Circa 1880. Tall ponderosa pines shade this rambling Spanish Pueblo Revival adobe, giving it the feeling of being in a mountain setting, although it's only blocks from the plaza. In the National Register, it was the home of poet and essayist Witter Bynner, when it hosted a myriad of celebrities including Edna St. Vincent Millay, Robert Frost, Ansel Adams, Rita Hayworth, Errol Flynn and Georgia O'Keeffe. The walled acre of grounds includes flagstone paths, wild roses, lilacs, rock terraces and stone benches and fountains. In a Southwest decor, there are kiva fireplaces and romantic courtyards. The Shaman room has a king bed, viga beams and a picture window with garden views. Guests are invited to enjoy wine and cheese in the afternoon. Museums, galleries, restaurants and shops are within walking distance. Among its accolades, the inn was the recipient of the City of Santa Fe's 1999 Heritage Preservation Award.

Historic Interest: Plaza of Santa Fe (6 blocks), Bandelier National Monument (40 miles).

Innkeeper(s): Robert Frost & Ralph Bolton. $95-195. MC, VISA, AX, DS, PC, TC. TAC10. 11 rooms, 7 with PB, 10 with FP, 1 suite and 1 conference room. Breakfast and snacks/refreshments included in rates. Type of meal: Cont plus. Beds: KQ. Cable TV, phone and VCR in room. Fax, library and child care on premises. Weddings, small meetings, family reunions and seminars hosted. Spanish, French, German and Norwegian spoken. Antiquing, art galleries, bicycling, canoeing/kayaking, fishing, golf, hiking, horseback riding, opera, live theater, museums, parks, shopping, downhill skiing, cross-country skiing, tennis and wineries nearby.

Pets allowed: small, well-behaved.

"Staying at your inn was a vacation and history lesson we will always remember!"

Santa Fe (Algodones)　　　D5

Hacienda Vargas

PO Box 307
Santa Fe (Algodones), NM 87001-0307
(505)867-9115 (800)261-0006 Fax:(505)867-1902

Circa 1840. Nestled among the cottonwoods and mesas of the middle Rio Grande Valley, Hacienda Vargas has seen two centuries of Old West history. It once served as a trading post for Native Americans as well as a 19th-century stagecoach stop between Santa Fe and Mesilla. The grounds contain an adobe chapel, courtyard and gardens. The main house features five kiva fireplaces, Southwest antiques, Spanish tile, a library, art gallery and suites with private Jacuzzis.

Historic Interest: Gronado Monument, Indian Ruins (5 miles), Bandelier National Park (40 miles).

Innkeeper(s): Paul & Jule De Vargas. $79-149. MC, VISA, PC, TC. TAC10. 7 rooms with PB, 7 with FP and 4 suites. Breakfast included in rates. Type of meal: Full bkfst. Beds: QT. Ceiling fan and spa in suites in room. Air conditioning. Weddings and family reunions hosted. Spanish and German spoken. Antiquing, fishing, live theater, shopping, downhill skiing, sporting events and water sports nearby.

Publicity: *Vogue, San Francisco Chronicle, Albuquerque Journal.*

"This is the best! Breakfast was the best we've ever had!"

Taos　　　B6

Casa Europa Inn & Gallery

HC 68, Box 3 F, 840 Upper Ranchito
Taos, NM 87571-9408
(505)758-9798 (888)758-9798
E-mail: casa-europa@travelbase.com
Web: www.travelbase.com/destinations/taos/casa-europa/

Circa 1700. Guests will appreciate both the elegance and history at Casa Europa. The home is a 17th-century pueblo-adobe creation with heavy beams, walls three-feet thick and a dining room with a massive kiva fireplace. Freshly baked pastries are served in the afternoons, and during ski season, hors d'oeuvres are provided in the early evening. European antiques fill the rooms, which are decorated in an elegant, Southwestern style. The French Room offers an 1860 bed, kiva fireplace and French doors opening onto the courtyard. Other rooms offer a fireplace, whirlpool tub or private hot tub. The five-room Apartment Suite includes a kitchen-dining room, sitting room with a kiva fireplace, bedroom and a private hot tub. The inn is 1.6 miles from Taos Plaza.

Innkeeper(s): Rudi & Marcia Zwicker. $75-135. MC, VISA, PC, TC. TAC10. 7 rooms with PB, 6 with FP, 2 suites and 2 conference rooms. Breakfast included in rates. Types of meals: Full gourmet bkfst and early coffee/tea. Afternoon tea and snacks/refreshments available. Beds: KQT. Cable TV, phone, turndown service and ceiling fan in room. Spa and sauna on premises. Small meetings and family reunions hosted. German and Spanish spoken. Antiquing, fishing, live theater, parks, shopping, downhill skiing, cross-country skiing and water sports nearby.

Pets allowed: Outside only.

Hacienda Del Sol

PO Box 177
Taos, NM 87571-0177
(505)758-0287 Fax:(505)758-5895
E-mail: sunhouse@newmex.com
Web: www.taoshaciendadelsol.com

Circa 1810. Mabel Dodge, patron of the arts, purchased this old hacienda as a hideaway for her Native American husband, Tony Luhan. The spacious adobe sits among huge cottonwoods, blue spruce, and ponderosa pines, with an uninterrupted view of the mountains across 95,000 acres of Native American Indian lands. Among Dodge's famous guests were Georgia O'Keefe, who painted here, and D. H. Lawrence. The mood is tranquil and on moonlit nights guests can hear Indian drums and the howl of coyotes.

Historic Interest: Taos Pueblo (2 miles), Bandelier National Monument (60 miles), Puye Cliffs (53 miles).

Innkeeper(s): Dennis Sheehan. $85-190. MC, VISA, PC, TC. TAC10. 11 rooms, 10 with PB, 10 with FP and 4 suites. Breakfast and snacks/refreshments included in rates. Types of meals: Full bkfst and early coffee/tea. Beds: KQT. Cassette player in room. Fax, spa and library on premises. Handicap access. Weddings, small meetings, family reunions and seminars hosted. Antiquing, fishing, museums, art galleries, 1000-year-old pueblo, art festivals, cultural programs, Indian ruins, live theater, parks, shopping, downhill skiing, cross-country skiing and water sports nearby.

Publicity: *Chicago Tribune, Los Angeles Daily News, Denver Post, Globe & Mail.*

"Your warm friendliness and gracious hospitality have made this week an experience we will never forget!"

La Posada De Taos

PO Box 1118
Taos, NM 87571-1118
(505)758-8164 (800)645-4803 Fax:(505)751-3294
E-mail: laposada@newmex.com
Web: newmex.com/laposada

Circa 1907. This secluded adobe is located just a few blocks from the plaza in the Taos historic district. Rooms are decorated in a romantic Southwestern style with country pine antiques, quilts and polished wood or tile floors. All but one of the guest rooms include a kiva fireplace, and some offer private patios. For those in search of solitude, ask about the innkeeper's separate honeymoon house. Guests can walk to galleries, museums, shops and restaurants.

Innkeeper(s): Bill & Nancy Swan. $80-135. MC, VISA, AX, DC, PC, TC. 6 rooms with PB, 5 with FP and 1 conference room. Breakfast included in rates. Type of meal: Full bkfst. Beds: KQ. TV and ceiling fan in room. VCR, fax, copier and library on premises. Handicap access. Weddings, small meetings and family reunions hosted. Antiquing, fishing, art galleries, live theater, parks, shopping, downhill skiing, cross-country skiing and water sports nearby.

Publicity: *New York Times, Bon Appetit, Country Inns, Glamour, Los Angeles Times.*

"I want to tell you how much we enjoyed our visit with you at La Posada De Taos in September. It was definitely the highlight of our trip."

Old Taos Guesthouse B&B

1028 Witt Rd, 6552 NDCBU
Taos, NM 87571
(505)758-5448 (800)758-5448
E-mail: oldtaos@newmex.com
Web: taoswebb.com/hotel/oldtaoshouse/

Circa 1850. This adobe hacienda sits on a rise overlooking Taos and is surrounded by large cottonwood, blue spruce, apple, apricot and pinon trees. This estate, which offers panoramic views, originally served as a farmer's home, but later was home to an artist. As the years went by, rooms were added.

Most rooms include special items such as kiva fireplaces, handwoven wall hangings, dried flowers, log four-poster beds and hand-painted vanities. The Southwestern-style rooms all have private entrances. The outdoor hot tub boasts a wonderful view. Healthy, homemade breakfasts are served in a room filled with antiques. The home is set on more than seven acres, located less than two miles from the Plaza.

Historic Interest: There is a historic acequia irrigation ditch that runs through the grounds. Nearby attractions include a 1,000-year-old Taos Pueblo, Martinez Hacienda, the Kit Carson House and St. Francis de Assisi church. The Bandelier National Monument Cliff Dwellings are about an hour from Taos.

Innkeeper(s): Tim & Leslie Reeves. $70-125. MC, VISA, PC, TC. 9 rooms with PB, 5 with FP and 2 suites. Breakfast included in rates. Types of meals: Cont plus and early coffee/tea. Beds: KQT. Spa, stables and library on premises. Spanish and German spoken. Antiquing, fishing, live theater, parks, shopping, downhill skiing and cross-country skiing nearby.

Publicity: *Denver Post Travel, Inn for the Night, Dallas Morning News, West, Country, Houston Chronicle.*

"We really enjoyed the authenticity of your guesthouse."

Inn on La Loma Plaza

PO Box 4159, 315 Ranchitos Rd
Taos, NM 87571
(505)758-1717 (800)530-3040 Fax:(505)751-0155
E-mail: laloma@taoswebb.com
Web: www.taos-nm.net

Circa 1800. Some of the walls of this hacienda were built originally as protection against Comanche, Apache and Ute Native American tribes. Located in the La Loma Plaza Historic District, the Pueblo Revival-style inn is in the National Register. Gardens, cottonwood trees and a spacious green lawn invite guests to enter. The inn's sunroom affords views of the mountains, and it is furnished with a kiva fireplace, benches and a fountain. This is where breakfast and refreshments are served. Southwestern fabrics, woven rugs, local art and hand-crafted furniture fill the rooms. Some accommodations offer private patios, and all have fireplaces. There are seven breakfast menus — one for each day of the week. For instance, if it's Tuesday, it must be Green Chile Strata. Sundays bring forth Breakfast Burritos with Jerry's green sauce and jack and cheddar cheeses. Visit some of the town's 80 art galleries, seven museums or nearby Taos Pueblo (resided in for more than 800 years). Other attractions include the Kit Carson House, the famous Saint Francis de Assisi Church and Taos Plaza and Historic District, two-and-one-half blocks away.

Innkeeper(s): Jerry & Peggy Davis. $75-195. MC, VISA, AX, DS, PC, TC. TAC10. 7 rooms with PB, 7 with FP, 2 suites and 1 conference room. Breakfast and snacks/refreshments included in rates. Types of meals: Full gourmet bkfst and early coffee/tea. Beds: KQ. Cable TV and phone in room. Air conditioning. VCR, fax, library and 6 person poured concrete hot tub on premises. Weddings, small meetings, family reunions and seminars hosted. Antiquing, fishing, golf, parks, shopping, downhill skiing, cross-country skiing, tennis and water sports nearby.

Publicity: *Outside, Chicago Tribune, Denver Post, Romantic Getaways, Sunset.*

"Your hospitality while we were there exceeded what we've ever experienced at a B&B."

Orinda B&B

461 Valverde
Taos, NM 87571
(505)758-8581 (800)847-1837

Circa 1935. Current innkeepers Adrian and Sheila Percival are only the fifth owners of this property, which was deeded to its original owners by Abraham Lincoln. The house itself, a traditional adobe with an outstanding view of Taos Mountain, was built years later, and features Southwestern touches such as kiva fireplaces, original art and turn-of-the century antiques. Sheila serves up a full breakfast such as green chile souffle (a John Wayne favorite), pecan French toast and bottomless cups of the inn's special coffee blend.

Historic Interest: The Kit Carson Home is a 15-minute walk from the bed & breakfast. Taos Pueblo and Martinez Hacienda are within easy driving distance, and the village of Taos offers many historic sites. Art galleries, museums, skiing, hiking, biking, riding, golf and fishing are all located nearby.

Innkeeper(s): Adrian & Sheila Percival. $80-145. MC, VISA, AX, DS, PC, TC. TAC10. 5 rooms with PB, 2 with FP and 1 suite. Breakfast included in rates. Type of meal: Full bkfst. Beds: KQD. One room has two person whirlpool in room. VCR on premises. Weddings and family reunions hosted. Antiquing, fishing, golf, hiking, museums, biking, shopping, downhill skiing and cross-country skiing nearby.

"It really is 'a B&B paradise' with your beautiful surroundings."

The Willows Inn

Box 6560 Ndcbu, 412 Kit Carson Rd
Taos, NM 87571
(505)758-2558 (800)525-8267 Fax:(505)758-5445
E-mail: willows@newmex.com
Web: www.willows-taos.com

Circa 1926. This authentic, Southwestern-style adobe was once home to artist E. Martin Hennings, a member of the Taos Society of Artists. Each of the rooms features a unique theme, including Hennings' Studio, which was the artist's workplace. The studio boasts a bed with a seven-foot headboard, high ceilings, a whirlpool tub and private patio. The Santa Fe Room is decked in contemporary, Southwestern style and has a sitting area. Each of the rooms includes a kiva fireplace. The Conquistador Room reflects old Spanish decor with an antique chest, equipale couch and ropero. The Cowboy and Anasazi rooms include artifacts such as a cowhide rug, handmade quilts, Zuni kachinas and hand-crafted pottery. Breakfasts are highlighted by fresh items right out of the inn's herb and vegetable gardens. Afternoon refreshments are served with lively conversation as guests browse through menus from various Taos eateries.

Historic Interest: The main house, studio and lap pool are listed in the National Registry of Historic Places. Taos Pueblo is less than two miles from the inn, and closer attractions include the Kit Carson Home & Museum, Mabel Dodge Luhan House, and the historic homes of several local artists.

Innkeeper(s): Janet & Doug Camp. $100-145. MC, VISA, AX, DS, PC, TC. TAC10. 5 rooms with PB, 5 with FP and 1 suite. Breakfast and snacks/refreshments included in rates. Types of meals: Full gourmet bkfst and early coffee/tea. Afternoon tea available. Beds: QT. Some desks, ceiling fans and Jacuzzi (in suite) in room. VCR, fax, copier and library on premises. Weddings, small meetings, family reunions and seminars hosted. Spanish spoken. Antiquing, fishing, golf, hiking, archeology studies, live theater, parks, shopping, downhill skiing, cross-country skiing and water sports nearby.

New York

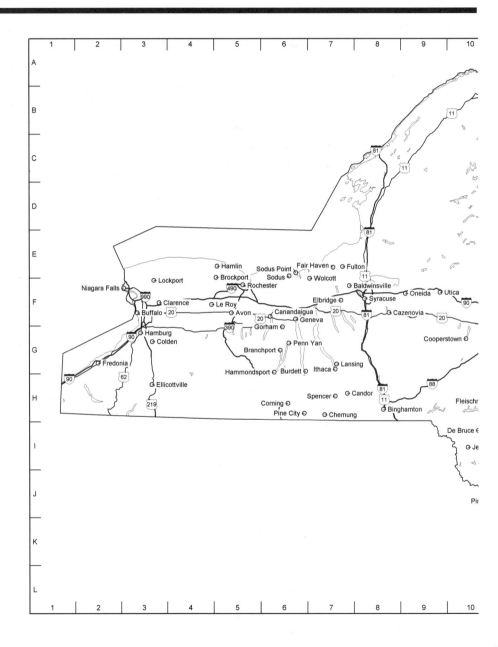

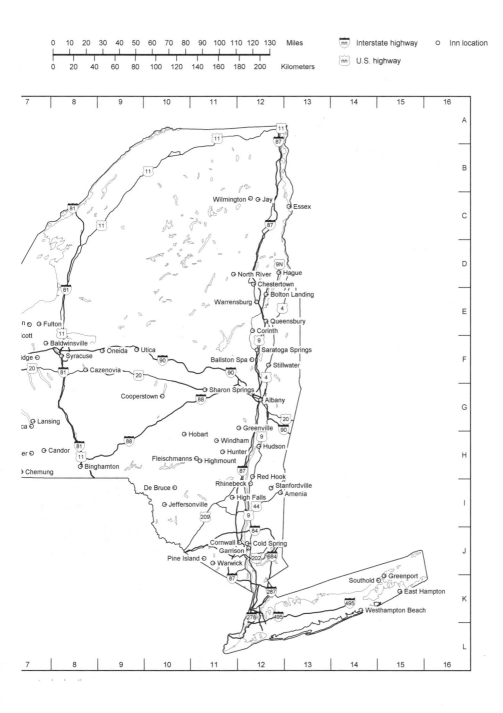

0 10 20 30 40 50 60 70 80 90 100 110 120 130 Miles

0 20 40 60 80 100 120 140 160 180 200 Kilometers

🛡 nn Interstate highway   ○ Inn location

⬡ nn U.S. highway

Albany
G12

Pine Haven B&B

531 Western Ave
Albany, NY 12203-1721
(518)482-1574

Circa 1896. This turn-of-the-century Victorian is located in Pine Hills, an Albany historic district. In keeping with this history, the innkeepers have tried to preserve the home's 19th-century charm. The rooms offer  old-fashioned comfort with Victorian influences. The Capitol Building and other historic sites are nearby.

Innkeeper(s): Janice Tricarico.
$64-79. MC, VISA, AX, PC, TC.
5 rooms, 2 with PB. Breakfast
included in rates. Types of meals:
Cont plus and early coffee/tea.
Beds: DT. Phone in room. Air conditioning. Weddings, small meetings, family reunions and seminars hosted. Antiquing, live theater, parks, shopping, cross-country skiing and sporting events nearby.

Amenia
I12

Troutbeck

Leedsville Rd
Amenia, NY 12501
(914)373-9681 Fax:(914)373-7080
E-mail: innkeeper@troutbeck.com
Web: www.troutbeck.com

Circa 1918. This English country estate on 442 wooded acres enjoyed its heyday in the '20s. The NAACP was conceived here and the literati and liberals of the period, including Teddy Roosevelt, were overnight guests. Weekend room rates, $650 to $1050, include six meals and an open bar as well as luxurious accommodations for two. On Sundays, brunch is served. The inn has a fitness center, billiard table, outdoor and indoor pools and tennis courts. During the week the inn is a corporate retreat and has been awarded Executive Retreat of the Year. In July, 1997, Troutbeck was the site of a United Nations Summit meeting. Many weddings are held here each year and a new Great Room/ballroom has been added, which accommodates weddings with up to 250 guests and corporate gatherings for about 70 people.

Innkeeper(s): Jim Flaherty & Garret Corcoran. $650-1050. MC, VISA, AX, PC, TC. TAC5. 42 rooms, 37 with PB, 9 with FP, 8 suites and 3 conference rooms. Breakfast and dinner included in rates. MAP. Types of meals: Full bkfst, cont and early coffee/tea. Picnic lunch, lunch, banquet service, catering service and room service available. Restaurant on premises. Beds: KQDT. Phone, turndown service and some ceiling fans in room. Air conditioning. VCR, fax, copier, spa, swimming, sauna, tennis and library on premises. Weddings, family reunions and seminars hosted. Spanish, Portuguese and Italian spoken. Antiquing, fishing, live theater, parks, shopping, downhill skiing, cross-country skiing and sporting events nearby.

"This 1920s-style estate makes you wish all life could be this way."

Avon
F5

Avon Inn

55 E Main St
Avon, NY 14414-1438
(716)226-8181 Fax:(716)226-8185

Circa 1820. This Greek Revival mansion, in both the state and national historic registers, has been providing lodging for more than a century. After 1866, the residence was turned into a health center that provided water cures from the local sulphur springs. The guest registry included the likes of Henry Ford, Thomas Edison and Eleanor Roosevelt. Though the inn is no longer a health spa, guests can still relax in the garden with its gazebo and fountain or on the Grecian-pillared front porch. A full-service restaurant and conference facilities are on the premises.

Historic Interest: 1820 Greek Revival initially the residence of Jonathan H. Gerry, a successful broom corn grower.

Innkeeper(s): Linda Reusch. $50-85. MC, VISA, AX, DC, CB, DS, TC. TAC10. 15 rooms with PB. Breakfast included in rates. Types of meals: Cont and early coffee/tea. Picnic lunch available. Restaurant on premises. Beds: KQD. Phone in room. Air conditioning. Fax and copier on premises. Weddings, small meetings, family reunions and seminars hosted. Amusement parks, antiquing, fishing, parks, shopping, downhill skiing and cross-country skiing nearby.

Baldwinsville
F7

Pandora's Getaway

83 Oswego St
Baldwinsville, NY 13027-1130
(315)635-9571 (888)638-8668

Circa 1845. Nestled amid large trees on a hill in a tranquil village setting, this Greek Revival inn is listed in the National Register of Historic Places. Homemade crafts are mingled with antiques and collectibles to decorate the inn. Families with children are welcomed with a variety of games and toys. Guests enjoy breakfasts of fresh fruit, homemade breads and quiche or a favorite family recipe in the formal dining room. The innkeeper collects  depression glassware and uses it in her special table settings. Rockers on the porch afford quiet reading and visiting while listening to the breeze rustle the trees. Located a block from the center of town, the inn provides easy access to all the village offerings, including restaurants, shops, a working river lock of the Barge Canal System and a bakery.

Historic Interest: St. Marie among the Indians (3 miles).

Innkeeper(s): Sandra Wheeler. $60-80. MC, VISA, DC, DS, PC, TC. TAC10. 4 rooms. Breakfast included in rates. Types of meals: Full gourmet bkfst and early coffee/tea. Beds: KQD. TV, phone and ceiling fan in room. VCR on premises. Family reunions and seminars hosted. Antiquing, bicycling, fishing, golf, hiking, horseback riding, museums, parks, shopping, cross-country skiing, sporting events, tennis and wineries nearby.

Binghamton H8

Pickle Hill B&B

795 Chenango St
Binghamton, NY 13901-1844
(607)723-0259

Circa 1890. This folksy B&B is a haven for those tired of endless motel nights. Guests feel as if they've stepped into the home of a good friend, and innkeepers Tom Rossi and Leslie Kiersted have made many friends over the last few years. The environment is comfortable country, highlighted by stained-glass windows and rich woodwork. The grounds are equipped for a game of basketball or badminton, and guests are often found gathered around the piano singing old songs.

Innkeeper(s): Tom Rossi & Leslie Kiersted Rossi. $45-50. PC, TC. 3 rooms. Breakfast and snacks/refreshments included in rates. Types of meals: Full bkfst and early coffee/tea. Room service available. Beds: DT. Radio and tapes in room. VCR, bicycles and piano on premises. Antiquing, fishing, live theater, parks, shopping, downhill skiing, cross-country skiing, sporting events and water sports nearby.

Bolton Landing E12

Hilltop Cottage B&B

4825 Lakeshore Dr
Bolton Landing, NY 12814
(518)644-2492

Circa 1924. Located on two acres, this country farmhouse was once a summer residence for music students at Marcella Sembrich Teaching Studio. It is located on the eight-mile stretch of what once was called "Millionaire's Row," on Lake George. There is a barn, greenhouse and ice house. Rooms are simply furnished in a homey, country style. The hosts speak German and enjoy offering German apple pancakes and a variety of other delicious breakfast selections. Breakfast is often served on the porch, which in summer is shaded by lavish vines.

Innkeeper(s): Anita & Charlie Richards. $65-85. MC, VISA, PC, TC. TAC10. 2 rooms with PB and 1 cottage. Breakfast included in rates. Type of meal: Full bkfst. Beds: QT. Ceiling fan in room. VCR on premises. German spoken. Amusement parks, antiquing, fishing, golf, hiking, parks, shopping, tennis and water sports nearby.

Branchport G6

Gone With The Wind on Keuka Lake

453 W Lake Rd, Rt 54 A
Branchport, NY 14418
(607)868-4603

Circa 1887. Breezes from Keuka Lake waft up to the front porch where guests often sit with a cup of coffee. The lakeside home, a Victorian, is decorated with an eclectic, uncluttered assortment of reproductions. Each of the bathrooms features unique decor, such as oak, brass or marble. One room includes

a fireplace. There's a hot tub in the solarium, and the grounds offer a gazebo by the inn's private beach cove.

Innkeeper(s): Linda & Robert Lewis. $70-125. PC, TC. 11 rooms, 3 with PB, 1 with FP. Breakfast included in rates. Type of meal: Full bkfst. Beds: KQ. Jacuzzi in room. Air conditioning. Fax, spa, swimming and tennis on premises. Weddings, small meetings, family reunions and seminars hosted. Antiquing, fishing, Curtis Museum, nine wineries, parks, shopping, cross-country skiing and water sports nearby.

"Thanks once again for a delightful stay. You have a little bit of heaven here."

Brockport E5

The Portico B&B

3741 Lake Rd N
Brockport, NY 14420-1415
(716)637-0220

Circa 1850. Named for its three porches, called porticos, this Greek Revival inn is situated amid blue spruce, maple and sycamore trees in a historic district. Tall columns and a cupola add to its charm. The interior features three fireplaces. Three antique-filled guest rooms are available to visitors, who enjoy a full Victorian breakfast and kettledrum, also known as afternoon tea. The inn is listed in

the National Register, as are several other structures in town. The surrounding area offers many attractions, including the Cobblestone Museum, Darien Lake Amusement Park, George Eastman House and Strasenburgh Planetarium. Several colleges, golf courses and parks are nearby. In winter, sleigh rides also are available nearby.

Innkeeper(s): Anne Klein. $60-70. PC, TC. 3 rooms with PB, 3 with FP. Breakfast included in rates. Types of meals: Full bkfst and early coffee/tea. Turndown service in room. VCR on premises. Amusement parks, antiquing, sleigh rides, live theater, shopping, downhill skiing, cross-country skiing and sporting events nearby.

The Victorian B&B

320 S Main St
Brockport, NY 14420-2253
(716)637-7519 Fax:(716)637-7519
E-mail: skehoe@po.brockport.edu
Web: www.victorianbandb.com

Circa 1890. Within walking distance of the historic Erie Canal, this Queen Anne Victorian inn and its sister house are located on Brockport's Main Street. Visitors select from eight second-floor guest rooms, all with phones, private baths and TVs. Victorian furnishings are found throughout the inn. A favorite spot is the solarium, with its three walls of windows and fireplace, perfect for curling up with a book or magazine. Two first-floor sitting areas with fireplaces also provide relaxing havens for guests. Lake Ontario is just 10 miles away, and visitors will find much to explore in Brockport and Rochester. Brockport is home to the State University of New York.

Innkeeper(s): Sharon Kehoe. $59-98. PC, TC. 8 rooms with PB. Breakfast and afternoon tea included in rates. Type of meal: Full bkfst. Beds: KQDT. Cable TV, phone and jacuzzi tub in room. Air conditioning. VCR, fax and e-mail access on premises. Small meetings, family reunions and seminars hosted. Antiquing, live theater, shopping, cross-country skiing and sporting events nearby.

"Memories of another time; hospitality of another era."

Buffalo   F3

Beau Fleuve B&B Inn

242 Linwood Ave
Buffalo, NY 14209-1802
(716)882-6116 (800)278-0245
E-mail: beaufleuve@buffnet.net
Web: www.beaufleuve.com

Circa 1881. Each of the five rooms in this Victorian setting celebrates ethnic groups that settled in the Buffalo area. In the French room, absolute comfort is complete with every touch,  from the feather bed that rests atop the Neoclassical king-size bed to Louis XV chairs that are covered with champagne damask with French blue highlights. The Irish room features an antique brass bed, Victorian seating and William Morris chrysanthemum wallcoverings in shades of sage and celery. Other elegant rooms mark the contributions of the German, Italian and Polish immigrants. Artifacts accented by stunning stained-glass windows render homage to the Western New York Native American tribes in the Native American common area. Set in the Linwood Preservation District, this inn is in the middle of everything. Millionaires' Row is only one block from the inn, and museums, art galleries, antique shops and a variety of restaurants are just steps away. A friendly ambiance will remind guests why Buffalo is known as the "City of Good Neighbors." Niagara Falls is a 25-minute drive.

Historic Interest: Buffalo's Allentown Historic District is less than one mile away and the magnificent Niagara Falls is 18 miles from the Beau Fleuve.

Innkeeper(s): Ramona Pando Whitaker & Rik Whitaker. $75-95. MC, VISA, AX, DS, TC. TAC10. 3 rooms with PB. Breakfast included in rates. Type of meal: Full bkfst. Gourmet dinner available. Beds: KQDT. Antiquing, fishing, concerts/music, live theater, downhill skiing, cross-country skiing, sporting events and water sports nearby.

"Relaxing, comfortable hospitality in beautiful surroundings."

Burdett   G6

The Red House Country Inn

4586 Picnic Area Rd
Burdett, NY 14818-9716
(607)546-8566

Circa 1844. Nestled within the 16,000-acre Finger Lakes National Forest, this old farmstead has an in-ground swimming pool, large veranda overlooking groomed lawns, flower gardens and picnic areas. Pet Samoyeds and goats share the seven acres. Next to the property are acres of wild blueberry patches and stocked fishing ponds. The Red House is near Seneca Lake, world-famous Glen Gorge, and Cornell University.

Historic Interest: Corning Glass Museum, Cornell University, Watkins Glen Gorge.

Innkeeper(s): Sandy Schmanke & Joan Martin. $59-89. MC, VISA, AX, DS. 5 rooms, 1 with FP. Breakfast and afternoon tea included in rates. Types of meals: Full bkfst and early coffee/tea. Beds: QDT. TV and phone in room. Small meetings, family reunions and seminars hosted. Antiquing, fishing, wineries, live theater, parks, shopping, cross-country skiing, sporting events and water sports nearby.

"An Inn-credible delight. What a wonderful place to stay and a difficult place to leave. It doesn't get any better than this."

Canandaigua   F6

The Sutherland House B&B Inn

3179 State Route 21 South
Canandaigua, NY 14424-8341
(716)396-0375 (800)396-0375 Fax:(716)396-9281
E-mail: goodnite@frontiernet.net
Web: www.sutherlandhouse.com

Circa 1885. Innkeepers Cor and Diane Van Der Woude refurbished this gracious home, adding more than 40 new windows, but leaving original elements such as a winding cherry staircase and marble  fireplaces. Their restoration effort has created a charming 19th-century atmosphere. Rooms feature elegant, Victorian decor, and some boast two-person whirlpool tubs. Diane serves up a bountiful breakfast each morning. The home is just a mile and a half from Main Street Canandaigua, and wineries, antique shopping and outdoor activities are nearby.

Innkeeper(s): Cor & Diane Van Der Woude. $95-175. MC, VISA, AX, PC. TAC10. 5 rooms with PB, 3 with FP, 1 suite and 1 conference room. Breakfast, afternoon tea and snacks/refreshments included in rates. Types of meals: Full gourmet bkfst, cont plus, cont and early coffee/tea. Gourmet dinner, lunch, banquet service, catered breakfast and room service available. Beds: KQ. Phone, ceiling fan and VCR in room. Air conditioning. Fax, copier and spa on premises. Weddings, small meetings, family reunions and seminars hosted. Dutch spoken. Antiquing, fishing, festivals, wine tours, live theater, parks, shopping, downhill skiing, cross-country skiing, sporting events and water sports nearby.

Candor   H7

The Edge of Thyme, A B&B Inn

6 Main St
Candor, NY 13743-1615
(607)659-5155 (800)722-7365 Fax:(607)659-5155

Circa 1840. Originally the summer home of John D. Rockefeller's secretary, this two-story Georgian-style inn offers gracious accommodations a short drive from Ithaca. The inn sports many interesting features, including an impressive stairway, marble fireplaces, parquet floors, pergola (arbor) and windowed porch with leaded glass. Guests may relax in front of the inn's fireplace, catch up with reading in  its library or watch television in the sitting room. An authentic turn-of-the-century full breakfast is served, and guests also may arrange for special high teas.

Innkeeper(s): Prof. Frank & Eva Mae Musgrave. $70-135. MC, VISA, AX, TC. 5 rooms, 2 with PB and 2 suites. Breakfast included in rates. Types of meals: Full gourmet bkfst and early coffee/tea. Afternoon tea available. Beds: KQDT. VCR on premises. Weddings, small meetings, family reunions and seminars hosted. Antiquing, fishing, live theater, parks, shopping, downhill skiing, cross-country skiing and sporting events nearby.

Cazenovia   F8

The Brewster Inn
PO Box 507, 6 Ledyard Ave
Cazenovia, NY 13035-0507
(315)655-9232 Fax:(315)655-2130
Web: www.cazenovia.com/brewster

Circa 1890. This large Victorian mansion is located on three acres and offers a terrace and two dining rooms with views of Cazenovia Lake. Originally, the home was constructed by Benjamin Brewster, a partner of John Rockefeller in Standard Oil. Some guest rooms offer fireplaces and Jacuzzi tubs. The inn's renown restaurant staffs seven chefs preparing gourmet meals with only the freshest ingredients. Dessert souffles are a specialty.
Innkeeper(s): Richard A. Hubbard. $60-225. MC, VISA, DC, CB, DS, PC, TC. 17 rooms with PB, 4 with FP and 1 suite. Breakfast included in rates. Types of meals: Cont plus and early coffee/tea. Gourmet dinner available. Restaurant on premises. Beds: KQD. Cable TV, phone and ceiling fan in room. Air conditioning. Fax, copier, swimming, library and child care on premises. Handicap access. Weddings, small meetings, family reunions and seminars hosted. Antiquing, fishing, golf, parks, shopping, downhill skiing, cross-country skiing, sporting events, tennis and water sports nearby.
Publicity: *New York Times, Conde Nast.*

Chemung   H7

Halcyon Place B&B
197 Washington St, PO Box 244
Chemung, NY 14825-0244
(607)529-3544

Circa 1820. The innkeepers chose the name "halcyon" because it signifies tranquility and a healing richness. The historic Greek Revival inn and its grounds offer just that to guests, who will appreciate the fine period antiques, paneled doors, six-over-six windows of hand-blown glass and wide plank floors. Two herb garden and screen porch also beckon visitors. Full breakfasts may include omelets with garden ingredients, raspberry muffins, rum

sticky buns or waffles. The inn's three guest rooms feature double beds, and one boasts a romantic fireplace. Fine antiquing and golfing are found nearby. During the summer months, the innkeepers host a Wednesday afternoon herb series and afternoon tea. Also ask about other special packages. The innkeepers opened an herb and antique shop in their restored barn.
Historic Interest: Sullivan's Monument (6 miles), Mark Twain's study and grave site (12 miles).
Innkeeper(s): Douglas & Yvonne Sloan. $55-75. MC, VISA, PC, TC. 3 rooms, 1 with PB, 1 with FP. Breakfast included in rates. Type of meal: Full gourmet bkfst. Afternoon tea available. Beds: D. Turndown service in room. Weddings hosted. German spoken. Antiquing, live theater, parks, shopping, cross-country skiing, sporting events and water sports nearby.

Chestertown   D12

Landon Hill B&B
10 Landon Hill Rd
Chestertown, NY 12817
(518)494-2599 (888)244-2599 Fax:(518)494-2599

Circa 1860. Built during Civil War times, this historic Victorian was once known as Sunset Camp. The home includes five guest rooms. Adirondack-style furnishings and wicker pieces

decorate the rooms. Beds are topped with quilts. Pedestal sinks in the bathrooms add to the historic flavor. Several rooms offer a view of the surrounding scenery. Guests can relax on the screened-in front porch, nap in the hammock or curl up in front of the fireplace in the living room. The acre-and-a-half of grounds includes a perennial rock garden and century-old maple trees. Adirondack quiche, eggs Benedict and blueberry pancakes are among the homemade entrees guests might enjoy during the morning breakfast service. Whatever the menu, the meal fortifies guests for a busy day in the Adirondacks. The innkeepers provide maps of the area, will make restaurant recommendations and offer several ski packages for nearby Gore and Whiteface ski areas.
Historic Interest: Fort William Henry,-15 miles, Fort Ticonderoga-35 miles.
Innkeeper(s): Judy & Carl Johnson. $70-120. MC, VISA, PC. TAC7. 5 rooms, 4 with PB. Breakfast included in rates. Types of meals: Full gourmet bkfst, cont, country bkfst, veg bkfst and early coffee/tea. Beds: KQ. Cable TV and ceiling fan in room. Air conditioning. Bicycles, library and refrigerator in common area on premises. Handicap access. Weddings, small meetings and family reunions hosted. Amusement parks, antiquing, art galleries, beaches, bicycling, canoeing/kayaking, fishing, golf, hiking, horseback riding, live theater, museums, parks, shopping, downhill skiing, cross-country skiing, tennis and water sports nearby.
Pets allowed: Must call first.

Clarence   F3

Asa Ransom House
10529 Main St
Clarence, NY 14031-1684
(716)759-2315 Fax:(716)759-2791
E-mail: info@asaransom.com
Web: www.asaransom.com

Circa 1853. Set on spacious lawns, behind a white picket fence, the Asa Ransom House rests on the site of the first grist mill built in Erie County. Silversmith Asa Ransom constructed an inn and grist mill here in response to the Holland Land Company's offering of free land to anyone who would start and

operate a tavern. A specialty of the dining room is "Veal Perrott" and "Pistachio Banana Muffins."

Historic Interest: Clarence Center Emporium (5 miles), Amherst Museum, Colony (8 miles), Theodore Roosevelt Inaugural National Historic Site (Wilcox Mansion) (16 miles).

Innkeeper(s): Robert & Judy Lenz. $95-155. MC, VISA, DS, PC, TC. TAC10. 9 rooms with PB, 7 with FP, 2 suites and 1 conference room. Breakfast included in rates. MAP, EP. Types of meals: Full bkfst and early coffee/tea. Dinner available. Restaurant on premises. Beds: KQDT. Phone, turndown service and old radio tapes in room. Air conditioning. Fax, copier and library on premises. Handicap access. Weddings and small meetings hosted. Antiquing, live theater, parks, shopping and cross-country skiing nearby.

Publicity: *Country Living. Country Inns.*

"Popular spot keeps getting better."

Cold Spring   J12

Pig Hill Inn
73 Main St
Cold Spring, NY 10516-3014
(914)265-9247 Fax:(914)265-4614
E-mail: pighillinn@aol.com
Web: www.pighillinn.com

Circa 1808. The antiques at this stately three-story inn can be purchased, and they range from Chippendale to chinoiserie style. Rooms feature formal English and Adirondack decor with special touches such
as four-poster or brass
beds, painted rockers
and, of course, pigs.
The lawn features a tri-
level garden. The deli-
cious breakfasts can be
shared with guests in
the Victorian conserva-
tory, dining room or garden, or you can take it in the privacy of your room. The inn is about an hour out of New York City, and the train station is only two blocks away.

Innkeeper(s): Kim Teng. $120-170. MC, VISA, AX, TC. 9 rooms, 5 with PB, 6 with FP and 1 conference room. Breakfast included in rates. Type of meal: Full bkfst. Afternoon tea and catering service available. Beds: QDT. Ceiling fan, tea, coffee, ice and glasses in room. Air conditioning. Weddings, small meetings, family reunions and seminars hosted. Antiquing, fishing, live theater, shopping and sporting events nearby.

"Some of our fondest memories of New York were at Pig Hill."

Cooperstown   G10

Angelholm
14 Elm Street
Cooperstown, NY 13326-0705
(607)547-2483 Fax:(607)547-2309
E-mail: anglholm@telenet.net
Web: angelholmbb.com

Circa 1805. Built at the turn of the 19th century, Angelholm was constructed on land that was part of historic Phinney's Farm. It was on this farmland that the game of baseball was first played. The National Baseball Hall of Fame is within walking distance. However, Angelholm is not just a place for baseball fans. The guest rooms are decorated in a nostalgic style. Rooms include items such as the four poster bed in the Elihu Phinney Room or the antique lace curtains in the Glimmerglass Room. Breakfast is a formal affair with entrees such as a souffle or pecan waffles. After a day exploring the Hall of Fame, shop-

ping, searching for antiques or perhaps golfing at a nearby course, return and enjoy afternoon tea on the veranda.

Innkeeper(s): Jan & Fred Reynolds. $80-120. MC, VISA, AX, DS, PC, TC. TAC10. 5 rooms with PB. Breakfast and afternoon tea included in rates. Types of meals: Full bkfst and early coffee/tea. Beds: KQT. Air conditioning. VCR and fax on premises. Weddings, small meetings and family reunions hosted. Antiquing, fishing, golf, Glimmerglass Opera, live theater, parks, shopping, cross-country skiing, sporting events and water sports nearby.

Publicity: *New York Times, Country Inns.*

Cooper Inn
Main & Chestnut Streets
Cooperstown, NY 13326
(607)547-2567 (800)348-6222 Fax:(607)547-1271

Circa 1812. This Federal-style brick house opened as an inn in 1927, although it was built more than a century before that. It has been restored to the elegance of when it was first designed in the early 1800s. Guests can relax in the inn's main parlor or visit the game room. Look for the penny embedded in the newel post of the elegant rounded staircase. Its significance remains a mystery, but visitors are welcome to offer a guess. Decorative period woodwork and paintings from the Fenimore House Museum adorn the main floor. Rooms have been redecorated recently, and the inn is within walking distance to most of Cooperstown's attractions.

Historic Interest: Cooperstown, N.Y., is an historic site, Cherry Valley (13 miles).

Innkeeper(s): Steve Walker. $155-230. MC, VISA, AX. TAC10. 20 rooms with PB, 5 suites and 1 conference room. Types of meals: Cont plus and early coffee/tea. Beds: QT. Cable TV and phone in room. Central air. Fax, copier, tennis and library on premises. Weddings, small meetings, family reunions and seminars hosted. Amusement parks, antiquing, art galleries, beaches, bicycling, canoeing/kayaking, fishing, golf, hiking, horseback riding, live theater, museums, parks, shopping, downhill skiing, cross-country skiing, sporting events, tennis, water sports and wineries nearby.

The Inn at Cooperstown
16 Chestnut St
Cooperstown, NY 13326-1006
(607)547-5756 Fax:(607)547-8779
E-mail: theinn@telenet.net
Web: www.cooperstown.net/theinn

Circa 1874. This three-story, Second Empire hotel features a graceful porch filled with wicker furniture and rocking chairs. The inn is located in the center of the Cooperstown National
Historic District. The guest
rooms are decorated tastefully and comfortably. A
block from Otsego Lake,
the inn is within walking
distance of most of
Cooperstown's attractions.
Historic Interest: Baseball Hall of
Fame (2 blocks), The Farmers'
Museum & Fenimore House Museum (1 mile), Glimmerglass Operal (8 miles).

Innkeeper(s): Michael Jerome. $89-165. MC, VISA, AX, DC, DS, PC, TC. 17 rooms with PB and 1 conference room. Breakfast included in rates. Type of meal: Cont. Beds: QT. Fax and library on premises. Handicap access. Small meetings hosted. Antiquing, fishing, museum, opera, lake, live theater, parks, shopping, cross-country skiing, sporting events and water sports nearby.

"An unpretentious country inn with 17 rooms, spotless on the inside and stunning on the outside. — Conde Nast Traveler."

Thistlebrook B&B

RR 1 Box 26
Cooperstown, NY 13326
(607)547-6093 (800)596-9305

Circa 1866. This sprawling red barn with its rustic appearance belies the spacious and elegant rooms awaiting discovery inside. Fluted columns in the living room enhance the inn's original architectural details. Furnishings include American and European pieces, an Egyptian Revival mirror, Oriental rugs and crystal chandeliers. Just up the wide stairway is a library from which the guest rooms are reached. Breakfasts are hearty and may include fresh fruit salad and three-cheese omelets with biscuits and ham. Enjoy valley vistas from the inn's deck. A variety of wildlife such as deer, bullfrogs, wood ducks and an occasional blue heron, gather around the pond.

Innkeeper(s): Paula & Jim Bugonian. $125-145. PC, TC. TAC10. 5 rooms with PB and 2 suites. Breakfast included in rates. Types of meals: Full bkfst and early coffee/tea. Beds: KQ. Ceiling fan in room. Air conditioning. Fax, library and hot tub on premises. Handicap access. Weddings, small meetings and family reunions hosted. Antiquing, fishing, golf, summer opera, live theater, shopping, sporting events, tennis and water sports nearby.

Publicity: *Country Inns.*

Cooperstown (Sharon Springs) *G10*

Edgefield

Washington St, PO Box 152
Cooperstown (Sharon Springs), NY 13459
(518)284-3339

Circa 1865. This home has seen many changes. It began as a farmhouse, a wing was added in the 1880s, and by the turn of the century, it sported an elegant Greek Revival facade.

Edgefield is one of a collection of nearby homes used as a family compound for summer vacations. The rooms are decorated with traditional furnishings in a formal English-country style. In the English tradition, afternoon tea is presented each day with scones, cookies and tea sandwiches. Sharon Springs includes many historic sites, and the town is listed in the National Register.

Historic Interest: Near Cooperstown, Glimmerglass Opera and Hyde Hall; Albany (45 miles away).

Innkeeper(s): Daniel Marshall Wood. $95-160. PC, TC. 5 rooms with PB. Types of meals: Full gourmet bkfst and early coffee/tea. Afternoon tea and snacks/refreshments available. Beds: QT. Turndown service and ceiling fan in room. VCR, library, drawing room and veranda on premises. Antiquing, golf, opera, live theater, parks, shopping and water sports nearby.

"Truly what I always imagined the perfect B&B experience to be!"

Corinth *E12*

Agape Farm B&B

4894 Rt 9N
Corinth, NY 12822-1704
(518)654-7777

Circa 1870. Amid 33 acres of fields and woods, this Adirondack farmhouse is home to chickens and horses, as well as guests seeking a refreshing getaway. Visitors have their

choice of six guest rooms, all with ceiling fans, phones, private baths and views of the tranquil surroundings. The inn's wrap-around porch lures many visitors, who often enjoy a glass of

icy lemonade. Homemade breads, jams, jellies and muffins are part of the full breakfast served here, and guests are welcome to pick berries or gather a ripe tomato from the garden. A trout-filled stream on the grounds flows to the Hudson River, a mile away.

Historic Interest: Built on the site of a hundred year old dairy farm, outbuildings and animals keep this atmosphere alive.

Innkeeper(s): Fred & Sigrid Koch. $75-175. MC, VISA, DS, PC, TC. 6 rooms with PB and 1 cottage. Breakfast, afternoon tea and snacks/refreshments included in rates. Types of meals: Full bkfst and early coffee/tea. Beds: KQDT. Phone and ceiling fan in room. VCR, library, child care and downstairs HC room and bath on premises. Small meetings hosted. Amusement parks, antiquing, fishing, live theater, parks, shopping, downhill skiing, cross-country skiing, sporting events and water sports nearby.

"Clean and impeccable, we were treated royally."

Corning *H6*

1865 White Birch B&B

69 E 1st St
Corning, NY 14830-2715
(607)962-6355

Circa 1865. This Victorian is a short walk from historic Market Street, the Corning Glass Museum and many restaurants. Guests will appreciate the detailed woodwork, hardwood floors, an impressive winding staircase and many antiques. The rooms are decorated in a cozy, country decor. Home-baked breakfasts provide the perfect start for a day of visiting wineries, antique shops or museums.

Innkeeper(s): Kathy Donahue. $55-85. MC, VISA, AX. 4 rooms, 2 with PB. Breakfast included in rates. Type of meal: Full bkfst. Beds: QT. TV, phone, window fans and comfortable chair in room. Antiquing, fishing, live theater, shopping, cross-country skiing and sporting events nearby.

"This is a beautiful home, decorated to make us feel warm and welcome."

Cornwall *J12*

Cromwell Manor Inn B&B

Angola Rd
Cornwall, NY 12518
(914)534-7136

Circa 1820. A descendant of Oliver Cromwell built this stunning Greek Revival home, which is set on seven lush acres boasting scenic views of mountains and a 4,000-acre forest preserve. The innkeepers refurbished the National Register manor, leaving original elements and adding period antiques and fine furnishings throughout. Relax by the fireplace or enjoy the inn's Jacuzzi and steam room. The innkeepers prepare a breakfast of

home-baked treats such as muffins, quiche, omelets, fruits and specialty breads. The innkeepers also offer a romantic cottage dating back to 1764, which boasts a fireplace and country antiques.

Historic Interest: West Point is only 10 minutes from the inn and the area offers plenty of historic homes, including the Vanderbilt Mansion. The Brotherhood Winery, the nation's oldest, is a nearby attraction.

Innkeeper(s): Dale & Barbara O'Hara. $135-275. MC, VISA, PC. TAC10. 13 rooms with PB, 7 with FP, 2 suites and 1 conference room. Breakfast included in rates. Types of meals: Full gourmet bkfst and early coffee/tea. Afternoon tea, picnic lunch, catering service and room service available. Beds: QD. Turndown service in room. Air conditioning. VCR and copier on premises. Handicap access. Weddings, small meetings, family reunions and seminars hosted. Antiquing, fishing, Hudson Valley Mansion, live theater, parks, shopping, downhill skiing, cross-country skiing, sporting events and water sports nearby.

De Bruce I10

De Bruce Country Inn on The Willowemoc

De Bruce Rd #982
De Bruce, NY 12758
(914)439-3900

Circa 1917. This inn is located on the banks of the Willowemoc stream, not far from where the first dry fly was cast in the United States. This early 20th-century retreat, with its excellent trout fishing, secluded woodlands, views of the valley and mountains continues to draw visitors today. The inn, situated in the Catskill Forest Preserve, offers wooded trails, wildlife and game, a stocked pond, swimming pool, sauna and whirlpool. Guests enjoy hearty breakfasts and fine dinners on the dining terrace and romantic evenings in the Dry Fly Lounge.

Innkeeper(s): Ron & Marilyn Lusker. $97-240. 13 rooms with PB and 2 suites. Breakfast and dinner included in rates. MAP. Type of meal: Full bkfst. Restaurant on premises. Beds: KQDT. Ceiling fan in room. VCR, fax, copier, spa, swimming, sauna, library, satellite TV in bar and wine cellar on premises. Weddings, small meetings, family reunions and seminars hosted. French, limited German and limited Italian spoken. Antiquing, golf and museums nearby.
Pets allowed: at inn owners' discretion.

East Hampton K15

Maidstone Arms

207 Main St
East Hampton, NY 11937-2723
(516)324-5006 Fax:(516)324-5037

Circa 1860. Situated on the village green, this classic inn has all the characteristics that epitomize this community of winding lanes and sandy white beaches. Turndown service is provided in the individually decorated rooms. The inn's restaurant houses a world-class selection of wines in its own climate-controlled underground wine cellar. Nearby activities include whale-watching expeditions and local winery tours.

Historic Interest: The Maidstone Arms is located on Long Island, which offers many historic buildings and sites. New York City is about two hours away.

Innkeeper(s): Coke Ann Saunders. $195-375. MC, VISA, AX. 19 rooms with PB, 6 suites, 3 cottages and 1 conference room. Breakfast included in rates. Types of meals: Full bkfst, cont plus, cont and early coffee/tea. Dinner, snacks/refreshments, picnic lunch, gourmet lunch, banquet service and room service available. Restaurant on premises. Beds: KQT. Cable TV, phone and turndown service in room. Air conditioning. Weddings, small meetings, family reunions and seminars hosted. Antiquing, fishing, live theater and water sports nearby.

Mill House Inn

33 N Main St
East Hampton, NY 11937-2601
(516)324-9766 Fax:(516)324-9793

Circa 1790. This Colonial house is just opposite the Old Hook Windmill. It is in the center of East Hampton, which has been called "America's most beautiful village." Guest rooms are decorated with a Hampton's theme in mind, sporting names such as Sail Away or Hampton Holiday. Romantic amenities abound, including fireplaces in six of the guest rooms. Several rooms also have whirlpool tubs. Families are welcome.

Innkeeper(s): Sylvia & Gary Muller. $185-425. MC, VISA, AX, DC, PC. 8 rooms with PB, 6 with FP. Breakfast and afternoon tea included in rates. Type of meal: Full bkfst. Beds: QD. Cable TV, phone, ceiling fan, VCR and refrigerator on porch in room. Air conditioning. Fax, copier and library on premises. Handicap access. Small meetings and family reunions hosted. Spanish spoken. Antiquing, fishing, fine dining, first run movies, live music, live theater, shopping and water sports nearby.

"Perfect everything, it's hard to leave."

The Pink House

26 James Ln
East Hampton, NY 11937-2710
(516)324-3400 Fax:(516)324-5254
E-mail: RoSo@hamptons.com
Web: thepinkhouse.net

Circa 1850. This pre-Civil War home is located in the East Hampton's historic district. The decor of this simple Victorian, originally owned by a whaling captain, has been greatly enhanced by a collection of architectural elements gathered from demolished buildings. The innkeeper has included scenic watercolors that were painted by his grandfather during his world travels. TVs, robes, in-room phones, designer sheets and evening chocolates are among the inn's amenities. A full breakfast is served on the porch overlooking the pool or in the dining room. There are three inn dogs. Celebrity guests include Jane Seymour, Martin Short, Robin Williams and Carly Simon.

Innkeeper(s): Ron Steinhilber. $135-375. MC, VISA, AX, PC, TC. 5 rooms with PB. Breakfast included in rates. Type of meal: Full bkfst. Beds: Q. Cable TV, phone and ceiling fan in room. Air conditioning. Fax, copier and swimming on premises. Antiquing, fishing, golf, shopping, tennis and water sports nearby.

Publicity: *New York Times.*

"I came jangeled and stressed and leave peaceful and calm."

Elbridge F7

Fox Ridge Farm B&B

4786 Foster Rd
Elbridge, NY 13060-9770
(315)673-4881 Fax:(315)673-3691

Circa 1910. Guests shouldn't be surprised to encounter deer or other wildlife at this secluded country home surrounded by woods. The innkeepers have transformed the former farmhouse into an inn with rooms boasting quilts, a four-poster bed and views of the woods or flower garden. Enjoy breakfasts in front of a fire in the large country kitchen. The innkeepers are happy to accommodate dietary needs. Snacks and refreshments always are available for hungry guests in the evening. Nearby Skaneateles Lake offers swimming, boating and other outdoor activities. Dinner cruises, touring wineries and antique shopping are other popular activities.

Historic Interest: The Canal Museum and The Creamery are five miles from the farm. The Harriet Tubman House is a 12-mile drive, as is the William Seward House.

Innkeeper(s): Marge Sykes. $55-85. MC, VISA, AX, DS, PC, TC. 3 rooms, 1 with PB. Breakfast and snacks/refreshments included in rates. Types of meals: Full gourmet bkfst, cont plus and early coffee/tea. Beds: QD. VCR, grand piano and wood stove on premises. Antiquing, fishing, live theater, parks, shopping, downhill skiing, cross-country skiing, sporting events and water sports nearby.

"If I could, I would take Marge Sykes home to Seattle with us. We stayed 7 days for a family reunion. Great company, marvelous hosts and the most delicious breakfasts everyday."

Ellicottville   H3

The Jefferson Inn of Ellicottville

3 Jefferson St, PO Box 1566
Ellicottville, NY 14731-1566
(716)699-5869 (800)577-8451 Fax:(716)699-5758
E-mail: jeffinn@eznet.net
Web: thejeffersoninn.com

Circa 1835. The Allegheny Mountains provide a perfect backdrop for this restored Victorian home built by Robert H. Shankland, an influential man who owned the local newspaper among his other duties. The home's 100-foot wraparound

Greek Revival porch was added in the 1920s and patterned after the summer home of President Woodrow Wilson. The quiet inn is located in the center of the village. Follow the tree-lined streets to 15 restaurants.

Historic Interest: Historic Ellicottville offers plenty of historic buildings and sites. Also offers a walking tour.

Innkeeper(s): Jim Buchanan & Donna Gushue. $65-175. MC, VISA, AX, DC, DS, PC, TC. TAC10. 7 rooms with PB, 3 with FP. Breakfast included in rates. Types of meals: Full gourmet bkfst and early coffee/tea. Picnic lunch available. Beds: KQDT. Cable TV and phone in room. Central air. VCR, fax and library on premises. Handicap access. Weddings, small meetings, family reunions and seminars hosted. Antiquing, art galleries, bicycling, fishing, golf, hiking, museums, parks, shopping, downhill skiing, cross-country skiing and tennis nearby.

Pets allowed: In efficiency units only.

"Even though we just met, we are leaving with the feeling we just spent the weekend with good friends."

Essex   C13

The Stone House

PO Box 43
Essex, NY 12936-0043
(518)963-7713 Fax:(518)963-7713

Circa 1826. Just a two-minute walk from the ferry that traverses Lake Champlain, this stately Georgian stone house offers a tranquil English country setting. Breakfast may be eaten in the elegant dining room or on the garden terrace, and guests also enjoy an evening snack and glass of wine by candlelight on the inn's porch. The charming hamlet of Essex, listed in the National Register, is waiting to be explored, and visitors may do so by borrowing one of the inn's bicycles. Antiquing, fine dining and shopping are found

in town, and Lake Champlain and nearby Lake George provide many recreational activities.

Historic Interest: Grounds include 1826 Georgian house, 1776 restored schoolhouse and 1850 converted barn.

Innkeeper(s): Sylvia Hobbs. $75-150. PC, TC. 4 rooms, 2 with PB, 1 suite and 1 cottage. Breakfast, afternoon tea and snacks/refreshments included in rates. Types of meals: Cont plus and early coffee/tea. Beds: QDT. Turndown service in room. VCR, bicycles, library and CD player on premises. Weddings, small meetings, family reunions and seminars hosted. German spoken. Antiquing, fishing, golf, live theater, parks, shopping, tennis and water sports nearby.

"Without a doubt, the highlight of our trip!"

Fair Haven   E7

Black Creek Farm B&B

PO Box 390
Fair Haven, NY 13064-0390
(315)947-5282

Circa 1888. Pines and towering birch trees frame this Victorian farmhouse inn, filled with an amazing assortment of authentic antiques. Set on 20 acres, Black Creek Farm is a refreshing escape from big-city life. Guests enjoy relaxing in a hammock on the porch or by taking a stroll along the peaceful back roads. A hearty country breakfast features seasonal fruit raised on the grounds as well as home baked date-nut, banana-nut or pumpkin-raisin bread. A new pond-side guest house is an especially popular accommodation for honeymooners and families, offering complete privacy. It features a gas  fireplace and double shower. Bring your own breakfast makings and enjoy breakfast sitting on the patio or the porch which overlooks the pond, with ducks and geese, bass and perch. Sometimes turkey or deer may be seen in the meadow. There's a peddle boat on the pond in summer. In winter sledding and snowmobiling are popular. The B&B is two miles from Lake Ontario, Fair Haven Beach State Park and minutes away from Sterling Renaissance Festival.

Innkeeper(s): Bob & Kathy Sarber. $60-125. MC, VISA, AX, DS, PC. 3 rooms with PB. Types of meals: Full bkfst and early coffee/tea. Beds: Q. Air conditioning. VCR, bicycles, paddle boat, satellite disc and movies available on premises. Family reunions hosted. Fishing, snowmobiling, cross-country skiing and water sports nearby.

Fleischmanns   H11

River Run

Main St, Box D4
Fleischmanns, NY 12430
(914)254-4884
E-mail: riverrun@catskill.net
Web: www.catskill.net/riverrun

Circa 1887. The backyard of this large three-story Victorian gently slopes to the river where the Bushkill and Little Red Kill trout streams meet. Inside, stained-glass windows surround the inn's common areas, shining on the oak-floored dining room and the book-filled parlor. The parlor also includes a fireplace and a piano. Adirondack chairs are situated comfortably on the front porch. Tennis courts, a pool, park, theater and restaurants are within walking distance, as is a country auction held each

Saturday night. The inn is two and a half hours out of New York City, 35 minutes west of Woodstock, and accessible by public transportation. Also, the inn was the recipient of the "Catskill Service Award" for best accommodations in the Belleayre Region.

Historic Interest: The Hudson River mansions are all located within one hour of the inn. Bethel, the site of the famed Woodstock concert is within an hour of the inn. Cooperstown is about an hour and a half away.

Innkeeper(s): Larry Miller. $70-115. MC, VISA, AX, PC. TAC10. 10 rooms, 6 with PB and 1 suite. Breakfast and afternoon tea included in rates. Types of meals: Cont plus and early coffee/tea. Beds: KQDT. TV in room. VCR, bicycles, library and refrigerator on premises. Small meetings and family reunions hosted. French and German spoken. Antiquing, fishing, golf, hiking, horseback riding, auctions, flea and farmers markets, live theater, parks, shopping, downhill skiing, cross-country skiing, tennis and water sports nearby.

Pets allowed: Well behaved, fully trained, over one year old.

"We are really happy to know of a place that welcomes all of our family."

Fredonia G2

The White Inn

52 E Main St
Fredonia, NY 14063-1836
(716)672-2103 (888)FRE-DONIA Fax:(716)672-2107
E-mail: inn@whiteinn.com
Web: www.whiteinn.com

Circa 1868. This 23-room inn is situated in the center of a historic town. The inn's rooms are pristinely furnished in antiques and reproductions and 11 are spacious suites. Guests, as well as the public may enjoy gourmet meals at the inn, a charter member of the Duncan Hines "Family of Fine Restaurants." In addition to fine dining and catered events, casual fare and cocktails are offered in the lounge or on the 100-foot-long veranda. Nearby the Chautauqua Institution operates during the summer offering a popular selection of lectures and concert performances. Fredonia State College is another avenue to cultural events as well as sporting events. Wineries, golfing, state parks and shops are nearby.

Innkeeper(s): Robert Contiguglia & Kathleen Dennison. $69-179. MC, VISA, AX, DC, DS, PC, TC. TAC10. 23 rooms with PB, 2 with FP, 11 suites and 4 conference rooms. Breakfast included in rates. EP. Type of meal: Full bkfst. Gourmet dinner, lunch, banquet service and catering service available. Restaurant on premises. Beds: KQD. Cable TV and phone in room. Air conditioning. VCR, fax and copier on premises. Handicap access. Weddings, small meetings, family reunions and seminars hosted. Antiquing, live theater, parks, shopping and cross-country skiing nearby.

Publicity: *Country Living, US Air Magazine.*

"The perfect mix of old-fashioned charm and modern elegance."

Fulton E7

Battle Island Inn

2167 State Route 48 N
Fulton, NY 13069-4132
(315)593-3699 Fax:(315)592-5071
E-mail: richard-rice@prodigy.net
Web: www.battle-island-inn.com

Circa 1840. Topped with a gothic cupola, this family farmhouse overlooks the Oswego River and a golf course. There are three antique-filled parlors. Guest accommodations are furnished in a variety of styles including Victorian and Renaissance Revival.

There are four wooded acres with lawns and gardens. Guests are often found relaxing on one of the inn's four porches and enjoying the views. The Honeymoon suite features a canopy bed, full bath and private Jacuzzi.

Innkeeper(s): Richard & Joyce Rice. $60-125. MC, VISA, AX, DS, PC, TC. 5 rooms with PB and 1 suite. Breakfast included in rates. AP. Types of meals: Full gourmet bkfst and early coffee/tea. Beds: QDT. Cable TV, phone, ceiling fan and refrigerator in 1 guest room in room. VCR, fax and copier on premises. Handicap access. Small meetings and seminars hosted. Fishing, golf, fort, live theater, parks, shopping, cross-country skiing and water sports nearby.

"We will certainly never forget our wonderful weeks at Battle Island Inn."

Garrison J12

The Bird & Bottle Inn

Old Albany Post Rd, Rt 9
Garrison, NY 10524
(914)424-3000 Fax:(914)424-3283

Circa 1761. Built as Warren's Tavern, this three-story yellow farmhouse served as a lodging and dining spot on the New York-to-Albany Post Road, now a National Historic Landmark. George Washington, Hamilton, Lafayette and many other historic figures frequently passed by.  The inn's eight acres include secluded lawns, a babbling stream and Hudson Valley woodlands. Timbered ceilings, old paneling and fireplace mantels in the inn's notable restaurant maintain a Revolutionary War-era ambiance. Second-floor guest rooms have canopied or four-poster beds and each is warmed by its own fireplace.

Innkeeper(s): Ira Boyar. $210-240. MC, VISA, AX, DC, PC, TC. 4 rooms with PB, 4 with FP, 1 suite and 1 cottage. Breakfast and dinner included in rates. MAP. Lunch available. Restaurant on premises. Beds: Q. Air conditioning. Fax and copier on premises. Weddings, small meetings, family reunions and seminars hosted. Antiquing, fishing, live theater, parks, shopping and cross-country skiing nearby.

Geneva F6

Geneva On The Lake

1001 Lochland Rd, Rt 14S
Geneva, NY 14456
(315)789-7190 (800)343-6382 Fax:(315)789-0322
E-mail: info@genevaonthelake.com
Web: www.genevaonthelake.com

Circa 1911. This opulent world-class inn is a replica of the Renaissance-era Lancellotti Villa in Frascati, Italy. It is listed in the National Register. Although originally built as a residence, it became a monastery for Capuchin monks. Now it is one of the finest resorts in the U.S. Recently renovated under the direction of award-winning designer William Schickel, there are 10 two-bedroom suites — some with views of the lake. Here, you may have an experience as fine as Europe can offer, without leaving the states. Some

compare it to the Grand Hotel du Cap-Ferrat on the French Riviera. The inn has been awarded four diamonds from AAA for more than a decade. Breakfast is available daily and on Sunday, brunch is served. Dinner is served each evening, and in the summer, lunch is offered on the terrace.

Historic Interest: The Corning Glass Center, where Steuben glass is created by hand, is nearby. The town of Elmira, another close attraction, is the site where "The Adventures of Tom Sawyer" and "Huckleberry Finn", were written by Mark Twain.

Innkeeper(s): William J. Schickel. $138-730. MC, VISA, AX, DS. TAC10. 30 suites, 3 with FP and 3 conference rooms. Breakfast included in rates. Types of meals: Full gourmet bkfst and cont. Gourmet dinner, banquet service and room service available. Restaurant on premises. Beds: KQDT. TV, phone and turndown service in room. Air conditioning. VCR, fax, copier, swimming, bicycles, sailing, fishing, lawn games and boats on premises. Weddings, small meetings, family reunions and seminars hosted. Antiquing, live theater, parks, shopping, downhill skiing, cross-country skiing, sporting events, water sports and wineries nearby.

"The food was superb and the service impeccable."

Gorham   G6

The Gorham House

4752 E Swamp Rd
Gorham, NY 14461
(716)526-4402 Fax:(716)526-4402
E-mail: gorham.house@juno.com
Web: www.angelfire.com/biz/GorhamHouse

Circa 1887. The Gorham House serves as a homey, country place to enjoy New York's Finger Lakes region. The five, secluded acres located between Canandaigua and Seneca lakes, include herb gardens, wildflowers and berry bushes. Part of the home dates back to the early 19th century, but it's the architecture of the 1887 expansion that accounts for the inn's Victorian touches. The interior is warm and cozy with comfortable, country furnishings. Some of the pieces are the innkeepers' family heirlooms. There are more than 50 wineries in the area, as well as a bounty of outdoor activities.

Innkeeper(s): Nancy & Al Rebmann. $89-120. PC, TC. 3 rooms, 1 with PB. Breakfast included in rates. Types of meals: Full gourmet bkfst and early coffee/tea. Beds: QD. Air conditioning. Library on premises. Family reunions hosted. Antiquing, fishing, live theater, parks, shopping, downhill skiing, cross-country skiing, sporting events and water sports nearby.

Greenport   K15

The Bartlett House Inn

503 Front St
Greenport, NY 11944-1519
(516)477-0371

Circa 1908. A family residence for more than 60 years and then a convent for a nearby church, this large Victorian house became a bed & breakfast in 1982. Features include corinthian columns, stained-glass windows, two fireplaces and a large front porch. Period antiques complement the rich interior. The inn is within walking distance of shops, restaurants, the harbor, wineries, the Shelter Island Ferry and train station.

Innkeeper(s): Michael & Patricia O'Donoghue. $95-125. MC, VISA, PC, TC. 10 rooms with PB, 1 with FP, 1 suite and 1 conference room. Breakfast included in rates. Types of meals: Cont plus and early coffee/tea. Beds: QDT. Air conditioning. Weddings, small meetings, family reunions and seminars hosted. Antiquing, fishing, maritime museum, outlet shopping, art galleries, golf, fine restaurants, parks, shopping and water sports nearby.

Greenville   G12

Greenville Arms

South St, PO Box 659
Greenville, NY 12083-0659
(518)966-5219 Fax:(518)966-8754

Circa 1889. William Vanderbilt had this graceful Victorian built with Queen Anne gables and cupolas. Seven acres of lush lawns are dotted with gardens, and there is a 50-foot outdoor pool. There are floor-to-ceiling fireplaces, chestnut woodwork, wainscoting and Victorian bead work over the doorways. Painting workshops are held in summer and fall. Dinner is served to inn guests seven nights a week.

Innkeeper(s): Eliot & Letitia Dalton. $125-165. MC, VISA, PC, TC. TAC10. 14 rooms with PB, 1 suite and 2 conference rooms. Breakfast and afternoon tea included in rates. MAP. Types of meals: Full bkfst and afternoon tea. Gourmet dinner and lunch available. Beds: KQDT. VCR, fax, swimming, library and air conditioning on premises. Weddings, small meetings, family reunions and seminars hosted. Amusement parks, antiquing, fishing, hiking, parks and water sports nearby.

"Just a note of appreciation for all your generous hospitality, and wonderful display of attention and affection!"

Hague   D12

Trout House Village Resort

PO Box 510
Hague, NY 12836-0510
(518)543-6088 (800)368-6088 Fax:(518)543-6124
E-mail: info@trouthouse.com
Web: www.trouthouse.com

Circa 1934. On the shores of beautiful Lake George is this resort inn, offering accommodations in the lodge, authentic log cabins or cottages. Many of the guest rooms in the lodge boast lake views, while the log cabins offer jetted tubs and fireplaces. The guest quarters are furnished comfortably. The emphasis here is on the abundance of outdoor activities. Outstanding cross-country skiing, downhill skiing and snowmobiling are found nearby. The inn furnishes bicycles, canoes, kayaks, paddle boats, rowboats, sleds, shuffleboard, skis and toboggans. Summertime evenings offer games of capture-the-flag and

soccer. Other activities include basketball, horseshoes, ping pong, a putting green and volleyball.

Historic Interest: Fort Ticonderoga (8 miles).

Innkeeper(s): Scott & Alice Patchett. $45-333. MC, VISA, AX, DS, PC, TC. TAC10. 13 rooms, 11 with PB, 15 with FP, 1 suite, 15 cottages and 2 conference rooms. AP. Type of meal: Cont plus. Banquet service available. Beds: QDT. Cable TV, phone and VCR in room. Swimming, bicycles, tennis, library and child care on premises. Handicap access. Weddings, small meetings, family reunions and seminars hosted. Amusement parks, antiquing, fishing, parks, shopping, downhill skiing, cross-country skiing and water sports nearby.

Pets allowed: During off season.

"My wife and I felt the family warmth at this resort. There wasn't that coldness you get at larger resorts."

Hamburg G3

Sharon's Lake House B&B

4862 Lake Shore Rd
Hamburg, NY 14075-5542
(716)627-7561

Circa 1935. This historic lakefront house is located 10 miles from Buffalo and 45 minutes from Niagara Falls. Overlooking Lake Erie, the West Lake Room and the Upper Lake Room provide spectacular views. The home's beautiful furnishings offer additional delights.

Innkeeper(s): Sharon & Vince Di Maria. $100-110. PC, TC. 2 rooms, 1 with PB. Breakfast included in rates. Type of meal: Full gourmet bkfst. Afternoon tea and gourmet dinner available. Beds: D. Cable TV, phone and ceiling fan in room. VCR, swimming and hot tub room & computer room at an hourly rate available on premises. Fishing, live theater, parks, shopping, downhill skiing, cross-country skiing and water sports nearby.

"Spectacular view, exquisitely furnished."

Hamlin E5

Sandy Creek Manor House

1960 Redman Rd
Hamlin, NY 14464-9635
(716)964-7528 (800)594-0400
E-mail: agreatbnb@aol.com
Web: www.sandycreekbnb.com

Circa 1910. Six acres of woods and perennial gardens provide the setting for this English Tudor house. Stained glass, polished woods and Amish quilts add warmth to the home. The innkeepers have placed many thoughtful amenities in each room, such as clock radios, fluffy robes, slippers and baskets of toiletries. Breakfast is served on the open porch in summer. Fisherman's Landing, on the banks of Sandy Creek, is a stroll away. Bullhead, trout and salmon are popular catches. There  is a gift shop, outdoor hot tub and deck on premises. Ask about murder-mystery, sweetheart dinner and spa treatment packages.

Innkeeper(s): Shirley Hollink & James Krempasky. $65-90. MC, VISA, AX, DS, PC, TC. TAC10. 4 rooms, 1 with PB. Breakfast, afternoon tea and snacks/refreshments included in rates. Types of meals: Full gourmet bkfst, cont plus, cont and early coffee/tea. Beds: KQDT. Cable TV and VCR in room. Air conditioning. Fishing, player piano and guest refrigerator on premises. Small meetings and family reunions hosted. Antiquing, fishing, farm markets, sky diving, gift shop on premises, parks, shopping, downhill skiing, cross-country skiing, sporting events and water sports nearby.

Pets Allowed.

Publicity: *Rochester Times Union.*

"Delightful in every way."

Hammondsport G6

The Amity Rose Bed & Breakfast

8264 Main St
Hammondsport, NY 14840-9701
(607)569-3408 (800)982-8818 Fax:(607)569-3483
E-mail: bbam@infoblvd.net
Web: www.amityroseinn.com

Circa 1900. This farmhouse Victorian has a two-story veranda and shuttered windows. Sweet Emma's Suite consists of two rooms, one a wicker-furnished sitting room. Two rooms offer whirlpool soaking tubs. There is a queen bed, and the decor is floral and stripes. Within walking distance is the village square with a bandstand from which summer concerts are held. There is a nearby trout stream, and across the street is a track for running.

Historic Interest: Corning Glass Museum, Winery Museum, Curtiss Museum, Warplane Museum.

Innkeeper(s): Ellen & Frank Lauferswiler. $85-125. PC, TC. 4 rooms with PB, 1 suite and 1 conference room. Breakfast and afternoon tea included in rates. Types of meals: Full bkfst, country bkfst, veg bkfst and early coffee/tea. Beds: Q. 2 whirlpool Jacuzzi's in room. Air conditioning. Fax, bicycles and tennis on premises. Small meetings and seminars hosted. Antiquing, art galleries, beaches, bicycling, canoeing/kayaking, fishing, golf, hiking, horseback riding, museums, parks, shopping, sporting events, tennis, water sports and wineries nearby.

"How nice, a bathroom big enough to waltz in, well almost!"

Blushing Rose B&B

11 William St
Hammondsport, NY 14840
(607)569-3402 (800)982-8818 Fax:(607)569-2504
E-mail: bbam@infoblud.net
Web: www.blushingroseinn.com

Circa 1843. This rose "Painted Lady" offers a large front porch and a Widow's Walk. Located at the southern tip of Keuka Lake in the Finger Lakes area, the inn is decorated with careful attention to detail. The Burgundy Room features burgundy walls, an antique armoire and a quilt. The Moonbeams Room boasts a skylight and a brass and iron bed. Breakfasts often feature  Belgian waffles, Southwest quiche and sticky buns. Enjoy homemade cookies with tea in the afternoon. Walk to the Historic Village Square for shops, restaurants and antiques. Nearby attractions include wineries, the Curtiss Aviation Museum, Corning Glass and Watkins Glen.

Historic Interest: Visit the historic Glen Curtiss Museum of Aviation and the Corning Glass Center.

Innkeeper(s): Ellen & Frank Lauferswiler. $85-105. PC, TC. 4 rooms with PB. Breakfast and afternoon tea included in rates. Type of meal: Full gourmet bkfst. Gourmet dinner available. Beds: KQ. Bicycles on premises. Antiquing, fishing and water sports nearby.

Publicity: *Dundee Observer.*

J.S. Hubbs B&B

17 Shether St, PO Box 366
Hammondsport, NY 14840-0428
(607)569-2440

Circa 1840. At the Southern tip of Keuka Lake is the village of Hammondsport, home to this Greek Revival inn, with its charming cupola. The village square and lake are just one-half block from the inn. Because of its interesting architecture, the inn has come to be known as the ink bottle house, one of the village's major landmarks. The inn offers four guest  rooms, including one in the cupola. Guests enjoy relaxing in the living room and parlor. Many fine wineries are found in the area, and the Greyton H. Taylor Wine Museum is nearby.

Innkeeper(s): Walter & Linda Carl. Call for rates. 1 suites. Ceiling fan in room. Air conditioning. Small meetings hosted. Antiquing and sporting events nearby.

High Falls *I11*

Locktender Cottage

Route 213
High Falls, NY 12440
(914)687-7700 Fax:(914)687-7073

Circa 1797. This quaint little Victorian-style cottage sits along-side the old Delaware and Hudson Canal. Guests can opt to stay in one of the two guest rooms, one of which features a fireplace, or in the Chef's

Quarters. The Chef's Quarters includes a full kitchen, washer and dryer and a relaxing Jacuzzi. Guests of the two guest rooms receive a discount on a gourmet dinner at the Depuy Canal House, an 18th-century home restored to house a four-star restaurant. Enjoy a seven-course meal of delectable appetizers, entrees, cheeses and desserts while surrounded by history. Gourmet cuisine is the ticket in nearby Hyde Park, which is home to the Culinary Institute of America.

Historic Interest: The Franklin D. Roosevelt Library & Museum, Hanford Museum, Hudson River Maritime Center and Huguenot Street, the oldest street in the United States, are among Hyde Park's historic attractions.

Innkeeper(s): John N. Novi. $95-951. VISA. 3 rooms with PB and 1 suite. Gourmet dinner available. Restaurant on premises. Beds: QD. Antiquing, fishing and cross-country skiing nearby.

Publicity: *Time Magazine, Hudson Valley Journal, Poughkeepsie Journal, Dupay Canal House.*

"A great home away from home!"

Highmount *H11*

Gateway Lodge

Rt 28 & Highlands Rd, PO Box 397
Highmount, NY 12441
(914)254-4084

Circa 1920. Gateway Lodge was built from the remains of a previous lodging, the Catskill Mountain Guest House. The 1920s-era lodge features a gambrel room and gingerbread trim done in shades of green. The guest rooms are furnished comfortably with antiques, quilts and country pieces. Breakfasts include a wide assortment of beverages, including cappuccino, herbal teas and the lodge's signature orange juice. An entrée, such as layers of French toast topped with cinnamon and powdered sugar, is served with breakfast sausage or bacon. The lodge is close to many outdoor activities, including hiking, fishing, tennis, boating, horseback riding and much more. Antique shops and flea markets also are nearby.

Historic Interest: Hudson Valley Mansions & Estates (40 miles).

Innkeeper(s): Isabella Young. $65-130. PC, TC. 5 rooms, 3 with PB and 1 suite. Breakfast and afternoon tea included in rates. Type of meal: Country bkfst. Beds: KQD. Cable TV in room. VCR on premises. Weddings, small meetings and family reunions hosted. Polish spoken. Antiquing, bicycling, canoeing/kayaking, fishing, golf, hiking, parks, shopping, downhill skiing, cross-country skiing and water sports nearby.

Hobart *H10*

Breezy Acres Farm B&B

RR 1 Box 191
Hobart, NY 13788-9754
(607)538-9338

Circa 1830. With 300 acres of meadows, woodlands and pastures, guests have plenty to explore and enjoy at this working crop farm. The historic farmhouse has been renovated and is decorated with family antiques. A homemade, country breakfast gets the day off to a perfect start. Enjoy the surrounding scenery or take a stroll along the nearby Catskill Scenic Trail.

Historic Interest: Hanford Mills Museum, National Baseball Hall of Fame & Museum, Howe Caverns.

Innkeeper(s): Joyce and David Barber. $60-75. MC, VISA, AX, DS, PC, TC. 3 rooms with PB. Breakfast included in rates. Type of meal: Full bkfst. Beds: KQ. VCR and copier on premises. Small meetings hosted. Antiquing, fishing, golf, downhill skiing, cross-country skiing and tennis nearby.

"Nicest people you'd want to meet. Perfect! Wonderful hosts, warm, friendly atmosphere. We will be back!"

Hudson *H12*

The Inn at Blue Stores

2323 Rt 9
Hudson, NY 12534-0099
(518)537-4277 Fax:(518)537-6608

Circa 1908. A rural Hudson Valley setting may seem an unusual place for a Spanish-style inn, but this former gentlemen's farm now provides a unique setting for those seeking a relaxing getaway. Visitors will enjoy the inn's clay tile roof and stucco exterior, along with its impressive interior, featuring black oak woodwork,

leaded-glass entry and stained glass. Visitors are treated to full breakfasts and refreshing afternoon teas. The spacious porch and swimming pool are favorite spots for relaxing and socializing.

Historic Interest: Olana, Clermont, Hyde Park, Shaker Museum, Montgomery Place.

Innkeeper(s): Linda & Robert. $99-175. MC, VISA, AX. 5 rooms, 2 with PB and 1 suite. Breakfast included in rates. Types of meals: Full gourmet bkfst and early coffee/tea. Afternoon tea available. Beds: KQT. TV and VCR in room. Air conditioning. Fax and swimming on premises. French spoken. Antiquing, art galleries, bicycling, canoeing/kayaking, fishing, golf, hiking, horseback riding, historic sites, OLANA, Hyde Park, Clermont Mills Estate, live theater, museums, parks, shopping, cross-country skiing, tennis and wineries nearby.

Hunter *H11*

Fairlawn Inn

PO Box 182, Main St
Hunter, NY 12442
(518)263-5025 Fax:(518)263-5025

Circa 1902. A three-story turret and a sweeping two-story covered veranda with a gazebo accentuate the exterior of this historic Victorian, which was built by a distinguished New York City businessman. The interior has been restored to its Victorian grandeur

and features period-style wallpapers and antiques. The original woodwork and light fixtures have been preserved, adding to the ambiance. Guest rooms include Victorian reproduction beds, and some include an over-sized clawfoot tub. Breakfasts feature fresh fruit, homemade breads, a savory egg dish and pancakes or French toast. The Catskill Mountains provide plenty of outdoor activities, as well as outstanding scenery. The Hunter Mountain Ski Area is a half-mile from the inn.

Historic Interest: Olana (30 miles).

Innkeeper(s): Kelly Coughlin. $75-110. MC, VISA, PC, TC. TAC10. 9 rooms with PB. Breakfast included in rates. Beds: Q. VCR, fax and copier on premises. Weddings, small meetings, family reunions and seminars hosted. Antiquing, bicycling, canoeing/kayaking, fishing, golf, hiking, horseback riding, parks, shopping, downhill skiing, cross-country skiing and tennis nearby.

"This was a wonderful romantic getaway as well as a great chance to meet and make new friends."

Ithaca   G7

Rose Inn

Rt 34N, Box 6576
Ithaca, NY 14851-6576
(607)533-7905 Fax:(607)533-7908
E-mail: roseinn@clarityconnect.com
Web: www.roseinn.com

Circa 1851. This classic Italianate mansion has long been famous for its circular staircase of Honduran mahogany. It is owned by Sherry Rosemann, a noted interior designer specializing in mid-19th-century architecture and furniture, and her husband Charles, a hotelier from Germany. On 14 landscaped acres with a large formal garden and wedding chapel, it is 10 minutes from Cornell University. The inn has been the recipient of many awards for its lodging and dining, including a four-star rating seven years in a row.

Historic Interest: National Women's Hall of Fame (1 hour), Steuben Glass (1 hour), Cornell University.

Innkeeper(s): Charles & Sherry Rosemann. $115-320. MC, VISA. TAC10. 21 rooms, 8 with FP, 11 suites and 1 conference room. Breakfast included in rates. Types of meals: Full bkfst and early coffee/tea. Gourmet dinner, banquet service and catering service available. Restaurant on premises. Beds: KQDT. Phone, turndown service, ceiling fan and ten rooms have Jacuzzi's in room. Air conditioning. Fax, copier and library on premises. Weddings, small meetings, family reunions and seminars hosted. Antiquing, art galleries, beaches, bicycling, canoeing/kayaking, fishing, golf, hiking, horseback riding, live theater, museums, parks, shopping, downhill skiing, cross-country skiing, sporting events, tennis, water sports and wineries nearby.

"The blending of two outstanding talents, which when combined with your warmth, produce the ultimate experience in being away from home. Like staying with friends in their beautiful home."

Ithaca (Spencer)   G7

A Slice of Home B&B

178 N Main St
Ithaca (Spencer), NY 14883
(607)589-6073

Circa 1850. This Italianate inn's location, approximately equidistant from Ithaca and Watkins Glen, offers a fine vantage point for exploring the Finger Lakes winery region. Although

the area is well-known for its scenery, many recreational opportunities also are available. The innkeeper is happy to help guests plan tours and has a special fondness for those traveling by bicycle.

The inn offers five guest rooms, one with hot tub. Rooms are furnished in country decor. Guests may relax by taking a stroll on the inn's 10 acres, mountain hiking, biking or having a cookout in the inn's backyard. Guests can begin a cross-country ski excursion right from the back porch.

Innkeeper(s): Bea Brownell. $45-130. MC, VISA. TAC10. 4 rooms with PB and 1 cottage. Types of meals: Full bkfst and early coffee/tea. Snacks/refreshments and picnic lunch available. Beds: KQD. Cable TV in room. Air conditioning. VCR, copier, bicycles, cross-country skiing, horseshoes and badminton on premises. Weddings, small meetings, family reunions and seminars hosted. Limited German spoken. Antiquing, fishing, swimming, live theater, parks, shopping, downhill skiing, sporting events, water sports and wineries nearby. Pets Allowed.

Jay   C12

Book and Blanket B&B

Rt 9N, PO Box 164
Jay, NY 12941-0164
(518)946-8323

Circa 1855. This Adirondack bed & breakfast served as the town's post office for many years and also as barracks for state troopers. Thankfully, however, it is now a restful bed & breakfast catering to the literary set. Guest rooms are named for authors and there are books in every nook and cranny of the house. Guests may even take a book home with them. Each of the guest rooms is comfortably furnished. The inn is a short walk from the Jay Village Green and the original site of the Historic Jay covered bridge.

Innkeeper(s): Kathy, Fred, Sam & Daisy the Basset Hound. $55-75. AX, PC, TC. 3 rooms, 1 with PB. Breakfast, afternoon tea and snacks/refreshments included in rates. Types of meals: Full bkfst and early coffee/tea. Beds: QDT. Turndown service in room. VCR and library on premises. Family reunions and seminars hosted. Antiquing, fishing, Olympic venues i.e. bobsled, luge, ski jump, ice skating, parks, shopping, downhill skiing, cross-country skiing, sporting events, tennis and water sports nearby.

Jeffersonville   I10

The Griffin House

RR 1 Box 178
Jeffersonville, NY 12748-9710
(914)482-3371
E-mail: info@griffin-house.com
Web: www.griffin-house.com

Circa 1895. Visitors are in for a visual treat when they enter this three-story Victorian inn. The inn, which required five years to complete at the turn of the century, remains a shining example of the master craftsmanship evident in those days. Filled with gorgeous examples of hand-carved American chestnut, including the main staircase, the inn also has brick fireplaces, stained-glass windows and wooden floors. Often, guests are treated to a sample of the talents of the innkeepers, both world-class musicians, and musical touches are found throughout, including in the guest rooms.

Call for rates. Breakfast included in rates. Turndown service and ceiling fan in room. VCR and piano on premises. Weddings, small meetings, family reunions and seminars hosted. Antiquing, live theater, shopping, downhill skiing, cross-country skiing and sporting events nearby.

Lansing   G7

The Federal House B&B

175 Ludlowville Rd
Lansing, NY 14882
(607)533-7362 (800)533-7362 Fax:(607)533-7899
E-mail: innkeeper@clarityconnect.com
Web: www.wordpro.com/fedh/fh.htm

Circa 1815. Salmon Creek Falls, a well-known fishing spot, is yards away from the inn. The rooms are furnished with antiques, which complement the original woodwork and hand-carved fireplace mantels. Each of the suites includes a television and a fireplace.

Innkeeper(s): Diane Carroll. $55-175. MC, VISA, AX, DS, PC, TC. 4 rooms with PB, 2 with FP and 2 suites. Breakfast included in rates. Type of meal: Full bkfst. Beds: KQT. Air conditioning. Fishing, biking, wineries, Cayuga Lake and State Parks nearby.

Publicity: *Ithaca Journal, Cortland Paper.*

"Your inn is so charming and your food was excellent."

LeRoy   F4

Hidden Gardens B&B

15 E Main St
LeRoy, NY 14482-1209
(716)768-2294 (800)724-1932 Fax:(716)768-9386

Circa 1802. Nestled on nearly two acres, this early 19th-century shingled home is bedecked with rosy trim and shutters, and a Colonial-era American flag waves from its front entrance. The home is decorated with a mix of Colonial, traditional, country and more modern furnishings. Two guest rooms include a claw-foot tub. Breakfasts with homemade baked goods, homemade jams and savory egg dishes or perhaps French toast or pancakes are served on tables set with china, silver and crystal. Museums, parks, wineries and plenty of outdoor activities are nearby. Niagara Falls and the Canadian border are an hour's drive from the home.

Historic Interest: Genesee Country Village, Letchworth State Park.

Innkeeper(s): Rita Filowick/Judy Manley. $65-85. MC, VISA, AX, DS, PC, TC. 4 rooms with PB. Breakfast and snacks/refreshments included in rates. Types of meals: Full bkfst, country bkfst and early coffee/tea. Beds: DT. Ceiling fan in room. VCR, fax, copier, spa and library on premises. Small meetings, family reunions and seminars hosted. Amusement parks, antiquing, canoeing/kayaking, fishing, golf, museums, parks, shopping, cross-country skiing, sporting events and tennis nearby.

Pets allowed: guests must care for.

Lockport   F3

Hambleton House B&B

130 Pine St
Lockport, NY 14094-4402
(716)439-9507

Circa 1850. A carriage maker was the first owner of this mid-19th-century home, and it remained in his family for several generations. The home maintains an old-fashioned appeal with its mix of country and traditional furnishings. Main

Street and the Erie Barge Canal locks are a short walk away, and Buffalo and Niagara Falls are within a half-hour drive.

Innkeeper(s): Ted Hambleton. $50-85. MC, VISA, PC, TC. TAC5. 3 rooms with PB. Breakfast included in rates. MAP. Type of meal: Cont plus. Beds: DT. Air conditioning. Weddings, small meetings and family reunions hosted. Antiquing, fishing, live theater, parks and water sports nearby.

Niagara Falls   F3

The Cameo Manor North

3881 Lower River Rd, Rt 18-F
Niagara Falls, NY 14174
(716)745-3034
E-mail: cameoinn@juno.com
Web: www.cameoinn.com

Circa 1860. This Colonial Revival inn offers a restful setting ideal for those seeking a peaceful getaway. The inn's three secluded acres add to its romantic setting, as does an interior that features several fireplaces. Visitors select from three suites, which feature private sun rooms, or two guest rooms that share a bath. Popular spots with guests include the library, great room and solarium. Fort Niagara and several state parks are nearby, and the American and Canadian Falls are within easy driving distance of the inn. The inn is actually located about eight miles north of Niagara Falls near the village of Youngstown.

Innkeeper(s): Gregory Fisher. $75-175. 5 rooms. Breakfast included in rates. Type of meal: Full bkfst. Beds: QDT. TV in room. Air conditioning. Amusement parks, antiquing, fishing, live theater, shopping, downhill skiing, cross-country skiing, sporting events and water sports nearby.

"I made the right choice when I selected Cameo."

Manchester House B&B

653 Main St
Niagara Falls, NY 14301-1701
(716)285-5717 (800)489-3009 Fax:(716)282-2144

Circa 1903. This turn-of-the-century home once was used to house doctors' offices. The home, just a mile from the famous falls, and the innkeepers are full of knowledge about their famous local attraction. The home is decorated with comfortable furnishings, family pieces and antiques. Prints and posters depicting scenes of the Niagara Falls area also decorate the home.

Innkeeper(s): Lis & Carl Slenk. $70-100. MC, VISA, TC. TAC10. 3 rooms with PB. Breakfast included in rates. Type of meal: Full bkfst. Beds: KQT. Ceiling fan in room. Air conditioning. VCR and library on premises. Weddings, small meetings, family reunions and seminars hosted. German spoken. Amusement parks, antiquing, fishing, parks and shopping nearby.

"Thanks for a wonderful stay. All your little extras make for a warm homey feeling. Breakfast knocked our socks off."

North River   D11

Highwinds Inn

Barton Mines Rd
North River, NY 12856
(518)251-3760 (800)241-1923
E-mail: highwinds@barton.com
Web: highwindsinn.com

Circa 1933. This mountain retreat offers panoramic views of the Siamese wilderness area and the Adirondacks. Every room has a view of the mountains. The inn offers a garnet stone fireplace and a view of the sunset on the dining porch.

Innkeeper(s): Holly Currier. $150-180. MC, VISA, DS. 4 rooms with PB. Breakfast and dinner included in rates. MAP. Type of meal: Full bkfst. Picnic lunch available. Restaurant on premises. Beds: KD. Cross country skiing and snowshoes on premises. Weddings, small meetings, family reunions and seminars hosted. Antiquing, fishing, golf, swimming, canoe, mountain bikes, & hiking, live theater, shopping, downhill skiing and tennis nearby.

Oneida Castle
F9

Governors House Bed & Breakfast

50 Seneca Ave
Oneida Castle, NY 13421-2558
(315)363-5643 (800)437-8177 Fax:(315)363-9568

Circa 1848. Built in the hopes of becoming the first residence for the Governor of New York State, this brick Federal house sits on two acres. The inn's finely crafted architecture includes features such as a mansard roof, elegant cupola and handsome porches. Antiques and canopy beds enhance most of the guest rooms, and there are two parlors, a library and a guest kitchen.
Innkeeper(s): Dawn E. Andrews. $76-143. MC, VISA, AX, DC, CB, DS, PC, TC. TAC15. 4 rooms with PB, 1 suite and 1 conference room. Breakfast, afternoon tea and snacks/refreshments included in rates. Types of meals: Full gourmet bkfst and early coffee/tea. Banquet service, catering service and catered breakfast available. Beds: KQT. Cable TV and phone in room. Air conditioning. VCR, bicycles, library, child care and complimentary guest kitchen on premises. Handicap access. Weddings, small meetings, family reunions and seminars hosted. Amusement parks, antiquing, fishing, golf, rural driving and walking routes, live theater, parks, shopping, downhill skiing, cross-country skiing, sporting events, tennis and water sports nearby.

Penn Yan
G6

Finton's Landing on Keuka Lake

661 E Lake Rd
Penn Yan, NY 14527-9421
(315)536-3146

Circa 1861. A delightful Victorian located on Keuka Lake, the inn features relaxing front porch rockers, whimsical period furnishings, painted wall murals and parlor fireplace. The sunny east shore has 165 feet of secluded beach, a restored lakeside gazebo and a hammock. A luscious two-course breakfast is served in the cozy dining room or on the wraparound porch with its views of the lake.
Historic Interest: Located close to the Curtiss Museum of Early Aviation.
Innkeeper(s): Doug & Arianne Tepper. $99. MC, VISA, PC, TC. 4 rooms with PB. Breakfast included in rates. Type of meal: Full bkfst. Beds: DT. Ceiling fan in room. Air conditioning. Antiquing, fishing, golf, parks, shopping, downhill skiing, cross-country skiing, tennis, water sports and wineries nearby.

The Wagener Estate B&B

351 Elm St
Penn Yan, NY 14527-1446
(315)536-4591

Circa 1794. Nestled in the Finger Lakes area on four shaded acres, this 15-room house features a wicker-furnished veranda where guests can relax in solitude or chat with others. Some of the early hand-hewn framing and the original brick fireplace and oven can be seen in the Family Room at the north end of the house. Most of the land, which is known as Penn Yan, was once owned by the original occupants of the home, David Wagener and his wife, Rebecca. David died in 1799, leaving this property to his son, Squire Wagener, who is considered to be the founder of Penn Yan. Some rooms include air conditioning and a television. Gift certificates are available.

Historic Interest: Near the Oliver House and Birkett Mills.

Innkeeper(s): Joanne & Scott Murray. $75-95. MC, VISA, AX, DS, PC, TC. 6 rooms, 4 with PB. Gourmet dinner available. Beds: KQDT. TV in some rooms in room. Antiquing, fishing, parks, cross-country skiing, water sports and wineries nearby.

"Thanks so much for the wonderful hospitality and the magnificent culinary treats."

Pine City
H6

Rufus Tanner House

60 Sagetown Rd
Pine City, NY 14871-9502
(607)732-0213

Circa 1864. This Greek Revival farmhouse sits among century-old sugar maple trees. The grounds boast gardens and a small orchard with fruit and nut trees. The spacious rooms are filled with antiques and other period furnishings that add greatly to the inn's ambiance. Each of the three air-conditioned guest rooms has been decorated individually. The Sleigh Room, located on the first floor, includes a sleigh bed, Victorian furnishings and a bath with a two-person shower, Jacuzzi tub and black marble floor. The Empire Room includes a fireplace. Guests can enjoy a cup of morning coffee in front of a crackling fire in the living room or perhaps on the plant-filled sun porch. The Elmira-Corning area near the inn offers many attractions, including Elmira College, Mark Twain's Burial Site, the Finger Lakes, wineries, Watkins Glen Raceway, the National Soaring Museum, the Corning Glass Museum and the National Warplane Museum.
Innkeeper(s): Donna & Rick Powell. $65-95. MC, VISA, PC, TC. TAC10. 3 rooms. Types of meals: Full bkfst and early coffee/tea. Beds: QD. VCR on premises. Weddings, small meetings, family reunions and seminars hosted. Antiquing, fishing, golf, hiking, parks and downhill skiing nearby.
"Lovely house! Wish we could stay longer!"

Pine Island
H11

The Glenwood House B&B

49 Glenwood Rd
Pine Island, NY 10969
(914)258-5066 Fax:(914)258-4226
E-mail: glenwood@warwick.net
Web: www.glenwoodhouse.com

Circa 1855. Built prior to the Civil War, this restored Victorian farmhouse is secluded on more than two picturesque acres in New York's Pochuck Valley. The spacious front veranda is filled with comfortable wicker furnishings, inviting guests to relax and enjoy the country setting. Guest rooms are decorated with a romantic flair. Three rooms include canopied beds. Deluxe cottage suites include a whirlpool tub for two and a fireplace. Seasonal, farm-fresh fruits start off the breakfast service, which might include an entrée such as Texas-style French toast or buttermilk pancakes accompanied by bacon or sausage. The home is close to ski areas, golf courses, wineries, historic home tours and antique stores. The Appalachian Trail, Hudson River and Greenwood Lake are other nearby attractions.
Historic Interest: Goshen Historic Track & Trotter Museum, Historic Warwick Village.
Innkeeper(s): Andrea & Kevin Colman. $110-250. MC, VISA, AX, TC. 5 rooms, 2 with PB, 2 with FP, 1 suite, 2 cottages and 1 conference room. Breakfast included in rates. Meals: Full gourmet bkfst, country bkfst and early coffee/tea. Picnic lunch and room service available. Beds: KQ. Cable TV, ceiling fan and VCR in room. Air conditioning. Fax, copier and library on premises. Weddings, small meetings, family reunions and seminars hosted. Italian and German spoken. Amusement parks, antiquing, art galleries, beaches, bicycling, canoeing/kayaking, fishing, golf, hiking, horseback riding, live theater, museums, parks, shopping, downhill skiing, cross-country skiing, tennis, water sports and wineries nearby.

Queensbury   E12

The Crislip's B&B

693 Ridge Rd
Queensbury, NY 12804-6901
(518)793-6869

Circa 1802. This Federal-style house was built by Quakers and was once owned by the area's first doctor, who used it as a training center for young interns. There's an acre of lawns and annual gardens and a Victorian Italianate veranda overlooks the Green Mountains. The inn is furnished with 18th-century antiques and reproductions, including four-poster canopy beds and highboys.

There's a keeping room with a huge fireplace. Historic stone walls flank the property.

Innkeeper(s): Ned & Joyce Crislip. $55-85. MC, VISA, TC. 3 rooms with PB. Breakfast included in rates. Types of meals: Full bkfst and early coffee/tea. Beds: KD. Air conditioning. Small meetings hosted. Amusement parks, antiquing, fishing, civic center, live theater, parks, shopping, downhill skiing, cross-country skiing, sporting events and water sports nearby.

Red Hook   H12

The Grand Dutchess

50 N Broadway
Red Hook, NY 12571-1403
(914)758-5818 Fax:(914)758-3143

Circa 1874. This Second Empire Victorian was originally built as the Hoffman Inn. It later served as the town school, a speakeasy and then a lonely hearts club. Twin parlors behind etched glass and wood sliding doors feature hardwood floors, antique chandeliers, arched marble fireplaces with massive carved mirrors, Oriental rugs and heirloom antiques. Lace curtains decorate the floor-to-ceiling windows. Most of the rooms have queen-sized beds and private baths and are located at the corners of the home to maximize the use of natural light. A full breakfast of homemade breads, a main dish, cereal and fruit is offered. For young guests, the innkeeper will prepare chocolate chip pancakes.

Innkeeper(s): Elizabeth Pagano & Harold Gruber. $85-125. AX, PC, TC. 6 rooms, 4 with PB, 1 suite and 1 conference room. Breakfast included in rates. Types of meals: Full gourmet bkfst and early coffee/tea. Snacks/refreshments available. Beds: KQDT. Air conditioning. VCR, fax, copier and library on premises. Weddings, small meetings and family reunions hosted. Antiquing, fishing, golf, historic homes, Rhinebeck Aerodrome, live theater, parks, shopping, cross-country skiing and tennis nearby.
Publicity: Northeast, Gazette Advertiser, Poughkeepsie Journal.
"This place is outrageous! We love this place!"

Rhinebeck   I12

Beekman Arms-Delamater House

Rt 9, 4 Mill St
Rhinebeck, NY 12572
(914)876-7077
E-mail: beekmanarm@aol.com
Web: www.beekmanarms.com

Circa 1766. Said to be the oldest landmark inn in America, some walls of the Beekman Arms are two-and three-feet-thick.

It has seen a variety of guests-including pioneers, trappers, Indians and Dutch farmers. Among the famous were Aaron Burr, William Jennings Bryan, Horace Greeley, Franklin Roosevelt, Neil Armstrong and Elizabeth Taylor. Like most old taverns and inns, it provided a meeting place for leaders of the day. Victorian furnishings are found throughout. Mr. LaForge is the 28th innkeeper at Beekman Arms.

Innkeeper(s): Charles LaForge. $85-140. MC, VISA, AX, DC. 63 rooms with PB, 25 with FP and 1 conference room. Breakfast included in rates. Type of meal: Cont. Restaurant on premises. Beds: KQDT. TV and phone in room. Handicap access.

"If this is any indication of your general hospitality, it is very easy to see why you have stayed in the business for so long."

Mansakenning Carriage House

29 Ackert Hook Rd
Rhinebeck, NY 12572
(914)876-3500 Fax:(914)876-6179
E-mail: Innpeople@aol.com
Web: MCHRhinebeck.com

Circa 1895. Guests are sure to find this National Register Colonial a perfect country inn. Take a walk along the five acres, and you'll find hammocks strung between trees and chairs placed here and there for guests who wish to relax and enjoy the fragrant grounds. Step into any one of the seven guest rooms, and you'll instantly feel as though you've entered a cozy, romantic haven. Ralph Lauren linens dress the beds, which are topped with fluffy comforters. Exposed beams, fireplaces, wood floors and quilts add to the decor of the individually appointed guest rooms. Guests will find robes, specialty bath soaps, a coffee maker, refrigerator,and satellite TV with VCR in their rooms. Innkeeper Michelle Dremann has had several recipes featured in cookbooks, and it is she or the managing innkeeper that prepare the decadent morning feast. Guests have breakfast delivered to their room along with the morning paper. Rhinebeck is full of historic houses and buildings, as well guests can visit antique shops, galleries, wineries, restaurants.

Innkeeper(s): Michelle Dremann. $150-395. PC, TC. TAC10. 7 rooms with PB, 5 with FP and 5 suites. Breakfast included in rates. Type of meal: Full gourmet bkfst. Beds: KQ. Cable TV, phone, ceiling fan and VCR in room. Air conditioning. Fax, copier and library on premises. Weddings, small meetings and family reunions hosted. Fishing, golf, live theater, parks, shopping, downhill skiing, cross-country skiing, sporting events, tennis and water sports nearby.
Pets allowed: Two rooms only.

Olde Rhinebeck Inn

37 Wurtemburg Rd
Rhinebeck, NY 12572
(914)871-1745
E-mail: innkeeper@rhinebeckinn.com
Web: www.rhinebeckinn.com

Circa 1745. Located on three acres, this is a beautifully maintained early colonial farmhouse. The original buttermilk blue finishes remain and there is original hardware throughout. The innkeeper provides fine linens, antiques, fresh flowers and a breakfast that is served in the historic dining room. Offerings include sweet potato frittata, baked French pear and apple butter maple pecan muffins. There are miniature goats and a bass-stocked pond on the property.

Innkeeper(s): Jonna Paolella. $195-295. MC, VISA, PC, TC. TAC5. 3 rooms with PB. Breakfast included in rates. Type of meal: Full bkfst. Afternoon tea available. Beds: Q. Cable TV and satellite TV in room. Air conditioning. VCR and fax on premises. Antiquing, golf, parks and shopping nearby.

Veranda House B&B

82 Montgomery St
Rhinebeck, NY 12572-1113
(914)876-4133 Fax:(914)876-4133
E-mail: veranda82@aol.com
Web: www.verandahouse.com

Circa 1845. For nearly a century, this Federal-style home served as the parsonage for an Episcopal church. The home is located in a Rhinebeck historic district among many notable houses. The home is decorated in a comfortable mix of styles, with a few antiques. If weather permits, breakfasts are served on the terrace, featuring items such as freshly baked pastries or maple walnut coffee cake and a daily entree. The scenic area offers much in the way of activities. Woodstock is a short drive away.
Innkeeper(s): Linda & Ward Stanley. $90-130. PC, TC. 4 rooms with PB. Breakfast included in rates. Type of meal: Full gourmet bkfst. Beds: QT. Ceiling fan and clocks in room. Air conditioning. VCR and library on premises. Small meetings, family reunions and seminars hosted. Some German spoken. Antiquing, fishing, golf, hiking, live theater, parks, shopping, downhill skiing, cross-country skiing, tennis and water sports nearby.

"Beautiful rooms, terrific breakfast! We will recommend you highly."

Rochester   F5

"428 Mt. Vernon" - A B&B Inn

428 Mount Vernon Ave
Rochester, NY 14620-2710
(716)271-0792 (800)836-3159

Circa 1917. Victorian furnishings and decor grace the interior of this stately Irish manor house. Set on two lush acres of shade trees and foliage, this secluded spot is perfect for guests in search of relaxation. Guests can create their morning meals from a varied breakfast menu. The inn is adjacent to Highland Park, a perfect spot for a picnic or birdwatching.
Innkeeper(s): Philip & Claire Lanzatella. $115. MC, VISA, AX, TC. 7 rooms with PB, 3 with FP and 1 conference room. Breakfast included in rates. Types of meals: Full gourmet bkfst and early coffee/tea. Catering service and room service available. Beds: QDT. Cable TV, phone, turndown service and ceiling fan in room. Air conditioning. Weddings, small meetings and seminars hosted. Amusement parks, antiquing, live theater, parks, shopping and cross-country skiing nearby.

"Everything was wonderful, they took care in every detail."

A Bed & Breakfast at Dartmouth House Inn

215 Dartmouth St
Rochester, NY 14607-3202
(716)271-7872 Fax:(716)473-0778
E-mail: stay@DartmouthHouse.com
Web: www.DartmouthHouse.com

Circa 1905. The lavish, four-course breakfasts served daily at this beautiful turn-of-the-century Edwardian home are unforgettable. Innkeeper and award-winning, gourmet cook Ellie Klein starts off the meal with special fresh juice, which is served in the parlor. From this point, guests are seated at the candlelit dining table to enjoy a series of delectable dishes, such as poached pears, a mouth-watering entree, a light, lemon ice and a rich dessert. And each of the courses is served on a separate pattern of Depression Glass. If the breakfast isn't enough, Ellie and husband,

Bill, an electrical engineer, have stocked the individually decorated bathrooms with fluffy towels and bathrobes and guests can soak in inviting clawfoot tubs. Each of the bedchambers boasts antique collectibles and fresh flowers. The inn is located in the prestigious turn-of-the-century Park Avenue Historical and Cultural District. The entire area is an architect's dream. Museums, colleges, Eastman School of Music, Highland Park, restaurants and antique shops are among the many nearby attractions.
Historic Interest: George Eastman's Mansion and International Museum of Photography is a 10-minute walk from the inn. The High Falls Brown's Race Historic Center is two miles, the graves of Susan B. Anthony and Frederick Douglass are two miles away at Mount Hope Cemetery. The Rochester Historical Society is a 10-minute walk.
Innkeeper(s): Elinor & Bill Klein. $85-125. MC, VISA, AX, PC, TC. TAC10. 4 rooms with PB. Breakfast included in rates. Types of meals: Full bkfst and early coffee/tea. Beds: KQT. TV, phone, ceiling fan, VCR, robe, tape deck and lighted makeup mirror in room. Air conditioning. Fax, bicycles and library on premises. Antiquing, complimentary pass to fitness club, museums, George Eastman Int'l Museum of Photography within walking distance, live theater, museums, parks and shopping nearby.

"The food was fabulous, the company fascinating, and the personal attention beyond comparison. You made me feel at home instantly."

Saratoga Springs   F12

Adelphi Hotel

365 Broadway
Saratoga Springs, NY 12866-3111
(518)587-4688 (800)860-4086 Fax:(518)587-4688

Circa 1877. This Victorian hotel is one of two hotels still remaining from Saratoga's opulent spa era. A piazza overlooking Broadway features three-story columns topped with Victorian fretwork. Recently refurbished with lavish turn-of-the-century decor, rooms are filled with antique furnishings, opulent draperies and wall coverings, highlighting the inn's high ceilings and ornate woodwork. Breakfast is delivered to each room in the morning. There is an inviting swimming pool in the back garden.
Innkeeper(s): Sheila Parkert. $95-300. MC, VISA, AX. TAC10. 39 rooms with PB, 18 suites and 1 conference room. Breakfast included in rates. Type of meal: Cont plus. Restaurant on premises. Beds: QDT. Cable TV, phone and turndown service in room. Air conditioning. Weddings and small meetings hosted. Antiquing, golf, live theater, parks and shopping nearby.
Publicity: *New York Times, Country Inns, Back Roads, Conde Nast, Victorian Homes.*

Chestnut Tree Inn

9 Whitney Pl
Saratoga Springs, NY 12866-4518
(518)587-8681

Circa 1870. Linger over breakfast as you sit and enjoy the view from a wicker-filled veranda at this Second Period Empire-style house. The grounds boast what is thought to be the last live chestnut tree in the city. The innkeepers are antique dealers, who operate a local group shop. They have filled the home with turn-of-the-century pieces and have won awards for the preservation of their inn and for having the "best front porch" in Saratoga. The home is within walking distance of the race track, downtown shopping, only a mile from the Saratoga Performing Arts Center and the State Park where guests can enjoy mineral baths.
Historic Interest: The Canfield Casino, a restored local gambling house with a museum on the second floor, is two blocks from the inn. Saratoga Battlefield is about 10 miles away.
Innkeeper(s): Cathleen & Bruce De Luke. $85-275. MC, VISA, PC. 10 rooms, 8 with PB. Breakfast included in rates. Type of meal: Cont plus. Beds: QDT. Antiquing, fishing, live theater and water sports nearby.
Publicity: *New York Times.*

Six Sisters B&B

149 Union Ave
Saratoga Springs, NY 12866-3518
(518)583-1173 Fax:(518)587-2470
E-mail: stay@sixsistersbandb.com
Web: www.sixsistersbandb.com

Circa 1880. The unique architecture of this Victorian home features a large second-story bay window, a tiger oak front door decked with stained glass and a veranda accentuated with rocking chairs. Inside, the marble and hardwoods combine with antiques and Oriental rugs to create an elegant atmosphere. During racing season, guests can rise early and take a short walk to the local race track to watch the horses work out. Upon their return,  guests are greeted with the aroma of a delicious, gourmet breakfast. A 10-minute walk to Saratoga Springs' downtown area offers antique shops, boutiques and many restaurants.

Historic Interest: Saratoga Battlefield (15 minutes), Spa State Park (5 minutes), Saratoga Racetrack (across street).

Innkeeper(s): Kate Benton. $75-300. MC, VISA, AX, DS, PC, TC. TAC10. 4 rooms with PB. Breakfast included in rates. Types of meals: Full gourmet bkfst and early coffee/tea. Beds: KQ. Cable TV, ceiling fan, three rooms with private balcony and whirlpool in room. Air conditioning. Fax on premises. Amusement parks, antiquing, fishing, spa and mineral baths, museums, live theater, parks, shopping, downhill skiing, cross-country skiing, sporting events and water sports nearby.

Publicity: *Gourmet, Country Inns, Country Folk Art, Country Victorian, McCalls, New York Times.*

Westchester House B&B

102 Lincoln Ave
Saratoga Springs, NY 12866-4536
(518)587-7613 (800)581-7613
E-mail: westchester@netheaven.com
Web: www.westchesterhousebandb.com

Circa 1885. This gracious Queen Anne Victorian has been welcoming vacationers for more than 100 years. Antiques from four generations of the Melvin family grace the high-ceilinged rooms. Oriental rugs top gleaming wood floors, while antique clocks and lace curtains set a graceful tone. Guests gather on the wraparound porch, in the parlors or gardens for an afternoon refreshment  of old-fashioned lemonade. Many attractions are within walking distance.

Historic Interest: Built by master carpenter Almeron King in 1885.

Innkeeper(s): Bob & Stephanie Melvin. $90-275. MC, VISA, AX, PC, TC. TAC10. 7 rooms with PB and 1 conference room. Breakfast and afternoon tea included in rates. Types of meals: Cont plus and early coffee/tea. Beds: KQT. TV and ceiling fan in room. Air conditioning. Fax, copier, library, baby grand piano, data ports, voice mail and on premises. Small meetings, family reunions and seminars hosted. Antiquing, fishing, opera, ballet, horse racing, race track, Saratoga Performing Arts Center, live theater, parks, shopping, cross-country skiing, sporting events and water sports nearby.

Publicity: *Getaways for Gourmets, Albany Times Union, Saratogian, Capital, Country Inns, New York Daily News, WNYT, Newsday, Hudson Valley.*

"I adored your B&B and have raved about it to all. One of the most beautiful and welcoming places we've ever visited."

Saratoga Springs (Ballston Spa) F12

Apple Tree B&B

49 W High St
Saratoga Springs (Ballston Spa), NY 12020-1912
(518)885-1113 Fax:(518)885-9758

Circa 1878. A pond, waterfall and a garden decorate the entrance to this Second Empire Victorian, which is located in the historic district of Ballston Spa, a village just a few minutes from Saratoga Springs. Guest rooms feature Victorian and French-country decor, and each has antiques and whirlpool tubs. Guests enjoy fresh fruit, homemade baked goods, a selection of beverages and a daily entree during the breakfast service.

Innkeeper(s): Dolores & Jim Taisey. $75-175. MC, VISA, AX, PC, TC. TAC10. 4 rooms with PB. Breakfast included in rates. Types of meals: Full bkfst and early coffee/tea. Beds: Q. Cable TV, VCR and whirlpool in room. Air conditioning. Small meetings and family reunions hosted. Amusement parks, antiquing, fishing, Saratoga Race Course, live theater, parks, shopping, downhill skiing, cross-country skiing, sporting events and water sports nearby.

Sodus   E6

Maxwell Creek Inn

7563 Lake Rd
Sodus, NY 14551-9309
(315)483-2222 (800)315-2206

Circa 1840. This historic cobblestone house rests on six acres with panoramic views of Lake Ontario, Maxwell Bay and Maxwell Creek. Its surrounded by a wooded wildlife preserve and apple orchards. Said to have been a part of the Underground Railroad, the property includes a historic flour mill where grains were ground and sent off to ships in Maxwell Bay, then traded for ale and wheat. There are hiking trails, a fishing stream, tennis courts and canoe rentals  on the premises. The accommodations include five guest rooms in the main house and Cobblestone Cottage, a former carriage house, which includes five single beds, a sofa bed, fireplace, fireside sitting area, dining area, kitchenette and bath. Guests are treated to a full breakfast served in a rustic wood-paneled dining room with a unique fireplace.

Innkeeper(s): Patrick & Belinda McElroy. $65-145. MC, VISA, DS, PC, TC. 6 rooms with PB, 2 suites, 1 cottage and 1 conference room. Breakfast included in rates. Type of meal: Full bkfst. Beds: KQDT. Tennis, library, fishing creek, hiking and player piano on premises. Weddings, small meetings, family reunions and seminars hosted. Amusement parks, antiquing, canoeing/kayaking, fishing, hiking, fall foliage train rides nearby, snowmobiling, parks, shopping, downhill skiing, cross-country skiing and water sports nearby.

Publicity: *Atlanta Journal, Newman Times.*

"The best food I've ever tasted."

Sodus Point

E6

Carriage House Inn

8375 Wickham Blvd
Sodus Point, NY 14555-9608
(315)483-2100 (800)292-2990 Fax:(315)483-2100

Circa 1870. The innkeeper at this inn offers accommodations in a historic Victorian home located on four acres in a residential area or in the stone carriage house on the shore of Lake Ontario. The carriage house overlooks the lake and Sodus Point historic lighthouse. The inn offers beach access, and guests can walk to restaurants and charter boats. For an additional cost, the inn will provide sandwiches and thermos.

Historic Interest: The Sodus Point historic lighthouse is adjacent to the inn.
Innkeeper(s): James Den Decker. $70-90. MC, VISA, AX, DC, DS, PC. 8 rooms with PB. Breakfast included in rates. Type of meal: Full bkfst. Beds: KT. Cable TV and telephone available in room. Antiquing, fishing, golf and water sports nearby.

Sodus Bay-Wolcott

F7

Bonnie Castle Farm B&B

PO Box 188
Sodus Bay-Wolcott, NY 14590-0188
(315)587-2273 (800)587-4006 Fax:(315)587-4003

Circa 1887. This large, waterfront home is surrounded by expansive lawns and trees, which overlook the east side of Great Sodus Bay, a popular resort at the turn of the century.

Accommodations include a suite and large guest rooms with water views. Other rooms feature wainscoting and cathedral ceilings. A full, gourmet breakfast includes a cereal bar, fresh fruit and juices and an assortment of entrees such as Orange Blossom French toast, sausages, a creamy potato casserole and fresh-baked pastries topped off with teas and Irish creme coffee. Guests can visit many nearby attractions, such as the Renaissance Festival, Erie Canal and Chimney Bluffs State Park.

Historic Interest: Dozens of historic sites await guests at the Bonnie Castle Farm, including the Everson Museum, Susan B. Anthony House, National Women's Hall of Fame, William Phelps General Store Museum, the Sodus Point Maritime Museum, Renaissance Faire and others.
Innkeeper(s): Eric & Georgia Pendleton. $85-160. MC, VISA, AX, DS, PC, TC. TAC10. 8 rooms with PB and 1 suite. Breakfast included in rates. Type of meal: Full gourmet bkfst. Beds: KQD. Cable TV, ceiling fan and VCR in room. Air conditioning. Fax, copier, spa and swimming on premises. Small meetings, family reunions and seminars hosted. Antiquing, fishing, live theater, parks, shopping, downhill skiing, cross-country skiing, sporting events and water sports nearby.

"We love Bonnie Castle. You have a magnificent establishment. We are just crazy about your place. Hope to see you soon."

Southold

K15

Goose Creek Guesthouse

1475 Waterview Dr, PO Box 377
Southold, NY 11971
(516)765-3356

Circa 1860. Grover Pease left for the Civil War from this house, and after his death, his widow, Harriet, ran a summer boarding house here. The basement actually dates from the 1780s and is constructed of large rocks. The present house was moved here and put on the older foundation. Southold has many beaches and historic homes (a guidebook is provided for visitors).

The inn is close to the ferry to New London and the ferries to the South Shore via Shelter Island.

Historic Interest: Hortons Point Lighthouse, Railroad and Maritime Museum.
Innkeeper(s): Mary Mooney-Getoff. $70-95. PC, TC. TAC10. 4 rooms. Breakfast and afternoon tea included in rates. Types of meals: Full gourmet bkfst, country bkfst and early coffee/tea. Picnic lunch available. Beds: KQDT. TV, phone, back rests and feather beds in room. Air conditioning. VCR, library and collection of local books on premises. Family reunions hosted. Spanish spoken. Amusement parks, antiquing, beaches, fishing, live theater, museums, parks, shopping and water sports nearby.

"We will be repeat guests. Count on it!!"

Stillwater

F12

Lee's Deer Run B&B

411 CR 71
Stillwater, NY 12170
(518)584-7722

Circa 1850. In an idyllic countryside setting between Saratoga Lake and Saratoga National Historic Park, this inn, crafted from an 18th-century barn, now is home to four guest rooms, some with four-poster beds. The inn's full breakfasts are served in the dining room or on a deck with a view of the surrounding area. Bennington Battlefield and the Willard Mountain Ski Area are nearby. Saratoga Springs is a 10-minute drive, and Saratoga National Veterans Cemetery is two minutes away.

Innkeeper(s): Rose & Don Lee. $85-250. PC. TAC10. 4 rooms with PB, 2 suites and 1 conference room. Breakfast included in rates. Types of meals: Full bkfst and early coffee/tea. Beds: KQ. Turndown service and ceiling fan in room. Air conditioning. VCR on premises. Amusement parks, antiquing, fishing, golf, Saratoga National Park - 2 minutes away, live theater, parks, shopping, downhill skiing, cross-country skiing, sporting events, tennis and water sports nearby.

Syracuse

F8

Giddings Garden Bed & Breakfast

290 W Seneca Tpke
Syracuse, NY 13207-2639
(315)492-6389 (800)377-3452
E-mail: giddingsb-b@webtv.net
Web: www.giddingsgarden.com

Circa 1810. Formerly Giddings Tavern, this historic federal-style home offers three guest rooms. The Honey Room features a white iron poster bed and a fireplace, as well as a unique private bath with a marble floor and a marble mirrored shower. The Executive Room is decorated in leather and black moiré fabric with mahogany furnishings, or you might prefer the Country Garden Room with a lace canopy and floral décor. All have marble baths, and there are fireplaces. In the morning, try the menu with Baked Apple Flowers and maple syrup, creamed eggs and hollandaise sauce in a filo cup, and strawberry-filled chocolate cups served with Grand Marnier. Afterwards, relax on the old stone patio that overlooks a fishpond or stroll around the inn's gardens.

Innkeeper(s): Pat & Nancy Roberts. $80-150. MC, VISA, AX, DS, TC. TAC5. 3 rooms with PB. Breakfast included in rates. Types of meals: Full gourmet bkfst and early coffee/tea. Beds: Q. Cable TV, phone and refrigerator in hall in room. Air conditioning. VCR on premises. Small meetings hosted. Antiquing, fishing, golf, live theater, parks, shopping, downhill skiing, cross-country skiing, sporting events, tennis and water sports nearby.

Utica
F9

Adam Bowman Manor

197 Riverside Dr
Utica, NY 13502-2322
(315)738-0276 Fax:(315)738-0276

Circa 1823. The founder of Deerfield, George Weaver, built this graceful brick Federal house for his daughter. It is said to have been a part of the Underground Railroad (there's a secret tunnel) and is in the National Register.
Handsomely landscaped grounds include a fountain, a gazebo, tall oaks and borders of perennials. The late Duke and Dutchess of Windsor were guests here and there are rooms named for them.

The Duke's room has French-country furniture, a hand-painted fireplace and a king bed. Enjoy the Drawing Room and library, and in the morning guests are offered a full breakfast in the dining room with china, crystal and silver.

Innkeeper(s): Marion & Barry Goodwin. $40-75. MC, VISA, PC, TC. TAC10. 4 rooms, 2 with PB, 2 with FP. Breakfast included in rates. Types of meals: Full bkfst, cont plus and cont. Beds: KQD. Air conditioning. VCR, fax and library on premises. Weddings, small meetings and family reunions hosted. Some French and Italian. some spanish spoken. Antiquing, golf, live theater, parks, shopping, downhill skiing, cross-country skiing, tennis and water sports nearby.

"Great company, good food and new friends for us."

Warrensburg
E12

Country Road Lodge B&B

115 Hickory Hill Rd
Warrensburg, NY 12885-3912
(518)623-2207 Fax:(518)623-4363
E-mail: parisibb@netheaven.com
Web: www.countryroadlodge.com

Circa 1929. This simple, rustic farmhouse lodge is situated on 35 acres along the Hudson River at the end of a country road. Rooms are clean and comfortable. A full breakfast is provided with homemade breads and muffins. The sitting room reveals panoramic views of the river and Sugarloaf Mountain. Bird watching, hiking and skiing are popular activities. Groups often reserve all four guest rooms.

Historic Interest: French and Indian War battlefields, Fort William Henry, Ticonderoga, and Defiance, Millionaire's Row on Lake George.

Innkeeper(s): Sandi & Steve Parisi. $55-62. PC. TAC10. 4 rooms, 2 with PB.

Breakfast included in rates. Types of meals: Full bkfst and early coffee/tea. Beds: DT. Ceiling fan in room. Air conditioning. Amusement parks, antiquing, fishing, live theater, parks, shopping, downhill skiing, cross-country skiing and water sports nearby.

Publicity: North Jersey Herald & News.

"Homey, casual atmosphere. We really had a wonderful time. You're both wonderful hosts and the Lodge is definitely our kind of B&B! We will always feel very special about this place and will always be back."

House on The Hill B&B

Rt 28 PO Box 248
Warrensburg, NY 12885
(518)623-9390 (800)221-9390 Fax:(518)623-9396
E-mail: mail@houseonthehillbb.com
Web: www.houseonthehillbb.com

Circa 1750. This historic Federal-style inn sits on a hill in the six million-acre Adirondack Park and offers four guest rooms with private jet tub baths and showers. After guests are treated to coffee and baked goods in their rooms, they enjoy the inn's full breakfasts in the sunroom, which offers wonderful views of the surrounding fields and woods from its many windows. Cross-country skiing, snowshoeing, biking and hiking may be enjoyed on the spacious grounds, covering 176 acres. Gore Mountain and Whiteface Olympic ski areas are close by, and Lake George is a 10-minute drive.

Historic Interest: The site for the novel "Last of the Mohicans," is nearby, as are French & Indian and Revolutionary war sites. Archaeological digs are in progress.

Innkeeper(s): Joe & Lynn Rubino. $99-149. MC, VISA, AX, DC, CB, DS, PC, TC. TAC4. 4 rooms, 3 with PB. Breakfast included in rates. Types of meals: Full bkfst and early coffee/tea. Beds: Q. Air conditioning. VCR and fax on premises. Handicap access. Weddings, small meetings, family reunions and seminars hosted. French and Italian also spoken spoken. Amusement parks, antiquing, fishing, live theater, parks, shopping, downhill skiing, cross-country skiing, sporting events and water sports nearby.

Publicity: Chronicle, Post Star, G.F. Business Journal, Country Victorian, Journal America.

Warwick
J11

Warwick Valley Bed & Breakfast

24 Maple Ave
Warwick, NY 10990-1025
(914)987-7255 Fax:(914)988-5318

Circa 1900. This turn-of-the-century Colonial Revival is located in Warwick's historic district among many of the town's other historic gems. The B&B includes four guest rooms decorated with antiques and country furnishings. Breakfasts are a treat with entrees such as eggs Benedict, apple pancakes or a savory potato, cheese and egg bake. Wineries, antique shops and many outdoor activities are nearby, and innkeeper Loretta Orenstein is happy to point guests in the right direction.

Innkeeper(s): Loretta Orenstein. $100-125. MC, VISA, AX, PC, TC. TAC15. 4 rooms with PB. Breakfast included in rates. Types of meals: Full gourmet bkfst and early coffee/tea. Beds: KQT. TV, phone and sitting area in room. Central air. VCR, fax, copier and bicycles on premises. Family reunions hosted. Amusement parks, antiquing, fishing, golf, wineries, live theater, parks, shopping, downhill skiing, cross-country skiing, sporting events, tennis and water sports nearby.

Westhampton Beach K14

1880 House Bed & Breakfast

PO Box 648
Westhampton Beach, NY 11978-0648
(516)288-1559 (800)346-3290 Fax:(516)288-7696

Circa 1880. On Westhampton Beach's exclusive Seafield Lane, this country estate includes a pool and tennis court, and it is just a short walk to the ocean. The inn is decorated with Victorian antiques, Shaker benches, and Chinese porcelain, creating a casual, country inn atmosphere.

Innkeeper(s): Elsie Collins.
$150-200. MC, VISA, AX.
3 suites. Breakfast included in rates. Type of meal: Full bkfst. Afternoon tea available. Beds: QD. Weddings, small meetings, family reunions and seminars hosted. Antiquing and live theater nearby.

"From the moment we stepped inside your charming home we felt all the warmth you sent our way which made our stay so comfortable and memorable."

Wilmington C12

Willkommen Hof

Rt 86, PO Box 240
Wilmington, NY 12997
(518)946-7669 (800)541-9119 Fax:(518)946-7626
E-mail: willkommenhof@whiteface.net
Web: lakeplacid.net/willkommenhof

Circa 1925. This turn-of-the-century farmhouse served as an inn during the 1920s, but little else is known about its past. The innkeepers have created a cozy atmosphere, perfect for relaxation after a day exploring the Adirondack Mountain area. A large selection of books and a roaring fire greet guests who choose to settle down in the reading room. The innkeepers also offer a large selection of movies. Relax in the sauna or outdoor spa or simply enjoy the comfort of your bedchamber.

Historic Interest: Visit a covered bridge in Jay, just four miles away or cruise the Whiteface Memorial Highway, which is just a few miles away. Lake Placid, the site of the 1932 and 1980 Olympics, offers much to see and do.
Innkeeper(s): Heike & Bert Yost. $57-154. MC, VISA, PC, TC. TAC7. 6 rooms, 3 with PB and 1 suite. Breakfast and afternoon tea included in rates. EP. Type of meal: Full bkfst. Gourmet dinner available. Beds: KQDT. Ceiling fan and one room with whirlpool bath in room. VCR, fax, spa, sauna, bicycles and pet boarding on premises. Weddings, small meetings and family reunions hosted. German spoken. Antiquing, fishing, rock climbing, mountain biking, parks, shopping, downhill skiing, cross-country skiing and water sports nearby.

Pets allowed: Pets must stay in kennel when guests are gone. Kennels available for rent.

"Vielen Dank! Alles war sehr schoen and the breakfasts were delicious."

Windham H11

Albergo Allegria B&B

Rt 296, PO Box 267
Windham, NY 12496-0267
(518)734-5560 Fax:(518)734-5570
E-mail: mail@albergousa.com
Web: www.albergousa.com

Circa 1892. Two former boarding houses were joined to create this luxurious, Victorian bed & breakfast whose name means "the inn of happiness." Guest quarters, laced with a Victorian theme, are decorated with period wallpapers and antique furnishings. One master suite includes an enormous Jacuzzi tub. There are plenty of relaxing options at Albergo Allegria, including a rustic lounge with a large fireplace and overstuffed couches. A second-story library, decorated with plants and wicker

furnishings, is still another location to relax with a good book. Guests also can choose from more than 300 videos in the innkeeper's movie collection. Located just a few feet behind the inn are the Carriage House Suites, each of which includes a double whirlpool tub, gas fireplaces, king-size beds and cathedral ceilings with skylights. The innkeepers came to the area to open LaGriglia, a deluxe, gourmet restaurant just across the way from the bed & breakfast. Their command of cuisine is evident each morning as guests feast on a variety of home-baked muffins and pastries, gourmet omelets, waffles and other tempting treats. The inn is a registered historic site.

Historic Interest: Blenheim Bridge, the longest covered wooden bridge of its kind in the United States, is about a half hour from the inn, as is Olana Castle.
Innkeeper(s): Vito & Lenore Radelich. $73-233. MC, VISA, TC. 21 rooms with PB, 8 with FP and 9 suites. Breakfast included in rates. Type of meal: Full gourmet bkfst. Afternoon tea and gourmet dinner available. Beds: KQT. Cable TV, phone, ceiling fan and VCR in room. Air conditioning. Fax, copier and bicycles on premises. Handicap access. Weddings, small meetings & seminars hosted. Italian, African & Croatin spoken. Amusement parks, antiquing, fishing, tennis, hiking, waterfalls, mountain biking, parks, shopping, skiing & water sports nearby.
Publicity: Yankee.

Danske Hus

361 South St, PO Box 893
Windham, NY 12496
(518)734-6335

Circa 1865. Located just across the road from Ski Windham and nestled between two golf courses, this farmhouse-style inn offers countryside and mountain views to its guests, as well as a taste of Scandinavian hospitality. Breakfast may be enjoyed in the heirloom-filled dining room or outside on a picturesque deck complete with the sounds of a babbling brook. Guests also enjoy a large living room, piano, wood-burning fireplace and a sauna. The Catskills provide many other tourist attractions, including caverns, fairs and ethnic festivals, as well as shopping, antiquing and sporting activities. The innkeeper welcomes families with children, and with prior arrangement, dogs may be allowed.
Innkeeper(s): Barbara Jensen. $65-95. AX, DS. 4 rooms, 3 with PB. Breakfast and afternoon tea included in rates. Meal: Full bkfst. Beds: KQDT. Air conditioning. Sauna and library on premises. Small meetings and family reunions hosted. Danish spoken. Amusement parks, antiquing, fishing, horseback riding, golf, hiking, parks, shopping, downhill skiing, cross-country skiing & water sports nearby.
Pets allowed: Dogs only.

"Your warm and cozy home is surpassed only by your warm and friendly smile. Breakfast - Wow - it can't be beat!"

North Carolina

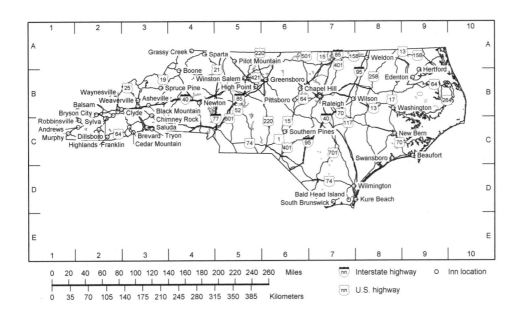

	1	2	3	4	5	6	7	8	9	10

Grassy Creek · Sparta · 220 · 501 · 15 · 85 · 158 · Weldon · 13 · 158
Boone · 21 · Pilot Mountain · 401 · 95 · Hertford
19 · Winston Salem · 421 · Greensboro · 258 · Edenton · 64
Spruce Pine · High Point · 85
Waynesville · 25 · Asheville · 40 · Chapel Hill · Wilson · 17 · Washington · 264
Balsam · Weaverville · Newton · 52 · Pittsboro · 64 · Raleigh · 70 · 13
Bryson City · Clyde · Black Mountain · 77 · 601 · 70
Robbinsville · Sylva · Chimney Rock · 220 · 15 · 40 · 117 · New Bern
Andrews · Saluda · 1 · Southern Pines · 70
Murphy · Dillsboro · 64 · Brevard · Tryon · 401 · 95 · Beaufort
Highlands · Franklin · Cedar Mountain · 74 · 701 · Swansboro
74 · Wilmington
Bald Head Island · Kure Beach
South Brunswick

0 20 40 60 80 100 120 140 160 180 200 220 240 260 Miles
0 35 70 105 140 175 210 245 280 315 350 385 Kilometers

(nn) Interstate highway   o Inn location
(nn) U.S. highway

Andrews   C2

The Cover House

173 Wilson St
Andrews, NC 28901-8657
(828)321-5302 (800)354-7642 Fax:(828)321-2145

Circa 1908. Mountain views and fine sunsets may be seen
from the porch of this large Four-Square house located on
almost two acres. There are polished hardwood floors, fireplaces with ornamental mantels and original woodwork.
Antique furnishings, Oriental rugs and a wonderful art collection fill the inn. A country breakfast of grits, homemade biscuits and gravy and scrambled eggs or quiche is served.

Innkeeper(s): Philip & Gayle Horton. $60-150. MC, VISA, AX, DC, DS, TC.
TAC15. 5 rooms, 3 with PB, 3 with FP and 1 cottage. Breakfast included in
rates. Types of meals: Full bkfst, cont and early coffee/tea. Beds: KQD.
Ceiling fan in room. Air conditioning. VCR and fax on premises. Handicap
access. Weddings, small meetings and family reunions hosted. Antiquing,
bicycling, fishing, golf, hiking, whitewater rafting and tennis nearby.

"A delightful place!! Wonderful place to visit."

Asheville   B3

Abbington Green B&B

46 Cumberland Cir
Asheville, NC 28801-1718
(828)251-2454 (800)251-2454 Fax:(828)251-2872

Circa 1908. Innkeeper Valerie Larrea has definitely put her
heart and soul into this bed & breakfast. When she discovered
the home, located in Asheville's Montfort Historic District, it
was desperately in need of a facelift. Through hard work, which
included putting in nine bathrooms and replacing the electrical
system and all the plumbing, she earned an award for the
restoration. The home sports an English-country decor, and
each guest room is named for a park or garden in England.
Antiques and reproductions furnish the home. An inventive
breakfast menu is pre-
pared each morning,
featuring gourmet tid-
bits such as home-
made pumpkin
bread, a warm cher-
ry soup and quiche
Florentine with

grilled sausage. The home was designed by a supervising architect during the building of the Biltmore Estate, which is nearby and open for tours. The inn also features award-winning gardens. The Blue Ridge Parkway and University of North Carolina also are near.

Innkeeper(s): Valerie, Julie & Gabrielle Larrea. $125-195. MC, VISA, AX, DS, PC, TC. TAC10. 6 rooms, 3 with FP and 1 cottage. Breakfast included in rates. Type of meal: Full bkfst. Beds: KQT. Ceiling fan in room. Air conditioning. VCR, fax, bicycles and library on premises. Antiquing, fishing, golf, white water rafting, live theater, parks, shopping, downhill skiing and tennis nearby.

"Our stay will always be a memorable part of our honeymoon. The breakfasts were outstanding."

Applewood Manor Inn

62 Cumberland Cir
Asheville, NC 28801-1718
(828)254-2244 (800)442-2197 Fax:(828)254-0899

Circa 1910. This is a spacious Colonial Revival house furnished comfortably with antiques. Guests can relax in front of the wood-burning fireplace or stroll the inn's two-acre grounds. Accommodations include four guest rooms and a cottage.

Cream-cheese omelets, orange French toast, blueberry pancakes or homemade waffles are some of the delectables that appear on the breakfast menu along with fresh fruits, juices and homemade breads.

Innkeeper(s): Coby & Johan Verhey. $95-115. MC, VISA, PC, TC. TAC10. 4 rooms with PB, 3 with FP and 1 cottage. Breakfast included in rates. Types of meals: Full bkfst and early coffee/tea. Beds: Q. Ceiling fan in room. Air conditioning. Fax, copier and bicycles on premises. Family reunions hosted. French, German and Dutch spoken. Antiquing, Biltmore Estate, live theater, parks and shopping nearby.

Publicity: *Country Inns, Innsider.*

"It goes without saying—the accommodations and breakfasts are outstanding!"

Asheville Accommodations Reservation Service

109 Circadian Way
Asheville, NC 27516
(919)929-5553 (800)770-9055 Fax:(919)929-5061
E-mail: carolinamorning@mindspring.com
Web: www.carolinamornings.com

This reservation service offers more than 100 lodging choices throughout North Carolina. More than a dozen lodgings are centered around Asheville and Great Smoky Mountains National Park. Other accommodations are located in the Raleigh-Durham and Winston-Salem areas. In addition to country inns and bed & breakfasts, also available are cabins, condominiums and lodges. Guest rooms range from deluxe suites with fireplaces and Jacuzzi tubs to more comfortable and economical accommodations. The service also offers a Biltmore Estate package where guests receive a two-night stay at a bed & breakfast, a tour of the Biltmore Estate, a guidebook written about the estate and a bottle of Biltmore Estate wine.

Historic Interest: Biltmore Estate.

$75-400. MC, VISA, AX, DS, PC, TC. Breakfast, afternoon tea and

snacks/refreshments included in rates. Types of meals: Full gourmet bkfst, cont plus, cont, country bkfst, veg bkfst and early coffee/tea. Restaurant on premises. Beds: KQDT. VCR, fax, copier, spa, swimming, sauna, stables, bicycles, tennis and library on premises. Handicap access. Weddings, small meetings and family reunions hosted. French spoken. Antiquing, art galleries, bicycling, canoeing/kayaking, fishing, golf, hiking, horseback riding, live theater, museums, parks, shopping, downhill skiing, cross-country skiing, tennis and wineries nearby.

Pets Allowed.

Beaufort House Victorian B&B

61 N Liberty St
Asheville, NC 28801-1829
(828)254-8334 (800)261-2221 Fax:(828)251-2082

Circa 1894. In the Queen Anne Victorian style, this inn rests on two acres of beautifully landscaped grounds, including a tea garden. Offering views of the mountains, the full wraparound porch is festooned with gingerbread trim. Most guest rooms feature Jacuzzi tubs. Ask for the Sarah Davidson Suite where light streams through a handsome fan window onto a king-size canopy bed decked in white Battenburg Lace. There is a sitting area with wing back chairs and a Queen Anne desk. Guests are pampered with a lavish, gourmet breakfast.

Innkeeper(s): Robert & Jacqueline Glasgow. $75-225. MC, VISA, PC, TC. TAC10. 11 rooms. Breakfast and afternoon tea included in rates. Types of meals: Full gourmet bkfst and early coffee/tea. Picnic lunch available. Beds: KQD. Cable TV, phone, ceiling fan and VCR in room. Air conditioning. Fax and bicycles on premises. Weddings, small meetings, family reunions and seminars hosted. Amusement parks, antiquing, fishing, golf, live theater, parks, shopping, downhill skiing, sporting events and tennis nearby.

Blake House Inn & Sycamore's Restaurant

150 Royal Pines Dr
Asheville, NC 28704
(828)681-5227 (888)353-5227 Fax:(828)681-0420
E-mail: blakeinn@aol.com
Web: www.blakehouse.com

Circa 1847. Built prior to the Civil War, this Gothic Italianate home was used as a Confederate field hospital during the Civil War. It also is rumored to have been a stop on the Underground Railroad. Each guest room is decorated with antiques, and three rooms include a fireplace. The Lilac Room includes both a fireplace and a clawfoot tub. Gourmet breakfasts include fresh fruit and homemade baked goods followed by an entrée such as egg-stuffed crepes in a tomato beurre blanc, sun-dried blueberry pancakes or perhaps Southern-style cheesy grits with bacon, sausage or country ham. In the evenings, guests are further pampered with hors d'oeuvres. Guests can enjoy a gourmet dinner at Sycamore's, the inn's restaurant. The inn is close to the Biltmore Estate and the scenic Blue Ridge Parkway.

Innkeeper(s): Nancy & Terry Rice. $95-225. MC, VISA, AX, DS, PC, TC. TAC10. 6 rooms, 5 with PB, 3 with FP, 1 suite and 3 conference rooms. Breakfast and snacks/refreshments included in rates. Types of meals: Full gourmet bkfst, cont, veg bkfst and early coffee/tea. Gourmet dinner, picnic lunch, banquet service, catering service and catered breakfast available. Restaurant on premises. Beds: KQD. Cable TV, phone and VCR in room. Fax and copier on premises. Weddings, small meetings, family reunions and seminars hosted. Amusement parks, antiquing, art galleries, bicycling, canoeing/kayaking, fishing, golf, hiking, horseback riding, live theater, museums, parks, shopping, downhill skiing, sporting events, tennis, water sports and wineries nearby.

Pets Allowed.

"Wonderful time, wonderful friends, and magnificent food every meal. This is a place to return to many times."

Cedar Crest Victorian Inns

674 Biltmore Ave
Asheville, NC 28803-2513
(828)252-1389 (800)252-0310 Fax:(828)253-7667
E-mail: Jack@cedarcrestvictorianinn.com
Web: www.cedarcrestvictorianinn.com

Circa 1891. This Queen Anne mansion is one of the largest and most opulent residences surviving Asheville's 1890s boom. A captain's walk, projecting turrets and expansive verandas wel-

come guests to lavish interior woodwork created by artisans employed by the Vanderbilts. All rooms are furnished in antiques with satin and lace trappings.

Historic Interest: The inn is in the National Register and is three blocks to the Biltmore Estate.

Innkeeper(s): Barbara & Jack McEwan. $145-210. MC, VISA, AX, DC, DS, PC, TC. 12 rooms with PB, 6 with FP, 3 suites and 1 cottage. Breakfast and snacks/refreshments included in rates. Type of meal: Full bkfst. Beds: QD. TV, phone, turndown service and ceiling fan in room. Air conditioning. Fax on premises. Amusement parks, antiquing, fishing, live theater, parks and shopping nearby.

Publicity: *New Woman, Southern Living, Good Housekeeping, House Beautiful, Country Inns, National Geographic Traveler.*

"Cedar Crest is a real beauty and will hold a special place in our hearts."

The Colby House

230 Pearson Dr
Asheville, NC 28801-1614
(828)253-5644 (800)982-2118

Circa 1924. This Dutch Colonial home, framed by a white picket fence, welcomes guests to the Montford Historic District, in the National Register. The first level offers a tradi-

tional decor with period antiques and hardwood floors. Guest rooms feature queen beds, pretty linens and antiques. The inn's colorful gardens are an inviting place for conversation. Local wildflowers grown within a rock-walled garden provide a setting for relaxation.

Innkeeper(s): Bonnie and Peter Marsh. $125-165. MC, VISA, AX, DS. 4 rooms with PB. Type of meal: Full bkfst. Beds: Q.
Publicity: *Asheville Citizen-Times.*

Corner Oak Manor

53 Saint Dunstans Rd
Asheville, NC 28803-2620
(704)253-3525 (888)633-3525

Circa 1920. Surrounded by oak, maple and pine trees, this English Tudor inn is decorated with many fine oak antiques and handmade items. Innkeeper Karen Spradley has hand-stitched something special for each room, and the house features handmade items by local artisans. Breakfast delights include entrees such as Blueberry Ricotta Pancakes, Four Cheese and Herb Quiche and Orange French Toast. When you

aren't enjoying local activities, you can sit on the shady deck, relax in the Jacuzzi, play a few songs on the piano or curl up with a good book.

Historic Interest: Biltmore House and Gardens (one-half mile).

Innkeeper(s): Karen & Andy Spradley. $100-160. MC, VISA, AX, DS, PC, TC. 3 rooms with PB, 1 with FP and 1 cottage. Breakfast included in rates. Type of meal: Full gourmet bkfst. Beds: Q. Ceiling fan and one cottage with fireplace in room. Air conditioning. Jacuzzi (outdoor) on premises. Family reunions hosted. Antiquing, fishing, live theater, parks, shopping and downhill skiing nearby.

"Great food, comfortable bed, quiet, restful atmosphere, you provided it all and we enjoyed it all!"

Dogwood Cottage

40 Canterbury Rd N
Asheville, NC 28801-1560
(828)258-9725

Circa 1910. This Carolina mountain home is located a mile-and-a-half from downtown Asheville, on Sunset Mountain. The veranda, filled with white wicker and floral chintz prints, is the focal point of the inn during summer. It affords tree-top views of the Blue Ridge Mountains. Wing chairs and country pieces accent the inn's gleaming hardwood floors. Breakfast is served in the formal dining room or on the covered porch.

Innkeeper(s): Joan & Don Tracy. $100-110. MC, VISA, AX, PC. TAC10. 4 rooms with PB, 3 with FP. Breakfast included in rates. Types of meals: Full gourmet bkfst and early coffee/tea. Beds: Q. Ceiling fan in room. Air conditioning. Swimming and pet boarding on premises. Handicap access. Weddings and family reunions hosted. Antiquing, fishing, live theater, parks, shopping, downhill skiing, sporting events and water sports nearby.
Pets Allowed.

"Cozy, warm and gracious."

The Lion & The Rose

276 Montford Ave
Asheville, NC 28801-1660
(828)255-7673 (800)546-6988
E-mail: info@lion-rose.com
Web: www.lion-rose.com

Circa 1895. Asheville's Montford Historic District wouldn't be complete without this Queen Anne Georgian, listed in the National Register. Innkeepers Lisa and Rice Yordy preserve the history of this home

with the period decor. The interior is gracious, showcasing the original leaded- and stained-glass windows and tiger oak wood. A wonderful afternoon tea is served each day, often on the inn's wraparound veranda. Lisa prepares the memorable breakfasts, which are served on English china with silver. Fresh flowers and chocolates welcome guests to their well-appointed rooms.

Innkeeper(s): Rice & Lisa Yordy. $135-225. MC, VISA, AX, DS, TC. 5 rooms with PB and 1 suite. Breakfast and afternoon tea included in rates. Type of meal: Full gourmet bkfst. Beds: QT. Cable TV, turndown service and ceiling fan in room. Air conditioning. Small meetings hosted. Antiquing, restaurants, live theater, parks, shopping and water sports nearby.

North Lodge on Oakland

84 Oakland Rd
Asheville, NC 28801-4818
(704)252-6433 (800)282-3602 Fax:(701)252-3034

Circa 1904. This inn was built by an old Asheville family, descendants of the owners of Smith Plantation. It is a three-story lodge that combines native stone work with cedar shingles. There are gables and a portico. Inside, guests enjoy a

front parlor, library and French-country dining room. Furnishings include English antiques and Oriental rugs mixed with contemporary pieces. Poached salmon souffle or German apple pancakes are specialties offered at breakfast.

Innkeeper(s): Herb & Lois Marsh. $95-130. MC, VISA, AX, DS, PC, TC. TAC10. 5 rooms with PB. Breakfast and afternoon tea included in rates. Type of meal: Full gourmet bkfst. Beds: QDT. Cable TV in room. Air conditioning. Fax on premises. Amusement parks, antiquing, fishing, golf, Biltmore Estate, live theater, parks, shopping, downhill skiing, cross-country skiing, sporting events, tennis and water sports nearby.

"The room was marvelous, breakfasts were delicious, and you certainly were gracious hosts."

The Old Reynolds Mansion

100 Reynolds Hgts
Asheville, NC 28804
(828)254-0496 (800)709-0496

Circa 1855. This handsome, three-story brick antebellum mansion is situated on a four-acre knoll of Reynolds Mountain. Rescued from near ruin by innkeepers Fred and Helen Faber, the home has been restored to its former glory as a gracious Southern

manor. Each of the guest quarters reflects a different style from early American to Oriental. Guests can enjoy mountain views from their own room, by a wood-burning fireplace or on a rocking chair on the inn's wraparound porch. The mansion offers use of a swimming pool set among pine trees.

Historic Interest: Several historic homes, including the Biltmore Estate, Thomas Wolfe home and Carl Sandburg home are a short drive.

Innkeeper(s): Fred & Helen Faber. $60-125. PC, TC. 10 rooms, 8 with PB, 5 with FP and 1 cottage. Breakfast and afternoon tea included in rates. Type of meal: Cont plus. Beds: QDT. Ceiling fan in room. Air conditioning. Swimming and library on premises. Antiquing, fishing, live theater, parks, shopping, downhill skiing, cross-country skiing and sporting events nearby.

Publicity: *Greensboro News & Record, Blue Ridge Country.*

"This was one of the nicest places we have ever stayed. We spent every sundown on the porch waiting for the fox's daily visit."

Richmond Hill Inn

87 Richmond Hill Dr
Asheville, NC 28806-3912
(828)252-7313 (800)545-9238 Fax:(828)252-8726
E-mail: info@richmondhillinn.com
Web: www.richmondhillinn.com

Circa 1889. This renovated Victorian mansion was designed for the Pearson family by James G. Hill, architect of the U.S. Treasury buildings. The elegant estate features a grand entry hall,

ballroom, library and 10 master fireplaces with Neoclassical mantels. Guests may choose from accommodations in the luxurious mansion, charming cottages on a croquet court, or the garden rooms amid a striking landscape and facing a waterfall. Gabrielle's Restaurant, which is on the premises, serves gourmet cuisine each evening. The inn is listed in the National Register of Historic Places.

Historic Interest: The Biltmore House and Gardens are 20 minutes away. The Thomas Wolfe Memorial is about 15 minutes from the home, while Carl Sandburg home is an hour away.

Innkeeper(s): Susan Michel. $135-375. MC, VISA, AX, PC, TC. 36 rooms with PB, 26 with FP, 3 suites and 3 conference rooms. Breakfast and afternoon tea included in rates. MAP. Type of meal: Full bkfst. Gourmet dinner available. Restaurant on premises. Beds: KQD. Fax and copier on premises. Handicap access. Croquet court nearby.

"A great adventure into history. I am moved to tell you how grateful we are that you had the foresight and courage to rescue this wonderful place. The buildings and grounds are elegantly impressive ... and the staff superb! You have created a total experience that fulfills and satisfies."

White Gate Inn & Cottage

173 E Chestnut St
Asheville, NC 28801-2339
(828)253-2553 (800)485-3045 Fax:(828)281-1883
E-mail: innkeeper@whitegate.net
Web: www.whitegate.net

Circa 1889. A white picket fence surrounds this historic brick home. Accommodations include rooms and suites named to honor American poets and decorated with antiques and collectibles. The WhiteGate Cottage includes a living room with a working fireplace and antique pine furnishings. White Gate Inn had its beginnings as a Victorian, including a three-story tower. In 1907, a new owner reconstructed the home, removing the tower and adding on to the home and transforming it into a shingle-style structure.

Guests can relax in front of a fire in the parlor or enjoy the warmth of the solarium, where wine is served in the evenings. In the mornings, a lavish, three-course breakfast is served. A sample menu might include a starter of homemade cinnamon biscuits, a second course of peaches and raisins baked with brown sugar and sherry, and a main course of crab and artichoke heart egg puff in a white wine and parsley sauce. After breakfast, guests can take a drive and enjoy the scenery of the Blue Ridge Mountains, visit the Biltmore Estate or explore downtown Asheville.

Historic Interest: Carl Sandburg house (10 miles), Grove Park Inn (1.5 miles), Thomas Wolfe house (2 blocks), Biltmore Estate and winery (3 miles).

Innkeeper(s): Frank Salvo & Ralph Coffey. $145-185. MC, VISA, AX, PC. TAC10. 4 rooms with PB, 3 with FP, 2 suites and 1 cottage. Breakfast included in rates. Types of meals: Full bkfst, cont, veg bkfst and early coffee/tea. Snacks/refreshments available. Beds: Q. Ceiling fan in room. Air conditioning. VCR, fax and copier on premises. Weddings, small meetings and family reunions hosted. Antiquing, art galleries, bicycling, canoeing/kayaking, fishing, golf, hiking, horseback riding, live theater, museums, parks, shopping, downhill skiing, cross-country skiing, tennis and wineries nearby.

Wright Inn & Carriage House

235 Pearson Dr
Asheville, NC 28801-1613
(828)251-0789 (800)552-5724 Fax:(828)251-0929
Web: www.wrightinn.com

Circa 1899. Located on a quiet, tree-lined street, this three-story gabled Queen Anne Victorian is the winner of two restoration awards and its gardens were judged Ashville's best.

An inviting wraparound porch with a built-in gazebo, balustrades and columns is a favorite place for morning coffee or evening chats. Guest rooms are furnished with antiques, family heirlooms and lovely linens. Two of the bedrooms feature fireplaces, and one has a balcony.

Guests staying in the inn rooms are treated to both afternoon tea and a breakfast of homemade breads, muffins, granola and tempting entrees. The Carriage House is a perfect place for families and includes a living room, dining room, kitchen, three bedrooms, two baths and the same carefully appointed decor evident in the main house.

Historic Interest: The inn and carriage house are listed in the local and national historic registers. The innkeepers will provide a Sony Walkman and tape for a walking tour of downtown Asheville. The Blue Ridge Parkway, Biltmore House and Smith-McDowell House are only minutes away.

Innkeeper(s): Carol & Art Wenczel. $110-235. MC, VISA, DS, PC, TC. 10 rooms with PB, 2 with FP, 1 suite and 1 cottage. Breakfast and afternoon tea included in rates. Types of meals: Full gourmet bkfst and early coffee/tea. Beds: KQDT. Cable TV and phone in room. Air conditioning. Fax, bicycles and library on premises. Small meetings and family reunions hosted. Antiquing, fishing, hiking, live theater, parks, shopping, downhill skiing, cross-country skiing, sporting events and water sports nearby.

Bald Head Island   D7

Theodosia's B&B

91 Keelson Row
Bald Head Island, NC 28461
(910)457-6563 (800)656-1812 Fax:(910)457-6055
E-mail: garrett.albertson@worldnet.att.net
Web: www.theodosias.com

Circa 1817. Although this inn is new, it was built in the grand style of the Victorian era. The home is named after Aaron Burr's daughter, Theodosia, which means "Gift of God," in Greek. The guest rooms are decorated in an eclectic mix of styles. Guests enjoy views of the ocean, harbor and river during their stay. The honeymoon suite offers a Jacuzzi tub and beautiful views. Cars are not allowed on the island, but the innkeepers provide guests with golf carts or bicycles, including tandem bikes. The island is a unique place, so small that residents have a key to the post office. Guests can enjoy a day at the beach or take a trip to the state's oldest lighthouse, which was built in 1817.

Innkeeper(s): Gary & Donna Albertson. $165-250. MC, VISA, DS, PC, TC. 13 rooms with PB and 1 suite. Breakfast included in rates. Type of meal: Full bkfst. Snacks/refreshments available. Beds: KQD. Cable TV and phone in room. Air conditioning. Fax and bicycles on premises. Handicap access. Weddings, small meetings and family reunions hosted. German and Lithuanian spoken. Fishing, golf, parks, tennis and water sports nearby.

Balsam   B2

Balsam Mountain Inn

Balsam Mountain Rd
Balsam, NC 28707-0040
(828)456-9498 (800)224-9498 Fax:(828)456-9298
E-mail: balsaminn@earthlink.net
Web: www.balsaminn.com

Circa 1905. This inn, just a quarter mile from the famed Blue Ridge Parkway, is surrounded by the majestic Smoky Mountains. The inn was built in the Neoclassical style and overlooks the scenic hamlet of Balsam. The inn is listed in the National Register of Historic Places and is designated a Jackson County Historic Site. It features a mansard roof and wrap-around porches with mountain views. A complimentary full breakfast is served daily, and dinner also is available daily.

Innkeeper(s): Merrily Teasley. $95-150. MC, VISA, DS, TC. TAC10. 50 rooms with PB and 8 suites. Breakfast included in rates. Types of meals: Full gourmet bkfst and early coffee/tea. Gourmet dinner, picnic lunch and banquet service available. Restaurant on premises. Beds: KD. Fax, copier, hiking trails and wildflower walks on premises. Handicap access. Weddings, small meetings, family reunions and seminars hosted. Antiquing, fishing, whitewater rafting, hiking, Blue Ridge Pkwy, parks, shopping and downhill skiing nearby.

"What wonderful memories we have of this beautiful inn."

Beaufort   C9

The Cedars Inn

305 Front St
Beaufort, NC 28516-2124
(252)728-7036 Fax:(252)728-1685
Web: www.cedarsinn.com

Circa 1768. The Cedars is comprised of two historic houses, of which the Main House dates back to 1768. Five of the guest rooms are located in the Main House, and an additional six are located in a restored 1851 house next door. The guest rooms include amenities such as fireplaces, clawfoot tubs, four-poster beds and antiques. All rooms include a private bath, and suites also have a sitting room. The innkeepers also have a honeymoon cottage, which includes a Jacuzzi tub. Both houses include front porches, lined with rocking chairs, on the first and second floors. Hearty breakfasts include such items as banana-walnut pancakes, French toast, croissants, pastries, country ham, bacon, fresh fruit, juices, coffee and tea. The inn has a wine bar featuring a variety of vintages, champagne, beer and non-alcoholic options. The Cedars is located in Beaufort's historic district, and bicycles are available for guests who wish to tour the state's third oldest town.

Historic Interest: The Beaufort Historical Association offers tours of a two-acre complex of historic buildings, including an 1829 jail and a 1796 county courthouse.

Innkeeper(s): Sam & Linda Dark. $95-165. MC, VISA, AX, DS, PC. 11 rooms with PB, 5 with FP, 1 cottage and 1 conference room. Type of meal: Full bkfst. Beds: KQDT. TV in room.

Publicity: *The Washington Post, Greensboro News & Record, Raleigh News & Observer, Chatham News.*

Delamar Inn

217 Turner St
Beaufort, NC 28516-2140
(252)728-4300 (800)349-5823
Web: www.bbonline.com/nc/delamarinn/

Circa 1866. The innkeepers, who have lived in Africa, Denmark, Hawaii and Scotland, lend an international touch to this hospitable two-story home, which features wide porches

on each level. Each of the guest rooms is decorated to reflect a different style. One of the rooms has an original clawfoot tub. The innkeepers keep plenty of coffee and tea around and stock comfortable sitting rooms with cookies and fruit for late-night snacking. They also can provide beach chairs and bicycles for guests heading to the beach.

Historic Interest: The Delamar Inn is located in North Carolina's third-oldest town, and historic Fort Macon, built in 1834, guards Beaufort's harbor. The inn is within walking distance of a collection of old buildings preserved by the local historical society. The Maritime Museum is another nearby historic attraction.

Innkeeper(s): Tom & Mabel Steepy. $78-116. MC, VISA, TC. 4 rooms with PB. Breakfast included in rates. Types of meals: Cont plus and early coffee/tea. Beds: KQ. Ceiling fan in room. Air conditioning. Bicycles, beach chairs and coolers and towels on premises. Small meetings and family reunions hosted. Antiquing, fishing, historic Beaufort-1709, parks, shopping and water sports nearby.

"We've come back here for the last four years. It's like coming home!"

Langdon House

135 Craven St
Beaufort, NC 28516-2116
(252)728-5499 Fax:(252)728-1717
E-mail: innkeeper@costalnet.com
Web: www.langdonhouse.com

Circa 1734. This three-story colonial house witnessed Beaufort pillaged by pirates in 1747, plundered by the British in 1782, occupied by the Union army in 1862, and pounded by the great hurricane of 1879. The atmosphere of the inn is enhanced by a 19th-century pump organ, an Empire secretary, and other antiques. A colonial garden features daisies, cabbage roses and a collection of herbs.

Historic Interest: Beaufort Historical Restoration, North Carolina Maritime Museum, Old Burying Grounds.

Innkeeper(s): Jimm & Lizzet Prest. $75-135. PC, TC. 4 rooms with PB and 1 conference room. Breakfast and snacks/refreshments included in rates. Types of meals: Full bkfst, cont plus, cont, veg bkfst and early coffee/tea. Beds: Q. Central air. Fax, bicycles, library and beach equipment on premises. Small meetings and family reunions hosted. Spanish spoken. Antiquing, art galleries, beaches, bicycling, canoeing/kayaking, fishing, golf, hiking, museums, parks, shopping, tennis and water sports nearby.

"Prest is a historian, a guide, a maitre'd', a confidant. Your friend."

Pecan Tree Inn B&B

116 Queen St
Beaufort, NC 28516-2214
(252)728-6733
E-mail: pecantreeinn@coastalnet.com
Web: www.pecantree.com

Circa 1866. Originally built as a Masonic lodge, this state historic landmark is in the heart of Beaufort's historic district. Gingerbread trim, Victorian porches, turrets and two-century-

old pecan trees grace the exterior. Guests can relax in the parlor, on the porches, or pay a visit to the flower and herb gardens. The Bridal Suite and "Wow" suite boast a king-size, canopied bed and two-person Jacuzzi.

Innkeeper(s): Susan & Joe Johnson. $75-140. MC, VISA, AX, DS, PC, TC. TAC8. 7 rooms with PB and 1 suite. Breakfast included in rates. Types of meals: Cont plus and early coffee/tea. Beds: KQ. Ceiling fan in room. Air conditioning. Bicycles and library on premises. Weddings, small meetings and family reunions hosted. Amusement parks, antiquing, fishing, jogging, biking, hiking, tennis, historical sites, parks, shopping and water sports nearby.

Publicity: *Sunday Telegram, This Week, Conde Nast Traveler, State.*

Black Mountain   B3

Red Rocker Country Inn

136 N Dougherty St
Black Mountain, NC 28711-3326
(828)669-5991 (888)669-5991 Fax:(828)669-5560
E-mail: redrockerinn.com
Web: www.redrockerinn.com

Circa 1896. An expansive wraparound porch surrounds this three-story country inn located on one acre of landscaped grounds. Guest rooms such as the Preacher's Room, the

Anniversary Room, Savannah and Elizabeth's Attic are part of the "grandma's place" feel to the inn. Mountain dinners served in the inn's restaurant include Carolina pot roast pie topped with puff pastry with fruit cobblers for dessert.

Innkeeper(s): Craig & Margie Lindberg. $80-145. PC, TC. TAC10. 18 rooms, 17 with PB, 3 with FP. Afternoon tea and snacks/refreshments included in rates. Types of meals: Full bkfst and early coffee/tea. Dinner, lunch, banquet service and catering service available. Restaurant on premises. Beds: KQD. Ceiling fan in room. Air conditioning. Fax and library on premises. Weddings, small meetings, family reunions and seminars hosted. Antiquing, fishing, golf, live theater, parks, shopping, downhill skiing, tennis and water sports nearby.

Brevard   C3

Red House Inn B&B

412 W Probart St
Brevard, NC 28712-3620
(828)884-9349

Circa 1851. Originally built as a trading post, this inn was also the county's first post office and railroad station. It survived the Civil War and years of neglect. Recently renovated, it is furnished with Victorian antiques. The center of town is four blocks away.

Innkeeper(s): Marilyn Ong. $59-99. MC, VISA, PC, TC. 5 rooms, 3 with PB, 1 with FP, 1 suite and 1 cottage. Breakfast included in rates. Type of meal: Full bkfst. Afternoon tea available. Beds: QDT. TV and ceiling fan in room. Air conditioning. VCR on premises. Handicap access. Weddings, small meetings and family reunions hosted. Antiquing, fishing, golf, horseback riding, hiking, live theater, parks and tennis nearby.

Publicity: *The Transylvania Times.*

"Lovely place to stay - clean and bright."

Womble Inn

301 W Main St
Brevard, NC 28712-3609
(704)884-4770

Circa 1958. Located in Brevard, Land of the Waterfalls, this New Orleans-style inn offers visitors a comfortable retreat in which to enjoy the many natural amenities that the North Carolina countryside has to offer, including hiking, trout fishing and swimming. Adding to the area's history is Goat Farm, Carl Sandburg's homestead, and the elegant Biltmore House. Guest rooms are individually decorated in antiques and offer private baths and air conditioning. A continental breakfast is served in the dining room.

Historic Interest: Located near Brevard Music Center, Brevard College and the Pisgah National Forest.

Innkeeper(s): Beth & Steve Womble. $58-72. MC, VISA, DS, PC, TC. 6 rooms with PB. Breakfast included in rates. Types of meals: Full bkfst, cont plus, cont and early coffee/tea. Picnic lunch and lunch available. Restaurant on premises. Beds: QDT. Ceiling fan in room. Air conditioning. Weddings, small meetings and family reunions hosted. Antiquing, fishing, golf, live theater, parks, shopping and tennis nearby.

Bryson City   B2

Folkestone Inn

101 Folkestone Rd
Bryson City, NC 28713-7891
(828)488-2730 (888)812-3385 Fax:(828)488-0722
E-mail: innkeeper@folkestone.com
Web: www.folkestone.com

Circa 1926. This farmhouse is constructed of local stone and rock. Pressed-tin ceilings, stained-glass windows and clawfoot tubs remain. The dining room, where breakfast is served, features floor-to-ceiling windows on all sides with views of the mountains. Afternoon refreshments also are served. There is a stream with a rock bridge on the property, and you can walk 10 minutes to waterfall views in the Great Smoky Mountains National Park.

Innkeeper(s): Ellen & Charles Snodgrass. $69-108. MC, VISA, AX, DS, PC, TC. TAC10. 10 rooms with PB. Breakfast included in rates. Types of meals: Full bkfst and early coffee/tea. Beds: QD. Central heat in room. Central air. Fax and copier on premises. Small meetings, family reunions and seminars hosted. Antiquing, fishing, tubing, rafting, hiking, scenic train, shopping and water sports nearby.

Publicity: *Asheville Citizen-Times, Atlanta Journal, Lakeland, Palm Beach Post.*

Randolph House Country Inn

223 Fryemont Rd PO Box 816
Bryson City, NC 28713-0816
(828)488-3472 (800)480-3472

Circa 1895. Randolph House is a mountain estate tucked among pine trees and dogwoods, near the entrance of Great Smoky Mountain National Park. Antiques, some original to the house, fill this National Register home. Each guest room is appointed in a different color scheme. The house provides an unforgettable experience, not the least of which is the gourmet dining provided on the terrace or in the dining room.

Historic Interest: In the National Register.

Innkeeper(s): Bill & Ruth Randolph Adams. $120-160. MC, VISA, AX, DS, PC, TC. TAC10. 7 rooms, 3 with PB, 2 with FP, 2 suites, 1 cottage and 1 conference room. Breakfast and dinner included in rates. MAP. Types of meals: Full bkfst and early coffee/tea. Restaurant on premises. Beds: KQDT. Cable TV in room. Air conditioning. Library on premises. Handicap access. Small meetings, family reunions and seminars hosted. Antiquing, fishing, parks, shopping and water sports nearby.

Publicity: *Tourist News, New York Times.*

"Very enjoyable, great food."

Chapel Hill   B6

The Inn at Bingham School

PO Box 267
Chapel Hill, NC 27514-0267
(919)563-5583 (800)566-5583 Fax:(919)563-9826
E-mail: fdeprez@aol.com
Web: www.chapel-hill-inn.com

Circa 1790. This inn served as one of the locations of the famed Bingham School. This particular campus was the site of a liberal arts preparatory school for those aspiring to attend the University at Chapel Hill. The inn is listed as a National Trust property and has garnered awards for its restoration. The property still includes  many historic structures including a 1790s log home, an 1801 Federal addition, an 1835 Greek Revival home, the headmaster's office, which was built in 1845, and a well house, smokehouse and milk house. Original heart of pine floors are found throughout the inn. Guests can opt to stay in the Log Room, located in the log cabin, with a tight-winder staircase and fireplace. Other possibilities include Rusty's Room with two antique rope beds. The suite offers a bedroom glassed in on three sides. A mix of breakfasts are served, often including pear almond Belgian waffles, quiche or souffles.

Historic Interest: The Orange County Historical Museum is 12 miles from the inn. The Durham Homestead is 20 miles away, and the Horace Williams House and North Carolina Collection Gallery are 10 miles away.

Innkeeper(s): Francois & Christina Deprez. $75-120. MC, VISA, AX, DS, PC, TC. TAC10. 5 rooms with PB, 4 with FP, 1 suite, 1 cottage and 1 conference room. Breakfast and snacks/refreshments included in rates. Types of meals: Full gourmet bkfst and early coffee/tea. Gourmet dinner available. Beds: QD. Phone, hair dryers and robes in room. Air conditioning. VCR, fax, library, trails and hammocks on premises. Weddings and small meetings hosted. Spanish and French spoken. Antiquing, fishing, live theater, parks, shopping, sporting events and water sports nearby.

Publicity: *Southern Inns, Mebane Enterprise, Burlington Times, Times News, Washington Post.*

Chimney Rock   B3

Esmeralda Inn & Restaurant

PO Box 57, Hwy 74A
Chimney Rock, NC 28720-0057
(828)625-9105
E-mail: esmeralda@blueridge.net
Web: www.esmeraldainn.com

Circa 1890. The Esmeralda Inn is located 27 miles east of Asheville in a village setting. The lobby is constructed with locally grown locust trees, and railings of mountain laurel lead to the second floor. The inn's restaurant is noted for its American regional cuisine and for its views through the expansive windows in the dining areas that overlook gardens, a waterfall, fountains, trees and Chimney Rock Park. Breakfast is

served in the lobby. The Lake Lure area offers both river and lake as well as mountain activities and its famous bottomless pools.

Innkeeper(s): Ackie & Jo Anne Okpych. $129. MC, VISA, AX, DS, TC. 14 rooms with PB. Breakfast included in rates. Type of meal: Cont. Dinner and lunch available. Restaurant on premises. Beds: Q. TV, phone and ceiling fan in room. Chimney Rock Park and Lake Lure nearby.

Dillsboro   C2

Squire Watkins Inn

657 Haywood Rd
Dillsboro, NC 28725
(828)586-5244 (800)586-2429

Circa 1880. Successful local businessman, J.C. Watkins, and his wife, Flora, built this Queen Anne Victorian to house their large family. The Watkins raised eight children in this historic mansion. Watkins, known by locals as the Squire, served in the Civil War and as mayor of Dillsboro. Flora was the granddaughter of the founder of nearby Cashiers. The home maintains many original features, including the woodwork, hardwood floors and leaded-glass windows. Rooms are decorated with antiques in English country style. Two acres of grounds surround the home, which rests on a hill overlooking Dillsboro. Guests are close to many popular attractions. Great Smoky Mountains National Park is 17 miles away, and the Biltmore Estate is about an hour's drive from the inn.

Historic Interest: Biltmore Estate (47 miles), Cherokee & Great Smokey Mountains National Park (17 miles).

Innkeeper(s): Tom & Emma Wertenberger. $65-85. PC, TC. 4 rooms with PB, 2 with FP and 2 cottages. Breakfast included in rates. Types of meals: Full bkfst and early coffee/tea. Beds: QD. Turndown service and ceiling fan in room. Air conditioning. Library on premises. Antiquing, bicycling, canoeing/kayaking, fishing, golf, hiking, horseback riding, railway excursion, live theater, museums, parks, shopping and tennis nearby.

Edenton   B9

Trestle House Inn

RR 4, Box 370, 632 Soundside Rd
Edenton, NC 27932-9668
(252)482-2282 (800)645-8466 Fax:(252)482-7003

Circa 1968. Trestle House is located on a six acres with a lake and a pond filled with large-mouth bass. The interior is unique as it features beams that were actually trestles that once belonged to the Southern Railway Company. Rooms are named for different birds, such as the Osprey and Mallard rooms. Two rooms have a sleigh bed. The morning meal includes homemade breads, breakfast casseroles and fresh orange juice.

Innkeeper(s): Peter L. Bogus. $80-95. MC, VISA, AX, PC, TC. 5 rooms with PB and 1 suite. Breakfast included in rates. Type of meal: Full bkfst. Beds: KQDT. Cable TV, phone, ceiling fan and VCR in room. Air conditioning. Fax,

swimming, bicycles and tennis on premises. Small meetings, family reunions and seminars hosted. Antiquing, fishing, golf, live theater, parks, shopping, sporting events, tennis and water sports nearby.

"We have stayed at many B&B, but yours is special because it brings us close to nature. Your breakfast are wonderful and relaxing while eating and watching wildlife in their natural habitat!"

Franklin   C2

Buttonwood Inn

50 Admiral Dr
Franklin, NC 28734-1981
(828)369-8985 (888)368-8985

Circa 1927. Trees surround this two-story batten board house located adjacent to the Franklin Golf Course. Local crafts and handmade family quilts accent the country decor. Wonderful breakfasts are served here—often eggs Benedict, baked peaches and sausage and freshly baked scones with homemade lemon butter. On a sunny morning, enjoy breakfast on the deck and savor the Smoky Mountain vistas. Afterward, you'll be ready for white-water rafting, hiking and fishing.

Innkeeper(s): Liz Oehser. $60-90. PC, TC. 4 rooms with PB. Breakfast and afternoon tea included in rates. Types of meals: Full bkfst and early coffee/tea. Beds: KDT. Ceiling fan in room. Family reunions hosted. Antiquing, fishing, parks and shopping nearby.

Grassy Creek   A4

River House

1896 Old Field Creek Rd
Grassy Creek, NC 28631
(336)982-2109

Circa 1870. This three-story farmhouse contains both guest rooms and a fine restaurant, located on 180 acres with a mile of river front. There is a guest cottage, barn, chicken house among the out buildings. Guest chambers are filled with antiques, paintings and have canopy beds, whirlpool tubs or private porches with views of the New River or the Blue Ridge Mountains. The fire-lit dining room, dressed in white linens, offers French-country cuisine with a regional influence. The innkeepers provide canoes and river tubes. Coffee is left outside your door in the morning, and there is a full American breakfast. The innkeeper, a former theatrical producer in New York, offers her guidance for weddings (held in the house or under the giant sycamore tree by the river) and business conferences.

Innkeeper(s): Gayle Winston, John Stewart. $115-150. MC, VISA, AX, DC, DS, PC, TC. TAC15. 9 rooms with PB, 6 with FP, 4 suites, 1 cottage, 2 cabins and 3 conference rooms. Types of meals: Full gourmet bkfst and early coffee/tea. Afternoon tea, gourmet dinner, picnic lunch, gourmet lunch, banquet service, catering service and room service available. Restaurant on premises. Beds: KQT. Turndown service, ceiling fan and whirlpool tubs in room. VCR, fax, copier, spa, swimming, tennis, library, pet boarding and child care on premises. Weddings, small meetings, family reunions and seminars hosted. French, Spanish and Italian spoken. Antiquing, canoeing/kayaking, fishing, golf, hiking, live theater, parks, shopping, downhill skiing, cross-country skiing, sporting events, tennis and water sports nearby.

Pets allowed: well-behaved.

Greensboro
B6

Biltmore Greensboro Hotel

111 W Washington St
Greensboro, NC 27401-2619
(336)272-3474 (800)332-0303 Fax:(336)275-2523

Circa 1895. The Biltmore offers all the amenities of a luxury hotel combined with the intimacy and ambiance of an inn. Guest rooms are appointed with elegant furnishings in European style. In-room amenities include hair dryers, modem jacks, refrigerators and mini bars. The hotel offers a concierge service, room service and a dry cleaning-laundry service. In the mornings, a continental buffet is presented, and in the evenings, a reception is held, featuring wine and hors d'oeuvres.

Innkeeper(s): Karl H. Lack. $75-125. MC, VISA, AX, DC, CB, DS, PC, TC. TAC10. 25 rooms with PB and 11 suites. Breakfast included in rates. EP. Type of meal: Cont plus. Beds: KQD. Cable TV, phone and VCR in room. Air conditioning. Fax, copier and library on premises. Weddings, small meetings, family reunions and seminars hosted. German spoken. Antiquing, golf, live theater, parks, shopping, sporting events and water sports nearby. Pets Allowed.

The Troy-Bumpas Inn B&B

114 S Mendenhall St
Greensboro, NC 27403
(336)370-1660 (800)370-9070 Fax:(336)274-3939
E-mail: www.ggbrowntbi@aol.com
Web: www.troy-bumpasinn.com

Circa 1847. As General Sherman marched through the South on his way to Atlanta, some of his Union soldiers occupied this home. The grand Greek Revival home was built by Rev. Sidney

Bumpas, and for 20 years, a Methodist newspaper was published here. The interior, often showcased on local historic home tours, has been restored to its former glory. The four guest rooms are decorated in a nostalgic, romantic style. One room contains a 19th-century mahogany bed with beautifully carved woodwork, another room offers a fireplace, clawfoot tub and bed draped in luxurious linens. The innkeepers offer two breakfast choices, one a light meal with fruits and homemade breads or a full Southern feast featuring items such as banana waffles topped with praline sauce. The home, listed in the National Register, is located in Greensboro's historic College Hill district.

Innkeeper(s): Charles & Gwen Brown. $95-125. MC, VISA, AX, DS, TC. TAC10. 4 rooms with PB, 1 with FP and 1 conference room. Breakfast and snacks/refreshments included in rates. Types of meals: Full bkfst and early coffee/tea. Beds: KQD. Phone and turndown service in room. Air conditioning. VCR on premises. Weddings, small meetings and family reunions hosted. Antiquing, golf, live theater, parks, shopping and sporting events nearby.

"You both know how to spoil people rotten."

Hertford
B9

1812 on The Perquimans B&B Inn

Rt 3, Box 10
Hertford, NC 27944-9502
(919)426-1812

Circa 1790. William and Sarah Fletcher were the first residents of this Federal-style plantation home, and the house is still in the family today. The Fletchers were Quakers and the first North Carolina residents to not only free their slaves, but also offered to pay the way for workers who wished to return to Africa. The farm rests along the banks of the Perquimans River, and the grounds retain many original outbuildings, including a brick dairy, smokehouse and a 19th-century frame barn. Inside, the mantels, marble and woodwork have been restored.

Historic Interest: Federal-style plantation dwelling.

Innkeeper(s): Peter & Nancy Rascoe. $75-85. MC, VISA. 5 rooms. Breakfast included in rates. Type of meal: Full bkfst.

Highlands
C2

Colonial Pines Inn

541 Hickory St
Highlands, NC 28741-8498
(828)526-2060

Circa 1937. Secluded on a hillside just half a mile from Highlands' Main Street, this inn offers relaxing porches that boast a mountain view. The parlor is another restful option, offering a TV, fireplace and piano. Rooms, highlighted by knotty pine, are decorated with an eclectic mix of antiques. The guest

pantry is always stocked with refreshments for those who need a little something in the afternoon. For breakfast, freshly baked breads accompany items such as a potato/bacon casserole and baked pears topped with currant sauce. In addition to guest rooms and suites, there are two cottages available, each with a fireplace and kitchen.

Innkeeper(s): Chris & Donna Alley. $85-145. MC, VISA, PC, TC. 8 rooms, 3 with PB, 3 suites and 2 cabins. Breakfast and afternoon tea included in rates. Type of meal: Full bkfst. Beds: KQDT. Guest pantry on premises. Antiquing, fishing, live theater, parks, shopping, downhill skiing and water sports nearby.

Publicity: *Greenville News, Atlanta Journal, Highlander.*

"There was nothing we needed which you did not provide."

High Point
B5

Bouldin House B&B

4332 Archdale Rd
High Point, NC 27263-3070
(336)431-4909 (800)739-1816 Fax:(336)431-4914

Circa 1915. This home, a unique example of American Four-Square architecture, is located a few miles outside of High Point, in the nearby village of Archdale. The innkeepers are only the second owners and have named their bed & breakfast for the family who built it. The house has been painstakingly

restored and now offers four guest rooms, with names such as Weekend Retreat or Warm Morning. Queen Anne chairs, pocket doors or a four-poster bed are among the features guests will discover in their rooms, and all guest quarters include a fireplace. Oatmeal currant scones topped with orange butter and pecan-basil pesto omelets and sage sausage are among the tempting treats served during the gourmet breakfasts.

Innkeeper(s): Larry & Ann Miller. $90-120. MC, VISA, AX, DS, PC, TC. TAC10. 4 rooms with PB, 4 with FP. Breakfast and snacks/refreshments included in rates. MAP. Types of meals: Full gourmet bkfst and early coffee/tea. Afternoon tea available. Beds: KT. Ceiling fan in room. Air conditioning. VCR, fax and library on premises. Small meetings and family reunions hosted. Amusement parks, antiquing, America's largest concentration of furniture showrooms, parks, shopping and sporting events nearby.

"Great place for a honeymoon."

Murphy C1

Huntington Hall B&B

500 Valley River Ave
Murphy, NC 28906-2829
(828)837-9567 (800)824-6189 Fax:(828)837-2527
E-mail: huntington@grove.net
Web: bed-breakfast-inn.com/

Circa 1881. This two-story country Victorian home was built by J.H. Dillard, the town mayor and twice a member of the House of Representatives. Clapboard siding and tall columns accent the large front porch. An English country theme is highlighted throughout. Afternoon refreshments and evening turndown service are included. Breakfast is served on the sun porch. Murder-mystery, summer-theater, and white-water-rafting packages are available.

Innkeeper(s): Curt & Nancy Harris. $65-125. MC, VISA, AX, DS, PC, TC. TAC10. 5 rooms with PB. Breakfast included in rates. MAP. Types of meals: Full gourmet bkfst and early coffee/tea. Beds: KQDT. Cable TV, turndown service and ceiling fan in room. Air conditioning. VCR, fax, copier, tennis and library on premises. Weddings, small meetings, family reunions and seminars hosted. Antiquing, fishing, live theater, parks, shopping and water sports nearby.

"A bed and breakfast well done."

New Bern C8

The Aerie

509 Pollock St
New Bern, NC 28562-5611
(252)636-5553 (800)849-5553

Circa 1882. This late Victorian home features an appealing three-sided bay that adds to the architecture of the downstairs parlor and an upstairs guest chamber. The innkeepers offer a choice of three entrees at breakfast. A huge herb and flower garden on the grounds is frequented by the cook and enjoyed by guests. Tryon Palace with its beautiful kitchen garden and ornamental garden is a one-block walk from the inn, and there are a variety of boutiques, shops and restaurants nearby.

Innkeeper(s): Doug & Donna Bennetts. $89-99. MC, VISA, AX, DS, PC. 7 rooms with PB, 5 with FP. Breakfast included in rates. Types of meals: Full bkfst and early coffee/tea. Snacks/refreshments available. Beds: KQT. TV and phone in room. Air conditioning. Fax, herbal/flower garden and player piano on premises. Antiquing, beaches, golf and museums nearby.

Newton B4

The Trott House Inn

802 N Main Ave
Newton, NC 28658-3148
(828)465-0404 Fax:(828)465-5753

Circa 1897. Trott House was built originally as a hunting lodge, the section that houses the inn guest rooms was part of a later addition. Room choices include three guest rooms decorated with Victorian accents and a spacious suite. The suite includes an in-room Jacuzzi. For honeymooners, the innkeepers can provide breakfast in the privacy of your bedchamber, as well as providing fresh flowers and champagne. In addition to the gourmet breakfasts, guests are pampered with afternoon refreshments and turndown service.

Innkeeper(s): Anne & Tom Stedman. $75-110. MC, VISA, PC. 4 rooms with PB and 1 suite. Breakfast and snacks/refreshments included in rates. Types of meals: Full gourmet bkfst and early coffee/tea. Catering service and catered breakfast available. Beds: KQT. Cable TV, phone and ceiling fan in room. Central air. Fax, copier and spa on premises. Small meetings, family reunions and seminars hosted. Antiquing, art galleries, fishing, golf, live theater, museums and parks nearby.

Pilot Mountain (Siloam) A5

The Blue Fawn B&B

3052 Siloam Rd
Pilot Mountain (Siloam), NC 27041
(336)374-2064 (800)948-7716

Circa 1892. This Greek Revival-style house, with its four two-story columns, is bordered by an old stone fence. Located 10 minutes from town, the Blue Fawn B&B offers a friendly stay in a small tobacco farming community. There are three porches, and one is off the second-story guest rooms, which are decorated comfortably with many quilts. Spinach blue cheese strudel, Irish soda bread and fruit or homemade biscuits served with sausage gravy, fried potatoes and baked garlic cheese grits are some of the breakfast offerings. It's a tenth of a mile to the Yadkin River.

Innkeeper(s): Geno & Terri Cella. $65-85. MC, VISA, PC. 3 rooms with PB and 1 suite. Breakfast, afternoon tea and snacks/refreshments included in rates. Types of meals: Full gourmet bkfst and early coffee/tea. Picnic lunch, catering service and room service available. Beds: KQDT. Cable TV, turndown service, ceiling fan, second story porch off rooms and quilts in room. Air conditioning. VCR, bicycles, library and three porches on premises. Weddings, small meetings, family reunions and seminars hosted. Antiquing, fishing, golf, horseback riding, hiking, live theater, parks, shopping and water sports nearby.

"Words could never express how welcome and at home you have made our family feel."

Pittsboro   B6

The Fearrington House Inn

2000 Fearrington Village Ctr
Pittsboro, NC 27312-8502
(919)542-2121 Fax:(919)542-4202
E-mail: fhouse@fearrington.com
Web: www.fearrington.com

Circa 1927. The Fearrington is an old dairy farm. Several of the original outbuildings, including the silo and barn, have been converted into a village with a potter's shop, bookstore, jewelry shop, and a Southern garden shop. The original homestead houses an award-winning restaurant. The inn itself is of new construction and its rooms overlook pasture land with grazing sheep, as well as a courtyard. Polished pine floors, fresh floral prints and amenity-filled bathrooms are among the inn's offerings.

Innkeeper(s): Richard Delany. $175-350. MC, VISA, AX, PC. TAC10. 31 rooms with PB, 3 with FP, 12 suites and 3 conference rooms. Breakfast and afternoon tea included in rates. Types of meals: Full gourmet bkfst and early coffee/tea. Gourmet dinner, snacks/refreshments, picnic lunch, lunch, catering service and room service available. Restaurant on premises. Beds: KQDT. Cable TV, phone, turndown service, VCR and heated towel racks in room. Air conditioning. Fax, copier, spa, swimming, bicycles and tennis on premises. Handicap access. Weddings, small meetings and seminars hosted. German and French spoken. Antiquing, fishing, golf, live theater, parks, shopping, sporting events, tennis and water sports nearby.

"There is an aura of warmth and caring that makes your guests feel like royalty in a regal setting!"

Raleigh   B7

The Oakwood Inn B&B

411 N Bloodworth St
Raleigh, NC 27604-1223
(919)832-9712 (800)267-9712 Fax:(919)836-9263

Circa 1871. Presiding over Raleigh's Oakwood Historic District, this lavender and gray Victorian beauty is in the National Register. A formal parlor is graced by rosewood and burgundy velvet, while guest rooms exude an atmosphere of vintage Victoriana.

Innkeeper(s): Bill & Darlene Smith. $85-135. MC, VISA, AX, DS. 6 rooms with PB, 6 with FP and 1 conference room. Type of meal: Full bkfst. Beds: KQD. Cable TV in room. Fax and copier on premises.

Publicity: *Business Digest, Connoisseur, Southern Living, The Inside Scoop.*

"Resplendent and filled with museum-quality antique furnishings."
—Kim Devins, Spectator.

The William Thomas House

530 N Blount St
Raleigh, NC 27604
(919)755-9400 (800)653-3466 Fax:(919)755-3966
E-mail: lofton@williamthomashouse.com
Web: www.williamthomashouse.com

Circa 1881. This Victorian home is located in downtown Raleigh, within walking distance of the Governor's mansion and the Capitol building. The interior, which boasts high ceilings, carved molding, hardwood floors, is decorated in an elegant style. Walls are painted in bright, cheerful hues, and the

furnishings include antiques. The grounds are decorated with flowers, foliage and shaded by trees, and guests can relax on a porch swing, hammock or rocking chairs. There is ample off-street parking located behind the house. Frances Gray Patton, who wrote the book, "Good Morning, Miss Dove," was born in the home.

Innkeeper(s): Jim & Sarah Lofton. $103-140. MC, VISA, AX, DC, CB, DS, PC, TC. 4 rooms with PB and 1 conference room. Breakfast and snacks/refreshments included in rates. Types of meals: Full bkfst and early coffee/tea. Beds: KQT. Cable TV, phone, turndown service, ceiling fan and VCR in room. Air conditioning. Fax, library and CD stereo player on premises. Weddings, small meetings, family reunions and seminars hosted. Antiquing, golf, live theater, parks, shopping and sporting events nearby.

Publicity: *News & Observer, WRAL-TV.*

"You have achieved a level of comfort, atmosphere and warmth that most B&Bs strive for."

Robbinsville   C2

Snowbird Mountain Lodge

275 Santeetlah Rd
Robbinsville, NC 28771-9712
(704)479-3433
E-mail: innkeeper@snowbirdlodge.com
Web: www.snowbirdlodge.com

Circa 1940. Panoramic, 40-mile views are one of the many reasons to visit this mountain-top lodge. One innkeeper is a trained chef, and the other a knowledgeable outdoorsman. So guests not only enjoy gourmet meals, but learn where to find the best hiking and nature trails in North Carolina. The lodge is decorated in a rustic style, with an emphasis on comfort. Guest rooms offer handmade quilts, ceiling fans, refrigerators and wood-paneled walls. Each room sports a different variety of wood and some rooms have whirlpool tubs, fireplaces or steam showers. Furnishings have been built by local craftsman using wood native to the area. A favorite place to relax is the 3,000-volume library/main lodge with its huge stone fireplace. Breakfast, lunch and a three-course gourmet dinner is included in the rates. The innkeepers offer many interesting activities, such as a dulcimer clinic, fly-fishing excursions, cooking seminars and nature walks or hikes led by experienced guides.

Innkeeper(s): Karen & Robert Rankin. $130-275. MC, VISA, PC, TC. 25 rooms with PB. Breakfast, dinner and picnic lunch included in rates. AP. Types of meals: Full bkfst and early coffee/tea. Beds: KQDT. Ceiling fan, whirlpool tubs, fireplaces and steam showers available in room. Library on premises. Handicap access. Weddings, small meetings, family reunions and seminars hosted. Bicycling, canoeing/kayaking, fishing, hiking and horseback riding nearby.

Saluda   C3

The Oaks

339 Greenville St
Saluda, NC 28773-9775
(704)749-9613 (800)893-6091

Circa 1894. The Oaks is a Victorian bed & breakfast furnished with American and Oriental antiques and original art work. Guests enjoy the mountain breezes from the wraparound porch and decks, playing croquet in the yard, reading by the fire in the library or chatting in the living room. The Oaks has four bedrooms, each with a private bath, cable TV and sitting area. All rooms are furnished with antiques and queen or double four-poster beds. A separate guest house is also available. A full breakfast is served family-style in the dining room.

Innkeeper(s): Crowley & Terry Murphy. $85-150. MC, VISA, AX, DS. 4 rooms with PB and 1 cottage. Breakfast included in rates. Types of meals: Full bkfst and early coffee/tea. Beds: QD. Cable TV in room. Weddings and family reunions hosted. Antiquing, fishing and shopping nearby.

"Everything about The Oaks was what we wanted it to be, lovely, comfortable, fun and the food delicious."

Southern Pines   C6

Knollwood House

1495 W Connecticut Ave
Southern Pines, NC 28387-3903
(910)692-9390 Fax:(910)692-0609
E-mail: knollwood@pinehurst.net
Web: www.knollwoodhouse.com

Circa 1925. Fairway dreams await golfers at this English-manor-style inn where upstairs sitting rooms overlook the 14th and 15th holes of the beautiful Mid-Pines golf course. The inn's lawns roll down 100 feet or so to the course, which is a masterpiece by Scottish golf course architect Donald Ross. More than 30 golf courses are within 20 miles. There have been many celebrations under the crystal chandelier and 10-foot ceilings, and the Glenn Miller Orchestra once played on the back lawn.

Innkeeper(s): Dick & Mimi Beatty. $100-170. MC, VISA, PC, TC. TAC10. 6 rooms with PB, 1 with FP and 4 suites. Breakfast included in rates. Type of meal: Full gourmet bkfst. Banquet service and catering service available. Beds: QDT. Turndown service in room. Air conditioning. VCR, fax, copier, swimming, tennis and library on premises. Weddings, small meetings and family reunions hosted. Antiquing, golf, live theater, parks, shopping and sporting events nearby.

Spruce Pine   B3

Richmond Inn B&B

51 Pine Ave
Spruce Pine, NC 28777-2733
(828)765-6993 (877)765-6993

Circa 1939. The scent of freshly baked muffins and steaming coffee serves as a pleasing wake-up call for guests staying at this country mountain home. More than an acre of wooded grounds surround the inn, which overlooks the Toe River valley. Rooms are decorated with family heirlooms and antiques. Several guest rooms include four-poster beds. Crackling flames from the stone fireplace warm the living room, a perfect place to relax. The innkeepers keep a guest refrigerator in the butler's pantry.

Innkeeper(s): Carmen Mazzagatt. $65-110. MC, VISA, DS, TC. 8 rooms with PB, 1 with FP and 1 suite. Breakfast included in rates. Types of meals: Full bkfst and early coffee/tea. Beds: QT. Ceiling fan and jacuzzi in suite in room. VCR and fax on premises. Small meetings and family reunions hosted. Antiquing, golf, gem mining, crafts, parks, shopping, downhill skiing and cross-country skiing nearby.

Sylva   C2

The Freeze House B&B

71 Sylvan Heights
Sylva, NC 28779-2523
(828)586-8161 Fax:(828)631-0714

Circa 1917. Two-hundred-year-old oak trees shade this brick cottage, one of the oldest buildings in the village. There's a comfortable porch for enjoying the relaxing views. Guests might enjoy water rafting or taking a train through the Tuckasiegee Valley or the Nantahala Gorge. Guests may breakfast on cheese grits, country sausage and scrambled eggs with sauteed mushrooms and tomatoes on the side.

Innkeeper(s): Patrick & Mary Ellen Montague. $65-100. PC, TC. TAC10. 4 rooms, 3 with PB and 1 cottage. Breakfast included in rates. Type of meal: Full gourmet bkfst. Beds: D. Cable TV in room. Air conditioning. VCR, fax and library on premises. French and German spoken. Antiquing, art galleries, bicycling, canoeing/kayaking, fishing, hiking, live theater, museums, parks, shopping, tennis and water sports nearby.

Mountain Brook

208 Mountain Brook Rd #19
Sylva, NC 28779-9659
(828)586-4329
E-mail: vacation@mountainbrook.com
Web: www.mountainbrook.com

Circa 1930. Located in the Great Smokies, Mountain Brook consists of 12 cottages on a hillside amid rhododendron, elm, maple and oak trees. The resort's 200-acre terrain is crisscrossed with brooks and waterfalls, contains a trout-stocked pond and nature trail. Two cottages are constructed with logs from the property, while nine are made from native stone. They feature fireplaces and porch swings and have brass, four-poster and canopy beds, quilts and rocking chairs, and some have bubble tubs.

Innkeeper(s): Gus & Michele McMahon. $80-130. TC. TAC10. 12 cottages with PB, 12 with FP. Type of meal: Early coffee/tea. Beds: KD. Sauna, game room and spa/sauna bungalow on premises. Handicap access. Weddings and family reunions hosted. Amusement parks, antiquing, fishing, golf, casino, Great Smokies National Park, railroad. nature trail, live theater, shopping, downhill skiing, sporting events, tennis and water sports nearby.

"The cottage was delightfully cozy, and our privacy was not interrupted even once."

Tryon   C3

Foxtrot Inn

PO Box 1561, 800 Lynn Rd
Tryon, NC 28782-2708
(828)859-9706 (888)676-8050
Web: www.foxtrotinn.com

Circa 1915. Located on six acres in town, this turn-of-the-century home features mountain views and large guest rooms.

There is a private guest cottage with its own kitchen and a hanging deck. The rooms are furnished with antiques. The Cherry Room in the main house has a four-poster, queen-size canopy bed with a sitting area overlooking the inn's swimming pool. The Oak Suite includes a wood-paneled sitting room. A cozy fireplace warms the lobby.

Innkeeper(s): Wim & Tiffany Woody. $75-125. PC. 4 rooms with PB, 2 suites and 1 cottage. Breakfast included in rates. Type of meal: Full bkfst. Beds: QDT. Air conditioning. Swimming on premises. Weddings, small meetings, family reunions and seminars hosted. Antiquing, fishing, parks, shopping and water sports nearby.

Pets allowed: Pets allowed in cottage by special arrangement.

Washington   B8

Pamlico House

400 E Main St
Washington, NC 27889-5039
(252)946-7184 (800)948-8507
E-mail: pamlicohouse@coastalnet.com
Web: www.bbonline.com/nc/pamlico

Circa 1906. This gracious Colonial Revival home once served as the rectory for St. Peter's Episcopal Church. A veranda wraps around the house in a graceful curve. Furnished in Victorian antiques, the inn has the modern convenience of air conditioning. Nearby is the city's quaint waterfront. Washington is on the Historic Albemarle Tour Route and within easy driving distance to the Outer Banks.

Historic Interest: The inn is in the National Register.
Innkeeper(s): George & Jane Fields. $75-95. MC, VISA, AX, DS, PC, TC. 4 rooms with PB. Type of meal: Full bkfst. Beds: KQT.

Waynesville   B2

Grandview Lodge

466 Lickstone Rd
Waynesville, NC 28786
(828)456-5212 (800)255-7826 Fax:(828)452-5432
Circa 1890. Grandview Lodge is located on two-and-a-half acres in the Smoky Mountains. The land surrounding the lodge has an apple orchard, rhubarb patch, grape arbor and vegetable garden for the inn's kitchen. Rooms are available in the main lodge and in a newer addition. The inn's dining room is known throughout the region and Linda, a home economist, has written "Recipes from Grandview Lodge," and its sequel, "More Recipes from Grandview Lodge."

Historic Interest: The Biltmore Estate (45 minutes), Cherokee Indian Reservation (45 minutes).
Innkeeper(s): Stan & Linda Arnold. $105-120. MC, VISA, PC, TC. TAC10. 9 rooms with PB, 3 with FP and 2 suites. Breakfast and dinner included in rates. MAP. Types of meals: Full bkfst and early coffee/tea. Lunch available. Restaurant on premises. Beds: KQDT. Cable TV, fans and refrigerator in apartments in room. Air conditioning. VCR, fax and library on premises. Weddings, small meetings, family reunions and seminars hosted. Polish, Russian and German spoken. Amusement parks, antiquing, fishing, golf, live theater, parks, shopping, downhill skiing, sporting events and water sports nearby.
Publicity: Asheville Citizen, Winston-Salem Journal, Raleigh News & Observer, Atlanta Journal & Constitution.

"It's easy to see why family and friends have been enjoying trips to Grandview."

Herren House

94 East St
Waynesville, NC 28786-3836
(828)452-7837 (800)284-1932
E-mail: herren@brinet.com
Web: www.circle.net/~herren

Circa 1897. Pink and white paint emphasize the Victorian features of this two-story inn with wraparound porch. Inside, the Victorian decor is enhanced with the innkeepers' paintings and handmade furniture. Soft music and candlelight set the tone for breakfast, which often features the inn's homemade chicken sausage and a baked egg dish along with freshly baked items such as apricot scones. A garden gazebo is

an inviting spot with an overhead fan and piped in music. A block away are galleries, antique shops and restaurants. The Great Smoky Mountains National Park and the Blue Ridge Parkway begin a few minutes from the inn.

Innkeeper(s): Jackie & Frank Blevins. $75-140. MC, VISA, AX, DS, PC, TC. 6 rooms with PB. Breakfast, afternoon tea and snacks/refreshments included in rates. Types of meals: Full gourmet bkfst and early coffee/tea. Beds: KQT. Cable TV, ceiling fan and VCR in room. Air conditioning. Fax, copier and library on premises. Handicap access. Small meetings hosted. Antiquing, fishing, golf, live theater, parks, shopping, downhill skiing, cross-country skiing and water sports nearby.

"The two of you have mastered the art of sensory pleasures! Nothing was left unattended."

The Old Stone Inn

109 Dolan Rd
Waynesville, NC 28786-2885
(828)456-3333 (800)432-8499

Circa 1946. Although The Old Stone Inn may be a post-World War II structure, its legacy of innkeeping stretches for more than 50 years. Surrounded by acres of woods and the scenic North Carolina Smokies, the lodge is an ideal location to commune with nature. Exposed-log beams, wooden floors and country furnishings add to the relaxing country atmosphere. Meals are served in the stone and log dining room in front of a crackling fire. The hearty breakfasts prepare guests for a day in the

mountains, with treats such as banana nut pancakes, Tennessee sausage pie, fresh fruit and egg dishes. Candle-lit dinners are romantic, with a Southern flair accompanied by freshly baked breads, distinctive appetizers and delectable desserts. The lodge porch is lined with rocking chairs, perfect for relaxing.

Innkeeper(s): Robert & Cindy Zinser. $94-164. MC, VISA, DS. 18 rooms with PB and 4 cottages. Breakfast included in rates. Type of meal: Full bkfst. Dinner and room service available. Restaurant on premises. Beds: KQD. Antiquing, fishing, live theater, downhill skiing and water sports nearby.

"The food was absolutely great and the treatment was top notch."

The Swag Country Inn

2300 Swag Rd
Waynesville, NC 28786-9623
(828)926-0430 Fax:(828)926-2036
E-mail: letters@theswag.com
Web: www.theswag.com

Circa 1795. The Swag is composed of six hand-hewn log buildings, one dating to 1795. They were moved to the site and restored. An old church was reassembled and became the cathedral-ceilinged common room. The fireplace in this room was constructed of fieldstones with no mortar to maintain authenticity. The inn's 250 acres feature a nature trail with five hideaways along the trail, a spring-fed pond, hammocks and thick forests. A two-and-a-half-mile gravel road winds through a heavily wooded hillside to the inn. In the evening, dinner is served on pewter ware at long walnut tables. Listening to folk music and mountain storytelling afterwards is popular. A full list of special events is available each month.

Innkeeper(s): Deener Matthews. $240-510. MC, VISA, AX, DS. 12 rooms with PB, 7 with FP, 3 suites and 1 conference room. AP. Type of meal: Full bkfst. Dinner, snacks/refreshments, picnic lunch and lunch available. Restaurant on premises. Beds: KQT. Phone in room. VCR, copier, spa and sauna on premises. Handicap access. Small meetings, family reunions and seminars hosted. Antiquing and shopping nearby.

"The Swag gives us both a chance to relax our bodies and revitalize our brains."

Weaverville   B3

Dry Ridge Inn

26 Brown St
Weaverville, NC 28787-9202
(828)658-3899 (800)839-3899
E-mail: dryridgeinn@msn.com
Web: www.bbonline.com/nc/dryridge

Circa 1849. This house was built as the parsonage for the Salem Campground, an old religious revival camping area. Because of the high altitude and pleasant weather, it was used as a camp hospital for Confederate soldiers suffering from pneumonia during the Civil War. The area was called Dry Ridge by the Cherokee Indians before the campground was established.

Innkeeper(s): Paul & Mary Lou Gibson. $95-135. MC, VISA, AX, PC, TC. 7 rooms with PB. Type of meal: Full bkfst. Beds: QD. Ceiling fan and outdoor hot tub in room. Air conditioning. VCR on premises. Antiquing, art galleries, hiking, Biltmore Estate, fine arts, white water rafting, gift shop, Blue Ridge Parkway outdoor spa and live theater nearby.

"Best family vacation ever spent."

Weldon   A8

Weldon Place Inn

500 Washington Ave
Weldon, NC 27890-1644
(252)536-4582 (800)831-4470 Fax:(252)536-4708

Circa 1913. Blueberry buckle and strawberry blintzes are a pleasant way to start your morning at this Colonial Revival home. Located in a National Historic District, it is two miles from I-95. Wedding showers and other celebrations are popular here. There are beveled-glass windows, canopy beds and Italian fireplaces. Most of the inn's antiques are original to the house,

including a horse-hair stuffed couch with its original upholstery. Select the Romantic Retreat package and you'll enjoy sweets, other treats, a gift bag, sparkling cider, a whirlpool tub and breakfast in bed.

Innkeeper(s): Bill & Cathy Eleczko. $65-89. MC, VISA, AX, DS, TC. 4 rooms with PB. Breakfast included in rates. Type of meal: Full bkfst. Beds: D. Cable TV and phone in room. Air conditioning. VCR on premises. Weddings and small meetings hosted. Antiquing, fishing, live theater and shopping nearby.

Wilmington   D7

Catherine's Inn

410 S Front St
Wilmington, NC 28401-5012
(910)251-0863 (800)476-0723

Circa 1883. This Italianate-style home features wrought-iron fences and a Colonial Revival wraparound porch in the front and a two-story screened porch in the back. The 300-foot pri-

vate garden overlooks a unique sunken garden and the Cape Fear River. Antiques and reproductions fill the interior, which includes 12-foot ceilings and an heirloom grand piano. Freshly brewed coffee is delivered to each room in the morning, followed by a full breakfast served on family collections of china, crystal and sterling silver in the dining room. Turndown service and complimentary refreshments are some of the other amenities offered by the innkeepers.

Historic Interest: Catherine's Inn is registered as a local, state and national landmark home and is located in the heart of Wilmington's historic district.

Innkeeper(s): Catherine & Walter Ackiss. $85-115. MC, VISA, AX. 5 rooms with PB. Breakfast and afternoon tea included in rates. Gourmet dinner available. Beds: KQT. Phone in room. Off-street parking on premises. Antiquing, fishing, live theater and water sports nearby.

"This is the best!"

Graystone Inn

100 S 3rd St
Wilmington, NC 28401-4503
(910)763-2000 (888)763-4773 Fax:(910)763-5555
E-mail: reservations@graystoneinn.com
Web: www.graystoneinn.com

Circa 1906. If you are a connoisseur of inns, you'll be delighted with this stately mansion in the Wilmington Historic District and in the National Register. Towering columns mark the balconied grand entrance. Its 14,000 square feet of magnificent space includes appropriate furnishings, art and amenities. A staircase of hand-carved red oak rises three stories. Guests lounge in the music room, drawing room and library. A conference room and reception area are on the third floor. The elegant guest rooms are often chosen for special occasions.

Innkeeper(s): Paul & Yolanda Bolda. $159-289. MC, VISA, AX, DC, CB, DS, PC, TC. TAC10. 7 rooms with PB, 6 with FP, 2 suites and 1 conference room. Breakfast included in rates. EP. Types of meals: Full gourmet bkfst and early coffee/tea. Beds: KQ. TV, phone, turndown service, ceiling fan and computer jacks many four-poster beds in room. Air conditioning. Fax, copier, library, weight training room and PC data ports on premises. Weddings, small meetings and family reunions hosted. Antiquing, fishing, golf, museums, live theater, parks, shopping, sporting events, tennis and water sports nearby.

Publicity: *Country Inns, TV series Young Indiana Jones, Matlock, Movie Rambling Rose, Mary Janes Last Dance and Cats Eye.*

Rosehill Inn

114 S 3rd St
Wilmington, NC 28401-4556
(910)815-0250 (800)815-0250 Fax:(910)815-0350
E-mail: rosehill@rosehill.com
Web: www.rosehill.com

Circa 1848. Architect Henry Bacon Jr., most famous for designing the Lincoln Memorial in Washington, D.C., lived here in the late 19th century. Located in the largest urban historic district in the country, this

Neoclassical Victorian was completely renovated in 1995. The guest rooms are spacious and decorated in period furnishings. Breakfast treats include eggs Benedict with Cajun Crab Hollandaise and stuffed French toast with orange syrup.

Innkeeper(s): Laurel Jones, Dennis Fietsch. $95-195. MC, VISA, AX, DS, TC. TAC10. 6 rooms with PB. Breakfast included in rates. Types of meals: Full gourmet bkfst, cont plus and early coffee/tea. Beds: KQD. Cable TV and phone in room. Fax on premises. Family reunions hosted. Antiquing, fishing, golf, battleship memorial, beaches, live theater, parks, shopping, sporting events, tennis and water sports nearby.

Verandas

202 Nun St
Wilmington, NC 28401-5020
(910)251-2212 Fax:(910)251-8932
Web: www.verandas.com

Circa 1854. It's difficult to believe that this graceful three-story Victorian ever featured shag carpeting and linoleum floors. Hardly a fitting ending for a home that once belonged to a Confederate ship-builder and blockade runner, who burned his shipyard rather than let Union soldiers capture it. Innkeepers Charles Pennington and Dennis Madsen transformed Verandas from an ill-decorated, fire-damaged wreck into an elegant bed & breakfast. The restoration process included two years of painstaking work. For their efforts, they have been awarded a historic preservation award from the Historic Wilmington Foundation. The romantic guest rooms are filled with American, French and English antiques. Most rooms include a fireplace, and the beds are topped with luxurious, hand-ironed linens. Bathrooms now feature oversized tubs and marble floors and vanities. Gourmet coffees and teas accompany the lavish breakfasts, which feature delectable entrees such as a croissant stuffed with smoked salmon and cream cheese and baked in an egg custard. There are many amenities for business travelers, including modem hook-ups, fax service and corporate midweek rates.

Historic Interest: Fort Fisher (15 miles).

Innkeeper(s): Charles Pennington & Dennis Madsen. $120-180. MC, VISA, AX, DS, PC, TC. 8 rooms with PB. Breakfast and snacks/refreshments included in rates. Types of meals: Full gourmet bkfst and early coffee/tea. Beds:

KQT. Cable TV, phone and VCR in room. Central air. Fax on premises. Family reunions hosted. Sign language spoken. Antiquing, art galleries, beaches, bicycling, canoeing/kayaking, fishing, golf, live theater, museums, parks, shopping, tennis and water sports nearby.

"You have done a magnificent job with your property, and you certainly make your guests feel welcome with your food and hospitality."

Wilson   B7

Miss Betty's B&B Inn

600 West Nash St
Wilson, NC 27893-3045
(252)243-4447 (800)258-2058 Fax:(252)243-4447

Circa 1858. Located in a gracious setting in the downtown historic district, the inn is comprised of several restored historic homes. Breakfast is served in the Victorian dining room of the main house, with its walnut antique furniture and clusters of roses on the wallpaper. All the extras, such as lace tablecloths and hearty meals, conjure up the Old South. Four golf courses and many fine restaurants are nearby. Wilson is known as the antique capitol of North Carolina.

Historic Interest: The inn is listed in the National Register and located on Nash Street, which once was described as one of the most beautiful streets in the country.

Innkeeper(s): Betty & Fred Spitz. $60-80. MC, VISA, AX, DC, CB, DS, PC, TC. 14 rooms with PB, 11 with FP and 3 suites. Breakfast included in rates. Type of meal: Full bkfst. Beds: KQDT. Cable TV, phone and ceiling fan in room. Air conditioning. Fax and copier on premises. Handicap access. Family reunions hosted. Antiquing, golf, four golf courses nearby, live theater, sporting events and tennis nearby.

Publicity: *Wilson Daily Times, Enterprise, Southern Living, Mid-Atlantic.*

"Yours is second to none. Everything was perfect. I can see why you are so highly rated."

Winston-Salem   B5

Augustus T. Zevely Inn

803 S Main St
Winston-Salem, NC 27101-5332
(336)748-9299 (800)928-9299 Fax:(336)721-2211
Web: www.winston-salem.inn.com

Circa 1844. The Zevely Inn is the only lodging in Old Salem. Each of the rooms at this charming pre-Civil War inn have a view of historic Old Salem. Moravian furnishings and fixtures permeate the decor of each of the guest quarters, some of which boast working fireplaces. The home's architecture is reminiscent of many structures built in Old Salem during the second quarter of the 19th century. The formal dining room and parlor have wood burning fireplaces. The two-story porch offers visitors a view of the period gardens and a beautiful magnolia tree. A line of Old Salem furniture has been created by Lexington Furniture Industries, and several pieces were created especially for the Zevely Inn.

Historic Interest: Winston-Salem abounds with historic activity. Old Salem, founded in 1766, is a restored, Moravian community. Among the sites are the Historic Bethabara Park, the Piedmont Craftsman, Inc. and Mesda, the nation's only museum dedicated to researching Southern materials and styles. The museum features a variety of furniture, textiles, ceramics and paintings dating back to the 17th century.

Innkeeper(s): Lori Long. $80-205. MC, VISA, AX, PC, TC. 12 rooms with PB, 3 suites and 1 suite. Breakfast and snacks/refreshments included in rates. Beds: KQDT. Cable TV, phone and whirlpool tub in room. Air conditioning. Fax and copier on premises. Antiquing, old Salem Historic District, live theater, shopping and sporting events nearby.

Publicity: *Washington Post Travel, Salem Star, Winston-Salem Journal, Tasteful, Country Living, National Trust for Historic Preservation, Homes and Gardens, Homes Across America, Southern Living.*

"Colonial charm with modern conveniences, great food. Very nice! Everything was superb."

Brookstown Inn B&B

200 Brookstown Ave
Winston-Salem, NC 27101-5202
(336)725-1120 (800)845-4262 Fax:(336)773-0147

Circa 1837. Originally constructed as a cotton mill, located on one acre, this three-story building now offers gracious accommodations to travelers. The old brick walls, exposed wood beams and high ceilings add warmth and character to all of the rooms, including the parlor and conference room. Guest rooms are decorated with attractive colonial reproductions such as poster beds, and there are spacious suites with decorative fireplaces, sitting areas and a garden tub or whirlpool bath. Breakfast is served in the dining room, which features a large colonial fireplace set against a sunny yellow wallcovering. Evening receptions offer wine and cheese in the parlor. Just a short walk away is Williamsburg-style Old Salem Moravian Village, built in 1766.

Historic Interest: Old Sales Moravan Village (.2 miles).

Innkeeper(s): Gary Colbert, GM. $125-155. MC, VISA, AX, DC, TC. TAC10. 71 rooms, 40 with PB, 31 suites and 2 conference rooms. Breakfast, afternoon tea and snacks/refreshments included in rates. Type of meal: Cont plus. Banquet service and catering service available. Restaurant on premises. Beds: KQD. Cable TV, phone, turndown service, garden tubs, hair dryers and iron & ironing board in room. Air conditioning. Fax and copier on premises. Weddings, small meetings, family reunions and seminars hosted. Antiquing, art galleries, live theater, museums, sporting events and wineries nearby.

Henry F. Shaffner House

150 S Marshall St
Winston-Salem, NC 27101-2833
(336)777-0052 (800)952-2256 Fax:(336)777-1188

Circa 1907. Located near the historic Old Salem area, this elaborate Queen Anne Tudor-style Victorian has been carefully renovated and was awarded the city's restoration award. Handsome gables, copper roof shingles and an elegant iron fence establish the house's unique appeal. Built by Henry Shaffner, one of the founders of Wachovia Bank, the mansion features tiger oak woodwork, fireplaces and several common rooms: the parlor, tea room, library and sun room. The inn is popular for holding special events and weddings. Each room is distinctively decorated with tastefully selected furnishings and fabrics. A favored guest room is the private top-floor Piedmont Room with Jacuzzi, wet bar, king-size bed and sitting room.

Breakfast features gourmet omelets and home-baked breads, fruits and specialty coffees. Murder-mystery weekends are also offered. Wine and cheese are offered in the evening. There is a horse-drawn carriage service available.

$99-239. MC, VISA, AX, PC. 9 rooms with PB, 3 suites and 2 conference rooms. Breakfast included in rates. Types of meals: Full bkfst and cont plus. Dinner, snacks/refreshments, banquet service, catering service and room service available. Beds: KQT. Cable TV, phone, turndown service, ceiling fan and whirlpool tubs in room. Air conditioning. Fax, copier, library and fitness club passes on premises. Weddings, small meetings, family reunions and seminars hosted. Antiquing, golf, live theater, parks, shopping, sporting events and tennis nearby.

Publicity: *Southern Living, Triad Business News, Winston-Salem Journal, Life & Leisure, Winston-Salem, Buena Vista, Great Country Inns.*

Lady Anne's Victorian B&B

612 Summit St
Winston-Salem, NC 27101-1117
(336)724-1074
Web: www.bbonline.com/nc/ladyannes

Circa 1890. Like the name indicates, this bed & breakfast is decked in Victorian tradition. Victorian antiques and treasures fill the rooms. Most of the guest quarters boast stained-glass windows and high ceilings. Three rooms include a balcony, patio or glassed-in porch. Most rooms also offer modern amenities such as refrigerators, coffee makers, stereos and double Jacuzzi tubs complete with romantic music. One offers a double garden

tub perfect for viewing a romantic sunset. A Victorian-style breakfast is served in the formal dining room or on the porch. Innkeeper Shelley Kirley offers a wealth of information about the history of her inn and the surrounding area.

Historic Interest: Lady Anne is located in Winston-Salem's historic West End neighborhood, one of the first streetcar suburbs in North Carolina. It's only three minutes by car to historic Salem and the Reynolds House, the summer residence of the R.J. Reynolds tobacco family.

Innkeeper(s): Shelley Kirley. $60-185. MC, VISA, AX, DS, TC. 4 rooms with PB and 3 suites. Breakfast and snacks/refreshments included in rates. AP. Types of meals: Full bkfst and early coffee/tea. Beds: QD. Cable TV, phone, ceiling fan, VCR and double Jacuzzis and double garden tub in room. Central air. Modem hookup on premises. Antiquing, fishing, old Salem Historic Village, Reynolds House, live theater, parks, shopping and sporting events nearby.

"We frequent B&Bs often and wanted to tell you that Lady Anne's is one of the finest that we've stayed in. We will be sure to tell all of our friends and family about your charming and friendly B&B."

North Dakota

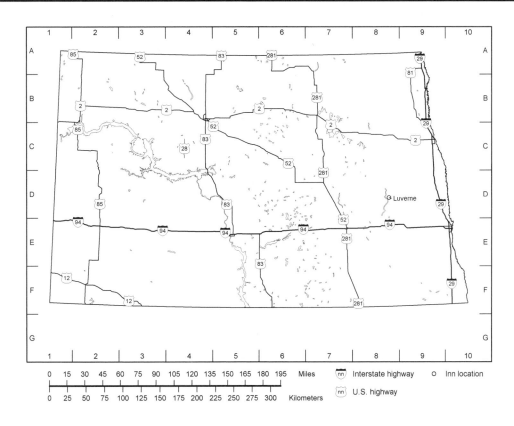

0 15 30 45 60 75 90 105 120 135 150 165 180 195 Miles

0 25 50 75 100 125 150 175 200 225 250 275 300 Kilometers

nn Interstate highway ○ Inn location

nn U.S. highway

Fessenden · *C6*

Beiseker Mansion
1001 2nd St NE
Fessenden, ND 58438-7409
(701)547-3411

Circa 1899. Situated on nearly a city block, this 15-room Queen Anne Victorian is bordered by an old-fashioned wrought iron fence. Features include a splendid wraparound veranda and two turrets. The original golden oak woodwork is seen in the staircase, fireplace and dining room wainscoting. The turret room, with its king-size sleigh bed and marble-topped dresser, is a favorite choice. A third-floor library, open to guests, contains 3,000 volumes. The house is in the National Register of Historic Places.

Innkeeper(s): Paula & Jerry Tweton. $55-95. MC, VISA. 6 rooms, 2 with PB. Breakfast included in rates. Types of meal: Full bkfst. Central air, TV and VCR in room.

Publicity: *Grand Forks Herald, Fessenden Herald Press.*

"What a beautiful house! The food and atmosphere were lovely."

Luverne · *D8*

Volden Farm
11943 County Rd 26
Luverne, ND 58056
(701)769-2275 Fax:(701)769-2610

Circa 1926. Perennial gardens and a hedge of lilacs surround this redwood house with its newer addition. A favorite room is the North Room with a lace canopy bed, an old pie safe and a Texas Star quilt made by the host's grandmother. Guests enjoy soaking in the clawfoot tub while looking out over the hills. There are two libraries, a music room and game room. The innkeepers also offer lodging in the Law Office, which dates to 1885 and is a separate little prairie house ideal for families. A stream, bordered by old oaks and formed by a natural spring, meanders through the property. The chickens here lay green and blue eggs. Dinner is available by advanced arrangement. Hiking, birdwatching, snowshoeing and skiing are nearby.

Innkeeper(s): Jim & JoAnne Wold. $60-95. PC. TAC10. 2 rooms and 1 cottage. Breakfast and snacks/refreshments included in rates. Types of meals: Full gourmet bkfst and early coffee/tea. Gourmet dinner and picnic lunch available. Beds: KDT. Bicycles and library on premises. Small meetings and seminars hosted. Limited Russian and limited Norwegian spoken. Antiquing, fishing, hiking, golf, canoeing, snowshoeing, bird watching, downhill skiing and cross-country skiing nearby.

Pets allowed: Outside.

"Very pleasant indeed! Jim & JoAnne make you feel good. There's so much to do, and the hospitality is amazing!"

Medora   E2

The Rough Riders Hotel B&B
Medora, ND 58645
(701)623-4444 Fax:(701)623-4494

Circa 1865. This old hotel has the branding marks of Teddy Roosevelt's cattle ranch as well as other brands stamped into the rough-board facade out front. A wooden sidewalk helps to maintain the turn-of-the-century cow-town feeling. Rustic guest rooms are above the restaurant and are furnished with homesteader antiques original to the area. In the summer, an outdoor pageant is held complete with stagecoach and horses. In October, deer hunters are accommodated. The hotel, along with two motels, is managed by the non-profit Theodore Roosevelt Medora Foundation.

Innkeeper(s): Randy Hatzenbuhler. $65-77. MC, VISA, AX. TAC10. 9 rooms with PB. Breakfast included in rates.

Mountain   B8

221 Melsted Place
PO Box 221
Mountain, ND 58262
(701)993-8257 Fax:(701)993-8257

Circa 1910. This handsome gabled estate is comprised of cast concrete blocks and offers three stories with a wide porch, stained and mullioned windows and inside, a grand staircase. Guest rooms feature antiques. At Christmas, the mansion is popular for tours because of its festive decorations. Candlelight and piano dinners and Victorian teas are held. Guests can arrange to play torchlight croquet or spend a morning picking berries. The area has an Icelandic heritage, and in August, an Icelandic Festival, the Deuce, is held.

Innkeeper(s): Lonnette Kelley. $65. MC, VISA, DS, PC, TC. 3 suites. Breakfast included in rates. Types of meals: Full breakfast and early coffee/tea. Dinner available. AP. Beds: KQT. Turndown service and ceiling fan in room. TV, VCR, fax, copier and bicycles on premises. Weddings, small meetings, family reunions and seminars hosted. Antiquing, fishing, parks, shopping, downhill skiing, cross-country skiing, golf, theater and watersports nearby.

Northwood   C8

Heritage House
440 34th St
Northwood, ND 58267
(701)587-5251

Circa 1914. Located on an 18-acre farm, the Heritage House has been the home to three generations of Thompsons. With two-and-a-half stories, the house offers bay windows and a steep mansard-like roof, which partially protects the third-story sun porch. In winter, the inn's country breakfasts are served in the formal dining room. Summertime breakfasts are provided poolside. Ask for the West Room and you'll enjoy French Country decor and a large bay window overlooking the farm's lawns and cottonwoods.

Innkeeper(s): Marjorie & David Thompson. $45-55. PC, TC. 4 rooms. Breakfast and evening snack included in rates. Types of meal: Early coffee/tea. Beds: QDT. Turndown service in room. TV, swimming and bicycles on premises. Weddings, small meetings and family reunions hosted. Antiquing, parks, shopping, cross-country skiing and golf nearby.

Ohio

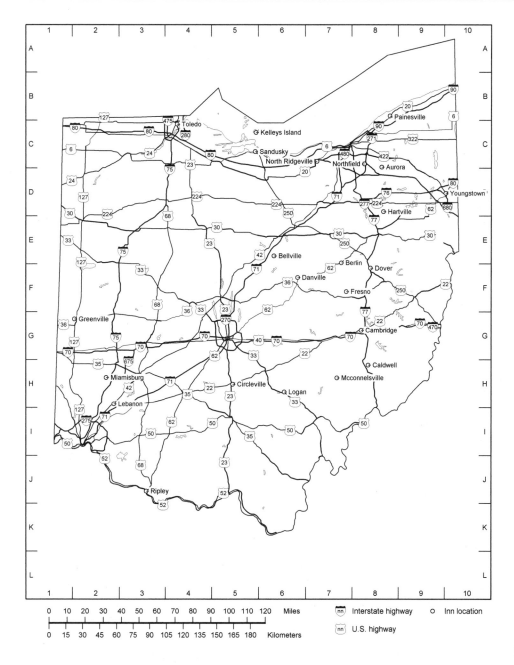

Bellville
E6

Frederick Fitting House, Ltd.

72 Fitting Ave
Bellville, OH 44813-1043
(419)886-2863 Fax:(419)886-2863

Circa 1863. This green and white Italianate Victorian house commands a corner of the town of Bellville. Rooms include the Colonial Room with a queen canopy bed and the Shaker Room with a queen Shaker bed. The Victorian Room includes a queen-size sleigh bed. Breakfast may be served in the Victorian dining room, garden gazebo or front porch. Guests can relax by a warming fire in the living room and enjoy the variety of books, CDs and movies found in the library. A bike trail, Malabar farms, Mohican River, skiing and antique shops are nearby.
Innkeeper(s): Barb & Jim Lomax. $69-83. 3 rooms with PB. Breakfast included in rates. Types of meals: Full bkfst and early coffee/tea. Gourmet dinner and snacks/refreshments available. Ceiling fan in room. Air conditioning. VCR on premises. Antiquing, shopping, downhill skiing, cross-country skiing and sporting events nearby.

Caldwell
H8

Harkins House Inn

715 West St
Caldwell, OH 43724-1230
(740)732-7347

Circa 1905. Innkeeper Stacey Lucas' great-grandfather built this turn-of-the-century home, which features many Victorian elements. He was a founder of the town's First National Bank. High ceilings, intricate moldings and original woodwork remain, as does the grand staircase. The decor includes brightly painted walls and flowery wallpapers. The second-story hall features Victorian furnishings, rose walls with teal stenciling and carpeting. Guests choose their own breakfast fare from a daily menu, which features items such as bacon, eggs, home-made muffins and coffee cake. State parks, antique shops and historic sites are nearby.
Innkeeper(s): Jeff & Stacey Lucas. $30-75. MC, VISA, AX, PC, TC. 2 rooms with PB. Breakfast included in rates. Types of meals: Full bkfst and early coffee/tea. Beds: DT. Cable TV in room. Air conditioning. VCR, library and child care on premises. Weddings and small meetings hosted. Antiquing, fishing, golf, live theater, parks and shopping nearby.

"Lucky for us we found your most interesting and beautiful home."

Cambridge
G8

Morning Glory B&B

5637 Fairdale Dr
Cambridge, OH 43725-9454
(740)439-2499

Circa 1859. This two-story farmhouse set on five acres along the Old National Road is conveniently located between Cambridge and New Concord. The original staircase, constructed of chestnut and walnut, leads to the three guest rooms that offer private baths and ceiling fans. The inn features hardwood floors, antiques and many handmade

items, influenced by the Amish, whose enclave is just an hour away. Guests can enjoy a full breakfast in the pantry kitchen by the warmth of the hearth or in the dining room. Shopping, antiques, crafts, museums and parks are located nearby.
Innkeeper(s): Jim & Jane Gibson. $65-75. MC, VISA, DS, PC, TC. 3 rooms with PB. Breakfast and snacks/refreshments included in rates. Types of meals: Full bkfst and early coffee/tea. Beds: Q. Ceiling fan in room. Air conditioning. Family reunions hosted. Antiquing, golf, "The Wild" animal preserve, glass factories, live theater, parks, shopping and tennis nearby.

"Outstanding, we give it '5 stars.'"

Circleville
H5

Penguin Crossing B&B

3291 SR 56 W
Circleville, OH 43113-9622
(740)477-6222 (800)736-4846 Fax:(740)420-6060
E-mail: innkeeper@penguin.cc
Web: www.penguin.cc

Circa 1820. Once a stagecoach stop, now a romantic country getaway, this B&B offers amenities in the rooms such as a wood-burning fireplace, brass bed or a heart-shaped Jacuzzi.
As the name might suggest, the innkeepers have a collection of penguins on display. Breakfasts include a selection of natural foods, and the innkeeper is happy to cater to special dietary needs.

Historic Interest: Ted Lewis Museum (4 miles), Circleville Pumpkin Show (4 miles), Deer Creek State Park (20 miles).
Innkeeper(s): Ross & Tracey Irvin. $100-225. MC, VISA, AX, DS, PC, TC. 5 rooms with PB, 2 with FP. Breakfast included in rates. Types of meals: Cont and early coffee/tea. Beds: KQDT. Phone and Jacuzzi (four rooms) in room. Air conditioning. VCR and fax on premises. Handicap access. Weddings, small meetings, family reunions and seminars hosted. Antiquing, fishing, live theater, parks, shopping and water sports nearby.

"If I had to describe this home in one word, it would be — enchanting."

Danville
F6

Red Fox Country Inn

26367 Danville Amity Rd, PO Box 717
Danville, OH 43014-0746
(740)599-7369

Circa 1830. This inn, located on 15 scenic central Ohio acres, was built originally to house those traveling on the Danville-Amity Wagon Road and later became a farm home. Amish woven rag rugs and country antiques decorate the guest rooms. Some of the furnishings belonged to early owners, and some date to the 18th century. Three rooms include Amish-made oak beds and the fourth an 1880s brass and iron double bed. Breakfasts

include fresh pastries, fruits, coffee and a variety of delectable entrees. Special dietary needs usually can be accommodated. There are books and games available in the inn's sitting room, and guests also are invited to relax on the front porch. Golfing, canoeing, fishing, horseback riding, hiking, biking, skiing and

Mohican State Park are nearby, and the inn is 30 minutes from the largest Amish community in the United States.

Historic Interest: Amish settlements, Malibar Farm, historic Roscoe Village and the National Heisey Glass Museum are less than an hour from the inn.

Innkeeper(s): Sue & Denny Simpkins. $75-85. MC, VISA, AX, DS, PC, TC. TAC10. 4 rooms with PB. Breakfast included in rates. Beds: QD. Air conditioning. Library on premises.

"Our dinner and breakfast were '5 star'. Thank you for the gracious hospitality and special kindness you showed us."

The White Oak Inn

29683 Walhonding Rd, SR 715
Danville, OH 43014
(740)599-6107
E-mail: yvonne@ecr.net
Web: whiteoakinn.com

Circa 1915. Large oaks and ivy surround the wide front porch of this three-story farmhouse situated on 13 green acres. It is located on the former Indian trail and pioneer road that runs along the Kokosing River, and an Indian mound has been discovered on the property. The inn's woodwork is all original white oak, and guest rooms are furnished in antiques. Visitors often shop for maple syrup, cheese and handicrafts at nearby Amish farms. Three cozy fireplace rooms provide the perfect setting for romantic evenings.

Historic Interest: Roscoe Village, restored Erie Canal Town (30 minutes).

Innkeeper(s): Yvonne & Ian Martin. $80-140. MC, VISA, AX, DS, PC, TC. TAC10. 10 rooms with PB, 3 with FP and 1 conference room. Breakfast and snacks/refreshments included in rates. MAP. Types of meals: Full bkfst and early coffee/tea. Gourmet dinner and catering service available. Beds: QDT. Phone, ceiling fan and TV jacks in room. Air conditioning. Bicycles, library, guest refrigerator and piano on premises. Weddings, small meetings, family reunions and seminars hosted. French spoken. Antiquing, fishing, Amish area/museums, horseback riding, parks, shopping and water sports nearby.

"The dinner was just fabulous and we enjoyed playing the antique grand piano."

Dover   F8

Olde World Bed & Breakfast

2982 State Route 516 NW
Dover, OH 44622-7247
(330)343-1333 (800)447-1273 Fax:(330)364-8022

Circa 1881. The five guest rooms at this red brick Victorian farmhouse have differing themes including Oriental, Parisian, Mediterranean and Alpine. Ask for the Victorian Room, which has a beautiful carved bed and a private bath with clawfoot tub. The parlor features beautifully preserved woodwork in its pocket doors and fireplace mantel. A chandelier, antique furnishings and floral wallpaper in the dining room add a Victorian atmosphere to the inn's full breakfast, which often includes Swiss Eggs, rhubarb muffins, cream scones and grilled local whole hog sausage. A favorite activity is retreating to the veranda

to munch on warm homemade cookies. The Amish countryside and an abundance of antiquing opportunities are nearby.

Innkeeper(s): Jonna Cranebaugh. $60-100. MC, VISA, DS. 5 rooms with PB, 1 suite and 1 conference room. Breakfast included in rates. Type of meal: Full gourmet bkfst. Afternoon tea, dinner, snacks/refreshments and lunch available. Beds: KQ. Air conditioning. VCR, fax and spa on premises. Family reunions and seminars hosted. Antiquing, fishing, golf, Amish country historical sites, live theater, shopping, tennis and water sports nearby.

Greenville   G2

Apple Blossom Inn

5842 State Route 571 E
Greenville, OH 45331-9612
(937)548-1223 Fax:(937)548-3314
E-mail: applewood@wesnet.com
Web: www.wesnet.com/applewood

Circa 1918. An apple orchard surrounds this aptly named inn. The 20-acre grounds boast 2,000 trees, as well as five gift shops, a bakery, candy store, car museum and a model log home. Each guest room has a private entrance, and each is decorated in a country Victorian style. Breakfasts feature homemade apple dumplings with fruit fresh from the orchard.

Historic Interest: Annie Oakley grave site and museum.

Innkeeper(s): Don & Marlyn Shellabarger. $69. PC, TC. 4 rooms. Breakfast included in rates. Type of meal: Cont plus. Beds: QDT. TV, ceiling fan and VCR in room. Air conditioning. Fax and copier on premises. Small meetings and family reunions hosted. Antiquing, golf, museums, parks, shopping and tennis nearby.

Hartville   D8

Ivy & Lace

415 S Prospect Ave
Hartville, OH 44632-9401
(330)877-6357

Circa 1920. Large trees shade the exterior of Ivy & Lace, a historic home built in the Mission and four-square architectural styles, both of which were popular when the property was being constructed. Hartville's blacksmith built this home. Guest rooms feature antique furnishings, including a few pieces from the innkeepers' family. Rates include a full breakfast, and the artfully presented morning specialties include garnishes of fresh flowers or fresh fruit. Crepes and French toast are among the entrees. Guests can walk from the home to the Town Square with its antique shops. Flea markets and Tessmer's General Store are other popular attractions.

Innkeeper(s): Sue & Paul Tarr. $65-75. AX, DS, PC. 3 rooms, 1 with PB. Breakfast included in rates. Type of meal: Full bkfst. Beds: QDT. Cable TV, ceiling fan and phones and TV can be arranged in room. Air conditioning. Antiquing, golf, live theater, museums, parks, shopping, cross-country skiing and sporting events nearby.

Kelleys Island   C5

Himmelblau B&B

337 Shannon Way
Kelleys Island, OH 43438
(419)746-2200

Circa 1893. This secluded Queen Anne Victorian on the Eastern Shore of Kellys Island rests on more than eight acres of lake front lawns and cedar groves. Its front yard tree swing and slate blue and white gabled entrance offer an inviting introduction to a pleasant stay. Once the summer home of an Ohio governor, the property was also an early 1900s vineyard. Inside are a screened porch and a second-floor reading corner, which offers expansive Lake Erie views. A favorite activity of guests is to walk along the pristine shoreline at sunrise. The more adventurous enjoy snorkeling around an old shipwreck yards from the shoreline. Watching for white-tail deer after a moonlight swim, sunbathing and stargazing are popular activities, as well.

Innkeeper(s): Marvin Robinson. Call for rates. 3 rooms. Beds: KD. Ceiling fan in room.

Lebanon   H2

Burl Manor

230 S Mechanic St
Lebanon, OH 45036-2212
(513)934-0400 (800)450-0401 Fax:(513)934-0402

Circa 1837. This handsome mansion was originally built for William Denney, an early editor and publisher for Ohio's oldest weekly newspaper, the Western Star. In addition to the parlors and formal dining room, the manor has an

unusual sunroom in the center staircase. There are Oriental rugs, period wallpapers and carved fireplaces. A swimming pool, lawn croquet, horseshoes, volleyball and basketball are among the activities that can be enjoyed on the premises. Guests can ride a bike or rent a canoe and enjoy the sites of the Little Miami River. Tennis and golf are just minutes away.

Innkeeper(s): Liz & Jay Jorling. $80. 3 rooms with PB, 3 with FP. Type of meal: Full bkfst. Beds: Q. TV and telephone available in room.

Logan   H6

The Inn At Cedar Falls

21190 SR 374
Logan, OH 43138
(740)385-7489 (800)653-2557 Fax:(740)385-0820

Circa 1987. This barn-style inn was constructed on 60 acres adjacent to Hocking State Parks and one-half mile from the waterfalls. The kitchen and dining room is in a 19th-century log house with a wood-burning stove and 18-inch-wide plank floor.

Accommodations in the new barn building are simple and comfortable, each furnished with antiques. There are also six, fully equipped log cabins available, each individually decorated. Verandas provide sweeping views

of woodland and meadow. The grounds include organic gardens for the inn's gourmet dinners, and animals that have been spotted include bobcat, red fox, wild turkey and whitetail deer.

Innkeeper(s): Ellen Grinsfelder. $75-240. MC, VISA, PC. 9 rooms with PB, 6 cabins and 2 conference rooms. Breakfast included in rates. Types of meals: Full gourmet bkfst and early coffee/tea. Gourmet dinner, picnic lunch and gourmet lunch available. Restaurant on premises. Beds: QT. Wood burning and gas log stoves in room. Air conditioning. Fax, copier and library on premises. Handicap access. Weddings, small meetings, family reunions and seminars hosted. Antiquing, fishing, live theater, parks, shopping and cross-country skiing nearby.

"Very peaceful, relaxing and friendly. Couldn't be nicer."

McConnelsville   H7

The Outback Inn

171 E Union Ave
McConnelsville, OH 43756-1373
(740)962-2158 (800)542-7171

Circa 1870. This Federalist-style home boasts many modern features, but the innkeepers have maintained much of its historic charm, retaining the original oak woodwork, pocket doors and the original gas fireplace, which dates to 1914. Each of the three guest rooms is

decorated with a specific theme in mind. In the Roadside Roost, parrot art objects, antique lamps and a 1930s-era double bed create a cozy atmosphere. The other comfortable rooms include the Queen's Chamber, which features a queen-size four-poster bed, and the Hooray for Hollywood room, which features an Art Deco bedroom set, including two twin beds. The home contains a variety of antiques, and many pieces of stained glass. The innkeepers prepare a hearty breakfast, and each meal includes gourmet coffee, fresh juices, a fresh fruit cup and mini muffins. The daily entrees vary; the meal might include a German apple puff pancake, a three-cheese egg puff with ham, or baked English breakfast pudding. The area offers many historic sites, including an 1890s opera house, a restored one-room schoolhouse and three covered bridges. Guests can take a historic walking tour of McConnelsville. The innkeepers are both professional actors (one is also a director), and they host a live radio show twice weekly from the inn.

Innkeeper(s): Bob & Carol Belfance. $65-70. PC, TC. 3 rooms with PB. Breakfast included in rates. Types of meals: Full bkfst, veg bkfst and early coffee/tea. Beds: QDT. Phone in room. Air conditioning. Private patio, garden and front porch with old fashioned swing on premises. Antiquing, art galleries, bicycling, canoeing/kayaking, fishing, golf, hiking, horseback riding, live theater, museums, parks, shopping, tennis and water sports nearby.

Miamisburg   H2

English Manor B&B

505 E Linden Ave
Miamisburg, OH 45342-2850
(937)866-2288 (800)676-9456

Circa 1924. This is a beautiful English Tudor mansion situated on a tree-lined street of Victorian homes. Well-chosen antiques combined with the innkeepers' personal heirlooms added to the inn's polished floors, sparkling leaded-and-stained-glass windows and shining silver, make this an elegant retreat. Breakfast is served in the formal dining room. Tea is served in the afternoon. Fine restaurants, a water park, baseball, air force museum and theater are close by, as is The River Corridor bikeway on the banks of the Great Miami River.

Historic Interest: 10 minutes south of Dayton.

Innkeeper(s): Ken & Jeannette Huelsman. $65-95. MC, VISA, AX, DC, CB, DS. 5 rooms and 1 conference room. Breakfast included in rates. Type of meal: Full bkfst. Phone and turndown service in room. Air conditioning. VCR on premises. Weddings, small meetings, family reunions and seminars hosted. Amusement parks, antiquing, live theater, shopping and sporting events nearby.

North Ridgeville C7

St. George House

33941 Lorain Rd
North Ridgeville, OH 44039-4231
(440)327-9354

Circa 1880. St. George House offers a restful alternative to staying in the city. The historic home is just 18 miles from Cleveland, but secluded on an acre and a half of grounds in the country. The guest rooms feature antiques and early American furnishings. After breakfast, guests can head out and take a short drive into the city where they'll find a variety of attractions. The Rock and Roll Hall of Fame, Great Lakes Science Center, antique shops, galleries and restaurants are among the many offerings. Oberlin College, an antique district and flea market are some of the local attractions. Guests also might arrange a ferry ride or 20-minute flight out to the Lake Erie Islands.
Innkeeper(s): Helen Bernardine & Muriel Dodd. $60-75. PC. 3 rooms, 1 with PB and 1 conference room. Breakfast included in rates. Types of meals: Cont plus, cont, veg bkfst and early coffee/tea. Room service available. Beds: QDT. Air conditioning. VCR, fax and bicycles on premises. Weddings and family reunions hosted. Amusement parks, antiquing, beaches, bicycling, fishing, golf, hiking, horseback riding, Baldwin-Wallace, Case Western Reserve, live theater, museums, parks, shopping, sporting events, water sports and wineries nearby. Pets allowed: confined to personal kennel.
"Your house is so beautiful and very relaxing."

Painesville B8

Rider's 1812 Inn

792 Mentor Ave
Painesville, OH 44077-2516
(216)354-8200

Circa 1812. In the days when this inn and tavern served the frontier Western Reserve, it could provide lodging and meals for more than 100 overnight guests. Restored in 1988, the pub features an original fireplace and wavy window panes. Most of the inn's floors are rare, long-needle pine. A passageway in the cellar is said to have been part of the Underground Railroad. An English-style restaurant is also on the premises. Guest rooms are furnished with antiques. Breakfast in bed is the option of choice.
Historic Interest: President Garfield's Home, Shadybrook.
Innkeeper(s): Elaine Crane & Judge Gary Herman. $75-99. MC, VISA, AX, DS. 1 suites and 3 conference rooms. Breakfast included in rates. Type of meal: Full bkfst. Afternoon tea, dinner, picnic lunch, lunch, banquet service, catering service and room service available. Restaurant on premises. Beds: KQDT. Cable TV, phone, turndown service, ceiling fan and VCR in room. Air conditioning. Fax, copier and child care on premises. Handicap access. Weddings, small meetings, family reunions and seminars hosted. Amusement parks, antiquing, live theater, shopping, cross-country skiing and water sports nearby. Pets allowed: limited.
Publicity: *Business Review, News-Herald, Channel 5, Midwest Living.*

Poland (Youngstown) D10

The Inn at the Green

500 S Main St
Poland(Youngstown), OH 44514-2032
(330)757-4688

Circa 1876. Main Street in Poland has a parade of historic houses including Connecticut Western Reserve colonials, Federal and Greek Revival houses. The Inn at the Green is a Classic Victorian Baltimore townhouse. Two of the common rooms, the greeting room and parlor have working marble fireplaces. Interiors evoke an authentic 19th-century atmosphere

with antiques and Oriental rugs that enhance the moldings, 12-foot ceilings and poplar floors.
Innkeeper(s): Ginny & Steve Meloy. $60. MC, VISA, DS. TAC10. 4 rooms with PB, 3 with FP. Breakfast included in rates. Type of meal: Cont. Beds: QDT. Cable TV and phone in room. Air conditioning. Antiquing, golf, biking trails and Amish country nearby, live theater, parks and shopping nearby.
"Thank you for a comfortable and perfect stay in your beautiful Victorian home."

Ripley J3

Misty River B&B

206 N Front St
Ripley, OH 45167-1015
(937)392-1556 Fax:(937)392-1556

Circa 1830. Ulysses S. Grant was a boarder here while he attended the Whittmore Private School in Ripley in the fall of 1838 and winter of 1839. This small 19th-century homestead-style house, located in the town's 55-acre historic district, is just across the road from the Ohio River. The bed & breakfast is decorated with a comfortable mix of country and antique furnishings. A cozy wood-burning fireplace in the living room warms guests in  the cooler evenings. The river offers guests a view of barges and boats, and wonderful sunsets. Ripley has many historic attractions, including Rankin House (of "Uncle Tom's Cabin" fame), the home of abolitionist Rev. John Rankin. Rankin and his family helped more than 1,000 slaves find their way to freedom.
Innkeeper(s): Dorothy Prevost & Lanny Warren. $75. PC, TC. TAC10. 2 rooms with PB. Breakfast included in rates. Types of meals: Full bkfst and early coffee/tea. Beds: D. Air conditioning. VCR, fax and books on Ulysses S. Grant on premises. Antiquing, fishing, biking, hiking, walking, shopping and water sports nearby.
Publicity: *Columbus Dispatch, Ripley Bee, Ohio.*
"It was like going back to "Grandmas". We enjoyed the simple beauty and pleasant atmosphere, the fire in the hearth, comfortable bed, and delicious home cooking. We are rested and refreshed. Thanks, Dotty, for your special touch!"

The Signal House

234 N Front St
Ripley, OH 45167-1015
(937)392-1640 Fax:(937)392-1640

Circa 1830. This Greek Italianate home is said to have been used to aid the Underground Railroad. A light in the attic told Rev. John Rankin, a dedicated abolitionist, that it was safe to transport slaves to freedom. Located within a 55-acre historical district, guests can take a glance back in time, exploring museums and antique shops. Twelve-foot ceilings with ornate plaster-work grace the parlor, and guests can sit on any of three porches anticipating paddlewheelers traversing the Ohio River.
Innkeeper(s): Vic & Betsy Billingsley. $75. MC, VISA, DS, PC, TC. TAC10. 2 rooms. Breakfast included in rates. Types of meals: Full bkfst and early coffee/tea. Snacks/refreshments available. Beds: Q. Ceiling fan in room. Central air. VCR, fax, copier and library on premises. Small meetings hosted. Antiquing, bicycling, canoeing/kayaking, fishing, golf, hiking, horseback riding, museums, parks, shopping, tennis, water sports and wineries nearby.

Sagamore Hills
D8

The Inn at Brandywine Falls
8230 Brandywine Rd
Sagamore Hills, OH 44067-2810
(330)467-1812

Circa 1848. Overlooking Brandywine Falls and situated snuggly on national parkland, this National Register Greek Revival farmhouse has been meticulously renovated. Antiques made in Ohio are featured in the Greek Revival-style rooms and include sleigh and four-poster beds. Some suites include a double whirlpool tub. The kitchen has been designed to allow guests to chat with the innkeepers while sipping coffee in front of a crackling fireplace and watching breakfast preparations. The Waterfall and hiking trails are just past the gate. Cleveland is a short drive, offering attractions such as the Rock 'n' Roll Hall of Fame and the Cleveland Orchestra.

Innkeeper(s): Katie & George Hoy. $98-225. MC, VISA, DS. 6 rooms with PB, 1 with FP and 3 suites. Breakfast included in rates. Type of meal: Full gourmet bkfst. Beds: KDT. Handicap access.

"The magic of the inn was not forgotten. We will be back to enjoy."

Sandusky
C5

The Red Gables
421 Wayne St
Sandusky, OH 44870-2710
(419)625-1189

Circa 1907. Nestled just blocks from Lake Erie, this beautifully appointed, red-trimmed Tudor home features polished natural woodwork, ornate ceilings and luxurious decor. Costume-maker

and innkeeper Jo Ellen Cuthbertson applied her skills as a seamstress to create a light, romantic atmosphere at Red Gables. Guests enjoy a breakfast of fresh muffins and fruit in the enormous great room, which features a huge fireplace and bay window. Red Gables is within walking distance of several island cruise ships and the island ferries. Two nearby nature preserves, wineries and antique shops offer other fun excursions.

Historic Interest: The Red Gables is located in Sandusky's historic Old Plat District. The Follett House Museum is just across the street from the B&B. The Merry-Go-Round Museum is just a few blocks away. Thomas Edison's birthplace and museum is about 10 miles away. Johnson's Island, a Civil War officer's prison camp, is another nearby attraction.

Innkeeper(s): Jo Ellen Cuthbertson. $75-100. MC, VISA. 4 rooms, 2 with PB. Breakfast included in rates. Type of meal: Cont plus. Beds: QDT. Antiquing, fishing, live theater and water sports nearby.

Publicity: *Ohio, Northern Ohio Live, Cuyahoga County Public Library, Ladies' Home Journal.*

Wagner's 1844 Inn
230 E Washington St
Sandusky, OH 44870-2611
(419)626-1726 Fax:(419)626-8465

Circa 1844. This inn originally was constructed as a log cabin. Additions and renovations were made, and the house evolved into Italianate style accented with brackets under the eaves and black shutters on the second-story windows. A wrought-iron fence frames the house, and there are ornate wrought-iron porch rails. A billiard room and screened-in porch are available to guests. The ferry to Cedar Point and Lake Erie Island is within walking distance.

Innkeeper(s): Walt & Barb Wagner. $70-120. MC, VISA, DS. 3 rooms with PB, 2 with FP. Breakfast included in rates. Type of meal: Cont. Beds: Q. TV in room. Air conditioning. Library on premises. Amusement parks, antiquing, fishing, Lake Erie Islands, golf, parks and shopping nearby.

Pets allowed: Some limitations.

"This B&B rates in our Top 10."

Toledo
C4

The William Cummings House B&B
1022 N Superior St
Toledo, OH 43604
(419)244-3219 (888)708-6998 Fax:(419)244-3219

Circa 1857. This Second Empire Victorian, which is listed in the National Register, is located in the historic Vistula neighborhood. The inn's fine appointments, collected for several years, include period antiques, Victorian chandeliers, mirrors, wallcoverings and draperies. The hosts are classical musicians of renown. Sometimes the inn is the location for chamber music, poetry readings and other cultural events.

Innkeeper(s): Lowell Greer, Lorelei Crawford. $40-90. PC, TC. 3 rooms and 1 suite. Breakfast and snacks/refreshments included in rates. Type of meal: Cont plus. Beds: KQDT. TV, ceiling fan, VCR, fresh flowers, robes and house chocolates in room. Air conditioning. Fax, copier, library, video library and refrigerator on premises. Weddings, small meetings, family reunions and seminars hosted. Spanish spoken. Amusement parks, antiquing, fishing, Toledo Art Museum, Toledo Zoo, science center, live theater, parks, shopping, sporting events and water sports nearby.

"We will never forget our wedding night at your B&B. We'll try to be in the area next anniversary."

Oklahoma

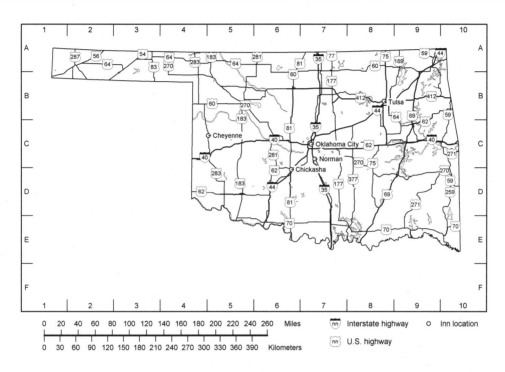

0 20 40 60 80 100 120 140 160 180 200 220 240 260 Miles

0 30 60 90 120 150 180 210 240 270 300 330 360 390 Kilometers

(nn) Interstate highway   o Inn location

(nn) U.S. highway

Cheyenne   C5

Ivy Rose Cottage B&B

210 South Cearlock
Cheyenne, OK 73628
(580)497-3508 (877)456-0403 Fax:(508)497-3611
E-mail: ivyrose@logixnet.net
Web: www.ivyrosecottage.com

Circa 1894. A perimeter of bright yellow, white and purple flowers surround the white columned wraparound veranda of this double gabled Victorian. Said to be the oldest home in town, it is painted a light robin's egg blue with white trim. White rocking chairs, ceiling fans and hanging flower baskets invite guests to relax. The innkeeper's country antique and quilt collection fill the rooms, and there are gas log fireplaces and queen beds in the four guest rooms. Breakfast might include mushroom and asparagus frittata served with raspberry jalapeno sauce and English muffins or red flannel hash, homemade biscuits and over-easy eggs followed by either strawberries or blueberries served with creme frece. There is a library and a gift shop on the premises.

Historic Interest: Antelope Hills-15 miles, Washita Battlefield-2.5 miles, Roll one room house, Strong City town site house, Santa Fe Depot.

Innkeeper(s): Steve & Becki Seay. $65. MC, VISA, AX, DS, PC. 4 rooms with PB, 4 with FP and 1 conference room. Breakfast and snacks/refreshments included in rates. Types of meals: Full gourmet bkfst and early coffee/tea. Beds: QD. Cable TV, phone, ceiling fan and VCR in room. Central air. Fax, copier and library on premises. Weddings, small meetings, family reunions and seminars hosted. Antiquing, art galleries, fishing, hiking, horseback riding, museums, parks and shopping nearby.

Chickasha   D6

Campbell-Richison House B&B

1428 Kansas
Chickasha, OK 73018
(405)222-1754

Circa 1909. Upon entering this prairie-style home, guests will notice a spacious entryway with a gracious stairway ascending to the second-floor guest rooms. The front parlor is a wonderful spot for relaxing, reading or just soaking up the history of the home. The dining room has a stained-glass window that gives off a kaleidoscope of beautiful colors when the morning sun shines through. A spacious yard encompasses one-quarter of a city block and has large shade trees that can be enjoyed from the wicker-lined porch.

Historic Interest: Grady County Historical Museum (less than a mile), Indian City, USA.

Innkeeper(s): David Ratcliff. $45-65. 3 rooms, 1 with PB. Breakfast included in rates. Types of meals: Full bkfst and early coffee/tea. Beds: QD. Phone and sitting area in room. Air conditioning. VCR on premises. Small meetings hosted. Antiquing, shopping and sporting events nearby.

Publicity: *Oklahoma Today, Chickasha Express, Cache Times Weekly, Chickasha Star.*

"We enjoyed our stay at your lovely B&B! It was just the getaway we needed to unwind from a stressful few weeks. Your hospitality fellowship and food were just wonderful."

Norman C7

Holmberg House B&B

766 Debarr Ave
Norman, OK 73069-4908
(405)321-6221 (800)646-6221 Fax:(405)321-6221
E-mail: holmberg@telepath.com

Circa 1914. Professor Fredrik Holmberg and his wife Signy built this Craftsman-style home across the street from the University of Oklahoma. Each of the antique-filled rooms has its own individual decor and style. The

Blue Danube and Bed & Bath rooms are romantic retreats and both include a two-person whirlpool tub. The Garden Room includes a clawfoot tub. The Sundance Room is ideal for friends traveling together, as it includes both a queen and twin bed. The parlor and front porch are perfect places to relax with friends, and the lush grounds include a cottage garden. Aside from close access to the university, Holmberg House is within walking distance to more than a dozen restaurants.

Historic Interest: The Oklahoma Museum of Natural History is six blocks from the inn. The Cleveland County Historical Society and Lindsey Moor House are about a mile from the home. Jacobson House, a Native American museum, is six blocks away.

Innkeeper(s): Jo Meacham & Michael Cobb. $65-120. MC, VISA, AX, DS, PC, TC. TAC10. 4 rooms with PB. Breakfast included in rates. Types of meals: Full gourmet bkfst and early coffee/tea. Beds: QT. Cable TV and ceiling fan in room. Air conditioning. Fax, copier and library on premises. Weddings, small meetings and family reunions hosted. Antiquing, live theater, parks, shopping and sporting events nearby.

Publicity: *Metro Norman, Oklahoma City Journal Record, Norman Transcript, Country Inns.*

"Your hospitality and the delicious food were just super."

Oklahoma City C7

The Grandison at Maney Park

1200 N Shartel Ave
Oklahoma City, OK 73103-2402
(405)232-8778 (800)240-4667 Fax:(405)232-5039
E-mail: grandison@juno.com
Web: www.bbonline.com/ok/grandison

Circa 1904. This spacious Victorian has been graciously restored and maintains its original mahogany woodwork,

stained glass, brass fixtures and a grand staircase. Several rooms include a Jacuzzi, and all have their own unique decor. The Treehouse Hideaway includes a queen bed that is meant to look like a hammock and walls are painted with a blue sky and stars. The Jacuzzi tub rests beneath a skylight. The home is located north of downtown Oklahoma City in a historic neighborhood listed in the National Register.

Historic Interest: Overholser Mansion (1/2 mile), Heritage Center (1 mile), Harn Homestead (2 miles), Bricktown (2 miles).

Innkeeper(s): Claudia & Bob Wright. $75-150. MC, VISA, AX, DS, PC, TC. TAC10. 9 rooms with PB, 3 suites and 1 conference room. Breakfast and snacks/refreshments included in rates. Types of meals: Full bkfst, cont plus and early coffee/tea. Banquet service, catering service and room service available. Beds: KQT. Cable TV, phone, ceiling fan and VCR in room. Air conditioning. Fax, copier, workout room and video library on premises. Handicap access. Weddings, small meetings, family reunions and seminars hosted. Antiquing, live theater, parks and sporting events nearby.

"Like going home to Grandma's!"

Tulsa B8

McBirney Mansion B&B

1414 S Galveston Ave
Tulsa, OK 74127-9116
(918)585-3234 Fax:(918)585-9377
Web: www.mcbirneymansion.com

Circa 1927. An oil baron built this immense Tudor mansion, which is listed in the National Register. The home rests on three acres, adjacent to Tulsa River Parks. The countryside, with its spring-fed ponds, was a common gathering spot for local native tribes and early settlers. Washington Irving once camped out on the grounds and later wrote about his experience in "Tour of the Prairies." Winding stone paths lead down to the banks of the Arkansas River, and the grounds are dotted with gardens. The manor's interior is equally impressive. Bedchambers boast fine antiques, some include a marble bath or whirlpool tub. The Author's Suite is ideal for couples traveling together, offering two rooms with a connecting bath. For a romantic getaway, consider the Carriage House Retreat, a private cottage with a bedroom, sitting room, small kitchen area and a bath with a jetted shower. Guests are treated to a multi-course, gourmet breakfast. The morning meal begins with fresh fruit, perhaps poached pears, strawberry compote or baked apple. The main course might include eggs Benedict, huevos rancheros, a spinach quiche served with cheese grits in a baked tomato and homemade English muffins. McBirney Mansion is close to museums, shops, antique stores, galleries, restaurants and Tulsa's business district and civic center.

Historic Interest: Tall Grass Prairie (80 miles), Council Oak Tree (3 blocks).

Innkeeper(s): Kathy Collins & Renita Shofner. $119-225. MC, VISA, AX, DS, PC, TC. 8 rooms with PB, 1 with FP, 3 suites and 3 conference rooms. Breakfast and snacks/refreshments included in rates. Types of meals: Cont plus, veg bkfst and early coffee/tea. Picnic lunch and catering service available. Beds: KQDT. Cable TV, phone and VCR in room. Central air. Fax, copier and library on premises. Weddings, small meetings, family reunions and seminars hosted. Amusement parks, antiquing, art galleries, bicycling, fishing, golf, hiking, live theater, museums, parks, shopping and tennis nearby.

Oregon

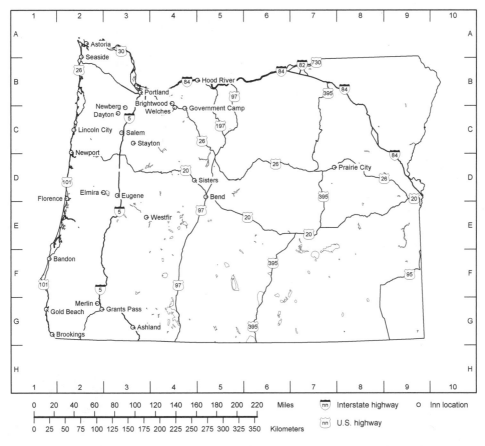

Map legend:
- ⬛ Interstate highway
- ○ Inn location
- nn U.S. highway

Miles: 0 20 40 60 80 100 120 140 160 180 200 220
Kilometers: 0 25 50 75 100 125 150 175 200 225 250 275 300 325 350

Ashland
G3

Iris Inn
59 Manzanita St
Ashland, OR 97520-2615
(541)488-2286 (800)460-7650 Fax:(541)488-3709

Circa 1905. The Iris Inn is a restored Victorian set on a large flower-filled yard. It features simple American country antiques. The upstairs guest rooms have views of the valley and mountains. Evening sips of wine often are taken out on the large deck overlooking a rose garden. Breakfast boasts an elegant presentation with dishes such as buttermilk scones and eggs Benedict.
Innkeeper(s): Vicki & Greg Capp. $60-115. MC, VISA. 5 rooms with PB.

Breakfast included in rates. Type of meal: Full bkfst. Gourmet dinner available. Beds: QT. Turndown service and ceiling fan in room. Air conditioning. Fax and large deck in garden on premises. Small meetings and seminars hosted. Antiquing, fishing, golf, live theater, shopping, downhill skiing, cross-country skiing, sporting events and water sports nearby.

Morical House Garden Inn
668 N Main St
Ashland, OR 97520-1710
(541)482-2254 (800)208-0960 Fax:(541)482-1775
E-mail: moricalhse@aol.com
Web: www.garden-inn.com

Circa 1882. The Morical House is a mile away from the Oregon Shakespeare festival, and blooming rose gardens frame this exquisitely restored Victorian farmhouse in summer. All guest

341

rooms are furnished with period antiques and handmade comforters, and most have a view of the Cascade Mountains. The inn's acre of grounds includes ponds, waterfalls and a large deck.

Innkeeper(s): Gary & Sandye Moore. $73-160. MC, VISA, AX, DS, PC, TC. TAC10. 7 rooms with PB, 2 with FP. Breakfast and afternoon tea included in rates. Types of meals: Full gourmet bkfst and early coffee/tea. Snacks/refreshments available. Beds: KQT. TV, phone, refrigerator two rooms and whirlpool tubs in room. Air conditioning. Fax on premises. Handicap access. Small meetings, family reunions and seminars hosted. Fishing, live theater, shopping, downhill skiing and cross-country skiing nearby.

Pinehurst Inn at Jenny Creek

17250 Hwy 66
Ashland, OR 97520-9406
(541)482-1873

Circa 1923. This lodge, built from logs harvested on the property, once accommodated travelers along the new state highway 66. The highway was built to replace the Southern Oregon

Wagon Road. As the name suggests, the inn is situated by the banks of Jenny Creek, and guests enjoy stunning canyon views from the upstairs sunroom. The lobby, with its huge stone fireplace, is a welcoming site. The inn also includes a restaurant open to guests and the public. The inn is about a half hour from Ashland, and Klamath Falls is 39 miles away.

Innkeeper(s): Don & Jean Rowlett. $69-89. MC, VISA, DS. 6 rooms with PB and 2 suites. Breakfast and dinner included in rates. Types of meals: Cont and early coffee/tea. Restaurant on premises. Beds: KQD. Ceiling fan in room. Weddings, small meetings and family reunions hosted. Antiquing, fishing, hiking, live theater, shopping, downhill skiing and cross-country skiing nearby.

Wolfe Manor Inn

586 B St
Ashland, OR 97520
(541)488-3676 (800)801-3676 Fax:(541)488-4567
E-mail: wolfebandb@aol.com
Web: www.wolfemanor.com

Circa 1910. A glass door with sidelights welcomes guests to this massive Craftsman-style home. A grand parlor/ballroom with original lighting fixtures and fine woodwork is the combination sitting area and dining room. Bedrooms offer views of the mountains or the inn's pleasantly landscaped lawns and gardens. Guests often enjoy relaxing on the inn's porches.

Innkeeper(s): Sybil & Ron Maddox. $89-139. MC, VISA, AX, DC, DS, PC, TC. TAC10. 5 rooms with PB. Breakfast and snacks/refreshments included in rates. Type of meal: Full bkfst. Beds: QD. Ceiling fan in room. Air conditioning. Fax, copier, library, refrigerator and snack bar on premises. Small meetings and family reunions hosted. Antiquing, fishing, golf, live theater, parks, shopping, downhill skiing, cross-country skiing, sporting events, tennis and water sports nearby.

The Woods House B&B

333 N Main St
Ashland, OR 97520-1703
(541)488-1598 (800)435-8260 Fax:(541)482-8027

Circa 1908. Built and occupied for almost 40 years by a prominent Ashland physician, each room of this Craftsman-style inn boasts special detail. Many guest rooms offer canopied beds and skylights. Full breakfasts are served either in the sunny dining room or in the garden under a spreading walnut tree. After breakfast, take a stroll through the half-acre of terraced, English gardens. Located in the historic district, the inn is four blocks from Ashland's Shakespearean theaters.

Historic Interest: Named after Dr. Ernest Woods, local physician.

Innkeeper(s): Francoise Roddy. $75-120. MC, VISA, DS. 6 rooms with PB. Breakfast included in rates. Types of meals: Full bkfst and early coffee/tea. Room service available. Beds: KQT. Books, magazines and shampoo in room. Air conditioning. VCR, fax, copier and garden for quiet parties on premises. Weddings, small meetings, family reunions and seminars hosted. Antiquing, live theater, shopping, downhill skiing and cross-country skiing nearby.

"Within this house lies much hospitality, friendship and laughter. What more could a home ask to be?."

Astoria   A2

Benjamin Young Inn

3652 Duane St
Astoria, OR 97103-2421
(503)325-6172 (800)201-1286
E-mail: benyoung@willapabay.org
Web: moriah.com/benjamin

Circa 1888. From this Queen Anne Victorian, guests can watch ships and boats travel along the Columbia River. The home is listed in the National Register of Historic Places, and

many of its period elements have been preserved and restored. Guest rooms are decorated in a comfortable, eclectic style with antiques, and all offer a river view. The spacious Fireplace Room

includes a fireplace, Jacuzzi tub, king-size bed and a bay window with a river view. It also has an adjoining room with a queen bed and two singles. Shops, museums and restaurants are just a mile and a half away in Astoria.

Innkeeper(s): Carolyn & Ken Hammer. $75-135. MC, VISA, AX, DS, PC, TC. TAC10. 5 rooms with PB, 1 with FP. Breakfast and afternoon tea included in rates. Types of meals: Full gourmet bkfst and early coffee/tea. Catering service available. Beds: KQT. Cable TV in room. Weddings, small meetings, family reunions and seminars hosted. French spoken. Antiquing, fishing, golf, live theater, parks, shopping, tennis and water sports nearby.

"Your home is absolutely gorgeous and the food and ambiance superb — so romantic, so wonderful!"

Grandview B&B

1574 Grand Ave
Astoria, OR 97103-3733
(503)325-0000 (800)488-3250 Fax:(707)982-8790
E-mail: grandviewbnb@freedom.usa.com
Web: www.pacifier.com/~grndview/

Circa 1896. To fully enjoy its views of the Columbia River, this
Victorian house has both a tower and a turret. Antiques and
white wicker furnishings contribute to the inn's casual, homey feeling. The Bird Meadow Room is particularly appealing to bird-lovers with its birdcage, bird books and bird wallpaper.
Breakfast, served in the main-floor
turret, frequently includes smoked
salmon with bagels and cream cheese.

Historic Interest: Flavel House (8 blocks), Heritage
Museum (1 block), Firefighters Museum (18 blocks).

Innkeeper(s): Charleen Maxwell. $55-98. MC, VISA, DS. 9 rooms, 7 with
PB, 3 with FP and 2 suites. Breakfast and snacks/refreshments included in
rates. Type of meal: Full bkfst. Beds: QT. Weddings, small meetings and family reunions hosted. Antiquing, fishing, Ecotown, historic homes tour, live theater, parks, shopping and water sports nearby.

Publicity: *Pacific Northwest Magazine, Northwest Discoveries, Los Angeles
Times, Oregonian, Daily Astorian.*

*"I have travelled all over the world and for the first time I found in
the country of the computers such a romantic house with such poetic rooms at the Grandview Bed & Breakfast." Thanks MD from
Paris, France.*

Bend   D5

The Sather House B&B

7 NW Tumalo Ave
Bend, OR 97701
(541)388-1065 (888)388-1065 Fax:(541)330-0591

Circa 1911. This Craftsman-style home is listed in the local,
county and national historic registers. One room includes a
clawfoot tub that dates to 1910. Period furnishings are found
in the nicely appointed guest rooms, which feature touches of
Battenburg and lace. The front porch is lined with wicker for
those who wish to relax and enjoy the surroundings. For breakfast, innkeeper Robbie Giamboi serves items such as pancakes
topped with her own homemade blackberry or apple syrup.
Guests also enjoy afternoon tea.

Innkeeper(s): Robbie Giamboi. $80-115. MC, VISA, DS, PC, TC. 4 rooms
with PB. Breakfast and afternoon tea included in rates. Types of meals: Full
gourmet bkfst and early coffee/tea. Beds: KQDT. Ceiling fan in room. VCR and
library on premises. Small meetings and family reunions hosted. Antiquing,
fishing, golf, live theater, parks, shopping, downhill skiing, cross-country skiing, sporting events, tennis and water sports nearby.

Publicity: *Bend Bulletin, Oregonian.*

Brightwood   B4

Brightwood Guesthouse B&B

64725 E Barlow Trail Rd
Brightwood, OR 97011-0189
(503)622-5783 (888)503-5783

Circa 1935. For a private romantic getaway, consider a trip to
this flower-filled cedar cottage, secluded on two acres. The
grounds include a waterfall and there's a Japanese water garden
that surrounds your private deck. Nearby is a mountain stream.

The cottage offers two sleeping areas — a cozy loft and the living room, as well as a kitchen/dining room and bath. Authentic
Japanese, Chinese and South Asian artifacts complement the
Oriental theme, and there are kimonos and slippers for everyone. Cupboards are stocked with gourmet coffee, tea and popcorn. The innkeepers have stocked the cottage with plenty of
items to help pass the time, such as games, books, videos, art
supplies and even mountain bikes and helmets. Breakfast is
served in the cottage or on the deck and may include Italian
scones, roasted potatoes, frittata and an Amaretto truffle for
dessert. Special beverages can be ordered for celebrations. The
innkeepers offer honeymoon, romance and ski packages.

Innkeeper(s): Jan Estep. $125-135. PC. TAC10. 1 cottages. Breakfast
included in rates. Type of meal: Full gourmet bkfst. Picnic lunch, catering service, catered breakfast and room service available. Beds: D. Phone and VCR
in room. Bicycles and library on premises. Family reunions hosted. Antiquing,
fishing, golf, kayaking, parks, shopping, downhill skiing, cross-country skiing,
sporting events, tennis and water sports nearby.

Brookings   G1

South Coast Inn B&B

516 Redwood St
Brookings, OR 97415-9672
(541)469-5557 (800)525-9273 Fax:(541)469-6615

Circa 1917. Enjoy panoramic views of the Pacific Ocean at this
Craftsman-style inn designed by renowned San Francisco architect Bernard Maybeck. All rooms are furnished with antiques,
ceiling fans, VCRs and TVs. Two guest rooms afford panoramic
views of the coastline and there is a separate cottage. A floor-to-
ceiling stone fireplace and beamed ceilings make the parlor a
great place to gather with
friends. There are sun
decks, a strolling garden,
and an indoor hot tub
and sauna. The Brookings
area offers something for
everyone. Outdoor activi-
ties include hiking, boating, golfing, digging
for clams or simply enjoying a stroll along the spectacular
coastline. Concerts, galleries, museums, antiques, specialty
shops and fine restaurants all can be found within the area.

Innkeeper(s): Ken Raith & Keith Pepper. $84-99. MC, VISA, AX, DS, PC, TC.
TAC10. 4 rooms with PB and 1 cottage. Breakfast included in rates. Types of
meals: Full gourmet bkfst and early coffee/tea. Beds: KQ. Cable TV, ceiling
fan, VCR and hair dryers in baths in room. Fax, spa, sauna and library on
premises. Weddings, small meetings, family reunions and seminars hosted.
Antiquing, fishing, live theater, parks, shopping and water sports nearby.

"Thank you for your special brand of magic. What a place!"

Dayton   C3

Wine Country Farm

6855 NE Breyman Orchards Rd
Dayton, OR 97114-7220
(503)864-3446 (800)261-3446 Fax:(503)864-3109

Circa 1910. Surrounded by vineyards and orchards, Wine
Country Farm is an eclectic French house sitting on a hill overlooking the Cascade Mountain Range. Arabian horses are raised
here, and five varieties of grapes are grown. Request the master
bedroom and you'll enjoy a fireplace. The innkeepers can arrange
for a horse-drawn buggy ride and picnic. There are outdoor wed-

ding facilities and a new wine tasting room. Downtown Portland and the Oregon coast are each an hour away.

Innkeeper(s): Joan Davenport. $85-125. MC, VISA, PC. 7 rooms with PB, 2 with FP, 1 suite and 1 conference room. Breakfast included in rates. Types of meals: Full gourmet bkfst and early coffee/tea. Banquet service, catering service and room service available. Beds: KQDT. Air conditioning. VCR, fax, copier, stables and library on premises. Weddings, small meetings, family reunions and seminars hosted. Antiquing, fishing, live theater, parks, shopping, downhill skiing, cross-country skiing, sporting events and water sports nearby.

Publicity: *Wine Spectator.*

Eugene
D3

Campbell House, A City Inn

252 Pearl St
Eugene, OR 97401-2366
(541)343-1119 (800)264-2519 Fax:(541)343-2258

Circa 1892. An acre of grounds surrounds this Victorian inn, built by a local timber owner and gold miner. The guest quarters range from a ground-level room featuring fly-fishing paraphernalia and knotty-pine panel-ing to an elegant two-room honeymoon suite on the second floor, complete with fireplace, jetted bathtub for two and a view of the mountains. The Campbell House, located in Eugene's historic Skinner Butte District, is within walking distance of restaurants, the Hult Center for the Performing Arts, the 5th Street Public Market and antique shops. Outdoor activities include jogging or biking along riverside paths.

Historic Interest: The historic Shelton McMurphy Johnson House, which was built in 1882 and now is owned by the city, is located at the base of the driveway and tours are available. The innkeepers will provide guests with walking maps of the historic district.

Innkeeper(s): Myra Plant. $86-350. MC, VISA, AX, DS, TC. TAC10. 18 rooms with PB, 7 with FP, 1 suite and 2 conference rooms. Breakfast included in rates. Types of meals: Full bkfst and early coffee/tea. Picnic lunch and room service available. Beds: KQDT. Cable TV, phone, turndown service, ceiling fan, VCR and jetted or clawfoot tubs in room. Air conditioning. Fax, copier and library on premises. Handicap access. Weddings, small meetings, family reunions and seminars hosted. Antiquing, fishing, golfing, rock climbing, hiking, bicycling, live theater, parks, shopping, sporting events and water sports nearby.

"I guess we've never felt so pampered! Thank you so much. The room is beautiful! We had a wonderful getaway."

Kjaer's House In Woods

814 Lorane Hwy
Eugene, OR 97405-2321
(541)343-3234 (800)437-4501

Circa 1910. This handsome Craftsman house on two landscaped acres was built by a Minnesota lawyer. It was originally accessible by streetcar. Antiques include a square grand piano of rosewood and a collection of antique wedding photos. The house is attractively furnished and surrounded by flower gardens.

Historic Interest: Wayne Moore Historical Park (4 blocks), covered bridges (3 miles).

Innkeeper(s): George & Eunice Kjaer. $65-80. PC, TC. TAC10. 2 rooms with PB and 1 conference room. Breakfast included in rates. Types of meals: Full gourmet bkfst, cont and early coffee/tea. Beds: Q. VCR and library on premises. Weddings, small meetings, family reunions and seminars hosted. Antiquing, fishing, live theater, parks, shopping and sporting events nearby.

"Lovely ambiance and greatest sleep ever. Delicious and beautiful food presentation."

Pookie's B&B on College Hill

2013 Charnelton St
Eugene, OR 97405-2819
(541)343-0383 (800)558-0383 Fax:(541)431-0967

Circa 1918. Pookie's is a charming Craftsman house with "yester-year charm." Surrounded by maple and fir trees, the B&B is located in an older, quiet neighborhood. Mahogany and oak antiques decorate the rooms. The innkeeper worked for many years in the area as a concierge and can offer you expert help with excursion planning or business needs.

Historic Interest: Historic downtown (1 1/2 mile).

Innkeeper(s): Pookie & Doug Walling. $70-115. PC, TC. 3 rooms, 2 with PB and 1 suite. Breakfast included in rates. AP. Types of meals: Full bkfst, cont plus, cont and early coffee/tea. Beds: KQT. Cable TV, phone and ceiling fan in room. VCR, fax and copier on premises. Antiquing, fishing, baseball stadium, live theater, parks, shopping, sporting events and water sports nearby.

"I love the attention to detail. The welcoming touches: flowers, the 'convenience basket' of necessary items . . . I'm happy to have discovered your lovely home."

Florence
D2

The Blue Heron Inn

6563 Hwy 126, PO Box 1122
Florence, OR 97439-0055
(541)997-4091 (800)997-7780

Circa 1940. From the porch of this bed & breakfast inn, guests can gaze at rolling, forested hills and watch as riverboats ease their way down the Siuslaw River. Aside from the spectacular view, the inn is located within a few yards of a marina where docking and mooring is available. The ocean, the dunes and historic Florence are just minutes away as well. The Bridal Suite offers king-size bed, sitting area, whirlpool tub and view of the river and grounds. Fresh, seasonal fare highlights the breakfast menu. Treats such as fresh fruit smoothies, muffins topped with homemade blackberry jam or a smoked salmon and avocado quiche are not uncommon.

Innkeeper(s): Maurice Souza. $55-120. MC, VISA, DS, PC, TC. TAC5. 5 rooms with PB. Breakfast and afternoon tea included in rates. Type of meal: Full bkfst. Beds: KQT. Ceiling fan and jetted tubs in room. VCR and library on premises. Weddings, small meetings and family reunions hosted. Antiquing, fishing, dune buggies, horseback riding, parks, shopping and water sports nearby.

"The entire place was decorated with great taste. Our room was beautiful and relaxing. It made us feel at ease and at peace."

Gold Beach   G1

Inn at Nesika Beach

33026 Nesika Rd
Gold Beach, OR 97444-9508
(541)247-6434

Circa 1992. Although this home is new, it sports the nostalgic Victorian design so popular with inngoers. The inn rests atop a bluff overlooking the ocean, and all of the romantic guest rooms offer water views. Two have decks facing the ocean. Bed chambers are dressed with down comforters, and there are whirlpool tubs and fireplaces. The innkeeper begins each day with a hearty breakfast. The inn is located a little more than five miles from the town of Gold Beach.
Innkeeper(s): Ann G. Arsenault. $100-130. PC. 4 rooms with PB, 3 with FP. Breakfast included in rates. Types of meals: Full gourmet bkfst and early coffee/tea. Beds: KQT. Ceiling fan, jacuzzi tubs and decks in room. VCR on premises. Weddings hosted. Fishing, golf, parks, tennis and water sports nearby.

"What a great surprise. The jewel of Nesika Beach."

Grants Pass   G2

Weasku Inn

5560 Rogue River Hwy
Grants Pass, OR 97527
(541)471-8000 (800)334-4567 Fax:(541)471-7038
E-mail: info@weasku.com
Web: www.weasku.com

Circa 1924. Built as a secluded fishing lodge, this historic inn once hosted the likes of President Herbert Hoover, Zane Grey, Walt Disney, Clark Gable and Carole Lombard. It is said that after Lombard's death, Gable spent several weeks here, lamenting the loss of his beloved wife. A complete restoration took place in the early 1990s, reviving the inn back to its former glory. The log exterior, surrounding by towering trees and 10 fragrant acres, is a welcoming site. Inside, crackling fires from the inn's rock fireplaces warm the common rooms. Vaulted ceilings and exposed log beams add a cozy, rustic touch to the pristine, airy rooms all decorated in Pacific Northwest style. Many rooms include a whirlpool tub and river rock fireplace, and several offer excellent views of the Rogue River, which runs through the inn's 10 acres. In addition to the inn rooms, there are riverfront cabins, offering an especially romantic setting. In the evenings, guests are treated to a wine and cheese reception, and in the mornings, a continental breakfast is served. The staff can help plan many activities, including fishing and white-water rafting trips.

Historic Interest: Applegate Trail and Interpretive Center (10 miles), historic downtown (6 miles).
Innkeeper(s): Dayle Sedgemore. $85-295. MC, VISA, AX, DC, CB, DS, TC. TAC10. 21 rooms, 19 with PB, 13 with FP, 3 suites, 12 cabins, 1 guest house and 1 conference room. Breakfast & snacks/refreshments included in rates. MAP. Meal: Cont plus. Beds: KQT. Cable TV, phone & ceiling fan in room. Central air. Fax on premises. Handicap access. Weddings, small meetings, family reunions & seminars hosted. Antiquing, canoeing/kayaking, fishing, golf, hiking, jetboat excursions/wildlife park, live theater, museums, parks, shopping, water sports & wineries nearby.

Hood River   B5

Avalon B&B

3444 Avalon Dr
Hood River, OR 97031
(541)386-2560 (888)386-3941

Circa 1906. Three comfortable, country-style rooms are available at this farmhouse homestay. The home offers a view of Mt. Adams on its deck and in the largest of the three guest rooms. After a breakfast that includes gourmet coffee, a fresh fruit course and an entrée, guests can head out and enjoy the bounty of outdoor activities the area has to offer. These activities include are skiing, hiking, as well as rafting and other watersports.
Innkeeper(s): Jim & Dorothy Tollen. $65-75. MC, VISA, DS, TC. 3 rooms and 1 conference room. Breakfast included in rates. Type of meal: Full gourmet bkfst. Beds: QT. Turndown service in room. VCR on premises. Small meetings and family reunions hosted. Antiquing, fishing, golf, hiking trails, mountains, parks, shopping, downhill skiing, cross-country skiing, tennis and water sports nearby.
Pets allowed: Outside only.

Columbia Gorge Hotel

4000 Westcliff Dr
Hood River, OR 97031-9799
(541)386-5566 (800)345-1921 Fax:(541)387-5414
E-mail: cghotel@gorge.net
Web: www.columbiagorgehotel.com

Circa 1921. This posh hotel is a gem among gems in the National Register of Historic Places. Idyllic guest quarters offer such ornate furnishings as a hand-carved canopy bed that once graced a French castle. The beautifully landscaped grounds, turndown service with rose and chocolates and a gourmet restaurant are favorite amenities. Last, but not least, are spectacular views of the majestic Columbia River. Guests are treated to the opulent "World Famous Farm Breakfast." The hotel is close to ski areas, golfing and popular windsurfing spots.
Innkeeper(s): Boyd & Halla Graves. $150-275. MC, VISA, AX, DC, CB, DS, TC. TAC10. 39 rooms with PB, 2 with FP and 3 conference rooms. Breakfast included in rates. Types of meals: Full bkfst and early coffee/tea. Gourmet dinner, picnic lunch, lunch, banquet service, catering service and room service available. Restaurant on premises. Beds: KQD. Cable TV, phone and turndown service in room. VCR, fax and copier on premises. Weddings, small meetings, family reunions and seminars hosted. Spanish, French and and Icelandic spoken. Antiquing, fishing, windsurfing, live theater, parks, shopping, downhill skiing, cross-country skiing and water sports nearby.
Pets allowed: $25 fee.

Hood River Hotel

102 Oak Ave
Hood River, OR 97031-2312
(541)386-1900 (800)386-1859 Fax:(541)386-6090
E-mail: HRHotel@gorge.net
Web: www.HoodRiverHotel.com

Circa 1913. This historic hotel was built as an annex to the Mount Hood Hotel, lodging established to serve railroad travelers coming through the area. The Hood River Hotel was an addition created to serve automobile traffic on the newly constructed highway that ran in front of the property. A grand piano and a fireplace grace the lobby, a perfect place to sit and read, play a

game or sip a cocktail. The main story includes the hotel's restaurant, which serves breakfast, lunch and dinner. Breakfast is included, and features such items as steak and eggs, eggs Benedict and fruit-topped waffles. Guest rooms are decorated with period reproductions and cherry and pine furnishings; some include a canopy bed. Some units include a kitchen, and there are toys and games available to occupy families. A private Jacuzzi and exercise facility is available, as well.

Historic Interest: Historic Columbia River Hwy (5 miles), Mt. Hood Railroad (one block).

Innkeeper(s): Jacquie & Pasquale Barone. $59-155. MC, VISA, AX, DC, DS, PC, TC. TAC10. 41 rooms with PB, 9 suites and 1 conference room. Breakfast included in rates. Types of meals: Full bkfst, cont plus and veg bkfst. Gourmet dinner, snacks/refreshments, picnic lunch, gourmet lunch, banquet service, catering service and room service available. Restaurant on premises. Beds: QD. Cable TV, phone, ceiling fan, VCR and full kitchen in room. Central air. Fax, copier, spa, restaurant and exercise facility on premises. Handicap access. Weddings, small meetings, family reunions and seminars hosted. Italian, Icelandic and Spanish spoken. Antiquing, art galleries, beaches, bicycling, canoeing/kayaking, fishing, golf, hiking, horseback riding, movie theater, concerts, live theater, museums, parks, shopping, downhill skiing, cross-country skiing, tennis, water sports and wineries nearby.

Pets allowed: $15 fee.

"I can say without reservation, this summer has been the best ever at your hotel."

Lincoln City C2

The Enchanted Cottage

4507 SW Coast Ave
Lincoln City, OR 97367
(541)996-4101 Fax:(541)996-2682

Circa 1940. This 4,000-square-foot house is 300 feet from the beach and a short walk from Siletz Bay with its herd of sea lions. Victoria's Secret is a favorite romantic guest room that features a queen canopy bed, antique furnishings and, best of all, the sounds of the Pacific surf. Ask for Sir Arthur's View if you must see and hear the ocean. This two-room suite also has a private deck and a living room with a fireplace and wet bar. Homemade breakfast casseroles are a specialty during the morning meal, which is served either in the dining room or on the deck overlooking the Pacific. Pets are allowed with some restrictions.

Innkeeper(s): David & Cynthia Gale Fitton. $100-175. MC, VISA, PC, TC. TAC10. 3 rooms with PB, 1 with FP and 1 suite. Breakfast and snacks/refreshments included in rates. Types of meals: Full gourmet bkfst and early coffee/tea. Gourmet dinner, catering service and room service available. Beds: KQ. Cable TV in room. VCR, fax, copier and library on premises. Handicap access. Weddings, small meetings, family reunions and seminars hosted. Some Spanish spoken. Amusement parks, antiquing, fishing, golf, Oregon Coast Aquarium, live theater, parks, shopping, tennis and water sports nearby.

Pets allowed: With some restrictions. Prefer small pets. Must have own pet bed.

Publicity: *Oregonian.*

Merlin G2

Morrison's Rogue River Lodge

8500 Galice Rd
Merlin, OR 97532-9722
(541)476-3825 (800)826-1963 Fax:(541)476-4953

Circa 1946. Many world travelers list Morrison's as one of their favorite places. The Rogue River wilderness that surrounds this handsome waterfront lodge provides scenic adventures up and down the river. Each cottage has its own balcony and fireplace, and the lodge is particularly noted for its excellent cuisine. In summer, a four-course, gourmet dinner is served on the deck

overlooking green lawns and the river. Breakfast and dinner are included in the summer rates. Breakfast, dinner and a picnic lunch are included in the fall rates.

Historic Interest: Crater Lake National Park (2-hour drive), Oregon Caves National Monument (1-1/2-hour drive), Ashland Shakespearean Festival (1-hour drive).

Innkeeper(s): Michelle Hanten. $160-260. MC, VISA, DS, PC, TC. TAC10. 13 rooms with PB, 9 with FP, 9 cottages and 1 conference room. Breakfast included in rates. MAP, AP. Restaurant on premises. Beds: KQT. TV, phone and VCR in room. Air conditioning. Fax, copier, swimming and library on premises. Weddings, family reunions and seminars hosted. Antiquing, fishing, white water rafting, live theater, parks, shopping and water sports nearby.

Publicity: *Los Angeles Times, Pacific Northwest, Bon Appetit, Orvis News.*

"The tales we heard of how delicious the food would be told nothing of how it really was! We were so delighted to find such marvelous home-cooked cuisine, and the family service was terrific!"

Newberg C3

Springbrook Hazelnut Farm

30295 N Hwy 99 W
Newberg, OR 97132
(503)538-4606 (800)793-8528

Circa 1912. An ancient silver maple tree shades the main house, one of four Craftsman-style buildings on this farm. There are 10 acres of gardens, a pool, tennis court and a 60-acre hazelnut orchard. A blue heron monitors the inn's pond and you may paddle around in the canoe. Walking through the orchard to the adjoining winery is a must, as is a bicycle ride to other wineries in the area. Ask

for the Carriage House or the Cottage, and you'll enjoy a pond and garden view. Two of the inn's cottages have private bathes. They also have kitchens, and if you eat in, you may choose from the garden's offerings for your dinner.

Historic Interest: Champoeg Park (6 miles).

Innkeeper(s): Charles & Ellen McClure. $95-175. 4 rooms, 2 with PB and 2 cottages. Breakfast included in rates. Type of meal: Full bkfst. Gourmet dinner available. Beds: QD. Air conditioning. VCR, orchard, pond and gardens on premises. Small meetings and seminars hosted. Antiquing, live theater, shopping, sporting events and water sports nearby.

"An incredible, wonderful refuge! We are beautifully surprised!"

Newport C2

Oar House

520 S W 2nd St
Newport, OR 97365-3907
(541)265-9571 (800)252-2358
E-mail: oarhouse@newpornet.com
Web: www.newportnet.com/oarhouse

Circa 1900. This Craftsman-style home was built using wood that washed ashore after a lumber schooner was abandoned by the crew during a fierce storm. It has a colorful history, serving as a boarding house and then as the Nye Beach bordello. One of the former occupants, a young woman, may still inhabit the house in ghostly form. Rooms feature nautical names, such as Captain's Quarters and Starboard Cabin. Guests are welcome to walk up the third-floor ship's ladder to the lighthouse tower and enjoy a panoramic view of the ocean, beach, mountains, lighthouses and sunsets. Freshly roasted coffee, orange juice, and seasonal fruit accompany an entree, such as lemon ricotta pancakes served with sauteed apples and smoked chicken sausage.

Innkeeper(s): Jan Le Brun. $95-125. MC, VISA, DS, TC. 5 rooms with PB and 1 suite. Breakfast included in rates. Types of meals: Full gourmet bkfst and early coffee/tea. Beds: Q. VCR, library, refrigerator and DMX music on premises. Antiquing, fishing, outstanding natural areas, live theater, parks, shopping and water sports nearby.

Ocean House B&B

4920 NW Woody Way
Newport, OR 97365-1328
(541)265-6158 (800)562-2632
E-mail: garrard@oceanhouse.com
Web: www.oceanhouse.com

Circa 1939. Simple but comfortable rooms provide magnificent views of the ocean and cozy spaces for storm watching at this homey bed and breakfast. A secluded, sheltered cliffside garden is terraced with tulips, azaleas and roses, providing a colorful setting to view the white waters of Agate Beach. A private path leads to the tide pools. Longtime Newport residents, the innkeepers know the area's most scenic spots.

Innkeeper(s): Bob & Marie Garrard. $90-150. MC, VISA, DS. 5 rooms with PB, 1 with FP. Breakfast and afternoon tea included in rates. AP. Types of meals: Full bkfst and early coffee/tea. Beds: KQ. TV, turndown service and ceiling fan in room. VCR, spa and library on premises. Antiquing, fishing, golf, live theater, parks, shopping, tennis and water sports nearby.

"This is the life. Don't change a single thing, because it's out of this world!"

Portland
B3

General Hooker's B&B

125 S W Hooker
Portland, OR 97201
(503)222-4435 (800)745-4135 Fax:(503)295-6410
E-mail: lori@generalhookers.com
Web: www.generalhookers.com

Circa 1888. This tastefully restored urban Queen Anne townhouse is a blend of comfort and informal charm. Situated in a Victorian village, Lair Hill, a tranquil and safe National Historic Register District, the inn has easy access to all of the city's attractions. (Park your car and take a stroll to Waterfront Park to enjoy the Saturday Market and whatever festival is being celebrated. If the weather is  inclement, shopping in sales-tax-free Portland is especially popular.) Guests are invited to take advantage of the inn's classic film and reference library. From the roof garden, guests can enjoy a view of the city, the river, bridges and mountains. The innkeeper, a fourth-generation Portlander, is active in city planning in the neighborhood and can recommend restaurants and special events. Try historic Lair Hill Market for lunch or dinner.

Historic Interest: Downtown Portland offers several historic districts and your host can direct you to many historic sites.

Innkeeper(s): Lori Hall. $75-125. MC, VISA, AX. 4 rooms, 2 with PB. Breakfast included in rates. Types of meals: Cont plus and veg bkfst. Beds: KQDT. TV, phone and VCR in room. Antiquing, concert hall and live theater nearby.

Terwilliger Vista B&B

515 SW Westwood Dr
Portland, OR 97201-2791
(503)244-0602 (888)244-0602 Fax:(503)293-8042

Circa 1940. Bay windows accentuate the exterior of this stately Georgian Colonial home. A mix of modern and Art Deco furnishings decorate the interior. The home has an airy, uncluttered feel with its polished floors topped with Oriental rugs and muted tones. There is a canopy bed and fireplace in the spacious Garden Suite, and the Rose Suite overlooks the Willamette Valley. Other rooms offer garden views, bay windows or wicker furnishings. There is a library, and an area set up with refreshments. The house is located in what will be the Historical Terwilliger Boulevard Preserve.

Innkeeper(s): Dick & Jan Vatert. $85-150. MC, VISA, PC, TC. TAC10. 5 rooms with PB, 1 with FP and 2 suites. Breakfast included in rates. Types of meals: Full bkfst and cont. Beds: KQT. Cable TV in room. Air conditioning. Refrigerator with sodas in bar area on premises. Family reunions hosted. Antiquing, wine country, live theater, parks, shopping and sporting events nearby.

"Like staying in House Beautiful."

Prairie City
D7

Strawberry Mountain Inn

HCR 77 Box 940
Prairie City, OR 97869
(541)820-4522 (800)545-6913 Fax:(541)820-4622
E-mail: linda@highdesertnet.com
Web: www.moriah.com/strawberry

Circa 1910. Vistas of Strawberry Mountain are a highlight of a getaway to this peaceful inn, set on three acres of farmland. The home, the largest in Grant County, was built by a man who bred and raised horses for the U.S. Cavalry. The interior is spacious and comfortable, a place where guests are made to feel at home. There is a library offering a wide selection of books, and guests can relax on the front porch or enjoy a game of chess in the parlor. 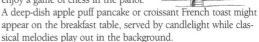 A deep-dish apple puff pancake or croissant French toast might appear on the breakfast table, served by candlelight while classical melodies play out in the background.

Innkeeper(s): Bill & Linda Harrington. $65-125. MC, VISA, AX, DS, PC, TC. TAC10. 4 rooms, 2 with PB. Breakfast included in rates. Type of meal: Full gourmet bkfst. Beds: KQDT. VCR, fax, copier, spa, stables, library, pet boarding and child care on premises. Weddings and small meetings hosted. Antiquing, fishing, golf, John Day Fossil Beds National Monument, historic museums, Kamwah Chung Chinese museums, parks, shopping, cross-country skiing and water sports nearby.

Pets allowed: Not inside the inn, separate facility.

Salem C3

A Creekside Inn, The Marquee House

333 Wyatt Ct NE
Salem, OR 97301-4269
(503)391-0837
E-mail: rickiemh@open.org
Web: www.marqueehouse.com/rickiemh

Circa 1938. Each room in this Mt. Vernon Colonial replica of George Washington's house is named after a famous old-time movie. Consider the Auntie Mame room. This gracious view room features a fireplace, fainting couch, costumes, collectibles and a private bath. The four other upstairs guest rooms offer similar themes. There are regular evening movie screenings complete with popcorn in the common  room. The extensive gardens offer guests an opportunity to stroll along historic Mill Creek or enjoy a round of croquet in the spacious backyard, weather permitting. Hazelnut waffles, confetti hash and oatmeal custard are a few of the breakfast specialties. The inn is just two blocks from the Chemeketa Historic District.

Historic Interest: Located close to the state capitol and Willamette University.
Innkeeper(s): Ms. Rickie Hart. $65-90. MC, VISA, DS, PC, TC. TAC10. 5 rooms, 3 with PB, 1 with FP. Breakfast and snacks/refreshments included in rates. Types of meals: Full gourmet bkfst and early coffee/tea. Beds: QT. VCR and bicycles on premises. Weddings, small meetings and family reunions hosted. Amusement parks, antiquing, golf, wine country tours, wineries, live theater, parks, shopping and sporting events nearby.

"We all agreed that you were the best hostess yet for one of our weekends!"

State House B&B

2146 State St
Salem, OR 97301-4350
(503)588-1340 (800)800-6712

Circa 1920. This three-story house sits on the banks of Mill Creek where ducks and geese meander past a huge old red maple down to the water. (A baby was abandoned here because the house looked "just right" and "surely had nice people there." The 12-year-old boy who found the baby on the side porch grew up to become a judge and legal counsel to Governor Mark Hatfield.) The inn is close to everything in Salem.
Innkeeper(s): Judy & Mike Winsett. $50-75. MC, VISA, DS. 4 rooms, 2 with PB. Breakfast included in rates. Type of meal: Full bkfst. Beds: QD. TV in room. Fax and copier on premises.

"You do a wonderful job making people feel welcome and relaxed."

Seaside A2

The Gilbert Inn, B&B

341 Beach Dr
Seaside, OR 97138-5707
(503)738-9770 (800)410-9770

Circa 1892. This yellow Victorian with its turret and third-story garret is framed with a white picket fence and gardens of lilies, roses and tulips. There are down quilts, antiques, and fresh

country fabrics in the guest rooms. A house specialty is stuffed French toast topped with apricot sauce. The ocean and the historic promenade, which stretches for a mile and a half along the sand, are a block away.

Innkeeper(s): Carole & Dick Rees. $89-125. MC, VISA, AX, DS. 10 rooms with PB. Type of meal: Full bkfst. Beds: QT. TV and phone in room.

Sand Dollar B&B

606 N Holladay Dr
Seaside, OR 97138-6926
(503)738-3491 (800)738-3491

Circa 1920. This Craftsman-style home looks a bit like a seashell, painted in light pink with dark pink trim. In fact, one of the guest rooms bears the name Sea Shell, filled with bright quilts and wicker. The Driftwood Room can be used as a two-bedroom suite for families, and there is also a cottage on the river. As the room names suggest, the house is decorated in a beach theme, graced by innkeeper Nita Hempfling's stained glasswork. Before breakfast is served, coffee or tea is delivered to the rooms.
Innkeeper(s): Robert & Nita Hempfling. $55-125. MC, VISA, AX, DS, TC. 3 rooms, 2 with PB and 1 suite. Breakfast and snacks/refreshments included in rates. Beds: KQT. Cable TV, ceiling fan and VCR in room. Bicycles and canoe on premises. Weddings and small meetings hosted. Antiquing, fishing, parks, shopping and water sports nearby.

Summer House - A Bed & Breakfast

1221 N Franklin St
Seaside, OR 97138-6242
(503)738-5740 (800)745-2378 Fax:(503)738-0172

Circa 1910. A few-minute stroll will take guests from this bed & breakfast to the beach. The cozy beach-style house is located just off the Promenade, a historic boardwalk running parallel to the beach. The inn's decor complements the peaceful, seaside surroundings. Each guest  room has been individually decorated in light, fanciful colors. Two rooms include a fireplace. Guests are pampered with an artfully presented gourmet breakfast.
Innkeeper(s): Jack & Leslie Palmeri. $79-159. MC, VISA, AX, DC, CB, DS, TC. 5 rooms with PB, 2 with FP and 1 conference room. Breakfast and snacks/refreshments included in rates. Types of meals: Full bkfst and early coffee/tea. Beds: KQT. Cable TV in room. Fax and copier on premises. Small meetings, family reunions and seminars hosted. Spanish spoken. Amusement parks, antiquing, fishing, golf, live theater, parks, shopping, tennis and water sports nearby.

Sisters D4

Conklin's Guest House

69013 Camp Polk Rd
Sisters, OR 97759-9705
(541)549-0123 (800)549-4262 Fax:(541)549-4481
Web: www.conklinsguesthouse.com

Circa 1910. The original portion of this Craftsman-style house was constructed in 1910, with later additions in 1938 and more recent changes in 1992 and 1996. Mountain views and four-and-a-half peaceful acres invite relaxation and romance. There are several ponds on the property stocked with trout for those wanting to try their hand at catch and release

fishing. There is also a heated swimming pool. Three guest rooms have clawfoot tubs, and the Suite and Forget-Me-Not rooms offer a pleasing view. For those in a larger group, the inn's Heather room includes a queen bed and two single beds, at a rate of $25 to $30 per person. Sisters' airport is across the street from the home.

Historic Interest: Camp Polk (U.S. Army) established 1865; Camp Polk cemetery remains (5 miles).

Innkeeper(s): Frank & Marie Conklin. $70-140. PC, TC. TAC10. 5 rooms with PB, 1 with FP and 1 suite. Breakfast and snacks/refreshments included in rates. Types of meals: Full gourmet bkfst, country bkfst, veg bkfst and early coffee/tea. Beds: QT. Phone and ceiling fan in room. Central air. Fax, copier and swimming on premises. Handicap access. Weddings, small meetings and family reunions hosted. Spanish spoken. Antiquing, art galleries, bicycling, canoeing/kayaking, fishing, golf, hiking, horseback riding, whitewater rafting, rock climbing, live theater, museums, parks, shopping, downhill skiing, cross-country skiing, tennis and water sports nearby.

Pets allowed: On leash outside.

"A wonderful and romantic time for our wedding anniversary. Thanks so much. Oh - great fishing too."

Stayton
C3

The Inn at Gardner House Bed & Breakfast

633 N 3rd Ave
Stayton, OR 97383-1731
(503)769-6331

Circa 1893. A former Stayton postmaster and city councilman built this home, which features a wraparound veranda. Accommodations include a suite with a small kitchen and dining room. Each guest room is comfortably furnished, with some antiques. The innkeeper prepares creative breakfasts with homemade breads, fresh fruit and entrees such as asparagus quiche or breakfast burritos topped with salsa.

Innkeeper(s): Dick Jungwirth. $55-65. MC, VISA, AX, DC, CB, DS, PC, TC. 2 rooms with PB and 1 suite. Breakfast included in rates. Types of meals: Full gourmet bkfst and early coffee/tea. Dinner and picnic lunch available. Beds: QT. Cable TV, phone and VCR in room. Copier and library on premises. Weddings, small meetings and family reunions hosted. Antiquing, fishing, live theater, parks, shopping, downhill skiing, cross-country skiing, sporting events and water sports nearby.

Pets Allowed.

Welches
C4

Old Welches Inn B&B

26401 E Welches Rd
Welches, OR 97067-9701
(503)622-3754 Fax:(503)622-5370

Circa 1890. This two-story colonial building, behind a picket fence, was originally the first hotel to be built in the Mt. Hood area. Reconstructed in the '30s, the building now has shutters and French windows. The inn's two acres offer a plethora of flower beds and views of the Salmon River and Hunchback

Mountain. Rooms are named for wildflowers and include antiques. If traveling with children or friends try Lilybank, a private cottage which overlooks the first hole of Three Nines. There are two bedrooms, a kitchen and a river rock fireplace.

Innkeeper(s): Judith & Ted Mondun. $75-130. MC, VISA, AX, DS, PC, TC. TAC10. 4 rooms and 1 cottage. Breakfast and snacks/refreshments included in rates. Types of meals: Full bkfst and early coffee/tea. Beds: QD. Turndown service in room. VCR, fax and pet boarding on premises. Weddings, small meetings and family reunions hosted. Antiquing, fishing, golf, parks, shopping, downhill skiing, cross-country skiing, sporting events and tennis nearby.

Pets allowed: House broken, well behaved in cottage only.

Westfir
E3

Westfir Lodge, A B&B Inn

47365 First St
Westfir, OR 97492
(541)782-3103

Circa 1923. Behind a white picket fence, this graceful Arts and Crafts house is near the longest covered bridge in Oregon. Once headquarters to a lumber company, the inn has English gardens and meandering stone paths that create an appealing setting from which to view the bridge. The inn's decor is English country with bright floral prints and antiques. Scones and crumpets, eggs, potatoes and broiled tomatoes comprise the full English breakfast.

Innkeeper(s): Ken Symons, Gerry Chamberlain. $50-85. PC. 9 rooms with PB. Breakfast and afternoon tea included in rates. Types of meals: Full bkfst and early coffee/tea. Beds: QT. Ceiling fan and robes in room. Air conditioning. VCR and copier on premises. Handicap access. Weddings, small meetings, family reunions and seminars hosted. Fishing, golf, parks, shopping, downhill skiing, cross-country skiing and tennis nearby.

Pennsylvania

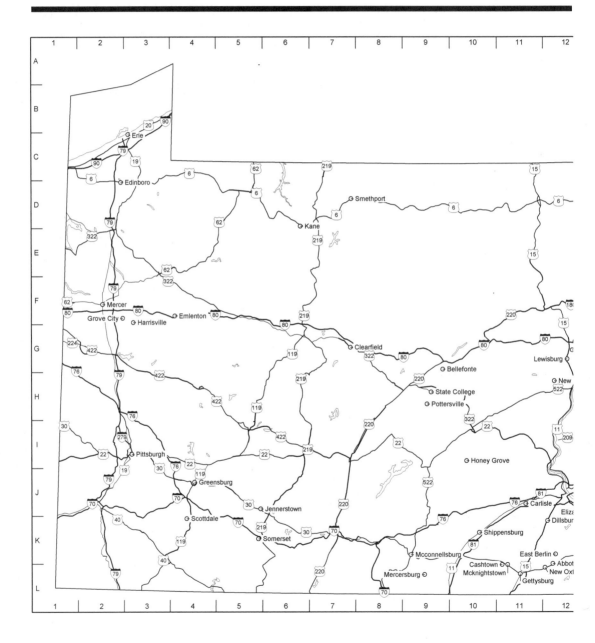

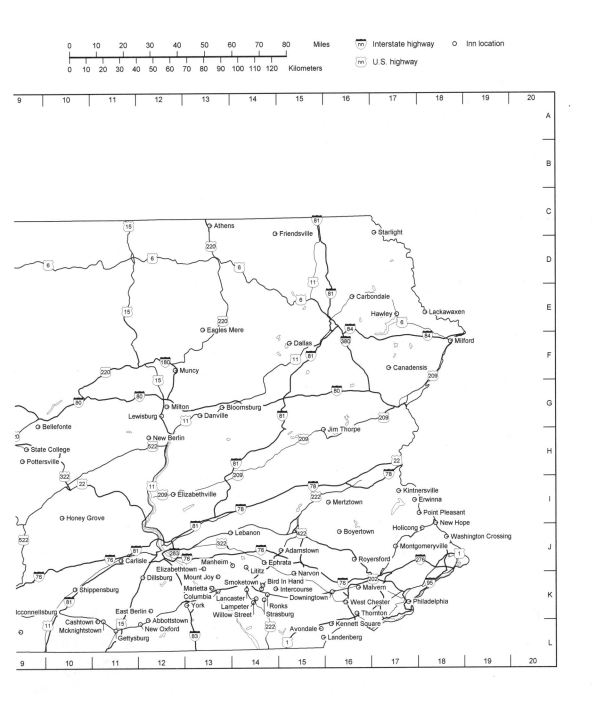

Miles

0 10 20 30 40 50 60 70 80

Kilometers

0 10 20 30 40 50 60 70 80 90 100 110 120

(nn) Interstate highway   o   Inn location

(nn) U.S. highway

Athens
Friendsville
Starlight
Carbondale
Hawley
Lackawaxen
Milford
Eagles Mere
Dallas
Canadensis
Muncy
Bloomsburg
Milton
Danville
Jim Thorpe
Lewisburg
Bellefonte
New Berlin
State College
Pottersville
Elizabethville
Kintnersville
Erwinna
Mertztown
Point Pleasant
Honey Grove
New Hope
Boyertown
Holicong
Washington Crossing
Lebanon
Montgomeryville
Adamstown
Royersford
Carlisle
Manheim
Ephrata
Shippensburg
Elizabethtown
Lititz
Narvon
Malvern
Dillsburg
Mount Joy
Smoketown
Bird In Hand
Marietta
Intercourse
Downingtown
Philadelphia
Columbia
Lancaster
West Chester
York
Lampeter
Ronks
Thornton
Icconnellsburg
Willow Street
Strasburg
Cashtown
East Berlin
Abbottstown
Kennett Square
Mcknightstown
New Oxford
Avondale
Landenberg
Gettysburg

351

Abbottstown
K12

The Altland House

Rt 30 Center Square
Abbottstown, PA 17301
(717)259-9535 Fax:(717)259-9956

Circa 1790. A French mansard roof sits atop this three-story country inn and tavern known for its cuisine and hospitality. Located halfway between York and Gettysburg, it is on an old Conestoga route. Two murals pay homage to the inn's historic presence in the town. With high ceilings and chestnut woodwork as a backdrop, the spacious rooms offer contemporary furnishings and several deluxe rooms have  whirlpools and fireplaces. The Cottage provides a kitchen, fireplace and private yard with hot tub. The inn's two restaurants present a variety of house specialties. The Underside Restaurant has a soup and salad bar and serves sandwiches and burgers, while the Berwick Room Restaurant is noted for a more elegant cuisine. The inn has a popular Sunday buffet.

Innkeeper(s): Mike Haugh. $89-125. MC, VISA, AX, DS, PC, TC. 9 rooms with PB, 1 suite, 1 cottage and 2 conference rooms. Breakfast included in rates. Types of meals: Cont plus and cont. Gourmet dinner, picnic lunch, lunch, banquet service, catering service and room service available. Beds: KQ. Cable TV, phone and whirlpool tubs in room. Air conditioning. Fax and copier on premises. Weddings and family reunions hosted. Antiquing, fishing, golf, history, history, history, live theater, shopping, downhill skiing and tennis nearby.

Adamstown
J15

Adamstown Inn

62 W Main St
Adamstown, PA 19501
(717)484-0800 (800)594-4808

Circa 1830. This square brick house, with its 1850s pump organ found in the large parlor and other local folk art, fits right into this community known as one of the antique capitals of America (3,000 antique dealers). Other decorations include family heirlooms, Victorian wallpaper, handmade quilts and lace curtains. Before breakfast, coffee, tea or hot chocolate is brought to your room. For outlet  mall fans, Adamstown is 10 miles from Reading, which offers a vast assortment of top-quality merchandise.

Historic Interest: The Ephrata Cloister is just seven miles away.

Innkeeper(s): Tom & Wanda Berman. $70-135. MC, VISA, PC, TC. 4 rooms with PB and 1 suite. Breakfast, afternoon tea and snacks/refreshments included in rates. Types of meals: Cont plus and early coffee/tea. Beds: Q. Ceiling fan and Jacuzzis (two rooms) in room. Air conditioning. Copier and library on premises. Small meetings, family reunions and seminars hosted. Amusement parks, antiquing, fishing, live theater, parks and shopping nearby.

Publicity: *Lancaster Intelligencer, Reading Eagle, Travel & Leisure, Country Almanac.*

"Your warm hospitality and lovely home left us with such pleasant memories."

Athens
C13

Failte Inn B&B and Antique Shoppe

RR #2 Box 323
Athens, PA 18810
(570)358-3899 Fax:(570)358-3387

Circa 1924. During its heyday, parties with hundreds of guests where not uncommon at this Gatsby-era estate. The inn's name derives from the innkeepers' Scottish heritage and means welcome in Gaelic. The inn is decorated with a variety of antiques, including some family pieces. One special decoration is an 18th-century quilt designed by the innkeeper's great-great-great-great grandmother. The innkeeper also has her father's World War I uniform on display and her mother's wedding dress. Complimentary wine, brandy and other beverages are provided in the inn's  pub, which formerly served as a speakeasy during the days of Prohibition. Breakfasts, served either in the formal dining room or on the screened wraparound verandas, include baked goods such as homemade sourdough bread, sticky buns or Amish friendship bread accompanied by homemade jams and jellies. The daily entrée might be cheesy eggs with Canadian bacon or perhaps thick slices of sourdough French toast with Pennsylvania maple syrup. The surrounding area offers lakes, parks and outdoor activities in the Endless Mountains, as well as antique shops, wineries and the Corning Glass Center.

Historic Interest: Covered bridge (10 miles), French Azilum (15 miles), PA grand canyon (40 miles), World's End State Park (40 miles), NY wine country, Corning, NY (40 miles), Finger Lakes & Watkins Glen (35 miles).

Innkeeper(s): Jim, Sarah & Jamie True. $65. MC, VISA, PC, TC. 5 rooms with PB. Breakfast and snacks/refreshments included in rates. Types of meals: Full bkfst, cont, veg bkfst and early coffee/tea. Beds: KQDT. Ceiling fan, Jacuzzi (one room) and wine in room. Air conditioning. VCR, fax, copier, library and huge screened veranda on premises. Handicap access. Weddings, small meetings, family reunions and seminars hosted. Antiquing, bicycling, canoeing/kayaking, fishing, golf, hiking, museums, parks, shopping, tennis and wineries nearby.

Bellefonte
G9

Reynolds Mansion B&B

101 W Linn St
Bellefonte, PA 16823-1622
(814)353-8407 (800)899-3929

Circa 1885. Bellefonte is a town with many impressive, historic homes, and this exquisite stone mansion is no exception. The home, a combination of late Victorian and Gothic styles, features extraordinary, hand-crafted woodwork and intricately laid wood floors, as well as 10 fireplaces. Five guest rooms include a fireplace and a Jacuzzi tub. All enjoy a romantic atmosphere, heightened by candles, fresh flowers and the poshest of furnishings and decor. There also is a bil-

liards room and library for guests to enjoy. Baked, stuffed French toast served with bacon or sausage is among the breakfast specialties accompanied by muffins, juices, cereals and a fruit compote created with more than a half dozen different fresh fruits. For an excellent lunch or dinner, the innkeepers suggest the nearby Gamble Mill Tavern, a 200-year-old mill listed in the National Register.

Historic Interest: Penn State University (10 miles).

Innkeeper(s): Joseph & Charlotte Heidt. $95-165. MC, VISA, AX, PC, TC. TAC10. 6 suites, 5 with FP. Breakfast included in rates. Types of meals: Full gourmet bkfst, cont plus and early coffee/tea. Beds: KQ. Jacuzzi tubs and Jacuzzi steam shower in room. VCR, fax, copier, library and billiards room on premises. Weddings, small meetings, family reunions and seminars hosted. Antiquing, fishing, golf, victorian architecture, live theater, parks, shopping, downhill skiing, cross-country skiing, sporting events and water sports nearby.

"Your bed & breakfast is such an inspiration to us."

Bird-in-Hand   K14

Mill Creek Homestead B&B

2578 Old Philadelphia Pike
Bird-in-Hand, PA 17505-9796
(717)291-6419 (800)771-2578 Fax:(717)291-2171

Circa 1790. This 18th-century fieldstone farmhouse is one of the oldest homes in Bird-in-the-Hand. Located in the

Pennsylvania Dutch Heartland, the inn is decorated for comfort with Amish influences represented throughout. There are two guest rooms with private baths and one two-room Victorian suite. Guests are invited to lounge by the pool or sit on the porch and watch the horse-drawn buggies go by. A full breakfast is served in the formal dining room, while afternoon refreshments are in the common rooms. The inn is walking distance from shops, museums, farmers market, antiques and crafts.

Historic Interest: James Buchannan's Wheatland, Rockford Plantation, Landis Valley Museum, Streisburg Railroad Museum, Americana Museum, Ephrata Cloister, Lancaster Heritage Museum.

Innkeeper(s): Vicki & Frank Alfone. $95-125. MC, VISA, DS, PC, TC. TAC10. 3 rooms, 2 with PB and 1 suite. Breakfast, afternoon tea and snacks/refreshments included in rates. Types of meals: Full bkfst and early coffee/tea. Beds: Q. Turndown service and ceiling fan in room. Air conditioning. Swimming and library on premises. Amusement parks, antiquing, fishing, golf, live theater, parks, shopping, tennis and water sports nearby.

"Thank you for sharing your wonderful home with us. I knew this place would be perfect!"

Bloomsburg   G13

Magee's Main Street Inn

20 W Main St
Bloomsburg, PA 17815-1703
(570)784-3500 (800)331-9815 Fax:(570)784-5517
E-mail: rusty@magees.com
Web: www.magees.com

Circa 1870. Magee's 43-room downtown inn offers regular rooms and deluxe double rooms with separate living rooms. An expansive breakfast is served, cooked to order in the restaurant, and coffee is available throughout the day. The inn boasts a

popular ballroom for wedding receptions and parties of 12 to 200 people. Harry's Grille, an adjoining casual-style restaurant, serves lunch and dinner in a cozy atmosphere.

Innkeeper(s): The Magee's. $57-93. MC, VISA, AX, DC, CB, DS. 43 rooms with PB, 6 suites and 1 conference room. Breakfast included in rates. Dinner and lunch available. Restaurant on premises. Beds: KQDT. Cable TV and phone in room. Air conditioning. VCR, fax and copier on premises. Weddings, small meetings, family reunions and seminars hosted. Amusement parks, antiquing, live theater, shopping, cross-country skiing and sporting events nearby.

The Inn at Turkey Hill

991 Central Rd
Bloomsburg, PA 17815-8990
(717)387-1500 Fax:(717)784-3718
E-mail: info@innatturkeyhill.com
Web: www.innatturkeyhill.com

Circa 1839. Turkey Hill is an elegant, white brick farmhouse. All the guest rooms are furnished with hand-crafted reproductions from Habersham Plantation in Georgia and most overlook the duck pond and gazebo. Two rooms provide wood-burning fireplaces and two-person whirlpool tubs. The five stable rooms also include a gas fireplace and two-person whirlpool tub. The mural room features hand-painted murals of the rolling Pennsylvania countryside.

Innkeeper(s): Babs & Andrew B. Pruden. $98-190. MC, VISA, AX, DC, CB, DS. 23 rooms with PB, 7 with FP and 2 conference rooms. Breakfast included in rates. Type of meal: Cont. Gourmet dinner and room service available. Restaurant on premises. Beds: KQD. Fax and copier on premises. Handicap access. Antiquing, fishing and live theater nearby.

Pets allowed: In some rooms.

"How nice to find an enclave of good taste and class, a special place that seems to care about such old-fashioned virtues as quality and the little details that mean so much— Art Carey, Philadelphia Inquirer."

Canadensis   F17

Brookview Manor B&B Inn

RR 1 Box 365
Canadensis, PA 18325-9740
(570)595-2451 (800)585-7974 Fax:(570)595-5065

Circa 1911. By the side of the road, hanging from a tall evergreen, is the welcoming sign to this forest retreat. There are brightly decorated common rooms and four fireplaces. The carriage house has three rooms. There are two rooms with Jacuzzi tubs. The innkeepers like to share a "secret waterfall" within a 30-minute walk from the inn.

Innkeeper(s): Mary Anne Buckley. $100-150. MC, VISA, AX, DS, PC, TC. TAC10. 10 rooms with PB, 1 with FP and 2 suites. Breakfast and afternoon tea included in rates. Types of meals: Full bkfst and early coffee/tea. Picnic lunch available. Beds: QD. Air conditioning. Fax and copier on premises. Weddings, small meetings and family reunions hosted. Amusement parks, antiquing, fishing, hiking, live theater, parks, shopping, downhill skiing, cross-country skiing and water sports nearby.

Publicity: *Mid-Atlantic Country, Bridal Guide.*

"Thanks for a great wedding weekend. Everything was perfect."

The Merry Inn

PO Box 757, Rt 390
Canadensis, PA 18325-0757
(717)595-2011 (800)858-4182

Circa 1942. Set in the picturesque Pocono Mountains, this bed & breakfast is a 90-minute drive from the metropolitan New York and Philadelphia areas. The turn-of-the-century, mountainside home was built by two sisters and at one time

was used as a boarding house. Current owners and innkeepers Meredyth and Chris Huggard have decorated their B&B using an eclectic mix of styles.

Each guest room is individually appointed, with styles ranging from Victorian to country. Guests enjoy use of an outdoor Jacuzzi set into the mountainside. Bedrooms are set up to accommodate families, and children are welcome here.

Innkeeper(s): Meredyth & Christopher Huggard. $75-95. MC, VISA, PC, TC. 6 rooms with PB. Breakfast included in rates. Type of meal: Full bkfst. Beds: KQDT. Cable TV, VCR and TV in room. Jacuzzi (outdoor) on premises. Small meetings and family reunions hosted. Antiquing, fishing, golf, live theater, parks, shopping, downhill skiing, cross-country skiing and water sports nearby.

Pets allowed: Dogs must be trained, $25 deposit.

Carbondale   E16

Heritage House on the Park

5 Park Place
Carbondale, PA 18407-2330
(570)282-7477 Fax:(570)282-8698

Circa 1912. Built in Victorian style, Heritage House offers four guest rooms all decorated with elegant, period décor. The Ivy Suite includes a fireplace and whirlpool tub. Lacy curtains, clawfoot tubs and roses are other romantic amenities. Breakfasts are served by candlelight and include homemade breads and muffins and items such as crepes with fresh fruit, oven-baked pancakes or baked oatmeal. The house overlooks Memorial Park and Carbondale's city hall. The inn offers close access to ski areas, golfing, hunting, fishing, horseback riding, tennis and snowmobiling.

Historic Interest: National Historic Steam Town, Anthricite Museum, Coal mine tour-16 miles.

Innkeeper(s): Darlene Ann Bednarczyk. $75-105. PC. 4 rooms, 3 with PB, 1 with FP and 1 suite. Breakfast and snacks/refreshments included in rates. Types of meals: Full gourmet bkfst and veg bkfst. Picnic lunch available. Beds: QD. Cable TV, phone and garden tub in room. Central air. Fax on premises. Antiquing, art galleries, bicycling, fishing, golf, hiking, horseback riding, live theater, museums, parks, shopping, downhill skiing, cross-country skiing, sporting events, tennis, water sports and wineries nearby.

Carlisle   J11

Line Limousin Farmhouse B&B

2070 Ritner Hwy
Carlisle, PA 17013-9303
(717)243-1281

Circa 1864. The grandchildren of Bob and Joan are the ninth generation of Lines to enjoy this 200-year-old homestead. A stone and brick exterior accents the farmhouse's graceful style,

while inside, family heirlooms attest to the home's longevity. This is a breeding stock farm of 110 acres and the cattle raised here, Limousin, originate from the Limoges area of France. Giant maples shade the lawn and there are woods and stone fences.

Innkeeper(s): Bob & Joan Line. $65-85. PC. 4 rooms, 2 with PB. Breakfast included in rates. Type of meal: Full bkfst. Beds: KQT. Cable TV and phone in room. Air conditioning. VCR and guest refrigerator on premises. Family reunions hosted. Amusement parks, antiquing, fishing, golf, live theater, parks, shopping, cross-country skiing and sporting events nearby.

"Returning to your home each evening was like returning to our own home, that's how comfortable and warm it was."

Pheasant Field B&B

150 Hickorytown Rd
Carlisle, PA 17013-9732
(717)258-0717 Fax:(717)258-0717

Circa 1800. Located on eight acres of central Pennsylvania farmland, this brick, two-story Federal-style farmhouse features wooden shutters and a covered front porch. Most rooms include a TV and telephone. An early 19th-century stone barn is on the property, and horse boarding often is available. The

Appalachian Trail is less than a mile away. Fly-fishing is popular at Yellow Breeches and Letort Spring. Dickinson College and Carlisle Fairgrounds are other points of interest.

Historic Interest: Gettysburg National Historical Park (32 miles), Molly Pitcher grave site.

Innkeeper(s): Denise Fegan. $85-120. MC, VISA, AX. 4 rooms with PB. Breakfast included in rates. Types of meals: Full bkfst and early coffee/tea. Beds: KQT. Cable TV and phone in room. Air conditioning. VCR, fax and piano on premises. Weddings, small meetings and family reunions hosted. Amusement parks, antiquing, fishing, live theater, downhill skiing and cross-country skiing nearby.

Publicity: *Outdoor Traveler, Harrisburg Magazine.*

"You have an outstanding, charming and warm house. I felt for the first time as being home."

Cashtown   L11

Cashtown Inn

1325 Old Rt 30, PO Box 103
Cashtown, PA 17310
(717)334-9722 (800)367-1797

Circa 1797. Cashtown Inn's history alone will inspire a visit. The inn was built as a stagecoach stop and has welcomed guests for more than two centuries. It also served as a stop along the Underground Railroad and curiously, also served as a Confederate headquarters prior to the Battle of Gettysburg. The inn's rooms are decorated in country Victorian style with four-poster beds. One room includes a lace canopy bed. In addition to the gourmet breakfasts, which are included in the rates, the inn also serves lunch and includes a renowned restaurant with dinners prepared by a chef who graduated from the Culinary Institute of America. Dinners are served in the rustic bar, which was the inn's original tavern. The chef's menus feature starters such as a baked brie in pastry or savory artichoke dip with foccacia bread. From there, guests can partake of homemade soups or salads with freshly prepared dressings. The menu is ever changing, but might include entrees such as pecan-crusted chicken with maple butter sauce or perhaps beef medallions with bourbon walnut sauce. The inn is eight miles from Gettysburg Military Park, and also offers close access to many historic sites, museums, a winery, art galleries and shopping.

Historic Interest: Gettysburg Military Park (8 miles).

Innkeeper(s): Dennis & Eileen Hoover. $76-145. MC, VISA, DS, PC, TC. 7 rooms, 4 with PB and 3 suites. Breakfast included in rates. Types of meals: Full gourmet bkfst and early coffee/tea. Dinner, lunch and banquet service available. Restaurant on premises. Beds: QD. Cable TV, ceiling fan and VCR in room. Central air. Fax and copier on premises. Weddings, small meetings, family reunions and seminars hosted. Antiquing, art galleries, golf, hiking, horseback riding, live theater, museums, parks, shopping, downhill skiing, sporting events and wineries nearby.

"We were impressed with your inn, but more importantly with your personal touch toward all your guests...many thanks for your generosity and hospitality."

Churchtown   J15

Churchtown Inn B&B

2100 Main St, Rt 23
Churchtown, PA 17555-9514
(717)445-7794 Fax:(717)445-0962

Circa 1735. This handsome, stone Federal house with its panoramic views was once known as the Edward Davies Mansion, but was also once a tinsmith shop and rectory. It has

heard the marching feet of Revolutionary troops and seen the Union Army during the Civil War. Tastefully furnished with antiques and collectables, the inn features canopy, pencilpost and sleigh beds. Breakfast is served in a new glass garden room. There is music everywhere, as the innkeeper directed choruses appearing at Carnegie Hall and the Lincoln Center. By prior arrangement, guests may dine in an Amish home.

Historic Interest: Located across the street from the Bangor Episcopal Church, the inn is listed in the National Register.

Innkeeper(s): Hermine & Stuart Smith, Jim Kent. $69-110. MC, VISA, DS, PC, TC. 8 rooms with PB and 1 suite. Breakfast included in rates. Type of meal: Full bkfst. Beds: Q. Cable TV in room. Air conditioning. VCR on premises. Small meetings, family reunions and seminars hosted. Antiquing, fishing, amish tourist area, parks and shopping nearby.

"Magnificent atmosphere. Outstanding breakfasts. Our favorite B&B."

Clearfield   G7

Christopher Kratzer House

101 E Cherry St
Clearfield, PA 16830-2315
(814)765-5024 (888)252-2632

Circa 1840. This inn is the oldest home in town, built by a carpenter and architect who also started Clearfield's first newspaper. The innkeepers keep a book of history about the house and town for interested guests. The interior is a mix of antiques from different eras, many are family pieces. There are collections of art and musical instruments. Two guest rooms afford views of the Susquehanna River. Refreshments and a glass of wine are served in the afternoons. The inn's Bridal Suite Special includes complimentary champagne, fruit and snacks, and breakfast may be served in the privacy of your room. Small wedding receptions, brunches and parties are hosted at the inn.

Innkeeper(s): Bruce & Ginny Baggett. $55-70. MC, VISA, DS, PC, TC. 4 rooms, 2 with PB. Breakfast, afternoon tea and snacks/refreshments included in rates. Types of meals: Full gourmet bkfst and early coffee/tea. Beds: KQT. Cable TV, phone and ceiling fan in room. Air conditioning. Library on premises. Antiquing, fishing, hiking, biking, playground across street, live theater, parks, shopping, cross-country skiing and sporting events nearby.

"Past and present joyously intermingle in this place."

Victorian Loft B&B

216 S Front St
Clearfield, PA 16830-2218
(814)765-4805 (800)798-0456 Fax:(814)765-9596

Circa 1894. Accommodations at this bed & breakfast are available in either a historic Victorian home on the riverfront or in a private, three-bedroom cabin. The white brick home is dressed with colorful, gingerbread trim, and inside, a grand staircase, stained glass and antique furnishings add to the Victorian charm. The suite is ideal for families as it contains two bedrooms, a living room, dining room, kitchen and a bath with a whirlpool tub. The cabin, Cedarwood Lodge, sleeps six and is located on eight, wooded acres near Parker Dam State Park and Elliot State Park. This is a favorite setting for small groups.

Innkeeper(s): Tim & Peggy Durant. $50-125. MC, VISA, AX, DS, PC, TC. TAC10. 3 rooms, 1 with PB, 2 suites and 1 cottage. Breakfast included in rates. Types of meals: Full bkfst and early coffee/tea. Beds: QD. Phone and VCR in room. Whirlpool on premises. Small meetings and family reunions hosted. Limited Spanish spoken. Antiquing, fishing, live theater, parks, shopping, cross-country skiing, sporting events and water sports nearby.

Pets allowed: By prior arrangement.

"A feeling of old-fashioned beauty. The elegance of roses and lace. All wrapped up into a romantic moment."

Columbia   K13

The Columbian

360 Chestnut St
Columbia, PA 17512-1156
(717)684-5869 (800)422-5869
E-mail: inn@columbianinn.com
Web: www.columbianinn.com

Circa 1897. This stately three-story mansion is a fine example of Colonial Revival architecture. Antique beds, a stained-glass window and home-baked breads are among its charms. Guests may relax on the wraparound sun porches.

Historic Interest: The National Watch and Clock Museum (one-half block), The Wrights Ferry Mansion (4 blocks), The Bank Museum (4 blocks).

Innkeeper(s): Chris & Becky Will. $75-125105. MC, VISA, PC, TC. 8 rooms with PB, 4 with FP and 2 suites. Breakfast included in rates. Type of meal: Full bkfst. Beds: KQT. Cable TV, ceiling fan and fruit/candy/flowers in room. Air conditioning. Ice cream parlor on premises. Weddings, small meetings and family reunions hosted. Amusement parks, antiquing, fishing, Elizabethtown, live theater, parks, shopping, downhill skiing, cross-country skiing, sporting events and water sports nearby.

"In a word, extraordinary! Truly a home away from home. First B&B experience but will definitely not be my last."

Dallas   F15

Ponda-Rowland B&B Inn

RR 1 Box 349
Dallas, PA 18612-9604
(570)639-3245 (800)854-3286 Fax:(570)639-5531
E-mail: bbres1@epix.net
Web: www.bnbcity.com/inns/20006

Circa 1850. Situated on a 130-acre farm, this historic house overlooks a 30-acre wildlife sanctuary with six ponds, and trails visited by whitetail deer, fox, turkeys, mallard ducks, Canadian

geese and, occasionally, blue herons. The home is filled with beautiful American country antiques and collections. There are beamed ceilings and a stone fireplace in the living room. The scenic setting, hospitable hosts, farm animals and hearty country breakfast make this a perfect place for a memorable vacation.
Historic Interest: French Azilium, farm museum, covered bridges, Steamtown National Park.

Innkeeper(s): Jeanette & Cliff Rowland. $85-115. MC, VISA, AX, DS, PC, TC. TAC10. 6 rooms with PB, 2 with FP. Breakfast and snacks/refreshments included in rates. Types of meals: Full bkfst and early coffee/tea. Beds: KDT. Ceiling fan in room. Air conditioning. VCR, fax, copier, canoe, toboggan, ice skates, fishing gear and guest refrigerator and microwave on premises. Antiquing, fishing, horseback riding, Steamtown National Park, live theater, parks, shopping, downhill skiing, cross-country skiing, sporting events and water sports nearby.

Danville   G13

The Pine Barn Inn

1 Pine Barn Pl
Danville, PA 17821-1299
(570)275-2071 (800)627-2276 Fax:(570)275-3248
E-mail: innkpr@pinebarninn.com
Web: pinebarninn.com

Circa 1860. The inn is a restored Pennsylvania German barn. Original stone walls and beams accent the restaurant and a large stone fireplace warms the tavern. It is believed to be the first all-electric residence in the state.

Innkeeper(s): Susan Dressler. $50-90. MC, VISA, AX, DC, CB, DS, TC. 102 rooms with PB and 2 conference rooms. Type of meal: Full bkfst. Restaurant on premises. Beds: KQDT.

"For four years we have stayed at the Pine Barn Inn. I thought then, and still think, it is truly the nicest inn I have been in and I've been in many."

Dillsburg   K12

Peter Wolford House

440 Franklin Church Rd
Dillsburg, PA 17019-9766
(717)432-0757 Fax:(717)432-0186

Circa 1797. A Federal farmhouse in the National Register, the Peter Wolford House was constructed of Flemish Bond brick by a prominent grist mill operator. A brick-patterned bank barn, a unique Pennsylvania and Maryland barn style, still stands. There are pine floors and many fireplaces, including a 10-foot-wide, walk-in fireplace used for  cooking. Antiques and handmade quilts fill the guest rooms. Outside on the 10 acres are meadows, an herb garden and perennial borders accented by a handmade picket fence. State game lands are adjacent to the inn.

Innkeeper(s): Ted & Loretta Pesano. $60-70. PC. 3 rooms, 2 with FP. Breakfast, afternoon tea and snacks/refreshments included in rates. Types of meals: Full bkfst and early coffee/tea. Beds: QD. Air conditioning. Jacuzzi on premises. Small meetings hosted. Amusement parks, antiquing, fishing, golf, downhill skiing and cross-country skiing nearby.

"Thank you for a splendid getaway."

Downingtown   K16

Glen Isle Farm

130 S Lloyd Ave
Downingtown, PA 19335-2239
(610)269-9100 (800)269-1730 Fax:(610)269-9191

Circa 1730. George Washington was a guest at this 18th-century farmhouse, as well as James Buchanan. Several members of the Continental Congress stayed here while on route to York. The home is a Revolutionary War site, as well as a stop on the Underground Railroad. Eight wooded acres ensure privacy and a relaxing stay. Guest rooms are decorated with antiques. The farm is within 10 miles of  Amish attractions, and a short drive from Valley Forge, Longwood Gardens and antique shops. Philadelphia is 30 miles away.

Historic Interest: Valley Forge (20 miles), Winterthur (25 miles), Underground Railroad site, Revolutionary War site, Longwood Gargens (20 miles), Amish (10 miles).

Innkeeper(s): Tim Babbage & Glenn Baker. $65-80. MC, VISA, DS, PC, TC. TAC10. 4 rooms, 1 with PB. Breakfast and snacks/refreshments included in rates. Types of meals: Full gourmet bkfst, cont and early coffee/tea. Catering service available. Beds: KQ. Air conditioning. VCR, fax, copier and library on premises. Weddings, small meetings, family reunions and seminars hosted. Antiquing, art galleries, bicycling, canoeing/kayaking, fishing, golf, hiking and horseback riding nearby.

"Our place to stay when next this way!"

Eagles Mere   E13

Crestmont Inn

Crestmont Dr
Eagles Mere, PA 17731
(570)525-3519 (800)522-8767
E-mail: crestmnt@epix.net
Web: www.crestmont-inn.com

Eagles Mere has been a vacation site since the late 19th century and still abounds with Victorian charm. The Crestmont Inn is no exception. The rooms are tastefully decorated with Oriental rugs, flowers and elegant furnishings. Suites include two-person whirlpool tubs, and one has a fireplace. A hearty country breakfast is served each morning, and guests also are treated to a five-course dinner in the candle-lit dining room. Savor a variety of mouth-watering entrees and finish off the evening with scrumptious desserts such as fresh fruit pies, English trifle or Orange Charlotte. The cocktail lounge is a perfect place to mingle and enjoy hors d'oeuvres, wines and spirits. The inn grounds offer a large swimming pool, tennis and shuffleboard courts. The Wyoming State Forest borders the property, and golfing is just minutes away.

Innkeeper(s): Karen Oliver & Doug Rider. $90-178. MC, VISA. 14 rooms. Breakfast included in rates. Type of meal: Full bkfst.

East Berlin (Gettysburg Area)   K12

Bechtel Victorian Mansion B&B Inn

400 W King St
East Berlin (Gettysburg Area), PA 17316
(717)259-7760 (800)579-1108
Web: www.bbonline.com/pa/bechtel/

Circa 1897. The town of East Berlin, near Lancaster and 18 miles east of Gettysburg, was settled by Pennsylvania Germans prior to the American Revolution. William Leas, a wealthy banker, built this many-gabled romantic Queen Anne mansion, now listed in the National Register. The inn is furnished with an abundance of museum-quality antiques and collections. Floral comforters top many of the handsome bedsteads.

Historic Interest: Gettysburg (18 miles).

Innkeeper(s): Richard & Carol Carlson. $70-150. MC, VISA, AX, DS, PC, TC. TAC10. 7 rooms and 2 suites. Breakfast included in rates. Types of meals: Full bkfst and early coffee/tea. Snacks/refreshments available. Beds: KQD. Turndown service in room. Air conditioning. VCR on premises. Weddings, small meetings and family reunions hosted. Amusement parks, antiquing, bicycling, fishing, golf, hiking, live theater, museums, shopping, downhill skiing and wineries nearby.

Edinboro   D2

Raspberry House B&B

118 Erie St
Edinboro, PA 16412-2209
(814)734-8997

Circa 1867. Raspberry gingerbread trim and stained glass are whimsical features of this early Victorian home, built by a doctor just a few years after the Civil War ended. The innkeepers

painstakingly restored the home, leaving many original elements, including chandeliers, pocket doors and wooden shutters. To keep the authentic Victorian flavor, reproduction wallpapers were used. Guest quarters are decorated in an eclectic style, intermingling country and modern pieces. As one might expect from the name, items such as raspberry muffins or baked apples with raspberries often find their way onto the breakfast table. Raspberry House is located in the center of downtown Edinboro and is near the university, restaurants, shopping and Edinboro Lake.

Innkeeper(s): Betty & Hal Holmstrom. $55-100. MC, VISA, AX, PC. 4 rooms with PB. Breakfast included in rates. Types of meals: Full gourmet bkfst and early coffee/tea. Beds: KQDT. Cable TV and ceiling fan in room. Air conditioning. Weddings, small meetings, family reunions and seminars hosted. Amusement parks, antiquing, fishing, live theater, parks, shopping, downhill skiing, cross-country skiing, sporting events and water sports nearby.

"The Raspberry House is exceptionally high on our list of pleasing and rewarding experiences."

Elizabethtown   J13

West Ridge Guest House

1285 W Ridge Rd
Elizabethtown, PA 17022-9739
(717)367-7783 (877)367-7783 Fax:(717)367-8468
E-mail: wridgeroad@aol.com
Web: www.westridgebandb.com

Circa 1890. Guests at this country home have many choices. They may opt to relax and enjoy the view from the gazebo, or perhaps work out in the inn's exercise room. The hot tub provides yet another soothing possibility. Ask about rooms with whirlpool tubs. The 20-acre grounds also include two fishing ponds. The innkeepers pass out a breakfast menu to their guests, allowing them to choose the time they prefer to eat and a choice of entrees. Along with the traditional fruit, muffins or coffeecake and meats, guests choose items such as omelets, waffles or pancakes.

Innkeeper(s): Alice P. Heisey. $60-120. MC, VISA, AX. 9 rooms with PB, 3 with FP and 2 suites. Breakfast included in rates. Type of meal: Full bkfst. Beds: KQ. Cable TV, phone, ceiling fan and VCR in room. Air conditioning. Fax, copier and spa on premises. Family reunions hosted. Antiquing, fishing, parks and shopping nearby.

Elizabethville   I12

The Inn at Elizabethville

30 W Main St, Box V
Elizabethville, PA 17023
(717)362-3476 Fax:(717)362-4571

Circa 1883. This comfortable, two-story house was owned by a Civil War veteran and founder of a local wagon company. The owners decided to buy and fix up the house to help support their other business, renovating old houses. The conference room features an unusual fireplace with cabinets and painted decorations. Rooms are filled with antiques and Mission oak-style furniture. County auctions, local craft fairs and outdoor activities entice guests. Comfortable living rooms, porches and a sun parlor are available for relaxation.

Innkeeper(s): Jennifer Kutzor. $49-65. MC, VISA, AX, TC. 7 rooms with PB and 1 conference room. Breakfast included in rates. AP. Type of meal: Cont. Beds: DT. Ceiling fan in room. Air conditioning. VCR, fax and copier on premises. Weddings, small meetings, family reunions and seminars hosted. Antiquing, fishing, parks, shopping and water sports nearby.

Publicity: *Harrisburg Patriot-News, Upper Dauphin Sentinel.*

Emlenton
F4

Apple Alley B&B

214 River Avenue, Box 130
Emlenton, PA 16373
(724)867-9636 (800)547-8499
Web: travel.to/emlenton/

Circa 1884. Located along the Allegheny River, this old Victorian offers hospitality and travel tips. (The innkeeper's travel writing and travel photography is highlighted at the B&B.) There are

quilts and collections of salt and pepper shakers and paperweights. A hearty breakfast is served and there is a gift shop on the premises. A large front porch and separate cottage are additional features.

Innkeeper(s): Dick Schnur and Terry Cooney. $40-60. MC, VISA, AX, DS, PC. 5 rooms, 2 with PB and 1 cottage. Breakfast and snacks/refreshments included in rates. Types of meals: Full bkfst and early coffee/tea. Beds: QDT. VCR, copier and library on premises. Weddings, small meetings and family reunions hosted. Antiquing, fishing, golf, parks, shopping, sporting events and water sports nearby.

Ephrata
J14

Doneckers, The Guesthouse, Inns

409 N State St
Ephrata, PA 17522
(717)738-9502 Fax:(717)738-9554

Circa 1777. Jacob Gorgas, a devout member of the Ephrata Cloister and a clock maker, noted for crafting 150 eight-day Gorgas grandfather clocks, built this stately Dutch Colonial-style home. Guests can opt to stay in one of four antique-filled homes. The 1777 House, which includes 12 rooms, features hand-sten-ciled walls, suites with whirlpool baths, fireplaces, orig-inal stone masonry and an antique tiled floor. The home served as a tavern in the 1800s and an elegant inn in the early 1900s. The Homestead

includes four rooms some with fireplaces and amenities such as Jacuzzis, sitting areas and four-poster beds. The Guesthouse fea-tures a variety of beautifully decorated rooms each named and themed in honor of local landmarks or significant citizens. The Gerhart House memorializes prominent innkeepers or hotel own-ers in Ephrata's history. All guests enjoy an expansive breakfast with freshly squeezed juice, fruits, breakfast cheeses and other delicacies. The homes are part of the Donecker Community, which features upscale fashion stores, art galleries and a restau-rant within walking distance of the 1777 House.

Historic Interest: The Ephrata Cloister, a communal religious society that was instrumental in the Colonial era's development of printing, music and Germanic architecture, is less than a mile away. Wheatland, the home of President James Buchanan, is nearby in Lancaster.

Innkeeper(s): Mary DeSimone. $65-210. MC, VISA, AX, DC, CB, DS, PC, TC. 40 rooms, 39 with PB and 13 suites. Breakfast included in rates. Types of meals: Full gourmet bkfst and cont plus. Gourmet dinner and gourmet lunch available. Restaurant on premises. Beds: KQDT. Phone and cable music in room. Central air. VCR and fax on premises. Weddings, small meet-ings, family reunions and seminars hosted. Amusement parks, antiquing, art galleries, golf, live theater, museums, parks, shopping and wineries nearby.

"A peaceful refuge."

358

Smithton Inn

900 W Main St
Ephrata, PA 17522-1328
(717)733-6094

Circa 1763. Henry Miller opened this inn and tavern on a hill overlooking the Ephrata Cloister, a religious society he belonged to, known as Seventh Day Baptists. Several of their medieval-style German build-ings are now a museum. This is a warm and wel-coming inn with canopy or four-poster beds, candlelight, fireplaces and night-shirts provided for each guest. If you desire, ask for a lavish feather bed to be put in your room. All rooms boast sitting areas with reading lamps, fresh flowers and the relaxing sounds of chamber music. The grounds include wonderful gardens.

Historic Interest: The Ephrata Cloister Museum is only one block away.

Innkeeper(s): Dorothy Graybill. $75-175. MC, VISA, AX, PC, TC. 8 rooms, 7 with PB, 8 with FP and 1 suite. Breakfast and snacks/refreshments included in rates. Type of meal: Full bkfst. Beds: KQDT. Candlelight - chamber music in room. Air conditioning. Flower gardens on premises. Amusement parks, antiquing, art galleries, golf, hiking, farmland, handcrafts, farmers market, live theater, museums, shopping, tennis and wineries nearby.

Pets allowed: No cats. Dogs, obedience trained, with owners at all times by previous arrangement.

"After visiting over 50 inns in four countries, Smithton has to be one of the most romantic, picturesque inns in America. I have never seen its equal!"

Erie
C3

Spencer House B&B

519 W 6th St
Erie, PA 16507-1128
(814)454-5984 (800)890-7263 Fax:(814)456-5091
E-mail: spencer@erie.net
Web: www.erie.net/~spencer

Circa 1876. This three-story Victorian Stick house features gabled windows and a wraparound porch. Original woodwork, is one of the inn's most outstanding features. Twelve-foot ceil-ings, interior folding shutters and a well-stocked library with black walnut bookshelves are other highlights. The Tree Top Room offers a ceiling-to-floor canopy and a reading nook.

Innkeeper(s): Pat & Keith Hagenbuch. $85-120. MC, VISA, AX, DS, PC, TC. 5 rooms with PB. Breakfast and afternoon tea included in rates. Types of meals: Full bkfst and early coffee/tea. Dinner and picnic lunch available. Beds: Q. Cable TV, phone and ceiling fan in room. Air conditioning. VCR, fax and copier on premises. Weddings, small meetings and family reunions host-ed. Amusement parks, antiquing, fishing, live theater, parks, shopping, down-hill skiing, cross-country skiing, sporting events and water sports nearby.

Erwinna 117

Golden Pheasant Inn

763 River Rd
Erwinna, PA 18920-9254
(610)294-9595 (800)830-4474 Fax:(610)294-9882
E-mail: barbara@goldenpheasant.com
Web: www.goldenpheasant.com

Circa 1857. The Golden Pheasant is well established as the location of a wonderful, gourmet restaurant, but it is also home to six charming guest rooms decorated by Barbara Faure. Four-poster canopy beds and antiques decorate the rooms, which offer views of the canal and river. The fieldstone inn was built as a mule-barge stop for travelers heading down the Delaware Canal. The five-acre grounds resemble a French-country estate, and guests can enjoy the lush

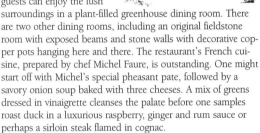

surroundings in a plant-filled greenhouse dining room. There are two other dining rooms, including an original fieldstone room with exposed beams and stone walls with decorative copper pots hanging here and there. The restaurant's French cuisine, prepared by chef Michel Faure, is outstanding. One might start off with Michel's special pheasant pate, followed by a savory onion soup baked with three cheeses. A mix of greens dressed in vinaigrette cleanses the palate before one samples roast duck in a luxurious raspberry, ginger and rum sauce or perhaps a sirloin steak flamed in cognac.

Historic Interest: Washington's Crossing (20 miles), Doylestown (10 miles), New Hope (13 miles).

Innkeeper(s): Barbara & Michel Faure. $95-175. MC, VISA, AX, DC, CB, DS, PC, TC. TAC10. 6 rooms with PB, 2 with FP, 1 suite, 1 cottage and 3 conference rooms. Breakfast included in rates. EP. Types of meals: Cont plus and early coffee/tea. Gourmet dinner, snacks/refreshments, picnic lunch, catering service and room service available. Restaurant on premises. Beds: Q. Phone, ceiling fan and jacuzzi tub/fireplaces in room. Air conditioning. Fax, copier, swimming, library and canal path for walking on premises. Small meetings, family reunions and seminars hosted. French and Spanish spoken. Antiquing, art galleries, bicycling, canoeing/kayaking, fishing, golf, hiking, horseback riding, historic Doylestown, New Hope, Washington Crossing, live theater, museums, parks, shopping, cross-country skiing, tennis, water sports and wineries nearby.

Pets allowed: cottage only.

"A more stunningly romantic spot is hard to imagine. A taste of France on the banks of the Delaware."

Erwinna (Bucks County) 117

Evermay-On-The-Delaware

River Rd, PO Box 60
Erwinna (Bucks County), PA 18920
(610)294-9100 Fax:(610)294-8249
E-mail: moffly@evemay.com
Web: www.evemay.com

Circa 1700. Twenty-five acres of Bucks County at its best — rolling green meadows, lawns, stately maples and the silvery Delaware River, surround this three-story manor. Serving as an inn since 1871, it has hosted such guests as the Barrymore family. Rich walnut wainscoting, a grandfather clock and twin fire-

places warm the parlor, scented by vases of roses or gladiolus. Antique-filled guest rooms overlook the river or gardens.

Historic Interest: Washington Crossing State Park, Mercer Museum, Pearl S. Buck House.

Innkeeper(s): Bill & Danielle Moffly. $135-350. MC, VISA, PC, TC. TAC10. 18 rooms with PB, 1 suite, 2 cottages and 2 conference rooms. Breakfast and afternoon tea included in rates. Type of meal: Cont plus. Gourmet dinner and picnic lunch available. Restaurant on premises. Beds: QD. Phone and turndown service in room. Air conditioning. VCR, fax, copier and library on premises. Handicap access. Weddings, small meetings and seminars hosted. Antiquing, fishing, live theater, parks, shopping, cross-country skiing, sporting events and water sports nearby.

Publicity: *New York Times, Philadelphia, Travel & Leisure, Food and Wine, Child, Colonial Homes, USAir Magazine.*

"It was pure perfection. Everything from the flowers to the wonderful food."

Friendsville C14

Addison House B&B

RR #1, Box 1586
Friendsville, PA 18818
(570)553-2682
E-mail: dm1000@epix.net

Circa 1811. Addison House was built by one of Friendsville's earliest settlers, an Irish immigrant who purchased the vast homestead for just under a dollar an acre. The early 19th-century house is built in Federal style, but its interior includes many Victorian features, from the rich décor to the hand-carved marble fireplaces. A creek rambles through the 260-acre property, and guests will enjoy the secluded, wilderness setting. In the guest rooms, fluffy comforters top antique beds and floral wallcoverings add

to the country Victorian ambiance. Breakfasts begin with items such as fresh berries with cream, followed by a rich entrée. The innkeepers are happy to help guests plan their days. The area offers a multitude of outdoor activities, as well as historic sites, antique shops, covered bridges and much more.

Historic Interest: Steamtown National Historic site (50 miles), Old Mill Village Museum (20 miles), Lackawanna Coal Mine Tour (50 miles), French Azilum Historic site (30 miles), Covered Bridges (30 miles), Pennsylvania Grand Canyon (100 miles), Finger Lakes (50 miles), Salt Springs State Park (10 miles).

Innkeeper(s): Dennis & Gloria McLallen. $65-95. PC. 4 rooms with PB and 1 suite. Breakfast included in rates. Types of meals: Full bkfst and early coffee/tea. Afternoon tea available. Beds: D. Turndown service, ice water and chocolates in room. Central air. VCR, swimming and library on premises. Weddings and small meetings hosted. Antiquing, art galleries, bicycling, canoeing/kayaking, fishing, golf, hiking, zoo, live theater, museums, parks, shopping, cross-country skiing, sporting events and wineries nearby.

Gettysburg *L11*

Appleford Inn

218 Carlisle St
Gettysburg, PA 17325-1305
(717)337-1711 (800)275-3373 Fax:(717)334-6228
E-mail: jwiley@cvn.net
Web: www.bbonline.com/pa/appleford

Circa 1867. Located in the historic district, this Italianate-style brick mansion offers a taste of 19th-century charm and comfort. Among its inviting features are a plant-filled sunroom and

a parlor with refurbished, 1918 grand piano. The innkeepers also display fine, linen needlework samplers and a collection of antique musical instruments. As the inn was built just following the Civil War, the innkeepers have tried to keep a sense of turbulent history present. Most of the guest rooms are named for Civil War generals, another for Abraham Lincoln. Breakfasts are a fashionable affair served on fine china in the inn's Victorian dining room.

Innkeeper(s): John & Jane Wiley. $90-160. MC, VISA, AX, DS, PC, TC. TAC10. 10 rooms with PB, 2 with FP and 1 suite. Breakfast and afternoon tea included in rates. Meals: Full bkfst and early coffee/tea. Catering service available. Beds: QD. Some desks in room. Air conditioning. Fax, library, refrigerator and snack bar in sunroom on premises. Weddings, small meetings and family reunions hosted. Amusement parks, antiquing, battlefield and historic attractions nearby, National Military Park, live theater, parks, shopping and downhill skiing nearby.
Publicity: *Innsider, Gettysburg Times, Baltimore Sun, Philadelphia Magazine.*

"Everything in your place invites us back."

Baladerry Inn at Gettysburg

40 Hospital Rd
Gettysburg, PA 17325
(717)337-1342
E-mail: baladerry@mail.wideopen.net
Web: www.baladerryinn.com

Circa 1812. The quiet and private setting on the edge of the Gettysburg Battlefield, this brick country manor was used as a hospital during the Civil War. Additions were added in 1830 and 1977, and the inn has been completely restored. Guests can snuggle up with a book in their comfortable rooms or in

the great room, which includes a fireplace. Two guest rooms include a private patio. The spacious grounds offer gardens, a gazebo, a tennis court and terraces. Guided tours of the battlefield can be arranged, and guests also can plan a horseback riding excursion on the battlefield.

Historic Interest: Gettysburg Battlefield National Park is just 100 yards from the inn. The area is full of historic sites, including the popular Eisenhower Farm tour.
Innkeeper(s): Caryl O'Gara. $105-150. MC, VISA, AX, DC, CB, DS, PC, TC. TAC10. 8 rooms with PB, 2 with FP and 3 conference rooms. Breakfast included in rates. Types of meals: Full bkfst and early coffee/tea. Snacks/refreshments and catering service available. Beds: KQT. Phone and private patio overlooking grounds in room. Air conditioning. VCR, fax and tennis on premises. Small meetings, family reunions and seminars hosted. Antiquing, fishing, golf, horseback riding, live theater, parks, shopping, downhill skiing, cross-country skiing and sporting events nearby.

Battlefield B&B

2264 Emmitsburg Rd
Gettysburg, PA 17325-7114
(717)334-8804 Fax:(717)334-7330
E-mail: battlefieldinn@hotmail.com
Web: www.gettysburgbattlefield.com

Circa 1809. Ponds, woods and streams fill the 46 acres of this historic estate. This stone farmhouse boasts four Confederate-themed guest rooms and four Union rooms. Hart's Battery provides a canopy bed and granite walls, while General Merritt's Headquarters takes up an entire floor of the Cornelius Houghtelin farmhouse and includes a fireplace and sitting

room. Daily programs offer history demonstrations such as firing muskets, handling cavalry equipment, loading artillery and Civil War gaming. Battlefield stories abound and daily carriage rides are offered, weather permitting. Friday night ghost stories are another activity. The farm was occupied by Union cavalry and artillery units during the Battle of Gettysburg.

Innkeeper(s): Charlie & Florence Tarbox. $75-165. MC, VISA, AX, DC, CB, DS, PC, TC. TAC10. 8 rooms with PB, 2 with FP, 2 suites and 2 conference rooms. Breakfast and snacks/refreshments included in rates. Types of meals: Full gourmet bkfst and early coffee/tea. Afternoon tea and room service available. Beds: QDT. Air conditioning. VCR, fax, copier, library, child care, carriage rides and living history presentations on premises. Small meetings, family reunions and seminars hosted. Some French and Spanish spoken. Antiquing, fishing, golf, battlefield, national park, live theater, parks, shopping, downhill skiing, cross-country skiing, sporting events and tennis nearby.

"An absolute gold mine of information in a beautiful setting."

The Brafferton Inn

44 York St
Gettysburg, PA 17325-2301
(717)337-3423

Circa 1786. Aside from its notoriety as the first deeded house in what became the town of Gettysburg, The Brafferton bears the mark of a bullet shot into the fireplace mantel during the Civil War battle. The rooms are appointed with 18th- and 19th-century antiques that belonged to the owners' ancestors. The dining room boasts a unique mural painted on all four walls depicting the early town of Gettysburg. Lavish breakfasts are served in the colorful room on tables set with English china, old silver and pineapple-pattern glass goblets. Guest quarters are available in the original house or in the old carriage house across the brick atrium. Carriage house rooms feature stenciling and skylights. The garden area offers a large wooden deck to relax on as guests take in a variety of spring and summer flowers. The National Register inn is near all of Gettysburg's historic attractions, including the Gettysburg National Military Park.

Historic Interest: The inn is listed in the National Register and Gettysburg, site of the Civil War's most infamous battles, offers much history.
Innkeeper(s): Maggie & Bill Ward. $90-150. MC, VISA, AX, DS, PC, TC. TAC10. 11 rooms with PB and 3 suites. Breakfast included in rates. Types of meals: Full bkfst and early coffee/tea. Beds: QDT. Alarm clocks in room. Air conditioning. Weddings, small meetings and family reunions hosted. Antiquing, fishing, Gettysburg National Park, live theater, parks, shopping, downhill skiing, cross-country skiing and sporting events nearby.
Publicity: *Early American Life, Country Living, Gettysburg Times.*

Brickhouse Inn

452 Baltimore St
Gettysburg, PA 17325-2623
(717)338-9337 (800)864-3464 Fax:(717)338-9265
E-mail: stay@brickhouseinn.com
Web: www.brickhouseinn.com

Circa 1898. A veranda, dressed in gingerbread trim, decorates the exterior of this red brick Victorian. The interior still maintains its original chestnut woodwork and pocket doors. Family heirlooms and antiques are featured in the guest rooms. One room offers walls in a deep burgundy hue and a bed topped with a colorful quilt. Another has a black iron bed, fine antiques and a bay window. Breakfasts,  with items such as shoo-fly pie or baked French toast topped with blueberries, are served on the brick patio, which overlooks the lawn. In the afternoons, cookies and lemonade also are served here. The home is located in Gettysburg's downtown historic district. The innkeepers keep a collection of Civil War books on hand for history buffs.

Innkeeper(s): Craig & Marion Schmitz. $75-140. MC, VISA, DS, PC, TC. TAC10. 7 rooms with PB and 1 suite. Breakfast and snacks/refreshments included in rates. Type of meal: Full bkfst. Beds: QD. Cable TV and ceiling fan in room. Air conditioning. Fax on premises. Weddings, small meetings, family reunions and seminars hosted. Amusement parks, antiquing, fishing, golf, parks, shopping, downhill skiing, cross-country skiing and tennis nearby.

Publicity: *Washington Post, Washington Flyer.*

"Wonderful, we loved the "19th-Century feel"."

The Doubleday Inn

104 Doubleday Ave
Gettysburg, PA 17325-8519
(717)334-9119

Circa 1929. This Colonial Inn is situated directly on the Gettysburg Battlefield. From its wooded grounds, flower gardens and patios, guests enjoy panoramic views of historic Gettysburg and the National Military Park. The innkeepers have a significant collection of Civil War relics and books on hand, and on selected evenings they feature presentations with battlefield historians. Rooms are furnished with antiques and decorated in  English-country style. A full, country-style breakfast is served by candlelight each morning, and the innkeepers offer a selection of teas in the afternoon.

Historic Interest: Aside from the inn's location on the battlefield, the inn is close to the General Dwight D. Eisenhower Farm.

Innkeeper(s): Ruth Anne & Charles Wilcox. $89-109. MC, VISA, DS. TAC10. 9 rooms, 5 with PB. Breakfast and afternoon tea included in rates. Types of meals: Full bkfst and early coffee/tea. Picnic lunch available. Beds: DT. Weddings, small meetings and family reunions hosted. Amusement parks, antiquing, fishing, battlefield tours, live theater, parks, shopping, downhill skiing, cross-country skiing and sporting events nearby.

"A beautiful spot on an historic site that we'll long remember."

The Gaslight Inn

33 E Middle St
Gettysburg, PA 17325
(717)337-9100
E-mail: gaslight@mail.cvn.net

Circa 1872. Gaslights illuminate the brick pathways leading to this 125-year-old Italianate-style, expanded farmhouse. The inn boasts two elegant parlors separated by original pocket doors, a spacious dining room and a first-floor guest room with wheelchair access that opens to a large, brick patio. An open switchback staircase leads to the second- and third-floor guest rooms, all individually decorated in traditional and European furnishings. Some of the rooms feature covered decks, whirlpool tubs and steam showers for two. Guests are invited to enjoy a hearty or heart-healthy breakfast and inn-baked cookies and brownies and  refreshments in the afternoon. Cooking classes are offered in the inn's professional kitchen year-round. Winter weekend packages are available and carriage rides, private guides and a variety of activities can be arranged with the help of the innkeepers.

Innkeeper(s): Denis & Roberta Sullivan. $95-165. MC, VISA, AX, DS, PC, TC. TAC10. 9 rooms with PB, 6 with FP and 1 conference room. Breakfast and snacks/refreshments included in rates. Types of meals: Full gourmet bkfst, cont and early coffee/tea. Beds: KQT. Cable TV, phone, ceiling fan and steam rooms in room. Air conditioning. VCR, spa and spa facilities on premises. Handicap access. Weddings, small meetings, family reunions and seminars hosted. Antiquing, fishing, golf, historic educational tours and lectures, live theater, parks, shopping, downhill skiing, cross-country skiing, tennis and water sports nearby.

Publicity: *Tyler Texas Times, Hanover Sun, Los Angeles Times, Southern Living, Country Inns.*

Inns of The Gettysburg Area

c/o The Brickhouse Inn 452 Baltimore St
Gettysburg, PA 17325
(717)624-1300 (800)549-2216
Web: www.gettysburg-bandb.com

Guests can choose from more than a dozen properties by using this reservation service. Among the choices are a pre-Civil War barn and homes that rest on the actual Gettysburg battlefield. All of the bed & breakfasts and inns are historic, and all offer close access to the many sites in the Gettysburg area. Choices range from cozy three-room bed & breakfasts to larger 12-room inns. At some locations, whirlpool tubs and fireplaces are available.

Historic Interest: Gettysburg battlefield and Eisenhower farm 10 miles.

Innkeeper(s): John Malpedi/Doris Martin. $60-170. Breakfast included in rates. Types of meals: Full gourmet bkfst, cont plus, country bkfst, veg bkfst and early coffee/tea. Afternoon tea and catering service available. Restaurant on premises. Beds: KQDT. Cable TV, phone, turndown service, ceiling fan, VCR and gift shops in room. Central air. Fax, spa, swimming, bicycles and library on premises. Weddings, small meetings, family reunions and seminars hosted. Antiquing, art galleries, bicycling, golf, hiking, horseback riding, live theater, museums, parks, shopping, downhill skiing and wineries nearby.

James Gettys Hotel

27 Chambersburg St
Gettysburg, PA 17325
(717)337-1334 Fax:(717)334-2103
E-mail: jghotel@mail.cvn.net
Web: www.jamesgettyshotel.com

Circa 1803. Listed in the National Register, this newly renovated four-story hotel once served as a tavern through the Battle of Gettysburg and was used as a hospital for soldiers. Outfitted with cranberry colored awnings and a gold painted entrance, the hotel offers a tea room, nature store and gallery on the street level. From the lobby, a polished chestnut staircase leads to the guest quarters. All accommodations are suites with living rooms appointed with home furnishings, and each has its own kitchenette. Breakfasts of home-baked scones and coffee cake are brought to your room.

Historic Interest: Gettysburg NMP/Eisenhower NHS.

Innkeeper(s): Stephanie McSherry. $125-145. MC, VISA, AX, DS, PC, TC. 11 suites. Breakfast included in rates. Type of meal: Cont. Beds: QD. Cable TV, phone and turndown service in room. Air conditioning. VCR and fax on premises. Handicap access. Weddings, small meetings and family reunions hosted. French spoken. Amusement parks, antiquing, art galleries, bicycling, fishing, golf, hiking, horseback riding, museums, parks, shopping, downhill skiing, cross-country skiing, tennis and wineries nearby.

Keystone Inn B&B

231 Hanover St
Gettysburg, PA 17325-1913
(717)337-3888

Circa 1913. Furniture maker Clayton Reaser constructed this three-story brick Victorian with a wide-columned porch hugging the north and west sides. Cut stone graces every door and window sill, each with a keystone. A chestnut staircase ascends the full three stories, and the interior is decorated with comfortable furnishings, ruffles and lace.

Historic Interest: National Military Park, Eisenhower Farm (1 mile).

Innkeeper(s): Wilmer & Doris Martin. $69-109. MC, VISA, DS. 5 rooms with PB and 1 suite. Breakfast and afternoon tea included in rates. Types of meals: Full bkfst and early coffee/tea. Beds: KQDT. Phone in room. Air conditioning. Library on premises. Family reunions hosted. Amusement parks, antiquing, fishing, Civil War Battlefield, historic sites, live theater, parks, shopping, downhill skiing and cross-country skiing nearby.

Publicity: *Gettysburg Times, Hanover Sun, York Sunday News, Pennsylvania, Lancaster Sunday News, Los Angeles Times.*

"We slept like lambs. This home has a warmth that is soothing."

Greensburg   J4

Huntland Farm B&B

RD 9, Box 21
Greensburg, PA 15601-9232
(724)834-8483 Fax:(724)838-8253

Circa 1848. Porches and flower gardens surround the three-story, columned, brick Georgian manor that presides over the inn's 100 acres. Corner bedrooms are furnished with English antiques. Fallingwater, the Frank Lloyd Wright house, is nearby. Other attractions include Hidden Valley, Ohiopyle water rafting, Bushy Run and Fort Ligonier.

Innkeeper(s): Robert & Elizabeth Weidlein. $75-85. AX, PC, TC. TAC10. 4 rooms, 2 with FP. Breakfast included in rates. Type of meal: Full bkfst. Beds: KQDT. Ceiling fan in room. VCR, fax, copier and library on premises. Small meetings and family reunions hosted. French spoken. Antiquing, live theater, parks and shopping nearby.

Mountain View Inn

1001 Village Dr
Greensburg, PA 15601-3797
(724)834-5300 (800)537-8709 Fax:(724)834-5304
E-mail: info@mountainviewinn.com
Web: www.mountainviewinn.com

Circa 1924. The Booher family has run this inn since 1940. The inn does, in fact, offer panoramic views of the Chestnut Ridge Mountains. In addition, there are 13 acres of grounds to enjoy, featuring a gazebo, gardens and a swimming pool. There are a variety of rooms to choose from, both in newer wings and in the original 1924 portion of the inn. Several suites include fireplaces and Jacuzzi tubs. There are several different meeting and banquet rooms available, and weddings often take place around the gazebo. There is a tavern providing light, casual meals, and the Candlelight Dining Room serves more formal fare and offers a wonderful view from its picture windows. Bushy Run Battlefield, Frank Lloyd Wright's "Fallingwater," museums and shops are all nearby.

Innkeeper(s): Vance & Vicki Booher. $69-310. MC, VISA, AX, DC, CB, DS, TC. TAC10. 93 rooms with PB, 7 with FP, 9 suites, 4 cottages and 7 conference rooms. Breakfast included in rates. Types of meals: Full bkfst, cont plus and cont. Dinner, lunch, catering service and room service available. Restaurant on premises. Beds: KQD. Cable TV and phone in room. Air conditioning. VCR, fax, copier, swimming, mineral water, chocolates, copy of USA Today and voice mail on premises. Handicap access. Weddings, small meetings, family reunions and seminars hosted. Amusement parks, antiquing, fishing, golf, live theater, parks, shopping, cross-country skiing, sporting events, tennis and water sports nearby.

Publicity: *Lodging Hospitality, Islander Magazine.*

Grove City   F2

Snow Goose Inn

112 E Main St
Grove City, PA 16127
(412)458-4644 (800)317-4644

Circa 1895. This home was built as a residence for young women attending Grove City College. It was later used as a family home and offices for a local doctor. Eventually, it was transformed into an intimate bed & breakfast, offering four homey guest rooms. The interior is comfortable, decorated in country style with stenciling, collectibles and a few of the signature geese on display. Museums, shops, Amish farms and several state parks are in the vicinity, offering many activities.

Innkeeper(s): Orvil & Dorothy McMillen. $65. MC, VISA. 4 rooms with PB. Breakfast and snacks/refreshments included in rates. Types of meals: Full gourmet bkfst and early coffee/tea. Beds: QD. Air conditioning. VCR on premises. Small meetings and family reunions hosted. Amusement parks, antiquing, fishing, golf, live theater, parks, shopping, downhill skiing, cross-country skiing, sporting events, tennis and water sports nearby.

Publicity: *Allied News.*

"Your thoughtful touches and "homey" atmosphere were a balm to our chaotic lives."

Harrisville F3

As Thyme Goes By B&B

214 N Main St, PO Box 493
Harrisville, PA 16038
(724)735-4003 (877)278-4963

Circa 1846. This country Victorian is furnished with a unique blend of antiques, Art Deco and Oriental decorative arts. The inn features movie memorabilia and guests can spend an

evening enjoying old films in the Bogart library or relaxing by the fire in the China Clipper parlor. Guest rooms are decorated with antique beds and offer private baths and air conditioning. A candlelight breakfast is highlighted by the innkeeper's homemade jams. Close to factory outlet shopping, local colleges and historic Volant Mills.

·Innkeeper(s): Susan Haas. $55-70. MC, VISA, PC. 3 rooms with PB. Breakfast and snacks/refreshments included in rates. Types of meals: Full bkfst and early coffee/tea. Afternoon tea available. Beds: KQD. Ceiling fan in room. Air conditioning. VCR and library on premises. Antiquing, fishing, golf, outlet mall, parks, shopping and cross-country skiing nearby.
Publicity: *Allied News, KDKA Pittsburgh.*

"We have been trying for years to make the time to get away for our first B&B experience and you have exceeded all of our expectations for the visit."

Hawley E17

Academy Street B&B

528 Academy St
Hawley, PA 18428-1434
(570)226-3430 Fax:(570)226-1910
E-mail: shlazan@worldnet.att.net
Web: www.academybb.com

Circa 1863. This restored Civil War Victorian home boasts a mahogany front door with the original glass paneling, two large fireplaces (one in mosaic, the other in fine polished marble)

and a living room with oak sideboard, polished marble mantel and yellow pine floor. The airy guest rooms have canopied brass beds. Guests are welcome to afternoon tea, which includes an array of cakes and pastries. Full, gourmet breakfasts are served on weekends.

Innkeeper(s): Judith Lazan. $65-90. MC, VISA. TAC10. 7 rooms, 4 with PB. Breakfast and afternoon tea included in rates. Type of meal: Early coffee/tea. Beds: QDT. Cable TV and ceiling fan in room. Air conditioning. VCR on premises. Weddings and family reunions hosted. Amusement parks, antiquing, fishing, live theater, parks, shopping and water sports nearby.
Publicity: *Wayne Independent, Citizens' Voice.*

"Truly wonderful everything!"

The Falls Port Inn & Restaurant

330 Main Ave
Hawley, PA 18428-1330
(717)226-2600

Circa 1902. Constructed by Baron von Eckelberg, this three-story grand brick Victorian is what one would expect to see in a city-center around the turn of the century. Named for its

magnificent nearby water falls, guests frequent the inn for both the elegance of its rooms and the fine dining in its well-established restaurant that boasts 20-foot-high original windows. Gourmet dinners include Chicken Remi and live lobster. Guest rooms are decorated in antiques, with polished brass fixtures and elegant window treatments. The inn is a favorite for weddings, family reunions and meetings.

Innkeeper(s): Dorothy Fenn. $75-100. MC, VISA, AX, TC. 9 rooms and 1 conference room. Breakfast included in rates. Type of meal: Cont. Gourmet dinner, lunch and banquet service available. Restaurant on premises. Beds: QD. Cable TV in room. Air conditioning. VCR on premises. Weddings, small meetings, family reunions and seminars hosted. Antiquing, fishing, golf, movie theater, live theater, parks, shopping, downhill skiing, tennis and water sports nearby.
Pets Allowed.

Holicong J18

Barley Sheaf Farm

5281 York Rd, Rt 202 Box 10
Holicong, PA 18928
(215)794-5104 Fax:(215)794-5332

Circa 1740. Situated on part of the original William Penn land grant, this beautiful stone house with ebony green shuttered windows and mansard roof is set on 30 acres of farmland. Once owned by noted playwright George Kaufman, it was the gathering place for the Marx Brothers, Lillian Hellman and S.J. Perlman. The bank barn, pond and majestic old trees round out a beautiful setting.

Innkeeper(s): Peter Suess. $105-235. MC, VISA, AX, PC, TC. TAC10. 12 rooms with PB, 3 with FP, 4 suites and 3 conference rooms. Breakfast and afternoon tea included in rates. Types of meals: Full bkfst and early coffee/tea. Catering service available. Beds: KQD. Phone in room. Air conditioning. VCR, fax, copier and swimming on premises. Handicap access. Weddings, small meetings, family reunions and seminars hosted. German and French spoken. Amusement parks, antiquing, fishing, museums, live theater, parks, shopping, downhill skiing, cross-country skiing and water sports nearby.

Honey Grove I10

The Inn at McCullochs Mills

RR 1, Box 194
Honey Grove, PA 17035-9801
(717)734-3628 (800)377-5106
Web: www.mcinn.com

Circa 1890. Innkeepers Verne and Christine Penner spent several years restoring their inn, once home to a local millmaster. The original home burned, and this charming 1882 Victorian was built in its place. The Penners offer a multitude of romantic amenities and extras that will make any getaway memorable. Carriage rides and moonlight sleigh rides are among the choices. Guests are pampered with gourmet breakfasts served by candlelight, chocolates, fresh flowers and more. Some rooms include clawfoot or Jacuzzi tubs.

Innkeeper(s): Verne & Christine Penner. $59-89. MC, VISA, DS, PC. TAC10. 5 rooms with PB. Breakfast, afternoon tea and snacks/refreshments included in rates. Types of meals: Full gourmet bkfst and early coffee/tea. Picnic lunch and catering service available. Beds: QD. Turndown service, ceiling fan and 2 private Jacuzzis for two in room. Air conditioning. Weddings, small meetings, family reunions and seminars hosted. Antiquing, canoeing/kayaking, fishing, golf, country sightseeing, shopping and cross-country skiing nearby.
Publicity: *Pennsylvania Magazine.*

Jennerstown   J5

The Olde Stage Coach B&B

1760 Lincoln Hwy
Jennerstown, PA 15547
(814)629-7440

Circa 1752. This renovated two-story Country Victorian farmhouse, located in the Laurel Mountains on historical Lincoln Highway, once served as a stagecoach rest stop. The yellow house has white trim and a wraparound porch overlooking the inn's acre. The common room features Victorian antiques, and guest rooms offer a fresh country decor. Blueberry French toast is a specialty of the innkeepers as well as home-baked breads and apple pancakes. The immediate area boasts the Mountain Playhouse, three golf courses within three miles, trout streams and lakes, hiking, skiing and outlet shopping — something for all generations.
Innkeeper(s): Carol & George Neuhof. $70. MC, VISA, PC, TC. 4 rooms with PB. Breakfast and snacks/refreshments included in rates. Types of meals: Full bkfst and early coffee/tea. Beds: QDT. Ceiling fan, chair and table in room. VCR, fax, library and wrap-around porch with swing on premises. Amusement parks, antiquing, fishing, golf, Nascar racing, live theater, parks, shopping, downhill skiing and cross-country skiing nearby.

Jim Thorpe   H15

Harry Packer Mansion

Packer Hill, PO Box 458
Jim Thorpe, PA 18229
(570)325-8566
E-mail: mystery@murdermansion.com
Web: www.murdermansion.com

Circa 1874. This extravagant Second Empire mansion was used as the model for the haunted mansion in Disney World. It

was constructed of New England sandstone, and local brick and stone trimmed in cast iron. Past ornately carved columns on the front veranda, guests enter 400-pound, solid walnut doors. The opulent interior includes marble mantels, hand-painted ceilings and elegant antiques. Murder-mystery weekends are a mansion specialty, and Victorian Balls are held in June and December.

Historic Interest: National Register. In historic district.
Innkeeper(s): Robert & Patricia Handwerk. $85-175. MC, VISA, TC. 13 rooms, 11 with PB, 3 suites and 3 conference rooms. Breakfast included in

rates. Types of meals: Full gourmet bkfst and early coffee/tea. Beds: QD. Turndown service and ceiling fan in room. Air conditioning. VCR on premises. Weddings, small meetings, family reunions and seminars hosted. Antiquing, fishing, parks, shopping, downhill skiing, cross-country skiing and water sports nearby.
Publicity: *Philadelphia Inquirer, New York, Victorian Homes, Washington Post.*

"What a beautiful place and your hospitality was wonderful. We will see you again soon."

The Inn at Jim Thorpe

24 Broadway
Jim Thorpe, PA 18229
(570)325-2599 (800)329-2599 Fax:(570)325-9145
E-mail: innjt@ptd.net
Web: www.innjt.com

Circa 1848. This massive New Orleans-style structure, now restored, hosted some colorful 19th-century guests, including Thomas Edison, John D. Rockefeller and Buffalo Bill. All rooms are appointed with Victorian furnishings and have private baths with pedestal sinks and marble floors. The suites include fireplaces and whirlpool tubs. Also on the premises are a Victorian dining Room, Irish pub and a conference center. The inn is situated in the heart of Jim Thorpe, a quaint Victorian town that was known at the turn of the century as the "Switzerland of America." Historic mansion tours, museums and art galleries are nearby, and mountain biking and whitewater rafting are among the outdoor activities.

Historic Interest: Switchboard Railroad, first railroad in U.S. (walking distance), Asa Packer Mansion, Millionaire's Row, Jim Thorpe final resting place (walking distance).
Innkeeper(s): David Drury. $65-250. MC, VISA, AX, DC, DS, TC. TAC10. 37 rooms with PB, 8 with FP, 8 suites and 2 conference rooms. Breakfast included in rates. MAP. Type of meal: Cont plus. Dinner, lunch and room service available. Beds: KQ. Cable TV, phone and 8 suites with whirlpools and fireplaces in room. Air conditioning. Fax, copier, game room and exercise room on premises. Handicap access. Weddings, small meetings, family reunions and seminars hosted. Antiquing, art galleries, bicycling, canoeing/kayaking, fishing, golf, hiking, horseback riding, museums, parks, shopping, downhill skiing and wineries nearby.

"We had the opportunity to spend a weekend at your lovely inn. Your staff is extremely friendly, helpful, and courteous. I can't remember when we felt so relaxed, we hope to come back again soon."

Kane   D6

Kane Manor Country Inn

230 Clay St
Kane, PA 16735-1410
(814)837-6522 Fax:(814)837-6664

Circa 1896. This Georgian Revival inn, on 250 acres of woods and trails, was built for Dr. Elizabeth Kane, the first female doctor to practice in the area. Many of the family's possessions dating back to the American Revolution and the Civil War remain. Decor is a

mixture of old family items in an unpretentious country style. There is a pub, popular with locals, on the premises. The building is in the National Register.

Innkeeper(s): Helen Johnson & Joyce Benek. $89-99. MC, VISA, AX, DS, PC, TC. TAC5. 10 rooms, 6 with PB. Breakfast included in rates. Types of meals: Full bkfst, cont plus, cont and early coffee/tea. Beds: DT. Cable TV in room. VCR, fax, copier and library on premises. Weddings, small meetings, family reunions and seminars hosted. Antiquing, fishing, parks, shopping, downhill skiing, cross-country skiing and water sports nearby.

Publicity: *Pittsburgh Press, News Herald, Cleveland Plain Dealer, Youngstown Indicator.*

"It's a place I want to return to often, for rest and relaxation."

Kennett Square L16

Meadow Spring Farm

201 E Street Rd
Kennett Square, PA 19348-1797
(610)444-3903 Fax:(610)444-7859

Circa 1836. You'll find horses grazing in the pastures at this 245-acre working farm, as well as colorful perennial flowers. The two-story, white-brick house is decorated with old family pieces and collections of  whimsical animals and antique wedding gowns. A Victorian doll collection fills one room. Breakfast is hearty country style, specialties include mushroom omelets and freshly baked breads. Afterwards, guests may gather eggs or feed rabbits and horses. Carriage rides, through the fields and back roads, are available.

Innkeeper(s): Anne Hicks. $85. PC, TC. TAC10. 6 rooms, 4 with PB, 2 with FP. Breakfast and afternoon tea included in rates. Type of meal: Full gourmet bkfst. Beds: QT. Ceiling fan in room. Air conditioning. Spa, swimming, child care, game room, ping pong and pool table on premises. Handicap access. Weddings, small meetings and seminars hosted. Antiquing, fishing, parks, shopping, cross-country skiing and sporting events nearby.

Scarlett House

503 W State St
Kennett Square, PA 19348-3028
(610)444-9592 (800)820-9592

Circa 1910. This granite American four-square home features an extensive wraparound porch, a front door surrounded by leaded-glass windows and magnificent chestnut woodwork. Beyond the foyer are two downstairs parlors with fireplaces, while a second-floor parlor provides a sunny setting for afternoon tea. Rooms are furnished in romantic Victorian decor with period antiques and Oriental carpets. An elegant gourmet breakfast is served with fine china, silver, crystal and lace linens. Mushroom-shaped chocolate chip scones are a novel breakfast specialty at the inn—a reminder that this is the acclaimed mushroom capital of the world.

Innkeeper(s): Jane & Sam Snyder. $89-139. MC, VISA, AX, DS, TC. 4 rooms, 2 with PB, 1 suite and 1 conference room. Breakfast, afternoon tea and snacks/refreshments included in rates. Types of meals: Full gourmet bkfst and early coffee/tea. Beds: QD. Phone and ceiling fan in room. Central air. Weddings, small meetings, family reunions and seminars hosted. Longwood Gardens, Brandywine Valley attractions and Amish country nearby.

"Truly an enchanting place."

Kennett Square (Avondale) L15

B&B at Walnut Hill

541 Chandler's Mill Rd
Kennett Square (Avondale), PA 19311-9625
(610)444-3703
E-mail: millsjt@magpage.com
Web: bbonline.com/pa/walnuthill

Circa 1840. The family who built this pre-Civil War home ran a grist mill on the premises. Innkeepers Sandy and Tom Mills moved into the home as newlyweds. Today, Sandy, a former caterer and Winterthur docent, serves up gourmet breakfasts such as cottage cheese pancakes with blueberry sauce and homemade teas, lemon butter and currant jam. Her cooking expertise  was recognized in Good Housekeeping's Christmas issue. The guest rooms are cozy, welcoming and filled with antiques. One room features a Laura Ashley canopy bed. Another boasts Victorian wicker. The house overlooks horses grazing in a meadow, and a nearby creek is visited by Canadian geese, deer and an occasional fox.

Historic Interest: Winterthur Museum, Brandywine Battlefield, Museum of Natural History, Longwood Gardens, Brandywine River Museum, Hagley Museum, Chaddsford Winery, Barnes Foundation.

Innkeeper(s): Tom & Sandy Mills. $75-95. PC, TC. TAC10. 2 rooms with PB. Breakfast and snacks/refreshments included in rates. Type of meal: Full gourmet bkfst. Afternoon tea available. Beds: KDT. Cable TV and turndown service in room. Central air. VCR, copier, spa and porch overlooking meadow and stream on premises. Family reunions hosted. Limited Spanish and French spoken. Canoeing/kayaking, golf, horseback riding, hot air balloons and shopping nearby.

Kintnersville I17

Bucksville House

4501 Durham Rd Rt 412
Kintnersville, PA 18930-1610
(610)847-8948 (888)617-6300 Fax:(610)847-8948

Circa 1795. For a century, Bucksville House served as a stagecoach stop. It also enjoyed use as a tavern and a speakeasy. For more than a decade, the historic Colonial-Federal home has welcomed guests in the form of a country inn. The five guest rooms have been appointed in a sophisticated style with Colonial and country furnishings. In one room, quilts are neatly stacked on armoire shelves. A quilt tops the bed and still another decorates a wall. Three rooms include a fireplace. Flowers decorate the exterior, and the grounds include a large deck and a gazebo where guests can enjoy breakfast. A pond and herb garden are other items guests will find while strolling the four-and-a-half-acre grounds. Several friendly, albeit somewhat mischievous, ghosts are said to haunt the inn.

Innkeeper(s): Barb & Joe Szollosi. $100-130. MC, VISA, AX, DS, PC, TC. 5 rooms with PB, 3 with FP and 1 suite. Breakfast and afternoon tea included in rates. Type of meal: Full bkfst. Beds: Q. Air conditioning. VCR, fax, copier, library, pond and water garden on premises. Handicap access. Amusement parks, antiquing, fishing, golf, live theater, parks, shopping, tennis and water sports nearby.

Lackawaxen
E18

Roebling Inn on The Delaware

Scenic Dr, PO Box 31
Lackawaxen, PA 18435-0031
(570)685-7900 Fax:(570)685-1718
E-mail: roebling@ltis.net
Web: www.roeblinginn.com

Circa 1870. In the National Register of Historic Places, this Greek Revival-style home was once the home of Judge Ridgway, tallyman for the Delaware and Hudson Canal Company. The

inn offers country furnishings and antiques. Guest rooms are comfortably furnished and some have fireplaces. There's a cottage, which is popular for families with children. The inn's long front

porch is the favorite place to relax, but the sitting room is inviting as well with its cozy fireplace. Full country breakfasts are provided. Afterward, ask the innkeepers for directions to nearby hidden waterfalls, or walk to the Zane Grey Museum. Roebling's Delaware Aqueduct is 100 yards downstream from the inn, now the oldest suspension bridge in North America. The scenic Delaware River is fun to explore, and there is a boat launch. Canoe, raft and tube rentals are available nearby. Fishing is a few steps from the inn's front porch or ask about guides for drift boat fishing. In the winter, look for bald eagles or ski at Masthope or Tanglewood. It's a two hour drive from New York City and two-and-a-half hours from Philadelphia.

Innkeeper(s): Don & JoAnn Jahn. $65-130. MC, VISA, AX, DS, TC. 6 rooms, 5 with PB and 1 cottage. Breakfast included in rates. Type of meal: Full bkfst. Beds: QDT. Cable TV and some rooms with fireplace and sitting room in room. Air conditioning. Fax on premises. Antiquing, fishing, live theater, parks, downhill skiing, cross-country skiing and water sports nearby.

Lampeter
K14

The Australian Walkabout Inn

837 Village Rd, PO Box 294
Lampeter, PA 17537-0294
(717)464-0707 Fax:(717)464-2501

Circa 1925. This inn offers hospitality Australian-style thanks to Australian Richard Mason, one of the innkeepers. Tea is imported from down under and breakfasts are prepared from

Australian recipes. The

inn, situated on beautifully landscaped grounds with an English garden and a lily pond, features a wraparound porch, where guests can watch Amish buggies pass by. Bedchambers

have antique furniture, Pennsylvania Dutch quilts and hand-painted wall stencilings. Each room is named from the image stenciled on its walls.

Historic Interest: The historic 1719 Hans Herr House is just one mile away.

Innkeeper(s): Richard & Margaret Mason. $99-199. MC, VISA, AX, PC, TC. TAC5. 5 rooms with PB, 5 with FP, 3 suites and 1 cottage. Breakfast included in rates. Type of meal: Full gourmet bkfst. Beds: Q. Cable TV in room. Air conditioning. VCR, fax, copier, spa, bicycles and library on premises. Family reunions hosted. Limited Spanish spoken. Amusement parks, antiquing, amish dinner, live theater, parks, shopping and sporting events nearby.

Publicity: *New York Post, Intelligencer Journal, Holiday Travel.*

"The "Walkabout Inn" itself & its surroundings are truly relaxing, romantic, & quaint. It's the kind of place that both of us wanted & pictured in our minds, even before we decided to make reservations."

Lancaster
K14

1725 Historic Witmer's Tavern Inn & Museum

2014 Old Philadelphia Pike
Lancaster, PA 17602-3413
(717)299-5305
Web: www.800padutch.com/1725histwit.html

Circa 1725. This pre-Revolutionary War inn is the oldest and most complete Pennsylvania inn still lodging travelers in its original building. Designated a Federal Landmark, the property has been restored to its original, pioneer style with hand-fashioned hardware and "bubbly" glass nine-over-six windows. There is even an Indian escape tunnel. Guest rooms feature antiques, fresh flowers, antique quilts and original wood-burning fireplaces. Revolutionary and Colonial dignitaries like Washington, Lafayette, Jefferson and Adams were entertained here. The Witmers provisioned hundreds of immigrants as they set up

Conestoga Wagon trains and headed for western and southern homestead regions. Amish farmland is adjacent to and in the rear of the inn, and a lovely park is located across the street. The innkeeper, native to the area, can provide an abundance of local information. He can also plan extra touches for a special occasion, and guests also can make an appointment for a therapeutic massage.

Historic Interest: Hans Herr House, Rockford Plantation, President Buchanan's House, Ephrata Cloister, Amish farms and villages are among the historic sites. Witmer's Heritage Tours provide interesting insight into Lancaster County.

Innkeeper(s): Brant Hartung. $65-110. PC. TAC10. 7 rooms, 2 with PB, 5 with FP. Breakfast included in rates. Type of meal: Cont plus. Beds: D. Air conditioning. Small meetings, family reunions and seminars hosted. Amusement parks, antiquing, fishing, nature preserves, Amish farms and villages, live theater, shopping, sporting events and water sports nearby.

Publicity: *Stuart News, Pennsylvania, Antique, Travel & Leisure, Mid-Atlantic, Country Living, Early American Life, Colonial Homes, USA Today.*

"Your personal attention and enthusiastic knowledge of the area and Witmer's history made it come alive and gave us the good feelings we came looking for."

Flowers & Thyme B&B

238 Strasburg Pike
Lancaster, PA 17602-1326
(717)393-1460 Fax:(717)399-1986

Circa 1941. This home was built by an Amish carpenter for a Mennonite minister and his family in a farming community. The innkeepers grew up among Amish and Mennonite commu-

nities and are full of knowledge about the area and its history. Fresh flowers from the inn's beautiful gardens are placed in the guest rooms in season. A country breakfast is served in the breakfast room overlooking the herb garden. The inn is only minutes away from outlet stores and plenty of outdoor activities.

Historic Interest: The Central Market in Lancaster is one of the oldest enclosed markets in the country featuring everything from fresh fruits and vegetables to flowers and baked goods. The Hans Herr House, the county's oldest building and second oldest Mennonite meeting house, is four miles from the home. For something unique, try the scenic 45-minute journey through Amish country on America's oldest short line, the Strasburg Railroad.

Innkeeper(s): Don & Ruth Harnish. $80-110. PC, TC. 3 rooms with PB. Breakfast included in rates. Type of meal: Full bkfst. Beds: Q. Ceiling fan in room. Air conditioning. Library and jacuzzi in one room on premises. Amusement parks, antiquing, live theater, parks, shopping, sporting events and water sports nearby.

Publicity: *Lancaster newspapers, Allentown Morning Call, Birds & Bloom Magazine.*

Gardens of Eden

1894 Eden Rd
Lancaster, PA 17601-5526
(717)393-5179 Fax:(717)393-7722

Circa 1867. Wildflowers, perennials and wooded trails cover the three-and-a-half-acre grounds surrounding Gardens of Eden. The home, which overlooks the Conestoga River, is an example of late Federal-style architecture with some early Victorian touches. The innkeepers have won awards for their restoration. Their guest cottage was featured on the cover of a decorating book. The interior, laced with dried flowers, handmade quilts, baskets and country furnishings, has the feel of a garden cottage. This cottage is ideal for families and includes a working fireplace and an efficiency kitchen. Gardens of Eden is within minutes of downtown Lancaster. The innkeepers can arrange for personalized tours of Amish and Mennonite communities and sometimes a dinner in an Amish home.

Innkeeper(s): Marilyn & Bill Ebel. $95-130. MC, VISA. 4 rooms with PB, 1 with FP and cottage. Breakfast included in rates. Type of meal: Full bkfst. Afternoon tea available. Beds: KQD. Phone and turndown service in room. Air conditioning. VCR, fax, copier, garden tours, canoe, rowboat, bicycling and museums on premises. Small meetings and family reunions hosted. Limited French spoken. Amusement parks, antiquing, fishing, amish culture, craft shows, live theater, shopping and cross-country skiing nearby.

The King's Cottage, A B&B Inn

1049 E King St
Lancaster, PA 17602-3231
(717)397-1017 (800)747-8717 Fax:(717)397-3447

Circa 1913. This Mission Revival house features a red-tile roof and stucco walls, common in many stately turn-of-the-century houses in California and New Mexico. Its elegant interiors include a sweeping staircase, a library with marble fireplace, stained-glass windows and a solarium. The inn is appointed

with Oriental rugs and antiques and fine 18th-century English reproductions. The Carriage House features the same lovely furnishings with the addition of a fireplace and Jacuzzi. The formal dining room provides the location for gourmet morning meals.

Historic Interest: Landis Valley Farm Museum (5 miles), Railroad Museum of Pennsylvania (8 miles), Hans Herr House (5 miles).

Innkeeper(s): Karen Owens. $100-205. MC, VISA, DS. 9 rooms with PB and 1 conference room. Breakfast and afternoon tea included in rates. Type of meal: Full bkfst. Gourmet dinner available. Beds: KQ. TV, turndown service and TV upon request in room. Small meetings and seminars hosted. Amusement parks, antiquing, fishing, live theater, shopping, cross-country skiing and sporting events nearby.

Publicity: *Country, USA Weekend, Bon Appetit, Intelligencer Journal, Times.*

"I appreciate your attention to all our needs and look forward to recommending your inn to friends."

Lincoln Haus Inn B&B

1687 Lincoln Hwy E
Lancaster, PA 17602-2609
(717)392-9412
Web: www.800padutch.com/linchaus.html

Circa 1915. A stained-glass entry greets guests as they enter this charming inn, located in the heart of Pennsylvania Dutch country. The home includes five comfortable rooms and two apartments, one a honeymoon suite perfect for romantic getaways and anniversary celebrations. Innkeeper Mary Zook is Amish and happy to provide a rich oral history of the area and Amish community over a hearty breakfast, served Monday through Saturday.

Historic Interest: Wheatland (President Buchanan's home) 5 miles, Lancaster Central Market (4 miles), Amish Country (5-10 miles).

Innkeeper(s): Mary Zook. $55-80. PC, TC. TAC10. 8 rooms with PB and 3 suites. Breakfast included in rates. Types of meals: Full bkfst and country bkfst. Beds: QDT. Ceiling fan in room. Air conditioning. Family reunions hosted. German spoken. Amusement parks, antiquing, art galleries, bicycling, fishing, golf, hiking, live theater, museums, parks, shopping, tennis and wineries nearby.

O'Flaherty's Dingeldein House B&B

1105 E King St
Lancaster, PA 17602-3233
(717)293-1723 (800)779-7765 Fax:(717)293-1947
E-mail: oflahbb@lancnews.infi.net
Web: www.800padutch.com/ofhouse.html

Circa 1910. This Dutch Colonial home was once residence to the Armstrong family, who acquired fame and fortune in the tile floor industry. Springtime guests will brighten at the sight of this home's beautiful flowers. During winter months, innkeepers Jack and Sue Flatley deck the halls with plenty of seasonal decorations. Breakfast by candlelight might include fresh-baked muffins, fruits, the innkeepers' special blend of coffee and mouth-watering omelets, pancakes or French toast. Cozy rooms include comfortable furnishings and cheery wall coverings. With advance notice, the innkeepers can arrange for guests to enjoy dinner at the home of one of their Amish friends.

Historic Interest: Lancaster offers several nearby historic sites and museums.

Innkeeper(s): Jack & Sue Flatley. $95-120. MC, VISA, DS, PC, TC. 4 rooms with PB and 1 suite. Breakfast included in rates. Types of meals: Full gourmet bkfst and early coffee/tea. Beds: QT. Ceiling fan in room. Air conditioning. VCR, fax, copier and library on premises. Family reunions hosted. Amusement parks, antiquing, fishing, live theater, parks, shopping and sporting events nearby.

Landenberg L15

Cornerstone B&B Inn

300 Buttonwood Rd
Landenberg, PA 19350-9398
(610)274-2143 Fax:(610)274-0734
E-mail: corner3000@aol.com
Web: www.belmar.com/cornerstone

Circa 1704. The Cornerstone is a fine 18th-century country manor house filled with antique furnishings. Two fireplaces make the parlor inviting. Wing chairs, fresh flowers and working fireplaces add enjoyment to the guest rooms. Perennial gardens, a water garden and swimming pool with hot tub are additional amenities.

Historic Interest: Brandywine River Museum, Brandywine Battlefield State Park, Franklin Mint, Valley Forge National Historical Park, Longwood Gardens, Winterthur Museum.

Innkeeper(s): Linda Chamberlin & Marty Mulligan. $75-250. MC, VISA, DS, PC, TC. TAC10. 8 rooms with PB, 5 with FP, 1 suite and 6 cottages. Breakfast included in rates. Types of meals: Full bkfst and early coffee/tea. Beds: KQT. Cable TV in room. Air conditioning. VCR, fax, spa and swimming on premises. Small meetings and family reunions hosted. Amusement parks, antiquing, live theater, parks, shopping and sporting events nearby.

Lebanon J13

Inn 422

1800 W Cumberland St, Rt 422
Lebanon, PA 17042
(717)274-3651 Fax:(717)372-5652
E-mail: inn422@lebmofo.com
Web: www.inn422.com

Circa 1880. This three-story slate gray Italianate Victorian constructed of wood and stone rests on more than an acre of beautifully landscaped grounds. Inside, a grand piano graces the parlor and there's a library, solarium and Jacuzzi. Breakfast is

served in the inn's dining rooms with fresh flowers, silver, china and linens. (The inn's highly rated dinner cuisine is also available here.) Traditionally furnished rooms are decorated with fine fabrics and offer TV, VCR, turndown service, robes and flowers. Afternoon tea and evening refreshments are offered. Allow for time to enjoy the secluded outdoor sitting areas, secret gardens, hammocks, birdbaths, arbors, rose trellises, bird feeders, waterfalls, fountains and gazebos. Banquets, weddings and corporate retreats are popular here. The inn's staff will help you organize activities such as antiquing, outlet shopping, dinner theater, flea markets, auctions, cave and cavern excursions, museums, wineries, pretzel or chocolate factory tours and many other area offerings.

Historic Interest: Cornwall Furnace (3 miles), Pennsylvania Dutch/Amish (12 miles).

Innkeeper(s): Scott & Crystal Aungst. $95-150. MC, VISA, AX, DC, CB, DS, PC, TC. TAC10. 5 rooms with PB, 1 with FP, 2 suites and 3 conference rooms. Breakfast included in rates. Types of meals: Full gourmet bkfst, cont plus, cont, country bkfst, veg bkfst and early coffee/tea. Gourmet dinner, snacks/refreshments, gourmet lunch, banquet service, catering service and room service available. Restaurant on premises. Beds: K. Cable TV, phone, turndown service and VCR in room. Central air. Fax, copier, spa and library on premises. Handicap access. Weddings, small meetings, family reunions and seminars hosted. Amusement parks, antiquing, art galleries, beaches, fishing, golf, hiking, horseback riding, live theater, museums, skiing, sporting events and wineries nearby.

Lewisburg G12

Anni's Inn & Outings

302 North Third St
Lewisburg, PA 17837
(570)523-7163
E-mail: anni@anni-bnb.com
Web: www.anni-bnb.com

Circa 1850. Built prior to the Civil War, Anni's has had a rich assortment of owners. For several decades, the home was owned by a native Indian medicine doctor who dried and prepared his own medicine on site, and his office still remains on the premises. The three guest rooms are named for members of the innkeeper's family and are decorated with antiques and some Asian influences. Guests have the option of enjoying a hearty, full breakfast or selecting lighter fare such as homemade muffins and fresh fruit. Historic Lewisburg offers unique shops and restaurants and is home to Bucknell University. Plenty of outdoor activities are available at the many state parks in the area. The innkeeper also helps guests plan interesting bicycle treks that range from 15 to 45 miles in length, taking in country farms, covered bridges and historic villages along the way.

Historic Interest: Joseph Priestly Museum (10 miles), Packwood house, Slifer house, buggy museum.

Innkeeper(s): Ann Longanbach. $65-80. PC. 3 rooms, 2 with PB. Breakfast included in rates. Types of meals: Full bkfst, cont plus, veg bkfst and early coffee/tea. Picnic lunch available. Beds: QT. Air conditioning. VCR on premises. Small meetings and seminars hosted. Amusement parks, antiquing, art galleries, bicycling, canoeing/kayaking, fishing, golf, hiking, live theater, museums, parks, shopping, cross-country skiing, sporting events, tennis and water sports nearby.

Linfield J16

Shearer Elegance

1154 Main St
Linfield, PA 19468-1139
(610)495-7429 (800)861-0308 Fax:(610)495-7814

Circa 1897. This stone Queen Anne mansion is the height of Victorian opulence and style. Peaked roofs, intricate trim and a stenciled wraparound porch grace the exterior. Guests enter the home via a marble entry, which boasts a three-story staircase. Stained-glass windows and carved mantels are other notable features. The Victorian furnishings and decor complement

the ornate workmanship, and lacy curtains are a romantic touch. The bedrooms feature hand-carved, built-in wardrobes. The grounds are dotted with gardens. The inn is located in the village of Linfield, about 15 minutes from Valley Forge.

Innkeeper(s): Shirley & Malcolm Shearer & Beth Smith. $90-140. AX, PC, TC. TAC10. 7 rooms with PB, 3 suites and 3 conference rooms. Types of meals: Full bkfst and early coffee/tea. Banquet service and catering service available. Beds: KQ. Cable TV, ceiling fan and VCR in room. Air conditioning. Fax, copier and library on premises. Weddings, small meetings, family reunions and seminars hosted. Amusement parks, antiquing, fishing, golf, outlets, live theater, parks, shopping, downhill skiing, sporting events and tennis nearby.

"Thank you for creating such a beautiful place to escape reality."

Lititz
J14

The Alden House

62 E Main St
Lititz, PA 17543-1947
(717)627-3363 (800)584-0753
E-mail: inn@aldenhouse.com
Web: www.aldenhouse.com

Circa 1850. For more than 200 years, breezes have carried the sound of church bells to the stately brick homes lining Main Street. The Alden House is a brick Victorian in the center of this historic district and within walking distance of the Pretzel House (first in the country) and the chocolate factory. A favorite room is the suite with a loft dressing room and private bath. A full breakfast is served, often carried to one of the inn's three porches.

Innkeeper(s): Tom & Lillian Vazquez. $90-120. MC, VISA, PC, TC. TAC10. 5 rooms with PB, 1 with FP and 3 suites. Breakfast included in rates. Type of meal: Full bkfst. Beds: Q. Cable TV and ceiling fan in room. Air conditioning. Small meetings hosted. Amusement parks, antiquing, live theater, parks and shopping nearby.

"Truly represents what bed & breakfast hospitality is all about. You are special innkeepers. Thanks for caring so much about your guests. It's like being home."

Casual Corners B&B

301 N Broad St
Lititz, PA 17543
(717)626-5299 (800)464-6764
E-mail: ccbb@redrose.net
Web: www.bbonline.com/pa/casual

Circa 1904. This three-story home has a dormer window, shutters and a wide wraparound porch filled with hanging ferns and wicker furnishings. There is a second-floor sitting room for guests. A country breakfast often includes poached pears and caramel apple French toast. Walk to the Wilbur Chocolate Company or the country's first pretzel bakery.

Historic Interest: PA Amish, Wilbur chocolate factory, oldest pretzel baker in U.S.
Innkeeper(s): Glenn & Ruth Lehman. $65-85. MC, VISA, PC, TC. 4 rooms, 2 with PB and 1 suite. Breakfast included in rates. Types of meals: Full bkfst, country bkfst, veg bkfst and early coffee/tea. Beds: QD. Turndown service and ceiling fan in room. Air conditioning. Amusement parks, antiquing, art galleries, bicycling, golf, hiking, live theater, museums, parks, shopping, tennis and wineries nearby.

Malvern
K16

General Warren Inne

Old Lancaster Hwy
Malvern, PA 19355
(610)296-3637 Fax:(610)296-8084
E-mail: suites@generalwarren.com
Web: www.generalwarren.com

Circa 1745. This 250-year-old inn, once owned by the grandson of William Penn, is surrounded by three wooded acres and is filled with 18th-century charm. The rooms are simple and elegant, featuring chandeliers, painted woodwork, quilts and period reproductions. Each of the guest rooms offers a special touch. The Presidential Suite features a sitting room with a fireplace, while the William Penn Suite boasts an original cathedral window. Other rooms include four-poster beds and fireplaces. Meals at the General Warren are a delight in one of the inn's three elegant candle-lit dining rooms. Start with a Caesar salad, prepared tableside or with a stuffed Portabello mushroom. Follow that with Beef Wellington and complete the meal with homemade Grand Marnier ice cream. Summer dishes feature locally grown produce and herbs from the inn's organic gardens. Gourmet magazine rated the inn's restaurant as one of Philadelphia's Top Tables.

Innkeeper(s): Karlie Davies. $110-160. MC, VISA, AX, DC. 8 suites. Breakfast included in rates. Type of meal: Cont. Gourmet dinner and lunch available. Restaurant on premises. Beds: KQD. Historical sites nearby and live theater nearby.

Manheim
J14

Penn's Valley Farm & Inn

6182 Metzler Rd
Manheim, PA 17545-8629
(717)898-7386

Circa 1826. This picture-perfect farm was purchased by the Metzler's ancestors in 1770, but it was originally owned by the three Penn brothers. The guest house, built in 1826, features stenciled farm animals painted along the winding stairway that leads to the bedrooms. An open hearth is in the living room. Breakfast is served in the dining room of the main farmhouse. There also is one room available in the farmhouse. It features a shared bath and a queen bed.

Innkeeper(s): Melvin & Gladys Metzler. $50-65. MC, VISA. 2 rooms and 1 guest house. Types of meals: Full bkfst and cont. Beds: QT. TV in room. Air conditioning. VCR on premises. Amusement parks, antiquing and shopping nearby.

Rose Manor B&B Tea Room and Herbal Gift Shop

124 S Linden St
Manheim, PA 17545-1616
(717)664-4932 (800)666-4932 Fax:(717)664-1611

Circa 1905. A local mill owner built this manor house, and it still maintains original light fixtures, woodwork and cabinetry. The grounds are decorated with roses and herb gardens. An herb theme is played out in the guest rooms, which feature names such as the Parsley, Sage, Rosemary and Thyme rooms. The fifth room is named the Basil, and its spacious quarters encompass the third story and feature the roof's angled ceiling. One room offers a whirlpool and another a fireplace. The decor is a comfortable Victorian style with some antiques. Afternoon tea is available by prior reservation and there is a gift shop on

the premises. The inn's location provides close access to many Pennsylvania Dutch country attractions.

Innkeeper(s): Susan & Anne Jenal. $70-120. MC, VISA, PC. TAC10. 5 rooms, 3 with PB, 1 with FP. Breakfast included in rates. Type of meal: Full bkfst. Afternoon tea and picnic lunch available. Beds: QDT. Cable TV, ceiling fan and one room with whirlpool in room. Air conditioning. Fax, copier and library on premises. Family reunions hosted. Amusement parks, antiquing, fishing, live theater, parks and shopping nearby.

Marietta   K13

Railroad House Restaurant B&B

280 W Front St
Marietta, PA 17547-1405
(717)426-4141
Web: www.lancnews.com/railroadhouse

Circa 1820. The Railroad House, a sprawling old hotel, conjures up memories of the days when riding the rail was the way to travel. The house was built as a refuge for weary men who were working along the Susquehanna River. When the railroad finally made its way through Marietta, the rail station's waiting room and ticket office were located in what's now known as the Railroad House. The restored rooms feature antiques, Oriental rugs, Victorian decor and rustic touches such as exposed brick walls. The chefs at the inn's restaurant create a menu of American and continental dishes using spices and produce from the beautifully restored gardens. The innovative recipes have been featured in Bon Appetit. The innkeepers also host a variety of special events and weekends, including murder mysteries and clambakes serenaded by jazz bands. Carriage rides and special walking tours of Marietta can be arranged.

Historic Interest: Wheatland, the home of President Buchanan, is 15 minutes from the Railroad House. The John Wright and Haldeman mansions are just 10 minutes away, and the Old Town Hall is a few blocks from the inn.

Innkeeper(s): Richard & Donna Chambers. $79-109. MC, VISA, TC. 10 rooms, 8 with PB, 1 cottage and 1 conference room. Breakfast included in rates. Meals: Full gourmet bkfst and early coffee/tea. Afternoon tea, gourmet dinner, snacks/refreshments, picnic lunch, gourmet lunch, banquet service, catering service and catered breakfast available. Restaurant on premises. Beds: QDT. Air conditioning. Copier, bicycles and gardens and yard games on premises. Weddings, small meetings, family reunions and seminars hosted. Spanish and French spoken. Amusement parks, antiquing, fishing, music box museum, live theater, parks, shopping, downhill skiing, sporting events and water sports nearby.

River Inn

258 W Front St
Marietta, PA 17547-1405
(717)426-2290 (888)824-6622 Fax:(717)426-2966

Circa 1790. This Colonial has more than 200 years of history within its walls. The home is listed in the National Register and located in Marietta's historic district. Herb and flower gardens

decorate the grounds. Relaxing in front of a fireplace is an easy task since the inn offers six, one of which resides in a guest room. Colonial decor and antiques permeate the interior. The inn is within walking distance to the Susquehanna River.

Innkeeper(s): Joyce & Bob Heiserman. $65-85. MC, VISA, DC, CB, DS, PC, TC. TAC10. 3 rooms with PB, 1 with FP. Breakfast included in rates. Types of meals: Full bkfst and early coffee/tea. Picnic lunch available. Beds: QT. Air conditioning. Bicycles and library on premises. Weddings hosted. Amusement parks, antiquing, fishing, museum, live theater, parks, shopping and water sports nearby.

Vogt Farm B&B

1225 Colebrook Rd
Marietta, PA 17547-9101
(717)653-4810 (800)854-0399
E-mail: vogtfarm@aol.com
Web: vogtfarmbnb.com

Circa 1868. Twenty-eight acres surround this farmhouse. There are three porches from which to enjoy the pastoral scene of cattle and sheep. Keith offers a walking tour of the farm, including the grain elevator. The innkeepers have hosted guests for 20 years and have created a comfortable setting for overnight stays. Private phones and a copier are available to business travelers.

Innkeeper(s): Keith & Kathy Vogt. $80-145. MC, VISA, AX, DC, DS, PC, TC. TAC10. 3 rooms and 1 suite. Breakfast and snacks/refreshments included in rates. Types of meals: Full bkfst and early coffee/tea. Beds: KQT. TV, phone, VCR and robes in room. Air conditioning. Copier and library on premises. Family reunions hosted. Amusement parks, antiquing, fishing, live theater, parks, shopping and sporting events nearby.

McConnellsburg   K9

The McConnellsburg Inn

131 W Market St
McConnellsburg, PA 17233-1007
(717)485-5495
E-mail: mcinn@cvn.net
Web: www.bbhost.com/mcinn

Circa 1903. This turn-of-the-century inn was built by a retired Union officer of the Civil War. Guest rooms include four-poster and canopy beds. Spiced apple crepes, savory ham and freshly baked fruit muffins are among the breakfast specialties. The inn is located in the McConnellsburg National Register Historic District. Gettysburg, East Broad Top Railroad, Cowans Gap State Park and Buchanan State Forest are nearby, as is Whitetail Ski Resort.

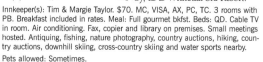

Innkeeper(s): Tim & Margie Taylor. $70. MC, VISA, AX, PC, TC. 3 rooms with PB. Breakfast included in rates. Meal: Full gourmet bkfst. Beds: QD. Cable TV in room. Air conditioning. Fax, copier and library on premises. Small meetings hosted. Antiquing, fishing, nature photography, country auctions, hiking, country auctions, downhill skiing, cross-country skiing and water sports nearby.

Pets allowed: Sometimes.

McKnightstown   **L11**

Country Escape

275 Old Rt 30, PO Box 195
McKnightstown, PA 17343
(717)338-0611 Fax:(717)334-5227
E-mail: merry@innernet.net

Circa 1868. This country Victorian, a brick structure featuring a porch decked in gingerbread trim, rests on the route that Confederate soldiers took on their way to nearby Gettysburg. The home itself was built

just a few years after the Civil War. There are three comfortable guest rooms, decorated in country style. For an extra fee, business travelers can use the inn's typing, copying, faxing or desktop publishing ser-

vices. All guests can enjoy the outdoor hot tub. There is also a children's play area outside. A traditional American breakfast is served, with such hearty items as eggs, pancakes, bacon and sausage. The inn offers close access to the famous battlefield, as well as other historic sites.

Innkeeper(s): Merry Bush & Ross Hetrick. $65-80. MC, VISA, AX, DS, PC, TC. TAC10. 3 rooms, 1 with PB. Breakfast included in rates. Type of meal: Full bkfst. Beds: Q. Air conditioning. VCR, fax, copier, spa, gift shop, children's play area and gardens on premises. Antiquing, battlefield - Gettysburg, live theater, parks, shopping, downhill skiing and water sports nearby.

Mercer   **F2**

The John Orr Guest House

320 E Butler St
Mercer, PA 16137
(724)662-0839 (877)849-0839 Fax:(724)662-3883
E-mail: jorrbandb@pathway.net
Web: www.pathway.net/jorrbandb

Circa 1905. A prominent local businessman built this turn-of-the-20th-century home, which is constructed in Greek Revival style. The home has been restored, leaving in place the original

woodwork and other architectural features. Guest rooms and common areas include period-style furnishings and some antiques. The front porch is set up for those who wish to relax, offering comfortable wicker chairs and a

porch swing. The innkeepers serve a full breakfast with items such as stuffed French toast, Belgian waffles, fruit bread pudding or a specialty egg dish. Mercer offers many historic homes and attractions to visit.

Historic Interest: Victorian town with historic homes and county courthouse.

Innkeeper(s): Ann & Jack Hausser. $65-80. MC, VISA, AX, DS, PC, TC. 3 rooms, 2 with PB, 2 with FP. Breakfast and snacks/refreshments included in rates. Types of meals: Full bkfst, veg bkfst and early coffee/tea. Beds: QD. Ceiling fan in room. Central air. VCR, fax, copier, CD player, stereo and refrigerator on premises. Small meetings and seminars hosted. Antiquing, art galleries, bicycling, canoeing/kayaking, fishing, golf, hiking, museums, parks, shopping, cross-country skiing and water sports nearby.

The Magoffin Inn

129 S Pitt St
Mercer, PA 16137-1211
(412)662-4611 (800)841-0824

Circa 1884. Dr. Magoffin built this house for his Pittsburgh bride, Henrietta Boulevard. The Queen Anne style is characterized by patterned brick masonry, gable detailing, bay windows and a wraparound porch. The technique of marbleizing was used on six of the nine fireplaces. Magoffin Muffins are featured each morning. Dinner is available Friday and Saturday.

Innkeeper(s): Jacque McClelland. $115-125. MC, VISA, AX, PC, TC. 5 rooms with PB, 5 with FP and 1 suite. Breakfast and snacks/refreshments included in rates. Types of meals: Full bkfst and early coffee/tea. Gourmet dinner available. Restaurant on premises. Beds: QD. Cable TV in room. Air conditioning. Weddings, small meetings and seminars hosted. Antiquing, parks and shopping nearby.

Publicity: *Western Reserve, Youngstown Vindicator.*

"While in Arizona we met a family from Africa who had stopped at the Magoffin House. After crossing the United States they said the Magoffin House was quite the nicest place they had stayed."

Mercersburg   **L9**

The Mercersburg Inn

405 S Main St
Mercersburg, PA 17236-9517
(717)328-5231 Fax:(717)328-3403
Web: www.mercersburginn.com

Circa 1909. Situated on a hill overlooking the Tuscorora Mountains, the valley and village, this 20,000-square-foot Georgian Revival mansion was built for industrialist Harry Byron. Six massive columns mark the entrance, which opens to a majestic hall featuring chestnut wainscoting and an elegant double stairway and rare scagliola (marbleized) columns. All the rooms are furnished with antiques and reproductions. A local craftsman built the inn's four-poster, canopied king-size beds. Many of the rooms have their own balconies and a few have fireplaces. During the weekends, the inn's chef prepares noteworthy, elegant five-course dinners, which feature an array of seasonal specialties.

Innkeeper(s): Walt & Sandy Filkowski. $120-235. MC, VISA, DS. 15 rooms with PB, 3 with FP and 1 conference room. Breakfast included in rates. Type of meal: Full gourmet bkfst. Gourmet dinner, picnic lunch and banquet service available. Restaurant on premises. Beds: KQT. TV and phone in room. Air conditioning. VCR and bicycles on premises. Weddings, small meetings, family reunions and seminars hosted. Antiquing, fishing, golf, live theater, shopping, downhill skiing, cross-country skiing and water sports nearby.

"Elegance personified! Outstanding ambiance and warm hospitality."

Mertztown   **I16**

Longswamp B&B

1605 State St
Mertztown, PA 19539-8912
(610)682-6197 Fax:(610)682-4854

Circa 1789. Country gentleman Colonel Trexler added a mansard roof to this stately Federal mansion in 1860. Inside is a magnificent walnut staircase and pegged wood floors. As the story goes, the colonel discovered his unmarried daughter having an affair and shot her lover. He escaped hanging, but it was said that after his death his ghost could be seen in the upstairs bedroom watching the road. In 1905, an exorcism was reported to have sent his spirit to a nearby mountaintop.

Innkeeper(s): Elsa Dimick. $83-88. MC, VISA, AX. 10 rooms, 6 with PB, 2 with FP and 2 suites. Breakfast and afternoon tea included in rates. Types of meals: Full gourmet bkfst and early coffee/tea. Gourmet dinner, picnic lunch and catering service available. Beds: QT. TV, phone and ceiling fan in room. Air conditioning. VCR and bicycles on premises. Weddings, small meetings, family reunions and seminars hosted. Antiquing, fishing, shopping, cross-country skiing and sporting events nearby.

Publicity: *Washingtonian, Weekend Travel, The Sun.*

"The warm country atmosphere turns strangers into friends."

Milford F18

Black Walnut Inn

179 Firetower Rd
Milford, PA 18337-9802
(570)296-6322 Fax:(570)296-7696
E-mail: stewart@theblackwalnutinn.com
Web: theblackwalnutinn.com

Circa 1897. Situated on 162 wooded acres, it's hard to imagine that this rustic English Tudor-style inn is less than two hours away from Manhattan. The woods, fields and four-acre lake offer guests a variety of on-site activities like picking fresh berries (in season), fishing for bass, horseback riding or mountain biking on endless trails. The grounds also include a petting zoo, a hot tub and paddle boats. The guest rooms are all furnished with brass beds and antique furniture. After a day of activities, guest can relax in front of the historic European fireplace or enjoy a drink while viewing the lake. There is also a game room. Guests begin their day with a hearty breakfast with items such as eggs, hot cakes, French toast, breakfast meats, fresh fruit salads and breads. The inn is often used for weddings, meetings and family reunions. Antique shopping, flea markets, museums, restaurants and canoeing down the Delaware are close by.

Historic Interest: Located near Grey Towers National Historic Landmark, the Applchian Trail and High Point Monument.

Innkeeper(s): Awilda Torres & Stewart Schneider. $60-175. MC, VISA, AX, DS. 12 rooms, 4 with PB and 1 cabin. Breakfast included in rates. Types of meals: Full bkfst and early coffee/tea. Afternoon tea available. Beds: QD. Cabin with full kitchen, full bathroom and living room with TV/VCR and fireplace in room. VCR, spa, swimming, paddle boats, horseback riding, petting zoo and game room on premises. Weddings, small meetings and family reunions hosted. Spanish spoken. Antiquing, bicycling, canoeing/kayaking, fishing, golf, hiking, horseback riding, boating (row and paddle), antique cars, rafting, lawn games, bird watching, overnight camp-out, museums, shopping, tennis and water sports nearby.

Milton G12

Pau-Lyn's Country B&B

RR 3 Box 676
Milton, PA 17847-9506
(570)742-4110

Circa 1850. This Victorian brick home offers a formal dining room with a fireplace and antique musical instruments. This restful haven with a porch and patio overlooking the large lawn. Nearby are working farms and dairies, covered bridges, mountains, rivers and valleys and underground railroad stops.

Innkeeper(s): Paul & Evelyn Landis. $60-65. 7 rooms and 2 suites. Breakfast included in rates. Type of meal: Full bkfst. Air conditioning. Large lawn and patio on premises. Amusement parks, antiquing, golf, hiking, biking, museum, underground railroad, little league field and shopping nearby.

Montgomeryville J17

Blue Skies Country Manor Estates

953 Horsham Rd
Montgomeryville, PA 18936
(215)872-0589

Circa 1723. This beautiful stone farmhouse is situated on six secluded acres. Allow plenty of time to meander around the inn's park-like grounds to enjoy the wildflowers and the spring-fed pond, or even to dangle a line and angle for bass. There's a wraparound porch for relaxing, reading or enjoying a cup of coffee in the early morning. Breakfast is either continental or a full menu such as eggs and French toast. A conference center at the inn is offered, as well. Restaurants abound in the area and nearby activities include miniature golf, theaters and shopping.

Historic Interest: 1723 all restored to original condition.. Valley Forge National Park (15 miles), Washington Crossing (15 miles).

Innkeeper(s): Maggie Eberhardt, Megan Murphy-Rose. $140. MC, VISA, AX, PC, TC. TAC10. 8 rooms. Breakfast and snacks/refreshments included in rates. Types of meals: Full bkfst and cont. Banquet service, catering service and room service available. Restaurant on premises. Beds: KQD. Cable TV, phone, turndown service and ceiling fan in room. Central air. VCR, fax, copier, library and pet boarding on premises. Weddings, small meetings, family reunions and seminars hosted. Amusement parks, antiquing, art galleries, canoeing/kayaking, fishing and golf nearby.

Pets allowed: Must be house trained and friendly and under 20 lbs.

Mount Joy K13

Cedar Hill Farm

305 Longenecker Rd
Mount Joy, PA 17552-8404
(717)653-4655 Fax:(717)653-9242
Web: www.800padutch.com/cedarhill.html

Circa 1817. Situated on 51 acres overlooking Chiques Creek, this stone farmhouse boasts a two-tiered front veranda affording pastoral views of the surrounding fields. The host was born in

the house and is the third generation to have lived here since the Swarr family first purchased it in 1878. Family heirlooms and antiques include an elaborately carved walnut bedstead, a marble-topped washstand and a "tumbling block" quilt. In the kitchen, a copper kettle, bread paddle and baskets of dried herbs accentuate the walk-in fireplace, where guests often linger over breakfast. Cedar Hill is a working poultry and grain farm.

Innkeeper(s): Russel & Gladys Swarr. $75-80. MC, VISA, AX, DS, PC, TC. 5 rooms with PB. Breakfast included in rates. Types of meals: Cont plus and early coffee/tea. Beds: KQDT. Whirlpool and hershey kisses in room. Air conditioning. VCR, fax and lawn Games on premises. Small meetings and family reunions hosted. Amusement parks, antiquing, fishing, amish country, live theater, parks, shopping, cross-country skiing, sporting events and water sports nearby.

"Dorothy can have Kansas, Scarlett can take Tara, Rick can keep Paris — I've stayed at Cedar Hill Farm."

Hillside Farm B&B

607 Eby Chiques Rd
Mount Joy, PA 17552-8819
(717)653-6697 (888)249-3406 Fax:(717)653-9775
E-mail: hillside3@juno.com
Web: www.hillsidefarmbandb.com

Circa 1863. This comfortable farm has a relaxing homey feel to it. Rooms are simply decorated and special extras such as handmade quilts and antiques add an elegant country touch. A

new guest cottage offers a king bed, whirlpool tub for two, fireplace, wet bar and deck overlooking a bucolic meadow. The home is a true monument to the cow. Dairy antiques, cow knick-

knacks and antique milk bottles abound. Some of the bottles were found during the renovation of the home and its grounds. Spend the day hunting for bargains in nearby antique shops, malls and factory outlets, or tour local Amish and Pennsylvania Dutch attractions. The farm is a good vacation spot for families with children above the age of 10.

Historic Interest: Home of President Buchanan (6 miles), Hans Herr House (10 miles), The Ephrata Cloister, Rockford Plantation (both 15 miles).

Innkeeper(s): Gary & Deborah Lintner. $65-175. MC, VISA, DS, PC, TC. TAC10. 5 rooms, 3 with PB and 1 cottage. Breakfast and snacks/refreshments included in rates. Types of meals: Full bkfst and early coffee/tea. Beds: KQDT. Ceiling fan, heat thermostats, magazines and wet bar in room. Central air. VCR, spa, library, barn to explore and balcony on premises. Small meetings, family reunions and seminars hosted. Amusement parks, antiquing, fishing, dinner with the Amish available with advance reservation. Hiking and biking trails, live theater, parks, shopping, downhill skiing, cross-country skiing and water sports nearby.

Muncy

F12

The Bodine House B&B

307 S Main St
Muncy, PA 17756-1507
(570)546-8949 Fax:(570)546-0607

Circa 1805. This Federal-style townhouse, framed by a white picket fence, is in the National Register. Antique and reproduction furnishings highlight the inn's four fireplaces, the parlor, study and library. A favorite

guest room features a walnut canopy bed, hand-stenciled and bordered walls, and a framed sampler by the innkeeper's great-great-great-grandmother. Candlelight

breakfasts are served beside the fireplace in a gracious Colonial dining room. Also available is a guest cottage with kitchenette.

Historic Interest: The Pennsdale Quaker Meeting House.

Innkeeper(s): David & Marie Louise Smith. $65-125. MC, VISA, AX, DS, PC, TC. TAC10. 3 rooms with PB, 1 with FP and 1 cottage. Breakfast included in rates. Types of meals: Full bkfst and early coffee/tea. Afternoon tea available. Beds: QDT. Cable TV and turndown service in room. Air conditioning. VCR, fax, bicycles and library on premises. Small meetings and family reunions hosted. Antiquing, fishing, parks, shopping, cross-country skiing and sporting events nearby.

Publicity: *Colonial Homes, Philadelphia Inquirer.*

"What an experience, made special by your wonderful hospitality."

New Berlin

H12

The Inn at Olde New Berlin

321 Market St
New Berlin, PA 17855-0390
(570)966-0321 (800)797-2350 Fax:(570)966-9557
E-mail: lodging@newberlin-inn.com
Web: www.newberlin-inn.com

Circa 1906. At this richly appointed Victorian inn, you can relax on the inviting front porch swing or in the step-down living room with its baby grand piano. Carved woodwork and high ceilings accentuate its antique-filled rooms. An herb garden in the patio area supplies seasonings for the acclaimed meals at the inn's restaurant named Gabriel's. Luscious soups, appetizers such as crisp duck won tons with a currant marmalade sauce, and a variety of salads begin a dinner of contemporary American cuisine. Scrumptious desserts such as Amaretto-Bailey's cheesecake and chocolate mousse cake follow dinner. Brunch, available at Gabriel's Restaurant, features unique omelets, fruit crepes, apple streusel French toast and drinks such as raspberry hot chocolate. Gabriel's Gift Collection features Radko collectible mouth-blown hand-painted ornaments and other unique gifts.

Historic Interest: The Slifer House Museum, Packwood House Museum, Mifflinburg Buggy Museum and Bucknell University are only a short drive away.

Innkeeper(s): Nancy & John Showers. $90-165. MC, VISA, DS, PC, TC. TAC10. 7 rooms with PB, 3 with FP, 2 suites and 1 conference room. Breakfast included in rates. Types of meals: Full bkfst and early coffee/tea. Gourmet dinner, lunch and catering service available. Restaurant on premises. Beds: QD. TV and phone upon request in room. Air conditioning. VCR, fax and copier on premises. Weddings, small meetings, family reunions and seminars hosted. Amusement parks, antiquing, fishing, golf, live theater, parks, shopping, sporting events and tennis nearby.

"I left feeling nurtured and relaxed. You've created a very caring, rich lodging as a perfect place for regenerating."

New Hope

I18

Centre Bridge Inn

2998 N River Rd
New Hope, PA 18938
(215)862-9139 Fax:(215)862-3244
E-mail: centreinn@aol.com
Web: www.letsmakeplans.com/centrebridgeinn

Circa 1705. This Williamsburg Colonial inn was rebuilt after a fire in 1959. The original inn was constructed in 1705. Canopy beds, colonial decor, and views of the Delaware River and Canal provide a romantic setting. The inn's dining areas include an outside dining terrace, a glass-enclosed garden dining room or the main dining room with an open-hearth fireplace. Two of the options boast a view of the river. Weddings and corporate gatherings are popular here.

Innkeeper(s): Stephen R. DuGan. $80-175. MC, VISA, AX. 10 rooms, 7 with PB and 3 suites. Breakfast included in rates. Type of meal: Cont. Dinner available. Restaurant on premises. Beds: KQD. TV in room. Air conditioning. Fax and copier on premises. Weddings, small meetings and family reunions hosted. Antiquing, fishing, live theater, parks, shopping and water sports nearby.

Hollileif B&B

677 Durham Rd (Rt 413)
New Hope, PA 18940
(215)598-3100

Circa 1700. This handsome former farmhouse sits on more than five rolling acres of scenic Bucks County countryside. The name "hollileif," which means "beloved tree," refers to the 40-foot holly trees that grace the entrance. Bedrooms are appointed with lace and fresh flowers. Afternoon refreshments in the parlor or patio are provided, as well as evening turndown service.

Historic Interest: Washington Crossing State Park (5 miles), Parry Mansion (6 miles), Pennsbury Manor (20 miles).

Innkeeper(s): Ellen & Richard Butkus. $85-160. MC, VISA, AX, DS, PC, TC. TAC10. 5 rooms with PB, 2 with FP. Breakfast and afternoon tea included in rates. Types of meals: Full gourmet bkfst and early coffee/tea. Beds: QD. Turndown service and ceiling fan in room. Air conditioning. VCR, fax, copier and library on premises. Family reunions hosted. Limited Spanish spoken. Antiquing, fishing, wineries, biking, live theater, parks, shopping, downhill skiing, cross-country skiing and water sports nearby.

Publicity: *Trentonian, Bucks County Courier Times, Philadelphia Inquirer.*

"The accommodations were lovely and the breakfasts delicious and unusual, but it is really the graciousness of our hosts that made the weekend memorable."

Pineapple Hill

1324 River Rd
New Hope, PA 18938
(215)862-1790
E-mail: ktriolo@pineapplehill.com
Web: www.pineapplehill.com

Circa 1790. The pineapple always has been a sign of friendship and hospitality, and guests at Pineapple Hill are sure to experience both. The inn is secluded on five private acres, yet it's just

four miles from town, antique shops, flea markets, auctions and plenty of outdoor activities. The inviting interior is filled with Colonial-style furnishings. All rooms include either a fireplace, private deck or living room. Guests enjoy everything from baked bananas to raspberry French toast during the romantic, candlelight breakfasts, which are served on tables set for two. Inside the walls of a stone barn, is a tiled swimming pool.

Innkeeper(s): Kathy & Charles. $94-182. MC, VISA, AX, DS, TC. TAC10. 8 rooms with PB, 3 suites and 1 conference room. Breakfast and afternoon tea included in rates. Types of meals: Full gourmet bkfst and early coffee/tea. Snacks/refreshments available. Beds: KQ. Cable TV, turndown service, private deck and living room in room. Air conditioning. VCR, fax and swimming on premises. Weddings, small meetings, family reunions and seminars hosted. Antiquing, fishing, museums, live theater, parks, shopping and water sports nearby.

"It was a delightful stay in every way. The clicking door latches and the smells of breakfast cooking wafting up to the bedroom were reminiscent of my childhood stays at my grandparents' farmhouse."

The Whitehall Inn

1370 Pineville Rd
New Hope, PA 18938-9495
(215)598-7945

Circa 1794. This white-plastered stone farmhouse is located on 13 country acres studded with stately maple and chestnut trees. Inside, a winding walnut staircase leads to antique-furnished guest rooms that offer wide pine floors, wavy-glass windows, high ceilings and some fireplaces. An antique clock collection, Oriental rugs and late Victorian furnishings are found throughout. Afternoon tea, evening chocolates and candlelight breakfasts served with heirloom china and sterling reflect the inn's many amenities. There are stables on the property and horseback riding may be arranged.

Innkeeper(s): Mike Wass. $140-200. MC, VISA, AX, DC, CB, DS. 6 rooms. Breakfast included in rates. Types of meals: Full bkfst and early coffee/tea. Turndown service and clocks in room. Air conditioning. Small meetings, family reunions and seminars hosted. Amusement parks, antiquing, live theater, shopping and cross-country skiing nearby.

New Oxford   L12

Flaherty House

104 Lincoln Way
New Oxford, PA 17350
(717)624-9494 (800)217-0618

Circa 1888. This three-story brick Victorian has a large bay, a wraparound porch, and stained-glass and shuttered windows.

Located in the middle of what is considered Pennsylvania's antique capital, there are more than 400 antique dealers within walking distance of the inn. Quilts and antiques are featured throughout the house. A full, three-course breakfast is served. The home is near to the Gettysburg battlefield.

Historic Interest: Gettysburg Battlefield Park (15-20 Minutes), Pfeiffer Medical Institute & College, Conewago Chapel (20 minutes).

Innkeeper(s): Bonnie Masslofsky. $60-200. MC, VISA. 5 rooms, 3 with PB and 2 suites. Breakfast included in rates. Type of meal: Full bkfst. Beds: QD. Antiquing nearby.

Philadelphia   K17

Gables B&B

4520 Chester Ave
Philadelphia, PA 19143-3707
(215)662-1918 Fax:(215)662-1935
E-mail: gablesbb@aol.com
Web: www.gablesbb.com

Circa 1889. Located in the University City section, this redbrick Queen Anne Victorian has three stories and offers off-street parking. Chestnut and cherry woodwork, a grand entry hall and sitting rooms furnished with antiques make this a popular site

for private affairs. A wraparound porch overlooks the inn's gardens of perennials, roses, dogwood and Japanese cherry and magnolia trees. The Christmas Room has mahogany antiques and a queen brass bed, while the Tower Room has a working fireplace and a settee tucked into the turret. Another room offers a soaking tub and sun porch. This inn received Philadelphia Magazine's four-heart award and the "Best of Philly 1996" award as an urban getaway.

Innkeeper(s): Don Caskey & Warren Cederholm. $60-100. MC, VISA, AX, PC, TC. 10 rooms, 8 with PB, 2 with FP and 1 suite. Breakfast included in rates. Type of meal: Full bkfst. Beds: QD. Cable TV and phone in room. Air conditioning. Fax and library on premises. Weddings, small meetings, family reunions and seminars hosted. Antiquing, live theater, parks, shopping and sporting events nearby.

The Penn's View Hotel

Front & Market Streets
Philadelphia, PA 19106
(215)922-7600 (800)331-7634 Fax:(215)922-7642
Web: www.pennsviewhotel.com

Circa 1828. The original portion of Penn's View Hotel dates to 1828. Today, the elegant hotel includes 40 guest rooms and suites, some of which include a fireplace and whirlpool tub. Ristorante Panorama, the hotel's gourmet restaurant, offers acclaimed Italian cuisine, as well as a wine bar with more than 120 different varieties. The hotel looks out to the Delaware River and is situated within walking distance to many historic sites.

Innkeeper(s): The Sena Family. $108-195. MC, VISA, AX, DC, CB, TC. TAC10. 40 rooms. Breakfast included in rates. Type of meal: Cont plus. Dinner and lunch available. Restaurant on premises. Beds: KQ. Cable TV, phone and lighted vanity mirror in room. Air conditioning. Fax, copier and child care on premises. Small meetings and family reunions hosted. Spanish and Italian spoken. Antiquing, live theater, parks, shopping, sporting events and tennis nearby.

Thomas Bond House

129 S 2nd St
Philadelphia, PA 19106-3039
(215)923-8523 (800)845-2663 Fax:(215)923-8504

Circa 1769. One way to enjoy the history of Philadelphia is to treat yourself to a stay at this Colonial-period, Georgian-style residence in Independence National Historical Park. White shutters and cornices accentuate the brick exterior, often draped in red, white and blue bunting. A finely executed interior renovation provides a handsome background for the inn's collection of Chippendale reproductions, four-poster beds and drop front desks. Working fireplaces, phones, hair dryers, television and whirlpool tubs provide additional comforts.

Innkeeper(s): Rita McGuire. $95-175. MC, VISA, AX, PC, TC. TAC7. 12 rooms with PB, 2 with FP, 2 suites and 1 conference room. Breakfast included in rates. Types of meals: Full bkfst, cont plus and early coffee/tea. Gourmet dinner, snacks/refreshments and catering service available. Beds: QDT. Phone and some with whirlpool tubs in room. Air conditioning. Fax and copier on premises. Weddings, small meetings, family reunions and seminars hosted. Amusement parks, antiquing, fishing, historic sites, live theater, parks, shopping and sporting events nearby.

Publicity: *Mid-Atlantic Country, Washingtonian, Washington Post, Philadelphia Inquirer, Home & Garden, Boston Globe.*

"Your service was excellent, congenial, made us feel comfortable and welcome."

Pittsburgh **13**

The Priory

614 Pressley St
Pittsburgh, PA 15212-5616
(412)231-3338 Fax:(412)231-4838

Circa 1888. The Priory, now a European-style hotel, was built to provide lodging for Benedictine priests traveling through Pittsburgh. It is adjacent to Pittsburgh's Grand Hall at the Priory in historic East Allegheny. The inn's design and maze of rooms and corridors give it a distinctly Old World flavor. All rooms are decorated with Victorian furnishings.

Historic Interest: Mexican War Streets Neighborhood, Fort Pitt Blockhouse & Point State Park.

Innkeeper(s): Ed & Mary Ann Graf. $114-150. MC, VISA, AX, DC, DS. 24 rooms with PB, 3 suites and 1 conference room. Breakfast included in rates. Type of meal: Cont plus. Beds: QDT. Handicap access. Live theater nearby.

Publicity: *Pittsburgh Press, US Air, Country Inns, Innsider, Youngstown Vindicator, Travel & Leisure, Gourmet, Mid-Atlantic Country.*

"Although we had been told that the place was elegant, we were hardly prepared for the richness of detail. We felt as though we were guests in a manor."

Point Pleasant **I18**

Tattersall Inn

16 Cafferty Rd, PO Box 569
Point Pleasant, PA 18950
(215)297-8233 (800)297-4988 Fax:(215)297-5093

Circa 1750. This Bucks County plastered fieldstone house with its 18-inch-thick walls, broad porches and wainscoted entry hall was the home of local mill owners for 150 years. Today it offers a peaceful place to relax, rebuild and enjoy the bucolic surroundings in Olde Bucks. Breakfast is served in the dining room or brought to your room. The Colonial-style common room features a beamed ceiling and walk-in fireplace where guests gather for apple cider, cheese and crackers and tea or coffee in the late afternoon.

Historic Interest: Washington Crossing Park (12 miles), William Penn's Pennsbury Manor (25 miles), Valley Forge (40 miles), 11 covered bridges (15 miles).

Innkeeper(s): Donna & Bob Trevorrow. $90-140. MC, VISA, DS. 6 rooms with PB, 2 with FP, 1 suite and 1 conference room. Breakfast and afternoon tea included in rates. Type of meal: Full bkfst. Beds: Q. Air conditioning. Fax, copier, library and refrigerator on premises. Small meetings and family reunions hosted. Antiquing, fishing, live theater, parks, shopping, cross-country skiing and water sports nearby.

"Thank you for your hospitality and warm welcome. The inn is charming and has a wonderful ambiance."

Pottersville   H9

Rest & Repast B&B Reservation Service (General Potter Farm)

RD1 Box 135, Rt 144
Pottersville, PA 16868-0126
(814)238-1484 Fax:(814)234-9890

Circa 1830. This is a reservation service with a collection of more than 50 homes offering guest rooms in private homes. There are several historic homes such as a restored mill with pond in Bellefonte, a cottage on 13 acres in Grove's Cottage, a horse farm on 60 acres, a limestone mansion, or a log home. Apartments and short-term cottages are also available. Ask to see the list or simply choose by area or amenities.

Innkeeper(s): Binky & Sam Lush. $100-120. PC, TC. 3 rooms, 1 with PB. Breakfast included in rates. Types of meals: Full bkfst and early coffee/tea. Beds: QD. Air conditioning. Weddings, small meetings and family reunions hosted. Antiquing, art galleries, bicycling, canoeing/kayaking, fishing, golf, hiking, horseback riding, live theater, museums, parks, shopping, downhill skiing, cross-country skiing, sporting events, tennis and wineries nearby.

Ronks   K14

Candlelight Inn B&B

2574 Lincoln Hwy E
Ronks, PA 17572-9771
(717)299-6005 (800)772-2635 Fax:(717)299-6397

Circa 1920. Located in the Pennsylvania Dutch area, this Federal-style house offers a side porch for enjoying the home's acre and a half of tall trees and surrounding Amish farmland. Guest rooms feature Victorian decor. Two rooms include a Jacuzzi tub and fireplace. The inn's gourmet breakfast, which might include a creme caramel French toast, is served by candlelight. The innkeepers are professional classical musicians. Lancaster is five miles to the east.

Innkeeper(s): Tim & Heidi Soberick. $79-139. MC, VISA, DS, PC, TC. TAC10. 7 rooms with PB, 2 with FP and 2 suites. Breakfast included in rates. Type of meal: Full gourmet bkfst. Beds: KQT. Amaretto, robes, Jacuzzi and fireplaces in room. Air conditioning. Fax, badminton and croquet on premises. Weddings, small meetings, family reunions and seminars hosted. French and Italian spoken. Amusement parks, antiquing, fishing, live theater, parks, shopping, downhill skiing, cross-country skiing, sporting events and water sports nearby.

Scottdale   K4

Zephyr Glen Bed & Breakfast

205 Dexter Rd
Scottdale, PA 15683-1812
(724)887-6577

Circa 1822. An inviting country theme permeates the atmosphere at this early 19th-century, Federal-style farmhouse. Rooms are filled with period antiques, quilts and a few carefully placed knickknacks and musical instruments. Several rooms are decorated with stencils created by innkeeper Noreen McGurl. She and husband, Gil, also run an antique store out of their inn. Guests are treated to breakfasts that include a fruit dish, jams made from berries on the property, freshly baked breads and a creative main course. The three-acres grounds are decorated with maples, oaks, fruit trees, berry bushes, herb gardens and a fish pond. Frank Lloyd Wright's masterpiece, Fallingwater, is nearby, and another Wright design also is near.

Historic Interest: Fort Necessity, Braddock's Grave, West Overton Museum, the Bushy Run Battlefield and Fort Ligonier are among the many historic sites in the area.

Innkeeper(s): Noreen & Gil McGurl. $75-80. MC, VISA, DS, PC, TC. TAC10. 3 rooms with PB, 1 with FP. Breakfast, afternoon tea and snacks/refreshments included in rates. Types of meals: Full bkfst and early coffee/tea. Beds: D. Turndown service, ceiling fan, fresh flowers and chocolates in room. Fax, library and musical instruments on premises. Amusement parks, antiquing, bicycling, fishing, hiking, steam train rides, historic sites, live theater, parks, shopping, downhill skiing, cross-country skiing and water sports nearby.

"We can't stop talking about the wonderful time we had at your lovely inn."

Shippensburg   K10

Field & Pine B&B

2155 Ritner Hwy
Shippensburg, PA 17257-9756
(717)776-7179
E-mail: fieldpine@aol.com
Web: cvbednbreakfasts.com

Circa 1790. Local limestone was used to build this stone house, located on the main wagon road to Baltimore and Washington. Originally, it was a tavern and weigh station. The house is surrounded by stately pines, and sheep graze on the inn's 80 acres. The bedrooms are hand-stenciled and furnished with quilts and antiques.

Innkeeper(s): Mary Ellen & Allan Williams. $70-80. MC, VISA, PC, TC. TAC10. 3 rooms, 1 with PB, 1 with FP and 1 suite. Breakfast and snacks/refreshments included in rates. Types of meals: Full gourmet bkfst and early coffee/tea. Beds: QDT. TV and turndown service in room. Air conditioning. VCR on premises. Weddings, small meetings and family reunions hosted. Antiquing, fishing, parks and shopping nearby.

"Our visit in this lovely country home has been most delightful. The ambiance of antiques and tasteful decorating exemplifies real country living."

Smethport   D7

Christmas Inn

911 W Main St
Smethport, PA 16749-1040
(814)887-5665 (800)653-6700

Circa 1900. The spacious front porch and ornate columns typify the detail and craftsmanship of this magnificent, turn-of-the-century, three-story mansion. Each guest room has its own

Christmas tree and innkeeper Connie Lovell was born on Christmas. Original woodwork and a marble fireplace are some of the features of the house. Guests are given a coupon for breakfast at the Smethport Diner, which was featured on the PBS diner series.

Innkeeper(s): Bob & Connie Lovell. $69-89. MC, VISA, AX, DS, PC, TC. TAC10. 7 rooms with PB, 4 with FP. Breakfast included in rates. Beds: Q. Phone and ceiling fan in room. Air conditioning. VCR and copier on premises. Antiquing, fishing, golf, parks, shopping and tennis nearby.

Somerset   K5

Glades Pike Inn

2684 Glades Pike
Somerset, PA 15501-8520
(814)443-4978 (800)762-5942 Fax:(814)443-2562
E-mail: fwmjj@sprynet.com
Web: www.gladespike.com

Circa 1842. This red brick Federal-style inn once served as a stagecoach stop along Glades Pike. The guest rooms feature period Federal décor, and three include a fireplace. In the

mornings, country breakfasts are served. The inn's rural setting includes 200 acres, and the surrounding area and Laurel Mountains offer a variety of outdoor activities. Guests

can trek along the Laurel Highlands Hiking Trail, fish or hunt in one of several state game lands, golf at a local course, or ski at nearby Seven Springs, Hidden Valley or Laurel Mountain. Historic forts and Frank Lloyd Wright's famous Fallingwater and Kentock Knob also are nearby.

Historic Interest: Somerset (6 miles), Fort Ligonier (20 miles), Fort Necessary (30 miles).

Innkeeper(s): Janet L Jones. $50-85. MC, VISA, AX, DS, PC, TC. TAC10. 5 rooms with PB, 3 with FP. Types of meals: Country bkfst and early coffee/tea. Beds: QD. TV and ceiling fan in room. Air conditioning. Fax, copier and bicycles on premises. Amusement parks, antiquing, art galleries, beaches, bicycling, canoeing/kayaking, fishing, golf, hiking, horseback riding, live theater, museums, parks, shopping, downhill skiing, cross-country skiing, tennis, water sports and wineries nearby.

Quill Haven Country Inn

1519 North Center Ave
Somerset, PA 15501-7001
(814)443-4514 Fax:(814)445-1376
E-mail: quill@quillhaven.com
Web: www.quillhaven.com

Circa 1918. Set on three acres that were once part of a chicken and turkey farm, this historic Arts & Crafts-style home offers guest rooms, each individually appointed. The Bridal Suite includes a four-poster wrought iron bed and sunken tub in the bath. The Country Room includes a decorative pot-bellied stove. Antiques, reproductions and stained-glass lamps decorate the rooms. Guests are treated to a full breakfast with items such

as baked grapefruit or apples, homemade breads and entrees such as stuffed French toast or a specialty casserole of ham, cheese and potatoes. Guests can spend the day boating or swimming at nearby Youghiogheny Reservoir, take a whitewater-rafting trip, bike or hike through the scenic countryside or

shop at antique stores and flea markets. Frank Lloyd Wright's Fallingwater is another nearby attraction.

Historic Interest: Somerset Historical Center (3 miles), Fallingwater & Kentuck Knob (40 miles).

Innkeeper(s): Carol & Rowland Miller. $75-95. MC, VISA, DS, PC. 4 rooms with PB. Breakfast and snacks/refreshments included in rates. Types of meals: Full bkfst, veg bkfst and early coffee/tea. Picnic lunch available. Beds: KQ. Cable TV, turndown service, ceiling fan, VCR and heated mattress pad in room. Air conditioning. Fax, copier, library and outdoor hot tub on premises. Small meetings and family reunions hosted. Amusement parks, antiquing, bicycling, canoeing/kayaking, fishing, golf, hiking, horseback riding, skiing at Seven Springs and Hidden Valley. Located in the Laurel Highlands, live theater, parks, shopping, downhill skiing, cross-country skiing, tennis, water sports and wineries nearby.

"What a beautiful memory we will have of our first B&B experience! We've never felt quite so pampered in all our 25 years of marriage."

Starlight   C17

The Inn at Starlight Lake

PO Box 27
Starlight, PA 18461-0027
(570)798-2519 (800)248-2519 Fax:(570)798-2672

Circa 1909. Acres of woodland and meadow surround the last surviving railroad inn on the New York, Ontario and Western lines. Originally a boarding house, the inn was part of a little village that had its own store, church, blacksmith shop and creamery. Platforms, first erected to accommodate tents for the summer season, were later replaced by three small cottage buildings that now includes a suite with a double whirlpool. A modern three-bedroom

house is available for family reunions and conferences. The inn is situated on the 45-acre, spring-fed Starlight Lake, providing summertime canoeing, swimming, fishing and sailing. (No motorboats are allowed on the lake.) Breakfast is served in the lakeside dining area where dinner is also available.

Innkeeper(s): Jack & Judy McMahon. $125-225. MC, VISA, PC. TAC10. 26 rooms, 22 with PB, 1 suite, 4 cottages and 1 conference room. Breakfast and dinner included in rates. MAP. Types of meals: Full gourmet bkfst and early coffee/tea. Picnic lunch, gourmet lunch and banquet service available. Restaurant on premises. Beds: KQDT. VCR, fax, copier, swimming, bicycles, tennis and library on premises. Weddings, small meetings, family reunions and seminars hosted. Antiquing, fishing, golf, live theater, parks, shopping, downhill skiing, cross-country skiing, tennis and water sports nearby.

Publicity: *New York Times, Philadelphia Inquirer, Newsday, Discerning Traveler, Freeman.*

State College   *H9*

Starry Night B&B

1170 W Branch Rd
State College, PA 16801-7653
(814)234-8111 Fax:(814)234-8111
E-mail: info@starrynightbandb.com
Web: starrynightbandb.com

Circa 1912. Forty acres of woodland and meadow surround this farmhouse. The decor is a combination of Scandinavian design, Persian rugs and antiques. Ask for Uncle George's Room and you'll climb atop a 100-year-old sleigh bed and warm to a gas fireplace. Watching the fireflies from the cedar screened-in porch is a favorite activity. A typical breakfast offers dishes such as vegetable tort, Mexican frittata, banana cinnamon pancakes, or Barbara's Blueberry Surprise. The nearby area offers Historic Boalsburg Village, Amish markets, local wineries, antiquing, fly fishing at Fisherman's Paradise, canoeing and kayaking. Penns Cave can be explored via boat or take tours through Indian Caverns and Woodward Cave.

Historic Interest: Historic Bellefonte, Boalsburg-10 miles.

Innkeeper(s): Chet & Alaina Esber. $55-140. PC, TC. 3 rooms with PB, 1 with FP and 1 conference room. Breakfast and snacks/refreshments included in rates. Types of meals: Full gourmet bkfst, cont plus, veg bkfst and early coffee/tea. Beds: QD. Air conditioning. VCR, fax and swimming on premises. Small meetings, family reunions and seminars hosted. Antiquing, art galleries, bicycling, fishing, golf, hiking, museums, parks, downhill skiing, cross-country skiing, sporting events, tennis and wineries nearby.

Strasburg   *K14*

Limestone Inn B&B

33 E Main St
Strasburg, PA 17579-1427
(717)687-8392 (800)278-8392 Fax:(717)687-8256

Circa 1786. The Limestone Inn housed the first Chief Burgess and later became the Headmaster's House for Strasburg Academy. It is a hand-some five-bay formal Georgian plan. Located in the Strasburg Historic District, the house is in the National Register. The surrounding scenic Amish farmlands offer sightseeing and antique and craft shopping.

Historic Interest: Lancaster Historic District (5 miles).

Innkeeper(s): Denise & Richard Waller & family. $75-105. MC, VISA, AX, PC, TC. 5 rooms with PB, 1 with FP. Breakfast and snacks/refreshments included in rates. Types of meals: Full gourmet bkfst and early coffee/tea. Beds: KQDT. Central air. Fax, copier and library on premises. Small meetings and family reunions hosted. Spanish spoken. Amusement parks, antiquing, golf, hiking, outlet shopping, live theater, museums, parks, shopping, sporting events, tennis and wineries nearby.

"A beautiful restoration, great innkeepers and a fantasy location."

Strasburg Village Inn

1 W Main St, Centre Sq
Strasburg, PA 17579
(717)687-0900 (800)541-1055
E-mail: foraroom@strasburg.com
Web: strasburg.com

Circa 1788. Located on historic Strasburg's Centre Square, this brick inn offers guests a glimpse of early Americana, in the center of the Amish country. Despite the old-fashioned charm, two suites offer the romantic, albeit modern, amenity of Jacuzzi tubs. The inn is adjacent to the Strasburg Country Store and Creamery, the town's oldest operating store. The shop offers a variety of baked goods, a 19th-century soda fountain, a deli with homemade ice cream, penny candy and plenty of collectibles. Guests are treated to a full breakfast at The Creamery. The inn is surrounded by many Pennsylvania Dutch sites, including Amish farms, antique stores and historic villages. Sight and Sound Theater, the Strasburg Railroad and Dutch Wonderland Amusement Park are nearby.

Innkeeper(s): Helen Pyott. $70-150. MC, VISA, AX, DS, PC, TC. TAC10. 10 rooms with PB and 2 suites. Breakfast included in rates. Types of meals: Full bkfst and early coffee/tea. Restaurant on premises. Beds: KQD. Cable TV in room. Air conditioning. Restaurant on premises. Weddings and family reunions hosted. Several outlet malls nearby nearby.

Thornton   *K16*

Pace One Restaurant and Country Inn

Thornton Rd & Glen Mills Rd
Thornton, PA 19373
(610)459-3702 Fax:(610)558-0825

Circa 1740. This beautifully renovated stone barn has two-and-a-half-foot-thick walls, hand-hewn wood beams and many small-paned windows. Just in front of the inn was the Gray family home used as a hospital during the Revolutionary War when Washington's army crossed nearby Chadd's Ford.

Innkeeper(s): Ted Pace. $95. MC, VISA, AX, DC, PC, TC. 6 rooms with PB and 3 conference rooms. Breakfast included in rates. Type of meal: Cont plus. Gourmet dinner, picnic lunch, lunch and banquet service available. Restaurant on premises. Beds: Q. Phone in room. Air conditioning. Fax and copier on premises. Weddings, small meetings, family reunions and seminars hosted. Antiquing, fishing, live theater, parks, shopping and sporting events nearby.

"Dear Ted & Staff, we loved it here!! The accommodations were great and the brunch on Sunday, fantastic. Thanks for making it a beautiful weekend."

West Chester   *K16*

Bankhouse B&B

875 Hillsdale Rd
West Chester, PA 19382-1975
(610)344-7388

Circa 1765. Built into the bank of a quiet country road, this 18th-century house overlooks a 10-acre horse farm and pond. The interior is decorated with country antiques, stenciling and folk art. Guests have a private entrance and porch. Two bedrooms share a common sitting room library. Hearty country breakfasts include German apple souffle pancakes, custard French toast and nearly 100 other recipes. West Chester and the Brandywine Valley attractions are conveniently close.

Historic Interest: Longwood Gardens, the Brandywine River Museum, Brandywine Battlefield (8 miles).

Innkeeper(s): Diana & Michael Bove. $70-90. TC. 2 rooms and 1 suite. Breakfast and snacks/refreshments included in rates. Types of meals: Full gourmet bkfst and early coffee/tea. Beds: DT. Phone in room. Central air. Antiquing, live theater, parks, shopping, cross-country skiing and sporting events nearby.

Publicity: *Philadelphia Inquirer, Mercury, Bucks County Town & Country Living, Chester County Living, Washington Post.*

"Everything was so warm and inviting. One of my favorite places to keep coming back to."

Willow Street K14

The Apple Bin Inn

2835 Willow Street Pike N
Willow Street, PA 17584-9501
(717)464-5881 (800)338-4296 Fax:(717)464-1818
E-mail: bininn@aol.com
Web: www.applebininn.com

Circa 1865. Once the village general store, the Apple Bin Inn has been restored and transformed into a cozy country getaway. The airy rooms are decorated with a mix of country furnishings and Colonial reproductions, creating a cheerful, romantic ambiance. There is also a restored carriage house, an ideal spot for a romantic occasion. The homemade breakfasts include fresh,

local ingredients, including fresh fruits. The innkeepers are both Lancaster County natives and can offer a bounty of information about this popular area. Lancaster County offers many historic sites, antique and craft shops, flea markets and many Amish sites.

Historic Interest: Oldest home in Lancaster County, Hann Herr House (1 mile).

Innkeeper(s): Debbie & Barry Hershey. $95-135. MC, VISA, AX, PC, TC. 5 rooms with PB and 1 guest house. Type of meal: Full bkfst. Beds: QD. Cable TV, phone and ceiling fan in room. Central air. Fax, copier and library on premises. Family reunions hosted. Amusement parks, antiquing, art galleries, beaches, bicycling, canoeing/kayaking, golf, hiking, live theater, museums, parks, shopping, tennis and wineries nearby.

York K13

Friendship House B&B

728 E Philadelphia St
York, PA 17403-1609
(717)843-8299

Circa 1897. A walk down East Philadelphia Street takes visitors past an unassuming row of 19th-century townhouses. The Friendship House is a welcoming site with its light blue shutters and pink trim. Innkeepers Becky Detwiler and Karen Maust have added a shot of Victorian influence to their charming townhouse B&B, decorating with wallcoverings and lacy curtains. A country feast is prepared some mornings with choices ranging from quiche to French toast accompanied with items such as baked apples, smoked sausage and homemade breads. Most items are selected carefully from a nearby farmer's market. Becky and Karen make sure guests never leave their friendly home empty-handed, offering a bottle of Pennsylvania's finest maple syrup upon departure.

Innkeeper(s): Becky Detwiler & Karen Maust. $55-65. 3 rooms, 2 with PB and 1 suite. Breakfast and snacks/refreshments included in rates. Types of meals: Full bkfst and cont plus. Beds: Q. Air conditioning. VCR on premises. Antiquing, fishing, museums, live theater, parks and shopping nearby.

Rhode Island

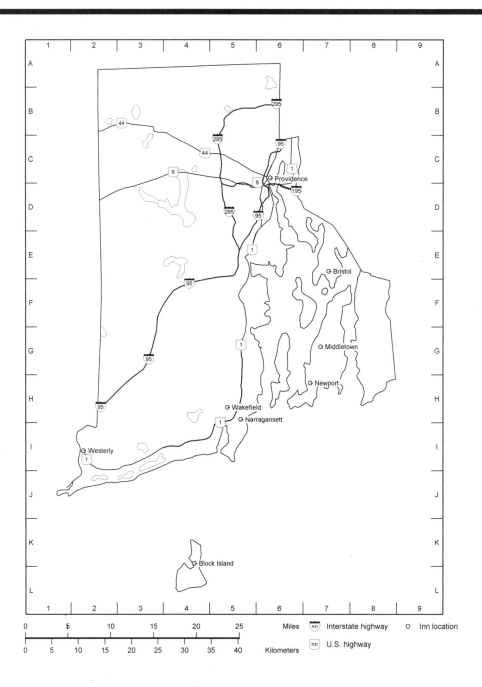

0 | 5 | 10 | 15 | 20 | 25 Miles
0 | 5 | 10 | 15 | 20 | 25 | 30 | 35 | 40 Kilometers

Interstate highway O Inn location
U.S. highway

Block Island K4

1661 Inn & Hotel Manisses

1 Spring St, PO Box 1
Block Island, RI 02807-0001
(401)466-2421 (800)626-4773 Fax:(401)466-2858
E-mail: biresorts@aol.com
Web: www.blockisland.com/biresorts

Circa 1875. Seven buildings comprise this island inn and overlook grassy lawns and the ocean. Common rooms and guest
rooms are furnished with antiques and art. The newest luxury
rooms in the
Nicholas Ball Cottage
(a replica of an
Episcopal church) offer
both Jacuzzis and fireplaces.
Dinner is available each night
in the summer. Visit the inn's
animal farm to watch the antics of the Indian runner ducks,
black swans, pygmy goats, llamas and Sicilian donkeys. Flower,
vegetable and herb gardens are adjacent to the farm.

Historic Interest: Historic Old Harbor.

Innkeeper(s): Joan & Justin Abrams. $60-335. MC, VISA, PC, TC. 60 rooms, 53
with PB and 5 conference rooms. Breakfast included in rates. Types of meals:
Full gourmet bkfst, cont plus, cont and early coffee/tea. Afternoon tea, gourmet
dinner, snacks/refreshments, picnic lunch, gourmet lunch, banquet service, catering service and catered breakfast available. Restaurant on premises. Beds: KQDT.
Child care on premises. Weddings, small meetings, family reunions and seminars
hosted. Antiquing, fishing, live theater, shopping and water sports nearby.

Publicity: *Newsday, New England Weekends, The Day, Detroit Free Press,
US Air, USA Today, Block Island, New England Travel, Yankee, Gourmet,
Bon Apetite.*

Atlantic Inn

PO Box 1788, High St
Block Island, RI 02807-1788
(401)466-5883 (800)224-7422 Fax:(401)466-5678
E-mail: atlanticinn@biri.com

Circa 1879. Guests first traveled up the long road to the
Atlantic Inn to enjoy its more than two acres of grassy slopes,
which overlook the ocean and Old Harbor Village. Today,
guests will experience much of the charm that lured vacation-

ers to this island spot
during the Victorian era.
The inn's 21 guest
rooms are individually
appointed with antiques
and period furnishings.
Inn guests enjoy use of
two tennis courts, a formal croquet court, a swing and gym set
for children as well as a playhouse, which is a replica of the
inn. Take a leisurely stroll around the landscaped grounds and
enjoy the gardens, which provide many of the herbs and vegetables used in meals at the inn's gourmet restaurant. President
and Mrs. Clinton recently dined here.

Historic Interest: The Block Island Historic District and Old Harbor Village
include many historic buildings.

Innkeeper(s): Brad & Anne Marthens. $125-235. MC, VISA, PC, TC. 21 rooms
with PB, 1 suite and 1 conference room. Breakfast and afternoon tea included in
rates. Types of meals: Cont plus and early coffee/tea. Picnic lunch available.
Restaurant on premises. Beds: QDT. Fax, copier, tennis and child care on premises. Weddings, small meetings, family reunions and seminars hosted. Antiquing,
fishing, beaches, biking, live theater, parks, shopping and water sports nearby.

The Bellevue House

PO Box 1198, High St
Block Island, RI 02807-1198
(401)466-2912

Circa 1882. Offering a hilltop perch, meadow-like setting and
ocean views, this Colonial Revival farmhouse inn in the Block
Island Historic District has served guests for more than a century. A variety of accommo-
dations includes eight guest
rooms, three with private
bath, four suites and two
cottages. The Old Harbor
Ferry, restaurants and shops
are just a five-minute walk
from the inn. Guests may
use ferries from New London, Conn., Montauk Point, N.Y., and
Newport, Point Judith and Providence, R.I., to reach the island.
Beaches, Block Island National Wildlife Reserve and Rodmans
Hollow Nature Area are nearby. Children are welcome.

Innkeeper(s): Neva Flaherty. $65-170. MC, VISA, PC, TC. 8 rooms, 4 suites
and 2 cottages. Breakfast included in rates. Type of meal: Cont. Beds: KQD.
Library, gas grills and picnic tables on premises. Family reunions hosted.
Fishing, parks, shopping and water sports nearby.

The White House

PO Box 447
Block Island, RI 02807-0447
(401)466-2653

Circa 1795. This Colonial-style bed & breakfast is furnished
with French Provincial antiques and has sweeping views of the
ocean, rolling lawns and gardens. The earliest portion of the
home dates back to
the 18th century. The
innkeepers have a col-
lection of presidential
autographs. Another
room, named for King
Louis Philippe of
France, contains French royal family pictures and autographs.
The Captain's Quarters has a bedroom-sitting room that encompasses the entire ocean side of the house. The room has a
canopied double bed and outdoor balcony. Guests have a private north portico entrance and main floor drawing room with
TV. Arrangements can be made to be met at the airport or ferry.

Innkeeper(s): Mrs. Joseph V. Connolly, Jr. $55-120. MC, VISA, PC, TC. 2
rooms. Type of meal: Full bkfst. Beds: DT. Library on premises. Weddings
hosted. Fishing, beaches and shopping nearby.

*"Your home is so fascinating and carries an international as well as
antique filled atmosphere."*

Bristol E7

Rockwell House Inn B&B

610 Hope St
Bristol, RI 02809-1945
(401)253-0040 (800)815-0040 Fax:(401)253-1811

Circa 1809. Situated on a half-acre with pond, this Federal and
Greek Revival home boasts eight-foot pocket doors, Italianate
mantels and working gas-log fireplaces. Double parlors open to
the dining room and its inlaid parquet floors. The sun porch fea-

tures a stone turret and leaded-glass windows. Two guest rooms include working fireplaces, and antiques abound in each of the elegant quarters. The inn is only one block from Narragansett Bay and a 15-mile bike path. Guests can walk to restaurants and museums.

Historic Interest: Historic Newport and Providence are 12 miles away. The Blithewold Mansion and Gardens, Americas' Cup Hall of Fame, Haffenreffer Museum of Anthropology, Linden Place and Coggeshall Historic Farm Museum are all within a mile and a half of Rockwell House.

Innkeeper(s): Debra & Steve Krohn. $90-150. MC, VISA, AX, DS, PC, TC. TAC10. 4 rooms with PB, 2 with FP and 1 conference room. Breakfast and afternoon tea included in rates. Types of meals: Full gourmet bkfst, cont plus and early coffee/tea. Catered breakfast available. Beds: KQT. Ceiling fan in room. VCR, fax, copier and guest refrigerator on premises. Small meetings and seminars hosted. Spanish spoken. Antiquing, fishing, museums, parks, shopping, cross-country skiing and water sports nearby.

William's Grant Inn

154 High St
Bristol, RI 02809-2123
(401)253-4222 (800)596-4222

Circa 1808. This handsome Federal Colonial home was built by Governor William Bradford for his grandson. There are two beehive ovens and seven fireplaces as well as original wide-board pine floors and paired interior chimneys. Antique furnishings and folk art make the guest rooms inviting. The backyard is an ideal spot for relaxation with its patios, water garden and quaint stone walls.

Historic Interest: The area offers many historic homes, the Blithewold Mansion and Gardens, Coggeshall Farm Museum and several other museums.

Innkeeper(s): Warren & Diane, Matthew & Janet Poehler. $95-105. MC, VISA, AX, DS, PC, TC. TAC10. 5 rooms, 3 with PB, 5 with FP. Breakfast included in rates. Type of meal: Full gourmet bkfst. Afternoon tea available. Beds: QD. Turndown service and ceiling fan in room. Bicycles and goldfish pond with waterfall on premises. Small meetings hosted. Antiquing, fishing, parks, shopping, sporting events and water sports nearby.

Publicity: *New York Times, Sun Sentinel, Providence Journal, Bristol Phoenix.*

"We felt better than at home with the wonderful treats (the breakfasts were fabulous), the lovely rooms, the inn is full of inspiration and innovation . . ."

Narragansett   H5

The 1900 House B&B

59 Kingstown Rd
Narragansett, RI 02882-3309
(401)789-7971

Circa 1900. For more than a century, Narragansett has been a hot spot for summer vacationers. Guests at the 1900 House enjoy both close access to the town's restaurants and shops as well as a nostalgic look back at the Victorian era. The innkeepers keep a stereoscope, hat boxes filled with antique post cards and other collectibles on hand for guests to discover. You might spot the

wedding certificate of the home's original owner. Waffles topped with fresh fruit and cream are typical of the rich treats served at breakfast.

Innkeeper(s): Sandra & Bill Panzeri. $75-85. PC, TC. 3 rooms, 1 with PB. Breakfast included in rates. Types of meals: Full gourmet bkfst and early coffee/tea. Beds: D. TV in room. Antiquing, fishing, Foxwoods Casino, bird sanctuary, South County Museum, live theater, parks, shopping, sporting events and water sports nearby.

"Wonderful! So relaxing and lovely, lovely breakfasts."

The Richards

144 Gibson Ave
Narragansett, RI 02882-3949
(401)789-7746

Circa 1884. J.P. Hazard, an influential member of one of the county's most prominent families, built this home, which resembles a English-country stone manor. The rooms are appointed with a beautiful collection of antiques, and each guest room has a fireplace and sitting area. Down comforters, carafes of sherry and candles are among the romantic amenities. After a restful night's sleep, guests are presented with a gourmet breakfast. French toast, made from Portuguese sweet bread, or rich, chocolate pancakes topped with an orange sauce might appear as the daily entree. The home is listed in the National Register of Historic Places.

Innkeeper(s): Nancy & Steven Richards. $85-165. PC, TC. 5 rooms, 4 with PB, 5 with FP and 2 suites. Breakfast included in rates. Type of meal: Full gourmet bkfst. Beds: KQ. Library and guest refrigerator on premises. Antiquing, fishing, golf, live theater, tennis and water sports nearby.

Stone Lea

40 Newton Ave
Narragansett, RI 02882-1368
(401)783-9546

Circa 1884. This rambling Victorian estate is situated on two magnificent oceanfront acres at the mouth of Narragansett Bay. One of a handful of summer homes built during the peak period of high society in Narragansett, it was designed by McKim, Mead & White of New York and is listed in the National Register. The inn is furnished in Victorian antiques and Oriental rugs. Waves crashing along the rocky shore may be seen and heard from most guest rooms.

Historic Interest: Newport Mansions (25 minutes), Smith's Castle, North Kingstown (25 minutes), Tower's (1 1/2 miles).

Innkeeper(s): Guy and Stephanie Lancellotti. $150-195. MC, VISA. 8 rooms with PB, 1 with FP. Breakfast included in rates. Type of meal: Full gourmet bkfst. Beds: QDT. TV in room. Library on premises. Weddings, small meetings, family reunions and seminars hosted. Antiquing, fishing, golf, live theater, parks, shopping, sporting events, tennis and water sports nearby.

Publicity: *New York Magazine.*

Newport   H7

Admiral Farragut Inn

31 Clarke St
Newport, RI 02840-3023
(401)846-4256
E-mail: 5star@admiralsinns.com
Web: www.admiralsinns.com

Circa 1702. General Rochambeau, commander of the French forces, quartered his personal staff at the Admiral Farragut house in 1776. The house had been expanded to two stories in

1755. Now framed by roses and a white picket fence, this yellow clapboard house showcases colonial cove moldings and 12-over-12 paned windows. In addition to the hand-crafted, reproduction Shaker four-poster beds, the inn features hand-painted armoires and a hand-painted fireplace mantel.

Innkeeper(s): Evelyn Echevarria. $65-185. MC, VISA, AX, DC. 9 rooms with PB. Type of meal: Full bkfst. Beds: QD. Fax and copier on premises.

Publicity: *Country Living, Country Inns.*

Beech Tree Inn

34 Rhode Island Ave
Newport, RI 02840-2667
(401)847-9794 (800)748-6565 Fax:(401)847-6824
E-mail: beechtreeinn.com
Web: www.beechtreeinn.com

Circa 1897. This inn's location in historic Newport offers close access to the famous local mansions, and the turn-of-the-century home is within walking distance of the harbor. Most of the guest rooms include a fireplace. Special furnishings include canopy or poster beds, and  suites offer the added amenity of a whirlpool tub. The innkeepers provide a breakfast feast, and guests enjoy made-to-order fare that might include eggs, pancakes, waffles, omelets, ham, bacon and more. In the winter months, guests are further pampered with homemade clam chowder in the evenings. Snacks, such as freshly baked cookies, are always on hand to curb one's appetite.

Innkeeper(s): Edwin & Kathy Wudyka. $70-275. MC, VISA, AX, DS, TC. TAC10. 5 rooms with PB, 1 suite, 2 guest houses and 1 conference room. Breakfast and afternoon tea included in rates. Types of meals: Full bkfst and early coffee/tea. Beds: KQT. Cable TV, phone, ceiling fan and fireplaces and jacuzzi in room. Air conditioning. Fax and copier on premises. Weddings, small meetings, family reunions and seminars hosted. Polish spoken. Antiquing, fishing, golf, live theater, parks, shopping, downhill skiing, cross-country skiing, sporting events, tennis and water sports nearby.

Black Duck Inn

29 Pelham St
Newport, RI 02840-3018
(401)841-5548 (800)206-5212 Fax:(401)846-4873
E-mail: mary@401@aol.com
Web: www.blackduckinn.com

Circa 1900. This inn derives its name from a ship that smuggled liquor into Newport during the days of Prohibition. The inn is located in the downtown area and within walking distance of the harbor and famed mansions of Newport. In the guest rooms, beds are topped with English country fabrics and coordinating curtains and wallcoverings complete the romantic look. For those celebrating a special occasion, the innkeeper offers rooms with whirlpool tubs and fireplaces. Six of the rooms include a private bath. Two other rooms are joined by a bathroom, creating an ideal family suite. One of the rooms includes a queen bed, the other includes two twin beds. The continental-plus breakfasts include cereals, granola, fresh fruit, croissants, muffins and coffee cake.

Innkeeper(s): Mary A. Rolando. $69-185. MC, VISA, AX, TC. TAC5. 8 rooms, 6 with PB, 2 with FP. Breakfast included in rates. Type of meal: Cont plus. Beds: Q. Cable TV and phone in room. Air conditioning. Fax and copier on premises. Antiquing, golf, parks, shopping, tennis and water sports nearby.

The Brinley Victorian Inn

23 Brinley St
Newport, RI 02840-3238
(401)849-7645 (800)999-8523
E-mail: thesweetmans@brinleyvictorian.com
Web: www.brinleyvictorian.com

Circa 1870. This is a three-story Victorian with a mansard roof and long porch. A cottage on the property dates from 1850. There are two parlors and a library providing a quiet haven from the bustle of the Newport wharfs. Each room is decorated with period wallpapers and furnishings. There are fresh flowers and mints on the pillows. The brick courtyard is planted with bleeding hearts, peonies and miniature roses, perennials of the Victorian era.

Historic Interest: Touro Synagogue (5-minute walk), Trinity Church (5-minute walk).

Innkeeper(s): John & Jennifer Sweetman. $75-199. MC, VISA, AX, TC. 15 rooms with PB and 3 suites. Breakfast included in rates. Beds: KQDT. TV and suite has Jacuzzi and fireplace in room.

"Ed and I had a wonderful anniversary. The Brinley is as lovely and cozy as ever! The weekend brought back lots of happy memories."

The Burbank Rose B&B

111 Memorial Blvd W
Newport, RI 02840-3469
(401)849-9457 (888)297-5800
E-mail: burbank@travelbase.com
Web: www.burbankrose.com

Circa 1850. The innkeepers of this cheery, yellow home named their B&B in honor of their ancestor, famed horticulturist Luther Burbank. As a guest, he probably would be taken by the bright, flowery hues that adorn  the interior of this Federal-style home. Rooms, some of which afford harbor views, are light and airy with simple decor. The innkeepers serve afternoon refreshments and a substantial breakfast buffet. The home is located in Newport's Historic Hill district and within walking distance of shops, restaurants and many of the seaside village's popular attractions.

Innkeeper(s): John & Bonnie McNeely. $69-149. AX, PC, TC. 3 rooms with PB and 2 suites. Breakfast and afternoon tea included in rates. Types of meals: Full bkfst and early coffee/tea. Beds: QT. Air conditioning. VCR and copier on premises. Antiquing, fishing, sailing, golf, tennis, live theater, shopping and water sports nearby.

Castle Hill Inn & Resort

Ocean Ave
Newport, RI 02840
(401)849-3800 (888)466-1355
E-mail: castlehill@edgenet.net
Web: www.castlehillinn.com

Circa 1874. A rambling Victorian, the Castle Hill Inn was built as a summer home for scientist Alexander Agassiz. A laboratory on the property was a forerunner of the Woods Hole Marine Laboratory. Many original furnishings remain, and there are spectacular views from every room. The inn's luxurious rooms and suites offer spacious whirlpool tubs, fireplaces, fine decor and lavish king beds. Some rooms have French doors that open to sweeping views of Narragansett Bay. A gourmet breakfast and complimentary afternoon tea are provided.

Innkeeper(s): Paul O'Reilly. $135-450. MC, VISA, AX, DS, TC. 35 rooms with PB and 10 cottages. Type of meal: Full bkfst. Afternoon tea, dinner and lunch available. Restaurant on premises. Beds: KD. Phone in room.

Clarkeston

28 Clarke St
Newport, RI 02840-3024
(401)848-5300 (800)524-1386 Fax:(401)847-7630

Circa 1705. Built at the turn of the 18th century, this charcoal-gray Colonial is one of the oldest in Newport. The inn features nine elegant guest rooms, each one individually decorated. Furnishings include sleigh, four-poster and canopy beds. Five of the rooms include a fireplace and whirlpool tub. Breakfasts include fresh fruit and entrees such as French toast or apple-cinnamon pancakes. The inn is just two blocks from the harbor.

Historic Interest: Trinity Church (1/4 mile).

Innkeeper(s): Ric Farrick. $95-265. MC, VISA, AX, PC, TC. 9 rooms with PB, 5 with FP. Breakfast included in rates. Types of meals: Full bkfst, veg bkfst and early coffee/tea. Beds: KQT. Cable TV in room. Air conditioning. Fax, copier and jacuzzi tubs on premises. Handicap access. Weddings, small meetings, family reunions and seminars hosted. Antiquing, art galleries, beaches, bicycling, canoeing/kayaking, fishing, golf, horseback riding, live theater, museums, shopping, tennis, water sports and wineries nearby.

Cliffside Inn

2 Seaview Ave
Newport, RI 02840-3627
(401)847-1811 (800)845-1811 Fax:(401)848-5850
E-mail: cliff@wsii.com
Web: www.cliffsideinn.com

Circa 1880. The governor of Maryland, Thomas Swann, built this Newport summer house in the style of a Second Empire Victorian. It features a mansard roof and many bay windows.
The rooms are decorated in a Victorian motif. Suites have marble baths, and all rooms have fireplaces. Fifteen rooms have a double whirlpool tub. The Cliff Walk is located one block from the inn.

Innkeeper(s): Stephan Nicolas. $195-480. MC, VISA, AX, DC, DS, PC, TC. TAC10. 15 rooms, 16 with PB, 16 with FP, 8 suites and 1 cottage. Breakfast and afternoon tea included in rates. Types of meals: Full gourmet bkfst and early coffee/tea. Beds: KQ. Cable TV, phone, turndown service, ceiling fan and VCR in room. Air conditioning. Fax on premises. French spoken. Antiquing, fishing, live theater, shopping and water sports nearby.

Publicity: Country Inns, Philadelphia, Discerning Traveler, New York, Boston, Good Morning America, Featured on "Great Country Inns."

"...it captures the grandeur of the Victorian age."

Francis Malbone House

392 Thames St
Newport, RI 02840-6604
(401)846-0392 (800)846-0392 Fax:(401)848-5956

Circa 1760. Newport, during the 18th century, was one of the busiest harbors in the Colonies. A shipping merchant, Colonel

Francis Malbone, built the historic portion of this home, which includes nine of the inn's 18 guest rooms. The newer addition was completed in 1996.
Fine furnishings fill the rooms, most of which offer a fireplace. Eleven rooms include a Jacuzzi tub. The inn's location, on the harborfront, is another wonderful feature. The breakfasts, heralded by Bon Appetit, include entrees such as pecan waffles with maple whipped cream or eggs Benedict with a roasted red pepper hollandaise. Guests are sure to be busy exploring Newport with its abundance of historic sites and spectacular mansions.

Innkeeper(s): Will Dewey & Mark & Jasminka Eads. $155-395. MC, VISA, AX. TAC10. 18 rooms with PB, 15 with FP, 2 suites and 5 conference rooms. Breakfast and afternoon tea included in rates. Type of meal: Full gourmet bkfst. Beds: KQ. Phone, turndown service and TV (most rooms) in room. Air conditioning. Fax on premises. Handicap access. Small meetings hosted. Antiquing, golf, mansion tours, parks, shopping and tennis nearby.

Hydrangea House Inn

16 Bellevue Ave
Newport, RI 02840-3206
(401)846-4435 (800)945-4667 Fax:(401)846-6602
E-mail: hydrangeahouse@home.com
Web: www.hydrangeahouse.com

The scent of fresh flowers welcomes guests into their cheery rooms at this B&B, which once housed a school of music. After abdicating his throne, King Edward was a guest at this home. Romance is emphasized by the decor in each of the individually appointed guest rooms, which feature wicker and antique furnishings. Breakfasts are served on the veranda, with its view of the gardens. In cooler weather, the breakfast buffet is set up in the art gallery, which features many original works.

Innkeeper(s): Grant Edmondson. $125-280. MC, VISA, AX. 6 rooms. Breakfast included in rates. Type of meal: Full bkfst. Afternoon tea available.

Inntowne Inn

6 Mary St
Newport, RI 02840-3028
(401)846-9200 (800)457-7803 Fax:(401)846-1534

Circa 1935. This Colonial-style inn is an elegant spot from which to enjoy the seaside town of Newport. Waverly and Laura Ashley prints decorate the individually appointed guest rooms, some of which have four-poster or canopy beds. The innkeeper serves an expanded continental breakfast with items such as fresh fruit, quiche and ham and cheese croissants. Afternoon tea also is served. A day in Newport offers many activities, including touring the Tennis Hall of Fame, taking a cruise through the harbor, shopping for antiques or perhaps taking a trek down Cliff Walk, a one-and-a-half-mile path offering the ocean on one side and historic mansions on the other. Parking is included in the rates.

Innkeeper(s): Carmella Gardner. $95-224. MC, VISA, AX. 26 rooms with PB and 1 suite. Afternoon tea included in rates. Type of meal: Cont plus. Beds: KQDT. Phone in room. Air conditioning. VCR, fax, copier and parking included in rates on premises. Weddings, small meetings and family reunions hosted. Antiquing, parks and shopping nearby.

"Thank you for your excellent service with a smile."

Marshall Slocum Guest House

29 Kay St
Newport, RI 02840-2735
(401)841-5120 (800)372-5120 Fax:(401)846-3787
E-mail: marshallslocuminn@edgenet.net
Web: www.marshallslocuminn.com

Circa 1855. Victorian homes line the streets in the Historic Hill District of Newport, where this two-and-a-half-story house is situated on an acre of grounds. Architectural features include shutters, a hip roof with dormer windows and a front porch. The inn is furnished with antiques and contemporary pieces. A favorite breakfast is Fluffy Belgian Waffles served with freshly picked strawberries and mountains of whipped cream. Don't miss the afternoon refreshments, and if you are staying longer than two nights ask about the innkeepers' Lobster Dinner Package. A five- to 10-minute walk will take you to the downtown area and the beach.

Innkeeper(s): Joan & Julie Wilson. $79-165. MC, VISA, AX, PC, TC. TAC10. 5 rooms with PB, 2 with FP. Breakfast and snacks/refreshments included in rates. Type of meal: Full gourmet bkfst. Dinner available. Beds: KQT. Ceiling fan in room. Air conditioning. VCR, fax, bicycles and library on premises. Weddings, small meetings and seminars hosted. Amusement parks, antiquing, fishing, golf, live theater, parks, shopping, sporting events, tennis and water sports nearby.

The Melville House

39 Clarke St
Newport, RI 02840-3023
(401)847-0640 Fax:(401)847-0956
E-mail: innkeeper@ids.net
Web: www.melvillehouse.com

Circa 1750. This attractive, National Register two-story Colonial inn once housed aides to General Rochambeau during the American Revolution. Early American furnishings decorate the interior. There is also an unusual collection of old appliances, including a cherry-pitter, mincer and dough maker. A full breakfast includes Portuguese Quiche, Jonnycakes, homemade bread and berry-stuffed French toast. The inn is a pleasant walk from the waterfront and historic sites.

Historic Interest: Vernon House (across the street).

Innkeeper(s): Vincent DeRico &Christine Leone. $85-165. MC, VISA, AX, DS, PC, TC. TAC10. 7 rooms, 5 with PB, 1 with FP and 1 suite. Breakfast and afternoon tea included in rates. Types of meals: Full gourmet bkfst and early coffee/tea. Picnic lunch available. Beds: KDT. Air conditioning. Fax and bicycles on premises. Small meetings, family reunions and seminars hosted. Antiquing, fishing, live theater, parks, shopping and water sports nearby.

"Comfortable with a quiet elegance."

Mill Street Inn

75 Mill St
Newport, RI 02840-3147
(401)849-9500 (800)392-1316 Fax:(401)848-5131
Web: www.millstreetinn.com

Circa 1820. Toil has given way to luxury in this converted 19th-century mill, decorated in an airy, ultra-modern design. All the rooms are suites, and many have decks with spectacular views of downtown Newport and the harbor. The exposed bricks and beams provide a rustic reminder of the mill's industrious past.

Historic Interest: Trinity Church, Newport History Museum, Newport Artillery Museum, International Tennis Hall of Fame (within blocks).

Innkeeper(s): Janice McHenry. $65-325. MC, VISA, AX, DC, CB, PC, TC. 23 suites and 1 conference room. Breakfast and afternoon tea included in rates. Type of meal: Cont plus. Catering service available. Beds: KQ. Fax and copier on premises. Handicap access. Antiquing, fishing and water sports nearby.

The Pilgrim House

123 Spring St
Newport, RI 02840-6805
(401)846-0040 (800)525-8373 Fax:(401)848-0357

Circa 1879. This Victorian inn, located in the heart of Newport, has a rooftop deck with a panoramic view of the harbor. The home is within walking distance of shops, restaurants, the Cliff Walk and the Newport mansions. In the afternoon, the innkeepers serve sherry and shortbread in the living room, which often is warmed by a crackling fire.

Historic Interest: Touro Synagogue, Trinity Church, Newport Harbor (1 block), Tennis Hall of Fame (3 blocks).

Innkeeper(s): Pam & Bruce Bayuk. $65-165. MC, VISA, PC. TAC10. 10 rooms, 8 with PB and 1 conference room. Breakfast and afternoon tea included in rates. Types of meals: Cont plus, cont and early coffee/tea. Beds: QDT. TV and phone in room. Air conditioning. Fax and copier on premises. Small meetings, family reunions and seminars hosted. Antiquing, fishing, live theater, parks, shopping and water sports nearby.

Publicity: *The Times.*

"What can I say, it's a perfect hideaway. Great time was had by all."

Queen Anne Inn

16 Clarke St
Newport, RI 02840-3024
(401)846-5676 (888)407-1616 Fax:(401)841-8509
E-mail: queenanne@prodigy.net
Web: www.queenanneinnnewport.com

Circa 1900. Located in one of Newport's oldest neighborhoods, this Victorian is just a few blocks from the waterfront and the downtown area. The garden-covered grounds and peaceful residential setting create a pleasing serenity for those in search of relaxation. Every home on the street is listed in the National Register. As it is just steps from the water, the innkeepers chose to decorate the inn in a nautical theme. In addition to the continental breakfast, which features items such as croissants and fresh pastries, afternoon tea is served each day. Museums and the famed mansions of Newport are among the town's attractions.

Historic Interest: Artillery, Touro Synagogue (2 blocks), Museum of Newport History (2 blocks), Fort Adams (5 miles).

Innkeeper(s): Flavia Gardiner. $110-175. MC, VISA, AX, PC, TC. 10 rooms, 6 with PB and 1 suite. Breakfast and afternoon tea included in rates. Types of meals: Cont and early coffee/tea. Beds: KQT. Air conditioning. VCR, fax, copier, modem hook-up and parking on premises. Weddings, family reunions and seminars hosted. Spanish and Portuguese spoken. Antiquing, art galleries, beaches, bicycling, canoeing/kayaking, fishing, golf, hiking, horseback riding, 12 meter sailing and power yachting, live theater, museums, parks, shopping, tennis, water sports and wineries nearby.

The Inn at Shadow Lawn

120 Miantonomi Ave
Newport, RI 02842-5450
(401)847-0902 (800)352-3750 Fax:(401)848-6529
E-mail: randy@shadowlawn.com
Web: www.shadowlawn.com

Circa 1855. This elegant, three-story Stick Victorian inn, listed in the National Register, offers a glimpse of fine living in an earlier age. The innkeepers' attention to detail is evident throughout, with French crystal chandeliers, stained-glass windows and parquet floors in the library as a few of the highlights. Parlors are found on each of the inn's floors. Newport's many attractions,

including the Art Museum, sailing and the world famous Newport mansions are just a short drive from the inn.

Historic Interest: Mansions from "Gilded Age" (5 minutes).

Innkeeper(s): Randy & Selma Fabricant. $85-195. MC, VISA, AX, TC. 8 rooms with PB, 8 with FP and 3 conference rooms. Breakfast included in rates. Type of meal: Full bkfst. Beds: KQ. Cable TV, phone and VCR in room. Air conditioning. Fax, copier and library on premises. Weddings, small meetings, family reunions and seminars hosted. Antiquing and mansions and sailing nearby.

"A dream come true! Thanks for everything! We'll be back."

Stella Maris Inn

91 Washington
Newport, RI 02840
(401)849-2862

Circa 1861. Made of stone with black walnut woodwork inside, this is a French Victorian with mansard roof and wraparound veranda. The inn's two acres are landscaped with flower beds. Bright yet elegant wall coverings and fabrics set off the antiques, paintings and interior architectural points of interest. In the National Register, the inn is an early Newport mansion that was originally called "Blue Rocks". It later became a convent at which time it was renamed Stella Maris, "star of the sea". Several of the inn's lavishly appointed rooms offer ocean views, and some have fireplaces.

Innkeeper(s): Dorothy & Ed Madden. $75-195. PC, TC. 9 rooms with PB, 4 with FP and 1 cottage. Breakfast and afternoon tea included in rates. Types of meals: Cont plus and early coffee/tea. Beds: KQDT. Ceiling fan and fireplace in four rooms in room. Library on premises. Small meetings and family reunions hosted. French spoken. Antiquing, fishing, golf, live theater, parks, shopping, tennis and water sports nearby.

"Rejuvenation for the soul!"

Victorian Ladies Inn

63 Memorial Blvd
Newport, RI 02840-3629
(401)849-9960 Fax:(401)849-9960

Circa 1850. Guests of this restored three-story Victorian building can stroll to Newport's beaches, the Cliff Walk, the Colonial town and the harbor front. At the Victorian Ladies, a charming latticed courtyard connects the main house to the smaller house in back. Reproduction period furniture, crystal and lush floral prints add to the Victorian ambiance in the rooms that innkeeper Helene O'Neill decorated.

Innkeeper(s): Donald & Helene O'Neill. $95-225. MC, VISA. 11 rooms with PB. Breakfast included in rates. Type of meal: Full gourmet bkfst. Beds: KQ. Cable TV and phone in room. Air conditioning. Fax and copier on premises. Weddings, small meetings and family reunions hosted. Antiquing, fishing, golf, live theater, parks, shopping, sporting events and tennis nearby.

"We want to move in!"

Willows of Newport - Romantic Inn & Garden

8-10 Willow St, Historic Point
Newport, RI 02840-1927
(401)846-5486 Fax:(401)849-8215
Web: www.newportri.com/users/willows

Circa 1740. There's little wonder why this inn is known as The Romantic Inn. The spectacular secret garden, with its abundance of foliage, colorful blooms and a heart-shaped fish pond, is a popular stop on Newport's Secret Garden Tour. The inn is a three-time recipient of the Newport Best Garden Award. The French Quarter Queen room and Canopy Room both boast views of the gardens, and guests awake to the fragrances of the many flowers. The romantic Victorian Wedding Room, decorated in pastel greens and rose, offers a queen canopy bed, hand-painted furniture and a fireplace. The Colonial Wedding Room features lace accents, a hand-crafted king bed and an original 1740s fireplace. A continental breakfast is delivered to your room on bone china with silver services. Innkeeper Pattie Murphy, aside from her gardening and decorating skills, is a native Newporter and is full of information about the city. Ask about the inn's new "Silk & Chandelier" collection.

Historic Interest: The home is listed as National Landmark. Newport is the home of the Touro Synagogue, the oldest Jewish house of worship in North America. The Tennis Hall of Fame and the nation's oldest library, Redwood, are popular attractions. Don't forget to visit the nation's oldest operating tavern, The White Horse Tavern, which first opened in 1687. Sunset sailing and a variety of popular restaurants are located nearby.

Innkeeper(s): Patricia 'Pattie' Murphy. $128-325. PC, TC. TAC10. 7 rooms with PB. Breakfast and snacks/refreshments included in rates. Type of meal: Cont plus. Beds: KQD. Air conditioning. Award-winning secret garden on premises. Antiquing, fishing, mansions, sunset sailing nearby, parks, shopping and water sports nearby.

"We enjoyed our getaway in your inn for its peace, elegance and emphasis on romance."

Providence
C6

Historic Jacob Hill Farm B&B/Inn

PO Box 41326
Providence, RI 02940
(508)336-9165 (888)336-9165 Fax:(508)336-0951

Circa 1722. This historic Colonial home overlooks 50 acres and is located three miles outside Providence. In the '20s and '30s, it was the Jacob Hill Hunt Club and hosted the

Vanderbilts during hunts and horse shows. Beamed ceilings, wall paintings of horse and hunting scenes and rare Southern long-

leaf pine floors create the gracious setting. Guest rooms may include a canopy bed, fireplace or whirlpool tub. Enjoy the inn's stable of horses or take a riding lesson, then relax in the gazebo at sunset. Stuffed French toast with whipped cream and strawberries is often served in the original kitchen area with its large beehive fireplace.

Innkeeper(s): Bill & Eleonora Rezek. $110-225. MC, VISA, AX, DS, PC, TC. TAC10. 6 rooms with PB, 3 with FP and 3 suites. Breakfast and snacks/refreshments included in rates. Types of meals: Full gourmet bkfst and early coffee/tea. Beds: KQDT. Cable TV, phone, turndown service, VCR and whirlpools in room. Air conditioning. Fax, swimming, stables, tennis and library on premises. Handicap access. Small meetings hosted. Polish spoken. Antiquing, fishing, golf, live theater, parks, sporting events and tennis nearby.

Old Court B&B

144 Benefit St
Providence, RI 02903-1226
(401)751-2002 Fax:(401)272-4830

Circa 1863. Adjacent to the historic Rhode Island Courthouse, this Italianate building originally served as an Episcopal rectory. Indoor shutters, chandeliers hanging from 12-foot ceilings and elaborate Italian marble mantelpieces provide the gracious setting for antique Victorian beds. Some rooms overlook the capitol. Brown University, Rhode Island School of Design and downtown Providence are a short walk away.

Innkeeper(s): Jon Rosenblatt. $115-260. TAC1. 10 rooms with PB. Breakfast included in rates. Type of meal: Full gourmet bkfst. Beds: KQDT. Phone and some refrigerators in room. Air conditioning. Fax and copier on premises. Weddings and small meetings hosted. Antiquing, live theater, parks, shopping and sporting events nearby.

Publicity: *New York Times.*

"My only suggestion is that you do everything in your power not to change it."

State House Inn

43 Jewett St
Providence, RI 02908-4904
(401)351-6111 Fax:(401)351-4261
E-mail: statehouseinn@edgenet.net
Web: www.providence-inn.com

Circa 1889. Shaker and Colonial furniture fill this turn-of-the-century home, located in the midst of a quaint and peaceful Providence neighborhood. The rooms provide amenities that will please any business traveler and have the country comfort and elegance of days gone by. The common room contains a

small library for guest use. A famed historic district, featuring restored homes and buildings, is three blocks away, and the capitol is a five-minute walk.

Innkeeper(s): Frank & Monica Hopton. $89-149. MC, VISA, AX, PC, TC. TAC10. 10 rooms with PB, 2 with FP. Breakfast included in rates. EP. Type of meal: Full bkfst. Afternoon tea available. Beds: KQ. Cable TV and phone in room. Air conditioning. Fax and copier on premises. Antiquing and parks nearby.

Publicity: *Providence Magazine.*

"Thank you again for the warm, comfortable and very attractive accommodations."

South Kingstown
H5

Admiral Dewey Inn

668 Matunuck Beach Rd
South Kingstown, RI 02879-7053
(401)783-2090 (800)457-2090
Web: www.admiraldeweyinn.com

Circa 1898. Although the prices have risen a bit since this inn's days as a boarding house (the rate was 50 cents per night), this Stick-style home still offers hospitality and comfort. The National Register inn is within walking distance of Matunuck Beach. Guests can enjoy the sea breeze from the inn's wraparound porch. Period antiques decorate the guest rooms, some of which offer ocean views.

Historic Interest: One half mile to Historic Theatre By The Sea.

Innkeeper(s): Joan Lebel. $100-150. MC, VISA, PC. 10 rooms, 8 with PB. Breakfast included in rates. Types of meals: Cont plus and early coffee/tea. Picnic lunch available. Beds: QDT. VCR, fax and copier on premises. Weddings, small meetings, family reunions and seminars hosted. Polish spoken. Antiquing, fishing, live theater, parks, shopping and water sports nearby.

Wakefield
H5

Larchwood Inn

521 Main St
Wakefield, RI 02879-4003
(401)783-5454 (800)275-5450 Fax:(401)783-1800
E-mail: larchwoodinn@xpos.com
Web: www.xpos.com/larchwoodinn.htm

Circa 1831. The Larchwood Inn and its adjacent sister inn, Holly House, were both constructed in the same era. The two are sprinkled with antiques and are family-run, with 20th-century amenities. Scottish touches are found throughout the inn and the Tam O'Shanter Tavern.

Three dining rooms offer breakfast, lunch and dinner. (Breakfast is an extra charge.) The tavern offers dancing on weekends. Beaches, sailing and deep sea fishing all are nearby.

Innkeeper(s): Francis & Diann Browning. $40-120. MC, VISA, AX, DC, CB, DS. 19 rooms, 13 with PB, 3 with FP and 1 conference room. Type of meal: Full bkfst. Dinner, lunch and banquet service available. Phone in room. Fax and copier on premises. Weddings, small meetings, family reunions and seminars hosted. Antiquing, live theater, shopping, downhill skiing and cross-country skiing nearby.

Westerly   I2

Kismet On-Park B&B

71 High St
Westerly, RI 02891-1812
(401)596-3237 Fax:(401)348-9988

Circa 1845. Book on just the right summer night at this inn
and you may find yourself listening to summer pops or an old-
time band concert from a ring-side seat. This Colonial home
boasts a long front veranda lined with rocking chairs and summer furnishings just across from Wilcox Park. The Victorian
home is filled with antiques and a collection of wicker furnishings and is in the National Register of Historic Places. A light
breakfast is served and the kitchen is open other times as well
to guests during their stay. Shakespeare in the Park and other
events are popular at the park or walk to nearby shops, galleries, the Colonial Theater or the train station. Rhode Island
beaches and water activities are close by.

Innkeeper(s): Cindy Slay. Call for rates. 4 rooms, 1 with PB, 1 suite and 1
conference room. Beds: KQDT.

Shelter Harbor Inn

10 Wagner Rd
Westerly, RI 02891-4701
(401)322-8883 (800)468-8883 Fax:(401)322-7907

Circa 1810. This farmhouse at the entrance to the community
of Shelter Harbor has been renovated and transformed to create
a handsome country inn. Rooms, many with fireplaces, are in
the main house, the
barn and a car-
riage house. A
third-floor deck
with a hot tub,
overlooks Block
Island Sound. The
dining room features local
seafood and other traditional New England dishes. Nearby are
secluded barrier beaches, stone fences and salt ponds.

Innkeeper(s): Jim Dey. $78-156. MC, VISA, AX, DC, CB, DS. 24 rooms with
PB and 1 conference room. Breakfast included in rates. Type of meal: Full
bkfst. Dinner, lunch and catering service available. Restaurant on premises.
Beds: QD. Phone in room. Air conditioning. VCR and spa on premises.
Weddings, small meetings and family reunions hosted. Amusement parks,
antiquing, fishing, golf, beach nearby, croquet, paddle tennis, shopping and
tennis nearby.

Publicity: *Rhode Island Monthly, The Day.*

"This inn was, on the whole, wonderful."

South Carolina

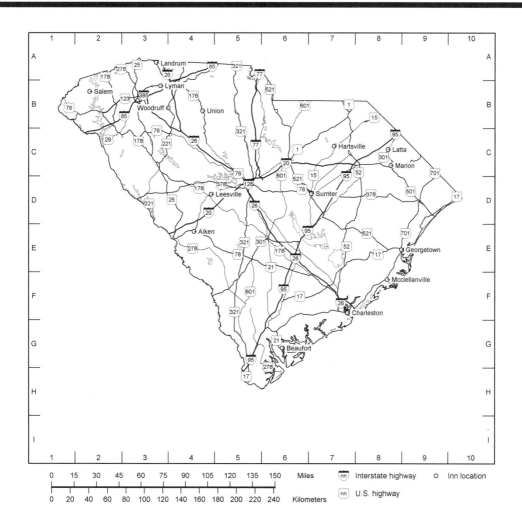

0 15 30 45 60 75 90 105 120 135 150 Miles

0 20 40 60 80 100 120 140 160 180 200 220 240 Kilometers

Interstate highway   o Inn location

U.S. highway

Aiken
E4

White House Inn

240 Newberry St SW
Aiken, SC 29801-3854
(803)649-2935

Circa 1924. History lovers will appreciate this inn's location, surrounded by three historic districts in the village of Old Aiken. The acre of grounds is dotted with many trees and a large gazebo, often the site for weddings. The Dutch Colonial is

furnished with antiques, and two rooms include a fireplace. Omelets, breakfast meats, freshly baked breads and seasonal fruit are among the morning offerings.

Innkeeper(s): Hal & Mary Ann Mackey. $70-225. MC, VISA, AX, DC, DS, PC, TC. TAC5. 4 rooms with PB, 2 with FP. Breakfast included in rates. Type of meal: Full bkfst. Beds: Q. Cable TV, phone, ceiling fan and fireplace two rooms in room. Air conditioning. Gazebo on premises. Weddings, small meetings, family reunions and seminars hosted. German, French and Spanish spoken. Antiquing, golf, golf, horseback riding, live theater, parks, shopping and water sports nearby.

"You should be congratulated. Keep it up."

Beaufort
G6

The Cuthbert House Inn B&B

1203 Bay St
Beaufort, SC 29902-5401
(843)521-1315 (800)327-9275 Fax:(843)521-1314
E-mail: cuthbert@hargray.com
Web: www.cuthberthouseinn.com

Circa 1790. This 18th-century waterfront mansion, listed in the National Register, boasts a veranda overlooking Beaufort Bay. The home was built during Washington's presidency, and General W.T. Sherman was once a guest here. The home has been lovingly restored to its original grandeur. Rich painted walls are highlighted by fine molding. Hardwood floors are topped with Oriental rugs and elegant 19th-century furnishings. The morning meal is served in a breakfast room that overlooks the water. The surrounding area offers plenty of activities in every season, and for those celebrating a new marriage, a honeymoon package is available.

Historic Interest: Located in the National Landmark district.

Innkeeper(s): Gary & Sharon Groves. $135-225. MC, VISA, AX, DS, PC, TC. TAC10. 7 rooms with PB, 2 suites and 2 conference rooms. Breakfast included in rates. Types of meals: Full bkfst, cont and early coffee/tea. Beds: KQDT. Cable TV, phone, turndown service, mini bar, robes and hair dryers in room. Air conditioning. VCR, fax, bicycles, library, modem, whirlpool, off street parking and beach towels on premises. Weddings, small meetings, family reunions and seminars hosted. Antiquing, fishing, Parris Island USMC Depot, Ace Basin Tours, parks and water sports nearby.

Publicity: *Atlanta Journal-Constitution, Glamour, Travel & Leisure, House & Garden Channel.*

The Rhett House Inn

1009 Craven St
Beaufort, SC 29902-5577
(843)524-9030 (888)480-9530 Fax:(843)524-1310

Circa 1820. Most people cannot pass this stunning two-story clapboard house without wanting to step up to the long veranda and try the hammock. Guest rooms are furnished in antiques,

with quilts, fresh flowers and eight of the rooms offer private Jacuzzi tubs. Many bedrooms have fireplaces and some have a history of famous guests such as Barbra Streisand, Dennis Quaid and Nick Nolte. Handsome gardens feature a fountain and are often the site for romantic weddings. Bicycles are available.

Historic Interest: The inn is listed in the National Register.

Innkeeper(s): Stephen Harrison. $150-250. MC, VISA, AX. 17 rooms with PB, 8 with FP. Breakfast and afternoon tea included in rates. Types of meals: Full bkfst and early coffee/tea. Snacks/refreshments, picnic lunch, catering service and room service available. Beds: KQ. Cable TV, phone, turndown service, ceiling fan and eight rooms with Jacuzzi tubs in room. Air conditioning. Fax on premises. Handicap access. Weddings, small meetings, family reunions and seminars hosted. Antiquing, fishing, golf, live theater, tennis and water sports nearby.

Publicity: *New York Times, Vogue, Elle, Conde Nast Traveler, Travel & Leisure, Self, Brides, Martha Stewart.*

TwoSuns Inn B&B

1705 Bay St
Beaufort, SC 29902-5406
(843)522-1122 (800)532-4244 Fax:(843)522-1122
E-mail: twosuns@islc.net
Web: www.twosunsinn.com

Circa 1917. The Keyserling family built this Neoclassical Revival-style home, which was later used by the local board of education as housing for single, female teachers. The home has been completely refurbished, a difficult task, considering the home had been the victim of two fires. The U.S. Department of the Interior noted the renovation with a Historic Building Certification in 1996. Guest rooms boast bay views, and each has its own theme. A gourmet breakfast and "Tea and Toddy Hour" are included in the rates.

Innkeeper(s): Ron & Carrol Kay. $105-155. MC, VISA, AX, DS, PC, TC. TAC10. 6 rooms with PB and 1 conference room. Breakfast and afternoon tea included in rates. Type of meal: Full bkfst. Beds: KQT. Phone, ceiling fan, tV available and hair dryer in room. Air conditioning. VCR, fax, copier, bicycles and library on premises. Handicap access. Antiquing, fishing, golf, live theater, parks, shopping and tennis nearby.

"One could not wish for a better experience."

Charleston F7

Antebellum B&B at The Thomas Lamboll House

19 King St
Charleston, SC 29401-2734
(803)723-3212 (888)874-0793 Fax:(803)723-5222

Circa 1735. A Colonial South Carolina judge, Thomas Lamboll, was the first resident of this impressive Colonial, located in Charleston's historic district. The home features two stories of piazzas set up with  wicker furnishings, where guests can catch a cool breeze in the afternoon. The rooms are appointed with fine antiques, including Chippendale chairs and an early 19th-century sideboard in the dining room. There are two guest rooms, each with French doors leading to the piazzas, that overlook rooftops and the river in the distance.

Innkeeper(s): Marie & Emerson Read. $100-155. MC, VISA, DS, PC, TC. 2 rooms with PB, 2 with FP and 1 suite. Breakfast included in rates. Type of meal: Cont. Beds: QT. Cable TV, phone and ceiling fan in room. Air conditioning. Amusement parks, antiquing, fishing, live theater, parks, shopping, sporting events and water sports nearby.

Ashley Inn B&B

201 Ashley Ave
Charleston, SC 29403-5810
(843)723-1848 (800)581-6658 Fax:(843)579-9080
E-mail: ashley@cchat.com
Web: www.charleston-sc-inns.com

Circa 1832. Pampering guests is the specialty of the house at this bed & breakfast. The rose exterior has green shutters and porches on the first and second stories. Bright, colorful rooms are accented by polished, hardwood floors, beautiful rugs and glorious furnishings and collectibles. Guest rooms boast antique four-poster, pencil-post or canopied rice beds. Breakfasts at Ashley Inn create culinary memories. Savory sausage pie,  Crunchy French Toast with orange honey sauce or Ashley Inn Welsh Rarebit are only a few of the mouth-watering specialties. An afternoon complete with plenty of homemade treats and evening sherry also is served. The innkeepers also provide bicycles for touring scenic Charleston.

Historic Interest: The inn is located in the Charleston historic district, full of interesting sites and shops. Ft. Sumter, The Battery, cabbage row, carriage tours are nearby.

Innkeeper(s): Sally & Bud Allen. $69-190. MC, VISA, AX, DS, PC, TC. TAC10. 7 rooms with PB and 1 suite. Breakfast and afternoon tea included in rates. Type of meal: Full bkfst. Gourmet dinner available. Beds: KQT. Antiquing, fishing, live theater and water sports nearby.

"A truly pampering experience for both of us!"

Battery Carriage House Inn

20 S Battery St
Charleston, SC 29401-2727
(803)727-3100 (800)775-5575 Fax:(803)727-3130

Circa 1843. Just outside the door of this antebellum house, guests can enjoy the serenity of a Charleston garden. And outside the wrought iron gates lies beautiful White Point Gardens, the Battery and Charleston Harbor. Renovations in many rooms have preserved the charm of the past, while increasing amenities, including cable television and steam baths or  Jacuzzis that add to the inn's romantic atmosphere. The inn was used in the filming of "North and South" and the interior rooms have been filmed for "Queen." In the afternoon, visitors can enjoy a glass of wine in the gardens.

Historic Interest: Fort Sumter and Plantations are nearby.

$129-250. MC, VISA, AX, DS, TC. 11 rooms with PB. Breakfast included in rates. Type of meal: Cont. Beds: KQT. Cable TV, phone, turndown service, ceiling fan and steam bath showers in room. Air conditioning. Fax on premises. Antiquing, fishing, live theater, parks, shopping, sporting events and water sports nearby.

Belvedere B&B

40 Rutledge Ave
Charleston, SC 29401-1702
(843)722-0973 (800)816-1664
Web: www.belvedereinn.com

Circa 1900. This Colonial Revival home with its semicircular portico, Ionic columns and four piazzas boasts a beautiful view of Charleston's Colonial Lake. Bright, airy rooms feature high ceilings with fans, polished wood floors, fireplaces, antique furnishings and Oriental rugs. Relax and enjoy the view on the piazzas or in one of the inn's public rooms. Belvedere B&B is close to many wonderful restaurants and shops.

Innkeeper(s): David S. Spell. $150-175. PC, TC. 3 rooms with PB. Breakfast included in rates. Type of meal: Cont plus. Beds: Q. Cable TV, ceiling fan and ornamental fireplaces in room. Air conditioning. VCR and refrigerator on premises. Antiquing, fishing, live theater, parks, shopping, sporting events and water sports nearby.

Publicity: *Discerning Traveler, Southern Brides.*

Cannonboro Inn

184 Ashley Ave
Charleston, SC 29403-5824
(803)723-8572 (800)235-8039 Fax:(803)723-8007
E-mail: Cannon@cchat.com
Web: www.charleston-sc-inns.com

Circa 1853. Enjoy a breakfast feast of Cannonboro Inn Eggs Benedict served with warm French puff muffins and local fresh fruit on the columned piazza overlooking the country garden and fountain. Guest rooms feature luxurious furnishings and antique four-poster and canopy beds. After a day in the city on the inn's touring bicycles, return for a scrumptious afternoon tea of home-baked treats and sherry. Cannonboro Inn has been rated as one of the best places to stay in the South.

Historic Interest: The Charleston Museum, Gibbes Museum and Rice Museum are nearby.

Innkeeper(s): Bud & Sally Allen, Lynn Bartosh. $69-190. MC, VISA, AX, DS, PC, TC. TAC10. 6 rooms with PB and 1 suite. Breakfast and afternoon tea included in rates. Type of meal: Full bkfst. Beds: KQD. Cable TV and ceiling fan in room. Air conditioning. Bicycles and free off street parking on premises. Antiquing, fishing, golf, carriage rides, harbor tours, live theater, parks, shopping, sporting events, tennis and water sports nearby.

"A brochure cannot convey the friendly, warm atmosphere created by Bud & Sally."

Charleston's Vendue Inn

19 Vendue Range
Charleston, SC 29401-2129
(843)577-7970 (800)845-7900
E-mail: vendueinn@navi-gator.com
Web: www.charlestonvendueinn.com

Circa 1864. Created from French Quarter warehouses, Vendue Inn is in the center of Charleston's historic district and one short block from the historic harbor and Waterfront Park. The bright lobby features polished pine floors, Oriental rugs, antiques and Low Country art. Fireplaces and marble Jacuzzi tubs with separate showers are offered in the spacious suites and many rooms offer harbor views. There are four-poster and canopy beds, luxurious bathrooms, French milled soaps, fresh flowers, two-line phones with data ports and many other amenities. The Garden Room with wicker furniture and lattice-work screens is the setting for afternoon wine and cheese and pleasant chamber music. Turndown service, a full Southern breakfast buffet, lunch and dinner are special features. (The inn's Library Restaurant offers American cuisine, and the Rooftop Terrace Bar is known for its beautiful sunset views of the harbor, passing sailboats and Ft. Sumter.) A friendly concierge can arrange carriage rides, historic walking tours and reservations for special events. Walk to fine antique shops, historic neighborhoods, art galleries and the Battery.

Innkeeper(s): Coyne & Linda Edmison. $120-275. MC, VISA, AX, DC, DS, PC, TC. 45 rooms with PB, 22 with FP. Breakfast included in rates. Type of meal: Full bkfst. Lunch and room service available. Restaurant on premises. Beds: KQD. Cable TV, turndown service and ceiling fan in room. Air conditioning. Fax, copier and fitness center on premises. Beaches, golf and live theater nearby.

East Bay B&B

301 E Bay St
Charleston, SC 29401-1532
(803)722-4186 Fax:(803)720-8528

Circa 1807. Acclaimed in Charleston as one of the most unique heritage properties in town, and located in the Historic District, East Bay is a Single House with a carriage house in the Federal style. Two large piazzas overlook the walled garden and the harbor. Phoebe Pember, Civil War heroine, was born here. Spacious guest rooms are filled with original art, antiques and fine fabrics. Some rooms offer canopied beds while others have a fully draped poster bed. Breakfast is provided on a silver tray

that may be enjoyed in the guest rooms, the dining room or on the piazza.

Innkeeper(s): Carolyn Rivers. $125-225. MC, VISA, PC. TAC10. 4 rooms, 2 suites, 2 cottages and 1 conference room. Breakfast included in rates. Types of meals: Cont plus and early coffee/tea. Room service available. Beds: KQT. Cable TV and phone in room. Air conditioning. VCR, fax and copier on premises. Small meetings hosted. Antiquing, fishing, medical University of SC, live theater, shopping and tennis nearby.

Fantasia B&B

11 George St
Charleston, SC 29401
(843)853-0201

Circa 1813. A hammock rests lazily at the edge of a covered veranda at this bed & breakfast, an invitation to guests that this is a place where they can relax and enjoy the Southern hospitality. Fantasia is located in Charleston's historic Ansonborough district, within walking distance to shops and historic homes and just two miles from Fort Sumter. The Greek Revival home dates prior to the Civil War. Two of the guest rooms include a fireplace. Each bedchamber is decorated with an eclectic mix of furnishings, including iron or four-poster beds. Breakfasts include a first course of fresh fruit followed by a special entrée, perhaps orange-yogurt pancakes served with a side of country bacon.

Historic Interest: Fort Sumter (2 miles), Patriots Point (2 miles).

Innkeeper(s): Martin & Catherine Riccio. $85-195. MC, VISA, AX, DS, PC. 6 rooms, 4 with PB, 2 with FP, 1 suite, 2 guest houses and 1 conference room. Breakfast included in rates. Type of meal: Cont. Beds: Q. Cable TV and ceiling fan in room. Central air. Piano on premises. Antiquing, art galleries, beaches, bicycling, canoeing/kayaking, fishing, golf, live theater, museums, parks, shopping and water sports nearby.

Fulton Lane Inn

202 King St
Charleston, SC 29401-3109
(843)720-2600 (800)720-2688 Fax:(843)720-2940

Circa 1870. The family of Confederate blockade runner John Rugheimer built this charming brick home after the Civil War ended. Bright cheery decor and fine furnishings highlight the architecture, which includes cathedral ceilings and several fireplaces. The inn affords views of the city skyline, full of historic sites and gracious, Southern buildings. Guest rooms boast canopy beds draped with hand-strung netting and large, whirlpool tubs. The innkeeper includes a stocked refrigerator in each room, and deliver breakfast on a silver tray. Wine and sherry are served in the lobby, and don't be surprised to find chocolates atop your pillow after you return from one of Charleston's many fine restaurants.

Historic Interest: Fulton Lane Inn is located in Charleston's historic district and the area abounds with historic sites.

Innkeeper(s): Beth Babcock. $130-285. MC, VISA, DC. TAC10. 27 rooms with PB, 8 with FP, 4 suites and 2 conference rooms. Breakfast included in rates. EP. Type of meal: Cont plus. Room service available. Beds: KQ. Cable TV, phone and turndown service in room. Air conditioning. Fax and child care on premises. Handicap access. Weddings, small meetings, family reunions and seminars hosted. Antiquing, fishing, live theater, parks, shopping and water sports nearby.

Historic Charleston B&B Reservation Service

57 Broad St
Charleston, SC 29401-2901
(843)722-6606 (800)743-3583 Fax:(843)722-9589

This bed & breakfast agency provides accommodations throughout Charleston's historic district. Rooms are located in private homes and carriage houses, offering a unique experience into the culture of Charleston. There are more than 50 different options; and guests can choose from accommodations such as two-bedroom cottages or romantic rooms with high-ceilings, fireplaces and family antiques. Some of the lodgings offer continental breakfasts, others might include a full breakfast. A member of the Historic Charleston Bed & Breakfast Reservation Service staff has inspected each of the locations.

$85-250. MC, VISA, PC. 50 rooms, 30 with PB, 6 with FP and 20 cottages. Breakfast included in rates. Types of meals: Full bkfst and cont. Beds: KQDT. TV and phone in room. Air conditioning. Bicycles are available at some locations on premises. Antiquing, fishing, parks, shopping and sporting events nearby.

John Rutledge House Inn

116 Broad St
Charleston, SC 29401-2437
(843)723-7999 (800)476-9741 Fax:(843)720-2615

Circa 1763. John Rutledge, first governor of South Carolina, Supreme Court Justice, and an author and signer of the Constitution of the United States, wrote first drafts of the document in the stately ballroom of his Charleston home. In 1791 George Washington dined in this same room. Both men would be amazed by the house's recent restoration, which includes three lavish suites with elaborately carved Italian marble fireplaces, personal refrigerators, spas, air conditioning and televisions along with fine antiques and reproductions. Exterior ironwork on the house was designed in the 19th century and features palmetto trees and American eagles to honor Mr. Rutledge's service to the state and country.

Innkeeper(s): Linda Bishop. $185-365. MC, VISA, AX, DC. TAC10. 19 rooms with PB, 8 with FP, 3 suites, 2 cottages and 1 conference room. Breakfast and afternoon tea included in rates. EP. Types of meals: Full bkfst and cont plus. Room service available. Beds: KQD. Cable TV, phone and turndown service in room. Air conditioning. Fax and child care on premises. Handicap access. Weddings, small meetings, family reunions and seminars hosted. Spanish spoken. Antiquing, fishing, live theater, parks, shopping and water sports nearby.

"Two hundred years of American history in two nights; first-class accommodations, great staff. John Rutledge should've had it so good!"

King George IV Inn

32 George St, Historic District
Charleston, SC 29401-1416
(843)723-9339 (888)723-1667 Fax:(843)723-7749

Circa 1792. This inn is a four-story Federal-style home with three levels of Charleston porches. All the rooms have decorative (non-working) fireplaces, high ceilings, original wide-planked hardwood floors and finely crafted original moldings and architectural

detail. Peter Freneau, who was a prominent Charleston journalist, merchant, ship owner and Jeffersonian politician, occupied the house for many years. The inn offers a hearty continental breakfast every morning. There is off-street parking available and King Street shopping and restaurants are just a short walk away.

Historic Interest: The inn is located in the United States' largest historic district with more than 3,000 historic homes and mansions.

Innkeeper(s): Debra, Terry. $89-169. MC, VISA, PC, TC. 10 rooms, 8 with PB, 9 with FP and 4 suites. Breakfast included in rates. Afternoon tea available. Beds: QDT. Phone and television in room. Air conditioning. Fax on premises. Small meetings and family reunions hosted. Antiquing, fishing, live theater, parks, shopping, sporting events and water sports nearby.

Kings Courtyard Inn

198 King St
Charleston, SC 29401-3109
(843)723-7000 (800)845-6119 Fax:(843)720-2608

Circa 1853. Having a Greek Revival style with unusual touches of Egyptian detail, this three-story building was designed by architect Francis D. Lee. The inn originally catered to plantation owners, shipping interests and merchant guests. Some of the rooms have fireplaces, canopied beds and views of the two inner courtyards or the garden. The building is one of historic King Street's largest and oldest structures and is at the center of Charleston's historic district.

Historic Interest: The home, which is listed in the National Register, is near all historic Charleston has to offer.

Innkeeper(s): Michelle Woodhull. $145-275. MC, VISA, AX, DC. TAC10. 41 rooms with PB, 13 with FP, 4 suites and 1 conference room. Breakfast included in rates. EP. Types of meals: Full bkfst and cont plus. Room service available. Beds: KQD. Cable TV, phone and turndown service in room. Air conditioning. Fax, copier, spa and child care on premises. Handicap access. Weddings, small meetings, family reunions and seminars hosted. Antiquing, fishing, live theater, parks, shopping and water sports nearby.

The Kitchen House

126 Tradd St
Charleston, SC 29401-2420
(843)577-6362 Fax:(843)965-5615

Circa 1732. This elegant, pre-Revolutionary War house was once the home of Dr. Peter Fayssoux, who served as Surgeon General in the Continental Army during the Revolutionary War. His descendant Bernard Elliot Bee became the Confederate general who bestowed the nickname of "Stonewall" to General Stonewall Jackson. The kitchen building has been restored around its four

original fireplaces using antique materials. The inn's patio overlooks a Colonial herb garden, pond and fountain. The pantry and refrigerator are stocked with breakfast items. Juice, cereals, eggs, fresh fruit, specialty teas and coffee are provided for guests. Afternoon sherry awaits guests on arrival and a concierge service is offered.

Historic Interest: Located in the heart of Charleston's historic district, the inn offers close access to many museum homes and antique shopping.

Innkeeper(s): Lois Evans. $150-250. MC, VISA, PC, TC. TAC5. 4 rooms with PB. Breakfast included in rates. Type of meal: Full bkfst. Beds: QT. Cable TV, phone and VCR in room. Air conditioning. Fax, copier, library and concierge Service on premises. Antiquing, fishing, golf, live theater, parks, shopping, sporting events, tennis and water sports nearby.

"By all comparisons, one of the very best."

Palmer Home

5 East Battery
Charleston, SC 29401-2740
(843)723-2308 (888)723-1574 Fax:(843)723-3904
E-mail: palmerbnb@aol.com

Circa 1849. With its magnificent view of the Charleston
Harbour and historic Fort Sumter, this pink and white
Italianesque mansion is one of 50 famous homes in the city.
The house features 30 rooms, 15 bedrooms, 10 fireplaces and
antiques dating back 200 years. The property includes the
main house, carriage house and pool. Little David, the first
submarine discharged during the war between the states was
invented in this house. Fresh-squeezed orange juice, croissants,
bagels and fresh fruit is offered each morning.

Innkeeper(s): Francess Palmer Hogan. $125-275. PC. 3 rooms with PB and
1 suite. Breakfast included in rates. Type of meal: Cont. Beds: KQD. Cable
TV, phone, ceiling fan and VCR in room. Air conditioning. Fax, swimming and
billiards on premises. Weddings and small meetings hosted. Antiquing, fishing, golf, live theater, parks, sporting events, tennis and water sports nearby.

Planters Inn

112 N Market St
Charleston, SC 29401-3118
(843)722-2345 (800)845-7082 Fax:(843)577-2125
E-mail: plantersinn@charleston.net
Web: www.plantersinn.com

Circa 1844. Prepare for a getaway of romance, elegance and
history at this opulent, four-diamond-rated inn, located in historic Charleston. Built decades prior to the Civil War, the inn
has watched Charleston grow and change. The interior displays
the height of Southern elegance and charm. Rooms are decorated with rich wallcoverings, elegant furnishings and four-poster
beds topped with the finest of linens. Breakfasts are delivered to
your door on a silver tray set with crystal, china and silver. The
inn's restaurant, Peninsula Grill, has been named one of the best
new restaurants in the country by Esquire magazine. Guests, if
they choose, may dine al fresco in a landscaped courtyard. The
innkeepers also offer romance and history packages.

Innkeeper(s): Larry Spelts, Jr. $125-350. MC, VISA, AX, DC, DS. 62 rooms
with PB. Type of meal: Cont. Restaurant on premises. Beds: KQ. Turndown
service in room. Air conditioning. Fax and copier on premises. Small meetings
hosted. Antiquing, live theater and shopping nearby.

Thirty Six Meeting Street

36 Meeting St
Charleston, SC 29401-2737
(843)722-1034 Fax:(843)423-0068

Circa 1740. The gracious craftsmanship of this Georgian
Charleston single house offers the best kind of Charleston experience. The historic home has a library, two piazzas with
columns and balusters and fine detailing in woodwork and staircase. The drawing room features a fireplace with mahogany fretwork. There's a two-bedroom suite in what was once the old
kitchen. It offers two fireplaces, including a 1740 fireplace with
finely carved mantel and molding. A mahogany four-poster rice
bed and European iron bed are the focal points of the bedrooms. The Pettigrew suite upstairs offers a Thomas Elfe rice
bed, a sitting area and a view of the garden of the former Royal
Governors House. Kitchenettes are in each suite and a continental breakfast is stocked in each room. There are bicycles to borrow, but walking offers a wealth of experience. Within a block

or two is the battery and White Point Gardens, the Nathaniel
Russell House Museum and the Calhoun Mansion House
Museum. The innkeepers are native Charlestonians.

Historic Interest: Fort Sumter.

Innkeeper(s): Vic & Anne Brandt. $85-160. MC, VISA, DS, PC, TC. 5 rooms,
1 with PB, 2 with FP and 2 suites. Breakfast included in rates. Type of meal:
Cont plus. Beds: Q. TV and phone in room. Central air. Fax and copier on
premises. Antiquing, art galleries, beaches, bicycling, canoeing/kayaking, fishing, golf, hiking, live theater, museums, parks, shopping, tennis and water
sports nearby.

Twenty Seven State Street B&B

27 State St
Charleston, SC 29401-2812
(843)722-4243

Circa 1800. Located in Charleston's distinctive French
Quarter, this inn offers comfort and the height of elegance at
the same time. Rooms are skillfully decorated with fine furnish-

ings. Polished wood floors are topped with
Oriental rugs. Rooms have four-
poster beds. The suites in
the carriage house overlook
the courtyard, and the rustic
interior features exposed
brick walls, antiques and
reproductions. Although the
inn does lend itself more
toward romance, the innkeepers happily provide for well-
behaved children in two of the suites. Breakfast is optional.

Innkeeper(s): Paul & Joye Craven. $110-180. PC, TC. 2 suites. Type of meal:
Cont plus. Beds: Q. Cable TV and phone in room. Air conditioning. Bicycles,
library and swimming nearby on premises. Antiquing, museums, live theater,
parks, shopping and sporting events nearby.

"We won't soon forget such a lovely retreat."

Victoria House Inn

208 King St
Charleston, SC 29401-3149
(843)720-2944 (800)933-5464 Fax:(843)720-2930

Circa 1898. Enjoy the gracious decor of the Victorian era while
staying at this Romanesque-style inn, located in the heart of
Charleston's historic district along King Street's
famed Antique Row. Some rooms boast working fireplaces, while others feature romantic whirlpool
baths. Champagne breakfasts are delivered to the bedchambers each morning, and the nightly turndown service
includes chocolates on your pillow.
Enjoy a glass of sherry before heading
out to one of Charleston's many fine
restaurants. The Victoria House Inn is
close to a variety of antique shops and
fashionable boutiques.

Historic Interest: The inn is within walking distance of plenty of historic
homes and museums, and walking tours are available.

Innkeeper(s): Beth Babcock. $150-255. MC, VISA, DC. TAC10. 18 rooms
with PB, 4 with FP, 4 suites and 1 conference room. Breakfast included in
rates. EP. Type of meal: Cont plus. Room service available. Beds: KD. Cable
TV, phone and turndown service in room. Air conditioning. Fax, copier and
child care on premises. Handicap access. Weddings, small meetings, family
reunions and seminars hosted. Antiquing, fishing, live theater, parks, shopping and water sports nearby.

Villa De La Fontaine B&B

138 Wentworth St
Charleston, SC 29401-1734
(843)577-7709
Web: charleston.cityinformation.com/villa/

Circa 1838. This magnificent Greek Revival manor is among Charleston's finest offerings. The grounds are lush with gardens and manicured lawns, and ionic columns adorn the impressive exterior. The innkeeper is a retired interior designer, and his elegant touch is found throughout the mansion, including many 18th-century antiques. A fully trained chef prepares the gourmet breakfasts, which are served in a solarium with a

hand-painted mural and 12-foot windows. The chef's recipe for cornmeal waffles was featured in a Better Homes & Gardens' cookbook. The inn is located in the heart of Charleston's historic district, three blocks from the market area.

Innkeeper(s): Aubrey Hancock. $125-150. PC, TC. 4 rooms with PB and 1 cottage. Breakfast included in rates. Type of meal: Full gourmet bkfst. Beds: KQT. TV in room. Central air. Antiquing, fishing, medical U, live theater, parks, shopping, sporting events and water sports nearby.

"What a wonderful vacation we had as recipients of your lavish hospitality."

Wentworth Mansion

149 Wentworth St
Charleston, SC 29401-1733
(843)853-1886 (888)466-1886

Circa 1886. This stately Second Empire mansion, designed originally as an opulent private residence for a wealthy cotton merchant, features the architectural details that one would expect to find in a home of this grandeur — hand-carved marble fireplaces, intricately detailed woodwork, Tiffany stained-glass windows and gleaming inlaid wood floors. Guest rooms have been historically restored and boast an elegant combination of antique furnishings and the modern comforts such as oversized whirlpools, most with a separate spacious shower, and working gas fireplaces. A breathtaking view of historic Charleston is accessible via the spiral staircase that leads to the towering cupola. Guests are invited to enjoy a complimentary breakfast buffet and afternoon tea or wine.

Innkeeper(s): Elizabeth Fisher. $295-695. MC, VISA, AX, DC, DS, PC, TC. TAC10. 21 rooms with PB, 19 with FP, 7 suites and 2 conference rooms. Breakfast and afternoon tea included in rates. Room service available. Restaurant on premises. Beds: K. Cable TV, phone and turndown service in room. Air conditioning. Fax, copier and library on premises. Handicap access. Weddings, small meetings and seminars hosted. Antiquing, fishing, golf, live theater, parks, shopping, tennis and water sports nearby.

Florence (Latta)   C8

Abingdon Manor

307 Church St
Florence (Latta), SC 29565-1359
(843)752-5090 (888)752-5090 Fax:(843)752-6034

Circa 1905. This 8,000-square-foot Greek Revival-style Victorian mansion offers another 2,000 square feet of wraparound porches and verandas. It is located on more than three acres with pecan,

chestnut and walnut trees. Once an opulent private residence, the inn is replete with beveled glass, marble window ledges, pier mirrors, pocket doors, 18-inch-thick walls, a winding staircase and interior arches and columns. Guest rooms offer period furnishings, feather beds and 12-foot-tall ceilings. The inn has a four-diamond rating. The inn is located six miles off Interstate 95.

Innkeeper(s): Michael & Patty Griffey. $105-140. MC, VISA, AX, DS, PC, TC. TAC10. 5 rooms with PB, 5 with FP, 1 suite and 1 conference room. Breakfast and snacks/refreshments included in rates. Types of meals: Full gourmet bkfst and early coffee/tea. Catering service available. Beds: KQD. Cable TV, turndown service, VCR, robes, feather beds, chocolates and bath amenities in room. Air conditioning. Fax, spa, bicycles and library on premises. Weddings, small meetings, family reunions and seminars hosted. Antiquing, fishing, golf, parks, shopping, tennis and water sports nearby.

Georgetown   E8

1790 House B&B Inn

630 Highmarket St
Georgetown, SC 29440-3652
(843)546-4821 (800)890-7432
E-mail: jwiley5211@aol
Web: www.1790house.com

Circa 1790. Located in the heart of a historic district, this beautifully restored West Indies Colonial just celebrated its 200th birthday. The spacious rooms feature 11-foot ceilings and seven fireplaces, three in the guest bedrooms. The inn's decor reflects the plantations of a bygone era. Guests can stay in former slave quarters, renovated to include a

queen bedroom and sitting area. Each of the romantic rooms features special touches, such as the Rice Planters' Room with its four-poster, canopy bed and window seat. The Dependency Cottage is a perfect honeymoon hideaway with a Jacuzzi tub and a private entrance enhanced with gardens and a patio. The inn is located one hour north of Charleston and 45 minutes south of Myrtle Beach.

Historic Interest: The Prince George Episcopal Church, the first church established in the district, is across the street from the home. The area offers several historic homes, some dating back to the 1740s, including the Kaminski House Museum and Hopsewee Plantation.

Innkeeper(s): John & Patricia Wiley. $95-135. MC, VISA, AX, DS, PC, TC. TAC10. 6 rooms with PB, 1 with FP and 1 cottage. Breakfast and snacks/refreshments included in rates. Type of meal: Full gourmet bkfst. Picnic lunch available. Beds: KQT. Cable TV, phone and ceiling fan in room. Air conditioning. VCR, bicycles, hammock, ping pong table and board games on premises. Weddings, small meetings and family reunions hosted. Antiquing, fishing, tours, boats, tram, live theater, parks and shopping nearby.

Publicity: *Georgetown Times, Sun News, Charlotte Observer, Southern Living. USAir, Augusta, Pee Dee, Sandlapper.*

"The 1790 House always amazes me with its beauty. A warm welcome in a lovingly maintained home. Breakfasts were a joy to the palate."

Du Pre House

921 Prince St
Georgetown, SC 29440-3549
(803)546-0298 (800)921-3877 Fax:(803)520-0771

Circa 1740. The lot upon which this pre-Revolutionary War gem stands was partitioned off in 1734, and the home built six years later. Three guest rooms have fireplaces, and all are decorated with a poster bed.
A full breakfast is prepared featuring such items as French toast, specialty egg dishes, fresh fruit and home-baked muffins. For those who love history,
Georgetown, South Carolina's third oldest city, offers more than 60 registered National Historic Landmarks.

Innkeeper(s): Marshall Wile. $75-115. MC, VISA, AX, PC, TC. 5 rooms with PB, 3 with FP. Breakfast, afternoon tea and snacks/refreshments included in rates. Types of meals: Full bkfst, cont plus and early coffee/tea. Picnic lunch available. Beds: Q. Turndown service, ceiling fan and bAthrobes in room. Air conditioning. Fax, copier, spa, swimming and library on premises. Weddings, small meetings and family reunions hosted. Amusement parks, antiquing, fishing, Myrtle Beach, plantation tours, live theater, parks, shopping and water sports nearby.

Mansfield Plantation B&B Country Inn

1776 Mansfield Rd
Georgetown, SC 29440-6923
(843)546-6961 (800)355-3223 Fax:(843)546-5235
E-mail: mansfield_plantation@prodigy.net
Web: www.bbonline.com/sc/mansfield/

Circa 1800. Listed in the National Register, Mansfield Plantation is a perfect respite for those in search of romance and history in a natural, secluded setting. In its days as a private plantation home, only the most elite aristocratic guests were invited. The home still maintains this elegant appeal. The dining room and sitting rooms are furnished with the owner's collections of 19th-century American antiques that include paintings, china, silver, furniture and gilt-framed mirrors. Accommodations include three guesthouses, each decorated in a romantic style and boasting fireplaces, hardwood floors, high ceilings, comfortable furnishings and collectibles. The vast grounds, shaded by moss-draped oaks, provide ideal spots for relaxing. Enjoy azalea and camellia gardens, as well as views of the surrounding marshlands. Guests can relax in hammocks or swings, watch for birds or enjoy a bike ride. Boating on the Black River is another possibility. Guests may bring their own boats or rent canoes or kayaks nearby. Among the plantation's notable historic features are a schoolhouse, kitchen, winnowing house, slave village and chapel, all of which predate the Civil War.

Historic Interest: The Rice Museum and Kaminski House Museum are among the historic sites in downtown Georgetown, which is 3.5 miles from the plantation. Brookgreen Gardens, which features a nationally known sculpture garden, is about a half hour away.

Innkeeper(s): Sally and James Cahalan. $95-115. PC, TC. TAC10. 8 rooms with PB, 8 with FP and 1 conference room. Breakfast included in rates. Type of meal: Full bkfst. Gourmet dinner available. Beds: KDT. TV and VCR in room. Central air. Fax, bicycles and library on premises. Weddings, small meetings, family reunions and seminars hosted. Antiquing, beaches, golf and live theater nearby.

Pets allowed: In room with prior approval.

"Handsome furnishings, wildlife walks, sports and hunting opportunities galore, and a sumptuous atmosphere all make for a weekend retreat to remember."

Hartsville   C7

Missouri Inn B&B

314 E Home Ave
Hartsville, SC 29550-3716
(843)383-9553 Fax:(843)383-9553

Circa 1901. It is from the third owners of this Federal-style inn that it derives its name. The home was at that time owned by the innkeepers' grandparents, F.E. and Emily Fitchett, and "Missouri" was the nickname given to Emily by her son-in-law. The entire house, including the five guest rooms, are decorated with antiques, and features wallpaper original to the home. The continental breakfasts are hearty and homemade. Don't forget to sample afternoon tea, which features scones, tarts, miniature quiche and tea sandwiches. The home, located in the town historic district, is across the street from Coker College and four blocks from downtown Hartsville.

Innkeeper(s): Kyle & Kenny Segars. $75-85. MC, VISA, AX, PC, TC. 5 rooms with PB, 3 with FP. Breakfast and afternoon tea included in rates. Types of meals: Full gourmet bkfst, cont plus and early coffee/tea. Gourmet dinner, lunch, catering service and catered breakfast available. Beds: KQT. Cable TV, phone, ceiling fan, robes, flowers, mints and heated towel racks in room. Air conditioning. VCR, fax, copier and library on premises. Handicap access. Weddings, small meetings, family reunions and seminars hosted. Antiquing, fishing, golf, parks, tennis and water sports nearby.

Landrum   A3

The Red Horse Inn

310 North Campbell Rd
Landrum, SC 29356
(864)895-4968 Fax:(864)895-4968
Web: www.theredhorseinn.com

Circa 1996. This collection of Victorian cottages is spread among nearly 200 acres with mountain views. The private, romantic cottages include kitchens, bedroom, bathroom and living room with a fireplace. Three of the elegant cottages also include a whirlpool tub. A breakfast basket with muffins, croissants, fresh fruit, juice, eggs, coffees, and teas. Golf courses and horseback riding are available nearby. The inn is a half-hour drive of Greenville, Spartanburg and Hendersonville.

Historic Interest: Campbell's Covered Bridge (1 mile), Cowpens National Battlefield (23 miles), Poinsett Bridge (8 miles).

Innkeeper(s): Mary & Roger Wolters. $110-155. MC, VISA, PC. 5 cottages. Breakfast included in rates. Types of meals: Cont plus and early coffee/tea. Picnic lunch and catering service available. Beds: Q. Cable TV, phone, turndown service, ceiling fan and satellite TV available in room. Central air. Fax, copier and massage on premises. Antiquing, art galleries, canoeing/kayaking, fishing, golf, hiking, horseback riding, live theater, museums, parks, shopping, sporting events, tennis and wineries nearby.

Pets allowed: Small/carriers $50 deposit.

Leesville   D4

The Able House Inn

244 E Columbia Ave
Leesville, SC 29070-9284
(803)532-2763 Fax:(803)532-2763

Circa 1939. This elegant, white brick home was built by a local druggist. Relax in the tastefully decorated living room or lounge on a comfy wicker chair among the large plants in the sunroom. Guest rooms, named after various relatives, boast beautiful

amenities such as a canopied bed or window seats. Jennifer's Room opens into a sitting room with a window seat so large, some guests have snuggled down for a restful night's sleep instead of the large, brass and enamel four-poster bed. Innkeepers offer guests a fresh fruit basket and turn-down service each night. Wake to freshly ground coffee before taking on the day. During the warmer months, innkeepers offer guests the use of their swimming pool.

Historic Interest: Historic Charleston is three hours from the inn.

Innkeeper(s): Jack & Annabelle Wright. $65-75. MC, VISA, PC, TC. 5 rooms with PB and 1 suite. Breakfast and snacks/refreshments included in rates. Meals: Cont plus and early coffee/tea. Beds: QD. Cable TV, phone, turndown service and ceiling fan in room. Air conditioning. VCR, fax, copier and swimming on premises. Weddings, small meetings and family reunions hosted. Antiquing, fishing, golf, live theater, shopping, sporting events, tennis and water sports nearby.

"Thank you for the warm Southern welcome. Your place is absolutely beautiful, very inviting. The food was extraordinary!"

Lyman
B3

Walnut Lane B&B

110 Ridge Rd
Lyman, SC 29365
(864)949-7230 Fax:(864)949-1633

Circa 1902. This three-story Greek Revival manor was once the headquarters for a working cotton plantation. Some of the home's original furnishings including mantel tops, a bed, and mirrors are mixed with other antique pieces in the parlor and

spacious guest rooms. There's a special suite available for families. Breakfast is offered in the formal dining room, which boasts vintage-style wallpapers, wood paneling, a fireplace and chandelier. A hearty Southern menu is served. The eight acres that surround the inn include a peach orchard as well as other fruit trees. Outlet shopping is particularly popular in the area, but there are also galleries, concerts and live theatre. The innkeepers can help with golf arrangements and reservations for country club dining.

Historic Interest: Cowpens Battleground (15 miles), Biltmore Estate (50 miles).

Innkeeper(s): Park & Marie Urquhart. $85-105. MC, VISA, AX, DS, PC, TC. 7 rooms with PB, 1 suite and 1 conference room. Breakfast included in rates. Types of meals: Full bkfst and early coffee/tea. Snacks/refreshments and catering service available. Beds: QDT. Cable TV and turndown service in room. Central air. VCR, fax, copier and library on premises. Weddings, small meetings, family reunions and seminars hosted. Antiquing, art galleries, bicycling, canoeing/kayaking, fishing, golf, hiking, horseback riding, live theater, museums, parks, shopping and sporting events nearby.

Marion
C8

Montgomery's Grove

408 Harlee St
Marion, SC 29571-3144
(843)423-5220 (877)646-7721

Circa 1893. The stunning rooms of this majestic Eastlake-style manor are adorned in Victorian tradition with Oriental rugs, polished hardwood floors, chandeliers and gracious furnishings.

High ceilings and fireplaces in each room complete the elegant look. Guest rooms are filled with antiques and magazines or books from the 1890s. Hearty full breakfasts are served each day, and candlelight dinner packages can be arranged. Guests will appreciate this inn's five acres of century-old trees and gardens. The inn is about a half-hour drive to famous Myrtle Beach and minutes from I-95.

Historic Interest: Brittons Neck (15 minutes), Camden, S.C., (40 minutes), Charleston (70 minutes).

Innkeeper(s): Coreen & Richard Roberts. $80-100. 5 rooms, 3 with PB and 1 suite. Breakfast included in rates. Type of meal: Full bkfst. Afternoon tea, gourmet dinner, picnic lunch, lunch and catering service available. Beds: KQ. Antiquing, fishing, live theater and water sports nearby.

McClellanville
F8

Laurel Hill Plantation

8913 N Hwy 17
McClellanville, SC 29458-9423
(843)887-3708 (888)887-3708

The wraparound porches at this plantation home provide a view of salt marshes, islands and the Atlantic Ocean. The home

was destroyed in 1989 by Hurricane Hugo, but has been totally reconstructed in its original Low Country style. It is furnished with antiques, local crafts and folk art.

Historic Interest: Historic Charleston is about 30 miles away.

Innkeeper(s): Jackie & Lee Morrison. $95-115. MC, VISA, AX, DC, DS, PC, TC. TAC10. 4 rooms with PB. Types of meals: Full bkfst and early coffee/tea. Beds: QT. Ceiling fan in room. Air conditioning. Antiquing, fishing, parks, shopping and water sports nearby.

Publicity: *Country Living, Seabreeze, Pee Dee, State.*

Salem
B2

Sunrise Farm B&B

325 Sunrise Dr
Salem, SC 29676-3444
(864)944-0121 (888)991-0121

Circa 1890. Situated on the remaining part of a 1,000-acre cotton plantation, this country Victorian features large porches with rockers and wicker. Guest rooms are furnished with period antiques, thick comforters, extra pillows and family heirlooms. The "corn crib" cottage is located in the original farm structure used for storing corn. It has a fully equipped kitchen, sitting area and bedroom with tub and shower. The June Rose Garden Cottage includes a river rock fireplace and full kitchen, as well as pastoral and mountain views. The inn offers a full breakfast and country picnic baskets.

Innkeeper(s): Barbara Laughter. $75-120. MC, VISA, PC, TC. TAC10. 4 rooms with PB and 2 cottages. Breakfast and snacks/refreshments included in rates. Types of meals: Full bkfst and cont plus. Picnic lunch available. Beds: Q. Cable TV, ceiling fan and VCR in room. Air conditioning. Antiquing, fishing, parks, sporting events and water sports nearby.

Pets allowed: With advanced notice.

"Saying thank you doesn't do our gratitude justice."

Sumter
D7

Calhoun Street B&B

302 W Calhoun St
Sumter, SC 29150-4512
(803)775-7035 (800)355-8119 Fax:(803)778-0934
E-mail: calhnbb@mindspring.com
Web: calhnbb.home.mindspring.com

Circa 1890. This home was built by innkeeper Mackenzie Sholtz's great-uncle, and she is the third generation to live in the clapboard Victorian. Guest rooms are well appointed with fine furnishings. For instance, the Audubon Room includes a canopy bed, a Victorian chair and loveseat and a polished hardwood floor topped with an Oriental rug. In the afternoon, refreshments are served, and in the mornings, guests enjoy a hearty, full breakfast. Eggs Calhoun, a unique twist on eggs Benedict, is a specialty served along with freshly squeezed orange juice and homemade breads or muffins. A phone, fax machine and copier are available for business travelers. Located in the historic district, this home borders a city park, and golfing and shopping are nearby.

Innkeeper(s): David & Mackenzie Sholtz. $65-85. MC, VISA, DS, PC, TC. 4 rooms with PB, 1 with FP. Breakfast and snacks/refreshments included in rates. Types of meals: Full gourmet bkfst and early coffee/tea. Beds: QT. Ceiling fan and portable phone in room. Air conditioning. VCR, fax and copier on premises. Weddings, small meetings, family reunions and seminars hosted. German and Italian spoken. Antiquing, fishing, 33 champion golf courses, live theater, parks and shopping nearby.

"This house gave us a good impression of uncompromised 1800s elegance."

Magnolia House

230 Church St
Sumter, SC 29150-4256
(803)775-6694 (888)666-0296

Circa 1907. Each room of this Greek Revival home with its five fireplaces is decorated in antiques from a different era. Also gracing the inn are inlaid oak floors and stained-glass windows.

Sumter's historic district includes neighborhood heroes such as George Franklin Haynesworth, who fired the first shot of The War Between the States. Guests may enjoy  an afternoon refreshment in the formal backyard garden. Breakfast is served in the large dining room with massive French antiques.

Innkeeper(s): Pierre & Liz Tremblay. $85-135. MC, VISA, AX, PC, TC. TAC10. 5 rooms, 4 with PB and 1 suite. Breakfast included in rates. Types of meals: Full gourmet bkfst and early coffee/tea. Beds: QDT. TV, phone, turndown service and ceiling fan in room. Air conditioning. VCR, bicycles and english gardens with fountains on premises. Weddings, small meetings and family reunions hosted. French spoken. Antiquing, fishing, golf, kayaking, canoeing, live theater, parks and shopping nearby.

Pets allowed: Call inn first.

Union
B4

The Inn at Merridun

100 Merridun Pl
Union, SC 29379-2200
(864)427-7052 (888)892-6020 Fax:(864)429-0373

Circa 1855. Nestled on nine acres of wooded ground, this Greek Revival inn is in a small Southern college town. During spring, see the South in its colorful splendor with blooming azaleas, magnolias and wisteria. Sip an iced drink on the inn's marble verandas and relive memories of a bygone era. Soft strains of Mozart and Beethoven, as well as the smell of freshly baked  cookies and country suppers, fill the air of this antebellum country inn. In addition to a complimentary breakfast, guest will enjoy the inn's dessert selection offered every evening.

Historic Interest: Rose Hill Plantation State Park (8 miles), historic Brattonsville (35 miles).

Innkeeper(s): Jim & Peggy Waller & JD the inn cat. $89-125. MC, VISA, AX, DS, PC, TC. TAC10. 5 rooms with PB and 3 conference rooms. Breakfast included in rates. Types of meals: Full gourmet bkfst and early coffee/tea. Afternoon tea, gourmet dinner, picnic lunch, gourmet lunch, banquet service, catering service, catered breakfast and room service available. Beds: KQT. Cable TV, phone, ceiling fan and hair dryers in room. Air conditioning. VCR, fax, copier, library, refrigerator on each floor for guest use, evening dessert and Miss Fannie's Tea Room on premises. Weddings, small meetings, family reunions and seminars hosted. Amusement parks, antiquing, fishing, parks, shopping, sporting events and water sports nearby.

Woodruff
B4

The Nicholls-Crook Plantation House B&B

120 Plantation Dr
Woodruff, SC 29388-9476
(864)476-8820 Fax:(864)476-8820
Web: www.bbonline.com/sc/nicholls/

Circa 1793. The innkeepers at this 18th-century home have restored the historic house with warmth and charm in mind. Period antiques, original mantels and the widest chimney in the upstate create a charming, rustic environment. The grounds boast 18th-century flowers, a white-rock courtyard and a pecan grove with  one of the largest pecan trees in South Carolina. Innkeepers Jim and Suzanne are full of information about the home's family history and the residents' ties to Revolutionary War heroes. A rich, plentiful breakfast is the perfect way to start off a day full of sightseeing and shopping or enjoying the area's many outdoor activities.

Historic Interest: The innkeepers can point guests in the direction of several battlefields. The Biltmore House is 60 miles from the home. Closer attractions include the Walnut Grove Plantation, only three miles away, and the Rose Hill Plantation, which is about 30 miles from the inn.

Innkeeper(s): Suzanne & Jim Brown. $85-150. AX, PC, TC. 3 rooms, 2 with PB and 1 suite. Breakfast included in rates. Type of meal: Full bkfst. Beds: KDT. Phone and turndown service in room. Air conditioning. Fax on premises. Weddings and small meetings hosted. Antiquing, golf and shopping nearby.

Publicity: *Herald Journal News, Country, Sandlapper, The Innside Scoop.*

"A beautiful, restful experience."

South Dakota

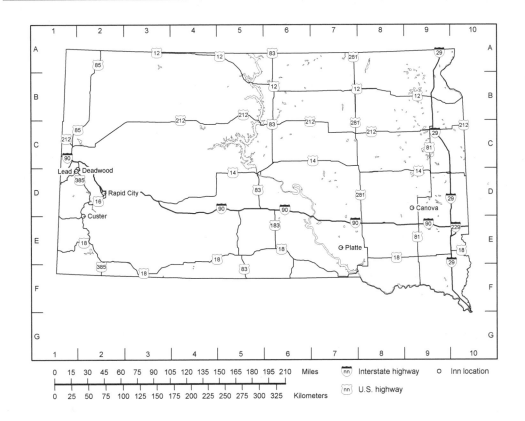

0 15 30 45 60 75 90 105 120 135 150 165 180 195 210   Miles

0 25 50 75 100 125 150 175 200 225 250 275 300 325   Kilometers

Interstate highway   Inn location

U.S. highway

Canova D9

B&B at Skoglund Farm

Rt 1 Box 45
Canova, SD 57321-9726
(605)247-3445

Circa 1917. This is a working farm on the South Dakota prairie. Peacocks stroll around the farm along with cattle, chickens, emu and other fowl. Guests can enjoy an evening meal with the family. The innkeepers offer special rates for families with children. The farm's rates are $30 per adult, $25 per teen-ager and $20 per child. Children age five and younger stay for free.

Innkeeper(s): Alden & Delores Skoglund. $60. PC. 4 rooms. Breakfast and dinner included in rates. Types of meals: Full bkfst and early coffee/tea. Snacks/refreshments available. Beds: QDT. TV in room. VCR and library on premises. Antiquing, fishing, parks, shopping, sporting events and water sports nearby.

Pets Allowed.

"Thanks for the down-home hospitality and good food."

Custer D2

State Game Lodge

HC 83 Box 74
Custer, SD 57730-9705
(605)255-4541 (800)658-3530 Fax:(605)255-4706

Circa 1921. The State Game Lodge is listed in the National Register of Historic Places. It served as the summer White House for presidents Coolidge and Eisenhower. Although not a bed and breakfast, the lodge boasts a wonderful setting in the Black Hills. Ask for a room in the historic lodge building. (There are cottages and motel units, as well.) A favorite part of the experience is rocking on the front

porch while watching buffalo graze. Breakfast is paid for separately in the dining room, where you may wish to order a pheasant or buffalo entree in the evening.

Innkeeper(s): Pat Azinger. $72-310. MC, VISA, AX, DS. 68 rooms with PB, 3 with FP. EP. Type of meal: Full gourmet bkfst. Dinner and lunch available. Restaurant on premises. Beds: QDT. Fishing and buffalo safari jeep tours nearby.

"Your staff's cheerfulness and can-do attitude added to a most enjoyable stay."

Platte E7

Grandma's House B&B

721 E 7th St
Platte, SD 57369-2134
(605)337-3589

Circa 1906. This Victorian farmhouse will stir memories of visits to Grandma. The interior is homey, done in a simple country style with antiques. The turn-of-the-century home maintains its original woodwork and a fireplace. The Prairie Queen room features a teal-blue satin bedspread with matching curtains of satin and white lace; an old sewing machine has been transformed into a sink. The Country Blue and Southern Rose rooms share a

bath with a clawfoot tub. Breakfast menus feature items such as pancakes or French toast with eggs and bacon. Parks and a swimming pool are nearby, and guests can fish at the Missouri River, which is a 20-minute drive from the home.

Innkeeper(s): Delores & Albert Kuipers. $40-50. PC. 3 rooms, 1 with PB. Breakfast included in rates. Types of meals: Full bkfst and early coffee/tea. Beds: QD. Ceiling fan in room. Air conditioning. VCR on premises. Small meetings and family reunions hosted. Fishing, golf, shopping and water sports nearby.

Pets allowed: Hunting dogs can stay in the garage.

Rapid City D2

Abend Haus Cottages & Audrie's B&B

23029 Thunderhead Falls Rd
Rapid City, SD 57702-8524
(605)342-7788
Web: www.audriesbb.com

Circa 1973. Whether guests stay in the innkeeper's country home, a historic powerhouse or in private cottages, they're sure to enjoy both the spectacular scenery and the comfortable rooms furnished with European antiques. The Old Powerhouse dates back to 1910 and was used to generate hydroelectricity. Its two suites both include a private hot tub. The suites in Abend Haus Cottage feature furnishings such as a mahogany sleigh bed and private hot tubs. The log

cottages and Cranbury House are other cozy options, also with hot tubs. Guests are provided with a full breakfast, which they can heat and enjoy in the privacy of their own suite and at their convenience. With all this pampering, one shouldn't forget to mention the seven acres of woods, a creek and mountain views.

Innkeeper(s): Hank & Audry Kuhnhauser. $95-145. PC, TC. 10 rooms with PB, 5 with FP, 6 suites and 4 cottages. Breakfast included in rates. Type of meal: Full bkfst. Beds: KQ. Cable TV, turndown service, ceiling fan and VCR in room. Air conditioning. Bicycles, fishing and hiking on premises. Antiquing, fishing, parks, shopping, downhill skiing, cross-country skiing and water sports nearby.

"I don't want to leave so I'm staying a few days longer! This is a wonderful place."

Tennessee

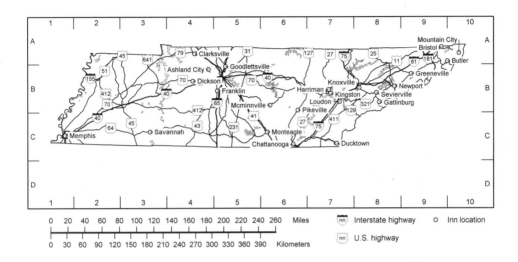

0 20 40 60 80 100 120 140 160 180 200 220 240 260   Miles

0 30 60 90 120 150 180 210 240 270 300 330 360 390   Kilometers

☒ Interstate highway ○ Inn location
☒ U.S. highway

Ashland City   B4

Birdsong Lodge - A Luxury Inn
1306 Hwy 49 E
Ashland City, TN 37015-2848
(615)792-1767 Fax:(615)792-1767
E-mail: rob.pilling@nashville.com
Web: www.birdsonglodge.com

Circa 1912. Listed in the National Register of Historic Places,
this lodge was built as the summer home for the Cheek family.
The family was responsible for building the Cheekwood
Botanical Gardens, as
well as the Museum
of Art. The guest
rooms feature four-
poster beds and chan-
deliers. Guests can
relax in front of the fireplace in the great room, enjoy
the swing on the porch or explore the 10-acre grounds. In addition to the lodge rooms, the innkeepers offer Lewis Cottage,
located just a few feet from the lodge. Breakfasts are served by
candlelight, and guests can arrange for gourmet dinners or picnic baskets. The lodge is a mere half-hour from downtown
Nashville. Boating, golfing, horseback riding, hiking and birdwatching are among the many local attractions. Private parties
are hosted by reservations, and children over 14 are welcome.
Innkeeper(s): Rob & Bett Pilling. $150-295. MC, VISA, TC. TAC10. 4 rooms

with PB, 1 suite and 1 cottage. Breakfast included in rates. Type of meal: Full
gourmet bkfst. Picnic lunch and catering service available. Beds: KQ. Cable
TV, phone and VCR in room. Spanish spoken. Antiquing, canoeing/kayaking,
fishing, golf, hiking, horseback riding, bird watching, Rails-to-Trails, Indian
Mounds, historic tours, parks, shopping and water sports nearby.

*"Hands down, the best inn we have ever stayed in! Wish we could
come back every weekend."*

Bristol   A9

New Hope B&B
822 Georgia Ave
Bristol, TN 37620-4024
(423)989-3343 (888)989-3343
E-mail: newhope@preferred.com
Web: www.bbonline.com/tn/newhope/

Circa 1892. Abram Reynolds, older brother of R.J. Reynolds,
once owned the property that surrounds this inn, and one of the
guest rooms is named in his honor. Each of the rooms has been
creatively decorated with bright prints and cheerful wallcoverings, emphasizing the high ceilings and wood floors. Clawfoot
tubs, transoms over the doors and distinctive woodwork are
some of the period elements fea-
tured in this late Victorian
home. Bristol is known as a
birthplace for country music,
and the innkeepers pay homage
to the history with the whimsically decorated Tennessee Ernie

401

Ford hallway. Ford got his start in Bristol, and pictures, record jackets, books and wallpaper fashioned from sheet music bedeck the hallway. The home is located in the historic Fairmount area, and a guided walking tour begins at New Hope. Half of the town of Bristol is located in Tennessee and the other half in Virginia.

Innkeeper(s): Tom & Tonda Fluke. $95-155. MC, VISA, AX, PC, TC. TAC10. 4 rooms with PB, 1 with FP. Breakfast & snacks/refreshments included. Meals: Full bkfst & early coffee/tea. Beds: KQT. Cable TV, phone, ceiling fan & whirlpool tub for two in room. Air conditioning. Library & large game room on premises. Antiquing, fishing, golf, live theater, parks, shopping & downhill skiing nearby.

Publicity: *Tennessee Getaways. Bristol Herald Courier.*

"It was like a second home in such a short time."

Chattanooga C6

Adams Hilborne Mansion Inn & Restaurant

801 Vine St
Chattanooga, TN 37403-2318
(423)265-5000 Fax:(423)265-5555
Web: www.innjoy.com

Circa 1889. This former mayor's mansion of Tudor and Romanesque design was presented with the 1997 award for Excellence in Preservation by the National Trust. The interior of

this gracious home boasts 16-foot ceilings and floors patterned from three different woods. The large entrance hall features carved cornices, a coiffured ceiling and a fireplace. Every room offers something special, from Tiffany windows and beveled glass to the mansion's eight fireplaces and luxurious ballroom. The cornerstone of the Fortwood Historic District, Chattanooga's finest historic residential area, the mansion has also received the coveted City Beautiful Award.

Historic Interest: The Chickamauga Battlefields are 15 minutes from the inn and other battle sites, museums and cemeteries are nearby.

Innkeeper(s): Wendy & Dave Adams. $100-275. MC, VISA, AX, TC. TAC10. 10 rooms with PB, 4 with FP and 3 suites. Breakfast included in rates. Types of meals: Cont plus and early coffee/tea. Gourmet dinner and banquet service available. Restaurant on premises. Beds: KQD. Cable TV, phone, turndown service and VCR in room. Air conditioning. Fax, copier, library and smoking pub bar on premises. Weddings, small meetings, family reunions and seminars hosted. Amusement parks, antiquing, fishing, live theater, parks, shopping, sporting events and water sports nearby.

Publicity: *National Geographic, Preservation Magazine, Traveler, News Free Press.*

Clarksville A4

Hachland Hill Inn

1601 Madison St
Clarksville, TN 37043-4980
(931)647-4084 Fax:(931)552-3454

Circa 1795. This log cabin contains a dining room and, in a stone-walled chamber, a place where pioneers sought refuge during Indian attacks. Three of Clarksville's oldest log houses have been reconstructed in the garden where old-fashioned barbeque suppers and square dances are held. Newly built rooms are available in the brick building, so request the log cabin if you want authentic historic atmosphere.

Innkeeper(s): Phila Hach. $65. MC, VISA, AX. 20 rooms, 10 with PB, 3 with FP and 1 conference room. Type of meal: Full bkfst. Beds: D. Fax on premises. Handicap access.

Ducktown C7

The White House B&B

104 Main St, PO Box 668
Ducktown, TN 37326-0668
(423)496-4166 (800)775-4166 Fax:(423)496-9778

Circa 1898. This Queen Anne Victorian boasts a wraparound porch with a swing. Rooms are decorated in traditional style with family antiques. Innkeepers pamper their guests with Tennessee hospitality, a hearty country breakfast and a mouthwatering sundae bar in the evenings. The innkeepers also help guests plan daily activities, and the area is bursting with possibilities. Hiking, horseback riding, panning for

gold and driving tours are only a few choices. The Ocoee River is the perfect place for a river float trip or take on the challenge of roaring rapids. The river was selected as the site of the 1996 Summer Olympic Whitewater Slalom events.

Historic Interest: The Ducktown Mining Museum is a popular local attraction. Fields of the Wood, a biblical theme park, is 20 minutes away and free of charge.

Innkeeper(s): Dan & Mardee Kauffman. $65-75. MC, VISA, DS, PC, TC. TAC10. 3 rooms, 1 with PB. Breakfast, afternoon tea and snacks/refreshments included in rates. Types of meals: Full gourmet bkfst and early coffee/tea. Catering service and catered breakfast available. Beds: QT. Ceiling fan and central heat in room. Central air. VCR, fax and library on premises. Weddings, small meetings and family reunions hosted. Antiquing, fishing, parks, shopping and water sports nearby.

Publicity: *Southern Living.*

"We wanted a relaxing couple of days in the mountains and that's what we got. Thank you."

Franklin B5

Magnolia House B&B

1317 Columbia Ave
Franklin, TN 37064-3620
(615)794-8178

Circa 1905. In summer, a blooming Magnolia tree shades the wicker-filled front porch of this gabled Craftsman cottage. The land is where the Battle of Franklin was fought. Furnishings range from 19th-century Victorian pieces to period antiques. Walk five blocks through a maple shaded neighborhood of historic houses to downtown Franklin, 15 blocks of which are in the National Register of Historic Places.

Innkeeper(s): Jimmy & Robbie Smithson. $80-95. 4 rooms. Breakfast included in rates. Types of meals: Full bkfst and early coffee/tea. Phone, turndown service and ceiling fan in room. Air conditioning. VCR on premises. Amusement parks, antiquing, live theater and shopping nearby.

Namaste Acres Country Ranch Inn

5436 Leipers Creek Rd
Franklin, TN 37064-9208
(615)791-0333

Circa 1993. This handsome Dutch Colonial is directly across the street from the original Natchez Trace. As the B&B is within walking distance of miles of hiking and horseback riding trails. Each of the suites includes private entrances and features individual themes. One room boasts rustic, cowboy decor with a clawfoot tub, hand-crafted furnishings, log and rope beds, and rough sawn lumber walls. The Franklin Quarters offers a sitting area where guests can settle down with a book from the large collection of historical material. The innkeepers chose the name Namaste from an Indian word, and carry an Indian theme in one of the guest rooms. Namaste Acres is just 12 miles outside of historic Franklin, which offers plenty of shops, a self-guided walking tour, Civil War sites and the largest assortment of antique dealers in the United States.

Innkeeper(s): Lisa Winters. $75-85. MC, VISA, AX, DS, PC. 4 rooms. Type of meal: Full bkfst. Beds: Q. Spa and swimming on premises. Guided trail rides nearby.

Publicity: *Southern Living, Western Horseman, Horse Illustrated.*

Gatlinburg   B8

Buckhorn Inn

2140 Tudor Mountain Rd
Gatlinburg, TN 37738-6014
(423)436-4668 Fax:(423)436-5009
E-mail: buckhorninn@msn.com
Web: www.buckhorninn.com

Circa 1938. Set high on a hilltop, Buckhorn is surrounded by more than 25 acres of woodlands and groomed meadows. There are inspiring mountain views and a spring-fed lake on the grounds.

Original paintings enhance the antique-filled guest rooms and the cottages and guest houses have working fireplaces.

Innkeeper(s): John & Lee Mellor. $95-250. MC, VISA, DS, PC, TC. 6 cottages with PB and 2 guest houses. Breakfast included in rates. Types of meals: Full gourmet bkfst and early coffee/tea. Afternoon tea, dinner, picnic lunch, lunch and catered breakfast available. Beds: KDT. TV in room. Air conditioning. VCR, fax, copier and library on premises. Weddings, small meetings, family reunions and seminars hosted. Amusement parks, antiquing, fishing, Great Smoky Arts & Crafts Community, live theater, parks, shopping, downhill skiing, cross-country skiing, sporting events and water sports nearby.

Publicity: *Atlanta Journal & Constitution, Country, Brides, British Vogue, Birmingham News, New York Times, Travel & Leisure, Travel Holiday.*

Goodlettsville   B5

Crocker Springs B&B

2382 Crocker Springs Road
Goodlettsville, TN 37072
(615)876-8502 Fax:(615)876-4083

Circa 1880. Once a working farm, the grounds that surround this historic home still include the old barn and outbuildings. Spacious, comfortable guest rooms are decorated with an elegant country style. Todd's Paisley Room includes a masculine paisley comforter atop an iron bed. Stefanie's Quilt Room includes antique furnishings and a feather bed topped with the room's namesake quilt. The Rose Room is especially spacious and can accommodate up to four guests. The aroma of freshly brewed coffee wafts throughout the house, a gentle promise to wonderful culinary things to come. The innkeepers prepare a variety of different breakfasts, all made with the finest farm-fresh ingredients. One guest favorite is a unique tomato pudding that is served along with egg dishes, homemade biscuits, potatoes, breakfast meats, orchard-fresh juice and a selection of fruit. Guests can stroll the 58 acres or take the short drive into Nashville where historic homes, Civil War battlefields and the Grand Old Opry await.

Historic Interest: Hermitage, Belle Meade Plantation, Civil War Battlefields.
Innkeeper(s): Jack & Bev Spangler. $100-145. MC, VISA, AX, DS, PC, TC. TAC10. 3 rooms with PB, 1 suite and 1 conference room. Breakfast and snacks/refreshments included in rates. Types of meals: Full bkfst, country bkfst, veg bkfst and early coffee/tea. Beds: QD. TV, ceiling fan, VCR and clawfoot tub in room. Central air. Fax, stables, tennis and library on premises. Weddings, small meetings, family reunions and seminars hosted. Antiquing, art galleries, canoeing/kayaking, fishing, golf, hiking, horseback riding, live theater, museums, parks, shopping, sporting events, water sports and wineries nearby.

Pets allowed: By prior arrangement.

Harriman   B7

Bushrod Hall B&B

422 Cumberland St, NE
Harriman, TN 37748
(423)882-8406 (888)880-8406 Fax:(423)882-6056

Circa 1892. Bushrod Hall was built as part of a competition to see which town resident could build the most beautiful home, so its original owners spared little expense. Among the home's most notable features are its exquisite restored woodwork and stained glass. Harriman was founded as a utopia for those following the Temperance Movement. Bushrod Hall once served as the Hall of Domestic Science for the American Temperance University. Period-era furnishings add to the historic ambiance. Gourmet breakfast entrees include items such as an egg soufflé or caramel French toast. Guests can take a guided walking tour and see some of the town's historic sites. Antique shops, museums and recreation areas offer other possibilities. Bushrod Hall is located in Harriman's Cornstalk Heights Historic District and is listed in the National Register of Historic Places.

Historic Interest: Ft SW Point (4 miles), Secret City Oak Ridge & Carbide Reactor (20 miles), Museum of Appalachia (30 miles), Ruby, Tenn. (20 miles).
Innkeeper(s): Nancy & Bob Ward. $75-100. MC, VISA, AX, PC, TC. 3 rooms with PB. Breakfast included in rates. Type of meal: Early coffee/tea. Snacks/refreshments and banquet service available. Beds: KQ. Ceiling fan in room. Air conditioning. VCR on premises. Weddings, small meetings and family reunions hosted. Antiquing, fishing, golf, hiking, live theater, museums, parks, shopping and water sports nearby.

Kingston   B7

Whitestone Country Inn

1200 Paint Rock Rd
Kingston, TN 37763-5843
(423)376-0113 (888)247-2464 Fax:(423)376-4454
E-mail: moreinfo@whitestones.com
Web: www.whitestones.com

Circa 1995. This regal farmhouse sits majestically on a hilltop overlooking miles of countryside and Watts Bar Lake. The inn is surrounded by 360 acres, some of which borders a scenic

lake, where guests can enjoy fishing or simply communing with nature. There are eight miles of hiking trails, and the many porches and decks are perfect places to relax. The inn's interior is as pleasing as the exterior surroundings. Guest rooms are elegantly appointed, and each includes a fireplace and whirlpool tub. Guests are treated to a hearty, country-style breakfast, and dinners and lunch are available by reservation. The inn is one hour from Chattanooga, Knoxville and the Great Smoky Mountains National Park.

Innkeeper(s): Paul & Jean Cowell. $105-200. MC, VISA, AX, DS, PC, TC. TAC10. 16 rooms with PB, 16 with FP and 2 conference rooms. Breakfast included in rates. EP. Type of meal: Full bkfst. Dinner and picnic lunch available. Restaurant on premises. Beds: KQ. Cable TV, phone, turndown service, ceiling fan and VCR in room. Air conditioning. Fax, copier, spa, sauna and library on premises. Handicap access. Weddings, small meetings, family reunions and seminars hosted. Antiquing, fishing, golf, shopping and water sports nearby.

"Not only have you built a place of beauty, you have established a sanctuary of rest. An escape from the noise and hurry of everyday life."

Knoxville   B8

Maplehurst Inn

800 W Hill Ave
Knoxville, TN 37902
(423)523-7773 (800)451-1562
E-mail: mplhrstinn@aol.com
Web: www.maplehurstinn.com

Circa 1917. This townhouse, located in the downtown neighborhood of Maplehurst, is situated on a hill that overlooks the Tennessee River. A parlor with fireplace and piano invites guests to mingle in the evening or to relax quietly with a book. The inn's favorite room is the Penthouse with king bed, cherry furnishings and a sky-lit Jacuzzi. The Anniversary Suite offers a double Jacuzzi and canopy bed. A light informal breakfast is served in the Garden Room overlooking the river, while breakfast casseroles, country potatoes, quiches and breads are offered buffet-style in the dining room. Check there for brownies and cookies if you come back in the middle of the day. The inn is within three blocks of the Convention Center and City Hall as well as several fine restaurants. The University of Tennessee and Neyland Stadium are nearby.

Historic Interest: James White Fort (1/2 mile), Mabry-Hazen House (1/2 mile). $59-149. MC, VISA, AX, PC, TC. TAC10. 11 rooms with PB and 2 suites. Breakfast and snacks/refreshments included in rates. Types of meals: Full bkfst, veg bkfst and early coffee/tea. Beds: KD. Cable TV and phone in room. Air conditioning. VCR, fax and spa on premises. Small meetings, family reunions and seminars hosted. Antiquing, art galleries, bicycling, canoeing/kayaking, fishing, golf, hiking, horseback riding, live theater, museums, parks, shopping, downhill skiing, sporting events, tennis, water sports and wineries nearby.

Pets Allowed.

Loudon   B7

The Mason Place B&B

600 Commerce St
Loudon, TN 37774-1101
(865)458-3921 Fax:(865)458-6092
E-mail: thempbb@aol.com
Web: www.themasonplace.com

Circa 1865. In the National Register, Mason Place is acclaimed for its award-winning restoration. In the Greek Revival style, the inn has a red slate roof and graceful columns. Three porches overlook three acres of lawns, trees and gardens. Inside, guests are welcomed to a grand entrance hall and tasteful antiques. There are 10 working fireplaces in the mansion's 7,000 square feet. Guests enjoy the Grecian swimming pool, gazebo and wisteria-covered arbor. A favorite honeymoon getaway has been created from the old smokehouse. It features brick walls and floors, a library loft, feather bed, wood burning Franklin fireplace and a tin bathtub (once feature in the movie Maverick).

Historic Interest: Fort Loudon Park & Museum, The Lost Sea, Sequoyah Museum.

Innkeeper(s): Bob & Donna Siewert. $96-135. PC, TC. 5 rooms with PB, 5 with FP. Breakfast included in rates. Types of meals: Full gourmet bkfst and early coffee/tea. Afternoon tea and picnic lunch available. Beds: Q. Air conditioning. Horseshoe and croquet on premises. Weddings, small meetings and seminars hosted. Amusement parks, antiquing, fishing, white water rafting, parks, shopping, tennis and wineries nearby.

Publicity: *Country Inn, Country Side, Country Travels, Tennessee Cross Roads, Antiquing in Tennessee, Knox-Chattanooga, Oak Ridge, Detroit Magazine.*

"Absolutely wonderful in every way. You are in for a treat! The best getaway ever!"

McMinnville   B6

Historic Falcon Manor

2645 Faulkner Springs Rd
McMinnville, TN 37110-1193
(931)668-4444 Fax:(931)815-4444
E-mail: falconmanor@falconmanor.com
Web: www.falconmanor.com

Circa 1896. Victorian glory is the theme at this restored mansion, right down to the period clothing worn by the owners during special tours. Museum-quality period furnishings fill each of the unique rooms, which are decorated in traditional Victorian style. High ceilings, a sweeping staircase, chandeliers and white oak hardwood floors accent the decor. Relax on the wraparound porch with its comfortable rockers or learn of home's past from innkeepers George and Charlien McGlothin, who can tell a few ghost stories along with providing ample historical detail. Glorious full breakfasts are served each morning and evening refreshments and desserts are offered. On weekends,

dinner is available by reservation. The inn was the 1st prize winner of the National Trust for Historic Preservation's American Home Restoration Award in 1997.

Historic Interest: Hermitage and Belle Meade mansions are 75 miles from the inn. The Chickamauga Battlefield is 71 miles. The Stones River Battlefield is 45 miles and Jack Daniels Country is found in Lynchburg about 50 miles from the inn. The Cumberland Caverns, a National Historic Landmark, is eight miles away.

Innkeeper(s): George & Charlien McGlothin. $95-120. MC, VISA, AX, DS, PC, TC. TAC10. 7 rooms with PB. Breakfast and snacks/refreshments included in rates. Types of meals: Full bkfst and early coffee/tea. Banquet service and catering service available. Beds: KQD. Ceiling fan in room. Air conditioning. VCR, fax, copier and library on premises. Handicap access. Weddings, family reunions and seminars hosted. Antiquing, Fall Creek Falls State Park, parks and water sports nearby.

"Everything, from the absolutely beautiful rooms to the wonderful breakfast to the kindness and sincerity of the hosts, made our stay wonderful!"

Memphis
C1

Bed and Breakfast in a Castle

217 N Waldran
Memphis, TN 38105
(901)527-7174 Fax:(901)527-9811

Circa 1898. Listed in the National Register, this Edwardian manor boasts 300-square feet of mahogany trim, two covered verandas and a covered gazebo on its third story. Antiques and reproductions decorate the rooms, which feature the home's rich original woodwork. Department-store owner Abraham Lowenstein built this Victorian, and it later became the Beethoven Music Club. In the '40s it was a boarding house, the Elizabeth Club for Girls, in the days before young ladies had their own apartments. The bed & breakfast is five minutes from downtown Memphis and close to attractions such as Dixon Gardens and Graceland.

Historic Interest: Victorian Village, Graceland.

Innkeeper(s): LIsa Lockett & Ora Simmons. $70-90. MC, VISA, PC, TC. 4 rooms with PB. Breakfast included in rates. Types of meals: Full bkfst and cont plus. Beds: Q. Cable TV in room. Central air. Weddings and family reunions hosted. Antiquing and art galleries nearby.

"We found it just lovely and enjoyed our stay very much."

Monteagle
C6

Adams Edgeworth Inn

Monteagle Assembly
Monteagle, TN 37356
(931)924-4000 Fax:(931)924-3236
E-mail: innjoy@blomand.com
Web: www.innjoy.com

Built in 1896 this National Register Victorian inn recently has been refurbished in a country-chintz style. Original paintings, sculptures and country antiques are found throughout. Wide verandas are filled with wicker furnishings and breezy hammocks, and there's an award-winning chef who will prepare candle-lit five-course dinners. You can stroll through the 96-acre Victorian village that surrounds the inn and enjoy rolling hills,

creeks and Victorian cottages. Waterfalls, natural caves and scenic overlooks are along the 150 miles of hiking trails of nearby South Cumberland State Park.

Historic Interest: University of the South, Jack Daniels Distillery, Civil War sites.

Innkeeper(s): Wendy Adams. $100-275. MC, VISA, AX. 12 rooms with PB, 4 with FP, 1 suite and 1 conference room. Breakfast included in rates. MAP, EP. Type of meal: Full bkfst. Gourmet dinner available. Beds: KQD. Phone, air-conditioning and ceiling fan and TV (some rooms) in room. VCR, fax and copier on premises. Weddings, small meetings, family reunions and seminars hosted. Antiquing, fishing, hiking, caving, historic architecture, live theater, parks, shopping and sporting events nearby.

Mountain City
A10

Prospect Hill B&B Inn

801 W Main St (Hwy 67)
Mountain City, TN 37683
(423)727-0139 (800)339-5084
E-mail: reserve@prospect-hill.com
Web: prospect-hill.com

Circa 1889. Fashioned from handmade bricks, this historic manor was once home to Joseph Wagner, a former Civil War major who, like his other neighbors in far northeastern Tennessee, served on the Union side. The restored home features five guest rooms. A 1910 oak Craftsman dining set complements the oak Stickley furniture (circa 1997) that decorates the living room. Fireplaces, whirlpools and stained glass add a romantic touch to the guest rooms. Prospect Hill boasts views of the Appalachian and Blue Ridge mountains. From the front window, guests can see three states: Tennessee, Virginia and North Carolina. The inn is within an hour of the Blue Ridge Parkway, Appalachian Trail and Roan and Grandfather mountains.

Innkeeper(s): Judy & Robert Hotchkiss. $89-200. MC, VISA, PC, TC. TAC10. 5 rooms with PB, 5 with FP and 1 conference room. Breakfast included in rates. Types of meals: Full bkfst, cont and early coffee/tea. Snacks/refreshments and picnic lunch available. Beds: KQ. Cable TV, phone, turndown service, ceiling fan and heat in room. Air conditioning. VCR, fax, copier, library and porch swing on premises. Handicap access. Weddings, small meetings, family reunions and seminars hosted. Antiquing, fishing, golf, mountain trails, bike trails, Eastern Tenn. State Univ, live theater, parks, shopping, downhill skiing, tennis and water sports nearby.

"The most wonderful thing I'll always remember about our stay is, by far, the wonderful home we came back to each night."

Newport
B8

Christopher Place - An Intimate Resort

1500 Pinnacles Way
Newport, TN 37821-7308
(423)623-6555 (800)595-9441 Fax:(423)613-4771
E-mail: thebestinn@aol.com
Web: www.christopherplace.com

Circa 1976. Although it was built in the mid-1970s, this mansion has the appearance of a great Antebellum estate. The inn is surrounded by more than 200 acres and offers views of the Great Smoky Mountains. The inn's interior, as well as its reputation for hospitality and service, earned it a four-diamond award. Country Inns magazine and Waverly chose Christopher Place's Stargazer as the 1995 Room of the Year. Each of the guest rooms is decorated with a different theme in mind. The Roman Holiday room is a romantic retreat with an iron canopy bed draped with a sheer, dramatic canopy. There is a fireplace and a whirlpool tub for two. Papaw's Suite is a rustic room with a hand-carved bed and hot tub. In addition to the inn's transfixing decor, guests are further pampered with on-site tennis courts, a sauna, swimming pool, billiards and library. As well, Gatlinburg and Pigeon Forge aren't far away.

Innkeeper(s): Tim Hall. $150-300. MC, VISA, AX, DS, PC, TC. TAC10. 8 rooms with PB, 2 with FP, 6 suites and 1 conference room. Breakfast included in rates. EP. Types of meals: Full bkfst and early coffee/tea. Dinner, picnic lunch and room service available. Beds: KQD. Cable TV, phone, turndown service, ceiling fan and VCR in room. Air conditioning. Fax, copier, swimming, sauna, tennis, library, billiard room and hiking trails on premises. Handicap access. Weddings, small meetings, family reunions and seminars hosted. Amusement parks, antiquing, fishing, golf, parks, shopping, downhill skiing, tennis and water sports nearby.

Savannah   C3

White Elephant B&B Inn
304 Church St
Savannah, TN 38372
(901)925-6410

Circa 1901. Guests will know they've arrived at the right place when they spot the white elephants on the front lawn of this Queen Anne Victorian. Listed in the National Register as part of the Savannah Historic District, it offers a wraparound veranda, back porch swing and shade from tall sugar maples. There are curved bay windows and, of course, a tower. Guest rooms feature antiques (ask for the Poppy Room) and bathrooms with clawfoot tubs. At breakfast, in addition to the silver, crystal and fine service, guests may find French toast made in the shape of an elephant. Afternoon

refreshments are served and include the innkeeper's award-winning cookies. Turndown service is another special addition. Innkeeper Ken Hansgen offers guided tours of nearby Shiloh National Military park.

Innkeeper(s): Ken & Sharon Hansgen. $90-110. PC, TC. TAC10. 3 rooms with PB. Breakfast and snacks/refreshments included in rates. Types of meals: Full bkfst and early coffee/tea. Picnic lunch available. Beds: Q. Ceiling fan in room. Central air. VCR, library, croquet, radio, CD player and pump organ on premises. Weddings and small meetings hosted. Antiquing, fishing, golf, Natchez Trace, live theater, museums, parks, shopping, sporting events, tennis and water sports nearby.

Sevierville   B8

Little Greenbrier Lodge
3685 Lyon Springs Rd
Sevierville, TN 37862-8257
(423)429-2500 (800)277-8100
E-mail: littlegreenbrier@worldnet.att.net
Web: www.bbonline.com/tn/lgl/

Circa 1939. The spectacular, forested setting at Little Greenbrier is worth the trip. The rustic lodge is set on five, wooded acres less than a quarter mile from Great Smoky Mountains National Park. Rooms have valley or mountain views and are decorated with Victorian-style furnishings and antiques. The lodge served guests from 1939 until the 1970s when it became a religious retreat. When the innkeepers purchased it in 1993, they tried to preserve some of its early history, including restoring original sinks and the first bathtub ever installed in the valley. A copy of the lodge's original "house rules" is still posted. Within 30 minutes are Dollywood, outlet malls, antiquing, craft stores and plenty of outdoor activities.

Innkeeper(s): Charles & Susan LeBon. $85-110. MC, VISA, DS, PC, TC. TAC10. 10 rooms, 8 with PB, 1 cabin and 1 conference room. Breakfast and snacks/refreshments included in rates. Types of meals: Full bkfst and early coffee/tea. Beds: QD. Ceiling fan in room. Air conditioning. VCR, fax and library on premises. Small meetings, family reunions and seminars hosted. Amusement parks, antiquing, fishing, golf, live theater, parks, shopping, downhill skiing, cross-country skiing, sporting events and tennis nearby.

"We had a relaxing holiday. Little Greenbrier is very special and we plan to return sometime soon."

Texas

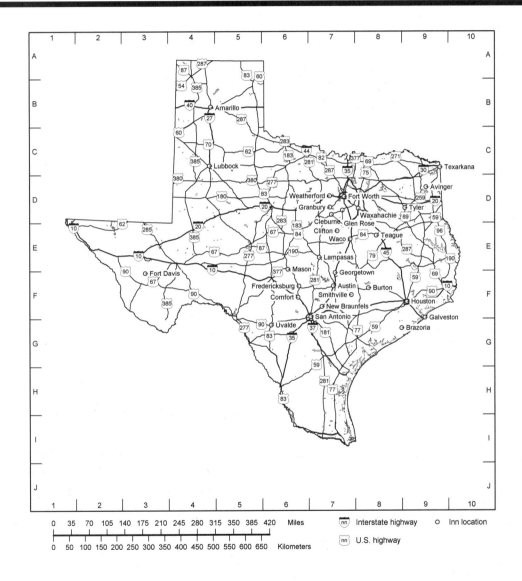

Amarillo B4

Parkview House B&B

1311 S Jefferson St
Amarillo, TX 79101-4029
(806)373-9464
E-mail: parkviewbb@aol.com
Web: hometown.aol.com/Parkviewbb/index.htm

Circa 1908. Ionic columns support the wraparound wicker-filled front porch of this prairie Victorian. Herb and rose gardens, highlighted by statuary and Victorian gazing ball, surround the property. Antique mahogany, walnut and oak pieces are found throughout. Guest rooms all feature draped bedsteads and romantic decor. A gourmet, full or continental-plus breakfast is served in an Andy Warhol-style kitchen or in the formal dining room. Guests can relax and enjoy the fireplaces, there's one in the kitchen and another in the common room. After a day of sightseeing, guests can enjoy a soak under the stars in the inn's hot tub or borrow a bicycle for a tour of the historic neighborhood. There are a multitude of area attractions, including shopping for antiques along historic Route 66, hiking in Palo Duro Canyon, touring historic homes and museums, hiking, birdwatching or perhaps attending the ballet, opera, symphony or a performance of "Texas," an outdoor musical drama presented nearby.

Historic Interest: Panhandle Plains Museum (15 minutes), Palo Duro State Park (23 miles), Alibates Flint Monument (16 miles).

Innkeeper(s): Carol & Nabil Dia. $65-135. MC, VISA, AX, PC, TC. TAC10. 5 rooms, 3 with PB, 1 suite and 1 cottage. Breakfast included in rates. Types of meals: Full gourmet bkfst, cont plus and early coffee/tea. Snacks/refreshments available. Beds: QD. TV, some ceiling fans, desks and telephones in room. Air conditioning. VCR, fax and bicycles on premises. Weddings and small meetings hosted. Arabic spoken. Amusement parks, antiquing, bicycling, hiking, horseback riding, bird watching, live theater, parks, shopping, tennis and water sports nearby.

"You are what give B&Bs such a wonderful reputation. Thanks very much for the wonderful stay! The hospitality was warm and the ambiance incredible."

Austin F7

Austin's Wildflower Inn B&B

1200 W 22 1/2 St
Austin, TX 78705-5304
(512)477-9639 Fax:(512)474-4188
E-mail: kjackson@io.com
Web: www.austinswildflowerinn.com

Circa 1936. This Colonial-style home fits right into its woodsy street, located in a quiet Austin neighborhood just a few blocks from the University of Texas. Three of the rooms are named for relatives of innkeeper Kay Jackson, who is related to a former president of the Republic of Texas. Lacy curtains, stenciling, pedestal sinks, quilts and antiques create a homey country atmosphere. One room has a canopy bed, another includes a four-poster, oak bed. Each morning, a new Wildflower specialty is served at breakfast, along with homemade breads or muffins and fresh fruit. The State Capitol Complex is a few minutes from the home.

Innkeeper(s): Kay Jackson. $79-94. MC, VISA, AX, PC, TC. 4 rooms, 2 with PB. Breakfast included in rates. Types of meals: Full bkfst and early coffee/tea. Beds: QD. Ceiling fan and telephones (two rooms) in room. Air conditioning. Fax on premises. Antiquing, fishing, live theater, parks, shopping, sporting events and water sports nearby.

"I was enchanted by your very friendly reception and personal care for my well-being."

Carrington's Bluff

1900 David St
Austin, TX 78705-5312
(512)479-0638 (800)871-8908 Fax:(512)476-4769

Circa 1877. Situated on a tree-covered bluff in the heart of Austin, this inn sits next to a 500-year-old oak tree. The innkeepers, one a Texan, the other British, combine down-home hospitality with English charm. The house is filled with English and American antiques and handmade quilts. Rooms are carefully decorated with dried flowers, inviting colors and antique beds, such as the oak barley twist bed in the Martha Hill Carrington Room. After a hearty breakfast, relax on a 35-foot-long porch that overlooks the bluff. The Austin area is booming with things to do.

Innkeeper(s): Lisa Kloss. $69-109. MC, VISA, AX, DC, CB, DS, PC, TC. 8 rooms with PB, 1 suite, 1 cottage and 1 conference room. Breakfast and snacks/refreshments included in rates. Types of meals: Full gourmet bkfst and early coffee/tea. Beds: KQDT. Cable TV, phone and ceiling fan in room. Air conditioning. VCR, fax, copier, library and child care on premises. Weddings, small meetings, family reunions and seminars hosted. Amusement parks, antiquing, fishing, live theater, parks, shopping, sporting events and water sports nearby.

Publicity: *PBS Special.*

"Victorian writer's dream place."

Fairview

1304 Newning Ave
Austin, TX 78704-1841
(512)444-4746 (800)310-4746 Fax:(512)444-3494
E-mail: fairview@io.com
Web: www.fairview-bnb.com

Circa 1910. Surrounded by huge live oak trees, this Texas Revival-style home has been designated an Austin historic landmark. Each of the four large guest rooms on the second floor has impressive antique beds and private baths. Some rooms also feature clawfoot tubs, screened porches and sun rooms. Two suites are offered in the Carriage House. Each has a private entrance, sitting room, full kitchen, eating area, bedroom and bath.

Historic Interest: Texas State Capitol (2 miles).

Innkeeper(s): Duke & Nancy Waggoner. $99-149. MC, VISA, AX, DC, CB, PC, TC. TAC10. 6 rooms, 3 with PB and 3 suites. Breakfast included in rates. Types of meals: Full bkfst and early coffee/tea. Beds: KQT. Cable TV, phone and ceiling fan in room. Air conditioning. Fax, copier and library on premises. Amusement parks, antiquing, fishing, live theater, parks, shopping, sporting events and water sports nearby.

"The meal was fantastic, the tour wonderful and your hospitality gracious."

Governors' Inn

611 W 22nd St
Austin, TX 78705-5115
(512)479-0638 (800)871-8908 Fax:(512)476-4769
E-mail: governorsinn@earthlink.net
Web: www.governorsinnaustin.com

Circa 1897. This Neoclassical Victorian is just a few blocks from the University of Texas campus and three blocks from the State Capitol. Guests can enjoy the view of two acres of trees and foliage from the porches that decorate each story of the inn. The innkeepers have decorated the guest rooms with antiques and named them after former Texas governors. Several of the bathrooms include clawfoot tubs.

Innkeeper(s): Lisa Kloss. $59-119. MC, VISA, AX, DC, CB, DS, TC. 10 rooms with PB, 5 with FP and 1 conference room. Breakfast, afternoon tea and snacks/refreshments included in rates. Types of meals: Full gourmet bkfst and early coffee/tea. Picnic lunch, banquet service and catering service available. Beds: KQ. Cable TV, phone, turndown service, ceiling fan, hair dryers and robes in room. Air conditioning. VCR, fax and copier on premises. Handicap access. Weddings, small meetings, family reunions and seminars hosted. Antiquing, fishing, live theater, parks, shopping, sporting events and water sports nearby. Pets Allowed.

Healthy Quarters

1215 Parkway
Austin, TX 78703-4132
(512)476-7484 (800)392-6566 Fax:(512)480-9356
E-mail: healthyquarters@webtv.net
Web: www.healthyquarters.com

Circa 1935. This homestay is located a half-mile from the Texas state capitol. The comfortable accommodations include the Sun Room, which features an arched ceiling, a quilt-topped bed and country décor. The Ivy Room also features country-style furnishings and plenty of sunlight, as a long series of windows adorns one wall. The guest refrigerators are stocked with milk, eggs, yogurt, English muffins and coffee. Juice and fresh fruit also is provided.

Historic Interest: State Capitol (1/2 mile), French Legation (1.5 mile), Museum (3 miles).

Innkeeper(s): Marilyn Grooms. $65-85. MC, VISA, AX, DS. 2 rooms with PB. Breakfast included in rates. Type of meal: Veg bkfst. Beds: QD. Cable TV, phone and VCR in room. Central air. Fax and copier on premises. Antiquing, art galleries, bicycling, canoeing/kayaking, golf, hiking, state Capitol, LBJ Library, live theater, museums, parks, shopping and sporting events nearby.

Burton   F8

Long Point Inn

3806 FM 390 West
burton, TX 77835-5584
(409)289-3171
E-mail: neins1@aol.com
Web: www.bbhost.com/longpointinnburtontx

Circa 1978. It might seem unusual to find a Bavarian chalet in Texas, but not when you consider that many German immigrants made the state their home after arriving in America. One of those immigrant families once lived in an 1840s log cabin that has been restored and added to the inn complex. This cabin has a stone fireplace and sleeps six.

Although this inn is newer, the innkeepers patterned their dream home in Old World style, including decorating it with treasures picked up during their global travels. The home rests on a 175-acre working cattle ranch that has been in the family for four generations. So, it's at this Bavarian inn and ranch where guests enjoy the best of Texas with a touch of Europe. Rooms are a little bit Old World and a little bit country. A hearty breakfast is served underneath a German crystal chandelier on a table set with fine china. Guests might partake of a savory egg dish, homemade German sausage, potatoes, freshly baked breads and a fresh fruit compote during their morning meal. The inn is located along FM 390, the only highway in Texas to be designated a historic, scenic highway and is midway between Houston and Austin.

Innkeeper(s): Bill & Jeannine Neinast. $80-130. AX. TAC10. 3 rooms, 2 with PB, 1 with FP and 1 cottage. Breakfast and snacks/refreshments included in rates. Type of meal: Full gourmet bkfst. Beds: QDT. Phone and ceiling fan in room. Air conditioning. VCR on premises. German spoken. Antiquing, classical music and Shakespeare, parks and shopping nearby.

"The wildflowers, Texas sunshine and the goodness of you two all created a warmth we dearly loved."

Cleburne   D7

Cleburne House

201 N Anglin St
Cleburne, TX 76031-4134
(817)641-0085
E-mail: jrb@digitex.net
Web: www.digitex.net/cleburnehouse/

Circa 1886. A sweeping wraparound veranda accented by gingerbread trim is one of the classic characteristics of this Queen Anne Victorian. Inside, visitors will find hardwood floors, stained-glass windows and comfortably appointed rooms decorated with antiques, lace and ceiling fans. Homemade cookies, ice cream, tea and coffee are served in the afternoon.

Innkeeper(s): Jan Bills. $95. 4 rooms, 2 with PB. Breakfast and snacks/refreshments included in rates. Types of meals: Full bkfst, cont and early coffee/tea. Beds: KD. Cable TV and ceiling fan in room. Air conditioning. Spa and library on premises. Weddings, small meetings and family reunions hosted. Amusement parks, antiquing, fishing, golf, live theater, parks, shopping, sporting events, tennis and water sports nearby.

"Never have we had such a good breakfast served with so much charm."

Comfort   F6

Idlewilde

115 Hwy 473
Comfort, TX 78013
(830)995-3844

Circa 1902. This Western-style farmhouse and its cottages have come to be known as "Haven in the Hills." The home and surrounding grounds were a girls' summer camp for more than 60 years. The inn has no set check-in or check-out times. The innkeepers offer breakfast either in the main house dining area or at your specified spot (which could be breakfast in bed). The large, unique hallways and center rooms are open and airy with

lots of windows. Antiques and country French furniture decorate the entire lodge.

Innkeeper(s): Hank Engel & Connie Engel. $77-93. 2 cottages. Breakfast included in rates. Type of meal: Full bkfst. Picnic lunch available. Beds: Q. Weddings, small meetings, family reunions and seminars hosted. Amusement parks, antiquing, fishing, golf, shopping, sporting events and water sports nearby. Pets Allowed.

Publicity: *Austin Chronicle, Hill Country Recorder.*

Fort Davis   F3

The Hotel Limpia

PO Box 1341
Fort Davis, TX 79734-1341
(915)426-3237 (800)662-5517 Fax:(915)426-3983

Circa 1912. Four buildings and three guest houses make up this restored hotel, located in the Davis Mountains. Favorite places for guests to relax include the courtyard garden with the

smell of roses and herbs, the glassed-in veranda with its plants and the porches with rocking chairs. The flavor of old Texas can be felt at this

inn, constructed of pink limestone quarried in town near Sleeping Lion Mountain. There are two gift shops on the premises, as well as a dining room and private club.

Historic Interest: The Fort Davis National Historic Site, Overland Trail Museum and Neill Doll Museum are nearby.

Innkeeper(s): Lanna & Joe Duncan. $79-150. MC, VISA, AX, DS, PC, TC. 39 rooms with PB. Type of meal: Early coffee/tea. Dinner and catering service available. Restaurant on premises. Beds: KQD. Cable TV and ceiling fan in room. Air conditioning. VCR, fax and copier on premises. Handicap access. Weddings, small meetings, family reunions and seminars hosted. Spanish spoken. Golf, McDonald Observatory, hiking, historic sites, parks and shopping nearby. Pets allowed: $10.00 per pet.

"Not many like this one left. Great."

The Veranda Country Inn B&B

PO Box 1238
Fort Davis, TX 79734-1238
(888)383-2847
E-mail: info@theveranda.com

Circa 1883. A mile above sea level sits this rustic historic inn, which first opened as the Lempert Hotel, a stopping point for travelers on the nearby Overland Trail. An owner later used the building for apartments, but current innkeepers Paul and Kathie Woods returned the home into a place for hospitality. Paul, who has a doctorate in design, and Kathie have restored their bed & breakfast's high ceilings, wood floors and beaded

wood ceilings back to their original condition. The interior is furnished with antiques and collectibles. All rooms have a private bath, and the separate Carriage House and Garden Cottage are available in addition to the 11 inn rooms. The grounds offer the serene setting of gardens and quiet courtyards.

Historic Interest: The Fort Davis area is full of historic places to visit, including the Fort Davis Historic Site, an 1854 restored frontier fort. The largest original unpaved portion of the Overland Trail is just a block away, and the Overland Trail Museum is another popular historic attraction. The Neill Doll Museum, which is located in a turn-of-the-century home, features more than 300 antique dolls.

Innkeeper(s): Paul & Kathie Woods. $80-115. MC, VISA, DS. 14 rooms with PB, 4 suites and 2 cottages. Breakfast included in rates. Type of meal: Full bkfst. Beds: KQ. Small meetings hosted. Antiquing, parks and shopping nearby.

Fort Worth   D7

Miss Molly's Hotel

109 1/2 W Exchange Ave
Fort Worth, TX 76106-8508
(817)626-1522 (800)996-6559 Fax:(817)625-2723

Circa 1910. An Old West ambiance permeates this hotel, which once was a house of ill repute. Miss Josie's Room, named for the former madame, is decked with elaborate wall and ceiling coverings and carved oak furniture. The Gunslinger Room is filled with pictures of famous and infamous gunfighters. Rodeo memorabilia deco-

rates the Rodeo Room, and twin iron beds and a pot belly stove add flair to the Cowboy's Room. Telephones and TV sets are the only things missing from the rooms, as the innkeeper hopes to preserve the flavor of the past.

Innkeeper(s): Mark & Alice Hancock. $75-170. MC, VISA, AX, DC, CB, DS, PC, TC. TAC10. 8 rooms, 1 with PB. Breakfast included in rates. Types of meals: Cont plus and early coffee/tea. Restaurant on premises. Beds: DT. Ceiling fan in room. Air conditioning. Fax and copier on premises. Small meetings, family reunions and seminars hosted. Amusement parks, antiquing, stockyards National Historic district, live theater, shopping and sporting events nearby.

Fredericksburg   F6

Alte Welt Gasthof (Old World Inn)

PO Box 628
Fredericksburg, TX 78624
(830)997-0443 (888)991-6749 Fax:(830)997-0040
E-mail: stay@texas-bed-n-breakfast.com
Web: www.texas-bed-n-breakfast.com

Circa 1915. Located on the second floor above a Main Street shop, Alte Welt is in a Basse Block building in the historic district. The entryway opens to an antique-filled foyer. A three-room suite offers a white sofa, silver accents including a silver, tin ceiling, wood floors and an antique iron four-poster bed draped in soft gauze. An armoire with TV and a small refrigerator and microwave add convenience. The innkeeper collects antique, crocheted and embroidered linens for the guest rooms. There is a spacious deck with hot tub adjoining one of the suites. Together, the two suites can accommodate as many as 10 people, so it is popular with families and small groups, who enjoy the freedom of simply going downstairs to Main Street and all its boutiques, shops and restaurants.

Innkeeper(s): Ron & Donna Maddux. $135-150. MC, VISA, AX, DS, PC, TC. 2 suites. Breakfast included in rates. Types of meals: Cont and early coffee/tea. Beds: Q. Cable TV, phone, ceiling fan, microwave, coffee bar and in room. Air conditioning. Small meetings, family reunions and seminars hosted. Antiquing, fishing, golf, museums, hunting, parks, shopping and tennis nearby.

Country Cottage Inn

405 E Main St
Fredericksburg, TX 78624
(830)997-8549
Web: www.countrycottageinn.com

Circa 1850. This beautifully preserved house was built by blacksmith and cutler Frederick Kiehne. With two-foot-thick walls and hand-hewn timbers, it was the first two-story limestone house in town. The Country Cottage holds a collection of antiques that are both

elegant and comfortable, accentuated by Ralph Lauren fabrics. Some of the baths include whirlpool tubs. The Oak Suite has a fireplace. Full breakfasts are left in each room for guests to enjoy at their leisure. Guests also enjoy swimming, tennis and exercise facility privileges at nearby Baron's Creek Racquet and Swim club. Main Street and the sites and shops of Fredericksburg are just steps from the inn.

Historic Interest: Nimitz Museum (within 10 miles), LBJ State Park (near), Johnson city (LBJ Ranch Stonewall, birthplace home), Pioneer Museum.

Innkeeper(s): Mary Lou Rodriquez. $85-145. MC, VISA, AX, DS, PC. TAC10. 4 rooms with PB, 1 with FP and 2 suites. Breakfast included in rates. Type of meal: Full bkfst. Beds: KQD. Cable TV, phone, Jacuzzi tubs, two-room suites and some fireplaces in room. Air conditioning. Antiquing, fishing, golf, festivals, bat cave, wildlife areas, museums, parks, shopping and water sports nearby.

"A step back in time in 1850 style."

Muncey Ranch Guest House

Ranch Rd 965 at Achtzehn Rd
Fredericksburg, TX 78624
(830)997-6015 (888)997-6015 Fax:(800)593-5085

Circa 1870. Built of thick stone walls and hand-hewn timber, this historic gem was restored completely by the innkeepers, one of whom is a retired architect. The interior features a fireplace and exposed beams, adding a rustic touch to elegant

rooms filled with antiques, Oriental rugs and artwork. Guests enjoy the run of the house, including a private porch and sitting room with wicker and bamboo furnishings. The home can accommodate up to three guests, and there is a kitchen for guest use. There are more than 100 acres to enjoy, complete with a waterfall and a spring-fed creek with a swimming hole.

Historic Interest: Nimitz Museum (5 miles), Enchanted Rock St Park (8 miles), LBJ Ranch National Park (15 miles).

Innkeeper(s): James & Virginia Muncey. $150. MC, VISA, TC. TAC7. 1 rooms with PB. Breakfast included in rates. Type of meal: Cont. Beds: Q. TV, phone and ceiling fan in room. Central air. Swimming on premises. Antiquing, art galleries, bicycling, fishing, golf, hiking, museums, parks, shopping, tennis and wineries nearby.

Galveston   F9

The Garden Inn, circa 1887

1601 Ball
Galveston, TX 77550
(409)770-0592
E-mail: as1231@aol.com
Web: www.galveston.com/gardeninn

The Garden Inn is located in the East End Historic District, a designated National Historic Landmark. The home features a unique style of architecture called High Victorian Chalet. Guests are immediately introduced to the European chalet influence with the double Dutch doors they enter. Family heirlooms, Victorian antiques and reproductions are found throughout the inn. The parlor with its beautiful cherry fireplace boasts furnishings that belonged to Angela's grandparents. Each guest room is named after a flower. Ask for the Rose Room and you'll enjoy an antique Rococo bedroom suite as well as nine-foot-high walk-through windows to a private balcony. Guests often use the pool and spa as well as the inn's library. Bishop's Palace is four blocks away and Moody Mansion a mile from the inn.

$70-165. 4 rooms.

Georgetown   F7

Claibourne House

912 Forest St
Georgetown, TX 78626-5524
(512)930-3934 Fax:(512)869-0202

Circa 1896. This turn-of-the-century Victorian was built by a local doctor to house his large family. The interior is decorated in an elegant mix of styles, with antiques, Southwestern and Oriental rugs and artwork. Each of the rooms is individually appointed and named. Two rooms have a marble bath and one bathroom features a skylight. Homemade breads, pastries and biscuits are the fare for the continental breakfasts. The B&B is just a few blocks from Georgetown's historic courthouse square.

Innkeeper(s): Clare Easley. $85-125. MC, VISA, PC, TC. TAC10. 4 rooms with PB, 2 with FP and 1 cottage. Breakfast included in rates. Types of meals: Cont plus and early coffee/tea. Beds: QDT. Ceiling fan in room. Air conditioning. Library on premises. Small meetings, family reunions and seminars hosted. Antiquing, fishing, golf, parks, shopping, sporting events and tennis nearby.

Pets Allowed.

Granbury   D7

Dabney House B&B

106 S Jones St
Granbury, TX 76048-1905
(817)579-1260 (800)566-1260

Circa 1907. Built during the Mission Period, this Craftsman-style country manor boasts original hardwood floors, stained-glass windows and some of the original light fixtures. The parlor and dining rooms have large, exposed, wooden beams and the ceilings throughout are 10-feet high. The Dabney Suite has

a private entrance into an enclosed sun porch with rattan table and chairs that allow for a private breakfast or a candlelight dinner by advance reservation. The bedroom of this suite is furnished with a four-post tester bed with drapes and an 1800 wardrobe.

Historic Interest: Historic Town Square (one-half mile), Dinosaur Valley State Park (18 miles), Texas Dr. Pepper Plant (45 miles), Elizabeth Crockett (5 miles).

Innkeeper(s): John & Gwen Hurley. $70-105. MC, VISA, AX, PC, TC. TAC10. 4 rooms with PB and 1 suite. Breakfast and snacks/refreshments included in rates. Type of meal: Full bkfst. Dinner available. Beds: Q. Ceiling fan in room. Air conditioning. VCR, spa, library, hot tub and evening beverage on premises. Small meetings, family reunions and seminars hosted. Antiquing, fishing, live theater, parks, shopping and water sports nearby.

Pearl Street Inn B&B

319 W Pearl St
Granbury, TX 76048-2437
(817)579-7465 (888)732-7578

Circa 1911. Known historically as the B. M. Estes House, the inn is decorated with a mix of English, French and American antiques. The Pearl Room boasts a king-size antique Victorian half canopy bed, a restored clawfoot tub and wall sink. The

water closet is a few steps from the guest room door. Other guest rooms include clawfoot tubs, crystal lamps and an outdoor hot tub.

Historic Interest: Town Square (3 blocks), Fort Worth Stockyards (40 minutes), Dinosaur Valley State Park (18 miles), Granbury Cemetery (2 miles), Fossil Rim (15 miles).

Innkeeper(s): Danette D. Hebda. $59-119. PC, TC. TAC10. 5 rooms with PB and 1 suite. Breakfast included in rates. Types of meals: Full gourmet bkfst and early coffee/tea. Beds: KD. Ceiling fan and table and chairs in room. Central air. VCR, copier, complimentary coffee and tea and cocoa on premises. Weddings and small meetings hosted. Antiquing, fishing, golf, drive-in movie, live theater, parks, shopping and water sports nearby.

"Needless to say, we want to stay forever! We had a grand time and highly enjoyed conversations and hospitality."

Houston   F9

Angel Arbor B&B Inn

848 Heights Blvd
Houston, TX 77007-1507
(713)868-4654 (800)722-8788

Circa 1922. Each of the rooms at Angel Arbor has a heavenly name and elegant decor. The Angelique Room offers a cherry sleigh bed and a balcony overlooking the garden. Canopy or poster beds grace the other rooms and suite, named Gabriel,

Raphael and Michael. The Georgian-style home is located in the historic Houston Heights neighborhood and was built by a prominent local family. The innkeeper, a cookbook author, prepares a mouthwatering homemade breakfast each morning. Ask about the innkeeper's special murder-mystery dinner parties.

Innkeeper(s): Marguerite Swanson. $95-125. MC, VISA, AX, DS, PC, TC. TAC10. 5 rooms with PB and 1 conference room. Breakfast included in

rates. Types of meals: Full gourmet bkfst and early coffee/tea. Afternoon tea available. Beds: Q. Cable TV, phone, turndown service, ceiling fan and VCR in room. Air conditioning. Fax and library on premises. Small meetings, family reunions and seminars hosted. Amusement parks, antiquing, fishing, jogging, live theater, parks, shopping, sporting events and water sports nearby.

Robin's Nest

4104 Greeley St
Houston, TX 77006-5609
(713)528-5821 (800)622-8343 Fax:(713)521-2154
E-mail: robin@hypercon.com
Web: www.houstonbnb.com

Circa 1898. Robin's Nest is the oldest home in Houston's historic Montrose District. A two-story wooden Queen Anne Victorian, the historic home features original pine hardwoods, tall windows, high ceilings and a wraparound veranda. Luxurious fabrics, all custom sewn, warm the interior, which also boasts wall murals. The home originally was a dairy farm and now rests on an urban lot surrounded by dozens of rose bushes and azaleas. Located in the city's museum and arts district, the inn offers close proximity to downtown Houston, theaters and gourmet restaurants. Galveston and Johnson Space Center are about an hour away.

Historic Interest: The San Jacinto Monument and Armannd Bayou are 30 minutes from the home. Bayou Bend Gardens are 15 minutes away, Theatre District, Port of Houston, Museum and Arts District.

Innkeeper(s): Robin Smith. $75-120. MC, VISA, AX, DS. 4 rooms with PB and 1 conference room. Breakfast included in rates. Type of meal: Full bkfst. Beds: QT. Cable TV, phone, ceiling fan and baths in room. Air conditioning. Weddings, small meetings, family reunions and seminars hosted. Amusement parks, antiquing, fishing, live theater, museums, shopping, sporting events and water sports nearby.

"Fanciful and beautiful, comfortable and happy. We saw a whole new side of Houston, thanks to you."

Sara's B&B Inn

941 Heights Blvd
Houston, TX 77008-6911
(713)868-1130 (800)593-1130 Fax:(713)868-3284

Circa 1898. This mauve and white, gingerbread Victorian is located in the Houston Heights, one of the first planned suburbs in Texas. Book the Tyler Room and climb the stairs that wind up to the cupola. In the Austin Suite in the turret and guests will enjoy a balcony overlooking the street. The rooms and suites are decorated with antiques and collectibles. Downtown Houston is five minutes away, and the inn is a good location to visit the Galleria, the museum district or the Arts and Medical center. The inn is a popular spot for retreats, weddings and business meetings.

Innkeeper(s): Connie & Bob McCreight. $70-150. MC, VISA, AX, DC, CB, DS. 13 rooms, 11 with PB and 4 suites. Breakfast included in rates. Type of meal: Full bkfst. Beds: KQDT. Fax on premises. Antiquing and museums nearby.

Lampasas   E7

Historic Moses Hughes B&B

RR 2 Box 31
Lampasas, TX 76550-9601
(512)556-5923

Circa 1856. Nestled among ancient oaks in the heart of the Texas Hill Country, this native stone ranch house rests on 45 acres that include springs, a creek, wildlife and other natural beauty. The ranch was built by Moses Hughes, the first white settler and founder of Lampasas. He and  his wife decided to stay in the area after her health dramatically improved after visiting the springs. Guests can join the innkeepers on the stone patio or upstairs wooden porch for a taste of Texas Hill Country life.

Historic Interest: Fort Hood, on the road to Colorado Bend State Park and Gorman Falls, Mission San Saba (within an hour), Vanishing Texas River Cruise.
Innkeeper(s): Al & Beverly Solomon. $75-90. MC, VISA, PC, TC. TAC10. 3 rooms with PB. Breakfast included in rates. Type of meal: Full gourmet bkfst. Beds: QD. Air conditioning. VCR, library and creek & springs on premises. Antiquing, fishing, birding, hiking,hunting, caves, parks and water sports nearby.

"What a delightful respite! Thank you for sharing your very interesting philosophies and personalities with us at this very special B&B. We hate to leave."

Lubbock   C4

Broadway Manor B&B

1811 Broadway St
Lubbock, TX 79401-3015
(806)763-0196 Fax:(806)763-0196

Circa 1926. Each of the guest rooms at Broadway Manor has been decorated in a different theme. Guest rooms feature names such as the Victorian Lady, the Wild West Show, the Salzburg Suite and the Garden of Siam. A prominent local banker, C.E. Maedgen, built Broadway Manor. The home is located in a historic, residential Lubbock neighborhood close to golf courses, Buffalo Springs Lake, wineries, museums and a science center. Texas Tech University is just a few blocks away.

Historic Interest: Depot Districts (1/2 mile).
Innkeeper(s): Hank & Lenora Browning. $55-95. MC, VISA, PC, TC. 4 rooms with PB. Breakfast and snacks/refreshments included in rates. Types of meals: Full bkfst and early coffee/tea. Beds: KQT. Ceiling fan in room. Central air. VCR, fax, copier and library on premises. Weddings, small meetings, family reunions and seminars hosted. Amusement parks, antiquing, art galleries, golf, live theater, museums, parks, shopping, sporting events and wineries nearby.

"You and your home have the same charm-friendship and an appreciation of life."

Mason   E6

Hasse House and Ranch

PO Box 779
Mason, TX 76856
(888)414-2773

Circa 1883. Guests may explore the 320-acre Hasse ranch, which is a working ranch where deer, wild turkey, feral hogs, quail and a bounty of wildflowers and bluebonnets are common sights. After purchasing the land, Henry Hasse and his wife lived in a log cabin on the property before building the sandstone home 23 years later. Three generations of Hasses have lived here, and today it is owned by a great-granddaughter who restored the home in 1980. The house is located in the small German village of Art, Texas, which is located six miles east of Mason. The innkeepers rent the two-bedroom National Register home out to only one group or guest at a time, host free. The home is filled with period furniture and accessories, yet offers the modern convenience of an on-site washer and dryer and a fully stocked kitchen. The ranch grounds include a two-mile nature trail perfect for nature lovers.

Innkeeper(s): Laverne Lee. $95. MC, VISA, PC, TC. 2 rooms with PB. Type of meal: Cont plus. Beds: D. TV, ceiling fan, dishwasher, microwave and etc in room. Air conditioning. Library, washer, dryer, stove, microwave and patio on premises. Handicap access. Weddings, small meetings and family reunions hosted. Antiquing, bicycle routes, 2 mile nature trail on ranch, bird-watching, wildflower viewing, parks, shopping and water sports nearby.

"We enjoyed every aspect of our stay; the atmosphere, sense of history, rustic setting with a touch of class. We would love to return the same time next year!"

New Braunfels   F7

Karbach Haus

487 W San Antonio St
New Braunfels, TX 78130-7901
(830)625-2131 (800)972-5941 Fax:(830)629-1126

Circa 1906. For six decades the Karbach family resided in this turn-of-the-century home, beginning with Dr. Hylmar Karbach and now with innkeepers Kathleen Karbach Kinney and her husband, Ben Jack. The Kinneys have restored the home to its original glory, filling it with family antiques and an eclectic assortment of pieces collected during Ben Jack's 30-year Naval career, which took the pair around the world. Particularly unique pieces include a 19th-century grandfather clock from Germany and many hand-painted porcelain pieces dated and signed by Dr. Karbach's mother. The family is always adding to their family homestead. Recent additions include a swimming pool and a whirlpool spa in the gardens. The family also remodeled the carriage house, and the spacious accommodations include Jacuzzi tubs and ceiling fans. The Karbachs serve an expansive, German-style breakfast each morning in the formal dining room or in the sun parlor. The multi-course feast begins with fresh fruit, a fruit sauce, cheese board and home-made sweet breads. A savory egg dish follows and lastly, a sweet dish is served. Pancakes, French toast, waffles and bread pudding are among the options.

Historic Interest: The oldest bakery in Texas, Hummel Museum and the Lindheimer Home are nearby. The oldest dance hall in Texas and a historic district are about three miles away, and the historic sites of San Antonio are 28 miles from the inn.

Innkeeper(s): Captain Ben Jack Kinney & Kathleen Kinney. $110-200. MC, VISA, DS. 6 rooms with PB and 2 suites. Breakfast included in rates. Type of meal: Full bkfst. Gourmet dinner available. Beds: KQ. Spa and swimming on premises. Antiquing, museums and water sports nearby.

"Many thanks for a very fine stay in your home. You are people of taste and graciousness, and your home reflects both those qualities. We've truly enjoyed being here."

San Antonio   F7

A. Beckmann Inn and Carriage House Bed and Breakfast

222 E Guenther
San Antonio, TX 78204-1405
(210)229-1449 (800)945-1449 Fax:(210)229-1061

Circa 1886. A wraparound porch with white wicker furniture warmly welcomes guests to the main house of this Victorian inn. Through the entrance and into the living room, guests  stand on an intricately designed wood mosaic floor imported from Paris. Arch-shaped pocket doors with framed opaque glass open to the formal dining room, where breakfast is served. All the guest rooms feature 12- to 14-foot ceilings with fans; tall, ornately carved queen-size antique Victorian beds; colorful floral accessories; and antiques.

Historic Interest: Alamo, Spanish Governor's Place, Riverwalk, missions, King William Historic District.

Innkeeper(s): Betty Jo & Don Schwartz. $99-150. MC, VISA, AX, DC, DS, PC. 5 rooms with PB, 2 with FP and 2 suites. Breakfast included in rates. Type of meal: Full gourmet bkfst. Beds: Q. Cable TV, phone, ceiling fan and robes in room. Air conditioning. Fax, copier, library and refrigerator on premises. Family reunions hosted. Amusement parks, antiquing, Alamo, Riverwalk, missions, Mexican market, Spanish Governor's Palace, live theater, parks, shopping and sporting events nearby.

"The Beckmann Inn & Carriage House is truly a home away from home for all who stay there. Don and Betty Jo put their heart and soul into making every guest's stay a memorable experience."

Adams House B&B

231 Adams St
San Antonio, TX 78210-1104
(210)224-4791 (800)666-4810 Fax:(210)223-5125

Circa 1902. Southern tradition and hospitality abound at this bed & breakfast, decorated with sweeping verandas on both its first and second stories. The historic home has been painstakingly restored, including Oriental rugs, period antiques and handmade reproductions. Adams House is located in the King William Historic District. The River Walk is just two blocks away, and The Alamo is a 15-minute walk.

Innkeeper(s): Nora Peterson & Richard Green. $99-149. PC, TC. Cable TV, phone and ceiling fan in room. Air conditioning. VCR and spa on premises. Weddings, small meetings and family reunions hosted. Amusement parks, golf, live theater, shopping and sporting events nearby.

A Victorian Lady Inn

421 Howard St
San Antonio, TX 78212-5531
(210)224-2524 (800)879-7116 Fax:(210)224-5123

Circa 1898. The innkeepers painstakingly restored this antebellum home back to its turn-of-the-century glory. The inn originally was built for a cattle rancher and his wife. The rancher's family occupied the home for more than seven decades. Today, the Victorian Lady features eight guest rooms, each boasting period antiques, lacy curtains and Victorian decor. Innkeeper Kathleen Bowski prepares a delightful full breakfast accompanied by home-baked breads, fruit and cereals. An outdoor hot tub and in-ground pool is secluded in a tropical setting with palms and banana trees.

Historic Interest: The Alamo, Monte Vista Historical District, San Antonio's Mission Trail and the King William Historic District are some of the nearby attractions.

Innkeeper(s): Joe & Kathleen Bowski. $89-135. MC, VISA, AX, DS. TAC10. 8 rooms with PB, 3 with FP, 2 suites and 1 conference room. Breakfast included in rates. Type of meal: Full bkfst. Beds: KQDT. Cable TV, phone and ceiling fan in room. Air conditioning. Fax, spa, library and swimming pool on premises. Small meetings, family reunions and seminars hosted. Amusement parks, antiquing, fishing, golf, live theater, parks, shopping, sporting events and tennis nearby.

"An oasis in the heart of San Antonio."

A Yellow Rose

229 Madison
San Antonio, TX 78204
(210)229-9903 (800)950-9903 Fax:(210)229-1691

Circa 1878. This historic Victorian is located in the quiet and elegant King William Historic District, adjacent to San Antonio's downtown area. There are five distinctly decorated and spacious guest rooms to choose from, each with beautiful furnishings and decor. Turn-of-the-century antiques add a nostalgic ambiance. A two-block walk will take guests to the River Walk, and it's just a block to the trolley. Guests also can walk five blocks to the downtown area, convention center and many restaurants.

Historic Interest: Alamo (8 blocks), St. Francis Church (8 blocks), San Antonio Riverwalk (2 blocks), Mission Trail (one-half mile).

Innkeeper(s): Kit Walker & Deb Walker. $100-175. MC, VISA, DS, PC, TC. TAC10. 5 rooms with PB, 1 suite and 1 conference room. Breakfast included in rates. Type of meal: Full gourmet bkfst. Beds: Q. Cable TV, phone, ceiling fan and robes in room. Air conditioning. VCR and library on premises. Small meetings, family reunions and seminars hosted. Amusement parks, antiquing, live theater, parks, shopping, sporting events and water sports nearby.

"Recommendations will be forthcoming. Best Christmas gift we gave ourselves coming here! Thanks."

Beauregard House B&B

215 Beauregard
San Antonio, TX 78204-1304
(210)222-1198 (800)841-9377 Fax:(210)492-0453
E-mail: beauregardbandb@hotmail
Web: beauregardbandb.com

Circa 1900. This historic Victorian is located on a quiet street within San Antonio's King William Historic District. The Riverwalk is just a block away, and the home is near to shops, restaurants and other attractions. Relaxation and a

step away from the fast pace of modern times is the theme at Beauregard House. Rooms aren't cluttered with modern amenities such as phones and TVs. Instead, period antiques decorate the bedchambers. Guests can relax on the front porch or play a game or watch TV in the home's living room. Homemade treats are served to guests upon arrival, and each morning brings with it the promise of a full, gourmet breakfast. Fresh fruit dishes and homemade breads accompany entrees such as baked French toast.

Innkeeper(s): Ann Trabal. $89-119. MC, VISA, PC, TC. TAC10. 4 rooms with PB, 1 with FP and 1 conference room. Breakfast included in rates. Types of meals: Full gourmet bkfst, veg bkfst and early coffee/tea. Snacks/refreshments and picnic lunch available. Beds: KQT. Ceiling fan in room. Central air. Library on premises. Weddings, small meetings and family reunions hosted. Amusement parks, antiquing, art galleries, bicycling, fishing, golf, horseback riding, live theater, museums, parks, shopping, sporting events, tennis and water sports nearby.

Bonner Garden

145 E Agarita Ave
San Antonio, TX 78212-2923
(210)733-4222 (800)396-4222 Fax:(210)733-6129

Circa 1910. Mary Bonner was internationally renowned for her etchings and printmaking skills. Selected Bonner prints and works by other artists, including the Bonner House's owner, are displayed throughout the house. This Italian Renaissance inn has a rooftop patio and wet bar. The house made history when it was constructed by Atlee Ayres, who was one of the foremost architects of the era. The home was built of concrete, reinforced with steel and cast iron, and clad in stucco. Exercise facilities

include a 50-foot pool, Nordic Track exerciser and bicycles.

Innkeeper(s): Jan & Noel Stenoien. $85-125. MC, VISA, AX, DC, CB, DS, PC, TC. TAC10. 5 rooms with PB, 3 with FP. Breakfast included in rates. Type of meal: Full bkfst. Beds: KQ. Cable TV, phone, ceiling fan and VCR in room. Air conditioning. Fax, copier, swimming, bicycles, library, exercise room and rooftop spa on premises. Small meetings and family reunions hosted. Amusement parks, golf, live theater, parks, shopping, sporting events and tennis nearby.

"Second time was as great as the first."

Brackenridge House

230 Madison
San Antonio, TX 78204-1320
(210)271-3442 (800)221-1412 Fax:(210)226-3139
E-mail: benniesueb@aol.com
Web: www.brackenridgehouse.com

Circa 1901. Each of the guest rooms at Brackenridge House is individually decorated. Clawfoot tubs, iron beds and a private veranda are a few of the items that guests might discover. Several rooms include kitchenettes. Blansett Barn, often rented by families or those on an extended stay, includes two bedrooms, a bathroom, a full kitchen and living and dining areas. Many of San Antonio's interesting sites are nearby. The San Antonio Mission Trail begins just a block away, and trolleys will take you to the Alamo, the River Walk, convention center and more. Coffeehouses, restaurants and antique stores all are within walking distance. Small pets are welcome in Blansett Barn.

Innkeeper(s): Bennie & Sue Blansett. $89-175. MC, VISA, DC, DS, PC, TC. TAC10. 6 rooms with PB, 2 suites and 1 cottage. Breakfast included in rates. Types of meals: Full gourmet bkfst and early coffee/tea. Beds: KQD. Cable TV, phone, ceiling fan, VCR, microwave, irons and ironing boards and hair dryers in room. Air conditioning. Fax, copier and spa on premises. Family reunions hosted. Amusement parks, antiquing, fishing, golf, live theater, parks, shopping, sporting events and tennis nearby.

Pets allowed: Small pets in carriage house.

"Innkeeper was very nice, very helpful."

Christmas House B&B

2307 McCullough
San Antonio, TX 78212
(210)737-2786 (800)268-4187 Fax:(210)734-5712

Circa 1908. Located in Monte Vista historic district, this two-story white inn has a natural wood balcony built over the front porch. The window trim is in red and green, starting the Christmas theme of the inn. (There's a Christmas tree decorated all year long.) Guest rooms open out to pecan-shaded balconies. The Victorian Bedroom offers pink and mauve touches mixed with the room's gold and black decor. The Blue & Silver Room is handicap accessible and is on the first floor. Antique furnishings in the inn are available for sale.

Historic Interest: Alamo (1.5 miles), Riverwalk (1.5 miles).

$75-125. MC, VISA, PC, TC. TAC10. 5 rooms with PB, 1 suite and 1 conference room. Breakfast and snacks/refreshments included in rates. AP. Types of meals: Cont plus, veg bkfst and early coffee/tea. Beds: KQ. Ceiling fan in room. Central air. Fax, library and ADA room on premises. Handicap access. Family reunions hosted. Amusement parks, antiquing, art galleries, bicycling, golf, live theater, museums, parks and shopping nearby.

"What a treat to rise to the sweet smell of candied pecans and a tasty breakfast."

The Columns on Alamo

1037 S Alamo St
San Antonio, TX 78210-1109
(210)271-3245 (800)233-3364 Fax:(210)271-3245

Circa 1892. This bed & breakfast is located in an impressive Greek Revival home and a 1901 guest house in the King William Historic District. Victorian antiques and reproductions decorate the guest rooms, including pieces such as brass beds and fainting couches, four-poster beds, gas log fireplaces and several two-person Jacuzzis. The trolley stops a half block from the house, transporting

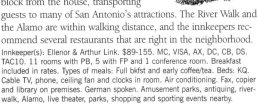

guests to many of San Antonio's attractions. The River Walk and the Alamo are within walking distance, and the innkeepers recommend several restaurants that are right in the neighborhood.

Innkeeper(s): Ellenor & Arthur Link. $89-155. MC, VISA, AX, DC, CB, DS. TAC10. 11 rooms with PB, 5 with FP and 1 conference room. Breakfast included in rates. Types of meals: Full bkfst and early coffee/tea. Beds: KQ. Cable TV, phone, ceiling fan and clocks in room. Air conditioning. Fax, copier and library on premises. German spoken. Amusement parks, antiquing, riverwalk, Alamo, live theater, parks, shopping and sporting events nearby.

"The house has been an inspiration. Very friendly and helpful host and hostess."

Noble Inns

107 Madison
San Antonio, TX 78204-1319
(210)225-4045 (800)221-4045 Fax:(210)227-0877
E-mail: nobleinns@aol.com
Web: www.nobleinns.com

Circa 1894. Two historic homes, both designated city historic structures, comprise the Noble Inns collection. Both are located in the King William Historic District. The Jackson House is a brick and limestone Victorian. It offers a conservatory of stained and leaded glass enclosing a heated spa. Breakfast is served in the dining room and there is a parlor. The Pancoast Carriage

House provides individual suites with full kitchens and stocked continental breakfasts. There is a swimming pool as well as spa. Both inns are furnished with Victorian-era antiques. There are fireplaces, marble baths, clawfoot tubs or whirlpools. Fresh flowers and fluffy monogrammed robes greet guests when they enter their rooms. Transportation in a classic 1960 Rolls Royce Silver Cloud II is available upon request. Call ahead for rates.

Innkeeper(s): Don & Liesl Noble. $130-190. MC, VISA, AX, DS, PC, TC. TAC10. 9 rooms with PB, 9 with FP and 4 suites. Breakfast and afternoon tea included in rates. Type of meal: Full bkfst. Beds: KQ. Cable TV, phone, turndown service and ceiling fan in room. Air conditioning. Fax, spa, library and voice mail on premises. Small meetings and family reunions hosted. Spanish spoken. Antiquing, live theater, parks, shopping and sporting events nearby.

"It couldn't have been better if we dreamed it! Thank you."

The Royal Swan B&B

236 Madison
San Antonio, TX 78204-1320
(210)223-3776 (800)368-3073 Fax:(210)271-0373
E-mail: theswan@onr.com
Web: www.royalswan.com

Circa 1892. This picture-perfect Victorian is filled with period furnishings that comfortably suit the handsome woodwork and polished floors. Crystal chandeliers, fireplaces and remarkable stained-glass windows add to the authentic atmosphere set by the foyer and a grand staircase, handsomely crafted out of pine. If you can't wait for the luscious peach or apple cobbler breakfast dessert, distract yourself with the quiche or crepes, bacon and fresh fruit, and the dessert will soon arrive. The Alamo, Riverwalk, restaurants and museums are all nearby.

Innkeeper(s): Curt & Helen Skredergard. $100-120. MC, VISA, AX, DS, PC, TC. 5 rooms with PB, 2 with FP. Breakfast and snacks/refreshments included in rates. Types of meals: Full gourmet bkfst and cont. Beds: Q. TV, phone and ceiling fan in room. Air conditioning. Fax and copier on premises. Antiquing, live theater and shopping nearby.

Smithville   F7

The Katy House

201 Ramona St, PO Box 803
Smithville, TX 78957-0803
(512)237-4262 (800)843-5289 Fax:(512)237-2239
E-mail: thekatyh@onr.com
Web: www.katyhouse.com

Circa 1909. Shaded by tall trees, the Katy House's Italianate exterior is graced by an arched portico over the bay-windowed living room. Georgian columns reflect the inn's turn-of-the-century origin. Long leaf pine floors, pocket doors and a graceful stairway accent the completely refurbished interior. The inn is decorated almost exclusively in American antique oak and railroad memorabilia. Historic Main Street is one block away with a fine collection of antique shops.

Also available are maps that outline walking or biking tours and point out scenic views such as that of the Colorado River from the city park. Guests usually come back from walking tours with pockets full of pecans found around town. Smithville was the hometown location for the movie "Hope Floats."

Innkeeper(s): Bruce & Sallie Blalock. $56-110. MC, VISA, AX, PC, TC. 5 rooms with PB, 1 suite and 2 cottages. Breakfast included in rates. Types of meals: Full bkfst and early coffee/tea. Beds: Q. TV, ceiling fan and VCR in room. Air conditioning. Fax and bicycles on premises. Family reunions hosted. Antiquing, fishing, parks and shopping nearby.
Pets allowed: With advance notice, in certain rooms.

Teague   E8

Hubbard House Inn B&B

621 Cedar St
Teague, TX 75860-1617
(254)739-2629

Circa 1903. Having served as the Hubbard House Hotel for railroad employees during part of its history, this red brick and white frame Georgian home is furnished mostly with early American antiques. There's a second-floor balcony porch with swings, which offer guests a place to relax. A country breakfast is served in the large formal dining room on a glass-topped antique pool table.

Innkeeper(s): John W. Duke. $65. PC, TC. TAC10. 6 rooms. Breakfast included in rates. Type of meal: Full bkfst. Beds: KD. Cable TV and ceiling fan in room. Air conditioning. VCR on premises. Handicap access. Weddings, small meetings and family reunions hosted. Antiquing, fishing, golf, B&RI Railroad Museum, Fort Parker State Park, parks and shopping nearby.

Texarkana   C9

Mansion on Main B&B

802 Main St
Texarkana, TX 75501-5104
(903)792-1835 Fax:(903)793-0878

Circa 1895. Spectacular two-story columns salvaged from the St. Louis World's Fair accent the exterior of this Neoclassical-style inn. Victorian nightgowns and sleepshirts are provided, and whether you are on a business trip or your honeymoon, expect to be pampered. Six bedchambers are furnished with antiques and period appointments. Awake to the aroma of dark roast cajun coffee, and then enjoy a full "gentleman's" breakfast in the parquet dining room. The inn is located in the downtown historic area. Enjoy a fireside cup of coffee or a lemonade on the veranda. The inn offers plenty of amenities for the business traveler, including fax machine, desks and modem connections.

Historic Interest: Old Washington, a town frequented by the likes of Davy Crockett, Jim Bowie and Sam Houston, is 35 miles away. The historic Perot Theater, which was restored by native son Ross Perot, offers many productions throughout the year. The town also offers a living museum, the Ace of Clubs House.

Innkeeper(s): Judge & Denise Canon. $60-109. MC, VISA, AX, PC, TC. TAC10. 6 rooms with PB. Breakfast included in rates. Types of meals: Full bkfst and early coffee/tea. Afternoon tea available. Beds: QD. Cable TV, phone, ceiling fan and Victorian sleepware in room. Air conditioning. Veranda, courtyard and gardens on premises. Handicap access. Weddings, small meetings, family reunions and seminars hosted. Cajun spoken. Antiquing, fishing, live theater and shopping nearby.

Tyler   D9

Chilton Grand

433 S Chilton Ave
Tyler, TX 75702-8017
(903)595-3270 Fax:(903)595-3270

Circa 1910. Tall pecan, maple, oak and magnolia trees shelter this red brick, Greek Revival home on a brick street in the Azalea District. (Tyler is considered by some to be the prettiest town in Texas.) Two-story columns and a crystal chandelier hanging from the front balcony and porch set the elegant tone. Inside,there are antiques and romantic touches such as a Jacuzzi tub and feather beds. Ivy Cottage features a canopied queen feather bed and a two-person whirlpool tub in the Gazebo Room. Breakfast is served with silver, crystal and china. Historic mansions, Brickstreet Playhouse, the mid-town Arts Center, Tyler's famous rose garden, tea rooms and downtown antique shops are all within walking distance.

Innkeeper(s): Jerry & Carole Glazebrook. $75-150. MC, VISA, AX, PC, TC. TAC7. 4 rooms with PB, 1 with FP, 2 suites and 1 cottage. Breakfast included in rates. Types of meals: Full gourmet bkfst and early coffee/tea. Beds: QD. Cable TV, phone, turndown service, ceiling fan and VCR in room. Air conditioning. Fax on premises. Antiquing, fishing, live theater, parks, shopping and water sports nearby.

"Wow, what a beautiful place you have. The food was simply the best."

Waco   E7

The Judge Baylor House

908 Speight Ave
Waco, TX 76706-2343
(254)756-0273 (888)522-9567 Fax:(254)756-0711

Circa 1940. This home was built by the head of the chemistry department at Baylor University, which is just one block away. There are five well-appointed guest rooms, each decorated with English antiques. Each room has something special. In one room, guests will discover French doors leading out to a patio. In another, there is a poster bed and hand-painted pedestal sink. Aside from the university and Elizabeth Barrett & Robert Browning Library, the home is near the Brazos Riverwalk, Lake Waco, the Texas Sports Hall of Fame, antique shops, historic homes and more.

Innkeeper(s): Bruce & Dorothy Dyer. $72-105. MC, VISA, AX, PC, TC. TAC10. 5 rooms, 4 with PB and 1 suite. Breakfast and afternoon tea included in rates. Types of meals: Full bkfst and early coffee/tea. Gourmet dinner available. Beds: KQT. Ceiling fan in room. Air conditioning. VCR, fax, copier and library on premises. Weddings, small meetings, family reunions and seminars hosted. Antiquing, fishing, golf, live theater, parks, shopping, sporting events and tennis nearby.

Waxahachie   D8

The BonnyNook

414 W Main St
Waxahachie, TX 75165-3234
(972)938-7207 (800)486-5936 Fax:(972)937-7700

Circa 1887. Each of the five guest rooms at this Queen Anne "Painted Lady" is filled with plants and antiques from around the world. The Sterling Room, a large octagon-shaped chamber, features a hand-carved mahogany canopy bed. The Morrow Room boasts a 100-year-old sleigh bed and an antique clawfoot tub with a shower. Three of the guest baths offer whirlpool tubs. Bon Appetit featured BonnyNook as part of an article on bed &

breakfasts. The hearty breakfasts feature such notable items as blueberry pudding coffeecake or Southern crepes filled with vegetables and eggs. Innkeeper Bonnie Franks keeps a special Coffee Nook filled with teas, coffee, hot cocoa and a refrigerator for her guests. Don't forget to ask about the inn's special cookies. BonnyNook is only two blocks from antique shops, boutiques and restaurants. Gourmet, six-course meals are available by reservation. Massage also is available by reservation.

Historic Interest: The Ellis County Museum and driving/walking tours are available to see Waxahachie's historic attractions.

Innkeeper(s): Vaughn & Bonnie Franks. $85-125. MC, VISA, AX, DC, DS. 5 rooms with PB. Breakfast and snacks/refreshments included in rates. Types of meals: Full bkfst, cont and early coffee/tea. Gourmet dinner available. Beds: KQD. Phone, ceiling fan and some rooms have Jacuzzis in room. Air conditioning. Fax, copier, coffee nook with refrigerator and ice buckets/ice on premises. Weddings, small meetings, family reunions and seminars hosted. Antiquing, parks and shopping nearby.

Publicity: *Texas Highways, Dallas Morning News, Forbes, Texas People & Places, Bon Appetit.*

"This was a wonderful retreat from the everyday hustle and bustle and we didn't hear a phone ring once!"

Weatherford   D7

St. Botolph Inn

808 S Lamar St
Weatherford, TX 76086
(817)594-1455 (800)868-6520 Fax:(817)594-1455

Circa 1897. Set on a five-acre hilltop, this fanciful Queen Anne Victorian offers a stunning exterior boasting elaborate gingerbread trim, a wraparound veranda and a two-story circular tower painted with light green stripes. The interior is equally enchanting, featuring a second-story ballroom with a domed ceiling and five original fireplaces. The King David Suite includes a whirlpool tub and a sitting room located in the home's turret. Other rooms include items such as an antique, four-foot clawfoot tub. Afternoon tea adds to the home's rich Victorian ambiance. Guests also are pampered with a gourmet breakfast. Freshly squeezed orange juice, Victorian shirred eggs and a bread basket filled with scones, homemade sourdough toast and muffins are some of the appetizing options. The home is a mile from Weatherford's historic city square.

Historic Interest: 1886 Courthouse (1 mile).

Innkeeper(s): Dan & Shay Buttolph. $85-175. MC, VISA, AX, DS, PC, TC. 6 rooms with PB, 1 with FP, 1 suite, 1 cottage and 1 conference room. Breakfast and afternoon tea included in rates. Types of meals: Full gourmet bkfst and early coffee/tea. Catered breakfast available. Beds: KQ. Cable TV, phone, turndown service, ceiling fan and VCR in room. Central air. Fax, copier, spa and swimming on premises. Handicap access. Weddings, small meetings, family reunions and seminars hosted. Antiquing, art galleries, bicycling, fishing, golf, hiking, horseback riding, live theater, museums, parks and shopping nearby.

"Come, let us pamper you."

Utah

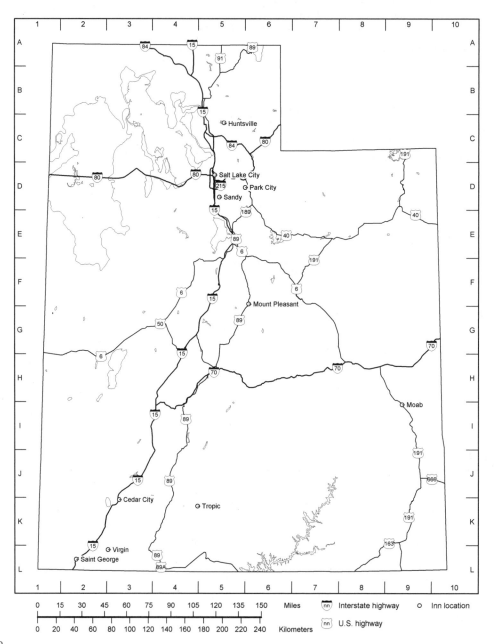

	Miles
0 15 30 45 60 75 90 105 120 135 150	
0 20 40 60 80 100 120 140 160 180 200 220 240	Kilometers

[nn] Interstate highway   ○ Inn location

[nn] U.S. highway

Cedar City K3

Paxman's House B&B

170 N 400 W
Cedar City, UT 84720-2421
(435)586-3755

Circa 1900. This steeply-gabled, turn-of-the-century Victorian offers a small veranda overlooking a residential street, two blocks from the Shakespearean Festival. Early Mormon pioneer pieces furnish the Pine Room, while walnut and marble Victorian furnishings fill the Walnut Room. Breakfast includes fruit, cereals, rolls and beverages. Brian Head Ski Resort and Zion National Park are a short drive away.

Innkeeper(s): Karlene Paxman. $69-85. MC, VISA, AX. 3 rooms. Breakfast included in rates. TV in room. Air conditioning. VCR on premises. Small meetings and family reunions hosted. Antiquing, live theater, shopping, downhill skiing, cross-country skiing and sporting events nearby.

Huntsville C5

Jackson Fork Inn

7345 E 900 S
Huntsville, UT 84317-9778
(801)745-0051 (800)255-0672

Circa 1938. This former dairy barn was named after the hay fork that was used to transport hay into the loft of the barn. The inn has eight guest rooms, all in a two-story configuration with lofts and spiral staircases. Four rooms include two-person Jacuzzi tubs, and all are cozy and comfortable. A self-serve continental breakfast is prepared each day with muffins and fresh coffee. There's a restaurant on the first floor that offers fish, chicken and steak. The inn is ideal for skiers with its location near Powder Mountain, Nordic Valley and Snowbasin ski resorts.

Innkeeper(s): Vicki Petersen. $60-120. MC, VISA, AX, DS, PC, TC. 8 rooms with PB. Breakfast included in rates. Type of meal: Cont. Restaurant on premises. Beds: Q. Ceiling fan in room. Full breakfast on Sunday on premises. Weddings and small meetings hosted. Fishing, parks, shopping, downhill skiing, cross-country skiing and water sports nearby.

Pets allowed: With $20 fee - must be kept on leash.

Moab I9

Sunflower Hill B&B

185 N 300 E
Moab, UT 84532-2421
(435)259-2974 (800)662-2786 Fax:(435)259-3065

Circa 1895. Guests at Sunflower Hill stay either in a restored adobe farmhouse or a garden cottage. The one-and-a-half-acre grounds, dotted with gardens and wooded pathways, create a secluded environment, yet the home is only three blocks from downtown Moab. Guest rooms are decorated in country style with antiques and stenciled walls. A hearty breakfast buffet is served on an antique sideboard. Guests choose from a multitude of items, such as a farmer's casserole, poached eggs with mushrooms and smoked turkey, lemon poppy seed scones, muffins, fresh fruit, honey-almond granola and more. There is an outdoor hot tub on the premises, as well as a laundry facility. Sunflower Hill is close to Arches and Canyonlands national parks.

Innkeeper(s): The Stucki Family. $65-165. MC, VISA, DS, PC, TC. TAC10. 11 rooms with PB and 2 suites. Breakfast included in rates. Types of meals: Full bkfst and early coffee/tea. Snacks/refreshments and picnic lunch available. Beds: QD. Cable TV, ceiling fan and deluxe rooms have jet tubs and private balconies or patios in room. Air conditioning. VCR, fax, copier, spa and library on premises. Fishing, golf, hiking, horseback riding, parks, shopping, cross-country skiing, tennis and water sports nearby.

"This place is awesome. We will be back."

Mt. Pleasant F6

Larsen House B&B

298 South State St
Mt. Pleasant, UT 84647
(435)462-9337 (800)848-5263 Fax:(435)462-2362
E-mail: larsenh@juno.com

Circa 1897. A white picket fence surrounds this two-and-a-half-story red brick Victorian. Bay windows and porches offer spots from which to enjoy the mountain views. A stained-glass window is the focal point of the foyer, which also features a hand-painted ceiling mural and a carved staircase. Victorian guest rooms are appointed with antiques, down comforters, stained-glass windows and Bradley and Bradley style wall paper borders. There are fireplaces and the bathrooms include jetted tubs. A sample breakfast is hot German pancakes served with fruit toppings, sausage, hot cocoa and coffee.

Historic Interest: Latter Day Saints Temple-22 miles, Restored train depot-1 mile.

Innkeeper(s): Sally East. $60-95. MC, VISA, AX, DS, PC. TAC10. 4 rooms, 3 with PB, 1 with FP, 2 suites and 1 cottage. Breakfast and snacks/refreshments included in rates. Types of meals: Full bkfst, country bkfst and early coffee/tea. Beds: QD. Cable TV, phone, ceiling fan, VCR, microwave and jetted tubs in room. Central air. Fax and copier on premises. Weddings and family reunions hosted. Antiquing, art galleries, bicycling, fishing, golf, horseback riding, museums, parks and cross-country skiing nearby.

Park City D6

The 1904 Imperial Hotel-A B&B

221 Main St, PO Box 1628
Park City, UT 84060-1628
(435)649-1904 (800)669-8824 Fax:(435)645-7421
E-mail: stay@1904imperial.com
Web: www.1904imperial.com

Circa 1904. The Imperial, a historic turn-of-the-century hotel, is decorated in a "Western" Victorian style. Several guest rooms include amenities like clawfoot or Roman tubs and sitting areas. A few overlook Park City's historic Main Street. The inn's largest suite includes a bedroom and a spiral staircase leading up to a cozy loft area. There are ski lockers and a Jacuzzi on-site. Transportation to area ski lifts are located nearby.

Innkeeper(s): Nancy McLaughlin & Karen Hart. $70-245. MC, VISA, AX, DS, TC. 10 rooms with PB and 2 suites. Breakfast included in rates. Type of meal: Full bkfst. Snacks/refreshments available. Beds: KQT. Cable TV and phone in room. Fax and copier on premises. Antiquing, fishing, live theater, parks, shopping, downhill skiing, cross-country skiing, sporting events and water sports nearby.

The Old Miners' Lodge - A B&B Inn

615 Woodside Ave, PO Box 2639
Park City, UT 84060-2639
(435)645-8068 (800)648-8068 Fax:(435)645-7420
E-mail: stay@oldminerslodge.com
Web: www.oldminerslodge.com

Circa 1889. This originally was established as a miners' boarding house by E. P. Ferry, owner of the Woodside-Norfolk silver mines. A two-story Victorian with Western flavor, the lodge is a significant structure in the Park City National Historic District. Just on the edge of the woods is a deck and a steaming hot tub.

Historic Interest: Mining artifacts from the silver mining industry.

Innkeeper(s): Susan Wynne & Liza Simpson. $70-275. MC, VISA, AX, DC, CB, DS, PC, TC. TAC10. 12 rooms with PB, 3 suites and 2 conference rooms. Breakfast and snacks/refreshments included in rates. Types of meals: Full bkfst and early coffee/tea. Banquet service and catering service available. Beds: KQDT. Turndown service, ceiling fan, robes and clock in room. Fax, copier, spa and library on premises. Small meetings, family reunions and seminars hosted. Antiquing, fishing, live theater, parks, shopping, downhill skiing and cross-country skiing nearby.

Publicity: *Boston Herald, Los Angeles Times, Detroit Free Press, Washington Post, Ski, Bon Appetit.*

"This is the creme de la creme. The most wonderful place I have stayed at bar none, including ski country in the U.S. and Europe."

Washington School Inn

544 Park Ave, PO Box 536
Park City, UT 84060-0536
(435)649-3800 (800)824-1672 Fax:(435)649-3802

Circa 1889. Made of local limestone, this inn was the former schoolhouse for Park City children. With its classic belltower, the four-story building is listed in the National Register. The inn is noted for its luxuriously appointed guest rooms. Drinks and appetizers are served each afternoon in front of an inviting fire. The inn's Jacuzzi and sauna are perfect places to relax. The hosts also offer the amenities of a concierge service and ski storage, which is helpful since the inn is only one block from ski lifts.

Innkeeper(s): Nancy Beaufait. $100-300. MC, VISA, AX, DC, DS, TC. TAC10. 12 rooms with PB, 2 with FP, 3 suites and 2 conference rooms. Breakfast, afternoon tea and snacks/refreshments included in rates. Type of meal: Full bkfst. Beds: KQT. Cable TV and phone in room. VCR, fax, spa and sauna on premises. Weddings, small meetings and family reunions hosted. Antiquing, fishing, live theater, parks, shopping, downhill skiing, cross-country skiing, sporting events and water sports nearby.

Publicity: *San Diego Magazine, Arizona Daily Star, Salt Lake Tribune.*

"The end of the rainbow."

Saint George   L2

Greene Gate Village Historic B&B Inn

76 W Tabernacle St
Saint George, UT 84770-3420
(435)628-6999 (800)350-6999 Fax:(435)628-6989

Circa 1876. This is a cluster of nine restored pioneer homes all located within one block. The Bentley House has comfortable Victorian decor. The Orson Pratt House and the Tolley House are other choices, all carefully restored. The fifth house contains three bedrooms each with private bath, a kitchen, living

room and two fireplaces. Six of the bedrooms have large whirlpool tubs.

Historic Interest: First Mormon Temple in the West (1 mile), first Cotton Mill in the West (1 mile), Mormon Tabernacle.

Innkeeper(s): Durk & Jane Johnson. $65-129. MC, VISA, AX, DC, DS, PC, TC. TAC10. 16 rooms with PB, 8 with FP, 6 suites, 1 cottage and 1 conference room. Breakfast included in rates. AP. Type of meal: Full bkfst. Dinner, snacks/refreshments, picnic lunch and lunch available. Restaurant on premises. Beds: KQDT. Cable TV, ceiling fan, courtyard and porches in room. VCR, fax, spa and swimming on premises. Handicap access. Weddings, small meetings, family reunions and seminars hosted. Portuguese spoken. Antiquing, art galleries, bicycling, fishing, golf, hiking, horseback riding, live theater, museums, parks, shopping, tennis and water sports nearby.

"You not only provided me with rest, comfort and wonderful food, but you fed my soul."

Salt Lake City   D5

The Anton Boxrud B&B

57 S 600 E
Salt Lake City, UT 84102-1006
(801)363-8035 (800)524-5511 Fax:(801)596-1316
E-mail: antonboxrud@earthlink.net
Web: www.netoriginals.com/antonboxrud/

Circa 1901. One of Salt Lake City's grand old homes, this Victorian home with eclectic style is on the register of the Salt Lake City Historical Society. The interior is furnished with antiques from around the country and Old World details. In the sitting and dining rooms, guests will find chairs with intricate carvings, a table with carved swans for support, embossed brass door knobs and stained and beveled glass. There is an out-door hot tub available to guests. The inn is located just a half-block south of the Utah Governor's Mansion in the historic district. A full homemade breakfast and evening snack are provided.

Innkeeper(s): Jane Johnson. $69-140. MC, VISA, AX, DC, DS. 7 rooms, 5 with PB and 1 suite. Breakfast included in rates. Types of meals: Full bkfst and early coffee/tea. Gourmet dinner and snacks/refreshments available. Beds: KQT. Small meetings, family reunions and seminars hosted. Amusement parks, antiquing, fishing, live theater, shopping, downhill skiing, cross-country skiing, sporting events and water sports nearby.

"Made us feel at home and well-fed. Can you adopt us?."

Armstrong Mansion Inn

667 E 100 S
Salt Lake City, UT 84102-1103
(801)531-1333 (800)708-1333 Fax:(801)531-0282
Web: www.Armstrong-BB.com

Circa 1893. A former Salt Lake City mayor built this Queen Anne-style home for his young bride. The mansion features the original carved-oak staircase, ornate woodwork and stained-glass windows. Guest rooms are decorated with Victorian furnishings and walls feature stenciling that the innkeepers designed after looking at old photographs of the home. Each

room is decorated to reflect a different month of the year. The home is within walking distance to downtown shopping, businesses and other attractions. The area offers many outdoor activities, such as hiking and skiing.

Historic Interest: The home is located in Salt Lake's historic district.

Innkeeper(s): Judy & Dave Savage. $89-239. MC, VISA, AX, DS, TC. 13 rooms with PB. Breakfast included in rates. Type of meal: Full bkfst. Gourmet dinner available. Beds: KQD. New historic Temple Square, close to ski resorts and summer watersports, live theater and shopping nearby.

Saltair B&B

164 S 900 E
Salt Lake City, UT 84102-4103
(801)533-8184 (800)733-8184 Fax:(801)595-0332
E-mail: saltair@saltlakebandb.com
Web: www.saltlakebandb.com

Circa 1903. The Saltair is the oldest continuously operating bed & breakfast in Utah and offers a prime location to enjoy Salt Lake City. The simply decorated rooms include light, airy window dressings, charming furnishings and special touches. Breakfasts, especially the delicious Saltair Eggs Benedict topped with avocado, sour creme and salsa, are memorable. The inn is

within walking distance to four historic districts and only one mile from Temple Square and the Governor's Mansion. Day trips include treks to several national and state parks and the Wasatch Front ski areas.

Innkeeper(s): Nancy Saxton & Jan Bartlett. $75-149. MC, VISA, AX, DC, CB, DS, TC. TAC10. 7 rooms, 4 with PB. Breakfast and snacks/refreshments included in rates. Types of meals: Full gourmet bkfst and early coffee/tea. Beds: QT. Fresh flowers in room. Air conditioning. VCR, fax and spa on premises. Seminars hosted. Antiquing, fishing, live theater, parks, shopping, downhill skiing, cross-country skiing, sporting events and water sports nearby.

"Your swing and Saltai Muffins were fabulous."

Tropic K4

Bryce Point B&B

61 N, 400 West
Tropic, UT 84776-0096
(801)679-8629 (888)200-4211 Fax:(435)679-8629

Circa 1941. The innkeepers of this comfortable bed & breakfast have owned the home since 1952 and renovated it in the late '80s and soon after opened for guests. Each of the guests rooms is named for the innkeepers' children and their spouses, and each room feature comfortable furnishings and large picture windows. Relax on the wraparound porch or pick a movie from the innkeepers' library and snuggle up in your room to watch an old favorite. Six national parks surround the Tropic area, offering plenty of seasonal activities.

Historic Interest: Historic Bryce Canyon Lodge is nearby and offers hiking, horseback riding, hunting and fishing.

Innkeeper(s): Lamar & Ethel LeFevre. $60-120. MC, VISA, AX. TAC10. 6 rooms, 5 with PB and 1 cottage. Breakfast included in rates. Type of meal: Full gourmet bkfst. Catered breakfast available. Beds: KQT. TV, phone, ceiling fan and VCR in room. Central air. Fax, spa and library on premises. Canoeing/kayaking, fishing, hiking, horseback riding, parks and cross-country skiing nearby.

"So many amenities abound: a comfortable, cheerful room, great sleeping, thoughtful touches, stargazing, scenery from your spacious deck, gracious hosts and so much more. We've been to many B&B's, Bryce Point is among the winners."

Vermont

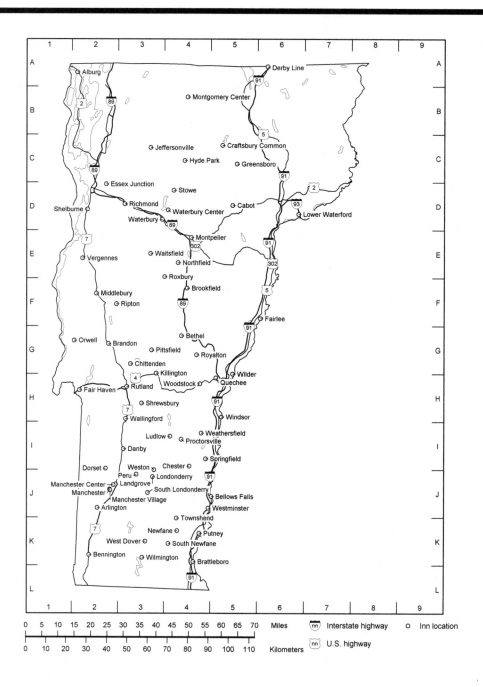

	Miles		Interstate highway		Inn location

0 5 10 15 20 25 30 35 40 45 50 55 60 65 70   Miles   Interstate highway   Inn location

0 10 20 30 40 50 60 70 80 90 100 110   Kilometers   U.S. highway

Alburg   A2

Thomas Mott Homestead B&B

63 Blue Rock Rd on Lake Champlain
Alburg, VT 05440-4002
(800)348-0843 Fax:(802)796-3736

Circa 1838. Each room in this restored farmhouse provides a special view of Lake Champlain, yet guests often may be found enjoying the view from the sitting room as they warm by the fireplace. There are also full views of Mt.
Mansfield and
nearby Jay Peak.
Montreal Island
is one hour away.
Guests are sure to

enjoy the complimentary Ben & Jerry's ice cream. Patrick is a noted wine consultant and holds Master's Degrees in criminology, sociology and the classical arts. A boat dock, extending 75 feet onto the lake, recently has been added to the property.
Historic Interest: Saint Anne's Shrine, Hyde Cabin, two presidential birthplaces.
Innkeeper(s): Patrick Schallert. $79-109. MC, VISA, AX, DC, CB, DS, PC, TC. TAC10. 5 rooms with PB, 1 with FP, 2 suites and 3 conference rooms. Breakfast and snacks/refreshments included in rates. Types of meals: Full gourmet bkfst and early coffee/tea. Beds: KQ. Turndown service and ceiling fan in room. Fax, copier and library on premises. Weddings, small meetings, family reunions and seminars hosted. Amusement parks, antiquing, fishing, live theater, parks, shopping, downhill skiing, cross-country skiing, sporting events and water sports nearby.
Publicity: *Los Angeles Times, St. Alban's Messenger, Yankee Traveler, Boston Globe, Elle, Outside, Prime Time, Vermont Life.*

"One of the greatest surprises was to open the freezer in the kitchen and find 15 flavors of Ben & Jerry's ice cream compliments of the host, available to anyone at anytime. We all enjoyed!"

Andover   I4

The Inn at High View

753 East Hill Rd
Andover, VT 05143
(802)875-2724 Fax:(802)875-4021
E-mail: hiview@aol.com
Web: www.innathighview.com

Circa 1789. Relaxation is stressed at this spacious farmhouse inn in the Green Mountains. A fireplace, rock garden, swimming pool and sauna add to guests' enjoyment. Cross-country ski trails are found on the grounds, hooking up with a series of others to provide up to 15 kilometers of uninterrupted skiing. The inn offers advance-reservation dinner service for its guests on weekends and specializes in Italian fare.

Innkeeper(s): Gregory Bohan & Salvatore Massaro. $95-155. MC, VISA. TAC10. 8 rooms with PB, 2 suites and 1 conference room. Breakfast included in rates. Types of meals: Full bkfst and early coffee/tea. Dinner and lunch available. Beds: KQD. Turndown service in room. VCR on premises. Weddings, small meetings, family reunions and seminars hosted. Italian, Spanish and English spoken. Antiquing, fishing, live theater, shopping, downhill skiing and cross-country skiing nearby.
Pets allowed: Special arrangements in suites only.

Arlington   J2

The Arlington Inn

Historic Rt 7A, PO Box 369
Arlington, VT 05250-0369
(802)375-6532 (800)443-9442
E-mail: arlington@sover.net
Web: www.arlingtoninn.com

Circa 1848. The Arlington Inn is one of Vermont's finest examples of Greek Revival architecture. Guest rooms are thoughtfully decorated in a traditional style with period antiques suiting the elegance of the inn. Marshall's Library, for instance, offers both a
tall canopy bed and
sofa, while Sylvester's
Study features a hand-
some fireplace, sitting
area, maple ceiling and a

private porch. Jacuzzi suites with fireplaces and private patios with pond views are very popular. Breakfast is served in the solarium with green lawn and flower garden stretching out before you. In the evening, candlelight dinners are available in the inn's fine dining room. Norman Rockwell once used the carriage house as a studio. Nearby activities include fishing, canoeing, downhill and cross-country skiing, snow shoeing and hiking. (Ask about the inn's fly fishing package that includes a visit to the American Museum of Fly Fishing and fishing venues at Batten Kill, Roaring Branch and Deerfield Rivers.)
Innkeeper(s): Bill & Sherrie Noonan. $100-265. MC, VISA, AX, DC, DS. 18 rooms with PB, 10 with FP, 5 suites and 1 conference room. Breakfast included in rates. MAP. Type of meal: Full gourmet bkfst. Gourmet dinner and picnic lunch available. Beds: KQDT. TV, phone and Jacuzzi in room. Air conditioning. VCR, fax, copier and bicycles on premises. Weddings, small meetings, family reunions and seminars hosted. Antiquing, fishing, live theater, shopping, downhill skiing, cross-country skiing, sporting events and water sports nearby.
Publicity: *San Diego Times, Bon Appetit, Country Inns, Vermont Life, Gourmet, New York Magazine.*

Arlington Manor House B&B

Cor. Buck Hill & Salter Hill Rd
Arlington, VT 05250-8648
(802)375-6784
E-mail: kitandal@arlingtonmanorhouse.com
Web: www.arlingtonmanorhouse.com

Circa 1908. A view of Mt. Equinox is enjoyed from the spacious terrace of this Dutch Colonial inn in the Battenkill River Valley. The inn also sports its own tennis court and is within easy walking distance
of the Battenkill River,
where canoeing, fish-
ing and river tubing
are popular activities.
A variety of accommo-
dations is offered, and

two of the inn's guest rooms have romantic fireplaces. A bikers' workshop and bench stand are on the premises.
Innkeeper(s): Al & Kit McAllister. $65-130. MC, VISA, AX, PC, TC. TAC10. 5 rooms, 3 with PB, 2 with FP, 1 suite and 2 conference rooms. Breakfast and afternoon tea included in rates. Types of meals: Full bkfst and early coffee/tea. Beds: KQDT. TV in room. Air conditioning. VCR, tennis, library, workbench, shops and satellite Prime-star on premises. Weddings, small meetings, family reunions and seminars hosted. Antiquing, fishing, live theater, parks, shopping, downhill skiing, cross-country skiing and water sports nearby.

The Inn on Covered Bridge Green

3587 River Rd
Arlington, VT 05250-9723
(800)726-9480
E-mail: cbg@sovernet.com
Web: www.coveredbridgegreen.com

Circa 1792. A quaint red covered bridge over the Battenkill River leads to this colonial inn, home to Norman Rockwell for 12 years. The artist was inspired by Arlington's scenes and people, and the five guest rooms at the inn are named for the framed Rockwell prints that adorn their walls. The rooms are filled with comfortable chairs, old-fashioned dressers, armoires, desks and fireplaces, all in a Norman Rockwell style. A hearty New England breakfast reinforces your enjoyment of the countryside. The artist's actual two-bedroom studio may be booked by the week.
Innkeeper(s): Clint & Julia Dickens. $125-160. 5 rooms, 4 with PB. Type of meal: Full gourmet bkfst. Beds: KQT. Fireplaces in room.

"We find it difficult to leave. Everything is perfect."

Ira Allen House

Rd 2, Box 2485
Arlington, VT 05250-9317
(802)362-2284 Fax:(802)362-0928
E-mail: stay@iraallenhouse.com
Web: www.iraallenhouse.com

Built by Ethan Allen's brother, this Colonial Revival inn is a state historic site. Hand-blown glass panes, hand-hewn beams, hand-made bricks and wide-board floors provide evidence of the inn's longevity. Surrounded by farms and forest, the inn's setting is

perfect for those searching for some peace and quiet. Plenty of recreational activities also are found nearby, including fine trout fishing in the Battenkill River just across the road, yet still on the property. Saturday-night dinners are available in winter, and guests are welcome to raid the living room fridge, where they will find soda and other refreshments.
Innkeeper(s): Sandy & Ray Walters. $75-100. 9 rooms and 2 suites. Breakfast included in rates. Type of meal: Full bkfst. Dinner available. Air conditioning. VCR on premises. Weddings and family reunions hosted. Antiquing, canoeing/kayaking, live theater, shopping, downhill skiing and cross-country skiing nearby.

West Mountain Inn

PO Box 481
Arlington, VT 05250-0481
(802)375-6516
E-mail: Info@WestMountainInn.com
Web: www.WestMountainInn.com

Circa 1849. Llamas graze the hillside of this sprawling New England farmhouse situated on 150 acres of meadows and woodland. The inn overlooks the Battenkill River. Each room boasts ameni-

ties such as a lace canopied bed, a balcony or a fireplace. The Rockwell Kent Suite graced with a cathedral ceiling, features a fireplace and king-size bed. Back porches and decks are filled with Adirondack lawn chairs. The innkeepers include a former school principal and a Vermont state senator.
Innkeeper(s): Wes & MaryAnn Carlson. $149-259. MC, VISA, AX, DS. 18 rooms with PB, 2 with FP, 6 suites and 1 conference room. Breakfast and dinner included in rates. MAP. Type of meal: Full bkfst. Restaurant on premises. Beds: KQ. TV and phone in room. Handicap access. Weddings, small meetings, family reunions and seminars hosted. Antiquing, bicycling, fishing, live theater, downhill skiing, cross-country skiing and water sports nearby.

"Excellent, warm, friendly, relaxing, absolutely the best!"

Bellows Falls   J5

River Mist B&B

7 Burt St
Bellows Falls, VT 05101-1401
(802)463-9023 (888)463-9023 Fax:(802)463-1571
E-mail: rmistbnb@vermontel.net
Web: www.river-mist.com

Circa 1880. The scenic village of Bellows Falls is home to this late 19th-century Queen Anne Victorian inn, with its inviting wraparound porch and country Victorian interior. Guests may

relax in any of three sitting rooms or in front of the fireplace. Enjoy a day of antiquing, skiing or just wandering around the picturesque environs. Be sure to take a ride on the Green Mountain Flyer before leaving town.
Innkeeper(s): John & Linda Maresca. $69-89. 3 rooms. Breakfast included in rates. Type of meal: Full bkfst. Amusement parks, antiquing, live theater, shopping, downhill skiing and cross-country skiing nearby.

Bennington   K2

Molly Stark Inn

1067 Main St
Bennington, VT 05201-2635
(802)442-9631 (800)356-3076 Fax:(802)442-5224
E-mail: mollyinn@vermontel.com
Web: www.mollystarkinn.com

Circa 1890. This attractive Queen Anne Victorian inn has been serving travelers for more than 50 years. Careful restoration has enabled it to retain its Victorian charm, while offering the comforts today's guests

have come to expect. Features include antique furnishings, clawfoot tubs, hardwood floors, handmade quilts and a wood stove. The inn's convenient Main Street location puts it within walking distance of many restaurants and shops and just minutes from Historic Old Bennington. The Bennington Museum boasts paintings by Grandma Moses.
Innkeeper(s): Reed & Cammi Fendler. $70-175. MC, VISA, AX, DS, PC, TC. TAC10. 7 rooms with PB, 1 with FP and 1 cottage. Breakfast and snacks/refreshments included in rates. Type of meal: Full gourmet bkfst.

Beds: KDT. Cable TV, phone and ceiling fan in room. Air conditioning. Bicycles and Jacuzzi on premises. Weddings, small meetings and family reunions hosted. Antiquing, fishing, live theater, parks, shopping, downhill skiing, cross-country skiing and water sports nearby.

Publicity: *Yankee Traveler, Colonial Homes, Albany Times Union, Saratogian.*

"...like my grandma's house, only better."

South Shire Inn

124 Elm St
Bennington, VT 05201-2232
(802)447-3839 Fax:(802)442-3547
E-mail: sshire@sover.net
Web: www.southshire.com

Circa 1850. Built prior to the Civil War, this inn boasts a mahogany-paneled library, soaring 10-foot ceilings, and three of the guest rooms include one of the home's original fireplaces. Guest rooms feature antiques and Victorian décor. Rooms in the restored carriage house include both a fireplace and a whirlpool tub. Guests are pampered with both a full breakfast, as well as afternoon tea. Local  attractions include the Bennington Museum, antique shops, craft stores, covered bridges and skiing.

Historic Interest: Bennington Museum and Monument-1 mile, Hildene (Lincoln Estate)-25 miles.

Innkeeper(s): George & Joyce Gocke. $105-180. MC, VISA, AX, PC, TC. TAC10. 9 rooms with PB, 7 with FP and 1 suite. Breakfast and afternoon tea included in rates. Types of meals: Full bkfst, veg bkfst and early coffee/tea. Beds: KQD. Cable TV, phone, ceiling fan, VCR and whirlpool tubs in room. Central air. Fax, copier, library and guest refrigerator on premises. Weddings, small meetings, family reunions and seminars hosted. Antiquing, art galleries, bicycling, canoeing/kayaking, fishing, golf, hiking, horseback riding, live theater, museums, shopping, downhill skiing and cross-country skiing nearby.

Bethel   G4

Greenhurst Inn

River St, Rd 2, Box 60
Bethel, VT 05032-9404
(802)234-9474 (800)510-2553

Circa 1890. In the National Register of Historic Places, Greenhurst is a gracious Victorian mansion built for the Harringtons of Philadelphia. Overlooking the White River, the inn's opulent interiors include etched windows once featured on the cover of Vermont Life. There are eight master-piece fireplaces and a north and south parlor.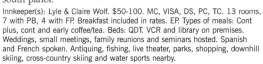

Innkeeper(s): Lyle & Claire Wolf. $50-100. MC, VISA, DS, PC, TC. 13 rooms, 7 with PB, 4 with FP. Breakfast included in rates. EP. Types of meals: Cont plus, cont and early coffee/tea. Beds: QDT. VCR and library on premises. Weddings, small meetings, family reunions and seminars hosted. Spanish and French spoken. Antiquing, fishing, live theater, parks, shopping, downhill skiing, cross-country skiing and water sports nearby.

Pets allowed: Dogs only.

"The inn is magnificent! The hospitality unforgettable."

Brandon   G2

Churchill House Inn

3128 Forest Dale Rd, Rte 73 E
Brandon, VT 05733-9202
(802)247-3078 (877)248-7444

Circa 1871. Caleb Churchill and his son, Nathan, first built a three-story lumber mill, a grist mill and a distillery here, all water powered. Later, with their milled lumber, they constructed this 20-room house. Because of its location, it became a stage-coach stop and has served generations of travelers with comfortable accommodations. The inn is adjacent to Green Mountain National Forest, and excellent hiking,  biking, skiing and fishing are just steps away. The inn serves a four-course dinner and a full breakfast.

Historic Interest: Shelburn Museum, Billings Farm, Fort Ticonderoga (less than 1 hour away).

Innkeeper(s): Linda & Richard Daybell. $80-120. MC, VISA, AX, PC, TC. 9 rooms with PB. Breakfast and dinner included in rates. Type of meal: Full bkfst. Picnic lunch available. Beds: QDT. Sauna on premises. Family reunions hosted. Antiquing, parks, shopping, downhill skiing, cross-country skiing and water sports nearby.

Publicity: *Country, Yankee.*

"We felt the warm, welcoming, down-home appeal as we entered the front hall. The food was uncommonly good — home cooking with a gourmet flair!"

Brattleboro   K4

1868 Crosby House

175 Western Ave
Brattleboro, VT 05301-3137
(802)257-4914 (800)528-1868

Circa 1868. Guests of this elegantly restored Italianate Victorian home with Victorian gardens, gazebo and woodland trails, remember it for its attention to detail and a feeling of being pampered. The Victorian theme is represented throughout the inn's fabric textures and soft colors. Each of the three guest rooms boasts family heirlooms and collected antiques, fireplaces and private baths, as well as four-poster,  canopy and paneled queen beds. There also is a two-bedroom apartment suite that is ideal for families. Bathrobes, specialty toiletries and luxurious bed and bath linens are provided. A full, gourmet breakfast is served in the oak-paneled dining room. The inn is a short walk from downtown.

$100-140. MC, VISA, AX, DS, PC, TC. 3 rooms with PB, 3 with FP and 1 suite. Breakfast included in rates. Types of meals: Full gourmet bkfst and early coffee/tea. Room service available. Beds: Q. Cable TV, phone, turndown service, ceiling fan, VCR and two-person whirlpool in room. Air conditioning. Fax and copier on premises. Weddings and small meetings hosted. Antiquing, fishing, golf, live theater, shopping, downhill skiing, cross-country skiing, tennis and water sports nearby.

40 Putney Road

40 Putney Rd
Brattleboro, VT 05301-2944
(802)254-6268 Fax:(802)258-2673

Circa 1931. The West River runs alongside this French Baronial estate. The inn's well-manicured lawn includes gardens and two fountains. The home is considered a town landmark. Antiques and Oriental rugs grace the interior. Guests are

pampered with chocolates, turndown service, fresh flowers and complimentary red wine. Additional amenities include hair dryers, ironing boards, refrigerators, TV, modem hookups and phones.

Innkeeper(s): Dan & Gwen Pasco. $90-170. MC, VISA, AX. 4 rooms. Breakfast included in rates. Type of meal: Full bkfst. Beds: QDT. TV, bathrobes, hair dryers and iron & ironing board in room.

Brookfield   F4

Green Trails Inn

PO Box 494
Brookfield, VT 05036-0494
(802)276-3412 (800)243-3412

Circa 1830. Two historic buildings, one constructed in 1790 and the other in 1830, comprise this inn. The innkeepers have an impressive clock collection, and clock sales, restoration and repair are located on the premises. Many guest rooms offer

views of the lake. One suite has a fireplace and others feature private Jacuzzis. The inn is across the street from Sunset Lake

and the Floating Bridge. Cross-country skiing, snowshoeing, hiking, biking and swimming are right outside the door, and there are a number of outdoor activities nearby.

Innkeeper(s): Sue & Mark Erwin. $79-130. MC, VISA, DS, PC, TC. TAC10. 13 rooms, 9 with PB, 1 with FP and 3 suites. Breakfast included in rates. Types of meals: Full bkfst and early coffee/tea. Gourmet dinner available. Beds: QDT. TV and Jacuzzi in room. VCR, fax, swimming, bicycles, library, cross-country skis and snowshoes on premises. Weddings, small meetings, family reunions and seminars hosted. Antiquing, fishing, golf, horseback riding, biking, tennis, hiking, canoeing, live theater, parks, shopping, downhill skiing and water sports nearby.

Pets allowed: Boarding nearby.

Publicity: *Sunday Republican, Yankee Magazine.*

"The inn is really lovely, the welcome very warm and food is scrumptious."

Cabot   D5

Creamery Inn

Cabot Rd & West Hill Pond Rd
Cabot, VT 05647-0187
(802)563-2819

Circa 1835. This white Federal-style home with green shutters is situated on two acres. A favorite guest room offers a canopy bed and stenciling. The home's original stenciling was discovered during the renovation; a section has been framed and the

rest carefully restored. Afternoon tea may be taken on the enclosed porch. Guests enjoy walking up the country road to see waterfalls or scenic views.

Candlelight dinners may be arranged by advance notice.

Innkeeper(s): Dan & Judy Lloyd. $55-75. PC, TC. 3 rooms with PB and 1 suite. Breakfast and afternoon tea included in rates. Types of meals: Full bkfst and early coffee/tea. Dinner available. Beds: KQDT. A/C and refrigerator (in suite) in room. Family reunions hosted. Antiquing, fishing, live theater, parks, shopping, downhill skiing, cross-country skiing and water sports nearby.

Chester   I4

Hugging Bear Inn & Shoppe

244 Main St
Chester, VT 05143
(802)875-2412 (800)325-0519 Fax:(802)875-3823

Circa 1850. Among the 9,000 teddy bear inhabitants of this white Victorian inn, several peek out from the third-story windows of the octagonal tower. There is a teddy bear shop on the premises and children and adults can borrow a bear to take to bed with them. Rooms are decorated with antiques and comfortable furniture. A bear puppet show is often staged during breakfast.

Innkeeper(s): Georgette Thomas. $60-125. MC, VISA, AX, DS, PC, TC. 6 rooms with PB. Breakfast included in rates. Types of meals: Full gourmet bkfst and early coffee/tea. Beds: QDT. TV and teddy bear in room. VCR and library on premises. Small meetings and family reunions hosted. Antiquing, fishing, golf, golf, parks, shopping, downhill skiing and cross-country skiing nearby.

Publicity: *Rutland Daily Herald, Exxon Travel, Teddy Bear Review, Teddy Bear Scene, Teddy Bear Tribune.*

Inn Victoria and Tea Pot Shoppe

On The Green, PO Box 788
Chester, VT 05143-0788
(802)875-4288 (800)732-4288 Fax:(802)875-4323

Circa 1820. High tea is one of the highlights for guests, who can keep the memory alive by purchasing from the innkeeper's Tea Pot Shoppe. This Second Empire Victorian is among several historic houses and seven churches found in Chester's On the Green area. Many weekends include Victorian fairs and festivals. Overture to Christmas is a festive time for townspeople and visitors who dress Victorian and carol door-to-door. Two summer theater groups are nearby.

Innkeeper(s): Tom & KC Lanagan. $90-325. MC, VISA, AX, CB, TC. 10 rooms with PB, 4 with FP. Breakfast and afternoon tea included in rates. Types of meals: Full gourmet bkfst and early coffee/tea. Beds: KQ. Cable TV and phone in room. Air conditioning. VCR, fax and spa on premises. Weddings, small meetings, family reunions and seminars hosted. Antiquing, fishing, special town-wide events, live theater, parks, shopping, downhill skiing, cross-country skiing, sporting events and water sports nearby.

Chittenden   G3

Tulip Tree Inn

Chittenden Dam Rd
Chittenden, VT 05737
(802)483-6213 (800)707-0017
E-mail: ttinn@sover.net
Web: tuliptreeinn.com

Circa 1830. Thomas Edison was a regular guest here when the house was the country home of William Barstow. The inn is surrounded by the Green Mountains on three sides with a stream flowing a few yards away. The guest rooms feature antiques and Vermont country decor. Most rooms offer Jacuzzis and some boast fireplaces. Guests enjoy both breakfast and dinner at the inn. Buttermilk pancakes topped with Vermont maple syrup are typical breakfast fare, and dinners include such items as medallions of pork topped with an orange-apricot sauce and white chocolate cheesecake.

Innkeeper(s): Ed & Rosemary McDowell. $150-400. MC, VISA, PC, TC. TAC10. 9 rooms with PB. Breakfast and dinner included in rates. MAP. Types of meals: Full bkfst and early coffee/tea. Restaurant on premises. Beds: KQ. Some with fireplaces and Jacuzzis in room. Library on premises. Weddings and small meetings hosted. Amusement parks, antiquing, fishing, live theater, parks, shopping, downhill skiing, cross-country skiing and water sports nearby.

Publicity: *New England Getaways.*

"Tulip Tree Inn is one of the warmest, friendliest and coziest country inns you'll find in New England. - New England Getaways."

Craftsbury Common   C5

The Inn on The Common

PO Box 75
Craftsbury Common, VT 05827-0075
(802)586-9619 (800)521-2233 Fax:(802)586-2249
E-mail: info@innonthecommon.com
Web: www.innonthecommon.com

Circa 1795. The Inn on the Common, built by the Samuel French family, is an integral part of this picturesque classic Vermont village. With its white picket fence and graceful white clapboard exterior, the inn provides a quietly elegant retreat. Pastoral views are framed by the inn's famous perennial gardens. The inn also includes a notable wine cellar.

Historic Interest: Stonehouse Museum (20 miles), Saint Johnsbury-Atheneum museum, Fairbanks Museum (25 miles).

Innkeeper(s): Michael & Penny Schmitt. $190-270. MC, VISA, AX, PC, TC. 16 rooms with PB, 2 suites and 1 conference room. Breakfast and dinner included in rates. MAP. Type of meal: Full bkfst. Picnic lunch available. Restaurant on premises. Beds: KQDT. Swimming and tennis on premises. Fishing, downhill skiing, cross-country skiing, tennis and water sports nearby.

Pets Allowed.

"The closest my wife and I came to fulfilling our fantasy of a country inn was at The Inn on the Common" — Paul Grimes.

Danby   I3

Quail's Nest B&B

81 S Main Street
Danby, VT 05739
(802)293-5099 (800)599-6444 Fax:(802)293-6300

Circa 1835. Located in the village, this Greek Revival inn features six guest rooms all with private baths and on each bed is found a handmade quilt. Full breakfasts are made to order by the innkeepers, and Nancy serves it in period clothing. Also provided is early morning coffee or tea, afternoon tea and an evening snack. The Green Mountain National Forest is just to the east of the inn, providing many outstanding recreational opportunities. Outlet shopping is found just a few miles south in Manchester, and Alpine skiing is enjoyed at Bromley, Killington, Okemo, Pico and Stratton ski areas, all within easy driving distance.

Historic Interest: 1835 Greek Revival house with original marble porches.

Innkeeper(s): Greg & Nancy Diaz. $60-120. MC, VISA, AX, DS, PC, TC. TAC10. 6 rooms with PB and 1 conference room. Breakfast and afternoon tea included in rates. Types of meals: Full bkfst and early coffee/tea. Beds: KQT. VCR on premises. Family reunions and seminars hosted. Antiquing, fishing, swimming, biking, hiking, live theater, shopping, downhill skiing, cross-country skiing, sporting events and water sports nearby.

Silas Griffith Inn

178 S Main St
Danby, VT 05739
(802)293-5567 (800)545-1509 Fax:(802)293-5559

Circa 1891. Originally on 55,000 acres, this stately Queen Anne Victorian mansion features solid cherry, oak and bird's-eye maple woodwork. Considered an architectural marvel, an eight-foot, round, solid-cherry pocket door separates the original music room from the front parlor.

Historic Interest: Hildene, Coolidge Homestead (30 minutes).

Innkeeper(s): George & Carol Gaines. $74-120. MC, VISA, PC, TC. TAC10. 15 rooms with PB. Breakfast and afternoon tea included in rates. Types of meals: Full gourmet bkfst and early coffee/tea. Gourmet dinner and picnic lunch available. Restaurant on premises. Beds: KQT. VCR, fax, swimming and library on premises. Weddings, small meetings, family reunions and seminars hosted. Antiquing, fishing, golf, live theater, parks, shopping, downhill skiing, cross-country skiing, tennis and water sports nearby.

Publicity: *Vermont Weathervane, Rutland Business Journal, Vermont, Country.*

"Never have I stayed at a B&B where the innkeepers were so friendly, sociable and helpful. They truly enjoyed their job."

Derby Line   A6

The Birchwood Bed & Breakfast

PO Box 550
Derby Line, VT 05830-0550
(802)873-9104 Fax:(802)873-9121

Circa 1920. Guests in search of a romantic atmosphere will have no trouble finding it at this cozy bed & breakfast. Fresh flowers, chocolates and luxury bath soaps are among the items waiting in bedchambers, which are decorated with antiques. The innkeeper also serves her gourmet breakfasts by candle-

light. Derby Line, located near the Canadian border in northern Vermont, offers beautiful scenery and close access to fishing, water sports, golf and many more outdoor activities. Sleigh rides are a popular winter activity.

Innkeeper(s): Dick & Betty Fletcher. $75. PC, TC. 3 rooms with PB. Breakfast included in rates. Type of meal: Full gourmet bkfst. Afternoon tea available. Beds: QDT. Designer soaps and lotions in room. Fax and library on premises. Small meetings, family reunions and seminars hosted. Antiquing, fishing, golf, tennis, hiking, cycling, live theater, parks, shopping, downhill skiing, cross-country skiing and water sports nearby.

"Heaven can wait. When I die I am going to Vermont and stay much longer at The Birchwood."

Derby Village Inn

440 Main St, PO Box 1085
Derby Line, VT 05830
(802)873-3604 Fax:(802)873-3047
E-mail: dvibandb@together.net
Web: www.together.net/~dvibandb

Circa 1900. This turn-of-the-century Neoclassical inn is just off the Canadian border in the village of Derby Line. Elegant rooms are individually decorated. Guests are pampered with a homemade breakfast. The inn is near to many activities, including downhill and cross-country skiing, hiking, snowmobiling, fishing and a variety of water sports. Antique shops are nearby, and an international library and opera house are within walking distance.

Innkeeper(s): Catherine McCormick & Sheila Steplar. $75-100. MC, VISA, AX, DS, PC, TC. 5 rooms with PB, 1 with FP, 1 suite and 1 conference room. Breakfast included in rates. Types of meals: Full bkfst and early coffee/tea. Beds: KQT. VCR, fax, copier and library on premises. Weddings, small meetings, family reunions and seminars hosted. Antiquing, bicycling, fishing, golf, snowmobiling, ice fishing, auctions, live theater, downhill skiing, cross-country skiing and water sports nearby.

Dorset   I2

Marble West Inn

PO Box 847, Dorset West Rd
Dorset, VT 05251-0847
(802)867-4155 (800)453-7629 Fax:(802)867-5731

Circa 1840. This historic Greek Revival inn boasts many elegant touches, including stenciling in its entrance hallways done by one of the nation's top craftspeople. Guests also will enjoy Oriental rugs, handsome marble fireplaces and polished dark oak floors. Visitors delight at the many stunning views enjoyed at the inn, including Green Peak and Owl's Head mountains, flower-filled gardens and meadows and two trout-stocked ponds. Emerald Lake State Park is nearby.

Historic Interest: Dorset (2 miles), Old Bennington

(30 miles), Norman Rockwell's West Arlington home (15 miles), Manchester Village (5 miles).

Innkeeper(s): Bonnie & Paul Quinn. $90-175. MC, VISA, AX, PC. 8 rooms with PB, 1 with FP and 1 suite. Breakfast and afternoon tea included in rates. Type of meal: Full bkfst. Beds: KQDT. Turndown service in room. Library on premises. Antiquing, fishing, designer outlet shopping, horseback riding, art galleries, biking, golf, tennis, fine dining, live theater, parks, shopping, downhill skiing, cross-country skiing and water sports nearby.

"A charming inn with wonderful hospitality. The room was comfortable, immaculate, and furnished with every imaginable need and comfort."

Essex Junction   D2

Allyn House B&B

57 Main Street
Essex Junction, VT 05452
(802)878-9408 Fax:(802)878-9408
E-mail: allynhouse@aolcom
Web: members.aol.com/allynhouse

Circa 1897. Built at the turn of the 20th century, the Allyn House features Queen Anne-style architecture. Rooms are decorated in Victorian style with antiques. Each room has a different theme. The Scottish Room includes a canopy bed with a handmade canopy, as well as old photographs of the Highlands. The Russian Room includes art from its namesake country. Other rooms evoke a French and Japanese ambiance. During the week, guests are served a continental breakfast with fresh fruit and baked goods. On the weekends, a full breakfast is served.

Historic Interest: Shelburne Museum (10 miles).

Innkeeper(s): AJ McDonald. $65-75. MC, VISA. 4 rooms, 3 with PB. Breakfast included in rates. Types of meals: Cont plus and country bkfst. Beds: QD. Air conditioning. VCR and library on premises. Small meetings and family reunions hosted. Antiquing, beaches, bicycling, canoeing/kayaking, golf, hiking, live theater, museums, shopping, sporting events, tennis and water sports nearby.

The Inn at Essex

70 Essex Way
Essex Junction, VT 05452-3383
(802)878-1100 Fax:(802)878-0063
E-mail: innfo@innatessex.com
Web: www.innatessex.com

Elegant furnishings and decor, each in a different style, grace the guest rooms at this luxurious Colonial inn, which carries a four-diamond rating. Several guest suites include whirlpool tubs, and 50 of the rooms include wood-burning fireplaces. The two restaurants are operated by New England Culinary Institute, one a gourmet restaurant and the other a more casual tavern. The inn also includes a swimming pool, library, art gallery and a bakery.

Historic Interest: New England Culinary Institute operates the two restaurants.
Innkeeper(s): Jim Lamberti. $175-499. MC, VISA, AX, DC, CB, DS. 120 rooms. Breakfast included in rates. Type of meal: Cont. Art gallery, ice skating in winter and volleyball in summer on premises.

Fair Haven   H2

Maplewood Inn

Rt 22A S
Fair Haven, VT 05743
(802)265-8039 (800)253-7729 Fax:(802)265-8210

Circa 1843. This beautifully restored Greek Revival house, which is in the National Register, was once the family home of the founder of Maplewood Dairy, Isaac Wood. Period antiques and reproductions grace
the inn's spacious
rooms and suites.
Some rooms boast fire-
places and all have sit-
ting areas. A collection

of antique spinning wheels and yarn winders is displayed. A porch wing, built around 1795, was a tavern formerly located down the road. Overlooking three acres of lawn, the inn offers an idyllic setting. The parlor's cordial bar and evening turndown service are among the many amenities offered by the innkeepers.

Historic Interest: Local historic attractions include the Vermont Maple Museum and Norman Rockwell Museum. Hubbardton Battlefield and Wilson Castle are within 20 minutes of the inn. Farther attractions include Fort Ticonderoga, which is 45 minutes away and the Shelburne Museum, an hour from the inn.

Innkeeper(s): Cindy & Doug Baird. $80-145. MC, VISA, AX, DS, PC, TC. TAC10. 5 rooms with PB, 4 with FP, 2 suites and 1 conference room. Breakfast included in rates. Beds: QD. Cable TV, phone and turndown service in room. Air conditioning. Fax, copier, library, complimentary cordial bar, hot beverage bar and snacks on premises. Small meetings and family reunions hosted. Amusement parks, antiquing, fishing, live theater, parks, shopping, downhill skiing, cross-country skiing, sporting events and water sports nearby.

Publicity: *Country, Insider, Americana, New England Getaways.*

"Your inn is perfection. Leaving under protest."

Fairlee   F6

Silver Maple Lodge & Cottages

520 US Rt 5 South
Fairlee, VT 05045
(802)333-4326 (800)666-1946
E-mail: scott@silvermaplelodge.com
Web: www.silvermaplelodge.com

Circa 1790. This old Cape farmhouse was expanded in the 1850s and became an inn in the '20s when Elmer & Della Batchelder opened their home to guests. It became so successful that several cottages, built from lumber on the property, were added. For 60 years, the Batchelder family continued the operation. They misnamed the lodge, however,
mistaking silver poplar trees
on the property for what
they thought were silver
maples. Guest rooms are
decorated with many of
the inn's original furnish-

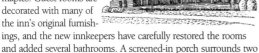

ings, and the new innkeepers have carefully restored the rooms and added several bathrooms. A screened-in porch surrounds two sides of the house. Three of the cottages include working fire-places and one is handicap accessible.

Historic Interest: The Quechee Gorge, Maple Grove Maple Museum, Billings Farm & Museum and the Saint Gauden's National Historic Site are among the area's historic sites.

Innkeeper(s): Scott & Sharon Wright. $56-86. MC, VISA, AX, DS, PC, TC. TAC10. 16 rooms, 14 with PB, 3 with FP and 8 cottages. Breakfast included in rates. Type of meal: Cont. Beds: KQDT. TV in room. VCR, copier and bicycles on premises. Handicap access. Small meetings and family reunions hosted. Antiquing, fishing, live theater, parks, shopping, downhill skiing, cross-country skiing and water sports nearby.

Pets allowed: Cottage rooms only.

Publicity: *Boston Globe, Vermont Country Sampler, Travel Holiday, Travel America, New York Times.*

"Your gracious hospitality and attractive home all add up to a pleasant experience."

Greensboro   C5

Highland Lodge

RR 1 Box 1290
Greensboro, VT 05841-9712
(802)533-2647 Fax:(802)533-7494

Circa 1865. With a private beach and 120 acres to enjoy, guests rarely have trouble finding a way to pass the time at this lodge. The lodge is located in a mid-19th-century farmhouse, and visitors either room here in country guest rooms or in a collection of cottages. The cottages have from one to three bedrooms, a living room, bathroom and a porch. All guests are welcome to use the lodge's common areas or simply relax on the porch, but there's sailing, swimming, fishing, boating and much more on the premises. In the winter, the lodge grooms 60 kilometers of cross-country ski trails and has a ski shop renting all the necessary gear. The breakfast choices might include French toast, waffles, pancakes, eggs or muffins, and at dinner, guests choose from four entrees accompanied by salad, homemade bread and dessert.

Historic Interest: Greensboro Historical Society.

Innkeeper(s): Wilhemina & David Smith. $194-240. MC, VISA, DS, PC, TC. TAC10. 11 cottages with PB. Breakfast and dinner included in rates. MAP. Types of meals: Full bkfst and early coffee/tea. Afternoon tea, picnic lunch and lunch available. Restaurant on premises. Beds: QDT. Fax, copier, swimming, bicycles, tennis, library, child care, sailing and cross-country skiing on premises. Handicap access. Weddings, small meetings, family reunions and seminars hosted. Dutch spoken. Antiquing, golf, live theater and downhill skiing nearby.

Publicity: *New England Skiers Guide, Vermont Magazine, Hardwick Gazette, Rural New England Magazine, Better Homes & Gardens, Providence Sunday Journal, Yankee.*

"We had a great time last weekend and enjoyed everything we did—hiking, climbing, swimming, canoeing and eating."

Hyde Park   C4

Fitch Hill Inn

258 Fitch Hill Rd
Hyde Park, VT 05655-9801
(802)888-3834 (800)639-2903 Fax:(802)888-7789

Circa 1797. This Federalist-style home sits on five acres of hill-top land overlooking the village and Green Mountains. There are three porches with spectacular
views. The five, second-floor guest
rooms share a period-fur-
nished living room, game
room and movie library.
There is a suite with a fireplace and Jacuzzi. There also
is a studio apartment available

with a whirlpool tub, fireplace, deck and kitchen. Gourmet breakfasts are served in the dining room. Gourmet, candlelight dinners can be arranged by advance reservation for six or more.

Historic Interest: Chester A. Arthur birthplace/home (20 miles), Shelburne Museum (40 miles).

Innkeeper(s): Richard A. Pugliese & Stanley E. Corklin. $85-189. MC, VISA, AX, DS, PC, TC. TAC10. 6 rooms with PB, 2 with FP, 2 suites and 1 conference room. Breakfast included in rates. Types of meals: Full gourmet bkfst and early coffee/tea. Afternoon tea, gourmet dinner and picnic lunch available. Beds: QDT. Cable TV, phone, ceiling fan, VCR and Jacuzzi in room. Air conditioning. Spa, bicycles and library on premises. Weddings, small meetings, family reunions and seminars hosted. English, Spanish and some French spoken. Amusement parks, antiquing, fishing, live theater, parks, downhill skiing, cross-country skiing and water sports nearby.

Jeffersonville   C3

Jefferson House

PO Box 288, Main St
Jeffersonville, VT 05464-0288
(802)644-2030 (800)253-9630

Circa 1910. Three comfortable guest rooms, decorated in a country Victorian style, are the offerings at this turn-of-the-century home. As one might expect, pancakes topped with Vermont maple syrup are often a staple at the breakfast table, accompanied by savory items such as smoked bacon. There is an antique shop on the premises. Each season brings a new activity to this scenic area. In the winter, it's just a few minutes to Smugglers' Notch ski area, and Stowe isn't far. Biking or hiking to the top of Mt. Mansfield are popular summer activities.

Innkeeper(s): Joan & Richard Walker. $55-75. MC, VISA, DS, PC, TC. 3 rooms with PB. Breakfast included in rates. Type of meal: Full bkfst. Beds: KQDT. Alarm clock in room. Air conditioning. VCR on premises. Antiquing, fishing, hiking, biking, canoeing. Antique shop on premises, live theater, parks, shopping, downhill skiing, cross-country skiing, sporting events and water sports nearby.

Pets allowed: By prior arrangement.

Killington   G3

Mountain Meadows Lodge

285 Thundering Brook Rd
Killington, VT 05751-9801
(802)775-1010 (800)370-4567 Fax:(802)773-4459

Circa 1850. Located in a pre-Civil War farmhouse, on Kent Lake and the Appalachian Trail, Mountain Meadows Lodge offers a multitude of amenities and services for guests. Rooms range from cozy standard rooms to suites and rooms with balconies or perhaps a fireplace. Guests enjoy a Vermont country breakfast with items such as blueberry pancakes and specialty omelets. Boxed lunches are prepared for guests who want to enjoy a picnic surrounded by Vermont's notable scenery. Dinners are served in a fire-lit dining room with starters such as a baked brie with a maple Scotch glaze and apple slices. From there, guests can choose from a number of main courses with everything from pan-seared hazelnut encrusted tuna to sirloin in puff pastry. A variety of vegetarian choices also are available. The lodge's state-licensed children center allows parents to leave children for an hour, half-day or all day. Activities at the center change each month and might include camp fires and marshmallow roasts or puppet-making classes and magic shows.

Innkeeper(s): Mark & Michelle Werle. $45-72. MC, VISA, AX, PC, TC. 18 rooms with PB, 1 with FP, 1 suite and 1 conference room. Breakfast, after-

noon tea, dinner and snacks/refreshments included in rates. Types of meals: Full gourmet bkfst and early coffee/tea. Picnic lunch, lunch, banquet service, catering service and catered breakfast available. Restaurant on premises. Beds: QDT. Phone in room. Air conditioning. VCR, fax, spa, swimming, sauna, library, child care, row boating and farm animals on premises. Handicap access. Weddings, small meetings, family reunions and seminars hosted. French, Spanish and German spoken. Antiquing, fishing, golf, Appalachian trail, hiking, waterfalls, live theater, parks, shopping, downhill skiing, cross-country skiing, sporting events, tennis and water sports nearby.

The Vermont Inn

Rt 4
Killington, VT 05751
(802)775-0708 (800)541-7795 Fax:(802)773-2440
E-mail: vtinn@together.net
Web: www.vermontinn.com

Circa 1840. Surrounded by mountain views, this rambling red and white farmhouse has provided lodging and superb cuisine for many years. Exposed beams add to the atmosphere in the living and game rooms. The award-winning dining room provides candlelight tables beside a huge fieldstone fireplace.

Historic Interest: Calvin Coolidge birthplace and Bennington, V.T., Civil War exhibits.

Innkeeper(s): Megan & Greg Smith. $50-185. MC, VISA, AX, DC, PC, TC. 18 rooms with PB, 2 with FP. Breakfast & afternoon tea included in rates. MAP, EP. Meals: Full bkfst & early coffee/tea. Gourmet dinner & banquet service available. Beds: QDT. TV and ceiling fan in room. Air conditioning. VCR, fax, copier, spa, swimming, sauna, tennis, library & screened porch on premises. Handicap access. Weddings, small meetings, family reunions & seminars hosted. Antiquing, fishing, live theater, parks, shopping, skiing and water sports nearby.

Publicity: *New York Daily News, New Jersey Star Leader, Rutland Business Journal, Bridgeport Post Telegram, New York Times, Boston, Vermont.*

"We had a wonderful time. The inn is breathtaking. Hope to be back."

Landgrove   J3

Landgrove Inn

Rd Box 215, Landgrove Rd
Landgrove, VT 05148
(802)824-6673 (800)669-8466 Fax:(802)824-3055
E-mail: vtinn@sover.net
Web: www.vermont.com/business/landgroveinn

Circa 1820. This rambling inn is located along a country lane in the valley of Landgrove in the Green Mountain National Forest. The Rafter Room is a lounge and pub with a fireside sofa for 12. Breakfast and dinner are served in the newly renovated and stenciled dining room. Evening sleigh or hay rides are often arranged. Rooms vary in style and bedding arrangements, including some newly decorated rooms with country decor, so inquire when making your reservation.

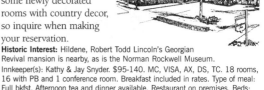

Historic Interest: Hildene, Robert Todd Lincoln's Georgian Revival mansion is nearby, as is the Norman Rockwell Museum.

Innkeeper(s): Kathy & Jay Snyder. $95-140. MC, VISA, AX, DS, TC. 18 rooms, 16 with PB and 1 conference room. Breakfast included in rates. Type of meal: Full bkfst. Afternoon tea and dinner available. Restaurant on premises. Beds: QD. Phone in room. VCR, fax, copier and spa on premises. Weddings, small meetings, family reunions and seminars hosted. Antiquing, fishing, live theater, parks, shopping, downhill skiing and cross-country skiing nearby.

"A true country inn with great food — we'll be back."

Lower Waterford D6

Rabbit Hill Inn

Lower Waterford Rd
Lower Waterford, VT 05848
(802)748-5168 (800)762-8669 Fax:(802)748-8342

Circa 1795. Above the Connecticut River overlooking the White Mountains, Samuel Hodby opened this tavern and provided a general store and inn to travelers. As many as 100 horse teams a day traveled by the inn. The ballroom, constructed in 1855, was supported by bentwood construction giving the dance floor a spring effect. The classic Greek Revival exterior features solid pine Doric columns. Romance abounds in every nook  and cranny. Rooms are decorated to the hilt with beautiful furnishings and linens. The Loft room, which overlooks the garden, includes cathedral ceilings and a hidden staircase. The Top-of-the-Tavern room boasts a Victorian dressing room with vintage clothing. Turndown service and afternoon tea are only a few of the amenities. Glorious breakfasts and gourmet, five-course, candle-lit dinners add to a memorable stay.

Historic Interest: There are several historic churches in the area. The Fairbanks Museum, Planetarium and Art Gallery is 10 minutes away, while the Robert Frost Museum is a 25-minute drive.

Innkeeper(s): Brian & Leslie Mulcahy. $235-370. MC, VISA, AX, PC. 21 rooms with PB, 12 with FP. Breakfast, afternoon tea and dinner included in rates. MAP. Types of meals: Full bkfst and early coffee/tea. Picnic lunch available. Restaurant on premises. Beds: KQT. Eight rooms with whirlpool tubs for two in room. Fax and copier on premises. Antiquing, bicycling, canoeing/kayaking, fishing, golf, hiking, horseback riding, sleigh rides, massage services, live theater, parks, shopping, downhill skiing and cross-country skiing nearby.

"It is not often that one experiences one's vision of a tranquil, beautiful step back in time. This is such an experience. Everyone was so accommodating and gracious."

Ludlow I4

The Governor's Inn

86 Main St
Ludlow, VT 05149-1113
(802)228-8830
E-mail: kubec@thegovernorsinn.com
Web: www.thegovernorsinn.com

Circa 1890. Governor Stickney built this house for his bride, Elizabeth Lincoln, and it retains the intimate feeling of an elegant country house furnished in the Victorian fashion. Antique-filled rooms are warmed by the crackling fires from slate fireplaces. In  addition to the full breakfast, the inn offers outstanding six-course, gourmet dinners.

Innkeeper(s): Cathy & Jim Kubec. $180-255. MC, VISA, AX. 8 rooms with PB and 1 suite. MAP. Type of meal: Full gourmet bkfst. Gourmet dinner available.

Manchester J2

The Battenkill Inn

PO Box 948
Manchester, VT 05254-0948
(802)362-4213 (800)441-1628 Fax:(802)362-0975
E-mail: info@battenkillinn.com
Web: www.battenkillinn.com

Circa 1840. There is something for everyone at this Victorian farmhouse inn. Guest rooms are filled with antiques, and four of them boast working fireplaces. Fine fishing is found in the Battenkill River on the inn's grounds, and guests also are welcome to stroll down to the pond to feed the ducks or play croquet on the lush lawns. Two sitting rooms with fireplaces are popular gathering areas.  Dining and shopping experiences await visitors in Manchester Village and Emerald Lake State Park is a short drive from the inn.

Innkeeper(s): Laine & Yoshi Akiyama. $95-165. MC, VISA, TC. 11 rooms with PB, 4 with FP. Breakfast and snacks/refreshments included in rates. Types of meals: Full bkfst and early coffee/tea. Beds: KQDT. Turndown service and ceiling fan in room. Air conditioning. VCR, fax, copier and library on premises. Handicap access. Small meetings hosted. Antiquing, fishing, outlet shopping, live theater, parks, shopping, downhill skiing, cross-country skiing and water sports nearby.

"The inn is beautiful and the atmosphere soothing."

The Inn at Manchester

PO Box 41, HR 7A
Manchester, VT 05254-0041
(802)362-1793 (800)273-1793 Fax:(802)362-3218
E-mail: iman@vermontel.com
Web: www.innatmanchester.com

Circa 1880. This restored Victorian and its carriage house are in the National Register. In a setting of beautiful gardens and meadows of wildflowers with a meandering brook, the inn offers an extensive art collection of old prints and paintings. Guest rooms have fine linens, bay windows and antiques. The inn was restored by the innkeepers. The guest pool is set in a secluded meadow.

Historic Interest: Robert Todd Lincoln's Estate and the Southern Vermont Art Center are within two miles of the inn. The Bennington Museum is 25 miles away.

Innkeeper(s): Amy, Dawn, Diane. $98-168. MC, VISA, AX, DS, PC, TC. TAC10. 18 rooms with PB, 3 with FP and 4 suites. Breakfast and afternoon tea included in rates. Type of meal: Full gourmet bkfst. Beds: KQDT. Clocks in room. Air conditioning. Fax, copier and swimming on premises. Small meetings and family reunions hosted. Antiquing, fishing, golf, outlet shopping, 100 shops, live theater, shopping, downhill skiing, cross-country skiing and tennis nearby.

Publicity: *New York Times, Boston Globe, Travel & Leisure, Gourmet, Newsday.*

Wilburton Inn

PO Box 468
Manchester, VT 05254-0468
(802)362-2500 (800)648-4944 Fax:(802)362-1107
E-mail: wilbuinn@sover.net
Web: www.wilburton.com

Circa 1902. Shaded by tall maples, this three-story brick mansion sits high on a hill overlooking the Battenkill Valley, which is set against a majestic mountain backdrop. In addition to the

mansion, the inn offers four villas and a seven-bedroom reunion house. Carved moldings, mahogany paneling, Oriental carpets and leaded-glass windows are complemented by carefully chosen antiques. The inn's 20 acres provide three tennis courts, a pool, green lawns and sculpture gardens. Country weddings are a Wiburton Inn's specialty. Gourmet dining is served in the billiard room with European ambiance. Two local country clubs provide the inn with golf privileges.

Innkeeper(s): Georgette Levis. $105-235. MC, VISA, AX. 35 rooms, 6 with FP and 1 conference room. Breakfast included in rates. MAP, AP. Type of meal: Full gourmet bkfst. Afternoon tea, gourmet dinner and room service available. Restaurant on premises. Beds: KQ. TV in room. Fax and copier on premises. Antiquing, fishing, golf, live theater, downhill skiing, cross-country skiing and water sports nearby.

Publicity: *Great Escapes TV, Travelhost, Getaways For Gourmets, Country Inns, Bed & Breakfast, Gourmet, Best Places to Stay In New England.*

"Simply splendid! Peaceful, beautiful, elegant. Ambiance & ambiance!"

Manchester Center   J2

Manchester Highlands Inn

Highland Ave, Box 1754A
Manchester Center, VT 05255
(802)362-4565 (800)743-4565 Fax:(802)362-4028
E-mail: relax@highlandsinn.com
Web: www.highlandsinn.com

Circa 1898. This Queen Anne Victorian mansion sits proudly on the crest of a hill overlooking the village. From the three-story turret, guests can look out over Mt. Equinox, the Green Mountains and the valley below. Feather beds and down comforters adorn the beds in the guest rooms. A game room with billiards and a stone fireplace are popular in winter, while summertime guests

enjoy the outdoor pool, croquet lawn and veranda. Gourmet country breakfasts and home-baked afternoon snacks are served.

Historic Interest: Hildene, summer home of Robert Todd Lincoln (1 mile), Bennington Monument (20 miles).

Innkeeper(s): Patricia & Robert Eichorn. $105-145. MC, VISA, AX, PC, TC. TAC10. 15 rooms with PB. Breakfast and afternoon tea included in rates. Type of meal: Full gourmet bkfst. Beds: QDT. TV in room. Air conditioning. VCR, fax, swimming, library, game room and guest bar on premises. Weddings, small meetings, family reunions and seminars hosted. Limited French and German spoken. Antiquing, fishing, golf, hiking, biking, fly fishing, canoeing, horseback riding, live theater, parks, shopping, downhill skiing and cross-country skiing nearby.

Publicity: *Toronto Sun, Vermont, Asbury Park Press, Vermont Weathervane, Yankee Traveler, Boston Globe, Cat Fanciers Magazine.*

"We couldn't believe such a place existed. Now we can't wait to come again."

The Inn at Ormsby Hill

1842 Main St
Manchester Center, VT 05255-9518
(802)362-1163 (800)670-2841 Fax:(802)362-5176
E-mail: ormsby@vermontel.com
Web: www.ormsbyhill.com

Circa 1764. During the Revolutionary War, hero Ethan Allen reportedly hid out in the smoke room at this Federal-style mansion. Robert Todd Lincoln and President Taft are among the

other notable guests at this historic treasure. The town's first jail cell still exists in the inn's basement, complete with steel bars and the marble slab where prisoners slept. The inn offers

beautiful views of the nearby Green Mountains. Inside, guests will marvel at the inn's conservatory, which was built to resemble a ship and looks out to the gardens and the mountains. Antique-filled rooms offer four-poster or canopy beds decked in fine linens. All rooms include fireplaces and two-person whirlpool tubs. Innkeeper Chris Sprague's culinary talents, in addition to writing a cookbook, have been heralded in such publications as Food & Wine, Yankee and Colonial Homes. Vermont is bustling with activities, dozens of which are just a short drive from the inn.

Historic Interest: The adjoining estate to the inn, which itself is listed in the Vermont Register of Historic Places, was home to Robert Todd Lincoln, the son of Abraham Lincoln.

Innkeeper(s): Ted & Chris Sprague. $165-325. MC, VISA, DS. TAC10. 10 rooms with PB, 10 with FP. Breakfast & afternoon tea included in rates. Beds: KQ. Two-person whirlpool in room. Air conditioning. Fax & library on premises. Antiquing, fishing, hiking, live theater, downhill skiing and cross-country skiing nearby.

"After 17 years of visiting B&Bs in Vermont, we can truly say you are the best. On a scale of 1-10, you are a 12."

River Meadow Farm

PO Box 822
Manchester Center, VT 05255-0822
(802)362-1602

Circa 1797. The oldest portion of this New England farmhouse was built in the late 18th century, and in keeping with that era, Colonial-style furnishings decorate the interior. During one part of its history, the home served as Manchester Poor Farm. The living room with its grand piano and fireplace is an ideal place for those seeking relaxation. At breakfast, fresh fruit, coffee, teas and juice accompany traditional entrees such as eggs and bacon or pancakes topped with blueberries. There are 90 acres to explore at this farm, some of which border the Battenkill River.

Historic Interest: Hildene, the summer home of Robert Todd Lincoln, can be seen from a hill on the farm. The 1906 home is open for tours from May to October.

Innkeeper(s): Patricia J. Dupree. $60. PC, TC. 5 rooms. Breakfast included in rates. MAP. Type of meal: Full bkfst. Beds: DT. VCR and library on premises. Antiquing, fishing, live theater, parks, shopping, downhill skiing, cross-country skiing and water sports nearby.

"We really loved our stay and are planning to return as soon as possible."

Manchester Village   J2

The Reluctant Panther Inn & Restaurant

17-39 West Rd
Manchester Village, VT 05254
(802)362-2568 (800)822-2331 Fax:(802)362-2586
E-mail: stay@reluctantpanthers.com
Web: www.reluctantpanther.com

Circa 1850. Elm trees line a street of manicured lawns and white clapboard estates. Suddenly, a muted purple clapboard house appears, the Reluctant Panther. The well-appointed guest rooms recently have been renovated and many include fireplaces, whirlpool tubs, cable TV and air conditioning. Guests will find a collection of gracious antique furnishings in their rooms. The inn offers two suites with double Jacuzzi tubs and fireplaces. The Greenhouse is a beautiful setting in which to enjoy a romantic dinner, on tables set with fine china and crystal. Breakfasts are served in the inn's private dining room, a bright room warmed by a crackling fire.

Historic Interest: Hildene (1 mile), Norman Rockwell Museum (8 miles), Bennington Monument and battlefield (20 miles).

Innkeeper(s): Robert & Maye Bachofen. $95-2388. MC, VISA, AX, DC, CB, DS, PC, TC. TAC10. 21 rooms, 10 with PB, 15 with FP, 11 suites and 1 conference room. Breakfast and dinner included in rates. MAP, AP, EP. Types of meals: Full gourmet bkfst, cont plus and cont. Banquet service available. Restaurant on premises. Beds: KQT. Cable TV, phone, turndown service, Jacuzzi and hair dryers in room. Central air. Fax and copier on premises. Handicap access. Family reunions hosted. German, Spanish and French spoken. Antiquing, art galleries, bicycling, canoeing/kayaking, fishing, golf, hiking, horseback riding, live theater, museums, parks, shopping, downhill skiing, cross-country skiing and tennis nearby.

"We enjoyed our stay so much that now we want to make it our yearly romantic getaway."

Middlebury   F2

Linens & Lace

29 Seminary St
Middlebury, VT 05753-1216
(802)388-0832 (800)808-3897

Circa 1820. Located within easy walking distance of the historic village and Middlebury College, this quaint Victorian inn provides guests with a comfortable respite whether they're in

town for the music festival, skiing, shopping or attending one of the many college functions. There are five guest rooms, all decorated in heirlooms and antiques.
Linen and lace, thus the name, fresh flowers and sterling silver add to the inn's ambiance. Afternoon tea is served on the porch overlooking the gardens, weather permitting, while a full breakfast of wild blueberry muffins, pancakes, bacon, orange juice and fresh fruit is offered in the dining room.

Innkeeper(s): Mary Botter. $89-129. PC, TC. 5 rooms, 3 with PB. Breakfast and afternoon tea included in rates. Types of meals: Full bkfst and early coffee/tea. Beds: QDT. Ceiling fan in room. Air conditioning. VCR on premises. Family reunions hosted. Antiquing, fishing, golf, hiking, bicycling, fine dining, parks, shopping, downhill skiing, cross-country skiing and tennis nearby.

Middlebury Inn

14 Courthouse Sq
Middlebury, VT 05753
(802)388-4961 (800)842-4666 Fax:(802)388-4563

Circa 1827. This red brick, white-shuttered inn that has hosted weary travelers for many generations, is celebrating its

173rd-year anniversary this year. Guests can choose from several options when selecting a room. The grounds include three different properties aside from the
Middlebury Inn, which is an amazing structure to behold. The Porter Mansion boasts a porch with wicker furnishings, marble fireplaces and a curving staircase. At the Middlebury Inn, guests enjoy delectable afternoon teas on the veranda while viewing the Village Greens. The innkeepers include plenty of special touches such as stocking rooms with books, bath soaps and lotions. Complimentary continental breakfast and afternoon tea is served daily. The inn offers ski and bicycle storage and will help guests make arrangements for walking tours, a popular activity.

Historic Interest: The Middlebury Inn is a community landmark, listed in the National Register, and in the center of Middlebury's historic district, which offers 155 architectural gems within walking distance. Vermont State Craft Center, museums and a waterfall are nearby.

Innkeeper(s): Frank & Jane Emanuel. $88-300. MC, VISA, AX, DS, PC, TC. TAC10. 80 rooms with PB and 3 conference rooms. Breakfast and afternoon tea included in rates. EP. Types of meals: Full bkfst, cont and early coffee/tea. Gourmet dinner, picnic lunch, lunch and banquet service available. Restaurant on premises. Beds: QDT. Cable TV, phone and hair dryers in bathroom in room. Air conditioning. VCR, fax, copier and library on premises. Handicap access. Small meetings, family reunions and seminars hosted. Antiquing, fishing, parks, shopping, downhill skiing, cross-country skiing, sporting events and water sports nearby.

Pets allowed: Limited, fee charged.

Montgomery Center   B4

Phineas Swan B&B

PO Box 43
Montgomery Center, VT 05471-0043
(802)326-4306

Circa 1889. Guests at this Victorian choose from cozy, antique-filled rooms in the main house or suites in the carriage house. The carriage house suites include Jacuzzi tubs and fire-

places. Guests enjoy both a gourmet breakfast and afternoon tea. The Jay Peak Ski Resort is nearby.
Innkeeper(s): Michael Bindler & Glen Bartolomeo. $69-145. MC, VISA, DS, TC. 6 rooms with PB. Breakfast and afternoon tea included in rates. Type of meal: Full gourmet bkfst. Beds: QDT. Turndown service and ceiling fan in room. VCR and library on premises. Small meetings, family reunions and seminars hosted. Antiquing, fishing, golf, live theater, parks, shopping, downhill skiing, cross-country skiing, tennis and water sports nearby.

Publicity: *Country Living, Boston Phinox, Boston Chronicle and Out Magazine.*

The Inn On Trout River

Main St, PO Box 76
Montgomery Center, VT 05471-0076
(802)326-4391 (800)338-7049
E-mail: info@troutinn.com
Web: www.troutinn.com

Circa 1895. Both a fine country inn and restaurant, The Inn on Trout River, offers an ideal location for enjoying Vermont's

Jay Peak region and the historic district of Montgomery Center. Antiques and comfortable furnishings decorate the inn. Feather pillows and down comforters top the queen-size beds. The innkeepers offer adventure packages and a "Teddy Bear Creation Weekend." New packages are added throughout the year. The inn's location provides close access to downhill and cross-country ski areas, snowmobiling, snowshoeing, hiking, biking, golf courses, swimming, fishing and hunting. Museums, shops, antique stores and auctions are other amusements. The area boasts seven covered bridges and endless acres of scenery perfect for shutterbugs and nature lovers alike.

Historic Interest: Covered bridges in Montgomery and within an hour circumference.

Innkeeper(s): Michael & Lee Forman. $58-113. MC, VISA, AX, DS. 10 rooms with PB, 1 with FP and 1 suite. Breakfast included in rates. MAP. Type of meal: Full bkfst. Gourmet dinner available. Restaurant on premises. Beds: KQT. Antiquing, bicycling, fishing, golf, hiking, snowmobiling, snowshoeing, snowboarding, museums, parks, downhill skiing, cross-country skiing and water sports nearby.

"A superb place to stay."

Montpelier   E4

Betsy's B&B

74 E State St
Montpelier, VT 05602-3112
(802)229-0466 Fax:(802)229-5412
E-mail: betsybb@together.net
Web: www.central-vt.com/web/betsybb

Circa 1895. Within walking distance of downtown and located in the state's largest historic preservation district, this Queen

Anne Victorian with romantic turret and carriage house features lavish Victorian antiques throughout its interior. Bay windows, carved woodwork, high ceilings, lace curtains and wood floors add to the authenticity. The full breakfast varies in content but not quality, and guest favorites include orange pancakes.

Innkeeper(s): Jon & Betsy Anderson. $55-95. MC, VISA, AX, DS, PC, TC. TAC10. 12 rooms with PB. Breakfast included in rates. Type of meal: Full bkfst. Beds: QDT. Cable TV and phone in room. VCR, fax and laundry on premises. Small meetings and family reunions hosted. Some Spanish spoken. Antiquing, fishing, art & history museums, live theater, parks, shopping, downhill skiing, cross-country skiing and water sports nearby.

Newfane   K4

West River Lodge & Stables

117 Hill Rd
Newfane, VT 05345-9606
(802)365-7745 Fax:(802)365-4450
E-mail: capite@artacseel.com
Web: westriverlodge.com

Circa 1829. West River Lodge includes a picturesque white farmhouse next door to a big red barn, surrounded by meadows and hills. Flower gardens in view of the long front porch invite guests to linger. Many enjoy horseback riding on the lodge's abundant trails. Horse boarding is offered and lessons and a riding ring are available. The home was built in the early 19th century as part of a horse farm, and it has served as a horse farm for nearly two centuries. The cozy farmhouse offers comfortable guest rooms decorated with country antiques. A hearty breakfast

with items such as blueberry pancakes, country sausage, eggs, homemade muffins and fresh fruit is included in the rates. Newfane offers everything from hiking to fishing, tubing, kayaking and canoeing, as well as antique shops and wonderful fall foliage. The West River is across the field from the lodge.

Innkeeper(s): Ellen & James Wightman. $85-95. MC, VISA, PC. 8 rooms, 2 with PB. Breakfast included in rates. Type of meal: Country bkfst. Beds: QDT. Turndown service in room. VCR, fax, copier, swimming, stables, tennis and pet boarding on premises. Weddings, small meetings, family reunions and seminars hosted. Antiquing, art galleries, beaches, bicycling, canoeing/kayaking, fishing, golf, hiking, horseback riding, live theater, museums, parks, shopping, downhill skiing, cross-country skiing, tennis and water sports nearby.

Pets allowed: In some rooms.

Northfield   E4

Northfield Inn

228 Highland Ave
Northfield, VT 05663-1448
(802)485-8558

Circa 1901. A view of the Green Mountains can be seen from this Victorian inn, which is set on a hillside surrounded by gardens and overlooking an apple orchard and pond. The picturesque inn also affords a view of the village of Northfield and historic Norwich University. Rooms are decorated with antiques and Oriental

rugs, and bedrooms feature European feather bedding and brass and carved-wood beds. Many outdoor activities are available on the three-acre property, including croquet, horseshoes, ice skating and sledding. Visitors may want to take a climb uphill to visit the Old Slate Quarry or just relax on one of the porches overlooking the garden with bird songs, wind chimes and gentle breezes.

Historic Interest: Norwich University, the oldest private military college in the country, is a half mile away. The state capitol is 10 miles away.

Innkeeper(s): Aglaia Stalb. $85-190. MC, VISA, PC, TC. 8 rooms with PB and 3 suites. Breakfast and snacks/refreshments included in rates. Type of meal: Full bkfst. Beds: QDT. Cable TV, phone, turndown service and ceiling fan in room. VCR, bicycles, library and lounge on premises. Weddings, small meetings, family reunions and seminars hosted. Greek spoken. Antiquing, fishing, golf, hiking, sledding, flying, live theater, parks, shopping, downhill skiing, cross-country skiing, sporting events and water sports nearby.

Publicity: Conde Nast Traveler, Gentlemen's Quarterly.

"There's no place like here."

Orwell   G2

Historic Brookside Farms
Country Inn & Antique Shop

PO Box 36, Route 22A
Orwell, VT 05760-9615
(802)948-2727 Fax:(802)948-2800
E-mail: hbfinnvt@aol.com
Web: brooksideinnvt.com

Circa 1789. Nineteen stately Ionic columns grace the front of this Neoclassical Greek Revival farmhouse, which was designed by James Lamb. This is a working farm with Hereford cattle, Hampshire sheep, maple syrup production and poultry. There are 300 acres of lush country landscape with several miles of cross-country skiing, plenty of places for hiking and a 26-acre pond for boating and fishing. Downhill skiing, tennis and skating are nearby. The farm is family owned and operated.

Historic Interest: Mount Independence (2 miles), Fort Ticonderoga (15 minutes).

Innkeeper(s): The Korda Family. $95-175. 7 rooms, 2 with PB, 1 suite and 1 conference room. Breakfast and afternoon tea included in rates. MAP, AP. Types of meals: Full gourmet bkfst and early coffee/tea. Gourmet dinner, snacks/refreshments, picnic lunch, gourmet lunch and banquet service available. Restaurant on premises. Beds: DT. Welcome tray w/ VT products in room. VCR, fax, copier, fishing, cross-country skiing and child care available on premises. Handicap access. Weddings, small meetings, family reunions and seminars hosted. Antiquing, live theater and downhill skiing nearby.

Publicity: *New York Times, Burlington Free Press, Los Angeles Times, Preservation Magazine Antiques.*

Peru J3

Wiley Inn

Rt 11 PO Box 37
Peru, VT 05152-0037
(802)824-6600 (888)843-6600 Fax:(802)824-4195

Circa 1835. The innkeepers at Wiley Inn offer guests a choice of rooms, from romantic bedchambers with canopy beds and clawfoot tubs to family suites that can accommodate up to five people. For honeymooners or those celebrating a special occasion, there are two luxury suites with a fireplace and double Jacuzzi. The nine-and-a-half acre grounds include a swimming pool and hot tub. The innkeepers offer special winter ski packages.

Innkeeper(s): Judy & Jerry Goodman. $75-185. MC, VISA, AX, DS, PC, TC. 16 rooms, 10 with PB, 3 with FP, 3 suites and 1 conference room. Breakfast and afternoon tea included in rates. EP. Types of meals: Full bkfst, cont plus, cont and early coffee/tea. Gourmet dinner available. Restaurant on premises. Beds: KQDT. Cable TV in room. VCR, fax, copier, spa, swimming, cybercafe and internet & e-mail on premises. Weddings, small meetings, family reunions and seminars hosted. Amusement parks, antiquing, fishing, golf, live theater, parks, shopping, downhill skiing, cross-country skiing, tennis and water sports nearby.

Pittsfield G3

The Pittsfield Inn

PO Box 685 Rt 100
Pittsfield, VT 05762-0685
(802)746-8943

Circa 1835. This inn was built as a stagecoach stop and has been serving guests as an inn ever since. Antiques and a country Colonial decor permeate the guest rooms, each has been individually appointed. There is a restaurant on the premises, serving gourmet fare such as grilled tuna steak with poppy seed goat cheese on a bed of cilantro pesto. The innkeepers offer special rates for children. Guests will find plenty to do in the area. Enjoy a tour of local historic sites, drive 15 minutes to skiing at Killington, play a game of golf or take a guided mountain bike or hiking tour.

Innkeeper(s): Tom Yennerell. $30-80. MC, VISA, TC. TAC10. 9 rooms with PB, 1 suite and 1 conference room. Breakfast included in rates. MAP, EP. Type of meal: Full gourmet bkfst. Gourmet dinner available. Restaurant on premises. Beds: QDT. VCR, bicycles and pet boarding on premises. Weddings, small meetings, family reunions and seminars hosted. Antiquing, fishing, golf, self-guided and guided outdoor activities, parks, shopping, downhill skiing, cross-country skiing, tennis and water sports nearby.

Pets allowed: One dog at the inn at any one time.

Proctorsville I4

The Golden Stage Inn

399 Depot St, PO Box 218
Proctorsville, VT 05153
(802)226-7744 (800)253-8226 Fax:(802)226-7882

Circa 1780. The Golden Stage Inn was a stagecoach stop built shortly before Vermont became a state. It served as a link in the Underground Railroad and was the home of Cornelia Otis Skinner. Cornelia's Room still offers its original polished wide-pine floors and view of Okemo Mountain, and now there's a four-poster cherry bed, farm animal border, wainscoting and a comforter filled with wool from the inn's sheep. Outside are gardens of wildflowers, a little pen with two sheep, a swimming pool and blueberries and raspberries for the picking. Breakfast offerings include an often-requested recipe, Golden Stage Granola. Home-baked breakfast dishes are garnished with jonny jumpups and nasturtiums from the garden. Guests can indulge anytime by reaching into the inn's bottomless cookie jar. Okemo Mountain Resort base lodge is four miles away and it's a 15 minute drive to Killington.

Innkeeper(s): Sandy & Peter Gregg. $99-169. MC, VISA, PC. TAC10. 6 rooms with PB and 1 suite. Breakfast and dinner included in rates. MAP. Type of meal: Full bkfst. Beds: QDT. VCR, fax, copier, swimming and library on premises. Weddings, small meetings and family reunions hosted. Antiquing, fishing, golf, live theater, shopping, downhill skiing and cross-country skiing nearby.

"The essence of a country inn!"

Whitney Brook B&B

2423 Twenty Mile Stream Rd
Proctorsville, VT 05153-9703
(802)226-7460

Circa 1870. Stone walls encompass the 10 acres that surround this historic farmhouse. The grounds include streams, meadows and woods. The guest rooms are decorated in country style. For example, the Newport room includes two poster beds topped with white and blue comforters. The walls are decorated with blue and white wallpaper and blue trim. The innkeepers keep books and games on hand, as well as information about local activities. The Vermont Country Store is a nearby attraction.

Innkeeper(s): Jim & Ellen Parrish. $55-95. MC, VISA, AX, DS, PC, TC. 4 rooms, 2 with PB. Breakfast included in rates. Type of meal: Full bkfst. Beds: QDT. Ceiling fan in room. VCR on premises. Antiquing, fishing, golf, live theater, shopping, downhill skiing, cross-country skiing and water sports nearby.

Putney K4

Hickory Ridge House

53 Hickory Ridge Rd S
Putney, VT 05346-9326
(802)387-5709 (800)380-9218 Fax:(802)387-4328
E-mail: mail@hickoryridgehouse.com
Web: www.hickoryridgehouse.com

Circa 1808. This brick Federal house originally was built as an elegant farmhouse on a 500-acre Merino sheep farm. Palladian windows, and six Rumford fireplaces are original features.

Rooms are painted in bright Federal colors, such as rose, salmon, blue and yellow. Hickory Ridge House is listed in the National Register of Historic Places.

Innkeeper(s): Linda & Jack Bisbee. $95-145. MC, VISA, AX, PC, TC. 6 rooms with PB, 5 with FP and 2 cottages. Breakfast included in rates. Type of meal: Full bkfst. Beds: KQ. TV and VCR in room. Air conditioning. Handicap access. Weddings hosted. Antiquing, canoeing/kayaking, crafts, live theater, shopping and cross-country skiing nearby.

"We love your serene and peaceful house and we thank you for your hospitality and warmth, good food and good company."

Quechee   H5

Parker House Inn

1792 Quechee Main St
Quechee, VT 05059
(802)295-6077

Circa 1857. State Sen. Joseph C. Parker built this riverside manor in 1857, and three of the guest rooms are named in honor of his family. Mornings at the inn begin with a delicious country breakfast served in the Parker House Restaurant's cozy  dining rooms. The chefs are justifiably proud of their "comfort food" cuisine. Guests can stroll next door to watch the art of glass blowing, or take a walk along the Ottauquechee River. The surroundings of this historic town provide hours of activity for nature-lovers and shutterbugs. Fall foliage, of course, is an autumnal delight.

Historic Interest: Calvin Coolidge's birthplace, the American Precision Museum and Dartmouth College are among the nearby historic attractions.

Innkeeper(s): Barbara & Walt Forrester. $100-135. MC, VISA, AX, PC, TC. 7 rooms with PB. Breakfast included in rates. MAP. Type of meal: Full gourmet bkfst. Gourmet dinner and banquet service available. Restaurant on premises. Beds: KQ. Ceiling fan in room. Air conditioning. VCR, fax and bicycles on premises. Weddings, small meetings, family reunions and seminars hosted. Antiquing, fishing, golf, live theater, downhill skiing, cross-country skiing and water sports nearby.

"The inn is lovely, the innkeepers are the greatest, excellent food and heavenly bed!"

Richmond   D3

The Richmond Victorian Inn

191 East Main St, Rt #2
Richmond, VT 05477-0652
(802)434-4410 (888)242-3362 Fax:(802)434-4411
E-mail: gailclar@together.net
Web: www.together.net/~gailclar/

Circa 1881. This Queen Anne Victorian, with a three-story tower, is accented with green shutters, a sunburst design, fish scale shingles and a gingerbread front porch. The Tower Room is filled with white wicker, delicate flowered wallpaper and an antique bed. The Rose Room offers two beds and white ruffled curtains, while the Pansy Room features an antique bed, white

walls and a stenciled pansy border. There are hardwood floors and leaded-glass windows throughout. From the tree-shaded porch, enjoy the inn's lawns and flower gardens after a full breakfast.

Innkeeper(s): Gail M. Clark. $70-110. MC, VISA, AX, PC, TC. 6 rooms with PB. Breakfast included in rates. Types of meals: Full bkfst and early coffee/tea. Beds: QD. VCR on premises. Small meetings, family reunions and seminars hosted. Some German spoken. Antiquing, fishing, golf, parks, shopping, downhill skiing, cross-country skiing, sporting events and water sports nearby.

"Thank you for being such a fabulous host. We loved your Victorian home & enjoyed your warm hospitality. We will definitely spread the word for you in Canada."

Ripton   F2

Chipman Inn

Rt 125
Ripton, VT 05766
(802)388-2390 (800)890-2390

Circa 1828. This was the home of Daniel Chipman, a prominent legislator and founder of Middlebury College. Chipman also managed the "Center Turnpike" (now Route 125) through the Green Mountains. A replica of the tariff board stands near the inn. The inn's lounge/bar is in the original kitchen, with its old fireplace and bread oven.

Historic Interest: Shelburne Museum (50 minutes), Fort Ticonderoga (1 hour).

Innkeeper(s): Joyce Henderson & Bill Pierce. $85-125. MC, VISA, AX, DS, TC. 8 rooms with PB. Breakfast included in rates. Type of meal: Full bkfst. Dinner available. Beds: QDT. Small meetings and family reunions hosted. Antiquing, fishing, parks, shopping, downhill skiing, cross-country skiing and water sports nearby.

Publicity: *Gourmet, Food & Wine, New York Times, Addison County Independent.*

"Cozy, warm and friendly."

Roxbury   E4

Johnnycake Flats

Carrie Howe Rd
Roxbury, VT 05669
(802)485-8961

Circa 1806. Johnnycake Flats is an unpretentious and delightfully small bed and breakfast that offers guests a quiet escape from the hectic pace of metropolitan life. The guest rooms in this registered historical site include family antiques, Shaker baskets and handmade quilts. The innkeepers can help you identify local wildflowers and birds. In winter, enjoy cross-country skiing or snowshoeing and come home to sip hot cider beside the fire.

Innkeeper(s): Debra & Jim Rogler. $65-85. DS, PC, TC. 4 rooms, 1 with PB. Breakfast and afternoon tea included in rates. Types of meals: Cont plus, cont and early coffee/tea. Beds: DT. Bicycles, library and snowshoes on premises. Small meetings and family reunions hosted. Antiquing, bicycling, fishing, snowshoeing, live theater, parks, shopping, downhill skiing, cross-country skiing, sporting events and water sports nearby.

"You've nurtured a bit of paradise here, thanks for the lovely stay."

Royalton
G4

Fox Stand Inn & Restaurant

Rt 14
Royalton, VT 05068
(802)763-8437

Circa 1818. This three-story brick tavern was built by Jacob Fox on the stage route between Boston and Montreal. The dining rooms are lit by oil lamps and there are fireplaces to complement the inn's cuisine. The innkeepers have hung paintings by local artists. Guest rooms on the second floor are simply furnished but comfortable. In the midst of Vermont Horse Country, shows and training events are frequent and the area offers abundant auctions, studios and antique shops.

Innkeeper(s): Jean & Gary Curley. $50-80. MC, VISA, PC, TC. 5 rooms. Breakfast included in rates. Type of meal: Full bkfst. Gourmet dinner available. Restaurant on premises. Beds: DT. Weddings, small meetings, family reunions and seminars hosted. Antiquing, fishing, golf, live theater, parks, shopping, downhill skiing, cross-country skiing, sporting events and water sports nearby.

Rutland
H3

The Inn at Rutland

70 N Main St
Rutland, VT 05701-3249
(802)773-0575 (800)808-0575

Circa 1890. This distinctive Victorian mansion is filled with many period details, from high, plaster-worked ceilings to leather wainscotting in the dining room. Leaded windows and interesting woodwork are found throughout. Guest rooms have been decorated to maintain Victorian charm without a loss of modern comforts. A wicker-filled porch and common rooms are available to guests. Located in central Vermont, The Inn at Rutland is only 15 minutes from the Killington and Pico ski areas.

Historic Interest: Wilson Castle (10 minutes), Coolidge birthplace (30 minutes), Hildene (30 minutes), Norman Rockwell Museum (5 minutes).

Innkeeper(s): Bob & Tanya Liberman. $59-209. MC, VISA, AX, DC, CB, DS, TC. 12 rooms with PB, 1 suite and 2 conference rooms. Breakfast included in rates. Type of meal: Full bkfst. Beds: KQD. Phone and clocks in room. Air conditioning. VCR, fax, copier and bicycles on premises. Weddings, small meetings and family reunions hosted. Antiquing, fishing, museum (Norman Rockwell), live theater, parks, shopping, downhill skiing, cross-country skiing, sporting events and water sports nearby.

"A lovely page in the 'memory album' of our minds."

Shelburne
D2

Elliot House B&B

5779 Dorset St
Shelburne, VT 05482-7307
(802)985-5497

Circa 1865. Panoramic views of the Green Mountains and Adirordaic Mountains surround this stately Greek Revival farmhouse nestled amidst perennial gardens, meadows and a pond. The Carriage House and the Milk House contain guest rooms, with maple beds and casual furnishings reminiscent of

Adirondack lodge-style pieces. Shelburne Farms and Museum are five minutes away. Other activities include picking blueberries, antiquing, and water sports on Lake Champlain. There are five ski areas within an hour. Families are welcome.

Innkeeper(s): Susan & Nicholas Gulrajani. $85-120. PC. 3 rooms with PB, 1 suite and 1 cottage. Breakfast included in rates. Type of meal: Full gourmet bkfst. Beds: QT. Books in room. Swimming on premises. Weddings, small meetings and family reunions hosted. Antiquing, fishing, golf, live theater, parks, downhill skiing, sporting events, tennis and water sports nearby.

"Two nights is not enough to enjoy everything you have to offer here."

Shrewsbury
H3

Crisanver House

1434 Crown Point Road
Shrewsbury, VT 05738
(802)492-3589 (800)492-8089 Fax:(802)402-3480

Circa 1850. Listed in the state historic register, this completely renovated inn offers an ideal location, boasting views of mountains and sunsets and surrounded by 117 acres. The guest rooms, decorated in an elegant country style, feature original artwork, down comforters and carefully chosen antiques. Breakfasts are healthy and scrumptious, often featuring low-fat and low-cholesterol fare. Homemade muffins, scones, entrees made from farm-fresh eggs, seasonal fruits and pancakes topped with Vermont maple syrup might appear on the breakfast table, set with English china, silver, crystal and fresh flowers from the inn's gardens.

Innkeeper(s): Carol & Michael Calotta. $90-140. PC, TC. 8 rooms, 6 with PB and 1 conference room. Breakfast, afternoon tea and snacks/refreshments included in rates. Types of meals: Full gourmet bkfst and early coffee/tea. Picnic lunch and banquet service available. Beds: QT. Robes in room. VCR, fax, copier, swimming, bicycles, tennis, library, lawn games, grand piano, player piano, ping pong and flower gardens on premises. Weddings, small meetings, family reunions and seminars hosted. Italian spoken. Antiquing, bicycling, fishing, golf, hiking, horseback riding, live theater, parks, shopping, downhill skiing, cross-country skiing, tennis and water sports nearby.

Pets allowed: Boarded at nearby kennel.

"Our expectation was great, but I must tell you the reality exceeded the expectation. I really cannot believe all the nice things you have done, big and small to make Crisanver House a comfortable, charming and elegant place to spend some quality time."

South Londonderry
J3

Londonderry Inn

PO Box 301-931, Rt 100
South Londonderry, VT 05155
(802)824-5226 Fax:(802)824-3146
E-mail: londinn@sover.net
Web: www.londonderryinn.com

Circa 1826. For almost 100 years, the Melendy Homestead, overlooking the West River and the village, was a dairy farm. In 1940, it became an inn. A tourist brochure promoting the area in 1881 said, "Are you overworked in the office, counting room or workshop and need invigorating influences? Come ramble over these hills and mountains and try

the revivifying effects of Green Mountain oxygen." Dinner is available weekends and holiday periods, in season.

Historic Interest: Home of Robert Todd Lincoln (20 minutes), Bennington Battle Monument (45 minutes), Bennington Museum with Grandma Moses exhibit (45 minutes).

Innkeeper(s): Jim & Jean Cavanagh. $41-116. 25 rooms, 20 with PB and 1 conference room. Breakfast included in rates. EP. Dinner available. Restaurant on premises. Beds: KQDT. VCR, fax and copier on premises. Weddings, small meetings, family reunions and seminars hosted. Antiquing, fishing, live theater, shopping, downhill skiing, cross-country skiing, sporting events and water sports nearby.

Publicity: *New England Monthly, Ski, McCall's.*

"A weekend in a good country inn, such as the Londonderry, is on a par with a weekend on the ocean in Southern Maine, which is to say that it's as good as a full week nearly anyplace else — The Hornet."

South Newfane   K4

The Inn at South Newfane

369 Dover Rd
South Newfane, VT 05351
(802)348-7191
E-mail: cullinn@sover.net
Web: www.innatsouthnewfane.com

Purchased by a wealthy Philadelphian in 1868 to use as a summer home, this charming turn-of-the-century manor house was converted to an inn in 1984. The inn is decorated in a comfortable style, with Oriental

rugs and traditional furnishings. The entry is painted an inviting shade of yellow and offers an assortment of chairs to relax on. The living room, with fireplace, invites reading, games and conversation. Guest rooms are cozy and distinctively decorated with floral wallcoverings and beds topped with quilts. Breakfasts are served in the morning room, which has a fireplace. The inn also has a restaurant, featuring a variety of gourmet fare. Guests might start off with a spinach and feta cheese tart or perhaps lobster bisque, then enjoy one of the evening's entrees. From there, desserts such as warm apple crisp with French vanilla ice cream, finish off the evening meal. Lunch is served summer through foliage. MAP rates are available.

Innkeeper(s): Neville & Dawn Cullen. $80-130. MC, VISA, AX, DS, TC. TAC10. 6 rooms with PB. Breakfast included in rates. Types of meals: Full bkfst and cont plus. Gourmet dinner, lunch, banquet service and catering service available. Restaurant on premises. Beds: KQT. Turndown service, ceiling fan, night stands and bureaus in room. Swimming, bocce, croquet, badminton, volleyball and horse shoes on premises. Weddings, small meetings, family reunions and seminars hosted. Antiquing, fishing, golf, music festival, Newfone Flea Market, horseback riding, live theater, parks, shopping, downhill skiing, cross-country skiing, tennis and water sports nearby.

"Wonderfully calm and peaceful. Loved every minute."

Springfield   I4

Hartness House Inn

30 Orchard St
Springfield, VT 05156-2612
(802)885-2115 (800)732-4789 Fax:(802)885-2207

Circa 1903. There are many inns where star-gazing is a popular nighttime activity. At Hartness House, it is taken to a whole new level. The original owner not only served as the state's governor, but inventor/astronomer James Hartness also created the historic observatory that remains at the home today. Aside from this uncommon amenity, the house itself is impressive. Guests who stay in the home's original portion reach their well-appointed rooms via a three-story staircase. Two newer wings also offer elegant accommodations. There is a Victorian-styled dining room on the premises as well, offering dinners by candlelight. The home is often the site of weddings, receptions and parties. Country Inns magazine chose Hartness House as one of its top inns, and in another article made note of the inn's wonderful holiday decorations and festivities.

Innkeeper(s): Brian Blair & Carolyn Blair Hofford. $89-150. MC, VISA, AX, PC, TC. TAC10. 40 rooms with PB, 1 suite and 3 conference rooms. Breakfast included in rates. Type of meal: Full bkfst. Gourmet dinner and banquet service available. Restaurant on premises. Beds: QDT. Cable TV and phone in room. Air conditioning. Fax, copier, swimming and library on premises. Weddings, small meetings, family reunions and seminars hosted. Antiquing, fishing, live theater, parks, shopping, downhill skiing, cross-country skiing and water sports nearby.

"A wonderful place to stop and remember simple elegance and all that is important."

Stowe   D4

Brass Lantern Inn

717 Maple St
Stowe, VT 05672-4250
(802)253-2229 (800)729-2980 Fax:(802)253-7425
E-mail: brasslntrn@aol.com
Web: www.brasslanterninn.com

Circa 1810. This rambling farmhouse and carriage barn rests at the foot of Mt. Mansfield. A recent award-winning renovation has brought a new shine to the inn, from the gleaming plank floors to the polished woodwork and crackling fireplaces and soothing whirlpool tubs. Quilts and antiques fill the guest rooms, and some, like the Honeymoon Room, have their own fireplace, whirlpool tub and mountain view. A complimentary afternoon and evening tea is provided along with a full Vermont-style breakfast. The inn is a multi-time winner of the Golden Fork Award from the Gourmet Dinners Society of North America.

Innkeeper(s): Andy Aldrich. $80-225. MC, VISA, AX. TAC10. 9 rooms with PB, 3 with FP. Breakfast and afternoon tea included in rates. Types of meals: Full bkfst and early coffee/tea. Beds: QDT. TV and whirlpool tubs in 6 rooms in room. Air conditioning. VCR, fax, copier, library, gardens and patio on premises. Weddings and small meetings hosted. Antiquing, fishing, tours, live theater, parks, shopping, downhill skiing, cross-country skiing, sporting events and water sports nearby.

Publicity: *Vermont, Vermont Life, Innsider, Discerning Traveler, Ski.*

"The little things made us glad we stopped."

Green Mountain Inn

PO Box 60, 1 Main St
Stowe, VT 05672-0060
(802)253-7301 (800)253-7302 Fax:(802)253-5096
E-mail: info@gminn.com
Web: www.greenmountaininn.com

Circa 1833. This early 19th-century inn is a member of the Historic Hotels of America. The inn has been restored completely and is decorated in early American style with antiques and reproductions. Original Walton Blodgett paintings also grace the interior. Guest rooms include amenities such as canopy beds, Jacuzzi and fireplaces. The main inn and the adjacent Depot Building are numbers 13 and 14 in the National Register of Historic Places. The Depot was constructed to house the Mount Mansfield Electric Railroad. Guests can uses the health club, which includes a sauna, steam room and Jacuzzi. There is also an outdoor pool and game room.

Historic Interest: The State House, Vermont's 114 covered bridges, Hubbardton Battlefield.

Innkeeper(s): Patricia Clark. $89-479. MC, VISA, AX, DS. 78 rooms with PB, 23 with FP and 1 conference room. AP, EP. Types of meals: Full gourmet bkfst, cont plus, cont and early coffee/tea. Afternoon tea, dinner, snacks/refreshments, picnic lunch, gourmet lunch, banquet service and catering service available. Restaurant on premises. Beds: KQDT. Cable TV and phone in room. Air conditioning. VCR, fax, copier, swimming, sauna, game room, health club and Jacuzzi on premises. Handicap access. Weddings, small meetings, family reunions and seminars hosted. Antiquing, bicycling, fishing, hiking, live theater, shopping, downhill skiing, cross-country skiing and water sports nearby.

Pets allowed: In annex rooms only.

Three Bears at The Fountain

1049 Pucker St Rt 100
Stowe, VT 05672-9802
(802)253-7671 (800)898-9634 Fax:(802)253-8804
E-mail: threebears@stowevt.net
Web: www.threebearsbandb.com

Circa 1820. A spring-fed fountain on the grounds and the innkeepers' Three Bears Restaurant inspired the name for this Vermont country inn. The historic home was built by the first couple married in the village of Stowe, and it is the oldest guest house in town, opening its doors for travelers in the 1920s. The main house dates to the 1820s, but an adjacent carriage house was built in 1796. Original fireplaces, restored wood floors and exposed beams add a historic ambiance. Guest rooms are decorated in country style with quilts and antiques. Vermont's highest peak, Mount Mansfield, is just six miles away and guests are afforded the wonderful views from the wraparound porch or while relaxing in the hot tub. The King Room includes a gas fireplace, cathedral ceilings and mountain views. The breakfast room is warmed by a fireplace; and the morning meal is served on country oak tables set with linen and fine china.

Innkeeper(s): Suzanne & Stephen Vazzano. $75-250. MC, VISA, AX, TC. TAC10. 4 rooms with PB, 2 with FP. Breakfast included in rates. Type of meal: Full bkfst. Beds: KQ. VCR, fax, copier, suite and two-bedroom apartment on premises. Small meetings and family reunions hosted. Antiquing, fishing, golf, live theater, shopping, downhill skiing, cross-country skiing and tennis nearby.

Winding Brook...
A Classic Mountain Lodge

199 Edson Hill Rd
Stowe, VT 05672
(802)253-7354 (800)426-6697 Fax:(802)253-8429

Circa 1939. Set beside a mountain stream on five wooded acres, Winding Brook is Stowe's oldest existing ski lodge. After skiing, relax in the living room with its inviting fieldstone fireplace or enjoy a long soak in the outdoor hot tub. During warmer months, guests can enjoy a swim in the pool. Stowe is famous for its skiing and Mount Mansfield, Vermont's highest mountain. The resort village also offers many shops, galleries and restaurants.

Innkeeper(s): Patrick J DiDomenico. $65-135. MC, VISA, AX, PC, TC. TAC10. 15 rooms with PB. Breakfast included in rates. Type of meal: Full bkfst. Beds: KQT. Air conditioning. VCR, copier, swimming, library, game room and pool table on premises. Weddings, small meetings, family reunions and seminars hosted. Antiquing, fishing, golf, parks, shopping, downhill skiing, cross-country skiing, tennis and water sports nearby.

Publicity: *Stowe Reporter.*

Ye Olde England Inne

433 Mountain Rd
Stowe, VT 05672-4628
(802)253-7558 (800)477-3771 Fax:(802)253-8944
E-mail: englandinn@aol.com
Web: www.oldeenglandinne.com

Circa 1890. Originally a farmhouse, Ye Olde England Inne has acquired a Tudor facade, interior beams and stone work. Each guest room is different. One cozy room includes hunter green carpeting and cheerful wallcoverings with red flowers. A matching comforter tops the lace canopy bed and a massive wardrobe further decorates the room. Other rooms are more traditional style. The

suites and cottages include a whirlpool tub, and many offer a mountain view and a private porch from which to enjoy it. The inn has a variety of getaway packages. A popular honeymoon package includes French champagne, a complete spa treatment and in winter, a sleigh ride. Mr. Pickwick's, which resembles an English pub, is an ideal spot to relax and enjoy ale or a glass or wine. The inn also offers Copperfields, where guests can enjoy a romantic dinner. Guests can spend their days hiking, skiing, relaxing by the inn's pool or exploring Stowe.

Innkeeper(s): Christopher Francis. $98-375. MC, VISA, AX. 30 rooms, 20 with PB, 4 with FP, 12 suites and 1 conference room. Breakfast included in rates. MAP. Type of meal: Full gourmet bkfst. Afternoon tea and gourmet lunch available. Restaurant on premises. Beds: QDT. Cable TV, phone and ceiling fan in room. Air conditioning. Fax, copier and spa on premises. Weddings, small meetings, family reunions and seminars hosted. Antiquing, live theater, parks, shopping, downhill skiing, cross-country skiing and sporting events nearby.

Townshend K4

Boardman House

PO Box 112
Townshend, VT 05353-0112
(802)365-4086

Circa 1840. This stately Greek Revival is located on the village green of Townshend in Southeast Vermont. Guests enjoy a full breakfast before beginning their day, which could include antiquing, canoeing or kayaking in the West River or skiing at Bromley, or Stratton ski areas, all within easy driving distance. The inn boasts a large, lush lawn and gar-

dens, a parlor with a library and a refreshing sauna. Early coffee or tea is served and picnic lunches are available.

Innkeeper(s): Paul Weber & Sarah Messenger. $70-80. PC, TC. 6 rooms, 5 with PB and 1 suite. Breakfast included in rates. Type of meal: Full gourmet bkfst. Beds: QT. Air conditioning. VCR, sauna and library on premises. Small meetings and family reunions hosted. Antiquing, fishing, golf, parks, shopping, downhill skiing, cross-country skiing, tennis and water sports nearby.

Pets allowed: Dogs only; by prior arrangement.

Redwing Farm B&B

157 Redwing Rd
Townshend, VT 05353
(802)365-4656 Fax:(802)365-4656
E-mail: info@redwingfarm.com
Web: redwingfarm.com

Circa 1780. Not only will guests learn all about organic farming when staying at this certified organic farm, but also if they arrive in the right season, they can watch draft horses helping to plow the land. The old farmhouse is set in a valley on the

West River, so guests can go tubing in the summer. (The hosts have tubes to lend.) Children might ask

to help pick the cantaloupe for breakfast, pull up carrots or select tomatoes, depending on the season. Breakfasts feature whole grain home-baked goods with farm-grown vegetables and fruits. The farmhouse features exposed hand-hewn beams and casual antiques. Townshend Dam Lake and Bald Mountain offer swimming and hiking opportunities.

Historic Interest: Hildene, Robert Todd Lincoln home (20 miles).

Innkeeper(s): Carol Rees & Joe Scanlon. $60. PC, TC. 3 rooms. Breakfast included in rates. Types of meals: Cont plus, veg bkfst and early coffee/tea. Beds: D. Fax and tubes for river tubing on premises. Family reunions hosted. Beaches, bicycling, canoeing/kayaking, fishing, golf, hiking, horseback riding, flea market, live theater, museums, parks, shopping, cross-country skiing and tennis nearby.

Pets allowed: With own dog-bed and leash.

Vergennes E2

Strong House Inn

94 W Main St
Vergennes, VT 05491-9531
(802)877-3337
E-mail: innkeeper@stronghouseinn.com
Web: www.stronghouseinn.com

Circa 1834. This Federal-style home boasts views of the Green Mountains and the Adirondac range. Several rooms offer working fireplaces and all are richly appointed. Country breakfasts and afternoon refreshments are served, and on selected Sundays don't miss the expansive afternoon tea, complete with pastries, tea sandwiches, and of

course, a wide selection of teas. Nearby Lake Champlain offers boating and fishing. Golf, hiking, skiing and some of the finest cycling in Vermont are all part of the area's myriad of outdoor activities. Innkeeper Mary Bargiel is an avid gardener and decorates the grounds with flowers and herb gardens. The innkeepers offer a selection of special weekends from a Valentine's Day to a quilter's weekend.

Historic Interest: The area has no shortage of antique shopping, and the inn itself is listed in the National Register of Historic Places.

Innkeeper(s): Mary Bargiel. $75-250. MC, VISA, AX. 14 rooms with PB, 6 with FP and 2 suites. Breakfast included in rates. Types of meals: Full gourmet bkfst and early coffee/tea. Afternoon tea available. Beds: KQT. Cable TV, phone, turndown service and VCR in room. Air conditioning. Weddings, small meetings, family reunions and seminars hosted. Antiquing, fishing, live theater, shopping, downhill skiing, cross-country skiing, sporting events and water sports nearby.

"Blissful stay...Glorious breakfast!"

Waitsfield E3

Lareau Farm Country Inn

PO Box 563, RT 100
Waitsfield, VT 05673-0563
(802)496-4949 (800)833-0766
E-mail: lareau@lareaufarminn.com
Web: www.lareaufarminn.com

Circa 1794. This Greek Revival house was built by Simeon Stoddard, the town's first physician. Old-fashioned roses, lilacs, delphiniums, iris and peonies fill the gardens. The inn sits in a wide meadow next to the crystal-clear Mad River. A canoe trip or a refreshing swim are possibilities here.

Innkeeper(s): Susan Easley.
$60-125. MC, VISA, PC, TC. 13 rooms, 11 with PB, 1 suite and 1 conference room. Breakfast included in rates. Types of meals: Full gourmet bkfst and early coffee/tea. Beds: QD. TV in room. Swimming and library on premises. Weddings, small meetings, family reunions and seminars hosted. Antiquing, fishing, live theater, shopping, downhill skiing and cross-country skiing nearby.

"Hospitality is a gift. Thank you for sharing your gift so freely with us."

Mad River Inn

Tremblay Rd, PO Box 75
Waitsfield, VT 05673
(802)496-7900 (800)832-8278 Fax:(802)496-5390

Circa 1860. Surrounded by the Green Mountains, this Queen Anne Victorian sits on seven scenic acres along the Mad River. The charming inn boasts attractive woodwork throughout, highlighted by ash, bird's-eye maple and cherry. Guest rooms feature European featherbeds and

include the Hayden Breeze Room, with a king brass bed, large windows and sea relics, and the Abner Doubleday Room, with a queen ash bed and mementos of baseball's glory days. The inn sports a billiard table, gazebo, organic gardens and a Jacuzzi overlooking the mountains. Guests can walk to a recreation path along the river.

Historic Interest: The Historic Round Barn and Shelbourne Farm & Museum are a short distance.

Innkeeper(s): Rita & Luc Maranda. $69-125. MC, VISA, AX. TAC10. 10 rooms with PB. Breakfast and afternoon tea included in rates. Type of meal: Full gourmet bkfst. Gourmet dinner available. Beds: KQ. Turndown service and ceiling fan in room. VCR, fax, spa, stables and child care on premises. Weddings, small meetings and family reunions hosted. French spoken. Antiquing, fishing, live theater, shopping, downhill skiing, cross-country skiing, sporting events and water sports nearby.

"Your hospitality was appreciated, beautiful house and accommodations, great food & friendly people, just to name a few things. We plan to return and we recommend the Mad River Inn to friends & family."

Waitsfield Inn

Rt 100, PO Box 969
Waitsfield, VT 05673-0969
(802)496-3979 (800)758-3801 Fax:(802)496-3970
E-mail: waitsfieldinn@madriver.com
Web: www.waitsfieldinn.com

Circa 1825. This Federal-style inn once served as a parsonage and was home to several state senators of the Richardson family. Pink and yellow flower beds frame the rambling inn. The 1839 barn offers a Great Room with fireplace and wood-plank floors, or in winter you may enjoy sipping spiced Vermont apple cider and munching on fresh cookies in the sitting room. Guest quarters are furnished with period antiques, quilts or comforters and some rooms have exposed beams or hand stenciling. A full breakfast is served in the dining room, with fresh-baked breads, fruit, muffins and a main dish. As the inn is in the village of Waitsfield, the entire town's sites are nearby including a beautiful covered bridge. Visit Glen Moss Waterfall, fly fish, canoe, try a glider, golf or watch a polo match. Snowshoeing, skiing and visits to the New England Culinary Institute and Ben & Jerry's Ice Cream Factory are popular activities.

Historic Interest: Ethan Allen's estate is 35 miles from the inn and Montpelier is 20 miles away.

Innkeeper(s): Jim & Pat Masson. $79-135. MC, VISA, AX, DS, PC, TC. 14 rooms with PB. Breakfast included in rates. Type of meal: Full bkfst. Beds: QDT. Small meetings, family reunions and seminars hosted. Antiquing, fishing, golf, canoeing, live theater, shopping, downhill skiing and cross-country skiing nearby.

Wallingford H3

I. B. Munson House

37 S Main St, PO Box 427
Wallingford, VT 05773-0427
(802)446-2860 (888)519-3771 Fax:(802)446-3336

Circa 1856. An Italianate Victorian bed & breakfast, the inn was meticulously restored as the innkeepers preserved many original elements, such as the wood floors, ornately carved mantels and woodwork. Period antiques and Waverly wallcoverings are featured in the guest rooms, two of which include a fireplace. All

seven guest rooms have private baths. Wallingford is a designated historic village, so there are many interesting old homes and buildings to see. Ski areas, shops and restaurants are within a couple of blocks.

Innkeeper(s): Tom & JoAnn Brem. $60-160. MC, VISA, AX, PC, TC. TAC15. 7 rooms with PB, 2 with FP and 2 suites. Breakfast included in rates. Types of meals: Full bkfst and early coffee/tea. Afternoon tea available. Beds: QDT. Turndown service and ceiling fan in room. VCR and fax on premises. Weddings, small meetings, family reunions and seminars hosted. Antiquing, fishing, parks, shopping, downhill skiing, cross-country skiing and water sports nearby.

"It was a pleasure to stay at your beautiful historic Bed and Breakfast. Wonderful hospitality! Delicious breakfast - a very special treat!! We will be back."

Waterbury D3

The Inn at Blush Hill

Blush Hill Rd, Box 1266
Waterbury, VT 05676
(802)244-7529 (800)736-7522 Fax:(802)244-7314
E-mail: innatbh@aol.com
Web: www.blushhill.com

Circa 1790. This shingled Cape-style house was once a stagecoach stop en route to Stowe and is the oldest inn in Waterbury. A 12-foot-long pine farmhand's table is set near the double fireplace and the kitchen bay window, revealing views of the Worcester Mountains. A

favorite summertime breakfast, served gardenside, is pancakes with fresh blueberries, topped with ice cream and maple syrup.

Historic Interest: The inn has a 1760 fireplace with adjacent brick oven.

Innkeeper(s): Pam Gosselin. $69-130. MC, VISA, AX, DS, PC, TC. TAC10. 5 rooms with PB, 1 with FP. Breakfast, afternoon tea and snacks/refreshments included in rates. Types of meals: Full gourmet bkfst and early coffee/tea. Beds: QDT. TV, turndown service and ceiling fan in room. Air conditioning. Fax and library on premises. Antiquing, fishing, golf, Ben & Jerry's ice cream factory, live theater, parks, shopping, downhill skiing, cross-country skiing and water sports nearby.

"Our room was wonderful — especially the fireplace. Everything was so cozy and warm."

Old Stagecoach Inn

18 N Main St
Waterbury, VT 05676-1810
(802)244-5056 (800)262-2206 Fax:(802)244-6956

Circa 1826. For many years, this inn served as both a stage-coach stop and meeting house. In the 1880s, an Ohio million-aire used the home as his summer retreat. He added the Victorian touches that are still present, including the polished woodwork, stained glass and elegant fireplaces. Today, guests stay in restored rooms decorated in Victorian style. Stowe, Sugarbush and Bolton Valley ski areas are nearby, and guests can also partake in fishing, swimming and water sports at Winooski River, Waterbury Reservoir or Lake Champlain.

Innkeeper(s): John & Jack Barwick. $45-150. MC, VISA, AX, DS, PC, TC. TAC10. 13 rooms, 10 with PB, 1 with FP and 3 suites. Breakfast and after-noon tea included in rates. Type of meal: Full bkfst. Dinner available. Beds: KQDT. Cable TV and ceiling fan in room. Air conditioning. Copier on premis-es. Weddings, small meetings and family reunions hosted. German and French spoken. Antiquing, fishing, Ben & Jerry's ice cream plant tours, live theater, parks, shopping, downhill skiing, cross-country skiing and water sports nearby.

Pets Allowed.

"This place was first class all the way."

Thatcher Brook Inn

PO Box 490, Rt 100 N
Waterbury, VT 05676-0490
(802)244-5911 (800)292-5911 Fax:(802)244-1294
E-mail: info@thatcherbrook.com
Web: www.thatcherbrook.com

Circa 1899. Listed in the Vermont Register of Historic Buildings, this restored Victorian mansion features a rambling porch with twin gazebos. A covered walkway leads to the his-toric Wheeler House. Guest rooms are decorated in clas-sic country style. Four rooms have fireplaces, and six have whirlpool tubs. The inn's restaurant and tavern are located in the main inn. Guests can dine fireside or by candlelight.

Historic Interest: The inn is listed in the National Register.

Innkeeper(s): Lisa & John Fischer. $80-185. MC, VISA, AX, DC, DS, PC, TC. TAC10. 22 rooms with PB, 4 with FP, 1 suite and 1 conference room. Breakfast included in rates. Type of meal: Full bkfst. Gourmet dinner and banquet service available. Restaurant on premises. Beds: KQDT. Phone, ceil-ing fan and 6 rooms have whirlpools in room. Air conditioning. Fax and copi-er on premises. Handicap access. Weddings, small meetings, family reunions and seminars hosted. Antiquing, bicycling, fishing, hiking, live theater, parks, shopping, downhill skiing, cross-country skiing and water sports nearby.

"I'd have to put on a black tie in Long Island to find food as good as this and best of all it's in a relaxed country atmosphere. Meals are underpriced."

Waterbury Center — D4

The Black Locust Inn

Rt 100
Waterbury Center, VT 05677
(802)244-7490 (800)366-5592 Fax:(802)244-8473
E-mail: info@blacklocustinn.com
Web: www.blacklocustinn.com

Circa 1832. Set on a hill graced with tall black locust trees is this recently restored three-gabled farmhouse. The home once presided over a 90-acre dairy farm and looks out to the Green Mountain range and Camel's Hump. Guest rooms offer inviting beds with duvets, down comforters, and piles of pillows. Bathrobes, thick towels and hand-made soaps are among the amenities. Wooden rocking chairs line the porch and situated in scenic spots are gatherings of Vermont-made country furni-ture. A hammock swings between two locust trees. Afternoon appetizers and drinks are served, and in the morning a three-course candlelight breakfast might offer items such as freshly baked oat honey bread, poached pear served with Ben & Jerry's sorbet and Vermont summer vegetable quiche with maple-cured sausage.

Innkeeper(s): Len, Nancy & Valerie Vignola. $100-150. MC, VISA, AX, DS, PC, TC. 6 rooms with PB. Breakfast and snacks/refreshments included in rates. Beds: Q.

"This is definitely the most welcoming and comfortable place we have ever stayed in. The breakfasts have been superb and your concern for our needs has been appreciated."

Weathersfield — I4

The Inn at Weathersfield

Rt 106 Box 165
Weathersfield, VT 05151-0165
(802)263-9217 (800)477-4828 Fax:(802)263-9219

Circa 1795. Built by Thomas Prentis, a Revolutionary War vet-eran, this was originally a four-room farmhouse set on 237 acres of wilderness. Two rooms were added in 1796 and a car-riage house in 1830. During the Civil War, the inn served as a station on the Underground Railroad. Six pillars give the inn a Southern Colonial look, and there are 12 fireplaces, a beehive oven, wide-plank floors and period antiques throughout.

Innkeeper(s): Mary & Terry Carter. $195-250. MC, VISA, AX, DS. 12 rooms with PB, 8 with FP, 3 suites and 1 conference room. MAP. Type of meal: Full bkfst. Afternoon tea and gourmet dinner available. Restaurant on premises. Beds: KQDT. VCR, fax, copier, sauna, sleigh and carriage rides and exercise equipment on premises. Handicap access. Weddings, small meetings, family reunions and seminars hosted. Antiquing, near Saint Gauden's Nat'l Historic Site & Calvin Coolidge Nat'l Historic Site, live theater, shopping, downhill ski-ing, cross-country skiing and sporting events nearby.

Publicity: *Boston Herald, Los Angeles Times, Country Inns, Colonial Homes, Better Homes & Gardens, National Geographic Traveler, Ladies Home Journal, Vermont Magazine, Westways Magazine.*

"There isn't one thing we didn't enjoy about our weekend with you and we are constantly reliving it with much happiness."

West Dover K3

Austin Hill Inn

Rt 100, Box 859
West Dover, VT 05356
(802)464-5281 (800)332-7352 Fax:(802)464-1229

Circa 1930. This family-owned and operated inn is situated between Mt. Snow and Haystack Mountains just outside the historic village of West Dover. Guest rooms feature country decor and furnishings.
Romantic amenities include in-room fireplaces and votive candles at turn-down. Guests are treated to a hearty New England breakfast, as well as after-noon wine and cheese or home-

baked treats. In cool weather, guests enjoy the warm glow of the inn's fireplaces in the common rooms. The Austin Hill Inn is notable for its attention to detail and superior hospitality.
Innkeeper(s): John & Deborah Bailey. $100-155. MC, VISA, DS, PC, TC. 12 rooms with PB and 1 conference room. Breakfast and afternoon tea included in rates. Type of meal: Full bkfst. Gourmet dinner, snacks/refreshments and catering service available. Beds: KQDT. Fax and copier on premises. Antiquing, bicycling, canoeing/kayaking, fishing, golf, hiking, chamber music, live theater, parks, downhill skiing and cross-country skiing nearby.

Deerhill Inn

Valley View Rd, PO Box 136
West Dover, VT 05356-0136
(802)464-3100 (800)993-3379 Fax:(802)464-5474

Circa 1954. Guests who wish to ski will be happy to note that Mt. Snow and Haystack ski areas are nearby, and all will delight in the inn's panoramic views of both places as well as other mountains. Rooms are inviting as this is a place for comfort and romance. Four rooms include a fireplace. Several rooms throughout the inn are decorated with hand-painted murals. Gourmet dinners are available, and guests can select the Modified American Plan, which will include both breakfast and dinner in the rates. For the dinners, guests might start off with Portabello mushrooms stuffed with crab and lobster. From there, veal medallions, grilled New York sirloin steak or perhaps a grilled stuffed chicken breast might suffice. At breakfast, items such as pancakes, French toast or omelets with sides of pota-toes, breads and bacon or sausage are served. The inn has been the site of weddings, and conference facilities are available.
Innkeeper(s): Michael & Linda Anelli. $86-220. MC, VISA, AX, PC, TC. 15 rooms with PB, 4 with FP and 2 suites. Breakfast included in rates. MAP. Type of meal: Full bkfst. Gourmet dinner available. Restaurant on premises. Beds: KQDT. Cable TV, turndown service and Jacuzzi (three rooms) in room. VCR, fax, copier, swimming and library on premises. Handicap access. Weddings, small meetings, family reunions and seminars hosted. Antiquing, fishing, music, live theater, parks, shopping, downhill skiing, cross-country skiing, sporting events and water sports nearby.

"A cozy fire, soft terry robes, warm flannel sheets, wonderful food and friendly innkeepers and staff - the perfect getaway place to be pampered."

Doveberry Inn

Rt 100 PO Box 1736
West Dover, VT 05356-7703
(802)464-5652 (800)722-3204 Fax:(802)464-6229
E-mail: duveberry@aol.com
Web: www.doveberryinn.com

Circa 1945. The Green Mountains and Vermont countryside provide the scenery at Doveberry Inn. The inn has been reno-vated and decorated in country style. One guest room includes a private sun deck.
Innkeepers Christine and Michael Fayette are both trained chefs and prepare the Northern Italian specialties at the inn's restaurant.
Michael creates starters

such as grilled shrimp with polenta or mixed vegetable risotto and entrees like tenderloin of beef on potato cakes with pancetta, tomatoes and herbs. Christine handles the rich, memorable desserts. The area boasts outstanding fall foliage, and the Mt. Snow Ski Area is less than two miles away.
Innkeeper(s): Christine & Michael Fayette. $75-150. MC, VISA, AX, PC. 8 rooms with PB. Breakfast and afternoon tea included in rates. Type of meal: Full bkfst. Dinner available. Restaurant on premises. Beds: KQDT. Cable TV, VCR and fans in room. Fax and library on premises. Weddings, small meet-ings and family reunions hosted. Antiquing, fishing, golf, live theater, shop-ping, downhill skiing, cross-country skiing and tennis nearby.

"Our room was spacious and pleasant. The food was unbelievable and the wine exquisite."

Snow Goose Inn

Rt 100, Box 366
West Dover, VT 05356
(802)464-3984 (888)604-7964 Fax:(802)464-5322

Circa 1959. Three acres of Vermont countryside create a secluded setting for the Snow Goose Inn. Renovations in 1998 include the addition of Southern pine floors and private decks.
Hand-hewn beams from an old country barn were fashioned into a new grand entry and a duplex honeymoon suite was created. (The

new suite offers two decks with mountain and valley views, a Jacuzzi tub, fireplace and sitting area.) Most of the other antique-filled rooms also include a fireplace, VCR, stereo and double Jacuzzi tub. Hypo-allergenic feather mattresses and comforters are additional features. Hearty breakfasts include cereals, fresh fruit, juices, breads and entrees such as wild mushrooms and herb scrambled eggs, French toast stuffed with bananas or fresh bagels imported from New York City. Evening wine and cheese is offered on one of the porches with views to the pond and flower gardens or by fireside in winter.
Innkeeper(s): Karen & Eric Falberg. $85-300. MC, VISA, AX, PC, TC. TAC10. 13 rooms with PB, 8 with FP. Breakfast included in rates. Type of meal: Full bkfst. Beds: KQDT. Cable TV, VCR, two-person Jacuzzis and fireplaces in room. Fax, copier and seven-foot Steinway Grand Piano on premises. Weddings, small meetings, family reunions and seminars hosted. Antiquing, fishing, hiking, live theater, parks, shopping, downhill skiing, cross-country skiing and water sports nearby.

West Dover Inn

Rt 100 Box 1208
West Dover, VT 05356
(802)464-5207 Fax:(802)464-2173

Circa 1846. This inn, which served originally as a stagecoach stop and tavern, has been hosting guests for more than 150 years. It features a Greek Revival facade with wide columns and porches. Located in the heart of the tiny village of West Dover, the inn offers a variety of amenities. Two guest rooms and each of the four suites include a fireplace. The suites also have whirlpool tubs. Handmade quilts and antiques add to the New England country appeal. During fall foliage season, guests can opt for breakfast-only rates or choose the Modified American Plan rates, which include breakfast and dinner. Dinner at the inn's restaurant, Gregory's, is a treat. The New American menu includes starters such as a Thai-barbecue shrimp or perhaps pan-seared scallops and lobster cakes. These are followed by entree selections such as Black Angus sirloin with a Gorgonzola cream sauce, a grilled salmon filet or perhaps Caribbean-style pork.

Innkeeper(s): Greg Gramas & Monique Phelan. $100-200. MC, VISA, AX, DS, PC, TC. TAC10. 12 rooms with PB, 6 with FP, 4 suites and 1 conference room. Breakfast included in rates. Type of meal: Full bkfst. Gourmet dinner available. Restaurant on premises. Beds: QDT. Cable TV in room. VCR, fax and library on premises. Weddings, small meetings, family reunions and seminars hosted. Antiquing, fishing, golf, mountain biking, golfing, hiking, live theater, parks, shopping, downhill skiing, cross-country skiing, tennis and water sports nearby.

Westminster   J4

Blue Haven Christian B&B

6963 US Rt 5
Westminster, VT 05158
(802)463-9008 (800)228-9008 Fax:(802)463-0669
E-mail: bluhaven@sover.net
Web: virtualvermont.com/bandb/bluehaven

Circa 1830. This Folk Victorian inn served as a school for nearly a century, until 1929. Guests will find the wide oak flooring used in the school and a crude stone fireplace added by the next owner. The visitors of today relax on canopied beds under goose-down quilts in air-conditioned guest rooms. Bathrobes and turndown service also are offered. Tea and scones are popular afternoon snacks, and homemade granola and freshly baked shortbreads often are served at breakfast. The Connecticut River is nearby.

Innkeeper(s): Helene Champagne. Call for rates. Type of meal: Early coffee/tea. Turndown service in room. Air conditioning. VCR on premises. Weddings, small meetings, family reunions and seminars hosted. Antiquing, live theater, shopping, downhill skiing and cross-country skiing nearby.

Weston   J3

Darling Family Inn

815 Rt 100
Weston, VT 05161-5404
(802)824-3223

This two-story inn also features two cottages. Located in the Green Mountains, just minutes from Bromley, Okemo, Magic and Stratton ski areas, the inn provides a taste of life from the early Colonial days. Guest rooms feature handmade quilts crafted locally. The cottages include kitchenettes, and pets are welcome

in the cottages if prior arrangements are made.

Innkeeper(s): Chapin & Joan Darling. $80-125. PC, TC. 5 rooms with PB and 2 cottages. Breakfast included in rates. Type of meal: Full bkfst. Turndown service in room. VCR and swimming on premises. Small meetings and family reunions hosted. Antiquing, live theater, shopping, downhill skiing and cross-country skiing nearby.

Wilder Homestead Inn

25 Lawrence Hill Rd
Weston, VT 05161-5600
(802)824-8172 Fax:(802)824-5054
E-mail: wilder@sover.net
Web: www.wilderhomestead.com

Circa 1827. Located in historic Weston and within walking distance of the Green Mountain National Forest, this inn has both Federal and Greek Revival stylings and features seven guest rooms, all with private baths and views. Five of the rooms have decorative fireplaces and three feature original Moses Eaton stenciling. Afternoon tea and romantic candlelight dinners are offered. Breakfast may include fresh fruit, eggs and homemade biscuits with jam, hot cakes with genuine Vermont maple syrup, Lumberjack mush or sausage. There's an old English pub and a craft shop is on the premises.

Innkeeper(s): Peter & Patsy McKay. $85-150. MC, VISA. 7 rooms with PB. Breakfast included in rates. MAP. Types of meals: Full bkfst and country bkfst. Afternoon tea available. Beds: KQDT. Ceiling fan in room. VCR on premises. Weddings, small meetings and family reunions hosted. Antiquing, fishing, live theater, shopping, downhill skiing, cross-country skiing and sporting events nearby.

Wilder   H5

Stonecrest Farm B&B

PO Box 504, 1187 Christian St
Wilder, VT 05088-0504
(802)296-2425 (800)730-2425 Fax:(802)295-1135

Circa 1810. Two acres of grounds and charming red barns create a secluded, country atmosphere at Stonecrest Farm, which is located three-and-a-half miles from Dartmouth College. The former dairy farm was owned by a prominent Vermont family and hosted notable guests such as Calvin Coolidge and Amelia Earhart. Guest rooms are decorated with antiques, and beds are topped with down comforters. Terry robes are placed in each room. The abundant breakfasts feature a different entree each morning. Orange French toast, vegetable frittatas, banana walnut pancakes and scones are some of the possibilities.

Innkeeper(s): Gail L. Sanderson. $129-144. MC, VISA, AX, PC, TC. TAC10. 6 rooms with PB. Breakfast and afternoon tea included in rates. Types of meals: Full bkfst and early coffee/tea. Beds: QDT. Down comforters and quilts in room. VCR, fax, copier and library on premises. Family reunions hosted. Limited German and French spoken. Antiquing, golf, museums, hiking (near Appalachian Trail), galleries, canoeing, live theater, parks, shopping, downhill skiing, cross-country skiing, sporting events, tennis and water sports nearby.

"Your house is enchanting. I especially liked your grandfather clock in the hallway."

Wilmington K3

Nutmeg Inn

Rt 9 W, Molly Stark Tr
Wilmington, VT 05363
(802)464-7400 (800)277-5402 Fax:(802)464-7331
E-mail: nutmeg@sover.net
Web: www.nutmeginn.com

Circa 1777. This red clapboard inn sits invitingly on a green lawn. Behind the inn, a forested hillside leads to a picturesque mountain brook. An extensive renovation has added to the charm of the inn. Quilts, four-poster and brass beds, rocking chairs and old-fashioned dressers maintain the Vermont country atmosphere. A hearty breakfast is provided in the dining room.

Historic Interest: Molly Stark Trail.

Innkeeper(s): Dave & Pat Cerchio. $89-299. MC, VISA, AX, DS. 10 rooms with PB, 10 with FP and 4 suites. Breakfast included in rates. Types of meals: Full bkfst and country bkfst. Afternoon tea available. Beds: KQ. Cable TV, phone, rooms have wood-burning fireplaces and suites have two-person whirlpools in room. Central air. German spoken. Antiquing, art galleries, bicycling, canoeing/kayaking, fishing, golf, hiking, horseback riding, sleigh rides, parks, shopping, downhill skiing, cross-country skiing, tennis and wineries nearby.

The Red Shutter Inn

PO Box 636
Wilmington, VT 05363-0636
(802)464-3768

Circa 1894. This colonial inn sits on a five-acre hillside amid maples, pin oaks and evergreens. Tucked behind the inn is the renovated carriage house; among its charms is a cozy fireplace suite. In the summer, guests can enjoy gourmet dining by candlelight on an awning-covered porch. The Red Shutter Inn, with its fireplaces in the sitting room and dining room, antique furnishings and view of a rushing river, provide a congenial atmosphere. Antique shops, galleries and craft shops are within walking distance.

Innkeeper(s): Renee & Tad Lyon. $100-200. MC, VISA, AX, DS, PC, TC. 9 rooms with PB, 3 with FP and 2 suites. Breakfast included in rates. Type of meal: Full bkfst. Gourmet dinner, picnic lunch and banquet service available. Restaurant on premises. Beds: QD. Cable TV and ceiling fan in room. VCR, fax, copier and library on premises. Weddings, small meetings, family reunions and seminars hosted. Antiquing, fishing, parks, shopping, downhill skiing, cross-country skiing and water sports nearby.

"You've made The Red Shutter Inn a cozy and relaxing hideaway."

Trail's End, A Country Inn

5 Trail's End Ln
Wilmington, VT 05363-7925
(802)464-2727 (800)859-2585

Circa 1956. The innkeepers transformed this rustic inn from its 1950s decor into a beautiful romantic bed & breakfast. The game room, where cookies and hot cider are served each day, features elegant wing-back chairs and a pool table, while the living room offers four overstuffed couches in front of a 22-foot Fieldstone fireplace. Each bedroom is decorated in a different color scheme

and utilizes brass, white wicker and family heirlooms for a chic country atmosphere.

Innkeeper(s): Debbie & Kevin Stephens. $105-195. MC, VISA, AX, PC, TC. TAC10. 15 rooms with PB, 6 with FP, 2 suites and 1 conference room. Breakfast and afternoon tea included in rates. Types of meals: Full bkfst and early coffee/tea. Beds: QDT. Cable TV, ceiling fan, clock and microwave in room. Copier, swimming, tennis, library and guest refrigerator on premises. Weddings, small meetings, family reunions and seminars hosted. Antiquing, fishing, Marlboro Music Festival, live theater, parks, shopping, downhill skiing, cross-country skiing and water sports nearby.

Publicity: *Inn Times, Snow Country, Sun Country, Changing Times.*

"Thank you again for an absolutely wonderful weekend."

White House of Wilmington

178 Rt 9 East
Wilmington, VT 05363
(802)464-2135 (800)541-2135 Fax:(802)464-5295
E-mail: whitehse@sover.net
Web: www.whitehouseinn.com

Circa 1915. The White House was built as a summer home for a wealthy lumber baron, and he spared no expense. The inn has 14 fireplaces, rich woodwork and hand-crafted French doors. Nine of the guest rooms include fireplaces, and some have a balcony, terrace or whirlpool tub. Seven guest rooms are located in an adjacent guest house. There is an outdoor swimming pool, and the spa includes an indoor pool, whirlpool and sauna. Guests are treated to breakfast, and award-winning, gourmet dinners are available in the dining rooms.

Innkeeper(s): Bob Grinold. $118-195. MC, VISA, AX, DC, DS, PC, TC. TAC10. 23 rooms with PB, 9 with FP, 1 suite and 2 conference rooms. Breakfast included in rates. MAP. Type of meal: Full bkfst. Gourmet dinner available. Restaurant on premises. Beds: KQDT. VCR, fax, copier, spa, swimming and sauna on premises. Handicap access. Weddings, small meetings, family reunions and seminars hosted. Antiquing, fishing, golf, live theater, parks, shopping, downhill skiing, cross-country skiing, tennis and water sports nearby.

Windsor H5

Juniper Hill Inn

153 Pembroke Road
Windsor, VT 05089
(802)674-5273 (800)359-2541 Fax:(802)674-5273

Circa 1902. This Colonial Revival mansion was built for Maxwell Evarts, who was the son of William Evarts, attorney general to Andrew Johnson. It was Maxwell's ties with the Union Pacific Railroad, which led to his familiarity with politicians and business leaders of the time. Teddy Roosevelt reportedly enjoyed the hospitality of the Evarts on a trip to Windsor. The common areas of the inn include a great hall with a massive fireplace, two dining rooms, a sitting parlor and a library.

Innkeeper(s): Robert & Susanne Pearl. $95-175. MC, VISA, DS. TAC10. 16 rooms with PB, 11 with FP. Breakfast included in rates. MAP. Types of meals: Full bkfst and early coffee/tea. Dinner available. Restaurant on premises. Beds: QD. Ceiling fan and fireplaces (some rooms) in room. VCR, fax, swimming, bicycles and library on premises. Weddings, small meetings, family reunions and seminars hosted. Antiquing, fishing, hiking, museums, shopping, downhill skiing, cross-country skiing and sporting events nearby.

"It was the charm of your place and your personal graciousness that made it such a pleasure."

Woodstock H4

Applebutter Inn

Happy Valley Rd
Woodstock, VT 05091
(802)457-4158 Fax:(802)457-4158

Circa 1850. Built prior to the Civil War, this Federal-style home rests on 12 acres that was once part of the Watson Jersey Farm. An old barn still remains. Guest rooms and common areas are decorated with period antiques, and the walls feature some of the home's original stenciling. Each bedchamber is named for a variety of apples. The

Pippin Room affords a view of the grounds, including the gardens and historic barn. The Granny Smith includes double and twin beds, a sitting area and ceiling with skylights. Other rooms feature names such as the Winesap Room, King David Room and Baldwin Room. Breakfast includes the inn's signature, homemade apple butter, as well as items such as raspberry bread pudding, crepes, granola and an assortment of beverages. The village of Woodstock is just three miles from the inn.

Historic Interest: Woodstock (3 miles), Quechee Gorge (5 miles), National Park (7 miles).

Innkeeper(s): Beverlee & Andy Cook. $75-150. MC, VISA, PC. 6 rooms with PB and 1 conference room. Breakfast and snacks/refreshments included in rates. Types of meals: Full bkfst, country bkfst, veg bkfst and early coffee/tea. Afternoon tea and catering service available. Beds: QDT. Cable TV and VCR in room. Air conditioning. Fax, copier and library on premises.

Ardmore Inn

23 Pleasant St
Woodstock, VT 05091
(802)457-3887 (800)497-9652 Fax:(802)457-9006

Circa 1850. This Greek Revival-style inn offers a gentle welcome with its pretty shutters and graceful entrance. Located on an acre in a village setting, it is furnished elegantly. For instance, the Tully Room has four eyebrow windows shedding sunlight on its four-poster queen bed, and there's a sitting area and marble bath. Enjoy breakfasts of Vermont flat bread served with truffle eggs, apple-smoked sausage and asparagus spears.

Innkeeper(s): Giorgio Ortiz. $110-175. MC, VISA, AX, PC, TC. TAC10. 5 suites, 1 with FP. Breakfast and afternoon tea included in rates. Type of meal: Full gourmet bkfst. Beds: KQD. Air conditioning. Fax, copier and bicycles on premises. Weddings, small meetings and family reunions hosted. Spanish spoken. Antiquing, fishing, golf, mountain biking, fly fishing, live theater, parks, shopping, downhill skiing, cross-country skiing and tennis nearby.

Canterbury House

43 Pleasant St
Woodstock, VT 05091-1129
(802)457-3077 (800)390-3077

Circa 1880. National Geographic tabbed Woodstock as one of America's most beautiful villages, and this Victorian inn offers a lovely stopping place for those exploring the area. Visitors find themselves within easy walking distance of antique stores, art galleries, museums, restaurants and shopping. Ski lifts at Killington, Pico and Okemo are only minutes away.

Historic Interest: The Dana Museum and Billings Farm Museum are some of

the historic sites. Walking tours are available.

Innkeeper(s): Bob & Sue Frost. $90-175. MC, VISA, AX, PC. TAC10. 8 rooms with PB, 1 with FP. Breakfast included in rates. Type of meal: Full gourmet bkfst. Beds: QDT. Air conditioning. VCR on premises. Weddings, small meetings and family reunions hosted. Antiquing, fishing, mountain bikes, live theater, parks, shopping, downhill skiing, cross-country skiing, sporting events and water sports nearby.

Charleston House

21 Pleasant St
Woodstock, VT 05091-1131
(802)457-3843
E-mail: nohl@together.net
Web: charlestonhouse.com

Circa 1810. This authentically restored brick Greek Revival town house, in the National Register, welcomes guests with shuttered many-paned windows and window boxes filled with pink blooms. Guest rooms are appointed with period antiques and reproductions, an art collection and Oriental rugs. Most of the rooms boast four-poster beds, and some feature fireplaces and Jacuzzis. A hearty full breakfast

starts off the day in the candle-lit dining room, and the innkeepers serve afternoon refreshments, as well. Area offerings include winter sleigh rides, snow skiing, auctions, fly fishing, golfing and summer stock theater, to name a few.

Historic Interest: The Billings/Marsh National Historic Park and Calvin Coolidge Homestead are nearby attractions.

Innkeeper(s): Dieter & Willa Nohl. $110-195. MC, VISA, AX. 9 rooms with PB. Breakfast included in rates. Type of meal: Full bkfst. Gourmet dinner available. Beds: QT. TV in room. Jacuzzis and fireplaces on premises. Antiquing, fishing, golf, downhill skiing and cross-country skiing nearby.

Publicity: *Harbor News, Boston Business Journal, Weekend Getaway, Inn Spots, Special Places.*

The Jackson House Inn & Restaurant

114 Senior Ln (Rt 4)
Woodstock, VT 05091-1247
(802)457-2065 (800)448-1890 Fax:(802)457-9290
E-mail: innkeepers@jacksonhouse.com
Web: www.jacksonhouse.com

Circa 1890. This beautifully restored late Victorian was built originally by Wales Johnson, a saw-mill owner and craftsman. The gleaming cherry and maple wood floors and moldings, exterior eaves and twin chimneys are a tribute to the original owner's attention to detail and workmanship. Although the inn passed hands a couple of times, the integrity of the interior and exterior

designs has never been compromised. Fine antique furnishings, decorative arts and Oriental rugs are a few of the elegant and sophisticated features that have been maintained throughout the years. French-cut crystal, a library of classics and a parlor with a welcoming fire add to the ambiance. Each guest room is inspired by a different style and period: French Empire, Brass and Bamboo inspired by Brighton Castle, and New England Country. A gourmet breakfast featuring house specialties such as Sante Fe omelets, fruit compote in champagne and poached eggs in puff pastry are offered daily. Listed in the National Register, the inn offers more than four lush acres of manicured gardens and pathways.

Innkeeper(s): Juan Florin. $180-340. MC, VISA, AX, PC. TAC10. 15 rooms, 6 with FP and 6 suites. Breakfast and snacks/refreshments included in rates. Type of meal: Full gourmet bkfst. Gourmet dinner available. Restaurant on premises. Beds: QT. Turndown service and ceiling fan in room. Air conditioning. VCR, fax, spa, swimming, library and steam room on premises. Weddings, small meetings, family reunions and seminars hosted. Spanish and French spoken. Antiquing, fishing, golf, live theater, parks, shopping, downhill skiing, cross-country skiing, tennis and water sports nearby.

Publicity: *Colonial Homes, Country Inns, Fitness Magazine, Travel & Leisure, New York Times, London Times.*

Kedron Valley Inn

Rt 106, Box 145
Woodstock, VT 05071
(802)457-1473 (800)836-1193 Fax:(802)457-4469

Circa 1828. Travelers have made this rustic, cozy inn a stopping point for 170 years. One of the guest buildings has a secret attic passageway and is rumored to have been a stop on the Underground Railway during the Civil War. A 60-piece quilt collection includes century-old quilts created by the hostess' great-grand-mothers. Guests need not leave the grounds

to enjoy a white-sand beach and swimming lake. A stable with horses is nearby. Seventeen of the rooms boast fireplaces, most rooms feature canopy beds and four rooms have large Jacuzzis. After feasting on a delectable breakfast, spend the day searching for antiques, hiking or viewing historic estates. The gourmet dinners are a treat.

Historic Interest: Home of Augustine Saint Gaudens (25 miles), Billings Farm & Museum (5 miles), Calvin Coolidge Homestead (20 miles), Marsh-Billings National Park (5 miles).

Innkeeper(s): Max & Merrily Comins. $120-270. MC, VISA, AX, DS, PC. TAC10. 28 rooms with PB, 17 with FP, 5 suites and 1 conference room. Breakfast included in rates. Type of meal: Full bkfst. Gourmet dinner available. Beds: QDT. TV, ceiling fan and four rooms with Jacuzzi in room. Air conditioning. Fax, copier and swimming on premises. Weddings, small meetings, family reunions and seminars hosted. Antiquing, art galleries, fishing, hiking, trail, surrey rides, fitness, parks, shopping, downhill skiing and cross-country skiing nearby.

"It's what you dream a Vermont country inn should be and the most impressive feature is the innkeepers ... outgoing, warm and friendly."

The Lincoln Inn at The Covered Bridge

530 Woodstock Rd, US Rt 4 W
Woodstock, VT 05091
(802)457-3312 Fax:(802)457-5808

Circa 1870. This admirable old farmhouse sits on six acres bordered by the Lincoln Covered Bridge and the Ottauquechee River. Lawns meander to a rise overlooking the water. A swing, park benches and a gazebo provide ample places from which to enjoy the view. Recent renovation has revealed hand-hewn beams in the library and a fireplace in the common room. The inn's world-class continental cuisine provides a memorable dinner.

Innkeeper(s): Kurt & Lori Hildbrand. $125-175. MC, VISA, DS, PC, TC. 6 rooms with PB and 1 conference room. Breakfast included in rates. Types of meals: Full gourmet bkfst and early coffee/tea. Gourmet dinner, snacks/refreshments, picnic lunch, lunch, banquet service and catering service available. Restaurant on premises. Beds: KQD. Air conditioning. VCR, fax, copier, swimming and library on premises. Weddings, small meetings, family reunions and seminars hosted. German spoken. Antiquing, fishing, live theater, parks, shopping, downhill skiing, cross-country skiing, sporting events and water sports nearby.

Publicity: *Travelhost.*

"Feels like family!"

Woodstocker B&B

61 River St
Woodstock, VT 05091-1227
(802)457-3896 Fax:(802)457-3897

Circa 1830. This early 19th-century, Cape-style inn is located at the base of Mt. Tom at the edge of the village of Woodstock. Hand-hewn wood beams create a rustic effect. The seven guest rooms and two suites are individually appointed. Buffet-style, full breakfasts get the day off to a great start. Guests can take a short walk across a covered

bridge to reach shops and restaurants. Hikers will enjoy trails that wind up and around Mt. Tom. After a busy winter day, come back and enjoy a soak in the five-person whirlpool.

Historic Interest: Billings Farm and Museum, the Calvin Coolidge Homestead and Dana House Museum are some of the historic sites. Four of Woodstock's churches boast bells made by Paul Revere.

Innkeeper(s): Tom & Nancy Blackford. $85-155. MC, VISA. 9 rooms with PB and 2 suites. Breakfast included in rates. Types of meals: Full bkfst and early coffee/tea. Beds: QD. Cable TV and ceiling fan in room. Air conditioning. VCR, fax and copier on premises. Weddings and family reunions hosted. Antiquing, fishing, live theater, shopping, downhill skiing, cross-country skiing, sporting events and water sports nearby.

"You have truly opened your home and heart to create a comfortable and memorable stay."

Virginia

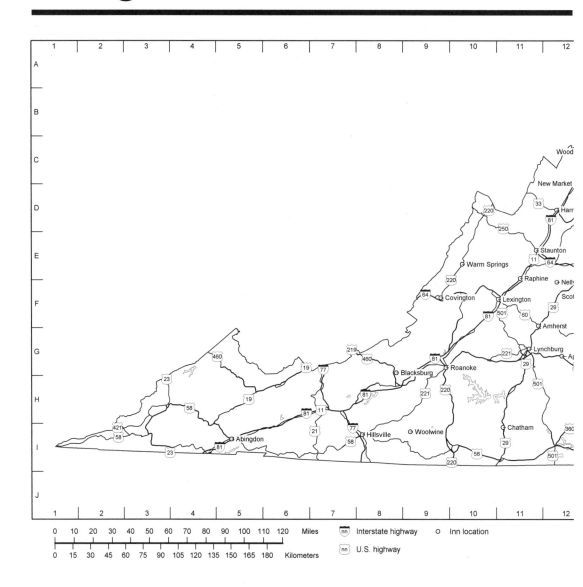

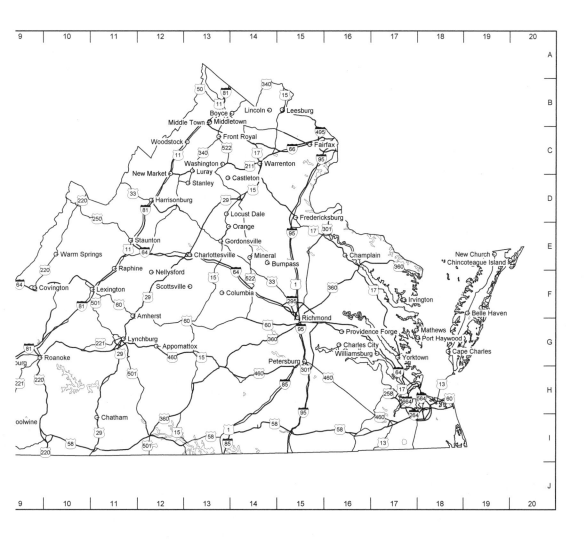

Abingdon   I5

Summerfield Inn

101 W Valley St
Abingdon, VA 24210
(540)628-5905 (800)668-5905 Fax:(540)628-7515
E-mail: stay@summerfieldinn.com
Web: www.summerfieldinn.com

Circa 1920. Located within Abingdon's Historic District,
Summerfield Inn is a graciously decorated three-story home.
The cheerful rooms are furnished with American and European
antiques, floral touches and
items such as brass and
four-poster beds, artwork,
Oriental rugs, wicker and
whirlpool baths. There are
two guest pantries for those
seeking a refreshment or

snack, and the innkeepers serve full breakfasts in the elegant
dining room or the sunroom. Specialties include freshly baked
cinnamon rolls, quiche and seasonal fruit. The inn's wraparound porch offers a swing and rocking chairs. Abingdon, the
oldest town west of the Blue Ridge Mountains, is the site of the
well-known Barter Theatre, a short walk from the inn. The
annual Virginia Highlands Festival, pleasant streets of historic
houses, local arts and crafts, an old mill and many excellent
restaurants are all nearby, as is the Virginia Creeper Trail.

Innkeeper(s): Janice & Jim Cowan. $90-130. MC, VISA, AX, PC, TC. TAC10.
7 rooms with PB. Breakfast included in rates. Type of meal: Full bkfst. Beds:
KQD. TV, phone, ceiling fan, whirlpool tubs, robes and chocolates in room.
Air conditioning. VCR and library on premises. Small meetings and family
reunions hosted. Antiquing, bicycling, hiking, historic tours, carriage rides,
hot air balloons, live theater and shopping nearby.

Amherst   F11

Dulwich Manor B&B Inn

550 Richmond Hwy
Amherst, VA 24521-3962
(804)946-7207 (800)571-9011
E-mail: mfarmer@iwinet.com
Web: thedulwichmanor.com

Circa 1912. This red Flemish brick and white columned
English Manor sits on five secluded acres at the end of a coun-
try lane and in the midst of 93 acres of woodland and meadow.
The Blue Ridge Parkway is minutes away. The entry features a

large center hall and a wide
oak staircase. Walls are 14
inches thick. The 18 rooms
include a 50-foot-long ballroom on the third floor. The
inn is decorated with a creative
mix of antiques, traditional
furniture and collectibles.

Innkeeper(s): Mike & Georgie Farmer. $80-110. MC, VISA, PC, TC. TAC10. 6
rooms with PB, 3 with FP. Breakfast included in rates. Types of meals: Full
bkfst and early coffee/tea. Beds: KQ. Phone, ceiling fan and two rooms with
whirlpool tub in room. Air conditioning. Spa on premises. Weddings, small
meetings, family reunions and seminars hosted. Antiquing, fishing, hiking,
historic sites, Monticello, Appomattox Court House and natural bridge nearby,
live theater, parks, shopping, downhill skiing, sporting events, water sports
and wineries nearby.

Appomattox   G12

Babcock House

RR 2 Box 822A
Appomattox, VA 24522
(804)352-7532 (800)689-6208 Fax:(804)352-5532

Circa 1884. This columned Greek Revival house occupies
more than an acre in the center of the town's 19th-Century
Homes Walking Tour. Dr. Havilah Babcock, English professor
and noted hunting and fishing author,
occupied the home with his family.
Once operated as a boarding house,
the home continues its tradition of
hospitality and comfort, but now
boasts cable television, private baths,
ceiling fans and air conditioning.

Guests still enjoy gathering at the end of the day on the back
porch to share their adventures, which many times includes
visiting Appomattox Courthouse National Historic Park where
General Robert E. Lee surrendered to General Grant. The
innkeepers offer regional dining in their restaurant with a daily
change of menu to reflect seasonal changes in ingredients.

Historic Interest: Boyhood home of Havilah Babcock-1884 classic example of
turn of the century architecture, Appomattox Courthouse National Historic Park.

Innkeeper(s): Deborah W Powell, Luella M Coleman. $95-120. MC, VISA,
AX, DS, PC, TC. TAC10. 6 rooms, 5 with PB, 1 with FP and 1 suite.
Breakfast and snacks/refreshments included in rates. Types of meals: Full
bkfst, country bkfst and veg bkfst. Gourmet dinner available. Restaurant on
premises. Beds: QT. Cable TV, phone and ceiling fan in room. Central air.
VCR on premises. Handicap access. Weddings, family reunions and seminars
hosted. Antiquing, bicycling, canoeing/kayaking, fishing and wineries nearby.

Belle Haven   F19

Bay View Waterfront B&B

35350 Copes Dr
Belle Haven, VA 23306-1952
(757)442-6963 (800)442-6966

Circa 1800. This rambling inn stretches more than 100 feet
across and has five roof levels. There are heart-pine floors, high
ceilings and several fireplaces. The hillside location affords bay
breezes and wide views of the Chesapeake, Occohannock
Creek and the inn's sur-
rounding 140 acres. The
innkeepers are descendants
of several generations who
have owned and operated
Bay View. If you come by
water to the inn's deep

water dock, look behind Channel Marker 16. Guests can
arrange to enjoy a boat tour along the Chesapeake Bay or
Atlantic Ocean led by the innkeepers' daughter, U.S. Coast
Guard-approved Capt. Mary.

Historic Interest: Kiptopeake State Park (30 miles), E.S. Historic Museum
(12 miles), Chincoteague Ponies (40 miles).

Innkeeper(s): Wayne & Mary Will Browning. $95. PC, TC. TAC10. 3 rooms,
1 with PB, 1 with FP. Breakfast included in rates. Type of meal: Full bkfst.
Beds: D. Phone in room. Air conditioning. VCR, swimming, bicycles and
library on premises. Weddings, small meetings and family reunions hosted.
Antiquing, fishing, live theater, parks, shopping and water sports nearby.

*"We loved staying in your home, and especially in the room with a
beautiful view of the bay. You have a lovely home and a beautiful
location. Thank you so much for your hospitality."*

Blacksburg   G8

Clay Corner Inn

401 Clay St SW
Blacksburg, VA 24060
(540)953-2604 Fax:(540)951-0541

Circa 1929. Clay Corner Inn is comprised of five houses on a corner one block from Virginia Tech and a couple blocks from downtown. There are 12 guest rooms, three of which are two-bedroom suites. Each
room is decorated with
a different theme, and
all guest rooms have
private baths, cable TV,
telephones and queen
or king beds. Two hous-
es were built early in the century, two are a decade old and another, circa 1940, is a private residence. A full breakfast is served in the main house or covered deck outside. The inn also features an on-site heated swimming pool and a hot tub.

Historic Interest: Smithfield Plantation is one mile away, Blacksburg is 200+ years old.

Innkeeper(s): Joanne Anderson. $74-115. MC, VISA, AX. 12 rooms with PB. Breakfast included in rates. Type of meal: Full bkfst. Swimming on premises. Antiquing, golf, wineries, hiking and tennis nearby.

Boyce   B14

L'Auberge Provencale

13630 Lord Fairfax Highway
Boyce, VA 22620
(540)837-1375 (800)638-1702 Fax:(540)837-2004

Circa 1753. This farmhouse was built with fieldstones gathered from the area. Hessian soldiers crafted the woodwork of the main house, Mt. Airy. As the name suggests, a French influence is prominent throughout the inn. Victorian and European antiques fill the elegant guest rooms, several of which include fireplaces. Innkeeper Alain Borel hails from a long line of master chefs, his expertise creates many happy culinary memories guests cherish. Many of the French-influenced items served at the inn's four-diamond restaurant, include ingredients from the inn's gardens, and Alain has been hailed by James Beard as a Great Country Inn Chef. The innkeepers also offer accommodations three miles away at Villa La Campagnette, an 1890 restored home. The home includes two suites and the Grand Master bedroom. Guests enjoy 18 acres with a swimming pool, hot tub and stables.

Historic Interest: Waterford, Luray Caverns, Holy Cross Abbey (Historic Long Branch).

Innkeeper(s): Alain & Celeste Borel. $145-250. MC, VISA, AX, DC, DS, PC, TC. TAC10. 11 rooms with PB, 6 with FP, 3 suites and 1 conference room. Breakfast included in rates. AP. Type of meal: Full gourmet bkfst. Gourmet dinner, picnic lunch and banquet service available. Restaurant on premises. Beds: KQD. Air conditioning. Fax and copier on premises. Weddings, small meetings and seminars hosted. French spoken. Antiquing, bicycling, canoeing/kayaking, fishing, golf, hiking, horseback riding, live theater, museums, parks, shopping, tennis and wineries nearby.

"Peaceful view and atmosphere, extraordinary food and wines. Honeymoon and heaven all in one!"

The River House

RR 1 Box 135
Boyce, VA 22620
(540)837-1476 Fax:(540)837-2399
E-mail: rvrhouse@visuallink.com
Web: www.bedand breakfast.com/bbc/p205577.asp

Circa 1780. This historic house is located on Shenandoah River frontage and 17 acres of woodlands. Grain from the neighboring mill (now restored) was once shipped from this
point on the river to Harpers
Ferry, and Stonewall Jackson
camped and crossed the river
here. Ask to stay in the original
1780 kitchen with its walk-in fireplace or the elegant master bedroom. Cornelia is a former actress
and organizes theatrical activities and house parties at the inn. A complimentary brunch is served every morning.

Historic Interest: Restored Belle Grove Plantation, George Washington HQ, Harpers Ferry (40 minutes).

Innkeeper(s): Cornelia Niemann. $90-150. MC, VISA, PC, TC. 5 rooms with PB, 5 with FP. Brunch available. Beds: KQDT. Fax and copier on premises. Handicap access. Antiquing, fishing, hiking, biking, live theater and downhill skiing nearby.

"A sure place to unwind for the weekend."

Bumpass   E14

Rockland Farm Retreat

3609 Lewiston Rd
Bumpass, VA 23024-9659
(540)895-5098

Circa 1820. The 75 acres of Rockland Farm include pasture land, livestock, vineyard, crops and a farm pond for fishing. The grounds here are said to have spawned Alex Haley's "Roots." Guests can study documents and explore local cemeteries describing life under slavery in the area surrounding this historic home and 18th-century farmlands.

Historic Interest: Some of the oldest slave cemeteries are nearby.

Innkeeper(s): Roy E. Mixon. $69-79. AX, PC. TAC10. 4 rooms, 3 with PB, 1 suite and 2 conference rooms. Breakfast included in rates. MAP. Type of meal: Full bkfst. Dinner, lunch, banquet service and catering service available. Beds: DT. Air conditioning. VCR on premises. Weddings, small meetings, family reunions and seminars hosted. French and Spanish spoken. Amusement parks, antiquing, fishing, parks, shopping and water sports nearby. Pets Allowed.

Cape Charles   G18

Cape Charles House

645 Tazewell Ave
Cape Charles, VA 23310-3313
(757)331-4920 Fax:(757)331-4960
E-mail: stay@capecharleshouse.com
Web: capecharleshouse.com

Circa 1912. A Cape Charles attorney built this Colonial Revival home on the site of the town's first schoolhouse. Each room is named for someone important to Cape Charles history. The Julia Wilkins Room is especially picturesque. Rich blue walls and white woodwork are accented by blue and white pastoral print draperies, a private bath with whirlpool and a balcony.

There is a seamstress dress form with an antique dress, rocking chair and chaise. Other rooms are decorated with the same skill and style, with fine window dressings, artwork and carefully placed collectibles. Oriental rugs top the wood floors, and among the fine furnishings are family heirlooms. Breakfasts are gourmet and served in the formal dining room. Innkeeper Carol Evans prepares breakfast items such as chilled melon with a lime glaze and lemon yogurt topping, egg quesadillas, rosemary roasted potatoes and freshly baked muffins. From time to time, cooking classes and murder-mystery events are available. There are many attractions in the area, including sunset sails, historic walking tour of Cape Charles, antique shops, golfing, beach and The Nature Conservancy.

Innkeeper(s): Bruce & Carol Evans. $85-120. MC, VISA, AX, DS, PC, TC. TAC10. 5 rooms with PB. Breakfast, afternoon tea and snacks/refreshments included in rates. Types of meals: Full gourmet bkfst and early coffee/tea. Gourmet dinner available. Beds: KQ. Ceiling fan and Jacuzzi (two rooms) in room. Air conditioning. VCR, fax, copier and bicycles on premises. Weddings, small meetings, family reunions and seminars hosted. Antiquing, fishing, golf, live theater, parks, shopping, tennis and water sports nearby.

Publicity: *Southern Inns.*

"Cape Charles House is first and foremost a home and we were made to feel 'at home'."

Castleton D13

Blue Knoll Farm

Box 110 Gore Rd
Castleton, VA 22716
(540)937-5234

Circa 1850. The original house of the Blue Knoll Farm is pre-Civil War, and many Civil War battles were fought in the area.

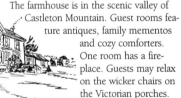

The farmhouse is in the scenic valley of Castleton Mountain. Guest rooms feature antiques, family mementos and cozy comforters. One room has a fireplace. Guests may relax on the wicker chairs on the Victorian porches.

Historic Interest: Shenandoah National Park (25 minutes), Charlottesville (1 hour).
Innkeeper(s): Mary & Gil Carlson. $95-125. MC, VISA, PC, TC. 4 rooms with PB, 1 with FP. Breakfast included in rates. Types of meals: Full bkfst and early coffee/tea. Beds: KQ. TV, alarm clocks, one fireplace and one with ceiling fan in room. Air conditioning. Antiquing, fine dining, live theater, parks and shopping nearby.

"Beautiful, charming inn. Delightful room, deep sleep and a delicious breakfast. Thank you. We will be back."

Champlain E16

Linden House B&B & Plantation

PO Box 23
Champlain, VA 22438-0023
(804)443-1170 (800)622-1202

Circa 1750. This restored planters home is designated a state landmark and listed in the National Register. The lush grounds boast walking trails, a pond, an English garden, patio with

fountain, gazebo, arbor and five porches. Each of the accommodations offers something special. The Carriage Suite features country decor, antiques, a private porch and a fireplace. The Robert E. Lee room has a

high-poster bed, fireplace and private bath. The Jefferson Davis room has a luxurious bath with a Jacuzzi and steam room. The fourth-floor Linden Room affords a view of the countryside and features a queen-size bed and an alcove with a day bed adjoining the private bath. Other rooms also promise an enchanting experience. All rooms have their own television and refrigerator. With its new reception hall and verandas, the inn is popular for weddings, conferences and meetings.

Innkeeper(s): Ken & Sandra Pounsberry. $85-135. MC, VISA, AX, PC, TC. TAC10. 7 rooms with PB and 2 suites. Breakfast included in rates. Types of meals: Full gourmet bkfst and early coffee/tea. Afternoon tea, gourmet dinner, snacks/refreshments, banquet service, catering service and catered breakfast available. Beds: Q. Phone, turndown service, ceiling fan and VCR in room. Air conditioning. Stables, bicycles and library on premises. Handicap access. Weddings, small meetings, family reunions and seminars hosted. Amusement parks, antiquing, fishing, boarding school, live theater, parks, shopping and water sports nearby.

Charles City G16

Edgewood Plantation

4800 John Tyler Memorial Hwy
Charles City, VA 23230
(804)829-6908 (800)296-3343 Fax:(804)829-2962

Circa 1849. Among its expansive 7,000 square feet, this Gothic Revival mansion includes high ceilings, a double parlor, 10 fireplaces and a double spiral staircase. The plantation has an incredible history. It rests along the oldest highway in the United States, and it was once part of the Berkeley Plantation, the ancestral home of President William Henry Harrison. The inn's Civil War history is as fascinating as the authentic Victorian decor. Both innkeepers are antique dealers, and among the vintage pieces they've included in the inn are canopy beds dating back to 1790, 1818 and 1820. Breakfasts are served with fine silver, china and pewter on a Queen Anne table surrounded by Chippendale chairs. The innkeepers attention to detail is impressive, especially during the Christmas season when 18 decorated trees are placed throughout the inn. A few yards from the inn is a three-story mill with an unusual inside mill wheel built in 1725.

Innkeeper(s): Dot & Julian Boulware. $125-198. MC, VISA, AX. 8 rooms, 6 with PB, 3 with FP, 2 suites, 2 cottages and 1 conference room. Breakfast included in rates. Types of meals: Full gourmet bkfst and early coffee/tea. Afternoon tea, gourmet dinner, picnic lunch and catering service available. Beds: KQD. TV, turndown service, ceiling fan and VCR in room. Fax and swimming on premises. Weddings, small meetings, family reunions and seminars hosted. Amusement parks, antiquing, fishing, horseback riding, live theater, parks, shopping, sporting events and water sports nearby.

Publicity: *Country Home, Southern Living, Country, Victoria, Country Inns.*

"A feast for the eyes and wonderful manner in which things are displayed and put together."

Charlottesville   E13

200 South Street Inn

200 W South St
Charlottesville, VA 22902-5041
(804)979-0200 (800)964-7008 Fax:(804)979-4403
E-mail: southst@cstone.net
Web: www.southstreetinn.com

Circa 1844. This house was built for Thomas Jefferson Wertenbaker, son of Thomas Jefferson's librarian at the University of Virginia. It is furnished with English and Belgian antiques. Guests may choose rooms with whirlpool baths, fireplaces and canopy beds.

Historic Interest: Jefferson Home, Monticello (4 miles), Monroe Home, Ashlawn (6 miles), Madison Home, Montpelier (20 miles).

Innkeeper(s): Brendan & Jenny Clancy. $115-230. MC, VISA, AX, DC, CB, PC, TC. TAC10. 20 rooms with PB, 11 with FP and 3 suites. Breakfast, afternoon tea and snacks/refreshments included in rates. Types of meals: Cont plus and early coffee/tea. Beds: QT. TV, phone and turndown service in room. Air conditioning. Fax and library on premises. Handicap access. Weddings, small meetings, family reunions and seminars hosted. Antiquing, fishing, live theater, parks, shopping, downhill skiing, sporting events and water sports nearby.

"True hospitality abounds in this fine inn which is a neatly turned complement to the inspiring history surrounding it."

Clifton- The Country Inn & Estate

1296 Clifton Inn Dr
Charlottesville, VA 22911-3627
(804)971-1800 (888)971-1800 Fax:(804)971-7098

Circa 1799. Thomas Mann Randolph, governor of the state of Virginia and son-in-law of Thomas Jefferson, built Clifton. One of the guest rooms boasts a winter view of Jefferson's estate, Monticello. Elegance and a careful attention to historical detail have enabled this historic country inn to garner national awards for its accommodations, cuisine and wine cellar. In addition to the main house, guests can choose Garden Rooms, Livery Suites or the two-level Carriage House. Aside from the abundance of history, Clifton also offers a variety of recreational facilities, including a clay tennis court, swimming pool with waterfall, year-round heated whirlpool spa and private lake. Ask for a gardener-led tour of the inn's 40 acres of landscaped grounds. Breakfast at Clifton is a treat with continental breakfast buffet and full breakfast. Afternoon tea is also served. Clifton operates a gourmet, four-diamond restaurant featuring five- and six-course dinners prepared by Executive Chef Rachel Greenberg.

Historic Interest: Monticello is only four miles away. Montpelier is about 30 miles from the inn and the University of Virginia is only a 10-mile journey.

Innkeeper(s): Keith Halford. $165-415. MC, VISA, AX, DC, PC. TAC10. 14 rooms with PB, 14 with FP, 7 suites and 2 conference rooms. Breakfast and afternoon tea included in rates. Types of meals: Full bkfst, cont plus and early coffee/tea. Gourmet dinner, banquet service and catering service available. Restaurant on premises. Beds: QD. Turndown service in room. Air conditioning. Fax, copier, spa, swimming, tennis, library and child care on premises. Handicap access. Weddings, small meetings, family reunions and seminars hosted. Antiquing, fishing, wineries, live theater, parks, shopping, downhill skiing, cross-country skiing and sporting events nearby.

Publicity: *International Living, Country Inns, Washington Post, Baltimore Sun, Richmond Times Dispatch, Rural Retreats, New York Times, Travel & Leisure.*

The Inn at the Crossroads

PO Box 6519
Charlottesville, VA 22906-6519
(804)979-6452
Web: www.crossroadsinn.com

Circa 1820. This four-story brick inn, which is listed in the National Register of Historic Places, was built as a tavern on the road from the Shenandoah Valley to the James River. It has been welcoming travelers since the early 1800s. The long front porch and straightforward, Federal-style architecture was common to ordinaries of that era. The four-acre grounds offer gardens of wild flowers and a swing hung under a grand oak tree, not to mention panoramic views of the foothills of the Blue Ridge Mountains. Country breakfasts are served in the inn's keeping room. The inn is nine miles south of Charlottesville, and Monticello and the University of Virginia are close by.

Innkeeper(s): Maureen & John Deis. $85-125. MC, VISA, PC, TC. 6 rooms with PB, 6 with FP, 1 suite and 1 cottage. Breakfast and afternoon tea included in rates. Types of meals: Full gourmet bkfst and early coffee/tea. Beds: KQD. Ceiling fan in room. Air conditioning. Weddings, small meetings and family reunions hosted. Antiquing, fishing, Monticello, Ash Lawn, Michie Tavern, live theater, parks, shopping, downhill skiing, cross-country skiing, sporting events, water sports and wineries nearby.

Guesthouses B&B Reservations

PO Box 5737
Charlottesville, VA 22905-5737
(804)979-7264
E-mail: guesthouses_bnb_reservations
Web: www.va-guesthouses.com

Guesthouses is thought to be America's first reservation service for bed & breakfast accommodations. It appropriately originated in an area with a centuries-old tradition of outstanding hospitality. Some of the homes are in the National Register. One, Carrsbrook, circa 1750 was built for Peter Carr, who was raised at Monticello and became Thomas Jefferson's secretary. Other homes are located near the University of Virginia and throughout Albemarle County and have been inspected carefully to assure a pleasant stay. Most accommodations offer one or two bedrooms in private homes or farms, but there is also a collection of private cottages including old renovated log houses. Mary Hill Caperton is the director.

Historic Interest: National Register.

Innkeeper(s): Mary Hill Caperton. $68-200. MC, VISA, AX.

Publicity: *Roanoke Times & World-News, Good Housekeeping.*

"The nicest B&B experience we had on our trip."

The Inn at Monticello

Rt 20 S, 1188 Scottsville Rd
Charlottesville, VA 22902
(804)979-3593
E-mail: innatmonticello@mindspring.com
Web: www.innatmonticello.com

Circa 1850. Thomas Jefferson built his own home, Monticello, just two miles from this gracious country home. The innkeepers have preserved the historic ambiance of the area. Rooms boast such pieces as four-poster beds covered with fluffy, down comforters. Some of the guest quarters have private porches or fireplaces. Breakfast at the inn is a memorable gourmet-appointed affair. Aside from the usual homemade rolls, coffee cakes and muffins, guests enjoy such entrees as pancakes or French toast with seasonal fruit, egg dishes and a variety of quiche. The front porch is lined with chairs for those who wish to relax, and the grounds feature several gardens to enjoy.

Historic Interest: Aside from its close access to Monticello, the inn is five miles from James Monroe's home, Ashlawn Highland. The historic Michie Tavern is just one mile from the inn, and the University of Virginia, which was founded by Jefferson, is about seven miles away.

Innkeeper(s): Norman & Rebecca Lindway. $110-145. MC, VISA, AX. TAC10. 5 rooms with PB, 2 with FP. Breakfast and afternoon tea included in rates. Types of meals: Full gourmet bkfst and early coffee/tea. Beds: KQT. Air conditioning. Fax on premises. Small meetings and family reunions hosted. Antiquing, Blue Ridge Parkway Sky Line Drive, wineries, live theater, parks, shopping, downhill skiing and sporting events nearby.

Publicity: *Gourmet, Country Inns, Bon Appetit.*

"What a magnificent room at an extraordinary place. I can't wait to tell all my friends."

The Quarters

611 Preston Pl
Charlottesville, VA 22903
(804)979-7264 Fax:(804)293-7799
E-mail: guesthouses_bnb_reservations@compuserve.com
Web: www.va-guesthouses.com

Circa 1815. This suite is in a cottage built to house slaves for John Kelly, who farmed about 500 acres. Thomas Jefferson wanted to buy the land, but built the University of Virginia on adjacent land instead. The suite is furnished with antiques, and there is a fireplace, TV and VCR in the sitting room. There are two bedrooms and one king bed and one single bed. Monticello is

five miles away. A sample breakfast menu is poached pears, cornbread, eggs, sausage, apple puffs and other hot breads. The innkeeper manages a reservation service and can offer a wide selection of B&B opportunities in the area.

Historic Interest: Jefferson designed University of Virginia (walking distance), Monticello (5 miles).

Innkeeper(s): Mary Hill Caperton. $100-150. MC, VISA, AX, DC, DS, PC, TC. TAC5. 3 rooms. Breakfast and snacks/refreshments included in rates. Type of meal: Full bkfst. Beds: King and twin.. Cable TV, phone, TV and VCR in room. Air conditioning. Library on premises. Antiquing, art galleries, bicycling, fishing, golf, hiking, horseback riding, U of Virginia college/university campus, historic sites, live theater, parks, shopping (local crafts), downhill skiing, sporting events, tennis and wineries nearby.

Pets Allowed.

Silver Thatch Inn

3001 Hollymead Dr
Charlottesville, VA 22911-7422
(804)978-4686 Fax:(804)973-6156
E-mail: info@silverthatch.com
Web: www.silverthatch.com

Circa 1780. This white clapboard inn, shaded by tall elms, was built by Hessian soldiers who were prisoners during the Revolutionary War. Before its present life as a country inn, Silver

Thatch was a boys' school, a melon farm and a tobacco plantation. Many additions have been made to the original house. The original 1780 section is now called the Hessian Room. The inn is filled with antiques. There are three intimate dining rooms featuring contemporary cuisine.

Historic Interest: Charlottesville, Thomas Jefferson's Monticello, James Madison's Montpelier, James Monroe's Ashlawn.

Innkeeper(s): Jim & Terri Petrovits. $130-160. MC, VISA, AX, DC, CB. 7 rooms with PB, 4 with FP. Breakfast included in rates. Types of meals: Full gourmet bkfst and country bkfst. Banquet service available. Restaurant on premises. Beds: QDT. Air conditioning. Antiquing, fishing, live theater, shopping and sporting events nearby.

Publicity: *Travel & Leisure, Washington Post, Los Angeles Times, New York Magazine.*

"Everything was absolutely perfect! The room, the food and above all, the people!"

Chatham   I11

Eldon, The Inn at Chatham

SR 685, 1037 Chalk Level Rd
Chatham, VA 24531
(804)432-0935

Circa 1835. Beautiful gardens and white oaks surround this former tobacco plantation home set among the backdrop of the Blue Ridge Mountains. Stroll the grounds and discover sculptures and an array of flowers and plants. Southern hospitality reigns at this charming home filled with Empire antiques. Guest rooms are light and airy and tastefully decorated with beautiful linens, Oriental rugs and antiques. Fresh flowers accentuate the bright, cheerful rooms. A lavish, Southern-style breakfast is served up each morning, and dinners at Eldon feature the gourmet creations of Chef Joel Wesley, a graduate of the Culinary Institute of America. Eldon is a popular location for weddings and parties.

Historic Interest: Danville, the last Confederate capital, is 17 miles, and a winery is 15 miles away. Day trips include treks to Lynchburg, Poplar Forest — the country home of Thomas Jefferson, the Roanoke Center Square and the scenic Blue Ridge Highway, Appomattox Courthouse (45 miles).

Innkeeper(s): Joy & Bob Lemm. $80-130. MC, VISA, PC, TC. 4 rooms, 3 with PB and 1 suite. Breakfast included in rates. Types of meals: Full gourmet bkfst, cont plus and early coffee/tea. Gourmet dinner available. Restaurant on premises. Beds: QDT. Cable TV, phone and turndown service in room. Air conditioning. Swimming and library on premises. Handicap access. Weddings, small meetings, family reunions and seminars hosted. Antiquing, Chatham Hall, parks, shopping and water sports nearby.

Publicity: *Richmond Times, Chatham Star Tribune.*

"The food, the ambiance, your wonderful hospitality made for a most charming weekend."

Chincoteague   E20

The Watson House

4240 Main St
Chincoteague, VA 23336-2801
(757)336-1564 (800)336-6787 Fax:(757)336-5776

Circa 1898. Situated in town, this "painted lady" Victorian has a large front porch overlooking Main Street. The porch is a favorite spot of guests and often the location for afternoon tea and refreshments. Beach towels, chairs and bicycles are complimentary, and there is an outdoor shower for cleaning up after sunning.

Innkeeper(s): Tom & Jacque Derrickson, David & Jo Anne Snead. $65-115. MC, VISA, PC, TC. TAC10. 6 rooms with PB and 2 cottages. Breakfast and afternoon tea included in rates. Beds: QD. Ceiling fan in room. Air conditioning. Fax and bicycles on premises. Antiquing, fishing, parks, shopping and water sports nearby.

Year Of The Horse Inn

3583 Main St
Chincoteague, VA 23336-1556
(757)336-3221 (800)680-0090
E-mail: rhebert@esva.net
Web: www.esva.net/~rhebert

Circa 1938. This inn overlooks Chincoteague Bay, and each room, except the two-bedroom apartment, has bay windows and sundecks from which to observe oyster catchers, snow geese, cormorants or a rare great blue heron. Watching sunsets over the marshes is also a regular activity. A serve-yourself-breakfast offers fruit, oatmeal, granola and homemade muffins. Chincoteague National Wildlife Refuge offers 16 miles of protected natural beach and Assateague's famous wild ponies, and it's only three miles from the inn.

Historic Interest: Chincoteague Lighthouse (3 miles).

Innkeeper(s): Richard Hebert. $55-135. MC, VISA, PC, TC. 5 rooms, 3 with PB. Breakfast included in rates. Types of meals: Cont plus and veg bkfst. Beds: KQDT. Cable TV in room. Central air. Library, outdoor grill, picnic decks and table for cookouts on premises. Weddings and family reunions hosted. French and Spanish spoken. Antiquing, art galleries, beaches, hiking, museums, parks, shopping, downhill skiing, cross-country skiing and sporting events nearby.

Columbia   F13

Upper Byrd Farm B&B

6452 River Rd W
Columbia, VA 23038-2002
(804)842-2240

Circa 1890. This 26-acre farm rests on top of a hill overlooking the James River. The scenic location is dotted with trees and wildflowers. Innkeeper Ivona Kaz-Jepsen, a native of Lithuania, had her work cut out for her when she began renovation of the house, which was inhabited by college students. She transformed the home into an artist's retreat, filling it with antiques and her own artwork. The breakfast table is set with a beautiful mix of china, and the meal is served by candlelight.

Innkeeper(s): Ivona Kaz-Jepsen. $70. 3 rooms, 2 with FP. Breakfast included in rates. Types of meals: Full gourmet bkfst and early coffee/tea. Beds: KT. Air conditioning. VCR on premises. Small meetings and seminars hosted. Antiquing, fishing and water sports nearby.

Covington   F9

Milton Hall B&B Inn

207 Thorny Ln
Covington, VA 24426-5401
(540)965-0196
E-mail: milton_h@cfw.com
Web: www.milton-hall.com

Circa 1874. This regal manor house, fashioned from handmade brick and boasting gothic details, is located in Virginia's

western highlands. The historic 44-acre estate adjoins the George Washington National Forest, where guests can enjoy hiking, biking and fishing. The home was

commissioned in 1874 by the Fitzwilliams, an English noble family. Guest rooms are furnished with Victorian antiques and reproductions, creating an authentic Victorian ambiance. Each guest room includes a sitting area and fireplace. Guests are treated to both a gourmet breakfast and afternoon refreshments. The grounds include an English country garden. Guests can peruse through gifts and antiques at Lady Milton's Attic, a shop located in the carriage house.

Historic Interest: Humpback Bridge (2 miles), Falling Springs Waterfall (5 miles), Natural Bridge (45 miles), Lost World Caverns (25 miles), Greenbrier Resort (16 miles), VMI (48 miles).

Innkeeper(s): Suzanne & Eric Stratmann. $95-150. MC, VISA, TC. TAC10. 6 rooms with PB, 6 with FP. Picnic lunch available. Beds: KQD. Turndown service in room. VCR and fax on premises. Antiquing, fishing, live theater, parks and downhill skiing nearby.

Pets allowed: Must have prior approval and requires a $100 advance deposit.

"A lovely place, a relaxing atmosphere, delicious breakfasts, gracious hospitality. We thank you."

Fairfax   C15

Bailiwick Inn

4023 Chain Bridge Rd
Fairfax, VA 22030-4101
(703)691-2266 (800)366-7666 Fax:(703)934-2112

Circa 1800. Located across from the county courthouse where George Washington's will is filed, this distinguished three-story Federal brick house recently has been renovated. The first Civil War casualty occurred on what is now the inn's lawn. The elegant, early Virginia decor is reminiscent of the state's fine plantation mansions. Ask to stay in the Thomas Jefferson Room, a replica of Mr. Jefferson's bedroom at Monticello.

Innkeeper(s): Bob & Annette Bradley. $135-309. MC, VISA, AX. 14 rooms with PB, 4 with FP, 1 suite and 1 conference room. Breakfast and afternoon tea included in rates. Types of meals: Full gourmet bkfst and early coffee/tea. Gourmet dinner available. Restaurant on premises. Beds: KQT. Cable TV, phone and turndown service in room. Air conditioning. VCR, fax and copier on premises. Weddings and small meetings hosted. Antiquing, live theater, parks, shopping and sporting events nearby.

Publicity: *Washington Post, Journal, Fairfax Connection, Inn Times, Mid-Atlantic Country, Victoria, Country Inns, Colonial Homes, Great Country Inns TV Program, Romancing America TV Program.*

"A visit to your establishment clearly transcends any lodging experience that I can recall."

Fredericksburg D15

La Vista Plantation

4420 Guinea Station Rd
Fredericksburg, VA 22408-8850
(540)898-8444 (800)529-2823

Circa 1838. La Vista has a long and unusual past, rich in Civil War history. Both Confederate and Union armies camped here, and this is where the Ninth Cavalry was sworn in. It is no won-

der then that the house is listed in the National Register of Historic Places. The house, a Classical Revival structure with high ceilings and wide pine floors, sits on 10 acres of pasture and woods. The grounds include a pond

stocked with bass. Guest quarters include a spacious room with a king-size, four-poster bed, fireplace and Empire furniture or a two-bedroom apartment that can accommodate up to six guests and includes a fireplace. Breakfasts feature homemade egg dishes from hens raised on the property.

Innkeeper(s): Michele & Edward Schiesser. $105. MC, VISA, PC, TC. TAC10. 1 rooms with PB. Breakfast included in rates. Types of meals: Full bkfst and early coffee/tea. Beds: KQDT. TV and phone in room. Air conditioning. Copier and library on premises. Amusement parks, antiquing, fishing, horseback riding, pond, rowboat and bird-watching, live theater, parks, shopping, sporting events and water sports nearby.

"Coming here was an excellent choice. La Vista is charming, quiet and restful, all qualities we were seeking. Breakfast was delicious."

The Richard Johnston Inn

711 Caroline St
Fredericksburg, VA 22401-5903
(540)899-7606

Circa 1770. Guests will find history in every nook and cranny of this 18th-century Colonial, which was built by John Tayloe. Elegant furnishings fill the tastefully decorated rooms. Guest quarters feature splendid pieces such as a pineapple-carved, four-poster bed with a matching dresser. Another guest room includes an oak bed with a scrolled six-foot headboard. The two third-floor rooms include cozy sitting areas and views of Caroline Street and the inn's courtyard. Beds are covered with fluffy pillows and comforters to ensure a restful night's sleep.

Innkeeper(s): Susan T. Williams. $95-145. MC, VISA, AX. 6 rooms with PB and 2 suites. Breakfast included in rates. Beds: KQD. Antiquing nearby.

Publicity: *Washingtonian, Rural Living, Washington Post, Philadelphia Inquirer, Fort Lauderdale Sun-Sentinel.*

Front Royal C13

Killahevlin B&B Inn

1401 N Royal Ave
Front Royal, VA 22630-3625
(540)636-7335 (800)847-6132 Fax:(540)636-8694
E-mail: kllhvln@shentel.net
Web: www.vairish.com

Circa 1905. This Edwardian Mansion is in the National Register due in part to its builder, William Carson, creator of Skyline Drive, Williamsburg, Jamestown and Yorktown. A Civil War encampment once was located on the property. Each guest room enjoys mountain views, handsome decor and a working

fireplace with antique mantels. Five rooms offer whirlpool tubs. The innkeeper shares a common Irish heritage with Will Carson. Nineteenth-century Irish cottage wallpapers and Waterford crystal add to the atmosphere. In addition to views of the Blue Ridge Mountains, the inn's three acres include two restored gazebos and an ornamental fish pool with a waterfall.

Innkeeper(s): Susan O'Kelly. $125-225. MC, VISA, AX, DC, DS, PC, TC. TAC10. 6 rooms with PB, 6 with FP, 2 suites and 1 conference room. Breakfast and snacks/refreshments included in rates. Types of meals: Full bkfst and early coffee/tea. Beds: Q. Phone, turndown service, ceiling fan, whirlpool baths and cable TV (in suites) in room. Air conditioning. Library and oriental fish pond on premises. Weddings, small meetings, family reunions and seminars hosted. Antiquing, canoeing/kayaking, fishing, golf, hiking, horseback riding, fine dining, live theater, parks, shopping, water sports and wineries nearby.

Gordonsville E13

Sleepy Hollow Farm B&B

16280 Blue Ridge Tpke
Gordonsville, VA 22942-8214
(540)832-5555 (800)215-4804 Fax:(540)832-2515
E-mail: sleepyhollowfarmbnb@ns.gemlink.com
Web: www.sleepyhollowfarmbnb.com

Circa 1785. Many generations have added to this brick farmhouse creating somewhat of an optical illusion, as the historic home appears much smaller from a distance. The pink and white room often was visited by a friendly ghost, believed to be a Red Cross nurse during the Civil War, according to local stories. She hasn't been seen since the house was blessed in 1959. Accommodations also are available in Chestnut Cottage, which offers two suites with downstairs sitting areas and bedrooms and baths upstairs. One suite has a fireplace. The other suite includes a deck, full kitchen, whirlpool room and Franklin wood stove. The grounds include abundant wildlife, flower gardens, an herb garden, a gazebo and pond for swimming and fishing.

Historic Interest: Montpelier (5 miles), James Madison Museum (6 miles), Wilderness Battlefields (30 miles), Civil War Exchange Hotel (4 miles), Fredericksburg (30 miles).

Innkeeper(s): Beverley Allison & Dorsey Comer. $65-150. MC, VISA, PC, TC. TAC10. 6 rooms with PB, 2 with FP, 2 suites and 1 cottage. Breakfast included in rates. Types of meals: Full bkfst and early coffee/tea. Snacks/refreshments available. Beds: QDT. Cable TV, phone and VCR in room. Air conditioning. Fax, swimming, library, two rooms with whirlpools. Cake and cookies available on sideboard on premises. Small meetings and family reunions hosted. Antiquing, art galleries, fishing, golf, hiking, steeplechase race, historic homes, live theater, museums, parks, shopping, downhill skiing, sporting events, tennis and wineries nearby.

Pets allowed: $10 first night, $5 each successive night. Cottage only.

"This house is truly blessed."

Harrisonburg   D12

Joshua Wilton House
412 S Main St
Harrisonburg, VA 22801-3611
(540)434-4464 Fax:(540)432-9525
E-mail: jwhouse@rica.net
Web: www.rica.net/jwhouse

Circa 1888. This beautifully restored Victorian has served as a variety of dwellings. First a family home, it was later used by a fraternity and then converted into apartments. Today, the inn offers a wonderful glimpse back into the Victorian era. Light, airy rooms are elegant, full of
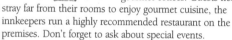
antiques, and each room includes access to a small reading area. Meals at the Wilton House are a treat. A typical breakfast at the home includes fresh fruit, pastries, delectable entrees and gourmet coffees. Guests need not stray far from their rooms to enjoy gourmet cuisine, the innkeepers run a highly recommended restaurant on the premises. Don't forget to ask about special events.

Historic Interest: The inn, surrounded by the Blue Ridge Mountains, is within walking distance of historic downtown Harrisonburg and James Madison University.

Innkeeper(s): Roberta & Craig Moore. $105-145. MC, VISA, AX, DC, DS, PC, TC. 5 rooms with PB, 1 with FP. Breakfast included in rates. Types of meals: Full gourmet bkfst, cont plus and early coffee/tea. Gourmet dinner available. Restaurant on premises. Beds: Q. Phone and ceiling fan in room. Air conditioning. Fax and copier on premises. Weddings, small meetings, family reunions and seminars hosted. Amusement parks, antiquing, fishing, parks, shopping, downhill skiing and sporting events nearby.

Irvington   F17

The Hope and Glory Inn
634 King Carter Dr
Irvington, VA 22480
(804)438-6053 (800)497-8228 Fax:(804)438-5362
Web: www.hopeandglory.com

Circa 1890. Checkerboard wood floors and interior columns add an elegant touch to this eclectic inn, which once served as a small school. A cheerful, yellow exterior with unique windows and second-story porch is accentuated by two front doors, one for the girls and one for the boys. The decor is whimsical and romantic. One guest room features a bed dressed with a flowery com-

forter and a headboard that appears as a picket fence. Another room has a hidden passageway, which leads to the private bath. Tucked behind the inn are five garden cottages, and a path leading to a private outdoor shower and secluded clawfoot tub. One of the cottages is the Meeting House, popular for small retreats and meetings. (Catered lunches and dinners are available for groups.) After enjoying a full breakfast, guests can partake in sailing, fishing, shopping and all the other surprises this Chesapeake Bay area town has to offer.

Innkeeper(s): Lizzie Wilkes. $95-175. MC, VISA, PC, TC. 7 rooms with PB, 2 suites and 4 cottages. Breakfast included in rates. Types of meals: Full bkfst and early coffee/tea. Beds: QD. VCR, fax, copier, bicycles and tennis on premises. Weddings, small meetings and family reunions hosted. Antiquing, bicycling, fishing, golf, horseback riding, sailing, bocce, croquet, historic tours, live theater, shopping and water sports nearby.

Pets allowed: in cottages.

Leesburg   B15

The Norris House Inn & Stone House Tea Room
108 Loudoun St SW
Leesburg, VA 20175
(703)777-1806 (800)644-1806 Fax:(703)771-8051
E-mail: inn@norrishouse.com
Web: norrishouse.com

Circa 1760. The Norris brothers, Northern Virginia's foremost architects and builders, purchased this building in 1850 and began extensive renovations several years later. They used the finest wood and brick available, remodeling the exterior to an Eastlake style. Beautifully restored, the inn features built-in bookcases in the library and a cherry fireplace mantel. Evening libations are served.

Historic Interest: Harpers Ferry (18 miles), Antietam Battlefield (30 minutes), Manassas Battlefield (30 minutes), Washington, D.C. (32 miles), Gettysburg (50 miles).

Innkeeper(s): Pamela & Don McMurray. $80-145. MC, VISA, AX, DC, CB, DS, PC, TC. TAC10. 6 rooms, 3 with FP and 3 conference rooms. Breakfast included in rates. Types of meals: Full bkfst and early coffee/tea. Afternoon tea available. Beds: QD. Turndown service in room. Air conditioning. Fax and library on premises. Weddings, small meetings, family reunions and seminars hosted. Antiquing, fishing, hiking, biking, parks, shopping and water sports nearby.

Publicity: *New York Times, Better Homes & Gardens, Washingtonian, Country Home.*

"Thank you for your gracious hospitality. We enjoyed everything about your lovely home, especially the extra little touches that really make the difference."

Lexington   F11

Stoneridge Bed & Breakfast
PO Box 38
Lexington, VA 24450
(540)463-4090 (800)491-2930 Fax:(540)463-6078
E-mail: rollo_va@cfw.com
Web: www.webfeat-inc.com/stoneridge

Circa 1829. The Shenandoah Valley is the setting for this bed & breakfast, located on 36 secluded acres of woods, streams and rolling fields. The inn was built using bricks made on the property, and once served as a plantation home and possibly a stagecoach stop. The home still

maintains original heart-of-pine floors, ornate mantels and other period features. Guest rooms feature antiques, some are family heirlooms. Four guest rooms include fireplaces, and three offer double Jacuzzi tubs. Several rooms have a mountain view. A variety of reading material is available in the library. Stoneridge offers a large selection of Virginia wines to its guests for purchase. The gourmet country breakfasts might include blueberry buckle, stuffed French toast and baked eggs. The meal is served either in the candle-lit dining room or on the back patio.

Innkeeper(s): Norm & Barbara Rollenhagen. $95-160. MC, VISA, AX, DS, PC, TC. TAC11. 5 rooms with PB, 4 with FP and 1 suite. Breakfast included in rates. Type of meal: Full bkfst. Afternoon tea available. Beds: Q. Turndown service, ceiling fan and jacuzzi tubs for two in room. Air conditioning. VCR, fax and library on premises. Antiquing, fishing, live theater, parks, shopping and cross-country skiing nearby.

Publicity: *News-Gazette, Blue Ridge Country.*

Lincoln   B14

Springdale Country Inn

Rt 2, Box 356
Lincoln, VA 20160
(540)338-1832 Fax:(540)338-1839
E-mail: springdale@vmcs.com
Web: www.springdalecountryinn.com

Circa 1832. Recently restored for historic certification, the Springdale Country Inn was once a schoolhouse, Civil War hospital and travelers' inn. The inn, with its high ceilings and windows, has richly burnished wide-board floors, reproduction wallpaper and period antiques. Guest rooms have fresh flowers, stenciled walls and four-poster canopy beds. Several offer private baths and fireplaces. Enjoy the sun and sitting porch, pleasant gardens and local folklore of the area and the school itself. Vineyards and Civil War battlefields are located nearby.

Innkeeper(s): Nancy & Roger Fones. $95-125. MC, VISA, PC. TAC8. 9 rooms, 6 with PB, 4 with FP, 2 suites and 2 conference rooms. Breakfast included in rates. Type of meal: Full bkfst. Catering service available. Beds: DT. TV in room. VCR, fax, copier and library on premises. Handicap access. Weddings, small meetings, family reunions and seminars hosted. Antiquing, live theater and shopping nearby.

Publicity: *Pamphlet, Washington Post.*

"Quaint setting and excellent meals."

Locust Dale   D13

The Inn at Meander Plantation

HC 5, Box 460A
Locust Dale, VA 22948-9701
(540)672-4912 (800)385-4936 Fax:(540)672-0405
E-mail: inn@meander.net
Web: www.meander.net

Circa 1766. This elegant country estate was built by Henry Fry, close friend of Thomas Jefferson, who often stopped here on his way to Monticello. Ancient formal boxwood gardens, woodland and meadows are enjoyed by guests as well as views

of the Blue Ridge Mountains from the rockers on the back porches. The mansion is decorated serenely with elegant antiques and period reproductions, including queen-

size, four-poster beds. The innkeeper is a food writer and will prepare special breakfasts for individual diets. Full dinner service and picnic baskets are available with advance reservations.

Historic Interest: Prehistoric Native American site on the property near the Robinson River. James and Dolley Madison's home (10 miles), Civil War battlefields: Cedar Mountain (4 miles), Brandy Station (15 miles), Manassas and Bull Run (50 miles).

Innkeeper(s): Bob & Suzie Blanchard, Suzanne Thomas. $110-200. MC, VISA, AX, PC, TC. TAC10. 8 rooms with PB, 5 with FP, 4 suites and 1 conference room. Breakfast included in rates. Types of meals: Full bkfst and early coffee/tea. Gourmet dinner, snacks/refreshments, picnic lunch and lunch available. Beds: KQD. Air conditioning. VCR, fax, stables, library, pet boarding and child care on premises. Weddings, small meetings, family reunions and seminars hosted. Antiquing, fishing, live theater, parks, shopping, downhill skiing, cross-country skiing and sporting events nearby.

Pets allowed: In dependencies only. Stabling for horses available.

"Staying at the Inn at Meander Plantation feels like being immersed in another century while having the luxuries and amenities available today."

Luray   C13

The Ruffner House

440 Ruffner House Rd
Luray, VA 22835-9704
(540)743-7855 (800)969-7855

Circa 1840. Situated on a farm nestled in the heart of the Shenandoah Valley, this stately manor was built by Peter Ruffner, the first settler of Page Valley and Luray. Ruffner family members discovered a cavern opposite the entrance to the Luray Caverns, which were found later. Purebred Arabian horses graze in the pasture on this 23-acre estate.

Innkeeper(s): Sonia Croucher. $98-150. PC, TC. 6 rooms with PB, 2 with FP. Breakfast included in rates. Types of meals: Full bkfst and early coffee/tea. Gourmet dinner, snacks/refreshments and picnic lunch available. Beds: QD. TV and ceiling fan in room. Air conditioning. VCR and spa on premises. Weddings, small meetings, family reunions and seminars hosted. Antiquing, canoeing/kayaking, fishing, golf, parks, shopping, downhill skiing, cross-country skiing and sporting events nearby.

Publicity: *Page News & Courier, Virginian Pilot.*

"This is the loveliest inn we have ever stayed in. We were made to feel very welcome and at ease."

Shenandoah River Inn

201 Stagecoach Ln
Luray, VA 22835
(540)743-1144 (888)666-6760 Fax:(540)743-9101

Circa 1812. This gracious two-and-a-half-story white colonial inn, located on four landscaped acres along the Shenandoah River, was once a stagecoach stop. Graceful walnut trees and fruit trees dot the property's wide lawns. There are three screened porches, all with water views. Guest rooms each have fireplaces, marble-floored baths and king or queen beds. Antiques, paintings, mirrors and a fireplace decorate the parlor. Gourmet candle-lit breakfasts may include Belgian waffles, fruit plate and breakfast meats. Seven-course dinners are available.

Picnic by the river or try your hand at smallmouth-bass fishing. The innkeepers also offer a secluded cabin surrounded by national forest and on top of a mountain with 50-mile views.

Innkeeper(s): Paul Bramell & Ann Merrigan. $135-145. MC, VISA, AX, PC, TC. TAC10. 4 rooms with PB, 4 with FP and 1 cabin. Breakfast and afternoon tea included in rates. Types of meals: Full gourmet bkfst and early coffee/tea. Gourmet dinner and picnic lunch available. Beds: KQ. Air conditioning. VCR, copier and swimming on premises. Handicap access. Weddings, small meetings, family reunions and seminars hosted. Antiquing, golf, horseback riding, parks, shopping, downhill skiing and water sports nearby.
Publicity: *Washingtonian.*

Woodruff House Collection

330 Mechanic St
Luray, VA 22835-1808
(540)743-1494 Fax:(540)743-1722
Web: www.woodruffinns.com

Circa 1882. Prepare to be pampered. The Woodruffs entered the B&B business after years of experience in hotel management and restaurant businesses. They have not missed a detail, ensuring a perfect, relaxing visit. The Rooftop Skylight Fireside Jacuzzi Suite is often the room of choice because of its interesting shape and architecture, located where the attic was before restoration. The suite boasts skylights, Jacuzzi tub for two and antique stained glass. Tasteful antiques and fresh bouquets of flowers framed by candlelight add a special ambiance.

Besides the extra attention and comfortable accommodations, the Woodruffs include afternoon dessert tea, early morning coffee or tea and a full fireside gourmet breakfast in the rates. Candlelight sets the mood for the gourmet dinner, and none of the spectacular meals are to be missed. A romantic finish to each evening is a private dip in one of the garden hot tubs.

Historic Interest: New Market Battlefield (20 minutes), the famous underground Luray Caverns discovered in the late 1800s (minutes away).
Innkeeper(s): Lucas & Deborah Woodruff. $135-295. MC, VISA, DS, PC, TC. TAC10. 5 rooms with PB, 9 with FP, 4 suites and 1 conference room. Breakfast, afternoon tea and dinner included in rates. MAP. Types of meals: Full gourmet bkfst and early coffee/tea. Catering service available. Beds: KQ. Ceiling fan and coffee makers (some rooms) in room. Air conditioning. Fax, spa, two outdoor gardens and Jacuzzi tubs for two on premises. Weddings, small meetings and family reunions hosted. Antiquing, fishing, caverns, Shenandoah River, Skyline Drive, parks, shopping, downhill skiing and water sports nearby.
Publicity: *Potomac Living, Cascapades Magazine, Blue Ridge Country Magazine.*

"The place is great. There aren't words to explain!"

Lynchburg   G11

Federal Crest Inn

1101 Federal St
Lynchburg, VA 24504-3018
(804)845-6155 (800)818-6155 Fax:(804)845-1445

Circa 1909. The guest rooms at Federal Crest are named for the many varieties of trees and flowers native to Virginia. This handsome red brick home, a fine example of Georgian Revival architecture, features a commanding front entrance flanked by

columns that hold up the second-story veranda. A grand staircase, carved woodwork, polished floors topped with fine rugs and more columns create an aura of elegance. Each guest room offers something special and romantic,

from a mountain view to a Jacuzzi tub. Breakfasts are served on fine china, and the first course is always a freshly baked muffin with a secret message inside.

Historic Interest: Appomattox Court House and Jefferson's Poplar Forest.
Innkeeper(s): Ann & Phil Ripley. $95-125. MC, VISA, AX, DS, PC, TC. 5 rooms, 4 with PB, 3 with FP, 2 suites and 1 conference room. Breakfast, afternoon tea and snacks/refreshments included in rates. Types of meals: Full bkfst and early coffee/tea. Beds: Q. Cable TV, turndown service, portable telephone and portable VCR in room. Air conditioning. Fax, copier, library, conference theater with 60-inch TV (Ballroom) with stage and 50's cafe with antique jukebox on premises. Weddings, small meetings, family reunions and seminars hosted. Antiquing, fishing, golf, live theater, parks, shopping, sporting events and tennis nearby.
Publicity: *Washington Post, News & Advance.*

"What a wonderful place to celebrate our birthdays and enjoy our last romantic getaway before the birth of our first child."

Lynchburg Mansion Inn B&B

405 Madison St
Lynchburg, VA 24504-2455
(804)528-5400 (800)352-1199 Fax:(804)847-2545
E-mail: mansioninn@aol.com
Web: www.lynchburgmansioninn.com

Circa 1914. This regal, Georgian mansion, with its majestic Greek Revival columns, is located on a brick-paved street in the Garland Hill Historic District. The grand hall showcases an oak and cherry staircase that leads up to the solarium. Breakfasts are served in the formal dining room on antique china. Romantic rooms feature inviting touches such as a four-poster beds, Laura Ashley and Ralph Lauren linens, Battenburg lace pillows and some include fireplaces. The Veranda Suite, as the name suggests, opens onto a romantic circular veranda and a treetop sunroom. The Garden Suite, with its private garden entrance, includes an original clawfoot tub. There is a hot tub on the back porch, and the innkeepers have added gardens full of perennials, herbs, edible flowers and more, including a picturesque gazebo. Lynchburg offers many exciting activities, including the unique Community Market and plenty of galleries, antique shops and boutiques. Ski areas are about 45 minutes from the inn.

Historic Interest: Poplar Forest, Thomas Jefferson's retreat and Appomattox Court House are among dozens of historic attractions in the area. The Old City Cemetery serves as the resting place for more than 2,500 Confederate soldiers. The home of acclaimed poet and figure of the Harlem Renaissance, Anne Spencer is nearby, as are five historic districts.
Innkeeper(s): Mauranna and Bob Sherman. $109-144. MC, VISA, AX, DC. 5 rooms with PB, 3 with FP, 2 suites and 1 conference room. Breakfast included in rates. Types of meals: Full gourmet bkfst and early coffee/tea. Gourmet dinner available. Beds: KQ. Cable TV, phone and turndown service in room. Air conditioning. Period library on premises. Handicap access. Weddings, small meetings, family reunions and seminars hosted. Antiquing, live theater, shopping, downhill skiing and sporting events nearby.
Publicity: *News & Advance, Roanoker.*

"The Lynchburg Mansion Inn is the creme de la creme. You have earned all sorts of pats on the back for the restoration and hospitality you offer. It is truly elegant."

Mathews G17

Ravenswood Inn

PO Box 1430
Mathews, VA 23109-1430
(804)725-7272

Circa 1913. This intimate waterfront home is located on five acres along the banks of the East River, where passing boats still harvest crabs and oysters. A long screened porch captures river breezes. Most rooms feature a river view and are decorated in Victorian, country, nautical or wicker. Williamsburg, Jamestown and Yorktown are within an hour.

Innkeeper(s): Mrs. Ricky Durham. $70-120. MC, VISA, TC. 5 rooms with PB. Breakfast included in rates. Types of meals: Full gourmet bkfst and early coffee/tea. Beds: KQ. Ceiling fan in room. Air conditioning. VCR and spa on premises. Weddings, small meetings and family reunions hosted. Amusement parks, antiquing, live theater, shopping, sporting events and water sports nearby.
Publicity: *Virginian Pilot, Daily Press.*

"While Ravenswood is one of the most beautiful places we've ever been, it is your love, caring and friendship that has made it such a special place for us."

Middletown B13

Wayside Inn Since 1797

7783 Main St
Middletown, VA 22645-9502
(703)869-1797 Fax:(703)869-6038
E-mail: waysiden@shentel.net
Web: www.waysideofva.com

Circa 1797. Head back to colonial times at this former stagecoach stop. The guest rooms are decorated tastefully with period furnishings, each is individually appointed. Some rooms include canopied beds. Fresh flowers add a special touch. The inn's ample collection of antiques is further displayed in the dining room, where guests enjoy breakfasts, lunch and perhaps a gourmet dinner. Coachyard Lounge offers a casual dinner choice in a pub setting. Conferences, receptions and weddings often are held at the inn's Larrick's Tavern, which dates back to 1724. Historians can spend the day on a tour of historic homes or at a Civil War battlefield. Museums, antique shops, wineries and ski areas are just a few of the other options.

Innkeeper(s): Jef Lindstrom & Diana Phillips. $95-150. MC, VISA, AX, DC, DS. 22 rooms with PB and 5 conference rooms. Breakfast, dinner and picnic lunch included in rates. Type of meal: Full gourmet bkfst. Lunch available. Beds: KQDT. Fax and copier on premises. Antiquing, beaches, canoeing/kayaking, fishing, golf, hiking, live theater, museums, parks, shopping, downhill skiing, cross-country skiing and wineries nearby.
Publicity: *Mid-Atlantic Country.*

Mineral E14

Littlepage Inn

15701 Monrovia Rd
Mineral, VA 23117-5011
(540)854-9861 (800)248-1803 Fax:(540)854-7998
E-mail: littlepage@earthlink.net
Web: www.littlepage.com

Circa 1811. Two old fieldstone posts mark the country lane to this large plantation home, on the National Register. Heart pine

floors and original glass window panes were preserved in a recent prize-winning restoration. The spacious rooms are filled with period furnishings, many original to the house. The inn's 125 acres offer gardens, fields, a wooded spring, a 19th-century smokehouse, ice house with Jacuzzi, barn and stable.

Innkeeper(s): Rob & Sarah Scardina. $99-145. 8 rooms with PB, 3 with FP. Type of meal: Full bkfst. Dinner and picnic lunch available. Phone and central air & heat in room. Weddings, small meetings, family reunions and seminars hosted. Antiquing and shopping nearby.

Nellysford F12

The Mark Addy

Rt 151 at Rt 613W, Box 375
Nellysford, VA 22958-9526
(804)361-1101 (800)278-2154
E-mail: markaddy@symweb.com
Web: www.symweb.com/rockfish/mark.html

Circa 1837. It's not hard to understand why Dr. John Everett, the son of Thomas Jefferson's physician, chose this picturesque, Blue Mountain setting for his home. Everett expanded the simple, four-room farmhouse already present into a gracious manor. The well-appointed guest rooms feature double whirlpool baths, double showers or a clawfoot tub. Beds are covered with vintage linens, feather pillows and cozy, down comforters. There are plenty of relaxing possibilities, including five porches and a hammock set among the trees.

Historic Interest: Dr. John Coleman Everett (son of Thomas Jefferson's physician) bought the estate in 1884.
Innkeeper(s): John Storck Maddox. $90-135. MC, VISA, PC, TC. TAC10. 9 rooms with PB and 1 suite. EP. Types of meals: Full gourmet bkfst, cont and early coffee/tea. Afternoon tea, gourmet dinner, picnic lunch, gourmet lunch, banquet service, catering service and catered breakfast available. Beds: KQDT. Ceiling fan and jacuzzi in room. Air conditioning. VCR and library on premises. Handicap access. Weddings, small meetings and family reunions hosted. German spoken. Antiquing, fishing, horseback riding, hiking, live theater, parks, shopping, downhill skiing and sporting events nearby.

The Meander Inn

3100 Berry Hill Rd
Nellysford, VA 22958-0443
(804)361-1121 Fax:(804)361-1380
E-mail: meanderinn@aol.com
Web: www.bbonline.com/va/meanderinn/

Circa 1913. Meander Inn rests on a hill overlooking the Blue Ridge Mountains and the inn's 40 picturesque acres with views of rolling meadows, horse pastures and woods. Inviting guest rooms are appointed with Victorian, French and Japanese furnishings and provide an elegant country experience. The innkeepers offer a special option for their farm-loving guests, which includes rising with the rooster's crow and helping to feed the horses and select eggs for the morning's hearty full breakfast. On weekends French Provencal cookery is featured at dinner if arranged in advance. Explore the idyllic grounds via hiking trails, enjoy the swimming hole or plan a picnic on the lush banks of Rockfish River, which winds its way through the property. Horse boarding is offered. The area offers many activities, including skiing, horseback riding, golf, tennis, fishing, biking and antique shopping or touring the local wineries.

Historic Interest: Monticello Ash Lawn (30 minutes).

Innkeeper(s): Alain & Francesca San Giorgio. $95-125. MC, VISA, AX, DC. 5 rooms with PB. Types of meals: Full gourmet bkfst and country bkfst. Dinner available. Beds: KQ. Ceiling fan in room. Air conditioning. VCR, spa, swimming, library and croquet on premises. Weddings hosted. French, Spanish, Italian and Japanese spoken. Antiquing, bicycling, fishing, golf, hiking, horseback riding, shopping, downhill skiing and tennis nearby.

"The setting was perfect. Your caring attitude was obvious, and you really made our first experience at a B&B memorable."

New Church   E19

The Garden and The Sea Inn

4188 Nelson Rd, #275
New Church, VA 23415-0275
(757)824-0672 (800)824-0672

Circa 1802. Gingerbread trim, a pair of brightly colored gables and two, adjacent verandas adorn the exterior of this Victorian. A warm, rich Victorian decor permeates the antique-filled guest rooms, an ideal setting for romance. Several rooms include whirlpool tubs. The inn's dining room serves gourmet dinners with an emphasis on fresh catch-es from the waters of the Eastern shore, but many continental items are featured as well.

Innkeeper(s): Tom & Sara Baker. $75-175. MC, VISA, AX, DS, PC, TC. TAC10. 6 rooms with PB and 1 conference room. Breakfast included in rates. Type of meal: Cont plus. Gourmet dinner, snacks/refreshments, picnic lunch, banquet service and catering service available. Restaurant on premises. Beds: Q. Ceiling fan in room. Air conditioning. VCR, fax, copier and library on premises. Handicap access. Antiquing, fishing, beach, parks, shopping and water sports nearby.

Pets allowed: quiet and leashed outside.

New Market   C12

Cross Roads Inn B&B

9222 John Sevier Rd
New Market, VA 22844-9649
(540)740-4157
E-mail: freisitz@shentel.net
Web: www.crossroadsinnva.com

Circa 1925. This Victorian is full of Southern hospitality and European charm. The innkeepers serve imported Austrian coffee alongside the homemade breakfasts, and strudel is served as an afternoon refreshment. The home is decorated like an English garden, laced with antiques, some of which are family pieces. Four-poster and canopy beds are topped with fluffy, down comforters. The historic downtown area is within walking distance.

Innkeeper(s): Mary Lloyd & Roland Freisitzer. $55-100. MC, VISA, TC. 6 rooms with PB, 1 with FP and 1 conference room. Breakfast, afternoon tea and snacks/refreshments included in rates. Meals: Full gourmet bkfst and early coffee/tea. Beds: KQDT. Turndown service in room. Air conditioning. VCR, fax and copier on premises. Handicap access. Weddings, small meetings, family reunions and seminars hosted. Antiquing, fishing, musical summer festivals, live theater, parks, shopping, downhill skiing, sporting events and water sports nearby.

Orange   E13

Hidden Inn

249 Caroline St
Orange, VA 22960-1529
(540)672-3625 Fax:(540)672-5029

Circa 1880. Acres of huge old trees can be seen from the wraparound veranda of this Victorian inn nestled in the Virginia countryside. Guests are pampered with afternoon tea, and a candlelight picnic can be ordered. Monticello, Montpelier, wineries, shopping and antiquing all are nearby. After a day of exploring the area, guests can return to the inn for afternoon refreshments and then head out for dinner at a local restaurant.

Historic Interest: The house was built by a descendent of Thomas Jefferson.

Innkeeper(s): Barbara & Ray Lonick, Chrys Dermody. $99-169. MC, VISA, AX, PC, TC. TAC10. 10 rooms with PB, 2 with FP and 2 cottages. Breakfast and afternoon tea included in rates. Types of meals: Full bkfst and early coffee/tea. Gourmet dinner available. Beds: KQDT. TV in room. Fax on premises. Weddings, small meetings, family reunions and seminars hosted. Spanish spoken. Antiquing, fishing, Monticello, Montpelier Civil War sites, wineries, live theater, shopping, sporting events and water sports nearby.

"It just doesn't get any better than this!"

Mayhurst Inn

12460 Mayhurst Ln
Orange, VA 22960
(540)672-5597 (888)672-5597 Fax:(540)672-7447
E-mail: bharmon527@aol.com
Web: www.bbonline.com/va/mayhurst

Circa 1859. The great-nephew of President James Madison, Col. John Willis built Mayhurst, an extravagant Italianate Victorian villa. It is noted for its fanciful architecture and oval spiral staircase ascending four floors to a rooftop tower. Thirty-seven acres of old oaks, cedars and magnolias surround the inn. The grounds also include a pond. Generals Lee, A. P. Hill and Stonewall Jackson were among the guests. During the winter of 1863-64, the army of Northern Virginia was head-quartered at Mayhurst and more than 18,000 men were commanded by General A. P. Hill from a tent in the home's front yard under the ash tree, still present.

Historic Interest: National Register, Virginia Historic Landmark.

Innkeeper(s): Bob & Peg Harmon. $115-200. MC, VISA, AX, DS, PC, TC. TAC10. 7 rooms with PB, 5 with FP and 2 suites. Breakfast and snacks/refreshments included in rates. Types of meals: Full bkfst and early coffee/tea. Beds: KQT. Phone in room. Air conditioning. VCR, fax and copier on premises. Handicap access. Weddings, small meetings, family reunions and seminars hosted. Antiquing, bicycling, fishing, golf, Civil War battlefields, Presidential homes and wineries nearby.

"The beauty of this Inn is exceeded only by the graciousness of Mayhurst hosts: Peg and Bob."

Petersburg G15

The High Street Inn

405 High St
Petersburg, VA 23803-3857
(804)733-0505 (888)733-0505 Fax:(804)861-2319
E-mail: highst@mail.ctg.net

Circa 1890. Victorians have a way of standing out, and this Queen Anne is particularly unique, fashioned from creamy, yellow bricks. The innkeepers have decorated the home with Victorian antique beds, dressers and Virginia period pieces. Among the impressive antiques is a carved walnut bed in the Sycamore Suite. The 7,000-square-foot home still has its original gaslight fixtures and eight fireplaces, each decorated with different tiles and mantels. Walk to restaurants and antique shops or enjoy the nearby Civil War battlefields and museums. The inn, which is close to Richmond and Williamsburg, is a two-and-a-half-hour drive from Washington, D.C., and just minutes from I-95 and I-85.

Innkeeper(s): Jim Hillier/Jon Hackett. $80-125. MC, VISA, DS, PC, TC. TAC10. 6 rooms, 4 with PB, 4 with FP and 2 suites. Breakfast included in rates. Type of meal: Full bkfst. Room service available. Beds: KQDT. Cable TV, phone and ceiling fan in room. Air conditioning. VCR and fax on premises. Weddings, small meetings, family reunions and seminars hosted. Antiquing, golf, parks and sporting events nearby.

Pets allowed: $10 per day.

Mayfield Inn

PO Box 2265
Petersburg, VA 23804-1565
(804)861-6775 (800)538-2381

Circa 1750. Mayfield Inn is the oldest existing brick building in Dinwiddie County, and although many records have been lost, its probable first resident was a member of the Virginia House of

Burgesses. During the Civil War, two Confederate defense lines were set up on the Mayfield Inn's grounds, and the battles were viewed by General Lee. Now where battles once raged, the grounds boast a swimming pool and large herb garden. The guests quarters feature pine floors, Oriental rugs, antiques and period reproductions. The dining room, where hearty country breakfasts are served, boasts Chippendale chairs, a fireplace and cupboards full of English china.

Historic Interest: Mayfield Inn is listed as a state and national landmark. The James River Plantations are within 30 minutes of the inn, and it's just a few miles to Petersburg's National Battlefield Park and Petersburg's historic district. Williamsburg and Jamestown are about an hour away.

Innkeeper(s): Cherry Turner. $69-95. MC, VISA, AX, PC, TC. 4 rooms with PB and 2 suites. Breakfast and afternoon tea included in rates. Type of meal: Full bkfst. Beds: Q. Antiquing, battlefields and historic sites nearby.

Publicity: *Richmond News Leader.*

"We did truly feel at home in your well restored surroundings."

Port Haywood G18

Tabb's Creek Inn

PO Box 219 Rt 14 Mathews Co
Port Haywood, VA 23138-0219
(804)725-5136 Fax:(804)725-5136

Circa 1820. Surrounded by 30 acres of woods and located on the banks of Tabb's Creek, this post-Colonial farm features a detached guest cottage. There are maple, elm, magnolia trees and 150 rose bushes on the property. The suites and guest rooms feature fireplaces and antiques. Boats for rowing and canoeing, docks, a swimming pool, and private waterview porches make this an especially attractive getaway for those seeking a dose of seclusion.

Historic Interest: Williamsburg (45 miles), Norfolk (50 miles), Yorktown (25 miles).

Innkeeper(s): Cabell & Catherine Venable. $125. PC, TC. 4 rooms with PB, 1 with FP and 2 suites. Breakfast included in rates. Types of meals: Full bkfst and early coffee/tea. Beds: KQD. Turndown service, ceiling fan and VCR in room. Air conditioning. Fax, copier, swimming, bicycles and library on premises. Weddings, small meetings and family reunions hosted. Antiquing, fishing and fine restaurants nearby.

Pets Allowed.

"A spot of tea with a bit of heaven. Truly exceptional hosts. The best B&Bs I've happened across!"

Providence Forge G16

Jasmine Plantation B&B Inn

4500 N Courthouse Rd
Providence Forge, VA 23140-3428
(804)966-9836 (800)639-5368 Fax:(804)966-5679

Circa 1750. Few travelers can boast that they have stayed at a mid-18th-century plantation. Jasmine Plantation is just such a place. Surrounded by more than 40 acres of Virginia countryside, it's not difficult to understand why the Morris family chose this spot for their home. The property's first dwelling was built as early as the 1680s. Several guest rooms are named for members of the Morris Family, and all are decorated with antiques. The Rose Room features Victorian furnishings and a whirlpool bath. The George Morris Room includes 19th-century pieces, a fireplace and clawfoot tub. Memorabilia from multiple centuries add special charm to the place. The innkeepers have antique irons, old books and magazines and a sampling of vintage advertising signs for Philip Morris or Coca-Cola. Breakfasts are a true Southern treat with items such as sweet potato biscuits and homemade jams and jellies.

Innkeeper(s): Howard & Joyce Vogt. $75-120. MC, VISA, AX, PC, TC. TAC10. 6 rooms, 5 with PB, 4 with FP. Breakfast and snacks/refreshments included in rates. Types of meals: Full bkfst and early coffee/tea. Beds: QD. Ceiling fan in room. Air conditioning. VCR on premises. Weddings, small meetings, family reunions and seminars hosted. Amusement parks, antiquing, fishing, golf, sporting clays, horse racing, parks, shopping and water sports nearby.

"We were charmed by the plantation accommodations and the kindness of the beautiful host and hostess."

Raphine E11

Willow Pond Farm Country House

137 Pisgah Rd
Raphine, VA 24472
(540)348-1310 (800)945-6763 Fax:(540)348-1359

Circa 1800. If visions of rolling hills, woods and the picturesque Shenandoah Valley are what you have in mind for a peaceful getaway, this Victorian farmhouse is an ideal location. Surrounded by more than 170 acres, guests are sure to enjoy this secluded bed & breakfast. There are four well-appointed, romantically styled guest rooms, featuring traditional furnishings and a few Victorian pieces. In addition, there are two suites available. The suites include double whirlpool tubs and private entrances that lead out to the pool and garden. The innkeepers pamper guests with a gourmet breakfast and afternoon tea. In addition, the hosts will arrange for guests to enjoy a five-course dinner served by candlelight on a table set with fine linens, china and crystal.

Innkeeper(s): Carol Ann & Walter P. Schendel. $115-190. MC, VISA, AX, PC, TC. 4 rooms with PB and 2 suites. Breakfast and afternoon tea included in rates. Types of meals: Full gourmet bkfst and early coffee/tea. Picnic lunch available. Beds: KQD. Turndown service and ceiling fan in room. Air conditioning. VCR, fax, copier and library on premises. Weddings and family reunions hosted. Antiquing, fishing, hiking, natural wonders, mountains, live theater, parks, shopping, downhill skiing, cross-country skiing, sporting events and water sports nearby.

"A jewel in the country! A perfect 10...many thanks!"

Richmond F15

The Emmanuel Hutzler House

2036 Monument Ave
Richmond, VA 23220-2708
(804)353-6900 Fax:(804)355-5053
E-mail: be.our.guest@bensonhouse.com
Web: www.bensonhouse.com

Circa 1914. This graciously restored Italian Renaissance home is a showcase of mahogany paneling and tastefully decorated rooms. Its 8,000 square feet includes a stunning parlor with handsome antiques, leaded-glass windows and a marble fireplace. The largest room boasts a four-poster mahogany bed, antique sofa and a private Jacuzzi tucked into an enormous bathroom. Breakfast is served in the formal dining room of this non-smoking inn. There is a resident cat at this home.

Innkeeper(s): Lyn M. Benson & John E. Richardson. $95-155. MC, VISA, AX, DC, DS, PC, TC. TAC7. 2 suites. Breakfast included in rates. AP. Types of meals: Full bkfst, cont plus and early coffee/tea. Beds: KQT. Cable TV and phone in room. Air conditioning. Fax and library on premises. Antiquing, live theater, parks and sporting events nearby.

"I'm glad there are still people like you who painstakingly restore great old houses such as this. A great job of reconstruction and beautifully decorated! Delightful hosts!"

Roanoke G9

The Inn at Burwell Place

601 W Main St
Roanoke, VA 24153-3515
(540)387-0250 (800)891-0250 Fax:(540)387-3279

Circa 1907. This Colonial Revival was built by a local industrialist, but it took its name from Nathanial Burwell, who owned the land prior to the home's construction. Antique cherry and walnut furnishings decorate guest rooms, and beds are covered with down comforters, designer linens and European bedspreads. Suites with a fireplace and whirlpool tub are offered. Robes and baskets with bath amenities are some of the thoughtful touches provided by the innkeepers.

Innkeeper(s): Cindi Lou MacMackin & Mark Bukowski. $90-130. MC, VISA, AX, DS, PC, TC. TAC10. 4 rooms with PB, 1 with FP and 2 suites. Breakfast included in rates. Types of meals: Full bkfst, cont and early coffee/tea. Banquet service and catering service available. Beds: Q. Cable TV, phone, ceiling fan, down comforters and newspapers in room. Air conditioning. VCR and fax on premises. Weddings hosted. Amusement parks, antiquing, fishing, live theater, parks, shopping, sporting events and water sports nearby.

"It was truly elegant, a day I will always remember!"

Scottsville F13

High Meadows Vineyard & Mtn Sunset Inn

Highmeadows Ln
Scottsville, VA 24590
(804)286-2218 (800)232-1832 Fax:(804)286-2124
E-mail: peterhmi@aol.com
Web: www.highmeadows.com

Circa 1832. Minutes from Charlottesville on the Constitution Highway (Route 20), High Meadows stands on 50 acres of gardens, forests, ponds, a creek and a vineyard. Listed in the National Register, it is actually two historic homes joined by a breezeway as well as a turn-of-the-century Queen Anne manor house. The inn is fur-nished in Federal and Victorian styles. Guests are treated to gracious Virginia hospitality in an elegant and peaceful setting with wine tasting and a romantic candlelight dinner every evening. There are two private hot tubs on the grounds.

Historic Interest: Jefferson, Monroe, Madison homes (15-20 miles), a Civil War trail site nearby.

Innkeeper(s): Peter Sushka & Mary Jae Abbitt. $84-195. MC, VISA, AX, DS. 14 rooms with PB, 12 with FP, 5 suites and 1 conference room. Breakfast included in rates. Type of meal: Full gourmet bkfst. Dinner available. Restaurant on premises. Beds: KQDT. Turndown service and ceiling fan in room. Air conditioning. Spa on premises. Handicap access. Weddings, small meetings, family reunions and seminars hosted. Antiquing, fishing, live theater, shopping, downhill skiing, cross-country skiing, sporting events and water sports nearby.

Stanley D13

Jordan Hollow Farm Inn

326 Hawkisbill Park Rd
Stanley, VA 22851-4506
(540)778-2285 (888)418-7000 Fax:(540)778-1759
E-mail: jhfc@jordanhollow.com
Web: jordanhollow.com

Circa 1790. Nestled in the foothills of the Blue Ridge Mountains, this delightful 145-acre horse farm is ideal for those who love riding and country living. The colonial farm house is decorated with antiques and country artifacts.
Gentle trail horses are available for guided one-hour rides. Horse boarding is available as is five miles of walking trails on the property.
Historic Interest: New Market Battlefield Museum, Luray Caverness, Skyline Drive.
Innkeeper(s): Gail Kyle & Betty Anderson. $140-190. MC, VISA, DC, CB, DS. 15 rooms with PB, 11 with FP and 1 conference room. Breakfast included in rates. Type of meal: Full bkfst. Dinner and picnic lunch available. Restaurant on premises. Beds: KQ. Fax and copier on premises. Parks, cross-country skiing and water sports nearby.

"I keep thinking of my day at your lovely inn and keep dreaming of that wonderful lemon mousse cake!"

Staunton E11

Ashton Country House

1205 Middlebrook Ave
Staunton, VA 24401-4546
(540)885-7819 (800)296-7819 Fax:(540)885-6029

Circa 1860. This Greek Revival home is surrounded by 25 explorable acres where cows roam and birds frolic in the trees. A mix of traditional and Victorian antiques grace the interior. Four of the guest rooms include a fireplace, and each is

appointed individually. The inn's porches, where afternoon tea often is served, are lined with chairs for those who seek relaxation and the scenery of rolling hills. Woodrow Wilson's birthplace is among the town's notable attractions.
Innkeeper(s): Dorie & Vince Di Stefano. $70-125. MC, VISA, AX, PC, TC. 6 rooms with PB. Breakfast, afternoon tea and snacks/refreshments included in rates. Beds: Q. Ceiling fan and fireplace (four rooms) in room. Central air. VCR on premises. Handicap access. Small meetings and family reunions hosted. Antiquing, fishing, museums, parks, shopping and water sports nearby.
Pets allowed: with prior arrangement.

Thornrose House at Gypsy Hill

531 Thornrose Ave
Staunton, VA 24401-3161
(540)885-7026 (800)861-4338

Circa 1912. A columned veranda wraps around two sides of this gracious red brick Georgian-style house. Two sets of Greek pergolas grace the lawns and there are gardens of azalea, rhododendron and hydrangea. The inn is furnished with a mix of antique oak and walnut period pieces and overstuffed English country chairs. Bircher muesli, and hot-off-the-griddle whole

grain banana pecan pancakes are popular breakfast items, served in the dining room (fireside on cool days). Across the street is a 300-acre park with lighted tennis courts, an 18-hole golf course and swimming pool.

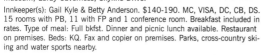

Historic Interest: Woodrow Wilson birthplace (8 blocks), Museum of American Frontier Culture.
Innkeeper(s): Otis & Suzy Huston. $69-89. 5 rooms with PB. Breakfast and afternoon tea included in rates. Type of meal: Full bkfst. Beds: KQDT. Turndown service and ceiling fan in room. Air conditioning. Weddings and family reunions hosted. Antiquing, fishing, live theater, shopping and sporting events nearby.

"We enjoyed ourselves beyond measure, the accommodations, the food, your helpfulness, but most of all your gracious spirits."

Warm Springs E10

Meadow Lane Lodge

HCR 01 Box 110
Warm Springs, VA 24484-9709
(540)839-5959 Fax:(540)839-2135
E-mail: meadowln@tds.net
Web: meadowlanelodge.com

Circa 1922. Meadow Lane Lodge boasts a colorful history. The lodge is located on a vast, 1,600-acre spread in the Allegheny Mountains, and its acreage was once part of a land grant made by King George III to Charles Lewis, a pioneer settler. The farm also is the site of Fort Dinwiddie, which was visited by George Washington on two occasions. Although the fort is no longer standing, a restored slave cabin still exists and is used as a reading room. An Indian village once rested on the property, and guests might discover an arrowhead while meandering the grounds. There are five guest rooms in the main lodge, decorated with a mix of comfortable furnishings and antiques. Guests will find walking and biking trails, a swimming hole and perhaps a beaver bog. Deer, fox and a variety of birds are other sites you're sure to see. In addition to the lodge, guests also can stay in nearby Warm Springs at a restored log house, which dates to 1820. A late 19th-century grain barn, located along the Jackson River, is another lodging option.
Innkeeper(s): Carter & Michelle Ancona. $105-260. MC, VISA. 11 rooms with PB, 3 with FP and 1 conference room. Type of meal: Full bkfst. Picnic lunch available. Beds: KQDT. Fishing on premises. Bicycling and fishing nearby.

"This 1600 acre farm was very private and nice."

Three Hills Inn

PO Box 9
Warm Springs, VA 24484-0009
(540)839-5381 (888)234-4557 Fax:(540)839-5199
E-mail: inn@3hills.com
Web: www.3hills.com

Circa 1913. Mary Johnston, who wrote the book "To Have and to Hold," built this inn, which rests on 38 mountainous acres. In 1917, Mary and her sisters opened the home to guests, earning a reputation for the home's view of the Allegheny Mountains and Warm Springs Gap. The innkeepers now offer lodging in the antique-filled main house or adjacent cottages. Some rooms include private decks, while others have fireplaces or clawfoot tubs. Each of the cottages includes a kitchen; one has a working fireplace, while another offers a wood-burning stove.

Innkeeper(s): Julie Miller. $69-189. MC, VISA, DS, PC, TC. TAC10. 10 rooms with PB, 3 with FP, 7 suites and 2 cottages. Breakfast included in rates. Type of meal: Full bkfst. Restaurant on premises. Beds: KQDT. Cable TV in room. VCR, fax, copier, child care, boardroom that seats 12, and a conference center that seats 80 and hiking on premises. Small meetings, family reunions and seminars hosted. Spanish spoken. Antiquing, fishing, hiking, thermal "spa" warm spring pools, live theater, parks, shopping, downhill skiing and cross-country skiing nearby.

Pets allowed: In rooms with outside door.

Publicity: *Listed on "Women of Virginia Historic Trail".*

Warrenton   C14

The Black Horse Inn

8393 Meetze Rd
Warrenton, VA 20187
(540)349-4020 Fax:(540)349-4242
E-mail: blackhrs@citizen.infi.net
Web: www.blackhorseinn.com

Circa 1850. One can easily imagine the days when gracious Southerners gathered at this home to celebrate a successful hunt. Rich in history, the inn is named after an elite Confederate cavalry unit. The home rests on 20 acres of rolling Virginia countryside. A hunt country theme is evident in the inn's decor. Romantic guest rooms are appointed with four-poster canopy beds, fireplaces and Jacuzzi tubs. One guest room alone has inspired more than three dozen marriage proposals. Upon check-in, guests are treated to an afternoon "hunt-country" tea with a sampling of local wines. Gourmet breakfasts include items such as Inn at Little Washington French toast, a rich entree stuffed with pecans and mascarpone cheese. Guests can spend the day hiking along the Appalachian Trail or perhaps enjoy some of the area's equestrian activities.
Historic Interest: Washington, D.C. (45 miles), Manassas battlefield (20 miles).
Innkeeper(s): Lynn A. Pirozzoli. $125-295. MC, VISA, AX. TAC10. 8 rooms with PB, 4 with FP, 2 suites and 2 conference rooms. Breakfast and afternoon tea included in rates. AP. Types of meals: Full bkfst and early coffee/tea. Snacks/refreshments, picnic lunch and catering service available. Beds: Q. Turndown service and ceiling fan in room. Air conditioning. Fax, copier, spa, stables, bicycles and library on premises. Weddings, small meetings and family reunions hosted. Antiquing, art galleries, bicycling, canoeing/kayaking, fishing, golf, hiking, horseback riding, health club, live theater, museums, parks, cross-country skiing, sporting events, tennis and wineries nearby.

Pets allowed: Horse boarding only.

Washington   C13

Caledonia Farm - 1812

47 Dearing Rd (Flint Hill)
Washington, VA 22627
(540)675-3693 (800)262-1812 Fax:(540)675-3693

Circa 1812. This gracious Federal-style stone house in the National Register is beautifully situated on 52 acres adjacent to Shenandoah National Park. It was built by a Revolutionary War officer, and his musket is displayed over a mantel. The house, a Virginia Historic Landmark, has been restored with the original Colonial color scheme retained. All rooms have working fireplaces and provide views of Skyline Drive and the Blue Ridge

Mountains. The innkeeper is a retired broadcaster.

Innkeeper(s): Phil Irwin. $140. MC, VISA, DS, PC, TC. TAC10. 2 suites, 3 with FP and 1 conference room. Breakfast and snacks/refreshments included in rates. Types of meals: Full gourmet bkfst and early coffee/tea. Beds: D. Phone, turndown service, VCR and skyline Drive View in room. Air conditioning. Fax, copier, spa, bicycles, library, hayride and lawn games on premises. Small meetings, family reunions and seminars hosted. German and Spanish spoken. Antiquing, fishing, wineries, caves, stables, battlefields, live theater, parks, shopping, downhill skiing, cross-country skiing and water sports nearby.

Publicity: *Country, Country Almanac, Country Living, Blue Ridge Country, Discovery, Washington Post, Baltimore Sun.*

"We've stayed at many, many B&Bs. This is by far the best!"

The Foster-Harris House

189 Main St
Washington, VA 22747
(540)675-3757 (800)666-0153

Circa 1900. This Victorian farmhouse stands on a lot laid out by George Washington and is located at the edge of the village. The streets of the town are exactly as surveyed 225 years ago. The village has galleries and craft shops as well as the Inn at Little Washington's five-star restaurant.
Historic Interest: Civil War battlefields & museums (less than an hour's drive).
Innkeeper(s): John & Libby Byam. $95-155. MC, VISA, DS. 5 rooms with PB, 2 with FP and 1 suite. Breakfast and afternoon tea included in rates. Type of meal: Full bkfst. Beds: QD. Ceiling fan in room. Air conditioning. Small meetings hosted. Antiquing, fishing, live theater, shopping and cross-country skiing nearby.

Publicity: *Culpeper News, Richmond Times-Dispatch.*

Gay Street Inn

160 Gay St
Washington, VA 22747
(540)675-3288 Fax:(540)675-1070

Circa 1855. After a day of Skyline Drive, Shenandoah National Park and the caverns of Luray and Front Royal, come home to this stucco, gabled farmhouse. If you've booked the fireplace room, a canopy bed will await you. Furnishings include period Shaker pieces. The innkeepers will be happy to steer you to the most interesting vineyards, organic "pick-your-own" fruit and veg-

etable farms and Made-In-Virginia food and craft shops. Breakfast and afternoon tea are served in the garden conservatory. Five-star dining is within walking distance at The Inn at Little Washington. The innkeepers can arrange for child care.
Historic Interest: Manassas Battlefield & Park and Chancellorsville are some of the area's many Civil War sites. The University of Virginia, historic Charlottesville and Monticello are other sites in the area.
Innkeeper(s): Robin & Donna Kevis. $95-135. MC, VISA, AX, PC, TC. TAC10. 4 rooms with PB, 1 with FP and 1 suite. Breakfast and afternoon tea included in rates. Types of meals: Full gourmet bkfst, cont plus and early coffee/tea. Picnic lunch available. Beds: Q. Air conditioning. Child care available and limited on premises. Handicap access. Weddings, small meetings and family reunions hosted. Antiquing, fishing, golf, horseback riding, vineyards, live theater, parks, shopping and water sports nearby.

Pets Allowed.

"Thank you for a wonderful visit. Your hospitality was superb."

Williamsburg G17

Candlewick B&B

800 Jamestown Rd
Williamsburg, VA 23185-3915
(757)253-8693 (800)418-4949 Fax:(757)253-6547
Web: www.candlewickinn.com

Circa 1946. Situated behind a white picket fence, this Colonial two-story house is close to the historic area and across the street from the College of William and Mary. Behind each shuttered window, a candle is lit at night to welcome guests, an old Virginia tradition. The inn is decorated with 18th-century antiques and reproductions and includes such features as indoor shutters, beamed ceilings, old latch doors and chair rails. Guest rooms all offer a beautifully draped canopy colonial bed, comfortable mattress and antique quilts. Cottage pancakes, French toast and homemade breads may be served at breakfast.

Innkeeper(s): Bernie & Mary Peters. $105-135. MC, VISA, AX, PC, TC. TAC10. 3 rooms with PB and 1 suite. Breakfast included in rates. AP. Types of meals: Full bkfst and early coffee/tea. Beds: KQT. Phone and turndown service in room. Air conditioning. Bicycles on premises. German spoken. Amusement parks, antiquing, fishing, golf, live theater, parks, shopping, sporting events, tennis and water sports nearby.

"Once again, our stay here was phenomenal."

Liberty Rose B&B

1022 Jamestown Rd
Williamsburg, VA 23185-3434
(757)253-1260 (800)545-1825
Web: www.libertyrose.com

Circa 1922. This cozy retreat, located on the historic corridor, is tucked among tall trees only a mile from Colonial Williamsburg. The owner of Jamestown constructed this two-story clapboard home. The entry porch is marked with the millstone from one of Williamsburg's old mills. Antiques and collectibles abound in each of the rooms. The innkeepers have merged modern amenities with turn-of-the-century atmosphere. All rooms include telephones, TVs and VCRs with an excellent selection of movies. A gourmet country breakfast is served each morning. Each of the romantic guest rooms features something unique such as a lush canopy bed. Honeymooners — the inn is often full of newlyweds — often return to celebrate their anniversaries.

Historic Interest: Colonial Williamsburg (1 mile), Jamestown 1607 (4 miles), Yorktown (12 miles), College of William & Mary (1/2 mile).
Innkeeper(s): Brad & Sandi Hirz. $145-225. MC, VISA, AX. 4 rooms with PB, 1 with FP and 3 suites. Breakfast included in rates. Type of meal: Full bkfst. Gourmet dinner available. Beds: QT. Cable TV, phone and VCR in room. Antiquing, live theater and water sports nearby.
Publicity: Country Inns, Washington Post, Rural Living, Los Angeles Times, Glamour, Country Victoria, Bedrooms & Baths, Travel Magazine (Romantic Weekends).

"More delightful than we could possibly have imagined. Charm & romance abounds when you walk into the house."

Newport House

710 S Henry St
Williamsburg, VA 23185-4113
(757)229-1775 Fax:(757)229-6408

Circa 1988. This neo-Palladian house is a 1756 design by Peter Harrison, architect of rebuilt Williamsburg State House. It features wooden rusticated siding. Colonial country dancing is held in the inn's ballroom on Tuesday evenings. Guests are welcome to participate. There are English and American antiques, and reproductions include canopy beds in all the guest rooms. The host was a museum director and captain of a historic tall ship.

Historic Interest: Newport House is within walking distance of Colonial Williamsburg. Jamestown is six miles, Yorktown is a 12-mile drive from the inn. The historic James River Plantations are scattered throughout the area.
Innkeeper(s): John & Cathy Millar. $125-160. PC, TC. TAC10. 2 rooms with PB and 1 conference room. Breakfast included in rates. Type of meal: Full bkfst. Beds: QT. Cable TV and VCR in room. Air conditioning. Fax and library on premises. Weddings, small meetings, family reunions and seminars hosted. French spoken. Amusement parks, antiquing, golf, historic buildings, parks, shopping, tennis and water sports nearby.
Publicity: Innsider, Mid-Atlantic Country.

"Host and hostess were charming and warm."

Williamsburg Manor B&B

600 Richmond Rd
Williamsburg, VA 23185-3540
(757)220-8011 (800)422-8011 Fax:(757)220-0245

Circa 1927. Built during the reconstruction of Colonial Williamsburg, this Georgian brick Colonial is just three blocks from the historic village. A grand staircase, culinary library, Waverly fabrics, Oriental rugs and antiques are featured. Breakfasts begin with fresh fruits and home-baked breads, followed by a special daily entree. Gourmet regional Virginia dinners also are available.

Historic Interest: Historic Williamsburg (3 blocks), Jamestown (5 miles), Yorktown (20 miles), William & Mary College (1 block).
Innkeeper(s): Laura Reeves. $75-150. MC, VISA, PC. TAC10. 5 rooms, 4 with PB and 1 suite. Breakfast included in rates. Types of meals: Full gourmet bkfst and cont plus. Gourmet dinner, picnic lunch, banquet service, catering service and catered breakfast available. Beds: QT. Cable TV and ceiling fan in room. Air conditioning. VCR and fax on premises. Weddings, small meetings, family reunions and seminars hosted. Amusement parks, antiquing, fishing, golf, live theater, parks, shopping, sporting events, tennis and water sports nearby.

"Lovely accommodations - scrumptious breakfast."

Williamsburg Sampler B&B Inn

922 Jamestown Rd
Williamsburg, VA 23185-3917
(757)253-0398 (800)722-1169 Fax:(757)253-2669
E-mail: WbgSampler@aol.com
Web: www.williamsburgsampler.com

Circa 1976. Although this 18th-century-style home was built in the year of the bicentennial, it captures the early American spirit of Colonial Williamsburg. The rooms serve as wonderful replicas of an elegant Colonial home, with antiques, pewter and framed American and English samplers found throughout the inn. Bedchambers, which include suites with fireplaces and "Roof Top Garden," are cozy with rice-carved, four-poster beds and Colonial decor. Guests can test their skill at checkers or curl up with a book in the 1827 armchair in the Tavern Reading Room, or watch premium cable TV in the Common

Keeping Room. The innkeepers term the morning meal at the Rooster's Den a "Skip Lunch® breakfast," an apt description of the colossal menu. If guests can move after this wonderful meal, they head out for a day exploring historic Williamsburg. Virginia's Governor has proclaimed Williamsburg Sampler as "Inn of the Year."

Innkeeper(s): Helen & Ike Sisane. $100-150. PC. TAC10. 4 rooms with PB, 2 with FP and 2 suites. Breakfast included in rates. Type of meal: Full bkfst. Beds: KQ. Cable TV, ceiling fan, VCR, refrigerator and fireplace (suites) in room. Air conditioning. Fax and copier on premises. Amusement parks, antiquing, fishing, golf, live theater, parks, shopping, sporting events, tennis and water sports nearby.

Publicity: *Washington Post.*

Woodstock   C13

The Inn at Narrow Passage

PO Box 608
Woodstock, VA 22664-0608
(540)459-8000 (800)459-8002 Fax:(540)459-8001
E-mail: innkeeper@innatnarrowpassage.com
Web: www.innatnarrowpassage.com

Circa 1740. This log inn has been welcoming travelers since the time settlers took refuge here against the Indians. Later, it
served as a stagecoach inn on the old Valley Turnpike, and in 1862, it was Stonewall Jackson's headquarters. Most guest rooms feature working fireplaces and views of the Shenandoah River and Massanutten Mountains.

Historic Interest: Shenandoah County Courthouse (5 minutes), Cedar Creek Battlefield (15 minutes), New Market Battlefield (20 minutes).

Innkeeper(s): Ellen & Ed Markel. $95-145. MC, VISA. 12 rooms with PB. Breakfast included in rates. Type of meal: Full bkfst. Beds: Q. TV and phone in room. Antiquing, fishing, horseback riding, hiking, caverns nearby and water sports nearby.

Publicity: *Southern Living, Washington Post, Washington Times, Richmond Times-Dispatch.*

Woolwine   I9

The Mountain Rose B&B Inn

1787 Charity Hwy
Woolwine, VA 24185
(540)930-1057 Fax:(540)930-2165
E-mail: mtrosein@swva.net
Web: www.swva.net/mtroseinn

Circa 1901. This historic Victorian inn, once the home of the Mountain Rose Distillery, sits on 100 acres of forested hills with plenty of hiking trails. A trout-stocked stream goes through the property and a swimming pool provides recreation.
Each room has an antique manteled fireplace, some of which have been converted to gas logs. Guests can relax by the pool or in rocking chairs on one of the six porches. The innkeepers look forward to providing guests with casually elegant hospitality in the

Blue Ridge Mountains. The Blue Ridge Parkway, Mabury Mill, The Reynolds Homestead, Laurel Hill J. EB Stuart Birthplace, Patrick County Courthouse and the Patrick County Historical Museum are located nearby. A three-course breakfast is offered every morning.

Innkeeper(s): Melodie Pogue & Reeves Simms. $79-99. MC, VISA, DS, PC, TC. TAC10. 5 rooms with PB, 5 with FP. Breakfast and afternoon tea included in rates. Types of meals: Full gourmet bkfst and early coffee/tea. Dinner and picnic lunch available. Beds: KQDT. Air conditioning. VCR, fax, copier, swimming, bicycles and trout-stocked creek on premises. Weddings, small meetings, family reunions and seminars hosted. Antiquing, fishing, golf, hiking, Nascar racing, parks, shopping, tennis, water sports and wineries nearby.

Yorktown   G17

Marl Inn B&B

220 Church St
Yorktown, VA 23690
(757)898-3859 (800)799-6207 Fax:(757)898-3587

Circa 1977. Although the Marl Inn is fairly new, built in 1978, the original structure that rested on this property dated back to 1716, and the land was surveyed in the 1690s. The inn includes four guest accommodations. There are two guest rooms and two spacious suites. The suites include a bedroom, living room, bathroom and kitchen. If you are a history buff in need of local information, look no further than the innkeeper of this bed & breakfast. A local resident for more than fifty years, innkeeper Eugene Marlin has lead historic walking tours of the historic village for several years. Guests may borrow an inn bicycle and explore the town. The inn is within walking distance to shopping, restaurants and is two blocks from York River. Historic battlefields and Revolutionary Army campgrounds also are nearby, as are the Colonial Parkway and NASA.

Historic Interest: Main Street Colonial Yorktown (1/2 block).

Innkeeper(s): Eugene C. Marlin. $85-125. MC, VISA, AX, PC, TC. TAC5. 4 rooms, 2 with PB and 2 suites. Types of meals: Cont plus and early coffee/tea. Beds: QD. Ceiling fan in room. Central air. VCR, fax, copier, bicycles and library on premises. Family reunions hosted. Amusement parks, antiquing, art galleries, beaches, bicycling, fishing, golf, hiking, live theater, museums, parks, shopping, sporting events and wineries nearby.

Washington

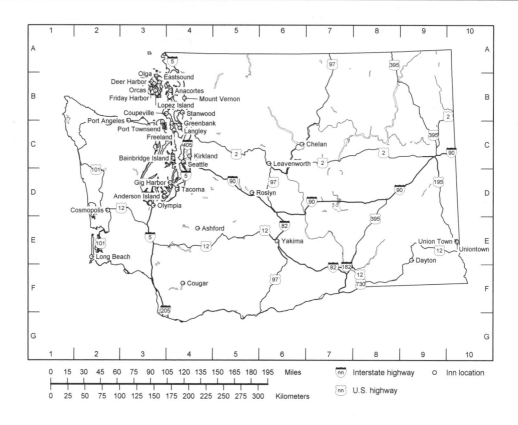

	1	2	3	4	5	6	7	8	9	10	

Map of Washington showing inn locations including Olga, Eastsound, Deer Harbor, Orcas, Anacortes, Friday Harbor, Mount Vernon, Lopez Island, Coupeville, Stanwood, Port Angeles, Greenbank, Port Townsend, Langley, Freeland, Chelan, Bainbridge Island, Kirkland, Seattle, Leavenworth, Gig Harbor, Tacoma, Roslyn, Anderson Island, Cosmopolis, Olympia, Ashford, Yakima, Union Town, Uniontown, Dayton, Long Beach, Cougar.

Scale:
0 15 30 45 60 75 90 105 120 135 150 165 180 195 Miles
0 25 50 75 100 125 150 175 200 225 250 275 300 Kilometers

Interstate highway o Inn location
U.S. highway

Anacortes B4

Albatross Bed & Breakfast

5708 Kingsway
Anacortes, WA 98221-2932
(360)293-0677 (800)622-8864

Circa 1927. This Cape Cod-style home is one of the last remaining relics of Anacortes' booming lumber days. The current bed & breakfast was built as a home for the mill manager at the E.K. Wood Mill Company. The popular Scarlett O'Hara Room is filled with unique pieces from a 19th-century Southern mansion. The home maintains many original elements, including beaded cedar ceilings and crystal chandeliers. Skyline Marina is adjacent to the home, and the San Juan ferry boat docks just one-half mile away.

Historic Interest: Historic San Juan Island, about 20 miles away by ferry, was the site of the Pig War, a conflict between the United States and Britain over the establishment of the border between Washington and British Colombia.

$70-95. MC, VISA, AX, DS, PC, TC. TAC10. 4 rooms with PB. Breakfast included in rates. Type of meal: Full gourmet bkfst. Afternoon tea available. Beds: KQ. TV, chairs, armoires and dressers in room. VCR, library and 46-foot sailboat on premises. Weddings, small meetings, family reunions and seminars hosted. Antiquing, fishing, sailing and crabbing, live theater, parks, shopping, downhill skiing, cross-country skiing, sporting events and water sports nearby.

Pets allowed: small pets.

"Our stay with you was a comfortable, enjoyable experience. Such cordiality!"

Ashford

E4

Storm King B&B, Spa and Cabins

37311 SR 706
Ashford, WA 98304
(360)569-2339 Fax:(360)569-2964

Circa 1890. Guests at Storm King will appreciate the cozy, rustic setting of this 100-year-old mountain home located a mile from the Nisqually entrance to Mt. Rainier National Park on Highway 706. Guest rooms are large and feature comfortable furnishings, quilts and fresh flowers. A full mountain breakfast is served each morning with fresh pastries. The breakfast is a great start to a day of hiking or cross-country skiing. The inn is an ideal location for park visitors and is four miles from the village of Ashford.

Innkeeper(s): Steve Brown & Deborah Sample. $85-110. MC, VISA, PC, TC. TAC10. 3 rooms, 1 with PB. Type of meal: Full bkfst. Spa and spa treatments and massage therapy on premises. Cross-country skiing nearby.

Bainbridge Island

C4

Buchanan Inn

8494 NE Oddfellows Rd
Bainbridge Island, WA 98110
(206)780-9258 (800)598-3926 Fax:(206)842-9458

Circa 1912. A short ferry ride will take you from Seattle's harbor to quaint Bainbridge Island and this New England-style barn house. The acre-and-a-half of grounds are dotted with gardens. Each of the guest rooms includes beds topped with luxurious Egyptian cotton linens, and two rooms include a fireplace. Guests are pampered with a glass of wine in the evenings and a full breakfast each morning. The breakfasts are served on  fine china and include gourmet coffee, fresh fruit, homemade baked goods and entrees such as Northwest Eggs Benedict or a ham and brie strata. Bainbridge Island offers many restaurants, shops and galleries. Guests can explore the island or head into Seattle. After a day in the city, return to the serenity of the island and inn, relaxing perhaps in the inn's hot tub, which is located in a little cedar cottage.

Innkeeper(s): Ron & Judy Gibbs. $109-159. MC, VISA, AX, DS, PC, TC. TAC10. 4 rooms with PB, 2 with FP and 2 suites. Breakfast and snacks/refreshments included in rates. Type of meal: Full gourmet bkfst. Catered breakfast available. Beds: KQ. Ceiling fan, hair dryers and robes in room. Fax, spa and library on premises. Weddings, small meetings and family reunions hosted. Antiquing, art galleries, beaches, bicycling, canoeing/kayaking, fishing, golf, hiking, live theater, museums, parks, shopping, cross-country skiing, tennis, water sports and wineries nearby.

"Would you adopt me so I can stay here?"

Camano Island

B4

Camano Island Inn

1054 S West Camano Dr
Camano Island, WA 98292
(360)387-0783 (888)718-0783 Fax:(360)387-4173
E-mail: rsvp@camanoislandinn.com
Web: camanoislandinn.com

Circa 1900. Built at the turn of the 20th century, this waterfront Craftsman-style inn features six guest rooms all individually decorated in a romantic style. The inn served originally as a boarding house for island mill workers. Today, its décor is undoubtedly far superior to its boarding house days. The rooms feature canopy featherbeds topped with a down comforter and plenty of pillows. Each room has a private deck offering an excellent view of the Saratoga Passage, Olympic Mountains and Whidbey Island. Full breakfasts are served in the dining room or delivered to rooms in baskets and can include homemade baked goods and fresh fruit, often from the inn's own orchard. The innkeepers can arrange massage services or provide a kayak for guests hoping to get a seaside view of the island. Camano Island is about an hour north of Seattle.

Innkeeper(s): Jon & Kari Soth. $108-160. MC, VISA, PC, TC. TAC10. 6 rooms with PB and 1 conference room. Breakfast, afternoon tea and snacks/refreshments included in rates. Types of meals: Full bkfst and early coffee/tea. Beds: KQ. Cable TV, phone and VCR in room. Fax, copier, spa, swimming, library, kayaks and massage on premises. Handicap access. Weddings, small meetings, family reunions and seminars hosted. Antiquing, art galleries, beaches, canoeing/kayaking, fishing, golf and hiking nearby.

Chelan

C6

A Quail's Roost Inn

121 E Highland Ave, PO Box 2089
Chelan, WA 98816
(509)682-2892 (800)681-2892

Circa 1902. Formerly named Highland Guest House, this turn-of-the-century Victorian is decorated in period style with antiques. Each of the guest rooms has its own theme. For instance, one room offers a romantic canopy bed topped with a quilt. The Rose & Wicker Room includes a private porch that affords a beautiful view of Lake Chelan. The inn's parlor and dining room feature hand-stenciled ceilings, which duplicate original turn-of-the-century painting done by the home's original owner. A number of collectibles, including a spinning wheel, decorate the common areas. Strawberries and cream French toast is a typical breakfast specialty. The innkeepers offer a variety of seasonal packages and can put together picnic and gift baskets. A Quail's Roost Inn is the site of a juried Victorian arts and crafts show, which takes place during the Christmas season.

Historic Interest: Listed in the National Register.

Innkeeper(s): Marilee & Brad Stolzenburg. $50-115. MC, VISA, PC. TAC10. 3 rooms with PB. Breakfast included in rates. Type of meal: Full gourmet bkfst. Picnic lunch and room service available. Beds: QD. Ceiling fan in room. Air conditioning. Library on premises. Small meetings, family reunions and seminars hosted. Amusement parks, antiquing, fishing, live theater, parks, shopping, cross-country skiing and water sports nearby.

"Always liked Chelan...now we love it! We'll be back!"

Cosmopolis

D2

Cooney Mansion B&B

PO Box 54, 1705 Fifth St
Cosmopolis, WA 98537-0054
(360)533-0602

Circa 1908. This former lumber magnate's home, in a wooded setting, boasts 37 rooms. In the National Register, it was built with a ballroom in the daylight basement, nine bedrooms and eight bathrooms. There are soaking tubs in all of the rooms.

The inn features original mission furnishings, and the Cooney suite has a fireplace, TV and VCR and original "rainfall" shower. Guests can enjoy the National Award Winning Lumber Baron's Breakfast.

Innkeeper(s): Judi & Jim Lohr. $75-185. MC, VISA, DC, DS. 8 rooms, 5 with PB, 1 with FP, 1 suite and 1 conference room. Breakfast and afternoon tea included in rates. Types of meals: Full bkfst and early coffee/tea. Banquet service and catering service available. Beds: KQDT. VCR, fax, spa, sauna and golf on premises. Weddings, small meetings, family reunions and seminars hosted. Antiquing, fishing, golf, whale watching, rain forest, live theater, parks, shopping, sporting events, tennis and water sports nearby.

"A good B&B should offer the comforts of home, serenity, relaxation and good company. You gave us all we expected and more. Thanks for a romantic weekend."

Coupeville

B4

Captain Whidbey Inn

2072 W Captain Whidbey Inn Rd
Coupeville, WA 98239
(360)678-4097 (800)366-4097 Fax:(360)678-4110

Circa 1907. Overlooking Whidbey Island's Penn Cove, this log inn has comfortable rooms featuring down comforters, feather beds and views of lagoons and gardens. The dining room also has

a magnificent view and guests can enjoy their meals by the fireplace. The chef utilizes local catches such as steelhead, salmon, spot prawns and Penn Cove mussels. The proprietor is also a sailing captain, and guests can

book an afternoon on his 52-foot ketch, Cutty Sark. The proprietor's family has run the inn for more than 30 years.

Innkeeper(s): Dennis A. Argent. $95-225. MC, VISA, AX, DC, DS. 32 rooms, 20 with PB, 7 with FP and 1 conference room. Breakfast included in rates. EP. Type of meal: Full bkfst. Gourmet dinner, snacks/refreshments, picnic lunch and lunch available. Restaurant on premises. Beds: KQD. Phone in room. Fax, copier, sailing and fishing on premises. Small meetings and family reunions hosted. Antiquing, museums and shopping nearby.

"I visit and stay here once a year and love it."

Dayton

E9

Weinhard Hotel

235 E Main St
Dayton, WA 99328-1352
(509)382-4032 Fax:(509)382-2640
Web: www.weinhard.com

Circa 1890. This luxurious Victorian bed & breakfast, tucked at the base of the scenic Blue Mountains, originally served up spirits as the Weinhard Saloon and Lodge Hall. Guests are transported back to the genteel Victorian era during their stay. After a restful sleep among period pieces, ornate carpeting and ceilings fans, guests might imagine the days when horses and buggies road through town. While the innkeepers have worked to preserve the history of the hotel, they didn't forget such modern luxuries as Jacuzzi tubs in the private baths. The hotel boasts a beautiful Victorian roof garden, a perfect place to relax with a cup of tea or gourmet coffee. For a unique weekend, try the hotel's special Romantic Getaway package. Guests are presented with sparkling wine or champagne and a dozen roses. The package also includes a five-course meal.

Historic Interest: If a stay at Weinhard Hotel doesn't take you back in time, a trip to Dayton will transport you to the Victorian Era. The town has 89 buildings in the National Register.

Innkeeper(s): Virginia Butler. $70-125. MC, VISA. 15 rooms with PB. Breakfast included in rates. Afternoon tea, gourmet dinner, lunch and catering service available. Restaurant on premises. Beds: Q.

Pets Allowed.

Publicity: *Seattle Times, Daily Journal of Commerce, Sunset Magazine, Lewiston Morning Tribune, San Francisco Examiner, Spokesman Review.*

"It's spectacular! Thank you so much for all your kindness and caring hospitality."

Eastsound

B3

Kangaroo House

1459 North Beach Rd, PO Box 334
Eastsound, WA 98245
(360)376-2175 (888)371-2175 Fax:(360)376-3604

Circa 1907. Guests can leave their busy lives behind at this island retreat. To reach the island, guests take a ferry from the town of Anacortes. The Craftsman-style home derives its name from a former owner who decided to bring a pet kangaroo back to the house after a trek to Australia. Interestingly enough, one of the current innkeepers hails from Australia. Period antiques and traditional furnishings decorate the interior. Guests can relax on the deck or in front of the fireplace in the living room. After a day of hiking, biking, kayaking or exploring nearby Moran State Park, return to the inn for a soak in the outdoor hot tub and count the stars.

Innkeeper Helen Allen

serves a savory, gourmet breakfast. Her recipe for portabella breakfast cups won first prize in the Jones Farm Recipe Contest. Other specialties include ginger-poached pears, sourdough pancakes, Challah bread French toast and vegetable frittatas.

Historic Interest: Moran Mansion.

Innkeeper(s): Peter & Helen Allen. $80-130. MC, VISA, AX, DS, PC, TC. TAC10. 5 rooms, 1 with PB, 1 suite and 1 conference room. Breakfast and snacks/refreshments included in rates. Types of meals: Full gourmet bkfst, veg bkfst and early coffee/tea. Beds: QDT. Fax, spa and library on premises. Weddings, small meetings, family reunions and seminars hosted. Antiquing, art galleries, beaches, bicycling, canoeing/kayaking, fishing, golf, hiking, horseback riding, live theater, museums, parks and shopping nearby.

Turtleback Farm Inn

1981 Crow Valley Rd
Eastsound, WA 98245
(360)376-4914 (800)376-4914

Circa 1895. Guests will delight in the beautiful views afforded from this farmhouse and the newly constructed Orchard House, which overlooks 80 acres of forest and farmland, duck ponds and Mt. Con-

stitution to the east. Rooms feature antique furnishings and many boast views of the farm, orchard or sheep pasture. Beds are covered with wool comforters made from sheep raised on the property. Bon Appetit highlighted some of the breakfast recipes served at Turtleback; a breakfast here is a memorable affair. Tables set with bone china, silver and fresh linens make way for a delightful mix of fruits, juice, award-winning granola, homemade breads and specialty entrees. Evening guests can settle down with a game or a book in the fire-lit parlor as they enjoy sherry, tea or hot chocolate.

Historic Interest: Orcas Island, once the apple capital of Washington, features many historic sites. The Orcas Island Historical Museum and Crow Valley School Museum are among several options.

Innkeeper(s): William & Susan C. Fletcher. $80-210. MC, VISA, DS, PC, TC. TAC10. 11 rooms with PB, 4 with FP. Breakfast included in rates. Types of meals: Full bkfst and early coffee/tea. Picnic lunch available. Beds: KQD. Library and refrigerator & self-serve beverage bar in dining room on premises. Handicap access. Weddings and family reunions hosted. Spanish and limited French spoken. Fishing, live theater, parks, shopping and water sports nearby.

"A peaceful haven for soothing the soul."

Friday Harbor   B3

States Inn

2039 W Valley Rd
Friday Harbor, WA 98250-9211
(360)378-6240 Fax:(360)378-6241

Circa 1910. This sprawling ranch home has ten guest rooms, each named and themed for a particular state. The Arizona and New Mexico rooms, often booked by families or couples travel-

ing together, can be combined to create a private suite with two bedrooms, a bathroom and a sitting area. The oldest part of the house was built as a country school and later used as a dance hall, before it was relocated to its current 60-acre spread.

Baked French toast, accompanied by fresh fruit topped with yogurt sauce and homemade muffins are typical breakfast fare.

Innkeeper(s): Alan & Julia Paschal. $85-125. MC, VISA, PC, TC. TAC10. 10 rooms, 8 with PB, 1 with FP and 1 suite. Breakfast included in rates. Type of meal: Full bkfst. Beds: KQDT. Fax and stables on premises. Handicap access. Weddings, small meetings and family reunions hosted. Antiquing, fishing, golf, kayaks, whale watching, live theater, parks, shopping and water sports nearby.

Publicity: *Glamour, Conde Nast, USA Today.*

Tucker House B&B With Cottages

260 B St
Friday Harbor, WA 98250-8074
(360)378-2783 (800)965-0123 Fax:(360)378-6437
E-mail: tucker@rockisland.com
Web: www.san-juan.net/tucker

Circa 1898. Only one block from the ferry landing, the white picket fence bordering Tucker House is a welcome sight for guests. The spindled entrance leads to the parlor. The home includes three guest rooms that share a bath. The rooms are decorated with antiques. The innkeepers also offer self-contained cottages that include private baths, kitchenettes, queen beds, TVs and VCRs. All guests enjoy use of the outdoor hot tub. The inn's breakfasts are served in the solarium.

Innkeeper(s): Skip & Annette Metzger. $75-225. MC, VISA, AX, DS, PC, TC. TAC10. 6 rooms and 3 cottages. Breakfast included in rates. Type of meal: Full bkfst. Beds: Q. Cable TV and VCR in room. Spa on premises. Family reunions hosted. Danish, German, Swedish and Norwegian spoken. Antiquing, fishing, live theater, parks, shopping and water sports nearby.

Pets allowed: Dogs under 40 pounds; $15 per evening per dog, limit two.

"A lovely place, the perfect getaway. We'll be back."

Greenbank   C4

Guest House Log Cottages

24371-SR 525, Whidbey Island
Greenbank, WA 98253
(360)678-3115
E-mail: guesthse@whidbey.net
Web: www.whidbey.net/logcottages

These storybook cottages and log home are nestled within a peaceful forest on 25 acres. The log cabin features stained-glass and criss-cross paned windows that give it the feel of a ginger-

bread house. Four of the cottages are log construction. Ask for the Lodge and enjoy a private setting with a pond just beyond the deck. Inside are two Jacuzzi tubs, a stone fireplace, king bed, antiques and a luxurious atmosphere.

Innkeeper(s): Don & Mary Jane Creger. $160-310. MC, VISA, AX, DS, PC, TC. 6 cottages. Breakfast included in rates. Type of meal: Full bkfst. Beds: KQ. Ceiling fan, VCR, kitchen and swimming pool in room. Air conditioning. Fax, copier, spa and swimming on premises. French spoken. Antiquing, fishing, golf, parks, shopping and tennis nearby.

Publicity: *Los Angeles Times, Woman's Day, Sunset, Country Inns, Bride's.*

"The wonderful thing is to be by yourselves and rediscover what's important."

Kirkland C4

Shumway Mansion

11410 99th Pl NE
Kirkland, WA 98033
(425)823-2303 Fax:(425)822-0421

Circa 1909. This resplendent 24-room, 10,000-square-foot mansion is situated on more than two acres overlooking Juanita Bay. With a large ballroom and veranda, few could guess that a short time ago, the building was hoisted on hydraulic lifts. It was then pulled three miles across town to its present site, near the beach. An athletic club just across the street offers inn guests privileges.

Innkeeper(s): Richard & Salli Harris, Julie Blakemore. $70-105. MC, VISA, AX. 7 rooms, 8 with PB and 1 suite. Breakfast included in rates. Type of meal: Full bkfst. Beds: Q. TV and fans in room. Weddings, family reunions and seminars hosted. Antiquing, fishing, live theater, shopping, sporting events and water sports nearby.

"Guests enjoy the mansion so much they don't want to leave — Northwest Living."

La Conner (Mt. Vernon) B4

The White Swan Guest House

15872 Moore Rd
La Conner (Mt. Vernon), WA 98273-9249
(360)445-6805

Circa 1898. Guests will marvel at innkeeper Peter Goldfarb's beautiful gardens as they wind up the driveway to reach this charming, yellow Victorian farmhouse. Inside, guests are greet-ed with luscious home-baked chocolate chip cookies in the bright, cheery kitchen and a vegetarian breakfast in the morning. Guest rooms are filled with comfortable, Victorian furnishings, and there's even a cozy Garden

Cottage to stay in, complete with its own kitchen and private sun deck. Each April, the area is host to the Skagit Valley Tulip festival. La Conner, a nearby fishing village, is full of shops and galleries to explore.

Historic Interest: The White Swan is only an hour from the historic sites of Seattle and about 90 miles from Vancouver. The new Museum of Northwest Art and the Skagit Historical Museum are both located in downtown La Conner.

Innkeeper(s): Peter Goldfarb. $75-150. MC, VISA, PC, TC. TAC10. 3 rooms and 1 cottage. Breakfast included in rates. Types of meals: Cont plus and early coffee/tea. Beds: KQD. Turndown service in room. Family reunions host-ed. Antiquing, fishing, art museum and galleries, parks and shopping nearby.

"This has been a very pleasant interlude. What a beautiful, comfort-able place you have here. We will be back."

Leavenworth C6

Mrs. Andersons Lodging House

917 Commercial St
Leavenworth, WA 98826-1413
(509)548-6173 (800)253-8990 Fax:(509)548-9113
E-mail: info@quiltersheaven.com
Web: www.quiltersheaven.com

Circa 1895. This historic home is named for the widow that purchased the place just a few years after its 1895 construc-tion. In order to support herself and two daughters, Mrs. Anderson transformed the place into a boarding house. Today, it still provides a cozy, relaxing haven for guests. Rooms feature whimsical names, such as the Double Wedding Ring, Grandmother's Flower Garden, Moon Over the Mountain and Leavenworth Nine Patch. As one might deduct, quilters are welcome here. In fact, quilting getaways are available and the home includes a shop filled with quilting supplies, quilting books, fabrics, stencils and other like items. Non-quilters can relax on the sun deck and enjoy the view. Leavenworth is known for its German heritage, and you'll find plenty of shops and boutiques, as well as many outdoor activities.

Innkeeper(s): Dee & Al Howie. $39-65. MC, VISA, DS. 9 rooms, 7 with PB and 1 conference room. Breakfast and afternoon tea included in rates. Types of meals: Cont plus and early coffee/tea. Beds: Q. Cable TV in room. Central air. Library on premises. Fishing, golf, hiking, horseback riding, live theater, museums, parks, shopping, downhill skiing and cross-country skiing nearby.

Long Beach E2

Boreas Bed & Breakfast Inn

607 Ocean Beach Blvd, PO Box 1344
Long Beach, WA 98631-1344
(360)642-8069 (888)642-8069 Fax:(360)642-5353
E-mail: boreas@boreasinn.com
Web: www.boreasinn.com

Circa 1920. This oceanfront inn started as a beach house and was remodeled eclectically with decks and a massive stone fire-place. There are two living rooms that offer views of the beach. All of the guest rooms feature ocean, gar-den or mountain views. Guests can enjoy private time in the hot tub in the enclosed gazebo, take the path that winds through the dunes to the surf or walk to the boardwalk,

restaurants and shopping. There is also a three-bedroom cottage available, and breakfast is not included in the cottage rates.

Innkeeper(s): Susie Goldsmith & Bill Verner. $125-135. MC, VISA, AX, DC, DS, PC, TC. 5 suites and 1 cottage. Type of meal: Full bkfst. Beds: KQT. VCR, fax, spa and library on premises. Weddings, small meetings and family reunions hosted. Limited Spanish spoken. Antiquing, fishing, golf, tennis, parks, shopping and water sports nearby.

Mount Ranier National Park E4

National Park Inn

Mt Rainer Guest Services PO Box 108
Mount Ranier National Park, WA 98304
(360)569-2275 Fax:(360)569-2770

Circa 1920. Mt. Rainier National Park boasts a spectacular
scenery of mountains and seemingly endless forests. For more
than half a century, visitors from around the world have chosen
National Park Inn for their park lodging. Old hickory and twig
furnishings decorate the rustic, comfortable guest rooms.
Lunch and dinner service are available at the inn's dining
room. From late October to May 1, rates include bed & breakfast. Breakfast is not included during the high season, from
May until about Oct. 19.

Innkeeper(s): James R. Sproatt. $69-96. MC, VISA, AX, DC, DS, PC, TC.
TAC5. 25 rooms, 18 with PB. Breakfast included in rates. AP. Types of
meals: Full bkfst, cont plus and cont. Afternoon tea, dinner and picnic lunch
available. Restaurant on premises. Beds: QDT. Coffee in room. Guided climbing on premises. Handicap access. Small meetings hosted. Hiking, mountain
climbing and cross-country skiing nearby.

Olga B3

Buck Bay Farm

716 Pt Lawrence Rd
Olga, WA 98279
(360)376-2908 (888)422-2825

Circa 1920. This farmhouse is secluded on five acres and is
decorated in country style. Down pillows and comforters are a
few homey touches. Homemade
breakfasts include items like freshly
baked muffins, scones and biscuits
still steaming from the oven.

Innkeeper(s): Rick & Janet Bronkey. $85-125.
MC, VISA, AX, DS, PC, TC. TAC10. 5 rooms,
4 with PB and 1 suite. Breakfast included in
rates. Types of meals: Full bkfst and early cof-
fee/tea. Beds: Q. Spa on premises. Handicap
access. Weddings, small meetings, family
reunions and seminars hosted. Antiquing, canoeing/kayaking, fishing, hiking,
whale watching, live theater, parks and shopping nearby.

Olympia D3

Puget View Guesthouse

7924 61st Ave NE
Olympia, WA 98516-9138
(360)413-9474

Circa 1930. This private, two-room waterfront cottage is located on Puget Sound. The innkeepers live on the property, but
not in the cottage, so guests have the run of the hideaway. The
country decor is simple and comfortable, and the cottage
includes a microwave and a small refrigerator. For a small extra
fee, the innkeepers will prepare a "Romantic Retreat" package.

Innkeeper(s): Dick & Barbara Yunker. $99-119. MC, VISA, PC, TC. TAC10. 1
cottages. Breakfast included in rates. Type of meal: Cont plus. Beds: QD.
Cable TV, phone and microwave in room. Deck, beach, BBQ and canoe on
premises. Shopping and water sports nearby.

Pets allowed: $10 per night fee. Pet accepted with hosts approval.

Orcas B3

Orcas Hotel

PO Box 155
Orcas, WA 98280-0155
(360)376-4300 (888)672-2792 Fax:(360)376-4399

Circa 1904. Listed in the National Register, this three-story
Victorian inn across from the ferry landing has been a landmark
to travelers and boaters since the early 1900s. The inn offers
scenic views of terraced lawns and
English gardens, as well as vistas
of the water and harbor, making it an ideal site for business meetings, retreats, wedding receptions and family
reunions. Breakfast, lunch and dinner are available in the
hotel's bakery, cafe and restaurant.

Innkeeper(s): Laura & Doug Tidwell. $79-180. MC, VISA, AX. 12 rooms, 5
with PB and 1 conference room. Types of meals: Full bkfst and cont. Dinner
and lunch available. Restaurant on premises. Beds: QT.

Port Angeles C3

Five SeaSuns B&B Inn

1005 S Lincoln St
Port Angeles, WA 98362-7826
(360)452-8248 (800)708-0777 Fax:(360)417-0465
E-mail: seasuns@olypen.com
Web: www.seasuns.com

Circa 1926. Five SeaSuns was built by a local attorney and later
purchased by a prominent area family who hosted many social
gatherings here. The restored home maintains much of its historic ambiance with guest rooms
decorated in 1920s style with
period antiques. Guest rooms
include amenities such as
whirlpool or soaking tubs, balconies and water or mountain
views. Picturesque gardens high-
light the estate like grounds. Artfully presented gourmet breakfasts are served with fine china, silver and candlelight.

Historic Interest: Federal building dedicated by Lincoln (1 mile), Port Angeles.
Innkeeper(s): Jan & Bob Harbick. $75-135. MC, VISA, AX, PC, TC. TAC10. 5
rooms with PB, 1 suite and 1 cottage. Breakfast, afternoon tea and
snacks/refreshments included in rates. Types of meals: Full bkfst, veg bkfst and
early coffee/tea. Picnic lunch available. Beds: QD. Turndown service in room.
VCR and fax on premises. Weddings and family reunions hosted. Antiquing, art
galleries, beaches, bicycling, canoeing/kayaking, fishing, hiking, live theater,
museums, parks, shopping, cross-country skiing and wineries nearby.

Port Townsend C3

Ann Starrett Mansion

744 Clay St
Port Townsend, WA 98368-5808
(888)385-3205
Web: www.starrettmansion.com

Circa 1889. George Starrett came from Maine to Port Townsend
and became the major residential builder. By 1889, he had constructed one house a week, totaling more than 350 houses. The
Smithsonian believes the Ann Starrett's elaborate free-hung spiral staircase is the only one of its type in the United States. A
frescoed dome atop the octagonal tower depicts four seasons

and four virtues. On the first day of each season, the sun causes a ruby red light to point toward the appropriate painting. The mansion won a "Great American Home Award" from the National Trust for Historic Preservation.

Historic Interest: The inn is located in the Port Townsend National Historic District near Fort Worden and Fort Townsend state parks.
Innkeeper(s): Edel Sokol. $133-225. MC, VISA, AX, DS, PC, TC. TAC10. 11 rooms with PB, 2 with FP, 2 suites, 2 cottages and 2 conference rooms. Breakfast included in rates. Type of meal: Full bkfst. Afternoon tea available. Beds: KQDT. Cable TV, phone and one room includes spa in room. VCR, fax, copier and spa on premises. German spoken. Antiquing, fishing, live theater, parks, shopping, cross-country skiing and water sports nearby.
Publicity: *Peninsula, New York Times, Vancouver Sun, San Francisco Examiner, London Times, Colonial Homes, Elle, Leader, Japanese Travel, National Geographic Traveler, Victorian, Historic American Trails.*

"Staying here was like a dream come true."

Chanticleer Inn

1208 Franklin St
Port Townsend, WA 98368-6611
(360)385-6239 (800)858-9421 Fax:(360)385-3377

Circa 1876. Located in the historic district, this is a Stick-style Victorian farmhouse. Guest rooms are in light colors and offer mountain and water views along with down comforters and feather beds. Comfortable parlors and sitting rooms include traditional

furnishings and Victorian antiques. The innkeepers create breakfasts of homemade granola and hot entrees such as blueberry-stuffed French toast or Mediterranean egg casserole with feta cheese, mushrooms and spinach. There are home-baked breads and muffins, as well. Ask for advice on kayaking, sailing and river rafting opportunities or take a sunset cruise, go whale watching or visit Point Wilson Lighthouse.

Historic Interest: The entire town is historic.
Innkeeper(s): Pattye O'Connor & Shirley O'Connor. $95-150. MC, VISA, DC, PC, TC. 5 rooms with PB and 1 guest house. Breakfast and afternoon tea included in rates. Types of meals: Full gourmet bkfst and veg bkfst. Catered breakfast available. Beds: KQ. Ceiling fan, one room w/Jacuzzi bath, full-equipped kitchen in guesthouse and TV (some rooms) in room. Central air. VCR on premises. Weddings, small meetings, family reunions and seminars hosted. Antiquing, art galleries, beaches, bicycling, canoeing/kayaking, fishing, golf, hiking, horseback riding, live theater, museums, parks, shopping, downhill skiing, cross-country skiing, sporting events, tennis, water sports and wineries nearby.

James House

1238 Washington St
Port Townsend, WA 98368-6714
(360)385-1238 (800)385-1238 Fax:(360)379-5551

Circa 1889. This Queen Anne mansion built by Francis James overlooks Puget Sound with views of the Cascades and Olympic mountain ranges. The three-story staircase was constructed of solid wild cherry brought around Cape Horn from Virginia. Parquet floors are composed of oak, cherry, walnut and maple, providing a suitable setting for the inn's collection of antiques.

Historic Interest: Located within the historic district and one mile from the Fort Worden State Park.
Innkeeper(s): Carol McGough. $75-185. MC, VISA, AX. 13 rooms, 11 with PB, 4 with FP, 3 suites and 2 cottages. Breakfast included in rates. Type of meal: Full bkfst. Gourmet dinner available. Beds: QD. Phone in room. Antiquing, fishing, live theater and cross-country skiing nearby.

"My dream house in a dream town."

Lizzie's

731 Pierce St
Port Townsend, WA 98368-8042
(360)385-4168 (800)700-4168
E-mail: wickline@olympus.net
Web: www.kolke.com/lizzies

Circa 1887. Named for Lizzie Grant, a sea captain's wife, this Italianate Victorian is elegant and airy. In addition to the gracious interiors, some rooms command an outstanding view of Port Townsend Bay, Puget Sound, and the Olympic and Cascade mountain ranges. Each room is filled with antiques dating from 1840 to the turn of the century. The grounds boast colorful gardens, and the dog's house is a one-quarter scale replica of the original house. Lizzie's is known for its elaborate breakfasts, where guests are encouraged to help themselves to seconds.
Innkeeper(s): Patricia Wickline. $70-135. MC, VISA, DS, PC, TC. 7 rooms with PB. Breakfast included in rates. Type of meal: Full bkfst. Beds: KQ.
Publicity: *Travel & Leisure, Victorian Homes.*

"As they say in show biz, you're a hard act to follow."

Manresa Castle

PO Box 564, 7th & Sheridan
Port Townsend, WA 98368-0564
(360)385-5750 (800)732-1281 Fax:(360)385-5883

Circa 1892. When businessman Charles Eisenbeis built the largest private residence in Port Townsend, locals dubbed it "Eisenbeis Castle," because it resembled the castles in Eisenbeis' native Prussia. The home is truly a royal delight to behold, both inside and out. Luxurious European antiques and hand-painted wall coverings decorate the dining room and many of

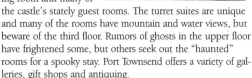

the castle's stately guest rooms. The turret suites are unique and many of the rooms have mountain and water views, but beware of the third floor. Rumors of ghosts in the upper floor have frightened some, but others seek out the "haunted" rooms for a spooky stay. Port Townsend offers a variety of galleries, gift shops and antiquing.

Historic Interest: Port Townsend and Manresa Castle are listed in the National Register. The town includes many examples of Victorian-style buildings and a historic district.
Innkeeper(s): Roger O'Connor. $70-175. MC, VISA, DS. 40 rooms with PB and 1 conference room. Breakfast included in rates. Types of meals: Full gourmet bkfst and cont. Dinner, banquet service and catered breakfast available. Restaurant on premises. Beds: KQDT. Cable TV and phone in room. Weddings, small meetings, family reunions and seminars hosted. Antiquing, fishing, live theater, shopping and water sports nearby.

Palace Hotel

1004 Water St
Port Townsend, WA 98368-6706
(360)385-0773 (800)962-0741 Fax:(360)385-0780

Circa 1889. This old brick hotel has been restored and refurbished in a Victorian style. The Miss Rose Room has a Jacuzzi tub and is on the third floor. Some rooms have kitchenettes. Miss Kitty's Room, with its antique bed and wood-burning stove has great views of Puget Sound and downtown.
Innkeeper(s): Phoebe Mason. $49-159. MC, VISA, AX, DS. 16 rooms. Breakfast included in rates. Type of meal: Cont plus. Restaurant on premises. Beds: KQDT. TV in room. Small conference room on premises. Pets Allowed.

Roslyn   D5

Hummingbird Inn

106 E Pennsylvania Ave PO Box 984
Roslyn, WA 98941
(509)649-2758

Circa 1890. This little blue house, located on an acre, has steep gables, a small front porch and a white picket fence. Once the local mine manager's house, it's decorated in country

Victorian furnishings in keeping with its architecture. Breakfast burritos and Dutch babies are served with homemade berry jam and baked goods. Both hosts are registered nurses.

Innkeeper(s): Roberta Spinazola. $60-75. MC, VISA, DS, PC, TC. 3 rooms, 1 with PB. Breakfast and snacks/refreshments included in rates. Types of meals: Full bkfst and early coffee/tea. Beds: Q. Child care, cd player & CDs, snow shoes and piano on premises. Weddings, small meetings and family reunions hosted. Antiquing, fishing, golf, national historic town, rodeo over labor day, small 50-seat movie house, parks, shopping, downhill skiing, cross-country skiing and water sports nearby.

"Your friendliness was infectious and we love the place. We will definitely be back."

Seattle   C4

Chelsea Station on The Park

4915 Linden Ave N
Seattle, WA 98103-6536
(206)547-6077 (800)400-6077 Fax:(206)632-5107

Circa 1929. Chelsea Station on the Park is a gracious Federal Colonial home nestled between Fremont and Woodland Park, just north of downtown. The inn's uniquely decorated rooms include some spacious suites with peek-a-boo mountain views. Antiques and Mission-style furnishings add to the atmosphere. Guests are treated to a full Northwest breakfast, and there's a bottomless cookie jar. Guests can walk to the park, Seattle's rose garden and excellent restaurants. It's ten minutes to the heart of the city.

Historic Interest: Minutes from Seattle's historic Pioneer Square district.

Innkeeper(s): Eric & Carolanne Watness. $75-135. MC, VISA, DC, DS, PC, TC. 9 rooms with PB and 7 suites. Breakfast included in rates. Type of meal: Full bkfst. Beds: KQT. Phone in room. Fax on premises. Museums and art galleries and live theater nearby.

"We're back...the food and lodging remains first class. We look forward to another visit soon."

Hill House B&B

1113 E John St
Seattle, WA 98102-5811
(206)720-7161 (800)720-7161 Fax:(206)323-0772

Circa 1903. Hill House is located on Capitol Hill, a historic section of Seattle. The guest rooms and suites have been decorated individually with antique beds. The Rose room includes a clawfoot tub original to the house. Breakfasts are served in the formal dining room, tables are set with fine china. Fresh fruit might be topped with a cinnamon wine sauce and accompa-

nied by an entree such as a smoked salmon omelet with mornay sauce. The inn is located near many downtown attractions, including shops, restaurants, Pike Place Market and the convention center.

Innkeeper(s): Heman & Alea Foster. $80-165. MC, VISA, AX, DC, DS, TC. 7 rooms, 3 with PB and 2 suites. Breakfast included in rates. Types of meals: Full gourmet bkfst and early coffee/tea. Dinner and picnic lunch available. Beds: QT. Cable TV, phone and down comforters in room. Fax and refrigerators on premises. Small meetings hosted. Antiquing, fishing, golf, live theater, parks, shopping, downhill skiing, cross-country skiing, sporting events, tennis and water sports nearby.

"Your cooking is out of this world and the whole house has an atmosphere which makes us wish we could stay longer."

Pioneer Square Hotel

77 Yesler Way
Seattle, WA 98104-3401
(206)340-1234 (800)800-5514 Fax:(206)467-9424
E-mail: sales@pioneersquare.com
Web: www.pioneersquare.com

Circa 1914. The estate of Seattle's founding father, Henry Yesler, built this historic waterfront hotel. The four-diamond hotel is well-appointed and elegant rooms feature coordinating prints. Business travelers will appreciate the direct dial telephones with data ports, and there are individual climate controls in each room. A continental breakfast is included in the hotel's rates. Restaurants and cafes are nearby, as is Historic Pioneer Square, ferries and shopping.

Innkeeper(s): Jo Thompson. $119-229. MC, VISA, AX, DC. 75 rooms with PB and 3 suites. Type of meal: Cont. Room service available. Beds: KQDT. Cable TV, phone and turndown service in room. Air conditioning. Fax, copier, library and child care on premises. Handicap access. Weddings, small meetings, family reunions and seminars hosted. Live theater, parks, shopping, downhill skiing, cross-country skiing, sporting events and water sports nearby.

Tugboat Challenger

1001 Fairview Ave N
Seattle, WA 98109-4438
(206)340-1201 Fax:(206)621-9208

Circa 1944. If you're a bit tired of the ordinary land-locked lodging, why not book a room and passage on this idyllic tugboat, docked in downtown Seattle's Chandler's Cove. The boat can sleep more than a dozen guests, in eight different cabins. The Admiral's Cabin is particularly suited to honeymooners, as it includes a four-poster bed, soaking tub and boasts city, lake and marina views. Not all rooms are as large and several main deck rooms include double or single bunks. The owners also have yachts available for renting, and each can accommodate four people. Tugboat guests enjoy a continental breakfast. The tug can be reserved for small parties and weddings.

Innkeeper(s): Rick Anderson. $55-170. MC, VISA, AX, DC, DS, PC, TC. TAC10. 10 rooms, 7 with PB and 3 suites. Breakfast included in rates. Type of meal: Cont plus. Beds: QD. Phone in room. VCR, fax, copier, video library and refrigerators on premises. Small meetings and family reunions hosted. Amusement parks, antiquing, fishing, live theater, parks, shopping, sporting events and water sports nearby.

"Our stay with you was the highlight of our accommodations. Your breakfast was terrific and the staff was even better."

Tacoma   D4

Blue Willow Cottage B&B

827 N Prospect St
Tacoma, WA 98406-7807
(253)383-9238

Circa 1903. Blue Willow Cottage offers two guest accommodations. Monet's Garden Suite is a spacious room with a private deck that looks out to the garden. Poet's Corner is a cozy retreat with a floral English country theme. Both rooms include country furnishings. The homestay is located in a historic Tacoma neighborhood, near to antique shops, restaurants, the waterfront, University of Puget Sound and the University of Washington's Tacoma campus.

Historic Interest: Steilacoom, Washington state's oldest incorporated town (1854) (10 miles).
Innkeeper(s): Barbara Vlcek. $75-95. PC, TC. 2 rooms, 1 with PB. Breakfast included in rates. Types of meals: Full bkfst, cont plus and veg bkfst. Beds: Q. Antiquing, art galleries, beaches, bicycling, live theater, museums, parks, shopping and water sports nearby.

Commencement Bay B&B

3312 N Union Ave
Tacoma, WA 98407-6055
(253)752-8175 Fax:(253)759-4025
E-mail: greatviews@aol.com
Web: www.great-views.com

Circa 1937. Watch boats sail across the bay while enjoying breakfast served with gourmet coffee at this Colonial Revival inn. All guest rooms feature bay views and each is unique and individually decorated. The surrounding area includes historic sites, antique shops, waterfront restaurants, wooded nature trails and Pt. Defiance Zoo and Aquarium. Relax in a secluded hot tub and deck area or in the fireside room for reading and the romantic view. The innkeepers also offer an exercise room and video/book library. Business travelers will appreciate amenities such as dataports, free e-mail and cable Internet access. The B&B is centrally located, 30 miles from both Seattle and Mt. Rainier park.

Historic Interest: Washington State Historical Museum (2 miles), Fort Nisqually first settlement in Washington, replica (2 miles), historic homes and buildings, driving tour (one-half mile) and Karples Manuscript Museum (1 mile).
Innkeeper(s): Sharon & Bill Kaufmann. $85-125. MC, VISA, AX, DS, PC, TC. TAC10. 3 rooms with PB and 2 conference rooms. Breakfast, afternoon tea and snacks/refreshments included in rates. AP. Types of meals: Full bkfst and early coffee/tea. Beds: Q. Cable TV, phone, VCR and robes in room. Fax, spa, bicycles, computer data ports, exercise room, massages and exercise room on premises. Small meetings hosted. Antiquing, fishing, Washington State Historic Museum, botanical parks, restaurants, live theater, parks, shopping, sporting events and water sports nearby.

"Perfect in every detail! The setting, breathtaking; the food, scrumptious and beautifully presented; the warmth and friendship here."

Uniontown   E10

Churchyard Inn

206 Saint Boniface St
Uniontown, WA 99179
(509)229-3200 Fax:(509)229-3213

Circa 1905. Not surprisingly, this historic inn is located adjacent to a church. From 1913 until 1972, the home served as a convent. The three-story brick home is adorned with a second-

story portico supported by two columns. The innkeepers restored the home to its turn-of-the-century grace and added a new wing. The inn's restored red fir woodwork is a highlight. The seven guest rooms include a spacious third-floor suite with a kitchen and fireplace. The home is listed in the National Register of Historic Places.

Innkeeper(s): Marvin J. & Linda J. Entel. $55-135. MC, VISA, DS. 7 rooms with PB, 1 with FP, 1 suite and 1 conference room. Breakfast included in rates. Types of meals: Full bkfst, cont and early coffee/tea. Beds: KQDT. Phone, ceiling fan and window fans in room. VCR and fax on premises. Handicap access. Weddings, small meetings, family reunions and seminars hosted. Antiquing, fishing, golf, parks, shopping, sporting events and water sports nearby.

"Beautiful property, location and setting. I would recommend this wonderful B&B to anyone coming to the area."

Yakima   E6

A Touch Of Europe™ B&B Inn Yakima

220 N 16th Ave
Yakima, WA 98902-2461
(509)454-9775 (888)438-7073
Web: www.winesnw.com/toucheuropeb&b.htm

Circa 1889. A lumber baron built this Queen Anne Victorian, which still maintains period elements such as stained glass and rich woodwork. Theodore Roosevelt was a guest of the home's second owner, who was the first woman to be a member of the Washington State House of Representatives. Roosevelt's portrait is displayed among other historical photographs. The guest rooms are elegant, featuring period decor and Victorian furnishings. Innkeeper, European chef and cookbook author  Erika Cenci prepares the multi-course breakfasts, which are served by candlelight. By prior request, guests and non-guests may arrange private luncheons, gracious high teas (for 6 to 20 guests) or memorable one-of-a-kind multi-course dinners (for 2 to 20 guests). Ask about the area's 27 highly acclaimed wineries. Maps are available for self-guided tours or the innkeepers can provide a private guide.

Innkeeper(s): Erika G. and James A. Cenci. $75-110. MC, VISA, AX, TC. TAC10. 3 rooms with PB, 1 with FP and 1 conference room. Breakfast included in rates. Type of meal: Full bkfst. Beds: QT. Phone in room. Air conditioning. Library on premises. Small meetings hosted. German and English spoken. Antiquing, fishing, golf, convention Center, skiing, parks, sporting events, tennis, water sports and wineries nearby.

"Thank you for your warmth and friendliness and outstanding food! Your home is beautiful."

Washington, D.C.

The Embassy Inn

1627 16th St NW
Washington, DC 20009-3063
(202)234-7800 (800)423-9111 Fax:(202)234-3309

Circa 1910. This restored inn is furnished in a Federalist style. The comfortable lobby offers books and evening sherry. Conveniently located, the inn is seven blocks from the Adams Morgan area of ethnic restaurants. The Embassy's philosophy of innkeeping includes providing personal attention and cheerful hospitality. Concierge services are available. The inn does not have an elevator.

Innkeeper(s): Susan Stiles. $79-150. MC, VISA, AX, DC, CB, TC. TAC10. 38 rooms with PB. Breakfast included in rates. Type of meal: Cont plus. Snacks/refreshments available. Beds: DT. Cable TV, phone and free HBO in room. Air conditioning. Fax, copier and Washington Post daily on premises. Antiquing, white House, live theater, museums and parks nearby.

"When I return to D.C., I'll be back at the Embassy."

Reeds B&B

PO Box 12011
Washington, DC 20005-0911
(202)328-3510 Fax:(202)332-3885

Circa 1887. This three-story Victorian townhouse was built by John Shipman, who owned one of the first construction companies in the city. The turn-of-the-century revitalization of Washington began in Logan Circle, considered to be the city's first truly residential area. During the house's restoration, flower gardens, terraces and fountains were added. Victorian antiques, original wood paneling, stained glass, chandeliers, as well as practical amenities such as air conditioning and laundry facilities, make this a comfortable stay. There is a furnished apartment available, as well.

Historic Interest: U.S. Capitol, Congress, Smithsonian Museums, White House, all national monuments.

Innkeeper(s): Charles & Jackie Reed. $65-150. MC, VISA, AX, DC, TC. TAC8. 6 rooms, 5 with PB, 3 with FP and 1 suite. Breakfast included in rates. Type of meal: Cont plus. Beds: QD. Cable TV, phone and player Piano in room. Air conditioning. Spa on premises. Weddings, small meetings and family reunions hosted. French and Spanish spoken. Antiquing, live theater, parks, shopping and sporting events nearby.

Publicity: *Philadelphia Inquirer, Washington Gardner, Washington Post, 101 Great Choices, Washington, DC.*

"This home was the highlight of our stay in Washington! This was a superb home and location. The Reeds treated us better than family."

Swann House

1808 New Hampshire Ave NW
Washington, DC 20009-3206
(202)265-4414 Fax:(202)265-6755
E-mail: stay@swannhouse.com
Web: www.swannhouse.com

Circa 1883. Swann House is a splendid example of Richardson Romanesque architecture and all its glory. The gothic brick home includes a turret and an arched, covered front porch and a lavish, second-story balcony. The interior includes the original crown moldings, hardwood floors, a carved marble fireplace and original doors and paneling. The guest rooms and suites are decorated with an eclectic mix of antiques and contemporary furnishings. Several include a fireplace. Guests can take in the city view from a rooftop deck or enjoy the backyard garden, which includes a fountain. The home is located in Dupont Circle, with Washington, D.C.'s, myriad of attractions all close by.

Historic Interest: White House, Arlington Cemetary, Mt. Vernon, National Mall.

Innkeeper(s): Mary & Richard Ross. $110-250. MC, VISA, AX, DC, DS, PC, TC. 12 rooms with PB, 6 with FP and 2 conference rooms. Breakfast and snacks/refreshments included in rates. Type of meal: Cont plus. Beds: KQ. Cable TV and phone in room. Central air. VCR, fax, copier, swimming, pool, roof deck, balconies and gardens on premises. Weddings, small meetings, family reunions and seminars hosted. Antiquing, art galleries, bicycling, Congress, memorials, historical attractions, live theater, museums, parks and shopping nearby.

The Windsor Inn

1842 16th St NW
Washington, DC 20009-3316
(202)667-0300 (800)423-9111 Fax:(202)667-4503

Circa 1910. Recently renovated and situated in a neighborhood of renovated townhouses, the Windsor Inn is the sister property to the Embassy Inn. It is larger and offers suites as well as a small meeting room. The refurbished lobby is in an Art Deco style and a private club atmosphere prevails. It is six blocks to the Metro station at Dupont Circle. There are no elevators.

Historic Interest: White House (12 blocks), Arlington House (3 miles), Hillwood House (2 miles), Mount Vernon (14 miles).

Innkeeper(s): Susan Stiles. $79-159. MC, VISA, AX, DC, CB, TC. TAC10. 45 rooms with PB, 2 suites and 1 conference room. Breakfast included in rates. Type of meal: Cont plus. Snacks/refreshments available. Beds: QDT. TV, phone and some refrigerators in room. Air conditioning. Fax, copier and Washington Post daily on premises. Weddings, small meetings and family reunions hosted. French and Spanish spoken. Antiquing, live theater and parks nearby.

"Being here was like being home. Excellent service, would recommend."

West Virginia

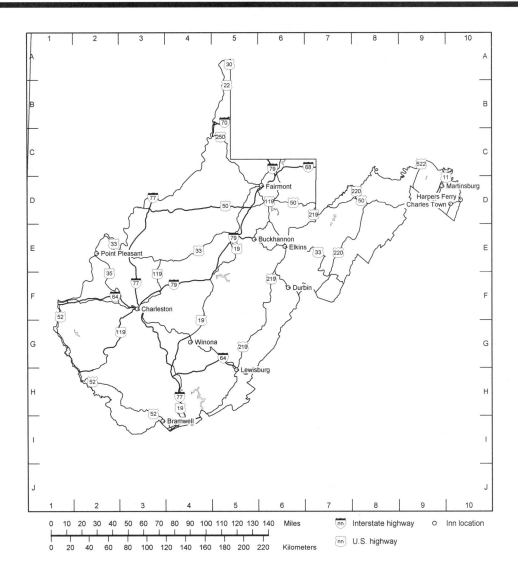

Bramwell 13

Perry House B&B

Main St, PO Box 188
Bramwell, WV 24715-0248
(304)248-8145 (800)328-0248

Circa 1902. This brick Victorian was built by a bank cashier and remained in the family for 80 years. The rooms are decorated in period style with antiques. Although a small village, Bramwell once was home to more than a dozen millionaires, and some of these families' homes are located on the town walking tour. The inn is listed in the National Register.
Innkeeper(s): Joyce & Jim Bishop. $55-85. MC, VISA, PC, TC. TAC10. 4 rooms, 1 with PB. Breakfast included in rates. Types of meals: Cont and early coffee/tea. Beds: QDT. Phone and ceiling fan in room. Air conditioning. Copier on premises. Weddings and family reunions hosted. Antiquing, fishing, live theater, parks, shopping, downhill skiing and water sports nearby.

Buckhannon E5

Post Mansion Inn Bed & Breakfast

8 Island Ave
Buckhannon, WV 26201-2822
(304)472-8959 (800)301-9309

Circa 1860. This massive Neoclassical Revival mansion is constructed of brick and precision-cut stone. An attached three-story stone tower resembles a medieval castle. Located on six acres, this National Register inn is bordered by the Buckhannon River on the front and back of the grounds. Victorian antiques furnish the inn. Children of all ages enjoy touring the slave quarters in the basement and barn, as well as the gymnasium.

Innkeeper(s): Lawrence & Suzanne Reger. $80. PC, TC. TAC10. 3 rooms, 1 with PB and 1 conference room. Breakfast and snacks/refreshments included in rates. Types of meals: Full bkfst and early coffee/tea. Beds: QD. Cable TV and ceiling fan in room. Air conditioning. VCR on premises. Weddings, small meetings, family reunions and seminars hosted. Antiquing, golf, parks, downhill skiing and water sports nearby.

"We were so pleased with everything and all the guests couldn't say enough about your beautiful home."

Charleston F3

Brass Pineapple B&B

1611 Virginia St E
Charleston, WV 25311-2113
(304)344-0748 (800)CAL-LWVA Fax:(304)344-0748
E-mail: pineapp104@aol.com
Web: www.wvweb.com/brasspineapplebandb

Circa 1910. This elegant smoke-free inn is situated in Charleston's historic district, one-half block from the Capitol Complex. Original oak paneling and leaded and stained glass are among the architectural highlights. Thoughtful amenities

such as terry robes and hair dryers have been placed in each guest room. In-room phones offer voice mail. For the extended-stay business traveler, there are one- and two-bedroom furnished apartments available. Guests can enjoy a gourmet breakfast or opt for lighter, low-fat continental fare. Honeymooners can have breakfast delivered to them on a silver tray. Limited airport pick-up and delivery is available, and the inn hosts small business meetings.
Innkeeper(s): Bill & Sue Pepper. $59-109. MC, VISA, AX, DC, PC, TC. TAC10. 6 rooms with PB, 1 suite and 3 cottages. Breakfast, afternoon tea and snacks/refreshments included in rates. Types of meals: Full bkfst, cont plus and early coffee/tea. Beds: KQT. Cable TV, phone, VCR, robes and voice mail in room. Air conditioning. Fax, copier and bicycles on premises. Small meetings hosted. Antiquing, fishing, golf, horseback riding, river cruises, live theater, parks, shopping, sporting events, tennis and water sports nearby.
Publicity: *Mid-Atlantic Country, Charlestonian, News 8 TV, Charleston Daily Mail, Gourmet, Southern Living, Recommended Country Inns.*

"Charming, convenient location, lovely antiques, appealing decor. Extremely clean; excellent service from Sue and her staff."

Historic Charleston B&B

110 Elizabeth St
Charleston, WV 25311-2117
(304)345-8156 (800)225-5982

Circa 1907. Located only one block from the state Capitol, this gray three-story French Country house is a city historical site, located in the historic district. The construction (balloon) creates many rounded corners in the inn's interior. There are long French windows, dormers on the third floor, six fireplaces and original cabinets in the kitchen. Furnishings include antiques, collectibles and country crafts. The Bridal Suite also offers a whirlpool tub. Breakfast treats may feature pecan pancakes, apple dumplings, or French toast, eggs and home-baked breads and muffins. Take a morning cup of coffee out to the six foot long swing on the front porch and relax and later enjoy a walk to the governor's mansion and the state cultural center on the capitol grounds.

Innkeeper(s): Robert & Jean Lambert. $65-95. 4 rooms with PB. Type of meal: Full bkfst.

Charles Town D10

Gilbert House B&B of Middleway

PO Box 1104
Charles Town, WV 25414-7104
(304)725-0637

Circa 1760. A magnificent graystone of early Georgian design, the Gilbert House is located in one of the state's oldest European settlements. Elegant appointments include fine Oriental rugs, tasteful art and antique furnishings. During restoration, graffiti found on the upstairs bedroom walls included an 1832 drawing of the future President James Polk and a child's growth chart from the 1800s. The inn is located in the Colonial era mill village of Middleway, which contains one of the country's best collections of log houses. The village is a mill site on the original settlers' trail into Shenandoah Valley ("Philadelphia Waggon Road" on Peter

Jefferson's 1755 map of Virginia). Middleway was also the site of "wizard clip" hauntings during the last decade of the 1700s. The region was home to members of "Virginia Blues," commanded by Daniel Morgan during the Revolutionary War.

Historic Interest: Charles Town, Bunker Hill, Leetown (10 minutes), Antietam Battlefield (20 minutes), Winchester, Va. (25 minutes), Harpers Ferry (20 minutes).

Innkeeper(s): Bernie Heiler. $100-140. MC, VISA, AX, PC, TC. TAC10. 3 rooms with PB, 2 with FP and 1 suite. Breakfast included in rates. Type of meal: Full gourmet bkfst. Beds: QT. Air conditioning. VCR and library on premises. German and Spanish spoken. Antiquing, sports car racing, live theater, parks and shopping nearby.

"We have stayed at inns for fifteen years, and yours is at the top of the list as best ever!"

The Washington House Inn

216 S George St
Charles Town, WV 25414-1632
(304)725-7923 (800)297-6957 Fax:(304)728-5150
E-mail: emailus@washingtonhouseinnwv.com
Web: www.washingtonhouseinnwv.com

Circa 1899. This three-story brick Victorian was built by the descendants of President Washington's brothers, John Augustine and Samuel. Carved oak mantels, spacious guest rooms, antique furnishings and refreshments served on the

wraparound veranda or gazebo make the inn memorable. For business travelers, dataports are available. Harpers Ferry National Historic Park, Antietam, and the Shenandoah and Potomac rivers are all within a 15-minute drive, as is Martinsburg outlet shopping. Thoroughbred racing and car racing are some of the popular area attractions.

Innkeeper(s): Mel & Nina Vogel. $75-125. MC, VISA, AX, DS, PC, TC. TAC10. 6 rooms with PB, 1 suite and 1 conference room. Breakfast and snacks/refreshments included in rates. Types of meals: Full bkfst, cont plus, cont and early coffee/tea. Beds: QT. Cable TV, phone and ceiling fan in room. Air conditioning. VCR, fax, copier, data ports, internet and antiques and collectibles for sale on premises. Small meetings, family reunions and seminars hosted. Antiquing, fishing, golf, history museums, horse racing, car racing, live theater, parks, shopping and water sports nearby.

Durbin   F6

Cheat Mountain Club

Rt 250 PO Box 28
Durbin, WV 26264-0028
(304)456-4627 (800)225-5982 Fax:(304)456-3192

Circa 1887. Built from hand-hewn logs, this historic lodge has served as an accommodation for such notable guests as Thomas Edison, Henry Ford and Harvey Firestone. These and

other guests have been drawn to the excellent fishing and outdoor activities available in the surrounding Monongahela National Forest. A trout stream runs past the inn. Guest rooms are decorated with antiques and maple furnishings; most have shared baths. The

rates include all three meals. A dinner menu might include cornish game hen with an apricot glaze, roasted garlic potatoes, salad, homemade bread and dessert.

$160-300. MC, VISA, PC, TC. TAC10. 10 rooms, 1 with PB and 2 conference rooms. Breakfast, dinner and picnic lunch included in rates. AP. Type of meal: Full bkfst. Afternoon tea, lunch and banquet service available. Beds: KQT. Fax, copier, hunting and fishing on premises. Weddings, small meetings, family reunions and seminars hosted. Antiquing, fishing, golf, mountain biking, national forest at your door, Cass scenic railroad, parks, shopping, downhill skiing and cross-country skiing nearby.

Elkins   E6

Tunnel Mountain B&B

Rt 1, Box 59-1
Elkins, WV 26241-9711
(304)636-1684 (888)211-9123

Circa 1938. Nestled on five acres of wooded land, this three-story Fieldstone home offers privacy in a peaceful setting. Rooms are tastefully decorated with antiques, collectibles and

crafts. Each bedroom boasts a view of the surrounding mountains. The chestnut and knotty pine woodwork accentuate the decor. The fireplace in the large common room is a great place for warming up after a day of touring or skiing. The area is home to a number of interesting events, including a Dulcimer festival.

Historic Interest: Rich Mountain Battlefield (20 miles), Halliehurst Mansion (4 miles), Beverly Museum (10 miles), Historic Elkins Walking Tour (4 miles), Beverly Historic Cemetery (10 miles), Old Mill (20 miles).

Innkeeper(s): Anne & Paul Beardslee. $70-80. PC, TC. 3 rooms with PB. Breakfast included in rates. Type of meal: Full bkfst. Beds: QD. Cable TV in room. Air conditioning. Antiquing, fishing, rock climbing, live theater, parks, shopping, downhill skiing, cross-country skiing and water sports nearby.

The Warfield House B&B

318 Buffalo St
Elkins, WV 26241
(304)636-4555 (888)636-4555
Web: www.bbonline.com/wv/warfield

Circa 1901. Restaurants, shops, boutiques, and theater are a five-minute stroll from the historic Warfield House, which is listed in the National Register. Guests can relax on the wraparound porch, in front of a fire in the library or strum the ivories on the parlor's piano. The turn-of-the-20th-century home features five guest rooms, each decorated with antiques and quilts. Two include a whirlpool tub. The home faces a city

park and is next to Davis and Elkins College. Elkins is the site of many annual festivals and events.

Innkeeper(s): Connie & Paul Garnett. $75-90. PC, TC. 5 rooms with PB. Breakfast included in rates. Type of meal: Full bkfst. Beds: QDT. Ceiling fan in room. Fax, bicycles and library on premises. Small meetings, family reunions and seminars hosted. Antiquing, bicycling, fishing, golf, hiking, historic attractions, battlefields, rock climbing, live theater, parks, shopping, downhill skiing, cross-country skiing, tennis and water sports nearby.

Fairmont
D6

Acacia House

158 Locust Ave
Fairmont, WV 26554-1630
(304)367-1000 (888)269-9541 Fax:(304)367-1000
E-mail: acacia@acaciahousewv.com
Web: www.acaciahousewv.com

Circa 1917. Two maple trees frame this four-story brown brick home built in the Neoclassical style. As an antique dealer, innkeeper Kathy Sprowls has filled her home with a memorable assortment of collectibles, including butter pats, pill boxes and stone eggs from around the world. There's an antique store on the premises and items found in the inn are also available for purchase. Guest rooms are handsomely furnished with antiques, of course. Kathy and her husband, George, serve a country breakfast in the dining room with Texas French toast or puffed pancakes, hot pepper bacon or West Virginia sausage and a fruit cup. As with most bed & breakfasts, smoking is not allowed.

Innkeeper(s): Kathy & George Sprowls. $45-70. MC, VISA, AX, DC, DS, PC, TC. TAC10. 4 rooms, 2 with PB. Breakfast included in rates. Types of meals: Full bkfst, cont plus, cont and early coffee/tea. Beds: QDT. TV in room. Air conditioning. VCR, fax and library on premises. Small meetings and family reunions hosted. Arabic spoken. Antiquing, bicycling, fishing, golf, live theater, parks, shopping, sporting events and water sports nearby.

Harpers Ferry
D10

Fillmore Street B&B

PO Box 34
Harpers Ferry, WV 25425-0034
(304)535-2619

Circa 1890. This two-story clapboard Victorian was built on the foundation of a Civil War structure on land deeded by Jefferson Davis, Secretary of War. The surrounding acreage was an encampment for both the Union and Confederate soldiers (at different times). Within walking distance of the inn are the national park, museums, shopping and dining.

Historic Interest: Harpers Ferry National Historic Park (two blocks), Potomac and Shenandoah Rivers.

Innkeeper(s): Alden & James Addy. $75-85. PC, TC. 2 rooms with PB. Breakfast included in rates. Types of meals: Full bkfst, cont plus and early coffee/tea. Beds: Q. Cable TV, turndown service and VCR in room. Air conditioning. Library on premises. Antiquing, hiking, bicycling, battlefields, historic exhibits, parks, shopping and water sports nearby.

"Delightful! What superb hosts you two are. We enjoyed ourselves luxuriously."

Lewisburg
H5

The General Lewis

301 E Washington St
Lewisburg, WV 24901-1425
(304)645-2600 (800)628-4454 Fax:(304)645-2600

Circa 1834. This gracious Federal-style inn boasts a columned veranda, flower gardens and long lawns. Patrick Henry and Thomas Jefferson registered at the inn's walnut desk, which was retrieved from an old hot springs resort in the area. A stagecoach that once delivered travelers to springs on the James River and Kanawha Turnpike, rests under an arbor. American

antiques are featured throughout the inn, and Memory Hall displays household items and tools once used by local pioneers. Nearby are state parks, national forests, streams and rivers, as well as sites of the Revolutionary and Civil wars.

Historic Interest: Civil War Cemetery, Carnegie Hall, Pearl S. Buck's Birthplace.

Innkeeper(s): Nan Morgan. $89-112. MC, VISA, AX, DS. TAC10. 26 rooms with PB and 2 suites. Type of meal: Early coffee/tea. Restaurant on premises. Beds: QD. Cable TV and phone in room. Air conditioning. Fax and copier on premises. Handicap access. Weddings hosted.

"Personality, charm and gracious service."

Martinsburg
D9

Boydville, The Inn at Martinsburg

601 S Queen St
Martinsburg, WV 25401-3103
(304)263-1448

Circa 1812. This Georgian estate was saved from burning by Union troops only by a specific proclamation from President Lincoln dated July 18, 1864. Tall maples line the long driveway leading up to the house. Guests can relax in rockers original to the inn on the spacious porch while gazing at 10 acres of lawns. The entry hall retains the original wallpaper brought from England in 1812 and hand-painted murals, fireplaces, and antiques adorn the spacious guest rooms. Sunlight filters through tree tops onto estate-sized lawns and gardens.

Historic Interest: Antietam Battlefield, Harpers Ferry, Berkeley Springs.

Innkeeper(s): LaRue Frye. $100-125. MC, VISA, PC. 7 rooms with PB and 1 conference room. Breakfast included in rates. Types of meals: Cont plus and early coffee/tea. Beds: QDT. Air conditioning. Library on premises. Weddings and family reunions hosted. Antiquing, Blue Ridge Outlet, golf, live theater, shopping and downhill skiing nearby.

"Your gracious home, hospitality and excellent amenities were enjoyed so much. Such a fine job of innkeeping."

Pulpit & Palette Inn

516 W John St
Martinsburg, WV 25401-2635
(304)263-7012

Circa 1870. Listed in the National Register, this Victorian inn is set off by a handsome iron fence. The interior is filled with a mix of American antiques, Tibetan rugs and art, setting off moldings and other architectural details in the library, drawing room and upstairs veranda. Your British-born innkeeper prepares afternoon tea for guests. The Blue Ridge Outlet Center is one block away.

Historic Interest: Harpers Ferry National Park (30 minutes), New Market Civil War Museum (80 minutes), Antietam Battlefield (20 minutes), Gettysburg National Park (80 minutes).

Innkeeper(s): Bill & Janet Starr. $80. MC, VISA, TC. 2 rooms. Breakfast, afternoon tea and snacks/refreshments included in rates. Types of meals: Full gourmet bkfst and early coffee/tea. Beds: Q. Turndown service in room. Air conditioning. Antiquing, canoeing, live theater, parks and shopping nearby.

"You have set an ideal standard for comfort and company."

Point Pleasant   E2

Stone Manor
12 Main St
Point Pleasant, WV 25550-1026
(304)675-3442 Fax:(304)675-7323

Circa 1887. This stone Victorian sits on the banks of the Kanawha River with a front porch that faces the river. Point Pleasant Battle Monument Park, adjacent to the inn, was built to commemorate the location of the first battle of the Revolutionary War. In the National Register, the inn was once the home of a family who ran a ferry boat crossing for the Ohio and Kanawha rivers. Now restored, the house is decorated with Victorian antiques and offers a pleasant garden with a Victorian fish pond and fountain.

Innkeeper(s): Janice & Tom Vance. $50. PC. 3 rooms, 3 with FP. Breakfast included in rates. Type of meal: Full bkfst. Beds: QD. VCR in room. Air conditioning.

Winona   G4

Garvey House
PO Box 98
Winona, WV 25942-0098
(304)574-3235 (800)767-3235
E-mail: garveyhs@cwv.net
Web: www.visitwv.com/garveyhouse

Circa 1916. Two mountainside, turn-of-the-century homes comprise this inn, which is surrounded by three lush acres decorated with trees, plants, flowers, a gazebo and goldfish pond. There is also an outdoor Jacuzzi. The secluded main house was built by a superintendent of the Maryland New River Coal Company. Guests sleep on antique beds, and there is an eclectic mix of antiques throughout the comfortable homes. A hearty homemade breakfast is served, and on request, dinners can be prepared. The area is known for its excellent white-water rafting, hiking and climbing.

Innkeeper(s): Christopher Terrafranca & Darrell Riedesel. $54-66. MC, VISA, TC. TAC10. 9 rooms, 6 with PB. Breakfast included in rates. Type of meal: Full bkfst. Dinner available. Beds: DT. Ceiling fan in room. Spa on premises. Weddings, small meetings, family reunions and seminars hosted. Antiquing, fishing, parks and shopping nearby.

Wisconsin

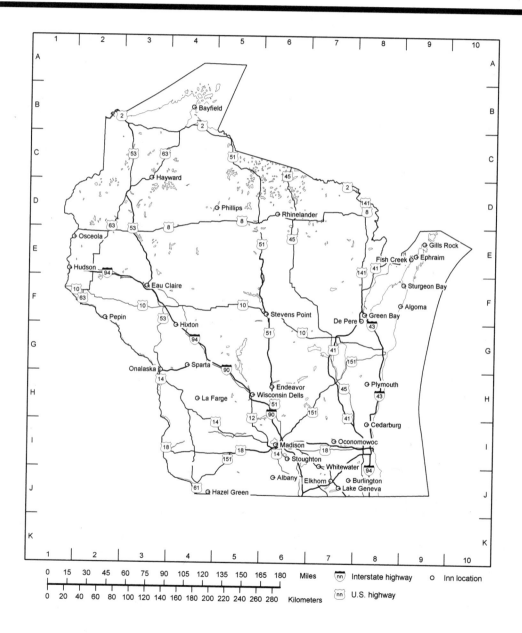

0 15 30 45 60 75 90 105 120 135 150 165 180   Miles

0 20 40 60 80 100 120 140 160 180 200 220 240 260 280   Kilometers

(nn) Interstate highway   o Inn location

(nn) U.S. highway

Albany
J6

Albany House

405 S Mill St
Albany, WI 53502-9502
(608)862-3636 Fax:(608)862-1837

Circa 1908. The brick walkway, French-tiled foyer, over-stuffed furniture and abundance of flowers both inside and out set the comfortable tone for this three-story inn. A baby grand piano in the large foyer and fireplace in the living room also add to the pleasant atmosphere. The guest rooms have large windows overlooking the garden and are furnished with many antiques and collectibles. Outside, maple and black walnut trees and various gardens grace the inn's two-acre property. Guests can tour New Glarus, a village known as America's Little Switzerland, which is a short drive away. Guests also can enjoy a bicycle ride on the nearby Sugar River Trail or canoe on the Sugar River.

Historic Interest: The Tallman House, the last existing house where Lincoln slept, is 25 miles away. The original Green County Courthouse with its restored clock tower is in Monroe, a 15-mile drive. The state capitol is 30 miles north.

Innkeeper(s): Ken & Margie Stoup. $65-95. MC, VISA, PC. 6 rooms, 4 with PB, 1 with FP. Breakfast included in rates. Types of meals: Full bkfst and early coffee/tea. Beds: KQD. Ceiling fan in room. Air conditioning. VCR, library, swings, hammock and horseshoe on premises. Small meetings, family reunions and seminars hosted. Antiquing, bicycling, canoeing/kayaking, fishing, parks and cross-country skiing nearby.

Publicity: *Silent Sports, Madison, Monroe Evening Times.*

"Was even more than I expected."

Algoma
F8

Amberwood Inn

N7136 Hwy 42, Lakeshore Dr
Algoma, WI 54201
(920)487-3471
E-mail: markrittle@itol.com
Web: www.amberwoodinn.com

Circa 1925. Amberwood Inn boasts 300 feet of Lake Michigan beachfront. Guests can enjoy the lake view from their rooms or

on a private deck. Jacuzzi tubs and fireplaces are among the amenities. Surrounding Door County offers a wide variety of outdoor activities.

Historic Interest: Historic Door County Wisconsin and Packer Hall of Fame are among the area's historic offerings.

Innkeeper(s): Mark & Karen Rittle. $80-115. MC, VISA, PC, TC. 5 rooms with PB, 5 with FP. Breakfast included in rates. Type of meal: Full bkfst. Beds: KQT. TV, whirlpool and wet bars in room. Refrigerators and private entrances on premises. Antiquing, fishing, live theater, parks, shopping and water sports nearby.

"Very personable, friendly, down-to-earth."

Bayfield
B4

Apple Tree Inn

Rt 1, Box 251, Hwy 135
Bayfield, WI 54814-9767
(715)779-5572 (800)400-6532

Circa 1911. The Apple Tree Inn is a fully restored farmhouse overlooking Lake Superior. It was once owned by a dairy farmer and landscape artist. A hearty, country-style breakfast is served in the sunroom, which boasts

a panoramic view of Madeline Island and Lake Superior. Guest rooms are furnished in early Americana style and three have lake views.

Historic Interest: Apostle Islands National Lakeshore Park (1 mile).

Innkeeper(s): Ellen & Rick Melcher. $85-95. MC, VISA, PC. TAC10. 5 rooms with PB. Breakfast included in rates. Types of meals: Full gourmet bkfst and early coffee/tea. Beds: KQD. Ceiling fan in room. Air conditioning. VCR on premises. Family reunions hosted. Antiquing, canoeing/kayaking, fishing, sailing, live theater, parks, shopping, downhill skiing, cross-country skiing and water sports nearby.

Pets allowed: Please check with innkeeper.

"You made us feel like old friends rather than guests."

Burlington
J7

The Hillcrest Inn & Carriage House

540 Storle Ave
Burlington, WI 53105-1030
(262)763-4706 (800)313-9030

Circa 1908. Romantic, luxurious and private, this stately Edwardian estate situated on four wooded acres offers visitors a magnificent view of two rivers, a lake, rolling farmlands and rustic countryside. An open staircase, beveled windows, homemade quilts and wood floors highlighted by a carefully furnished antique-filled interior are just a few of the inn's amenities. Guests have the option of staying in the main house or the elegantly restored original carriage house. Guests may relax and enjoy the sights from one of the historic estate's two porches while comfortably seated on antique wicker furniture.

Innkeeper(s): Gayle & Mike Hohner. $90-170. MC, VISA. 6 rooms with PB, 3 with FP. Type of meal: Full bkfst. Beds: Q. Fishing, golf, cross-country skiing and tennis nearby.

"We had a delightful time, absolutely beautiful home and gardens."

Cedarburg
I8

Stagecoach Inn B&B

W 61 N 520 Washington Ave
Cedarburg, WI 53012
(262)375-0208 (888)375-0208 Fax:(262)375-6170
E-mail: info@stagecoach-inn-wi.com
Web: www.stagecoach-inn-wi.com

Circa 1853. This historic Greek Revival inn has been welcoming travelers since its earliest days, when it served as a stagecoach stop between Milwaukee and Green Bay. The innkeepers used 19th-century photographs to help authenticate the inn's meticulous restoration. In addition to the nine guest rooms, the inn houses a pub where the continental-plus breakfasts are served in the mornings and complimentary wine in the afternoon. The innkeepers have owned Stagecoach Inn since the early 1980s. In 1991, they restored Weber Haus, an 1847 house across the street from the inn. Weber Haus offers three suites with whirlpool tubs. Two of the suites include a fireplace, and there is a secret garden to explore and enjoy. Many attractions are within walking distance, including a historic district, antique shops, galleries, a winery and restaurants.

Historic Interest: Cedarburg, known as the antique capital of Wisconsin, is listed in the National Register. Milwaukee, about 20 minutes north of the inn, offers many museums and historic buildings.

Innkeeper(s): Brook & Liz Brown. $75-140. MC, VISA, AX, DC, DS. 12 rooms with PB, 2 with FP, 6 suites and 1 conference room. Breakfast included in rates. Type of meal: Cont plus. Room service available. Beds: QDT. TV, phone and suite has whirlpool tub in room. Air conditioning. Antiquing, art galleries, cedar Creek Settlement, Pioneer village, shopping and wineries nearby.

"Cedarburg is a lovely town and this is a great place from which to explore it. We hope to return."

The Washington House Inn

W 62 N 573 Washington Ave
Cedarburg, WI 53012-1941
(414)375-3550 (800)554-4717 Fax:(414)375-9422
E-mail: whinn@execpc.com
Web: www.washingtonhouseinn.com

Circa 1886. Completely renovated, this three-story cream city brick building is in the National Register. Rooms are appointed in a country Victorian style and feature antiques, whirlpool baths, vases of flowers and fireplaces. The original guest registry, more than 100 years old, is displayed proudly in the lobby, and a marble trimmed fireplace is often lit for the afternoon wine and cheese hour. Breakfast is continental and is available in the gathering room, often including recipes from a historic Cedarburg cookbook for items such as homemade muffins, cakes and breads.

Historic Interest: National Register.

Innkeeper(s): Wendy Porterfield. $75-205. MC, VISA, AX, DC, DS, TC. 34 rooms with PB, 3 suites and 1 conference room. Breakfast included in rates. MAP. Type of meal: Cont plus. Snacks/refreshments available. Beds: KQD. Cable TV, phone, ceiling fan and VCR in room. Air conditioning. Fax, copier and sauna on premises. Weddings, small meetings, family reunions and seminars hosted. Antiquing, fishing, live theater, parks, shopping, cross-country skiing and sporting events nearby.

Publicity: *Country Home, Chicago Sun-Times.*

De Pere
F8

James St. Inn

201 James St
De Pere, WI 54115-2562
(920)337-0111 (800)897-8483 Fax:(920)337-6135
E-mail: jamesst@netnet.net
Web: www.jamesstreetinn.com

Circa 1995. In 1858, a flour mill sat where the James St. Inn now stands. The mill later burned and the inn was built in its place. Set alongside the Fox River, the water still flows beneath the structure as it did when it powered the mill more than a century before. The inn appears more as a creation of the 19th century than a modern building. Traditional and Shaker furnishings appear in the guest rooms. Some rooms also include whirlpool tubs, fireplaces or balconies with river views. The inn is located in the heart of downtown De Pere, so there's plenty to do. Shops, restaurants, a railroad museum and the Green Bay Packer Hall of Fame are just minutes away.

Innkeeper(s): Kevin Flatley & Joan Pruner. $69-139. MC, VISA, AX, DS, PC, TC. TAC10. 30 rooms with PB, 4 with FP, 27 suites and 1 conference room. Breakfast and snacks/refreshments included in rates. Types of meals: Cont plus and early coffee/tea. Beds: Q. Cable TV, phone, VCR, decks over the river and data port on phones in room. Air conditioning. Fax and copier on premises. Handicap access. Small meetings, family reunions and seminars hosted. Amusement parks, antiquing, fishing, live theater, parks, shopping, cross-country skiing, sporting events and water sports nearby.

Eau Claire
F3

Fanny Hill Inn

3919 Crescent Ave
Eau Claire, WI 54703-9170
(715)836-8184 (800)292-8026 Fax:(715)836-8180

Circa 1989. This modern inn, built in the Queen Anne Victorian style, provides an elegant lodging experience with its well-appointed guest rooms and dinner theater. Many of the romantic rooms boast fireplaces and whirlpool baths. Each offers Victorian furnishings, but still retains its own unique ambiance, including several with city, garden, woods or river views. Special dinner/theater packages are available.

Innkeeper(s): Dennis & Carol Heyde. $89-189. MC, VISA, AX, DS, PC. 2 rooms with PB and 1 conference room. Dinner, banquet service and catering service available. Beds: KQ. Cable TV, phone and ceiling fan in room. Air conditioning. VCR on premises. Weddings, small meetings, family reunions and seminars hosted. Antiquing, shopping, downhill skiing, cross-country skiing and sporting events nearby.

Otter Creek Inn

2536 Hwy 12. PO Box 3183
Eau Claire, WI 54702-3183
(715)832-2945 Fax:(715)832-4607

Circa 1920. On a hillside overlooking a creek is this Tudor-style inn, surrounded by oaks and pines. Visitors immediately feel welcome as they make their way up the inn's curved pebblestone walk and step into a house with country Victorian decor. Each of the guest rooms includes a double whirlpool tub, and many have a fireplace. The Rose Room, often the choice of honeymooners, features a cloverleaf-shaped whirlpool tub that overlooks the gardens and gazebo. The spacious inn provides many spots for relaxation, including a gazebo, the great room with its inviting fireplace and a roomy patio surrounding the in-ground heated swimming pool.

Innkeeper(s): Shelley & Randy Hansen. $79-169. MC, VISA, AX, DC, CB, DS, PC, TC. 6 rooms with PB and 1 suite. Breakfast and afternoon tea included in rates. Types of meals: Full bkfst and early coffee/tea. Beds: KQ. Cable TV, phone and double whirlpools in room. Air conditioning. Refrigerator on premises. Weddings and small meetings hosted. Antiquing, fishing, golf, live theater, parks, shopping, cross-country skiing, tennis and water sports nearby.

"This is the perfect place to recharge your 'couple batteries.'"

Elkhorn   J7

Ye Olde Manor House

N7622 US Hwy 12
Elkhorn, WI 53121
(414)742-2450 Fax:(414)742-2450

Circa 1905. Located on three tree-shaded acres, this country manor house offers travelers all the simple comforts of home. The guest rooms, living room and dining room are decorated with a variety of antiques and comfortable furniture that inspires a family atmosphere. One room offers a porch and views of Lauderdale Lakes. The B&B offers a full gourmet break-fast each morning.

Innkeeper(s): Babette & Marvin Henschel. $50-100. MC, VISA, AX, PC, TC. TAC10. 4 rooms, 2 with PB, 1 suite and 1 conference room. Breakfast included in rates. Types of meals: Full gourmet bkfst and early coffee/tea. Beds: QDT. Cable TV in room. VCR, fax and copier on premises. Small meetings, family reunions and seminars hosted. Antiquing, fishing, golf, live theater, parks, shopping, downhill skiing, cross-country skiing and water sports nearby.

Endeavor   H6

Neenah Creek Inn & Pottery

W7956 Neenah Rd
Endeavor, WI 53930-9308
(608)587-2229 Fax:(608)587-2229

Circa 1900. Wildlife-lovers will enjoy the creekfront setting of this turn-of-the-century Portage brick farmhouse. The Victorian Room offers a view of the creek and orchard. Other rooms include special touches such as a quilt-topped canopy bed. Country furnishings are found throughout the inn. Guests enjoy relaxing in the common room,

on the outdoor porch, in the solarium and in the spacious din-ing-living room. The inn's 11 acres are filled with walking paths. Don't be shy about asking for a demonstration of the potter's wheel. Wisconsin Dells is an easy drive away.

Innkeeper(s): Pat & Doug Cook. $75-115. MC, VISA, DS, TC. 4 rooms with PB and 1 suite. Breakfast and snacks/refreshments included in rates. MAP. Types of meals: Full gourmet bkfst and early coffee/tea. Beds: QT. Air conditioning. VCR, fax, copier, bicycles and sun-room and resident potter on premises. Amusement parks, antiquing, fishing, golf, live theater, parks, shopping, downhill skiing, cross-country skiing and water sports nearby.

Ephraim   E9

Eagle Harbor Inn

9914 Water St
Ephraim, WI 54211-0072
(920)854-2121 (800)324-5427 Fax:(920)854-2121

Circa 1946. The Eagle Harbor Inn is located in the historic district and offers a variety of accommodations. There are one and two-bedroom suites with six-foot whirlpool tubs and two-sided fireplaces, full kitchens and private decks. Rooms in the inn are

decorated with antiques.
Breakfast (optional for guests in the suites) is home cooked and served in the garden in summer-time. Afternoon refreshments are offered to all guests. There is an indoor current pool, sauna and

fitness room. A scenic sandy beach is a block away. Nearby are shops and galleries, and a half-hour drive leads guests to Rock Island, home of Wisconsin's first settlers. Door County Peninsula offers the largest selection of lighthouses in any U.S. county.

Innkeeper(s): Nedd & Natalie Neddersen. $64-199. MC, VISA, PC, TC. 41 rooms, 9 with PB, 32 with FP and 32 suites. Breakfast and afternoon tea included in rates. EP. Types of meals: Full gourmet bkfst and early coffee/tea. Banquet service and catering service available. Beds: Q. Cable TV, phone, ceiling fan and VCR in room. Air conditioning. Fax, copier, spa, swimming, sauna, library, child care, gardens, croquette, playground and picnic areas with woods and stream on premises. Handicap access. Weddings, small meetings, family reunions and seminars hosted. Antiquing, fishing, golf, his-toric walking tours, horse-drawn carriage rides, live theater, parks, shopping, downhill skiing, cross-country skiing, tennis and water sports nearby.

"From the friendly greeting when we arrived, to the elegant room, to the wonderful four-poster bed, our stay has been everything we hoped."

Fish Creek   E9

Thorp House Inn & Cottages

4135 Bluff Ln, PO Box 490
Fish Creek, WI 54212
(920)868-2444
E-mail: innkeeper@thorphouseinn.com
Web: www.thorphouseinn.com

Circa 1902. Freeman Thorp picked the site for this home because of its view of Green Bay and the village. Before his house was finished, however, he perished in the bay when the Erie L. Hackley sank. His wife completed it as a guest house. Each room is decorated with English or Victorian antiques. A stone fire-place is the focal point of the par-lor, and four of the cottages on the property have fireplaces. Some cot-

tages have whirlpools and all have kitchens, cable TVs and VCRs. Listed in the National Register of Historic Places, everything upon which the eye might rest in the inn must be "of the era." Breakfast is not included in the rates for cottage guests.

Historic Interest: The Asa Thorp Log Cabin and Noble House Museum are one block away. The Church of the Atonement is three blocks away, and the Peninsula Park Lighthouse is four miles from the inn.

Innkeeper(s): Christine & Sverre Falck-Pedersen. $85-185. PC, TC. 6 cottages with PB. Breakfast included in rates. Types of meals: Cont plus and early coffee/tea. Beds: KQDT. Ceiling fan and Jacuzzi (some rooms) in room. Bicycles on premises. Norwegian spoken. Antiquing, fishing, summer art school, music festival, live theater, parks, shopping, cross-country skiing and water sports nearby.

Publicity: *Madison PM, Green Bay Press-Gazette, Milwaukee Journal/Sentinel, McCall's, Minnesota Monthly.*

"Amazing attention to detail from restoration to the furnishings. A very first-class experience."

Gills Rock E9

Harbor House Inn

12666 Hwy 42
Gills Rock, WI 54210
(920)854-5196 Fax:(920)854-9717

Circa 1904. Gills Rock, a fishing village on the northern tip of Door County, is the home of the Harbor House Inn. The inn has been in the Weborg family since its inception, and the innkeepers recently restored the home to reflect its original Victorian elegance. Also on the grounds is Troll cottage, a nautical Scandinavian dwelling. The inn's guest rooms all feature private baths, microwave ovens and refrigerators. Guests will enjoy the inn's period furniture, sauna cabin, whirlpool and gorgeous sunsets over the waters of Green Bay. Many of the rooms are done in a Scandinavian country decor. A recently added lighthouse suite is a favorite among guests, and a private beach is within walking distance.

Historic Interest: Nautical Museum, many lighthouses.

Innkeeper(s): David & Else Weborg. $34-149. MC, VISA, AX, PC, TC. 15 rooms with PB, 2 with FP and 2 cottages. Breakfast included in rates. Types of meals: Cont plus and early coffee/tea. Beds: KQDT. Cable TV, ceiling fan, microwaves, kitchenettes and decks in room. Air conditioning. Fax, spa, sauna, bicycles, beach and gas grills on premises. Handicap access. Danish spoken. Antiquing, art galleries, beaches, bicycling, fishing, golf, hiking, island ferry, sunset cruise, live theater, museums, parks, shopping, tennis and water sports nearby.

Pets allowed: Please inquire.

"Lovely inn. Thank you for your hospitality."

Green Bay F8

The Astor House B&B

637 S Monroe Ave
Green Bay, WI 54301-3614
(920)432-3585 (888)303-6370
E-mail: astor@execpc.com
Web: www.astorhouse.com

Circa 1888. Located in the Astor Historic District, the Astor House is completely surrounded by Victorian homes. Guests have their choice of five rooms, each uniquely decorated for a range of ambiance, from the Vienna Balconies to the Marseilles Garden to the Hong Kong Retreat. The parlor, veranda and many suites feature a grand view of City Centre's lighted church towers. This home is also the  first and only B&B in Green Bay and received the Mayor's Award for Remodeling and Restoration. Business travelers should take notice of the private phone lines in each room, as well as the ability to hook up a modem.

Historic Interest: Green Bay City Centre (8 blocks), Lambeau Field, 1837 Hazelwood Historic Home museum.

Innkeeper(s): Doug Landwehr. $109-149. MC, VISA, AX, DC, DS. 5 rooms with PB, 4 with FP and 3 suites. Breakfast included in rates. Type of meal: Cont plus. Beds: KQDT. Cable TV, phone, VCR, gas fireplaces and double whirlpool tub (four rooms) in room. Air conditioning. Amusement parks, antiquing, fishing, live theater, parks, shopping, cross-country skiing, sporting events and water sports nearby.

Hayward C3

Ross' Teal Lake Lodge & Golf Club

12425 N Ross Rd
Hayward, WI 54843
(715)462-3631
E-mail: rossteal@win.bright.net
Web: www.rossteal.com

Circa 1908. Located on 250 acres bordering Teal Lake and Teal River, this is a great vacation spot for families, golfers and fishermen. Most of the Northwoods cabins here are of vertical log construction, and most feature fireplaces and kitchens. There are two beds in each room. Most rooms offer ceiling fans. Fishing guides and a fishing school for both children and adults offers fishing expertise and local folklore. (You'll learn how to catch the prized muskie, a fierce freshwater game fish.) An 18-hole golf course winds through the woods and has been recognized by Wisconsin Golf Magazine as one of the upper Midwest's best courses. Bicycles, tricycles and water bicycles are available to use. A family of eagles nest on the island, and you can watch them feed and learn to fly. Early springtime guests enjoy the otters that scramble around the inn's docks. Picnic and basket lunches are available. Breakfast and dinner are available in the lodge's dining room.

Innkeeper(s): Prudence & Tim Ross. $110-520. MC, VISA, PC, TC. TAC10. 25 rooms, 3 suites, 22 cottages and 1 conference room. MAP, AP, EP. Types of meals: Full bkfst and cont. Dinner and picnic lunch available. Restaurant on premises. Beds: KDT. Some with ceiling fans in room. Swimming, sauna, bicycles, tennis and library on premises. Small meetings and family reunions hosted. Antiquing, fishing, golf, parks, shopping, cross-country skiing and water sports nearby.

Pets Allowed.

Hazel Green J4

Wisconsin House Stagecoach Inn

2105 Main, PO Box 71
Hazel Green, WI 53811-0071
(608)854-2233
E-mail: wishouse@mhtc.net
Web: wisconsinhouse.com

Circa 1846. Located in southwest Wisconsin's historic lead mining region, this one-time stagecoach stop will delight antique-lovers. The spacious two-story inn once hosted Ulysses S. Grant, whose home is just across the border in Illinois. One of the inn's guest rooms bears his name and features a walnut four-poster bed. Don't miss the chance to join the Dischs on a Saturday evening for their gourmet dinner, served by reservation only.

Innkeeper(s): Ken & Pat Disch. $55-110. MC, VISA, AX, DS, PC. TAC10. 8 rooms, 6 with PB and 2 suites. Breakfast included in rates. Types of meals: Full gourmet bkfst and early coffee/tea. Gourmet dinner available. Beds: KQDT. Air conditioning. Copier, bicycles and library on premises. Weddings, small meetings, family reunions and seminars hosted. Antiquing, fishing, live theater, parks, downhill skiing and cross-country skiing nearby.

Hudson   E1

Jefferson-Day House

1109 Third St
Hudson, WI 54016-1220
(715)386-7111
E-mail: jeffersn@pressenter.com
Web: www.jeffersondayhouse.com

Circa 1857. Near the St. Croix River and 30 minutes from Mall
of America, the Italianate Jefferson-Day House features five guest
rooms with both double whirlpool tubs and gas fireplaces.
Antique art and furnishings fill the rooms, and there is a formal
dining room and living room. Ask for the Captain's Room and
you'll be rewarded with a cedar-lined bathroom, over-sized
shower, antique brass bed, and a gas fireplace visible from the
whirlpool tub for two. A four-course breakfast is served fireside
every morning, and complimentary spirits are offered.

Innkeeper(s): Tom & Sue Tyler. $99-179. MC, VISA, DS, PC, TC. 5 rooms
with PB, 5 with FP and 1 suite. Breakfast and snacks/refreshments included
in rates. Type of meal: Full bkfst. Beds: Q. Weddings, small meetings and
family reunions hosted. Amusement parks, antiquing, fishing, live theater,
parks, shopping, downhill skiing, cross-country skiing, sporting events and
water sports nearby.

Pets allowed: With advance notice; some restrictions apply.

*"Absolute perfection! That's the only way to describe our stay in the
wonderful St. Croix suite!"*

The Phipps Inn

1005 3rd St
Hudson, WI 54016-1261
(715)386-0800 (888)865-9388
Web: www.phippsinn.com

Circa 1884. In the National Register of Historic Places, Phipps
Inn is an outstandingly beautiful example of delicate Queen
Anne Victorian architecture. The mansion offers wraparound
porches, fluted pilasters, gabled dormers and
an octagonal tower that rises three stories
high. Located on a historic street in
Wisconsin's St. Croix Valley, an
appropriate Victorian decor compliments the interior's oak and
maple woodwork. Guest rooms
and suites offer romantic furnishings and amenities such as
brass, canopy or four-poster
feather beds, and all feature large whirlpool tubs and fireplaces. There are a variety of rooms to wander into and enjoy,
including the music room, billiard room and the inn's two
parlors. Four-course breakfasts include a fresh fruit course, a
pastry course, an entrée and a dessert. Antique shops, galleries, boutiques and a good selection of restaurants are nearby, as are parks, the St. Croix River and a dog-racing track.
Octagon House, a museum in an 1855 house, is across the
street from the inn.

Innkeeper(s): Todd Jadwin & Susan Jadwin. $99-189. 6 rooms with PB. Types
of meals: Full gourmet bkfst and early coffee/tea. Beds: Q. Double whirlpool
and fireplaces in room. Air conditioning. Bicycles on premises. Antiquing, art
galleries, dog races, museums, parks, shopping and water sports nearby.

Lake Geneva   J7

Eleven Gables Inn on Lake Geneva

493 Wrigley Dr
Lake Geneva, WI 53147-2115
(262)248-8393
E-mail: egi@lkgeneva.com
Web: www.lkgeneva.com

Circa 1847. Built as a summer estate, this Carpenter Gothic inn
does feature nearly a dozen of its namesake gables.
Accommodations include rooms in the main house, as well as the
restored coach house that is ideal for families or couples traveling
together. The innkeeper has lived in the house since the 1950s
and has decorated the historic home with what she describes as
"Jackie O"-era furnishings. The innkeeper has been opening her
home to guests since the 1960s. The homemade breakfasts
include entrees such as a soufflé or perhaps eggs Benedict.

Historic Interest: Peterson House, Yerkes Observatory, Stone Manor.

Innkeeper(s): A.F. Milliette. $105-219. MC, VISA, AX, DC, CB, DS, TC.
TAC10. 8 rooms with PB, 8 with FP, 2 suites, 2 cottages, 2 guest houses and
2 conference rooms. Breakfast included in rates. Types of meals: Full bkfst,
cont plus and veg bkfst. Beds: KQ. Cable TV, ceiling fan and VCR in room.
Central air. Fax, copier and swimming in lake on premises. Handicap access.
Weddings, small meetings and seminars hosted. Amusement parks, antiquing,
beaches, bicycling, canoeing/kayaking, fishing, golf, hiking, horseback riding,
parks, shopping, cross-country skiing, tennis and water sports nearby.

Pets allowed: In some rooms with prior approval.

Madison   I6

Arbor House, An Environmental Inn

3402 Monroe St
Madison, WI 53711-1702
(608)238-2981

Circa 1853. Nature-lovers not only will enjoy the inn's close
access to a 1,280-acre nature preserve, they will appreciate the
innkeepers' ecological theme. Organic sheets and towels are
offered for guests as well as environmentally safe bath products.
Arbor House is one of Madison's
oldest existing homes and features plenty of historic features,
such as romantic reading chairs
and antiques, mixed with modern amenities and unique touch-
es. Five guest rooms include a whirlpool tub and three have fireplaces. The Annex guest rooms include private balconies. The
innkeepers offer many amenities for business travelers, including
value-added corporate rates. The award-winning inn has been
recognized as a model of urban ecology. Lake Wingra is within
walking distance as are biking and nature trails, bird watching
and a host of other outdoor activities. Guests enjoy complimentary canoeing and use of mountain bikes.

Historic Interest: Frank Lloyd Wright designed many homes in Madison, and
the Mansion Hill Historic District is nearby.

Innkeeper(s): John & Cathie Imes. $85-205. MC, VISA, AX, PC, TC. 8 rooms
with PB, 3 with FP, 1 suite and 1 conference room. Breakfast included in
rates. Types of meals: Full bkfst and cont plus. Beds: KQ. Cable TV, phone,
ceiling fan and VCR in room. Air conditioning. Fax and copier on premises.
Handicap access. Weddings, small meetings, family reunions and seminars
hosted. Antiquing, fishing, parks, shopping, cross-country skiing, sporting
events and water sports nearby.

*"What a delightful treat in the middle of Madison. Absolutely,
unquestionably, the best time I've spent in a hotel or otherwise.
B&Bs are the only way to go! Thank you!"*

The Livingston

752 E Gorham St
Madison, WI 53703
(608)257-1200 Fax:(608)257-1145
E-mail: reservations@thelivingston.com
Web: www.thelivingston.com

Circa 1856. This pre-Civil War inn, a locally and nationally recognized historic landmark, was built from native sandstone and features classic Gothic Revival architecture. The interior boasts nine fireplaces, five in guest rooms. The historic ambiance is enhanced by the Victorian decor. The spacious William T. Leitch Suite includes a sitting room and bedroom, as well as two fireplaces and whirlpool tub. The suite is named after the inn's builder, once mayor of Madison. The innkeepers offer an assortment of amenities designed to please guests in town either for business or pleasure. Fax service, voice mail, cable TV, daily newspapers and laundry service are available, and guests are pampered with a continental-plus breakfast and afternoon refreshments. The inn is close to the airport, state capitol and University of Wisconsin.

Innkeeper(s): Rosalind Anderson. $149-600. MC, VISA, AX, PC. TAC10. 4 rooms with PB, 5 with FP and 2 suites. Breakfast and snacks/refreshments included in rates. Types of meals: Full bkfst, cont plus and early coffee/tea. Beds: QD. Cable TV, phone and turndown service in room. Fax and library on premises. Small meetings and family reunions hosted. Antiquing, fishing, golf, live theater, parks, shopping and sporting events nearby.

Mansion Hill Inn

424 N Pinckney St
Madison, WI 53703-1472
(608)255-3999 (800)798-9070 Fax:(608)255-2217
Web: www.mansionhillinn.com

Circa 1858. The facade of this Romanesque Revival sandstone mansion boasts magnificent arched windows, Swedish railings, verandas and a belvedere. There are marble floors, ornate moldings and a magnificent mahogany and walnut staircase that winds up four stories. Lovingly restored and lavishly decorated, the inn easily rivals rooms at the Ritz for opulence. A special occasion warrants requesting the suite with the secret passageway behind a swinging bookcase.

Historic Interest: State Capitol (3 blocks).

Innkeeper(s): Janna Wojtal. $120-320. MC, VISA, AX, PC, TC. TAC10. 11 rooms with PB, 4 with FP, 2 suites and 1 conference room. Breakfast and snacks/refreshments included in rates. Types of meals: Cont plus and early coffee/tea. Room service available. Beds: KQ. Cable TV, phone, turndown service, VCR and whirlpool bath in room. Air conditioning. Fax, copier and library on premises. Weddings and small meetings hosted. Fishing, state Capitol, live theater, parks, shopping and sporting events nearby.

Publicity: *Chicago Tribune, New York Times, Country Inns, Americana, Glamour, Conde Nast Traveler.*

"The elegance, charm and superb services made it a delightful experience."

Oconomowoc   I7

The Inn at Pine Terrace

351 E Lisbon Rd
Oconomowoc, WI 53066-2838
(414)567-7463 (888)526-0588

Circa 1879. This inn's convenient location, two hours from Chicago, midway between Madison and Milwaukee and just north of the interstate that connects them, makes it equally appealing to business travelers and those seeking a romantic retreat. The innkeepers bill the inn as a combination of a Victorian mansion and a small European hotel. Some rooms boast whirlpool tubs, and visitors are welcome to the inn's in-ground swimming pool. A conference room is available for meetings, seminars and special occasions.

Innkeeper(s): Rich Borg. $65-150. MC, VISA, AX, DS, PC, TC. 13 rooms with PB and 1 conference room. Breakfast included in rates. Type of meal: Cont plus. Beds: QT. Cable TV and phone in room. Air conditioning. Copier, swimming and heated pool in summer on premises. Weddings, small meetings, family reunions and seminars hosted. Antiquing, fishing, golf, excellent dining, nature trails, live theater, parks, shopping, downhill skiing, cross-country skiing, sporting events and water sports nearby.

Onalaska   G3

Rainbow Ridge Farms B&B

N5732 Hauser Rd
Onalaska, WI 54650-8912
(608)783-8181

Circa 1902. Horses, llamas, goats, sheep and ducks are the primary occupants of Rainbow Ridge's 35 acres. Pleasant pond-view guest rooms are offered in the old farmhouse. Woodland, meadow and surrounding wooded bluffs create a picturesque setting and explains why this was the site for one of Onalaska's original farms. Guests are offered the opportunity to enjoy the working farm with a hands-on experience by feeding the animals and collecting eggs. A hearty farm breakfast is offered on weekends and an expanded continental during the week. The farm is popular for family reunions and weddings.

Historic Interest: Hixon House-8 miles, Museum-8 miles, Norskedalen-25 miles, St Rose Convent Chapel-12 miles, Trempealeau Hotel-14 miles.

Innkeeper(s): Donna Murphy & Cindy Hoehne. $65-105. MC, VISA, PC, TC. TAC10. 4 rooms with PB. Breakfast and snacks/refreshments included in rates. Types of meals: Cont plus, country bkfst, veg bkfst and early coffee/tea. Beds: QDT. Central air. VCR, spa, bicycles, library, satellite dish, fire pit, refrigerator and grill on premises. Weddings and family reunions hosted. Antiquing, art galleries, beaches, bicycling, canoeing/kayaking, fishing, golf, hiking, horseback riding, live theater, museums, parks, shopping, downhill skiing, cross-country skiing, sporting events, tennis and water sports nearby.

Osceola   E1

St. Croix River Inn

305 River St, PO Box 356
Osceola, WI 54020-0356
(715)294-4248

Circa 1910. This stone house is poised on a bluff overlooking the St. Croix River. The sitting room overlooks the river. All guest rooms have whirlpool baths. Rooms feature such ameni-

ties as four-poster canopy beds, a tile fireplace, a Palladian window that stretches from floor to ceiling, stenciling, bull's-eye moldings and private balconies. Breakfast is served in room.

Innkeeper(s): Bev Johnson. $100-200. MC, VISA, DS. 7 rooms with PB, 2 with FP. Breakfast included in rates. Type of meal: Full bkfst. Beds: Q. Fishing and parks nearby.

Pepin   F2

A Summer Place

106 Main St
Pepin, WI 54759
(715)442-2132 Fax:(715)442-2132

Circa 1911. Guests rooms at this intimate bed & breakfast look out to Lake Pepin. All three rooms include a double whirlpool tub. Guests are treated to appetizers and a glass of wine upon arrival. Breakfasts include items such as quiche with homemade breads and fresh fruit, sometimes hand-picked berries. The inn is open from May until the beginning of November. Pepin was the birthplace of Laura Ingalls Wilder, and aside from sites related to her, the town offers galleries, shops and restaurants.

Innkeeper(s): Nancy & Bill Henderson. $105-120. PC. 3 rooms with PB. Breakfast included in rates. Type of meal: Full bkfst. Beds: Q. Ceiling fan in room. Air conditioning. VCR, fax, copier, library and refrigerator on premises. Family reunions hosted. Spanish, French and Dutch spoken. Antiquing, fishing, golf, live theater, parks, shopping and water sports nearby.

Phillips   D5

East Highland School House B&B

West 4342, Hwy D
Phillips, WI 54555
(715)339-3492

Guests are invited to ring the bell at this restored one-room schoolhouse. An addition to the building in 1920 features rooms with rustic exposed beams, brick walls and original light fixtures. Innkeepers Jeanne and Russ Kirchmeyer filled the home with family antiques and turn-of-the-century pieces. Lacy curtains, doilies and hand-hooked rugs lend to the romantic, country atmosphere. Two museums featuring a 1900s kit area, school area and old logging and farming tools have been added to the inn; one in the basement and one in the barn across the street. The kitchen, which once served as a stage for the school, is now where Jeanne prepares the expansive morning meals.

Innkeeper(s): Russ & Jeanne Kirchmeyer. $45-60. 4 rooms. Breakfast included in rates. Type of meal: Full bkfst.

Plymouth   H8

Yankee Hill Inn B&B

405 Collins St
Plymouth, WI 53073-2361
(920)892-2222

Circa 1870. Two outstanding examples of 19th-century architecture comprise this inn, one a striking Italianate Gothic listed in the National Register, and the other a Queen Anne Victorian with many custom touches. Between the two impressive structures, vis-

itors will choose from 12 spacious guest rooms, featuring antique furnishings and handmade quilts. Visitors can walk to downtown, where they will find an antique mall, shopping and fine dining.

Historic Interest: The Wade House, a state historical site, is five miles from the inn. Plymouth Historical Museum is within walking distance. Sheboygan County offers more than 200 locally landmarked buildings. The Historic Plymouth Walking Tour features 50 early Plymouth buildings.

Innkeeper(s): Peg Stahlman. $78-106. MC, VISA. 12 rooms with PB. Breakfast included in rates. Types of meals: Full bkfst and early coffee/tea. Beds: QD. VCR on premises. Small meetings, family reunions and seminars hosted. Antiquing, fishing, bicycling, hiking, shopping and cross-country skiing nearby.

"You have mastered the art of comfort. All the perfect little touches make this a dream come true. I only regret that we cannot stay forever."

Rhinelander   D6

Cranberry Hill B&B

209 E Frederick St
Rhinelander, WI 54501-3222
(715)369-3504

Circa 1892. This grand 9,000-square-foot, pink and white Queen Ann Victorian commands three acres of landscaped grounds. E. O. Brown, who helped develop the town, built the inn. He was also instrumental in starting Merchants State Bank and the Rhinelander Paper Mill. Now, guests can enjoy the fine detailing of the home in one of seven guest rooms. The Peter Pan Nursery is a large accommodation suitable for families. Some rooms feature fireplaces and some have brass beds. Breakfast offerings include homemade muffins and entrees such as eggs Benedict.

$65-125. PC. 7 rooms and 1 conference room. Breakfast, afternoon tea and snacks/refreshments included in rates. Types of meals: Full gourmet bkfst, cont plus, country bkfst, veg bkfst and early coffee/tea. Catered breakfast available. Beds: KQDT. Cable TV, turndown service and ceiling fan in room. Small meetings and family reunions hosted. Amusement parks, antiquing, art galleries, beaches, bicycling, fishing, golf, hiking, horseback riding, boating, carriage and sleigh rides, live theater, museums, parks, shopping, downhill skiing, tennis, water sports and wineries nearby.

Sparta   G4

The Franklin Victorian

220 E Franklin St
Sparta, WI 54656-1804
(608)269-3894 (800)845-8767

Circa 1800. Built for a banker when Sparta was the hub of social life, this house still boasts of such splendid woods as black ash, curly birch, quarter-cut white oak and red oak. Features include leaded windows in the library and dining room, many of the original filigreed brass light fixtures, and a magnificent sunset stained-glass window. Sparta is nestled

among the hills of Wisconsin's Coulee Region. Area attractions include rivers, trout streams, 130 miles of bike trails, craft and antique shops.

Innkeeper(s): Lloyd & Jane Larson. $70-95. MC, VISA, PC, TC. 4 rooms, 2 with PB, 1 with FP and 1 conference room. Breakfast included in rates. Types of meals: Full gourmet bkfst and early coffee/tea. Beds: KQ. Ceiling fan in room. Air conditioning. Small meetings hosted. Antiquing, fishing, parks, shopping, downhill skiing, cross-country skiing and sporting events nearby.

Justin Trails B&B Resort

7452 Kathryn Ave
Sparta, WI 54656-9729
(608)269-4522 (800)488-4521 Fax:(608)269-3280
E-mail: justntrailsbb@centuryinter.net
Web: www.justintrails.com

Circa 1920. Nestled in a scenic valley sits this 200-acre farm. Guests are encouraged to explore the hiking, snowshoe and cross-country ski trails. The innkeepers offer ski and snowshoe rentals and lessons for both adults and children. In addition to delightfully decorated rooms in the farmhouse, there are two Scandinavian log houses and a plush, restored granary for those desiring more privacy. Each of these cottages includes a whirlpool bath and a fireplace. There also is a suite in the farmhouse with a fireplace and whirlpool. The well-cared-for grounds and buildings reflect the innkeepers' pride in their home, which was built by Don's grandfather. Guests will find cats, kittens, rabbits, chickens, a pygmy goat named Peter, and Heidi, a Siberian Husky dog on the premises.

Innkeeper(s): Don & Donna Justin. $80-300. MC, VISA, AX, DS, PC, TC. TAC10. 7 rooms with PB, 5 with FP, 3 cottages and 1 conference room. Breakfast included in rates. Type of meal: Full bkfst. Beds: KQT. Ceiling fan in room. Air conditioning. Disc golf on premises. Weddings, small meetings, family reunions and seminars hosted. Antiquing, fishing, golf, amish, snowshoe trails, parks, shopping, downhill skiing and cross-country skiing nearby.

Pets allowed: $10 per pet per day.

Publicity: *Milwaukee Journal/Sentinel, Wisconsin Trails, Travel America, Family Fun, Family Life.*

Stevens Point   F6

A Victorian Swan on Water

1716 Water St
Stevens Point, WI 54481-3550
(715)345-0595 (800)454-9886

Circa 1889. This Victorian is located a block and a half from the Wisconsin River. Black walnut inlays in the wood floors, crown moldings, walnut paneling and interior shutters are among the inn's architectural elements. The suite features a mural of a pastoral Mediterranean scene, a ceiling fan, whirlpool tub, fireplace and a balcony overlooking the garden. There are antique furnishings and lace curtains. Breakfast items may include rum-baked fresh pineapple and "turtle" French toast stuffed with chocolate and pecans and served with caramel sauce.

Innkeeper(s): Joan Ouellette. $60-130. MC, VISA, AX, DS, PC, TC. TAC5. 4 rooms, 3 with PB, 1 with FP and 1 suite. Breakfast included in rates. Types of meals: Full gourmet bkfst and early coffee/tea. Beds: KQDT. Ceiling fan and whirlpool and fireplace in suite in room. Air conditioning. VCR and library on premises. Weddings, small meetings, family reunions and seminars hosted. Antiquing, fishing, live theater, parks, shopping, downhill skiing, cross-country skiing, sporting events and water sports nearby.

"Our first white Christmas...what a wonderful time we had here in your home. Breakfast was great. We can't thank you enough for your warm hospitality."

Dreams of Yesteryear B&B

1100 Brawley St
Stevens Point, WI 54481-3536
(715)341-4525 Fax:(715)344-3047
E-mail: bonnie@dreamsofyesteryear.com
Web: dreamsofyesteryear.com

Circa 1901. This elegant, three-story, 4,000-square-foot Queen Anne home is within walking distance of downtown, the

Wisconsin River and the University of Wisconsin. The inn features golden oak woodwork, hardwood floors and leaded glass. Each guest room offers exquisite decor; the third-floor Ballroom Suite boasts a whirlpool. Gourmet breakfasts are served in the inn's formal dining room. An excellent hiking trail is just a block from the inn.

Historic Interest: Historic downtown Stevens Point is nearby, and the inn is only a short trip from dozens of historical sites.

Innkeeper(s): Bonnie & Bill Maher. $58-142. MC, VISA, AX, DS, PC, TC. TAC5. 6 rooms, 4 with PB and 2 suites. Breakfast, afternoon tea and snacks/refreshments included in rates. Types of meals: Full gourmet bkfst and early coffee/tea. Beds: KQDT. Cable TV and phone in room. Air conditioning. VCR, library, piano and victrolas on premises. Weddings, small meetings and family reunions hosted. Amusement parks, antiquing, fishing, historical attractions, hiking trails, live theater, parks, shopping, downhill skiing, cross-country skiing, sporting events and water sports nearby.

"Something from a Hans Christian Anderson fairy tale."

Stoughton   I6

Naeset-Roe B&B

126 E Washington St
Stoughton, WI 53589
(608)877-4150 Fax:(608)877-4155
E-mail: ejquamme@naesetroe.com
Web: www.naesetroe.com

Circa 1878. A prominent local architect built this historic Italianate home, which is listed in the National Register. The brick exterior is decked with goldenrod trim with scarlet accents. Guest rooms are decorated with antiques. Two rooms include a whirlpool tub, one has a clawfoot tub and the other offers a large soaking tub. Beds are dressed with fine, hand-ironed linens. The Victorian décor is accentuated by the soft glow of candlelight. Massage service is available, as are honeymoon packages. The library offers a large selection of

books and magazines, as well as some antique books. Three-course breakfasts are served by candlelight and might begin with a baked grapefruit with a chocolate cherry liqueur sauce. From there, guests partake of an asparagus quiche with a side of fresh salsa, potatoes and homemade bread. Lastly, guests are treated to pecan rolls and a plate featuring a selection of the state's famous cheeses. The town of Stoughton offers close access to Madison, Cambridge and Janesville.

Innkeeper(s): Edward & Sally Jo Quamme. $55-145. MC, VISA, PC, TC. 4 rooms with PB, 2 with FP and 1 conference room. Breakfast included in rates. Types of meals: Full gourmet bkfst, cont plus and early coffee/tea. Snacks/refreshments and catered breakfast available. Beds: Q. Some rooms with fireplaces in room. Central air. VCR, fax, copier, bicycles and library on premises. Weddings, small meetings, family reunions and seminars hosted. Antiquing, art galleries, beaches, bicycling, canoeing/kayaking, fishing, golf, hiking, horseback riding, live theater, museums, parks, shopping, cross-country skiing, sporting events, tennis, water sports and wineries nearby.

"You have not missed an item to make your B&B welcoming!"

Sturgeon Bay
F9

The Inn at Cedar Crossing

336 Louisiana St
Sturgeon Bay, WI 54235-2422
(920)743-4200 Fax:(920)743-4422
E-mail: innkeeper@innatcedarcrossing.com
Web: www.innatcedarcrossing.com

Circa 1884. This historic hotel, in the National Register, is a downtown two-story brick building that once housed street-level shops with second-floor apartments for the tailors, shopkeepers and pharmacists who worked below. The upstairs, now guest rooms, is decorated with rich fabrics and wallpapers and fine antiques. The Anniversary Room has a mahogany bed, fireplace and double whirlpool tub.  The Victorian-era dining room and pub, both with fireplaces, are on the lower level. The waterfront is three blocks away.

Historic Interest: Door County Historical and Maritime Museums.

Innkeeper(s): Terry Smith. $99-169. MC, VISA, AX, DS, PC, TC. 9 rooms with PB, 6 with FP. Breakfast and snacks/refreshments included in rates. Types of meals: Full gourmet bkfst, cont plus and early coffee/tea. Gourmet dinner, picnic lunch, lunch, catering service, catered breakfast and room service available. Restaurant on premises. Beds: KQ. Cable TV, phone, VCR, double whirlpool tubs and some fireplaces in room. Air conditioning. Fax, copier and library on premises. Small meetings hosted. Antiquing, fishing, art galleries, great biking, live theater, parks, shopping, downhill skiing, cross-country skiing and water sports nearby.

"The second-year stay at the inn was even better than the first. I couldn't have found a more romantic place."

Chanticleer Guest House

4072 Cherry Rd (Hwy HH)
Sturgeon Bay, WI 54235
(920)746-0334 Fax:(920)746-1368
E-mail: chanticleer@itol.com
Web: www.chanticleerguesthouse.com

Circa 1916. Although Chanticleer is secluded on 30 acres boasting woods and fields of wildflowers, the home is just one mile from Sturgeon Bay. Each of the eight guest rooms has a fireplace and double whirlpool tub. Poster and sleigh beds are topped with country comforters. Delicate floral wallcoverings, exposed wood beams and paneled wood walls accentuate the elegant country decor. Breakfast is brought to your door, including such items as homemade muffins and a cold fruit soup. Door County offers a multitude of attractions, including theater productions, musical festivals, watersports and hiking on trails in one of five state parks.

Innkeeper(s): Darrin Day & Bryon Groeschl. $120-190. MC, VISA, DS, PC, TC. 8 suites, 8 with FP. Breakfast and snacks/refreshments included in rates. Types of meals: Cont plus, veg bkfst and early coffee/tea. Beds: KQ. TV, ceiling fan, VCR and antiques in room. Central air. Fax, copier, swimming and sauna on premises. Handicap access. Antiquing, art galleries, beaches, bicycling, canoeing/kayaking, fishing, golf, hiking, horseback riding, live theater, museums, parks, shopping, downhill skiing, cross-country skiing, sporting events, tennis, water sports and wineries nearby.

Hearthside B&B Inn

2136 Taube Rd
Sturgeon Bay, WI 54235
(920)746-2136
E-mail: hearthside@itol.com
Web: www.hearthside-farm-bb.com

Circa 1880. Quilts and country furnishings decorate the guest rooms at this bed & breakfast, located in a historic home. Among the interesting architectural features is a fireplace with a mirrored mantel that reaches to the ceiling. The inn's suite is ideal for families and offers two guest rooms, one with twin beds and the other with a double bed. Breakfast includes American staples such as pancakes or eggs, sausage and potatoes. The inn is two miles from Lake Michigan, where guests can enjoy a myriad of watersports. Hiking, restaurants and shops also are nearby.

Innkeeper(s): Don & Lu Klussendorf. $45-75. PC. 4 rooms with PB, 1 suite and 1 cottage. Breakfast included in rates. Type of meal: Full gourmet bkfst. Beds: QDT. Cable TV and VCR in room. Air conditioning. Stables on premises. Weddings, small meetings, family reunions and seminars hosted. Antiquing, golf, Green Bay Packers, live theater, parks, shopping, cross-country skiing, sporting events and water sports nearby.

The Little Harbor Inn

5100 Bay Shsore Dr
Sturgeon Bay, WI 54234
(920)743-3789 Fax:(920)743-3789
E-mail: littleharborinn@dcwis.com
Web: www.littleharborinn.com

Circa 1997. Innkeeper John Borkovetz built this handsome Victorian-style inn located on two waterfront acres in historic downtown Sturgeon Bay in 1997. All eight rooms have a water view of Lake Michigan, and four boast double whirlpools and fireplaces. Some rooms feature four-poster beds and sofas, as well. Breakfast, served buffet style or delivered to your room, offers freshly baked breads and quiche. The inn's lawn slopes down to the waterside where lounge chairs and tables are set up for guests. Ask for the winter Sleigh Ride Package that includes a prime rib dinner for two.

Historic Interest: Downtown Sturgeon Bay.

Innkeeper(s): John Borkovetz. $95-165. MC, VISA, PC, TC. TAC5. 8 rooms with PB, 8 with FP. Breakfast included in rates. Type of meal: Cont plus. Beds: Q. TV, phone and VCR in room. Central air. Fax, swimming and bicycles on premises. Handicap access. Family reunions hosted. Antiquing, art galleries, beaches, bicycling, canoeing/kayaking, fishing, golf, hiking, horseback riding, boating, snowmobiling, live theater, museums, parks, shopping, downhill skiing, cross-country skiing, tennis, water sports and wineries nearby.

The Reynolds House B&B

111 So 7th Ave
Sturgeon Bay, WI 54235
(920)746-9771 Fax:(920)746-9441

Circa 1900. A three-story, red-roofed Queen Anne Victorian house, the Reynolds House is painted in two shades of teal and yellow with white trim on its  balustrades and brackets. Leaded-glass windows and a stone veranda that wraps around the front of the house are features. Rooms are cheerfully decorated and offer antique beds, attractive bed coverings and wallpapers. Tucked under the gable, the Winesap Suite includes a whirlpool, sitting room and fireplace. The innkeeper's kitchen garden furnishes fresh herbs to accent breakfast dishes, as well as flowers for the table.

Historic Interest: Door County lighthouses (30 miles), Sturgeon Bay.

Innkeeper(s): Stan & Jan Sekula. $75-155. MC, VISA, AX, PC. 4 rooms, 3 with PB, 2 with FP and 1 suite. Breakfast and snacks/refreshments included in rates. Types of meals: Full gourmet bkfst and early coffee/tea. Beds: Q. Cable TV and ceiling fan in room. Central air. VCR, fax, copier and library on premises. Weddings and family reunions hosted. Antiquing, art galleries, beaches, bicycling, fishing, golf, hiking, horseback riding, live theater, museums, parks, shopping, cross-country skiing, tennis and wineries nearby.

"Sometimes the last minute things in life are the best!"

Sturgeon Bay (Door County) F9

Scofield House B&B

908 Michigan St
Sturgeon Bay (Door County), WI 54235-1849
(920)743-7727 (888)463-0204 Fax:(920)743-7727
E-mail: scofhse@mail.wiscnet.net
Web: www.scofieldhouse.com

Circa 1902. Mayor Herbert Scofield, prominent locally in the lumber and hardware business, built this late-Victorian house with a sturdy square tower and inlaid floors that feature intri-

cate borders patterned in cherry, birch, maple, walnut, and red and white oak. Oak moldings throughout the house boast raised designs of bows, ribbons, swags and flowers. Equally lavish

decor is featured in the guest rooms with fluffy flowered comforters and cabbage rose wallpapers highlighting romantic antique bedsteads. Baked apple-cinnamon French toast is a house specialty. Modern amenities include many suites with fireplaces and double whirlpools. "Room at the Top" is a sky-lit 900-square-foot suite occupying the whole third floor and furnished with Victorian antiques.

Historic Interest: Door County Lighthouses, Maritime Museum, Door County Museum (within walking distance).

Innkeeper(s): Mike & Carolyn Pietrek. $95-198. PC, TC. 6 rooms with PB, 5 with FP. Breakfast and afternoon tea included in rates. Type of meal: Full gourmet bkfst. Beds: Q. Cable TV, ceiling fan, VCR and double whirlpools in room. Air conditioning. Fax, copier and movie library (free) on premises. Amusement parks, antiquing, fishing, live theater, parks, shopping, downhill skiing, cross-country skiing, sporting events and water sports nearby.

"You've introduced us to the fabulous world of B&Bs. I loved the porch swing and would have been content on it for the entire weekend."

Whitewater I7

Victoria-On-Main B&B

622 W Main St
Whitewater, WI 53190-1855
(414)473-8400

Circa 1895. This graceful Queen Anne Victorian, shaded by a tall birch tree, is in the heart of Whitewater National Historic District, adjacent to the University of Wisconsin. It was built for Edward Engebretson, mayor of Whitewater. Yellow tulip and sunny daffodils fill the spring flower beds, while fuchsias and geraniums

bloom in summertime behind a picket fence. The inn's gables, flower-filled veranda and three-story turret feature a handsome green tin roof. Each guest room is named for a Wisconsin hardwood. The Red Oak Room, Cherry Room and Bird's Eye Maple Room all offer handsome antiques in their corresponding wood, Laura Ashley prints,

antique sheets, pristine heirloom-laced pillowcases and down comforters. A hearty breakfast is sometimes served on the wraparound veranda, and there are kitchen facilities available for light meal preparation. Whitewater Lake and Kettle Moraine State Forest are five minutes away.

Innkeeper(s): Nancy Wendt. $65-75. MC, VISA. 3 rooms, 1 with PB, 1 with FP. Breakfast included in rates. Types of meals: Full bkfst and early coffee/tea. Beds: D. Ceiling fan in room. Air conditioning. Antiquing, fishing, live theater, parks, shopping, cross-country skiing and water sports nearby.

"We loved it. Wonderful hospitality."

Wisconsin Dells H5

Wisconsin Dells Thunder Valley B&B Inn

W15344 Waubeek Rd
Wisconsin Dells, WI 53965-9005
(608)254-4145

Circa 1870. As the area is full of both Scandinavian and Native American heritage, and the innkeeper of this country inn has tried to honor the traditions. The inn even features a Scandinavian gift shop. Chief Yellow Thunder, for whom this inn is named, often camped out on the grounds and surrounding area. The inn's restaurant is highly acclaimed. Everything is fresh, including the wheat the innkeepers grind for the morning pancakes and rolls. There is a good selection of Wisconsin beer and wine, as well. Guests can stay in the farmhouse, which offers a microwave and refrigerator for guest use, or spend the night in one of two cottages. The Guest Hus features gable ceilings and a knotty pine interior. The Wee Hus is a smaller unit, and includes a refrigerator.

Historic Interest: Chief Yellow Thunder, a Winnebago Indian Chief, had a pow-wow behind the barn. He is buried nearby.

Innkeeper(s): Anita, Kari & Sigrid Nelson. $65-95. MC, VISA. 4 rooms with PB and 1 cottage. Breakfast included in rates. Type of meal: Full bkfst. Beds: KQD. Air conditioning. Handicap access. Weddings, small meetings, family reunions and seminars hosted. Norwegian spoken. International Crane Foundation, Circus Museum, House on Rock, casino and farm animals and dairy close by nearby.

"Thunder Valley is a favorite of Firstar Club members — delicious food served in a charming atmosphere with warm Scandinavian hospitality."

Wyoming

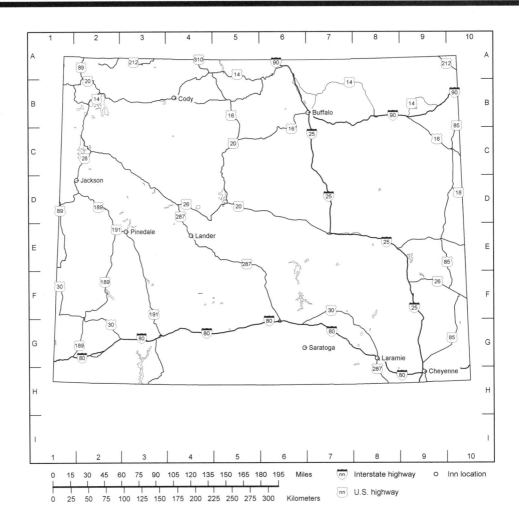

Buffalo   *B7*

Cloud Peak Inn

590 N Burritt Ave
Buffalo, WY 82834-1610
(307)684-5794 (800)715-5794 Fax:(307)684-7653

Circa 1906. Built at the turn of the century by a wealthy rancher, this inn features a graceful staircase, elegant parlor and spacious bedrooms. At the end of the day, guests can relax in

front of the "fossilized" fireplace, soak in the Jacuzzi or unwind on the porch or balcony. Arrangements can be made for dinner although there are some

excellent restaurants in the area. A fine golf course is only two blocks from the inn. The innkeepers will tell you about the secret fishing spots in the mountains that are sure bets. Geologic tours of the area can be arranged with prior notice.

Historic Interest: Fort Phil Kearney (10 miles), Fort Fetterman (11 miles), Bozeman Trail (1 mile), Fort McKinney (2 miles).

Innkeeper(s): Rick & Kathy Brus. $55-85. MC, VISA, AX, PC, TC. TAC15. 5 rooms, 3 with PB and 1 conference room. Breakfast included in rates. Types of meals: Full gourmet bkfst and early coffee/tea. Beds: KQDT. Ceiling fan in room. VCR, fax, copier, spa and library on premises. Weddings, small meetings, family reunions and seminars hosted. Amusement parks, antiquing, fishing, parks, shopping, downhill skiing, cross-country skiing and water sports nearby.

Cheyenne   *H9*

Nagle Warren Mansion B&B

222 E 17th St
Cheyenne, WY 82001
(307)637-3333 (800)811-2610 Fax:(307)638-6879
E-mail: josterfoss@aol.com
Web: www.naglewarrenmansion.com

Circa 1888. When this Victorian mansion was constructed, Cheyenne was the richest town in the world for its size. The home's brilliant architecture serves as a reminder of this grand time in the city's history. The home boasts meticulously restored woodwork, including a grand staircase adorned with an ornate gaslight. The cast bronze fireplaces are topped with mirrors that reach the ceilings. Bronze medallions were set in the front doors, and guests will find stained glass throughout the home. The home's parlor still includes two paintings commissioned by the home's first owner, Erasmus Nagle. Nagle made his fortune in both the grocery and cattle businesses. From 1915 until 1933, the home belonged to Senator F.E. Warren and his wife. The mansion is in the National Register as well as being listed in the Smithsonian Guide to Historic America.

$98-125. MC, VISA, AX, PC, TC. TAC10. 12 rooms with PB, 6 with FP, 1 suite and 3 conference rooms. Breakfast and afternoon tea included in rates. Beds: KQD. Cable TV, phone and iron and ironing board in room. Air conditioning. Fax, copier, spa and library on premises. Handicap access. Weddings, small meetings and family reunions hosted. Spanish and German spoken. Antiquing, golf, live theater, parks and shopping nearby.

"Thanks so much for your attention to the fine details of beauty in an old house. The food was great, the atmosphere was romantic."

Cody   *B4*

Parson's Pillow B&B

1202 14th St
Cody, WY 82414-3720
(307)587-2382 (800)377-2348 Fax:(307)587-6372

Circa 1991. This historic building originally served as the Methodist-Episcopal Church, Cody's first church. Guests are free to practice a tune on the piano in the home's parlor, which also offers a TV and VCR. Guest rooms feature antiques and quilts. Clawfoot and oak-framed prairie tubs add to the nostalgia. The Buffalo Bill Historical Center and the Cody Historic Walking Tour are nearby.

Historic Interest: Buffalo Bill Historical Center, Old West Miniature Village & Museum, Cody Night Rodeo.

Innkeeper(s): Lee & Elly Larabee. $65-85. MC, VISA, AX, DS, PC. TAC10. 4 rooms with PB. Breakfast included in rates. Types of meals: Full gourmet bkfst and early coffee/tea. Beds: Q. Turndown service and ceiling fan in room. VCR, library and computer port on premises. Antiquing, fishing, golf, white water rafting, parks, shopping, downhill skiing, cross-country skiing, tennis and water sports nearby.

Jackson   *D2*

The Huff House Inn

240 E Deloney, PO Box 1189
Jackson, WY 83001-1189
(307)733-4164 (307)739-9091 Fax:(307)739-9091

Circa 1917. Originally built for the town's first medical doctor and town mayor, this Craftsman-style home served as both an office for seeing patients and a residence. The innkeepers have dedicated themselves to retaining the inn's historic character. Beveled-glass doors, chandeliers, antiques and brocade fabrics add to the inn's comfortable atmosphere. In addition to the five guest rooms in the main house, the inn features four separate cottages that boast hand-stenciled walls and Jacuzzi tubs. Breakfast is served in the formal dining room or breakfast room. Baked apple French toast with a spicy applesauce topping is a house favorite. The inn is a block from the historic district, restaurants, shops and museums.

Innkeeper(s): Jackie & Weldon Richardson. $109-205. MC, VISA, DS, PC, TC. TAC10. 9 rooms, 5 with PB and 4 cottages. Breakfast included in rates. Types of meals: Full gourmet bkfst and early coffee/tea. Beds: KQT. Cable TV, phone, VCR and cottages have fireplaces and whirlpool tubs in room. Air conditioning. Fax, copier, spa and library on premises. Small meetings and family reunions hosted. German/English spoken. Antiquing, fishing, golf, dog sledding, snowmobiling, horse back riding, hiking, live theater, parks, shopping, downhill skiing, cross-country skiing, tennis and water sports nearby.

"Our honeymoon could not have been nicer! The food was incredible and the cottage was perfect."

Lander
E4

Blue Spruce Inn

677 S 3rd St
Lander, WY 82520-3707
(307)332-8253

Circa 1920. Five blue spruce trees mark this large Arts and Crafts influenced home. Original chandeliers, stained glass, oak crown molding and woodwork add to the house's appeal.

Mission-style furnishings are in keeping with the house's period. Ask for the Spotted Elk Room for a Native American-themed accommodation. There is a sun porch and front porch, and a block away is a mountain trout stream. Lander is adjacent to the Wind River Indian Reservation, and it is on this reservation where the grave site of Sacajawea is located.

Historic Interest: In addition to small museums and cultural sites on the Wind River Indian Reservation, South Pass, a significant portion of the Oregon Trail is nearby. The Oregon/Mormon/California Trail is about 20 miles away. Historic South Pass City, a Wyoming State Historic Site, is 45 minutes away.

Innkeeper(s): Marvin & JoAnne Brown. $80. MC, VISA, AX, DS, PC, TC. 4 rooms with PB. Breakfast included in rates. Types of meals: Full bkfst and early coffee/tea. Beds: QT. Two rooms with phone in room. VCR, bicycles and library on premises. Small meetings and family reunions hosted. Limited German spoken. Antiquing, fishing, Wind River Indian Reservation, museum, parks, shopping and cross-country skiing nearby.

Laramie
G8

Prairie Breeze B&B

718 Ivinson Ave
Laramie, WY 82070-3245
(307)745-5482 (800)840-2170 Fax:(307)745-5341
E-mail: prairiebrz@vcn.com
Web: prairiebreezebandb.com

Circa 1888. In the National Register, this three-story yellow Victorian was built by Professor John Conley, once vice-president of the University of Wyoming. The inn is furnished with antiques including a wind-up Victrola and old piano. Kirsten's Suite offers an upper balcony, a four-poster bed, antiques, a clawfoot tub, and dressing area. The university is a two-block walk.

Innkeeper(s): Anne & George Cowardin-Bach. $60-80. MC, VISA, AX, DC, CB, DS, PC, TC. TAC5. 3 rooms with PB and 1 suite. Breakfast included in rates. Types of meals: Cont plus, cont and early coffee/tea. Turndown service and ceiling fan in room. Fax, copier and bicycles on premises. Weddings, small meetings, family reunions and seminars hosted. French spoken. Antiquing, fishing, golf, four museums, live theater, parks, shopping, downhill skiing, cross-country skiing, sporting events and tennis nearby.

Pets allowed: small under control; owner responsible for damage.

Vee Bar Guest Ranch

2091 State Hwy 130
Laramie, WY 82070-9734
(307)745-7036 (800)483-3227 Fax:(307)745-7433

Circa 1896. Experience the Old West on this 800-acre guest ranch nestled on Little Laramie River at the base of the Snowy Range Mountains. Once the private residence of an English cattle baron, the main lodge was the home station for a stage-

coach company. Today, the authentic western character of the lodge and its log cabins are preserved in the Ralph Lauren-style rustic furnishings, wood floors and stone fireplaces. A full country breakfast is included. The inn offers a variety of on-site recreational activities.

Innkeeper(s): Jim "Lefty" & Carla Cole. $100-150. MC, VISA, PC, TC. TAC10. 9 cabins and 1 conference room. Breakfast included in rates. AP. Type of meal: Full bkfst. Lunch and banquet service available. Restaurant on premises. Beds: KQDT. Fax, copier, spa, stables and library on premises. Handicap access. Weddings, small meetings, family reunions and seminars hosted. Fishing, snowmobiling, horseback riding, downhill skiing and cross-country skiing nearby.

Publicity: Log Home Design Ideas Magazine, National Geographic Traveler.

Saratoga
G6

Far Out West B&B

304 N Second St
Saratoga, WY 82331
(307)326-5869 Fax:(307)326-9864

Circa 1920. Winters in Wyoming can be harsh, so Minnie Sears built this home in town to make it easier for her children to attend school during the cold months. The home is a small-

er replica of Sears' ranch, which was out in the country. The main house still maintains many original features, and there are two guest rooms located in this historic section. As well, there is a unique room accessible only by a tiny, four-foot-high door. Inside, children will find toys, books and other goodies. Out back, there are several accommodations with special names such as The Calamity Jane or The James Gang. The Hideout, located in a separate house, includes a kitchen, dining room and living room. Breakfast entrees, such as Gunfighter eggs, are accompanied by freshly baked biscuits, sausage, bacon and fresh fruit.

Innkeeper(s): Bill & BJ Farr. $75-125. MC, VISA, AX, DS, PC. TAC10. 5 rooms with PB and 1 cottage. Breakfast included in rates. Types of meals: Full bkfst and early coffee/tea. Beds: KDT. Cable TV, ceiling fan and robes in room. VCR, fax, copier and library on premises. Handicap access. Weddings, small meetings, family reunions and seminars hosted. Antiquing, fishing, golf, snowmobiling, natural hot springs, parks, shopping, cross-country skiing, tennis and water sports nearby.

Pets allowed: Boarding at vet's office and kennel nearby.

"An absolutely wonderful place for comfort, friendliness and food."

U.S. Territories

Puerto Rico

San Juan

El Canario Inn
1317 Ashford Ave
San Juan, PR 00907
(787)722-3861 (800)533-2649 Fax:(787)722-0391
E-mail: canariopr@aol.com
Web: www.canariohotels.com

Circa 1938. This three-story inn is only a block from San Juan's glorious white-sand beaches. Rooms are decorated in a tropical theme with rattan and wicker furnishings and Bermuda ceiling fans. Guests can relax on one of the patios. The inn is a charming escape from the multitude of high rise hotels along the coast. Casinos and discotheques are nearby, and sightseeing tours and boating trips can be arranged at the hotel.

Historic Interest: Old San Juan is only three miles away, and features forts, a museum, cathedrals and plenty of gracious Spanish architecture set among cobblestone streets.

Innkeeper(s): Jude & Keith Olson. $75-114. MC, VISA, AX, DC, DS. TAC10. 25 rooms with PB. Breakfast included in rates. Types of meals: Cont plus and early coffee/tea. Beds: DT. Cable TV, phone and ceiling fan in room. Air conditioning. Fax on premises. Fishing, parks, shopping and water sports nearby.

Canada

Alberta

Banff

Pension Tannenhof

121 Cave Ave
Banff, AB T0L 0C0
(403)762-4636 Fax:(403)762-5660
E-mail: riedinger@hotmail.com
Web: www.pensiontannenhof.com

Circa 1942. This English country-style inn was built in the early 1940s. The inn's huge outdoor barbecue is made from petrified dinosaur bones. Aside from this unique feature, guests also enjoy beautiful views of the Rockies. Guest rooms are spacious and comfortably furnished. Three rooms include a fireplace. Skiing, hiking, fishing, and horseback riding are among the many nearby activities. The Cave and Basin Hot Springs are within walking distance.

Innkeeper(s): Herbert & Fannye Riedinger. $95-165. MC, VISA, TC. 10 rooms, 9 with PB, 2 with FP and 2 suites. Breakfast included in rates. Types of meals: Full bkfst and early coffee/tea. Beds: KQT. Cable TV and turndown service in room. VCR, fax, copier, sauna and library on premises. Weddings, small meetings and family reunions hosted. German, Spanish and French spoken. Fishing, golf, hiking, horseback riding, live theater, parks, shopping, downhill skiing, cross-country skiing and sporting events nearby.

Okotoks

Lineham House B&B & Historic Site

33 Elma St SS 3
Okotoks, AB T0L 1T3
(403)938-6182

Circa 1906. This turn-of-the-20th-century Victorian was the home of W.D. Lineham, one of Okotoks' founding fathers. The innkeepers searched at auctions and flea markets to decorate their historic home, and the furnishings include antiques and period pieces. The  three guest rooms share a bath with an enormous clawfoot tub, perfect for a long, relaxing soak. In the mornings, guests are treated to a hearty breakfast with items such as eggs Benedict, crepes or French toast topped with strawberries. Okotoks is located ten minutes from Calgary, and the home is close to shops, restaurants and parks.

Historic Interest: Heritage walking tour of historic homes.

Innkeeper(s): Lynn & Ian Turner. $60-75. VISA. 3 rooms and 1 conference room. Breakfast included in rates. Types of meals: Full bkfst, cont plus, cont, country bkfst, veg bkfst and early coffee/tea. Snacks/refreshments, picnic lunch, lunch, banquet service, catering service and catered breakfast available. Beds: DT. Cable TV, phone, turndown service and ceiling fan in room. VCR on premises. Weddings, small meetings and family reunions hosted. Amusement parks, antiquing, art galleries, bicycling, canoeing/kayaking, fishing, golf, hiking, horseback riding, live theater, museums, parks, shopping, downhill skiing, cross-country skiing, sporting events, tennis and water sports nearby.

Pets allowed: On prior arrangements.

"The best place to run to when you're running away from home."

Oyen

Prairie Bells B&B

416 2 St W, Box 25
Oyen, AB T0J 2J0
(403)664-2355

Circa 1917. Originally an early pre-fab house purchased from a catalog and then shipped by both train and horse and buggy, this seven-bedroom house served for 30 years as a home for the sisters of St. Benedict. A wide veranda stretches across the front of the two-story house. The inn is named for the innkeeper's collection of more than 300 bells, and bell-shaped chocolates are offered in the guest rooms, carrying out the bell theme. Homemade pies and desserts are served with coffee and tea for evening snacks, while breakfast offerings include cinnamon buns, sausage and eggs and fruit trays followed by mints and chocolates. The innkeepers plan to build a two-level solarium to house a hot tub in the future, as well as a gazebo. Ask about the area's buffalo rodeo and "pick your own" produce at Prairie Orchard.

Historic Interest: Indian head rock (40 miles), Dinosaur par (120 miles), Stone house (60 miles).

Innkeeper(s): Manfred & Cheryle Schroeder. $65-75. MC, VISA, PC, TC. 6 rooms, 3 with PB. Breakfast and snacks/refreshments included in rates. Types of meals: Full bkfst and country bkfst. Beds: QDT. VCR and library on premises. Weddings and small meetings hosted. German spoken. Fishing, golf, museums and shopping nearby.

British Columbia

Ladner

Primrose Hill Guest House

4919 48 Ave
Ladner, BC V4K 1V4
(604)940-8867 Fax:(604)940-0234
E-mail: primrose@intouch.bc.ca
Web: www.primrose-hill.com

Circa 1913. Primrose Hill is a historic Craftsman-style house located a half hour from Vancouver. The innkeepers restored the home, filling it with 1920s-era furnishings. Some rooms include a canopy bed or bath with a clawfoot tub. The home is 10 minutes from the ferry terminal and less than a half hour from the airport and U.S. border. Local attractions include a bird sanctuary and walking/biking trails along the Fraser River.

Innkeeper(s): Christine & James. $85-135. MC, VISA, AX, TC. TAC10. 6 rooms with PB. Breakfast included in rates. Type of meal: Full bkfst. Catering service available. Beds: KQDT. VCR, fax, bicycles and library on premises. Weddings, small meetings and family reunions hosted. Fishing, golf, parks, shopping, tennis and water sports nearby.

North Vancouver

Grand Manor

1617 Grand Blvd
North Vancouver, BC V7L 3Y2
(604)988-6082 Fax:(604)988-4596

Circa 1912. Located across from a city park, this four-story stone and shingled Edwardian house offers guest rooms with water or mountain views. There is also a guest house with kitchen, two bedrooms and garden. Breakfast specialities are pancakes and omelettes. It's 20 minutes to the ferries to Vancouver Island and 10 minutes to Capilano Suspension Bridge.

Innkeeper(s): Donna Patrick. $60-130. VISA. 4 rooms, 2 with PB, 1 with FP, 1 suite and 1 cottage. Breakfast included in rates. Types of meals: Full bkfst and cont. Beds: KQT. Cable TV in room. VCR, fax, copier and library on premises. Small meetings and family reunions hosted. Amusement parks, hospital on bus route to Lonsdale Quay and downtown Vancouver, live theater, parks, shopping, downhill skiing, cross-country skiing, sporting events and tennis nearby.

Sue's Victorian Guesthouse

152 E 3rd
North Vancouver, BC V7L 1E6
(604)985-1523 (800)776-1811 Fax:(604)985-1868

Circa 1904. This turn-of-the-century home has seen more than 4,000 guests in its 10-plus years as a guesthouse. The home has been restored, maintaining its veranda and original staircases. Rooms are decorated with antiques. There are four rooms in the guest house (two with a private bath and Victorian soaking

tubs). Guests have use of a shared kitchen, where they can prepare their own breakfasts. Several local eateries are nearby. There also are six apartments, four include two bedrooms and a sitting room. The other two have one bedroom and a sitting room. Each of the apartments includes a full bathroom and a kitchen. The apartments are located in a 1949 salt box-style structure adjacent to the guest house. The rooms and apartments are located four blocks from the waterfront.

Historic Interest: Gastown, Capilano suspension bridge, steam train.
Innkeeper(s): Jen Lau/Sue Chalmers. $60-75. TC. 10 rooms, 8 with PB. Type of meal: Early coffee/tea. Afternoon tea available. Beds: KQDT. Cable TV, phone, ceiling fan and VCR in room. Antiquing, art galleries, beaches, bicycling, canoeing/kayaking, fishing, golf, hiking, horseback riding, suspension bridge, steam train, live theater, museums, parks, shopping, downhill skiing, cross-country skiing, tennis and water sports nearby.

Shawnigan Lake

Marifield Manor, an Edwardian B&B

2039 Merrifield Lne, RR 1
Shawnigan Lake, BC V0R 2W0
(250)743-9930 Fax:(250)743-1667
E-mail: mariman@pccinternet.com
Web: www.marifieldmanor.com

Circa 1910. Overlooking Shawnigan Lake, this Edwardian mansion features wraparound verandas. Guest rooms offer clawfoot tubs, antiques and fine, old linens. Most have views of the mountains and lake through the trees. Tea is served fireside or on the veranda, if weather permits. Tapestries and antiques are found throughout. The inn's artfully presented, gourmet breakfasts are served in the dining room or al fresco. The inn has become popular for meetings, workshops and retreats as well as receptions and family gathering, recently hosting visitors on Heritage House Tour.

Innkeeper(s): Cathy Basskin. $75-175. TC. 6 rooms with PB, 2 suites and 1 conference room. Breakfast and afternoon tea included in rates. Types of meals: Full gourmet bkfst, cont plus and early coffee/tea. Banquet service and room service available. Beds: QDT. Turndown service in room. Air conditioning. VCR, fax, copier, sauna, bicycles, library and e-mail on premises. Weddings, small meetings, family reunions and seminars hosted. French spoken. Antiquing, bicycling, canoeing/kayaking, golf, rowing, host of Shawnigan Lake Writers Village, boarding schools, live theater, parks, downhill skiing, water sports and wineries nearby.

"To a new and wonderful friend. Thank you for sharing your little slice of paradise."

Sooke

Ocean Wilderness Inn & Spa Retreat

109 W Coast Rd, RR 2
Sooke, BC V0S 1N0
(250)646-2116 (800)323-2116 Fax:(250)646-2317
E-mail: ocean@sookenet.com
Web: www.sookenet.com/ocean

Circa 1940. The hot tub spa of this log house inn is in a Japanese gazebo overlooking the ocean. Reserve your time for a private soak, terry bathrobes are supplied. Experience massage and mud treatments, ocean treatments and herbal wraps while meditation enhances your creative expression. The inn will arrange fishing charters, nature walks and beachcombing. Coffee is delivered to your room each morning on a silver service. Guests are invited to enjoy breakfast in their room or in the dining lounge. Rooms include antiques, sitting areas and canopy beds. Two of the rooms have hot tubs for two with spectacular ocean and Olympic Mountain views.

Historic Interest: Botanical Beach and Hatley Castle are 15 miles from the inn, while Moss Cottage is only eight miles away. Butchart Gardens and the Royal B.C. Museum are within 35 miles.

Innkeeper(s): Marion J. Rolston. $85-175. MC, VISA, AX, TC. TAC10. 9 rooms with PB. Breakfast included in rates. Types of meals: Full bkfst and early coffee/tea. Beds: KQT. Fax and copier on premises. Handicap access. Weddings, small meetings, family reunions and seminars hosted. Antiquing, fishing, whale watching, live theater, parks and shopping nearby.

Pets allowed: By arrangement.

"Thank you for the most wonderful hospitality and accommodations of our entire vacation."

Vancouver

The Albion Guest House

592 W 19th Ave
Vancouver, BC V5Z 1W6
(604)873-2287 Fax:(604)879-5682

Circa 1906. Close to Vancouver's popular West End, Wreck Beach, Stanley Park and other attractions, this Victorian inn boasts window boxes, porches, and a colorful front flower garden. Guest rooms feature antiques, fresh flowers, feather mattresses, fine linens and wrought iron queen-size beds topped with down comforters. Complimentary drinks, fruit and cookies are offered. In the morning, early coffee and the daily newspaper are followed by a three-course gourmet breakfast. West Coast Eggs Benedict accompanied by homemade tomato chutney is a favorite dish. Breakfast-to-go is offered to early risers and business folks. Try the inn's hot tub or walk to the theater, casino or restaurants. Boating, kayaking and other watersports are available. The Vancouver International Airport is 12 minutes away, and guests can walk to Vancouver's famous gardens.

Innkeeper(s): Lise & Richard. $115-155. MC, VISA, AX. 3 rooms, 1 with PB. Breakfast included in rates. Types of meals: Full gourmet bkfst and early coffee/tea. Afternoon tea available. Beds: Q. Fax, copier, spa and tennis on premises. Weddings, small meetings, family reunions and seminars hosted. Antiquing, golf, live theater, parks, shopping, downhill skiing, cross-country skiing, sporting events and water sports nearby.

"Everything was fantastic! The room, food, flowers & hospitality. See you after our cruise, again with joy and anticipation at returning."

Johnson Heritage House

2278 W 34th Ave
Vancouver, BC V6M 1G6
(604)266-4175 Fax:(604)266-4175
E-mail: fun@johnsons-inn-vancouver.com
Web: www.johnsons-inn-vancouver.com

Circa 1920. One of the first things guests will notice as they enter this Craftsman-style home is the ornate woodwork. Different patterns and a variety of woods have been used in the moldings, walls, floors and staircase. There is a pressed tin ceiling decorating the kitchen. Country antiques, Oriental rugs and collectibles also fill the whimsical interior. Brass beds, canopy beds, quilts and carousel horses are among the items guests might discover in their rooms. The Carousel Suite is especially impressive and romantic with a fireplace, a natural-wood cathedral ceiling, canopy bed, sitting area with a loveseat, mountain views and a bathroom with a mermaid theme and a Jacuzzi tub. The home is within walking distance of small parks, shops, city bus lines and restaurants. The University of British Columbia, Anthropology Museum, Queen Elizabeth Park, Granville Island and the Van Dusen Gardens are nearby.

Innkeeper(s): Sandy & Ron Johnson. $85-185. PC, TC. TAC10. 3 rooms, 2 with PB, 2 with FP and 1 suite. Breakfast included in rates. Type of meal: Full bkfst. Beds: KQDT. Phone in room. VCR, fax and library on premises. Some French spoken. Amusement parks, antiquing, fishing, museums, ice skating, rollerblading, biking, hiking, live theater, parks, shopping, sporting events and water sports nearby.

"Wonderful place, great hosts, great food. We'll be back and we'll recommend to others."

Kenya Court Ocean Front Guest House

2230 Cornwall Ave
Vancouver, BC V6K 1B5
(604)738-7085

Circa 1927. Enjoy a piping hot cup of fresh, gourmet coffee as you gaze out over the ocean at this scenic bed & breakfast. Innkeeper Dorothy Mae Williams not only provides a delectable spread of fresh breads, croissants, cereals and fruits, she serves it in a rooftop solarium. Williams, in charge of the piano department at Vancouver Academy, will serenade guests with piano concerts on some days. Roomy suites feature antiques, separate entrances and boast ocean views. The home is within walking distance to the Granville Market, the planetarium, city centres, 10 minutes from the University of British Columbia and 20 miles from the U.S. border. The athletically inclined will enjoy the use of tennis courts, walking and jogging trails and a heated outdoor saltwater pool across the street.

Historic Interest: A maritime museum is a five-minute walk from the bed & breakfast. An anthropology museum is 10 minutes by car.

Innkeeper(s): Dr. & Mrs. H. Williams. $95-110. PC, TC. 7 rooms with PB, 4 with FP and 5 suites. Breakfast included in rates. Types of meals: Full gourmet bkfst and early coffee/tea. Beds: KQT. Cable TV and phone in room. VCR and library on premises. Weddings and family reunions hosted. Italian, French and German spoken. Antiquing, fishing, live theater, parks, shopping, downhill skiing, cross-country skiing and water sports nearby.

"Beautiful home; we enjoyed the unsurpassed hospitality."

The Manor Guest House

345 W 13th Ave
Vancouver, BC V5Y 1W2
(604)876-8494 Fax:(604)876-5763
E-mail: manorguesthouse@bc.sympatico.ca
Web: www.manorguesthouse.com

Circa 1902. This turn-of-the-century Edwardian still features many original elements, including carved banisters, polished wood floors and ornate wainscoting. The home is one of the city's oldest. The innkeeper has deco-
rated it with a collection of English antiques. The penthouse suite, which includes a bedroom, loft, deck and kitchen, boasts a spectacular view of the city. Fresh fruits, home-baked breads and specialties such as a cheese and mushroom souffle or blueberry cobbler highlight the breakfast menu.

Innkeeper(s): Brenda Yablon. $65-125. MC, VISA, TC. TAC10. 10 rooms, 6 with PB, 1 with FP, 1 suite and 1 conference room. Type of meal: Full gourmet bkfst. Beds: KQDT. Cable TV in room. VCR, fax and copier on premises. Weddings, small meetings, family reunions and seminars hosted. French and German spoken. Antiquing, live theater, parks, shopping, downhill skiing, sporting events and water sports nearby.

O Canada House

1114 Barclay St
Vancouver, BC V6E 1H1
(604)688-0555 (877)688-1114 Fax:(604)488-0556
Web: vancouver-bc.com/ocanadahouse

Circa 1897. The first version of the Canadian national anthem was written in this Queen Anne Victorian, thus its unusual name. The home is furnished with an upscale mix of Arts and Crafts and Victorian pieces. The richly painted walls, fine woodwork and luxurious carpeting add to the elegant interior.

In addition to the guest rooms, there is a private cottage available. The innkeepers offer many amenities for busi-
ness travelers, including fax and copy services. A pantry is stocked with snacks and refreshments, and break-
fasts include gourmet coffee, homemade muffins, croissants or scones, fresh fruit and entrees such as seafood crepes or eggs Florentine. The home is minutes from many of Vancouver's popular attractions, including shopping, restaurants, Stanley Park and the beach.

Historic Interest: Gastown 1 mile.

Innkeeper(s): Jim Britten. $125-215. MC, VISA. TAC10. 6 rooms with PB, 1 with FP and 1 cottage. Breakfast, afternoon tea and snacks/refreshments included in rates. Types of meals: Veg bkfst and early coffee/tea. Catered breakfast available. Beds: QD. Cable TV, phone, ceiling fan and VCR in room. Central air. Fax, copier and library on premises. Antiquing, art galleries, beaches, bicycling, canoeing/kayaking, fishing, golf, hiking, live theater, museums, parks, shopping, downhill skiing, cross-country skiing, sporting events, tennis and water sports nearby.

Victoria

Abigail's Hotel

906 McClure St
Victoria, BC V8V 3E7
(250)388-5363 (800)561-6565 Fax:(250)388-7787
E-mail: innkeeper@abigailshotel.com
Web: www.abigailshotel.com

Circa 1930. Abigail's, a Tudor-style hotel, boasts three gabled stories, stained-glass windows, crystal chandeliers and tasteful decor. It holds a five-star rating as a heritage inn with Canada Select. Complimentary hors d'oeuvres and beverages are offered in the library, also a popular area for small weddings. Rooms feature a variety of ameni-
ties such as canopied beds, fireplaces, Jacuzzi baths and antiques. The inn is located three blocks from Victoria's inner harbor, shops and restaurants.

Innkeeper(s): Daniel & Frauke Behune. $119-329. MC, VISA, AX, TC. TAC10. 22 rooms with PB, 14 with FP and 6 suites. Breakfast and snacks/refresh-ments included in rates. Types of meals: Full gourmet bkfst and coffee/tea. Beds: KQD. Phone in room. Fax, copier and library on premises. Weddings, small meetings, family reunions and seminars hosted. German spo-ken. Antiquing, fishing, live theater, parks, shopping and water sports nearby.

Beaconsfield Inn

998 Humboldt St
Victoria, BC V8V 2Z8
(250)384-4044 Fax:(250)384-4052
E-mail: beaconsfield@islandnet.com
Web: www.islandnet.com/beaconsfield/

Circa 1905. Beautiful grounds accentuate this turn-of-the-cen-tury English manor. Rooms are light and airy with antiques, original woodwork, Oriental carpets and stained-glass windows. Many of the rooms feature fireplaces and Jacuzzi tubs and all include cozy, down comforters. A luxurious gourmet breakfast is served in the dining room or sunroom and afternoon tea is sure to delight. Evening sherry is served in the library. There's plenty to do in this seaside town, and The Beaconsfield is only four blocks from downtown and the oceanfront.

Historic Interest: Butchart Gardens are 25 miles away, and Victoria has many historic buildings, homes and other sites. Old Town and several muse-ums are close by.

Innkeeper(s): Con & Judi Sollid. $200-350. MC, VISA. 6 rooms with PB and 3 suites. Breakfast and afternoon tea included in rates. Type of meal: Full bkfst. Gourmet dinner available. Beds: Q. Antiquing, fishing, live theater and water sports nearby.

"This place is about as close to heaven as one can get."

Dashwood Seaside Manor

One Cook St
Victoria, BC V8V 3W6
(800)667-5517 Fax:(250)383-1760
E-mail: reservations@dashwoodmanor.com
Web: www.dashwoodmanor.com

Circa 1912. Dashwood Manor is a historic listed Edwardian Tudor Revival mansion with a rare oceanfront location. Choose between a first-floor suite with a fireplace, chandelier and beamed ceilings; a second-story "special occasion" suite; or a top-floor suite for spectacular balcony views of the ocean and the Olympic Mountains. Some suites include a Jacuzzi tub. To reach downtown Victoria, take a short walk through the park. The inn offers a self-catered full breakfast.

Innkeeper(s): Derek Dashwood Family & Staff. $75-285. MC, VISA, AX, DC. 14 suites, 3 with FP. Breakfast included in rates. Type of meal: Full bkfst. Beds: Q. Cable TV in room. Antiquing, fishing, live theater and shopping nearby.

Pets allowed: Small pets with kennel.

Publicity: San Francisco Chronicle.

"Enchanting, very soothing."

Dreemskerry Heritage Home

1509 Rockland Ave
Victoria, BC V8S 1W3
(250)384-4014 Fax:(250)598-4239
E-mail: dreemskerry@msn.com
Web: www.dreemskerry.bc.ca

Circa 1920. Three blocks from the water, this Georgian Revival mansion is located in a beautiful old historic neighborhood. Guest rooms and baths are spacious and include large beds, Jacuzzi tubs, and some offer splendid views of sea and mountain. The Coach House Suite includes a private balcony. The family is retired from hotel management and now enjoys guests in the gracious setting of their own dining room at their English style-breakfast. Enjoy the garden with its flowers, water gardens and park-like grounds or stroll past other estate homes on a walk to Craigdarroch Castle, Antique Row or the gardens of Government House, all nearby.

Historic Interest: Lt. Governor's Residence-1/8 miles, Craigdarroch Castle-1/4 mile.

Innkeeper(s): Bryan & Maureen Stoodlry. $85-150. MC, VISA, PC, TC. TAC10. 4 rooms with PB. Breakfast included in rates. Beds: KQ. Fans in room. Central air. VCR, fax, copier, spa, swimming, sauna, stables, bicycles, tennis, library, pet boarding, child care and e-mail links on premises. Handicap access. Amusement parks, antiquing, art galleries, beaches, bicycling, canoeing/kayaking, fishing, golf, hiking, horseback riding, live theater, museums, parks and tennis nearby.

"Thank you for letting us share this dream house with you; beautiful!"

Elk Lake Chalet B&B

5275 Patrice Bay Hwy
Victoria, BC V8Y 1S8
(250)658-8999 (800)601-8999 Fax:(250)658-8999

Circa 1904. As one might gather, this bed & breakfast provides a view of Elk Lake and its cedar exterior evokes images of a mountain chalet. Located midway between Victoria and the Swartz Bay Ferry Terminal, guests are just minutes from many popular attractions. The interior is comfortably furnished with a mix of contemporary, traditional and some Victorian pieces. The grounds include a deck with a hot tub. Golfing, tennis and watersports are among the local offerings, and the home is 10 minutes from Butchart Gardens.

Historic Interest: Craigdarroch Castle (8 miles), Parliament building (10 miles), Hatney Castle (10 miles).

Innkeeper(s): Gil & Pam Parsons. $55-70. MC, VISA, TC. TAC10. 6 rooms, 5 with PB, 1 with FP and 1 suite. Breakfast included in rates. Types of meals: Full bkfst, veg bkfst and early coffee/tea. Beds: QT. Fax, spa, bicycles and library on premises. Small meetings, family reunions and seminars hosted. Antiquing, art galleries, beaches, bicycling, canoeing/kayaking, fishing, golf, hiking, horseback riding, live theater, museums, parks, shopping, tennis, water sports and wineries nearby.

Gregory's Guest House

5373 Patricia Bay Hwy
Victoria, BC V8Y 2N9
(250)658-8404 (888)658-8404 Fax:(250)658-4604
E-mail: gregorys@direct.ca
Web: www.bctravel.com/gregorys.html

Circa 1919. The two acres of this historic hobby farm are just across the street from Elk Lake, six miles from Victoria near Butchart Gardens. All the rooms are decorated in antiques and duvets, and they feature garden and lake views. The grounds include water gardens, a waterfall and a pond. A traditional, full Canadian breakfast is served, and after the meal, guests can enjoy the hobby farm and animals or perhaps rent a boat at the lake.

Innkeeper(s): Paul & Elizabeth Gregory. $79-89. MC, VISA, PC, TC. TAC10. 3 rooms, 2 with PB. Breakfast included in rates. Type of meal: Full bkfst. Beds: DT. Fax and library on premises. Antiquing, fishing, Victoria Butchart Gardens, live theater, parks, sporting events and water sports nearby.

"Our family felt very welcome, loved the house and especially liked the super breakfasts."

Holland House Inn

595 Michigan St
Victoria, BC V8V 1S7
(250)384-6644 (800)335-3466 Fax:(250)384-6117
E-mail: stay@hollandhouse.victoria.bc.ca
Web: hollandhouse.victoria.bc.ca

Circa 1915. Refurbished in a pristine English country style, the three-story Holland House Inn is accentuated with a white picket fence, pillared balconies and colorful flower boxes. Luxurious accommodations have been designed individually and include fireplaces, sitting areas, a balcony or patio, handsome antiques and unique pieces, matching wallpapers and draperies, goose down duvets and full baths (four with double soaking tubs). The Conservatory or patio is the site for the inn's lavish breakfast. Victoria's Inner Harbor, downtown and the Seattle and Port Angeles ferry terminals are within three blocks.

Innkeeper(s): Margaret & Harry Brock. $68-172. MC, VISA, AX. 14 rooms. Breakfast included in rates. Type of meal: Full bkfst. Beds: KQT. Cable TV and phone in room. Weddings, small meetings and family reunions hosted. Antiquing, live theater and shopping nearby.

Oak Bay Guest House

1052 Newport Ave
Victoria, BC V8S 5E3
(250)598-3812 (800)575-3812 Fax:(450)598-0369

Circa 1912. Said to be the oldest continuously operated bed & breakfast in Victoria, Oak Bay is an English Tudor-style inn on a half acre of grounds. Features of the inn include beamed ceilings, diamond-shaped leaded-glass windows, built-in cupboards, a sun lounge and a parlor. Furnishings include antiques. Breakfasts are served  in the dining room, complete with fireplace. There are four courses, including favorites as eggs Benedict and freshly baked muffins such as cranberry-walnut or rhubarb muffins. The inn's gardens are inviting, but so is downtown Victoria, a double-decker bus away (or you can walk). There are tea rooms, antique shops and turn-of-the-century Victorian homes in the gracious tree-shaded neighborhood. The ocean and beach walks are a block away.

Historic Interest: Hudson Bay Post in Canada's early days.

Innkeeper(s): Jackie & Karl Morris. $60-170. MC, VISA, AX, TC. TAC10. 11 rooms, 9 with PB, 2 suites and 1 conference room. Breakfast included in rates. Types of meals: Full bkfst, country bkfst and early coffee/tea. Gourmet lunch available. Beds: KQDT. Cable TV, phone and VCR in room. Fax, copier, bicycles and library on premises. Weddings, family reunions and seminars hosted. German, French and Czech spoken. Antiquing, beaches, bicycling, canoeing/kayaking, fishing, golf, shopping, tennis and water sports nearby.

Scholefield House B&B

731 Vancouver St
Victoria, BC V8V 3-V4
(250)385-2025 (800)661-1623 Fax:(250)383-3036
E-mail: mail@scholefieldhouse.com
Web: scholefieldhouse.com

Circa 1892. The innkeeper at this two-story Queen Anne Victorian is an author, who enjoys the connection to the original owner of the house who founded the library in the Legislature Building. Located on a tree-lined street a short walk from the Empress Hotel, a picket fence and gabled front entrance welcome guests. Rooms are furnished with antiques, elegant draperies and period decor, and  there are clawfoot soaker tubs. Edible flowers decorate the abundant servings of eggs Florentine, french toast with Brie, smoked salmon and other entrees of the five-course champagne breakfasts served fireside in the parlor. The house is listed in the historical heritage register.

Innkeeper(s): Tana Dineen. $100-150. MC, VISA, PC, TC. TAC10. 3 rooms with PB, 1 with FP and 1 suite. Breakfast included in rates. Type of meal: Full gourmet bkfst. Beds: KQ. Turndown service and ceiling fan in room. VCR, fax and library on premises. Antiquing, fishing, golf, whale watching, hiking, live theater, parks, shopping and water sports nearby.

New Brunswick

Edmundston

Auberge-LeFief Inn

87 Rue De L'Eglise
Edmundston, NB E3V 1J6
(506)735-0400 Fax:(506)735-0402

Circa 1920. This red brick Victorian offers rooms decorated in a variety of cultural themes, reflecting the pioneer heritage of New Brunswick. There's Irish Mist, The Highland, The French Vineyard and The Malobiannah, to name a few. Fine dining is offered in the evening and includes a four-course dinner with choice of three entrees such as Salmon in Champagne Sauce, Filet of Beef in Portal and Bernaise Sauce and Citrus Chicken. Among the inn's regional dishes is the local "ploye," a buckwheat type crepe occasionally offered at breakfast. The inn has a four-star rating from Mobile.

Historic Interest: King Landing (200 km).

Innkeeper(s): Sharon Belanger. $60-95. MC, VISA, TC. 8 rooms and 1 conference room. Breakfast, afternoon tea and snacks/refreshments included in rates. Meal: Early coffee/tea. Gourmet dinner available. Beds: KQD. Cable TV, phone, ceiling fan and VCR in room. Air conditioning. Fax, copier and library on premises. Weddings, small meetings, family reunions and seminars hosted. French spoken. Amusement parks, antiquing, art galleries, bicycling, canoeing/kayaking, golf, hiking, horseback riding, live theater, museums, parks, shopping, downhill skiing, cross-country skiing, sporting events, tennis and water sports nearby.

Nova Scotia

Canning

The Farmhouse Inn

1057 Main St
Canning, NS B0P 1H0
(902)582-7900 (800)928-4346 Fax:(902)582-7900

Circa 1840. Located 75 minutes from Halifax, this renovated farmhouse offers a welcoming front porch accentuated by colorful flower beds. Guest rooms inside offer fireplaces, ceiling fans, cable television and air conditioning. Some rooms include double whirlpool tubs. (Ask for the Fundy Suite.) A pressed tin ceiling and pine floors add to the character of the dining room. Afternoon tea is served with freshly baked goodies, and in the morning a full breakfast features homemade bread, French toast, apple sausage and "Blueberry Grunt". The inn offers an exercise room. In the winter, sleigh rides are available. If you drive eight minutes up to the Look-Off, you'll enjoy panoramic views of the valley and Minas Basin. Other popular activities include cycling along Fundy Shore, watching the spectacularly fast tides at Kingsport Beach or visiting Blomidon Park's red cliffs.

Historic Interest: Grand Pre-15 miles, Fort Anne-60 miles.

Innkeeper(s): Doug & Ellen Bray. $69-119. MC, VISA, TC. TAC10. 6 rooms, 3 with PB, 3 with FP, 3 suites and 1 conference room. Breakfast and afternoon tea included in rates. Types of meals: Full bkfst and early coffee/tea. Beds: KQDT. Cable TV, phone, ceiling fan and VCR in room. Air conditioning. Fax, copier and library on premises. Small meetings, family reunions and seminars hosted. Amusement parks, antiquing, art galleries, beaches, bicycling, golf, hiking, horseback riding, live theater, museums, parks, shopping, downhill skiing, cross-country skiing and wineries nearby.

Chester

Mecklenburgh Inn

78 Queen St
Chester, NS B0J 1J0
(902)275-4638

Circa 1906. Guests to this Edwardian Mission-style inn have plenty to see and do in the seaside village, which has catered to summer visitors for more than 150 years. Favorite activities include touring the historic streets, watching a yacht race, tennis, golf, and browsing the craft shops and boutiques. The living room is a popular place for sitting by the fireplace to talk and read  from the selection of travel books and magazines. Local theater productions can be seen at the Chester Playhouse. Guests will be happy to know that the innkeeper is a Cordon Bleu chef.

Historic Interest: Oak Island (5 miles).

Innkeeper(s): Suzi Fraser. $55-75. VISA, AX. 4 rooms. Breakfast and afternoon tea included in rates. Types of meals: Full bkfst and afternoon tea. Beds: QDT. VCR on premises. Weddings and family reunions hosted. Antiquing, fishing, live theater, shopping, sporting events and water sports nearby.

"Lovely experience, great hospitality, yummy breakfast."

Clyde River

Clyde River Inn

10525 Highway 103
Clyde River, NS B0W 1R0
(902)637-3267 (877)262-0222 Fax:(902)637-1512

Circa 1874. This beautifully restored Victorian, once a stage-coach stop, features an inviting red exterior trimmed in a creamy shade of saffron. The interior is decorated with antiques in period, Victorian style. Guests are treated to an evening snack, as well as a full breakfast with items such as fresh fruit, homemade muffins and croissants, homemade preserves, yogurt and entrees such as blueberry pancakes. Golfing, fishing and beaches all are nearby.

Historic Interest: Black Loyalist Landing 1783 (8 miles), Old meeting house and woollen mill (10 miles).

Innkeeper(s): Michael & Pat Nickerson. $45-90. MC, VISA, TC. TAC10. 4 rooms, 3 with PB and 1 suite. Breakfast and snacks/refreshments included in rates. Types of meals: Full bkfst and early coffee/tea. Beds: QDT. Ceiling fan in room. VCR, fax, library and pet boarding on premises. Antiquing, beaches, bicycling, canoeing/kayaking, fishing, golf, museums, parks and shopping nearby.

Pets allowed: CAll ahead.

Middleton

Fairfield Farm Inn

10 Main St
Middleton, NS B0S 1P0
(902)825-6989 (800)237-9896 Fax:(902)825-6989
E-mail: griffith@glinx.com
Web: www.valleyweb.com/fairfieldfarminn

Circa 1886. Nova Scotia's picturesque Annapolis Valley creates the peaceful surroundings at this restored Victorian farmhouse. The inn is located on a 110-acre estate on the Annapolis River that offers woodland, mountain and meadow views. Guest rooms feature period antiques, as do the library, parlor and solarium. Guests have a wide range of breakfast items to choose from.  Dinner is served at 7 p.m. by reservation. Seasonal fruits and vegetables are freshly picked from the inn's extensive gardens. The innkeepers' latest plans include the addition of an on-site pitch and putt golf century, as well as more suites. A historic church, museum, galleries, shops and restaurants are all within walking distance, and a short drive will take you to the Bay of Fundy, national parks and historic sites.

Innkeeper(s): Richard & Shae Griffith. $55-90. MC, VISA, AX, DC, DS, TC. TAC10. 5 rooms with PB and 1 conference room. Breakfast included in rates. Types of meals: Full bkfst and early coffee/tea. Dinner and picnic lunch available. Beds: KQD. Cable TV, ceiling fan and hair dryer in room. Air conditioning. VCR, fax, copier and library on premises. Weddings, small meetings, family reunions and seminars hosted. French and English spoken. Amusement parks, antiquing, fishing, golf, national Parks, live theater, parks, shopping, cross-country skiing, sporting events and water sports nearby.

Ontario

Gananoque

Manse Lane B&B

465 Stone St S
Gananoque, ON K7G 2A7
(613)382-8642 (888)565-6379

Circa 1860. Four comfortable guest rooms, two with a private bath, are available at this bed & breakfast. Breakfasts include items such as cereal, fruit, yogurt, cheeses, breads, bacon and eggs. Guests are within walking distance of local attractions.

Innkeeper(s): Jocelyn & George Bounds. $53-130. MC, VISA, AX, TC. TAC10. 4 rooms, 2 with PB. Breakfast included in rates. MAP. Types of meals: Full bkfst and early coffee/tea. Afternoon tea and room service available. Beds: QT. Air conditioning. Swimming on premises. Antiquing, fishing, golf, boat cruises, festivals, live theater, parks, cross-country skiing, tennis and water sports nearby.

"Thoroughly enjoyed the stay. It was great to see you again."

Kingston

Hotel Belvedere

141 King St E
Kingston, ON K7L 2Z9
(613)548-1565 (800)559-0584 Fax:(613)546-4692
E-mail: ian@hotelbelvedere
Web: www.hotelbelvedere.com

Circa 1880. Hotel Belvedere began its life as a private mansion, built in the Georgian style of architecture. Eventually, it was transformed into a hotel and then into a boarding house. Thankfully, it has been restored and refurbished back to its original state. The interior boasts the fine woodwork, carved mantels and marble floors one expects in a grand mansion. Elegant guest rooms are decorated in period style with antiques, and beds are dressed with fine white linens. In warm weather, the innkeepers serve a continental breakfast on the private terrace. Guests can enjoy the morning fare in their room or in front of a warm fire in the living room. Secluded three hours from Toronto along the shores of Lake Ontario, Kingston is a charming site for a getaway. Historic homes, museums and dinner cruises are among the offerings in town. The town once served as the capital of Canada.

Historic Interest: Bellvue House, Fort Henry (1 mile), 1000 Island tours (1 block), Marine Museum (1 block).

Innkeeper(s): Donna Mallory & Ian Walsh. $110-225. MC, VISA, AX, DC, PC, TC. 20 rooms with PB, 2 suites and 1 conference room. Breakfast included in rates. Types of meals: Cont plus and early coffee/tea. Catering service available. Beds: KQDT. TV and phone in room. Air conditioning. Fax, copier and library on premises. Weddings, small meetings, family reunions and seminars hosted. French, Dutch and Portuguese spoken. Antiquing, art galleries, beaches, bicycling, canoeing/kayaking, fishing, golf, hiking, live theater, museums, parks, shopping, cross-country skiing, sporting events, tennis and water sports nearby.

The North Nook B&B

83 Earl St
Kingston, ON K7L 2G8
(613)547-8061 Fax:(613)547-2818

Circa 1849. Recently restored, this two-story limestone house has exposed stone and brick walls, gleaming pine floors and original tin ceilings and a tin roof. It was originally built as a market. Antiques now fill the rooms. Breakfast is served in the dining room and often includes orange French toast.

Innkeeper(s): Mary Ellen North. $85-135. MC, VISA, AX. 4 rooms with PB. Breakfast and afternoon tea included in rates. Types of meals: Cont plus and early coffee/tea. Beds: QD. Cable TV, phone, turndown service, ceiling fan and VCR in room. Air conditioning. Fax on premises. Antiquing, fishing, golf, live theater, parks, shopping, downhill skiing, cross-country skiing, tennis and water sports nearby.

Painted Lady Inn

181 William St
Kingston, ON K7L 2E1
(613)545-0422

Circa 1872. Built as a church manse, the inn still maintains its original features, including an idyllic veranda and second-story balcony. Rooms are decorated in Victorian style. Three guest rooms feature a double Jacuzzi tub and fireplace. Freshly baked croissants, homemade waffles and omelets made with Canadian cheddar cheese are just a few of the breakfast possibilities. Kingston offers many historic things to do, from Thousand Islands boat cruises to visiting Fort Henry and 17 museums. The town also boasts dozens of restaurants, pubs and shops.

Historic Interest: Fort Henry (1 mile), Bellevue House (one-fourth mile), Kingston Prison Museum (one-fourth mile).

Innkeeper(s): Carol Franks. $75-140. MC, VISA, AX. 7 rooms, 4 with PB, 3 with FP. Breakfast included in rates. Type of meal: Full bkfst. Beds: QT. Jacuzzi and fireplace suites in room. Central air. Veranda, parking and balcony on premises. Antiquing, art galleries, beaches, bicycling, canoeing/kayaking, fishing, golf, hiking, horseback riding, open air summer market, live theater, museums, parks, shopping, cross-country skiing, tennis and water sports nearby.

Ottawa

Auberge McGEE's Inn [Est. 1984]

185 Daly Ave
Ottawa, ON K1N 6E8
(613)237-6089 (800)262-4337 Fax:(613)237-6201
E-mail: aubmcgeesinn@webtv.net
Web: www.coatesb.demon.co.uk/McGees

Circa 1886. The home was built for John McGee, Canada's first Clerk of Privy Council. The portico of this restored Victorian mansion is reminiscent of McGee's Irish roots featuring pillars that were common in Dublin architecture. Rooms are comfortable and decorated in soft, pleasing colors. Amenities such as mounted hair dryers add a touch of modern convenience. The two Jacuzzi suites are decorated with a special theme in mind.

One is named the Victorian Roses Suite, and the other is The Egyptian Room. For extended stays, the inn provides the use of laundry facilities and a guest kitchenette. The

innkeepers celebrate 17 years of award-winning hospitality. Business travelers will appreciate items such as in-room phones with computer modem hook-ups and voice mail. There is no end to what guests can see and do in Ottawa. Visit the Byward Market, the many museums or the 230-store Rideau Center.

Historic Interest: Walking distance to Congress Centre, University of Ottawa, Parliament Hill, War Memorial at Confederation Square and Rideau Canal.

Innkeeper(s): Anne Schutte & Mary Unger. $88-198. MC, VISA, AX. 14 rooms with PB, 3 with FP, 2 suites and 1 conference room. Breakfast included in rates. Type of meal: Full bkfst. Beds: KQDT. Cable TV, phone, some fireplaces and ceiling fans and hair dryers in room. Air conditioning. Limited free parking on premises. Small meetings and family reunions hosted. Spanish, French and English spoken. Antiquing, live theater, parks, shopping, downhill skiing, cross-country skiing, sporting events and water sports nearby.

Gasthaus Switzerland Inn

89 Daly Ave
Ottawa, ON K1N 6-E6
(613)237-0335 (888)663-0000 Fax:(613)594-3327

Circa 1872. This historic structure, built from natural stone, was originally a private home and later served as a military rehabilitation facility during World War I. The accommodations include guest rooms and four suites. Two of the suites include a poster bed and Jacuzzi tub. Breakfasts, as the name might suggest, consist of a Swiss buffet with items such as croissants, eggs, cheese and the inn's specialty, Birchermuesli.

Innkeeper(s): Sabina & Josef Sauter. $78-198. MC, VISA, AX, DC, CB, TC. TAC10. 22 rooms, 18 with PB, 4 with FP and 4 suites. Breakfast included in rates. Type of meal: Full bkfst. Beds: KQDT. Cable TV and phone in room. Air conditioning. Fax on premises. Swiss, German and French spoken. Fishing, golf, parks, shopping, downhill skiing, cross-country skiing, sporting events, tennis and water sports nearby.

Peterborough

King Bethune Guest House

270 King St
Peterborough, ON K9J 2S2
(705)743-4101 (800)574-3664 Fax:(705)743-8446

Circa 1893. This brick Victorian is downtown on a quiet tree-shaded street. Restored hardwood floors, original trim throughout, tall ceilings and handsome windows grace the interiors. Guest rooms are large and offer antiques, as well as desks, data ports, TVs and VCRs. The Executive Suite has a king bed and private entrance as well as a private hot tub, sauna and steam bath. There's a private walled garden with reflecting pool, fountain and fireplace, a favorite spot for breakfast. Plan ahead, and you can arrange for a roast beef dinner complete with yorkshire pudding.

Innkeeper(s): Marlis Lindsay. $74-156. MC, VISA, AX, PC, TC. TAC10. 3 rooms with PB. Breakfast included in rates. Types of meals: Full gourmet bkfst and early coffee/tea. Afternoon tea, gourmet dinner, picnic lunch, lunch and room service available. Beds: KQ. Cable TV, phone, turndown service, ceiling fan, VCR, sauna and garden hot tub in room. Fax, spa, sauna, bicycles, library and english courtyard garden on premises. Small meetings and family reunions hosted. Amusement parks, antiquing, fishing, golf, live theater, parks, shopping, downhill skiing, cross-country skiing, sporting events, tennis and water sports nearby.

Pets allowed: owner supervised.

Publicity: *Canadian Country, Examiner.*

"We still have not found better accommodations anywhere."

Port Hope

Butternut Inn B&B

36 North St
Port Hope, ON L1A 1T8
(905)885-4318 (800)218-6670 Fax:(905)885-5464
E-mail: info@butternutinn.com
Web: www.butternutinn.com

Circa 1847. The original portion of Butternut Inn was built in the late 1840s. A Neo-classical addition was added in 1878. The home's most notable resident has been "The Great Farini," the renowned impressario and 19th-century circus performer. The grounds include a croquet area and a perennial secret garden. Rooms are decorated with romance in mind. The hardwood floors are  topped with Oriental rugs, and furnishings include brass iron beds topped with opulent linens and soft comforters. Guests can relax in the solarium, which offers comfortable wicker furnishings, a warm fireplace and a view of the garden. Breakfasts are served in the formal dining room. A typical menu might include a starter of strawberries and grapefruit with candied ginger, followed by an entrée of an asparagus and goat cheese frittata with fresh herbs, salsa, potatoes and sourdough biscuits. The innkeepers offer gourmet getaway packages where guests get to enjoy the inn's fine cuisine, as well as take part in a cooking class led by a local chef. Port Hope offers an assortment of antique shops, as well as golfing, hiking, skiing and fishing.

Historic Interest: Town of Port Hope.

Innkeeper(s): Bonnie & Bob Harrison. $80-95. MC, VISA, TC. TAC10. 4 rooms with PB. Breakfast included in rates. Types of meals: Full gourmet bkfst and early coffee/tea. Beds: QT. Cable TV, turndown service, ceiling fan and whirlpool tubs in room. Air conditioning. Fax, bar refrigerator, patio and secret garden on premises. Weddings, small meetings, family reunions and seminars hosted. Some french spoken. Antiquing, art galleries, beaches, bicycling, fishing, golf, hiking, horseback riding, live theater, shopping, downhill skiing, cross-country skiing and tennis nearby.

Toronto

Aberdeen Guest House

52 Aberdeen Ave
Toronto, ON M4X 1A2
(416)922-8697 Fax:(416)922-5011
E-mail: aberinn@interlog.com
Web: www.interlog.com/~aberinn

Circa 1907. Nestled in the heart of Toronto's historic Cabbagetown, Aberdeen Guest House provides accommodations within walking distance to many Toronto attractions. The Victorian Row House is located in a neighborhood filled with historic Victorian homes. Guest rooms are decorated in a cheerful, cozy style featuring names such as the Magnolia Room or the Water Lily Room. The Sunflower Room includes artwork representing the  signature flower, a sunflower comforter atop a four-poster bed, sunflower curtains and walls painted in a warm saffron tone. During the week, a continental breakfast is provided. On weekends, a full breakfast is served in the home's dining room.

Innkeeper(s): Gary Stothers. $90-125. MC, VISA, AX, TC. 4 rooms, 1 with PB, 1 with FP and 1 conference room. Breakfast included in rates. Types of meals: Full gourmet bkfst, cont plus, cont and early coffee/tea. Catering service available. Beds: KQT. TV and ceiling fan in room. Central air. Fax and copier on premises. Weddings, small meetings, family reunions and seminars hosted. Japanese and French spoken. Amusement parks, antiquing, art galleries, beaches, bicycling, golf, hiking, live theater, museums, parks, shopping, sporting events, tennis, water sports and wineries nearby.

Quebec

Montreal

Auberge De La Fontaine

1301 E Rachel St
Montreal, PQ H2J 2K1
(514)597-0166 (800)597-0597 Fax:(514)597-0496

Circa 1910. Located just across the street from a lovely 80-acre park, accommodations at this historic stone Victorian are the piece de resistance. Auberge's location is in the heart of the Plateau Mont-Royal quarter, a trendy Montreal area packed with restaurants, cafes and boutiques. The award-winning inn offers individually decorated, sound-proofed rooms, all in a modern style. Some rooms have exposed brick walls, a sitting area, a terrace or a balcony, and the three suites include a whirlpool. Guests have access to the kitchen, where they can find a snack. Continental breakfast is served each morning. Breads, muffins, cereals, cheeses, cold cuts, yogurt and fresh fruit fill the buffet in the inn's dining room. The staff is happy to help guests find their way to attractions in Montreal, and parking at the back of the inn and nearby streets is free.

Historic Interest: Old Montreal (4 miles).

Innkeeper(s): Jean LaMothe & Celine Boudreau. $94-233. MC, VISA, AX, DC, DS, TC. TAC10. 18 rooms with PB, 3 suites and 1 conference room. Breakfast and snacks/refreshments included in rates. EP. Types of meals: Cont plus and early coffee/tea. Afternoon tea available. Beds: QDT. Cable TV, phone and access to kitchen in room. Air conditioning. VCR, fax and terrace on premises. Handicap access. Small meetings, family reunions and seminars hosted. French and English spoken. Amusement parks, antiquing, art galleries, bicycling, golf, casino and underground city, live theater, museums, parks, shopping, downhill skiing, cross-country skiing, sporting events, tennis and water sports nearby.

"Breakfast was superb and we enjoyed the quietness of the room."

Inns of Interest

African-American History

Munro House B&B . . . . .Jonesville, Mich.
Wooden Rabbit . . . . .Cape May, N.J.
Troubeck . . . . .Amenia, N.Y.
Signal House . . . . .Ripley, Ohio
1790 House B&B Inn . .Georgetown, S.C.
Golden Stage Inn . . . . . .Proctorsville, Vt.
Kedron Valley Inn . .South Woodstock, Vt.
Inn at Weathersfield . . .Weathersfield, Vt.
Rockland Farm Retreat . . . . .Bumpass, Va.
Sleepy Hollow Farm . . . .Gordonsville, Va.

Barns

Old Church House Inn . . . . .Mossville, Ill.
Brickyard Barn Inn . . . . . . .Topeka, Kan.
Watchtide, B&B By the Sea
. . . . .Searsport, Maine
Brannon-Bunker Inn . . . . .Walpole, Maine
Candlelite Inn . . . . .Bradford, N.H.
Lee's Deer Run B&B . . . . .Stillwater, N.Y.
Inn at Cedar Falls . . . . .Logan, Ohio
Pine Barn Inn . . . . .Danville, Pa.
Cornerstone B&B Inn . . .Landenberg, Pa.
Pace One Restaurant and Country Inn
. . . . .Thornton, Pa.
Jackson Fork Inn . . . . . .Huntsville, Utah
Waitsfield Inn . . . . .Waitsfield, Vt.

Boats

Dockside Boat & Bed . . . .Oakland, Calif.
Tugboat Challenger . . . . . .Seattle, Wash.

Castles

Castle Marne- A Luxury Urban Inn
. . . . .Denver, Colo.
Castle Inn Riverside . . . . . . .Wichita, Kan.
Manresa Castle . . . .Port Townsend, Wash.

Churches & Parsonages

The Parsonage . . . . . . .Nevada City, Calif.
The Parsonage . . . . .Santa Barbara, Calif.
Old Church House Inn . . . . .Mossville, Ill.
Churchtown Inn . . . . . .Churchtown, Pa.
Parsonage Inn . . . . . . .St. Michaels, Md.
The Beechcroft Inn . . . . .Brewster, Mass.
The Parsonage Inn . . .East Orleans, Mass.
The Parsonage on the Green . . .Lee, Mass.
The Abbey . . . . .Cape May, N.J.
Parson's Pillow . . . . .Cody, Wyo.

Civil War

Mansion Bed & Breakfast . .Bardstown, Ky.
Myrtledene . . . . .Lebanon, Ky.
Old Manse Inn . . . . .Brewster, Mass.
Munro House . . . . .Jonesville, Mich.
Anchuca . . . . .Vicksburg, Miss.
Dunleith . . . . .Natchez, Miss.
Cedar Grove Mansion Inn
. . . . .Vicksburg, Miss.
Wooden Rabbit . . . . .Cape May, N.J.
Goose Creek Guesthouse . .Southold, N.Y.
Red House Inn B&B . . . . .Brevard, N.C.
Troy-Bumpass Inn . . . .Greensboro, N.C.
Misty River B&B . . . . .Ripley, Ohio
Churchtown Inn B&B . . .Churchtown, Pa.
Baladerry Inn at Gettysburg Gettysburg, Pa.
Brafferton Inn . . . . .Gettysburg, Pa.
Doubleday Inn . . . . .Gettysburg, Pa.
Inns of the Gettysburg Area
. . . . .Gettysburg, Pa.
James Getty Hotel . . . . . .Gettysburg, Pa.
Kedron Valley Inn . .South Woodstock, Vt.
Inn at Weathersfield . . .Weathersfield, Vt.
River House . . . . .Boyce, Va.
Edgewood Plantation . . . .Charles City, Va.
Inn at La Vista Plantation
. . . . .Fredericksburg, Va.
Springdale Country Inn . . . . .Lincoln, Va.
Mayhurst Inn . . . . .Orange, Va.
Mayfield Inn . . . . .Petersburg, Va.
Inn at Narrow Passage . . . .Woodstock, Va.
Fillmore Street B&B
. . . . .Harpers Ferry, W.Va.
Boydville, Inn at Martinsburg
. . . . .Martinsburg, W.Va.

Cookbooks Written By Innkeepers

Old Yacht Club Inn . .Santa Barbara, Calif.
"The Old Yacht Club Inn Cookbook"
Sea Holly B&B Inn . . . . . .Cape May, N.J.
"Sea Holly Bed and Breakfast, A Sharing of Secrets"
Grandview Lodge . . . . . .Waynesville, N.C.
"Recipes from Grandview Lodge"
The Old Stone Inn . . . .Waynesville, N.C.
"The Old Stone Inn Cookbook"
Ravenscroft Inn . . .Port Townsend, Wash.
"Something's CookInn"
A. Drummonds Ranch . .Cheyenne, Wyo.
"With Lots of Love"

Farms and Orchards

Apple Lane Inn . . . . .Aptos, Calif.
Scarlett's Country Inn . . . .Calistoga, Calif.
Brookside Farm . . . . .Dulzura, Calif.
Inn at Shallow Creek Farm .Orland, Calif.
Howard Creek Ranch . . . .Westport, Calif.
Black Forest B&B .Colorado Springs, Colo.
Apple Orchard Inn . . . . . .Durango, Colo.
Applewood Farms Inn . . . .Ledyard, Colo.
1810 West Inn . . . . .Thomson, Ga.
Kaia Ranch & Co . . . . .Kona, Hawaii
Kingston 5 Ranch B&B . .Kingston, Idaho
Canaan Land Farm B&B . .Harrodsburg, Ky.
Maple Hill Farm B&B Inn
. . . . .Hallowell/Augusta, Maine
Summer Hill Farm . . . . . .Lenox, Mass.
On Cranberry Pond B&B
. . . . .Middleboro, Mass.
Gilbert's Tree Farm B&B . .Rehoboth, Mass.
Steep Acres Farm . . .Williamstown, Mass.
Horse & Carriage B&B . .Jonesville, Mich.
Four Columns Inn . . . . .Sherburn, Minn.
Caverly Farm & Orchard . . . . .Bland, Mo.
Grandpa's Farm . . . . .Lampe, Mo.
Old Pioneer Garden Guest Ranch
. . . . .Unionville, Nev.
Rockhouse Mountain Farm Inn
. . . . .Eaton Center, N.H.
Colby Hill Inn . . . . .Henniker, N.H.
Ellis River B&B . . . . .Jackson, N.H.
Olde Orchard Inn . .Moultonborough, N.H.
Apple Valley Inn B&B and Antiques
. . . . .Glenwood, N.J.
Agape Farm B&B . . . . .Corinth, N.Y.
Breezy Acres Farm B&B . . . .Hobart, N.Y.
Fearrington House Inn . . . .Pittsboro, N.C.
Volden Farm . . . . .Lucerne, N.D.
Wine Country Farm . . . . .Dayton, Ore.
Springbrook Hazelnut Farm . .Newberg, Ore.
Line Limousin Farmhouse B&B
. . . . .Carlisle, Pa.
Ponda-Rowland B&B Inn . . . . .Dallas, Pa.
Glen Isle Farm . . . . .Downington, Pa.
Huntland Farm . . . . .Greensburg, Pa.
Barley Sheaf Farm . . . . .Holicong, Pa.
Meadow Spring Farm . .Kennett Square, Pa.
Vogt Farm B&B . . . . .Marietta, Pa.
Cedar Hill Farm . . . . .Mount Joy, Pa.
Field & Pine B&B . . . . .Shippensburg, Pa.
B&B at Skogland Farm . . . .Canova, S.D.

507

River Meadow Farm
.... Manchester Center, Vt.
West River Lodge & Stables . . Newfane, Vt.
Historic Brookside Farms ..... Orwell, Vt.
Redwing Farm .... Townshend, Vt.
Stonecrest Farm B&B .... Wilder, Vt.
Rockland Farm Retreat .... Bumpass, Va.
Blue Knoll Farm .... Castleton, Va.
Upper Byrd Farm .... Columbia, Va.
Turtleback Farm .... Eastsound, Wash.
Just-N-Trails B&B .... Sparta, Wis.

French and Indian War

Summer Hill Farm .... Lenox, Mass.

Gold Mines & Gold Panning

Julian Gold Rush Hotel .... Julian, Calif.
Dunbar House, 1880 ..... Murphys, Calif.
Hotel Nipton .... Nipton, Calif.

Hot Springs

Rainbow Tarns B&B at Crowley Lake
.... Mammoth/Crowley Lake, Calif.
Vichy Hot Springs Resort ... Ukiah, Calif.
Idaho Rocky Mountain Ranch
.... Stanley, Idaho
Boulder Hot Springs ..... Boulder, Mont.
Soldier Meadows Guest Ranch
.... Gerlach, Nev.

Inns Built Prior to 1799

1649 Three Chimneys Inn . . Durham, N.H.
1690 Jonas Green House B&B
.... Annapolis, Md.
1690 Penny House Inn ... Eastham, Mass.
1692 The Dan'l Webster Inn
.... Sandwich, Mass.
1699 Ashley Manor Inn
.... Barnstable, Cape Cod, Mass.
1700 Elias Child House B&B
.... Woodstock, Conn.
1700 Casa Europa Inn & Gallery
.... Taos, N.M.
1700 Evermay-On-The-Delaware
.... Erwinna, Pa.
1700 Hollileif B&B ...... New Hope, Pa.
1702 Admiral Farragut Inn . Newport, R.I.
1704 Stumble Inne .... Nantucket, Mass.
1704 Cornerstone B&B Inn
.... Landenberg, Pa.
1705 Centre Bridge Inn ... New Hope, Pa.
1705 Clarkeston .... Newport, R.I.
1709 The Woodbox Inn . Nantucket, Mass.
1710 The Robert Morris Inn . . Oxford, Md.
1710 The Stockton Inn ... Stockton, N.J.
1720 Butternut Farm . Glastonbury, Conn.
1722 Historic Jacob Hill Farm B&B/Inn
.... Providence, R.I.
1723 Blue Skies Country Manor Estates
.... Montgomeryville, Pa.
1725 1725 Historic Witmer's Tavern Inn & Museum
.... Lancaster, Pa.
1730 Glen Isle Farm ... Downingtown, Pa.

1732 Under Mountain Inn
.... Salisbury, Conn.
1732 Armitage Inn ..... New Castle, Del.
1732 The Kitchen House . . Charleston, S.C.
1734 Langdon House ..... Beaufort, N.C.
1735 Churchtown Inn B&B
.... Churchtown, Pa.
1735 Antebellum B&B at the Thomas
Lamboll House ..... Charleston, S.C.
1738 Brown's Historic Home B&B
.... Salem, N.J.
1740 Red Brook Inn . . . Old Mystic, Conn.
1740 High Meadows B&B . . . Eliot, Maine
1740 The Lamb & Lion . . Barnstable, Mass.
1740 Red Maple Farm .... Princeton, N.J.
1740 The Galisteo Inn .... Santa Fe, N.M.
1740 Barley Sheaf Farm .... Holicong, Pa.
1740 Pace One Restaurant and Country Inn
.... Thornton, Pa.
1740 Willows of Newport - Romantic Inn
& Garden .... Newport, R.I.
1740 Thirty Six Meeting Street
.... Charleston, S.C.
1740 Du Pre House LLC
.... Georgetown, S.C.
1740 The Inn at Narrow Passage ....
Woodstock, Va.
1741 The Dunbar House . . Sandwich, Mass.
1742 The Kelley House . . Edgartown, Mass.
1743 The Inn at Mitchell House
.... Chestertown, Md.
1745 Olde Rhinebeck Inn Rhinebeck, N.Y.
1745 General Warren Inne . . Malvern, Pa.
1746 Deacon Timothy Pratt House B&B
.... Old Saybrook, Conn.
1749 Adams House ...... Mystic, Conn.
1750 Candleberry Inn .... Brewster, Mass.
1750 Isaac Hilliard House, LLC
.... Pemberton Boro, N.J.
1750 House on The Hill B&B
.... Warrensburg, N.Y.
1750 Tattersall Inn ... Point Pleasant, Pa.
1750 The Melville House . . . Newport, R.I.
1750 Linden House B&B & Plantation
.... Camplain, Va.
1750 Mayfield Inn ...... Petersburg, Va.
1750 Jasmine Plantation B&B Inn
.... Providence Forge, Va.
1752 The Olde Stage Coach B&B
.... Jennerstown, Pa.
1753 L'Auberge Provencale .... Boyce, Va.
1756 Bee and Thistle Inn
.... Old Lyme, Conn.
1758 Captain Folsom Inn
.... Greenland, N.H.
1760 Edgewater B&B ... Fairhaven, Mass.
1760 Mountain Lake Inn . . Bradford, N.H.
1760 Francis Malbone House
.... Newport, R.I.
1760 The Norris House Inn & Stone House
Tea Room .... Leesburg, Va.
1760 Gilbert House B&B of Middleway
.... Charles Town, W.Va.

1761 The Bird & Bottle Inn
.... Garrison, N.Y.
1763 Casa De Solana, B&B Inn
.... Saint Augustine, Fla.
1763 The Squire Tarbox Inn
.... Wiscasset, Maine
1763 Smithton Inn .... Ephrata, Pa.
1763 John Rutledge House Inn
.... Charleston, S.C.
1764 Colonel Spencer Inn Plymouth, N.H.
1764 The Inn at Ormsby Hill
.... Manchester Center, Vt.
1765 Bankhouse B&B .. West Chester, Pa.
1766 Beekman Arms-Delamater House
.... Rhinebeck, N.Y.
1766 The Inn at Meander Plantation
.... Locust Dale, Va.
1767 Lakeshore Inn Bed & Breakfast
.... Rockland, Maine
1767 Birchwood Inn .... Lenox, Mass.
1767 Highland Lake Inn B&B
.... East Andover, N.H.
1768 The Cedars Inn ..... Beaufort, N.C.
1769 Thomas Bond House
.... Philadelphia, Pa.
1770 The Parsonage Inn
.... East Orleans, Mass.
1770 The Richard Johnston Inn
.... Fredericksburg, Va.
1771 The Village Inn ..... Lenox, Mass.
1771 Publick House Historic Inn & Country
Motor Lodge ... Sturbridge, Mass.
1772 The Bagley House . . Durham, Maine
1773 The Red Lion Inn
.... Stockbridge, Mass.
1775 Todd House ...... Eastport, Maine
1775 Colonel Roger Brown House
.... Concord, Mass.
1776 Griswold Inn .... Essex, Conn.
1776 Chase House B&B Inn
.... Cornish, N.H.
1777 Doneckers, The Guesthouse, Inns
.... Ephrata, Pa.
1777 Nutmeg Inn ...... Wilmington, Vt.
1778 The Inn at Chester .. Chester, Conn.
1780 Mill Pond Inn
.... Damariscotta Mills, Maine
1780 Catoctin Inn and Conference Center
.... Buckeystown, Md.
1780 Cumworth Farm Cummington, Mass.
1780 Garden Gables Inn .... Lenox, Mass.
1780 Ivanhoe Country House
.... Sheffield, Mass.
1780 Egremont Inn South Egremont, Mass.
1780 Hacienda Antigua B&B
.... Albuquerque, N.M.
1780 The River House .... Boyce, Va.
1780 The Golden Stage Inn
.... Proctorsville, Vt.
1780 Redwing Farm B&B . Townshend, Vt.
1780 Silver Thatch Inn
.... Charlottesville, Va.
1782 Abel Darling B&B . Litchfield, Conn.
1783 The Towers B&B ..... Milford, Del.

1785 Weathervane Inn
. . . . .South Egremont, Mass.
1785 Oakland Plantation . . .Natchez, Mo.
1785 The 1785 Inn . .North Conway, N.H.
1785 Sleepy Hollow Farm B&B
. . . . .Gordonsville, Va.
1786 Gibson's Lodgings . . .Annapolis, Md.
1786 Windsor House . .Newburyport, Mass.
1786 The Brafferton Inn . .Gettysburg, Pa.
1786 Limestone Inn B&B . .Strasburg, Pa.
1788 Strasburg Village Inn . .Strasburg, Pa.
1789 Captain Josiah Mitchell House B&B
. . . . .Freeport, Maine
1789 Stevens Farm B&B . . . .Barre, Mass.
1789 The Azubah Atwood Inn
. . . . .Chatham, Mass.
1789 Miles River Country Inn
. . . . .Hamilton, Mass.
1789 Longswamp B&B . . .Mertztown, Pa.
1789 The Inn at High View . .Andover, Vt.
1789 Historic Brookside Farms Country Inn
& Antique Shop . . . . . . .Orwell, Vt.
1790 Riverwind . . . . . .Deep River, Conn.
1790 Silvermine Tavern . .Norwalk, Conn.
1790 Tolland Inn . . . . . . .Tolland, Conn.
1790 Benjamin F. Packard House
. . . . .Bath, Maine
1790 Fairhaven Inn . . . . . . .Bath, Maine
1790 Currier House . Havre de Grace, Md.
1790 Corner House . . . .Nantucket, Mass.
1790 Tuck Inn B&B . . . . .Rockport, Mass.
1790 The Southern Hotel
. . . . .Sainte Genevieve, Mo.
1790 1812 on The Perquimans B&B Inn
. . . . .Hertford, N.C.
1790 Nestlenook Farm Resort
. . . . .Jackson, N.H.
1790 Olde Orchard Inn
. . . . .Moultonborough, N.H.
1790 The Inn at Pleasant Lake
. . . . .New London, N.H.
1790 Stepping Stones B&B
. . . . .Wilton Center, N.H.
1790 Mill House Inn . .East Hampton, N.Y.
1790 The Inn at Bingham School
. . . . .Chapel Hill, N.C.
1790 Jacobs Resting Place . . . .Carlisle, Pa.
1790 The Altland House
. . . . .Abbottstown, Pa.
1790 Mill Creek Homestead B&B
. . . . .Bird-in-Hand, Pa.
1790 River Inn . . . . .Marietta, Pa.
1790 Pineapple Hill . . . . . .New Hope, Pa.
1790 Field & Pine B&B . .Shippensburg, Pa.
1790 The Cuthbert House Inn B&B
. . . . .Beaufort, S.C.
1790 1790 House B&B Inn
. . . . .Georgetown, S.C.
1790 Silver Maple Lodge & Cottages
. . . . .Fairlee, Vt.
1790 The Inn at Blush Hill . .Waterbury, Vt.
1790 Jordan Hollow Farm Inn . .Stanley, Va.
1791 St. Francis Inn . .Saint Augustine, Fla.

1791 The Inn on Cove Hill
. . . . .Rockport, Mass.
1792 King George IV Inn
. . . . .Charleston, S.C.
1792 The Inn on Covered Bridge Green
. . . . .Arlington, Vt.
1793 Pepper House Inn . . .Brewster, Mass.
1793 Bullard Farm B&B
. . . . .North New Salem, Mass.
1793 The Historic Temperance Tavern
. . . . .Gilmanton, N.H.
1793 The Nicholls-Crook Plantation
House B&B . . . . .Woodruff, S.C.
1794 Historic Merrell Inn
. . . . .Stockbridge, Mass.
1794 The Wagener Estate B&B
. . . . .Penn Yan, N.Y.
1794 The Whitehall Inn . .New Hope, Pa.
1794 Lareau Farm Country Inn
. . . . .Waitsfield, Vt.
1795 Canaan Land Farm B&B
. . . . .Harrodsburg, Ky.
1795 Watchtide...B&B by the Sea
. . . . .Searsport, Maine
1795 Shiretown Inn on the Island of
Martha's Vineyard . .Edgartown, Mass.
1795 The Swag Country Inn
. . . . .Waynesville, N.C.
1795 Bucksville House . .Kintnersville, Pa.
1795 The White House . .Block Island, R.I.
1795 Hachland Hill Inn . .Clarksville, Tenn.
1795 The Inn on The Common
. . . . .Craftsbury Common, Vt.
1795 Rabbit Hill Inn
. . . . .Lower Waterford, Vt.
1795 The Inn at Weathersfield
. . . . .Weathersfield, Vt.
1796 Myrtles Plantation
. . . . .Saint Francisville, La.
1796 Hodgdon Island Inn
. . . . .Boothbay, Maine
1796 Summer Hill Farm . . . .Lenox, Mass.
1797 Hannah Dudley House Inn
. . . . .Leverett, Mass.
1797 Williamsville Inn
. . . . .West Stockbridge, Mass.
1797 Colby Hill Inn . . . . .Henniker, N.H.
1797 Applebrook B&B . . . .Jefferson, N.H.
1797 Locktender Cottage . High Falls, N.Y.
1797 Cashtown Inn . . . . . .Cashtown, Pa.
1797 Peter Wolford House . .Dillsburg, Pa.
1797 Fitch Hill Inn . . . . .Hyde Park, Vt.
1797 River Meadow Farm
. . . . .Manchester Center, Vt.
1797 Wayside Inn Since 1797
. . . . .Middletown, Va.
1798 The House on Bayou Road
. . . . .New Orleans, LA

Jail House

Jailer's Inn . . . . .Bardstown, Ky.
Inn at Ormsby Hill
. . . . .Manchester Center, Vt.

Lighthouse

Light House Retreat
. . . . Sooke, British Columbia
Keeper's House . . . . .Isle Au Haut, Maine

Literary Figures Associated With Inns

Louisa May Alcott
Hawthorne Inn . . . . .Concord, Mass.
Susan B. Anthony
The Park House . . . . . .Saugatuck, Mich.
Devoe Mansion B&B . . . . .Tacoma, Wash.
Rachel Carson
Newagen Seaside Inn . . .Newagen. Maine
Ralph Waldo Emerson
Island House . . .Southwest Harbor, Maine
Hawthorne Inn . . . . .Concord, Mass.
Ralph Waldo Emerson Inn
. . . . .Rockport, Mass.
Frances Grey Patton
William Thomas House . . . .Raleigh, N.C.
Nathaniel Hawthorne
Hawthorne Inn . . . . .Concord, Mass.
D.H. Lawrence
Hacienda del Sol . . . . .Taos, N.M.
Jack London
Vichy Hot Springs Resort Inn Ukiah, Calif.
James A. Michener
Robert Morris Inn . . . . .Oxford, Md.
Becky Thatcher, Mark Twain/Samuel Clemens
Fifth Street Mansion B&B . .Hannibal, Mo.
Mark Twain/Samuel Clemens
Vichy Hot Springs Resort Inn
. . . . .Ukiah, Calif.
Garth Woodside Mansion . .Hannibal, Mo.
Edith Wharton
The Gables Inn . . . . .Lenox, Mass.

Llama Ranches

Canaan Land Farm B&B . .Harrodsburg, KY
Rockhouse Mountain Farm Inn
. . . . .Eaton Center, N.H.
1661 Inn & Hotel Manisses
. . . . .Block Island, R.I.
Rainbow Ridge . . . . .Onalaska, Wisc.

Log Houses/Cabins

Ocean Wilderness Country Inn & Spa
Retreat . . . . .Sooke, British Columbia
Anniversary Inn . . . . . .Estes Park, Colo.
Sandusky House & O'Neal Log Cabin
. . . . .Nicholasville, Ky.
The Log House . . . . .Russellville, Ky.
Log Cabin Lodging
. . . . .Bailey Island, Maine
Trout House Village . . . . . . .Hague, N.Y.
Log Country Inn-B&B of Ithaca
. . . . .Ithaca, N.Y.
Inn at Cedar Falls . . . . .Logan, Ohio
Pinehurst Inn at Jenny Creek
. . . . .Ashland, Ore.
Cheat Mountain Club . . . . .Durbin, W.Va.
Bad Rock Country B&B
. . . . .Columbia Falls, Mont.

Trout House Village Resort . . .Hague, N.Y.
Inn at Cedar Falls . . . . .Logan, Ohio
West Mountain Inn . . . . . .Arlington, Vt.
Inn at Narrow Passage . . . .Woodstock, Va.
The Inn at Burg's Landing
. . . . .Anderson Island, Wash.
A. Drummonds Ranch . . .Cheyenne, Wyo.

Movie Locations

Eden House . . . . .Key West, Fla.
"Criss Cross"
Goldsmith's B&B Inn . . .Missoula, Mont.
"A River Runs Through It"

Old Mills

Silvermine Tavern . . . . .Norwalk, Conn.
Arbor Rose B&B . . . . .Stockbridge, Mass.
Twin Gables Country Inn Saugatuck, Mich.
Brookstown Inn . . . .Winston-Salem, N.C.
Asa Ransom House . . . . . .Clarence, N.Y.
Edgewood Plantation . . . Charles City, Va.

Oldest Continuously Operated Inns

Historic National Hotel B&B
. . . . .Jamestown, Calif.
Julian Gold Rush Hotel . . . .Julian, Calif.
Griswold Inn . . . . .Essex, Conn.
1857 Florida House Inn
. . . . .Amelia Island, Fla.
Cranberry Inn at Chatham
. . . . .Chatham, Mass.
Ralph Waldo Emerson Inn
. . . . .Rockport, Mass.
Candlelite Inn . . . . .Bradford, N.H.
Wakefield Inn . . . . .Wakefield, N.H.
Ebbie Guest House . . . . .Ocean City, N.J.
Stockton Inn, Colligan's . . .Stockton, N.J.
The Bellevue House . . . .Block Island, R.I.
Kedron Valley Inn . . . . . . .Woodstock, Vt.

Plantations

Little St. Simons Island
. . . . .St. Simons Island, Ga.
Melhana . . . . .Thomasville, Ga.
The House on Bayou Road
. . . . .New Orleans, La.
Madewood Plantation . .Napoleonville, La.
Merry Sherwood Plantation . . .Berlin, Md.
Mostly Hall B&B . . . . . .Falmouth, Mass.
Monmouth . . . . .Natchez, Miss.
Oakland Plantation . . . . . .Natchez, Miss.
Mansfield Plantation . . .Georgetown, S.C.
Laurel Hill Plantation
. . . . .McClellanville, S.C.
Nicholls-Crook Plantation House B&B
. . . . .Woodruff, S.C.
Edgewood Plantation . . . .Charles City, Va.
Inn at La Vista Plantation
. . . . .Fredericksburg, Va.
Inn at Meander Plantation
. . . . .Locust Dale, Va.

Ranches

Rancho DeLa Osa . . . . .Sasabe, Ariz.
Howard Creek Ranch . . . .Westport, Calif.
Wit's End Guest Ranch . . .Bayfield, Colo.
Kaia Ranch & Co . . . . .Kona, Hawaii
Idaho Rocky Mountain Ranch
. . . . .Stanley, Idaho
Meadow View Ranch B&B Bunkhouse
. . . . .Gordon, Neb.
Soldier Meadows Guest Ranch
. . . . .Gerlach, Nev.
Pinehurst Inn at Jenny Creek
. . . . .Ashland, Ore.
Wine Country Farm . . . . . .Dayton, Ore.
Hasse House and Ranch . . .Mason, Texas
A. Drummonds Ranch . . .Cheyenne, W.Y.

Revolutionary War

Robert Morris Inn . . . . .Oxford, Md.
Captain Samuel Eddy House
. . . . .Auburn, Mass.
Ashley Manor Inn
. . . . .Barnstable/Cape Cod, Mass.
Colonel Roger Brown House
. . . . .Concord, Mass.
Village Green Inn . . . . .Falmouth, Mass.
Dan'l Webster Inn . . . . .Sandwich, Mass.
Pace One Restaurant & Country Inn
. . . . .Thornton, Pa.
The Melville House . . . . . .Newport, R.I.
Kitchen House . . . . .Charleston, S.C.
John Rutledge House Inn . .Charleston, S.C.
Inn at Ormsby Hill
. . . . .Manchester Center, Vt.
Inn at Weathersfield . . .Weathersfield, Vt.
Silver Thatch Inn . . . . .Charlottesville, Va.
Gilbert House B&B of Middleway
. . . . .Charles Town, Va.

Schoolhouses

The Roosevelt . . . . .Coeur d'Alene, Idaho
Bagley House . . . . .Durham, Maine
Old Sea Pines Inn . . . . . .Brewster, Mass.
School House B&B Inn . .Rocheport, Mo.
The Inn at Bingham School
. . . . .Chapel Hill, N.C.
Washington School Inn . . .Park City, Utah
Springdale Country . . . . . . .Lincoln, Va.
Blue Haven Christian B&B
. . . . .Westminster, Vt.
East Highland School House B&B
. . . . .Phillips, Wis.

Stagecoach Stops

Simpson House Inn . .Santa Barbara, Calif.
Maple Hill Farm B&B Inn
. . . . .Hallowell/Augusta, Maine
Alden Country Inn . . . . .Lyme, N.H.
Wakefield Inn . . . . .Wakefield, N.H.
Hacienda Antigua B&B
. . . . .Albuquerque, N.M.
Hacienda Vargas
. . . . .Algodones/Santa Fe, N.M.
Inn at Bingham School . .Chapel Hill, N.C.

Penguin Crossing B&B . .Circleville, Ohio
The Olde Stage Coach B&B
. . . . .Jennerstown, Pa.
Churchill House Inn . . . . . .Brandon, Vt.
Pittsfield Inn . . . . .Pittsfield, Vt.
The Golden Stage Inn . . .Proctorsville, Vt.
Inn at Blush Hill . . . . .Waterbury, Vt.
Old Stagecoach Inn . . . . . .Waterbury, Vt.
West Dover Inn . . . . .West Dover, Vt.
Inn at Narrow Passage . . .Woodstock, Va.
Stagecoach Inn B&B . . . .Cedarburg, Wis.
Wisconsin House Stagecoach Inn
. . . . .Hazel Green, Wis.
General Lewis . . . . .Lewisburg, W.Va.

Still in the Family

The Sherwood Inn . . . . . .New Haven, Ky.
Oakland House Seaside Inn & Cottages
. . . . .Brooksville, Maine
The Grey Havens . . .Georgetown, Maine
Jonas Green House B&B . .Annapolis, Md.
Sanders - Helena's Bed & Breakfast
. . . . .Helena, Mont.
Rockhouse Mountain Farm Inn
. . . . .Eaton Center, N.H.
Chalfonte . . . . .Cape May, N.J.
Line Limousin Farmhouse . . . .Carlisle, Pa.
Cedar Hill Farm . . . . . . .Mount Joy, Pa.
Castle Hill Inn . . . . .Newport, R.I.
Hasse House and Ranch . . . .Mason, Texas
Bay View Waterfront B&B
. . . . .Belle Haven, Va.
The General Lewis . . . . .Lewisburg,, W.Va.

Taverns

Red Brook Inn . . . . . . .Old Mystic, Conn.
Silvermine Tavern . . . . . .Norwalk, Conn.
Alden Country Inn . . . . .Lyme, N.H.
Birchwood Inn . . . . .Lenox, Mass.
Kendall Tavern . . . . .Freeport, Maine
The Historic Temperance Tavern
. . . . .Gilmanton, N.H.
Bird & Bottle Inn . . . . . . .Garrison, N.Y.
Giddings . . . . .Syracuse, N.Y.
Rider's 1812 Inn . . . . . . .Painesville, Ohio
Smithton Inn . . . . .Ephrata, Pa.
James Getty Hotel . . . . . .Gettysburg, Pa.
1725 Historic Witmer's Tavern
. . . . .Lancaster, Pa.
Rabbit Hill Inn . . . . .Lower Waterford, Vt.
Fox Stand Inn . . . . .Royalton, Vt.

Train Stations & Renovated Rail Cars

Inn at Depot Hill
. . . . .Capitola-by-the-Sea, Calif.
Varner's Caboose . . . . . . .Montpelier, Iowa
Red House Inn . . . . .Brevard, N.C.
Green Mountain Inn . . . . .Stowe, Vt.
Mountain Meadows Inn B&B
. . . . .Ashford, Wash.

Tunnels, Secret Passageways, Caves

Ashley Manor
.......Barnstable/Cape Cod, Mass.
Merry Sherwood Plantation .Berlin, Maine
Munro House ....Jonesville, Mich.
Lehrkind Mansion .....Bozeman, Mont.
Colonel Spencer Inn ....Plymouth, N.H.
1725 Historic Witmer's Tavern
.................Lancaster, Pa.
Kedron Valley Inn .South Woodstock, Vt.
Lynchburg Mansion Inn ...Lynchburg, Va.
Mansion Hill Inn ....Madison, Wisc.

Unusual Sleeping Places

On a yacht
Dockside Boat & Bed ....Oakland, Calif.
Above a gold mine
Chichester-McKee House B&B
.................Placerville, Calif.
By waterfalls
Inn at Brandywine Falls
............Sagamore Hills, Calif.
In a caboose
Varners Caboose .....Montpelier, Iowa
In a bank
Landmark Inn at the Historic Bank of Oberlin
.................Oberlin, Kan.
In a bunkhouse
Meadow View Ranch .....Gordon, Neb.
In a trading post
Hacienda Vargas ....Santa Fe, N.M.
On or next to an archaeological dig site
The White Oak Inn .....Danville, Ohio
In a tinsmith shop
Churchtown Inn ....Churchtown, Pa.
Historic powerhouse
Abend Haus ....Rapid City, S.C.

Waterfalls

Inn at Cedar Falls ....Logan, Ohio
Inn at Brandywine Falls
............Sagamore Hills, Ohio
Creamery Inn ....Cabot, Vt.

Who Slept/Visited Here

John Adams
1725 Historic Witmer's Tavern
.................Lancaster, Pa.
Ethan Allen
Inn at Ormsby Hill
.........Manchester Center, Vt.
Neil Armstrong
Beekman Arms ....Rhinebeck, N.Y.
John James Audubon
Weston House ....Eastport, Maine
Mary Hunter Austin
Victoria Tyme House .....Carlinville, Ill.
Barrymore family
Evermay-on-the-Delaware
........Erwinna/Bucks County, Pa.
Sarah Bernhardt
Abigail's "Elegant Victorian Mansion"
.................Eureka, Calif.
Clara Bow
Hotel Nipton ....Nipton, Calif.

Aaron Burr
Beekman Arms ....Rhinebeck, N.Y.
Margaret Chase Smith
Peacock House ....Lubec, Maine
Salmon Chase
Chase House B&B Inn ....Cornish, N.H.
Winston Churchill
Bayview Inn ....Bar Harbor, Maine
Henry Clay
Monmouth Plantation ....Natchez, Miss.
Samuel Clemens
Garth Woodside Mansion ..Hannibal, Mo.
Grover Cleveland
Cordova ....Ocean Grove, N.J.
Calvin Coolidge
State Game Lodge ....Custer, S.D.
Jefferson Davis
Monmouth Plantation ....Natchez, Miss.
Anchuca ....Vicksburg, Miss.
Thomas Edison
Tulip Tree Inn ....Chittenden, Vt.
Dwight D. Eisenhower
State Game Lodge ....Custer, S.D.
Clark Gable
Gold Mountain Manor Historic B&B
.................Big Bear, Calif.
Cary Grant
Mulburn Inn ....Bethlehem, N.H.
Ulysses S. Grant
Thayers Inn ....Littleton, N.H.
Misty River B&B ....Ripley, Ohio
Alexander Hamilton
Bird & Bottle Inn ....Garrison, N.Y.
Mrs. Warren Harding
Watchtide, B&B By the Sea
.................Searsport, Maine
Lillian Hellman
Barley Sheaf Farm ....Holicong, Pa.
Patrick Henry
General Lewis ....Lewisburg, Va.
Bob & Delores Hope
Greenfield Inn ....Greenfield, N.H.
Mrs. Herbert Hoover
Watchtide, B&B By the Sea
.................Searsport, Maine
Howard Hughes
Colonial Inn of Martha's Vineyard
.................Edgartown, Mass.
Barbara Hutton
Mulburn Inn ....Bethlehem, N.H.
Andrew Jackson
Oakland Plantation .....Natchez, Miss.
General Stonewall Jackson
Inn at Narrow Passage ....Woodstock, Va.
Thomas Jefferson
1725 Historic Witmer's Tavern
.................Lancaster, Pa.
General Lewis ....Lewisburg, Va.
Inn at Meander Plantation
.................Locust Dale, Va.
General Lafayette
The Bird & Bottle Inn ....Garrison, N.Y.
Lillie Langtry
Abigail's "Elegant Victorian Mansion"
.................Eureka, Calif.
D.H. Lawrence
Hacienda Del Sol ....Taos, N.M.

Robert E. Lee
The President's Quarters
.................Savannah, Ga.
Wooden Rabbit ....Cape May, N.J.
Robert Todd Lincoln
Inn at Ormsby Hill
..........Manchester Center, Vt.
Carole Lombard
Gold Mountain Manor Historic B&B
.................Big Bear, Calif.
Marx brothers
Barley Sheaf Farm ....Holicong, Pa.
Somerset Maugham
Colonial Inn of Martha's Vineyard
.................Edgartown, Mass.
Captain Cornelius J. Mey
Captain Mey's B&B Inn ...Cape May, N.J.
Edmund Muskey
Peacock House ....Lubec, Maine
Captain Ezra Nye
Captain Ezra Nye House .Sandwich, Mass.
Georgia O'Keefe
Hacienda del Sol ....Taos, N.M.
S.J. Perlman
Barley Sheaf Farm ....Holicong, Pa.
General Quitman
Monmouth Plantation ....Natchez, Miss.
Eleanor Roosevelt
Watchtide, B&B By the Sea
.................Searsport, Maine
Franklin Roosevelt
Beekman Arms ....Rhinebeck, N.Y.
Theodore Roosevelt
Troutbeck ....Amenia, N.Y.
A Touch of Europe B&B Inn
.................Yakima, Wash.
Jane Seymour
The Pink House .....East Hampton, N.Y.
General W.T. Sherman
Cuthbert House Inn B&B ..Beaufort, S.C.
Carly Simon
The Pink House .....East Hampton, N.Y.
Martin Short
The Pink House .....East Hampton, N.Y.
J William Taft
Inn at Ormsby Hill .Manchester Center, Vt.
Elizabeth Taylor
Beekman Arms ....Rhinebeck, N.Y.
Martin Van Buren
Old Hoosier House ....Knightstown, Ind.
George Washington
Jonas Green House B&B ..Annapolis, Md.
Dan'l Webster Inn ......Sandwich, Mass.
Bird & Bottle Inn ....Garrison, N.Y.
Jacob's Resting Place ....Carlisle, Pa.
Glen Isle Farm ....Downington, Pa.
1725 Historic Witmer's Tavern
.................Lancaster, Pa.
John Rutledge House Inn .Charleston, S.C.
Robin Williams
The Pink House .....East Hampton,
Stanford White
Inn at Jackson ....Jackson, N.H.
Woodrow Wilson
Cordova ....Ocean Grove, N.J.
Woolworth family
Mulburn Inn ....Bethlehem, N.H.

INN EVALUATION FORM

Please copy and complete this form for each stay and mail to the address shown. Since 1981 we have maintained files that include thousands of evaluations from inngoers who have sent this form to us. This information helps us evaluate and update the inns listed in this guide.

Name of Inn: _____

City and State: _____

Date of Stay: _____

Your Name: _____

Address: _____

City/State/Zip: _____

Phone: (__ __ __) __ __ __ – __ __ __ __

Please use the following rating scale for the next items.
1: Outstanding.   2: Good.   3: Average.   4: Fair.   5: Poor.

	1	2	3	4	5
Location	1	2	3	4	5
Cleanliness	1	2	3	4	5
Food Service	1	2	3	4	5
Privacy	1	2	3	4	5
Beds	1	2	3	4	5
Bathrooms	1	2	3	4	5
Parking	1	2	3	4	5
Handling of reservations	1	2	3	4	5
Attitude of staff	1	2	3	4	5
Overall rating	1	2	3	4	5

Comments on Above: _____

_____

_____

_____

_____

MAIL THE COMPLETED FORM TO:
American Historic Inns, Inc.
PO Box 669
Dana Point, CA 92629-0669
(949) 499-8070
http://bnbinns.com
E-mail: comments@bnbinns.com

INN EVALUATION FORM

Please copy and complete this form for each stay and mail to the address shown. Since 1981 we have maintained files that include thousands of evaluations from inngoers who have sent this form to us. This information helps us evaluate and update the inns listed in this guide.

Name of Inn: _____

City and State: _____

Date of Stay: _____

Your Name: _____

Address: _____

City/State/Zip: _____

Phone: (__ __ __) __ __ __ – __ __ __ __

Please use the following rating scale for the next items.
1: Outstanding.   2: Good.   3: Average.   4: Fair.   5: Poor.

Location	1	2	3	4	5
Cleanliness	1	2	3	4	5
Food Service	1	2	3	4	5
Privacy	1	2	3	4	5
Beds	1	2	3	4	5
Bathrooms	1	2	3	4	5
Parking	1	2	3	4	5
Handling of reservations	1	2	3	4	5
Attitude of staff	1	2	3	4	5
Overall rating	1	2	3	4	5

Comments on Above: _____

_____

_____

_____

_____

MAIL THE COMPLETED FORM TO:
American Historic Inns, Inc.
PO Box 669
Dana Point, CA 92629-0669
(949) 499-8070
http://bnbinns.com
E-mail: comments@bnbinns.com

Publications From American Historic Inns

Bed & Breakfast and Country Inns, 11th Edition

By Deborah Edwards Sakach

Imagine the thrill of receiving this unique book with its FREE night certificate as a gift. Now you can let someone else experience the magic of America's country inns with this unmatched offer. *Bed & Breakfasts and Country Inns* is the most talked about guide among inngoers.

This fabulous guide features more than 1,600 inns from across the United States and Canada. Best of all, no other bookstore guide offers a FREE night certificate.* This certificate can be used at any one of the inns featured in the guide.

American Historic Inns, Inc. has been publishing books about bed & breakfasts since 1981. Its books and the FREE night offer have been recommended by many travel writers and editors, and featured in: *The New York Times, Washington Post, Los Angeles Times, Boston Globe, Chicago Sun Times, USA Today, Orange County Register, Baltimore Sun, McCalls, Good Housekeeping, Cosmopolitan, Consumer Reports* and more.

*With purchase of one night at the regular rate required. Subject to limitations.

448 pages, paperback, 700 illustrations.　　　　　　　　　　　**Price $21.95**

The Official Guide to American Historic Inns

Completely Revised and Updated, Seventh Edition

By Deborah Sakach

Open the door to America's past with this fascinating guide to historic inns that reflect our colorful heritage. From Dutch Colonials to Queen Anne Victorians, these bed & breakfasts and country inns offer experiences of a lifetime.

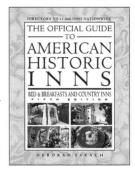

This special edition guide includes certified American Historic Inns that provide the utmost in hospitality, beauty, authentic restoration and preservation. Inns have been carefully selected so as to provide readers with the opportunity to visit genuine masterpieces.

With Inns dating back to as early as 1649, this guide is filled with treasures waiting to be discovered. Full descriptions, illustrations, guest comments and recommendations all are included to let you know what's in store for you before choosing one of America's Historic Inns.

528 pages, paperback, 1,000 illustrations.　　　　　　　　　　　**Price $15.95**

The Bed & Breakfast Encyclopedia

Completely Revised and Updated, Second Edition

By Deborah Edwards Sakach & Tiffany Crosswy

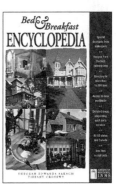

This massive guide is the most comprehensive guide on the market today. Packed with detailed listings to more than 2,300 bed & breakfasts and country inns, the Encyclopedia also includes an index to an additional 13,000 inns, detailed state maps and more than 1,200 illustrations. Recipes, helpful phone numbers, information about reservation services and informative articles about bed & breakfast hot spots, the best bed & breakfasts, inns of interest, how to start your own B&B and much, much more.

If you're planning a getaway, this all-inclusive guide is a must!

992 pages, paperback, 1,200 illustrations   **Price $18.95**

Bed & Breakfast and Country Inn Travel Club
Membership From American Historic Inns, Inc.

SAVE! SAVE! SAVE! We offer an exclusive discount club that lets you enjoy the excitement of bed & breakfast and country inn travel again and again. As a member of this once-in-a-lifetime offer you'll receive benefits that include savings of 25% to 50% off every night's stay!

Your membership card will entitle you to tremendous savings at some of the finest inns in America. <u>Members receive a guide with more than 1,200 participating bed & breakfasts and country inns to choose from.</u> Plan affordable getaways to inns nearby or visit an area of the country you've always wanted to experience.

The best part of being an American Historic Inns Travel Club Member is that the card can be used as many times as you like.

In addition to your card, you will get a FREE night's stay certificate—truly a club membership that's hard to pass up!

All travel club members receive:
- Travel club card entitling holder to 25% to 50% off lodging.
- FREE night's stay certificate.
- Guide to more than 1,200 participating inns across America.

Membership is good for one year. Free night's stay with purchase of one night at the regular rate. Discount and certificate cannot be combined.

Introductory price with full benefits (Reg. $59.95)   **$49.95**

How To Start & Run Your Own Bed & Breakfast Inn

By Ripley Hotch & Carl Glassman

In this book you'll discover the secrets of the best inns. Learn how to decide whether owning or leasing an inn is right for you. Find out what business strategies characterize a successful inn and learn how to incorporate them in your own business.

If you've always dreamed of owning a bed & breakfast, then this book is for you!

182 pages, paperback.   **Price $15.95**

AMERICAN HISTORIC INNS
INCORPORATED

PO Box 669
Dana Point
California
92629-0669
(949) 499-8070
Fax (949) 499-4022
http://bnbinns.com

Order Form

Date: __ __ / __ __ / __ __   Shipped: __ __ / __ __ / __ __

Name: _____

Street: _____

City/State/Zip: _____

Phone: (__ __ __) __ __ __ __ – __ __ __ __

QTY.	Prod. No.	Description	Amount	Total
_____	AHI11	Bed & Breakfasts and Country Inns	$21.95	_____
_____	AHIH7	The Official Guide to American Historic Inns	$15.95	_____
_____	AHIE2	Bed & Breakfast Encyclopedia	$18.95	_____
_____	AHIC2	Bed & Breakfast and Country Inn Travel Club	$49.95	_____
_____	CB03	How to Start Your Own B&B	$15.95	_____

Subtotal _____

California buyers add 7.75% sales tax _____

Shipping and Handling on Encyclopedia Book Orders
STANDARD (10-20 days): $3 for first book. Add $1 for each additional copy.
PRIORITY (3-5 days): $5. Add $2 each add'l copy. 2ND-DAY AIR: $7.50. Add $4.50 each add'l copy.

Shipping and Handling on Other Book and Travel Club Orders
STANDARD (10-20 days): $2.25 for first book. Add 75¢ for each additional copy.
PRIORITY (3-5 days): $3.75. Add $2 each add'l copy. 2ND-DAY AIR: $7.50. Add $4.50 each add'l copy _____

TOTAL _____

❏ Check/Money Order   ❏ Discover   ❏ Mastercard   ❏ Visa   ❏ American Express

Account Number __ __ __ __ __ __ __ __ __ __ __ __ __ __ __ __   Exp. Date __ __ / __ __

Name on card _____

Signature _____

516

AMERICAN HISTORIC INNS
I N C O R P O R A T E D

PO Box 669
Dana Point
California
92629-0669
(949) 499-8070
Fax (949) 499-4022
http://bnbinns.com

Order Form

Date: __ __ / __ __ / __ __   Shipped: __ __ / __ __ / __ __

Name: _____

Street: _____

City/State/Zip: _____

Phone: (__ __ __) __ __ __ - __ __ __ __

QTY.	Prod. No.	Description	Amount	Total
_____	AHI11	Bed & Breakfasts and Country Inns	$21.95	_____
_____	AHIH7	The Official Guide to American Historic Inns	$15.95	_____
_____	AHIE2	Bed & Breakfast Encyclopedia	$18.95	_____
_____	AHIC2	Bed & Breakfast and Country Inn Travel Club	$49.95	_____
_____	CB03	How to Start Your Own B&B	$15.95	_____
			Subtotal	_____
		California buyers add 7.75% sales tax		_____

Shipping and Handling on Encyclopedia Book Orders
STANDARD (10-20 days): $3 for first book. Add $1 for each additional copy.
PRIORITY (3-5 days): $5. Add $2 each add'l copy. 2ND-DAY AIR: $7.50. Add $4.50 each add'l copy.

Shipping and Handling on Other Book and Travel Club Orders
STANDARD (10-20 days): $2.25 for first book. Add 75¢ for each additional copy.
PRIORITY (3-5 days): $3.75. Add $2 each add'l copy. 2ND-DAY AIR: $7.50. Add $4.50 each add'l copy   _____

TOTAL   _____

❏ Check/Money Order   ❏ Discover   ❏ Mastercard   ❏ Visa   ❏ American Express

Account Number __ __ __ __ __ __ __ __ __ __ __ __ __ __ __ __   Exp. Date __ __ / __ __

Name on card _____

Signature _____

bnbinns.com

"The only online bed & breakfast guide you will ever need.™"

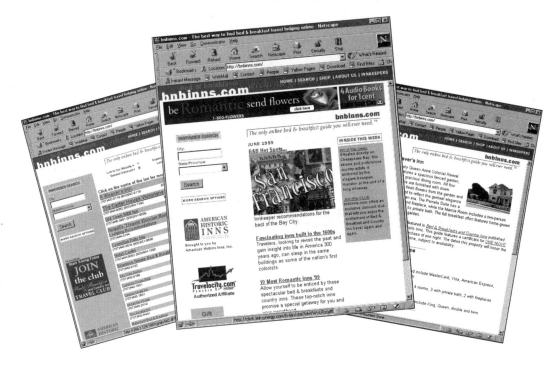

- More than 15,000 bed & breakfasts and country inns.

- Color photos and line illustrations.

- Use our easy Innfinder Search to quickly access inns near your destination.

- Or use our Advanced Search to look for inns that meet your specific needs.

- Search for inns in our Free Night program.

- Make reservations via e-mail.

- See our specially selected Inn of the Week.

- Learn about bed & breakfast hot spots across the country.

- Find out where the top inns are, including our famous picks for the 10 Most Romantic Inns.